Chambers
Essential Learners'
Dictionary

For elementary learners of English

Chambers Essential Learners' Dictionary

For elementary learners of English

Chambers

CHAMBERS
An imprint of Chambers Harrap Publishers Ltd
7 Hopetoun Crescent, Edinburgh, EH7 4AY

Chambers Harrap is an Hachette UK company

© Chambers Harrap Publishers Ltd 2009

Images reproduced with the permission of QA International, www.qa-international.com from the book "The Visual Dictionary". © QA International. 2009. All rights reserved

Chambers® is a registered trademark of Chambers Harrap Publishers Ltd

First published by Chambers Harrap Publishers Ltd 2009

A CIP catalogue record for this book is available from the British Library.

Main edition ISBN 978 0550 10478 6
French edition ISBN 978 0245 50980 3   Dépôt légal: juillet 2009

10 9 8 7 6 5 4 3 2 1

We have made every effort to mark as such all words which we believe to be trademarks. We should also like to make it clear that the presence of a word in the dictionary, whether marked or unmarked, in no way affects its legal status as a trademark.

Publishing Manager
Morven Dooner

Editors
Pat Bulhosen
Penny Hands
Lucy Hollingworth
Ginny Klein
Alison Macaulay
Julie Moore
Elizabeth Walter
Kate Woodford

www.chambersharrap.co.uk

Designed by Sharon Mcteir
Typeset in Bliss by Charlesworth
Printed and bound in Italy by Legoprint

Contents

Preface

The *Chambers Essential Learners' Dictionary* is a new dictionary for anyone learning English. It contains all the important words you will need for study, work or simply for life, explained in a clear, simple way, using words you will already know.

When you open the book, you will probably notice the symbol 🔁, which appears at many entries. This is the sign we have used to show one of the most important aspects of English: collocation. Collocation means the way words go together. For example, if there are a lot of cars on the road, we say there is '**heavy traffic**', and if someone does something illegal, we say they '**commit a crime**'. These word combinations can often be impossible to guess, but learning them is probably the most important thing you can do to make your English sound fluent and natural, and this dictionary will help you to do it.

Unlike many learners' dictionaries, the *Chambers Essential Learners' Dictionary* does not have complicated grammar codes, but the most important and common words all have examples which show clearly how to use them. Because the book has been written by experienced teachers, you will also find special notes to help you avoid common mistakes.

The information in this dictionary is based on the evidence provided by the *Chambers Harrap Corpus*, a collection of millions of words of English, taken from all types of language, from newspapers to novels to ordinary conversation. It helps us to see how words are used in real life and to make sure that the dictionary is completely up-to-date.

You will also find a useful Study Section, which gives information and help with English grammar.

We hope you enjoy using the *Chambers Essential Learner's Dictionary* at home, in the classroom or wherever you may be!

How to use

Entry words are in alphabetical order.

Numbers show where a word has different **meanings**.

Common **idioms** are shown, usually at the entry for their first word.

laugh¹ /lɑːf/ VERB [laughs, laughing, laughed] to make a sound of enjoyment when you think something is funny □ **+ at** *She laughed at my jokes.* □ **+ about** *We can laugh about the whole thing now.* 🖫 *It really made me laugh.* 🖫 *They burst out laughing* (= suddenly laughed loudly).
♦ PHRASAL VERB **laugh at someone/something** to laugh or say something rude because you think someone or something is stupid □ *Wallis just laughed at the suggestion.*

laugh² /lɑːf/ NOUN [plural laughs]
1 when you laugh, or the sound that you make when you laugh 🖫 *He gave a nervous laugh.* □ *He has a very loud laugh.*
2 **have a laugh** an informal phrase that means to have fun and enjoy yourself □ *We all have such a laugh together.*

laughter /ˈlɑːftə(r)/ NOUN, NO PLURAL when someone laughs or the sound that they make when they laugh □ *I could hear laughter in the next room.*

All **verb inflections** are shown.

Phrasal verbs are shown after the other verbs in an entry.

The **plural** of all nouns is shown.

Every word has a **part of speech**, showing if it is a noun, verb, adjective, etc. For an explanation of these words, see page 10.

Entry words like this are the **most common and useful** words to learn and use.

Every word has a **pronunciation** using the International Phonetic Alphabet. You can find an explanation of these symbols inside the front cover.

eager /ˈiːɡə(r)/ ADJECTIVE wanting very much to do or have something □ **+ to do something** *Imran seems eager to learn.*

Simple **grammar patterns** are shown for these common words. They are always attached to an example, showing you clearly how to use the word. For an explanation of all the grammar codes, see page 11.

Words belonging to the same **word families** are shown under the main entry if they are in alphabetical order.

thoughtful /ˈθɔːtfʊl/ ADJECTIVE
1 a thoughtful person is kind and thinks of other people □ *It was very thoughtful of you to phone.*
2 if someone looks thoughtful, they look as if they are thinking
• **thoughtfully** /ˈθɔːtfʊli/ ADVERB in a thoughtful way □ *She stared thoughtfully at the letter.* □ *She'd very thoughtfully left drinks and sandwiches on the kitchen table for us.*

This dictionary has thousands of **example sentences** showing typical uses of the entry words.

Some words have more than one possible **spelling**.

hairdryer *or* **hairdrier** /ˈheədraɪə(r)/ NOUN [plural hairdryers *or* hairdriers] a piece of electrical equipment that dries your hair by blowing hot air over it

Collocations (words that go together) are a very important feature of this dictionary. For more information, see page 13.

lonely /ˈləʊnli/ ADJECTIVE [lonelier, loneliest] unhappy because you are alone, with no friends around you 🔁 *She suddenly felt very lonely.* 🔁 *I get lonely at the weekends.*

The **comparative** and **superlative** forms of adjectives and adverbs are shown. These are used when you want to say that something or someone has more of a quality or most of a quality, compared to other things or people.

Because this dictionary is for use at school as well as at home, words used in the **school subjects** maths, physics, chemistry, biology, geography and computing are shown.

desktop /ˈdesktɒp/ NOUN [plural desktops] a computer screen that shows the icons (= small pictures) for programs you can use. A computing word.

This dictionary uses simple words in all the entries, but where a more difficult word is necessary, a **short explanation** is given.

microscope /ˈmaɪkrəskəʊp/ NOUN [plural microscopes] a piece of equipment with lenses (= curved pieces of glass) that makes very small objects look much larger so that you can study them closely

If a word is always used in a particular **phrase**, that phrase is shown before the explanation, and the explanation describes the whole phrase.

beg /beg/ VERB [begs, begging, begged]
1 to ask someone for something in an eager or emotional way because you want it very much □ *I begged him to come home.*
2 to ask people for money in the street because you are very poor
3 I beg your pardon (a) a formal way of saying sorry when you have made a mistake □ *Oh, I beg your pardon, I didn't realize this pen was yours.* (b) a formal way of asking someone to repeat what they have just said because you did not hear it □ *'I'm going now.' 'I beg your pardon.' 'I said, I'm going now.'*

If you need to be careful using a word, for instance because it is formal or informal, this is shown in the explanation. For a list of words that describe these characteristics, see 12.

Usage notes give advice about using words. In particular, they help you avoid mistakes which learners of English often make.

picnic[1] /ˈpɪknɪk/ NOUN [plural picnics] a meal that you take with you to eat outdoors 🔁 *We had a picnic on the beach.* 🔁 *There's a beautiful picnic area in the forest.*

➤ Note that you **have** a picnic. You do not 'make' a picnic: ✓ *We had a picnic in the park.* ✗ *We made a picnic in the park.*

diaper /ˈdaɪəpə(r)/ NOUN [plural diapers] the US word for **nappy**

This dictionary is written in British English. The spellings in explanations and examples are British. However, US spellings and common US words are shown.

Thesaurus notes help you learn more about alternative words

➤ **THESAURUS:** If you are absent, you are not at a place where you are expected to be. For example, you might be absent from school or work because you are ill. If you are away from work, you might be out of the office on business or on holiday. If a person is missing, they are not where you expect them to be, and you do not know where they are. If a person or thing has gone, it was in a place, but now it is no longer there.

Parts of speech

These are the parts of speech used in this dictionary:

abbreviation	a short form of a word or words, using their first letters	l (litre), UK (United Kingdom)
adjective	a word that describes a noun	pretty, hot, uncomfortable
adverb	a word that describes a verb or an adjective	slowly, extremely, well
auxiliary verb	a verb used to make tenses, negatives and questions	be, do, have
conjunction	a word that connects parts of a sentence	but, however
determiner	a word used before a noun to show how the noun is being used	the, this, those
exclamation	something you say suddenly or loudly	hey, ouch
modal verb	a verb used to show ideas such as being possible, necessary, certain, etc.	might, ought, will
noun	a word that refers to a person, a thing, or a quality	dog, table, car
noun no plural	a noun that cannot be used in a plural form	air, happiness, ham
number	a number	eleven, twenty, million
past participle	the part of the verb that indicates the past	sung, watched, eaten
past tense	the word you use to talk about the past	sang, watched, ate
plural noun	a noun that often refers to several things and needs a plural verb	trousers, outskirts
prefix	letters added to the beginning of a word to make another meaning	anti-, eco-, hydro-
preposition	a word used to show things such as position, time or method	by, under, with
pronoun	a word that can be used in place of a noun	they, it, those
suffix	letters added to the end of word to make another word	-ful, -able
verb	a word that says what something or someone does	speak, increase, allow

Grammar in the dictionary

In order to make this dictionary as easy to use as possible, grammar codes are used only on the most important and common words. That is because these are the words you are most likely to use and not just want to understand.

You will see that wherever there is a grammar code, there is also an example which shows you what it means.

This is a list of the codes that are used in this dictionary:

+ ing	the word is followed by a verb using an –ing form	e.g. + ing: *I like playing computer games*
+ question word	the word is followed by a word such as *who, what, why*	e.g. + question word: *I don't understannd why he is so upset*
+ that	the word is followed by part of a sentence beginning with that	e.g. + that: *I promise that I'll pay you back later*
+ to do something	the word is followed by an infinitive verb	e.g. + to do something: *I forgot to lock the door*
no plural	this meaning of the word cannot be used in a plural form even though other meanings of the same word can	e.g. no plural: *all the hairs that grow on your head*
+ in/over/up etc.	this word is followed by a preposition	e.g.: truth + about: *We're determined to learn the truth about his disapearance*

Special use of words

Sometimes a word that can be used in one situation is not suitable for another situation. (We do not use the same language when we are talking to our friends as we do when we are writing an essay.)

These differences are clearly shown in the explanations of words in this dictionary. These are the words we use to describe them:

formal formal words are suitable for serious writing and official situations. They would sound slightly strange if you used them in an ordinary conversation.

furthermore /ˌfɜːðəˈmɔː(r)/ ADVERB a formal word
used when you are adding something to what you
have already said □ *His plans will be very expensive.*
Furthermore, they will cause a lot of disruption.

informal informal words are not suitable for serious writing or official situations. They are more likely to be used with people you know well.

dumb /dʌm/ ADJECTIVE [dumber, dumbest]
1 stupid. An informal word □ *He kept asking me*
dumb questions.
2 not able to speak

old-fashioned This dictionary does not include words which are not used any more, but there are some words which are still in use, but not used much by young people.

centigrade /ˈsentɪɡreɪd/ ADJECTIVE an old-
fashioned word for **Celsius** □ *forty degrees centigrade*

literary literary words are usually found in poetry or novels.

riches /ˈrɪtʃɪz/ PLURAL NOUN a word used in stories
meaning a lot of money and expensive things

> ➤ THESAURUS: Money is a general word for
> coins and paper notes that you use for buying
> things. Riches is a literary word meaning a lot
> of money and expensive things. For example,
> you might talk about a king's riches in a story.
> Someone's wealth is all the money and
> expensive things that they have. A fortune
> is a very large amount of money.

British and US English

This dictionary is written in British English. The spelling and words in the explanations and the example sentences are British. However, common US words have also been included:

sidewalk /ˈsaɪdwɔːk/ NOUN [*plural* sidewalks] the
US word for **pavement**

Sometimes just one meaning of a word is US, for instance meaning number 4 here:

regular /'regjʊlə(r)/ ADJECTIVE
1 happening often or doing something often ⊞ *We
all know the benefits of regular exercise.* ⊞ *I keep in
regular contact with my family.* ⊞ *He writes to me
on a regular basis.* □ *She was a regular visitor to the
museum.*
2 having the same amount of time or space
between each thing □ *He has a regular heartbeat.*
⊞ *I still see the doctor at regular intervals.*
3 following the usual rules of grammar □ *'Cat' has a
regular plural.* ⊞ *'Pick' is a regular verb.*
4 a US word meaning usual □ *My regular doctor
was away.*

Many words have a different spelling in British and US English, and this is explained in the
dictionary:

cancel /'kænsəl/ VERB [cancels, cancelling/*US*
canceling, cancelled/*US* canceled] to say that a
planned event will not happen □ *The match was
cancelled because of the snow.*

Increasing your vocabulary

English has a very large vocabulary, and this dictionary can help you to increase your
vocabulary. Some entries have **Thesaurus** boxes. These boxes tell you about words that are
similar to the headword. Often, the thesaurus boxes tell you about words that have a less
general meaning than the headword. Using words like these can make your english more
interesting and accurate:

> ➤ THESAURUS: If you are happy or cheerful, you
> are pleased, and feel that a situation is good.
> Delighted means very happy. If you are glad,
> you are happy because of something that has
> happened. Often you are glad because a bad or
> difficult situation has ended or because some-
> thing bad has not happened. For example, you
> might be glad to be home after a long journey,
> or glad that your exams are finished.

Sometimes, the thesaurus boxes explain the differences between words that learners find
confusing:

> ➤ THESAURUS: To leave means to go away from
> a place. The words depart and set off have a
> similar meaning, but are especially used to
> describe the start of a journey. For example we
> can ssay that a train departs at a particular
> time. Depart is a more formal word than set
> off.

Collocations

What are collocations?

Collocations are sometimes known as 'word partners' because they are the words that go together with the word you are using. For instance, if it is raining a lot, we talk about '*heavy* rain', and if two people love each other very much, we say they are '*madly* in love'.

These words appear together more often than they would do just by chance, or just because of their meanings. For instance, it is correct to say that someone can 'steal a car', but this is not a collocation because 'steal' can be used with many different nouns. However, if we talk about someone '*committing* a crime', we are using a collocation because those words go together so strongly, and if you need a verb to go with 'crime' it *has* to be 'commit' – a verb like 'do' would not be correct.

Sometimes we can guess the collocations we want, but often it is difficult. Why do we '*pay* attention' or '*draw* conclusions'? Why do we '*tell* lies' but '*make* promises'?

That is why we have been careful to show the most useful collocations of words in this dictionary. Collocations are shown ⊞, to make it easy for you to see the words you need to learn together with the word you have looked up.

Why is it so important to learn collocations?

Words are not usually used on their own. As well as learning just one word, you need to learn the words that go around it; the words that allow you to use your word in a clear and natural way.

Knowing collocations will help you to speak and write more fluent and natural English. For example, you may know the meaning of a word like 'exam', but it is also important to know which verbs to use with it. Although it is possible to say 'I have to do an exam at the end of the year', it is much more natural to say 'I have to *take* an exam at the end of the year'. And although people will understand if you say 'I was successful in my exam', a native speaker of English would not be likely to say that. They would say 'I *passed* my exam'.

Knowing collocations will make your English more interesting and help you to express yourself better. For instance, it is fine to say 'I was very disappointed', but if you know how to say 'I was *bitterly* disappointed', your sentence has much more force, and sounds more impressive.

Knowing collocations will help you avoid mistakes. Although it is sometimes possible to guess which words to use, it is also easy to make mistakes. For instance, many learners of English say things like 'We decided to make a party for him'. This is not correct English: you should say 'We decided to *have* a party for him', or even better 'We decided to *throw* a party for him'.

Knowing collocations will improve your exam results. Many common English exams test your knowledge of collocation. You will lose marks if you use the wrong ones, and gain marks if you use correct, interesting ones.

Finding and learning collocations

Collocations are such an important part of learning a language, it is a good idea to try to learn them right from the beginning.

Look at the following simple sentences, for instance, to see how important they are, even for the type of ideas and activities we talk about nearly every day:

- I **brush** my **teeth** every morning.
- I need to **do** my **homework**.
- He **watches TV** every evening.
- It was **raining heavily** yesterday.
- My sister **wears glasses**.

When you look up a word in the dictionary, try to look for its collocations and learn them together with the word.

What sort of collocations are there?

adjective + noun	e.g. **strong accent, detailed account, heavy traffic**
verb + noun	e.g. **gain acceptance, open an account, commit a crime**
verb + adverb	e.g. **go abroad, chop finely**
noun + verb	e.g. **standards slip, war breaks out**
adverb + adjective	e.g. **hopelessly lost, pleasantly surprised**
verb + adjective	e.g. **fall asleep, get married**
noun + preposition + noun	e.g. **a sense of achievement, a piece of advice**
noun + noun	e.g. **travel arrangements, management skills**

Intensifying adverb collocations

If you look in the dictionary, you will see that there is often a much more interesting way of saying 'very' or 'extremely'.

For instance, if someone is very ill, we can say they are *seriously ill*, and if someone is very shy, we can say they are *painfully shy*. Adverbs like 'seriously' and 'painfully' are called 'intensifying adverbs' because they make words more intense, or stronger in meaning. They are useful collocations to learn, because they can make your English more interesting.

Essential Learners' Dictionary: Study Pages

Regular verb tables

Present simple tense:

I	look
you	look
he/she/it	looks
we	look
they	look

*They **work** in my office.*
*I **enjoy** swimming.*
*Yukiko **wants** to make a phone call.*

Remember to add an –s to the end of verbs in the present simple in the 3rd person (*he/she/it*).

Negative form:

I	don't look
you	don't look
he/she/it	doesn't look
we	don't look
they	don't look

*I **don't like** eggs.*
*He **doesn't speak** English.*
*We **don't want** to buy it.*

Question form:

Do	I	look?
Do	you	look?
Does	he/she/it	look?
Do	we	look?
Do	they	look?

***Do** you **work** on Saturdays?*
***Does** Carlos **want** a drink?*
***Do** you **like** football?*

Use the present simple tense:

- to talk about things that are always true or things that always happen:

  *The Earth **moves** round the sun.*

*If you **heat** water to 100°C, it **boils**.*
*My birthday **is** in April.*

- to talk about things that continue for a long time:

*Maria **wears** nice clothes.*
*We **live** in London.*
*He **works** in an office.*
*Sara **is** a doctor.*

- to talk about habits, routines and timetables:

*Juan always **goes** to the gym after work.*
*They **collect** the rubbish on Mondays.*
*The train **arrives** at 8.30.*

- with certain verbs. We do not usually use these verbs in continuous tenses, but there are exceptions:

verbs that describe feelings and ideas: *believe, dislike, feel, forget, hate, know, like, look, love, mean, need, prefer, remember, seem, think, understand, want*

*I **think** your mum is very friendly.*
*I **like** her very much.*

verbs of the senses: *taste, hear, see*

*This meat **tastes** strange.*
*I **hear** the phone ringing.*

verbs to do with possession: *have* (when it means 'possess'), *own, belong*

*Pablo **has** two sisters.*
*They **own** five cars and a motorbike.*
*That phone **belongs** to me.*

Present continuous tense:

I	am	looking
you	are	looking
he/she/it	is	looking
we	are	looking
they	are	looking

We often use the short forms *I'm, you're, he's, she's, it's, we're, they're* with this tense.

*I**'m reading** a good book.*
*He**'s working** at the moment.*

Negative form:

I	am not	looking
you	are not	looking
he/she/it	is not	looking
we	are not	looking
they	are not	looking

*I'm **not staying** in this hotel.*
*John's **not living** here at the moment – he's away at university.*

Question form:

Am	I	looking?
Are	you	looking
Is	he/she/it	looking?
Are	we	looking
Are	they	looking

*Are you **working**?*
*Is Sally **watching** TV?*

We use the present continuous tense:

- to talk about things that are happening now:

  *He's **listening** to the radio.*
  *Where is Jenny? She's **brushing** her teeth..*

- to talk about temporary situations:

  *I'm **living** in London for 6 months.*
  *I'm **studying** at Manchester University.*

- to talk about arrangements:

  *I'm **seeing** John tonight.*
  *We're **meeting** the bank manager on Friday.*

Present perfect tense:

I	have	looked
you	have	looked
he/she/it	has	looked
we	have	looked
they	have	looked

We often use the short forms *I've, you've, he's, we've* and *they've* with this tense.

*I've **lived** in New York since September.*
*Anna **has travelled** all over the world.*

Negative form:

I	have not	looked
you	have not	looked
he/she/it	has not	looked
we	have not	looked
they	have not	looked

*I can't go out. I **haven't finished** my homework yet.*
*They **haven't visited** me for a long time.*

Question form:

Have	I	looked?
Have	you	looked?
Has	he/she/it	looked?
Have	we	looked?
Have	they	looked?

> **Have** you ever **visited** this museum?
> **Has** your brother **finished** his breakfast yet?

We use the present perfect tense:

- to talk about actions which started in the past and are still continuing:

  I've lived here for 5 years. (= and I still live here now)
  I haven't done the washing-up yet. (the dishes are still dirty)

- to talk about actions that are finished, with a result in the present:

  I've finished my homework. (= so now we can go out)

- to talk about experiences, with reference to the present:

  Have you ever been to New York? (= can you tell me about it now?)

Past simple tense:

I	looked
you	looked
he/she/it	looked
we	looked
they	looked

Remember that if the verb ends in –e, you just add –d to form the past simple tense:

> *I **lived** in Rome for many years.*

Negative form:

I	didn't look
You	didn't look
He/she/it	didn't look
We	didn't look
They	didn't look

> They **didn't phone** me.
> I **didn't want** to go to the party.
> He **didn't help** me.

Question form:

Did	I	look?
Did	you	look?

Did	he/she/it	look?
Did	we	look?
Did	they	look?

Did you enjoy the film?
Did Lola come to the party?

We use the past simple tense:

- to talk about actions and situations that started and finished in the past:

I walked to the supermarket.
Marco lived in Paris for 3 years.

Past continuous tense:

I	was	looking
you	were	looking
he/she/it	was	looking
we	were	looking
they	were	looking

I was walking down the road when I saw her.
He was having a bath when the phone rang.

Negative form:

I	was not	looking
you	were not	looking
he/she/it	was not	looking
we	were not	looking
they	were not	looking

We often use the short forms *wasn't* and *weren't* in this tense.

It wasn't raining, so we didn't take our coats.
Helena wasn't expecting to see him at the party.

Question form:

Was	I	looking?
Were	you	looking?
Was	he/she/it	looking?
Were	we	looking?
Were	they	looking?

Were you eating dinner when I called?
Was Abdul listening to the teacher?

We use the past continuous tense:

- to talk about something that was happening when another action happened, or at a particular time in the past:

*While I **was watching** TV the doorbell rang.*
*We **were waiting** for a bus when it started to rain.*
*At midnight, Miguel **was** still **playing** games on the computer.*

- to say that two actions were happening at the same time:

  *While I **was cooking**, my mother **was looking after** the children.*
  ***Were** you **listening** to what I **was saying**?*

Future simple tense:

I	will	look
you	will	look
he/she/it	will	look
we	will	look
they	will	look

We often use the short forms *I'll, you'll, he'll, we'll* and *they'll* with this tense.

*I**'ll help** you to look for the book.*
*It **will be** an interesting trip.*

Negative form:

I	will not	look
you	will not	look
he/she/it	will not	look
we	will not	look
they	will not	look

We often use the short form *won't* with this tense.

*They **won't come** with me.*
*I **won't tell** anyone your secret.*

Question form:

Will	I	look?
Will	you	look?
Will	he/she/it	look?
Will	we	look?
Will	they	look?

***Will** you **call** me when you arrive?*
***Will** he **go away** for a long time?*

We use the simple future tense:

- to say that something will happen in the future:

  *I**'ll do** it later.*
  *Jack **will be** back this afternoon.*
  *The wedding **will begin** at 4 o'clock.*

- to talk about promises:

*I'll **love** you forever.*
*He'll never **forget** your kindness.*

- to talk about offers or requests:

*I'll **help** you carry that box.*
***Will** you **open** a window, please?*

- to make predictions about the future (often when there is no evidence in the present):

*I'm sure this **will be** a good year.*

Common irregular verbs:

infinitive	past tense	past participle
be	was/were	been
beat	beat	beaten
become	became	become
begin	began	begun
bend	bent	bent
bite	bit	bitten
bleed	bled	bled
blow	blew	blown
break	broke	broken
bring	brought	brought
build	built	built
burn	burned/burnt	burned/burnt
buy	bought	bought
catch	caught	caught
choose	chose	chosen
come	came	come
cost	cost	cost
cut	cut	cut
dig	dug	dug
do	did	done
draw	drew	drawn
drink	drank	drunk
drive	drove	driven
eat	ate	eaten
fall	fell	fallen
feel	felt	felt
fight	fought	fought
find	found	found
fly	flew	flown
forbid	forbade	forbidden
forget	forgot	forgotten
freeze	froze	frozen
get	got	got (US: gotten)
give	gave	given
go	went	gone
grow	grew	grown
have	had	had
hear	heard	heard

infinitive	past tense	past participle
hide	hid	hidden
hit	hit	hit
hold	held	held
hurt	hurt	hurt
keep	kept	kept
know	knew	known
lay	laid	laid
learn	learned/learnt	learned/learnt
leave	left	left
lend	lent	lent
let	let	let
lose	lost	lost
make	made	made
mean	meant	meant
meet	met	met
pay	paid	paid
put	put	put
read	read	read
ride	rode	ridden
ring	rang	rung
rise	rose	risen
run	ran	run
say	said	said
see	saw	seen
sell	sold	sold
send	sent	sent
set	set	set
shake	shook	shaken
shine	shone	shone
show	showed	shown
shut	shut	shut
sing	sang	sung
sink	sank	sunk
sit	sat	sat
sleep	slept	slept
smell	smelt	smelt
speak	spoke	spoken
spend	spent	spent
spoil	spoiled/spoilt	spoiled/spoilt
stand	stood	stood

infinitive	past tense	past participle
steal	stole	stolen
swim	swam	swum
take	took	taken
teach	taught	taught
tell	told	told
think	thought	thought
throw	threw	thrown
understand	understood	understood
wake	woke	woken
wear	wore	worn
win	won	won
write	wrote	written

Dictionary skills

Alphabetical order

This is alphabetical order:

ABCDEFGHIJKLMNOPQRSTUVWXYZ
abcdefghijklmnopqrstuvwxyz

All of the words in the dictionary are in alphabetical order. The words you look for in a dictionary are called **headwords**. When the first letters of two headwords are the same, the second letter, and then the third letter are also in alphabetical order. So *apple* comes before *carrot*, and *carrot* comes before *potato*. *Animal* comes before *apple*, and *apricot* comes after *apple* in the dictionary.

Exercise 1
Put the following words in alphabetical order. Then check your answers by finding the headwords in the dictionary.

teacher
sun
keyboard
cat
goose
American
microphone
wind
bicycle
burglar

Exercise 2
Put the following words in alphabetical order. Then check your answers by finding the headwords in the dictionary.

bouquet
birthday
broccoli
ballet
building
bridge
blouse
biology
biscuit
box

Some headwords are made of two or more words. These are called **compounds**. Just like normal headwords, compounds come in alphabetical order in the dictionary.

Exercise 3
Put the following words in alphabetical order. Then check your answers by finding the headwords in the dictionary.

mineral water
midnight
modal verb
MP3 player
make-up
mother-in-law
mobile phone
microwave oven
middle class
moonlight

Some headwords are abbreviations (short forms of longer words). These also come in alphabetical order.

Exercise 4

Put the following words in alphabetical order. Then check your answers by finding the headwords in the dictionary.

Christmas tree
certificate
traffic lights
ID
traffic jam
cm
mm
Boxing Day
HQ
BBC

Phrasal verbs are verbs which consist of two or more words, a verb and a preposition or an adverb. You have to understand the phrasal verb as a whole in order to understand its meaning. *Get up* and *find out* are phrasal verbs. Phrasal verbs come after the main verb entry, and are organised in alphabetical order.

Exercise 5

Put the following phrasal verbs in alphabetical order, and then find them in the dictionary to check your answers.

get through
get through something
get up
get round to doing something
get on
get out of something
get over something
get away with

Homonyms

Some words have more than one **part of speech.** For example, the word *record* can be a noun (*He has a criminal **record***) and a verb (*The band **are recording** a new album*). *Record* can also be an adjective (*He ran the race in **record** time*). Each of these is called a **homonym.** You need to know which part of speech a word is to help you find it in the dictionary. In this dictionary, each homonym is usually a separate headword. So *record* has three homonym headwords, one for the noun, one for the verb and one for the adjective.

Exercise 6
Look at the following sentences. For each sentence, choose the correct part of speech for the word in **bold**.

a	The loud noise **alarmed** him.	noun/verb
	My **alarm** goes off at 6 o'clock.	noun/verb
b	He has an **American** accent	noun/adjective
	Junko is an **American**, but her parents are Japanese.	noun/adjective
c	I received a job **offer** this morning.	noun/verb
	Ricardo **offered** to help me with my work.	noun/verb
d	I only went to his house **once**.	conjunction/adverb
	Once you finish your homework, you can watch TV.	conjunction/adverb
e	Could you **peel** the potatoes for me, please?	noun/verb
	Put the **peel** in the bin when you've finished.	noun/verb

Exercise 7
In the following sentences, decide what part of speech the word in **bold** is. Write *n* for a noun, *v* for a verb or *a* for an adjective. Then look up the words and decide which homonym number is the correct one for each headword.

Example:

   I'll **phone** you in the morning. v, phone 2
   I can't talk at the moment, I'm on the **phone**. n, phone 1

a   Maria **picked** some flowers from the garden. _____
   There are three dresses – please take your **pick**. _____

b   The soldiers **pinned** him to the ground. _____
   There are some **pins** by the sewing machine. _____

c   Oscar came in third **place** in the race. _____
   Nadia **placed** the cup carefully on the table. _____

d   Have you got any **plastic** bags? _____
   These chairs are made of **plastic**. _____

e   He was **presented** with a gold medal. _____
   Ana gave me a lovely **present** for my birthday. _____
   The **present** system for organizing the files works very well. _____

Homophones

In English, some words sound the same as other words, but are spelled differently. These words are called **homophones**. You need to make sure that you know how to spell a word correctly before you look it up in the dictionary.

Exercise 8

In each sentence below, choose the correct word to fill the gap. Each pair of words is pronounced the same way. Check your answers by looking up each word in the dictionary.

a   Would you like an apple or a _____?   pair/pear
    I've just bought a new _____ of trousers.   pair/pear

b   Would you like some more _____ on your pasta?   sauce/source
    The country's main _____ of energy is oil.   sauce/source

c   _____ coat is yours?   which/witch
    The _____ in the story wore a big black hat.   which/witch

d   My _____ leaves at 4.30, so I must leave now.   plain/plane
    We've painted the walls _____ white.   plain/plane

e   Yukiko loves _____ music.   sole/soul
    The _____ of my shoe is worn out.   sole/soul

f   There's a _____ in my new jumper.   hole/whole
    The economic problems are affecting the _____   hole/whole
    world.

Finding the right definition

A **definition** is the explanation of a word's meaning in the dictionary. When you have found the correct headword, you may find more than one definition. In this dictionary, the definitions are in order of frequency, so the most common definition comes first and so on.

Exercise 9
Look again at the sentences in exercise 7 above. For each one, write down the correct definition number. If there is only one definition, write *1*.

Some words have many definitions, so it can be difficult to find the right information.

Exercise 10
Look at the following sentences. Then look up the word *set¹* in the dictionary and decide which definition best matches each sentence.

a   Our teacher has set us some exercises for homework.

b   The sun sets at 8pm.

c   Wait for the glue to set before you paint it.

d   When are you going to set a date for your wedding?

e   I have to catch a plane tomorrow, so I've set my alarm for 7am.

f   The film is set in Rome and New York.

g   I set up my business in 1995.

h   He was set free after 15 years in prison.

Using the dictionary to find out about words

A dictionary entry can often give you more information about a word. For example, you can find out which other words are used with a headword, and grammatical information about a word. You can look in the definitions, but also in the boxes in some entries.

Exercise 11

Use your dictionary to find the answers to these questions. The word you need to look up to find the answer is in **bold**.

a Which of these sentences is wrong, and why?
Our holiday was **absolutely** wonderful.
Our holiday was **absolutely** OK.

b Which word is needed to complete the sentence below?
He told me the secret _____ **accident**.

c What is wrong with the following sentence?
We **accompanied** him at the airport.

d Find three things that you can **protect** somebody from.

e What is the difference between a **hedge** and a **fence**?

f Find two things that can be **first-class**.

g Name two things that you can **roast**.

h Does the Earth **roll**, spin or revolve around the sun?

i Which is bigger, a **van** or a truck?

j What is the plural of the word **accommodation**?

k Which word completes the following sentence?
I'm going to _____ a **rest** before I go to the shops.

l Name three places where you might make a **reservation**.

m Complete the following sentences using expressions with the word **hand**.
They walked _____ _____ _____ down the street.
You must _____ _____ with your mother when you cross the road.
Let me _____ you a _____ with that heavy suitcase.
You should _____ _____ with him when you meet him for the first time.

Exercise 12

The dictionary can also help you to find the correct prepositions to use with words. Look up the following verbs in the dictionary and choose the correct preposition to fill the gaps. Use the same preposition to fill the gaps in the example sentences.

VERB + PREPOSITION

a accuse someone _____ sth
The police accused him _____ murder.

b   agree _____ someone
    Janet agrees _____ me.

c   apply _____ something
    I have applied _____ a job in Australia.

d   approve _____ something
    They didn't approve _____ my behaviour.

e   argue _____ someone
    Katerina argues _____ her boyfriend about everything!

f   ask _____ something
    Shall I ask the waiter _____ some water?

g   blame someone _____ something
    Alex blamed me _____ the accident.

h   borrow something _____ someone
    Can I borrow £10 _____ you?

i   hope _____ something
    I'm hoping _____ good weather for our holidays.

j   insist _____ something
    His parents always insist _____ good behaviour.

k   lend something _____ someone
    It was raining, so Max lent his umbrella _____ me.

l   listen _____ something/someone
    Please listen _____ me when I'm talking!

m   pay _____ something
    My uncle paid _____ my plane ticket and hotel room.

n   prepare _____ something
    We need to prepare _____ the bad weather.

o   prevent someone _____ doing something
    The police prevented them _____ entering the building.

p   provide someone _____ something
    The hotel provides its guests _____ all meals.

q   suffer _____ something
    He's suffered _____ a bad back for many years.

r   talk _____ someone
    If you need to talk _____ someone, please call me.

s   thank someone _____ something
    I thanked them _____ their kindness.

t   wait _____ someone/something
    I'll wait _____ you outside the cinema.

u   worry _____ something
    Susie's very worried _____ her exams, but she'll be fine!

Exercise 13
ADJECTIVE + PREPOSITION
Look up the following adjectives in the dictionary and choose the correct preposition to fill the gaps. Use the same preposition to fill the gaps in the example sentences.

a afraid _____ something/someone
The children are afraid _____ the dark.

b ashamed _____ someone/something
You behaved very badly, and I'm ashamed _____ you.

c aware _____ something
Mina was not aware _____ the time and missed her train.

d different _____ something
I like this dress – it's different _____ all the others.

e fond _____ something/someone
Mr Morrison is very fond _____ his grandchildren.

f good _____ something
Elizabeth is very good _____ maths.

g guilty _____ something
He told the judge that he was not guilty _____ the crime.

h interested _____ something
Mia is very interested _____ horses.

i keen _____ something
Joe is keen _____ riding his bike.

j proud _____ something/someone
Cathy's son came first in the exam. She's very proud _____ him.

k sick _____ something
I'm sick _____ this terrible weather!

l similar _____ something
Your shoes are very similar _____ mine.

m tired _____ something
We're tired _____ going to the same place on holiday every year. We want to go somewhere different.

Exercise 14
NOUN + PREPOSITION
Look up the following nouns in the dictionary and choose the correct preposition to fill the gaps. Use the same preposition to fill the gaps in the example sentences.

a answer _____
Do you know the answer _____ question 3?

b attack _____
There has been an attack _____ the airport.

c _____ average
_____ average, I get about 7 hours' sleep every night.

d   decrease _____
     There has been a decrease _____ unemployment this month.

e   disadvantage _____
     One disadvantage _____ living here is that the weather is terrible.

f   _____ a hurry
     I was _____ such a hurry that I forgot my keys.

g   increase _____
     There's been a big increase _____ the number of homeless people.

h   need _____
     There is a need _____ more food for the people in the earthquake area.

i   reaction _____
     What was her reaction _____ the news?

j   reason _____
     Noriko didn't give any reason _____ her behaviour.

k   result _____
     Have you got the result _____ your tests yet?

l   solution _____
     There is no easy solution _____ this problem.

Exercise 15

The dictionary can also tell you about other words which go together. The words *make* and *do* often cause problems for learners of English because in some languages only one word is used for both of these verbs. Look up the following words in your dictionary and decide if each word is used with *make* or with *do*.

a   _____ an **arrangement**

b   _____ your **best**

c   _____ **business**

d   _____ a **decision**

e   _____ someone a **favour**

f   _____ **friends**

g   _____ **homework**

h   _____ a **job**

i   _____ a **mess**

j   _____ a **mistake**

k   _____ **money**

l   _____ a **noise**

m   _____ a **phone call**

n   _____ the **washing-up**

Pronunciation

The dictionary can tell you about the pronunciation of a word. After each headword you will see the pronunciation symbols. There is a full table of these symbols on **the inside front cover**. This is useful, because it can be difficult to see how a word is pronounced from its spelling.

Exercise 16

Using the pronunciation table on **the inside front cover**, decide what the following words are. Be careful with spellings, especially with the vowel sounds.

a   /blæk/ _____

b   /'zebrə/ _____

c   /sʌm/ _____

d   /'kɑːpɪt/ _____

e   /pleɪt/ _____

f   /ə'bʌv/ _____

g   /dʒiːnz/ _____

h   /'jeləʊ/ _____

i   /ʃɔːt/ _____

j   /'iːzɪ/ _____

Different sound, same spelling

Exercise 17

The following words have exactly the same spelling, but have different pronunciations for different meanings. Use the pronunciation guide on **the inside front cover** and the dictionary to help you decide on the correct pronunciation.

a   /liːd/ /led/

The inside of your pencil is called the **lead**. _____
You must keep your dog on a **lead** in the park. _____

b   /kləʊz/ /kləʊs/

Please **close** the door behind you. _____
Don't sit too **close** to the fire. _____

c   /wɪnd/ /waɪnd/

Wind the scarf around your neck to keep you warm. _____
Listen to the **wind** in the trees. _____

d   /tɪə(r)z/ /teə(r)z/

There were large **tears** in the curtains. _____
Magda burst into **tears** when she heard the news. _____

e   /rəʊ/ /raʊ/

Jack and Sophie had a huge **row** last night. _____
There was a **row** of empty seats in front of us. _____

Exercise 18

The following pairs of words have similar spellings but very different pronunciations. For each word, decide which vowel sound the letters in **bold** have. Check your answers by looking up the word in the dictionary. Use the pronunciation guide on **the inside front cover** to help you.

comb, bomb
break, weak
now, low
pose lose
shoe toe
lord word
cough tough
meat great
work fork

a   /ɒ/ _____

b   /ʌ/ _____

c   /ɜː/ _____

d   /iː/ _____

e   /ɔː/ _____

f   /uː/ _____

g   /aʊ/ _____

h   /əʊ/ _____

i   /eɪ/ _____

Different spelling, same sound

Exercise 19

You can see from exercise 8 above that some sounds have different possible spellings. Choose two words for each of the vowel sounds below. The vowel sounds in the words are in **bold**.

bird
day
blue
flood
greet
neat
pain
run
through
word

a   /ʌ/ _____

b   /ɜː/ _____

c　/iː/ _____

d　/uː/ _____

e　/eɪ/ _____

Shifting stress

The dictionary can also tell you where the stress (the emphasis) in a word falls. The symbol ['] shows you that the stress falls on the next syllable (= part of a word) after the mark. For example, if you look at the pronunciation for the word *abandon,* you can see that the stress falls on the second syllable:

/ə'bændən/ = a-**ban**-don

Exercise 20

Some words with more than one part of speech have the same sounds, but different stress for the different parts of speech. In the following sentences, find the correct part of speech for the word in **bold**, and then write down the correct pronunciation (including the stress marks) in the table.

	part of speech	**pronunciation**

I　I gave her a Christmas **present**.

2　Who is going to **present** the prize?

3　He visited the **desert** when he was in Morrocco.

4　How could he **desert** his family?

5　He broke the world **record**.

6　You need to **record** the results in this chart.

7　The countries of the Middle East **produce** much of the world's oil.

8　They sell their **produce** at local markets.

Silent letters

Exercise 21

Some words in English have letters which are not pronounced at all. For example, the 'b' in the word *thumb* is silent. For each of the following words, decide which letter is silent. Check the dictionary pronunciations to find out the answers.

a　castle

b　comb

c　honest

d　listen

e　wrong

Phrasal verbs

Phrasal verbs are verbs made of a verb and one or more other words. *Get up* is a phrasal verb. In exercise 5, we explained that the phrasal verbs come after the main verb entry, in alphabetical order.

Phrasal verbs can be difficult for learners to use properly, but the dictionary can help you. There are different kinds of phrasal verbs, and they work in different ways. Look at the phrasal verbs in the entry for *get* for example:

♦ PHRASAL VERBS **get away with something** to avoid being punished or criticized □ *I'm hoping to miss the next meeting, if I can get away with it.* **get on 1** to make progress □ **+ with** *I need to get on with my work.* □ *How are you getting on in your new job?* **2** to be friendly □ *Pierre and Alex don't really get on.* **get out of something** to avoid doing something □ *He'll do anything to get out of the washing up.* **get over something** to feel better after being ill or unhappy □ *He never really got over his wife's death.* **get round to doing something** to do something that you have been intending to do □ *I'd like to do more exercise, but I never seem to get round to it.* **get through** to manage to talk to someone on the telephone □ *I tried to ring her, but I couldn't get through.* **get through something** to reach the end of a difficult situation □ *It was a terrible illness, but his determination helped to get him through it.* **get (someone) up** to wake up and get out of bed □ *I always get up early.* □ *My Dad gets me up in the morning.*

a. intransitive phrasal verbs

get through (manage to talk to someone on the telephone) is an intransitive verb; it does not take a direct object. We do not say that you *get through something* or *get through someone*. In the dictionary, you can see the intransitive phrasal verbs because they do not have *someone* or *something* in the headword.

Which other *get* phrasal verbs are intransitive?

b. transitive phrasal verbs

Other phrasal verbs are **transitive**; they take a direct object. There are three main types of transitive phrasal verbs:

> **get over something** is an **inseparable** phrasal verb. The object (*something*) always comes **after** the phrasal verb. You **get over an illness**, you do not ~~get an illness over~~.

You can see the inseparable phrasal verbs in the dictionary because they have *something* or *someone* **after** the phrasal verb.

Which other *get* phrasal verbs are inseparable?

Other phrasal verbs are **separable**. The object of these verbs can go in the middle of the phrasal verb or after it. When the object is a pronoun (*it/he/she* etc), it always goes in the middle of the phrasal verb. There are no separable phrasal verbs in *get*. However, if you look at the entry for *do* you can see a separable phrasal verb:

♦ PHRASAL VERBS **do something up**
 1 to fasten a piece of clothing □ *Do your jacket up.*
 2 to repair or decorate a room or building **do without (something)** to manage without something

do something up is a separable phrasal verb. You can see this in the dictionary, because *something* comes in the middle of the phrasal verb headword. So you can say *'Do your jacket up'* or *'Do up your jacket'*, but you always say *'Do it up'*, not *'Do up it'*.

Some phrasal verbs can be used with or without a direct object. In these verbs, the object is in brackets () in the headword. *Get (someone) up* is an example. You can also see that when this verb has an object, it is separable, because *someone* is in the middle of the phrasal verb. You can see from the examples how we use this verb:

   I always get up early. (no object)
   My Dad gets me up in the morning. (object)

do without is also used with and without an object, but this time it is inseparable, so the object always comes after the phrasal verb.

   We didn't have much money for luxuries, so we did without. (no object)
   We didn't have much money, so we did without a car. (object after phrasal verb)
   We couldn't afford the car, so we did without it. (pronoun object after phrasal verb)
   We couldn't afford the car, so we did it without.

Exercise 22
Look at the phrasal verbs section in the verb *take* in your dictionary. Use the information above and in the dictionary entries to decide whether the sentences below are correct or incorrect. If they are incorrect, correct the mistakes. The phrasal verbs are in **bold** in the sentences below.

a   The plane **took off** the ground.

b   Noah **took off** his shoes and sat down.

c   He **takes** his father **after**. They both have a great sense of humour.

d   I love riding horses. I **took up** it when I was a child.

e   I **took up** yoga when I had a bad back.

f   Oh that's the doorbell. Could you **take** this **over** while I answer it?

g   I **took** his phone number **down** on a piece of paper.

h   The police **took down** our names.

i   What time does your flight **take off**?

j   Are you hot in your coat? Why don't you **take** it **off**?

Cross references

In some entries, you will find **cross references**. These show you where in the dictionary you can find more information about a word. One kind of cross reference shows you where to find information about idioms and phrases. These can be difficult to find if you don't know which word to look up. For example, in entry **have** there is a cross reference to **cake**:

---

have[3] /hæv/ VERB [has, having, had]
1 used for describing someone or something □ *He has got black hair.* □ *The room had patches of damp on the walls.* □ *The soup had a delicious flavour.*
2 to own something □ *He has a house in Spain.* □ *I have got three brothers.* □ *She has the determination to win.*
➡ *go to* **have your** cake **and eat it**

This tells you to look for the idiom *have your cake and eat it* at the headword **cake**. If you then look up **cake**, you can find out the meaning of this expression:

---

cake /keɪk/ NOUN [*plural* cakes] a sweet food made from a baked mixture, usually of flour, sugar, butter and eggs 🔁 *a birthday cake* 🔁 *He made a cake for the school fair.* 🔁 *Would you like another slice of chocolate cake?*
◆ IDIOM **have your cake and eat it** to get all the advantages of a situation in a way that is unfair

---

Exercise 23
Look up each of the following words in your dictionary. In each entry, you will find a cross reference to an idiom. Write down the idiom, and then use the cross reference to find a definition for the idiom.

	idiom	definition
heart		
catch		
pull		
take		
turn[1]		

Some cross references tell you about American words. American and British English speakers sometimes use different words to describe the same thing. If you look up an American word in this dictionary, you will usually find a cross-reference to a British word, where you can find the definition.

Exercise 24
Use your dictionary to find the British word for the following American words.

a   candy

b   chip

c   grade

d   homicide

e   jelly

f   line

Exercise 25

Sometimes, the cross reference or the definition tells you that the spelling is different in British English. Again, the main information will be at the British English entry. What is the British spelling of the following words? Use your dictionary to help you.

a   favorite

b   gray

c   theater

KEY

Exercise 1

American

bicycle

burglar

cat

goose

keyboard

microphone

sun

teacher

wind

Exercise 2

ballet

biology

birthday

biscuit

blouse

bouquet

box

bridge

broccoli

building

Exercise 3

make-up

microwave oven

middle class

midnight

mineral water

mobile phone

modal verb

moonlight

mother-in-law

MP3 player

Exercise 4

BBC

Boxing Day

certificate

Christmas tree

cm

HQ

ID

mm

traffic jam

traffic lights

Exercise 5

get away with

get on

get out of something

get over something

get round to doing something

gct through

get through something

get up

Exercise 6

a   verb
    noun

b   adjective
    noun

c   noun
    verb

d   adverb
    conjunction

e   verb
    noun

Exercise 7

a   v, pick 1
n, pick 2

b   v, pin 2
n, pin 1

c   n, place 1
v, place 2

d   a, plastic 2
n, plastic 1

e   v, present 3
n, present 1
a, present 2

Exercise 8

a   Would you like an apple or a pear?
I've just bought a new pair of
trousers.

b   Would you like some more sauce
on your pasta?
The country's main source of energy
is oil.

c   Which coat is yours?
The witch in the story wore a big
black hat.

d   My plane leaves at 4.30, so I must
leave now.
We've painted the walls plain white.

e   Yukiko loves soul music.
The sole of my shoe is worn out.

f   There's a hole in my new jumper.
The economic problems are
affecting the whole world.

Exercise 9

a   definition 2, definition 1

b   definition 2, definition 1

c   definition 6, definition 1

d   definition 1, definition 1

e   definition 1, definition 1, definition 2

Exercise 10

a   7

b   6

c   10

d   2

e   5

f   4

g   phrasal verb *set something up*

h   9

Exercise 11

a   Sentence 2 is wrong. 'Absolutely'
meaning 'extremely' is only used
before adjectives with very strong
meanings. So *'absolutely wonderful'* is
OK, but *'absolutely OK'* is not.

b   by accident (sense 2)

c   The correct preposition is *to* (sense 1):
*We accompanied him **to** the airport*.

d   harm, danger (in definition), frost (in
example)

e   a hedge is made of bushes or trees,
a fence is made of wood or metal.

f   a ticket, a stamp (in examples)

g   meat, vegetables (in definition)

h   The Earth *revolves* around the sun
(see the Thesaurus box).

i   a truck (in definition)

j   it has no plural (in part of speech and
in usage box)

k *I'm going to have a rest.* (in example for definition 2)

l *a restaurant, a hotel, a plane* (in definition)

m *hand in hand, hold hands, give you a hand, shake hands*

Exercise 12

a	of	g	for	m	for	s	for
b	with	h	from	n	for	t	for
c	for	i	for	o	from	u	about
d	of	j	on	p	with		
e	with	k	to	q	from		
f	for	l	to	r	to		

Exercise 13

a	of	e	of	i	on	m	of
b	of	f	at	j	of		
c	of	g	of	k	of		
d	from	h	in	l	to		

Exercise 14

a	to	d	in	g	in	j	for
b	on	e	of	h	for	k	of
c	on	f	in	i	to	l	to

Exercise 15

a	make	f	make	k	make
b	do	g	do	l	make
c	do	h	do	m	make
d	make	i	make	n	do
e	do	j	make		

Exercise 16

a	black	e	plate	i	short
b	zebra	f	above	j	easy
c	sum	g	jeans		
d	carpet	h	yellow		

Exercise 17

a /led/, /liːd/

b /kləʊz/, /kləʊs/

c /waɪnd/, /wɪnd/

d /teə(r)z/, /tɪə(r)z/

e /raʊ/, /rəʊ/

Exercise 18

a bomb, cough

b tough

c word, work

d weak, meat

e lord, fork

f lose, shoe

g now

h comb, low, pose, toe

i break, great

Exercise 19

a flood, run

b bird, word

c greet, neat

d blue, through

e day, pain

Exercise 20

		part of speech	pronunciation
1	I gave her a Christmas **present**.	noun	/'prezənt/
2	Who is going to **present** the prize?	verb	/prɪ'zent/
3	He visited the **desert** when he was in Morrocco.	noun	/dɪ'zɜːt/
4	How could he **desert** his family?	verb	/'dezət/
5	He broke the world **record**.	noun	/'rekɔːd/
6	You need to **record** the results in this chart.	verb	/rɪ'kɔːd/
7	The countries of the Middle East **produce** much of the world's oil.	verb	/prə'djuːs/
8	They sell their **produce** at local markets.	noun	/'prɒdjuːs/

Exercise 21

a castle – silent t

b comb – silent b

c honest – silent h

d listen – silent t

e wrong – silent w

Exercise 22

a *The plane took off.* (*take off* is intransitive, so doesn't take a direct object)

b correct (*take off* is separable with this meaning, so the object goes in the middle of or after the phrasal verb when it is not a pronoun)

c *He takes after his father.* (*take after* is inseparable, so the object goes after the phrasal verb).

d *I took it up when I was a child.* (*take up* is separable, so the pronoun *it* always goes in the middle of the phrasal verb)

e correct (the object can go in the middle or after the verb if it is not a pronoun)

f *Could you take over while I answer it?* (*take over* is intransitive, so doesn't take a direct object)

g correct (*take down* is separable so the object can go in the middle or after the verb if it is not a pronoun)

h correct (*take down* is separable so the object can go in the middle or after the verb if it is not a pronoun)

i correct (*take off* is intransitive with this meaning, so no direct object)

j correct (*take off* is separable, so the pronoun *it* always goes in the middle of the phrasal verb)

Exercise 23

	idiom	definition
heart	break someone's heart	to make someone very unhappy
catch	catch someone's eye	if something catches your eye, you notice it
pull	pull your socks up	to try to improve your behaviour or work
take	take your breath away	to surprise you very much
turn¹	turn your nose up at something	to refuse to accept something because you do not think it is good enough for you

Exercise 24

a	sweet	**c**	form	**e**	jam
b	crisp	**d**	murder	**f**	queue

Exercise 25

a	favourite	**b**	grey	**c**	theatre

A*a*

A *or* **a** /eɪ/ the first letter of the alphabet

a *or* **an** /ən/ DETERMINER
1 used before a noun to refer to one person or thing but not a particular person or thing □ *I need a pen.* □ *I'd love to have a baby.*
2 one □ *a hundred miles*
3 each or every □ *He gets £5 a week.*

➤ Remember to use **an** (and not **a**) before a word that begins with a vowel, or a word that sounds as if it begins with a vowel □ *a bag* □ *an apple* □ *an hour*

abandon /ə'bændən/ VERB [abandons, abandoning, abandoned] to leave someone or something, often not intending to go back □ *He abandoned the car and walked the rest of the way.* □ *How could she abandon her family like that?*

abbreviation /ə,briː'vɪ'eɪʃən/ NOUN [plural abbreviations] a short form of a word or phrase □ **+ of** *UK is an abbreviation of United Kingdom.*

ABC /,eɪbiː'siː/ NOUN [plural ABCs] the alphabet □ *The children were learning their ABC.*

abdomen /'æbdəmən/ NOUN [plural abdomens] the part of an animal or person's body that contains the stomach

abduct /æb'dʌkt/ VERB [abducts, abducting, abducted] to take someone away by using force □ *Two more tourists have been abducted from their hotel room.*

ability /ə'bɪlɪti/ NOUN [plural abilities] someone who has the ability to do something is able to do it or has the skill to do it □ **+ to do something** *Not everyone has the ability to play a musical instrument.*

➤ Remember that **ability** is followed by the structure **to do something**:
✓ *her ability to drive*
✗ *her ability of driving*

able /'eɪbəl/ ADJECTIVE able to do something if you are able to do something, you can do it □ *He wasn't able to run fast enough.* □ *Will you be able to help me?*

abnormal /æb'nɔːməl/ ADJECTIVE not normal, especially in a way that worries you □ *This is abnormal behaviour for a five-year-old.*

abolish /ə'bɒlɪʃ/ VERB [abolishes, abolishing, abolished] to get rid of a rule or a way of doing something □ *The school has abolished its uniform.*

abolition /,æbə'lɪʃən/ NOUN, NO PLURAL getting rid of a law or a way of doing something □ *the abolition of slavery*

about¹ /ə'baʊt/ PREPOSITION
1 on the subject of □ *a book about bats* □ *a talk about Spain*
2 in different parts of a place □ *Clothes were scattered about the room.*
3 What about/How about something? used to make a suggestion □ *How about going for a walk?*

about² /ə'baʊt/ ADVERB
1 not exactly but almost the number or amount given □ *about five years ago* □ *about four centimetres*
2 in or to different parts of a place □ *We started moving things about.* □ *They were running about all day.*
3 about to do something if you are about to do something, you are going to do it very soon □ *I was about to leave when the phone rang.* □ *I think it's about to rain.*

above /ə'bʌv/ PREPOSITION, ADVERB
1 in a higher position than something else □ *the shelf above the sink* □ *clouds in the sky above*
2 more than an amount or level □ *two degrees above zero* □ *in the class above me*
3 above all more than anything else □ *Above all, I'm grateful to my parents.*

abroad /ə'brɔːd/ ADVERB in or to a foreign country ⊞ *We always go abroad for our holidays.* □ *She's abroad at the moment.*

abrupt /ə'brʌpt/ ADJECTIVE
1 sudden and unexpected □ *The driver made an abrupt change of direction.*
2 rude and unfriendly ⊞ *She has rather an abrupt manner.*

absence /'æbsəns/ NOUN [plural absences] being away from a place □ *Your absence from the meeting was noticed.*

absent /ˈæbsənt/ ADJECTIVE not at a place where you are expected to be □ + *from* She has been absent from school twice this week. □ Is anyone absent today?

➤ THESAURUS: If you are **absent**, you are not at a place where you are expected to be. For example, you might be absent from school or work because you are ill. If you are **away** from work, you might be out of the office on business or on holiday. If a person is **missing**, they are not where you expect them to be, and you do not know where they are. If a person or thing has **gone**, it was in a place, but now it is no longer there.

absolute /ˈæbsəluːt/ ADJECTIVE complete □ I have absolute trust in her. □ That's absolute rubbish!

absolutely /ˈæbsəluːtlɪ/ ADVERB
1 completely □ Are you absolutely sure you locked the door?
2 extremely □ This cake is absolutely delicious! □ That's absolutely ridiculous!
3 used to agree or to give permission □ 'We should write and thank them'. 'Absolutely'.

➤ **Absolutely** meaning 'extremely' is only used before adjectives with very strong meanings:
✓ That's absolutely crazy.
✗ That's absolutely silly.
✓ She's absolutely beautiful.
✗ She's absolutely pretty.

absorb /əbˈsɔːb/ VERB [absorbs, absorbing, absorbed] to take up liquid and keep it inside □ The bath mat will absorb the splashes.

absorbent /əbˈsɔːbənt/ ADJECTIVE an absorbent material is able to take up liquid and keep it inside □ absorbent kitchen towels
absorbing /əbˈsɔːbɪŋ/ ADJECTIVE very interesting and taking all your attention □ an absorbing puzzle
absurd /əbˈsɜːd/ ADJECTIVE very silly □ What an absurd idea!
abuse¹ /əˈbjuːs/ NOUN [plural abuses]
1 using something the wrong way for a bad reason □ This is an abuse of power. □ alcohol abuse (= drinking too much alcohol)
2 violence or bad treatment □ child abuse
3 insults □ They shouted abuse at us.
• **abusive** /əˈbjuːsɪv/ ADJECTIVE rude or insulting □ abusive language
abuse² /əˈbjuːz/ VERB [abuses, abusing, abused]
1 to use something the wrong way for a bad purpose □ She abused people's trust in order to steal money from them.
2 to hurt someone or to treat them badly □ He was abused in prison.

➤ The noun **abuse** ends with an **ss** sound. The verb **abuse** ends with a **z** sound.

academic /ˌækəˈdemɪk/ ADJECTIVE to do with studying and education □ academic qualifications □ the academic year

academy /əˈkædəmɪ/ NOUN [plural academies]
1 a school or college where you learn about a particular subject □ a science academy
2 an organization that supports a particular subject □ the Academy of Ancient Music
accelerate /əkˈseləreɪt/ VERB [accelerates, accelerating, accelerated] to drive faster □ She accelerated round the corner.

accent /ˈæksent/ NOUN [plural accents]
1 the way people from a particular area pronounce words □ I have a Scottish accent. 🔊 I speak German with a strong English accent.
2 a mark over a letter that shows how to pronounce it, for example in the word 'café'

➤ THESAURUS: Your **accent** is the way that you say words, according to where you come from. For example, you may speak English with a Scottish accent or a German accent. **Pronunciation** is the sound of a word or a letter. **Tone** refers to the feeling with which you speak a word, for example, your tone of voice may be angry or kind.

accept /əkˈsept/ VERB [accepts, accepting, accepted]
1 to take something that someone offers you □ + *from* He accepted some food from us. □ She won't accept help from anyone.
2 to say yes to an invitation □ We've accepted his invitation to lunch.
3 to agree that something is true □ + *that* I accept that I was wrong and I'm sorry.

acceptable /əkˈseptəbəl/ ADJECTIVE good enough □ This kind of behaviour isn't acceptable!

acceptance /əkˈseptəns/ NOUN, NO PLURAL
1 taking something that is given or offered to you □ We are delighted about her acceptance of the job.
2 when you agree that something is true, good or necessary 🔊 His ideas on education never gained acceptance.

access /ˈækses/ NOUN, NO PLURAL
1 when you are able to see or use something □ + *to* They don't have access to a doctor. 🔊 Do you have Internet access?
2 a way of getting to or entering a place □ + *to* The builders will need access to the house while you're out at work.
• **accessible** /əkˈsesəbəl/ ADJECTIVE
1 easy to get to □ The house is not very accessible.
2 easy to see and use □ We make the information accessible to the public.
3 easy to understand □ Make sure you use clear, accessible language.

accident /ˈæksɪdənt/ NOUN [plural accidents]
1 a bad thing that happens that is not intended
🔁 *Don's had an accident.* 🔁 *a serious/fatal accident*
□ *She was injured in a road traffic accident.* □ *I'm sorry I broke your clock – it was an accident.*
2 by accident if something happens by accident, it is not intended □ *I dropped the glass by accident and it smashed.*

accidental /ˌæksɪˈdentəl/ ADJECTIVE not intended
🔁 *There was a lot of accidental damage.*
accidentally /ˌæksɪˈdentəlɪ/ ADVERB by accident
□ *I accidentally shut the car door and locked my keys inside.*
accommodate /əˈkɒmədeɪt/ VERB
[accommodates, accommodating, accommodated]
1 to find someone a place to stay □ *The whole group can be accommodated in the same hotel.*
2 to be big enough for someone or something
□ *This room could easily accommodate ten people.*

accommodation /əˌkɒməˈdeɪʃən/ NOUN, NO PLURAL somewhere to stay or live 🔁 *She's staying in rented accommodation.* 🔁 *Does the college provide accommodation?*

> ➤ In UK English **accommodation** is never used in the plural:
> ✓ *Accommodation is very expensive.*
> ✗ Accommodations are very expensive.

accompany /əˈkʌmpənɪ/ VERB [accompanies, accompanying, accompanied]
1 to go with someone □ *+ to* *We accompanied him to the station.*
2 to play an instrument, especially the piano, while someone else sings a song or plays another instrument □ *Her sister usually accompanies her on the piano.*

accomplish /əˈkʌmplɪʃ/ VERB [accomplishes, accomplishing, accomplished] to manage to do something □ *The children accomplished the task in a few minutes.*
accomplishment /əˈkʌmplɪʃmənt/ NOUN [plural accomplishments] when you finish something successfully

according to /əˈkɔːdɪŋ tuː/ PREPOSITION
1 as said or written by someone □ *Hannah's ill, according to Lucy.* □ *According to the dictionary, there are two m's in 'accommodation'.*
2 using a particular measurement or system
□ *You'll be paid according to how much work you have done.* 🔁 *Everything went according to plan (– happened as intended).*

account /əˈkaunt/ NOUN [plural accounts]
1 a description of something that has happened
🔁 *He gave an account of his journey.*
2 an arrangement with a bank to keep money there
🔁 *I opened a savings account.* □ *Which account do you want to pay this cheque into?*

3 take something into account to consider something when you are thinking about a situation or a decision □ *Will they take my age into account when they decide who can go?*
4 on no account certainly not □ *On no account are you to stay out after ten o'clock.*

> ➤ **THESAURUS:** An account or a description is something you write or say. A report is usually more formal and may be spoken (for example, a news report) or written. For example, teachers write reports on their students. A statement is an official report of something, which is often written. For example, a witness might make a statement to the police describing what they saw.

◆ PHRASAL VERB [accounts, accounting, accounted]
account for something to be the reason for something □ *The fact that it's her birthday accounts for all the visitors she's had today.*

accounts /əˈkaunts/ PLURAL NOUN written records of the money received and spent by a person or organization
accumulate /əˈkjuːmjuleɪt/ VERB [accumulates, accumulating, accumulated] to collect a number or amount of something, or to increase in number or amount □ *Greenhouse gases are accumulating in the Earth's atmosphere.*
accuracy /ˈækjurəsɪ/ NOUN, NO PLURAL being exactly correct □ *Please check the accuracy of this measurement.*
accurate /ˈækjurət/ ADJECTIVE exactly correct 🔁 *an accurate description* 🔁 *accurate measurements*
🔁 *What they said was pretty accurate.*
accusation /ˌækjuːˈzeɪʃən/ NOUN [plural accusations] a statement saying that someone has done something bad 🔁 *She has made some accusations against me.* 🔁 *These are serious accusations.*

accuse /əˈkjuːz/ VERB [accuses, accusing, accused] to say that someone has done something bad □ *+ of* *He was accused of murder.* □ *Are you accusing me of lying?*

ace /eɪs/ NOUN [plural aces] a playing card with one symbol on it which has the highest or lowest value in games □ *the ace of spades*

ache[1] /eɪk/ NOUN [plural aches] a pain which is not strong but continues for a long time 🔁 *I started getting aches and pains.* □ *She could feel an ache in her back.*

ache[1] /eɪk/ VERB [aches, aching, ached] to hurt for a long time, especially in a way which is not strong □ *My arm aches from playing too much tennis.*

achieve /əˈtʃiːv/ VERB [achieves, achieving, achieved] to succeed in doing or getting something good, especially by trying hard □ *We have achieved everything we wanted to do.* □ *She has achieved a very high standard.*

achievement /əˈtʃiːvmənt/ NOUN [plural achievements] a success or a good result □ *Reaching the finals is a great achievement.*

acid /ˈæsɪd/ NOUN [plural acids] a type of chemical. Strong acids can dissolve metals. A chemistry word.

acknowledge /əkˈnɒlɪdʒ/ VERB [acknowledges, acknowledging, acknowledged]
1 to admit that something is true □ *I acknowledge that you were right.*
2 to tell someone that you have got something they sent you □ *They never acknowledge my letters.*

acquire /əˈkwaɪə(r)/ VERB [acquires, acquiring, acquired] a formal word meaning to get or to buy something □ *I managed to acquire a copy of the tape.* □ *A Russian billionaire recently acquired 25% of the company.*

acre /ˈeɪkə(r)/ NOUN [plural acres] a unit for measuring the area of land, equal to 4047 square metres

acrobat /ˈækrəbæt/ NOUN [plural acrobats] someone who performs skilful physical movements, like jumping and balancing, to entertain people

across /əˈkrɒs/ PREPOSITION, ADVERB
1 from one side of something to the other □ *a bridge across the river* □ *I ran across the road.* □ *Don't run, but walk across quickly.* □ *clouds moving across the sky*
2 on the opposite side □ *Their house is across the river from ours.*

act¹ /ækt/ VERB [acts, acting, acted]
1 to behave in a particular way 🔁 *Stop acting like a baby!* 🔁 *Police thought the man was acting suspiciously.*
2 to do something 🔁 *The hospital acted quickly to solve the problem.* □ *We must act now to save the planet!*
3 to perform in a film or in the theatre □ *+ in He has acted in more than 50 films.*
◆ PHRASAL VERB **act as something** to have a particular effect or to do a particular job □ *Our driver also acted as interpreter.* □ *The sheet acted as a curtain.*

act² /ækt/ NOUN [plural acts]
1 something that someone does 🔁 *a terrorist act* 🔁 *He was accused of committing a criminal act.* □ *+ of an act of kindness*
2 a part of a theatre performance □ *He appears in the third act of the play.*
3 a short performance, or the people in the performance □ *a comedy act*

acting /ˈæktɪŋ/ NOUN, NO PLURAL performing in films or in the theatre □ *There was some brilliant acting in the film.*

action /ˈækʃən/ NOUN [plural actions]
1 something you do 🔁 *We must take action to prevent a disaster.* 🔁 *They need to decide on a course of action* (= what to do). □ *He has to take responsibility for his actions.*
2 the action what happens in the story of a film, book or theatre play □ *Most of the action takes place in America.*
3 out of action not working □ *My car's out of action at the moment.*

activate /ˈæktɪveɪt/ VERB [activates, activating, activated] to make something start working □ *Someone activated the fire alarm.*

active /ˈæktɪv/ ADJECTIVE
1 busy doing things or involved in an activity □ *+ in Her mum's very active in the drama club.* 🔁 *He remained politically active throughout his life.* 🔁 *Fathers are taking a more active role in their children's lives.*
2 moving around a lot 🔁 *She's still physically active.* 🔁 *Try to keep active as you grow older.*
3 in grammar, an active verb or sentence has a subject that performs the action of the verb, for example in the sentence 'The cat chased the mouse '.

activist /ˈæktɪvɪst/ NOUN [plural activists] someone who tries to change society by doing things that people notice □ *animal rights activists*

activity /ækˈtɪvəti/ NOUN [plural activities]
1 something you do, especially something you do for fun, in an organized way 🔁 *Outdoor activities include sailing and horse riding.* 🔁 *a variety of sporting activities*
2 no plural being active or busy generally 🔁 *Children need regular physical activity.* 🔁 *There was a flurry of activity* (= a lot of things happening) *for a few days.*

actor /ˈæktə(r)/ NOUN [plural actors] someone who performs in a film or in the theatre

actress /ˈæktrɪs/ NOUN [plural actresses] a woman who performs in a film or in the theatre

actual /ˈæktʃuəl/ ADJECTIVE really true or exact 🔁 *We guessed there were about 100 people but the actual number was 110.*

➤ **Actual** means 'true' or 'exact'. It does not mean 'existing now'. Adjectives that mean 'existing now' are 'present' and 'current':
✓ *My current job involves a lot of travel.*
✗ *My actual job involves a lot of travel.*

actually /ˈæktʃuəli/ ADVERB
1 used to emphasize what is true □ *Actually, I haven't read any of his books.* □ *We haven't actually chosen a name yet.*
2 used to emphasize something surprising □ *Instead of improving, things have actually got worse.*

acute /əˈkjuːt/ ADJECTIVE
1 an acute problem, especially an illness, is very bad □ *acute appendicitis*
2 an acute angle is less than 90°. A mathematics word.

AD /ˌeɪˈdiː/ ABBREVIATION used before or after a date to show that the date was after the birth of Jesus Christ □ *95 AD*
➡ *go to BC*

ad /æd/ NOUN [plural ads] an informal short way to say or write **advertisement**

adapt /əˈdæpt/ VERB [adapts, adapting, adapted]
1 to change so that you become more happy or comfortable in a new situation □ *It didn't take long to adapt to the heat.*
2 to change something to make it more suitable □ *The design can be adapted for use in a variety of situations.*

adaptable /əˈdæptəbəl/ ADJECTIVE able to deal with new or different situations

add /æd/ VERB [adds, adding, added]
1 to put things together □ *+ to Add the sugar to the egg mixture.*
2 to put two or more numbers or amounts together □ *Add two and two.*
3 to say or write something more □ *'You could take the letter yourself – if you don't mind?' he added.* □ *+ that A police spokesman added that the two arrests weren't linked.*
◆ PHRASAL VERB **add (something) up** to find the total of numbers put together □ *Can you add these numbers up in your head?*

addict /ˈædɪkt/ NOUN [plural addicts] someone who cannot stop taking a drug 🔁 *a drug addict*

addiction /əˈdɪkʃən/ NOUN [plural addictions] not being able to stop taking a drug □ *alcohol addiction*

addition /əˈdɪʃən/ NOUN [plural additions]
1 in addition (to something) extra or added to something □ *The schools offer extra subjects in addition to the basic curriculum.*
2 no plural the process of adding numbers together □ *The pupils are learning simple addition.*
3 something that has been added or when something is added 🔁 *There are four new additions to our menu.* 🔁 *The changes include the addition of a swimming pool.*

address¹ /əˈdres/ NOUN [plural addresses]
1 the details of the building, the street and the town where someone lives □ *I'll give you my address and telephone number.* 🔁 *Here is a list of the names and addresses of all the members.*
2 the numbers, letters and symbols that are used to send e-mails or to find pages on the Internet. A computing word 🔁 *What's your e-mail address?* 🔁 *Our web address is in the brochure.*

address² /əˈdres/ VERB [addresses, addressing, addressed]

1 to write an address on an envelope
2 to speak to someone □ *Were you addressing me?*

adequate /ˈædɪkwət/ ADJECTIVE enough □ *Three rooms should be adequate for our family.* □ *There's an adequate supply of clean water.*

adjective /ˈædʒɪktɪv/ NOUN [plural adjectives] a word that tells you something about a noun. For example, *difficult, good* and *stupid* are adjectives.

adjust /əˈdʒʌst/ VERB [adjusts, adjusting, adjusted]
1 to change something slightly □ *I adjusted the clock by two minutes.*
2 to get used to a new situation □ *It was difficult to adjust to living in a flat.*

admiral /ˈædmərəl/ NOUN [plural admirals] one of the most important officers in the navy

admiration /ˌædməˈreɪʃən/ NOUN, NO PLURAL a feeling of admiring someone or something □ *+ for I have great admiration for her work.*

admire /ədˈmaɪə(r)/ VERB [admires, admiring, admired]
1 to like and respect someone or something very much □ *He was someone I admired greatly.* □ *+ for I admired her for her courage in speaking out.*
2 to enjoy looking at something 🔁 *We stopped at the top of the hill to admire the view.*

admission /ədˈmɪʃən/ NOUN [plural admissions]
1 when someone goes into a place or joins a university or other organization □ *A sign on the door said 'No admission'.* □ *the university admissions process*
2 no plural the cost of going into a place □ *We don't charge admission here.* □ *Adult admission is £10.*

admit /ədˈmɪt/ VERB [admits, admitting, admitted]
1 to agree that you have done something bad □ *+ (that) I admit that I should have told you sooner.* □ *+ to She admitted to cheating.* □ *He admitted his mistake.*
2 to agree that something is true □ *I admit that this is a difficult exercise, but do your best.*
3 to allow someone to go into a place or to take someone to hospital □ *They won't admit anyone wearing trainers.* □ *+ to The next morning he was admitted to hospital.*

adolescence /ˌædəˈlesəns/ ADJECTIVE to do with the period of your life between being a child and becoming an adult □ *Martha had a difficult adolescence.*

adolescent /ˌædəˈlesənt/ NOUN [plural adolescents] someone older than a child, but not yet an adult □ *adolescent girls/boys*

adopt /əˈdɒpt/ VERB [adopts, adopting, adopted] to take someone else's child into your family and legally become their parent □ *I always knew I had been adopted.*

adore /ə'dɔ:(r)/ VERB [adores, adoring, adored] to love something or someone very much □ *She adores her father.*

adult[1] /'ædʌlt/ NOUN [plural adults] someone who is no longer a child □ *The activity is suitable for adults and children.*

adult[2] /'ædʌlt/ ADJECTIVE to do with or for adults □ *adult sizes* □ *The film is aimed at an adult audience.*

advance[1] /əd'va:ns/ NOUN [plural advances]
1 in advance before something is needed or before a particular time □ *I arrived in advance to make sure everything was ready.* □ *We prepared all the food in advance.*
2 progress or new things □ *technological advances* □ *We have to keep up with the latest advances in medicine.*
3 a movement towards a place by an army □ *The troops continued their advance on the city.*

advance[2] /əd'va:ns/ VERB [advances, advancing, advanced]
1 to make progress □ *Technology is advancing rapidly.*
2 to move forwards □ *The crowd advanced towards us.* □ *The army is advancing on our borders.*

advanced /əd'va:nst/ ADJECTIVE
1 the newest or most developed □ *the most technologically advanced facilities*
2 at a high academic level □ *an advanced Spanish course* □ *advanced students*

advantage /əd'va:ntɪdʒ/ NOUN [plural advantages]
1 something good or helpful about a situation □ **+ of** *the advantages of working from home* □ *Being tall does have some advantages.*
2 something that helps you to succeed □ **+ over** *Max had an advantage over the others as he already spoke Italian.* 🖻 *Her long legs give her an advantage in the high jump.* 🖻 *an unfair advantage*
3 take advantage of something to use a situation well □ *We took advantage of the sunshine to get the clothes dry.*
4 take advantage of someone to get what you want from someone in an unfair way □ *She's very generous and her children take advantage of her.*

adventure /əd'ventʃə(r)/ NOUN [plural adventures] something exciting that happens to you □ *A visit to the jungle would be a real adventure for us.*

adventurous /əd'ventʃərəs/ ADJECTIVE an adventurous person likes to do exciting new things □ *He's more adventurous than his brother.*

adverb /'ædvɜ:b/ NOUN [plural adverbs] a word that you use to describe a verb or an adjective. For example, *really*, *badly*, *abroad* and *often* are adverbs.

advert /'ædvɜ:t/ NOUN [plural adverts] a short word for an **advertisement**

advertise /'ædvətaɪz/ VERB [advertises, advertising, advertised] to tell people about something in order to persuade them to buy it or use it □ *They advertise their products in magazines.*

advertisement /əd'vɜ:tɪsmənt/ NOUN [plural advertisements] a picture, short article or film about something to persuade people to buy it or use it 🖻 *a television/newspaper advertisement* □ **+ for** *I saw an advertisement for a new chocolate bar.*

advertising /'ædvətaɪzɪŋ/ NOUN, NO PLURAL the business of making advertisements □ *She works in advertising.* 🖻 *an advertising campaign*

advice /əd'vaɪs/ NOUN, NO PLURAL suggestions about what you think someone should do 🖻 *She gave me some good advice.* 🖻 *I decided to take Jane's advice and go to the doctor's.* 🖻 *May I offer a piece of advice?* □ **+ on** *They provide expert advice on career development.*

► Remember that **advice** with a **c** is a noun and **advise** with an **s** is a verb □ *Can you give me some advice?* □ *Can you advise me?*

► Remember also that you say **any/some advice** and not 'an advice':
✓ *Can I give you some advice?*
✗ *Can I give you an advice?*
To talk about one particular suggestion, use **piece of advice**: □ *Can I give you a piece of advice?*

advise /əd'vaɪz/ VERB [advises, advising, advised] to tell someone what you think they should do □ **+ to do something** *They are advising motorists to drive carefully.* □ **+ against** *We advise against all travel to the region.* □ **+ on** *He advises us on financial matters.*

aerial /'eərɪəl/ NOUN [plural aerials] a piece of metal equipment for getting or sending radio or television signals 🖻 *a television aerial*

aerobics /eə'rəubɪks/ PLURAL NOUN exercises for the whole body that make your heart and lungs work hard

aeroplane /'eərəpleɪn/ NOUN [plural aeroplanes] a flying vehicle that has wings and an engine □ *The aeroplane took off at midday.*

aerosol /'eərəsɒl/ NOUN [plural aerosols] a container with a part that you press to force out very small drops of liquid

affair /ə'feə(r)/ NOUN [plural affairs]
1 affairs events or activities in a particular area of life, business, politics, etc. 🖻 *He is very interested in foreign affairs* (= international politics). 🖻 *She was responsible for the financial affairs of the club.*

2 a situation or an event, especially a problem or something bad □ *Some people have criticized the way he handled the affair.*
3 a sexual relationship between two people, especially when one or both of them is married to someone else 🔁 *She had an affair with an older man.*

affect /əˈfekt/ VERB [affects, affecting, affected]
to change, influence or cause harm to someone or something □ *The accident affected his eyesight.*
□ *Were you affected by the floods?*

> ➤ Be careful not to confuse **affect**, which is a verb, with **effect**, which is a noun □ *One thing affects another.* □ *One thing has an effect on another.*

affection /əˈfekʃən/ NOUN, NO PLURAL a strong feeling of liking someone or something □ *I have great affection for the town.* □ *My father rarely showed his affection.*

affectionate /əˈfekʃənət/ ADJECTIVE showing that you like or love someone □ *Her mother gave her an affectionate kiss.*

afford /əˈfɔːd/ VERB [affords, affording, afforded] if you can afford something, you have enough money to pay for it □ *I can't afford a new dress.* □ **+ to do something** *We couldn't afford to go abroad.*

afraid /əˈfreɪd/ ADJECTIVE
1 frightened or worried □ *There's no need to be afraid.* □ **+ of** *Small children are often afraid of dogs.* □ **+ that** *I was afraid that I'd fall.* □ **+ to do something** *Don't be afraid to tell me if you don't understand.*
2 I'm afraid used to tell someone in a polite way that you cannot do something, or to give them bad news □ *I'm afraid I don't know.* □ *Helen can't come, I'm afraid.* □ **+ that** *I'm afraid that I can't tell you any more now.*

African[1] /ˈæfrɪkən/ ADJECTIVE belonging to or from Africa □ *an African country*

African[2] /ˈæfrɪkən/ NOUN [plural Africans] a person from Africa

after[1] /ˈɑːftə(r)/ PREPOSITION
1 when something has happened □ *I'll do it after dinner.* □ *It rained day after day.*
2 after an hour/three days, etc. when an hour/three days, etc. have passed
3 following in order □ *Your name's after mine on the list.*
4 following someone or something □ *We ran after the man.*
5 after all used to talk about something that happened or was true although you did not expect it to be □ *I decided to go to the party after all.*

after[2] /ˈɑːftə(r)/ CONJUNCTION when something has happened □ *Mrs Shaw died after we*

moved. □ *After we'd said goodbye, we felt quite sad.*

> ➤ Use the phrases **a week/month, etc. from now** or **in a week's/month's, etc. time** to talk about a time in the future that you are measuring from now. Do not say 'after a week/month, etc.' to mean this:
> ✓ *A week from now my exams will all be finished.*
> ✓ *In a week's time my exams will all be finished.*
> ✗ *After a week my exams will all be finished.*

after[3] /ˈɑːftə(r)/ ADVERB following in time □ *Can you come the week after?*

afternoon /ˌɑːftəˈnuːn/ NOUN [plural afternoons]
1 the time between the middle of the day and the evening □ *I saw him on Monday afternoon.* □ *We finish at 4 o'clock in the afternoon.* 🔁 *What are you doing this afternoon?*
2 Good afternoon used to say 'hello' when you meet someone in the afternoon

afterwards /ˈɑːftəwədz/ ADVERB later or after something else □ *He's busy now but I'll speak to him afterwards.* □ *They moved to Paris and soon afterwards they got married.*

again /əˈgen/ ADVERB
1 once more □ *Do it again!* □ *Will I see you again?*
2 in the same place or situation as before □ *Can we go home again now?*
3 again and again many times □ *I've told you again and again to tidy your room!*

> ➤ Remember that **again** meaning 'once more' usually comes after the object in a sentence:
> ✓ *I'd like to visit France again.*
> ✗ *I'd like to visit again France.*
> ✓ *We could have pizza again.*
> ✗ *We could have again pizza.*

against /əˈgenst/ PREPOSITION
1 leaning on, touching or hitting something □ *She was throwing a ball against the wall.* □ *He was sitting with his back against a tree.*
2 competing or fighting with someone □ *Liverpool are playing against Barcelona.* □ *We all support the fight against racism.*
3 disagreeing with a plan or situation □ *I'm against the ban on hunting.*
4 against the law/rules not allowed by the laws/rules □ *Smoking on the train is against the law.*

age /eɪdʒ/ NOUN [plural ages]
1 how old someone or something is 🔁 *Zoe will start school at the age of four.* 🔁 *He's 19 years of age.* □ **+ of** *Do you know the age of the building?* 🔁 *It's suitable for children of all ages.*

2 ages an informal word meaning a very long time □ *I haven't seen Alex for ages.* 🔁 *You took ages to finish.* □ *The tickets sold out ages ago.*
3 a period of time in history □ *the Stone Age*
• **aged** /eɪdʒd/ ADJECTIVE used to say how many years old someone is □ *They have two children aged eight and three.* 🔁 *young people aged between 18 and 25*

agency /'eɪdʒənsɪ/ NOUN [plural agencies] a business that provides a particular service □ *an employment agency* □ *an advertising agency*

agenda /ə'dʒendə/ NOUN [plural agendas] a list of things to be discussed at a meeting 🔁 *What's on the agenda today?*

agent /'eɪdʒənt/ NOUN [plural agents]
1 someone who does business for another person or company □ *Our agents sell the books for us.*
2 someone who collects secret information for a government 🔁 *a secret agent*
➔ go to **travel agent, estate agent**

aggression /ə'greʃən/ NOUN, NO PLURAL behaviour that is angry and threatening

aggressive /ə'gresɪv/ ADJECTIVE angry and threatening 🔁 *aggressive behaviour*

ago /ə'gəʊ/ ADVERB used to say how long in the past something happened □ *I last saw Lily ten years ago.* 🔁 *That all seems a long time ago.*

agony /'æɡənɪ/ NOUN, NO PLURAL very great pain □ *You could see he was in agony.*

agree /ə'griː/ VERB [agrees, agreeing, agreed]
1 to have the same opinion as someone else about something □ **+ with** *She never agrees with him about anything.* □ **+ about** *I'm glad we agree about something.*
2 to say that you will do what someone has asked you to □ **+ to do something** *I only agreed to come if you came too.*
3 to decide something together with someone □ **+ on** *They couldn't agree on a name for the baby.* □ *Doctors have agreed a pay deal.*

agreement /ə'griːmənt/ NOUN [plural agreements]
1 a decision or a promise between two or more people □ **+ between** *a trade agreement between Canada and the US* □ **+ with** *We have an agreement with the local sports club.* 🔁 *The two companies have reached an agreement.*
2 no plural when people have the same opinion □ *There was no agreement about what to do.*
3 in agreement if people are in agreement, they agree with each other

agriculture /'æɡrɪˌkʌltʃə(r)/ NOUN, NO PLURAL the work of farming

ahead /ə'hed/ ADVERB
1 in front □ *Run on ahead and tell them we're coming.* 🔁 *Our house is straight ahead.*
2 in the future □ **+ of** *We've got a long journey ahead of us.* 🔁 *We're planning for the year ahead.*
3 in a better position in a race, competition, etc. □ **+ of** *They are four points ahead of their main rivals.* □ *United were ahead after a goal in the first half.*

aid¹ /eɪd/ NOUN [plural aids]
1 help 🔁 *He can walk with the aid of a stick.* 🔁 *Mr Oliver came to our aid* (= helped us).
2 money, food, etc. that is sent to places that need it □ *Many countries will send aid to the disaster area.*
aid² /eɪd/ VERB [aids, aiding, aided] to help someone □ *Gentle exercise will aid your recovery.*

AIDS or **Aids** /eɪdz/ ABBREVIATION Acquired Immune Deficiency Syndrome; an illness that makes the body unable to fight disease

aim¹ /eɪm/ VERB [aims, aiming, aimed]
1 to intend or to hope to do something □ **+ to do something** *We aim to help all our customers.* □ **+ for** *She's aiming for a medal at the next Olympics.*
2 to point a weapon at someone or something □ **+ at** *Paul was aiming at the target but missed it completely.*

aim² /eɪm/ NOUN [plural aims]
1 what you are trying to achieve □ **+ of** *The aim of the project is to encourage healthy eating.* 🔁 *My main aim is to get fit.* 🔁 *We have achieved our aim.*
2 take aim to point a weapon at someone or something □ **+ at** *He took aim at the open window.*

ain't /eɪnt/ an informal short way to say and write 'am not', 'are not', 'is not', 'has not' or 'have not' □ *Ain't he clever?* □ *You ain't lived yet.*

air¹ /eə(r)/ NOUN
1 no plural the gases around us that we breathe in 🔁 *Kelly went outside to get some fresh air.* □ *The air carries the seeds for miles.*
2 the air the space above you □ *He put his hand in the air.* □ *Police fired into the air.*
3 no plural travel in an aircraft □ *The food is transported by air.* 🔁 *air travel*

air² /eə(r)/ VERB [airs, airing, aired] to allow some fresh air into a room

aircraft /'eəkrɑːft/ NOUN [plural aircraft] a vehicle that can fly 🔁 *a commercial aircraft* 🔁 *a military aircraft*

air force /'eə ˌfɔːs/ NOUN [plural air forces] a military organization that uses aircraft

airline /'eəlaɪn/ NOUN [plural airlines] a company that takes people or goods to places by plane 🔁 *an airline ticket* 🔁 *an airline pilot*

airmail /'eəmeɪl/ NOUN, NO PLURAL the system of sending letters and packages by aeroplane □ *I'll send you the book by airmail.*

airport /ˈeəpɔːt/ NOUN [plural airports] a place where passengers get on and off aircraft □ She arrived at the city's international airport.

aisle /aɪl/ NOUN [plural aisles] the space that you can walk along between rows of seats or shelves in a church, supermarket, etc.

alarm¹ /əˈlɑːm/ NOUN [plural alarms]
1 a loud noise to warn people about something 🔁 the fire alarm 🔁 My alarm goes off at 7 o'clock.
2 no plural a sudden feeling of fear and worry □ He jumped back in alarm. 🔁 Everyone stay calm, there's no cause for alarm.

alarm² /əˈlɑːm/ VERB [alarms, alarming, alarmed] to frighten and worry someone suddenly □ It's okay, don't be alarmed.

alarm clock /əˈlɑːm ˈklɒk/ NOUN [plural alarm clocks] a clock that makes a noise to wake you up 🔁 His alarm clock went off (= rang) at 6 am.

alarming /əˈlɑːmɪŋ/ ADJECTIVE frightening and making you worry □ alarming reports

album /ˈælbəm/ NOUN [plural albums]
1 a book for keeping photographs, stamps, etc. 🔁 a photo album
2 a collection of songs or pieces of music on a CD, record, etc. □ the band's new album

alcohol /ˈælkəhɒl/ NOUN, NO PLURAL
1 drinks like wine and beer that can make you drunk 🔁 He doesn't drink alcohol.
2 a substance in wine and beer that is also in some chemicals and medicines. A chemistry word.

alcoholic /ˌælkəˈhɒlɪk/ ADJECTIVE containing alcohol 🔁 alcoholic drinks

alert¹ /əˈlɜːt/ ADJECTIVE quick to notice what is around you and to react to it □ Stay alert – the enemy could attack at any time.

alert² /əˈlɜːt/ NOUN [plural alerts]
1 a warning about something 🔁 Weather experts issued a flood alert.
2 on alert ready to deal with problems 🔁 Security forces are on full/high alert.

alert³ /əˈlɜːt/ VERB [alerts, alerting, alerted] to warn someone about a danger □ If you see a suspicious package, alert the police at once.

alien¹ /ˈeɪliən/ NOUN [plural aliens]
1 a creature from another planet
2 someone who is not from the country they are living in 🔁 an illegal alien

alien² /ˈeɪliən/ ADJECTIVE
1 strange and not familiar □ The idea of taking orders from a woman was totally alien to him.
2 to do with creatures from another planet □ an alien spaceship

alike¹ /əˈlaɪk/ ADJECTIVE like one another □ The twins aren't alike in character.

alike² /əˈlaɪk/ ADVERB in the same way □ Dad treats us both alike.

alive /əˈlaɪv/ ADJECTIVE living □ He was seriously injured, but still alive. □ She didn't know whether he was alive or dead.

all¹ /ɔːl/ PRONOUN, DETERMINER
1 every one □ All the children stood up. □ I want to see them all. □ **+ of** All of the animals were healthy.
2 every part □ We ate all the cake. □ Don't spend it all. □ We've been working all day.
3 the only thing □ All he's interested in is football.
4 at all used to emphasize a negative statement □ You haven't eaten anything at all.

all² /ɔːl/ ADVERB
1 completely □ His shirt was all dirty.
2 all over (a) in every place or part of something □ His clothes were all over the place. (b) finished □ I'll be glad when it's all over.

Allah /ˈælə/ NOUN the Muslim name for God

allege /əˈledʒ/ VERB [alleges, alleging, alleged] to say that someone has done something wrong or illegal □ The police allege that he stole the car.

allergic /əˈlɜːdʒɪk/ ADJECTIVE having a condition where your body reacts badly to something you touch, breathe, eat or drink 🔁 an allergic reaction □ I'm allergic to cats.

allergy /ˈælədʒi/ NOUN [plural allergies] a condition where your body reacts badly to something you touch, breathe, eat or drink □ a peanut allergy 🔁 I have an allergy to dairy products.

alley /ˈæli/ or **alleyway** /ˈæliweɪ/ NOUN [plural alleys] a narrow passage between buildings

alliance /əˈlaɪəns/ NOUN [plural alliances] an agreement between organizations or countries to work together 🔁 The US car maker has formed an alliance with a Chinese manufacturer.

alligator /ˈælɪɡeɪtə(r)/ NOUN [plural alligators] a large reptile with thick skin, a long body and a big mouth with sharp teeth

allow /əˈlaʊ/ VERB [allows, allowing, allowed]
1 to give permission for something □ **+ to do something** Will you allow me to come in now? □ We do not allow smoking in the house. □ Prisoners are allowed out to exercise.
2 to make something possible □ **+ to do something** The new technology allows them to stay in touch with their families.

➤ Do not use the phrase it is not allowed to do something as this is not correct English. Instead use either of these phrases □ You are not allowed to talk in a written exam. □ Talking is not allowed in a written exam.

all right¹ /ˈɔːl ˈraɪt/ ADJECTIVE, ADVERB
1 quite good but not very good □ The party was all right I suppose.

2 safe or well □ *I'm all right. How are you?* □ *I'm glad you're all right – we heard there was an accident.*
3 acceptable or not a problem □ *Is it all right if I go out tonight?* □ *It's all right – it wasn't your fault.*
4 That's all right. used when someone has thanked you for something

all right² /ɔːl ˈraɪt/ EXCLAMATION used to agree to something □ *All right, I'll go then.*

ally NOUN /ˈælaɪ/ [allies] a person or country that supports another ⌗ *He is one of the president's closest allies.* □ *Britain has been a strong political ally of the United States.*

almost /ˈɔːlməʊst/ ADVERB not quite or not completely □ *She is almost ten years old.* ⌗ *Almost all the children go to state schools.* □ *He's almost as tall as his father.* □ *It's almost impossible to predict.* □ *I almost missed my flight.*

alone /əˈləʊn/ ADJECTIVE, ADVERB
1 without anyone else □ *I live alone.* ⌗ *I was all alone with no one to talk to.* □ *A young woman sat alone in the waiting room.* □ *I felt completely alone.*
2 used to emphasize that only one person or thing is involved □ *The ticket alone will use up all my money.*
3 leave something alone to not touch something □ *Leave my sweets alone!*
4 leave someone alone to not talk to or annoy someone □ *Leave her alone – she's had enough of your complaints.*

➤ Note that **alone** only means 'without anyone else'. It does not mean 'feeling sad because you are without other people'. The word for this is **lonely** □ *I was alone in the house.* □ *I felt lonely without my family around me.*

along¹ /əˈlɒŋ/ PREPOSITION
1 from one part of something to another □ *Shona walked along the street.*
2 by the side of something long □ *Hari's house is somewhere along this street.*

along² /əˈlɒŋ/ ADVERB
1 forwards □ *Move along, please.* □ *He was driving along, singing.*
2 with someone ⌗ *We're going swimming – why don't you come along?* ⌗ *Adam brought a friend along.*
3 along with together with □ *We'd packed drinks along with the sandwiches.*

aloud /əˈlaʊd/ ADVERB so that other people can hear ⌗ *She almost laughed aloud.* ⌗ *Edith read the letter aloud to the boys.*

alphabet /ˈælfəbet/ NOUN [plural alphabets] all the written letters of a language ⌗ *Z is the last letter of the alphabet.*

alphabetical /ˌælfəˈbetɪkəl/ ADJECTIVE with the first letters in the order of the alphabet ⌗ *The books are in alphabetical order.* □ *an alphabetical index*

already /ɔːlˈredɪ/ ADVERB
1 before now or before a particular time □ *I had already gone when Bob arrived.* □ *We've already booked our summer holiday.*
2 now, before the expected time □ *Is he here already?* □ *I'm already tired.*

also /ˈɔːlsəʊ/ ADVERB in addition □ *Bernie speaks French and also Italian.* □ *My sister also attends this school.* ⌗ *The process is not only slow, but also very expensive.*

altar /ˈɔːltə(r)/ NOUN [plural altars] a special table used for religious ceremonies in a church

alter /ˈɔːltə(r)/ VERB [alters, altering, altered] to change, or to change something □ *The town has altered a lot recently.* □ *Can you alter this skirt to fit me?*

alteration /ˌɔːltəˈreɪʃən/ NOUN [plural alterations] a change, or the process of being changed □ *There have been a few alterations to our plans.* □ *The museum is closed for alteration.*

alternate¹ /ɔːlˈtɜːnət/ ADJECTIVE
1 happening on one day, week, etc. but not the next □ *I have to work on alternate Saturdays.*
2 with one thing, then another, then the first thing again, in a repeated pattern □ *alternate stripes of red and green*

alternate² /ˈɔːltəneɪt/ VERB [alternates, alternating, alternated] if two things alternate, one happens or is used first, then the other, then the first again, etc. □ *She alternates between being too strict and being too soft.* □ *He alternates between the guitar and the violin.*

alternative¹ /ɔːlˈtɜːnətɪv/ ADJECTIVE giving you another choice or possibility □ *If you cannot come on Tuesday you can suggest an alternative day.* □ *Drivers are advised to use an alternative route.*

alternative² /ɔːlˈtɜːnətɪv/ NOUN [plural alternatives] another possibility or choice □ *Is there an alternative to chips on the menu?* □ *There are cheaper alternatives.*

although /ɔːlˈðəʊ/ CONJUNCTION
1 despite the fact that □ *Although he was a clever boy, he didn't do well in exams.* □ *I went to the show, although I had said I wouldn't.*
2 but □ *He's retired from professional athletics, although he's still very fit.*

altogether /ˌɔːltəˈgeðə(r)/ ADVERB
1 completely □ *Finally, he stopped altogether.* ⌗ *I'm not altogether happy.*
2 in total □ *We raised £100 altogether.* □ *There are six of us altogether.*

aluminium /ˌælju'mɪnɪəm/ NOUN, NO PLURAL a very light metal that is a silver colour

aluminum /ə'luːmɪnəm/ NOUN, NO PLURAL the US word for **aluminium**

always /'ɔːlweɪz/ ADVERB

1 at all times □ *I always work hard.* 🔁 *You look lovely, as always.*

2 at all times in the past □ *She's always lived in the same village.* □ *He hasn't always been so successful.*

3 forever □ *I'll always remember that day.*

4 repeatedly □ + *ing I'm always getting this wrong.*

> — THESAURUS: Always means 'at all times'. For example, if you are very careful about your appearance, you might always look smart. If you do something regularly, or if something happens regularly, it happens often, and often with the same amount of time between each thing. For example, you might go swimming regularly. If you do something repeatedly, you do it many times. This word is often used to describe something which is bad or annoying. For example, you might say that you complain about something repeatedly.

am¹ /æm/ VERB the present tense of the verb **be** when it is used with with I □ *I am happy.*

> — Note that instead of **I am**, people often say and write the short form **I'm** □ *I'm very pleased.*

am² /eɪ'em/ or **a.m.** ABBREVIATION used after the time to show that it is in the morning □ *My flight is at 6 am.*

amateur¹ /'æmətə(r)/ NOUN [plural amateurs] someone who does something because they enjoy it, not for money □ *The team is made up of enthusiastic amateurs.*

amateur² /'æmətə(r)/ ADJECTIVE doing something for fun and not to be paid □ *an amateur photographer* □ *amateur athletics*

amaze /ə'meɪz/ VERB [amazes, amazing, amazed] to surprise someone very much □ *It amazes me how stupid you can be.*

amazed /ə'meɪzd/ ADJECTIVE very surprised □ + *at We were all amazed at how easy it was.* □ + *that I'm amazed that no one was hurt.* □ *Mum looked amazed when he walked in.*

amazement /ə'meɪzmənt/ NOUN, NO PLURAL great surprise 🔁 *To my amazement, Dad agreed with me.* □ *He shook his head in amazement.*

amazing /ə'meɪzɪŋ/ ADJECTIVE

1 very surprising □ *an amazing sight* □ *It's amazing how quickly the weather can change.*

2 very pleasant, exciting or enjoyable □ *We saw an amazing sunset.* □ *It's a pretty amazing feeling.*

ambassador /æm'bæsədə(r)/ NOUN [plural ambassadors] someone who officially represents their government in a foreign country □ *the British ambassador to Japan*

ambition /æm'bɪʃən/ NOUN [plural ambitions]

1 something that you want to achieve 🔁 *I have an ambition to see the pyramids.* 🔁 *He achieved his ambition of becoming a doctor.*

2 no plural wanting to be very successful □ *He shows a lack of ambition.*

ambitious /æm'bɪʃəs/ ADJECTIVE wanting to be very successful in life □ *an ambitious and talented young player*

ambulance /'æmbjʊləns/ NOUN [plural ambulances] a vehicle for taking ill or injured people to hospital

American¹ /ə'merɪkən/ ADJECTIVE belonging to or from America, especially the United States of America □ *an American accent*

American² /ə'merɪkən/ NOUN [plural Americans] a person from America, especially the United States of America

ammunition /ˌæmjʊ'nɪʃən/ NOUN, NO PLURAL bullets or bombs that you can fire from a weapon

among /ə'mʌŋ/ or **amongst** /ə'mʌŋst/ PREPOSITION

1 surrounded by or in the middle of □ *You are among friends.*

2 between people in a group □ *Divide the chocolate among yourselves.*

3 in a group of □ *The band is popular among teenagers.*

amount /ə'maʊnt/ NOUN [plural amounts] a quantity □ + *of a small amount of money* □ *These drinks contain large amounts of sugar.*

> — Remember that 'large' and 'small' are used before the word **amount**, but not 'big' or 'little' □ *A large amount of this food is wasted.* □ *A small amount of salt is necessary.*

ample /'æmpəl/ ADJECTIVE enough or more than enough □ *We had ample opportunity to ask questions.* □ *an ample supply of water*

amuse /ə'mjuːz/ VERB [amuses, amusing, amused] to make someone smile or laugh □ *He told jokes to amuse his classmates.*

amused /ə'mjuːzd/ ADJECTIVE finding something funny □ *He smiled, amused at John's silly mistake.* □ *an amused expression*

amusement /ə'mjuːzmənt/ NOUN [plural amusements] the feeling that makes you smile or laugh □ *He smiled with obvious amusement.*

amusing /ə'mju:zɪŋ/ ADJECTIVE making you want to smile or laugh □ *an amusing story* 🔁 *She found the whole thing quite amusing.*

an /ən/ DETERMINER used instead of a before words beginning with a vowel, or before words beginning with 'h' when it is not pronounced □ *an apple* □ *an elephant* □ *an honest person*

analysis /ə'næləsɪs/ NOUN [plural analyses] when you examine something carefully in order to understand it 🔁 *a statistical analysis* 🔁 *We carried out a detailed analysis of the project.*

analyze or **analyse** /'ænəlaɪz/ VERB [analyzes, analyzing, analyzed] to examine something carefully in order to understand it 🔁 *We need to analyze the data.* □ *Researchers analyzed a thousand samples.*

ancestor /'ænsestə(r)/ NOUN [plural ancestors] a member of your family who lived in the past □ *His distant ancestors came from India.*

anchor[1] /'æŋkə(r)/ NOUN [plural anchors] a heavy piece of metal attached to a boat that is dropped into the water to stop it from moving away

anchor[2] /'æŋkə(r)/ VERB [anchors, anchoring, anchored] to drop the anchor of a boat to stop it moving away □ *The ship is anchored in Sydney harbour.*

ancient /'eɪnʃənt/ ADJECTIVE from a very long time ago 🔁 *ancient history* 🔁 *the remains of an ancient civilization*

and /ænd/ CONJUNCTION
1 a word that is used to join parts of sentences □ *bread and butter* □ *I saw Alice and Peter.* □ *Go and get ready.*
2 added to □ *Two and two make four.*

angel /'eɪndʒəl/ NOUN [plural angels] a creature, usually shown like a person with wings, which is believed to bring messages from God

anger /'æŋgə(r)/ NOUN, NO PLURAL the strong, bad feeling you get about someone or something that annoys you □ *The fans expressed their anger at the decision.* □ *There's a lot of anger among local people.* □ *He was shaking with anger.*

angle /'æŋgəl/ NOUN [plural angles] the shape that is made at the point where two straight lines meet, measured in degrees □ *a 90-degree angle*

angrily /'æŋgrəlɪ/ ADVERB in an angry way □ *A young woman came in, shouting angrily.* □ *He reacted angrily.*

angry /'æŋgrɪ/ ADJECTIVE [angrier, angriest] very annoyed □ **+ about** *They're angry about the way they were treated.* □ **+ with** *I'm not angry with you.* □ *an angry crowd* □ *Then Mike got very angry.* 🔁 *That kind of thing makes me so angry.*

> **THESAURUS:** If you are **angry**, you dislike something or feel very impatient about it. **Annoyed** and **cross** have a similar meaning, but are not so strong. If you are **furious**, you are very angry. For example, you might be **annoyed** if a train is 5 minutes late, **angry** if you miss a meeting because your train doesn't arrive, and **furious** if you lose your job because you miss the meeting.

animal /'ænɪməl/ NOUN [plural animals] a living creature that is not a human 🔁 *a wild animal* 🔁 *a farm animal* □ *The charity helps to protect endangered animals.*

ankle /'æŋkəl/ NOUN [plural ankles] the place where your foot joins your leg □ *She fell over and broke her left ankle.*

annex[1] or **annexe** /'æneks/ NOUN [plural annexes] an extra part of a building that is added on to it

annex[2] /æ'neks/ VERB [annexes, annexing, annexed] to take control of an area or country next to your own □ *After the war, the region was annexed by the Soviet Union.*

anniversary /ænɪ'vɜ:sərɪ/ NOUN [plural anniversaries] a date when you celebrate something that happened on the same date in the past 🔁 *a wedding anniversary* □ **+ of** *Today is the anniversary of the King's death.* 🔁 *The celebrations will mark the 60th anniversary of the country's independence.*

announce /ə'naʊns/ VERB [announces, announcing, announced] to tell people something, especially loudly or forcefully 🔁 *The government has announced plans to build four new hospitals.* 🔁 *Have they announced their engagement yet?* □ **+ that** *The minister has announced that he is retiring.*

announcement /ə'naʊnsmənt/ NOUN [plural announcements] something that people are told, especially publicly or officially 🔁 *I want to make an announcement.* 🔁 *a formal/official announcement*

announcer /ə'naʊnsə(r)/ NOUN [plural announcers] someone who introduces programmes on television or the radio

annoy /ə'nɔɪ/ VERB [annoys, annoying, annoyed] to make someone angry □ *It really annoys me when she wastes food.*

annoyed /ə'nɔɪd/ ADJECTIVE angry □ **+ with** *I could see that he was annoyed with me.*

annoying /ə'nɔɪɪŋ/ ADJECTIVE making you feel annoyed 🔁 *an annoying habit* □ *Jo can be so annoying!*

annual¹ /'ænjuəl/ ADJECTIVE an annual event happens once every year □ *an annual meeting of shareholders*
• **annually** /'ænjuəlɪ/ ADVERB happening once every year

annual² /'ænjuəl/ NOUN [*plural* annuals] a book that is published every year

another /ə'nʌðə(r)/ DETERMINER, PRONOUN
1 one more person or thing □ *Have another piece of chocolate.* □ *He had two gold medals and now he has another.*
2 a different person or thing □ *We'll finish this game another time.* □ *If that pen's broken, use another one.* □ *I lost my coat and I haven't got another.*

answer¹ /'ɑːnsə(r)/ VERB [answers, answering, answered]
1 to reply when someone asks you a question or sends you a letter □ *I waited for him to answer.* □ *She tried to answer truthfully.* □ *I'm just going to answer his letter.*
2 to pick up the telephone when it rings, or to open the door when someone is there □ *A child answered the telephone.* □ *I knocked at the door and an old woman answered.*

answer² /'ɑːnsə(r)/ NOUN [*plural* answers]
1 a reply □ + **to** *I couldn't find an answer to my question.* 🔃 *He gave a detailed answer.*
2 the solution to a problem □ *If you can't afford a car, a car sharing scheme could be the answer.*
3 what you write or say to answer a question in an exam or a competition 🔃 *the correct/wrong answer*

➤ Remember to use the preposition **to** after the noun **answer**:
✓ *What's the answer to question six?*
✗ *What's the answer for question six?*

answerphone /'ɑːnsə.fəʊn/ or **answering machine** /'ɑːnsərɪŋ mə'ʃiːn/ NOUN [*plural* answerphones or answering machines] a machine that automatically answers your telephone and records messages for you

ant /ænt/ NOUN [*plural* ants] a small, usually black, insect that lives in organized groups

Antarctic¹ /ænt'ɑːktɪk/ NOUN the Antarctic the area of the world round the South Pole

Antarctic² /ænt'ɑːktɪk/ ADJECTIVE to do with the Antarctic □ *Antarctic exploration* □ *the Antarctic winter*

antenna /æn'tenə/ NOUN [*plural* antennae or antennas]
1 one of two long thin parts on the head of an insect or a sea animal, used for feeling
2 a thin piece of metal that is used for getting television or radio signals

anthem /'ænθəm/ NOUN [*plural* anthems] a song that praises a country or an organization, for example a football team

anti- /'æntɪ/ PREFIX anti- is added to the beginning of words to mean 'against' or 'preventing'
□ *antisocial* □ *antifreeze*

antibiotic /ˌæntɪbaɪ'ɒtɪk/ NOUN [*plural* antibiotics] a medicine that kills bacteria that can cause infections □ *The doctor's put me on antibiotics.*

anticipate /æn'tɪsɪˌpeɪt/ VERB [anticipates, anticipating, anticipated] to expect something to happen, and often to prepare for it □ *We don't anticipate any problems.*

antique¹ /æn'tiːk/ NOUN [*plural* antiques] an object that is old and valuable □ *a collector of antiques*

antique² /æn'tiːk/ ADJECTIVE old and valuable
□ *antique jewellery*

➤ Remember that **antique** is used for old objects, such as furniture and jewellery. It is not used for old buildings. For buildings, use **old** or **ancient** □ *They have a lot of very valuable antique furniture.* □ *We visited the ancient monuments.*

antonym /'æntənɪm/ NOUN [*plural* antonyms] a word that means the opposite of another word

anxiety /æŋ'zaɪətɪ/ NOUN [*plural* anxieties] a feeling of worry □ *The parents of these soldiers suffered a lot of anxiety.*

anxious /'æŋkʃəs/ ADJECTIVE worried □ + **about** *He's anxious about missing his train.* □ *She gave me an anxious glance.*

any¹ /'enɪ/ DETERMINER, PRONOUN
1 used in questions and negative statements to mean 'some' □ *Have we got any sweets?* □ *We had lots of food, but there isn't any left now.*
2 one or a piece of something, but not a particular one □ *Let me know if you have any questions.* □ *Choose any colour you like.* □ *The children all know the answers – ask any of them.*

any² /'enɪ/ ADVERB
1 at all □ *Are you feeling any better?* □ *Can't you walk any faster?*
2 any more if something does not happen any more, it has stopped happening □ *Ricky doesn't work here any more.* □ *The children don't get free milk any more.*

anybody /'enɪˌbɒdɪ/ PRONOUN
1 used in questions and negatives to mean 'a person' or 'people' □ *Has anybody seen my glasses?*
□ *I didn't speak to anybody.*
2 any person □ *Anybody is allowed to enter.*

anyhow /'enɪhaʊ/ ADVERB
1 used to add another reason to what you have just said □ *I missed lunch but I wasn't hungry anyhow.*
2 despite that □ *Two of our players are injured, but anyhow we have a very good team.*

anyone /'enɪwʌn/ PRONOUN
1 used in questions and negatives to mean 'a person' or 'people' □ *Has anyone got a mobile?* □ *There isn't anyone left.*
2 any person □ *Anyone can bake a cake.* □ *He'll talk to anyone.*

➤ Remember that 'anyone' is singular so the verb following it must be singular □ *If anyone calls, tell them I'll be back in ten minutes.* □ *Anyone is welcome to come.*

anything /'enɪθɪŋ/ PRONOUN
1 used in questions and negative statements to mean 'something' □ *We didn't have anything to eat.* □ *Is there anything I can do to help?* 🕭 *Is there anything else I should know?*
2 something of any type □ *He's capable of anything.* □ *We can do anything we like while our teacher is away.*

anyway /'enɪweɪ/ ADVERB
1 used to add another reason to what you have just said □ *I can give you a lift. I'm going that way anyway.*
2 despite that □ *Leon couldn't go with me but I enjoyed the party anyway.*
3 used to start a new part of a conversation □ *Anyway, how have you been lately?*

anywhere /'enɪweə(r)/ ADVERB
1 in or to any place □ *I'm willing to travel anywhere.* □ *You can buy these anywhere in the world.* □ *Don't go anywhere near Dad – he's in a terrible mood.*
2 used in questions and negative statements to mean 'a place' □ *Have you got anywhere to stay?* □ *There isn't anywhere to hide.*

apart /ə'pɑːt/ ADVERB
1 separated by distance or time □ *Stand with your feet apart.* □ *We had two classes, a week apart.*
2 into pieces 🕭 *The seams of this jacket have come apart.* □ *We had to take the lamp apart to mend it.*
3 apart from except for □ *Apart from us, nobody's interested.* □ *I've had nothing to eat apart from a biscuit.*
4 tell apart if you cannot tell two people apart, you cannot see any differences in their appearance

apartment /ə'pɑːtmənt/ NOUN [*plural* apartments] a mainly US word for **flat** (= set of rooms on one level) □ *an apartment block*

ape /eɪp/ NOUN [*plural* apes] a large animal like a monkey with no tail

apologize *or* **apologise** /ə'pɒlədʒaɪz/ VERB [apologizes, apologizing, apologized] to say sorry for doing something wrong □ *+ for* *I had to apologize for being late.*

apology /ə'pɒlədʒɪ/ NOUN [*plural* apologies] when someone says sorry for doing something wrong 🕭 *He made a public apology.* 🕭 *She demanded an apology from the newspaper's editor.* □ *+ for* *I owe you an apology for forgetting your birthday again.*

apostrophe /ə'pɒstrəfɪ/ NOUN [*plural* apostrophes]
1 the symbol (') that shows where a letter or letters have been missed out □ *Jane's* (= Jane is) *late again.* □ *I think it'll* (= it will) *rain later.*
2 the symbol (') that is used before the letter s to show who something belongs to □ *I borrowed Ralf's bicycle.*

apparatus /ˌæpə'reɪtəs/ NOUN, NO PLURAL the equipment that you need for a particular task □ *breathing apparatus*

apparent /ə'pærənt/ ADJECTIVE easy to see 🕭 *Then, for no apparent reason, he began to cry.*

apparently /ə'pærəntlɪ/ ADVERB used to tell people about something you have been told, although you are not sure if it is true □ *Apparently there's going to be an announcement later.*

appeal[1] /ə'piːl/ VERB [appeals, appealing, appealed]
1 to ask for something, often forcefully or publicly □ *The police have appealed to the public for more information.*
2 if something appeals to you, you think you would enjoy it □ *Diving doesn't appeal to me at all.*

appeal[2] /ə'piːl/ NOUN [*plural* appeals]
1 when someone asks for something, often forcefully or publicly □ *Their appeals for calm were ignored.* □ *Their appeal raised £3,000 for the hospital.*
2 the quality that makes something attractive □ *I don't understand the appeal of stamp collecting.*

appear /ə'pɪə(r)/ VERB [appears, appearing, appeared]
1 to seem □ *+ that* *It appears that his wife knew nothing of his crimes.* □ *+ to do something* *The man appeared to hit his victim.* 🕭 *I appear to be the only one who has read the book.* □ *He appears determined to win.*
2 to arrive or start to be able to be seen □ *Greta appeared round the corner.* □ *A car appeared in the distance.*
3 if an actor appears in a film or a play, they are in it

appearance /ə'pɪərəns/ NOUN [plural appearances]
1 the way someone or something looks □ He was of Asian appearance. □ We thought carefully about the appearance of the room.
2 when someone appears in public 🔁 He is making his first appearance for AC Milan. 🔁 This is her first public appearance since her divorce.
3 when someone or something arrives or starts to be seen □ We were thrilled by the appearance of dolphins near our boat. □ The appearance of a police officer frightened the youths away.

appendix¹ /ə'pendɪks/ NOUN [plural appendixes] a small body part that has no purpose, just below the stomach. A biology word.

appendix² /ə'pendɪks/ NOUN [plural appendices] an extra part at the end of a book or document that gives more details about something

appetite /'æpɪtaɪt/ NOUN [plural appetites] the feeling of being hungry 🔁 Elly has lost her appetite since she's been ill. 🔁 You'll spoil your appetite if you eat all those biscuits.

applaud /ə'plɔːd/ VERB [applauds, applauding, applauded] to hit your hands together to show that you enjoyed something □ The audience applauded loudly.

> **THESAURUS:** When you clap, you hit your hands together to show appreciation, or to get someone's attention. To applaud means to clap in order to show appreciation, for example in a theatre or at a concert. If you cheer, you shout to show appreciation, or to encourage or praise someone. You might cheer at a rock concert, or at a sports event. When you congratulate someone, you tell them that you are happy about something that has happened to them. You might congratulate someone on getting married, passing an exam, or having a baby.

applause /ə'plɔːz/ NOUN, NO PLURAL when people hit their hands together to show that they enjoyed something

apple /'æpəl/ NOUN [plural apples] a hard, round fruit with red, green or yellow skin
♦ IDIOM the apple of someone's eye if someone is the apple of your eye, you love them and are very proud of them

appliance /ə'plaɪəns/ NOUN [plural appliances] a piece of electrical equipment 🔁 kitchen appliances

applicant /'æplɪkənt/ NOUN [plural applicants] someone who applies for something such as a job or university place

application /ˌæplɪ'keɪʃən/ NOUN [plural applications] a written document asking for something such as a job

apply /ə'plaɪ/ VERB [applies, applying, applied]
1 to officially ask for something, especially a job or a place on a course □ **+ for** I've applied for a new job. □ **+ to** Maria's applying to university this year.
2 to spread a substance on a surface □ Apply the cream to your skin three times a day.
3 to affect a particular person or people □ **+ to** Do these rules apply to all of us?

appoint /ə'pɔɪnt/ VERB [appoints, appointing, appointed] to officially give someone a job □ The committee has appointed Mark Burns as manager.

appointment /ə'pɔɪntmənt/ NOUN [plural appointments] a time when you have arranged to meet someone 🔁 I've made an appointment with the nurse. 🔁 I have a doctor's appointment. 🔁 I've arranged a dental appointment.

> ➤ An **appointment** is an arranged meeting with a doctor, dentist, etc. It is not a meeting with a friend. To say that you are meeting a friend, say **I'm seeing x** or **I have arranged to see x**:
> ✓ I'm seeing Maria this afternoon.
> ✗ I have an appointment with Maria this afternoon.

> **THESAURUS:** A date is an arrangement to see someone that you are having a romantic relationship with. A meeting is a time when people come together to discuss something, for example at work. An interview is a meeting where you answer questions to find out if you are suitable for a job. You can also use interview to describe a meeting between a journalist and a famous person, where the famous person answers questions about their life or work.

appreciate /ə'priːʃieɪt/ VERB [appreciates, appreciating, appreciated] to feel grateful for something □ I really appreciate all the time you've spent on this.

appreciation /əˌpriːʃi'eɪʃən/ NOUN, NO PLURAL when you are grateful to someone □ Here's a little gift to show our appreciation of all your help.

apprentice /ə'prentɪs/ NOUN [plural apprentices] someone who is learning how to do a skilled job from someone who can already do it

approach¹ /ə'prəʊtʃ/ VERB [approaches, approaching, approached]
1 to come towards a place, person or thing □ Approach the animals very slowly. □ The plane was approaching Paris from the south.
2 to deal with something □ What's the best way to approach the problem?

approach² /ə'prəʊtʃ/ NOUN [plural approaches]
1 a way of trying to deal with something □ **+ to** It's

a sensible approach *to the problem.* 🔁 *We could take a different* approach.

2 when something or someone gets closer □ *the approach of spring* □ *At the approach of the train, everyone pushed forward.*

appropriate /əˈprəʊprɪət/ ADJECTIVE suitable □ *Please wear appropriate clothing.*

approval /əˈpruːvəl/ NOUN, NO PLURAL when someone thinks something is good □ *I've always wanted my father's approval.*

approve /əˈpruːv/ VERB [approves, approving, approved] approve of something/someone to think something or someone is good □ *They don't approve of her boyfriend.*

approximate /əˈprɒksɪmət/ ADJECTIVE not exact but close □ *Can you tell me the approximate number of chairs we'll need?* □ *This is the approximate size of the rug.*

approximately /əˈprɒksɪmətlɪ/ ADVERB not exactly although close to □ *There will be approximately sixty people there.*

apricot /ˈeɪprɪkɒt/ NOUN [plural apricots] a small light orange fruit with a soft skin and a stone inside

April /ˈeɪprəl/ NOUN [plural Aprils] the fourth month of the year, after March and before May □ *We're getting married in April.*

apron /ˈeɪprən/ NOUN [plural aprons] something that you wear over your normal clothes, especially when you are cooking, which keeps your clothes clean

arch[1] /ɑːtʃ/ NOUN [plural arches] a curved structure that sometimes gives support to something, for example a bridge

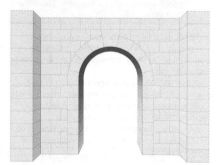

arch[2] /ɑːtʃ/ VERB [arches, arching, arched] to make a curved shape □ *The cat arched its back.*

archaeologist /ˌɑːkɪˈɒlədʒɪst/ NOUN [plural archaeologists] someone who studies things from ancient societies that have been found

archaeology /ˌɑːkɪˈɒlədʒɪ/ NOUN, NO PLURAL the study of ancient societies by looking at things from that time that have been found

archbishop /ˌɑːtʃˈbɪʃəp/ NOUN [plural archbishops] the most important priest in some Christian churches

architect /ˈɑːkɪtekt/ NOUN [plural architects] someone whose job is to design buildings

architecture /ˈɑːkɪtektʃə(r)/ NOUN, NO PLURAL **1** designing buildings □ *He studied architecture.* **2** a style of building □ *modern architecture*

Arctic[1] /ˈɑːktɪk/ NOUN the Arctic the area of the world around the North Pole

Arctic[2] /ˈɑːktɪk/ ADJECTIVE to do with the Arctic □ *the Arctic Ocean*

are /ɑː(r)/ VERB the present tense of the verb **be** when it is used with **you**, **we** and **they** □ *They are hungry.* □ *Are we late?*

> ➤ Note that instead of **you are**, **we are** and **they are**, people often say or write the short forms, **you're**, **we're** and **they're** □ *You're late.* □ *We're here!* □ *They're over there.*

area /ˈeərɪə/ NOUN [plural areas] **1** a part of a place □ *There are a lot of farms in this area.* □ *We work with children from poor areas of the city.* **2** the size of a surface, that you measure in square units of measurement □ *A carpet that is 5 metres by 5 metres has an area of 25 square metres.*

arena /əˈriːnə/ NOUN [plural arenas] a large space for sports or concerts with seats all around it

aren't /ɑːnt/ a short way to say and write 'are not' □ *These aren't my boots.*

argue /ˈɑːgjuː/ VERB [argues, arguing, argued] to speak in an angry way with someone because you disagree with them □ **+ with** *The children never stop arguing with each other.* □ **+ about/over** *They were arguing about where to go on holiday.*

argument /ˈɑːgjʊmənt/ NOUN [plural arguments] an angry discussion 🔁 *The kids were having an argument.* 🔁 *a heated argument* (= a very angry argument) □ **+ about** *an argument about money*

> ➤ **THESAURUS:** A discussion is when two people talk about something. An argument is an angry discussion about something. Quarrel has a similar meaning, but a quarrel is usually less serious than an argument. For example, two children might have a quarrel about toys. A dispute is a serious argument. We often use this word to describe an argument about work, for example between managers and workers in a company. A debate is a formal discussion about something, for example between politicians.

arise /əˈraɪz/ VERB [arises, arising, arose, arisen] to happen □ *A small problem has arisen.*

arithmetic /əˈrɪθmətɪk/ NOUN, NO PLURAL
mathematics that involves processes such as
adding and multiplying □ *simple
arithmetic*

arm¹ /ɑːm/ NOUN [*plural* arms]
1 the part of your body between your shoulder and
your hand □ *I put my arm round his shoulder.* 🗣 *She
folded her arms* (= crossed one over the other close
to her body).
2 arm in arm holding someone's arm □ *They
walked arm in arm along the beach.*

arm² /ɑːm/ VERB [arms, arming, armed] to give
someone a weapon to fight with □ *The crowd was
armed with sticks and knives.*

armchair /ˈɑːmtʃeə(r)/ NOUN [*plural* armchairs]
a comfortable chair with sides for resting your arms
on

armed /ɑːmd/ ADJECTIVE carrying a weapon
🗣 *heavily armed* 🗣 *armed robbery/burglary*

armed forces /ɑːmd ˈfɔːsɪz/ PLURAL NOUN the
armed forces the military groups of a country, for
example its army
armour /ˈɑːmə(r)/ NOUN, NO PLURAL metal covers
worn by soldiers in the past to protect their bodies
🗣 *a suit of armour*
armpit /ˈɑːmpɪt/ NOUN [*plural* armpits] the
part under your arm where it joins your
body

army /ˈɑːmɪ/ NOUN [*plural* armies] an
organization of soldiers 🗣 *He joined the army
after leaving school.* □ *the US army* □ *an army
officer*

arose /əˈrəʊz/ PAST TENSE OF **arise**

around /əˈraʊnd/ PREPOSITION, ADVERB
1 on all sides □ *We were sitting around the
table.*
2 in or to different parts of a place □ *We walked
around the city.* □ *There were clothes lying around
everywhere.* □ *The children are allowed to run
around all over the place.*
3 to several different people □ *We passed the drinks
around.*
4 about □ *They should arrive at around 4 o'clock.*
□ *I weigh around sixty kilos.*
5 to face the opposite direction □ *He turned around
and pointed the gun at me.*
6 in a circular movement □ *Twist the knife around in
the hole.*
7 near □ *Is there a teacher around?*

arrange /əˈreɪndʒ/ VERB [arranges, arranging,
arranged]
1 to make plans to prepare for something □ *Who is
arranging the wedding?* □ **+ to do something**
He's arranged to go out with his friends tonight. □ **+**

for *I've arranged for a taxi to pick him up
later.*
2 to put things in a particular order □ *Arrange the
flowers in the vase.* □ *All his books are arranged in
alphabetical order.*

arrangement /əˈreɪndʒmənt/ NOUN [*plural*
arrangements] a plan that is made so that
something can happen the way you want it to
🗣 *They made arrangements to meet back at the car.*
□ *If he's not back in time, we'll have to make other
arrangements.*

array /əˈreɪ/ NOUN [*plural* arrays] a large group of
things □ *He owns a vast array of electronic
equipment.*

arrest¹ /əˈrest/ VERB [arrests, arresting, arrested]
if the police arrest someone, they take them
to the police station because they may have
committed a crime □ **+ for** *He was arrested for
robbery.*

➤ THESAURUS: If the police **arrest** someone,
they take them to the police station to ask
them questions. We use **charge** when the
police officially accuse someone of committing a crime. **Capture** is a more general word
to describe catching someone or something
and not letting it go. For example, you might
capture an animal, or a soldier.

arrest² /əˈrest/ NOUN [*plural* arrests]
1 when the police arrest someone 🗣 *Police
have made three arrests in connection with the
murder.*
2 under arrest someone is under arrest when the
police are keeping them because they may have
committed a crime

arrival /əˈraɪvəl/ NOUN [*plural* arrivals] **no plural**
when someone reaches a place □ *We are all looking
forward to Alice's arrival.*

arrive /əˈraɪv/ VERB [arrives, arriving, arrived] to
reach a place □ **+ at** *Please arrive at the station by
5.30.* □ **+ in** *We arrived in Warsaw on Friday.* □ *If
they don't arrive soon, we'll have to go without
them.*

➤ Remember that you **arrive in** a city or country:
✓ *We arrived in Madrid at 10 o'clock that night.*
✗ *We arrived to Madrid at 10 o'clock that
night.*

➤ THESAURUS: If you **arrive** somewhere, you
reach that place. For example, you can arrive
at a party, or in a city, or at work. If you **enter**
a place, you go into a place, often a building or
a room. If you **turn up** at a place, you arrive
there, often unexpectedly, or very late.

arrow /ˈærəʊ/ NOUN [plural arrows]
1 a pointed shape used to show a particular direction □ *Follow the red arrows to the X-ray department.*
2 a thin, pointed stick that is used as a weapon

art /ɑːt/ NOUN [plural arts]
1 *no plural* the beautiful things that people make and invent in painting, music, writing, etc.
2 a skill that you use to do or make something □ *the art of conversation*
3 the arts subjects that you can study that are not sciences

artery /ˈɑːtəri/ NOUN [plural arteries] a tube that takes blood from your heart to the rest of your body. A biology word.

article /ˈɑːtɪkəl/ NOUN [plural articles]
1 a piece of writing in a magazine or newspaper 🔁 *Maya wrote an article for the school magazine.* 🔁 *I read an interesting article in the newspaper.* □ *+ about/on* an article about farming
2 a thing 🔁 *There were a few articles of clothing on the floor.*
3 in grammar, the words 'a', 'an' and 'the'

> ➤ **THESAURUS:** An article is a piece of writing for a newspaper or a magazine. An essay is a piece of writing by a student about a particular subject. A story is a piece of writing, often about invented things. For example, we often read stories to children before they go to bed. Story can also be used to describe a report in a newspaper or on television about something that has happened.

artificial /ˌɑːtɪˈfɪʃəl/ ADJECTIVE looking natural, but made by a person or machine □ *artificial snow*

artist /ˈɑːtɪst/ NOUN [plural artists]
1 someone who paints or draws things □ *the well-known French artist, Claude Monet*
2 a performer, for example a singer or a dancer

artistic /ɑːˈtɪstɪk/ ADJECTIVE
1 to do with art □ *The ballet was one of his greatest artistic achievements.*
2 good at art □ *Emma's very artistic.*

as /əz/ CONJUNCTION, PREPOSITION
1 as ... as used to compare things □ *Are you as tall as me?* □ *This restaurant's not as cheap as the other one.*
2 while □ *As we climbed, the air got colder.*
3 used to talk about the purpose or job of something

or someone □ *She works as a teacher.* □ *I use this room as my study.*
4 as if/as though used to talk about how something seems □ *He looks as if he's going to faint.* □ *She cried as though her heart was broken.*
5 because □ *I went first as I was the youngest.*

ash /æʃ/ NOUN [plural ashes] the white powder that remains after something is burnt

ashamed /əˈʃeɪmd/ ADJECTIVE feeling embarrassed or guilty about something □ *+ of* I am deeply ashamed of everything I said, and I apologize. 🔁 *You should be ashamed of yourself, behaving like that.* □ *+ that* I felt ashamed that I had never visited him in hospital.

ashore /əˈʃɔː(r)/ ADVERB onto the land at the edge of a sea, river, etc. □ *We went ashore for dinner and returned to the ship later.*

Asian[1] /ˈeɪʒən, ˈeɪʃən/ ADJECTIVE to do with Asia, or from Asia □ *Asian art*
Asian[2] /ˈeɪʒən, ˈeɪʃən/ NOUN [plural Asians] someone who comes from Asia

aside /əˈsaɪd/ ADVERB to or on one side 🔁 *Please stand aside and let us through.*

ask /ɑːsk/ VERB [asks, asking, asked]
1 to say something as a question □ *She asked how old I was.* □ *+ about* They asked us about our families.
2 to say that you want someone to give you something □ *+ for* I asked Joanne for some food.
3 to say that you want someone to do something □ *+ to do something* He asked me to close the door.
4 to invite □ *+ to* We've asked twenty people to our party.

> ➤ Remember that you **ask someone**. You do not **ask to someone**:
> ✓ *He asked me the time.*
> ✗ *He asked to me the time.*

> ➤ **THESAURUS:** Ask is a general word. Inquire is a more formal word, and is used if you ask for information about something. For example, you might inquire about a job. If you have a query, you ask questions about something, often because you think that there has been a mistake or because you need more information. For example, you might have a query about a bill. If you question someone, you ask them questions, often officially. For example, the police might question someone about a crime.

asleep /ə'sli:p/ ADJECTIVE

1 if you are asleep, you are sleeping □ *Don't wake her if she's asleep.* 🔸 *The baby was fast asleep* (= deeply asleep) *in her pram.* 🔸 *She got out of bed, still half asleep* (= very tired).
2 fall asleep to start sleeping □ *He fell asleep in front of the television.*

aspect /'æspekt/ NOUN [plural aspects] a part of a situation or subject □ *Newspapers have examined every aspect of her life.*

aspiration /ˌæspə'reɪʃən/ NOUN [plural aspirations] a hope that you will get or achieve something □ *She has aspirations to be a lawyer.*

aspirin /'æsprɪn/ NOUN [plural aspirin or aspirins]

1 no plural a medicine that stops pain 🔸 *He takes aspirin every day.*
2 a pill that contains this medicine 🔸 *I've taken a couple of aspirins for my headache.*

assassin /ə'sæsɪn/ NOUN [plural assassins] someone who kills an important person, for example a politician

assassinate /ə'sæsɪneɪt/ VERB [assassinates, assassinating, assassinated] to kill a famous person

assassination /əˌsæsɪ'neɪʃən/ NOUN [plural assassinations] the murder of a famous person

assault[1] /ə'sɔ:lt/ NOUN [plural assaults] an attack 🔸 *It was a violent assault on an elderly woman.*

assault[2] /ə'sɔ:lt/ VERB [assaults, assaulting, assaulted] to attack someone

assemble /ə'sembəl/ VERB [assembles, assembling, assembled]

1 to bring several things or people together □ *We've assembled a choir for the concert.*
2 to make something by putting several parts together □ *Where are the instructions for assembling the bookcase?*

assembly /ə'semblɪ/ NOUN [plural assemblies]

1 a regular meeting for everyone in a school
2 a group of people who make decisions for a country or an organization □ *the General Assembly of the United Nations*

assess /ə'ses/ VERB [assesses, assessing, assessed] to examine something and make a judgment about it □ *One of our agents will assess the damage to your car.*

assignment /ə'saɪnmənt/ NOUN [plural assignments] a job someone has given you to do □ *I've got three homework assignments to finish by Friday.*

assist /ə'sɪst/ VERB [assists, assisting, assisted] to help □ *Villagers assisted in the search for the girl.*

assistance /ə'sɪstəns/ NOUN, NO PLURAL help 🔸 *The charity provides financial assistance to people in need.* 🔸 *Can I be of any assistance* (= can I help)?

assistant /ə'sɪstənt/ NOUN [plural assistants]

1 someone whose job is to help someone else

🔸 *She's a teaching assistant at the local school.*
🔸 *You can speak to the assistant manager.*
2 someone who works in a shop 🔸 *She worked as a shop assistant.*

> ➤ **THESAURUS:** An assistant is someone who helps you to do a job. For example, a teaching assistant helps a teacher in a classroom. A shop assistant helps customers in a shop. A supporter is someone who wants someone else to succeed. For example, you can be a supporter of a politician, or of a football team. A colleague is a person that you work with. An ally is a person or a country that supports another person or country.

associate VERB /ə'səʊʃɪeɪt/ [associates, associating, associated] to be related to or caused by something □ *Heavy pollution is associated with increased road travel.*

association /əˌsəʊsɪ'eɪʃən/ NOUN [plural associations] an organization for people with similar interests □ *a professional association for teachers*

assume /ə'sju:m/ VERB [assumes, assuming, assumed] to think something is true, although you have no proof □ *Oh sorry, I assumed that you had met each other before.*

assure /ə'ʃʊə(r)/ VERB [assures, assuring, assured] to tell someone that something is certainly true or will certainly happen □ *Mr Harris has assured us that the car will be ready tomorrow.*

asthma /'æsmə/ NOUN, NO PLURAL an illness that makes breathing difficult

astonish /ə'stonɪʃ/ VERB [astonishes, astonishing, astonished] to surprise someone very much □ *His arrest astonished his neighbours and friends.*

astonishment /ə'stonɪʃmənt/ NOUN, NO PLURAL the state of being very surprised □ *To my astonishment, she agreed that I could stay.* □ *We stared in astonishment at the painting.*

astronaut /'æstrənɔ:t/ NOUN [plural astronauts] someone who travels into space

astronomer /ə'stronəmə(r)/ NOUN [plural astronomers] someone who studies stars and planets

astronomy /ə'stronəmɪ/ NOUN, NO PLURAL the study of stars and planets

asylum /ə'saɪləm/ NOUN, NO PLURAL when someone is allowed to stay in a country because they are in danger in their own country 🔸 *Many people seek asylum in this country.* 🔸 *He was granted asylum in 2006.*

at /ət/ PREPOSITION

1 used to show the position of someone or something □ *Meet me at the station.* □ *The car is at Clara's house.* □ *He's still at work.*
2 used to show the time or period that something happens □ *School finishes at 4 o'clock.* □ *Will you be here at the weekend?* □ *I always visit my parents at Christmas.*

3 towards □ *He threw a bucket of water at me.* □ *Look at me!* □ *She drove the car straight at him.*
4 bad/good at something used to show someone's level of ability □ *He's good at football.*
5 used to show the price, speed, level, etc. of something □ *We bought four bottles at 75p each.* □ *The car was travelling at 70 miles an hour.*
6 used to describe someone's reaction □ *He broke down at the news.*
7 at all used for emphasis, for example when talking about something that does not exist □ *Doesn't he have any friends at all?* □ *I'm not looking forward to the party at all.*

ate /eɪt/ PAST TENSE OF **eat**

athlete /ˈæθliːt/ NOUN [plural athletes] someone who is good at sports such as running 🔁 *She is one of the country's top athletes.* 🔁 *He was an Olympic athlete in 1928.*

athletics /æθˈletɪks/ NOUN, NO PLURAL the sports that include running, jumping and throwing □ *Lee is very good at athletics.*

atlas /ˈætləs/ NOUN [plural atlases] a book of maps

atmosphere /ˈætməˌsfɪə(r)/ NOUN [plural atmospheres]
1 the feeling that a place or situation has □ *The atmosphere in the company was very friendly.* □ **+ of** *Increased crime is creating an atmosphere of fear.*
2 the air around a planet □ *the Earth's atmosphere*

atom /ˈætəm/ NOUN [plural atoms] the smallest part of a chemical element □ *Water contains two hydrogen atoms and one oxygen atom.*

atomic /əˈtɒmɪk/ ADJECTIVE using the power that is created when atoms are broken 🔁 *an atomic bomb* 🔁 *atomic energy*

attach /əˈtætʃ/ VERB [attaches, attaching, attached]
1 to join one thing to another thing □ **+ to** *They attached a rope to the car.*
2 if you attach a document to an e-mail, you send the document with the e-mail. A computing word.

attachment /əˈtætʃmənt/ NOUN [plural attachments] a document or picture that you send with an e-mail. A computing word. 🔁 *Don't open an attachment if you don't know who it's from.*

attack¹ /əˈtæk/ VERB [attacks, attacking, attacked]
1 to suddenly try to hurt someone □ **+ with** *He attacked her with a knife.* □ *A man was attacked and robbed on Friday.*
2 to try to destroy a place using weapons □ *A violent crowd tried to attack the embassy.*
3 to criticize someone or something □ *He attacked*

the government for failing to improve standards in schools.

attack² /əˈtæk/ NOUN [plural attacks]
1 a violent act against a place or person 🔁 *The attack was carried out by four men.* 🔁 *Terrorist attacks have killed thousands of people.* □ **+ on** *The attack on police officers began when an angry crowd started throwing bottles.*
2 strong criticism □ **+ on** *He launched a personal attack on the President.*

> ➤ **THESAURUS:** An attack may involve any number of people. An invasion is when the army of one country enters another country. A raid is a short or sudden attack, usually with a particular purpose. For example, a bank raid is an attack on a bank to steal money, and in a police raid, the police visit a place without warning and often use force to enter it.

attacker /əˈtækə(r)/ NOUN [plural attackers] a person who tries to hurt someone violently □ *Ravi was able to describe his attacker to police.*

attempt¹ /əˈtempt/ VERB [attempts, attempting, attempted] to try to do something □ **+ to do something** *He attempted to explain what he meant.*

attempt² /əˈtempt/ NOUN [plural attempts] when you try to do something 🔁 *Doctors made a desperate attempt to save her life.* 🔁 *She made no attempt to escape.* □ **+ to do something** *His attempt to climb Mount Everest failed.*

attend /əˈtend/ VERB [attends, attending, attended] to go to an event. A formal word. □ *More than 100 people attended the meeting.*

> ➤ People **attend** formal meetings but people usually **come to** or **go to** parties, friends' houses, football matches, etc:
> ✓ *Did Jamie come to the wedding?*
> ✗ *Did Jamie attend the wedding?*

attendance /əˈtendəns/ NOUN, NO PLURAL being present somewhere □ *She was given an award for 100% attendance at school.*

attention /əˈtenʃən/ NOUN, NO PLURAL
1 pay attention to listen or watch carefully □ **+ to** *Pay attention to what I'm saying, please.*
2 interest and thought that you give to something 🔁 *The story attracted attention from all over the world.*
3 get someone's attention to make someone notice you □ *I waved at her to get her attention.*

attic /ˈætɪk/ NOUN [plural attics] the space in the roof of a house

attitude /'ætɪtjuːd/ NOUN [plural attitudes] the way someone thinks about something ▢ He has a very positive attitude. ▢ He needs to change his attitude and start working hard. □ + to/towards Jane has a relaxed attitude to life.

attract /ə'trækt/ VERB [attracts, attracting, attracted]
1 to make someone feel interested in or like someone or something □ It was his smile that first attracted me. □ + to They were attracted to the idea of filming in Sydney because of the weather.
2 to make people come somewhere or do something □ The museum attracts visitors from all around the world. □ The programme attracted 15 million viewers.

attraction /ə'trækʃən/ NOUN [plural attractions]
1 no plural a feeling of liking someone and finding them physically attractive □ + between The attraction between them was immediate.
2 something that people want to visit or do ▢ The Eiffel Tower is a popular tourist attraction. ▢ The town's main attraction is its castle.

attractive /ə'træktɪv/ ADJECTIVE nice to look at □ She was an attractive woman. □ The hotel is set in attractive gardens.

> THESAURUS: Attractive means 'pleasant to look at', and we use it to describe people and things. For example, a building may be attractive. Both men and women can be attractive. Good-looking can also be used to talk about men and women who have attractive faces. Pretty is usually used to talk about women and girls, and handsome is usually used to talk about men.

attribute¹ /ə'trɪbjuːt/
♦ PHRASAL VERBS [attributes, attributing, attributed]
attribute something to someone to think that something was made, painted, written, etc. by a particular person □ The statue had been wrongly attributed to Bernini. **attribute something to something** to say that something is caused by something □ He attributed his success to determination.

attribute² /'ætrɪbjuːt/ NOUN [plural attributes] a quality or feature □ He was chosen for his physical attributes rather than his acting ability.

auction /'ɔːkʃən/ NOUN [plural auctions] a sale in which the person who offers the most money buys something

audience /'ɔːdɪəns/ NOUN [plural audiences] the people who listen to or watch a performance ▢ My father was in the audience tonight. ▢ Many audience members left before the end of the show.

> THESAURUS: The audience is all the people who listen to or watch a performance, for example in the theatre or the cinema. A spectator is a person who watches an event, often a sports event such as a football match. A fan is someone who likes a person or thing very much. For example, you can be a fan of a football team, or of a pop star. A viewer is a person who watches television.

audition /ɔː'dɪʃən/ NOUN [plural auditions] a short performance that an actor, dancer, etc. does so that someone else can decide if they are good enough to be in a play, musical group, etc. ▢ They're holding auditions for the show next week.

August /'ɔːgəst/ NOUN [plural Augusts] the eighth month of the year, after July and before September □ We'll visit you in August.

aunt /ɑːnt/ or **auntie** or **aunty** /'ɑːntɪ/ NOUN [plural aunts or aunties]
1 the sister of one of your parents □ My aunt and uncle live in Canada. □ Auntie Emily came to stay.
2 your uncle's wife

authentic /ɔː'θentɪk/ ADJECTIVE real □ an authentic wartime uniform

author /'ɔːθə(r)/ NOUN [plural authors] a writer □ Atkinson is the author of four novels.

authority /ɔː'θɒrətɪ/ NOUN [plural authorities]
1 no plural power and control ▢ People who are in a position of authority must behave appropriately. □ + to do something The chairman has the authority to make decisions. □ + over This law gives the government more authority over the police force.
2 an official organization or government department that controls something ▢ Some local authorities do not have enough money for repairing roads.
3 the authorities the police and people who have the power to make people obey laws □ The British authorities raised concerns over the deal.

auto /'ɔːtəʊ/ ADJECTIVE to do with cars □ the American auto industry

autograph /'ɔːtəgrɑːf/ NOUN [plural autographs] the name of a famous person, written by them ▢ Please can I have your autograph?

automatic /ˌɔːtə'mætɪk/ ADJECTIVE
1 an automatic machine works without a person operating it ▢ automatic doors ▢ Our heating system is fully automatic.
2 an automatic action is something you do without thinking □ My automatic response was to cover my face.

automatically /ˌɔːtə'mætɪkəlɪ/ ADVERB
1 without a person operating something □ The doors open automatically.

2 without thinking □ *When I saw the stone coming I automatically ducked.*

autumn /ˈɔːtəm/ NOUN [*plural* autumns] the season after summer, when the leaves change colour and fall □ *I love the colours of autumn leaves.*

availability /əˌveɪləˈbɪlətɪ/ NOUN, NO PLURAL
1 how possible it is to get something □ *Please can you check the availability of tickets for Thursday?*
2 the times when someone is free to do something

available /əˈveɪləbəl/ ADJECTIVE
1 if something is available, you can get it or buy it ⊞ *Guns are readily available* (= easy to get) *here.* ⊞ *The government plans to make more college places available to poor students.*
2 if someone is available, they are free to do something □ **+ to do something** *I'm sorry, there's nobody available to help you at the moment.*

avalanche /ˈævəlɑːnʃ/ NOUN [*plural* avalanches] a large amount of snow and rocks sliding down the side of a mountain

avenue /ˈævənjuː/ NOUN [*plural* avenues] a wide street, usually with trees on both sides

average¹ /ˈævərɪdʒ/ ADJECTIVE
1 usual or ordinary □ *How much do you earn in an average week?*
2 an average amount is the amount you get by adding amounts together and dividing by the number of amounts □ *average temperatures* □ *the average wage*

average² /ˈævərɪdʒ/ NOUN [*plural* averages]
1 the amount you get by adding amounts together and dividing by the number of amounts.
2 on average usually, or based on an average amount □ *On average, adults in this country watch three hours of TV every day.*
3 above/below average more/less than the average amount □ *Temperatures are below average for the time of year.*

avoid /əˈvɔɪd/ VERB [avoids, avoiding, avoided] to stay away from somewhere or someone □ *Have you been avoiding me?* □ *I left early to avoid the rush hour traffic.*

await /əˈweɪt/ VERB [awaits, awaiting, awaited] to wait for something or someone ⊞ *He is in prison, awaiting trial for murder.*

awake /əˈweɪk/ ADJECTIVE not sleeping ⊞ *I tried to stay awake.* ⊞ *Stop talking – you're keeping me*

awake. ⊞ *She's wide awake* (= completely awake) *by six every morning.*

➤ **Awake** is used mainly as an adjective. The verb **awake** is formal and not often used. Instead, use the phrasal verb **wake up**:
✓ *I woke up early this morning.*
✗ *I awoke early this morning.*

award¹ /əˈwɔːd/ NOUN [*plural* awards] a prize for someone who has achieved something ⊞ *Joe won an award for his contribution to football.*
award² /əˈwɔːd/ VERB [awards, awarding, awarded] to give someone a prize or something good because of what they have achieved □ *She was awarded the Nobel Prize for literature.*

aware /əˈweə(r)/ ADJECTIVE if you are aware of something, you know about it □ **+ of** *Katya became aware of someone else in the room.* □ **+ that** *I'm perfectly aware that you've been waiting a long time.*

away¹ /əˈweɪ/ ADVERB
1 to a different place or in a different place □ *He walked away.* □ *We'll be away for three weeks.*
2 at a distance □ *How far away is the school?* □ *The exam is only a week away.*
3 not at work or school □ *Tina was away today.*
4 in the place where something is kept □ *Could you put the books away, please?*

away² /əˈweɪ/ ADJECTIVE an away game or match is one a team has to travel to

awful /ˈɔːfʊl/ ADJECTIVE
1 very bad □ *an awful headache* ⊞ *The food was absolutely awful.*
2 very great □ *There is an awful lot of ice on the roads.* □ *Looking after their dogs is an awful nuisance.*

awkward /ˈɔːkwəd/ ADJECTIVE
1 difficult to manage or use □ *I find this keyboard a bit awkward.*
2 embarrassed or embarrassing □ *I feel really awkward when she asks me for money.* □ *an awkward silence*
3 awkward movements are not easy and relaxed

awoke /əˈwəʊk/ PAST TENSE OF awake
awoken /əˈwəʊkən/ PAST PARTICIPLE OF awake
axe¹ /æks/ NOUN [*plural* axes] a tool for cutting wood
axe² /æks/ VERB [axes, axing, axed] to stop a plan or a service, close a business or get rid of workers □ *Thousands of jobs were axed.*

B or **b** /biː/ the second letter of the alphabet

baby /ˈbeɪbɪ/ NOUN [*plural* babies] a very young child 🖼 *Paola has had a baby.* □ *a baby boy*

babysit /ˈbeɪbɪˌsɪt/ VERB [babysits, babysitting, babysat] to look after a baby or child when its parents are not in the house □ *Could you babysit for me on Saturday?*
babysitter /ˈbeɪbɪˌsɪtə(r)/ NOUN [*plural* babysitters] someone who looks after a baby or a child when its parents are not in the house
bachelor /ˈbætʃələ(r)/ NOUN [*plural* bachelors] a man who has never married

back¹ /bæk/ NOUN [*plural* backs]
1 the part of something that is furthest away from the front □ *Nina hid her diary at the back of a drawer.*
2 the part of the body that goes from the shoulders to the bottom □ *I always sleep on my back.*
◆ IDIOM **back to front** the wrong way, so that the part that should be at the back is now at the front □ *You've got your sweater on back to front!*

back² /bæk/ VERB [backs, backing, backed]
1 to support or help someone or something ■ *He is backing the female candidate in the election.*
2 to move backwards, usually in a car □ *She backed into the drive.*
◆ PHRASAL VERBS **back someone up** to support someone □ *If you complain to the teacher, I'll back you up.* **back something up** to make an extra

copy of information on a computer. A computing word. □ *Are the files all backed up?* **back down** to admit that you are wrong □ *He backed down when I showed him that his calculations were wrong.*

back³ /bæk/ ADVERB
1 to the place where a person or thing was before □ *What time is he coming back?* □ *Could you give Marla her book back, please?*
2 in the direction that is the opposite of forwards □ *I stood back to let her pass.* □ *She sat back in her chair.*
3 as a reply to something □ *Can I call you back in an hour?*
4 to the condition someone or something was in before □ *I went back to sleep.*
5 to an earlier time □ *Thinking back to that day, she was obviously unhappy.*

back⁴ /bæk/ ADJECTIVE away from the front □ *Ben's had one of his back teeth taken out.*

backbone /ˈbækbəʊn/ NOUN [*plural* backbones] the row of bones down the middle of your back
backdrop /ˈbækdrɒp/ NOUN [*plural* backdrops]
1 the things you can see behind the main thing you are looking at □ *The hotel is set against a backdrop of beautiful mountains.*
2 a cloth with a picture on it that is hung at the back of a stage in a theatre

background /ˈbækɡraʊnd/ NOUN [*plural* backgrounds]
1 the part of a picture which is behind the main people or objects 🖼 *Here's a photo of us with Mount Fuji in the background.*
2 a person's background is their family and the things they have done in the past □ *These children are from very poor backgrounds.*
3 the background of an event is all the things that happened before it and caused it to happen □ **+ to** *the background to the English civil war.*

backpack /ˈbækpæk/ NOUN [*plural* backpacks] a large bag that you carry on your back □ *I was carrying the tent in my backpack.*

backspace /ˈbækspeɪs/ VERB [backspaces, backspacing, backspaced] to move back one space by pressing a key on a computer. A computing word.

backup /'bækʌp/ NOUN [*plural* backups] an extra copy of information on a computer. A computing word.

backward /'bækwəd/ ADJECTIVE towards the back □ *a backward look*

backwards /'bækwədz/ ADVERB

1 in the direction behind you □ *I stepped backwards to give her some room.*
2 in the wrong position, with the back part at the front □ *I think my skirt is on backwards.*
3 in the opposite way to the usual way □ *Tom can say the alphabet backwards.*

bacon /'beɪkən/ NOUN, NO PLURAL thin pieces of salty meat from a pig

bacteria /bæk'tɪərɪə/ PLURAL NOUN very small living things that sometimes cause disease in humans and animals

bad /bæd/ ADJECTIVE [worse, worst]

1 not of a good standard □ *I've had a really bad haircut.* □ *The food was so bad I couldn't eat it.*
2 unpleasant, causing problems or worry □ *Bad weather can spoil a holiday.* □ *I had some bad news this morning.*
3 not bad satisfactory or good enough □ *We made over three hundred pounds so that's not bad.* □ *'How are you doing, Maria?' 'Not bad, thanks.'*
4 bad for someone harmful to your body, making you not healthy □ *It's bad for you to eat too much sugar.*
5 bad at something not able to do something well □ *I'm very bad at maths.*
6 food which is bad does not taste or smell good because it is old □ *This meat is bad – throw it away.*
7 evil or cruel □ *He's not a bad man.*

> ► Remember that **bad** is an adjective and not an adverb. To describe the way that someone does something, use the adverb **badly**:
> ✓ *He behaved very badly.*
> ✗ *He behaved very bad.*

bade /bæd, beɪd/ PAST TENSE OF **bid²** □ *I bade him goodbye.*

badge /bædʒ/ NOUN [*plural* badges] a small object with words or pictures that you put on your clothes to show something, for example your name

badly /'bædlɪ/ ADVERB [worse, worst]

1 seriously □ *The car was badly damaged in the crash.*
2 in a way that is not good □ *Both children behaved badly.*
3 very much □ *I badly wanted a new pair of shoes.*

bag /bæg/ NOUN [*plural* bags] an object that you put things in and carry with you □ *a leather bag* □ *a bag of crisps*

> ► THESAURUS: Bag is a general word for an object that you use for carrying things. A backpack is a large bag that you carry on your back. For example, you might use a backpack if you go camping. A handbag is a bag that a woman uses to carry things like money and keys. We use a suitcase to carry our clothes in when we are travelling.

baggage /'bægɪdʒ/ NOUN, NO PLURAL the cases and bags that a person takes with them when they travel □ *The baggage is stored in the back of the coach.*

> ► Remember that the noun **baggage** is never used in the plural:
> ✓ *I had so much baggage.*
> ✗ *I had so many baggages.*

bail¹ /beɪl/ NOUN, NO PLURAL money that must be paid to a court so that someone who has been arrested for a crime can leave a prison until their trial ⊞ *He was released on bail.*

bail² /beɪl/ VERB [bails, bailing, bailed] to allow someone to go free because bail has been paid

bait /beɪt/ NOUN, NO PLURAL food that you use for catching a fish or an animal

bake /beɪk/ VERB [bakes, baking, baked] to cook things like bread, cakes or biscuits in an oven □ *I baked a cake this afternoon.* □ *I love to bake with the children.*

balance¹ /'bæləns/ NOUN, NO PLURAL

1 when you have the same amount of weight on each side of the body so that you do not fall over ⊞ *I lost my balance and fell over.* ⊞ *I find it hard to keep my balance in high heels.*
2 a good situation in which you have or do the right amount of two or more things □ *I try to achieve a balance between work and family life.*
3 the amount of money that is in a bank account

balance[2] /ˈbæləns/ VERB [balances, balancing, balanced] to stay in a position where you do not fall to either side, or to put something in a position where it will not fall □ *Lisa balanced the book on her head.*

balcony /ˈbælkənɪ/ NOUN [plural balconies]
1 a part of a high building which is on the outside wall. You can sit or stand in it □ *We sat on the balcony and watched the sun go down.*
2 in a theatre, the area upstairs where the seats are above the rest of the audience

bald /bɔːld/ ADJECTIVE [balder, baldest] with little or no hair on the head ⊕ *He's going bald.*

ball /bɔːl/ NOUN [plural balls]
1 a round object that you use for playing games like football and tennis
2 anything that has a round shape □ *a ball of string*
□ *The hedgehog rolled itself into a ball.*
3 a big formal party where people dance

ballet /ˈbæleɪ/ NOUN [plural ballets]
1 *no plural* a type of dancing that tells a story and uses smooth, attractive movements which are very difficult to do ⊕ *a ballet dancer* □ *Sarah does ballet and tap dancing.*
2 a story which is told using ballet □ *My favourite ballets are The Nutcracker and Swan Lake.*

balloon /bəˈluːn/ NOUN [plural balloons] a very light, round, rubber object that is filled with air or gas □ *The children were holding balloons.*

ballot /ˈbælət/ NOUN [plural ballots] a way of voting in secret by marking a paper and putting it into a special box ⊕ *They held a ballot to decide who would be leader.*

bamboo /bæmˈbuː/ NOUN, NO PLURAL a tall grass that has hard, hollow stems that are used to make furniture

ban /bæn/ NOUN [plural bans] an order that people are not allowed to do something □ *There's a ban on smoking in public places.*

banana /bəˈnɑːnə/ NOUN [plural bananas] a long, curved, yellow fruit which is white inside ⊕ *I watched him peel a banana.*

band /bænd/ NOUN [plural bands]
1 a group of musicians who play together □ *a rock band*
2 a long, thin piece of material used for putting round something ⊕ *a rubber band*
3 a group □ *a band of robbers*

bandage[1] /ˈbændɪdʒ/ NOUN [plural bandages] a long piece of cloth that you put around a part of your body that has been cut or hurt □ *He had a bandage around his arm.*

bandage[2] /ˈbændɪdʒ/ VERB [bandages, bandaging, bandaged] to put a bandage around a part of your body □ *The nurse bandaged his wrist.*

bandit /ˈbændɪt/ NOUN [plural bandits] someone who attacks people who are travelling and takes money and possessions from them

bang[1] /bæŋ/ NOUN [plural bangs]
1 a sudden loud noise □ *There was a loud bang and all the lights went out.*
2 when you knock part of your body against something □ *She's had a bang on the head and is feeling a bit dizzy.*

bang[2] /bæŋ/ VERB [bangs, banging, banged]
1 to make a sudden loud noise by hitting against something □ *The door banged shut in the wind.*
2 to knock part of your body against something □ *Neil banged his head on the shelf.*

banish /ˈbænɪʃ/ VERB [banishes, banishing, banished] to make someone leave their country or their home as a punishment

bank[1] /bæŋk/ NOUN [plural banks]
1 a business that looks after other people's money and also lends money ⊕ *I must go to the bank.*
2 an area of ground which is next to a river or lake □ *We camped on the banks of Loch Lomond.*

➤ **THESAURUS:** The bank of a river or a lake is the area of land next to it. The area of land next to the sea is called the shore. A slope is the side of a hill or mountain. Side and edge are more general words. You can talk about the side of a river, but also the side of a building or a road. Edge is often used to talk about the very end or outer part of something. For example, you might talk about the edge of a cliff or the edge of a city.

---

bank[2] /bæŋk/ VERB [banks, banking, banked] to have a bank account with a particular bank □ *I've banked with them for years.*
♦ PHRASAL VERB **bank on something** to depend on something □ *He might help you but don't bank on it.*

bank account /ˈbæŋk əˈkaʊnt/ NOUN [plural bank accounts] an arrangement that you have with a bank for keeping money there, and for taking it out when you need it ⊕ *I must open a bank account.*

bank balance /ˈbæŋk ˈbæləns/ NOUN [plural bank balances] the amount of money you have in a bank account

banking /ˈbæŋkɪŋ/ NOUN, NO PLURAL the business that banks do

banknote /ˈbæŋknəʊt/ NOUN [plural banknotes] a piece of paper money □ *a £20 banknote*

bankrupt /ˈbæŋkrʌpt/ ADJECTIVE if a person or business is bankrupt, they are not able to pay the money they owe ⊕ *The business went bankrupt because costs rose.*

banner /'bænə(r)/ NOUN [plural banners] a large piece of cloth with writing on it which people carry on poles □ The anti-war protesters were carrying banners.

bar¹ /bɑː(r)/ NOUN [plural bars]
1 a place that sells alcoholic drinks □ The city is full of cafés and bars.
2 a long narrow piece of metal □ an iron bar
3 a large piece of something such as chocolate or soap □ + of a bar of chocolate

bar² /bɑː(r)/ VERB [bars, barring, barred]
1 if someone is barred from a place or barred from doing something, they are not allowed in or are not allowed to do it □ + from Anyone over the age of 12 is barred from the competition.
2 to prevent someone from going somewhere by standing in their way □ Over a hundred protestors barred the entrance to the building.
3 to lock a door or window by putting a metal bar across it

barbecue¹ /'bɑːbɪkjuː/ NOUN [plural barbecues]
1 a piece of equipment used for cooking food outdoors □ She was trying to light the barbecue. 🔁 Put some more sausages on the barbecue.
2 a party or meal outdoors where food is cooked on a barbecue 🔁 We're having a barbecue tonight.

barbecue² /'bɑːbɪkjuː/ VERB [barbecues, barbecuing, barbecued] to cook food on a barbecue

barber /'bɑːbə(r)/ NOUN [plural barbers]
1 a man whose job is to cut men's hair
2 barber's a shop where men have their hair cut

bare /beə(r)/ ADJECTIVE [barer, barest] not covered with anything 🔁 It's too cold to go out with bare legs. □ The wall looks really bare without any pictures on it.

barely /'beəlɪ/ ADVERB almost not □ She was old and barely able to walk. □ They had barely arrived when they had to leave again.

bargain /'bɑːɡɪn/ NOUN [plural bargains]
1 something that is cheap or cheaper than usual □ These jeans were a real bargain.
2 an agreement in which each person or group promises to do something 🔁 She tried to strike a bargain with (= make an agreement with) him.

barge /bɑːdʒ/ NOUN [plural barges] a boat with a flat bottom, used on canals (= passages of water) and rivers

bark¹ /bɑːk/ NOUN [plural barks]
1 the short, loud sound that a dog makes
2 the rough wood on the outside of a tree

bark² /bɑːk/ VERB [barks, barking, barked] when a dog barks, it makes a short, loud sound

barn /bɑːn/ NOUN [plural barns] a large building on a farm, for keeping crops or animals in

barracks /'bærəks/ PLURAL NOUN a group of buildings where soldiers live and work

barrel /'bærəl/ NOUN [plural barrels]
1 a wooden or metal container with curved sides, used for holding liquids such as beer
2 the barrel of a gun is the metal tube through which the bullet is fired

barrier /'bærɪə(r)/ NOUN [plural barriers]
1 a gate or fence used to stop people getting past □ There is a barrier at the exit of the car park, and you need a ticket to get out.
2 something that stops you from making progress or stops you from being successful □ Nowadays, being a woman isn't a barrier to a career in the navy.

> ➤ **THESAURUS:** A barrier is a thing which stops people moving forward. For example, there might be a barrier at the entrance or exit of a car park or a station to check tickets. A wall is a structure that separates two areas or goes round an area. You might have a wall around your garden. Walls are usually made of something hard such as brick or concrete. A fence goes around land, and is usually made of wood or metal. You might have a fence around a garden or a field. A railing is a fence made of vertical metal bars. You often see railings around parks in cities.

barrister /'bærɪstə(r)/ NOUN [plural barristers] a lawyer who works in a court

base¹ /beɪs/ NOUN [plural bases]
1 the lowest part of something □ + of He broke a bone at the base of his spine.
2 something which is under something else and which supports it □ The shed stood on a concrete base.
3 the main place where someone works or stays □ + for The hotel is an ideal base for walking holidays.

base² /beɪs/ VERB [bases, basing, based] if a person or organization is based in a particular place, that is where they live or do their work □ **usually passive** The company is based in Moscow.
◆ PHRASAL VERB **base something on something** to use an idea, situation, fact etc. as the thing that you develop something else from □ **often passive** The court's decision was based on facts.

baseball /'beɪsbɔːl/ NOUN [plural baseballs]
1 no plural a game for two teams who hit a ball with a long bat (= wooden stick) and run to four different places 🔁 He taught me how to play baseball. □ a baseball game
2 a small ball used in the game of baseball

basement /'beɪsmənt/ NOUN [plural basements] the lowest level of a building, under the ground □ There is a restaurant in the basement. □ a basement flat

bases /'beɪsiːz/ PLURAL OF basis and base

basic /'beɪsɪk/ ADJECTIVE
1 being the main or most important part of something □ *He taught us the basic principles of karate.* □ *basic training/skills*
2 without any extra or special features □ *The cottage was pretty basic – it didn't even have a proper bath.*

basin /'beɪsən/ NOUN [plural basins]
1 a bowl with taps (= objects you turn to get water) for washing your hands and face in
2 a bowl used in the kitchen for holding food □ *a pudding basin*

> ► THESAURUS: We usually call the bowl that we use for washing in the bathroom a basin. The bowl which we use for washing things in the kitchen is usually called a sink. Basin is also a word for a bowl that we use for preparing food. Bowl is a more general word, and a bowl can be large or small. We use bowls for eating from and also for cooking. Dish is also a general word, and can be a **plate** or a **bowl**.

basis /'beɪsɪs/ NOUN [plural bases]
1 on a regular/part-time/unpaid, etc. basis used to express the method or system used for arranging or organizing something □ *The team meets on a weekly basis.* □ *I work there on a voluntary basis.*
2 the thing on which something is based 🕮 *Sweets can be eaten occasionally but should not form the basis of your diet.*

basket /'bɑːskɪt/ NOUN [plural baskets] a container for storing or carrying things, made of thin pieces of material such as wood or plastic 🕮 *a shopping basket* □ *+ of a basket of fruit*

basketball /'bɑːskɪtbɔːl/ NOUN [plural basketballs]
1 no plural a game played by two teams who try to throw a ball through a net
2 a large ball used to play basketball

bat¹ /bæt/ NOUN [plural bats]
1 a piece of wood used for hitting the ball in sports such as cricket and baseball
2 an animal that flies around at night, and looks like a mouse with wings

bat² /bæt/ VERB [bats, batting, batted] to use the bat in games such as cricket and baseball □ *It's Gary's turn to bat next.*

batch /bætʃ/ NOUN [plural batches] several people or things that are dealt with as a group □ *He tied a batch of papers together.*

bath¹ /bɑːθ/ NOUN [plural baths]
1 a long container that you fill with water and sit or lie in to wash yourself □ *Russell's in the bath.* 🕮 *She went upstairs and ran a bath* (= put water in it).

2 when you sit or lie in a long container filled with water so that you can wash yourself 🕮 *I think I'll have a bath.*

bath² /bɑːθ/ VERB [baths, bathing, bathed] to wash someone in a bath

bathroom /'bɑːθrum/ NOUN [plural bathrooms] the room that you wash yourself in □ *The hotel rooms all have a private bathroom.* □ *a bathroom mirror*

batsman /'bætsmən/ NOUN [plural batsmen] a man who is hitting the ball in cricket

batter¹ /'bætə(r)/ VERB [batters, battering, battered] to hit someone or something very hard several times □ *He was battered to death with a hammer.* □ *Waves battered the shore.*
• **battered** /'bætəd/ ADJECTIVE damaged □ *a battered leather suitcase*

batter² /'bætə(r)/ NOUN, NO PLURAL a mixture of flour, milk and eggs, used for covering food before it is fried
• **battered** /'bætəd/ ADJECTIVE covered in batter □ *battered cod*

battery /'bætərɪ/ NOUN [plural batteries] a device used to supply electrical power to things like watches, cameras and car engines 🕮 *The car wouldn't start because the battery was flat* (= the battery did not work).

battle /'bætəl/ NOUN [plural battles] a fight between two armies □ *the Battle of Hastings* □ *His father was killed in battle.*

> ► THESAURUS: A battle is a fight between two armies. A war describes a longer period of fighting between two armies, groups or countries. A war may include a number of different battles. Fight is a more general word. A fight can be a situation where people use force to hurt each other, or an argument between people.

battlefield /'bætəlfiːld/ NOUN [plural battlefields] a place where armies fight

bay /beɪ/ NOUN [plural bays] a piece of land on the coast that curves in □ *the Bay of Biscay*

BBC /ˌbiːbiːˈsiː/ ABBREVIATION British Broadcasting Corporation; the television and radio company paid for by the public in the UK

BC /ˌbiːˈsiː/ ABBREVIATION before Christ; used after a date to show that it was before the birth of Jesus Christ. □ *450 BC*
➜ *go to* **AD**

be¹ /biː/ VERB
1 used for giving information about someone or something □ *He's French.* □ *Are you hungry?* □ *Her brother's an accountant.*
2 there are/is/were, etc. used for saying

that something exists or existed □ *There are a lot of people here.* □ *Is there anything else to eat?*

be² /bi:/ AUXILIARY VERB

1 used with the present participle of another verb to talk about actions that were or are continuous □ *I am enjoying my course.* □ *What are you doing?* □ *He is not doing very well at school*

2 used with the present participle of another verb to talk about actions in the future □ *He is going to London next week.* □ *They are opening a new shop.* □ *I am coming back again later.*

3 used with the past participle of another verb to make passive sentences □ *She was taken to hospital.* □ *They have been warned before.* □ *The animals will be kept in a zoo.*

beach /bi:tʃ/ NOUN [*plural* beaches] an area of sand or stones at the edge of the sea □ *We spent the day on the beach.* 🔁 *The town has a beautiful sandy beach.*

➤ **THESAURUS:** A beach is an area of sand or stones next to the sea. People often go to a beach to play or swim. The shore describes the area of land where water such as sea or a lake reaches the land. People may not be able to go on a particular part of a shore, for example if it is very rocky. Coast describes any area next to the sea and involves a bigger area than shore. For example, we can say that a town is on the coast, or that a road travels along a coast.

bead /bi:d/ NOUN [*plural* beads] a small round piece of glass, plastic or wood with a hole through it, used for making jewellery

beak /bi:k/ NOUN [*plural* beaks] a bird's beak is its hard pointed mouth

beam¹ /bi:m/ NOUN [*plural* beams]
1 a line of light □ *the beam of the car's headlights*
2 a long thick piece of wood or metal that is used to support the weight of a building
3 a big smile
beam² /bi:m/ VERB [beams, beaming, beamed] to smile a big smile □ *Meg beamed at him gratefully.*

bean /bi:n/ NOUN [*plural* beans] a vegetable that is the large seed of some plants □ *kidney beans*

bear¹ /beə(r)/ VERB [bears, bearing, bore, born *or* borne]
1 to accept something unpleasant or painful 🔁 *I can't bear the thought of him suffering.* □ *+ to do something Stephanie can't bear to leave her children.* □ *Can you bear to wait a bit longer for dinner?*
2 bear something in mind to remember that something is important □ *Please bear in mind that you only have an hour to write your essay.*

3 to carry something in your hand □ *Hassan appeared, bearing a cup of coffee.*
• **bearable** /'beərəbəl/ ADJECTIVE if something is bearable, you can accept it, despite the fact that it is bad □ *The warmer weather made life a bit more bearable.*

bear² /beə(r)/ NOUN [*plural* bears] a large, strong animal with thick fur

beard /bɪəd/ NOUN [*plural* beards] the hair that grows on a man's chin 🔁 *He wanted to grow a beard.* 🔁 *Dieter shaved off his beard.*

beast /bi:st/ NOUN [*plural* beasts]
1 an animal, especially a large one
2 an old-fashioned word meaning a cruel person

beat¹ /bi:t/ VERB [beats, beating, beat, beaten]
1 to defeat someone in a game or competition □ *England were beaten 3-0 by Italy.* □ *+ at She beat me at squash.*
2 to hit someone or something many times □ *He was beaten and robbed by two men.*
3 to make a regular sound or movement □ *He could hear his heart beating.*
4 to mix food together very quickly □ *Beat the eggs.*
♦ PHRASAL VERB **beat someone up** to hit or kick someone until they are badly injured □ *He was beaten up by some boys in his class.*

beat² /bi:t/ NOUN [*plural* beats]
1 a regular sound or movement like that made by your heart □ *+ of I could hear the rapid beat of her heart.*
2 a regular rhythm in music

beautiful /'bju:tɪfʊl/ ADJECTIVE
1 very attractive □ *She was a very beautiful young woman.* 🔁 *She looked beautiful in her long blue dress.* □ *beautiful countryside* □ *beautiful music*
2 very sunny and bright □ *It was a cold but beautiful day.*

beauty /'bju:tɪ/ NOUN, NO PLURAL the quality of being very attractive 🔁 *The area is noted for its natural beauty.* □ *+ of the beauty of her face*

became /bɪ'keɪm/ PAST TENSE OF **become**

because /bɪ'kɒz/ CONJUNCTION
1 used for giving the reason for something □ *We chose the hotel because it was easy for everyone to get to.* □ *You can't borrow my bike because there's something wrong with the brakes.*
2 because of as a result of □ *Because of your rudeness, we've lost the job.* □ *We decided not to go because of the rain.*

become /bɪ'kʌm/ VERB [becomes, becoming, became, become]
1 to begin to be something □ *She'd become old and frail.* □ *He became prime minister in 1997.*

2 what became of someone/something used to ask what has happened to someone or something □ *Do you remember the woman with the pink coat? I wonder what became of her?*

bed /bed/ NOUN [*plural* beds]
1 a piece of furniture that you sleep on □ *He was ill and spent the day in bed.* 🔊 *I got out of bed and went downstairs.* 🔊 *What time do you usually go to bed?* 🔊 *I need to make the bed (= put the sheets on it).* 🔊 *The room had a double bed (= bed for two people) in it.*
2 the bottom of a river, a lake or the sea 🔊 *the sea bed*
3 an area in a garden that contains flowers and other plants 🔊 *He was weeding the flower bed.*

> ➤ THESAURUS: Bed is a general word for the piece of furniture that you sleep on. A single bed is a bed for one person. A double bed is a bed for two people. A cot is a bed with high sides that a baby sleeps in. The mattress is the soft part of the bed, that you lie on.

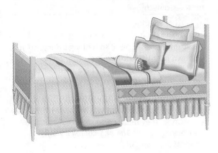

bedroom /'bedrʊm/ NOUN [*plural* bedrooms] a room that you sleep in 🔊 *We have a spare bedroom so you can come and stay.* □ *bedroom furniture*

bee /biː/ NOUN [*plural* bees] a black and yellow insect that makes honey

beef /biːf/ NOUN, NO PLURAL meat from a cow 🔊 *We had roast beef for dinner.*

been /biːn/ PAST PARTICIPLE OF be □ *I have been thinking.*

beer /bɪə(r)/ NOUN [*plural* beers]
1 NO PLURAL an alcoholic drink made from a type of grain 🔊 *He had a pint of beer in his hand.* 🔊 *empty beer bottles*
2 a glass of this drink □ *I'll have a beer please.*

beetle /'biːtəl/ NOUN [*plural* beetles] a black insect with a hard back

before¹ /bɪ'fɔː(r)/ PREPOSITION
1 earlier than something 🔊 *He lost his job just before Christmas.* □ *I posted the letter the day before yesterday.* □ *+ ing He tidied the house before going to bed.*
2 if one place is before another place, you get to that place first □ *Our house is just before the turning on the left.*
3 before long soon □ *Before long, we became good friends.*

before² /bɪ'fɔː(r)/ CONJUNCTION earlier than the time when something will happen □ *Wash your hands before you come to the table.*

before³ /bɪ'fɔː(r)/ ADVERB at an earlier time □ *I don't think we've met before.* 🔊 *We had all been to the beach the day before.*

beg /beg/ VERB [begs, begging, begged]
1 to ask someone for something in an eager or emotional way because you want it very much □ *I begged him to come home.*
2 to ask people for money in the street because you are very poor
3 I beg your pardon (a) a formal way of saying sorry when you have made a mistake □ *Oh, I beg your pardon, I didn't realize this pen was yours.* (b) a formal way of asking someone to repeat what they have just said because you did not hear it □ *'I'm going now.' 'I beg your pardon.' 'I said, I'm going now.'*

began /bɪ'gæn/ PAST TENSE OF begin

beggar /'begə(r)/ NOUN [*plural* beggars] someone who asks people for money in the street

begin /bɪ'gɪn/ VERB [begins, beginning, began, begun]
1 to start □ *The concert began at 7.30 and finished at 9.30.* □ *+ to do something I was beginning to feel better.* □ *+ ing She began walking towards the door.* □ *+ with The year began with a big disappointment.*
2 to begin with at the start of something □ *Lorna didn't like her new school to begin with.*

beginner /bɪ'gɪnə(r)/ NOUN [*plural* beginners] someone who has just started to do or to learn something □ *a guitar class for beginners*

> ➤ THESAURUS: A beginner is someone who is starting to do or learn something. A learner is also learning to do something, but a learner may or may not be a beginner. For example, you can be a language learner for many years. A recruit is someone who has just joined a company or an organization. New soldiers are also called recruits.

beginning /bɪ'gɪnɪŋ/ NOUN, NO PLURAL the start of something or the first part of something 🔊 *My birthday is at the beginning of July.* 🔊 *He led from* the beginning of the race. 🔁 In the beginning, I didn't like her very much.

begun /bɪˈɡʌn/ PAST PARTICIPLE OF **begin**

behalf /bɪˈhɑːf/ NOUN on someone's behalf /on behalf of someone else □ Petra spoke on behalf of the other students.

behave /bɪˈheɪv/ VERB [behaves, behaving, behaved]
1 to do things in a particular way 🔁 I'm sorry – I've behaved badly. 🔁 He was behaving like a child!
2 to be polite and not do anything that you should not do □ Did the children behave? 🔁 I hope Harry behaved himself.

behavior /bɪˈheɪvjə(r)/ NOUN, NO PLURAL the US spelling of **behaviour**

behaviour /bɪˈheɪvjə(r)/ NOUN, NO PLURAL the way you behave 🔁 Children should be rewarded for good behaviour. 🔁 I've never seen such bad behaviour. □ + **towards** His behaviour towards Sarah was appalling.

➤ Remember that the noun **behaviour** is never used in the plural:
✓ The children's behaviour was awful.
✗ The children's behaviours were awful.

behind[1] /bɪˈhaɪnd/ PREPOSITION
1 at the back of something or someone □ Look behind the sofa. □ Rachel peeped out from behind the curtains. □ Shut the door behind you, please.
2 making less progress than other people 🔁 Roberto's fallen behind the rest of the class
3 behind someone's back without someone knowing □ I don't like people talking about me behind my back.

behind[2] /bɪˈhaɪnd/ ADVERB
1 at the back 🔁 The car was hit from behind.
2 late in doing something □ I'm behind with my work.
3 in the place where you were 🔁 I stayed behind after the class to talk to my teacher. 🔁 I left my bag behind.

beige /beɪʒ/ ADJECTIVE having a light brown colour □ They chose a beige carpet.

being[1] /ˈbiːɪŋ/ VERB the present participle of the verb be □ Help! I'm being attacked!

being[2] /ˈbiːɪŋ/ NOUN [plural beings] a person or creature □ a being from another planet

belief /bɪˈliːf/ NOUN [plural beliefs] something you believe, especially something that you think is true or something that you think exists 🔁 religious beliefs □ + **that** There is a widespread belief that the economy will improve. □ + **in** His belief in God remained with him all his life.

believe /bɪˈliːv/ VERB [believes, believing, believed]
1 to think that something is true □ I believed his story. □ I found his excuses difficult to believe. □ + **that** I can't believe that you did that!
2 to think that something is true although you are not completely sure. A formal word. □ + **that** I believe that they're getting married.
♦ PHRASAL VERB **believe in something**
1 to think that something exists □ I don't believe in ghosts. **2** to think that something is important or acceptable □ I don't believe in hitting children.

believer /bɪˈliːvə(r)/ NOUN [plural believers] someone who believes something, especially someone who believes in a particular religion

bell /bel/ NOUN [plural bells]
1 a hollow metal object that makes a ringing sound when it moves 🔁 The church bells were ringing.
2 a device that makes a ringing sound when you press it □ a bicycle bell 🔁 She walked up to the front door and rang the bell.

belly /ˈbeli/ NOUN [plural bellies] an informal word for the stomach

belong /bɪˈlɒŋ/
♦ PHRASAL VERBS [belongs, belonging, belonged]
belong to someone if something belongs to you, you own it □ Who does this suitcase belong to?
belong to something to be a member of an organization □ Peter belongs to the local tennis club.

belongings /bɪˈlɒŋɪŋz/ PLURAL NOUN the things you own 🔁 They returned to the hotel to collect their belongings. 🔁 The bag contained a few personal belongings.

➤ THESAURUS: Your belongings are the things that you own, especially when you are carrying them with you. Possessions and property are more general words to describe the things that you own. Your stuff or your things are more informal words for this. Goods are things that have been made to sell. For example, a lorry delivers goods to a shop.

beloved /bɪˈlʌvɪd/ ADJECTIVE loved very much □ I lost my beloved old teddy bear.

below[1] /bɪˈləʊ/ PREPOSITION
1 in a lower place or position □ The plane was flying below the clouds. □ Simon was in the class below me in school.
2 less than a particular amount or level □ Audience numbers never fell below 1000. 🔁 The results were below average.

below[2] /bɪˈləʊ/ ADVERB at or to a lower place □ We climbed to the top of the hill and looked down *on the valley below.* □ *Write your name and address below.*

belt /belt/ NOUN [plural belts] a narrow piece of leather or cloth that you wear around your waist 🔀 *Karim undid his belt.*

bench /bentʃ/ NOUN [plural benches] a long seat 🔀 *a park bench*

> ➤ THESAURUS: A bench is a long seat which may have arms and a back. We often see benches outdoors, for example in a park. A sofa is a long comfortable seat for more than one person. A chair is a piece of furniture for one person, with a back. It may be hard or soft. A stool is a seat without a back. You sit on a stool to play the piano. Seat is a more general word to describe any object that you sit on. A seat may be a chair, a bench outside, or it may be the place where you sit in a vehicle such as a car or a plane.

bend¹ /bend/ VERB [bends, bending, bent]
1 to move the top part of your body to a lower position □ *She bent down to pick up some paper she'd dropped.*
2 to move a part of your body so that it is no longer straight 🔀 *Bend your knees slightly.*
3 to curve □ *He bent the wire around the post.* □ *The road bends to the right up ahead.*

bend² /bend/ NOUN [plural bends] a curve 🔀 *There was a sharp bend in the road.*

beneath /bɪˈniːθ/ PREPOSITION, PREPOSITION below or under something □ *He lay on the ground beneath the tree.* □ *I didn't realize there was another layer of chocolates beneath.*

beneficial /ˌbenɪˈfɪʃəl/ ADJECTIVE having a good effect on someone or something 🔀 *Improved diet had a beneficial effect on patients.*

benefit¹ /ˈbenɪfɪt/ NOUN [plural benefits] an advantage that you get from something 🔀 *Most patients get some benefit from the treatment.* 🔀 *The centre is run for the benefit of (= in order to help) the community.*

benefit² /ˈbenɪfɪt/ VERB [benefits, benefiting/US benefitting, benefited/US benefitted] if you benefit from something, or if something benefits you, it helps you □ **+ from** *I think you'll benefit from the extra lessons.*

bent¹ /bent/ PAST TENSE AND PAST PARTICIPLE OF **bend¹**
bent² /bent/ ADJECTIVE not straight □ *a bent pin*
berry /ˈberi/ NOUN [plural berries] a small soft fruit containing seeds □ *Holly has red berries.*

beside /bɪˈsaɪd/ PREPOSITION next to or at the side of someone or something □ *There was a chair beside the bed.* □ *Go and stand beside Billy.*

besides¹ /bɪˈsaɪdz/ PREPOSITION as well as □ *Besides playing the piano, she sings in a choir.*
besides² /bɪˈsaɪdz/ ADVERB also □ *It's too wet to go out. Besides, I'm really tired.*

best¹ /best/ ADJECTIVE better than everyone or everything else 🔀 *Mia is my best friend.* 🔀 *What's the best way to cook this fish?* □ *It is probably best to arrive a little early.*

best² /best/ NOUN
1 the best the person or thing that is better than all others □ *Which of these computers is the best?*
2 do/try your best to do something as well as you can □ *It doesn't matter if you don't win, just do your best.*

best³ /best/ ADVERB
1 more than everything else 🔀 *What food do you like best?* 🔀 *The area is best known for its wine.*
2 in the most satisfactory way □ *She performs best when she is slightly nervous.*

bet¹ /bet/ VERB [bets, betting, bet or betted]
1 I bet (a) used for saying what you think will happen or what you think is true □ *I bet he'll forget to come.* □ *I bet Jane wasn't pleased about that.* (b) used for saying that you understand why someone feels the way they do □ *'I was really upset when he told me.' 'I bet you were!'*
2 to try to win money by guessing the result of a competition, etc. □ *My uncle bets on horse races.* □ *I bet him 50p that I could climb the tree.*

bet² /bet/ NOUN [plural bets] money that you risk by trying to guess the result of a competition 🔀 *I put a bet on the winning horse.*

betray /bɪˈtreɪ/ VERB [betrays, betraying, betrayed] to do something which harms someone who trusts you □ *He betrayed me by telling everyone my secret.*

better¹ /ˈbetə(r)/ ADJECTIVE
1 of a higher standard or more suitable or enjoyable □ *I want to buy a better computer.* 🔀 *Is his work getting any better?* 🔀 *His French is much better than mine.* □ *It's better to buy spices from an Asian shop.*
2 not as ill 🔀 *I hope you get better soon.* 🔀 *Are you feeling better now?*
3 the bigger/faster, etc. the better the more big/fast, etc. something is, the more you will like it

better² /ˈbetə(r)/ ADVERB
1 in a more enjoyable or suitable way or to a higher standard □ *Which do you like better, the green one or the blue one?* □ *Try to do better next time.* □ *I wish I could swim better.*

2 I/he, etc. had better used to say that someone ought to do something □ *I'd better hurry, or I'll be late.* □ *I think you had better apologize.*
3 better off **(a)** richer □ *We're better off now than we were ten years ago.* **(b)** in a better situation □ *You'd be better off hiring a car rather than buying one.*

between /bɪ'twiːn/ PREPOSITION, ADVERB
1 in the area that divides two people, things or places □ *What letter comes between Q and S in the alphabet?* □ *I had to stand between Dan and Shona.* □ *We were on the road between San Francisco and Los Angeles.*
2 in the period of time that separates two times □ *The shop is closed between 2 and 3.* □ *There was only a week between the wedding and their house move.*
3 used to show a range of amounts or measurements □ *We usually have between 2 and 4 centimetres of rainfall in January.*
4 used to show the people or groups involved in something □ *There was an interesting discussion between Angela and Kim.* □ *The match between Leeds and Arsenal has been cancelled.* □ *Between us, we cleaned the whole house.*
5 used to show the differences of two things, people or groups □ *Can you see the difference between the real jewels and the fakes?*
6 used to show how something is divided □ *Russell and Colin divided the work between them.*

beware /bɪ'weə(r)/ VERB used for warning someone about something □ *The sign on the gate said 'Beware of the dog'.*

➤ The verb **beware** does not have different forms or tenses like other verbs, because it is only used when you are telling people what to do or giving them a warning.

beyond /bɪ'jɒnd/ PREPOSITION, ADVERB
1 on the other side of something □ *Turn right just beyond the bridge.* □ *She had never travelled beyond Europe.* □ *I stared out of the window at the hills beyond.*
2 after a particular time □ *The strike is likely to continue beyond Christmas.*

bias /'baɪəs/ NOUN [*plural* biases] when someone supports one person or thing in a way that is unfair □ *She felt there was a bias against female employees.*

Bible /'baɪbəl/ NOUN [*plural* Bibles] the holy book of the Christian religion

biblical /'bɪblɪkəl/ ADJECTIVE to do with the Bible, or in the Bible □ *a biblical character*

bicycle /'baɪsɪkəl/ NOUN [*plural* bicycles] a vehicle you sit on and turn the wheels by pressing the pedals (= parts your feet go on) ⊕ *I learned to ride a bicycle when I was six.*

bid¹ /bɪd/ NOUN [*plural* bids] an amount of money that you offer to pay for something that a lot of people want to buy ⊕ *The highest bid for the house was £300,000.*
bid² /bɪd/ VERB [bids, bidding, bid] to offer to pay a particular amount of money for something ⊕ *Will someone bid £5 for this beautiful old chair?*
bid³ /bɪd/ VERB [bids, bidding, bid or bade, bidden or bid] to say something such as 'good morning' or 'good night' to someone. An old-fashioned word. □ *He bade me goodnight.*

big /bɪg/ ADJECTIVE [bigger, biggest]
1 large in size □ *a big car* □ *It was the biggest fish he'd ever seen.* ⊕ *They live in a great big* (= very big) *house.*
2 important and having a large effect □ *a big decision* □ *a big mistake* □ *There's a big match on TV tonight.*
3 big brother/sister a brother or sister who is older than you □ *I've got a big sister and a little brother.*

bike /baɪk/ NOUN [*plural* bikes] a bicycle ⊕ *Can you ride a bike?* ⊕ *We went on a bike ride.* ⊕ *The road has a separate bike lane.*

bikini /bɪ'kiːnɪ/ NOUN [*plural* bikinis] a piece of clothing in two parts that women wear for swimming

bill /bɪl/ NOUN [*plural* bills]
1 a piece of paper showing how much you must pay for something ⊕ *Have you paid the phone bill?* □ *a gas bill*
2 a suggestion for a new law that people in a government vote for or against ⊕ *The government have passed a bill* (= made a law) *which will restrict Internet gambling.*
3 the US word for **note¹** (= piece of paper money) □ *a $100 bill*

➤ **THESAURUS:** A bill is a piece of paper which tells you how much money you must pay for something such as electricity or the telephone. An account is an arrangement with a bank to keep your money there. A statement is a piece of paper which tells you how much money you have in your bank account.

billion /ˈbɪljən/ NUMBER [*plural* billions] the number 1,000,000,000 □ *The government gets billions of pounds a year from taxes.*

billionaire /ˌbɪljəˈneə(r)/ NOUN [*plural* billionaires] someone who has a billion pounds or a billion dollars or more

bin /bɪn/ NOUN [*plural* bins] a container for putting rubbish in 🔁 *a rubbish bin* 🔁 *You should put paper in the recycling bin.*

bind /baɪnd/ VERB [binds, binding, bound] to tie something together □ *The robbers bound his hands and feet with tape.*

bingo /ˈbɪŋgəʊ/ NOUN, NO PLURAL a game in which you mark numbers on a card when someone shouts those numbers. You win if you are the first person to mark all the numbers on your card.

binoculars /bɪˈnɒkjʊləz/ PLURAL NOUN a piece of equipment that you hold up to your eyes to help you see things that are a long way away □ *She was watching the birds with a pair of binoculars.*

biography /baɪˈɒgrəfɪ/ NOUN [*plural* biographies] a book about a real person's life □ + *of She wrote a biography of Napoleon.*

biological /ˌbaɪəˈlɒdʒɪkəl/ ADJECTIVE to do with living things and the way they grow and behave □ *a biological process*

biologist /baɪˈɒlədʒɪst/ NOUN [*plural* biologists] a person who studies biology

biology /baɪˈɒlədʒɪ/ NOUN, NO PLURAL the study of living things

bird /bɜːd/ NOUN [*plural* birds] a creature with wings and feathers that produces eggs □ *wild birds* □ *There was a bird's nest in the tree.*

birth /bɜːθ/ NOUN [*plural* births]
1 the time when someone is born □ *He was there at the births of all his children.* 🔁 *What is your date of birth* (= the date when you were born)?
2 give birth if a woman gives birth, a baby comes out of her body □ *She gave birth to a healthy baby boy.*

birthday /ˈbɜːθdeɪ/ NOUN [*plural* birthdays] the date you were born which happens each year □ *It's my mother's 60th birthday next week.* 🔁 *Happy Birthday, John!* 🔁 *I'm going to his birthday party.* 🔁 *Did you get a lot of birthday presents?*

biscuit /ˈbɪskɪt/ NOUN [*plural* biscuits] a flat hard cake □ *He was eating a chocolate biscuit.* 🔁 *a packet of biscuits*

bishop /ˈbɪʃəp/ NOUN [*plural* bishops] an important priest in some Christian churches

bit¹ /bɪt/ NOUN [*plural* bits]
1 a bit (a) slightly □ *I'm a bit tired today.* 🔁 *He looks a bit like David Beckham.* (b) a short time □ *We had to wait a bit for the bus.* 🔁 *I don't mind looking after her for a bit.* (c) a small amount □ *'Would you like some more fish?' 'Yes, just a bit, please.'* □ + *of I need a bit of help with my homework.*
2 a piece or part of something bigger □ + *of There were some bits of the book that I enjoyed.*
3 quite a bit a lot □ *He's quite a bit taller than his wife.*

➤ The phrase **a bit** meaning 'slightly' is used a lot in spoken English but is too informal for formal written English. If you are writing an essay, it is better to use the words **slightly** or **a little**:
✓ *Attitudes to this subject have changed slightly.*
✗ *Attitudes to this subject have changed a bit.*

bit² /bɪt/ PAST TENSE OF **bite¹**

bite¹ /baɪt/ VERB [bites, biting, bit, bitten]
1 to use your teeth to cut through something □ + *into Guy bit into the apple.* 🔁 *A lot of people bite their nails.*
2 if an animal bites, it injures someone with its teeth □ *She was badly bitten by a dog.*

bite² /baɪt/ NOUN [*plural* bites]
1 when you bite food with your teeth 🔁 *Ali took a bite of the sausage.*
2 an injury on your skin where an animal or insect has bitten you 🔁 *an insect bite* □ *a mosquito bite*

bitten /ˈbɪtən/ PAST PARTICIPLE OF **bite¹**

bitter /ˈbɪtə(r)/ ADJECTIVE
1 angry because you feel someone has treated you badly □ *He turned into a bitter old man.*
2 having a strong taste such as you find in strong coffee □ *Dark chocolate is too bitter for me.*
3 if the weather is bitter, it is extremely cold □ *It's bitter out there!*

black¹ /blæk/ ADJECTIVE
1 having the colour of coal or the sky at night □ *I bought a black coat.*
2 black people are of a race that have dark brown skin □ *We need more black police officers.*
3 black tea or coffee has no milk in it

black² /blæk/ NOUN, NO PLURAL the colour of coal or the sky at night

blackboard /'blæk,bɔ:d/ NOUN [plural blackboards] a dark board that a teacher writes on in a classroom

black hole /,blæk 'həʊl/ NOUN [plural black holes] an area in outer space that pulls everything into it. Nothing can escape from a black hole.

blade /bleɪd/ NOUN [plural blades]
1 the sharp part of a knife or tool which cuts 🏷 a razor blade
2 a blade of grass a long thin piece of grass

blame[1] /bleɪm/ VERB [blames, blaming, blamed] to say that something is someone's fault □ + for He blamed me for the accident.

blame[2] /bleɪm/ NOUN, NO PLURAL responsibility for something bad that has happened 🏷 Why do I always get the blame for everything? 🏷 I'm not going to take the blame for someone else's mistake.

blank /blæŋk/ ADJECTIVE
1 with no writing on, or with no sound or pictures on 🏷 a blank sheet of paper □ a blank CD
2 showing no emotion or no understanding 🏷 She gave me a blank stare.

blanket /'blæŋkɪt/ NOUN [plural blankets]
1 a cover for a bed, usually made of wool □ a wool blanket
2 a layer that covers everything □ + of A blanket of snow covered the roads.

> ► THESAURUS: A blanket is a cover for a bed and is usually made of wool. A sheet is also used on a bed, but is thin, and is usually made of cotton. A duvet is a cotton bag, usually filled with feathers. A cover is something that you put on the top of something else to protect it. A duvet cover is a bag made of cotton that you put around a duvet to protect it and for decoration.

blast[1] /blɑ:st/ NOUN [plural blasts]
1 an explosion 🏷 They were killed in a bomb blast. □ Three people survived the blast.
2 a sudden strong movement of air □ The door opened, letting in a blast of freezing air.
3 a loud sound from something such as a horn □ The lorry driver gave a couple of blasts on his horn.

blast[2] /blɑ:st/ VERB [blasts, blasting, blasted]
1 to make a lot of loud noise □ Music was blasting out of the open windows.
2 to use explosives to break up something such as rock
♦ PHRASAL VERB **blast off** if a rocket (= type of spacecraft) blasts off, it starts to go up into the air

blaze[1] /bleɪz/ NOUN [plural blazes] a big fire 🏷 Firefighters put out the blaze.

blaze[2] /bleɪz/ VERB [blazes, blazing, blazed] to burn or shine brightly □ Her eyes were blazing with anger.

bleak /bli:k/ ADJECTIVE [bleaker, bleakest]
1 without hope or happiness □ The economic situation looks bleak. 🏷 a bleak future/outlook
2 a bleak place is cold, empty and not pleasant □ a bleak winter landscape

bleed /bli:d/ VERB [bleeds, bleeding, bled] when you bleed, blood comes out of a cut on your body □ He was bleeding from a cut on his head. 🏷 My head was bleeding profusely (= very much).

blend[1] /blend/ VERB [blends, blending, blended] to mix things together completely □ Blend the butter and the sugar.

blend[2] /blend/ NOUN [plural blends] a mixture of two or more things □ Banana milkshake is a blend of milk, banana and ice cream.

blender /'blendə(r)/ NOUN [plural blenders] a machine used for mixing food

bless /bles/ VERB [blesses, blessing, blessed] to ask God to protect someone or to make something holy □ The priest blessed the bread and the wine.
♦ IDIOM **Bless you!** something you say when someone sneezes (= suddenly blows out air from their nose and mouth in a way that they cannot control)

blew /blu:/ PAST TENSE OF blow[1]

blind[1] /blaɪnd/ ADJECTIVE not able to see 🏷 He went blind (= became blind) at the age of five.

blind[2] /blaɪnd/ NOUN [plural blinds]
1 the blind people who are blind
2 a covering that you pull down over a window

blink /blɪŋk/ VERB [blinks, blinking, blinked] to close and open your eyes quickly □ He was blinking in the strong sunlight. □ Emma tried to blink away the tears.

blister /'blɪstə(r)/ NOUN [plural blisters] a swollen area filled with liquid on your skin where it has been burned or rubbed

blizzard /'blɪzəd/ NOUN [plural blizzards] a storm with strong winds and snow

block[1] /blɒk/ NOUN [plural blocks]
1 a solid, usually square piece of something □ Cut the wood into blocks. □ + of a block of ice
2 a large building with a lot of offices or homes in it 🏷 a block of flats 🏷 a fifteen-storey office block

block[2] /blɒk/ VERB [blocks, blocking, blocked]
1 to stop people or things from getting through □ The road was blocked by a tree. 🏷 A large police officer blocked our path/exit. □ + up The stream was blocked up with sticks.
2 to be in front of someone so that they cannot see something or light cannot get to them 🏷 A tall man in front was blocking my view.
♦ PHRASAL VERB **block something off** to close

something such as a path or an entrance by placing something across it □ *The police had blocked off the road.*

blog[1] /blɒg/ NOUN [*plural* blogs] a record of someone's activities and opinions that they put on the Internet for other people to read. A computing word.

blog[2] /blɒg/ VERB [blogs, blogging, blogged] to write a blog. A computing word.

blogger /'blɒgə(r)/ NOUN [*plural* bloggers] someone who writes a record of their activities and opinions and puts it on the Internet for other people to read. A computing word.

bloke /bləʊk/ NOUN [*plural* blokes] an informal word meaning man □ *He's a nice bloke.*

blond[1] or **blonde** /blɒnd/ ADJECTIVE [blonder, blondest] blond hair is pale yellow □ *She had long blonde hair.*

blond[2] or **blonde** /blɒnd/ NOUN [*plural* blonds or blondes] a person with pale yellow hair

blood /blʌd/ NOUN, NO PLURAL the red liquid that is inside your body □ *Your heart pumps blood around your body.* 🔁 *A blood test will show if you have an infection.*

bloom[1] /bluːm/ NOUN [*plural* blooms] a flower □ *The stems are covered in large white blooms.*

bloom[2] /bluːm/ VERB [blooms, blooming, bloomed] to produce flowers □ *A lot of plants have bloomed early this year.*

blossom[1] /'blɒsəm/ NOUN [*plural* blossoms] the flowers that appear on a fruit tree before the fruit grows

> ➤ THESAURUS: Blossom is the flowers that appear on fruit trees such as apples and cherries before the fruit grows. A bud is the part of a plant that the flower grows from. Flower is a more general word to describe the coloured part of a plant that turns into fruit and where seeds are produced.

blossom[2] /'blɒsəm/ VERB [blossoms, blossoming, blossomed] to produce blossom

blouse /blaʊz/ NOUN [*plural* blouses] a woman's shirt □ *a school blouse*

blow[1] /bləʊ/ VERB [blows, blowing, blew, blown]
1 wind when it moves around □ *A cold wind was blowing from the east.*
2 to push out air from your mouth onto something or into something □ *Blow on your soup — it's hot.*
3 to breathe into something such as a musical instrument in order to make a sound □ *When I blow this whistle, I want you all to stop.*
4 blow your nose to get the liquid out of your nose by forcing air through it

◆ PHRASAL VERBS **blow over** if an argument blows

over, people forget about it **blow something up** to destroy something with an explosion □ *He was planning to blow up the aeroplane and all its passengers.*

blow[2] /bləʊ/ NOUN [*plural* blows]
1 a hard knock □ + *to* *He suffered a blow to the face.*
2 something disappointing that happens □ *It was a blow not being able to go to the concert.*

blown /bləʊn/ PAST PARTICIPLE OF **blow**[1]

blue[1] /bluː/ ADJECTIVE having the colour of the sky 🔁 *She was wearing a dark blue dress.* 🔁 *He has a pale blue shirt on.*

blue[2] /bluː/ NOUN [*plural* blues] the colour of the sky □ *The sea was a deep blue.*
◆ IDIOM **out of the blue** not expected at all □ *Out of the blue, he announced that he was leaving.*

blunt /blʌnt/ ADJECTIVE [blunter, bluntest] with an edge or point that is not sharp □ *This knife is blunt.*

blush /blʌʃ/ VERB [blushes, blushing, blushed] to start to have a red face because you are embarrassed □ *Everyone turned to look at Philip, who blushed.*

board[1] /bɔːd/ NOUN [*plural* boards]
1 a flat piece of wood 🔁 *Please use a bread board for cutting on.* 🔁 *I lifted the carpets to look at the floor boards.*
2 a flat piece of wood or cardboard with marks on it, used to play a game □ *a chess board*
3 a surface on the wall of a classroom where the teacher writes □ *The answers are on the board.*
4 a group of people who control a company or other organization 🔁 *the board of directors* 🔁 *a board meeting*
5 **on board** on a ship, aircraft or other vehicle □ *There were 197 passengers on board.*

board[2] /bɔːd/ VERB [boards, boarding, boarded] to get on a ship or an aeroplane □ *Could all remaining passengers please board the plane.*

boarder /'bɔːdə(r)/ NOUN [*plural* boarders] a student who lives at his or her school □ *The school has day students and boarders.*

boarding pass /'bɔːdɪŋ ˌpɑːs/ or **boarding card** /'bɔːdɪŋ ˌkɑːd/ NOUN [*plural* boarding passes or boarding cards] a card that you need to show someone before you can get on an aeroplane or a ship □ *Passengers should have their boarding passes ready.*

boarding school /'bɔːdɪŋ ˌskuːl/ NOUN [*plural* boarding schools] a school in which students can live

boast /bəʊst/ VERB [boasts, boasting, boasted] to talk proudly about yourself in a way that other people find annoying □ *He's always boasting about the famous people he knows.*

boastful /'bəustful/ ADJECTIVE often talking proudly about the good things you have done or the expensive things you own

boat /bəut/ NOUN [plural boats] a vehicle for travelling over water □ *a fishing boat*

♦ IDIOM in the same boat having the same problems as other people □ *Don't worry, we're all in the same boat.*

> ➤ THESAURUS: Boat is a general word to describe any vehicle that travels on water. Very large boats are usually called ships. For example, ships transport goods around the world. A ferry is a boat which carries passengers between two places, and can be large or small. A barge is a long, narrow boat used to carry goods on a canal. A yacht is a boat with sails. We use yachts for racing or for pleasure.

bob /bɒb/ VERB [bobs, bobbing, bobbed] to move up and down quickly □ *She watched the little boats bobbing on the lake.*

body /'bɒdɪ/ NOUN [plural bodies]
1 the whole physical form of a person or animal □ *I had red spots all over my body.*
2 a dead person □ *His body was never found.*

bodyguard /'bɒdɪgɑːd/ NOUN [plural bodyguards] someone whose job is to protect an important or famous person

boil /bɔɪl/ VERB [boils, boiling, boiled]
1 a liquid boils when it is heated until it produces bubbles and turns into gas □ *Is the water boiling yet?* □ *Boil some water in a pan and add the pasta.*
2 to cook food in boiling water □ *I'm going to boil some eggs.*
3 to heat a container of liquid until it is boiling □ *Shall I boil the kettle?*

bold /bəuld/ ADJECTIVE [bolder, boldest]
1 not afraid to take a risk □ *Calling an election was a bold move* (= a brave thing to do) *for the president.* □ *It was rather bold of him to ask that question.*
2 bold type or print is thick dark letters **like this** □ *Her name is written in bold type at the top of the page.*

bolt¹ /bəult/ NOUN [plural bolts]
1 a metal bar that you push across a door to lock it □ *She slid back the bolts and opened the door.*
2 a metal object with small, raised lines that you use with a nut (= metal object with a hole in the middle) to fasten pieces of wood or metal together
bolt² /bəult/ VERB [bolts, bolting, bolted]
1 to lock a door using a bolt □ *We bolted all the doors before we went to bed.*

2 to run away very fast □ *Beth's horse bolted when it heard the noise.*

bomb¹ /bɒm/ NOUN [plural bombs] a weapon that explodes to cause serious damage to buildings, people, etc. □ *The bomb went off in a crowded market.*

bomb² /bɒm/ VERB [bombs, bombing, bombed] to attack a place using bombs □ *Enemy aircraft bombed every town and village in the area.*

bone /bəun/ NOUN [plural bones] one of the hard parts that form the frame inside the body of an animal or person □ *Brian broke a bone in his arm.*

bonnet /'bɒnɪt/ NOUN [plural bonnets]
1 the part at the front of a car that covers the engine
2 a woman's or child's hat that you tie under the chin
bonus /'bəunəs/ NOUN [plural bonuses]
1 something good that you get in addition to something else good □ *The food is great, and has the added bonus of being healthy too.*
2 extra money that people sometimes get in addition to their usual payment □ *a Christmas bonus*

> ➤ THESAURUS: A bonus is extra money that you sometimes get at work, in addition to your usual payment. You might get a bonus if your work is very good. A reward is money that you get for doing something good. You might get a reward if you help to catch a criminal. A tip is money that you get for helping someone as part of your job, for example if you are a waiter. A prize is something that you get for winning a competition. A gift or a present is something that you give to someone, for example because it is their birthday.

boo /buː/ VERB [boos, booing, booed] people in an audience boo when they make loud noises because they do not think the performance is good

book¹ /buk/ NOUN [plural books] a set of pages joined together inside a cover □ *a library book* □ *Have you read Dan Brown's new book?* □ *I'm reading a really interesting book about Mexico.*

> ➤ THESAURUS: Book is a general word for pages joined together inside a cover. An atlas is a book of maps. A guidebook is a book that contains information for people visiting a place. It might contain maps and information about things to see. A manual is a book that tells you how to do something. We use manuals to help us use machines. A textbook is a book that students use to help them with their studies. For example, you might have a geography textbook.

book² /buk/ VERB [books, booking, booked] to buy tickets for something or to arrange to have or use something in the future □ *I'd like to book a* table for four, please. □ *We've booked a family holiday in Majorca.*

► **THESAURUS:** If you book something or reserve something, you buy tickets or arrange to use something in the future. For example, you can reserve seats on a train, or you can book a holiday. If you order something, you pay for it and arrange for someone to deliver it to you. For example you order food in a restaurant and you can order a book on the Internet.

bookshop /ˈbʊkʃɒp/ NOUN [*plural* bookshops] a shop that sells books

boom[1] /buːm/ NOUN [*plural* booms]
1 a situation in which a company or country sells a lot of products and makes a lot of money □ *an economic boom*
2 a loud noise like the sound of a big drum

boom[2] /buːm/ VERB [booms, booming, boomed]
1 if a business or the economy booms, it becomes very successful
2 to make a loud noise like the sound of a drum

boost[1] /buːst/ NOUN [*plural* boosts] something that makes something larger or more successful □ *The school funds got a boost from the money raised at the summer fair.*

boost[2] /buːst/ VERB [boosts, boosting, boosted] to make something larger or more successful □ *Extra lessons will help to boost her confidence.*

boot /buːt/ NOUN [*plural* boots]
1 a type of shoe that covers the ankle and often part of the leg
2 the covered place at the back of a car for storing bags, etc.

booth /buːð/ NOUN [*plural* booths] a small place with walls around it where you can do something privately, for example make a telephone call

border /ˈbɔːdə(r)/ NOUN [*plural* borders]
1 the line which separates two countries or areas □ *They lived near the Canadian border.*
2 a strip around the edge of something, often for decoration □ *a pillowcase with a pretty lace border*

bore[1] /bɔː(r)/ VERB [bores, boring, bored]
1 to make someone feel bored □ *The speech bored him.*
2 to make a hole in something with a sharp tool
• **boredom** /ˈbɔːdəm/ NOUN, NO PLURAL the feeling of being bored

bore[2] /bɔː(r)/ PAST TENSE OF bear[1]

bored /bɔːd/ ADJECTIVE feeling that something is not interesting or that you have nothing to do □ + **with** *I'm really bored with my clothes.* ⊞ *The others enjoyed the show, but I was bored stiff* (= extremely bored).

boring /ˈbɔːrɪŋ/ ADJECTIVE not at all interesting □ *My course is really boring.*

► Remember the difference between the words **boring** and **bored**. **Boring** means 'not interesting'. **Bored** is how you feel when something is not interesting □ *What a boring film!* □ *I was so bored during the film, I fell asleep.*

born[1] /bɔːn/ VERB be born (a) a person or animal is born when it comes out of its mother's body □ *My sister was born in 1989.* □ *He was born with a heart problem.* (b) something is born when it starts to exist □ *The idea for the film was born over dinner at Jack's house.*

► Remember that the verb is **be born** and not just **born**:
✓ *I was born in Germany.*
✗ *I born in Germany.*

born[2] /bɔːn/ ADJECTIVE a born leader/performer, etc. is a very good leader/performer, etc. □ *Zoe's a born entertainer.*

borne /bɔːn/ PAST PARTICIPLE OF bear[1]

borrow /ˈbɒrəʊ/ VERB [borrows, borrowing, borrowed] to use something that belongs to someone else and give it back to them later □ *Can I borrow your pencil for a minute, please?* □ + **from** *She borrowed £100 from her Dad.*

► Remember that when you **borrow** something, you use something that belongs to someone else. When you give something to someone else to use, the verb is **lend** □ *I borrowed Dan's mobile.* □ *Dan lent me his mobile.*

boss /bɒs/ NOUN [*plural* bosses] someone who is in charge of other people at work □ *I'm going to ask my boss for a pay rise.*
♦ PHRASAL VERB [bosses, bossing, bossed] boss someone around/about to tell other people what to do, in a way that annoys them □ *I wish Amy would stop bossing us all around.*

bossy /ˈbɒsɪ/ ADJECTIVE always telling other people what to do □ *Stop being so bossy – you're not in charge here.*

both /bəʊθ/ PRONOUN, DETERMINER used for saying the same thing is true for two people or things □ *She ate both cakes, and I didn't get one.* □ + **of** *Both of the boys are good at tennis.* □ *Both the men wore black suits.* □ *We both like classical music.* □ *The book is both interesting and informative.*

bother /'bɒðə(r)/ VERB [bothers, bothering, bothered]
1 to do something that annoys or interrupts someone □ *Stop bothering me, I'm busy.*
2 can't be bothered if you can't be bothered to do something, you feel too lazy to do it □ *I can't be bothered to cook just for myself.*
3 to make you feel unhappy or worried □ *He said that losing the match didn't bother him.*
4 to take the time or make an effort to do something □ *Don't bother tidying up yet.*

bottle /'bɒtəl/ NOUN [plural bottles] a glass or plastic container used for holding liquids, often with a narrow part at the top □ *+ of a bottle of mineral water* □ *a wine bottle*

bottom[1] /'bɒtəm/ NOUN [plural bottoms]
1 the lowest part of something □ *+ of He stood at the bottom of the stairs* □ *the bottom of the sea*
2 the surface on the lowest part of something □ *There were holes in the bottom of his shoes.*
3 the lowest level of success □ *My team is at the bottom of the league.*
4 the part of something that is furthest away □ *the bottom of the road/garden*
5 the part of your body that you sit on □ *Always keep your baby's bottom clean and dry.*

bottom[2] /'bɒtəm/ ADJECTIVE
1 in the lowest position □ *Put the biggest books on the bottom shelf.*
2 at the lowest level of success ⊞ *She came bottom in the exam.*

bought /bɔːt/ PAST TENSE AND PAST PARTICIPLE OF **buy**
boulder /'bəʊldə(r)/ NOUN [plural boulders] a very big stone
bounce /baʊns/ VERB [bounces, bouncing, bounced]
1 to hit a hard surface and move away again □ *The ball bounced high into the air.*
2 to jump up and down on a soft surface □ *The children were bouncing on the bed.*
bouncy /'baʊnsɪ/ ADJECTIVE [bouncier, bounciest]
1 able to hit a hard surface and move away again easily □ *a bouncy ball*
2 a bouncy surface moves up and down when you move or jump on it
bound[1] /baʊnd/ VERB [bounds, bounding, bounded] to run with long jumping steps □ *The dogs bounded into the room, barking excitedly.*
bound[2] /baʊnd/ NOUN [plural bounds]
1 a jump □ *The deer jumped over the fence in a single bound.*
2 out of bounds if a place is out of bounds, you are not allowed to go there
bound[3] /baʊnd/ PAST TENSE AND PAST PARTICIPLE OF **bind**

boundary /'baʊndərɪ/ NOUN [plural boundaries] a line that divides two places □ *We live on the boundary between the city and the countryside.*
bouquet /bu'keɪ/ NOUN [plural bouquets] flowers that have been tied together in an attractive way
bow[1] /baʊ/ VERB [bows, bowing, bowed] to bend your head or the top part of your body forward to say hello to someone politely or to show them respect □ *Everyone bowed to the king and queen.*
bow[2] /baʊ/ NOUN [plural bows]
1 when you bow ⊞ *The pianist came back on stage to take a bow.*
2 the pointed front part of a ship
bow[3] /bəʊ/ NOUN [plural bows]
1 a knot with two circular ends, used to tie shoes or for decoration □ *Tie the ribbon in a bow.*
2 a weapon made from a long piece of wood, used for shooting arrows
3 a long, straight piece of wood with horse hair stretched along it, used for playing some musical instruments □ *a violin bow*

bowl /bəʊl/ NOUN [plural bowls] a round, open container, used for holding food □ *a soup bowl* □ *a bowl of cornflakes*

bowler /'bəʊlə(r)/ NOUN [plural bowlers] the person who bowls in sports such as cricket and baseball
bowling /'bəʊlɪŋ/ NOUN, NO PLURAL a game in which players roll a large heavy ball along a track and try to knock over objects shaped like bottles
box[1] /bɒks/ NOUN [plural boxes]
1 a container, sometimes with a lid, used for holding or storing things
2 a small square on a page with information in it or with a space where you must write ⊞ *Tick the relevant box.*
box[2] /bɒks/ VERB [boxes, boxing, boxed] to take part in the sport of boxing
• **boxer** /'bɒksə(r)/ NOUN [plural boxers] someone who takes part in the sport of boxing

boxing /'bɒksɪŋ/ NOUN, NO PLURAL a sport in which two people fight by hitting each other while wearing heavy gloves (= coverings for your hands)

Boxing Day /'bɒksɪŋ ˌdeɪ/ NOUN the day after Christmas Day

box office /'bɒks ˌɒfɪs/ NOUN [plural box offices] the place at a theatre or cinema where you buy tickets

boy /bɔɪ/ NOUN [plural boys] a male child □ a six-year-old boy □ They've got two boys and a girl. □ When I was a little boy I wanted to be a train driver.

boycott[1] /'bɔɪkɒt/ VERB [boycotts, boycotting, boycotted] to refuse to take part in an activity or to buy a particular product

boycott[2] /'bɔɪkɒt/ NOUN [plural boycotts] a situation in which someone boycotts an activity or product

boyfriend /'bɔɪˌfrend/ NOUN [plural boyfriends] a man or boy who you are having a romantic relationship with □ Emily has got a new boyfriend.

bra /brɑː/ NOUN [plural bras] a piece of underwear that women wear to support their breasts

brace /breɪs/ NOUN [plural braces] a piece of wire that you have on your teeth to pull them into a straight position

bracelet /'breɪslɪt/ NOUN [plural bracelets] a piece of jewellery that you wear around your arm □ a diamond bracelet

bracket /'brækɪt/ NOUN [plural brackets] one of a pair of marks ( ) or [ ], used to separate information from the main text ⊞ She added her own comments in brackets after each point.

brag /bræg/ VERB [brags, bragging, bragged] to talk about your achievements or possessions in a proud way that annoys people □ Kate's always bragging about the expensive gifts he gives her.

brain /breɪn/ NOUN [plural brains] the organ inside your head that controls all the other parts of your body, and that you think with □ the human brain

brake[1] /breɪk/ NOUN [plural brakes] the part in a vehicle that you press to stop the vehicle or make it go slower □ Have you checked your brakes? ⊞ a brake pedal

brake[2] /breɪk/ VERB [brakes, braking, braked] to use a brake to stop a vehicle or make it go slower □ Dad braked suddenly and we were all thrown forward.

branch /brɑːntʃ/ NOUN [plural branches]
1 one of the smaller parts of a tree that grow out from the main straight part □ Crows build their nests high in the branches of trees.
2 one of the shops or businesses that belong to a larger organization ⊞ the local branch of the bank ⊞ They're opening a new branch in Livingston.

brand /brænd/ NOUN [plural brands] a product that has a particular name, and that is made by a particular company □ This isn't my usual brand of shampoo.

brand-new /'brænd,njuː/ ADJECTIVE completely new □ a brand-new car

brass[1] /brɑːs/ NOUN, NO PLURAL a yellow metal used for making things such as musical instruments

brass[2] /brɑːs/ ADJECTIVE made of brass □ a brass candlestick

brave /breɪv/ ADJECTIVE [braver, bravest] able to deal with danger without being afraid, or able to suffer pain without complaining □ + of It was very brave of her to jump in the water and save the child. □ This might hurt a little – just try to be brave.
♦ IDIOM put a brave face on something to behave as if you are not afraid or worried, although you feel afraid or worried

bravery /'breɪvəri/ NOUN, NO PLURAL being brave □ an award for bravery

bread /bred/ NOUN, NO PLURAL a basic food made with flour and water that is baked in an oven. It is often sold in a large piece and then cut into smaller pieces. ⊞ a loaf of bread ⊞ a slice of bread ⊞ brown/white bread

break[1] /breɪk/ VERB [breaks, breaking, broke, broken]
1 to separate into pieces or to make something separate into pieces □ The vase fell to the floor and broke. □ Be careful, you'll break that glass. □ + off I broke a piece off the biscuit. □ + up The company was broken up and sold in several parts.
2 to damage something or to become damaged □ My camera broke. □ I've broken my umbrella.

3 break your arm/leg, etc to damage a bone so that it cracks

4 break the rules/the law/your promise, etc. to not do what you should do, for example because it is a rule or you have made a promise

• **breakable** /'breɪkəbəl/ ADJECTIVE able to be broken easily

♦ IDIOM **break someone's heart** to make someone very unhappy □ *It breaks my heart to see the children suffer.*

♦ PHRASAL VERBS **break down** if a machine or vehicle breaks down, it stops working □ *Sorry I'm late; the car broke down.* **break in** to get into a place by using force □ *Thieves broke in using a hammer.* **break out** to start suddenly 🔂 *Fighting broke out during a football match.* 🔂 *Fire broke out in the factory.* **break up 1** if two people break up, they end their relationship □ *She's broken up with her boyfriend.* **2** a school breaks up when the term finishes and the holiday starts

> ➤ **THESAURUS:** Break is a general word. If you break something into small pieces, for example by dropping it, you can use the words **smash** and **shatter**. For example, you might smash or shatter a plate if you drop it. If you damage something thin such as paper or cloth by pulling it apart, you use the word **tear**. If something **splits** or if you split it, it breaks apart. For example, you might split a piece of wood with an axe.

break² /breɪk/ NOUN [*plural* breaks]

1 a short period of time in which someone stops an activity 🔂 *Shall we have/take a break?* 🔂 *What time is your lunch break?* □ **+ from** *I need a break from the children.*

2 an opening or crack in something □ **+ in** *a break in the clouds* □ *She suffered a nasty break in her leg.*

breakdown /'breɪkdaʊn/ NOUN [*plural* breakdowns]

1 when a machine or vehicle stops working □ *We had a breakdown on the motorway.*

2 when something fails in a situation □ *a breakdown in communication* □ *Stress contributed to the breakdown of his marriage.*

3 a period of mental illness when someone is too upset or sad to deal with life 🔂 *She suffered a breakdown after her divorce.* 🔂 *a nervous breakdown*

breakfast /'brekfəst/ NOUN [*plural* breakfasts] the first meal that you eat in the morning □ *What do you usually have for breakfast?*

breast /brest/ NOUN [*plural* breasts]

1 one of the two organs on the front of a woman's body that produce milk when she has a baby 🔂 *breast milk* 🔂 *breast cancer*

2 the front part of a bird's body, or the meat from this part 🔂 *chicken breasts*

breath /breθ/ NOUN [*plural* breaths]

1 when you fill your lungs with air and then allow the air out again 🔂 *Take a deep breath.*

2 the air that comes out of your mouth □ *We could see our breath in the freezing air.*

3 be out of breath to be breathing fast because you have been running or working hard □ *You shouldn't be out of breath after walking upstairs.*

4 hold your breath to breathe in but not breathe out again □ *They have to hold their breath for a long time under the water.*

5 under your breath if you say something under your breath, you say it very quietly

♦ IDIOM **take your breath away** to surprise you very much □ *His kindness took my breath away.*

breathe /briːð/ VERB [breathes, breathing, breathed] to take air into and out of your lungs □ *He was so quiet, I thought he had stopped breathing.* □ *It feels good to breathe some clean air again.*

♦ PHRASAL VERBS **breathe in** to take air into your lungs □ *Breathe in through your nose.* **breathe out** to allow air out of your lungs □ *Now breathe out through your mouth.*

> ➤ Remember that the verb **breathe** has an **e** at the end, while the noun **breath** does not. Be careful not to confuse the spellings of the verb **breathes** and the noun plural **breaths**.

breed¹ /briːd/ VERB [breeds, breeding, bred]

1 when animals breed they produce young animals □ *The birds breed across Europe and Asia.*

2 to produce young animals from dogs, cows, sheep, etc. □ *These dogs are bred for hunting.*

breed² /briːd/ NOUN [*plural* breeds] a particular type of animal □ *The Aberdeen Angus is a famous Scottish breed of cattle.*

breeze /briːz/ NOUN [*plural* breezes] a light wind □ *a cool/gentle breeze*

bribe /braɪb/ NOUN [*plural* bribes] money that is offered to someone so that they will do something dishonest 🔂 *accept/take a bribe*

brick /brɪk/ NOUN [*plural* bricks] a block used for building walls □ *Someone threw a brick through the window.* 🔂 *a brick wall*

bride /braɪd/ NOUN [plural brides] a woman who is getting married

bridge /brɪdʒ/ NOUN [plural bridges]
1 a structure that is built over a river or a road to allow people or vehicles to cross from one side to the other □ *We drove across the bridge.* ☝ *a railway bridge*
2 a card game for four people playing in pairs

brief /briːf/ ADJECTIVE [briefer, briefest] short □ *We had a brief telephone conversation.* □ *He wrote her a brief note.*

briefcase /ˈbriːfkeɪs/ NOUN [plural briefcases] a flat case for carrying business documents

briefly /ˈbriːflɪ/ ADVERB in or for a short amount of time □ *Tell us briefly what you want us to do.* □ *They stopped briefly to get petrol.*

brigade /brɪˈgeɪd/ NOUN [plural brigades] a group of soldiers that forms part of a group in the army
→ go to **fire brigade**

bright /braɪt/ ADJECTIVE [brighter, brightest]
1 producing a lot of light □ *We could see the bright lights of the city.*
2 full of light □ *This is a nice bright bedroom.*
3 a bright colour is strong and clear □ *His eyes were bright blue.*
4 clever □ *He was always the brightest child in our family.*

brighten /ˈbraɪtən/ VERB [brightens, brightening, brightened] to become brighter or to make something brighter □ *The weather brightened up and we went out for a walk.* □ *A coat of paint would brighten the walls.*

brilliant /ˈbrɪljənt/ ADJECTIVE
1 very clever, or showing great skill □ *Fiona gave a brilliant speech.*
2 very bright ☝ *brilliant sunshine*

bring /brɪŋ/ VERB [brings, bringing, brought]
1 to take or carry a person or thing with you when you go somewhere □ **+ to** *You can bring all your friends to the party.* □ *He brought a couple of jigsaws downstairs.* □ **+ back** *He never brought back the book he borrowed.*
2 to cause a feeling or a situation □ **+ to** *The new leaders brought peace to the area.* □ *Our grandchildren have brought us great happiness.*

> ➤ Use **bring** when you are talking about taking a person or thing towards you (the person speaking). Use **take** when you are talking about taking a person or thing away from you (the person speaking), or away from the place where you are now □ *Could you bring my mobile when you come?* □ *I'll take some flowers to the hospital.*

♦ PHRASAL VERBS **bring something about** to cause something to happen □ *Motherhood had brought about enormous changes.* **bring something up**
1 to mention a subject □ *Did anyone bring up the subject of payment?* **2** to make food come up from your stomach and out of your mouth **bring someone up** to look after a child until they are old enough to look after themselves □ *My parents brought me up to be polite and considerate.*

brink /brɪŋk/ NOUN on the brink of something if you are on the brink of something, it is going to happen very soon □ *Noreen was on the brink of tears.*

Brit /brɪt/ NOUN [plural Brits] a British person. An informal word □ *There are a lot of Brits in Majorca in the summer.*

Britain /ˈbrɪtən/ NOUN England, Scotland and Wales

British[1] /ˈbrɪtɪʃ/ ADJECTIVE belonging to or coming from Britain □ *British industry*

British[2] /ˈbrɪtɪʃ/ NOUN the British the people who come from Britain

Briton /ˈbrɪtən/ NOUN [plural Britons] a person who comes from Britain □ *Several Britons were killed in the accident.*

broad /brɔːd/ ADJECTIVE [broader, broadest]
1 wide ☝ *He was a tall man with broad shoulders.* ☝ *She gave us a broad smile.*
2 including many different things ☝ *We discussed a broad range of subjects.*

broadcast[1] /ˈbrɔːdkɑːst/ NOUN [plural broadcasts] a programme sent out on television or radio ☝ *We watched a live broadcast of the World Cup Final.*

broadcast[2] /ˈbrɔːdkɑːst/ VERB [broadcasts, broadcasting, broadcast] to send out information or programmes on television or radio □ *The interview was broadcast on Sunday.* □ *The BBC broadcast the event live.*

broaden /ˈbrɔːdən/ VERB [broadens, broadening, broadened]
1 to become wider, or to make something wider □ *They've broadened the road.* □ *Her smile broadened.*
2 to include more things or people □ *The socialist party will have to broaden its appeal.*
♦ IDIOM **broaden your mind** to give you more knowledge about the world and make you accept different people more □ *They say that travel broadens the mind.*
→ go to **broaden your horizon**

broccoli /ˈbrɒkəlɪ/ NOUN, NO PLURAL a vegetable with a lot of very small green or purple flowers growing from a thick stem

brochure /ˈbrəʊʃə(r)/ NOUN [plural brochures] a small book containing information about particular products or services, often with pictures □ a holiday brochure

broke /brəʊk/ PAST TENSE OF break¹

broken¹ /ˈbrəʊkən/ PAST PARTICIPLE OF break¹

broken² /ˈbrəʊkən/ ADJECTIVE
1 damaged, and often in several pieces ⧉ broken glass ⧉ a broken bone
2 if a machine is broken, it is not working □ The washing machine is broken.
3 if someone's heart is broken, they are very sad, especially because someone they loved has gone away or died ⧉ They say she died of a broken heart.

bronze /brɒnz/ NOUN [plural bronzes]
1 a dark red-brown metal □ The statue was made of bronze.
2 a bronze medal (= prize for coming third in a competition or race) □ Williams came first, Miller came second, and Lewis got the bronze.

brooch /brəʊtʃ/ NOUN [plural brooches] a piece of jewellery with a pin on the back that you fasten to the front of a dress or jacket

brother /ˈbrʌðə(r)/ NOUN [plural brothers] a boy or man who has the same parents as you ⧉ I share a bedroom with my little brother. ⧉ Do you have any brothers and sisters?

brother-in-law /ˈbrʌðərɪnlɔː/ NOUN [plural brothers-in-law] your sister's husband or the brother of your husband or wife

brought /brɔːt/ PAST TENSE AND PAST PARTICIPLE OF bring

brow /braʊ/ NOUN [plural brows] the part of your face above your eyes □ She wrinkled her brow in confusion.

brown¹ /braʊn/ ADJECTIVE having the colour of soil or wood ⧉ She has light brown hair. ⧉ They painted the walls dark brown.

brown² /braʊn/ NOUN [plural browns] the colour of soil or wood □ We chose a dark brown for the sofa.

bruise¹ /bruːz/ NOUN [plural bruises] a dark mark that you get on your skin if it is hit □ Joe's got a big black bruise under his eye.

bruise² /bruːz/ VERB [bruises, bruising, bruised] to make a bruise on someone's skin □ Daniel bruised his knee when he fell.

brush¹ /brʌʃ/ VERB [brushes, brushing, brushed] to make something tidy or clean using a brush ⧉ Have you brushed your teeth? ⧉ Make sure you brush your hair before you go out.

brush² /brʌʃ/ NOUN [plural brushes] an object with short hairs or thin pieces of plastic, wire, etc. fixed to a handle, used for tidying your hair, painting or cleaning □ You'll need a brush to get the mud off

those shoes. □ An artist needs a range of different brushes.

brutal /ˈbruːtəl/ ADJECTIVE very cruel □ a brutal murder

bubble¹ /ˈbʌbəl/ NOUN [plural bubbles] a very thin light ball of liquid filled with air ⧉ soap bubbles ⧉ The children were blowing bubbles in the garden.

bubble² /ˈbʌbəl/ VERB [bubbles, bubbling, bubbled] liquid bubbles when small balls of air form in it, usually because it is boiling □ A big pot of soup was bubbling on the stove.

bucket /ˈbʌkɪt/ NOUN [plural buckets] a round open container with a handle, used for carrying water, or substances such as soil or sand ⧉ a bucket of water □ You'll need about four buckets of water to wash the car.

buckle¹ /ˈbʌkəl/ NOUN [plural buckles] a metal object on the end of a belt, used for fastening it
buckle² /ˈbʌkəl/ VERB [buckles, buckling, buckled] to fasten something with a buckle □ She buckled her belt tightly around her waist.

bud /bʌd/ NOUN [plural buds] the part of a plant from which a leaf or flower develops

Buddhism /ˈbʊdɪzəm/ NOUN, NO PLURAL a religion that is practised in many parts of the world, which follows the teaching of Buddha □ He gave up politics, and went to Tibet to study Buddhism.

Buddhist¹ /ˈbʊdɪst/ NOUN [plural Buddhists] someone who practises Buddhism

Buddhist² /ˈbʊdɪst/ ADJECTIVE to do with Buddhism or Buddhists ⧉ a Buddhist monk

budget¹ /ˈbʌdʒɪt/ NOUN [plural budgets] an amount of money that a person, company or government has available to spend □ We offer holidays to suit all budgets. ⧉ They were on a tight budget (= did not have much money). □ The company is cutting its marketing budget. □ the education budget

budget² /'bʌdʒɪt/ ADJECTIVE cheap □ budget flights

buffet¹ /'bufeɪ/ NOUN [plural buffets] a meal where different types of food are put on a table from which people can choose what they want

buffet² /'bʌfɪt/ VERB [buffets, buffeting, buffeted] to knock someone or something about roughly □ The little boat was buffeted by the storm.

bug /bʌg/ NOUN [plural bugs]
1 an informal word for an infectious illness 🔂 She's got a tummy bug.
2 a fault in a computer program 🔂 She is trying to fix a bug in the program.
3 a small insect

build /bɪld/ VERB [builds, building, built] to make something by putting materials or parts together □ He's planning to build his own house. □ The walls are built of wood.

builder /'bɪldə(r)/ [plural builders] someone whose job is to build and repair houses and other structures

building /'bɪldɪŋ/ [plural buildings]
1 a structure with walls and a roof, for example a house or a church □ What's the tallest building in the world?
2 no plural the activity of building houses and other structures □ There is a lot of building going on in this street.

— THESAURUS building is a general word for any structure with a roof and walls. A house is a general word for a place where people live, often for one family. A flat is a set of rooms that someone lives in, which is part of a larger building. Flats usually have no stairs inside. A set of flats in a building is called a block of flats. Flats are sometimes called apartments, especially in American English. A cottage is a small house in the countryside or in a village.

building society /'bɪldɪŋ sə'saɪətɪ/ NOUN [plural building societies] an organization similar to a bank, from which people can borrow money to buy a house

built /bɪlt/ PAST TENSE AND PAST PARTICIPLE OF build

bulb /bʌlb/ NOUN [plural bulbs] a glass object that you put in an electric light to make it work □ I need a new bulb for my lamp.

bulge /bʌldʒ/ VERB [bulges, bulging, bulged]
1 if someone's eyes or muscles bulge, they stick out □ His eyes bulged in horror.
2 if a container is bulging, it is very full □ His sack was bulging with presents.

bulk /bʌlk/ NOUN
1 the bulk of something most of something

□ The bulk of his pocket money was spent on computer games.
2 in bulk you buy in bulk when you buy something in large quantities □ It's much cheaper to buy household goods in bulk.

bull /bʊl/ NOUN [plural bulls]
1 an adult male cow
2 the male of some other animals, such as the elephant

bulldozer /'bʊldəʊzə(r)/ NOUN [plural bulldozers] a large vehicle with a heavy metal container at the front, used for moving large amounts of earth and stones

bullet /'bʊlɪt/ NOUN [plural bullets] a small piece of metal that is shot from a gun □ a bullet wound 🔂 Several people were in the room when the bullets were fired.

bully¹ /'bʊlɪ/ NOUN [plural bullies] a person who frightens or hurts people who are smaller or weaker than they are

bully² /'bʊlɪ/ VERB [bullies, bullying, bullied] to frighten or hurt smaller or weaker people
• **bullying** /'bʊlɪɪŋ/ NOUN, NO PLURAL when someone bullies another person

bump¹ /bʌmp/ VERB [bumps, bumping, bumped] to knock against something by accident □ The baby bumped her head on the table. □ I bumped into the wall.
◆ PHRASAL VERB **bump into someone** to meet someone by chance □ I bumped into Sarah in town today.

bump² /bʌmp/ NOUN [plural bumps]
1 a raised part on a surface □ He had a nasty bump on the back of his head. □ There were a lot of bumps in the road.
2 a knock □ I felt a gentle bump against my leg.

bumper¹ /'bʌmpə(r)/ NOUN [plural bumpers] a long bar fixed to the front and back of a car that protects it if it hits something

bumper² /'bʌmpə(r)/ ADJECTIVE bigger than usual 🔂 We had a bumper crop of tomatoes this year.

bun /bʌn/ NOUN [plural buns]
1 a small round sweet cake □ a currant bun
2 bread in the form of a round shape □ a hamburger in a bun
3 a hairstyle in which the hair is twisted into a tight ball and fixed at the back of the head

bunch /bʌntʃ/ NOUN [plural bunches]
1 a group of things tied or held together 🔊 a bunch of flowers ☐ The caretaker has a big bunch of keys.
2 a group of things that grow together ☐ a bunch of grapes/bananas

bundle /'bʌndəl/ NOUN [plural bundles] a group of things fastened together ☐ a bundle of newspapers

bungalow /'bʌŋgələu/ NOUN [plural bungalows] a house that is all on one level

buoy /bɔɪ/ NOUN [plural buoys] a large object that floats in the sea, used to warn people or ships of danger

burden /'bɜ:dən/ NOUN [plural burdens] something unpleasant or difficult that someone has to deal with 🔊 He offered to share the burden of the work. ☐ Running two homes is a big financial burden.

burger /'bɜ:gə(r)/ NOUN [plural burgers] a type of flat round food made from small pieces of meat that have been pressed together ☐ I'll have a burger with fries and a coke, please.

burglar /'bɜ:glə(r)/ NOUN [plural burglars] someone who illegally enters a building in order to steal things ☐ The burglars broke in through a downstairs window.

burglary /'bɜ:glərɪ/ NOUN [plural burglaries] the crime of going into a building and stealing things ☐ He called the police to report a burglary.

burial /'berɪəl/ NOUN [plural burials] when a dead person is put in the ground

burn¹ /bɜ:n/ VERB [burns, burning, burnt or burned]
1 to destroy something by setting fire to it, or to be destroyed in this way ☐ We burn all our garden waste. 🔊 Both houses burnt to the ground.
2 to be on fire ☐ We could see the grass burning from miles away.
3 to injure yourself by touching fire or heat ☐ I burnt my hand on the cooker.
♦ PHRASAL VERB **burn down** if a building burns down, it is completely destroyed in a fire ☐ The old school burnt down.

burn² /bɜ:n/ NOUN [plural burns] an injury or mark left after touching fire or something very hot

burst /bɜ:st/ VERB [bursts, bursting, burst]
1 to break or tear, especially from having too much pressure inside ☐ The pipe had burst and water was running everywhere. ☐ He was bursting all the balloons with a pin.
2 burst into flames to suddenly start to burn a lot
3 burst into tears to suddenly start to cry
♦ PHRASAL VERB **burst out crying/laughing** to suddenly start to cry or laugh

bury /'berɪ/ VERB [buries, burying, buried] to put something in the ground, especially a dead person ☐ She was buried in the village where she was born. ☐ They buried the treasure.

bus /bʌs/ NOUN [plural buses] a large vehicle with a lot of seats for passengers 🔊 I caught the bus into town. 🔊 a school bus 🔊 a bus driver

bush /buʃ/ NOUN [plural bushes] a type of small tree ☐ a rose bush

business /'bɪznɪs/ NOUN [plural businesses]
1 no plural buying and selling, and the work of producing things that people will buy 🔊 He went into business (= started buying and selling) with his brother. 🔊 In 2004 her company went out of business (= ended because they had no money). 🔊 They do a lot of business with Asia (= They sell a lot to Asia).
2 a company that makes and sells goods, or that sells services 🔊 He runs the business with his wife.
3 on business working ☐ He travels a lot on business.

➤ Remember that you travel/go somewhere **on business**:
✓ I was recently in Paris on business.
✗ I was recently in Paris for business.

♦ IDIOM **Mind your own business!** used as a rude way of refusing to answer a personal question ☐ 'What's your boyfriend's name?' 'Mind your own business!'

businessman /'bɪznɪsmæn/ NOUN [plural businessmen] a man who works in business, usually in a high position

businesswoman /'bɪznɪsˌwumən/ NOUN [plural businesswomen] a woman who works in business, usually in a high position

bus stop /'bʌs ˌstɒp/ NOUN [plural bus stops] a place where a bus stops to allow passengers to get on or off ☐ I saw Fiona standing at the bus stop.

busy /'bɪzɪ/ ADJECTIVE [busier, busiest]
1 doing a lot of things ☐ + **with** They're busy with wedding preparations. ☐ + **doing something** I was

busy getting dinner ready. 🔁 That report should keep
him busy today. 🔁 I've had a very busy day.
2 full of people or traffic 🔁 We live on a busy street.
□ Were the shops busy this morning?

but /bʌt/ CONJUNCTION used for joining two parts
of a sentence which say different or opposite things
□ She eats fish but not meat. □ He's not very
attractive but he's a nice guy. □ I can cycle but I
can't drive. □ I'd like to come but I haven't got time.

butcher /'bʊtʃə(r)/ NOUN [plural butchers]
1 someone whose job is to cut up and sell raw meat
2 butcher's a shop that sells raw meat

butter /'bʌtə(r)/ NOUN, NO PLURAL a yellow food
made from milk, used for spreading on bread or for
cooking 🔁 a slice of bread and butter

butterfly /'bʌtəflaɪ/ NOUN [plural butterflies] a
type of insect with large brightly coloured wings
♦ IDIOM get/have butterflies (in your stomach) to
have an uncomfortable feeling in your stomach
because you are nervous

button /'bʌtən/ NOUN [plural buttons]
1 a small object that you press in order to make a
machine work 🔁 I pressed the button to call the lift.
□ Press the start button.
2 a small round object used for fastening clothes
🔁 He did up/undid (= fastened/unfastened) his
buttons.

buy /baɪ/ VERB [buys, buying, bought] to get
something by giving money for it □ I've bought the
tickets. □ Have you bought him a present? □ **+
from** We buy most of our food from the
supermarket.

buyer /'baɪə(r)/ NOUN [plural buyers] someone
who buys something □ Have they found a buyer for
their house?

buzz[1] /bʌz/ NOUN, NO PLURAL the continuous sound
that a large flying insect makes □ The constant buzz
of insects disturbed his sleep.

buzz[2] /bʌz/ VERB [buzzes, buzzing, buzzed] to make
a continuous sound like a large flying insect □ Flies
buzzed round our heads.

by[1] /baɪ/ PREPOSITION
1 shows who or what does something □ a painting
by Picasso □ The house was built by her grandfather.
2 near or next to something □ There's a café by the
station.
3 using something □ We came by train. □ All their
clothes are made by hand. □ Can I pay by credit
card? □ **+ doing something** By buying food from
local shops you are supporting your community.
4 past □ A tall boy ran by me.
5 by accident/chance without intending to □ We
met by chance. □ I only discovered it by accident.
6 by 20%/£500, etc. shows how much something
has increased or decreased □ Prices have risen by 20
percent.
7 by the arm/coat, etc. shows which part of
someone you take in your hand □ She grabbed me
by the hand.
8 before □ I'll be home by 7.30.
9 used when giving measurements of length and
width □ The room is 5 metres by 3 metres.

by[2] /baɪ/ ADVERB past □ A car went speeding by.
♦ IDIOM by the way used before you say something
that is not related to what you were saying
before

bye /baɪ/ EXCLAMATION an informal word that
means goodbye □ Bye – see you later!
bypass /'baɪpɑːs/ NOUN [plural bypasses] a road
around a town or city

Cc

C¹ *or* **C** /siː/ the third letter of the alphabet

C² /siː/ ABBREVIATION
1 Celsius
2 centigrade

cab /kæb/ NOUN [*plural* cabs] a taxi ⊞ *We took a cab to the airport.*

cabbage /ˈkæbɪdʒ/ NOUN [*plural* cabbages] a large round green vegetable formed of tight layers of leaves

cabin /ˈkæbɪn/ NOUN [*plural* cabins]
1 a simple wooden house ⊞ *He built a log cabin in the forest.*
2 a small room for sleeping in on a ship
3 the part of an aeroplane which the passengers sit in

cabinet /ˈkæbɪnɪt/ NOUN [*plural* cabinets]
1 Cabinet a group of people with important government jobs who decide what the government will do □ *She became a member of the Cabinet in 1990.* □ *a Cabinet meeting*
2 a cupboard with shelves, used for storing things or for showing attractive objects □ *a bathroom cabinet*

cable /ˈkeɪbəl/ NOUN [*plural* cables]
1 a tube containing wires that carry electricity or electronic signals □ *a telephone cable*
2 thick, strong metal rope □ *Miles of cable were used to build the bridge.*
3 *no plural* a television service in which programmes are sent along underground wires □ *We can't get cable or satellite here.*

café /ˈkæfeɪ/ NOUN [*plural* cafés] a small restaurant that serves drinks and things to eat

cafeteria /ˌkæfɪˈtɪərɪə/ NOUN [*plural* cafeterias] a restaurant where the customers buy food and drink and take it to a table to eat it

cage /keɪdʒ/ NOUN [*plural* cages] a box or an area with bars around it for keeping birds or animals in □ *The pet shop sells bird cages and hamster cages.*

cake /keɪk/ NOUN [*plural* cakes] a sweet food made from a baked mixture, usually of flour, sugar, butter and eggs ⊞ *a birthday cake* ⊞ *He made a cake for the school fair.* ⊞ *Would you like another slice of chocolate cake?*

♦ IDIOM **have your cake and eat it** to get all the advantages of a situation in a way that is unfair

calculate /ˈkælkjuleɪt/ VERB [calculates, calculating, calculated] to find out an amount by using mathematics □ *One apple costs 13p. Calculate the cost of 174 apples.* □ *Do you understand how they calculate tax?*

calculation /ˌkælkjuˈleɪʃən/ NOUN [*plural* calculations] when you use mathematics to find out an amount ⊞ *I did some quick calculations to work out the total cost.* □ *By my calculation, we should finish by Tuesday.*

calculator /ˈkælkjuleɪtə(r)/ NOUN [*plural* calculators] an electronic machine that you use for doing mathematical calculations ⊞ *a pocket calculator*

calendar /ˈkælɪndə(r)/ NOUN [*plural* calendars] something that shows all the days, weeks and months of the year □ *She looked on the calendar to see what date it would be on Monday.*

calf /kɑːf/ NOUN [*plural* calves]
1 the back part of your leg below the knee
2 a young cow

call¹ /kɔːl/ VERB [calls, calling, called]
1 if a person or thing is called something, that is their name □ *He's called Jonathan James.*
2 to shout □ *I heard him calling my name.*
3 to ask someone to come to you □ *Call the children in from the garden.*
4 to telephone someone □ *Have you called your mother yet?*
5 to visit someone □ *+ in* *We called in to see Maria this morning.*

> ➤ Remember that the verb **call** meaning 'telephone' is used without 'to':
> ✓ *I called my brother to wish him happy birthday.*
> ✗ *I called to my brother to wish him happy birthday.*

♦ PHRASAL VERBS **call for someone** to go to someone's house in order to go somewhere with them □ *I'll call for you at seven.* **call something off** to stop a plan or an activity □ *The search has* *been called off.* **call someone up** a US word meaning to telephone someone □ *He called me up in the middle of the night.*

call² /kɔ:l/ NOUN [plural calls]
1 when you contact someone by telephone 🗫 *Give me a call tomorrow.* 🗫 *I'm sure I can find someone to fix you car – let me make a few calls.*
2 a shout □ *They ignored his calls for help.*
3 a short visit 🗫 *I thought I might pay you a call tomorrow.*

calm¹ /kɑ:m/ ADJECTIVE [calmer, calmest]
1 not nervous, excited or upset □ *Try to stay calm.* □ *'Yes', he said in a calm voice.*
2 if the sea is calm, it is flat with no big waves

calm² /kɑ:m/
♦ PHRASAL VERB [calms, calming, calmed] **calm (someone) down** to stop someone being angry, excited or upset, or to stop being angry, excited or upset □ *She took a couple of deep breaths to calm herself down.* □ *Just calm down! Nobody's going to hurt you.*

calmly /'kɑ:mlɪ/ ADVERB without seeming nervous or excited □ *Grace walked calmly on to the stage.*

calves /kɑ:vz/ PLURAL OF calf
came /keɪm/ PAST TENSE OF come

camel /'kæməl/ NOUN [plural camels] a large animal that lives in the desert and has one or two humps (= tall rounded parts) on its back

camera /'kæmərə/ NOUN [plural cameras] a device for taking photographs, or for making television programmes or films 🗫 *I have a digital camera.* 🗫 *He's very confident in front of the television cameras.*

camp¹ /kæmp/ NOUN [plural camps] a place where people live in tents or temporary shelters, usually for a short time 🗫 *a holiday camp* 🗫 *a refugee camp*

camp² /kæmp/ VERB [camps, camping, camped] to stay somewhere for a short time in a tent or caravan (= vehicle for living in) □ *We camped next to the lake.*

campaign /kæm'peɪn/ NOUN [plural campaigns] a series of activities designed to achieve something □ *an advertising campaign* □ *an election campaign*

camping /'kæmpɪŋ/ NOUN, NO PLURAL the activity of staying in a tent 🗫 *We went camping in France last summer.* 🗫 *The boys are on a camping trip.*

campsite /'kæmpsaɪt/ NOUN [plural campsites] a place where people stay in tents for a holiday □ *We found a good campsite near the river.*

campus /'kæmpəs/ NOUN [plural campuses] the land and buildings that form a university or college

can¹ /kæn/ MODAL VERB
1 to be able to do something □ *Can you swim? Yes, I can.* □ *Can you see my keys anywhere?*
2 to be allowed to □ *Can I go swimming? Yes, you can.*
3 used to ask someone to do something or give you something □ *Can you open the window, please?* □ *Can you lend me some money?*
4 used to say if something is possible or not □ *Can you buy tickets here?* □ *Tiredness can cause accidents.*

➤ **Can** is the present tense form. Use **could** for the past tense.

➤ To ask for something politely, do not use **can** but instead use **could** □ *Could I use this chair, please?*

can² /kæn/ NOUN [plural cans]
1 a closed metal container that keeps food or drink fresh 🗫 *a beer can* 🗫 *Do you recycle your tin cans?* □ *She opened a can of beans.*
2 a container used for liquid or other substances □ *a paint can*

can³ /kæn/ VERB [cans, canning, canned] to put food or drink in closed metal cans that keep it fresh

canal /kə'næl/ NOUN [plural canals] a long passage filled with water, made for boats to travel along □ *the Panama Canal*

cancel /'kænsəl/ VERB [cancels, cancelling/US canceling, cancelled/US canceled] to say that a planned event will not happen □ *The match was cancelled because of the snow.*

cancer /'kænsə(r)/ NOUN, NO PLURAL a serious disease in which some cells in the body start to grow very quickly □ *Smoking can cause lung cancer.* 🗫 *Use sun cream – you don't want to get skin cancer.* 🗫 *The drug is used to treat cancer patients.*

candidate /'kændɪdət/ NOUN [plural candidates]
1 someone who is trying to get a job □ + **for** There are three candidates for the job. □ *The Democratic candidate for the US presidency is Barack Obama.*
2 someone who is taking an exam □ *All our GCSE candidates were successful.*

candle /'kændəl/ NOUN [plural candles] a stick of wax with a piece of string through the middle which produces a flame when you burn it 🗫 *I must light the candles on the dinner table.* 🗫 *Don't forget to blow out the candle.*

candy /'kændɪ/ NOUN [plural candies] the US word for **sweet²** (sense 1)
cane /keɪn/ NOUN [plural canes] a stick that someone uses to help them walk

cannon /ˈkænən/ NOUN [plural cannons] a large gun that fires big metal balls or other large explosives

cannot /ˈkænɒt/ MODAL VERB the negative form of can □ I just cannot do it.

➤ In spoken English, **can't** is usually used instead of 'cannot' □ I can't come tonight.

canoe /kəˈnuː/ NOUN [plural canoes] a light boat with pointed ends which you move through the water using a paddle (= stick with wide flat ends)

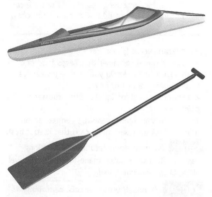

can't /kɑːnt/ a short way to say and write **cannot** □ I can't hear you.

canteen /ˌkænˈtiːn/ NOUN [plural canteens] a restaurant in a school or work place □ I had lunch with my friends in the school canteen.

canvas /ˈkænvəs/ NOUN [plural canvases]
1 a piece of strong cloth stretched on a frame for an artist to paint on
2 strong cloth used to make tents and sails

canyon /ˈkænjən/ NOUN [plural canyons] a deep valley with steep sides. A geography word □ the Grand Canyon

cap /kæp/ NOUN [plural caps]
1 a soft hat, often with a flat part that sticks out at the front □ a baseball cap
2 a small top for a bottle, tube or pen □ The pen will dry up if you leave the cap off.

capability /ˌkeɪpəˈbɪlətɪ/ NOUN [plural capabilities] ability or power to do something ⊞ The task is simply beyond his capabilities.

capable /ˈkeɪpəbəl/ ADJECTIVE
1 if you are capable of something, you are able to do it □ The old lady isn't capable of looking after herself any more.
2 able to do things and deal with problems without help □ She's a very capable person.

➤ Note that the structure that comes after **capable** is of doing something:
✓ She isn't capable of looking after a small child.
✗ She isn't capable to look after a small child.

capacitor /kəˈpæsɪtə(r)/ NOUN [plural capacitors] a device used to store electrical charge. A physics word.

capacity /kəˈpæsɪtɪ/ NOUN [plural capacities]
1 the total amount that a container or building will hold ⊞ The hall has a seating capacity of 300. □ Each barrel has a capacity of 100 litres.
2 someone's ability to do or experience something □ Flynn has the capacity to be a great leader.

capital /ˈkæpɪtəl/ NOUN [plural capitals]
1 the city where the government of a state or country is □ + of London is the capital of England.
2 a large letter such as B that you write at the beginning of a sentence, or at the beginning of a name □ Write your name in capitals at the top of the page. ⊞ The notice was typed in capital letters.

captain /ˈkæptɪn/ NOUN [plural captains]
1 the person in charge of a ship or an aircraft □ Everyone must obey the captain's orders.
2 the person in charge of a sports team □ He is the new England captain.
3 a person of middle rank in the army, high rank in the navy or high rank in the US police □ Captain Jones

captive /ˈkæptɪv/ NOUN [plural captives] a prisoner

captivity /kæpˈtɪvətɪ/ NOUN, NO PLURAL when a person or animal is kept in a place which they are not allowed to leave □ The bear spent its whole life in captivity.

capture¹ /ˈkæptʃə(r)/ VERB [captures, capturing, captured]
1 to catch an animal or person and not allow them to escape □ Many soldiers were captured by the enemy.
2 to get control of a place or equipment by force □ Armed soldiers have captured the airport.

capture² /ˈkæptʃə(r)/ NOUN, NO PLURAL
1 when you catch someone or something ⊞ How long can the killer avoid capture?
2 when you take or get control of a place or equipment □ the capture of enemy tanks

car /kɑː(r)/ NOUN [plural cars] a vehicle with an engine and seats for a small number of passengers □ Many children travel to school by car. ⊞ You need a licence before you can drive a car. ⊞ Where did you park the car? ⊞ I've lost the car keys.

caravan /ˈkærəvæn/ NOUN [plural caravans] a vehicle for living in, especially on holiday, which can be pulled behind a car

carbohydrate /ˌkɑːbəʊˈhaɪdrɒɪt/ NOUN [*plural* carbohydrates] a substance in foods such as potatoes and bread which gives your body energy

carbon /ˈkɑːbən/ NOUN, NO PLURAL a chemical element which is in all living things and in substances such as coal and oil. A chemistry word.

carbon dioxide /ˈkɑːbən daɪˈɒksaɪd/ NOUN, NO PLURAL a gas that is produced when people and animals breathe out and when carbon is burned. A chemistry word.

card /kɑːd/ NOUN [*plural* cards]
1 a piece of stiff paper with a picture and a message 🔁 *a birthday/Christmas card* 🔁 *I must send her a card.*
2 *no plural* thick stiff paper □ *coloured card*
3 a small flat piece of plastic that you can use in shops and machines to pay for things □ *Can I pay by card?* 🔁 *a bank card*
4 a small piece of stiff paper or plastic with information on it □ *a library card* □ *Here's my business card.*
5 one of a set of rectangular pieces of card used for playing games 🔁 *I bought a pack of cards.*
6 cards games that are played with a set of cards 🔁 *Do you like playing cards?*

cardboard /ˈkɑːdbɔːd/ NOUN, NO PLURAL very stiff thick paper used to make boxes and packages for goods 🔁 *a cardboard box*

cardiac /ˈkɑːdɪæk/ ADJECTIVE to do with the heart. A biology word □ *a cardiac surgeon*

cardigan /ˈkɑːdɪɡən/ NOUN [*plural* cardigans] a piece of clothing for your upper body that is made from wool and fastens with buttons down the front

cardinal[1] /ˈkɑːdɪnəl/ NOUN [*plural* cardinals] a priest of high rank in the Roman Catholic Church

cardinal[2] /ˈkɑːdɪnəl/ ADJECTIVE cardinal numbers are numbers like one, two, three, not first, second, third. A mathematics word.

care[1] /keə(r)/ NOUN, NO PLURAL
1 looking after someone 🔁 *They need urgent medical care.* 🔁 *The care he received in hospital was excellent.*
2 take care of someone/something to look after someone or something □ *Their aunt took care of them after their parents died.*
3 when you give something a lot of attention or effort 🔁 *Meg does her work with great care.* 🔁 *She took a lot of care over her appearance.*
4 take care to be careful not to have an accident or make a mistake □ *You must take care to lock all the doors.* □ *Take care, the roads are very icy!*

care[2] /keə(r)/ VERB [cares, caring, cared]
1 to think that something is interesting or important □ *+ question word He said he didn't care what happened.* □ *+ about I don't care about your holiday plans – we've got work to do!*
2 to feel love or affection for someone □ *+ for He really cares for his staff.*
♦ PHRASAL VERB **care for someone/something** to look after a person or an animal □ *Sarah wants to be a vet so that she can care for sick animals.*

career /kəˈrɪə(r)/ NOUN [*plural* careers] a job or type of work that you train for and continue doing for a long time □ *+ in a career in the police force* □ *a teaching career* □ *We both chose law as a career.*

➤ **THESAURUS:** A career is something that you train for and do for a long time. The word **profession** is similar, and is usually used for jobs which need special qualifications. For example, medicine, teaching and law are all **professions**. A **trade** is a job using your hands that involves special skills or training. Plumbers work in a **trade**. **Job** is a general word to describe the work that someone does for money.

careful /ˈkeəfʊl/ ADJECTIVE making sure that you do something correctly or safely 🔁 *Be careful when you cross the road.* □ *+ to do something Dad is always careful to lock all the doors.*

carefully /ˈkeəfʊli/ ADVERB without making mistakes or causing damage □ *Greta wrapped up the glass carefully in tissue paper.*

careless /ˈkeəlɪs/ ADJECTIVE not being careful 🔁 *a careless mistake* □ *Alex is a bit careless with his money.*

carelessly /ˈkeəlɪsli/ ADVERB in a careless way □ *He threw the letter aside carelessly.*

cargo /ˈkɑːɡəʊ/ NOUN [*plural* cargoes] the things that a vehicle is carrying □ *The ship had a cargo of sugar and coffee.*

carnival /ˈkɑːnɪvəl/ NOUN [*plural* carnivals] a celebration when people sing and dance outdoors wearing special clothes

carp[1] /kɑːp/ NOUN [*plural* carp] a large fish that lives in lakes and rivers

carp[2] /kɑːp/ VERB [carps, carping, carped] to complain a lot in a way that is annoying □ *He was carping about the cost of everything.*

car park /ˈkɑːr ˌpɑːk/ NOUN [*plural* car parks] a building or place where cars can be left □ *The car park was full.*

carpenter /ˈkɑːpəntə(r)/ NOUN [*plural* carpenters] someone whose job is to make things from wood

carpentry /ˈkɑːpəntri/ NOUN, NO PLURAL making things from wood

carpet /ˈkɑːpɪt/ NOUN [*plural* carpets] a covering for a floor made of wool or a similar material □ *Don't get mud on the carpet.*

carriage /'kærɪdʒ/ NOUN [plural carriages]
1 one of the long parts of a train where passengers sit
2 a vehicle with wheels that is pulled by horses

► THESAURUS: A carriage is one of the parts of a train where people sit. The words carriage and coach also describe vehicles that are pulled by horses. People used carriages and coaches for travelling in the past. Coaches were usually used for long journeys. Nowadays, a coach is a bus for long journeys. Note that a car is a vehicle with an engine and seats for a small number of passengers. Vehicle is a general word for something that carries people or goods. Cars, buses and trains are all vehicles.

carrot /'kærət/ NOUN [plural carrots] a long orange vegetable that grows under the ground

carry /'kærɪ/ VERB [carries, carrying, carried]
1 to pick something up and take it somewhere □ This suitcase is too heavy for me to carry. □ You may only carry one bag onto the plane.
2 to have something with you in your hand, your pocket, etc. □ The robber was carrying a gun. □ Why were you carrying so much cash on you? □ + around Do you have to carry that umbrella around with you?
♦ PHRASAL VERBS **carry on** to continue □ + with Carry on with your work while I go and see the headmaster. □ + ing When the noise stopped, our guide was able to carry on speaking. **carry out something 1** to do a task □ carry out research/an experiment **2** to do something that you have said you will do 🕀 Will the terrorists manage to carry out their threat?

cart /kɑ:t/ NOUN [plural carts] a vehicle for goods which is pulled by a horse 🕀 a horse and cart
carton /'kɑ:tən/ NOUN [plural cartons] a box for food or drink that is made of cardboard □ a carton of milk
cartoon /kɑ:'tu:n/ NOUN [plural cartoons]
1 a funny drawing or series of drawings in a newspaper or magazine
2 a film made from a long series of drawings 🕀 Mickey Mouse is a cartoon character.
carve /kɑ:v/ VERB [carves, carving, carved]
1 to make something by cutting wood, stone, etc. □ There are angels carved out of stone.
2 to cut meat into thin flat pieces using a sharp knife

► THESAURUS: If you cut something, you use a knife to divide it into pieces. Cut is a general word. If you cut thin pieces from a large piece of meat, such as a chicken, you can use the word carve. Slice has a similar meaning, but we usually use slice when a whole thing is cut into thin, flat pieces. For example, you can slice a loaf of bread or an onion. When you cut something into lots of small pieces you use the word chop.

case /keɪs/ NOUN [plural cases]
1 a situation or an example of a particular situation □ Inspectors are examining several cases of cruelty to animals. 🕀 You haven't got any money? In that case, you'd better get a job.
2 (just) in case because of the possibility of something □ I don't think it's going to rain, but I'll take my umbrella just in case.
3 a crime that the police are trying to solve □ a murder case
4 something that is being decided in a court 🕀 a court case
5 a container for something □ a violin case □ The crown jewels are in a glass case.
6 a suitcase (= large container for carrying clothes on holiday) 🕀 Have you packed your case yet?

cash¹ /kæʃ/ NOUN, NO PLURAL
1 money in the form of paper money and coins □ The gardener likes to be paid in cash.
2 money 🕀 I'm rather short of cash (= I haven't got much money).

► THESAURUS: You use money for buying things. Cash is a word to describe money in the form of notes and coins. A note is a piece of paper money. A coin is a piece of metal money, which is usually round. Change is extra money which is given back to you when you pay for something. For example, if you are buying something that costs £4.50 and you use a £5.00 note to pay for it, you will get 50p change.

cash² /kæʃ/ VERB [cashes, cashing, cashed] to cash a cheque is to change it for paper money or coins

cashpoint /'kæʃpɔɪnt / NOUN [plural cashpoints] a machine, usually in the wall outside a bank, where you can get money using a small plastic card
casino /kə'si:nəʊ/ NOUN [plural casinos] a building where people play games in which they lose or win money
cast¹ /kɑ:st/ VERB [casts, casting, cast]
1 to choose the actors who will be in a play or a film □ He was cast as Hamlet.
2 if something casts light or a shadow somewhere, it makes it go there □ The lamp cast light onto the desk.
3 when you cast your vote, you vote for someone or something
4 cast a spell on someone/something to use magic on someone or something
cast² /kɑ:st/ NOUN [plural casts]
1 the actors in a play or a film □ a member of the cast
2 a hard covering that is put on a broken arm or leg

castle /'kɑːsəl/ NOUN [plural castles] a large building with high walls and towers, which was built to protect people from attack □ *Edinburgh Castle stands high above the city.* □ *We visited a ruined castle.*

casual /'kæʒuəl/ ADJECTIVE
1 not formal □ *casual clothes* □ *She runs the hotel in quite a casual and relaxed style.*
2 not serious □ *He has had several casual relationships since his divorce.* □ *I worry about Sarita's casual attitude to her work.*

casualty /'kæʒjuəltɪ/ NOUN [plural casualties] someone who has been injured or killed □ *Ambulances rushed the casualties to hospital.*

cat /kæt/ NOUN [plural cats]
1 an animal which people keep as a pet, which catches mice and birds □ *I stroked the cat and it purred happily.*
2 a wild animals such as a lion, that belongs to the same family as the cat ⏚ *One of my favourite big cats is the leopard.*
➡ *go to* let the cat out of the bag

catalog /'kætəlɒg/ NOUN [plural catalogs] the US spelling of **catalogue**

catalogue /'kætəlɒg/ NOUN [plural catalogues]
1 a book that shows the products you can buy from a company ⏚ *Mum got me some jeans from a mail order catalogue.*
2 a list of all the books or objects in a collection

> ► THESAURUS: There are several words to describe books that contain lists of useful information. A **catalogue** is a book that shows products that you can buy from a company. A **brochure** is similar, and is often used for selling holidays, or other things that you do not buy in a shop and take home, such as kitchens. A **directory** is a book that contains a list of names and telephone numbers in alphabetical order. An **index** is the section at the end of a book which tells you which page to look for information.

catastrophe /kə'tæstrəfɪ/ NOUN [plural catastrophes] an event that causes a lot of damage or suffering □ *The government has plans for dealing with floods and other natural catastrophes.*

catch[1] /kætʃ/ VERB [catches, catching, caught]
1 to stop and hold something that is moving through the air □ *Throw the ball and I'll try to catch it.*
2 to stop a person or animal from escaping □ *James caught a huge fish.* □ *Police managed to catch the escaped prisoners.*
3 to get an illness □ *Most people catch between two and four colds a year.*
4 to get on a bus, train, etc. □ *I left early so that I could catch the 8.30 train.*
5 to become stuck on something, or to make something become stuck on something else □ *Sam caught his sleeve on the door handle.*
6 catch fire to start burning □ *The plane caught fire after its tyre burst on landing.*
7 catch sight of someone/something to see someone or something for a short time □ *I just managed to catch sight of the queen.*
➡ *go to* catch someone's eye
♦ PHRASAL VERB catch (someone/something) up
1 to reach someone or something that is in front of you by moving faster than them □ *We ran to catch the others up.* **2** to get to the same level as someone or something □ *When children miss a lot of school, it can be difficult for them to catch up with the others.*

catch[2] /kætʃ/ NOUN [plural catches] when someone stops and holds something that was moving through the air □ *That was a brilliant catch!*

category /'kætə,gərɪ/ NOUN [plural categories] a group of people or things of the same type ⏚ *Our members tend to fall into one of three categories.*

cathedral /kə'θiːdrəl/ NOUN [plural cathedrals] a large and important church □ *St Paul's Cathedral in London*

Catholic[1] /'kæθəlɪk/ ADJECTIVE to do with, or belonging to, the Roman Catholic Church □ *a Catholic priest*
● **Catholicism** /kə'θɒlɪ,sɪzəm/ NOUN, NO PLURAL the beliefs and practices of Catholics

Catholic[2] /'kæθəlɪk/ NOUN [plural Catholics] a member of the Roman Catholic Church

cattle /'kætəl/ PLURAL NOUN male and female cows on a farm □ *cattle farmers*

caught /kɔːt/ PAST TENSE AND PAST PARTICIPLE OF catch[1]

cauliflower /ˈkɒlɪˌflaʊə(r)/ NOUN [plural cauliflowers] a round vegetable with green leaves around a hard white centre

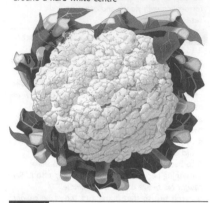

cause¹ /kɔːz/ VERB [causes, causing, caused] to make something happen □ Do they know what caused the accident? □ Strong winds caused problems on the roads. □ **+ to do something** Unfortunately the delay caused me to miss my appointment.

cause² /kɔːz/ NOUN [plural causes]
1 what makes something happen □ There are many causes of poverty. □ The engineer can't find the cause of the problem.
2 something that people support because they believe it is good or useful ⏍ She collects money for many good causes.

caution /ˈkɔːʃən/ NOUN, NO PLURAL when you take care to avoid danger or risk □ Please drive with caution.

cautious /ˈkɔːʃəs/ ADJECTIVE very careful to avoid danger or risk □ He's very cautious with his money.

cave /keɪv/ NOUN [plural caves] a large hole in a mountain or under the ground □ The cave was dark and damp.

CD /ˌsiːˈdiː/ ABBREVIATION compact disc; a disc with sound recorded on it □ He bought a CD of Scottish folk songs.

CD-ROM /ˌsiːdiːˈrɒm/ ABBREVIATION compact disc read-only memory; a type of CD that stores a lot of information which you play on a computer □ The dictionary is available on CD-ROM.

cease /siːs/ VERB [ceases, ceasing, ceased] a formal word meaning to stop

ceasefire /ˌsiːsˈfaɪə(r)/ NOUN [plural ceasefires] an agreement between two armies to stop fighting for a period of time

ceiling /ˈsiːlɪŋ/ NOUN [plural ceilings] the surface at the top of a room □ This house has very high ceilings.

celebrate /ˈselɪbreɪt/ VERB [celebrates, celebrating, celebrated] when you celebrate an event you have a party or do other special things because of it ⏍ Dad took a day off work to celebrate his 50th birthday. ⏍ We like to celebrate Christmas in a traditional way. □ Mark passed his driving test, so we're going out to celebrate!

celebration /ˌselɪˈbreɪʃən/ NOUN [plural celebrations] a party or something special that is done to celebrate an event □ a wedding celebration

➤ **THESAURUS:** Celebration is a general word for a party or other event that is held to celebrate a special event. An anniversary is a date when you celebrate something that happened on the same date in the past. For example, you might celebrate your wedding anniversary. Note that in English, the celebration of the date of your birth is called your birthday, not your anniversary. A party is a special event where people get together to dance, drink and eat.

celebrity /sɪˈlebrətɪ/ NOUN [plural celebrities] someone who is famous □ Will there be any celebrities at the party?

celery /ˈselərɪ/ NOUN, NO PLURAL a vegetable with long, pale green stems, usually eaten raw

cell /sel/ NOUN [plural cells]
1 the smallest part of a living thing □ cancerous cells
2 a small room that a prisoner is kept in or that a monk (= religious man) lives in

cellar /ˈselə(r)/ NOUN [plural cellars] an underground room used for storing things

cellphone /ˈselfəʊn/ NOUN [plural cellphones] the US word for **mobile phone**

Celsius /ˈselsɪəs/ ADJECTIVE measured using the temperature measurement at which water freezes at 0 degrees and boils at 100 degrees □ 57 degrees Celsius

cement /sɪˈment/ NOUN, NO PLURAL a grey powder that is mixed with sand and water for use in building

cemetery /ˈsemɪtərɪ/ NOUN [plural cemeteries] a place where dead people are buried

cent /sent/ NOUN [plural cents] a unit of money worth 1/100 of a dollar

center /ˈsentə(r)/ NOUN [plural centers] the US spelling of **centre**

centigrade /ˈsentɪɡreɪd/ ADJECTIVE an old-fashioned word for **Celsius** □ forty degrees centigrade

centimetre /ˈsentɪˌmiːtə(r)/ NOUN [plural centimetres] a unit for measuring length, equal to 10 millimetres. This is often written **cm** □ The card measures eight centimetres across. □ These heels are 8cm high.

central /ˈsentrəl/ ADJECTIVE near or in the centre of an object or a place □ He works in central London.

central heating /ˌsentrəl ˈhiːtɪŋ/ NOUN, NO PLURAL a system used for heating houses where heated water goes through pipes to each room

centre /ˈsentə(r)/ NOUN [plural centres]
1 the middle point or part of something □ It is difficult to park in the city centre. □ These chocolates have soft centres. □ + of He stood in the centre of the field.
2 the most important part of something □ + of The woman at the centre of the dispute is refusing to speak to journalists. □ The idea is at the centre of the project.
3 a place or a building used for a particular activity □ a sports centre □ The centre carries out research into breast cancer.

century /ˈsentʃʊri/ NOUN [plural centuries] a hundred years □ She lived in the fifteenth century. □ a twentieth-century building

cereal /ˈsɪəriəl/ NOUN [plural cereals]
1 a plant such as rice, that is grown in order to use the grains for food □ Wheat is a cereal used for making bread and pasta.
2 food made from cereal crops, especially one eaten for breakfast ⊞ breakfast cereals

ceremony /ˈserɪməni/ NOUN [plural ceremonies] a formal event where special or traditional words or actions are used ⊞ a wedding ceremony ⊞ The graduation ceremony was held at the cathedral. ⊞ Who will be attending the award ceremony this year?

certain /ˈsɜːtən/ ADJECTIVE
1 with no doubts □ + about Dad wasn't certain about the time of the train. □ + question word I'm not certain how it works. □ + that I'm certain that I saw someone in the garden.
2 sure to happen or be true □ + that It seems certain that he will get the job. ⊞ Make certain that the rope is tight. □ + to do something She says you're certain to pass the exam.
3 used to talk about someone or something without saying exactly which person or thing you are talking about □ There are certain rules which you must obey. □ Certain people have been asked to leave.

certainly /ˈsɜːtənli/ ADVERB
1 used to show that there is no doubt about something □ Joe certainly knows a lot about birds. ⊞ 'Can I stay up until midnight?' 'Certainly not!'
2 used to agree to something □ 'May I borrow your lawnmower?' 'Certainly.'

certificate /səˈtɪfɪkət/ NOUN [plural certificates] an official document that shows something is true ⊞ They asked to see my birth certificate. □ We each received a certificate for completing the course.

> ► **THESAURUS:** A document is a general word for a piece of paper with official information on it. For example, travel documents might include passport, tickets and visas. A certificate is an official piece of paper that shows that something is true. For example, you get a certificate to show that you have passed an examination. A licence is a document which gives you official permission to do something. A driving licence shows that you are allowed to drive a car. A passport is an official document which you carry with you when you travel to other countries to show who you are.

chain[1] /tʃeɪn/ NOUN [plural chains]
1 metal rings that are connected in a line □ He wore a gold chain around his neck. □ The chain came off my bicycle.
2 a group of similar shops, restaurants, etc. that have the same owner □ + of She owns a chain of restaurants.

chain[2] /tʃeɪn/ VERB [chains, chaining, chained] to fasten something or someone with a chain
□ often passive The bicycle was chained to the fence.

chair[1] /tʃeə(r)/ NOUN [plural chairs]
1 a piece of furniture that has a back and which one person sits on
2 the person who is in charge of a meeting, business or organization

chair[2] /tʃeə(r)/ VERB [chairs, chairing, chaired] to be officially in charge of a meeting

chairman /ˈtʃeəmən/ NOUN [plural chairmen]
1 the person who is in charge of a company, group or organization □ the chairman of the board
2 the person who is in charge of a meeting

chairwoman /'tʃeəwumən/ NOUN [plural chairwomen]
1 a woman who is in charge of a company, group or organization
2 a woman who is in charge of a meeting

chalk /tʃɔːk/ NOUN, NO PLURAL
1 a type of soft white stone □ crumbling chalk cliffs
2 pieces of this stone that you use to draw with □ She wrote on the blackboard with chalk.

challenge¹ /'tʃælɪndʒ/ NOUN [plural challenges]
1 something that is difficult to do ⊞ The world faces a huge challenge in tackling climate change. ⊞ Crime poses/presents a serious challenge to our community.
2 when you try to change a rule, or do not accept a decision or someone's authority ⊞ There is likely to be a legal challenge to this decison.
3 when you ask someone to fight or compete with you □ The approach of their army was a clear challenge.

challenge² /'tʃælɪndʒ/ VERB [challenges, challenging, challenged]
1 to try to change a rule, or to say that you do not accept a decision or someone's authority □ We will challenge this decision in the courts.
2 to ask someone to compete or fight □ + to He challenged his enemy to a fight.
3 if something challenges you, you find it difficult to do □ This exam will challenge even our best pupils.
• **challenger** /'tʃælɪndʒə(r)/ NOUN [plural challengers] someone who wants to try and beat another person in a game, election, etc.

champagne /ʃæm'peɪn/ NOUN, NO PLURAL a pale French wine with lots of bubbles, often drunk to celebrate something □ Let's open a bottle of champagne.

champion /'tʃæmpɪən/ NOUN [plural champions] a person or team that has beaten all the others in a competition □ He became world boxing champion at twenty-six.

championship /'tʃæmpɪənʃɪp/ NOUN [plural championships] a competition to decide who is the best at a game or sport

chance /tʃɑːns/ NOUN [plural chances]
1 a possibility that something will happen □ + that There is a good chance that she is still alive. □ + of Our school has no chance of winning the match.
2 an opportunity □ + to do something I haven't had a chance to check yet. ⊞ You didn't give me a chance to answer. ⊞ This is your last chance to buy a ticket.
3 by chance in a way that is not planned or expected □ I saw him by chance at the supermarket.

4 take a chance to take a risk □ I took a chance on the weather staying dry and left my coat at home.

► Note that **chance** meaning 'a possibility that something will happen' is followed by **that** or **of doing something** □ What are the chances that they will win? □ What are the chances of them winning?

chancellor /'tʃɑːnsələ(r)/ NOUN [plural chancellors]
1 the British government official who is in charge of finance
2 the leader of the government of some European countries □ the German chancellor

change¹ /tʃeɪndʒ/ VERB [changes, changing, changed]
1 to become different, or to make something different □ + into It has changed from a liquid into a gas. □ + from The leaves changed from green to gold.
2 to stop having or using one thing and start having or using another instead □ We need to change the batteries. □ My daughter changed schools last term. ⊞ Don't try to change the subject (= start talking about something else). □ + to I'm changing to a new dentist.
3 to put on different clothes ⊞ I must get changed (= change my clothes) for work. □ + into I will just change into my jeans.
4 change your mind to start to think or plan something different from before □ I've changed my mind – I'll have soup not pasta, please.

► THESAURUS: Change is a general word to talk about when you stop using one thing and start using something else. You can also use that word swap when you stop having or using one thing and take or use something else instead. For example, you might swap a book with a friend (you give a book to your friend and your friend gives you another book in return). Replace is used when you put one thing in the place of another. For example, if the batteries in a radio run out, you replace them with new batteries.

change² /tʃeɪndʒ/ NOUN [plural changes]
1 a difference ⊞ I have made some changes to the timetable. □ + in Let's wait until there is a change in the weather.
2 a change something that is enjoyable because it is new and different □ I didn't hate my old job – I just fancied a change.
3 for a change instead of the usual thing □ Could you just stop complaining for a change?
4 no plural the extra money that is given back to you when you have paid for something ⊞ I told the taxi driver to keep the change.

channel /ˈtʃænəl/ NOUN [plural channels]
1 a television or radio station 🔊 May I change channels, or are you watching this?
2 a narrow piece of sea □ the English Channel

chant /tʃɑːnt/ VERB [chants, chanting, chanted] to shout or sing something repeatedly

chaos /ˈkeɪɒs/ NOUN, NO PLURAL great confusion □ There was chaos in town when the traffic lights stopped working.

chap /tʃæp/ NOUN [plural chaps] an informal word for a man □ He's a nice chap.

chapel /ˈtʃæpəl/ NOUN [plural chapels] a small church, or a room used as a church □ the hospital chapel

chapter /ˈtʃæptə(r)/ NOUN [plural chapters] one of the parts that a book is divided into □ Turn to Chapter 3 in your history books. □ Can I just finish (= finish reading) this chapter?

character /ˈkærəktə(r)/ NOUN [plural characters]
1 what someone or something is like and the qualities that they have □ Can you describe her character? Is she reliable? □ It isn't in his character to stay angry for long.
2 a person in a story, film or play □ Harry Potter is a fictional character. □ Who is your favourite character in the book?

charge¹ /tʃɑːdʒ/ VERB [charges, charging, charged]
1 to ask a particular amount of money for something □ + for How much do you charge for a haircut? □ The shopkeeper charged me $20 too much.
2 if the police charge someone with a crime, they accuse them officially □ + with He was charged with murder.
3 to move forward quickly and suddenly □ The boys came charging into the room. □ We charged down the hill towards them.
4 to fill a battery or piece of electrical equipment with electricity □ Where can I charge my phone?

charge² /tʃɑːdʒ/ NOUN [plural charges]
1 the amount of money that you have to pay 🔊 You can have another cup of coffee free of charge (= without paying). □ There will be a small charge for postage and packing.
2 in charge controlling or managing something or someone □ I am in charge while the boss is away. □ Ms Handy is in charge of the sales department.
3 take charge to take control of something or someone □ Can you take charge of the food preparation?
4 when someone is accused of a crime □ He was arrested on a charge of robbery.

▶ THESAURUS: The charge for something is the amount of money that you have to pay for it. We usually use charge to talk about a service and price to talk about goods. So, we talk about the price of goods in shops, but the charge for supplying electricity to your house. A fee is an amount of money that you pay for a particular service. You use rate to talk about how much you pay someone for a service. For example, a lawyer's rate is how much they cost per hour or per day, but their fee is the total amount you pay them for a particular job.

charity /ˈtʃærəti/ NOUN [plural charities] an organization that gives money or other help to people who need it

charm /tʃɑːm/ NOUN [plural charms]
1 a quality that makes someone pleasant and attractive to other people
2 an object that is believed to be lucky

charming /ˈtʃɑːmɪŋ/ ADJECTIVE extremely pleasant □ What a charming young man your son is.

chart /tʃɑːt/ NOUN [plural charts]
1 a drawing that shows information □ This chart shows the population growth over the last fifty years.
2 the charts a list of the most popular music □ Their new record went straight to the top of the charts.
3 a map of the sea used by sailors

▶ THESAURUS: Chart and diagram are words for a drawing that shows information. Diagrams often show how something works, for example a machine. A graph is a chart which shows how things compare to each other or how something changes. A graph is usually made of lines between different points. A map is a drawing of a particular area which shows rivers, roads and hills. You can use a map to help you find your way. A plan is a drawing to show you how to build something. For example, architects draw plans when they are designing a new house.

chase¹ /tʃeɪs/ VERB [chases, chasing, chased] to run after someone or something to try and catch them □ A police officer chased the thief down the High Street. □ Our dog was chasing a rabbit.

▶ THESAURUS: If you chase someone, you run after them and try to catch them. If you follow someone, you go where they go, moving behind them. You can follow someone in secret. If you look for something or someone, you can use the word hunt. For example, the police might hunt a criminal, or you might hunt for something that you have lost. We also use hunt to talk about chasing and killing an animal for sport or for food.

chase² /tʃeɪs/ NOUN [plural chases] when someone or something is chased 🔊 A man was arrested following a high-speed car chase.

chat¹ /tʃæt/ VERB [chats, chatting, chatted] to talk to someone in a friendly way □ *+ to* *She was chatting to her friend on the phone.*

chat² /tʃæt/ NOUN [plural chats] a friendly talk 🔁 *Come round later and we can have a chat.*

cheap /tʃiːp/ ADJECTIVE [cheaper, cheapest] not costing a lot □ *a cheap air ticket* □ *It is cheaper to buy vegetables at the market.*

➤ THESAURUS: Cheap is a general word to describe something which does not cost a lot of money. A bargain is something which costs less than usual. Your budget is the total amount of money that you can spend on something. For example, you might have a budget for a holiday.

cheat¹ /tʃiːt/ VERB [cheats, cheating, cheated] to behave dishonestly in order to succeed at something or get something □ *It's cheating to look at someone else's cards.* □ *Hey, you're cheating! That is against the rules.*

cheat² /tʃiːt/ NOUN [plural cheats] someone who cheats

check¹ /tʃek/ VERB [checks, checking, checked]
1 to make sure that something is correct □ *Please check your work carefully before you hand it in.* □ *I think my appointment is at 10.30, but I'll check in my diary.*
2 to find out □ *+ question word* *Could you check whether the post has arrived?* □ *He is just checking how many copies we need.*
3 to make sure that something is working correctly □ *The engineer came to check the fire alarm.*
♦ PHRASAL VERBS **check in** to tell the people at a hotel or airport that you have arrived □ *Please check in two hours before the flight.* **check out** to pay for your stay at a hotel and leave □ *You must check out before 10 am.*

check² /tʃek/ NOUN [plural checks]
1 a test to see that something is correct or is working correctly 🔁 *a health/safety check* 🔁 *The police did fingerprint checks on the document.*
2 a pattern of squares □ *black-and-white check*
3 the US spelling of **cheque**
4 the US word for **tick¹** (sense 1)
5 the US word for a **bill** in a restaurant

➤ THESAURUS: A check or a test is something you do to find out if something is working properly or that it is correct. An inspection is an official visit by a person to check that a place is working properly. For example, restaurants have inspections to make sure that the kitchens are clean and safe. An examination is a test of someone's knowledge about a subject. Most students take examinations.

check-in /tʃekɪn/ NOUN [plural check-ins]
1 a desk at an airport where passengers' tickets are checked
2 *no plural* the process that happens when you arrive at an airport

checkout /tʃekaʊt/ NOUN [plural checkouts]
1 the place where you pay at a supermarket □ *There was a big queue at the checkout.*
2 the place on a website where you pay for things you have bought. A computing word.

checkpoint /tʃekpɔɪnt/ NOUN [plural checkpoints] a place where soldiers or police stop vehicles or people

cheek /tʃiːk/ NOUN [plural cheeks] one of the two areas on each side of your face below your eyes 🔁 *She has lovely rosy cheeks.*

cheeky /tʃiːkɪ/ ADJECTIVE [cheekier, cheekiest] a bit rude, often in a funny way □ *You cheeky boy!* □ *a cheeky grin*

cheer¹ /tʃɪə(r)/ VERB [cheers, cheering, cheered] to shout loudly to praise or encourage someone □ *We cheered loudly when he came onto the stage.* □ *The spectators cheered each runner as they ran past.*
♦ PHRASAL VERB **cheer (someone) up** to feel happier, or to make someone feel happier □ *Cheer up! Don't look so miserable!* □ *I've got some news that will cheer you up.*

cheer² /tʃɪə(r)/ NOUN [plural cheers] a loud shout to show that you are pleased □ *When he caught the ball there was a big cheer from the crowd.*

cheerful /tʃɪəfʊl/ ADJECTIVE happy □ *You're very cheerful this morning.*

cheerio /ˌtʃɪərɪˈəʊ/ EXCLAMATION an informal word meaning goodbye □ *Cheerio, see you tomorrow.*

cheers /tʃɪəz/ EXCLAMATION
1 a word used to express your good wishes to other people when you are drinking alcohol together □ *Cheers, everyone. Happy New Year!*
2 an informal word meaning thank you □ *'Here's your book back'. 'Cheers'.*

cheese /tʃiːz/ NOUN [plural cheeses] a solid white or yellow food made from milk □ *cheese sauce* 🔁 *Would you like some cheese and biscuits?* 🔁 *Sprinkle some grated cheese on the top.*

chef /ʃef/ NOUN [plural chefs] someone whose job is to cook in a restaurant or a hotel □ *Please tell the chef that was delicious.*

chemical¹ /ˈkemɪkəl/ NOUN [plural chemicals] a substance that is formed by or used in chemistry 🔁 *The lorry contained dangerous chemicals.* □ *The hydrochloric acid and other chemicals are kept in the laboratory.*

chemical² /ˈkemɪkəl/ ADJECTIVE involving or produced by chemistry 🔁 *a chemical reaction*

chemist /'kemɪst/ NOUN [plural chemists]
1 someone who prepares medicines □ Could you ask the chemist if my prescription is ready?
2 chemist's a shop where medicines and products for washing, etc. are sold
3 someone who studies chemistry

chemistry /'kemɪstri/ NOUN, NO PLURAL the study of chemical elements and how they react with each other □ She studied physics and chemistry at A level.

cheque /tʃek/ NOUN [plural cheques] a piece of printed paper that you sign and use as a way of paying for things ⌹ I wrote him a cheque for £50. ⌹ Our last customer paid by cheque.

cherry /'tʃeri/ NOUN [plural cherries] a small round red fruit with a hard seed inside

chess /tʃes/ NOUN, NO PLURAL a game where two players move pieces on a board with black and white squares ⌹ a chess board ⌹ Tom plays chess almost every day.

chest /tʃest/ NOUN [plural chests]
1 the front of your body between your neck and your stomach □ a hairy chest □ chest pains
2 a large box for storing things □ a treasure chest

chew /tʃu:/ VERB [chews, chewing, chewed] to break up food inside your mouth with your teeth □ My tooth is sore and it hurts to chew. □ He bit off a piece of bread and chewed it slowly.

chewing gum /'tʃu:ɪŋ ˌgʌm/ NOUN, NO PLURAL a sweet substance that you chew but do not swallow

chick /tʃɪk/ NOUN [plural chicks] a baby bird

chicken /'tʃɪkɪn/ NOUN [plural chickens]
1 a bird that is kept on farms to produce eggs and to be eaten ⌹ The farmer keeps a few chickens. ⌹ This chicken has stopped laying (= producing eggs).
2 no plural the meat from this bird □ roast chicken

chief[1] /tʃi:f/ ADJECTIVE biggest or most important □ the chief city of the region □ My chief worry is the cost.

chief[2] /tʃi:f/ NOUN [plural chiefs]
1 a person in charge of a group or organization □ We heard a speech by the new police chief. □ Industry chiefs met today in London.
2 a ruler of a tribe (= large group of related people) □ an African tribal chief

child /tʃaɪld/ NOUN [plural children]
1 a young human □ When my Dad was a child, he lived in New York. □ There are thirty children in my class.
2 a son or daughter ⌹ Sue never had (= gave birth to) any children. □ Our children are grown up now.

➤ **THESAURUS:** Child is a general word to describe someone who is not an adult. We usually use the word **teenager** to describe older children aged between 13 and 19. A very young child who cannot walk is a **baby**. Kid is an informal word for a child.

---

childhood /'tʃaɪldˌhʊd/ NOUN, NO PLURAL the time in your life when you are a child □ My memories of childhood are very happy.

children /'tʃɪldrən/ PLURAL OF child

chilly /'tʃɪli/ ADJECTIVE [chillier, chilliest] cold □ It's a bit chilly in here.

chimney /'tʃɪmni/ NOUN [plural chimneys] a pipe above a fire that allows smoke to escape □ a factory chimney

chimpanzee /ˌtʃɪmpæn'zi:/ NOUN [plural chimpanzees] a small African ape (= large monkey) with black fur, a flat face and large brown eyes

chin /tʃɪn/ NOUN [plural chins] the part of your face that is below your mouth

china /'tʃaɪnə/ NOUN, NO PLURAL
1 clay used for making things like cups and plates
2 cups, plates, etc. which are made from this clay

chip[1] /tʃɪp/ NOUN [plural chips]
1 a long thin piece of potato that is fried and eaten hot ⌹ fish and chips
2 the US word for crisp[2] (= a very thin piece of potato cooked in oil and eaten cold) □ a bag of chips
3 a small piece broken off a hard object, or the place where a small piece has broken off □ The plate had a chip in it.
4 a very small part in a computer or other electronic equipment that contains a circuit (= system of wires) and stores information

chip[2] /tʃɪp/ VERB [chips, chipping, chipped] to break a small piece off something □ Roy chipped one of his teeth playing rugby.

chocolate /'tʃɒkələt/ NOUN [plural chocolates]
1 no plural a sweet brown food made from the seeds of a tropical tree ⌹ milk/dark chocolate ⌹ a bar of chocolate
2 one of many small sweets made with chocolate that are sold together ⌹ a box of chocolates
3 a sweet drink made with chocolate ⌹ a hot chocolate

choice /tʃɔɪs/ NOUN [plural choices]
1 when you can choose between different things ⌹ If I had a choice, I'd work from home. ⌹ I had to leave – I had no choice.
2 a decision to choose a person or thing ⌹ In the end I had to make a choice. ⌹ It was a hard choice to make.

3 the different things you can choose from □ **+ of** We were given a choice of meat or fish. ⊞ The bag is available in a wide choice of colours.

choir /'kwaɪə(r)/ NOUN [plural choirs] a group of singers □ She sings in the church choir.

choke /tʃəʊk/ VERB [chokes, choking, choked] to not be able to breathe because something is blocking your throat □ She choked on a fish bone.

choose /tʃuːz/ VERB [chooses, choosing, chose, chosen] to take one particular thing or person from a group of people or things □ Can you help me choose a present for grandma? □ Kitty chose a slice of chocolate cake. □ **+ between** I can't choose between the red one and the pink one. □ **+ question word** How do you choose which charity to give money to? □ **+ to do something** She chose to attend a university near home.

chop[1] /tʃɒp/ VERB [chops, chopping, chopped] to cut something into pieces □ Chop the onion into large chunks. □ He was chopping wood for the fire.
♦ PHRASAL VERBS **chop something down** to cut the main part of a tree or big plant so that it falls down **chop something off** to remove a part of something by cutting it □ He accidentally chopped his finger off.

chop[2] /tʃɒp/ NOUN [plural chops] a piece of meat, usually with a bone □ lamb chops

chorus /'kɔːrəs/ NOUN [plural choruses]
1 the part of a song that you repeat several times □ We all joined in with the chorus.
2 a large group of people who regularly sing together

chosen /'tʃəʊzən/ PAST PARTICIPLE OF **choose**

Christ /kraɪst/ NOUN Jesus Christ, the holy man that Christians believe is the Son of God

Christian[1] /'krɪstʃən/ NOUN [plural Christians] someone who is a member of the religion that is based on the ideas of Jesus Christ and the Bible

Christian[2] /'krɪstʃən/ ADJECTIVE to do with Christianity or Christians

Christianity /ˌkrɪstɪ'ænəti/ NOUN, NO PLURAL the religion that is based on the ideas of Jesus Christ and the Bible

Christmas[1] /'krɪsməs/ NOUN, NO PLURAL 25 December, the day Christians celebrate the birth of Christ each year □ Happy Christmas!

Christmas[2] /'krɪsməs/ ADJECTIVE for or to do with Christmas ⊞ Christmas decorations/presents

Christmas Day /ˌkrɪsməs 'deɪ/ NOUN, NO PLURAL 25 December, the day on which Christmas is celebrated

Christmas Eve /ˌkrɪsməs 'iːv/ NOUN, NO PLURAL 24 December, the day before Christmas Day

Christmas tree /'krɪsməs ˌtriː/ NOUN [plural Christmas trees] a tree that you cover with decorations and lights and put in your house during the Christmas period

chronic /'krɒnɪk/ ADJECTIVE a chronic disease is one that continues for a long time

chuckle /'tʃʌkəl/ VERB [chuckles, chuckling, chuckled] to laugh quietly □ The story made me chuckle to myself.

chunk /tʃʌŋk/ NOUN [plural chunks] a thick piece of something □ a chunk of cheese □ pineapple chunks

church /tʃɜːtʃ/ NOUN [plural churches] a building where people, especially Christians, go to pray ⊞ Do you go to church?

cigar /sɪ'gɑː(r)/ NOUN [plural cigars] a thick tube made from dried tobacco leaves that people smoke

cigarette /ˌsɪgə'ret/ NOUN [plural cigarettes] a thin tube of paper filled with tobacco that people smoke

cinema /'sɪnəmə/ NOUN [plural cinemas] a place where you go to watch a film on a big screen □ We went to the cinema last night.

circle[1] /'sɜːkəl/ NOUN [plural circles]
1 a flat shape whose outside edge is a continuous curved line which is always the same distance away from a central point □ Draw one circle for the head and another for the body. □ Form a circle in the centre of the room.
2 a group of people who know each other or do a particular activity together □ a sewing circle □ He's not part of my circle of friends.
3 the circle the upper area of seats in a theatre or cinema

circle[2] /'sɜːkəl/ VERB [circles, circling, circled]
1 to move in a circle □ Birds circled overhead. □ Several planes were circling the airport.
2 to draw a circle around something □ She circled the area on the map with a red pen.

circuit /'sɜːkɪt/ NOUN [plural circuits]
1 a path, route or track that forms a circle □ He drove five laps of the circuit.
2 the path that electricity goes along between two points

circular[1] /'sɜːkjʊlə(r)/ ADJECTIVE
1 in the shape of a circle □ a circular window
2 a circular journey or route finishes in the same place that it started

circular[2] /'sɜːkjʊlə(r)/ NOUN [plural circulars] a letter or advertisement that is sent to a lot of different people

circulate /'sɜːkjʊleɪt/ VERB [circulates, circulating, circulated] to move around or through something □ *Water circulates in the central heating system.* □ *Details of the meeting will be circulated to all members of staff.*

circulation /ˌsɜːkjʊ'leɪʃən/ NOUN, NO PLURAL
1 the movement of blood around your body. A biology word □ *I have very poor circulation.*
2 movement around or through something □ *This system controls the circulation of air.*

circumstances /'sɜːkəmˌstənsɪz/ PLURAL NOUN
1 the events or conditions that affect or cause a particular situation 🔄 *His reaction was understandable under the circumstances* (= when you consider the situation).
2 under no circumstances used for saying that something must not happen □ *Under no circumstances should you attempt to climb without a rope.*

circus /'sɜːkəs/ NOUN [plural circuses] a show performed in a big tent by people and often trained animals □ *We're taking the children to the circus tonight.*

citizen /'sɪtɪzən/ NOUN [plural citizens] someone who has the right to live in a particular country permanently □ *He lives in Singapore but he's an Australian citizen.*

city /'sɪti/ NOUN [plural cities] a large, important town 🔄 *Paris is the capital city of France.* □ *the city streets*

civic /'sɪvɪk/ ADJECTIVE to do with a city or the people who live in it □ *civic pride*

civilian /sɪ'vɪljən/ NOUN [plural civilians] a person who is not a member of a military organization or the police

civilization or **civilisation** /ˌsɪvɪlaɪ'zeɪʃən/ NOUN [plural civilizations] a society that has its own culture and organizations □ *ancient civilizations*

civil rights /ˌsɪvəl 'raɪts/ PLURAL NOUN your basic rights to be treated fairly in society, to express yourself, and to practise your religion

civil servant /ˌsɪvəl 'sɜːvənt/ NOUN [plural civil servants] someone who works in the government departments of a country

civil service /ˌsɪvəl 'sɜːvɪs/ NOUN the civil service all the departments of the government and the people who work in them

civil war /ˌsɪvəl 'wɔː(r)/ NOUN [plural civil wars] a war between different groups within the same country

claim[1] /kleɪm/ VERB [claims, claiming, claimed]
1 to say that something is true, although there is no clear proof □ *Marco claims he saw a flying saucer.* □ *The group claims to have over a million workers.*
2 to officially ask for something as your right or to say that it is yours □ *You'll need to fill in this form to claim unemployment benefit.* □ *If no one claims the lost items they will be sold for charity.*

claim[2] /kleɪm/ NOUN [plural claims]
1 a statement that something is true although it has not been proved 🔄 *The government has rejected claims that pensions will fall.* 🔄 *He denied claims of racism.*
2 when you ask for something that you have a right to or that you say is yours 🔄 *compensation claims* 🔄 *insurance claims*

clap[1] /klæp/ VERB [claps, clapping, clapped] to hit your hands together, especially to show that you like or admire someone or something □ *The audience clapped and cheered.* □ *We all clapped in time to the music.*

clap[2] /klæp/ NOUN [plural claps]
1 when you clap your hands 🔄 *Let's all give Adam a clap.*
2 a clap of thunder a sudden very loud sound made by thunder

clarify /'klærɪfaɪ/ VERB [clarifies, clarifying, clarified] to make something clearer or easier to understand □ *I asked her to clarify her remarks.*

clash[1] /klæʃ/ VERB [clashes, clashing, clashed]
1 if two people or groups clash, they fight or disagree angrily with each other □ *Protesters clashed with the police.*
2 if two events clash, they happen at the same time □ *Unfortunately the meeting clashes with my piano exam.*
3 if two colours clash, they do not look good together □ *The purple clashes with the red.*

clash[2] /klæʃ/ NOUN [plural clashes]
1 an angry disagreement or fight □ *There were violent clashes between students and the police today.*
2 a sound made when two metal objects hit against each other

clasp /klɑːsp/ VERB [clasps, clasping, clasped] to hold something or someone tightly □ *Jenny was clasping a baby in her arms.*

class /klɑːs/ NOUN [plural classes]
1 a group of students who are taught together, or a period of time during which a particular subject is taught □ *Hannah's in my class at school.* □ *I'm going to my aerobics class tonight.*
2 one of the social groups into which people can be divided according to their family, income, job, etc. □ *the working class*
3 a group of animals or plants that are related to each other or have similar qualities

classic[1] /'klæsɪk/ NOUN [plural classics] a great book or other work of art that is admired for a long time after it was written or made □ *great film classics*

classic[2] /ˈklæsɪk/ ADJECTIVE very good and popular for a long time □ *classic children's stories*

classical /ˈklæsɪkəl/ ADJECTIVE
1 belonging to the style or culture of ancient Greece or Rome □ *classical architecture*
2 traditional □ *classical ballet*

classical music /ˈklæsɪkəl ˈmjuːzɪk/ NOUN, NO PLURAL traditional, serious music written by people like Beethoven and Verdi

classify /ˈklæsɪfaɪ/ VERB [classifies, classifying, classified] to put people or things into groups or classes according to what qualities they have □ *The books are classified by subject.*

classmate /ˈklɑːsmeɪt/ NOUN [plural classmates] someone in your school or college class

classroom /ˈklɑːsruːm/ NOUN [plural classrooms] a room where students have lessons

clause /klɔːz/ NOUN [plural clauses] a group of words that makes up a sentence or part of a sentence □ *a relative clause*

claw /klɔː/ NOUN [plural claws]
1 one of the long pointed nails on the toes of some animals and birds
2 a long part at the end of the leg of some sea creatures and insects, that is used for holding things

clay /kleɪ/ NOUN, NO PLURAL a soft sticky substance in the ground that goes hard when it is baked and is used for making cups and bowls □ *clay pots*

clean[1] /kliːn/ ADJECTIVE [cleaner, cleanest] not dirty □ *clean hands* □ *a clean kitchen* □ *clean air* □ *clean drinking water* ⊞ *Everywhere looked clean and tidy.*
• **cleanly** /ˈkliːnli/ ADVERB if something breaks cleanly, it breaks completely and in a tidy way □ *The log split cleanly in half.*

clean[2] /kliːn/ VERB [cleans, cleaning, cleaned] to remove the dirt from something □ *I've just been cleaning the kitchen.* □ *Have you cleaned your teeth?*
• PHRASAL VERB **clean (something) up** to make a place clean and tidy, removing any rubbish □ *I'll start cleaning up this mess.*

> ➤ **THESAURUS:** Clean is a general word to describe removing dirt from something. If you clean something with a brush, you can use the word sweep. If you rub the surface of something to clean it, you can use the word wipe. For example, you wipe the table after a meal. If you scrub something such as a dirty pan, you rub it very hard to get it clean. If something has a layer of fine powder on it, you might dust it with a cloth.

cleaner /ˈkliːnə(r)/ NOUN [plural cleaners] someone whose job is to clean places □ *The cleaner comes in once a week.*

clear[1] /klɪə(r)/ ADJECTIVE [clearer, clearest]
1 easy to understand □ *I gave clear instructions.* □ *He drew a very clear map.*
2 obvious □ **+ that** *It was clear that she wasn't happy.* ⊞ *Sally made her feelings very clear.*
3 easy to see or hear □ *The recording wasn't very clear.* □ *The pictures were very clear.*
4 transparent □ *clear glass*
5 not blocked or covered by anything □ *a clear sky* □ *a clear view of the stage* □ **+ of** *The road was clear of traffic.*

clear[2] /klɪə(r)/ VERB [clears, clearing, cleared] to remove people or things from a place □ *I'll just clear these dishes.* □ *Police cleared the streets around the car bomb.*
• PHRASAL VERBS **clear something away** to remove things that you have finished using in order to make a place tidy □ *I'll just clear away my papers.* **clear (something) up** to make a place tidy □ *I helped to clear up after the party.* **clear up** to get better □ *Her skin problem has cleared up.* □ *The weather has cleared up.*

clearly /ˈklɪəli/ ADVERB
1 in a way that is easy to see, hear, or understand □ *You can see it quite clearly in the photo.* □ *She explained it very clearly.*
2 obviously □ *Clearly, we can't do the job without enough people.*

cleric /ˈklerɪk/ NOUN [plural clerics] a member of the clergy (= priests)

clerk /klɑːk/ NOUN [plural clerks] an office worker whose job is to write letters, store documents, or keep financial records

clever /ˈklevə(r)/ ADJECTIVE [cleverer, cleverest] good at learning and understanding things □ *He was a very clever boy.*

click[1] /klɪk/ VERB [clicks, clicking, clicked]
1 to press a button on a computer mouse in order to make the computer do something. A computing word □ *Just type your message and click 'Send'.* □ **+ on** *Click on the icon to open the program.*
2 to make a short, sharp sound □ *We could hear her heels clicking on the stone floor.*

click[2] /klɪk/ NOUN [plural clicks]
1 a short, sharp sound □ *The box closed with a click.*
2 when you press a button on a computer mouse to make the computer do something. A computing word □ *You can place your order with just one click.*

client /ˈklaɪənt/ NOUN [plural clients] someone who pays someone else for a service

cliff /klɪf/ NOUN [*plural* cliffs] the high, steep side of a piece of land, usually next to the sea

climate /ˈklaɪmɪt/ NOUN [*plural* climates] the type of weather that a country or area usually gets □ *These plants only grow in hot climates.*

➤ THESAURUS: The climate of a place is the type of weather that it usually gets. For example, a place might have a wet climate if it often rains there. Weather describes the particular conditions in a place at a particular time, for example how hot it is, or whether it is raining. The temperature of a place is how hot or cold it is. We usually measure temperature in degrees Celsius.

climb[1] /klaɪm/ VERB [climbs, climbing, climbed]
1 to go up or to go towards the top, often using your hands and feet □ *He likes to climb trees.* □ *It's a very difficult mountain to climb.*
2 to increase in number □ *Last year, the number of people without a job climbed to 2 million.*

climb[2] /klaɪm/ NOUN [*plural* climbs] an act of climbing or the distance you climb □ *We had a steep climb to the top.*

climber /ˈklaɪmə(r)/ NOUN [*plural* climbers] someone who climbs, often as a hobby or sport □ *a very experienced climber*

cling /klɪŋ/ VERB [clings, clinging, clung] to hold on to something tightly, usually because you are afraid □ *The child clung to her mother.*

clinic /ˈklɪnɪk/ NOUN [*plural* clinics] a place where people can see doctors to get treatment and advice □ *an eye clinic*

clip[1] /klɪp/ VERB [clips, clipping, clipped]
1 to cut small or short parts off something □ *He was busy clipping the hedge.*
2 to fasten something to something else with a pin □ *He had a badge clipped to his lapel.*
clip[2] /klɪp/ NOUN [*plural* clips] a small object that fastens something together or to something else □ *a paper clip* □ *a hair clip*

cloak /kləʊk/ NOUN [*plural* cloaks] a loose coat without sleeves that hangs down from the shoulders

cloakroom /ˈkləʊkruːm/ NOUN [*plural* cloakrooms] a room or area in a building where visitors can leave their coats, hats and bags

clock /klɒk/ NOUN [*plural* clocks] an object which shows the time □ *an alarm clock* □ *There's a clock on the kitchen wall.*

close[1] /kləʊz/ VERB [closes, closing, closed]
1 to shut □ *Could you close the door, please?* □ *The door closed behind him.* □ *Close your eyes and go to sleep.*

2 if a shop, restaurant, etc. closes, it stops serving people, for example at the end of a day □ *Supermarkets close around 8 o'clock.*
3 to stop operating as a business, permanently □ *A lot of shops in this area have closed.*
4 to finish using a computer program or document and make it go off your screen. A computing word.
♦ PHRASAL VERB **close (something) down** to stop operating as a business, or make something stop operating as a business □ *A lot of small businesses are closing down.*
close[2] /kləʊz/ NOUN, NO PLURAL the end of something □ *The pound was weak at the close of trading.* □ *She quickly brought the meeting to a close.*

close[3] /kləʊs/ ADJECTIVE [closer, closest]
1 near in distance or time □ *+ to The flat is close to the shops.* □ *It was close to midnight when he got back.*
2 if you are close to someone, you know and like them well □ *+ to I'm very close to my younger sister.* □ *We invited a few close friends.*
3 a close relation is someone such as your mother, father, sister or brother
4 looking or listening carefully □ *Pay close attention to what he says.* □ *I kept a close eye on the time.*

close[4] /kləʊs/ ADVERB [closer, closest]
1 near □ *Her mother was standing close by.*
2 be/come close to doing something to almost do something □ *He came close to winning.*

close[5] /kləʊs/ NOUN [*plural* closes] a street that cars can go into only at one end □ *They live at 16 Cathedral Close.*

closed /kləʊzd/ ADJECTIVE not open □ *Laura kept her eyes closed.* □ *The banks are closed on Sundays.*

closely /ˈkləʊslɪ/ ADVERB
1 carefully □ *Police are examining the scene closely.*
2 with little distance between two things □ *He entered, closely followed by his parents.*
3 if two things are closely connected, they are very similar or have a strong connection □ *Humans are very closely related to apes.*

closure /ˈkləʊʒə(r)/ NOUN [*plural* closures] when a business, organization, etc. stops operating □ *school closures*

cloth /klɒθ/ NOUN [*plural* cloths]
1 *no plural* material made of wool, cotton, etc., used for making clothes etc. □ *cotton cloth* □ *a cloth bag*
2 a piece of cloth used for cleaning or drying □ *She wiped the table with a damp cloth.*

clothes /kləʊðz/ PLURAL NOUN the things people wear to cover their bodies □ *She wears very interesting clothes.* □ *baby clothes* □ *a clothes shop*

➤ **THESAURUS:** Clothes is a general word. An outfit is a set of clothes that go together. You might buy a new outfit to wear to a party. A costume is a set of clothes that you wear to make you look like another person, an animal or another creature. Children often dress up in costumes. A disguise is something you wear so that people will not know who you are, or to make you look like someone else. A famous person might wear a disguise so that people will not know who she is. Garment is a word for a piece of clothing. It is quite a formal word.

clothing /ˈkləʊðɪŋ/ NOUN, NO PLURAL clothes, especially for a particular activity □ *waterproof clothing* □ *Please bring a change of clothing.* 🔁 *a piece of clothing*

cloud /klaʊd/ NOUN [*plural* clouds]
1 a white or grey mass of small water drops that is in the sky □ *rain clouds* □ *dark clouds*
2 a mass of smoke, dust, sand, etc. in the air □ *a cloud of flies* □ *Clouds of smoke were pouring out of the factory.*

➤ **THESAURUS:** A cloud is a white or grey mass of small water drops in the sky. Rain falls from clouds. Mist is small drops of water in the air that make it difficult to see. If mist is very thick, we call it fog.

cloudy /ˈklaʊdɪ/ ADJECTIVE [cloudier, cloudiest] full of clouds 🔁 *a cloudy sky*

clown /klaʊn/ NOUN [*plural* clowns] someone who wears funny clothes, has a painted face, and does silly things to make people laugh

club /klʌb/ NOUN [*plural* clubs]
1 an organization of people who meet regularly to do a particular activity, or the place where they meet 🔁 *She belongs to a golf club.* 🔁 *I've joined a tennis club.*
2 a place where people go at night to dance and drink
3 one of the sticks used in golf to hit the ball
4 clubs one of the four types of playing card, which have the symbol (♣) printed on them □ *the four of clubs*

clue /kluː/ NOUN [*plural* clues] a sign or piece of information that helps solve a problem, mystery or crime □ *a crossword clue* □ *The police are looking for clues.*
♦ IDIOM **not have a clue** an informal phrase meaning to know or understand nothing about something □ *I didn't have a clue what she meant.*

clumsy /ˈklʌmzɪ/ ADJECTIVE [clumsier, clumsiest] a clumsy person is awkward in the way they move, often dropping things or knocking into things

clung /klʌŋ/ PAST TENSE AND PAST PARTICIPLE OF cling

clutch /klʌtʃ/ VERB [clutches, clutching, clutched] to hold something tightly in your hand or hands □ *She clutched her mother's hand.*

cm ABBREVIATION centimetre *or* centimetres

Co ABBREVIATION company, used in the name of a business □ *Smith, Jenkins and Co.*

coach¹ /kəʊtʃ/ NOUN [*plural* coaches]
1 a comfortable bus for long journeys □ *a coach station* 🔁 *a coach trip*
2 someone who helps people to improve a skill, often a sport, or who gives extra teaching in a school subject □ *a rugby coach* □ *a singing coach*
3 in the past, a vehicle that was pulled by horses

coach² /kəʊtʃ/ VERB [coaches, coaching, coached] to help someone to improve a skill, often a sport, or to give extra teaching to someone in a school subject □ *He's being coached by an ex-Olympic champion.*

coal /kəʊl/ NOUN, NO PLURAL a hard black substance that is dug out of the ground and burnt to give heat

coast /kəʊst/ NOUN [*plural* coasts] the area of land next to the sea □ *It's a town on the west coast of Ireland.* □ *They've gone for a trip to the coast.*
♦ IDIOM **the coast is clear** if the coast is clear, there is no one around to see you or stop you doing something

coastline /ˈkəʊstlaɪn/ NOUN [*plural* coastline] the edge of a coast □ *the beautiful Scottish coastline*

coat /kəʊt/ NOUN [*plural* coats]
1 a piece of clothing with sleeves that you wear over your other clothes when you go out □ *He was wearing a thick winter coat.*
2 a layer of a substance 🔁 *a coat of paint*
3 the fur of an animal

cockpit /ˈkɒkpɪt/ NOUN [*plural* cockpits] the area in an aeroplane where the pilot sits

cocktail /ˈkɒkteɪl/ NOUN [*plural* cocktails] an alcoholic drink made with two or more types of drink mixed together

cocoa /ˈkəʊkəʊ/ NOUN, NO PLURAL
1 a brown powder made from the seeds of a tropical tree, used to make chocolate
2 a hot drink made from cocoa powder mixed with milk

coconut /ˈkəʊkəˌnʌt/ NOUN [*plural* coconuts] a large nut with a brown outer part with hair on, and white flesh and liquid inside 🔊 *coconut milk*

cod /kɒd/ NOUN [*plural* cod] a large sea fish that you can eat

code /kəʊd/ NOUN [*plural* codes]
1 a set of signs or letters used instead of normal writing to send a secret message □ *The letter was written in code.* 🔊 *They managed to break the code* (= understand it).
2 the first part of a telephone number that tells you the area or the country □ *What's the code for the UK?*

coffee /ˈkɒfɪ/ NOUN [*plural* coffees]
1 *no plural* a drink made from the beans of a tropical plant □ *I don't drink coffee.* 🔊 *Let's have a cup of coffee.* 🔊 *black/white coffee* (= coffee without/with milk)
2 a cup of this drink □ *Two black coffees, please.*

coffin /ˈkɒfɪn/ NOUN [*plural* coffins] a long wooden box that a dead body is put into to be buried

coin /kɔɪn/ NOUN [*plural* coins] a round, flat piece of metal money 🔊 *a gold coin* 🔊 *a pound coin*

coincide /ˌkəʊɪnˈsaɪd/ VERB [coincides, coinciding, coincided] when events coincide with each other, they happen at the same time □ *The carnival will coincide with the beginning of the school holidays.*

coincidence /kəʊˈɪnsɪdəns/ NOUN [*plural* coincidences] when two things happen at the same time by chance □ *It was coincidence that I was on the train that day.* □ *By coincidence, his father had also worked in China.*

cola /ˈkəʊlə/ NOUN [*plural* colas] a dark brown, sweet fizzy (= with bubbles) drink

cold¹ /kəʊld/ ADJECTIVE [colder, coldest] low in temperature □ *a cold drink* □ *She hated cold weather.* 🔊 *It's freezing cold outside.* □ *His hands felt cold.*

▶ **THESAURUS:** Cold is a general word to talk about things that are low in temperature. If you say that something such as the weather or a room is chilly, you mean that it is quite cold, in an unpleasant way. If something is quite cold in a pleasant way, you use the word cool. For example, people might enjoy a cool breeze in a very hot place. If something is freezing, it is very cold.

cold² /kəʊld/ NOUN [*plural* colds]
1 a common illness that makes you cough and blocks your nose 🔊 *Hannah's got a cold.* 🔊 *I caught a cold while I was away.*
2 the cold cold weather or a low temperature □ *We waited around in the cold for an hour.*

collapse¹ /kəˈlæps/ VERB [collapses, collapsing, collapsed]
1 if a building or structure collapses, it falls down because it is too weak □ *The bridge collapsed under the lorry's weight.*
2 if a person collapses, they fall down because they are ill or very tired □ *He collapsed from exhaustion.* □ *I put down my bags and collapsed on the sofa.*
collapse² /kəˈlæps/ NOUN [*plural* collapses]
1 when a building, structure or person falls down □ *After her collapse, she went to Switzerland to recover.*
2 when a business, government, plan, etc. fails □ *The country faces economic collapse.*

collar /ˈkɒlə(r)/ NOUN [*plural* collars]
1 the piece of material on a shirt or jacket that fits round your neck □ *I unbuttoned my shirt collar.*
2 a piece of leather or other material fastened round an animal's neck

colleague /ˈkɒliːg/ NOUN [*plural* colleagues] a person who you work with □ *A colleague of mine told me about it.*

collect /kəˈlekt/ VERB [collects, collecting, collected]
1 to get things from different places and put them together □ *The survey collected data from 500 people.* □ *+ up* *Could you collect up all the plates, please?*
2 to get and keep things of a particular type as a hobby □ *Ted collects unusual postcards.*
3 to go to a place to get someone or something □ *George collected me from the airport.* □ *The following items are collected for recycling.*
4 to take money from people □ *I'm collecting donations for charity.*

collection /kəˈlekʃən/ NOUN [*plural* collections]
1 things that have been collected together 🔊 *a private art collection* □ *+ of* *a collection of rare photographs* □ *The book is a collection of short stories.*

2 when you go to get something from a place □ There were two parcels waiting for collection. □ weekly rubbish collections
3 money collected from different people □ We had a collection for Bob's retirement.

college /'kɒlɪdʒ/ NOUN [plural colleges] in the UK, a place where people go to learn after they have left school ⊞ She went to college to do catering.

collide /kə'laɪd/ VERB [collides, colliding, collided] when moving objects collide, they hit each other □ The bus collided with a car.

collision /kə'lɪʒən/ NOUN [plural collisions] a crash between moving vehicles or objects □ A collision between two lorries has closed the road.

colon /'kəʊlən/ NOUN [plural colons] a mark (:) used to separate parts of a sentence or used before a list

colonel /'kɜ:nəl/ NOUN [plural colonels] an officer with a high rank in the army or air force

colony /'kɒlənɪ/ NOUN [plural colonies] a country or area that is controlled by another country ⊞ The French established a colony there in the 19th century.

colour¹ /'kʌlə(r)/ NOUN [plural colours] red, blue, green, black, etc. □ + of Look at the colour of the sky. □ What colour are your eyes? □ The sea was a lovely colour. ⊞ There is a range of designs in bright colours.

➤ When you say the colour of something or ask about the colour of something, remember to use the verb **be** and not **have**:
✓ Your jacket is a lovely colour.
✗ Your jacket has a lovely colour.
✓ What colour is your coat?
✗ What colour has your coat?

➤ Note also that when you say the colour of something, you do not usually use the word 'colour' after the name of the colour:
✓ My new car is red.
✗ My new car is red colour.

colour² /'kʌlə(r)/ VERB [colours, colouring, coloured] to make something a particular colour or to become a particular colour □ Does she colour her hair? □ Colour the sun yellow. □ + in Would you like to colour in your picture?

colour³ /'kʌlə(r)/ ADJECTIVE having or using colour □ a colour TV □ a colour photograph

coloured /'kʌləd/ ADJECTIVE having a colour or colours, not just black and white ⊞ a brightly coloured scarf □ Use different coloured pens.

colourful /'kʌləfʊl/ ADJECTIVE having lots of bright colours □ dancers in colourful costumes □ The garden was full of colourful flowers.

colourless /'kʌləlɪs/ ADJECTIVE having no colour □ Water is a colourless liquid.

column /'kɒləm/ NOUN [plural columns]
1 a tall, thick post, usually made of stone □ Huge columns support the roof.
2 a piece of writing in a newspaper that appears regularly and is usually written by the same person ⊞ He writes a weekly newspaper column.
3 numbers or words written one under the other on a page □ + of a column of figures □ Add up the numbers in the right-hand column.
4 something with a long or tall narrow shape □ + of Columns of smoke and dust rose from the erupting volcano.

comb¹ /kəʊm/ NOUN [plural combs] an object with a row of very narrow parts along one side that you use to tidy your hair

comb² /kəʊm/ VERB [combs, combing, combed] to tidy your hair using a comb □ She combed her hair.

combat¹ /'kɒmbæt/ NOUN, NO PLURAL fighting, especially in a war □ The two soldiers died in combat.
combat² /'kɒmbæt/ VERB [combats, combatting, combatted] to try to stop something bad or harmful □ The government brought in new laws to combat terrorism. □ He will receive treatment to combat the infection.

combination /ˌkɒmbɪ'neɪʃən/ NOUN [plural combinations] several things that have been joined or mixed together □ + of The problem is due to a combination of factors.

combine /kəm'baɪn/ VERB [combines, combining, combined] to join or mix things together □ Combine all the ingredients in a mixing bowl. □ + with Carbon dioxide combines with water to form an acid.

come /kʌm/ VERB [comes, coming, came, come]
1 to move towards someone or a place □ Come here! □ Here comes Julia. □ He came back to see me later. □ She came in and said hello.
2 to go with someone □ + with Are you coming with us or not? □ We're going swimming – do you want to come?
3 to arrive □ Has my parcel come yet?
4 to move in a particular direction or to a particular level □ Prices have come down. □ All the flowers have come up. □ We watched the sun come up.
5 come second/last/before, etc. to have a particular position in a competition or a list □ P comes before Q in the alphabet. □ Philippe came first in the English exam.
6 come apart/off, etc. to become separated from something □ I picked up the jug and the handle came off.
7 How come ...? used to ask for an explanation □ How come Penny isn't here?

➤ Remember that the verb **come** means 'to move towards the speaker' or 'to move with the speaker'. For movements away from the speaker, use **go** □ *Come here!* □ *Eva came to see us last night.* □ *Are you coming to the supermarket with me?*

◆ PHRASAL VERBS **come along** 1 to arrive □ *Luckily a police officer came along at that moment.* 2 to go with someone □ *Do you mind if I come along?* **come from somewhere** to be born somewhere or to live somewhere □ *She comes from Brazil.* **Come on!** used to encourage someone or to make them go faster □ *Come on, we're going to be late for school!* **come round** to become conscious again □ *When he came round, he could remember nothing about the accident.* **come to something** to be a particular amount of money □ *Six bananas and a bag of apples – that comes to £2.80, please.* **come up** to happen □ *If the opportunity to travel comes up, you should take it.* □ *If any problems come up, just phone me.*

comedian /kə'mi:dɪən/ NOUN [plural comedians] a performer who tells jokes and funny stories

comedy /'kɒmədɪ/ NOUN [plural comedies] entertainment that makes you laugh □ *His latest movie is a comedy.* □ *a comedy sketch*

comet /'kɒmɪt/ NOUN [plural comets] a type of star that travels across the sky with a line of light behind it

comfort¹ /'kʌmfət/ NOUN, NO PLURAL a feeling of being relaxed and without pain or other unpleasant feelings □ *I prefer to travel in comfort, flying first class.* □ *When I buy shoes, I choose comfort before fashion* 🔁 *People can now shop online in the comfort of their own home.*

comfort² /'kʌmfət/ VERB [comforts, comforting, comforted] to make someone feel happier by saying or doing nice things □ *After she heard the news, she was being comforted by relatives.*

comfortable /'kʌmfətəbəl/ ADJECTIVE
1 relaxed and without pain □ *Are you comfortable there?* 🔁 *I was in a lot of pain and couldn't get comfortable.* 🔁 *He immediately made me feel comfortable.*
2 feeling pleasant and not causing any pain □ *a comfortable chair* □ *They're the most comfortable shoes I've got.*

comic¹ /'kɒmɪk/ ADJECTIVE to do with comedy 🔁 *a comic actor* □ *He has great comic timing.*

comic² /'kɒmɪk/ NOUN [plural comics]
1 a magazine, especially for children, that has picture stories
2 someone whose job is to tell jokes and make people laugh

comma /'kɒmə/ NOUN [plural commas] a mark (,) used to separate parts of a sentence

command¹ /kə'mɑ:nd/ VERB [commands, commanding, commanded]
1 to be in control of someone or something, especially in a military organization □ *He eventually commanded the regiment.*
2 to order someone to do something □ *'Stand up straight!' he commanded.* □ **+ to do something** *An officer commanded him to go back to his unit.*
● **commander** /kə'mɑ:ndə(r)/ NOUN [plural commanders] someone who is in charge, especially in the police or a military organization

command² /kə'mɑ:nd/ NOUN [plural commands]
1 an order to do something 🔁 *You must obey commands.* 🔁 *He gave the command to shoot.*
2 *no plural* control of someone or something □ **+ of** *He took command of the expedition.*
3 **in command** in control of a group of people □ *Who's the officer in command?*

comment¹ /'kɒment/ NOUN [plural comments] something you say to give your opinion □ *I'd welcome any comments about the revised schedule.* 🔁 *He made the comments in a meeting.*
comment² /'kɒment/ VERB [comments, commenting, commented] to give your opinion about something □ *'That was a waste of time', Sally commented.* □ *A spokesman refused to comment on the reports.*
commentary /'kɒməntərɪ/ NOUN [plural commentaries] a description or explanation of an event as it happens □ *There will be live radio commentary of every match.*
commentator /'kɒmənteɪtə(r)/ NOUN [plural commentators] someone who gives a description or explanation of an event as it happens □ *a football commentator*

commerce /'kɒmɜːs/ NOUN, NO PLURAL the buying and selling of goods and services □ *international commerce*

commercial /kə'mɜːʃəl/ ADJECTIVE to do with business and selling things □ *commercial and residential buildings* □ *a commercial airline*

commit /kə'mɪt/ VERB [commits, committing, committed] to do something bad or illegal ⊞ *He went on to commit more serious crimes.* ⊞ *What makes people commit murder?* ⊞ *to commit suicide*

commitment /kə'mɪtmənt/ NOUN [plural commitments]
1 a promise to do something ⊞ *Viran made a definite commitment to be there.*
2 *no plural* strong support, effort and enthusiasm for something ⊞ *She has demonstrated great commitment to the job.*

committee /kə'mɪti/ NOUN [plural committees] a group of people chosen to do a particular job or to make decisions about something □ *I'm on the committee for the summer fair.*

common /'kɒmən/ ADJECTIVE [commoner, commonest]
1 existing or happening often and in many places ⊞ *Traffic jams are a common occurrence in cities.*
□ *+ among* The condition is common among older people.* □ *Chickenpox is one of the commonest childhood diseases.*
2 shared by several people ⊞ *We share a common language.* ⊞ *It's common knowledge* (= everyone knows) *that Ann's leaving.*

common sense /ˌkɒmən 'sens/ NOUN, NO PLURAL the ability to think and behave in a sensible, practical way ⊞ *Use your common sense.* □ *He tries to take a common sense approach to his work.*

communicate /kə'mjuːnɪkeɪt/ VERB [communicates, communicating, communicated] to share information, opinions, feelings, etc. with other people by speaking, writing, etc. □ *+ with* We are looking for new ways to communicate with our customers.* □ *+ by* We communicate mainly by telephone and e-mail.* □ *He failed to communicate important information.*

communication /kəˌmjuːnɪ'keɪʃən/ NOUN, NO PLURAL sharing of information ⊞ *Text messaging is a common form of communication.* □ *+ with* We want to improve communication with the public.*
□ *+ between* There was poor communication between departments.*

communism /'kɒmjuˌnɪzəm/ NOUN, NO PLURAL a political system in which the government owns all industry and everyone is treated equally

community /kə'mjuːnəti/ NOUN [plural communities] people living in a particular area ⊞ *The school serves the local community.* □ *He grew up in a small fishing community.*

compact /kəm'pækt/ ADJECTIVE small and taking up very little space □ *a compact camera* □ *The equipment is very compact and easy to carry.*

compact disc /ˌkɒmpækt 'dɪsk/ NOUN [plural compact discs] a disc with sound recorded on it

companion /kəm'pænjən/ NOUN [plural companions] someone who is with you □ *Who is her companion?*

company /'kʌmpəni/ NOUN [plural companies]
1 a business organization □ *an insurance company* □ *He works for a small web design company.*
2 *no plural* being with other people or the people you spend time with ⊞ *He's very good company* (= fun to spend time with).
3 keep someone company to stay with someone or go somewhere with them □ *Jon came along to keep me company.*

comparative[1] /kəm'pærətɪv/ ADJECTIVE in grammar, a comparative adjective or adverb usually ends with -er or is used with *more*. For example *better*, *happier* and *more dangerous* are comparative forms.

comparative[2] /kəm'pærətɪv/ NOUN [plural comparatives] a comparative form of an adjective or adverb

compare /kəm'peə(r)/ VERB [compares, comparing, compared] to consider how two or more things are similar or different, or which is better □ *+ to* The weather today is lovely compared to last week.* □ *+ with* The figure is slightly low compared with the national average.* □ *Researchers compared the performance of the four groups.*

comparison /kəm'pærɪsən/ NOUN [plural comparisons] when you compare things ⊞ *Many people have drawn a comparison between the two players.* □ *+ between* Teachers were always making comparisons between me and my brother.* ⊞ *There's no comparison between shop cakes and homemade cakes* (= homemade cakes are much better).
⊞ *Taxes are low in comparison with other countries.*

compartment /kəm'pɑːtmənt/ NOUN [plural compartments]
1 a separate part within a container, piece of furniture, etc. □ *There was a secret compartment at the back of the desk.*
2 a separate area, especially in a train ⊞ *the first-class compartment*

compass /'kʌmpəs/ NOUN [plural compasses]
1 a piece of equipment that shows the direction of north, which you can use to find your way
2 compasses a piece of equipment used for drawing circles

compel /kəm'pel/ VERB [compels, compelling, compelled] a formal word meaning to force someone to do something ⏹ I felt compelled to get involved.

compensate /'kɒmpənseɪt/ VERB [compensates, compensating, compensated] to pay someone money in exchange for something they have lost or suffered ⏹ We were compensated for the extra hours we had to work.

compete /kəm'pi:t/ VERB [competes, competing, competed] to take part in a race, competition, etc. ⏹ + *in* I always dreamed of competing in the Olympics. ⏹ + *against* We'll be competing against some top teams. ⏹ + *for* Twenty-five players are competing for the title. ⏹ He has the ability to compete at the highest level.

competition /ˌkɒmpɪ'tɪʃən/ NOUN [plural competitions] an event at which people try to win or to be better than the others ⏹ She entered a competition to win a holiday. ⏹ He won a singing competition.

> ▶ **THESAURUS:** A competition or a contest is an event in which people try to win something or be better than others. A match is a sports competition between two players or two teams. A game is more general, and is any activity with rules that people do for enjoyment. A race is a competition to see who can do something fastest or get somewhere fastest.

competitive /kəm'petɪtɪv/ ADJECTIVE
1 to do with or involving competition ⏹ a competitive sport
2 liking to compete and win ⏹ I'm a very competitive person.

competitor /kəm'petɪtə(r)/ NOUN [plural competitors] someone taking part in a competition ⏹ He's the oldest competitor in the race.

> ▶ **THESAURUS:** A competitor or contestant is a person who takes part in a competition. A candidate is a person who takes part in an examination or someone who is trying to get a job or win an election.

complain /kəm'pleɪn/ VERB [complains, complaining, complained] to say that you are not happy or satisfied about something ⏹ + *that* He complained that it was too hot. ⏹ + *about* Our neighbours complained about the noise.

complaint /kəm'pleɪnt/ NOUN [plural complaints] when you complain about something ⏹ + *about* We've received several complaints about his behaviour. ⏹ I wish to make a complaint.

complete¹ /kəm'pli:t/ VERB [completes, completing, completed] to finish something ⏹ You must complete the test in 15 minutes. ⏹ She completed a 10-week English course. ⏹ The work should be completed by the end of March. ⏹ Complete the sentence using one word in each gap.

complete² /kəm'pli:t/ ADJECTIVE
1 including all parts ⏹ a complete set of golf clubs ⏹ Here's the complete list of winners. ⏹ + *with* It's a 5-star hotel complete with indoor pool and spa.
2 used to emphasize what you are saying ⏹ I felt a complete fool. ⏹ It was a complete surprise to me. ⏹ She received a letter from a complete stranger.

completely /kəm'pli:tlɪ/ ADVERB in every way or with every part finished ⏹ I agree completely. ⏹ The whole day was completely ruined. ⏹ This job is completely different from what I did before. ⏹ They had completely cleaned the whole house.

> ▶ Note that **completely** comes before adjectives that have strong meanings. Before adjectives that are less strong, use **very** or **extremely** ⏹ It's completely ridiculous. ⏹ It's very silly. ⏹ It's completely exhausting. ⏹ It's very tiring.

complex /'kɒmpleks/ ADJECTIVE with many different parts and difficult to understand ⏹ These are complex issues. ⏹ The situation has become increasingly complex.

complicated /'kɒmplɪkeɪtɪd/ ADJECTIVE difficult to understand or to deal with ⏹ a complicated calculation ⏹ The situation has become more complicated.

compliment /'kɒmplɪmənt/ NOUN [plural compliments] something that you say that praises someone ⏹ Otto paid me a compliment for once.

> ➤ THESAURUS: Praise is when you tell someone
> that they have done something well. A
> compliment is what you say to praise some-
> one. Congratulations are what you say to tell
> someone that you are happy about their good
> news. For example, you might say 'Congratu-
> lations' to someone if they have a new baby or
> if it is their birthday. Admiration is what you
> feel when you have great respect for someone
> or if you think that they have done something
> very special.

compose /kəm'pəuz/ VERB [composes,
composing, composed]
1 to write a piece of music □ *He has composed the
music for a number of movies.*
2 if something is composed of something, it is
formed of it □ *The team is composed of three men
and three women.*

composer /kəm'pəuzə(r)/ NOUN [plural
composers] someone who writes music

composition /ˌkɒmpə'zɪʃən/ NOUN [plural
compositions]
1 a piece of music
2 an essay □ *We had to write a composition on the
nature of love.*

compound /'kɒmpaund/ NOUN [plural
compounds]
1 a substance formed from two or more parts or
substances. A chemistry word 🖥 *a chemical compound*
2 a word made of two or more other words. The
words *airport* and *car park* are compounds.

comprehensive /ˌkɒmprɪ'hensɪv/ NOUN [plural
comprehensives] a comprehensive school

compromise /'kɒmprəmaɪz/ VERB
[compromises, compromising, compromised] to
give up some part of what you want so that an
agreement can be made □ *I'm not willing to
compromise on this issue.*

computer /kəm'pju:tə(r)/ NOUN [plural
computers] an electronic machine that can store
and deal with very large amounts of information
🖥 *a personal computer* 🖥 *I mostly use my computer
to send emails.*

computing /kəm'pju:tɪŋ/ NOUN, NO PLURAL the
use of computers or the skill of working with
computers □ *He studied computing.*

conceal /kən'si:l/ VERB [conceals, concealing,
concealed] to hide something or to keep it secret
□ *She concealed herself behind a bush.* □ *He
couldn't conceal his disappointment.*

concentrate /'kɒnsəntreɪt/ VERB
[concentrates, concentrating, concentrated] to
give all your attention to something □ **+ on** *Try to
concentrate on one thing at a time.* 🖥 *I had to
concentrate hard to understand what he said.*

concept /'kɒnsept/ NOUN [plural concepts] an
idea or principle □ *the concept of democracy* □ *We
teach some of the basic concepts of web design.*

concern[1] /kən'sɜːn/ VERB [concerns, concerning,
concerned]
1 to worry someone □ *His disappearance was
beginning to concern us.* □ *Which issue concerns you
most right now?*
2 to affect or to be important to someone □ *Don't
interfere in things that don't concern you.*
3 to be about something □ *The research concerns
the long-term effects of poor diet.*

concern[2] /kən'sɜːn/ NOUN [plural concerns]
1 something that worries you or a feeling of worry
□ *If you have any concerns about the exam, speak to
your teacher.* 🖥 *He expressed concern about the safety
of the vehicle.* 🖥 *There is widespread concern about
fuel shortages.* □ *They showed no concern for the law.*
2 something that affects you or is important to you
🖥 *My main concern is getting a job.*

concerned /kən'sɜːnd/ ADJECTIVE
1 worried or caring about someone or something
□ *concerned parents* □ *Many people are concerned
about the environmental impact of flying.*
2 as far as I'm/he's, etc. concerned used to show
someone's opinion □ *As far as I'm concerned, he
can go ahead.*

concerning /kən'sɜːnɪŋ/ PREPOSITION about or
involving someone or something □ *There are serious
allegations concerning his behaviour.*

concert /'kɒnsət/ NOUN [plural concerts] a
musical performance 🖥 *a rock concert*

conclude /kən'klu:d/ VERB [concludes,
concluding, concluded]
1 to decide something after thinking carefully about
it □ *He concluded that she was lying.* □ *The
researchers concluded that the risk is very low.*
2 a formal word meaning to end □ *The drama
course concluded with a performance.*

conclusion /kən'klu:ʒən/ NOUN [plural
conclusions]
1 a decision you make after thinking carefully about
something □ **+ of** *What was the main conclusion of
the study?* 🖥 *I've come to the conclusion that she
just doesn't care.* 🖥 *You can reach your own
conclusion about that.* 🖥 *It's difficult to draw any
conclusions from one small survey.*
2 the last part of something □ **+ of** *I just have to
write the conclusion of my essay.* □ *He spoke to
reporters at the conclusion of the meeting.*

concrete /'kɒŋkri:t/ NOUN, NO PLURAL a strong,
hard building material made by mixing sand, cement
(= grey powder), small stones and water □ *a slab of
concrete*

condemn /kən'dem/ VERB [condemns,
condemning, condemned]

1 to say that someone or something is wrong or bad □ *The President has condemned the violence.*
2 if someone is condemned to a serious punishment, they are given it by a court 🖭 *He was condemned to death.*

condition /kənˈdɪʃən/ NOUN [plural conditions]
1 the state that someone or something is in □ *+ of There were concerns over the condition of the plane.* 🖭 *He was taken to hospital in a critical condition.* 🖭 *The house was in a poor condition.* 🖭 *The flight was cancelled due to bad weather conditions.*
2 something that has to happen before something else does, especially as part of an agreement □ *+ of He broke the conditions of his licence.* 🖭 *I'll go on the condition that you come too.*

conduct¹ VERB /kənˈdʌkt/ [conducts, conducting, conducted]
1 to organize or do something 🖭 *Doctors are conducting further tests.* □ *We are conducting a full investigation into the accident.*
2 to stand in front of an orchestra (= large group of musicians) to control their performance □ *Sarah Hobbs conducted the orchestra.*

conduct² NOUN, NO PLURAL /ˈkɒndʌkt/
1 the way someone behaves □ *Their reckless conduct was the cause of the accident.*
2 the way something is organized or done □ *An independent body is supervising the conduct of the election.*

conductor /kənˈdʌktə(r)/ NOUN [plural conductors] someone who stands in front of an orchestra (= large group of musicians) to control their performance

cone /kəʊn/ NOUN [plural cones]
1 a solid shape with a round base and sides that slope up to a point at the top, or an object with this shape 🖭 *a traffic cone*
2 a hard fruit of some trees □ *a pine cone*

conference /ˈkɒnfərəns/ NOUN [plural conferences] a large meeting of people to discuss a particular subject □ *+ on a UN conference on climate change* 🖭 *The union is holding its annual conference this week.*

confess /kənˈfes/ VERB [confesses, confessing, confessed] to admit to other people that you have done something wrong □ *He confessed to stealing the money.* □ *'I forgot his name', she confessed.*

confession /kənˈfeʃən/ NOUN [plural confessions] when you admit that you are guilty of a crime or something wrong 🖭 *I've got a confession to make.* 🖭 *He made a full confession to the police.*

confidence /ˈkɒnfɪdəns/ NOUN, NO PLURAL being sure of yourself and your abilities □ *+ to do something It gave me the confidence to try again.* 🖭 *We're growing in confidence.* 🖭 *I totally lost my confidence.*

confident /ˈkɒnfɪdənt/ ADJECTIVE sure of yourself or your abilities □ *+ in I'm confident in my own ability.* 🖭 *I'm feeling pretty confident.* □ *She's a very confident swimmer.*

confidential /ˌkɒnfɪˈdenʃəl/ ADJECTIVE secret or private 🖭 *He had access to confidential information.* 🖭 *highly/strictly confidential*

confine /kənˈfaɪn/ VERB [confines, confining, confined] to keep someone or something within limits or shut inside a place □ *The soldiers were confined to barracks.* □ *Please confine your remarks to the subject under discussion.*

confirm /kənˈfɜːm/ VERB [confirms, confirming, confirmed]
1 to say or to make sure that something is correct or true □ *Police would not confirm the identity of the woman.* □ *+ that A company spokesman confirmed that the director had resigned.* □ *+ question word She refused to confirm whether the rumour was true.* □ *+ as Robinson was confirmed as England captain yesterday.*
2 to say that something will happen as arranged □ *+ that Please confirm that you will be able to come to the meeting.* □ *I'm writing to confirm the booking.*

conflict /ˈkɒnflɪkt/ NOUN [plural conflicts] an argument or a disagreement 🖭 *We help to resolve conflicts between neighbours.* 🖭 *There is an armed conflict in the region.*

confront /kənˈfrʌnt/ VERB [confronts, confronting, confronted] if you are confronted with a problem or a difficult situation, it appears and you have to deal with it □ *She was confronted with a difficult choice.* □ *How would you react if you were confronted by a real emergency?*

confuse /kənˈfjuːz/ VERB [confuses, confusing, confused]
1 to make someone unable to think clearly or to understand something □ *I think it will confuse people if we make changes.*
2 to think one thing or person is something or someone else □ *I think you're confusing the two brothers.* □ *+ with A podcast should not be confused with a webcast.*

confusion /kənˈfjuːʒən/ NOUN, NO PLURAL a feeling of being confused 🖭 *The new rules caused confusion among tourists.* □ *I saw the look of confusion on her face.*

congratulate /kənˈɡrætʃʊˌeɪt/ VERB [congratulates, congratulating, congratulated] to tell someone you are happy about their achievements or their good news □ *I congratulated her on her exam results.*

congratulations /kənˌɡrætʃʊˈleɪʃənz/ PLURAL NOUN something you say to someone to show that you are happy about their achievements or their

good news □ *Congratulations! That's great news.*
□ + *on Congratulations on passing your exams.*

> ➤ Remember that the preposition you use after
> the noun **congratulations** is on □ *Congratula-*
> *tions* **on** *your marriage!* □ *Congratulations* **on**
> *passing your driving test!*

conjunction /kən'dʒʌŋkʃən/ NOUN [*plural*
conjunctions] in grammar, a word that connects
other words or parts of a sentence. For example,
and, but and *or* are conjunctions.

connect /kə'nekt/ VERB [connects, connecting,
connected] to join two things together □ *The*
Channel Tunnel connects Britain and France. □ *The*
two parts of the building are connected by a corridor.

connection /kə'nekʃən/ NOUN [*plural*
connections]
1 the relationship between two people, things or
events □ + *between They researched the*
connection between diet and certain diseases. □ +
with There is a possible connection with corruption.
□ + *to I have a personal connection to the town.*
2 something that connects telephones, computers,
etc. □ *a high-speed broadband connection* □ *a*
wireless Internet connection
3 something that joins two things together ⌨ *a*
loose electrical connection

conquer /'kɒŋkə(r)/ VERB [conquers, conquering,
conquered] to take control of a country or an area,
especially in a war □ *Napoleon tried to conquer Egypt.*
conqueror /'kɒŋkərə(r)/ NOUN [*plural*
conquerors] someone who takes control of a
country or an area, especially in a war
conquest /'kɒŋkwest/ NOUN [*plural* conquests]
when someone takes control of a country or an area,
especially in a war □ *the Spanish conquest of Mexico*
conscience /'kɒnʃəns/ NOUN [*plural* consciences]
your feeling of what is right and wrong □ *You*
should follow your conscience. ⌨ *Now I can relax*
with a clear conscience (= without feeling guilty).
⌨ *He clearly had a guilty conscience.*

conscious /'kɒnʃəs/ ADJECTIVE awake and aware
of what is around you ⌨ *He is now fully conscious*
following the operation. □ *He had to fight to*
remain conscious.

consent /kən'sent/ NOUN, NO PLURAL when you
agree to or allow something ⌨ *Patients must give*
their consent for the treatment.
consequence /'kɒnsɪkwəns/ NOUN [*plural*
consequences] something that is the result of
something else □ *She didn't realize the*
consequences of her actions. ⌨ *If you eat too much,*
you'll suffer the consequences. ⌨ *They could face*
serious health consequences if they don't change
their lifestyles.

consequently /'kɒnsɪkwəntlɪ/ ADVERB as a result
□ *He injured his ankle and, consequently, he had to*
withdraw from the match.
conservation /ˌkɒnsə'veɪʃən/ NOUN, NO PLURAL
looking after something to prevent it being damaged
or destroyed ⌨ *nature conservation*
conservative /kən'sɜːvətɪv/ ADJECTIVE a
conservative person does not like changes or new
ideas □ *He's a very conservative dresser.*

consider /kən'sɪdə(r)/ VERB [considers,
considering, considered]
1 to think about something carefully □ *I'll consider*
your idea. □ *We're considering all the options.* □ +
whether I'm considering whether to go or not. □ +
ing Have you considered hiring a car?
2 to have a particular opinion about someone or
something □ *I consider him to be a true friend.*
□ *We will delete anything we consider*
inappropriate. □ *I consider myself to be very lucky.*

> ➤ Note that when **consider** (meaning 'to think
> about something carefully') is followed by a
> verb, that verb is in the -ing form:
> ✓ *She's considering leaving her job.*
> ✗ *She's considering to leave her job.*

considerable /kən'sɪdərəbəl/ ADJECTIVE quite
large or important □ *a considerable distance*
□ *We've spent a considerable amount of money*
already.
consideration /kənˌsɪdə'reɪʃən/ NOUN [*plural*
considerations]
1 thinking carefully about things ⌨ *The idea*
deserves serious consideration. ⌨ *We will give*
consideration to the request.
2 take something into consideration to think
about something while you are making a decision or
a plan □ *We will take all views into consideration.*
3 thinking about other people and what they want □ *We*
all want to be treated with consideration and respect.
□ *They showed little consideration for her privacy.*

consist /kən'sɪst/
◆ PHRASAL VERB [consists, consisting, consisted]
consist of something to be made of two or
more things □ *It was a simple meal, consisting of*
bread and cheese. ⌨ *His diet consists mainly of meat*
and potatoes.

console¹ /kən'səʊl/ VERB [consoles, consoling,
consoled] to make someone who is sad or
disappointed feel better
console² /'kɒnsəʊl/ NOUN [*plural* consoles] a
piece of equipment that you connect to a television
to play video games on ⌨ *a games console*

consonant /'kɒnsənənt/ NOUN [*plural*
consonants] any letter of the alphabet except *a, e, i,*
o, or *u*
➡ *go to* **vowel**

constant /'kɒnstənt/ ADJECTIVE never stopping □ He was in constant pain. □ The city is under constant threat of attack.

constituency /kən'stɪtjuənsɪ/ NOUN [plural constituencies] a part of a country that elects someone to a parliament

construct /kən'strʌkt/ VERB [constructs, constructing, constructed] to build something □ The building was constructed in 1974.

construction /kən'strʌkʃən/ NOUN [plural constructions] the process of building something □ The substance is used in road construction.

consul /'kɒnsəl/ NOUN [plural consuls] a government official who works in a foreign city and helps visitors from his or her own country □ The British consul in Barcelona arranged for him to have a temporary passport.

consult /kən'sʌlt/ VERB [consults, consulting, consulted] to speak to someone or to look at something in order to get information or advice □ If symptoms persist, consult a doctor. □ Anna stopped to consult the map.

consume /kən'sju:m/ VERB [consumes, consuming, consumed] to use something such as energy or time □ Cities consume 75% of the world's energy.

consumer /kən'sju:mə(r)/ NOUN [plural consumers] someone who buys and uses things □ Consumers want choice and competitive prices.

consumption /kən'sʌmpʃən/ NOUN, NO PLURAL the use of things such as energy, fuel, water, etc. ⊞ The newer model of car offers better fuel consumption. □ The programme suggests ways of reducing water consumption.

contact¹ /'kɒntækt/ NOUN, NO PLURAL
1 when you write to someone or speak to them by telephone □ +with I've had no contact with my brother for over a year. ⊞ I've lost contact with most of the people I went to school with. ⊞ I keep in contact with all my ex-colleagues.
2 in contact if you are in contact with someone, you write to them or speak to them by telephone □ Have you been in contact with Adrian recently?
3 when two things or people touch each other ⊞ There was no physical contact between them. ⊞ She became ill after coming into contact with infected chickens.

contact² /'kɒntækt/ VERB [contacts, contacting, contacted] to write to someone or to speak to them on the telephone □ Anyone with information about the fire should contact police.

contain /kən'teɪn/ VERB [contains, containing, contained]
1 to include something or have it as a part □ The document contained important personal information. □ Oranges contain a lot of vitamin C.

2 to have something inside □ The bag contained some money.

► Note that the verb **contain** is never used in the -ing form. It is always used in simple tenses:
✓ The bag contained my passport.
✗ The bag was containing my passport.

---

container /kən'teɪnə(r)/ NOUN [plural containers] something for putting things in, for example a box ⊞ She put the food in a plastic container. □ + of a container of milk

contemplate /'kɒntəmpleɪt/ VERB [contemplates, contemplating, contemplated] to think seriously about something □ We're contemplating moving to France

content¹ /'kɒntent/ NOUN, NO PLURAL
1 the subject or ideas that a magazine, television programme, etc. deals with □ The content is not suitable for children.
2 the amount of a substance that something contains ⊞ Pizzas have a very high fat content.
➔ go to **contents**

content² /kən'tent/ ADJECTIVE happy □ Tatsuya was quite content to let Mai help him.

● **contented** /kən'tentɪd/ ADJECTIVE happy and satisfied □ a contented smile □ Gemma was a contented baby.

contents /'kɒntentz/ PLURAL NOUN the things that are inside something □ She emptied the contents of her bag onto the table. □ The newspaper revealed the contents of the Prince's letter.

► **THESAURUS:** The contents of a something are the things that are inside it. For example, you can talk about the contents of a bag or the contents of a book. The parts of a thing are all of the different small things that you use to make a bigger thing, such as a machine. For example, you can talk about the parts of a car. Ingredients are the different foods that you use to cook something. For example the ingredients of a cake include flour, butter and eggs.

contest /'kɒntest/ NOUN [plural contests] a competition 🖾 *She entered a singing contest.*

contestant /kən'testənt/ NOUN [plural contestants] someone who is taking part in a competition

context /'kɒntekst/ NOUN [plural contexts]
1 the situation in which something happens and all the events that caused it 🖾 *These events need to be seen in the context of the decade in which they happened.*
2 the words before and after a word which help you to understand its meaning

continent /'kɒntɪnənt/ NOUN [plural continents] one of the large areas that the Earth's land is divided into. The continents are Africa, Antarctica, North America, South America, Asia, Australia and Europe
• **continental** /ˌkɒntɪ'nentəl/ ADJECTIVE to do with continents

continue /kən'tɪnjuː/ VERB [continues, continuing, continued]
1 to keep happening, existing, or doing something without stopping □ + *for* *This disagreement has continued for many years.* □ + *to do something* *Jake continued to do well at school.* *She continued working past retirement age.* □ + *with* *He said he would continue with his campaign.*
2 to start doing something again □ *Police will continue the search in the morning.*
3 to go further in the same direction □ + *along* *They continued along the road until they reached the village.*

continuous /kən'tɪnjuəs/ ADJECTIVE
1 existing or happening without stopping □ *There has been a continuous improvement in exam results.*
2 in grammar, the continuous form of a verb shows that something is continuing to happen □ *The sentence 'They are playing football' is in the continuous form.*

contract /'kɒntrækt/ NOUN [plural contracts] an official written agreement 🖾 *She signed a contract to design clothes for a top store.* 🖾 *The company has won a contract to supply books to schools.*

contrary[1] /'kɒntrərɪ/ ADJECTIVE completely different to something else □ *They have contrary views on the subject.* 🖾 *Contrary to popular belief* (= although many people believe this), *hair does not grow quicker if you cut it.*

contrary[2] /'kɒntrərɪ/ NOUN, NO PLURAL
1 the contrary the opposite □ *He's not a nervous person. Quite the contrary, in fact.*
2 on the contrary used for emphasizing that the opposite is true □ *The situation isn't depressing. On the contrary, there's a new feeling of hope.*

contrast[1] /'kɒntrɑːst/ NOUN [plural contrasts] a big difference □ *The contrast between the two men could not be greater.*

contrast[2] /kən'trɑːst/ VERB [contrasts, contrasting, contrasted]
1 if two things contrast, they are very different from each other 🖾 *His comments contrast sharply with those of his colleagues.*
2 to compare two things and show the differences between them □ *She contrasted her experiences of working in China with her time in India.*

contribute /kən'trɪbjuːt, 'kɒntrɪbjuːt/ VERB [contributes, contributing, contributed] to give something in order to buy or achieve something together with other people □ *We all contributed towards Paul's present.* □ *He contributed a lot to the discussion.*

contribution /ˌkɒntrɪ'bjuːʃən/ NOUN [plural contributions] something that you give or do to help achieve something 🖾 *She has made a significant contribution to the project.*

control[1] /kən'trəʊl/ NOUN [plural controls]
1 *no plural* the power or ability to make someone or something do what you want □ + *over* *He has no control over his children.* 🖾 *Brock lost control of the car and it hit a tree.* 🖾 *The army has taken control of the city.*
2 in control having the power to make decisions in an organization, country etc. □ *He remains in control of the company.*
3 under control if something is under control, someone is dealing with it □ *The situation is under control.* □ *It took three hours to get the fire under control.*
4 out of control unable to be controlled □ *The situation is getting out of control.*
5 controls the handles, buttons etc. you use to make a vehicle or machine work

control[2] /kən'trəʊl/ VERB [controls, controlling, controlled]
1 to have the power to make decisions □ *Congress was controlled by the Democrats.*
2 to make someone or something do what you want □ *To be a good football player you must be able to control the ball.*

controversial /ˌkɒntrə'vɜːʃəl/ ADJECTIVE causing disagreement 🖾 *Nuclear power is a highly controversial issue.*

convenience /kən'viːnjəns/ NOUN, NO PLURAL the state of being easy to use, reach or do □ *I like the convenience of living so close to the shops.* □ *For everyone's convenience, we will meet after school.*

convenient /kən'viːnjənt/ ADJECTIVE
1 suitable and easy □ *Drinking fruit juice is a convenient way for children to get vitamin C.*
2 very close and easy to get to □ + *for* *Our house is very convenient for the school.*

conversation /ˌkɒnvəˈseɪʃən/ NOUN [plural conversations] a talk between people ◻ We had a long conversation about music. ◻ + **with** I had a nice conversation with my Dad last night. ◻ I overheard a conversation between my brother and his girlfriend.

converse¹ /kənˈvɜːs/ VERB [converses, conversing, conversed] when people converse, they talk to each other. A formal word.

converse² /ˈkɒnvɜːs/ NOUN, NO PLURAL the converse the opposite of a statement, fact etc.

• **conversely** /kənˈvɜːslɪ/ ADVERB in the opposite way, or from the opposite point of view

conversion /kənˈvɜːʃən/ NOUN [plural conversions]
1 when you change something from one thing to another ◻ the conversion from analogue to digital television
2 when someone changes to a different religion ◻ her conversion from Christianity to Islam

convert /kənˈvɜːt/ VERB [converts, converting, converted]
1 to change something into something else ◻ Convert this sum of money from pounds into dollars.
2 to change from one religion to another one

convey /kənˈveɪ/ VERB [conveys, conveying, conveyed] to communicate information, ideas or feelings ◻ What are you trying to convey in this poem?

convict /ˈkɒnvɪkt/ NOUN [plural convicts] someone who has been found guilty of a crime and sent to prison

convince /kənˈvɪns/ VERB [convinces, convincing, convinced] to make someone believe that something is true ◻ Vijay tried to convince his parents that he was too ill to go to school.

convoy /ˈkɒnvɔɪ/ NOUN [plural convoys] a line of vehicles which are travelling together

cook¹ /kʊk/ VERB [cooks, cooking, cooked]
1 to prepare and heat food so that it is ready to eat ◻ I offered to cook a meal for her. ◻ Ben was cooking dinner. ◻ Cook the pasta in a pan of boiling water.
2 food cooks when it heats up and becomes ready to eat ◻ While the potatoes are cooking, prepare the other vegetables.

➤ THESAURUS: Cook is a general word. If you bake something, you cook it in an oven. You bake cakes and bread. When you cook meat or vegetables in an oven, using fat, you use the word **roast**. When you **grill** food, you cook it on a barbecue or under direct heat. If you cook food in fat in a pan, you **fry** it. When you use hot water to cook food in a pan, you **boil** it. To **simmer** food means to boil it very gently.

cook² /kʊk/ NOUN [plural cooks] someone who prepares and cooks food ◻ Emma's a really good cook. ◻ He works as a hospital cook.

cooker /ˈkʊkə(r)/ NOUN [plural cookers] a piece of kitchen equipment used for cooking food ◻ a gas cooker

➤ Note that a **cook** is someone who prepares and cooks food and a **cooker** is a piece of equipment used for cooking food.

cookery /ˈkʊkərɪ/ NOUN, NO PLURAL the skill or activity of cooking food ◻ She's doing a cookery course.

cookie /ˈkʊkɪ/ NOUN [plural cookies] a biscuit ◻ a chocolate chip cookie

cooking /ˈkʊkɪŋ/ NOUN, NO PLURAL
1 when someone cooks food ◻ Cooking is my main interest.
2 the type of food that is cooked ◻ I love my grandma's cooking.

cool¹ /kuːl/ ADJECTIVE [cooler, coolest]
1 slightly cold ◻ There was a cool breeze. ◻ I need a cool drink.
2 an informal word meaning great ◻ He has a really cool haircut. ◻ 'I've got a new mobile'. 'Cool!'
3 calm ◻ Try to stay cool in a dangerous situation.

cool² /kuːl/ VERB [cools, cooling, cooled] to become cooler or to make something cooler ◻ Have a drink to help you cool down.

cooperate /kəʊˈɒpəˌreɪt/ VERB [cooperates, cooperating, cooperated] to work together with other people to achieve something ◻ The two countries are cooperating with each other in the fight against terrorism.

cooperation /kəʊˌɒpəˈreɪʃən/ NOUN, NO PLURAL working with others so that something can be done or achieved

cooperative /kəʊˈɒpərətɪv/ ADJECTIVE willing to do what someone asks you to do

coordinate /kəʊˈɔːdɪneɪt/ VERB [coordinates, coordinating, coordinated] to organize all the different parts of something ◻ He is coordinating the research project.

cop /kɒp/ NOUN [plural cops] an informal word for a police officer ◻ a New York cop

copper[1] /'kɒpə(r)/ NOUN, NO PLURAL a red-brown metal

copper[2] /'kɒpə(r)/ ADJECTIVE
1 made of copper □ *a copper kettle*
2 having the colour of copper □ *She had beautiful copper hair.*

copy[1] /'kɒpɪ/ NOUN [plural copies]
1 something that is made so that it looks exactly the same as something else 🕀 *Rick bought a CD and made a copy from that.* □ **+ of** *He sent a copy of her death certificate.*
2 one book, magazine, etc. from many the same that have been produced □ **+ of** *I bought a copy of her new book.*

copy[2] /'kɒpɪ/ VERB [copies, copying, copied]
1 to make something that is exactly the same as something else □ *She copied the file onto a CD.*
2 to write down words or information that you have found somewhere □ *I copied the train times into my notebook.* □ *She tried to copy my answers in the exam.*
♦ PHRASAL VERB **copy something down** to write something that someone has told you or that is written somewhere □ *Copy down these questions and do them for homework.*

copyright /'kɒpɪˌraɪt/ NOUN, NO PLURAL the legal right to copy or use a book, film, etc. 🕀 *The company owns the copyright to thousands of songs.*

coral[1] /'kɒrəl/ NOUN, NO PLURAL a hard pink or white substance formed from the bones of small sea creatures

coral[2] /'kɒrəl/ ADJECTIVE made of coral □ *a coral island* □ *a coral necklace*

cord /kɔːd/ NOUN [plural cords]
1 a piece of thick string □ *The prisoner's hands were tied with cord.*
2 wire covered with plastic that connects a piece of equipment to an electrical supply

core /kɔː(r)/ NOUN [plural cores]
1 the most important part of something 🕀 *This area is at the core of the Chinese manufacturing industry.*
2 the hard part with seeds in the middle of fruit like apples □ *an apple core*

cork /kɔːk/ NOUN [plural corks]
1 *no plural* a light material from the outside part of a tree
2 a piece of cork, which is put inside the top of a wine bottle

corn /kɔːn/ NOUN, NO PLURAL a crop that is grown for grain

corner /'kɔːnə(r)/ NOUN [plural corners]
1 a point where two walls, edges or lines meet 🕀 *It was a large room with a table in the corner.* □ **+ of** *The corner of the page was torn.*
2 the point where two roads meet 🕀 *There's a hairdresser's on the corner.* 🕀 *The school is just*

round the corner. □ **+ of** *I'll meet you at the corner of George Street and Alexander Road.*

coronation /ˌkɒrə'neɪʃən/ NOUN [plural coronations] a ceremony in which someone becomes a king or queen

corporation /ˌkɔːpə'reɪʃən/ NOUN [plural corporations] a large company

corpse /kɔːps/ NOUN [plural corpses] a dead body

correct[1] /kə'rekt/ ADJECTIVE right, not wrong
🕀 *The correct answer is 15.* □ *What is the correct pronunciation of that word?*
• **correctly** /kə'rektlɪ/ ADVERB in a way that is correct □ *Make sure you enter your password correctly.*

correct[2] /kə'rekt/ VERB [corrects, correcting, corrected]
1 to make something right □ *He had an operation on his ankle to correct the problem.*
2 to show someone the mistakes they have made in speaking or writing □ *He interrupted me to correct my grammar.*

correction /kə'rekʃən/ NOUN [plural corrections] a change that makes something right
🕀 *They have made corrections to their report.*

correspond /ˌkɒrɪ'spɒnd/ VERB [corresponds, corresponding, corresponded]
1 if two things correspond, they are the same □ *Let's see if what he told you corresponds with what he told me.*
2 if people correspond, they write to each other. A formal word.

correspondence /ˌkɒrɪ'spɒndəns/ NOUN, NO PLURAL letters that people write to each other, or the activity of writing letters

correspondent /ˌkɒrɪ'spɒndənt/ NOUN [plural correspondents] someone who writes news reports about a particular subject □ *a political correspondent*

corridor /'kɒrɪdɔː(r)/ NOUN [plural corridors] a passage in a building with doors on one or both sides 🕀 *a long corridor* □ *I was chatting to her in the corridor.*

corrupt /kə'rʌpt/ ADJECTIVE being dishonest in order to get money or power □ *corrupt officials*

cost[1] /kɒst/ VERB [costs, costing, cost] to have a particular price □ *The ticket cost £35.* □ *How much does a litre of milk cost?* □ *This coat cost me a lot of money.* □ **+ to do something** *It cost £10,000 to fix the roof.*

cost[2] /kɒst/ NOUN [plural costs]
1 the amount of money that you need in order to buy or do something □ **+ of** *The average cost of a house in this area is £350,000.* 🕀 *the high cost of*

fuel ⊞ There has been an increase in the cost of living (= the price of food, clothes, etc.).
2 damage that is done to someone or something □ **+ to** There's a great cost to the environment when we burn carbon fuels.

♦ IDIOM at all costs used for saying that you will do something even if it is difficult or even if people suffer □ Yushi was determined to succeed at all costs.

co-star /ˈkəʊˌstɑː(r)/ NOUN [plural co-stars] one of two famous actors in a film or play
costly /ˈkɒstlɪ/ ADJECTIVE expensive □ The building was costly to repair.

costume /ˈkɒstjuːm/ NOUN [plural costumes]
1 a set of clothes that you wear to make you look like a different person or like an animal or other creature □ The costumes in the film were beautiful. □ He was in a clown's costume at Amy's party.
2 the traditional clothes from a country or from a time in the past ⊞ The children were dressed in national costume for the parade. □ Elizabethan costumes

cosy /ˈkəʊzɪ/ ADJECTIVE [cosier, cosiest] warm and comfortable □ a cosy little bedroom □ I'm nice and cosy sitting here by the fire.
cot /kɒt/ NOUN [plural cots] a bed with high sides that a baby sleeps in

cottage /ˈkɒtɪdʒ/ NOUN [plural cottages] a small house in the countryside or in a village □ They've bought one of the cottages in the village.

cotton /ˈkɒtən/ NOUN, NO PLURAL
1 a common type of cloth made from a plant □ a white cotton shirt □ cotton sheets
2 a plant that produces a soft white substance, used for making cloth □ cotton farmers

couch /kaʊtʃ/ NOUN [plural couches] a long, comfortable chair that two or more people can sit on

cough[1] /kɒf/ VERB [coughs, coughing, coughed] to make a loud rough sound in your throat as air comes out of your lungs □ He was coughing and sneezing.

cough[2] /kɒf/ NOUN [plural coughs]
1 the noise you make when you cough ⊞ She gave a little cough and looked up.
2 an illness that causes you to cough ⊞ I have got a bad cough. ⊞ You need some cough medicine.

could /kʊd/ MODAL VERB
1 used as the past tense of **can**[1] □ We could see into the building. □ He could run very fast when he was young. □ He said we could go.
2 used to ask for something or to ask someone to do something □ Could I have a glass of water, please? □ Could you pass me the butter?

3 used to make a suggestion □ You could try texting her. □ We could go for a walk.
4 used to say that something is possible □ The weather could get better later. □ The disease could be prevented with good hygiene.

couldn't /ˈkʊdənt/ a short way to say and write 'could not'
could've /ˈkʊdəv/ a short way to say and write 'could have'
council /ˈkaʊnsəl/ NOUN [plural councils] a group of people who are elected to control a town or city ⊞ Local councils are responsible for repairing roads. □ council leaders

count[1] /kaʊnt/ VERB [counts, counting, counted]
1 to find out the total of something □ He was busy counting his money.
2 to say numbers in order □ Can you count backwards from 10?
3 to be important □ He played well when it counted.

♦ PHRASAL VERBS count on someone to depend on someone □ I was counting on him to help. count up something to find out the total of something □ She counted up how many people there were.

count[2] /kaʊnt/ NOUN [plural counts]
1 the process of counting, or the total you get ⊞ She did a quick count of the people present.
2 keep count to know how many of something there is
3 lose count to stop knowing how many of something there is

countable noun /ˌkaʊntəbəl ˈnaʊn/ NOUN [plural countable nouns] in grammar, a noun that can form a plural, e.g. dog, table or car
countdown /ˈkaʊntˌdaʊn/ NOUN, NO PLURAL
1 the time just before something important and exciting happens □ The countdown to the World Cup has begun.
2 when people count backwards to zero before something happens

counter /ˈkaʊntə(r)/ NOUN [plural counters]
1 the place where people are served in a shop or bank □ She worked on the perfume counter.
2 a small plastic disc used in some games that are played on a board

count noun /ˈkaʊnt ˌnaʊn/ NOUN [plural count nouns] in grammar, a noun that can form a plural, e.g. dog, table or car

country[1] /ˈkʌntrɪ/ NOUN [plural countries]
1 an area of land with its own government and national borders □ We don't have the death penalty in this country. ⊞ Have you ever lived in a foreign country?
2 the country areas that are away from towns and cities □ I prefer living in the country.

country[2] /'kʌntrɪ/ ADJECTIVE in or from the countryside □ *country lanes* □ *The Prime Minister's country house is located on Lake Mousseau.*

countryside /'kʌntrɪsaɪd/ NOUN, NO PLURAL land that is away from towns and cities ⌗ *The hotel is surrounded by open countryside.*

> ➤ THESAURUS: The countryside or the country is land that is away from towns and cities. Scenery is what you can see when you look around, especially natural things such as trees and rivers in the countryside. A landscape is a view of a large area of land, and may be in a city or in the country.

county /'kaʊntɪ/ NOUN [*plural* counties] an area of a country or state that has its own local government □ *Yorkshire is a huge county.*

coup /ku:/ NOUN [*plural* coups] when a group of people suddenly take control of a country without an election ⌗ *a military coup*

couple /'kʌpəl/ NOUN [*plural* couples]
1 two or approximately two □ + *of* *I haven't seen him for a couple of months.* □ *She relaxed after the first couple of games.* □ *Who ate all the chocolates? I only had a couple.*
2 a husband and wife, or two people who have a similar close relationship ⌗ *Most people on the holiday were married couples.* ⌗ *Many young couples can't afford to buy a house.*

courage /'kʌrɪdʒ/ NOUN, NO PLURAL the ability to do difficult or frightening things ⌗ *He didn't have the courage to tell her what he really thought.* ⌗ *John showed great courage throughout his ordeal.* ⌗ *I haven't plucked up the courage (= found the courage) to leave my job yet.*

courageous /kə'reɪdʒəs/ ADJECTIVE brave □ *a courageous decision*

course /kɔ:s/ NOUN [*plural* courses]
1 of course (a) used for saying yes □ *'Can I borrow your pen?' 'Of course you can'.* (b) used for saying that what happened was what you expected □ *We went on holiday and of course it rained the whole time.*
2 of course not used for emphasizing the word no □ *'Did you leave the keys in the car?' 'No, of course not'.*
3 a set of lessons on a particular subject ⌗ *I'm doing a French course.* ⌗ *There was a four-year training course to become a teacher.* □ + *in* *a part-time course in business studies*
4 one of the parts of a meal ⌗ *For the main course we had roast chicken.*
5 the direction that a vehicle is travelling in ⌗ *The pilot had to change course and land in Berlin.*
6 a piece of land that a race is run on or a game of golf is played on □ *a golf course*

> ➤ Remember that **course** (sense 3) is followed by the preposition **in** □ *She's doing a four-day course in travel writing.*

> ➤ THESAURUS: A class or a lesson is a period of time when a group of students learn something from a teacher. A set of lessons on a subject is called a course. A lecture is a talk by a teacher, particularly for older students. Often, a large number of students listen to a lecture together.

court /kɔ:t/ NOUN [*plural* courts]
1 the room where legal trials take place ⌗ *He will appear in court charged with murder.*
2 an area where you play sports such as tennis □ *an indoor basketball court*
3 the home of a king or queen and the people who live with them

courtyard /'kɔ:tjɑ:d/ NOUN [*plural* courtyards] an open area that is surrounded by walls, usually next to a building

cousin /'kʌzən/ NOUN [*plural* cousins] the son or daughter of your aunt or uncle □ *Clare and I are cousins.*

cover[1] /'kʌvə(r)/ VERB [covers, covering, covered]
1 to put something over something else to hide or protect it □ + *with* *Mum had covered the table with a clean cloth.* □ + *up* *We covered up the broken window with a board.* □ *Cover your mouth when you cough, please.*
2 to form a layer on the surface of something □ *The mountains were covered in snow.* □ *The carpets are covered in mud.*
3 to deal with or to include a subject or some information □ *The local newspaper covered the story.* □ *The course covers every aspect of childcare.* □ *This law only covers UK residents.*
♦ PHRASAL VERB **cover something up** to stop people from discovering something bad you have done □ *He set fire to the house in an attempt to cover up his crime.*

cover[2] /'kʌvə(r)/ NOUN [*plural* covers]
1 something that you put on top of or around something to protect it □ *a duvet cover*
2 the outer part of a book or magazine ⌗ *There was a photograph of him on the front cover.*
3 no plural protection from attack or bad weather ⌗ *We took cover in an old church.*

cow /kaʊ/ NOUN [*plural* cows] a large animal kept on farms for its milk or meat ⌗ *The farmer had a large herd of cows.*

coward /'kaʊəd/ NOUN [*plural* cowards] someone who has no courage

cowardly /'kauədlɪ/ ADJECTIVE behaving like a person who has no courage

cowboy /'kaubɔɪ/ NOUN [plural cowboys] a man who rides a horse and looks after cows in the US

crab /kræb/ NOUN [plural crabs] a sea creature with a round shell and ten legs, whose pink meat is eaten

crack[1] /kræk/ VERB [cracks, cracking, cracked]
1 to break something so that a line appears on the surface, or to break in this way □ I'm sorry, I've cracked this cup. □ The ice had started to crack.
2 if you crack an egg or a nut, you break it open

crack[2] /kræk/ NOUN [plural cracks]
1 a narrow break □ This mug has a crack in it. □ The ceiling had lots of cracks in it.
2 a narrow space between two parts of something □ The sun was coming in through a crack in the curtain.
3 a sudden short sound □ the crack of a whip

cracker /'krækə(r)/ NOUN [plural crackers]
1 a paper tube with a toy inside that you pull apart at Christmas
2 a plain, dry biscuit that you eat with cheese

cradle /'kreɪdəl/ NOUN [plural cradles] a baby's bed that can move from side to side

craft[1] /krɑːft/ NOUN [plural crafts] a skill in which you make something with your hands □ They teach traditional crafts such as pottery and sewing.

craft[2] /krɑːft/ VERB [crafts, crafting, crafted] to make something using skill □ The statues were crafted from marble.

craft[3] /krɑːft/ NOUN [plural craft] a boat

cram /kræm/ VERB [crams, cramming, crammed] to push people or things into a small space □ Elizabeth tried to cram everything into her bags. □ We all crammed into the car.

crane /kreɪn/ NOUN [plural cranes] a tall machine used to lift and move heavy things

crash[1] /kræʃ/ VERB [crashes, crashing, crashed]
1 if a vehicle crashes, or you crash it, it hits something by accident □ A plane had crashed into the mountain. □ Jane crashed her car last night.
2 to make a loud noise, often by hitting something □ The crystal vase crashed to the floor. □ The waves were crashing against the rocks.

3 if a computer crashes, it suddenly stops working. A computing word.

crash[2] /kræʃ/ ADJECTIVE done in a short time to get results quickly ⊞ a crash diet ⊞ I took a crash course in French.

crash[3] /kræʃ/ NOUN [plural crashes]
1 an accident in which a vehicle hits something □ Her parents were killed in a plane crash.
2 a loud noise made when something breaks or falls □ the crash of breaking glass

crawl /krɔːl/ VERB [crawls, crawling, crawled]
1 to move on your hands and knees □ The baby has just learnt to crawl.
2 insects crawl when they move around on their legs □ There's a spider crawling up the wall behind you.

crayon /'kreɪɒn/ NOUN [plural crayons] a stick of coloured wax or a coloured pencil for drawing with

crazy /'kreɪzɪ/ ADJECTIVE [crazier, craziest]
1 silly or stupid □ a crazy idea ⊞ Have you gone crazy?
2 angry ⊞ Mum will go crazy when she finds out. ⊞ His stupid questions drive me crazy.
3 be crazy about someone/something to like someone or something very much □ As a child, she was crazy about horses.

creak /kriːk/ VERB [creaks, creaking, creaked] if a door or a piece of wood creaks, it makes a long low sound □ The floorboards creaked as he crossed the room.

cream[1] /kriːm/ NOUN [plural creams]
1 no plural a thick yellow-white liquid that forms on top of milk □ strawberries and cream
2 a soft substance that you put on your skin or hair □ suntan cream
3 no plural a yellow-white colour

cream[2] /kriːm/ ADJECTIVE having a yellow-white colour □ a cream leather sofa

create /kriː'eɪt/ VERB [creates, creating, created] to make something happen or exist □ We are hoping to create an environmentally friendly building. □ Snow created problems for drivers today. □ He hoped to create a good impression by arriving on time.

creation /kriː'eɪʃən/ NOUN [plural creations]
1 the act or process of creating something □ He opposed the creation of a new department.
2 something that has been made □ This dress is one of the designer's latest creations.

creative /kriː'eɪtɪv/ ADJECTIVE good at imagining and making new things, especially works of art □ She's a very creative artist.

creature /'kri:tʃə(r)/ NOUN [plural creatures] any living thing that is not a plant

credible /'kredəbəl/ ADJECTIVE able to be believed □ a credible story

credit¹ /'kredɪt/ NOUN, NO PLURAL
1 a way of buying goods or services and paying for them later □ I bought the car on credit.
2 praise that people give you for something you have done 卷 We all worked hard but Ben got most of the credit. 卷 I can't take all the credit for the success of the film.
3 in credit your bank account is in credit when you have money in it

credit² /'kredɪt/ VERB [credits, crediting, credited] to put some money into a bank account

credit card /'kredɪt ˌkɑːd/ NOUN [plural credit cards] a small plastic card that allows you to buy things when you want them and to pay for them later □ Can I pay by credit card?

creep /kri:p/ VERB [creeps, creeping, crept] to move slowly and quietly so that nobody hears you □ He crept downstairs in the middle of the night.

crept /krept/ PAST TENSE AND PAST PARTICIPLE OF **creep**

crest /krest/ NOUN [plural crests]
1 the highest point of a hill or wave
2 the feathers that point upwards on the top of some birds' heads

crew /kru:/ NOUN [plural crews] a group of people who work together on a ship, aeroplane or train □ The lifeboat has a crew of five.

cricket /'krɪkɪt/ NOUN [plural crickets]
1 no plural a game played outdoors between two teams of eleven players who score points by hitting a ball □ a cricket bat
2 a small insect that lives in grass and makes a noise by rubbing its wings together

cried /kraɪd/ PAST TENSE AND PAST PARTICIPLE OF **cry¹**

crime /kraɪm/ NOUN [plural crimes]
1 no plural illegal activities □ a life of crime 卷 The government is introducing new measures to fight crime. 卷 Violent crime is increasing.
2 an illegal activity □ minor crimes like shoplifting 卷 Have you ever committed a crime? 卷 The police never managed to solve the crime (= discover who did it).

➤ Note that a person **commits** a crime. A person does not **make** or **do** a crime.

criminal¹ /'krɪmɪnəl/ NOUN [plural criminals] someone who has committed a crime □ a dangerous criminal

criminal² /'krɪmɪnəl/ ADJECTIVE to do with crime or criminals 卷 He has a criminal record.

crisis /'kraɪsɪs/ NOUN [plural crises] a very difficult or dangerous time or event □ a financial crisis □ the growing crisis in the housing market

crisp¹ /krɪsp/ ADJECTIVE [crisper, crispest]
1 crisp food is pleasantly hard or fresh □ crisp salad leaves □ crisp pastry
2 crisp weather is cold and dry □ a crisp spring morning

crisp² /krɪsp/ NOUN [plural crisps] a very thin piece of potato that is cooked in oil and eaten cold 卷 a bag of crisps

critic /'krɪtɪk/ NOUN [plural critics] someone whose job is to give their opinion of new books, films, plays, etc. □ He was the film critic for the Times.

critical /'krɪtɪkəl/ ADJECTIVE
1 saying that you think something is bad or wrong 卷 The report was highly critical of her work. □ critical remarks/comments
2 very important □ The talks have reached a critical stage. □ Good hygiene is of critical importance.

criticism /'krɪtɪsɪzəm/ NOUN, NO PLURAL when you say what is bad about someone or something 卷 There has been widespread criticism of the new laws. 卷 The company has faced criticism from environmental campaigners.

criticize or **criticise** /'krɪtɪsaɪz/ VERB [criticizes, criticizing, criticized] to say what you think is bad about someone or something □ It always hurts when you criticize me. □ + for They were criticized for leaving the children alone.

crockery /'krɒkəri/ NOUN, NO PLURAL plates, bowls, cups, etc.

crocodile /'krɒkədaɪl/ NOUN [plural crocodiles] a large reptile with a long tail and a big mouth that lives in rivers and lakes

crook /krʊk/ NOUN [plural crooks] an informal word for a criminal or someone who tricks people

crooked /'krʊkɪd/ ADJECTIVE
1 not straight or even □ crooked teeth □ That picture's crooked.
2 an informal word meaning not honest □ crooked cops

crop /krɒp/ NOUN [plural crops] a plant that is grown for food □ They grow crops such as corn and maize.

cross¹ /krɒs/ NOUN [plural crosses]
1 the symbol 'x', used to show when an answer is wrong, or used to show someone where to write something on a document
2 a symbol used in the Christian religion to represent the cross on which Christ died

cross² /krɒs/ ADJECTIVE [crosser, crossest] angry □ **+ with** I got very cross with him for not doing his homework.

cross³ /krɒs/ VERB [crosses, crossing, crossed]
1 to go from one side of something to the other 🖫 Find a safe place to cross the road. □ A bridge crosses the river at that point. □ Troops crossed the border at dawn.
2 if two things cross, they go across each other □ The accident happened where the road and railway line cross.
3 cross your arms/fingers/legs to put one arm/finger/leg over the top of the other □ She was sitting quietly, with her arms crossed.
♦ PHRASAL VERB cross something out to draw a line through something, usually because it is wrong □ He crossed out his answer and started again.

crossing /'krɒsɪŋ/ NOUN [plural crossings] a place where you can cross a road or a river □ Be sure to cross at the crossing.

crossroads /'krɒsrəʊdz/ NOUN [plural crossroads] a place where two roads meet and cross each other □ Turn left at the crossroads up ahead.

crouch /kraʊtʃ/ VERB [crouches, crouching, crouched] to bend your legs and back so that your body is close to the ground □ She crouched down to tie her shoe lace.

crow /krəʊ/ NOUN [plural crows] a large black bird that makes a loud, rough sound

crowd¹ /kraʊd/ NOUN [plural crowds] a large number of people or things together in one place □ a football crowd □ crowds of shoppers 🖫 A crowd had gathered at the scene.

crowd² /kraʊd/ VERB [crowds, crowding, crowded] if a large number of people crowd somewhere, they fill that place □ People crowded the streets.

crowded /'kraʊdɪd/ ADJECTIVE full of people □ crowded shops

crown /kraʊn/ NOUN [plural crowns] a circle made of gold and valuable stones that a king or queen wears on their head at formal occasions

crucial /'kruːʃəl/ ADJECTIVE very important □ The talks are now at a crucial stage. □ crucial information
crude /kruːd/ ADJECTIVE [cruder, crudest]
1 made or done in a simple, rough way showing little skill □ I had a rather crude map that Josh had quickly drawn.
2 rude □ a crude joke

cruel /krʊəl/ ADJECTIVE [crueller, cruellest] causing pain or suffering to people or animals without caring □ **+ to** It's cruel to keep an animal in such a small cage. □ **+ to** He was cruel to his children.

cruelty /'kruːəltɪ/ NOUN, NO PLURAL when someone is cruel □ They were accused of cruelty to animals.

cruise¹ /kruːz/ VERB [cruises, cruising, cruised] to travel in a car, boat, etc. at the same speed

cruise² /kruːz/ NOUN [plural cruises] a holiday spent on a ship, travelling to a lot of different places

crumble /'krʌmbəl/ VERB [crumbles, crumbling, crumbled] to break into very small pieces □ The walls of the old house were crumbling. □ Crumble the biscuit on top of the fruit.

crunch /krʌntʃ/ VERB [crunches, crunching, crunched]
1 to make a noise as you bite and eat something hard □ She was crunching on a carrot stick.
2 to make the sound of something being crushed □ The snow crunched under our feet.

crunchy /'krʌntʃɪ/ ADJECTIVE [crunchier, crunchiest] crunchy food is pleasantly hard and makes a noise when you bite it □ a crunchy biscuit

crush /krʌʃ/ VERB [crushes, crushing, crushed] to press something so that it is broken or in small pieces □ His leg was crushed by a falling rock. □ Crush two cloves of garlic.

crust /krʌst/ NOUN [plural crusts] the hard surface on the outside of bread or some other baked foods □ Cut the crusts off two slices of bread.

cry¹ /kraɪ/ VERB [cries, crying, cried]
1 to produce liquid from your eyes because you are sad or in pain □ I could hear a baby crying in the next room.
2 to shout □ **+ out** She cried out in pain.

cry² /kraɪ/ NOUN [plural cries] a shout □ **+ for** No one heard her cries for help.

crystal /'krɪstəl/ NOUN [plural crystals]
1 a small regular shape that some substances form when they become solid, for example salt, ice or a mineral □ sugar crystals
2 no plural a type of high quality glass □ crystal wine glasses

cub /kʌb/ NOUN [plural cubs] a baby animal, for example a lion or bear

cube /kjuːb/ NOUN [plural cubes] a solid shape with six equal square sides □ sugar cubes

cucumber /'kjuːkʌmbə(r)/ NOUN [plural cucumbers] a long vegetable with a green skin that you eat raw in salads

cuddle /'kʌdəl/ VERB [cuddles, cuddling, cuddled] to hold someone in your arms to show that you love them □ They were kissing and cuddling on the sofa.
cultivate /'kʌltɪˌveɪt/ VERB [cultivates, cultivating, cultivated]

1 to prepare land so that you can grow crops on it □ *Peasants used to cultivate the land.*
2 to grow a crop to eat or to sell □ *Rice is cultivated in India.*

cultivation /ˌkʌltɪˈveɪʃən/ NOUN, NO PLURAL
1 the process of preparing land to grow crops
2 the process of growing crops

cultural /ˈkʌltʃərəl/ ADJECTIVE to do with culture, especially art, music and literature □ *cultural activities*

culture /ˈkʌltʃə(r)/ NOUN [plural cultures]
1 the customs and beliefs of a particular group or society that make it different from other people or societies □ *The school has students from many different cultures.*
2 no plural music, literature, art, etc.

cunning /ˈkʌnɪŋ/ ADJECTIVE clever in a dishonest way □ *I have a cunning plan.*

cup /kʌp/ NOUN [plural cups]
1 a small container with a handle that you drink from □ *cups and saucers* □ *Let's have a cup of tea.*
2 a metal cup given as a prize in a competition, or the competition itself □ *the World Cup*
♦ IDIOM not be someone's cup of tea if something is not your cup of tea, you do not like it or are not interested in it □ *Graphic novels aren't my cup of tea.*

cupboard /ˈkʌbəd/ NOUN [plural cupboards] a piece of furniture with shelves and a door, used to store things in □ *a kitchen cupboard* □ *The plates are in the cupboard.*

cure¹ /kjʊə(r)/ VERB [cures, curing, cured] to make someone with an illness healthy again □ *+ of The treatment cured her of her insomnia.*

cure² /kjʊə(r)/ NOUN [plural cures] something that makes an illness end or go away □ *+ for a cure for cancer*

curfew /ˈkɜːfjuː/ NOUN [plural curfews] a law that says that people must stay in their houses after a particular time

curiosity /ˌkjʊərɪˈɒsətɪ/ NOUN, NO PLURAL the feeling of wanting to discover facts about something □ *Children have a natural curiosity about the world.*

curious /ˈkjʊərɪəs/ ADJECTIVE wanting to know about something □ *+ about He was very curious about my past.*

curl¹ /kɜːl/ NOUN [plural curls] a piece of hair that forms a curved shape □ *blonde curls*

curl² /kɜːl/ VERB [curls, curling, curled] to form curves or to make something form curves □ *Do you curl your hair or is it natural?*
♦ PHRASAL VERB curl up to sit or lie with your arms and legs close to your body □ *Jenny curled up on the sofa and fell asleep.*

curly /ˈkɜːlɪ/ ADJECTIVE [curlier, curliest] shaped like a curl or with a lot of curls ⊞ *curly hair* □ *a curly tail*

currency /ˈkʌrənsɪ/ NOUN [plural currencies] the money used in a particular country ⊞ *foreign currency* □ *The euro is the European currency.*

current¹ /ˈkʌrənt/ ADJECTIVE existing or happening now □ *The current situation is not acceptable.*

current² /ˈkʌrənt/ NOUN [plural currents]
1 a flow of water or air going in one direction ⊞ *Strong currents swept them out to sea.*
2 a flow of electricity through a wire

curriculum /kəˈrɪkjələm/ NOUN [plural curriculums or curricula] a course of study or all the courses of study at a school or college

curry /ˈkʌrɪ/ NOUN [plural curries] a type of food cooked with spices □ *chicken curry*

curse¹ /kɜːs/ NOUN [plural curses] magic words which are intended to make someone have bad luck ⊞ *She put a curse on the family.*
curse² /kɜːs/ VERB [curses, cursing, cursed]
1 to use rude words
2 to say angry things about someone or something □ *I was cursing him for leaving the car so dirty.*

curtain /ˈkɜːtən/ NOUN [plural curtains] a long piece of material that can be pulled across a window ⊞ *Could you draw the curtains (= open or close the curtains), please?*

curve¹ /kɜːv/ NOUN [plural curves] a line that bends

curve² /kɜːv/ VERB [curves, curving, curved] to form a curve or make something form a curve □ *The wall curves round the end of the garden.*

cushion /'kuʃən/ NOUN [plural cushions] a cloth bag filled with something soft that you sit on or rest against to be comfortable □ *There were some cushions on the sofa.*

custody /'kʌstədɪ/ NOUN, NO PLURAL
1 when someone is kept in prison until their trial for a crime 🔁 *He was held in custody for several weeks.* **2** the legal right to have a child living with you, especially after parents separate 🔁 *She lost/won custody of the children.*

custom /'kʌstəm/ NOUN [plural customs] something that people usually do or that is a tradition □ *Japanese customs* □ *It is my custom to walk to the station each morning.*

customer /'kʌstəmə(r)/ NOUN [plural customers] a person who buys things or services from a shop or business □ *The business attracts customers from all over the country.* □ *This office handles customer complaints.*

customs /'kʌstəmz/ NOUN, NO PLURAL the place at an airport or port where officials check your bags to make sure they do not contain anything illegal □ *a customs officer*

cut^1 /kʌt/ VERB [cuts, cutting, cut]
1 to use a knife or a sharp tool to divide something or remove a piece from something □ *Cut the cake into six pieces.* □ *Ben tried to cut the wood in two.* □ **+ off** *She's cut off all her hair.* □ **+ up** *Shall I help you cut up your food?* **2** to injure yourself by rubbing or hitting your skin with something sharp □ *I cut my finger on the can lid.* **3** to reduce the amount or level of something □ *Mum and Dad have cut my allowance.* **4** to remove an amount of text from a computer document
♦ PHRASAL VERBS **cut down (on something)** to reduce the amount or number of something or to do something less □ *The doctor told her to cut down*

on red meat. **cut someone off** if you are cut off on the telephone, the connection is broken before the call ends **cut someone/something off**
1 to stop people from leaving a place □ *The whole town was cut off by the flooding.* **2** to stop the supply of something □ *If you don't pay your bill, the electricity will be cut off.* **cut something out** to stop eating or drinking something □ *I feel much better since I cut meat out of my diet.*

cut^2 /kʌt/ NOUN [plural cuts]
1 an opening or injury made by something sharp □ *She's got a nasty cut on her forehead.* □ *He made two cuts in the fabric.* **2** a reduction in something □ *a price cut* □ *job cuts*

cute /kjuːt/ ADJECTIVE [cuter, cutest] attractive or pretty □ *a cute little puppy*

cutlery /'kʌtlərɪ/ NOUN, NO PLURAL knives, forks and spoons

cycle^1 /'saɪkəl/ NOUN [plural cycles]
1 a series of things that happen one after the other and then start again □ *He seems to be trapped in a cycle of stealing and prison.* **2** a bicycle

cycle^2 /'saɪkəl/ VERB [cycles, cycling, cycled] to ride a bicycle □ *I always cycle to school.*

cyclist /'saɪklɪst/ NOUN [plural cyclists] someone who rides a bicycle

cyclone /'saɪkləʊn/ NOUN [plural cyclones] a large storm that happens in tropical countries, with strong winds moving in a circle

cylinder /'sɪlɪndə(r)/ NOUN [plural cylinders] a solid shape with a circular top and bottom and long straight sides

cylindrical /sɪ'lɪndrɪkəl/ ADJECTIVE having a circular top and bottom and long straight sides

Dd

D *or* **d** /diː/ the fourth letter of the alphabet

dad *or* **Dad** /dæd/ NOUN [*plural* dads *or* Dads] an informal word that means father and that you use for talking to your father □ *Hey Dad, I scored a goal today!* □ *It was really nice of your dad to help.*

daddy *or* **Daddy** /ˈdædɪ/ NOUN [*plural* daddies *or* Daddies] a word that children use for talking to or about their father □ *Read me another story, Daddy!* □ *I gave my daddy a big hug.*

daft /dɑːft/ ADJECTIVE [**dafter, daftest**] silly □ *What a daft thing to do.* □ *Don't be daft – you can't do that!*

dagger /ˈdægə(r)/ NOUN [*plural* daggers] a small knife that is used as a weapon

daily¹ /ˈdeɪlɪ/ ADJECTIVE happening or done every day 🔁 *Exercise is part of my daily routine.* □ *Two tablets is the correct daily dose.*

daily² /ˈdeɪlɪ/ ADVERB every day □ *We have fresh bread delivered daily.*

dairy¹ /ˈdeərɪ/ ADJECTIVE
1 to do with keeping cows to produce milk 🔁 *a dairy farmer*
2 dairy foods contain milk or are made from milk 🔁 *She can't eat dairy products.*

dairy² /ˈdeərɪ/ NOUN [*plural* dairies] a place where foods such as butter and cheese are made from milk

dam /dæm/ NOUN [*plural* dams] a wall across a river that holds a lot of the water back

damage¹ /ˈdæmɪdʒ/ NOUN, NO PLURAL harm that is done by something 🔁 *The storm caused a lot of damage.* □ **+ to** *The storm did some damage to the roof.*

> ➤ Note the verbs that are used with the noun **damage**. Something **causes** damage or **does** damage:
> ✓ *The fire caused a lot of damage.*
> ✗ *The fire made a lot of damage.*

damage² /ˈdæmɪdʒ/ VERB [damages, damaging, damaged] to spoil or break something □ *The book was damaged in the post.*

> ➤ Note that the verb **damage** is used for *things* and not *people*. For people, use **hurt** or **injure**
> □ *The car was badly damaged in the accident.*
> □ *Both men were injured in the accident.*

damp /dæmp/ ADJECTIVE [**damper, dampest**] slightly wet □ *Wipe with a damp cloth.*

dance¹ /dɑːns/ VERB [**dances, dancing, danced**] to move your feet and body to music □ *Let's dance!* □ *She danced with her boyfriend all evening.* □ *Will you teach me how to dance the tango?*

dance² /dɑːns/ NOUN [*plural* dances]
1 when you dance 🔁 *Why don't you have a dance with your dad?*
2 a particular set of steps that you do to music □ *The first dance we learnt was the waltz.*
3 a party for dancing

dancer /ˈdɑːnsə(r)/ NOUN [*plural* dancers] someone who dances

dancing /ˈdɑːnsɪŋ/ NOUN, NO PLURAL the activity of moving your feet and body to music □ *I love dancing.*

danger /ˈdeɪndʒə(r)/ NOUN [*plural* dangers]
1 a situation where something may harm you □ *Danger! Keep out!*
2 in danger in a situation where something could harm you □ *He wasn't in danger at any point.*
3 something or someone that may harm you □ **+ of** *the dangers of smoking* □ **+ to** *This man is a serious danger to the public.*

dangerous /ˈdeɪndʒərəs/ ADJECTIVE if something is dangerous, it may harm you □ *a dangerous substance*

dangerously /ˈdeɪndʒərəslɪ/ ADVERB in a dangerous way □ *He was driving dangerously close to the edge.*

dare /deə(r)/ VERB [**dares, daring, dared**]
1 dare (to) do something to be brave enough to do something □ *Rachel wouldn't dare argue with the boss.* □ *I never thought I'd dare to jump out of a plane.*
2 to ask someone to do something dangerous or frightening 🔁 *I dare you to climb to the top.*

3 How dare you/he, etc. do something!
something you say when someone has done
something that upsets you very much □ *How dare
you speak to me like that!*
4 Don't you dare! used to tell someone that if
they do something you will be very angry with them
□ *Don't you dare throw that at me!*

daring /'deərɪŋ/ ADJECTIVE brave □ *a daring rescue
attempt*

dark¹ /dɑːk/ ADJECTIVE [darker, darkest]
1 without light ⌷ *When we looked outside it was
getting dark.* ⌷ *All of a sudden it went dark.*
2 not light in colour and nearer to black than to
white □ *dark blue* □ *Ruth has dark hair.*

dark² /dɑːk/ NOUN, NO PLURAL
1 where there is no light □ *I'm not afraid of the dark.*
2 the time when it becomes dark outside ⌷ *Don't go
out after dark without a torch.*

darkness /'dɑːknɪs/ NOUN, NO PLURAL where there
is no light

darling /'dɑːlɪŋ/ NOUN [plural darlings] a word
used for talking to someone you love □ *What's the
matter, darling?*

dart /dɑːt/ VERB [darts, darting, darted] to move
somewhere fast □ *A child darted out of the door as I
came in.*

dash¹ /dæʃ/ VERB [dashes, dashing, dashed] to
hurry somewhere □ *I've got to dash to the shops.*
□ *Mary came in but then she dashed off again.*

dash² /dæʃ/ NOUN [plural dashes]
1 a line '–' that is sometimes used in writing
between parts of a sentence
2 when you hurry to get somewhere ⌷ *The two
boys made a dash for the door.* ⌷ *In our mad dash to
catch the plane we forgot the presents.*

data /'deɪtə/ NOUN, NO PLURAL information ⌷ *The
hospital keeps a lot of personal data on its patients.*
□ *We collected data over a five-year period.*

database /'deɪtəbeɪs/ NOUN [plural databases]
information that is stored on a computer in an
organized form □ *Details of known criminals are
stored on a national computer database.*

date¹ /deɪt/ NOUN [plural dates]
1 the number of the day of the month, the month
and the year □ *The date today is 30 July.*
2 a particular day of a particular month and year
⌷ *What is your date of birth?* ⌷ *Shall we fix/set a
date for our next meeting?*
3 an arrangement to meet someone that you are
having a romantic relationship with or who you may
start a romantic relationship with □ *Polly's got
another date with Chris tonight.*
4 a small, brown, sticky fruit

date² /deɪt/ VERB [dates, dating, dated]
1 to write a date on a letter or other document
□ *The letter was dated 3rd May.*

2 to have a romantic relationship with someone and
meet them regularly □ *How long have you and Kelly
been dating?*

daughter /'dɔːtə(r)/ NOUN [plural daughters]
someone's female child □ *She was the daughter of a
poet.* □ *Dave and Maria have a new baby daughter.*

daughter-in-law /'dɔːtərɪn,lɔː/ NOUN [plural
daughters-in-law] your son's wife □ *Have you met
my daughter-in-law, Sandra?*

dawn /dɔːn/ NOUN [plural dawns] the beginning of
the day, when it gets light

day /deɪ/ NOUN [plural days]
1 the twenty-four hours between one midnight
(= 12 am) and another □ *There are 365 days in a
year.* □ *I do five hours' work a day.* ⌷ *I try to do
some exercise every day.*
2 the time when there is light from the sun, or when
you are awake □ *We spent the whole day on the
beach.* □ *I spent all day cleaning the house.* □ *Did
you have a good day at work?*
3 a time or period □ *in my grandfather's day* ⌷ *In
those days we didn't have computers.*
4 one day used to talk about something that
happened in the past or something that will happen
in the future □ *One day I came home to discover my
car had been stolen.* □ *I hope to have my own
business one day.*
5 the other day a few days ago □ *I saw Julio the
other day.*
6 these days used to talk about what things are
like now □ *These days I don't play much tennis.*

daylight /'deɪlaɪt/ NOUN, NO PLURAL
1 the light that comes from the sun during the day
□ *In the daylight she looked pale.*
2 the part of the day when there is light □ *I'd like to
get home in daylight.*

day-to-day /,deɪtə'deɪ/ ADJECTIVE happening or
done regularly, every day ⌷ *These attacks now
happen on a day-to-day basis* (= every day).
⌷ *Diane is in charge of the day-to-day running of
the department.*

dead¹ /ded/ ADJECTIVE
1 not now living □ *I could see he was dead.* ⌷ *He
dropped dead* (= died suddenly) *on the tennis court.*
□ *a dead body*
2 no longer working ⌷ *My phone's gone dead.*
□ *The batteries are dead.*

dead² /ded/ NOUN the dead people who have
died

dead³ /ded/ ADVERB
1 exactly □ *They were standing dead in the centre
of the circle.*
2 an informal word meaning very □ *dead boring/
easy*

deadline /'dedlaɪn/ NOUN [plural deadlines] the time when something must be finished 🔁 *You'll miss the deadline if you delay.*

deadly /'dedlɪ/ ADJECTIVE [deadlier, deadliest] able to kill 🔁 *a deadly weapon* 🔁 *a deadly poison*

deaf /def/ ADJECTIVE [deafer, deafest] not able to hear, or not able to hear well □ *Grandma is getting a bit deaf.*

• **deafness** /'defnɪs/ NOUN, NO PLURAL being deaf

deal¹ /diːl/ NOUN [plural deals]
1 an agreement, especially in business or politics 🔁 *make/strike a deal* 🔁 *We are about to sign a deal with a major record producer.* 🔁 *I got a good deal* (= a cheap price) *on my new car.*
2 a great deal a large amount □ *We spent a great deal of money on solar panels.*

deal² /diːl/ VERB [deals, dealing, dealt] to give cards to players in a game □ *You deal the cards this time.*
♦ PHRASAL VERB **deal with something/someone**
1 to take action, especially to solve a problem or to get something done □ *New houses were built to deal with the problem of homelessness.* □ *You take the boy to another room – I'll deal with his father.* □ *I need to deal with all these letters.* **2** to learn to accept a difficult situation □ *I'm finding it hard to deal with his death.* **3** to be about a particular subject □ *The programme deals with the true cost of cheap labour.*

dealer /'diːlə(r)/ NOUN [plural dealers] someone who buys and sells things □ *an antiques dealer*

dear¹ /dɪə(r)/ ADJECTIVE [dearer, dearest]
1 Dear the word you use with a name or title at the beginning of a letter □ *Dear Max* □ *Dear Sir*
2 loved 🔁 *a very dear friend*
3 expensive □ *The shoes were beautiful but very dear.*

dear² /dɪə(r)/ EXCLAMATION **Oh dear!** something you say when something slightly bad has happened □ *Oh dear! I'm late again.*

death /deθ/ NOUN [plural deaths] the time when a person or animal stops living □ *He wrote this just before his death in 1875.* □ **+ from** *The number of deaths from cancer is decreasing all the time.* 🔁 *The cause of death was unknown.*

death penalty /'deθ ˌpenəltɪ/ NOUN [plural death penalties] when someone is killed as a legal punishment for a crime

debate¹ /dɪ'beɪt/ NOUN [plural debates] a big or formal discussion about something □ *a parliamentary debate*

debate² /dɪ'beɪt/ VERB [debates, debating, debated] to have a debate about something

debris /'deɪbriː/ NOUN, NO PLURAL the parts of something that has broken into pieces □ *Debris from the crashed aircraft lay all around.*

debt /det/ NOUN [plural debts]
1 an amount of money that one person owes to another 🔁 *I always pay off my debts.*
2 in debt owing someone money

decade /'dekeɪd/ NOUN [plural decades] a period of ten years □ *This is the first decade of the twenty-first century.*

decay¹ /dɪ'keɪ/ NOUN, NO PLURAL when something becomes rotten or breaks into pieces 🔁 *This toothpaste helps prevent tooth decay.*

decay² /dɪ'keɪ/ VERB [decays, decaying, decayed] to go rotten or break into pieces □ *The bins were full of decaying food.*

deceive /dɪ'siːv/ VERB [deceives, deceiving, deceived] to make someone believe something that is not true □ **+ by** *Don't be deceived by his friendly manner.* □ **+ into** *She was deceived into thinking she'd won a holiday.* □ *If she thinks Keith actually loves her, she's deceiving herself.*

December /dɪ'sembə(r)/ NOUN [plural Decembers] the twelfth month of the year, after November and before January □ *Her birthday is in December.*

decent /'diːsənt/ ADJECTIVE
1 acceptable or good enough □ *Is there a decent butcher's near here?* 🔁 *I think they have a decent chance of winning.*
2 good, honest and of a high moral standard □ *He's a very decent bloke.*

decide /dɪ'saɪd/ VERB [decides, deciding, decided] to choose what you are going to do □ **+ to do something** *Greg decided to buy a computer.* □ **+ that** *She decided that she would go with him.* □ *I can't decide what to do.*

decimal¹ /'desɪml/ ADJECTIVE a decimal system is a way of counting based on the number ten

decimal² /'desɪml/ NOUN [plural decimals] a fraction (= number that is less than a whole number) written as a decimal point (.) followed by numbers. A mathematics word □ *A half, written as a decimal, is 0.5.*

decision /dɪ'sɪʒən/ NOUN [plural decisions] when you decide something 🔁 *I will let you know when I have made my decision.* 🔁 *Finally we took the difficult decision to sell the house.* 🔁 *Most of us think the directors came to the right decision.*

► **THESAURUS:** When you choose what you are going to do, you make a decision. A conclusion is a decision that you make after you have thought about it very carefully. You also write a conclusion at the end of an essay. A verdict is the decision that a jury or a judge makes in a court when they decide if someone is guilty of a crime.

deck /dek/ NOUN [plural decks]
1 the flat part that you walk on on the outside of a boat □ Let's take a walk up on deck.
2 one of the levels of a boat or bus 🔁 There are more seats on the upper deck.

declaration /ˌdeklə'reɪʃən/ NOUN [plural declarations] an announcement □ a declaration of war

declare /dɪ'kleə(r)/ VERB [declares, declaring, declared] to announce something firmly or officially 🔁 Britain declared war on Germany. □ She suddenly declared that she was leaving.

decline /dɪ'klaɪn/ VERB [declines, declining, declined]
1 to become weaker or smaller □ His popularity has declined sharply.
2 a formal word that means to refuse □ I'm afraid I must decline your kind invitation. □ The minister declined to comment.

decorate /'dekəreɪt/ VERB [decorates, decorating, decorated]
1 to put things on or around something to make it look more attractive □ We'll decorate the cake with sugar roses.
2 to put paint or paper on the inside walls of a room □ We've just decorated the dining room.

decoration /ˌdekə'reɪʃən/ NOUN [plural decorations]
1 when you add something to make something more attractive, or the thing you add 🔁 Christmas/party decorations
2 no plural putting paint or paper on the inside walls of a room □ The whole house is in need of decoration.

decorator /'dekəreɪtə(r)/ NOUN [plural decorators] someone whose job is to decorate rooms

decrease¹ /dɪ'kriːs/ VERB [decreases, decreasing, decreased] to make something less or to become less □ A healthy diet helps to decrease the risk of heart disease. □ Josh's interest in football decreased as he got older.

decrease² /'diːkriːs/ NOUN [plural decreases] an amount by which something is smaller □ + in There was a decrease in violent crime in the area. □ + of They saw a decrease of 5% in sales.

dedicate /'dedɪkeɪt/ VERB [dedicates, dedicating, dedicated] to spend a particular amount of time doing something □ She dedicated her whole life to music.

deep¹ /diːp/ ADJECTIVE [deeper, deepest]
1 going a long way down from the top □ Is the pond very deep? □ The sea was 30 metres deep at that point.
2 deep feelings and emotions are very strong □ I have a deep dislike of dogs.

3 deep colours are strong and dark □ I painted the walls deep blue.
4 a deep sound is very low 🔁 a deep voice
5 a deep breath a big breath that fills your lungs □ Take a deep breath then jump into the water.

deep² /diːp/ ADVERB [deeper, deepest] a long way from the top of something □ They swam deep beneath the ocean.

deeply /'diːpli/ ADVERB
1 very much □ I deeply regret my actions.
2 if you breathe deeply, you take a lot of air into your lungs

deer /dɪə(r)/ NOUN [plural deer] a large wild animal that has antlers (= parts like branches) on the head of the males

defeat¹ /dɪ'fiːt/ VERB [defeats, defeating, defeated] to beat someone in a war or competition 🔁 We shall defeat the enemy and restore peace. □ The visiting team were defeated 3-0.

defeat² /dɪ'fiːt/ NOUN [plural defeats] a game, fight, war, etc. that you have lost 🔁 The king suffered a defeat by the rebel army. 🔁 England had another heavy defeat in the cricket.

defect¹ /'diːfekt/ NOUN [plural defects] a fault that stops something from working correctly □ He has a serious heart defect.

➤ THESAURUS: A defect is a problem or a fault which stops something from working properly. For example, you can have a defect in your body or in a machine. A flaw is a bad quality in a person or a thing. You might talk about a flaw in someone's character or a flaw in the design of a building. An error or a mistake is something wrong that you do. Usually, a mistake is smaller or less important than an error.

defect² /dɪ'fekt/ VERB [defects, defecting, defected] to leave a country or organization and go to live or work in an enemy country or organization □ The spy defected to the United States.
• **defection** /dɪ'fekʃən/ NOUN [plural defections] when someone defects □ There were three more defections when the athletes were in Canada.

defence /dɪ'fens/ NOUN [plural defences]
1 no plural the act of protecting someone or something from attack, harm, criticism, etc. 🔁 His bodyguards leaped to his defence. 🔁 The prime minister spoke out in defence of the chancellor.
2 something that protects something or someone from attack, harm, criticism, etc. □ They have built massive defences against the tide.

defend /dɪˈfend/ VERB [defends, defending, defended] to protect someone or something from attack, harm, criticism, etc. □ + *against* *Heavy armour on the tanks defends them against gunfire.* □ *Kim always defends his brother if people say he's too quiet.*

defense /dɪˈfens/ NOUN [plural defenses] the US spelling of **defence**

define /dɪˈfaɪn/ VERB [defines, defining, defined] to show or explain exactly what something is □ *Researchers have defined the problem.* □ *The aims of the project were poorly defined.*

definite /ˈdefɪnɪt/ ADJECTIVE certain □ *It's not definite, but the wedding will probably be in August.* □ *I've noticed a definite improvement in his condition.*

definite article /ˈdefɪnɪt ˈɑːtɪkəl/ NOUN [plural definite articles] the name used in grammar for the word **the**

> ➤ There are two kinds of article in English grammar: **the** is the *definite article* and **a** or **an** is the *indefinite article.*

definitely /ˈdefɪnɪtlɪ/ ADVERB certainly □ *We'll definitely be back by 10 o'clock.* □ *'Do you think she'll pass the exam?' 'Oh yes, definitely'.* □ *I definitely want to go back there.*

definition /ˌdefɪˈnɪʃən/ NOUN [plural definitions] an explanation of the meaning of a word or phrase □ *Look up the definition of 'magic' in your dictionary.*

defy /dɪˈfaɪ/ VERB [defies, defying, defied] to refuse to obey someone or something □ *Defying his mother, he left the house.*

degree /dɪˈɡriː/ NOUN [plural degrees]
1 a unit for measuring temperature, shown by the symbol ° □ *It's 30° (degrees) here today.*
2 a unit for measuring angles, shown by the symbol ° □ *An angle of 90° (degrees) is a right angle.*
3 a qualification that students can study for at a university or college □ *He's got a degree in German.* 🔁 *He did his degree at Cambridge.*

delay[1] /dɪˈleɪ/ NOUN [plural delays] the extra time you have to wait if something happens later than expected □ *There was a delay of half an hour before take-off.* 🔁 *Please return to your seats without delay.*

delay[2] /dɪˈleɪ/ VERB [delays, delaying, delayed]
1 to do something or make something happen later than was planned or expected □ *We delayed our holidays until after the strike.* □ *Buy now! Don't delay!*
2 to make someone or something late □ *I was delayed by the arrival of an unexpected visitor.*

> ➤ THESAURUS: To delay or postpone something means to decide to do it later than planned. You could postpone a meeting or a holiday, for example. Put off has the same meaning, but is less formal. To cancel something means to stop something from happening as planned. You might cancel a football match if it is snowing, for example. Call off has the same meaning, but is less formal.

delegate /ˈdelɪɡət/ NOUN [plural delegates] someone who goes to a meeting to represent someone else

delete /dɪˈliːt/ VERB [deletes, deleting, deleted]
1 to remove something from a piece of writing □ *Someone has deleted your name from the list.* □ *I think we should delete the last paragraph.*
2 to remove something such as a file that is stored on a computer. A computing word □ *I've accidentally deleted all their addresses.*

deliberate[1] /dɪˈlɪbərət/ ADJECTIVE done on purpose □ *He said it was an accident, but I'm sure it was deliberate.* 🔁 *It was a deliberate attempt to confuse his opponent.*

deliberate[2] /dɪˈlɪbəreɪt/ VERB [deliberates, deliberating, deliberated] to think carefully about something □ *They deliberated for three hours over their decision.*

deliberately /dɪˈlɪbərətlɪ/ ADVERB on purpose □ *You deliberately dropped that so that you wouldn't have to eat it!*

delicate /ˈdelɪkət/ ADJECTIVE
1 easily damaged □ *This china is very delicate.* 🔁 *We must respect the delicate balance between humans and nature.*
2 not strong 🔁 *a delicate flavour* 🔁 *a delicate fragrance*

delicious /dɪˈlɪʃəs/ ADJECTIVE tasting very good 🔁 *Mum's homemade soup tastes absolutely delicious.* □ *That was a delicious meal.*

delight[1] /dɪˈlaɪt/ NOUN [plural delights] great pleasure □ *The baby squealed with delight when he saw his mother.* □ *It was such a delight to see her.*

delight[2] /dɪˈlaɪt/ VERB [delights, delighting, delighted] to please someone very much

delighted /dɪˈlaɪtɪd/ ADJECTIVE very pleased 🔁 *That's great news – I'm absolutely delighted!* □ + *to do something* *We'd be delighted to come to the party.*

delightful /dɪˈlaɪtfʊl/ ADJECTIVE very pleasant □ *What a delightful surprise!*
• **delightfully** /dɪˈlaɪtfʊlɪ/ ADVERB in a delightful way □ *a delightfully funny book*

deliver /dɪˈlɪvə(r)/ VERB [delivers, delivering, delivered]

1 to take something, especially letters, packages or something you have bought, to a place □ *We're delivering leaflets to all the houses in this area.* □ *Our new washing machine is being delivered next week.*
2 if someone delivers a baby, they help the baby to be born

> ► **THESAURUS:** To deliver something means to take it to a place. Deliver is usually used to talk about letters, parcels and things that you have bought. If you **send** something to a place, you arrange for it to go there. For example, you can send a letter or an email. To **supply** something means to provide it. For example, you can say that a company supplies a shop with bread. If you **give** someone something, you let them have it.

delivery /dɪˈlɪvərɪ/ NOUN [*plural* deliveries]
1 *no plural* when something is delivered ⊞ *The price includes free delivery.*
2 something that has been delivered or will be delivered □ *We are expecting a delivery of bricks.*
3 when a baby is born □ *It was a straightforward delivery.*

demand¹ /dɪˈmɑːnd/ VERB [demands, demanding, demanded] to ask for something in a forceful way that shows you do not expect to be refused □ *They are demanding the release of all political prisoners.* ⊞ *He demanded an apology from the journalist.* □ *+ to do something* I demanded to see the manager. □ *+ that* The group is demanding that the law should be changed.

demand² /dɪˈmɑːnd/ NOUN [*plural* demands]
1 when someone asks for something in a very forceful way □ *+ for* I gave in to his demands for a new computer. ⊞ *Employers say they can't meet the union's demands.*
2 **in demand** wanted by a lot of people □ *His skills are in demand all over the world.*

democracy /dɪˈmɒkrəsɪ/ NOUN [*plural* democracies] a form of government or a country where people elect their leaders □ *The allies plan to introduce democracy to the country.* □ *We live in a democracy.*

democratic /ˌdeməˈkrætɪk/ ADJECTIVE based on a form of government where people elect their leaders □ *democratic elections*

demolish /dɪˈmɒlɪʃ/ VERB [demolishes, demolishing, demolished] to destroy something, especially a building □ *The flats will be demolished immediately.*

demolition /ˌdeməˈlɪʃən/ NOUN, NO PLURAL when something is destroyed, especially a building □ *We watched the demolition of the old sports centre.*

demon /ˈdiːmən/ NOUN [*plural* demons] an evil spirit

demonstrate /ˈdemənstreɪt/ VERB [demonstrates, demonstrating, demonstrated]
1 to show that something exists or is true □ *Her success demonstrates that women can do well in business.*
2 to show someone how to do something or how something works □ *Can you demonstrate how the ice cream maker works?*
3 to march or stand with a group of other people to show that you support or disagree with something □ *They are demonstrating against the war.*

demonstration /ˌdemənˈstreɪʃən/ NOUN [*plural* demonstrations]
1 an event where a group of people stand or march together to show that they support or disagree with something ⊞ *Supporters of the prisoners held a demonstration outside the court.* ⊞ *Over 5,000 people took part in the demonstration.* □ *+ against* They organized a peaceful demonstration against the war.
2 when someone shows you how to do something or how something works □ *a cookery demonstration* ⊞ *The sales assistant gave us a demonstration of the phone's features.*

den /den/ NOUN [*plural* dens] the home of a wild animal □ *a lion's den*

denial /dɪˈnaɪəl/ NOUN [*plural* denials] when you say that something is not true □ *He repeated his denial of his guilt.*

denim /ˈdenɪm/ NOUN, NO PLURAL a strong cotton cloth, usually blue, that is used to make clothes □ *Joe was wearing a denim jacket.*

dense /dens/ ADJECTIVE [denser, densest]
1 containing a lot of people or things very close together □ *a dense forest*
2 thick and difficult to see through □ *Dense fog filled the valley.*

dent /dent/ NOUN [*plural* dents] a hollow in a hard surface where it has been hit □ *There's a dent in the car bumper.*

dental /ˈdentəl/ ADJECTIVE to do with teeth □ *Children get free dental care.*

dentist /ˈdentɪst/ NOUN [*plural* dentists] someone whose job is to look after people's teeth

deny /dɪˈnaɪ/ VERB [denies, denying, denied] to say that something is not true □ *+ that* Nina denied that she had stolen the bag. □ *+ ing* He denies doing anything wrong. □ *She denied any involvement in the crime.*

> ► **THESAURUS:** To **deny** doing something means to say that something is not true. For example a criminal might deny committing a crime. To **oppose** means to disagree with someone's plans or ideas and try to stop or change them. For example, a group of people might oppose plans to build a factory in their village. To **disagree** means to have a different opinion from someone else.

depart /dɪ'pɑ:t/ VERB [departs, departing, departed] to leave a place, especially to start a journey □ *Flight BA123 is now departing.* □ **+ from** *The Oxford train departs from platform 8.*

department /dɪ'pɑ:tmənt/ NOUN [plural departments] a part of a school, shop, business or government that deals with a particular subject or area of work □ *the sales department* □ *The college has a very fine modern languages department.*

department store /dɪ'pɑ:tmənt ˌstɔ:(r)/ NOUN [plural department stores] a large shop that has different departments which sell different types of product

departure /dɪ'pɑ:tʃə(r)/ NOUN [plural departures] when someone or something leaves a place □ *All departures are shown on the timetable.* □ *We were shocked by her sudden departure from the school.*

depend /dɪ'pend/ VERB [depends, depending, depended] it/that depends used to say that you are not certain because something else affects the situation □ *'Do you want to come to the film?' 'It depends how late it goes on'.* □ *'Are you going to invite Rick?' 'That depends. I think he's still angry with me'.*
- PHRASAL VERB **depend on someone/something** **1** to need the help of someone or something □ *Millions of children depend on charity for their education.* □ *The farm depends on government subsidies.* **2** if what happens depends on something else, it is affected by it and may change because of it □ *A lot will depend on how well you do in your exams.* **3** to be able to trust someone to do what you want or need □ *I can depend on my family to help me.*

dependant /dɪ'pendənt/ NOUN [plural dependants] someone whose food, clothes, house, etc. you have to pay for □ *Fill in the names of all your dependants.*

dependent[1] /dɪ'pendənt/ ADJECTIVE needing something or someone to live or exist □ *She's totally dependent on her car to get around.*

dependent[2] /dɪ'pendənt/ NOUN [plural dependents] the US spelling of **dependant**

deport /dɪ'pɔ:t/ VERB [deports, deporting, deported] to force a foreign person to leave a country □ *He will be deported when he finishes his prison sentence.*

deposit[1] /dɪ'pɒzɪt/ NOUN [plural deposits] **1** part of the price of something that you pay before you buy the thing, and that you will lose if you do not buy it 🔁 *We've put down a deposit on a flat.* **2** an amount of money that you pay into a bank account 🔁 *He made several large deposits.*

3 an amount of money that you pay when you rent something, that you get back if you return the thing without any damage

deposit[2] /dɪ'pɒzɪt/ VERB [deposits, depositing, deposited] to put money into a bank account □ *I'm hoping to deposit £50 a month into a savings account.*

depot /'depəʊ/ NOUN [plural depots] **1** a place where vehicles like buses or trains are kept when they are not being used **2** a building where goods are stored □ *a weapons depot*

depressed /dɪ'prest/ ADJECTIVE unhappy □ *I felt a bit depressed about how much weight I'd put on.*

deprive /dɪ'praɪv/ VERB [deprives, depriving, deprived] to take something important or necessary away from someone □ *She's been deprived of sleep for days.*

depth /depθ/ NOUN [plural depths] **1** the distance from the top to the bottom of something □ *This instrument measures the depth of the water.* □ **+ of** *We dug down to a depth of around 2 metres.* □ *The swimming pool was only 2 metres in depth.* **2** in depth in a lot of detail □ *We discussed the situation in great depth.*

deputy /'depjʊtɪ/ NOUN [plural deputies] someone who has the job that is next in importance to another job □ *He is deputy sales manager.*

descend /dɪ'send/ VERB [descends, descending, descended] to go or climb down. A formal word □ *They descended the stairs.* □ *The road descended steeply.*

descendant /dɪ'sendənt/ NOUN [plural descendants] someone who is related to a person who lived in the past □ *a direct descendant of Genghis Khan*

descent /dɪ'sent/ NOUN [plural descents] a movement down □ *the descent of the mountain* □ *The plane started its descent.*

describe /dɪ'skraɪb/ VERB [describes, describing, described] to say what happened or what someone or something is like □ *A reporter described the scene in detail.* □ **+ question word** *Can you describe what you saw?* □ **+ as** *He described his daughter as kind and caring.* 🔁 *She describes herself as a feminist.*

description /dɪ'skrɪpʃən/ NOUN [plural descriptions] when you describe someone or something □ **+ of** *There's a description of the hotel.* 🔁 *She gave a detailed description of the man.* 🔁 *He fitted the general description of the attacker* (= his appearance was the same as what was described). 🔁 *a job description*

desert[1] /dɪˈzɜːt/ VERB [deserts, deserting, deserted] to go away and leave someone or something, especially the army □ The soldier was shot for deserting. □ She deserted her young family.

desert[2] /ˈdezət/ NOUN [plural deserts] an area of land where it rains very little so the ground is very dry □ the Sahara desert

deserve /dɪˈzɜːv/ VERB [deserves, deserving, deserved] if you deserve something, you should have it because of your behaviour □ I'm pleased Molly won the prize – she deserves it. □ + to do something Samir deserves to be promoted.

design[1] /dɪˈzaɪn/ VERB [designs, designing, designed] to plan something before it is built or made □ The concert hall was designed by architect Frank Gehry. □ She designs clothes for a top fashion store. □ We design software to control robots.

design[2] /dɪˈzaɪn/ NOUN [plural designs]
1 a plan or drawing of something that could be made □ + for a design for a new racing car □ She has won awards for her designs.
2 a pattern □ They wore dresses in bright floral designs.

designer[1] /dɪˈzaɪnə(r)/ NOUN [plural designers] someone whose job is to design things ⊞ a fashion designer □ a web designer
designer[2] /dɪˈzaɪnə(r)/ ADJECTIVE expensive and fashionable and made by a famous company □ designer clothes □ designer sunglasses

desire[1] /dɪˈzaɪə(r)/ NOUN [plural desires] a strong feeling of wanting something ⊞ He had a burning desire (= very much wanted) to become a doctor. □ We respect his desire for privacy.
desire[2] /dɪˈzaɪə(r)/ VERB [desires, desiring, desired] to want something very much. A formal word □ You can have any model you desire.

desk /desk/ NOUN [plural desks] a table for writing or working at ⊞ Andrew sat at his desk. □ There was a big pile of papers on her desk.

desktop /ˈdesktop/ NOUN [plural desktops] a computer screen that shows the icons (= small pictures) for programs you can use. A computing word.

despair /dɪˈspeə(r)/ NOUN, NO PLURAL a feeling of having no hope ⊞ We were in deep despair. ⊞ There's a growing sense of despair among local people.

desperate /ˈdespərət/ ADJECTIVE
1 feeling very worried and that you will do anything to improve your situation ⊞ He made a desperate attempt to escape.
2 needing something very much □ Farmers are desperate for workers. □ He was desperate to win.

despise /dɪˈspaɪz/ VERB [despises, despising, despised] to hate someone or something very much □ The two men despised each other.

despite /dɪˈspaɪt/ PREPOSITION used to say that something happens or is true, although something else makes it seem unlikely □ Despite the rain, we enjoyed the picnic. ⊞ I think that she'll be very good, despite the fact that she doesn't have much experience. □ + ing The team remained positive, despite losing their first two games.

dessert /dɪˈzɜːt/ NOUN [plural desserts] sweet food eaten at the end of a meal □ We had ice cream for dessert.

destination /ˌdestɪˈneɪʃən/ NOUN [plural destinations] the place someone is travelling to ⊞ We were very tired when we finally reached our destination. ⊞ The town is a popular tourist destination.

destroy /dɪˈstrɔɪ/ VERB [destroys, destroying, destroyed] to damage something so badly that it no longer exists or cannot be used □ Thousands of homes were destroyed by the earthquake. □ A fire destroyed dozens of paintings at the museum.

destruction /dɪˈstrʌkʃən/ NOUN, NO PLURAL when something is destroyed □ + of We need to stop the destruction of the rainforest. □ The storms caused widespread destruction.

detail /ˈdiːteɪl/ NOUN [plural details]
1 a small part, fact or piece of information about something □ + of They provided details of the plans. □ + about We learnt more details about the incident. ⊞ For further details, see our website. ⊞ She didn't give any details.
2 in detail including all the information or facts about something □ She described in detail what had happened. □ We need to examine it in detail.

detect /dɪˈtekt/ VERB [detects, detecting, detected] to discover something that is difficult to find □ The dogs are trained to detect explosives. □ The test can detect cancer at an early stage.

detective /dɪˈtektɪv/ NOUN [plural detectives] someone whose job is to try to find out information about a crime ⊞ a private detective ⊞ a retired police detective □ She told detectives that she'd seen a man leaving the building.

deteriorate /dɪˈtɪəriəreɪt/ VERB [deteriorates, deteriorating, deteriorated] to get worse □ Joe's health is deteriorating rapidly.

determination /dɪˌtɜːmɪˈneɪʃən/ NOUN, NO PLURAL a strong feeling that you want to do something, even when it is difficult □ They showed great determination. □ + to do something He has a determination to win.

determined /dɪˈtɜːmɪnd/ ADJECTIVE having or showing determination □ + to do something The team was determined to finish first. □ She's a very determined young woman. 🔁 He's made a determined effort to lose weight.

detonate /'detəneɪt/ VERB [detonates, detonating, detonated] to explode or to make something explode □ The bomb was detonated from across the street.

devastate /'devəsteɪt/ VERB [devastates, devastating, devastated] to destroy something or damage it very badly □ The storm devastated much of the city.

devastated /'devəsteɪtɪd/ ADJECTIVE
1 very shocked and upset □ We were absolutely devastated by the news.
2 completely destroyed □ The minister visited the devastated area.

devastating /'devəsteɪtɪŋ/ ADJECTIVE
1 making someone very shocked and upset □ devastating news
2 causing a lot of damage □ devastating floods

develop /dɪ'veləp/ VERB [develops, developing, developed]
1 to grow or change, or to make something grow bigger, better or more advanced □ The young animals develop very quickly. □ **+ into** The eggs develop into adult insects. □ There are plans to develop tourism in the area. □ The process has developed over time.
2 to design and create something new □ Researchers are developing new technologies. □ We need to develop strategies to deal with this problem.
3 to start to happen or exist □ The disease develops gradually. □ A close friendship developed between the two women.
4 to make a photograph on a film into a picture

developing /dɪ'veləpɪŋ/ ADJECTIVE
1 a developing country is quite poor and its economy is not very advanced
2 in the process of happening or growing □ We're reporting on two developing news stories.

development /dɪ'veləpmənt/ NOUN [plural developments]
1 when something becomes bigger, better or more advanced 🔁 There has been rapid economic development. □ **+ of** The condition affects the normal development of the brain.
2 when something new is created □ **+ of** This research may aid the development of new treatments. □ The project is still in the early stages of development. 🔁 New developments in mobile phone technology have made communication easier.

device /dɪ'vaɪs/ NOUN [plural devices] a tool or piece of equipment □ a device for cleaning keyboards

➤ **THESAURUS:** A tool is a thing that you use to do a particular job. Hammers and drills are tools. A device is a tool or a piece of equipment that you use to do something. For example, a remote control is a device for changing the television channel. An instrument is a tool that you use for doing a particular task, particularly in science or medicine.

devil /'devəl/ NOUN [plural devils]
1 the Devil the most powerful evil spirit in some religions
2 an evil spirit

devise /dɪ'vaɪz/ VERB [devises, devising, devised] to design a plan or way of doing something 🔁 We need to devise a plan. 🔁 He devised a method of measuring earthquakes.

devote /dɪ'vəʊt/
♦ PHRASAL VERB [devotes, devoting, devoted]
devote yourself to someone/something to give all your time and interest to someone or something □ She devoted herself to helping the poor.

diabetes /ˌdaɪə'biːtiːz/ NOUN, NO PLURAL a serious illness in which your body cannot control the amount of sugar in your blood

diagnose /'daɪəgnəʊz/ VERB [diagnoses, diagnosing, diagnosed] to decide what is wrong with a person or a piece of equipment □ She was diagnosed with cancer last year. □ It's important to diagnose the disease early. □ An engineer diagnosed the problem and fixed it.

diagram /'daɪəgræm/ NOUN [plural diagrams] a drawing that explains something 🔁 He drew a diagram of the building.

dial¹ /'daɪəl/ NOUN [plural dials]
1 the round part on a clock or a machine that shows the time or a measurement
2 a round control on a radio or other machine that you turn to operate it □ I turned the radio dial.

dial² /'daɪəl/ VERB [dials, dialling/US dialing, dialled/US dialed] to call a telephone number 🔁 She picked up the phone and dialled the number. □ In an emergency, dial 999.

➤ **THESAURUS:** When you dial a telephone number, you put the number into your telephone and start making a call. If you call someone, ring someone, or phone someone, you make a telephone call to them. These words all have the same meaning. When you put the phone down at the end of your conversation, you hang up.

dialogue /'daɪəlɒg/ NOUN [plural dialogues] the words or conversation of characters in a book, film, etc.

diameter /daɪˈæmɪtə(r)/ NOUN [plural diameters] a straight line from one side of a circle to the other through its centre, or this measurement. A mathematics word □ the diameter of the pipe

diamond /ˈdaɪəmənd/ NOUN [plural diamonds]
1 a very hard, clear stone that is very valuable □ a diamond ring
2 a four-sided pointed shape (♦)
3 diamonds one of the four types of playing card, with a diamond symbol printed on them □ the eight of diamonds

diaper /ˈdaɪəpə(r)/ NOUN [plural diapers] the US word for **nappy**

diary /ˈdaɪərɪ/ NOUN [plural diaries] a book with spaces for all the dates of the year where you can write things down □ I've put the appointment in my diary. □ I'll check my diary. ⊞ He kept a diary.

dice /daɪs/ NOUN [plural dice] a small object with six square sides with different numbers of small round marks on each side that you use in games ⊞ Each player rolls the dice.

dictate /dɪkˈteɪt/ VERB [dictates, dictating, dictated] to say words for someone to write down □ I have to type the letters that my boss dictates.

dictation /dɪkˈteɪʃən/ NOUN [plural dictations] a piece of text that a teacher reads for students to write down, or the process of doing this

dictator /dɪkˈteɪtə(r)/ NOUN [plural dictators] a person who has complete power over a country □ a fascist dictator

dictionary /ˈdɪkʃənərɪ/ NOUN [plural dictionaries] a book that gives words in alphabetical order and their meanings □ a French dictionary □ + of a dictionary of medical terms

did /dɪd/ PAST TENSE OF **do**

didn't /ˈdɪdənt/ a short way to say and write 'did not'

die /daɪ/ VERB [dies, dying, died]
1 to stop living □ Her father died suddenly at the age of 56. □ Six people died in the crash. □ + of He died of heart failure. □ + from He was taken to hospital, but died from his injuries.
2 to disappear or stop existing □ My love for him will never die.
♦ IDIOM be dying for something/to do something an informal phrase meaning you want to have something or do something very much and you do not want to wait □ I'm dying for a cold drink. □ The kids were dying to get outside.
♦ PHRASAL VERB **die down** to gradually become quieter or less active □ She waited until the applause had died down. □ All the attention seems to have died down now.

diesel /ˈdiːzəl/ NOUN, NO PLURAL a heavy type of oil that is used as fuel

diet¹ /ˈdaɪət/ NOUN [plural diets]
1 the food that a person eats ⊞ Do you have a healthy diet? ⊞ You need to eat a balanced diet. □ + of They live on a basic diet of rice and beans.
2 a limited amount or range of foods that someone eats, for example to lose weight ⊞ Maybe you need to go on a diet.

diet² /ˈdaɪət/ VERB [diets, dieting, dieted] to eat less food in order to lose weight □ I've never dieted, but I do do a lot of exercise.

differ /ˈdɪfə(r)/ VERB [differs, differing, differed] to not be the same as something else □ + from His working methods differ from other TV producers. □ + in The males and females differ in size.

difference /ˈdɪfrəns/ NOUN [plural differences]
1 the way in which two people or things are not the same □ + between Is there a difference between male and female players? □ + in There was a difference in the children's behaviour. ⊞ There are big differences between the two cultures. ⊞ They don't know the difference between right and wrong.
2 make a difference to have an effect on something □ + to This will make a difference to people's lives. □ Working harder didn't make any difference – we still couldn't manage.

different /ˈdɪfrənt/ ADJECTIVE not the same as someone or something else □ + from He seems quite different from the rest of the boys. □ + in The two girls are very different in appearance and personality. ⊞ Each case is completely different. □ We listen to different types of music.

difficult /ˈdɪfɪkəlt/ ADJECTIVE
1 not easy to do or understand □ That's a very difficult question. □ + to do something It's becoming increasingly difficult to find a parking space. □ + for It's difficult for anyone to understand. ⊞ Many people are finding it difficult to get jobs.
2 not friendly or easy to please □ a difficult customer

difficulty /ˈdɪfɪkəltɪ/ NOUN, NO PLURAL when something is difficult to do or understand □ You should be able to do this without difficulty. □ + ing She has difficulty sleeping. □ + in He was having difficulty in breathing. □ + with My grandmother now has difficulty with everyday tasks. ⊞ With great difficulty, he managed to pull himself out of the water.

dig /dɪg/ VERB [digs, digging, dug]
1 to make a hole, especially in the ground ⊞ They dug a hole in the snow. □ They're digging a tunnel.
2 to lift up and turn over soil with a spade (= tool with a flat, metal part that you push into the soil) □ He's digging in the garden.
♦ PHRASAL VERB **dig something up** to remove

something from under the ground by digging □ *We dug up some vegetables.*

> ► THESAURUS: If you dig, you make a hole, usually in the ground. For example, you might dig in your garden when you are planting something. When you scoop, you lift something in your curved hands, or with a spoon or similar tool. You might scoop ice cream out of a container, for example. When someone digs a big hole in the ground in order to get something out, we use the word mine. You mine diamonds and coal, for example.

digest /daɪˈdʒest/ VERB [digests, digesting, digested] when the body digests food, it changes it into substances that it can use 🔂 *Bacteria in the stomach help to digest food.*

digital /ˈdɪdʒɪtəl/ ADJECTIVE
1 storing information, sounds and pictures as sets of numbers or electronic signals 🔂 *a digital camera* 🔂 *a digital radio* 🔂 *There's been a growth in digital music sales.*
2 a digital clock or watch shows the time as numbers

dignity /ˈdɪɡnəti/ NOUN, NO PLURAL calm, controlled behaviour, especially in a difficult situation □ *She showed great dignity through a difficult period.*

dilemma /dɪˈlemə/ NOUN [plural dilemmas] when you have to decide which of two or more things to do and you are finding this decision difficult 🔂 *I'm in a dilemma over whether to go or not.* 🔂 *a moral dilemma*

dim /dɪm/ ADJECTIVE [dimmer, dimmest] not bright or clear 🔂 *We couldn't see much in the dim light.* □ *I made my way along the dim corridor.*

diminish /dɪˈmɪnɪʃ/ VERB [diminishes, diminishing, diminished] to become less or smaller, or to make something less or smaller □ *I don't want to diminish the importance of this meeting.* □ *Recently, their power has diminished.*

dine /daɪn/ VERB [dines, dining, dined] to eat dinner (= main meal). A formal word □ *They regularly dine at the best restaurants.*

dining room /ˈdaɪnɪŋ ˌruːm/ NOUN [plural dining rooms] the room in a house or hotel where you have your meals

dinner /ˈdɪnə(r)/ NOUN [plural dinners] a main meal in the evening or in the middle of the day □ *We had fish for dinner.* 🔂 *We sat down to eat dinner.* 🔂 *Alice is cooking dinner.*

dinosaur /ˈdaɪnəsɔː(r)/ NOUN [plural dinosaurs] a very large type of animal that lived millions of years ago and no longer exists

dip /dɪp/ VERB [dips, dipping, dipped] to put something in and out of a liquid quickly □ *Dip the clothes in the dye.* □ *She dipped a toe into the water.*

diploma /dɪˈpləʊmə/ NOUN [plural diplomas] a qualification that someone can study for in a particular subject □ *+ in* *She has a diploma in Journalism Studies.*

dire /ˈdaɪə(r)/ ADJECTIVE very bad, serious or extreme 🔂 *a dire warning* 🔂 *These people are in dire need of help.* 🔂 *If these spending cuts go ahead, they will have dire consequences.*

direct¹ /dɪˈrekt/ ADJECTIVE
1 straight from one place to another 🔂 *It's the shortest, most direct route.* 🔂 *a direct flight between London and Beijing*
2 involving two people or things with nothing else between 🔂 *We had no direct contact with Mr Ellis.* 🔂 *They found a direct link between computer usage and back pain.*

direct² /dɪˈrekt/ VERB [directs, directing, directed]
1 to tell the actors in a film or play what to do 🔂 *The film was directed by Clint Eastwood.* □ *She directed the new production of the musical.*
2 to tell someone how to get somewhere □ *Could you direct me to the post office, please?*

direction /dɪˈrekʃən/ NOUN [plural directions]
1 the place or point a thing or person is going or facing towards □ *In which direction was she going – towards town or away?* □ *+ of* *He pointed in the direction of the kitchen.* 🔂 *The bus was travelling in the opposite direction.* 🔂 *They all walked off in different directions.* 🔂 *The wind has changed direction.*
2 directions instructions for getting somewhere or doing something 🔂 *I followed his directions as we drove out of town.* □ *Make sure you read the directions for use carefully.*

> ► THESAURUS: A direction is the place or point a thing or person is moving or pointing towards. Your route is the way you take to get somewhere. So, a bus route is the roads that the bus uses to get from the start to the end of its journey. Way is a more general word, which can have a similar meaning to direction: □ *Which way did she go? North or south?*, or a similar meaning to route: □ *What is the best way to get to the station?* Note that in English, the surface that vehicles travel on is called a road.

directly /dɪˈrektli/ ADVERB with no other person or thing between or involved □ *It plugs directly into your computer.* □ *Did you talk directly to him?* 🔂 *He wasn't directly involved in the project.* 🔂 *She wasn't directly responsible for the error.*

direct object /dɪˌrekt ˈɒbdʒɪkt/ NOUN [plural direct objects] the noun or pronoun that is affected by the action of a verb. For example, in *He gave the boy a book*, the direct object is *a book*.

director /dɪˌrektə(r)/ NOUN [plural directors]
1 the manager of a business, organization or department □ **+ of** the director of the CIA ⊞ the institute's executive director ⊞ the supermarket's finance director
2 someone who makes a film or organizes a stage show ⊞ a Hollywood film director □ **+ of** She's the artistic director of the Sydney Theatre Company.

directory /dɪˈrektərɪ/ NOUN [plural directories]
a book containing an alphabetical list of names, numbers or other information ⊞ a telephone directory

direct speech /dɪˌrekt ˈspiːtʃ/ NOUN, NO PLURAL in a story or report, the exact words that a person said

dirt /dɜːt/ NOUN, NO PLURAL any substance that is not clean or that makes something become not clean □ Rinse under water to remove any dirt. □ She brushed the dirt from the surface.

dirty /ˈdɜːtɪ/ ADJECTIVE [dirtier, dirtiest] not clean □ dirty hands □ I cleared all the dirty dishes. ⊞ Try not to get your clothes dirty. ⊞ a pile of dirty laundry

disability /ˌdɪsəˈbɪlətɪ/ NOUN [plural disabilities]
a physical or mental problem that makes some parts of life difficult ⊞ a physical disability □ Buildings should be accessible to people with disabilities.

disabled[1] /dɪsˈeɪbəld/ ADJECTIVE having a disability ⊞ We provide support for disabled people. ⊞ Our son is severely disabled.

disabled[2] /dɪsˈeɪbəld/ NOUN the disabled people who are disabled

disadvantage /ˌdɪsədˈvɑːntɪdʒ/ NOUN [plural disadvantages] something that makes something less attractive, less successful or more difficult □ **+ of** The only disadvantage of the plan is that it could be too expensive. □ The advantages outweigh the disadvantages.

disagree /ˌdɪsəˈɡriː/ VERB [disagrees, disagreeing, disagreed] to have a different opinion from someone else about something □ **+ with** I completely disagree with you about that. □ **+ about** Doctors disagree about how effective the treatment is. □ **+ over** Ministers disagree over who is to blame. □ **+ on** They disagree on almost everything.
♦ PHRASAL VERB **disagree with something** to disapprove of something □ Many people disagree with the death penalty.

disagreement /ˌdɪsəˈɡriːmənt/ NOUN [plural disagreements] when people have different opinions or argue ⊞ We've had several disagreements on this subject. □ There are still some areas of disagreement. □ **+ between** There was some disagreement between John and Robert. □ **+ over** There are disagreements over money.

disappear /ˌdɪsəˈpɪə(r)/ VERB [disappears, disappearing, disappeared]
1 if someone or something disappears, they go somewhere where they cannot be seen or found □ **+ from** The woman disappeared from her home in April. □ He disappeared into the crowd. □ The car disappeared down the street.
2 to stop existing □ The symptoms usually disappear within a couple of days. □ Finally the light disappeared altogether.

disappoint /ˌdɪsəˈpɔɪnt/ VERB [disappoints, disappointing, disappointed] to make someone feel unhappy because something is not how they had hoped or expected □ I'm sorry to disappoint you, but I can't come to your party. □ We don't want to disappoint our fans.

disappointed /ˌdɪsəˈpɔɪntɪd/ ADJECTIVE
unhappy because something is not how you had hoped or expected □ **+ that** I'm disappointed that he can't come. □ **+ with** I'm very disappointed with the result.

disappointing /ˌdɪsəˈpɔɪntɪŋ/ ADJECTIVE not as good as you hoped or expected ⊞ It was a disappointing performance by the team. □ It's extremely disappointing that we haven't made any progress.

disappointment /ˌdɪsəˈpɔɪntmənt/ NOUN [plural disappointments] a feeling of being disappointed or something that makes you disappointed ⊞ The hotel was a big disappointment. ⊞ She expressed her disappointment at the decision.

disapproval /ˌdɪsəˈpruːvəl/ NOUN, NO PLURAL when you think something is bad, wrong or not suitable □ **+ of** She ignored the disapproval of her family. ⊞ His parents expressed their disapproval of the planned marriage.

disapprove /ˌdɪsəˈpruːv/ VERB [disapproves, disapproving, disapproved] to think that something or someone is bad, wrong or not suitable □ **+ of** My parents definitely disapproved of my new friend. □ We were wearing short skirts and he clearly disapproved.

disaster /dɪˈzɑːstə(r)/ NOUN [plural disasters]
something that causes a lot of damage, injuries or deaths ⊞ They help victims of natural disasters such as earthquakes. ⊞ The flight had just taken off when disaster struck.

disc /dɪsk/ NOUN [plural discs]
1 something flat and round □ a small metal disc □ a disc of yellow plastic
2 a record (= flat plastic object with music recorded on it) or CD (= small flat metal object with music or information recorded on it)

discard /dɪˈskɑːd/ VERB [discards, discarding, discarded] to throw something away □ a discarded wrapper □ Discard the herbs before serving.

discipline[1] /'dɪsɪplɪn/ NOUN, NO PLURAL when people are made to obey rules and behave in a particular way □ We're concerned about the lack of discipline in the school.

discipline[2] /'dɪsɪplɪn/ VERB [disciplines, disciplining, disciplined] to punish someone □ Parents were asked how they discipline their children.

disc jockey /'dɪsk ˌdʒɒkɪ/ NOUN [plural disc jockeys] someone who plays recorded music on the radio or at a club

disco /'dɪskəʊ/ NOUN [plural discos] a place or party where people dance to recorded music

discount /'dɪskaʊnt/ NOUN [plural discounts] a reduction in the price of something □ + on There's a 10% discount on all goods. 🖻 I got a £5 discount. 🖻 The company offers discounts to students.

discourage /dɪ'skʌrɪdʒ/ VERB [discourages, discouraging, discouraged] to try to stop something happening or to persuade someone not to do something □ They introduced new laws to discourage smoking. □ We want to discourage people from driving into the city centre.

discover /dɪ'skʌvə(r)/ VERB [discovers, discovering, discovered] to find information, a place or an object, especially for the first time □ The settlers discovered gold in the mountains. □ The man's body was discovered yesterday. □ She finally discovered the truth. □ + that We discovered that the paint wouldn't mix with water. □ + question word Scientists hope to discover why numbers of the birds have dropped.

discovery /dɪ'skʌvərɪ/ NOUN [plural discoveries] when someone discovers something, or the thing they discover □ + of the discovery of America 🖻 He made a surprising discovery.

discriminate /dɪs'krɪmɪneɪt/ VERB [discriminates, discriminating, discriminated] to treat someone unfairly because of their colour, religion, sex, etc. □ Some employers were accused of discriminating against women.

discrimination /dɪsˌkrɪmɪ'neɪʃən/ NOUN, NO PLURAL treating people unfairly because of their colour, religion, sex, etc. 🖻 racial discrimination 🖻 They have suffered discrimination.

discuss /dɪs'kʌs/ VERB [discusses, discussing, discussed] to talk about something □ You should try to discuss these issues with your wife. □ + question word We have been discussing what to do.

> ► Note that when you use the verb **discuss**, you must say what you are discussing:
> ✓ I must discuss the problem with Angela.
> ✗ I must discuss with Angela.

discussion /dɪs'kʌʃən/ NOUN [plural discussions] when people discuss something □ + about We got into a discussion about politics. □ + between There have been weeks of discussion between US and Chinese officials. 🖻 The two sides have agreed to hold discussions next week.

disease /dɪ'ziːz/ NOUN [plural diseases] an illness 🖻 He developed heart disease. 🖻 The infection can cause liver disease.

> ► THESAURUS: Disease and illness are similar in meaning, but disease is more general. A disease can affect a person, an animal or a plant. An illness affects a person. An infection is a disease that is caused by bacteria or a virus. For example, you might have an ear infection or a skin infection. The word sickness is usually used in a general way. For example you can say that someone has time off work because of sickness (the person may have several different illnesses or infections).

disgrace[1] /dɪs'greɪs/ NOUN, NO PLURAL
1 when someone loses respect because of something they have done □ It's no disgrace to come last if you tried hard. □ You have brought disgrace to your family.
2 in disgrace if you are in disgrace, other people are angry with you □ Debbie's in disgrace for staying out all night.

disgrace[2] /dɪs'greɪs/ VERB [disgraces, disgracing, disgraced] to lose other people's respect because of your behaviour □ I disgraced myself and my family.

disgraceful /dɪs'greɪsful/ ADJECTIVE very bad or shocking 🖻 Their behaviour was absolutely disgraceful.
• **disgracefully** /dɪs'greɪsfulɪ/ ADVERB very badly □ They treated him disgracefully.

disguise[1] /dɪs'ɡaɪz/ NOUN [plural disguises] something you wear to change your appearance so that people do not recognize you □ He left the hotel in disguise.

disguise[2] /dɪs'ɡaɪz/ VERB [disguises, disguising, disguised] to make something or someone look, sound or seem like something or someone else □ He had a bomb disguised as a laptop computer. □ She disguised herself as a tourist.

disgust[1] /dɪs'ɡʌst/ NOUN, NO PLURAL a strong feeling that you do not like or approve of something □ The sight of the worms filled Luisa with disgust.

disgust[2] /dɪs'ɡʌst/ VERB [disgusts, disgusting, disgusted] to make someone feel disgust □ They were disgusted by what they saw. □ It disgusts me that people can behave that way.

disgusting /dɪs'ɡʌstɪŋ/ ADJECTIVE extremely bad or unpleasant □ a disgusting mess 🖻 It tasted absolutely disgusting. □ disgusting behaviour

dish /dɪʃ/ NOUN [plural dishes]
1 a plate or bowl for food □ Cover the dish with a

lid. 🖃 *a pile of dirty dishes* 🖃 *I'll wash the dishes.*
2 food that has been prepared for eating □ *a fish dish* 🖃 *The restaurant serves traditional dishes.*

dishonest /dɪs'ɒnɪst/ ADJECTIVE not telling the truth, or doing things that are wrong or illegal □ *I didn't do anything dishonest.* □ *It would be dishonest to hide it from him.*

dishwasher /'dɪʃwɒʃə(r)/ NOUN [plural dishwashers] a machine for washing things such as plates, cups, etc. after a meal

disk /dɪsk/ NOUN [plural disks]
1 a round flat object that computers use to store information on. A computing word □ *Insert a disk into drive D.* 🖃 *It requires at least 600MB of disk space.*
2 the US spelling of **disc**

dislike[1] /dɪs'laɪk/ VERB [dislikes, disliking, disliked] to not like someone or something □ *She disliked the idea of the children travelling alone.* □ *He disliked dentists intensely.* □ *+ ing I dislike getting up early.*

dislike[2] /dɪs'laɪk/ NOUN [plural dislikes] something you dislike or the feeling of disliking something or someone □ *He had a dislike of crowds.* 🖃 *They took an instant dislike to each other.*

dismay /dɪs'meɪ/ NOUN, NO PLURAL an unpleasant feeling of surprise and worry □ *We watched in dismay as Ted fell into the water.* 🖃 *To her dismay, she found her foot was stuck.* 🖃 *Campaigners expressed dismay at the decision.*

dismiss /dɪs'mɪs/ VERB [dismisses, dismissing, dismissed]
1 to make someone leave their job □ *She was dismissed for misconduct.* □ *He was dismissed from the army.*
2 to send someone away □ *The class were dismissed by the teacher early today.*

> ➤ **THESAURUS:** If you fire someone, you tell someone that they must leave their job. Dismiss has a similar meaning to fire, but is more formal. You can also say that someone gets the sack. These words are all used when someone has done something wrong or if their work is not good enough.

dispatch /dɪ'spætʃ/ VERB [dispatches, dispatching, dispatched] a formal word meaning to send something or someone somewhere □ *The parcel was dispatched on the 29th.* □ *The navy dispatched a helicopter to help in the search.*

display[1] /dɪ'spleɪ/ NOUN [plural displays]
1 things which are arranged or presented for people to look at □ *+ of a display of the children's work* 🖃 *a fireworks display*
2 on display arranged for people to look at □ *The painting is on display at the National Gallery.*

display[2] /dɪ'spleɪ/ VERB [displays, displaying, displayed] to arrange things for people to look at □ *The treasure will be displayed in the museum for two months.* □ *All offices must display no smoking signs.*

disposal /dɪ'spəʊzəl/ NOUN, NO PLURAL getting rid of something 🖃 *We are using new methods of waste disposal.* □ *There are strict regulations about the disposal of chemicals.*

dispose /dɪ'spəʊz/
◆ PHRASAL VERB [disposes, disposing, disposed]
dispose of something to get rid of something □ *Where can I dispose of my old fridge?*

dispute[1] /dɪ'spjuːt/ NOUN [plural disputes] a serious disagreement about something □ *They went on strike in a dispute over pay.* 🖃 *They are trying to resolve their dispute.*

dispute[2] /dɪ'spjuːt/ VERB [disputes, disputing, disputed] to say that something is not true or correct □ *They dispute that they have been treated fairly.*

disrupt /dɪs'rʌpt/ VERB [disrupts, disrupting, disrupted] to stop something continuing as usual □ *Traffic was disrupted because of the march.*

dissolve /dɪ'zɒlv/ VERB [dissolves, dissolving, dissolved] to melt or be melted in liquid □ *Keep stirring until the sugar dissolves completely.* □ *Stir to dissolve the sugar.*

> ➤ **THESAURUS:** If a solid dissolves, it disappears when you mix it with water. Salt and sugar dissolve in water. If something melts, or if you melt it, it changes from a solid to a liquid when you heat it. Snow melts in the sun, and you can melt butter in a pan. If you soften something, or if it softens, it becomes soft, but not liquid. You can soften butter by keeping it out of the fridge.

distance /'dɪstəns/ NOUN [plural distances]
1 the space between things □ *+ between Measure the distance between the lines.* □ *+ from The hotel is only a short distance from the city centre.* 🖃 *He doesn't like driving long distances.*
2 in the distance if you see or hear something in the distance you see or hear it but it is a long way away □ *I could hear the sound of a train in the distance.*

distant /'dɪstənt/ ADJECTIVE far away in space or time □ *He heard distant voices which were getting closer.* 🖃 *The holiday seems like a distant memory now.* 🖃 *the distant past*

distinct /dɪ'stɪŋkt/ ADJECTIVE
1 easy to see, hear, smell etc. □ *Green tea has a distinct flavour.*
2 different □ *The two languages are quite distinct.*

distinguish /dɪ'stɪŋgwɪʃ/ VERB [distinguishes, distinguishing, distinguished] to see a difference between things □ *If you're colour blind, you have difficulties distinguishing green from red.*

distract /dɪ'strækt/ VERB [distracts, distracting, distracted] to take someone's attention away from something □ *Advertisements at the side of the road can distract drivers.*

distress /dɪ'stres/ NOUN, NO PLURAL when someone is upset □ *I didn't want to cause them any distress.*

distressing /dɪ'stresɪŋ/ ADJECTIVE making someone feel very upset □ *It has been a very distressing time for me and my family.*

distribute /dɪ'strɪbjuːt/ VERB [distributes, distributing, distributed] to give something to a lot of people or places □ *Please distribute the leaflets to your friends.* □ *The company manufactures and distributes drinks.*

distribution /ˌdɪstrɪ'bjuːʃən/ NOUN, NO PLURAL the process of giving something to a group of people □ *He organized the distribution of food among the refugees.*

district /'dɪstrɪkt/ NOUN [plural districts] a part of a country or city □ *Shanghai's business district*

disturb /dɪ'stɜːb/ VERB [disturbs, disturbing, disturbed]
1 to interrupt what someone is doing □ *I'm sorry to disturb you, but I need to ask you a question.*
2 to upset or worry someone □ *The incident disturbed him.*
3 to move something and change its position □ *Someone had disturbed the papers at my desk.*

ditch /dɪtʃ/ NOUN [plural ditches] a long narrow hole at the side of a field or road

dive¹ /daɪv/ VERB [dives, diving, dived]
1 to jump into water with your arms and head first □ *+ into Sasha dived into the pool.*
2 to swim under water using special equipment
• **diver** /'daɪvə(r)/ NOUN [plural divers] someone who swims under water using special equipment

dive² /daɪv/ NOUN [plural dives]
1 a jump into water with your arms and head first
2 a time when you swim under water using special equipment

diverse /daɪ'vɜːs/ ADJECTIVE of very different types □ *He has appeared in a diverse range of films.*

diversion /daɪ'vɜːʃən/ NOUN [plural diversions] a different route for traffic because the usual one is closed

diversity /daɪ'vɜːsəti/ NOUN, NO PLURAL when there are many different types of people or things □ *Australia's cultural diversity*

divert /daɪ'vɜːt/ VERB [diverts, diverting, diverted] to make something go in a different direction □ *Traffic was diverted because of an accident.*

divide /dɪ'vaɪd/ VERB [divides, dividing, divided]
1 to separate into parts, or to separate something into parts □ *+ into Divide the class into teams of five.* □ *The cell divides and becomes two cells.*
2 to separate something and give a part of it to several people □ *+ up They divided up the money.* □ *+ between She divided the cake between the children.*
3 to find how many times one number contains another number. A mathematics word □ *+ by If you divide 12 by 3, you get 4.* □ *12 divided by 3 is 4.*

divine /dɪ'vaɪn/ ADJECTIVE coming from God, or to do with God □ *divine punishment*

division /dɪ'vɪʒən/ NOUN [plural divisions]
1 no plural the process of separating people or things into groups or parts □ *cell division*
2 no plural the way something is shared between people □ *+ of We need a more equal division of power between governments.*
3 no plural when you calculate how many times one number contains another number. A mathematics word.
4 a group within a large organization □ *He heads the company's sales and marketing division.*

divorce¹ /dɪ'vɔːs/ NOUN [plural divorces] the legal ending of a marriage 🔁 *We're getting a divorce.*

divorce² /dɪ'vɔːs/ VERB [divorces, divorcing, divorced] to end your marriage legally □ *His parents divorced when he was six.* □ *Julia is divorcing her husband.*

DIY /ˌdiːaɪ'waɪ/ ABBREVIATION do-it-yourself; when you make or repair things in the home yourself □ *DIY stores*

dizzy /'dɪzi/ ADJECTIVE [dizzier, dizziest] feeling as if everything around you is moving and you are going to fall 🔁 *You'll get dizzy if you spin round like that.*

DJ /ˌdiː'dʒeɪ/ ABBREVIATION disc jockey; someone who plays music in a club or on the radio

do¹ /duː/ AUXILIARY VERB [does, doing, did, done]
1 used with another verb to make questions and negative sentences □ *Do you want another drink?* □ *I don't* (= do not) *like her husband.* □ *She doesn't* (= does not) *play tennis.*
2 used to avoid repeating a verb □ *'I love chocolate'. 'So do I'.* □ *They spent a lot more money than I did.*
3 used to emphasize the main verb □ *I do love Paris.* □ *She does want to come, but she's very busy.*
4 used at the end of a sentence to make it into a question □ *Lucy goes to this school, doesn't she?*

► Notice that instead of **do not**, people often say or write the short form **don't** and instead of **does not**, people often say or write the short form **doesn't**.

do² /duː/ VERB [does, doing, did, done]
1 to perform an action □ *What are you doing?* □ *Make sure you do your homework.* □ *What does your mother do* (= what is her job)? □ **+ with** *What have you done with the map* (= where is it)?
2 to study a subject □ *I'm doing English and French.*
3 do badly/well to make bad/good progress □ *Oleg's doing well with his swimming.*
4 How are you doing? an informal way of asking someone about their health and situation □ *Hi Carlos – how are you doing?*
5 something will do something will be enough or be suitable □ *If you haven't got walking boots, trainers will do.*
6 to do with something connected with something □ *He's writing a book – something to do with astronomy.*
7 someone could do with something someone needs something. An informal phrase □ *I could do with a hot drink.*
♦ PHRASAL VERBS **do something up**
1 to fasten a piece of clothing □ *Do your jacket up.*
2 to repair or decorate a room or building **do without (something)** to manage without something

dock¹ /dɒk/ NOUN [plural docks] the place where ships stop so goods can be taken on and off
dock² /dɒk/ VERB [docks, docking, docked] a ship docks when it goes into a dock

doctor /ˈdɒktə(r)/ NOUN [plural doctors]
1 someone whose job is to treat people who are ill 🖫 *You should see a doctor if your symptoms don't improve.* □ *Could I make an appointment with Doctor Kennedy, please?*
2 the doctor's the place where a doctor works □ *Go to the doctor's if your cough isn't any better.*

document /ˈdɒkjʊmənt/ NOUN [plural documents]
1 a paper with official information on it □ *Make sure you have all your travel documents with you.* 🖫 *She had to sign some legal documents.*
2 something that you write and keep on a computer. A computing word 🖫 *How do I open a new document?*

documentary¹ /ˌdɒkjʊ'mentərɪ/ NOUN [plural documentaries] a film or television programme about real people or real events □ *They made a documentary on global warming.*
documentary² /ˌdɒkjʊ'mentərɪ/ ADJECTIVE a documentary programme or film is about real people or real events 🖫 *It's a new documentary series set in a school.*

dodge /dɒdʒ/ VERB [dodges, dodging, dodged]
1 to move quickly to avoid something □ *Graeme managed to dodge out of the way before the ball hit him.*
2 to avoid doing something or talking about something 🖫 *He dodged questions about his private life.*

does /dəz/ VERB the form of the verb **do** that is used with **he, she** and **it**
doesn't /ˈdʌzənt/ a short way to say and write 'does not'

dog /dɒg/ NOUN [plural dogs] an animal with four legs that is kept as a pet, for hunting or for guarding buildings 🖫 *The dog barks whenever anyone comes to the house.* 🖫 *He walks the dog every evening.*

doll /dɒl/ NOUN [plural dolls] a toy in the shape of a person

dollar /ˈdɒlə(r)/ NOUN [plural dollars] the unit of money in many countries including the US, Canada, Australia and New Zealand. The written symbol is $ □ *They've spent millions of dollars on the project.*

dolphin /ˈdɒlfɪn/ NOUN [plural dolphins] an intelligent sea mammal that has grey skin and a long pointed mouth

dome /dəʊm/ NOUN [plural domes] a raised round roof on a building
domestic /də'mestɪk/ ADJECTIVE
1 to do with your home, or happening in your home □ *I hate domestic tasks like cleaning and cooking.* 🖫 *She was the victim of domestic violence.*
2 to do with one particular country and not international □ *the government's domestic policies* 🖫 *At Boston, he took a domestic flight to Seattle.*
3 a domestic animal is kept as a pet or on a farm

dominance /'dɒmɪnəns/ NOUN, NO PLURAL
when someone has more influence, power, and
control than other people □ *The company's
dominance of the home phone market is
declining.*

dominate /'dɒmɪneɪt/ VERB [dominates,
dominating, dominated] to have more influence,
power, or success than others □ *The company
dominates the insurance market.* □ *He dominated to
conversation.*

donate /də'neɪt/ VERB [donates, donating,
donated] to give something, especially money, to
someone who needs it □ *He donated money to a
local charity.*

donation /də'neɪʃən/ NOUN [plural donations]
something, especially money, that you
give to help a person or an organization
□ *He was asked whether he would like to make a
donation.* 🔁 *She made generous donations to
various charities.*

> ➤ THESAURUS: A donation is something,
> especially money, that you give to help a
> person or organization. A **contribution** is
> something that you give or do to help to
> achieve something. You might make
> a **contribution** to a project, or you might
> make a **contribution** of money to help
> to buy something. **Gift** and **present** are
> words to describe a thing that you give
> to someone. For example, you might give
> someone a **gift** or a **present** on their
> birthday.

done /dʌn/ PAST PARTICIPLE OF **do**

donkey /'dɒŋkɪ/ NOUN [plural donkeys] an
animal that looks like a small horse with
long ears

donor /'dəʊnə(r)/ NOUN [plural donors] someone
who gives something to help a person or
organization 🔁 *An anonymous donor has offered
£5,000 to help find the girl's killer.* 🔁 *Blood donors
are urgently needed.*

don't /dəʊnt/ a short way to say and write 'do
not'

door /dɔː(r)/ NOUN [plural doors]
1 the thing you open to get into a building,
room, cupboard or vehicle 🔁 *Janie opened
the door and went in.* 🔁 *She quickly closed
the door.* 🔁 *There was a bell by the front door.*
🔁 *Just go and knock on the door.* □ *She closed the
car door.*
2 the space in a wall where you go into a building or
room □ *He was so fat he could barely get through
the door.*
3 at the door if there is someone at the door,
someone is waiting for you to open the door so they
can come inside □ *Mum, there's someone at the
door.*

doorbell /'dɔːbel/ NOUN [plural doorbells] a
button on the door of a building that you press
to ring a bell to tell the people inside that you are
there

doorway /'dɔːweɪ/ NOUN [plural doorways] the
entrance to a room or building □ *He was standing in
the doorway.*

dose /dəʊs/ NOUN [plural doses] an amount of
medicine that you take at one time 🔁 *You
may get problems if you take a high dose of the
drug.*

dot¹ /dɒt/ NOUN [plural dots]
1 a small round mark
2 the symbol . in an Internet or
email address □ *Is it 'al dot wood?'* (= Is it
'al. wood?')

dot² /dɒt/ VERB [dots, dotting, dotted]
if a large area is dotted with things, there
are a lot of them with spaces between
each thing □ *The hillside was dotted with
sheep.*

double¹ /'dʌbəl/ ADJECTIVE
1 twice as much or twice as many
□ *He was given a double dose of
medicine.*
2 having or involving two parts or things which are
the same □ *double doors* □ *She's a double Olympic
medallist.*
3 suitable for two people 🔁 *It costs £100 a night for
a double room.*
4 used when you are saying that a particular
number or letter is repeated □ *You spell 'marry' m-
a-double-r-y.*

double² /'dʌbəl/ DETERMINER twice as big or
twice as much □ *She earns double the amount
I do.*

double³ /'dʌbəl/ VERB [doubles, doubling,
doubled] to become twice as big, or to make
something become twice as big □ *+ in*
The shares have doubled in value. □ *The
drug doubles your risk of having a heart
attack.*

doubt¹ /daʊt/ NOUN [plural doubts]
1 a feeling of not being certain about
something 🔁 *Leo had serious doubts about
the plan.* 🔁 *I have no doubt that you will
succeed.*
2 be in doubt if something is in doubt,
it is not certain that it will succeed or
continue to exist □ *His future at the club
is in doubt.*
3 no doubt used for emphasizing that something
seems very certain □ *No doubt he'll be late as
usual.*

doubt² /daʊt/ VERB [doubts, doubting, doubted]
to think that something is probably not true or will

probably not happen □ + *that* *I doubt that he will agree.* 🔁 *'Do you think Rebecca will come?' ' I doubt it'*.

doubtful /'dautfʊl/ ADJECTIVE probably not true, or probably not going to happen 🔁 *It's doubtful whether she'll take the job.*

dough /dəʊ/ NOUN, NO PLURAL a mixture of flour and water for making bread

dove /dʌv/ NOUN [plural doves] a white bird, used as a sign of peace

down¹ /daʊn/ ADVERB
1 towards or in a lower position □ *He was sitting down.* □ *She bent down to speak to the child.* □ *I'll put the box down here.*
2 to a smaller size, amount or level □ *He cut the picture down to fit the frame.* □ *Can you turn the television down, please?*
3 along □ *I'm just going down to the post office.*
4 In or towards the south □ *We're driving down from Edinburgh tonight.*

down² /daʊn/ ADJECTIVE
1 unhappy. An informal word □ *You seem a bit down.*
2 if a computer or website is down, it is not working. A computing word □ *I can't book the tickets because the website's down.*

down³ /daʊn/ PREPOSITION
1 towards or in a lower part □ *There were tears running down his face.*
2 along □ *Rachel was walking down the road.*

downhill /ˌdaʊn'hɪl/ ADVERB down a slope □ *The car rolled downhill.*

download¹ /'daʊnləʊd/ VERB [downloads, downloading, downloaded] to copy information, such as pictures or music, onto your computer from the Internet or another computer. A computing word □ *You can download music for free.* □ *The file is downloading now.*

download² /'daʊnləʊd/ NOUN [plural downloads] something that you have copied onto your computer from the Internet or another computer. A computing word.

downstairs¹ ADVERB /ˌdaʊn'steəz/ to or on a lower level of a building 🔁 *He went downstairs to get breakfast.* □ *The kids were all downstairs.*

downstairs² ADJECTIVE /'daʊnˌsteəz/ on a lower level in a building □ *a downstairs bathroom*

downward /'daʊnwəd/ ADJECTIVE towards a lower place or position □ *a downward slope*
downwards /'daʊnwədz/ or **downward** /'daʊnwəd/ ADVERB towards a lower place or position □ *The path winds downwards to the lake.*

dozen /'dʌzən/ NOUN [plural dozens]
1 twelve □ *a dozen eggs* 🔁 *There were about two dozen (= 24) people at the party.* 🔁 *I read half a dozen (= 6) pages.*
2 dozens of something a lot of something. An informal phrase □ *He's been in dozens of films.*

Dr ABBREVIATION doctor. The abbreviation is used in writing □ *Dr Smith*

draft /drɑːft/ VERB [drafts, drafting, drafted] to write something that you will change before you finish it □ *He was drafting a letter to his boss.*

drag /dræg/ VERB [drags, dragging, dragged]
1 to pull something along the ground □ *Thomas came out of school, dragging his school bag behind him.*
2 to move words or pictures on a computer screen by pulling them with a mouse. A computing word.

➤ THESAURUS: Pull is a general word to describe the action of holding something and moving it towards you. If you drag something, you pull it along the ground, often because it is heavy. If you tow something, you pull it along behind you with a rope or a chain. Tow is often used to talk about vehicles. If you tug something, you pull it suddenly and firmly. For example, a child might tug another child's hair.

dragon /'drægən/ NOUN [plural dragons] a big imaginary animal with wings, that breathes fire from its mouth

drain¹ /dreɪn/ VERB [drains, draining, drained]
1 to make the liquid in something flow away □ *They had to drain the tank.* □ *Drain the pasta and serve with the sauce.*
2 if a liquid drains, it flows away □ *She watched the water drain down the sink.*

drain² /dreɪn/ NOUN [plural drains] a pipe or hole that allows waste water to flow away □ *The drain was blocked.*

➤ THESAURUS: A pipe is a metal or plastic tube that water or gas can flow through. A drain is a pipe or a hole that takes waste water away. For example, sinks have a drain, and there are drains in the street to take rain water away. A ditch is a long narrow hole at the side of a road or a field to collect waste water.

drainpipe /'dreɪnpaɪp/ NOUN [plural drainpipes] a pipe on the outside of a building, that takes waste water down into the ground

drama /'drɑːmə/ NOUN [plural dramas]
1 a play at the theatre or on television 🔁 *a TV drama* 🔁 *an Australian drama series*
2 no plural plays and acting in general □ *Dan studied drama at Birmingham University.* 🔁 *She went to drama school.*
3 something exciting which happens 🔁 *They watched the drama unfold (= happen) from her bedroom window.*

dramatic /drə'mætɪk/ ADJECTIVE
1 sudden, exciting or unexpected 🔁 *There has been*

a dramatic increase in the number of exam passes.
🔁 Computers have led to dramatic changes in work
habits. □ He described his dramatic rescue from the
sinking boat.
2 to do with plays and the theatre □ the dramatic
works of an author

drank /dræŋk/ PAST TENSE OF **drink**[1]

draught /drɑːft/ NOUN [plural draughts]
1 a movement of air in a room which feels cold
2 draughts a game for two people who move flat,
round pieces on a board that has black and white
squares on it

draw[1] /drɔː/ VERB [draws, drawing, drew, drawn]
1 to make a picture with a pencil or pen □ Ellie was
drawing. 🔁 She drew a lovely picture of a horse.
2 to pull something from somewhere or pull
something in a particular direction. A literary
word □ He drew a small piece of paper from his
pocket.
3 to score the same number of points as someone
else in a game □ We drew 2-2.
4 draw closer/near to move closer in time or
distance □ As they drew closer she saw a path.
□ Election day is drawing near.
5 draw the curtains to pull curtains so that they
cover a window or do not cover a window
♦ PHRASAL VERB **draw up** if a vehicle draws up, it
stops □ A taxi drew up outside the house.

draw[2] /drɔː/ NOUN [plural draws] a game that
ends with both players or teams having the same
score 🔁 The game ended in a draw.

drawer /drɔː(r)/ NOUN [plural drawers] a part of
a piece of furniture that you pull out and keep things
in 🔁 He opened the drawer and got out some paper.
🔁 The pens are in the top drawer.

drawing /ˈdrɔːɪŋ/ NOUN [plural drawings]
1 a picture done with a pencil or pen 🔁 She did a
few drawings. □ + of a drawing of a house
2 no plural making pictures using a pencil or pen
□ Most children like drawing.

drawn /drɔːn/ PAST PARTICIPLE OF **draw**[1]

dreadful /ˈdredfʊl/ ADJECTIVE very bad □ dreadful
news □ a dreadful film

dream[1] /driːm/ NOUN [plural dreams]
1 the things you think and see in your mind while
you sleep 🔁 I had a very strange dream last night.
□ + about I had a dream about you. 🔁 a bad dream
2 something you hope will happen □ It was always
her dream to go to Hollywood.

dream[2] /driːm/ VERB [dreams, dreaming, dreamt
or dreamed]
1 to think about and see something in your mind
while you sleep □ + that Last night I dreamt that I
was lying on a beach. □ + about I often dream
about flying.

2 to imagine something that you would like to
happen □ + of I've always dreamt of moving to the
coast.

> ► Note that sense 2 of the verb **dream** is
> followed by **of** + the ing-form of the verb:
> ✓ I've always dreamt of owning a restaurant.
> ✗ I've always dreamt to own a restaurant.

dress[1] /dres/ NOUN [plural dresses]
1 a piece of clothing for girls or women like a top
and skirt joined together □ She was wearing a black
dress. 🔁 a wedding dress
2 no plural clothes of a particular type 🔁 The
dancers were wearing traditional Highland
dress.

dress[2] /dres/ VERB [dresses, dressing, dressed]
1 to put clothes on yourself or someone else 🔁 She
got dressed and had breakfast. □ I'll dress the
children.
2 to wear a particular style of clothes □ She always
dresses smartly.

> ► Note that when you put clothes on yourself,
> you **get dressed**:
> ✓ I get dressed in the dark.
> ✗ I dress myself in the dark.

♦ PHRASAL VERB **dress up**
1 to put on clothes that make you look like
someone else □ Oliver is going to dress up as a
pirate. **2** to wear clothes that are more formal than
the clothes you usually wear □ Can I go in jeans, or
do I need to dress up?

dresser /ˈdresə(r)/ NOUN [plural dressers] a piece
of furniture with a cupboard at the bottom and
shelves above for keeping plates on

dressing /ˈdresɪŋ/ NOUN [plural dressings] a
sauce for a salad 🔁 a salad dressing.

drew /druː/ PAST TENSE OF **draw**[1]

dried[1] /draɪd/ PAST TENSE AND PAST PARTICIPLE OF
dry[2] □ Jill dried the glasses with a soft cloth.

dried[2] /draɪd/ ADJECTIVE dried food or flowers
have had the water taken out of them 🔁 dried fruit
□ dried herbs

drift /drɪft/ VERB [drifts, drifting, drifted] to move
with a current of water or air □ Smoke drifted over
the city.

drill[1] /drɪl/ NOUN [plural drills] a tool for making
holes in something hard, such as stone □ an electric
drill

drill[2] /drɪl/ VERB [drills, drilling, drilled] to make a
hole in something hard 🔁 She drilled a hole in the
wall. □ They had to drill through rock.

drink[1] /drɪŋk/ VERB [drinks, drinking, drank, drunk]
1 to swallow a liquid □ *I drink a lot of coffee.* 🔊 *I'll get you something to drink.*
2 to drink alcohol □ *Mark doesn't drink.*

► **THESAURUS:** If you swallow food or drink, you make it go down your throat. Drink is a general word for swallowing a liquid. If you sip, you drink something slowly, taking only a small amount at a time. For example, you might sip a drink which is very hot.

drink[2] /drɪŋk/ NOUN [plural drinks] a liquid that you swallow 🔊 *Can I have a drink, please?* □ *+ of* Would you like a drink of water?

drip /drɪp/ VERB [drips, dripping, dripped]
1 if a liquid drips, it falls in drops □ *Water was dripping from the trees.*
2 to produce drops of liquid □ *I can hear a tap dripping somewhere.*

► **THESAURUS:** If a liquid drips, it falls in small drops. If a liquid splashes, or if you splash it, it hits something with a quick movement, often making a noise. Children enjoy splashing in water, and you might splash water on your face. If a liquid trickles, it flows in a slow, thin stream. For example, blood might trickle down your arm if you cut yourself. If a liquid or gas leaks, it escapes from the place where it should be. For example, a pipe might leak in your house.

drive[1] /draɪv/ VERB [drives, driving, drove, driven] to make a car, bus, etc. move and control where it goes and how fast it moves □ *Can you drive?* □ *I had to drive my mother's car.* □ *We drove to Spain.* □ *She drove me to the airport.*

drive[2] /draɪv/ NOUN [plural drives]
1 a journey in a car 🔊 *We went for a drive in the country.* 🔊 *He began the long drive home.* □ *It's a two-hour drive to the coast.*

2 an area in front of a house where you can put your car □ *There were two cars on the drive.*
3 a part of a computer that stores information. A computing word □ *The PC has a standard DVD drive.*

driven /ˈdrɪvən/ PAST PARTICIPLE OF **drive**[1]

driver /ˈdraɪvə(r)/ NOUN [plural drivers] a person who drives a car, etc. □ *a taxi driver* □ *She's a good driver.*

driving /ˈdraɪvɪŋ/ NOUN, NO PLURAL when you drive a car, etc. or the way that you drive 🔊 *Jane's having driving lessons.* □ *He was arrested for dangerous driving.*

driving licence /ˈdraɪvɪŋ ˌlaɪsəns/ NOUN [plural driving licences] an official document that shows you are allowed to drive □ *He didn't have a driving licence.* 🔊 *A clean driving licence (= showing that you have never done anything wrong while driving) is essential for the job.*

droop /druːp/ VERB [droops, drooping, drooped] to hang down □ *The flowers were starting to droop.* □ *Her head drooped slightly forwards.*

drop[1] /drɒp/ VERB [drops, dropping, dropped]
1 to fall to the ground, or to allow something to fall to the ground □ *She tripped and dropped her glass.* □ *The ball dropped into the hole.*
2 to change to a lower level or amount □ *The temperature drops at night.* □ *+ from* The exam pass rate has dropped from 75% to 60%.
3 if you drop someone somewhere, you take them there in your car, and then drive somewhere else yourself □ *I'll drop you at the doctor's on my way to the supermarket.*
♦ **PHRASAL VERBS drop by/in/round** to visit someone for a short time □ *Why don't you drop round for a coffee later?* **drop someone/something off** to take someone or something to a place □ *I've got to drop this bag off at my Mum's house.* **drop out** to stop doing something before you have finished □ *She dropped out of school at the age of fifteen.*

drop[2] /drɒp/ NOUN [plural drops]
1 a very small amount of a liquid □ *+ of* Was that a drop of rain? □ *There were some drops of blood on the floor.*
2 *no plural* a decrease 🔊 *There has been a sharp drop (= big decrease) in profits.* □ *+ in* There was a small drop in the number of tourists last year.

drought /draʊt/ NOUN [plural droughts] a time when very little rain falls 🔊 *The country is currently suffering from a severe drought.*

drove /drəʊv/ PAST TENSE OF **drive**[1]

drown /draʊn/ VERB [drowns, drowning, drowned] to die because of being under water and not able to breathe □ *Three soldiers drowned when their truck fell into a river.*

drug /drʌg/ NOUN [plural drugs]
1 a medicine ⬧ Doctors usually prescribe the drug for children.
2 an illegal substance that people take to change the way they feel ⬧ He was on drugs (= regularly taking drugs). ⬧ I've never taken drugs. ⬧ a drug addict

drum¹ /drʌm/ NOUN [plural drums]
1 an instrument that is round and has a skin stretched over it that you hit to make a rhythm ⬧ He plays the drums in a band. ⬧ a drum kit (= a set of drums)
2 a tall round container for liquids ⬧ an oil drum

drum² /drʌm/ VERB [drums, drumming, drummed] to hit something in a regular rhythm □ Rain was drumming on the roof. □ He was drumming impatiently on the table.

drummer /ˈdrʌmə(r)/ NOUN [plural drummers] someone who plays the drums

drunk¹ /drʌŋk/ PAST PARTICIPLE OF **drink¹**

drunk² /drʌŋk/ ADJECTIVE having drunk too much alcohol ⬧ He got drunk at the party.

drunken /ˈdrʌŋkən/ ADJECTIVE having drunk too much alcohol, or involving people who have drunk too much alcohol □ a drunken brawl

dry¹ /draɪ/ ADJECTIVE [drier, driest]
1 not wet □ Are the clothes dry yet?
2 with little rain ⬧ dry weather □ a hot, dry summer

dry² /draɪ/ VERB [dries, drying, dried] to make something dry, or to become dry □ He dried his hands on the towel. □ She hung the clothes out to dry.
♦ PHRASAL VERB **dry (something) up** to dry plates, bowls, etc. after someone has washed them

dry-clean /ˌdraɪˈkliːn/ VERB [dry-cleans, dry-cleaning, dry-cleaned] to clean clothes with chemicals instead of water

dry cleaner /ˌdraɪ ˈkliːnə(r)/ NOUN [plural dry cleaners] a shop where clothes are cleaned with chemicals instead of water

dry cleaning /ˌdraɪ ˈkliːnɪŋ/ NOUN, NO PLURAL
1 clothes that are cleaned with chemicals instead of water
2 cleaning clothes using chemicals instead of water

dual /ˈdjuːəl/ ADJECTIVE having two parts ⬧ Hening has dual Belgian/French nationality.

dub /dʌb/ VERB [dubs, dubbing, dubbed] to change the language in a film or television programme into a different language □ The film has been dubbed into Russian.

duck¹ /dʌk/ NOUN [plural ducks]
1 a water bird with short legs and a wide, flat beak □ wild ducks
2 no plural the meat from a duck □ roast duck

duck² /dʌk/ VERB [ducks, ducking, ducked] to lower your head or body so that you are not hit or seen ⬧ Hamish ducked his head to get through the low doorway. □ **+ behind** He ducked behind a car when the shooting began.

due /djuː/ ADJECTIVE
1 expected to arrive or happen □ **+ at** The train is due at 10:15. □ **+ in** Their baby is due in March. □ **+ to do something** The project is due to start next month.
2 needing to be paid □ The rent is due at the beginning of the month.
3 due to something because of something □ The plane was delayed due to bad weather.
4 be due for something if you are due for something, it is time for you to have that thing □ I'm due for a pay rise.

dug /dʌg/ PAST TENSE AND PAST PARTICIPLE OF **dig**

duke /djuːk/ NOUN [plural dukes] a title for a man with a very high social rank

dull /dʌl/ ADJECTIVE [duller, dullest]
1 boring □ It was the dullest job you could imagine. □ Life is never dull when John's around.
2 not bright □ It was a dull, grey day.

dumb /dʌm/ ADJECTIVE [dumber, dumbest]
1 stupid. An informal word □ He kept asking me dumb questions.
2 not able to speak

dump¹ /dʌmp/ VERB [dumps, dumping, dumped]
1 to put something somewhere quickly □ He dumped his bag in the hall and ran upstairs.
2 to leave something somewhere because you do not want it □ It is not acceptable to dump toxic waste in the sea.

dump² /dʌmp/ NOUN [plural dumps] a place where people can leave things they do not want □ I'm going to take the old sofa to the dump.

dune /djuːn/ NOUN [plural dunes] a hill of sand

duo /ˈdjuːəʊ/ NOUN [plural duos] two people who perform together ⬧ a comedy duo

duplicate¹ /ˈdjuːplɪkət/ NOUN [plural duplicates] an exact copy □ She sent a duplicate of the photo.

duplicate² /ˈdjuːplɪkət/ ADJECTIVE exactly the same □ a duplicate key

duration /djuˈreɪʃən/ NOUN, NO PLURAL the length of time that something continues. A formal word ⬧ Hotel guests are offered a car for the duration of their stay.

during /ˈdjʊərɪŋ/ PREPOSITION
1 at one point in a period of time □ My grandfather was killed during the war.
2 through the whole of a period of time □ The garden looks beautiful during the summer.

➤ Remember that **during** is not used to talk about how long something happens. Use **for** for this:
✓ I studied English **for** three years.
✗ I studied English during three years.

dusk /dʌsk/ NOUN, NO PLURAL the time in the evening when it starts to get dark 🔁 Dusk was falling.

dust¹ /dʌst/ NOUN, NO PLURAL a powder of dirt on a surface or in the air 🔁 A thin layer of dust covered the desk. 🔁 The horses kicked up a cloud of dust.

dust² /dʌst/ VERB [dusts, dusting, dusted] to clean dust from something using a cloth ◻ I've dusted the shelves.

dustbin /'dʌstbɪn/ NOUN [plural dustbins] a container for rubbish, which is outside your house ◻ She threw the empty boxes in the dustbin.

dusty /'dʌstɪ/ ADJECTIVE [dustier, dustiest] covered with dust ◻ a dusty floor ◻ Children played in the dusty streets.

duty /'dju:tɪ/ NOUN [plural duties]
1 something that you do because other people expect you to do it or because it is morally right to do it 🔁 He felt he had a moral duty to help her. ◻ + **to do something** Society has a duty to protect children.
2 on/off **duty** if someone such as a doctor, police officer etc. is on duty, they are working, and if they are off duty, they are not working ◻ Which doctor is on duty tonight?

duty-free /ˌdju:tɪ'fri:/ ADJECTIVE duty-free products are cheaper because you can bring them into a country without paying tax ◻ duty-free perfume 🔁 We went to the duty-free shop at the airport.

duvet /'du:veɪ/ NOUN [plural duvets] a thick warm cover for your bed ◻ He pulled the duvet over his head. 🔁 a duvet cover

DVD /ˌdi:vi:'di:/ ABBREVIATION digital versatile disk; a type of disk with pictures and sound recorded on it ◻ The movie is available on DVD. 🔁 a DVD player 🔁 The children were watching a DVD.

dwarf¹ /dwɔ:f/ NOUN [plural dwarfs or dwarves] an imaginary creature in children's stories, which looks like a very small man

dwarf² /dwɔ:f/ ADJECTIVE dwarf plants are much smaller than the usual type ◻ dwarf apple trees

dye¹ /daɪ/ NOUN [plural dyes] a substance used for changing the colour of cloth or hair

dye² /daɪ/ VERB [dyes, dyeing, dyed] to use a substance to change the colour of cloth or hair ◻ Emma dyed her hair red.

dynamic /daɪ'næmɪk/ ADJECTIVE full of energy and new ideas ◻ a dynamic young manager

E*e*

E¹ or **e** /iː/ the fifth letter of the alphabet

E² /iː/ ABBREVIATION **east**²

e- /iː/ PREFIX **e-** is added to the beginning of words to mean 'electronic' or to do with the Internet □ *e-commerce*

---

each /iːtʃ/ DETERMINER, PRONOUN

1 every separate person or thing □ *We had to pay £5 each.* □ **+ of** *Each of the soldiers was given a gun.* □ *He had a heavy suitcase in each hand.*
2 each other used to show that each person or thing in a group of two or more does something to the others □ *The team all hugged each other.* □ *The cat and dog don't like each other much.*

> ➤ Remember that **each** is followed by a singular noun: □ *Each person starts the game with five cards.*

---

eager /ˈiːɡə(r)/ ADJECTIVE wanting very much to do or have something □ **+ to do something** *Imran seems eager to learn.*

---

eagle /ˈiːɡəl/ NOUN [*plural* **eagles**] a large bird with a curved beak that hunts small birds and animals

---

ear /ɪə(r)/ NOUN [*plural* **ears**]

1 one of the two parts on each side of your head that you hear with □ *He whispered something in my ear.*
2 the part at the top of the stem of some plants where the grains grow □ *an ear of corn*

---

earache /ˈɪəreɪk/ NOUN, NO PLURAL pain inside your ear

---

early /ˈɜːlɪ/ ADJECTIVE, ADVERB [**earlier, earliest**]

1 happening or arriving before others or before the expected or normal time □ *Nick had taken an earlier train.* □ *I'm tired so I'm going to bed early tonight.*
2 near the beginning of something □ *It's so quiet here in the early morning.* □ *She showed musical talent early in life.* ⊞ *The police were in the early stages of the investigation.*
3 early on in the first part of something □ *He played really well early on in the match.*

---

earn /ɜːn/ VERB [**earns, earning, earned**]

1 to get money for work that you do □ *He earns about £45,000 a year.* ⊞ *Does she earn her living (= get all the money she needs to live) as an artist?*
2 to get something good, such as praise, because you have done something well □ *He worked hard and earned the respect of his colleagues.*

> ➤ Remember that you **earn** money for work that you do. You **win** money in a competition: □ *He earns a very good salary.* □ *He won a million pounds on the lottery.*

---

earnings /ˈɜːnɪŋz/ PLURAL NOUN money that you get from working

---

earring /ˈɪərɪŋ/ NOUN [*plural* **earrings**] a piece of jewellery for the ear □ *a pair of earrings* □ *diamond earrings*

---

earth /ɜːθ/ NOUN [*plural* **earths**]

1 Earth the planet we live on ⊞ *life on Earth* □ *The Earth rotates around the sun.*
2 *no plural* soil □ *a pile of earth*
♦ IDIOM **how/what/where/why on earth?** used to emphasize a question, usually when you are very surprised □ *How on earth did that happen?* □ *What on earth was he wearing?*

---

earthquake /ˈɜːθkweɪk/ NOUN [*plural* **earthquakes**] when the ground suddenly moves, often causing serious damage to buildings

ease¹ /iːz/ NOUN, NO PLURAL

1 with ease easily □ *She won the race with ease.*
2 at ease relaxed □ *He's never completely at ease talking to strangers.*

ease² /i:z/ VERB [eases, easing, eased] to become less difficult or painful, or to make something less difficult or painful ⊞ *These tablets should ease the pain.* □ *Tensions in the area have gradually eased.*

easily /'i:zɪlɪ/ ADVERB with no effort or difficulty □ *Chelsea won easily.*

east¹ /i:st/ NOUN, NO PLURAL the direction that you look towards to see the sun rise □ *Which way is east?* □ *York is to the east of Harrogate.*

east² /i:st/ ADJECTIVE, ADVERB in or towards the east □ *the east coast* □ *East London* □ *We headed east.*

Easter /'i:stə(r)/ NOUN, NO PLURAL a Christian holiday in March or April to celebrate when Christ came back to life from the dead □ *the Easter holidays* □ *Easter Sunday*

eastern /'i:stən/ ADJECTIVE in or from the east part of a country or area □ *the eastern coast of America* □ *Eastern England*

easy¹ /'i:zɪ/ ADJECTIVE [easier, easiest] not difficult to do □ *an easy exam paper*

easy² /'i:zɪ/ ADVERB [easier, easiest] take it easy to relax and not work hard □ *Grandad's taking it easy in the garden.*
◆ IDIOMS **Easier said than done.** used to say that something is difficult to do □ *I know I should get the kids to help but that's easier said than done.* **go easy on someone** to treat someone more gently □ *Go easy on Matt, he's having a hard time at the moment.* **go easy on something** to eat or use only a little of something □ *My doctor said I should go easy on the red meat.*

eat /i:t/ VERB [eats, eating, ate, eaten]
1 to put food in your mouth and swallow it □ *We've eaten all the bread.* □ *He ate a huge meal.* ⊞ *Do you fancy something to eat?*
2 to have a meal □ *What time would you like to eat?*
◆ PHRASAL VERBS **eat out** to have a meal in a restaurant □ *We eat out about twice a month.* **eat something up** to eat all of an amount of food □ *Eat up your vegetables, Maisie.*

eBay /'i:beɪ/ NOUN, NO PLURAL a website where you can buy and sell things. A trademark. ⊞ *She buys a lot of clothes on eBay.*

echo¹ /'ekəʊ/ VERB [echoes, echoing, echoed] a sound echoes when it comes back and you hear it again □ *Their laughter echoed in the empty concert hall*

echo² /'ekəʊ/ NOUN [plural echoes] a sound that you hear again after it is sent back off a surface such as a wall

ecology /ɪ'kɒlədʒɪ/ NOUN, NO PLURAL the study of how plants and animals exist together and how their environment affects them

economic /ˌi:kə'nɒmɪk/ ADJECTIVE to do with money, business and industry ⊞ *More economic growth is predicted.* ⊞ *economic development* □ *an economic forecast*

economics /ˌi:kə'nɒmɪks/ NOUN, NO PLURAL the study of how money, business and industry are organized □ *a degree in economics*

economy /ɪ'kɒnəmɪ/ NOUN [plural economies] all the money a country or area creates through producing and selling goods and services, and the way that money is used □ *Canada's economy grew fast.* □ *Tourism benefits the local economy.*

ecosystem /'i:kəʊˌsɪstəm/ NOUN [plural ecosystems] all the plants and animals in an area and the way they depend on each other and on their environment to live

edge /edʒ/ NOUN [plural edges]
1 the outer part or end of something □ *We stood on the edge of the cliff.* □ *I live on the outer edge of the city.* □ *Trim off all the rough edges.*
2 a side of something that is sharp enough to cut
3 on edge nervous and slightly bad-tempered

edit /'edɪt/ VERB [edits, editing, edited] to prepare a book, document, film, etc. by correcting mistakes and making any changes that are needed

edition /ɪ'dɪʃən/ NOUN [plural editions] the copies of a book, newspaper, etc. that are printed at the same time □ *The story was in the early editions of the newspaper.* □ *I bought the hardback edition of her first novel.*

editor /'edɪtə(r)/ NOUN [plural editors] someone whose job is to prepare a book, document, newspaper, etc. to be published by correcting mistakes and making any changes that are needed □ *He thanked his editor for all her help.*

educate /'edjʊkeɪt/ VERB [educates, educating, educated]
1 to teach someone □ *He was educated at the local school.*
2 to give people information about something so that they understand it more □ **+ about** *We need to educate people about the importance of exercise.*

education /ˌedjʊ'keɪʃən/ NOUN, NO PLURAL the process of teaching, especially in schools or colleges □ *Our students receive a good standard of education.* □ *secondary education*

> ► THESAURUS **Education** is a general word for the process of teaching and learning things. **Teaching** is the work that a teacher does. **Training** is the process of teaching someone how to do something. For example, you might get **training** in how to use a computer or how to do a new job.

educational /ˌedjuˈkeɪʃənəl/ ADJECTIVE to do with teaching and learning ⊞ *She organized an educational visit to the museum.* □ *He works for a company which makes educational toys.*

effect /ɪˈfekt/ NOUN [plural effects] if one thing has an effect on another, it influences it or causes something to happen to it □ **+ on** *His asthma has no effect on his ability as a footballer.* □ *She was suffering from the effects of a long plane journey.*

➤ Be careful not to confuse **effect**, which is a noun, with **affect**, which is a verb: □ *One thing has an effect on another.* □ *One thing affects another.*

effective /ɪˈfektɪv/ ADJECTIVE working well or producing the results you want □ *This is an effective treatment for the common cold.* □ *Do you know of an effective way of removing chewing gum from a carpet?*

➤ THESAURUS: You might describe a medicine as effective if it makes you feel better. If something is efficient, it works well and does not waste time or energy. You might describe a factory as efficient if it produces things that are good quality in a short time. If a teacher describes your work as adequate, it is good enough, but not very good. If something is useful, it helps you to do something. For example, a map is useful in a city that you do not know.

efficient /ɪˈfɪʃənt/ ADJECTIVE working well and not wasting any time or energy □ *The questionnaire was an efficient method of collecting information.* □ *This is not an efficient use of resources.*

effort /ˈefət/ NOUN [plural efforts] the physical or mental energy that you need to do something ⊞ *She made a real effort to be friendly.* ⊞ *You must put some more effort into your school work.* □ **+ to do something** *It takes a lot of effort to be an athlete.*

eg *or* **e.g.** /ˌiːˈdʒiː/ ABBREVIATION for example □ *The zoo specializes in African animals, eg the lion and the giraffe.*

egg /eg/ NOUN [plural eggs]
1 an oval object with a shell or case, in which a baby bird, reptile or fish develops ⊞ *The cuckoo lays its eggs in another bird's nest.*
2 an oval object with a shell produced by a chicken or similar bird that we eat as food ⊞ *a boiled/fried egg* ⊞ *Beat two egg yolks with a little milk.*

ego /ˈiːɡəʊ/ NOUN [plural egos] the opinion you have of yourself □ *All the attention and praise was good for her ego.*

eight /eɪt/ NUMBER [plural eights] the number 8

eighteen /ˌeɪˈtiːn/ NUMBER the number 18
eighteenth /ˌeɪˈtiːnθ/ NUMBER 18th written as a word

eighth[1] /eɪtθ/ NUMBER 8th written as a word
□ *the eighth book in the series* □ *Our team finished eighth.*

eighth[2] /eɪtθ/ NOUN [plural eighths] 1/8; one of eight equal parts of something

eightieth /ˈeɪtɪəθ/ NUMBER 80th written as a word
eighty /ˈeɪtɪ/ NUMBER [plural eighties] the number 80

either[1] /ˈaɪðə(r)/ ADVERB used in negative sentences to mean 'as well' □ *If you don't go, I won't go either.* □ *Dan doesn't like cheese either.*

either[2] /ˈaɪðə(r)/ DETERMINER, PRONOUN
1 one or the other □ *She can write with either hand.*
□ **+ of** *I can't afford either of them.*
2 both ⊞ *They stood on either side of the Queen.*

either[3] /ˈaɪðə(r)/ CONJUNCTION either ... or used to show a choice □ *You can have either a video game or a CD.*

elaborate /ɪˈlæbərət/ ADJECTIVE involving complicated detail or decoration □ *an elaborate plan* □ *elaborate costumes*
elbow /ˈelbəʊ/ NOUN [plural elbows] the part in the middle of your arm where it bends
elder[1] /ˈeldə(r)/ ADJECTIVE older □ *She has an elder brother.*
elder[2] /ˈeldə(r)/ NOUN, NO PLURAL the elder the older of two people □ *She's the elder of two sisters.*
elderly[1] /ˈeldəlɪ/ ADJECTIVE old □ *an elderly lady*

► THESAURUS: Old is a general word to describe people or things that have existed for a long time. When you are talking about people, the word elderly is more polite than the word old. We do not use elderly to talk about things. Aged is used to say how old a person is. To talk about how old a thing is, we usually use the word old. For example, you can say that a child is aged three, or that he is three years old. You say that a house is ten years old, not aged ten.

elderly² /ˈeldəlɪ/ NOUN the elderly people who are old □ *Sarah works in a care home for the elderly.*

eldest¹ /ˈeldɪst/ ADJECTIVE oldest □ *Alex is my eldest child.*

eldest² /ˈeldɪst/ NOUN, NO PLURAL the eldest the person who is the oldest □ *Fiona is the eldest of three sisters.*

elect /ɪˈlekt/ VERB [elects, electing, elected] to choose someone for a particular job or position in an organization by voting □ *The committee has to elect a chairperson.* □ *The president was elected in 2004.*

► THESAURUS: If you elect a person, you choose them to do a job, by voting. For example, we elect politicians. If you appoint someone, you officially give that person a job. Pick and choose are more general words to describe taking one thing or person from a group. For example, you might pick or choose paint for your kitchen, or people to invite to a party.

election /ɪˈlekʃən/ NOUN [plural elections] when people choose someone by voting 🔊 *Nobody knows when he will decide to hold the election.* 🔊 *Her party won the election.*

electric /ɪˈlektrɪk/ ADJECTIVE made or worked by electricity □ *an electric spark* □ *an electric light* □ *electric current*

electrical /ɪˈlektrɪkəl/ ADJECTIVE to do with electricity □ *She's studying electrical engineering.* □ *The shop sells small electrical appliances like kettles and irons.*

electricity /ˌɪlekˈtrɪsətɪ/ NOUN, NO PLURAL a type of energy used to make light and heat and to make machines work □ *We're trying to save electricity by turning off our computers at night.*

electron /ɪˈlektrɒn/ NOUN [plural electrons] one of the parts of an atom that move around the nucleus and have a negative electrical charge. A chemistry and physics word.

electronic /ˌɪlekˈtrɒnɪk/ ADJECTIVE using electricity and very small electrical parts to work

🔊 *an electronic device* 🔊 *They sell computers and other electronic equipment.*

electronics /ˌɪlekˈtrɒnɪks/ NOUN, NO PLURAL the study of how electricity flows and how it can be used in machinery

element /ˈelɪmənt/ NOUN [plural elements]
1 a part of something □ *They are unhappy about some elements of the course.* □ *His work has a political element.*
2 a substance that cannot be divided into smaller chemical substances, for example oxygen and carbon. A chemistry word.

elementary /ˌelɪˈmentərɪ/ ADJECTIVE basic □ *You have forgotten the elementary principles of journalism.* □ *He makes too many elementary mistakes.* □ *elementary maths* □ *students at elementary level*

elephant /ˈelɪfənt/ NOUN [plural elephants] a very large animal with a long nose, large ears and thick grey skin

eleven /ɪˈlevən/ NUMBER [plural elevens] the number 11

eleventh /ɪˈlevənθ/ NUMBER 11th written as a word

eliminate /ɪˈlɪmɪneɪt/ VERB [eliminates, eliminating, eliminated] to get rid of something completely □ *We aim to eliminate poverty.* 🔊 *The new technology eliminates the need for ID cards and passwords.*

elite¹ /ɪˈliːt/ NOUN [plural elites] the best, most important or most powerful people in a society or group □ *the country's ruling elite* □ *the sporting elite*

elite² /ɪˈliːt/ ADJECTIVE of very high quality □ *an elite athlete*

else /els/ ADVERB
1 as well as the thing or person that has been talked about 🔊 *Promise not to tell anyone else.* 🔊 *You must wait in the queue, the same as everybody else.* 🔊 *There's something else I need to tell you.*
2 different from something or someone 🔊 *I had to leave. What else could I do?* 🔊 *I hate swimming. Can we do something else instead?* 🔊 *He must be angry. Why else would he react like that?*
3 or else used to say that a bad thing will happen if another thing does not happen □ *Put on a jumper or else you'll get cold.*

elsewhere /ˌelsˈweə(r)/ ADVERB in or to another place □ *It's too expensive here, we'll have to look elsewhere.*

e-mail¹ or **email** /ˈiːmeɪl/ NOUN [plural e-mails or emails]
1 no plural the system for sending messages between computers □ *They keep in touch by*

e-mail. □ *Are you on e-mail?* 🔁 *What's your e-mail address?*
2 a written message sent between computers 🔁 *He sends me an e-mail every day.*

e-mail[2] *or* **email** /ˈiːmeɪl/ VERB [e-mails, e-mailing, e-mailed *or* emails, emailing, emailed] to send someone an e-mail □ *I'll e-mail you the address.*

embarrass /ɪmˈbærəs/ VERB [embarrasses, embarrassing, embarrassed] to make someone feel ashamed or stupid □ *Stop it! You're embarrassing me!* □ *The information could embarrass the president if it gets out.*

embarrassed /ɪmˈbærəst/ ADJECTIVE looking or feeling ashamed or stupid □ *an embarrassed silence* 🔁 *Quinn felt embarrassed.* □ **+ about** *They're very embarrassed about what's happened.* □ **+ by** *She looked a little embarrassed by all the attention.*

➤ **THESAURUS:** If you are **embarrassed**, you feel ashamed or silly about something that you have done or said. If you feel **shy**, you do not feel comfortable or confident when you speak to other people. If someone **humiliates** you, they make you feel stupid or ashamed about something, and you feel **humiliated**. This is a stronger word than embarrassed.

embarrassing /ɪmˈbærəsɪŋ/ ADJECTIVE making you feel embarrassed □ *It was an embarrassing moment.* 🔁 *a highly embarrassing photo* □ **+ for** *The incident was very embarrassing for the government.*

embarrassment /ɪmˈbærəsmənt/ NOUN, NO PLURAL a feeling of being embarrassed 🔁 *Check the price in advance to avoid embarrassment.* 🔁 *I don't want to cause her any embarrassment.*

embassy /ˈembəsi/ NOUN [*plural* embassies] a group of officials who represent their government in a foreign country, or the building where they work □ *the Australian embassy in Washington*

embrace /ɪmˈbreɪs/ VERB [embraces, embracing, embraced] to put your arms around someone and hold them as a sign of love or being friends □ *The two friends embraced warmly.*

embryo /ˈembriəʊ/ NOUN [*plural* embryos] a baby or animal when it starts growing inside its mother's body. A biology word.

emerge /ɪˈmɜːdʒ/ VERB [emerges, emerging, emerged] to come out of something or from behind something □ *The baby crocodiles emerge from the eggs.* □ *Al emerged from the tent.*

emergency[1] /ɪˈmɜːdʒənsi/ NOUN [*plural* emergencies] a sudden, unexpected and usually dangerous event that needs immediate action 🔁 *In*

an emergency, call my husband's number.* 🔁 *I always take my mobile with me in case of emergencies.* 🔁 *a medical emergency*

emergency[2] /ɪˈmɜːdʒənsi/ ADJECTIVE to do with an emergency □ *emergency surgery* □ *The plane made an emergency landing.*

emit /ɪˈmɪt/ VERB [emits, emitting, emitted] to send light, heat, gas or a sound out into the air. A formal word. □ *The substance emits light.* □ *The machine emitted a high-pitched noise.*

emotion /ɪˈməʊʃən/ NOUN [*plural* emotions] a feeling, such as love, hate, fear or anger 🔁 *He showed no emotion throughout the trial.* □ *Anya struggled to control her emotions.* 🔁 *I've got mixed emotions* (= good and bad feelings) *about the place.*

emotional /ɪˈməʊʃənəl/ ADJECTIVE showing or having strong feelings □ *an emotional speech* 🔁 *I get emotional just talking about it.* □ *He was in a highly emotional state.*

emperor /ˈempərə(r)/ NOUN [*plural* emperors] the ruler of a group of countries governed by one leader or government

emphasis /ˈemfəsɪs/ NOUN [*plural* emphases] special importance or attention you give to something 🔁 *Schools put too much emphasis on exams.*

emphasize *or* **emphasise** /ˈemfəsaɪz/ VERB [emphasizes, emphasizing, emphasized] to give special importance or attention to something 🔁 *I want to emphasize the importance of road safety.* □ *She emphasized that she had been treated very well.*

empire /ˈempaɪə(r)/ NOUN [*plural* empires] a group of countries governed by one leader or government □ *the Roman empire*

employ /ɪmˈplɔɪ/ VERB [employs, employing, employed] to pay someone to work for you □ *The company employs skilled workers.* □ **+ as** *He was employed as a teacher.* □ **+ to do something** *We employed a local builder to do the work.*

employee /ɪmˈplɔɪiː/ NOUN [*plural* employees] someone who works for a company or another person 🔁 *The company has 16 full-time employees.* □ **+ of** *We spoke to a former employee of the firm.*

employer /ɪmˈplɔɪə(r)/ NOUN [*plural* employers] a company or person who employs people □ *It's a chance for students to meet potential employers.* □ *The factory is the area's largest employer.*

employment /ɪmˈplɔɪmənt/ NOUN, NO PLURAL paid work for a company or person 🔁 *Are you in* full-time employment? 🖥 He found employment as a security guard.

empty¹ /'emptɪ/ ADJECTIVE [emptier, emptiest] containing nothing or no one □ an empty box 🖥 There was an empty space between the two buildings. □ The restaurant was almost empty. □ + of The streets were empty of traffic.

empty² /'emptɪ/ VERB [empties, emptying, emptied] to become empty, or to make something empty □ Empty your pockets. □ The theatre slowly emptied.

enable /ɪ'neɪbəl/ VERB [enables, enabling, enabled] to make it possible for someone to do something □ The software enables users to download music.

enclose /ɪn'kləuz/ VERB [encloses, enclosing, enclosed]
1 to put something in an envelope with a letter □ I'm enclosing a copy of the certificate.
2 to be all around something □ The children's play area is enclosed by a wooden fence.

encourage /ɪn'kʌrɪdʒ/ VERB [encourages, encouraging, encouraged] to support someone and make them feel confident about doing something □ + to do something We encourage students to work together. □ My parents encouraged me to write. □ We have been encouraged by recent successes.

encouragement /ɪn'kʌrɪdʒmənt/ NOUN, NO PLURAL when you encourage someone or something □ The crowd shouted encouragement to the team. □ + to do something She needed no encouragement to dive into the pool.

end¹ /end/ NOUN [plural ends]
1 the last part of something □ The end of the book is very sad. □ I'll come back at the end of the week.
2 the part of something that is furthest away from the middle □ He poked me with the end of a stick. 🖥 There is a church at the other end of this street. 🖥 We sat at opposite ends of the table.
3 when something does not exist any more 🖥 We were sad when our holiday came to an end.
4 in the end after a long period of time □ The train was delayed, but we got there in the end.

end² /end/ VERB [ends, ending, ended] to finish □ Our holiday ends tomorrow. □ + with He ended his speech with a joke. □ The word cough ends with a 'f' sound.
♦ PHRASAL VERB **end up somewhere/doing something** to have to do something or to finish in a bad situation □ I knew he'd end up in prison. □ I ended up catching a later train.

endanger /ɪn'deɪndʒə(r)/ VERB [endangers, endangering, endangered] to cause someone to be in a dangerous situation 🖥 His actions could have

endangered the lives of people nearby. □ These chemicals could endanger public health.

ending /'endɪŋ/ NOUN [plural endings] the last part of a story 🖥 The story had a happy ending. □ + of I don't want to spoil the ending of the film.

endless /'endlɪs/ ADJECTIVE seeming to never finish □ The task seemed endless. 🖥 There's an endless supply of cheap workers.

enemy /'enɪmɪ/ NOUN [plural enemies]
1 someone who is against you and wants to harm you 🖥 He made a few enemies while he was there. □ + of They are viewed as enemies of the regime.
2 the enemy in a war, the people or country you are fighting against □ We will defend ourselves and defeat the enemy.

➤ THESAURUS: An enemy is someone who is trying to harm you, or a country that is fighting against yours. An opponent is someone that you compete against in a competition or game. For example, you might have an opponent in an election, or in a boxing match. A rival is a person or an organization that is competing against you, for example in business.

energetic /ˌenə'dʒetɪk/ ADJECTIVE very active and full of energy □ an energetic dance □ I feel a lot more energetic.

energy /'enədʒɪ/ NOUN [plural energies]
1 the strength or power you have to work or to be active □ Young children have loads of energy. □ My boss has tremendous energy and enthusiasm. □ + to do something I didn't have the energy to walk home.
2 a form of power, such as heat or electricity 🖥 Turn off lights to save energy. 🖥 nuclear energy 🖥 renewable sources of energy □ energy efficiency

engaged /ɪn'geɪdʒd/ ADJECTIVE
1 if two people are engaged, they have promised to marry each other □ + to She's engaged to actor Alex Donovan. 🖥 The couple got engaged last month.
2 if a telephone or toilet is engaged, it is being used

engine /'endʒɪn/ NOUN [plural engines] a part of a machine that uses energy to produce movement □ a car with a diesel engine 🖥 He closed the door and started the engine.

engineer /ˌendʒɪ'nɪə(r)/ NOUN [plural engineers] someone who designs, makes or repairs things like bridges, roads or machines □ a telephone engineer

engineering /ˌendʒɪ'nɪərɪŋ/ NOUN, NO PLURAL the study or work of designing and making machines, roads, bridges, etc. 🖥 He graduated in mechanical engineering.

English¹ /'ɪŋglɪʃ/ ADJECTIVE
1 belonging to or from England □ *the English countryside*
2 to do with the English language □ *an English translation*

English² /'ɪŋglɪʃ/ NOUN
1 *no plural* the main language of Britain, North America and Australia, and an official language in some other countries □ *She speaks English very well.*
2 the English people from England

Englishman /'ɪŋglɪʃmən/ NOUN [*plural* Englishmen] a man who comes from England, or who has English parents

enhance /ɪn'hɑ:ns/ VERB [enhances, enhancing, enhanced] to improve something □ *He has never used drugs to enhance his performance.*

enjoy /ɪn'dʒɔɪ/ VERB [enjoys, enjoying, enjoyed]
1 to like doing something □ *They seemed to enjoy the concert.* □ *Enjoy your meal!* □ *+ ing I enjoy playing tennis.*
2 enjoy yourself to have a good time doing something □ *We enjoyed ourselves at the party.* □ *He was clearly enjoying himself.*

enjoyable /ɪn'dʒɔɪəbəl/ ADJECTIVE fun and giving you pleasure □ *The whole trip was a really enjoyable experience.*

enjoyment /ɪn'dʒɔɪmənt/ NOUN, NO PLURAL when you enjoy something 🕮 *I get tremendous enjoyment out of the sport.* □ *+ of I don't let the illness affect my enjoyment of life.*

enormous /ɪ'nɔ:məs/ ADJECTIVE very big or great □ *an enormous tree* 🕮 *It cost an enormous amount of money.* □ *The staff were under enormous pressure.*

enough¹ /ɪ'nʌf/ DETERMINER, PRONOUN as much or as many as you need or want □ *Have you all had enough to eat?* □ *We need some more oil – there isn't enough here.* □ *I've got enough problems without this!*

enough² /ɪ'nʌf/ ADVERB as much as is needed or wanted □ *She's not pretty enough to be a model.* □ *Stop when you think you've written enough.*

enquiry /en'kwaɪərɪ/ NOUN [*plural* enquiries] another spelling of **inquiry**

enter /'entə(r)/ VERB [enters, entering, entered]
1 to go into a place □ *A tall man entered the room.* □ *He entered hospital at 3pm.* □ *The bullet entered his chest.* □ *They entered the country illegally.*
2 to put information in a book, document, computer, etc. □ *Enter your name here.* □ *The data is stored in a special computerized system.*
3 to take part in a competition or an exam □ *My mum agreed to enter the mother's race.*

entertain /ˌentə'teɪn/ VERB [entertains, entertaining, entertained]
1 to do something which people find interesting and enjoyable □ *Emily entertained us by telling a few jokes.* □ *A band entertained the crowd.*
2 to invite people as your guests for a meal or a drink □ *Tom tends to cook when we're entertaining.*

entertaining /ˌentə'teɪnɪŋ/ ADJECTIVE interesting and enjoyable □ *She gave an entertaining account of her trip.* □ *It was a highly entertaining match.*

entertainment /ˌentə'teɪnmənt/ NOUN [*plural* entertainments] something that entertains people □ *There's live entertainment every night.* 🕮 *Traditional dancers provided the entertainment.* 🕮 *There are new forms of entertainment developing on the Internet.*

enthusiasm /ɪn'θju:zɪæzəm/ NOUN, NO PLURAL when you are very interested in something or want to do it very much □ *+ for Her enthusiasm for her subject remains strong.* 🕮 *There was a general lack of enthusiasm for the project.*

enthusiastic /ɪnˌθju:zɪ'æstɪk/ ADJECTIVE showing enthusiasm □ *+ about Not everyone is enthusiastic about the idea.* □ *You don't sound very enthusiastic.*

entire /ɪn'taɪə(r)/ ADJECTIVE all of something □ *He lived his entire life in the same town.*

entrance /'entrəns/ NOUN [*plural* entrances] the part of a building where you go into it 🕮 *I'll meet you outside the main entrance.* □ *+ of There are security staff at the entrance of the building.* □ *+ to There were clear signs at the entrance to the tunnel.*

➤ **THESAURUS:** An entrance is the way into a building. A door is the thing that you open in order to go into a building, a room, a cupboard or a car. A gate is part of a fence or a wall that opens like a door. You might go through a gate to get into a garden, for example.

entrepreneur /ˌɒntrəprə'nɜ:(r)/ NOUN [*plural* entrepreneurs] a person who starts a business using their own ideas and usually their own money □ *China's young entrepreneurs*

entry /'entrɪ/ NOUN [*plural* entries]
1 when you go into a place 🕮 *They were refused entry into the country.* 🕮 *We gained entry (= got in) through an open window.* □ *+ to This card gives you free entry to most museums.* □ *+ into They were allowed entry into the area.*
2 no entry a phrase used on signs to show that you must not go into a place.
3 something that you have done to try to win a competition 🕮 *The winning entries will be announced next week.*

envelope /ˈenvələup/ NOUN [plural envelopes]
a folded paper cover for a letter, especially one that
is sent by post □ a brown A4 envelope ⊞ You
haven't opened the envelope.

environment /ɪnˈvaɪərənmənt/ NOUN [plural
environments]
1 the environment all the things, such as air, land,
sea, animals and plants, that make up the natural
world around us ⊞ Our main aim is to protect the
environment.
2 the things that surround you where you live, work
or do something ⊞ We want to create a positive
working environment. □ It provides a safe
environment for young children to play.

➤ THESAURUS: The environment is all of the
things that make up the world around us, such
as the air, land and sea. Your surroundings are
the area around a person or a place. Nature
describes everything in the world that was not
made or changed by man such as animals and
plants.

envoy /ˈenvɔɪ/ NOUN [plural envoys] a
government official sent to another country to meet
with a foreign government □ the United Nations
envoy to Bosnia

envy¹ /ˈenvɪ/ NOUN, NO PLURAL a feeling of wanting
what someone else has □ I felt a little envy at her
success.

envy² /ˈenvɪ/ VERB [envies, envying, envied] to
want what someone else has □ We envied him
because he didn't have to go to school.

enzyme /ˈenzaɪm/ NOUN [plural enzymes] a
chemical substance made in both animals and
plants, which causes chemical changes. A biology
word.

epic /ˈepɪk/ NOUN [plural epics] a long story, poem
or film about great events or exciting adventures
□ His new film is a historical epic.

epidemic /ˌepɪˈdemɪk/ NOUN [plural epidemics] a
situation in which a disease spreads quickly and

many people become ill at the same time □ a flu
epidemic

episode /ˈepɪsəud/ NOUN [plural episodes] one
separate part of a story that is broadcast on the
radio or television over a period of time

➤ THESAURUS: An episode is one part of a longer
story that is shown on the television or the
radio. A chapter is one of the parts that a book
is divided into. A scene is a short part of a play,
book or film that happens in one place. A
passage is a short part of a piece of writing or
music.

equal¹ /ˈiːkwəl/ ADJECTIVE
1 of the same size, value or amount □ Cut the cake
into four roughly equal slices.
2 having or deserving the same rights as other
people □ Men and women were finally regarded as
equal. ⊞ equal rights for all

equal² /ˈiːkwəl/ NOUN [plural equals] someone
who has the same rights or importance as another
person □ The women expect to be treated as equals.

equal³ /ˈiːkwəl/ VERB [equals, equalling/US
equaling, equalled/US equaled]
1 to be the same in size, value or amount □ Two
plus two equals four.
2 to achieve as much as someone else □ She
equalled the world record.

equality /iˈkwɒlɪtɪ/ NOUN, NO PLURAL when
everyone has the same rights and importance
⊞ racial equality ⊞ sexual equality

equation /ɪˈkweɪʒən/ NOUN [plural equations] a
mathematical statement that shows that two sets
of numbers are equal

equator /ɪˈkweɪtə(r)/ NOUN, NO PLURAL the
equator the line drawn on maps that goes around
the middle of the Earth □ Kampala is just north of
the equator.

equipment /ɪˈkwɪpmənt/ NOUN, NO PLURAL the
machines, furniture, etc. that you need in order to
do a particular activity or job □ camping equipment
□ office equipment ⊞ a piece of equipment

➤ Remember that **equipment** is never used in the
plural:
✓ We need more equipment.
✗ We need more equipments.

equivalent¹ /ɪˈkwɪvələnt/ NOUN [plural
equivalents] something that has the same value,
use, meaning or effect as something else □ The
Internet has become the modern equivalent of a
telephone or a daily newspaper. □ Children eat the
equivalent of almost twelve bags of sugar every year.

equivalent² /ɪˈkwɪvələnt/ ADJECTIVE having the
same value, use, meaning or effect □ The average

temperature of Mars is roughly equivalent to the temperature in Antarctica.

-er /-ər/ SUFFIX
1 -er is added to the end of words to mean 'a person or thing that does something' □ *teacher*
2 -er is added to the end of some adjectives to make a comparative form □ *brighter*

era /ˈɪərə/ NOUN [plural eras] a period of time 🔁 *The country is entering a new era of peace.*

erase /ɪˈreɪz/ VERB [erases, erasing, erased] to remove information or files from a computer □ *The file had somehow been erased.*

eraser /ɪˈreɪzə(r)/ NOUN [plural erasers] a small piece of rubber used to remove pencil marks from paper

erect /ɪˈrekt/ VERB [erects, erecting, erected] to build something or put it together. A formal word. □ *They erected a monument to their leader.* □ *A barrier was erected around the area.* □ *We had to erect the tent in the dark.*

erode /ɪˈrəʊd/ VERB [erodes, eroding, eroded] if something erodes or is eroded, its surface is gradually removed by wind or water, for example □ *Houses are falling into the sea as the coastline erodes.*

error /ˈerə(r)/ NOUN [plural errors] a mistake 🔁 *He admits making some errors.* 🔁 *The report blamed human error for the air crash.*

erupt /ɪˈrʌpt/ VERB [erupts, erupting, erupted] a volcano erupts when hot rocks, flames and dust suddenly come out of it

> ► **THESAURUS:** We usually use erupt to talk about volcanoes. If something explodes, it breaks open suddenly so that parts fly out, making a loud noise. For example, you say that a bomb explodes. If something bursts, it also breaks open suddenly, but with less violence. A water pipe might burst, or a balloon.

escalate /ˈeskəleɪt/ VERB [escalates, escalating, escalated] to make or become worse or more serious □ *The violence has escalated in recent weeks.*

escalator /ˈeskəleɪtə(r)/ NOUN [plural escalators] a set of moving stairs for carrying people between the levels of a building 🔁 *Shall we take the escalator?*

escape¹ /ɪˈskeɪp/ VERB [escapes, escaping, escaped]
1 to get away from a place where you are being kept □ **+ from** *The lion had escaped from its cage.*
2 to get away from a dangerous place or situation □ **+ from** *He escaped from the country hidden in a lorry.* □ *When fire broke out, we managed to escape through the window.*

escape² /ɪˈskeɪp/ NOUN [plural escapes] when someone gets away from a place or a bad situation

□ **+ from** *He wrote a book about his daring escape from prison.*

escort¹ /ɪˈskɔːt/ VERB [escorts, escorting, escorted] to go somewhere with someone in order to look after them □ *Airport staff will escort your child to the boarding gate.*

escort² /ˈeskɔːt/ NOUN [plural escorts] someone who goes somewhere with another person in order to look after them 🔁 *The players needed a police escort to get to the bus.*

especially /ɪˈspeʃəli/ ADVERB
1 very, more than anything or anyone else □ *I was especially impressed by the food.* □ *He wasn't especially clever.* □ *The children, especially the younger ones, were tired.*
2 for one person or purpose only □ **+ for** *I bought it especially for you.* □ **+ to do something** *I came here especially to see you.*

essay /ˈeseɪ/ NOUN [plural essays] a piece of writing by a student about a particular subject □ **+ on** *Students are required to write a 4,000-word essay on a topic of their choice.*

essence /ˈesəns/ NOUN, NO PLURAL the essence of something the most important part of something, or its true character □ *The film captures the essence of life in 18th-century Paris.*

essential /ɪˈsenʃəl/ ADJECTIVE if something is essential, you must do it or have it □ **+ that** *It is essential that we all stay together.* 🔁 *Fat is an essential part of our diet.* □ *A car is useful, but not essential.*

establish /ɪˈstæblɪʃ/ VERB [establishes, establishing, established] to start an organization or business □ *He established a small bakery.*

estate /ɪˈsteɪt/ NOUN [plural estates] a large area with a lot of buildings on it 🔁 *an industrial estate* 🔁 *a housing estate*

estate agent /ɪˈsteɪt ˌeɪdʒənt/ NOUN [plural estate agents] someone whose job is to help people to buy and sell houses and apartments

estimate¹ /ˈestɪmeɪt/ VERB [estimates, estimating, estimated] to try to judge the size, amount or value of something, using the information that you have □ *The government estimated the cost at over £5 million.* □ *Experts estimate that thousands of deaths every year are caused by unhealthy diets.*

estimate² /ˈestɪmət/ NOUN [plural estimates] when you estimate something

etc or **etc.** /ɪtˈsetərə/ ABBREVIATION used after a list to show that there are other similar things that you have not mentioned □ *The art shop sells paints, canvases, brushes, etc.*

ethnic /'eθnɪk/ ADJECTIVE to do with a group of people who have the same race and culture ⊞ *The Pashtuns form the main ethnic group of Afghanistan.*

EU /,i:'ju:/ ABBREVIATION the EU the European Union; a political and economic organization of European countries

euro /'juərəʊ/ NOUN [plural euros] the main unit of money in many European countries □ *There are 100 cents in a euro.*

European¹ /,juərə'pi:ən/ ADJECTIVE belonging to or from Europe

European² /,juərə'pi:ən/ NOUN [plural Europeans] a person from Europe

European Union /,juərə,pi:ən 'ju:njən/ NOUN, NO PLURAL the European Union a political and economic organization of European countries

evacuate /ɪ'vækjueɪt/ VERB [evacuates, evacuating, evacuated] to leave a place because it is dangerous, or to make people leave a place because it is dangerous □ *Hundreds of people had to evacuate their homes during the floods.* □ *Residents were evacuated from the areas affected by the fires.*

eve /i:v/ NOUN [plural eves]
1 the day or evening before a particular day □ *He died on the eve of his 80th birthday.*
2 Eve used in the names of some days that come before an important day □ *Christmas Eve* □ *New Year's Eve*

even¹ /'i:vən/ ADVERB
1 used to emphasize another word □ *It was even colder the next morning.* □ *Max is even better than Adam at football.* □ *Even Pia seemed to be enjoying herself.*
2 even though although □ *She still tried to help him, even though he was so rude to her.*
3 even if used to say that what you are going to say next would not change anything □ *Grandad wouldn't go on holiday even if we paid for it.*

even² /'i:vən/ ADJECTIVE
1 an even surface is level and smooth
2 equal □ *The scores were even.*
3 an even number is one that can be divided by 2

evening /'i:vnɪŋ/ NOUN [plural evenings] the last part of the day, before the night begins ⊞ *What are you doing this evening?* ⊞ *We're going to the cinema on Friday evening.* ⊞ *They usually watch TV in the evening.* ⊞ *What time do you usually have your evening meal?*

event /ɪ'vent/ NOUN [plural events] something that happens ⊞ *These events occurred in the 19th century.* ⊞ *Recent events have made it necessary to introduce new rules.* ⊞ *Millions of people watched the events unfold (= happen) on TV.*

eventual /ɪ'ventʃuəl/ ADJECTIVE happening at the end of a period of time or as a result of a process □ *They lost the match to the eventual winners, Liverpool.*

ever /'evə(r)/ ADVERB
1 at any time or at all □ *Have you ever been to France?* □ *Nobody ever offers to help me.* □ *It was the most delicious meal ever.* □ *If you are ever in Edinburgh, do come and see me.*
2 ever since since the time when □ *He's been unhappy ever since he started at his new school.*
3 for ever for all future time □ *I'm sure we'll be friends for ever.*

every /'evrɪ/ DETERMINER
1 all the people or things □ *Every runner will get a medal for taking part.* □ *There were eight cakes on the plate, and she ate every one.*
2 every day/week/three hours, etc. used to show how often something happens □ *He does 200 press-ups every day.*

➤ Remember that **every** is followed by a singular noun: □ *Every student in the group owns a mobile phone.*

everybody /'evrɪ,bɒdɪ/ PRONOUN everyone □ *I thought everybody liked ice cream.* □ *Could everybody listen, please?*

everyone /'evrɪwʌn/ PRONOUN every person □ *Everyone likes Jonathan.* □ *I know everyone at the party.* ⊞ *Everyone else (= all other people) had left by this point.*

everything /'evrɪθɪŋ/ PRONOUN all the things in a place or situation □ *Everything in the room was covered in dust.* ⊞ *We kept the books, and threw everything else in the bin.*

everywhere /'evrɪweə(r)/ ADVERB in or to every place □ *We looked everywhere but couldn't find it.* □ *They go everywhere together.*

evidence /'evɪdəns/ NOUN, NO PLURAL facts or objects that help to prove something □ *His body was examined and no evidence of the disease found.*

evident /'evɪdənt/ ADJECTIVE obvious or easy to understand □ *It was evident that she was unhappy.*

evil¹ /'i:vəl/ ADJECTIVE morally very bad and cruel □ *an evil man* □ *This was an evil act.*

evil² /'i:vəl/ NOUN, NO PLURAL evil actions generally □ *So are we all capable of evil?*

evolution /,i:və'lu:ʃən/ NOUN, NO PLURAL the process by which animals and plants change over many thousands of years in order to suit their environment

exact /ɪgˈzækt/ ADJECTIVE accurate in every way □ *Those were his exact words.* □ *I don't recall the exact date.* □ *They never mentioned the exact amount of money.* □ *This is an exact copy of the document.*

exactly /ɪgˈzæktlɪ/ ADVERB
1 used when saying prices, amounts, the time, etc. that are completely accurate □ *That comes to £10 exactly.* □ *It's five o'clock exactly.*
2 in every way □ *That's exactly what I was thinking.* □ *He looks exactly like his father.* ☐ *The coats look exactly the same to me.*
3 used for agreeing strongly with what someone has said □ *'She should be pleased she's got a job.' 'Exactly.'*

exaggerate /ɪgˈzædʒəreɪt/ VERB [exaggerates, exaggerating, exaggerated] to say that something is more extreme than it really is □ *He's not that fat – you're exaggerating!* □ *The media have exaggerated the problem.*

exam /ɪgˈzæm/ NOUN [plural exams] an important test of someone's knowledge or ability ☐ *I'm taking my final exams in June* ☐ *She passed her exams.* ☐ *What if he fails his exams?*

examination /ɪgˌzæmɪˈneɪʃən/ NOUN [plural examinations]
1 a formal word that means exam
2 no plural when someone looks carefully at something □ *On closer examination, the painting turned out to be a copy.*

examine /ɪgˈzæmɪn/ VERB [examines, examining, examined]
1 to look at something carefully □ *The sample was examined under a microscope.*
2 if a doctor examines you, he or she looks carefully at your body to see if there is anything wrong □ *The doctor examined her throat and ears.*

example /ɪgˈzɑːmpəl/ NOUN [plural examples]
1 something which has all the features or qualities of the type of thing that you are talking about □ *This is a typical example of a building from this period.* ☐ *Let me give you an example of what I mean.*
2 for example used for giving an example of something □ *People drive unnecessarily. Jo, for example, drives to her friend's house which is 10 minutes' walk away.*

exceed /ɪkˈsiːd/ VERB [exceeds, exceeding, exceeded] to be greater than a particular limit or amount □ *He exceeded the speed limit by 30 kilometres per hour.*

excellent /ˈeksələnt/ ADJECTIVE extremely good or of a very high standard □ *Her work is excellent.*

except /ɪkˈsept/ PREPOSITION, CONJUNCTION not including something □ *He works every day except Sunday.* □ *+ that* *I feel better now, except that my*
head still hurts a bit. □ *+ for* *Everyone stayed, except for the children.*

exception /ɪkˈsepʃən/ NOUN [plural exceptions]
1 something that is not the same as the others in a group, and so cannot be included in a statement about them □ *With a few exceptions, the people were very friendly.* □ *There is one exception to this rule.*
2 make an exception to say that one person does not have to follow a particular rule □ *You're not supposed to leave the room during the lesson, but I'll make an exception for you.*

excess[1] /ɪkˈses/ NOUN [plural excesses] too much of something □ *There was an excess of fat in his blood.*

excess[2] /ˈekses/ ADJECTIVE more than you want, or more than is allowed ☐ *Many airlines charge you for excess baggage.*

exchange[1] /ɪksˈtʃeɪndʒ/ VERB [exchanges, exchanging, exchanged] to give someone something and take something from them □ *We exchanged rings as a sign of our friendship.* □ *They exchanged phone numbers.* □ *We only exchanged a few words* (= spoke for a short time). □ *This website enables us to exchange information.*

exchange[2] /ɪksˈtʃeɪndʒ/ NOUN [plural exchanges]
1 in exchange for something if you do something or give something in exchange for something, you do it or give it to get that thing □ *He took money in exchange for passing on information.*
2 when you give something to someone and take something from them □ *+ of* *The exchange of food is a symbol of our community.*

excite /ɪkˈsaɪt/ VERB [excites, exciting, excited] to make someone feel excited

excited /ɪkˈsaɪtɪd/ ADJECTIVE feeling very happy and not calm because something good is going to happen ☐ *He was getting excited about the party.* □ *+ about* *It was my first trip to the US and I was really excited about it.* □ *+ to do something* *I'm excited to be part of the team.*

excitement /ɪkˈsaɪtmənt/ NOUN, NO PLURAL the feeling of being excited ☐ *The news caused great excitement.* □ *In her excitement, she forgot something important.* □ *+ of* *I still remember the excitement of winning the competition.*

exciting /ɪkˈsaɪtɪŋ/ ADJECTIVE making you feel excited □ *an exciting opportunity* □ *+ to do something* *The game was exciting to watch.*

➤ Remember the difference between the words **excited** and **exciting**. If you are **excited**, you are very happy because something good is going to happen. Something that is **exciting** makes you feel excited: □ *I was so* **excited** *during that game.* □ *It was such an* **exciting** *game.*

exclaim /ɪkˈskleɪm/ VERB [exclaims, exclaiming, exclaimed] to say something suddenly and loudly because you are surprised, angry, etc. □ '*What a wonderful surprise!' she exclaimed.*

exclude /ɪkˈskluːd/ VERB [excludes, excluding, excluded]
1 to not allow someone to take part in something or go into a place □ *Paul was excluded from school for a week as a punishment.*
2 to deliberately not include something □ *The figures exclude children under the age of twelve.*

excuse¹ /ɪkˈskjuːs/ NOUN [plural excuses] a reason you give to explain why you did something wrong or did not do something 🕭 *I'm sick of you making excuses about your work.* 🕭 *He's late again – he'd better have a good excuse this time!* □ + **for** *There's no excuse for this sort of behaviour.*

excuse² /ɪkˈskjuːz/ VERB [excuses, excusing, excused]
1 excuse me (a) something that you say to get someone's attention □ *Excuse me, could you tell me the way to the library?* □ *Excuse me, Susan, there's someone on the phone for you.* (b) used to say sorry □ *Oh, excuse me, I didn't realize this seat was taken.*
2 to forgive someone for doing something, especially something that is not serious □ *Please excuse the mess in here.* □ *I hope you'll excuse us being late.*
3 if you are excused something, you are allowed not to do it □ + **from** *Could I be excused from tennis today, as I don't feel well?*

execute /ˈeksɪkjuːt/ VERB [executes, executing, executed] to kill someone as an official punishment □ *Many of the prisoners were executed.*

execution /ˌeksɪˈkjuːʃən/ NOUN [plural executions] killing someone as an official punishment □ *He is facing execution for his role in the terrorist bombings.*

exercise¹ /ˈeksəsaɪz/ NOUN [plural exercises]
1 *no plural* physical activities done to keep your body strong and healthy 🕭 *We should all take more exercise.* 🕭 *Regular exercise will help to control your weight.*
2 a particular movement done to make your body strong and healthy □ *We did some stretching exercises.* □ *This exercise works the stomach muscles.*
3 a piece of written work you do when you are studying □ *Please do exercise 4 in your grammar book.* □ *This exercise deals with prepositions.*

exercise² /ˈeksəsaɪz/ VERB [exercises, exercising, exercised] to do exercises to make you strong and healthy 🕭 *I try to exercise regularly.* □ *You should try to exercise the damaged joints.*

exhaust¹ /ɪgˈzɔːst/ VERB [exhausts, exhausting, exhausted] to make someone very tired □ *That jog exhausted me.*

exhaust² /ɪgˈzɔːst/ NOUN [plural exhausts]
1 the pipe on a vehicle which waste gas come out of
2 *no plural* the waste gas that comes out of a vehicle 🕭 *exhaust fumes*

exhausted /ɪgˈzɔːstɪd/ ADJECTIVE extremely tired □ *She was completely exhausted by the time she got home.*

exhausting /ɪgˈzɔːstɪŋ/ ADJECTIVE making you feel extremely tired □ *It was an exhausting climb.*

exhaustion /ɪgˈzɔːstʃən/ NOUN, NO PLURAL a feeling of extreme tiredness □ *The singer cancelled his tour because of stress and exhaustion.*

exhibit /ɪgˈzɪbɪt/ VERB [exhibits, exhibiting, exhibited] to show something in a place such as a museum □ *Julia exhibits her paintings at a small local gallery.*

exhibition /ˌeksɪˈbɪʃən/ NOUN [plural exhibitions] a show where people go to see paintings, photographs, etc. 🕭 *an art exhibition* □ + **of** *The museum will be holding an exhibition of works by Monet.*

➤ **THESAURUS:** An exhibition is a show where people go to see paintings, photographs etc. A **demonstration** is when someone shows you how to do something or how it works. For example, you might go to a cookery demonstration. A **presentation** is a talk to a group of people to explain or describe something. For example, you might give a presentation to the people you work with.

exile¹ /ˈeksaɪl/ NOUN [plural exiles]
1 someone who has been forced to leave their country, usually for political reasons
2 in exile if someone is in exile, they have been forced to live in a country that is not their own, for political reasons □ *The former leader is now living in exile in Japan.*

exile² /ˈeksaɪl/ VERB [exiles, exiling, exiled] if you are exiled, you are forced to leave your own country and live somewhere else, for political reasons

exist /ɪgˈzɪst/ VERB [exists, existing, existed] to be real, or to happen □ *Does God really exist?* □ *Similar problems exist in Britain.*

existence /ɪgˈzɪstəns/ NOUN, NO PLURAL when someone or something exists □ *The rule was in existence for almost 40 years.* □ + **of** *We can no longer deny the existence of global warming.*

exit /ˈeksɪt/ NOUN [plural exits] a door you go through to leave a public building or vehicle 🕭 *The bus has an emergency exit at the back.*

exotic /ɪgˈzɒtɪk/ ADJECTIVE interesting and unusual, and often to do with a foreign country □ *exotic animals* □ *exotic holidays*

expand /ɪkˈspænd/ VERB [expands, expanding, expanded] to become bigger, or to make something become bigger □ *Many cities are expanding very rapidly.* □ *The company plans to expand its range of products.*

expansion /ɪkˈspænʃən/ NOUN, NO PLURAL when something increases in size or amount □ *The rapid expansion of the airline industry has led to cheap flights.*

expect /ɪkˈspekt/ VERB [expects, expecting, expected]
1 to think that something will happen or be true □ *We're expecting an announcement soon.* □ *I expect he's forgotten the meeting.* □ *I didn't expect anything like this to happen.* □ **+ to do something** *Sales are expected to fall next month.* □ **+ that** *I expect that it will be hot in Portugal.*
2 to think that something or someone will arrive □ *I'm expecting a phone call from Mary.*
3 to think that something ought to happen or that you have a right to it □ **+ to do something** *I expect you to behave better than this.* □ *Our customers expect a first class service.*
4 if you are expected to do something, you have to do it □ *We are expected to do 3 hours' homework a day.*

expedition /ˌekspɪˈdɪʃən/ NOUN [plural expeditions] a long journey, especially to a dangerous place or to a place that has not been visited before □ *The group went on an expedition to the South Pole.*

expel /ɪkˈspel/ VERB [expels, expelling, expelled] to make someone leave a school, country or organization because they have done something wrong □ *John was expelled from school for hitting a teacher.*

expense /ɪkˈspens/ NOUN [plural expenses] the money that you pay for something 🔁 *medical/legal expenses* 🔁 *The money he gave me will cover the expense of the transport.* 🔁 *We have to pay our own travelling expenses.*

expensive /ɪkˈspensɪv/ ADJECTIVE costing a lot of money □ *These clothes are too expensive for me.* □ *expensive gifts/equipment*

experience¹ /ɪkˈspɪəriəns/ NOUN [plural experiences]
1 *no plural* knowledge and skill that you get by doing something or by something happening to you 🔁 *The players have been gaining experience over the last four years.* 🔁 *She had no experience of looking after children.* □ **+ of** *The company is looking for someone with experience of managing people.*
2 something that happens to you 🔁 *We had a bad experience on holiday.* 🔁 *The whole experience was*

terrifying. □ *Watching a baby being born was an amazing experience.*

experience² /ɪkˈspɪəriəns/ VERB [experiences, experiencing, experienced] if you experience something, it happens to you or you feel it □ *Many customers were experiencing problems with Internet access.* □ *He had never experienced such pain.*

experienced /ɪkˈspɪəriənst/ ADJECTIVE having skill and knowledge because you have done something for a long time □ *an experienced teacher*

experiment¹ /ɪkˈsperɪmənt/ NOUN [plural experiments] a scientific test to discover or prove something 🔁 *Two experiments were conducted, using children suffering from heart problems.* 🔁 *The experiment shows that lack of sleep affects people's performance of basic tasks.*

experiment² /ɪkˈsperɪment/ VERB [experiments, experimenting, experimented] to do scientific tests to discover or prove something □ **+ on** *The team experimented on rats.*

expert¹ /ˈekspɜːt/ NOUN [plural experts] someone who knows a lot about something □ *legal/health experts* □ **+ on/in** *She's an expert on Middle East politics.*

expert² /ˈekspɜːt/ ADJECTIVE very good at something, or knowing a lot about something □ *expert skiers*

expire /ɪkˈspaɪə(r)/ VERB [expires, expiring, expired] if an official document or agreement expires, the time when you can use it ends □ *Your passport expired last month.*

explain /ɪkˈspleɪn/ VERB [explains, explaining, explained]
1 to give someone more or simpler information so that they can understand something □ **+ question word** *Could you explain what you mean?* □ **+ to** *She explained the rules of the game to me.*
2 to give or to be a reason for something □ *He was asked to explain his absence.* □ *Having a bad childhood can explain the behaviour of some criminals.* □ **+ that** *She explained that she had lost her keys.*

➤ Note that you cannot *explain someone something*. You must *explain something to someone*:
✓ *She explained the rules to me.*
✗ *She explained me the rules.*

explanation /ˌekspləˈneɪʃən/ NOUN [plural explanations]
1 something you say or write to make something easy to understand 🔁 *She gave an explanation of how to do it.* □ **+ of** *The teacher started with an explanation of why plants are green.*

2 a reason for something ▣ *The research offers several explanations for this behaviour.* □ *+ for Is there a scientific explanation for this?*

explicit /ɪk'splɪsɪt/ ADJECTIVE clear and exact □ *Michael gave me explicit instructions about how to do it.*

explode /ɪk'spləud/ VERB [explodes, exploding, exploded] to burst (= break suddenly so the parts fly out) and make a very loud noise ▣ *A bomb exploded in the centre of the city.* □ *The car exploded, killing two police officers.* □ *Fireworks exploded in every direction.*

➤ Note that a bomb **explodes**. When people make a bomb explode in a building, aeroplane, etc. they **blow up** that building, aeroplane, etc: □ *The bomb exploded in the centre of the building.* □ *They blew up the building*

exploit /ɪk'splɔɪt/ VERB [exploits, exploiting, exploited] to use someone unfairly to help you get what you want □ *These people are often exploited as they will work for very little money.*

exploration /ˌeksplə'reɪʃən/ NOUN [plural explorations] going to a place to find out about it □ *space exploration*

explore /ɪk'splɔː(r)/ VERB [explores, exploring, explored] to travel around a place and find out what it is like □ *The hotel is a good base for exploring the region.* □ *Radar technology will help us to explore the planet Mars.*

explorer /ɪk'splɔːrə(r)/ NOUN [plural explorers] someone who travels to places that people have not been to before □ *a Polar explorer*

explosion /ɪk'spləuʒən/ NOUN [plural explosions] when something such as a bomb explodes □ *The explosion happened inside the building.* ▣ *Two soldiers were killed in a roadside bomb explosion.* ▣ *He was seriously injured in a gas explosion.*

explosive¹ /ɪk'spləusɪv/ ADJECTIVE able to cause an explosion □ *a highly explosive gas* ▣ *an explosive device*

explosive² /ɪk'spləusɪv/ NOUN [plural explosives] a substance that can cause an explosion

export¹ /ɪk'spɔːt/ VERB [exports, exporting, exported] to sell goods to another country □ *India exports rice and wheat to many countries.*
➔ *go to import*

export² /'ekspɔːt/ NOUN [plural exports]
1 a product that a country sells to another country □ *Syria's main export is oil.*
2 *no plural* the process of selling goods to another country □ *The country relies on the export of wool.*
➔ *go to import*

expose /ɪk'spəuz/ VERB [exposes, exposing, exposed] to show something that was covered or hidden □ *He pulled up his shirt to expose his stomach.*

express¹ /ɪk'spres/ VERB [expresses, expressing, expressed] to show or tell people what you are thinking or feeling ▣ *He expressed his concerns about the safety of the equipment.* ▣ *She expressed strong views about education.* ▣ *Amy expressed surprise at his comments.* □ *He was unable to express himself clearly.*

express² /ɪk'spres/ NOUN [plural expresses] a train or bus that is fast because it does not stop at many places □ *We caught the express to Leeds.*

express³ /ɪk'spres/ ADJECTIVE travelling fast from one place to another ▣ *an express train* □ *The package arrived express delivery.*

expression /ɪk'spreʃən/ NOUN [plural expressions]
1 a look on your face that shows what you are thinking or feeling ▣ *I could tell by the expression on his face that he didn't believe me.* ▣ *I couldn't read her facial expression.*
2 a word or phrase ▣ *Dieter always uses very old-fashioned expressions.*

extend /ɪk'stend/ VERB [extends, extending, extended]
1 to make something bigger □ *We're having our kitchen extended.* □ *The airport has plans to extend the runway.*
2 to make something continue for longer □ *The contract was extended by three months.*

extension /ɪk'stenʃən/ NOUN [plural extensions]
1 a part added to a building □ *They're building an extension at the side of the house.*
2 a telephone line to a particular person in an office □ *Can I have extension 4321, please?*

extensive /ɪk'stensɪv/ ADJECTIVE large in size or amount ▣ *The fire caused extensive damage.* ▣ *He has an extensive collection of rare books.*

extent /ɪk'stent/ NOUN, NO PLURAL
1 the size or degree of something □ *What's the extent of the damage?*
2 *to some extent/to a certain extent* in some ways □ *The situation has improved to some extent.*

exterior /ɪk'stɪərɪə(r)/ NOUN [plural exteriors] the outside of something □ *The house had a very impressive exterior.*
➔ *go to interior¹*

external /ɪk'stɜːnəl/ ADJECTIVE on the outside of a person or thing □ *The building has external lighting.*

extinct /ɪk'stɪŋkt/ ADJECTIVE a type of animal or plant which is extinct no longer exists □ Many types of frog have already become extinct.

extinguish /ɪk'stɪŋgwɪʃ/ VERB [extinguishes, extinguishing, extinguished] a formal word meaning to make a fire stop burning or to make a light stop shining □ Firefighters tried to extinguish the flames.

extra¹ /'ekstrə/ ADJECTIVE more or more than usual □ The extra money will be used to buy books. □ The teacher gives Raj extra help with maths. □ The room is £70 but meals are extra (= meals are not included in the price).

extra² /'ekstrə/ ADVERB more than usual □ I get paid extra for working at weekends. □ I bought an extra large box of chocolates.

extract /ɪk'strækt/ VERB [extracts, extracting, extracted] a formal word meaning to remove something from a place □ No dentist will extract a tooth that could be saved.

extraordinary /ɪk'strɔːdənrɪ/ ADJECTIVE very special, unusual or surprising □ Ann told me the most extraordinary story. ᵬ He knew he had seen something quite extraordinary (= very extraordinary). □ + that It's extraordinary that he survived the accident.

extravagant /ɪk'strævəgənt/ ADJECTIVE spending or costing too much money, or using too much of something □ an extravagant lifestyle □ Don't be too extravagant with the paper – we haven't much left.

extreme /ɪk'striːm/ ADJECTIVE
1 very great ᵬ The roads are icy, and motorists should drive with extreme caution. □ We were working under extreme pressure.
2 very unusual or severe ᵬ Planes cannot take off or land in extreme weather conditions. ᵬ In extreme cases, the illness can cause death.
3 at the furthest edge of something □ My mother is on the extreme right of the picture.

extremely /ɪk'striːmlɪ/ ADVERB very □ He found it extremely difficult to relax. □ Education is extremely important. □ Ben did extremely well in the test.

➤ **Extremely** is not used before adjectives which have a strong meaning:
✓ It was extremely difficult to hear.
✗ It was extremely impossible to hear. If you are using an adjective with a strong meaning, put an adverb such as **completely** or **absolutely** before it: □ It was absolutely impossible to hear.

eye /aɪ/ NOUN [plural eyes]
1 one of the two things on your face which you see with □ I have blonde hair and blue eyes. ᵬ John closed his eyes and tried to sleep. ᵬ When she opened her eyes again, he'd gone.
2 the hole in a needle that you put the thread through
♦ IDIOMS catch someone's eye if something catches your eye, you notice it □ A sudden movement caught my eye. keep an eye on someone/something to look after someone or something to make sure they are safe □ Could you keep an eye on the children for me? not see eye to eye to disagree with someone about something □ We don't see eye to eye about religion.

eyebrow /'aɪbraʊ/ NOUN [plural eyebrows] one of the two lines of hair above your eyes
eyelash /'aɪlæʃ/ NOUN [plural eyelashes] one of the many hairs round the edges of your eyes
eyelid /'aɪlɪd/ NOUN [plural eyelids] one of the pieces of skin that cover your eyes when your eyes are closed

F¹ *or* **f** /ef/ the sixth letter of the alphabet

F² /ef/ ABBREVIATION **Fahrenheit**

fabric /'fæbrɪk/ NOUN [*plural* fabrics] cloth □ *They are made of natural fabrics such as cotton or linen.*

fabulous /'fæbjʊləs/ ADJECTIVE extremely good □ *The weather was fabulous.* □ *You look fabulous in that dress.*

face¹ /feɪs/ NOUN [*plural* faces]
1 the front of your head where your eyes, nose, and mouth are □ *She had a huge smile on her face.*
2 the part of a clock or watch where the numbers are

face² /feɪs/ VERB [faces, facing, faced]
1 to be in a particular direction □ *My house faces the park.* □ *She turned to face him.*
2 to have to deal with a difficult situation □ *She has faced many difficulties in her life.*
3 can't face doing something if you can't face doing something, it is too unpleasant for you to do □ *I just can't face cooking this evening.*

facility /fə'sɪlətɪ/ NOUN [*plural* facilities]
facilities buildings, rooms or equipment that you can use for doing something ➕ *The university has excellent sports facilities.* □ *The company provides childcare facilities for employees.*

fact /fækt/ NOUN [*plural* facts]
1 something that you know is true □ **+ about** *We don't yet know all the facts about the accident.* ➕ *I know for a fact (= I'm certain) that he was in London last week.* ➕ *The fact is, I'm too scared to talk to him.* ➕ *The fact that she's ill means she can't work full-time.*
2 in fact/as a matter of fact used to give more information about something □ *They know each other well; in fact they went to school together.*
3 in fact used to say what is really true □ *He said he was ill, when in fact he was at the football match.*

faction /'fækʃən/ NOUN [*plural* factions] a group that is part of a larger group but has different opinions from others in that group

factor /'fæktə(r)/ NOUN [*plural* factors] something that causes or influences a situation □ *The weather is often one of the main factors in choosing where to go for a holiday.* ➕ *Price is an important factor for many people.*

factory /'fæktərɪ/ NOUN [*plural* factories] a building where something is made in large quantities □ *a chocolate factory*

fade /feɪd/ VERB [fades, fading, faded]
1 to disappear or become less strong gradually □ *Hopes of finding him were starting to fade.* □ *His smile faded.* □ *Their voices faded into the background.*
2 to lose colour and become less bright □ *These jeans have faded.* □ *The light was fading.*

Fahrenheit /'færənhaɪt/ NOUN, NO PLURAL a system for measuring temperature in which water freezes at 32 degrees and boils at 212 degrees

fail¹ /feɪl/ VERB [fails, failing, failed]
1 to not be successful □ **+ in** *They failed in their attempt to sail round the world.* □ **+ to do something** *The business failed to attract enough customers.* □ *After four years, the marriage failed.*
2 if you fail an exam or test, you do not pass it □ *My brother failed his driving test.*
3 to not do something that is expected or needed □ **+ to do something** *The parcel failed to arrive.* □ *Yesterday's announcement failed to address the main problems.* □ *They failed to provide enough food for the animals.*

fail² /feɪl/ NOUN, NO PLURAL **without fail** (a) used to show that something always happens in a particular way or at a particular time □ *He visits me every day, without fail* (b) used to emphasize that something must be done □ *I want your homework in tomorrow, without fail!*

failure /'feɪljə(r)/ NOUN [*plural* failures]
1 when something is not successful ➕ *Their first attempt ended in failure.* □ **+ of** *After the failure of his business, he went to live abroad.*
2 someone or something that is not successful □ *She felt like a failure.* □ *The party was a complete failure.*

faint¹ /feɪnt/ ADJECTIVE [fainter, faintest]
1 difficult to see, hear or smell □ *There's a faint mark on the carpet.* □ *the faint sound of footsteps* □ *He gave a faint smile.*
2 if you feel faint, you feel that you might become unconscious ➕ *I suddenly felt faint.*
• **faintly** /'feɪntlɪ/ ADVERB in a way that is difficult

to see, hear or smell □ *'Yes,'* she said faintly. □ *The room smelled faintly of smoke.*

faint² /feɪnt/ VERB [faints, fainting, fainted] to suddenly become unconscious and fall to the ground □ *Richard fainted when he saw the blood.*

fair¹ /feə(r)/ ADJECTIVE [fairer, fairest]
1 treating everyone in the same, reasonable way 🖐 *It's not fair! Ella got more cake than me.* 🖐 *a fair trial/election* 🖐 *Make sure Patsy does her fair share of the work.*
2 fair skin or hair is light in colour
3 fair weather is pleasant, with no rain
4 quite good but not very good □ *Joe's work is only fair.*
• **fairly** /'feəlɪ/ ADVERB
1 quite a lot, but not extremely □ *He is fairly well paid.* □ *It's fairly obvious that she is lying.*
2 in a fair way □ *They treat their staff fairly.* □ *The money was divided fairly between them.*

fair² /feə(r)/ NOUN [plural fairs] an event held outdoors, where you can ride on machines, play games, etc.

fairy /'feərɪ/ NOUN [plural fairies] an imaginary creature which looks like a small person with wings
faith /feɪθ/ NOUN [plural faiths]
1 *no plural* great trust and belief in someone or something 🖐 *I have a lot of faith in him.* 🖐 *I've lost faith in the whole system.*
2 a religion □ *the Christian faith* □ *people of different faiths*
3 *no plural* religious belief generally □ *He was a man of deep faith.*
faithful /'feɪθful/ ADJECTIVE loyal and keeping your promises □ *a faithful friend* □ *He was faithful to his wife.*

faithfully /'feɪθfulɪ/ ADVERB Yours faithfully something you write at the end of a formal letter that begins with 'Dear Sir' or 'Dear Madam'

fake /feɪk/ ADJECTIVE not real, but copying something else □ *fake fur* □ *He was travelling on a fake passport.*

fall¹ /fɔːl/ VERB [falls, falling, fell, fallen]
1 to drop down to the ground □ *The apples fell from the tree.* □ *Snow fell all morning.*
2 to suddenly go down to the ground by accident □ *Ben fell downstairs.* □ *+ off He fell off a fence and broke his arm.*
3 fall apart/off/out, etc. to become separated □ *The doll's arms fell off.* □ *All his hair fell out.*
4 if an amount, price or temperature falls, it goes down □ *+ by The temperature has fallen by several degrees.* □ *+ to Prices fell to their lowest levels since June.*
5 to start being in a particular state 🖐 *They fell in*

love. 🖐 *I often fall asleep at the cinema.* 🖐 *He fell ill on holiday.*
♦ PHRASAL VERBS **fall for someone** to start to love someone **fall for something** to be tricked by something □ *I told her I'd give her the money later and she fell for it!* **fall over** to fall to the ground or onto one side □ *I fell over and cut my knee.* **fall out** to stop being friends □ *Carlos and Sergei have fallen out.* **fall through** to fail or not happen □ *Their plans for a holiday have fallen through.*

➤ THESAURUS: If you fall, or fall over, you drop to the ground. If you trip, you hit your foot on something and fall, or almost fall. For example, you might trip on a carpet. If you collapse, you fall over because you are ill or very tired.

fall² /fɔːl/ NOUN [plural falls]
1 when someone falls by accident □ *My grandmother had a serious fall last week.*
2 a decrease in a price, amount or temperature □ *+ in There has been a fall in unemployment.*
3 the US word for **autumn**

false /fɔːls/ ADJECTIVE
1 not true or based on information that is not correct □ *He made a false statement to the police.* □ *These claims are completely false.* 🖐 *We had a false sense of security.* 🖐 *We don't want to give people false hope.*
2 not real or natural 🖐 *false teeth* □ *a false passport*

fame /feɪm/ NOUN, NO PLURAL the state of being known by a lot of people 🖐 *She found fame in a hit TV series.* 🖐 *He achieved international fame as a novelist.* 🖐 *Young actors go to Hollywood seeking fame and fortune (= fame and money).*

familiar /fə'mɪljə(r)/ ADJECTIVE
1 known to you □ *His voice sounded familiar.* 🖐 *There were a few familiar faces (= people you know) at the party.*
2 be familiar with something to have seen or used something before □ *I'm not familiar with this software.* □ *If you're familiar with the area, it's just next to the big park.*

family /'fæmlɪ/ NOUN [plural families] a group of people who are related to each other 🖐 *I invited my whole family to the wedding.* 🖐 *I met her parents and several other family members.* 🖐 *She discussed the decision with family and friends.* □ *The minister met the families of the victims.*

➤ Family can be used with a singular or plural verb in British English: □ *The family next door has a dog.* □ *The family next door have a dog.*

famine /'fæmɪn/ NOUN [plural famines] a situation in which many people in an area do not have enough food and may die □ *The country was hit by a severe drought and famine.*

famous /'feɪməs/ ADJECTIVE known by a lot of people □ *a famous actor* □ *a famous painting* □ **+ for** *She is most famous for her role in Star Wars.* □ **+ as** *He later became famous as a children's writer.*

fan[1] /fæn/ NOUN [*plural* fans]
1 someone who likes or admires a person or thing very much □ *football fans* □ *She's a big fan of Madonna.*
2 a machine with thin blades that turn round and make the air cooler □ *There was a ceiling fan in our room.*
3 something that you move in front of your face to make you feel cooler
fan[2] /fæn/ VERB [fans, fanning, fanned] to move something in front of your face to make you feel cooler □ *He fanned himself with his cap.*
fancy[1] /'fænsɪ/ VERB [fancies, fancying, fancied]
1 an informal word meaning to want to have or do something □ *Do you fancy going to the cinema?* □ *I really fancy a curry.*
2 an informal word meaning to be attracted to someone □ *My friend fancies you.*
fancy[2] /'fænsɪ/ ADJECTIVE [fancier, fanciest]
fashionable or expensive □ *fancy clothes* □ *We went for a meal at a fancy restaurant.*

fantastic /fæn'tæstɪk/ ADJECTIVE an informal word meaning extremely good □ *We had a fantastic time in Rome.* □ *This is a fantastic opportunity for us.* □ *You look fantastic!*

far[1] /fɑː(r)/ ADVERB [farther *or* further, farthest *or* furthest]
1 a long distance □ *Don't go too far.* □ **+ away** *Is the hotel very far away?* □ **+ to** *It's not far to Paris.* □ **+ from** *He lives not far from the church.*
2 much □ *She's a far better swimmer than I am.* □ *He's far more interested in football.* □ *These trousers are far too small for me.*
3 as far as I know/can remember, etc.
used to say what you think is true □ *As far as I can remember, there aren't any very steep hills.*
4 by far used to emphasize the quality you are talking about □ *He's by far the most talented of our dancers.*
5 so far until now □ *So far, there haven't been any accidents.*

> ➤ Note that **far**, meaning 'a long distance', is mainly used in questions and in negative sentences: □ *How far is it to the town centre?* □ *It's not far from the town centre.* In positive sentences, we usually say **a long way**: □ *It's a long way from the town centre.*

far[2] /fɑː(r)/ ADJECTIVE the far part of something is the part that is the greatest distance from you ⊞ *The house is on the far side of the lake.*

fare /feə(r)/ NOUN [*plural* fares] the price of a journey by bus, train, aeroplane, etc. ⊞ *The train fare to London is £33.* ⊞ *Cheap air fares make travel much easier.*

farm[1] /fɑːm/ NOUN [*plural* farms] an area of land where crops are grown and animals are kept ⊞ *a dairy farm* (= which keeps cows for milk) ⊞ *a farm animal* □ *He works on a farm.*

farm[2] /fɑːm/ VERB [farms, farming, farmed] to use land for growing crops or keeping animals for meat □ *They have farmed the land here for generations.*

farmer /'fɑːmə(r)/ NOUN [*plural* farmers] someone who owns and works on a farm □ *a local sheep farmer*

farmhouse /'fɑːmhaʊs/ NOUN [*plural* farmhouses] a house on a farm where the farmer lives

farming /'fɑːmɪŋ/ NOUN, NO PLURAL the activity or business of working on and managing a farm □ *The organization promotes organic farming.* ⊞ *He grew up in a small farming community.*

fascinate /'fæsɪneɪt/ VERB [fascinates, fascinating, fascinated] to interest and attract someone very much □ *The story of Tutankhamun has fascinated people for many years.* □ *The thing that fascinates me is the variety of shapes and colours.*

fascinated /'fæsɪneɪtɪd/ ADJECTIVE very interested and attracted by something □ *As a kid I was fascinated by the stars.* □ *She watched the fascinated expressions of the children.*
fascinating /'fæsɪneɪtɪŋ/ ADJECTIVE very interesting ⊞ *a fascinating story* □ *It's the island's wildlife that I find fascinating.*

fashion /'fæʃən/ NOUN [*plural* fashions] something, especially a piece of clothing, that is very popular at a particular time □ **+ for** *There was a fashion for tight jeans.* □ *Short skirts were in fashion then.* ⊞ *She wears all the latest fashions.*

fashionable /'fæʃənəbəl/ ADJECTIVE popular with many people at a particular time □ *a fashionable restaurant* ⊞ *The area has become fashionable with students.* □ **+ to do something** *It's fashionable to play team sports again.*

fast[1] /fɑːst/ ADJECTIVE [faster, fastest]
1 quick □ *a fast car* □ *He was the fastest runner.*
2 if a clock or watch is fast, it shows a time that is later than the correct time

fast² /fɑːst/ ADVERB [faster, fastest]
1 quickly □ *She can run very fast.* □ *We're working as fast as we can.* □ *The population has grown faster than in any other region.*
2 fast asleep completely asleep □ *The boys are fast asleep.*
3 firmly or tightly ⊞ *The door was stuck fast.*

fast³ /fɑːst/ VERB [fasts, fasting, fasted] to not eat any food for a period of time, often for religious reasons □ *I am fasting because it is Ramadan.*

fast⁴ /fɑːst/ NOUN [plural fasts] a time when you fast

fasten /'fɑːsən/ VERB [fastens, fastening, fastened] to join or fix two things or parts together ⊞ *Please fasten your seat belts.* □ **+ to** *The phone was fastened to the wall.* □ *She fastened the papers together with a stapler.* □ *The dress fastens at the back.*

fastener /'fɑːsənə(r)/ NOUN [plural fasteners] something that is used to join two things together

fast food /ˌfɑːst 'fuːd/ NOUN, NO PLURAL food that is prepared and served quickly in a restaurant, often to take away

fat¹ /fæt/ ADJECTIVE [fatter, fattest]
1 a fat person has too much flesh, usually because they eat too much ⊞ *George is getting fat, isn't he?* ⊞ *Do these jeans make me look fat?* □ *Fat children are often teased.*
2 thick or large □ *a big, fat book*

➤ It is not polite to describe someone as **fat**. To sound less rude, use the words **big** or **overweight**: □ *She's quite big at the moment and unhappy about it.*

fat² /fæt/ NOUN [plural fats]
1 *no plural* a soft white substance that forms a layer under your skin ⊞ *Can exercise reduce body fat?*
2 a substance like oil that is in food or used in cooking □ *Limit the amount of fat you eat.* ⊞ *Hard cheese has a higher fat content.*

fatal /'feɪtəl/ ADJECTIVE causing someone's death ⊞ *a fatal accident*

fate /feɪt/ NOUN, NO PLURAL
1 the things that happen to someone, especially bad things ⊞ *I hope that the others don't suffer the same fate.* ⊞ *The High Court will decide the fate of the three men.*
2 a power that seems to control what happens □ *She believes that fate brought them together.*

father /'fɑːðə(r)/ NOUN [plural fathers] your male parent □ *I'll speak to my father.*

➤ **Father** is a formal way of speaking or referring to your male parent. Most young people use the word **Dad** instead and young children often use the word **Daddy**.

Father Christmas /ˌfɑːðə 'krɪsməs/ NOUN an imaginary old man with a white beard in a red coat who children believe brings presents on Christmas Eve

father-in-law /'fɑːðərɪnˌlɔː/ NOUN [plural fathers-in-law] the father of your wife or husband

fatigue /fə'tiːɡ/ NOUN, NO PLURAL extreme tiredness □ *The illness can cause fatigue.*

fault /fɔːlt/ NOUN [plural faults]
1 the fact of being responsible for something bad or wrong □ *Sorry, that's my fault – I left it unlocked.* □ **+ of** *This is not the fault of the teachers.* □ *The driver was not at fault.*
2 a mistake, problem or bad feature □ *The plane developed a technical fault.* □ **+ with** *There was a fault with the design.*

faulty /'fɔːltɪ/ ADJECTIVE not working correctly □ *a faulty computer*

favor /'feɪvə(r)/ NOUN [plural favors], VERB [favors, favoring, favored] the US spelling of **favour**

favorite /'feɪvrɪt/ ADJECTIVE, NOUN [plural favorites] the US spelling of **favourite**

favour /'feɪvə(r)/ NOUN [plural favours]
1 something you do for someone to help them ⊞ *Could you do me a favour and check my homework?* ⊞ *I need to ask you a favour.* ⊞ *As a special favour, Bill's fixing my car.*
2 in favour of something supporting something as a good idea □ *I'm in favour of higher pay for nurses.* □ *Workers have voted in favour of strike action.*

favourite¹ /'feɪvrɪt/ ADJECTIVE your favourite person or thing is the one you like best □ *My favourite colour is purple.* □ *Who's your favourite player?*

favourite² /'feɪvrɪt/ NOUN [plural favourites] the person or thing you like best □ *I love all cheese, but brie is my favourite.*

fax¹ /fæks/ NOUN [plural faxes]
1 a written message that is sent by a machine over a telephone line ⊞ *I sent a fax to the bank.*
2 a machine used for sending a fax message

fax² /fæks/ VERB [faxes, faxing, faxed] to send someone a fax

fear¹ /fɪə(r)/ NOUN [plural fears]
1 *no plural* the feeling of being very frightened □ *She was shaking with fear.* ⊞ *They live in constant fear of attack.*
2 a feeling of being frightened or worried about a particular thing □ **+ of** *John has a fear of spiders.* □ **+ about** *He has raised fears about the future of the company.* □ **+ for** *She expressed fears for their safety.* ⊞ *The news confirmed her worst fears.*

fear² /fɪə(r)/ VERB [fears, fearing, feared] to be afraid of or worried about someone or something □ *Experts fear the virus could spread.* □ **+ that** *She feared that she was already too late.* □ **+ for** *He feared for his safety.* ⊞ *She feared for her life* (= thought she might die).

fearless /'fɪələs/ ADJECTIVE not frightened by anything □ *a fearless fighter*

feast /fiːst/ NOUN [plural feasts] a large meal for a special occasion

feat /fiːt/ NOUN [plural feats] something someone does that needs a lot of skill, strength or courage □ *a feat of strength and endurance*

feather /'feðə(r)/ NOUN [plural feathers] one of the long light things that cover a bird's body

feature /'fiːtʃə(r)/ NOUN [plural features]
1 a part or quality of something □ **+ of** *One of the key features of the system is its flexibility.* ⊞ *The phone's other features include a camera, radio and MP3 player.* ⊞ *The school buses have special safety features.*
2 a part of your face, such as your eyes, nose or mouth ⊞ *She described the man's hair colour and facial features.*

February /'febrʊəri/ NOUN [plural Februarys] the second month of the year, after January and before March □ *I started my new job in February.*

fed /fed/ PAST TENSE AND PAST PARTICIPLE OF **feed**

federal /'fedərəl/ ADJECTIVE to do with a group of states which make some of their own laws but also have a national government □ *a federal system*

fed up /ˌfed 'ʌp/ ADJECTIVE annoyed or bored with something that has been happening for a long time □ *I've been peeling potatoes all morning and I'm fed up now.* □ *We're fed up with your moaning.*

fee /fiː/ NOUN [plural fees] an amount of money that you pay for a service □ **+ for** *They charge a monthly fee for unlimited Internet access.* ⊞ *Companies pay a fee to advertise on the site.*

feed /fiːd/ VERB [feeds, feeding, fed] to give food to a person or an animal □ *Dad was feeding the baby.* □ *I don't earn enough money to feed my family.* □ *Can you feed my cat while I'm on holiday?*

feedback /'fiːdbæk/ NOUN, NO PLURAL opinions from people about work you are doing or have done, intended to help you do it better ⊞ *It's always good to get feedback from customers.*

feel /fiːl/ VERB [feels, feeling, felt]
1 to have an emotion or to be in a particular state □ *I feel tired.* □ *Do you feel better today?* □ *How are you feeling?* □ *I don't feel any anger towards them.*

2 to touch something with your fingers to see what it is like □ *Feel how soft her fur is!*
3 to experience something touching you or happening to you □ *Suddenly, she felt a hand on her shoulder.* □ *He could feel himself falling.* □ *I felt a pain in my leg.*
4 if something feels a certain way, that is how it seems to you □ *Your forehead feels hot.* □ *It feels strange to be back here.* □ *It feels as though nobody is interested.*
5 to think or believe something □ *I feel I should have asked my opinion first.*
6 **feel like something** to want something or want to do something □ **+ ing** *Do you feel like going for a swim?*

feeling /'fiːlɪŋ/ NOUN [plural feelings]
1 an emotion □ *There was a feeling of excitement amongst the children.*
2 something that you experience physically, or the ability to experience it □ *I don't like the feeling of being under water.* ⊞ *I lost the feeling in my toes.*
3 a belief that something is true ⊞ *I have the feeling that she's avoiding me.*
➡ *go to* **hurt¹ someone's feelings**

feet /fiːt/ PLURAL OF **foot**

fell¹ /fel/ PAST TENSE OF **fall¹**

fell² /fel/ VERB [fells, felling, felled] if you fell a tree, you cut it down

fellow¹ /'feləʊ/ NOUN [plural fellows] an old-fashioned word for a boy or man □ *He's an unusual fellow.*

fellow² /'feləʊ/ ADJECTIVE used to refer to a person who is similar to you in some way □ *He chatted with fellow passengers.*

felt¹ /felt/ NOUN, NO PLURAL a type of cloth made of rolled and pressed wool

felt² /felt/ PAST TENSE AND PAST PARTICIPLE OF **feel**

female¹ /'fiːmeɪl/ ADJECTIVE belonging to the sex which can give birth or lay eggs □ *a female athlete* □ *She won the award for best female artist.* □ *A female lion is called a lioness.*

female² /'fiːmeɪl/ NOUN [plural females] a female animal or person □ *We saw an adult female with three cubs.*

feminine /'femɪnɪn/ ADJECTIVE
1 to do with women, or having qualities that are typical of a woman □ *a feminine voice* □ *This outfit feels more feminine.*
2 in English grammar, feminine forms of words refer to females. For example, *she* is a feminine pronoun.

fence /fens/ NOUN [plural fences] a wooden or metal structure that goes around or separates land □ *He put up a fence around the garden.*

ferocious /fə'rəʊʃəs/ ADJECTIVE extremely violent, strong or dangerous □ *a ferocious dog* □ *a ferocious storm*

ferry /'ferɪ/ NOUN [*plural* ferries] a boat that carries people and vehicles 🔁 *a passenger ferry* 🔁 *We took a ferry to a smaller island.*

fertile /'fɜːtaɪl/ ADJECTIVE
1 fertile land is good for growing crops on □ *fertile soil*
2 a fertile person or animal is able to produce children or young animals

fertilizer *or* **fertiliser** /'fɜːtɪlaɪzə(r)/ NOUN [*plural* fertilizers] a substance you put on soil to make plants grow better

festival /'festɪvəl/ NOUN [*plural* festivals]
1 a series of special events of a particular type 🔁 *a film festival* 🔁 *a five-day music festival* □ *+ of* an *annual festival of traditional music*
2 a special time or day when people celebrate something 🔁 *a religious festival* □ *+ of* the *Muslim festival of Eid*

fetch /fetʃ/ VERB [fetches, fetching, fetched] to go somewhere and bring something or someone back with you □ *Could you fetch the newspaper for me, please?* □ *I'll come and fetch you.* □ *The women fetch water from the river.*

fever /'fiːvə(r)/ NOUN [*plural* fevers] if you have a fever, your body temperature is higher than normal because you are ill 🔁 *He had a high fever.*

few /fjuː/ DETERMINER, PRONOUN [fewer, fewest]
1 a small number □ *I packed a few apples and some bread.* □ *A few people tried to help him.* □ *I visit her every few days.* □ *The past few weeks have been very difficult.*
2 some but not many □ *We only had a few replies to our advert.* □ *Few of the children had seen a cow before.* 🔁 *Very few people know her real name.*
3 quite a few quite a lot □ *There were quite a few mistakes in his work.*

fiancé /fɪ'ɒnseɪ/ NOUN [*plural* fiancés] a woman's fiancé is the man she has promised to marry □ *She will marry her fiancé in April.*

fiancée /fɪ'ɒnseɪ/ NOUN [*plural* fiancées] a man's fiancée is the woman he has promised to marry □ *Tom's fiancée is a teacher.*

fibre /'faɪbə(r)/ NOUN [*plural* fibres]
1 a substance in food which your body cannot digest, and which helps your bowels work well □ *Brown bread is high in fibre.*
2 a thin thread of something □ *Fibres from the girl's clothing were found in his car.*

fiction /'fɪkʃən/ NOUN, NO PLURAL books about imaginary people and situations 🔁 *He enjoys reading*

crime fiction. 🔁 *JK Rowling is one of the most famous children's fiction writers.*

field /fiːld/ NOUN [*plural* fields] an area of land used for growing crops or keeping animals on □ *There were lots of cows in the field.* □ *+ of* We *saw a lovely field of poppies.*

fierce /fɪəs/ ADJECTIVE [fiercer, fiercest] violent and angry □ *a fierce animal* □ *fierce fighting*
fifteen /ˌfɪf'tiːn/ NUMBER the number 15
fifteenth /ˌfɪf'tiːnθ/ NUMBER 15th written as a word

fifth^1 /fɪfθ/ NUMBER 5th written as a word □ *Today is their fifth wedding anniversary.*

fifth^2 /fɪfθ/ NOUN [*plural* fifths] 1/5; one of five equal parts of something □ *A fifth of the money is mine.*

fiftieth /'fɪftɪəθ/ NUMBER 50th written as a word
fifty /'fɪftɪ/ NUMBER [*plural* fifties]
1 the number 50
2 the fifties the years between 1950 and 1959

fight^1 /faɪt/ VERB [fights, fighting, fought]
1 to use your body or weapons to try to defeat someone □ *They started fighting.* □ *My great-grandfather fought in the second world war.* □ *Troops fought a fierce battle in the desert.*
2 to argue with someone □ *+ about* They're *fighting about who should do the washing up.* □ *+ over* They're *fighting over her money* (= arguing about who should have it).

fight^2 /faɪt/ NOUN [*plural* fights]
1 when people use physical force to hurt each other □ *+ between* There was a fight between local gangs.
2 when people argue with each other □ *I had a fight with my Mum about staying out late.* 🔁 *Josh is always trying to pick a fight* (= start an argument).
3 when people try hard to achieve something □ *+ for* His *book describes the long fight for justice.*

fighter /'faɪtə(r)/ NOUN [*plural* fighters] someone who is fighting

figure /'fɪɡə(r)/ NOUN [*plural* figures]
1 a number that tells you an amount, especially in official documents 🔁 *official/government figures* 🔁 *The latest unemployment figures were released* (= told to the public) *today.* 🔁 *Figures show that unemployment has increased.*
2 a number □ *He paid a four figure sum* (= over £1,000). 🔁 *The number of deaths has reached double figures* (= is at least 10).
3 the shape of your body □ *She's got a lovely figure.*
4 a person that you do not know or cannot see clearly □ *There was a shadowy figure in the doorway.*

file^1 /faɪl/ NOUN [*plural* files]
1 a place for storing information on a computer. A

computing word. □ *I've created a new file for the accounts.* □ *I downloaded some image files.*
2 a piece of folded card for keeping documents in
3 a tool with a rough edge for making things smooth

file² /faɪl/ VERB [files, filing, filed]
1 to put documents into a file □ *Please file these application forms under 'rejects'.*
2 to walk somewhere, one person behind another □ *The children filed into the hall.*
3 to make something smooth using a file

fill /fɪl/ VERB [fills, filling, filled]
1 to make a container or space full □ **+ with** *The waiter filled our glasses with wine.* □ *The room was filled with smoke* □ **+ up** *She filled up the pan with water.*
2 to become full □ **+ with** *The concert hall quickly filled with people.* □ **+ up** *The room had filled up by the time we got back.*
♦ PHRASAL VERB **fill something in/out** to write information in the spaces on an official document ◨ *To apply for a place on the course, you need to fill in this form.*

filling /'fɪlɪŋ/ ADJECTIVE food that is filling makes your stomach feel full

film¹ /fɪlm/ NOUN [plural films]
1 a story that you watch in a cinema or on television ◨ *Have you seen this James Bond film?* ◨ *He was watching a film on television.* ◨ *They made a film about his life.* ◨ *a film star* (= a famous actor who has been in many films)
2 something you put inside a camera so you can take photographs ◨ *I need a new roll of film.*

> ➤ THESAURUS: A film or a movie is a general word for a story that you watch in a cinema or on television. Movie is the usual word in American English. A documentary is a film about real people or real events. A cartoon is a film made from a long series of drawings.

film² /fɪlm/ VERB [films, filming, filmed] to make a film of something □ *They were filming scenes for her new movie.* □ *'Brokeback Mountain' was filmed in Canada.*

filter¹ /'fɪltə(r)/ NOUN [plural filters] a device that you put a liquid or gas through in order to remove solid substances □ *a water filter*
filter² /'fɪltə(r)/ VERB [filters, filtered, filtering] to put something through a filter

final¹ /'faɪnəl/ ADJECTIVE coming at the end □ *I'm reading the final chapter of the book.* □ *On the final day of his tour, the Prime Minister visited a school.*

final² /'faɪnəl/ NOUN [plural finals] the last game in a competition, which decides who will win □ *Federer will play Henman in the final.* □ *The team are through to the finals.*

finale /fɪ'nɑːlɪ/ NOUN [plural finales] the last part of a show or piece of music

finally /'faɪnəlɪ/ ADVERB
1 after a long time □ *When he finally arrived, it was after midnight.*
2 used to introduce the last in a list of things □ *Finally, I would like to thank everyone who has helped.*

finance¹ /'faɪnæns/ NOUN [plural finances] things that are to do with money, especially in a government or company □ *John is an expert in finance.* ◨ *She's the company's finance director.*

finance² /faɪ'næns/ VERB [finances, financing, financed] to provide the money for something, especially in business □ *They took out a loan to finance the project.*

financial /faɪ'nænʃəl/ ADJECTIVE to do with money ◨ *banks and other financial institutions* ◨ *Many companies are facing financial difficulties.*

find /faɪnd/ VERB [finds, finding, found]
1 to discover or see something or someone you have been looking for □ *I can't find my pencil case.* □ *The murderer was never found.*
2 to discover something by chance □ *A jogger found the body by the river last night.* □ *I found a beetle in my soup.*
3 to discover that something has happened or that something is true □ *The survey found a link between birth weight and intelligence.* □ **+ that** *I find that it is best to call her in the mornings.* □ *I found I had forgotten my phone.*
4 to discover an answer, a reason or a way of doing something ◨ *We found a way to stop the leak.* ◨ *We are trying to find a solution to the problem of litter.*
5 find someone guilty/not guilty to say that someone is guilty/not guilty in a court □ *He was found guilty of murder and sentenced to life in prison.*
♦ PHRASAL VERB **find out (something)** to discover information or the truth about something □ **+ that** *We found out that they had been stealing from us.* □ **+ about** *She used the Internet to find out about bees.* □ *I need to find out how to set up a website.*

fine¹ /faɪn/ ADJECTIVE [finer, finest]
1 good or acceptable □ *'Let's meet at seven.' 'OK, that sounds fine.'* □ *'Is the water hot enough?' 'Yes, it's fine, thanks.'*
2 healthy or happy □ *'How are you?' 'I'm fine, thanks.'* ◨ *Don't worry, I'm absolutely fine.*
3 of a very good quality □ *The museum has many fine examples of Japanese art.* □ *It was a fine performance.*
4 very thin, or made of very small pieces □ *a fine needle* □ *fine powder*
5 sunny, with no rain ◨ *The fine weather brought many people to the coast.*
● **finely** /'faɪnlɪ/ ADVERB
1 into very thin small pieces ◨ *Chop the onion finely.*

2 in a beautiful way □ *The palace was finely decorated.*

> ➤ Note that the adjective **fine**, meaning 'healthy or happy' never has the word 'very' before it:
> ✓ 'How are you, Lilia?' 'I'm fine, thanks.'
> ✗ 'How are you, Lilia?' 'I'm very fine, thanks.'

fine² /faɪn/ VERB [fines, fining, fined] to make someone pay a fine □ *He was fined for dropping litter.*

fine³ /faɪn/ NOUN [*plural* fines] money that someone must pay as a punishment ⊞ *He was given a parking fine.* ⊞ *She was ordered to pay a fine of £60 for speeding.*

finger /'fɪŋɡə(r)/ NOUN [*plural* fingers] one of the five long parts at the end of your hand ⊞ *Sam had a cut on his little finger* (= smallest finger).
♦ IDIOMS **(keep your) fingers crossed** used for saying that you hope something will happen □ *We're keeping our fingers crossed that he passes the exam.* □ *Fingers crossed the train arrives on time.* **put your finger on something** to understand exactly what is wrong, different etc. □ *Something wasn't right but I couldn't put my finger on it.*

fingernail /'fɪŋɡəneɪl/ NOUN [*plural* fingernails] the hard part at the top of each finger □ *He bites his fingernails.*

fingerprint /'fɪŋɡəprɪnt/ NOUN [*plural* fingerprints] the mark that your finger leaves when you touch something □ *The police took his fingerprints.*

fingertip /'fɪŋɡətɪp/ NOUN [*plural* fingertips] the top end of each finger

finish¹ /'fɪnɪʃ/ VERB [finishes, finishing, finished]
1 to complete something □ *Have you finished your homework?* □ **+ ing** *I've finished cleaning the bathroom.*
2 to come to an end □ *What time did the film finish?*
3 to use, eat or drink all of something □ *I've finished the bread.*
♦ PHRASAL VERBS **finish something off 1** to complete the last part of something □ *I just need to finish off the housework.* **2** to eat, drink or use the last part of something □ *The children finished off all the sausages.* **finish with something** to stop using or needing something □ *Have you finished with the bread knife?*

finish² /'fɪnɪʃ/ NOUN [*plural* finishes] the last part of something ⊞ *The course was badly planned from start to finish.*

fire¹ /'faɪə(r)/ NOUN [*plural* fires]
1 *no plural* flames and heat that are caused by something burning □ *The building was destroyed by fire.*
2 when something burns in a way that is not intended ⊞ *Fire broke out* (= started) *in the warehouse.* ⊞ *We used buckets of water to put out the fire.* ⊞ *The curtains caught fire* (= started to burn).
3 **on fire** burning □ *Soon the whole building was on fire.*
4 **set fire to something** to make something burn
5 a pile of wood, coal, etc. that is burned to provide heat ⊞ *I lit a fire in the bedroom.*

> ➤ THESAURUS: A **fire** is the heat and flames caused by burning something. You can have a fire in your house to keep you warm, or it can be an accident. A **flame** is the hot orange gas that you see in a fire. A **blaze** is a big fire.

fire² /'faɪə(r)/ VERB [fires, firing, fired]
1 to fire a gun is to shoot a bullet from it
2 an informal word meaning to tell someone that they must leave their job □ *She was fired for bullying her colleagues.*

firearm /'faɪərɑːm/ NOUN [*plural* firearms] a formal word meaning a gun

fire brigade /'faɪə brɪ,ɡeɪd/ NOUN [*plural* fire brigades] the group of people whose job is to stop fires burning

fire engine /'faɪər ,endʒɪn/ NOUN [*plural* fire engines] a vehicle that carries fire fighters and their equipment

firefighter /'faɪə,faɪtə(r)/ NOUN [*plural* firefighters] someone whose job is to stop fires burning □ *Firefighters battled for two hours to get the blaze under control.*

fireman /'faɪəmən/ NOUN [*plural* firemen] a man whose job is to stop fires burning

fireplace /'faɪəpleɪs/ NOUN [*plural* fireplaces] the space for a fire in the wall of a room, or the frame around this space

firework /'faɪəwɜːk/ NOUN [*plural* fireworks] something which explodes and makes bright lights in the sky for entertainment ⊞ *The festival ended with a spectacular fireworks display.*

firm¹ /fɜːm/ ADJECTIVE [firmer, firmest]
1 not soft □ *a firm bed*
2 showing that you are in control and that you mean what you say □ *She spoke in a quiet but firm voice.* □ *She is a very firm leader.* □ **+ with** *You should be more firm with the children.*
3 tight, strong and not going to move □ *Betsy took a firm hold on the tray.*

firm² /fɜːm/ NOUN [*plural* firms] a company □ *Sally works for a law firm.* □ *a software firm*

first¹ /fɜːst/ DETERMINER, NUMBER
1 coming before everyone or everything else □ *His was the first name on the list.* □ *The first time I went skiing, I hated it.* □ *Take the first road on the left.*
2 1ˢᵗ written as a word

first² /fɜːst/ PRONOUN, NOUN, NO PLURAL the person or thing that comes before all others □ *She was the first to realise how the drug could be used.* □ *This is the first in a series of Beethoven concerts.* □ *The doctor's ready now. Who's first?*

first³ /fɜːst/ ADVERB
1 before anyone or anything else □ *You can phone Josh, but eat your dinner first.* □ *First you need to dig the foundations.*
2 for the first time □ *We first met at university.* □ *I first became aware of the problem last week.*
3 doing better than everyone else in a competition, exam, etc. 🔁 *Philip came first in the cookery competition.*
4 at first at the beginning □ *At first I couldn't speak French at all.*

first-class¹ /ˌfɜːstˈklɑːs/ ADJECTIVE used about travel when you pay for a better seat etc., and about post when you pay more for a quicker service □ *a first-class train ticket* □ *a first-class stamp*
first-class² /ˌfɜːstˈklɑːs/ ADVERB using the best or most expensive type □ *Len always travels first-class.*
first name /ˌfɜːst ˈneɪm/ NOUN [*plural* first names] the name that comes before your family name □ *Her first name's 'Jane' and her surname is 'Smith'.*

fish¹ /fɪʃ/ NOUN [*plural* fish or fishes]
1 an animal that lives and swims in water 🔁 *They were trying to catch fish in the stream.*
2 *no plural* the meat from this animal eaten as food □ *We had fish for dinner.*

> Note that the plural form of **fish** is usually **fish**. **Fishes** is not common but is sometimes used when talking about different types of fish:
> ✓ We caught a lot of **fish**.
> ✗ We caught a lot of **fishes**.

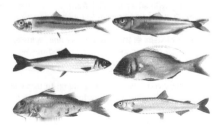

fish² /fɪʃ/ VERB [fishes, fishing, fished] to try to catch fish □ *+ for* *The men were fishing for salmon.*

fisherman /ˈfɪʃəmən/ NOUN [*plural* fishermen] someone who catches fish as a job or sport

fishing /ˈfɪʃɪŋ/ NOUN, NO PLURAL the sport or job of catching fish 🔁 *We're going fishing at the weekend.* 🔁 *the fishing industry*

fist /fɪst/ NOUN [*plural* fists] your hand when it is closed tightly □ *Don't shake your fist at me!*

fit¹ /fɪt/ VERB [fits, fitting, fitted]
1 to be the right shape or size for someone or something □ *The dress fits you perfectly.* □ *The cupboard will fit in the corner.*
2 to have enough room to put something or someone somewhere, or to be small enough to go somewhere □ *I can't fit any more documents in this file.* □ *We tried to get the piano up the stairs, but it wouldn't fit.*
3 to fix something in a place □ *We're having a new kitchen fitted next week.* □ *+ with* *He was fitted with a pacemaker.*
♦ PHRASAL VERBS **fit in** to become accepted by a group of people □ *They were all very sporty, and I didn't really fit in.* **fit someone/something in** to have time to see someone or do something □ *We can fit you in to see the doctor at ten.*

fit² /fɪt/ ADJECTIVE [fitter, fittest]
1 healthy, especially because of doing exercise 🔁 *I'm trying to get fit.*
2 suitable or good enough □ *+ to do something* *This food isn't fit to eat.*

five /faɪv/ NUMBER [*plural* fives] the number 5

fix /fɪks/ VERB [fixes, fixing, fixed]
1 to attach something to something else □ *+ to* *She fixed the shelves to the wall.*
2 to repair something □ *He's trying to fix the roof.* 🔁 *I need to get the car fixed.* 🔁 *All our staff are working to fix the problem.*
3 to decide something 🔁 *Have you fixed a date for the wedding?*
♦ PHRASAL VERB **fix something up** to arrange something such as a meeting or visit □ *They fixed up a meeting for the following week.*

> THESAURUS: If you **fix** or **mend** something you repair it. If you **adjust** something, you change it slightly. For example, you might adjust a clock if it is fast or slow. If you **correct** something, you make it right or show someone the mistakes that they have made. For example, a teacher might correct a student's writing.

flag /flæg/ NOUN [*plural* flags] a piece of cloth with a pattern on it, used as the symbol of a country or organization □ *The American flag has stars and stripes on it.* 🔁 *Hundreds of people were waving flags as the Queen arrived.* 🔁 *Flags were flying on the castle.*

flame /fleɪm/ NOUN [plural flames]
1 the hot orange gas you see in a fire 🔁 *Flames leapt from the roof.* 🔁 *Firefighters tried to put out the flames.*
2 in flames burning □ *The building was in flames.*
3 burst into flames/go up in flames to suddenly start burning □ *The plane skidded off the runway and burst into flames.*

flap[1] /flæp/ VERB [flaps, flapping, flapped] if a bird flaps its wings, it moves them up and down
flap[2] /flæp/ NOUN [plural flaps] a piece of something that hangs down over an opening □ *He closed the tent flaps.*

flash[1] /flæʃ/ VERB [flashes, flashing, flashed]
1 if a light flashes, it goes on and off quickly □ *The warning light was flashing.* 🔁 *a flashing light*
2 to make a light go on and off quickly □ *He flashed his car lights to warn other drivers of the danger.*
3 to appear for a short time and then disappear □ *Some important news suddenly flashed up on the screen.*

flash[2] /flæʃ/ NOUN [plural flashes]
1 a sudden bright light 🔁 *a flash of lightning*
2 a light on a camera that you use when you are taking photographs indoors
3 in a flash an informal phrase meaning very quickly □ *She was out of the door in a flash.*

➤ **THESAURUS:** A flash is a sudden bright light. For example, we talk about a flash of lightning. If something shines with small flashes of light, we can say that it glitters. Diamonds glitter, for example. A spark is a small burning piece that is sent out of a fire. A glow is a warm or soft light. A fire might glow, especially if it is not burning very strongly.

flat[1] /flæt/ ADJECTIVE [flatter, flattest]
1 level, smooth and not sloping □ *a flat roof* □ *Place the box on a flat surface.* □ *I'd like to have a flatter stomach.*
2 a flat tyre does not have enough air in it

flat[2] /flæt/ ADVERB in a way that is level, smooth and not sloping □ *I spread the carpet flat on the floor.* □ *Omar was lying flat on his back.*

flat[3] /flæt/ NOUN [plural flats] a set of rooms that someone lives in, which are part of a larger building

flatten /'flætən/ VERB [flattens, flattening, flattened] to make something become flat

flatter /'flætə(r)/ VERB [flatters, flattering, flattered] to say nice things to someone because you want to please them, especially when you are not being sincere □ *I'm sure he's just flattering me when he said he enjoyed reading my article.*

flavour /'fleɪvə(r)/ NOUN [plural flavours] the taste that something has □ *Chocolate is my favourite ice cream flavour.* □ *Brown rice has a wonderful nutty flavour.*

flaw /flɔː/ NOUN [plural flaws] a fault in someone or something □ *The building has some serious design flaws.*

fled /fled/ PAST TENSE AND PAST PARTICIPLE OF **flee**

flee /fliː/ VERB [flees, fleeing, fled] a formal word meaning to run away or to escape □ *Nina turned and fled.*

fleet /fliːt/ NOUN [plural fleets] a group of ships or vehicles □ *a fleet of boats*

flesh /fleʃ/ NOUN, NO PLURAL the part of a person's or animal's body between the skin and the bones □ *The salmon's flesh should be pink and firm.*

flew /fluː/ PAST TENSE OF **fly**[1]

flexibility /ˌfleksə'bɪlətɪ/ NOUN, NO PLURAL
1 the quality of being able to change to suit different people or situations □ *We appreciate your flexibility about the time of the meeting.*
2 the quality of being easy to bend

flexible /'fleksəbəl/ ADJECTIVE
1 able to change to suit different people or situations □ *flexible arrangements*
2 easy to bend □ *flexible wires*

flick /flɪk/ VERB [flicks, flicking, flicked] to send something through the air quickly and suddenly, often with your fingers □ *She flicked the fly off her coat.* □ *He flicked the ball back to me.*
♦ PHRASAL VERB **flick through something** to look quickly at each page in a magazine, book, etc.

flight /flaɪt/ NOUN [plural flights]
1 a journey in an aircraft □ *+ from* *a direct flight from Heathrow to Singapore* 🔁 *He boarded a flight to Tokyo.*
2 a set of stairs 🔁 *We walked up several flights of stairs.* 🔁 *a flight of steps* □ *She climbed the five flights to her apartment.*

fling /flɪŋ/ VERB [flings, flinging, flung] to throw or move something using a lot of force □ *He flung his racket down.* □ *She flung her arms round him.* □ *She flung herself down in the chair, completely exhausted.*

flip /flɪp/ VERB [flips, flipping, flipped] to turn over quickly or to make something turn over quickly □ *The car ran off the road and flipped over.* □ *After a couple of minutes, flip the fish over to cook the other side.*

flirt /flɜːt/ VERB [flirts, flirting, flirted] to behave as if you think someone is attractive □ *Emma was flirting with her sister's boyfriend.*

float /fləʊt/ VERB [floats, floating, floated]
1 to move slowly or to stay on the surface of a liquid and not sink □ *Leaves were floating on the surface of the lake.* □ *The boat floated slowly down the river.*
2 to stay in the air or to move slowly through the air □ *He let go of the balloon and it floated away.* □ *Voices floated down the stairs.*

flock /flɒk/ NOUN [plural flocks] a group of sheep or birds

flood¹ /flʌd/ NOUN [plural floods] a lot of water covering a place that is usually dry □ *Two days of heavy rain caused floods.*

flood² /flʌd/ VERB [floods, flooding, flooded] if water floods a place or if a place floods, it becomes covered in a lot of water □ *Large parts of the town were flooded.* □ *The river has flooded its banks.*

floor /flɔː(r)/ NOUN [plural floors]
1 the surface that you stand on in a room □ *There were toys all over the kitchen floor.* □ *The hall has a wooden floor.*
2 one of the levels in a building □ *Which floor is your apartment on?* □ *Our office is on the top floor of the building.*

floppy disk /ˌflɒpɪ ˈdɪsk/ NOUN [plural floppy disks] a disk inside a flat piece of plastic that is used for copying information from a computer. A computing word

flour /ˈflaʊə(r)/ NOUN, NO PLURAL powder made from wheat (= grain), used for making bread and cakes

flourish /ˈflʌrɪʃ/ VERB [flourishes, flourishing, flourished] to develop quickly and well □ *Her new business is flourishing.* □ *Wildlife is once again flourishing in the area.*

flow¹ /fləʊ/ VERB [flows, flowing, flowed] if a liquid flows, it moves along □ **+ through** *The River Thames flows through London.* □ **+ into** *The water flows into the sea.* □ *Tears flowed down her face.*

flow² /fləʊ/ NOUN [plural flows] a continuous movement of something □ **+ of** *We used bandages to stop the flow of blood.* 🖰 *a steady flow of tourists*

> ► THESAURUS: A **flow** is a continuous movement of something, especially liquid. A **current** is a flow of water or air moving in one direction. A **tide** is the regular rise and fall of the level of the sea. At high **tide**, the sea covers the beach. At low **tide**, the sea does not cover the beach. A **flood** is a lot of water covering a place that is usually dry. If there is a lot of rain, it can cause a **flood**.

flower /ˈflaʊə(r)/ NOUN [plural flowers] the coloured part of a plant □ *Tulips are my favourite flower.* 🖰 *We picked some wild flowers.* 🖰 *They gave her a bunch of flowers.*

flown /fləʊn/ PAST PARTICIPLE OF **fly**¹

flu /fluː/ NOUN, NO PLURAL an illness like a very bad cold which makes you feel hot and tired 🖰 *Last month she caught flu.* □ *I had a bad bout of flu.*

fluent /ˈfluːənt/ ADJECTIVE able to speak a language easily and well □ *She speaks fluent German.*

fluid¹ /ˈfluːɪd/ NOUN [plural fluids] a liquid □ *Runners should drink plenty of fluids.*

fluid² /ˈfluːɪd/ ADJECTIVE able to flow like a liquid □ *Blood is a fluid substance.*

flung /flʌŋ/ PAST TENSE AND PAST PARTICIPLE OF **fling**

flush /flʌʃ/ VERB [flushes, flushing, flushed]
1 to press or pull a handle to make water go down a toilet 🖰 *I can't flush the toilet.*
2 to become red in the face □ *He flushed with embarrassment.*

flute /fluːt/ NOUN [plural flutes] a musical instrument you play by holding it sideways against your mouth and blowing into it

flutter /ˈflʌtə(r)/ VERB [flutters, fluttering, fluttered] to move quickly up and down or from side to side □ *Her eyelids fluttered.* □ *The flags fluttered in the breeze.*

fly¹ /flaɪ/ VERB [flies, flying, flew, flown]
1 to travel in an aircraft □ **+ to** *He flew to Miami.* □ *She flew in by helicopter.*
2 to move through the air using wings □ *A robin flew across the garden.* □ *A plane flew overhead.*
3 to control an aircraft □ *She learned to fly a helicopter.*
4 to move very quickly □ *A bullet flew past my head.* 🖰 *The door flew open.*

► **THESAURUS:** Fly is a general word for moving above the earth. Planes and birds can fly. To float means to stay in the air or move slowly through the air. A balloon floats in the air. If something hovers, it stays still in the air. A helicopter can hover, and some birds can hover.

fly² /flaɪ/ NOUN [plural **flies**] a small insect that flies

foam /fəʊm/ NOUN, NO PLURAL a mass of small bubbles on top of a liquid □ I like to eat the foam off my coffee with a spoon.

focus¹ /'fəʊkəs/ VERB [focuses, focusing, focused]
1 to concentrate on one particular thing □ The report focused on the need to improve standards. ⬧ She wants to focus attention on the problem.
2 to make small changes to equipment such as a camera so that you get a clear picture

focus² /'fəʊkəs/ NOUN, NO PLURAL
1 when you focus on one thing, or the thing you focus on ⬧ My main focus is to play well. ⬧ She soon became the focus of media attention.
2 in focus if an image is in focus, it can be seen clearly □ Make sure the faces are in focus.
3 out of focus if an image is out of focus, it cannot be seen clearly □ Some of the photos were out of focus.

foe /fəʊ/ NOUN [plural **foes**] a formal word for an enemy □ The two men are old foes.

fog /fɒg/ NOUN, NO PLURAL thick, low cloud that makes it difficult to see ⬧ The flight was delayed due to thick fog. □ The fog lifted slightly.

foggy /'fɒgi/ ADJECTIVE [foggier, foggiest] having a lot of fog □ a foggy day □ foggy weather
♦ IDIOM **not have the foggiest (idea)** used to emphasize that you do not know anything about something □ I haven't got the foggiest idea where he is.

fold¹ /fəʊld/ VERB [folds, folding, folded]
1 to bend one part of something so that it covers another part □ Dan folded the letter and put it in the envelope. □ He folded the clothes neatly.
2 to make something smaller by bending parts of it □ **+ up** He folded up his laptop and put it in his bag. □ The back seats fold down to give more luggage space.
3 fold your arms to cross your arms over your chest

fold² /fəʊld/ NOUN [plural **folds**] a line or mark where something is folded

folder /'fəʊldə(r)/ NOUN [plural **folders**]
1 a cardboard or plastic cover for holding papers

2 a place where you keep documents on a computer. A computing word.

folk¹ /fəʊk/ PLURAL NOUN people □ He has more money than most folk around here. ⬧ Babies and old folk are most at risk.

folk² /fəʊk/ ADJECTIVE to do with the traditions and culture of the people of a country or area ⬧ an Irish folk song ⬧ Russian folk tales

folk music /'fəʊk ˌmjuːzɪk/ NOUN, NO PLURAL traditional music from a particular country or area

follow /'fɒləʊ/ VERB [follows, following, followed]
1 to go behind someone or something and go where they go □ He followed her down the street.
2 to happen after something □ The meal was followed by a dance.
3 to do what a person or a rule, law, etc. says you should do ⬧ We decided to follow his advice and catch the train. ⬧ Just open the letter and follow the instructions in it.
4 if you follow a road, you go along it □ Follow the path to the end and turn right.
5 to understand what someone is saying □ Do you follow me?

following /'fɒləʊɪŋ/ ADJECTIVE the following day, week, year, etc. is the next one □ I finished work on Friday and we went on holiday the following Wednesday.

fond /fɒnd/ ADJECTIVE [fonder, fondest] **fond of someone/something** liking someone or something □ **+ ing** We're very fond of walking in the countryside. □ He is particularly fond of chocolate. ⬧ I've grown very fond of the children.

food /fuːd/ NOUN [plural **foods**] **no plural** things that people and animals eat □ They didn't have enough food. □ We often eat Chinese food. ⬧ pet food

► Note that **food** is not usually used in the plural. **Foods** is sometimes used when talking about different types of food but is not common:
✓ I buy most of our food at the supermarket.
✗ I buy most of our foods at the supermarket.

fool¹ /fuːl/ NOUN [plural **fools**]
1 a stupid or silly person □ I'm not a complete fool. □ I didn't want to look a fool.
2 make a fool of yourself to do something that makes people think you are silly □ They're going to make fools of themselves.

fool² /fuːl/ VERB [fools, fooling, fooled] to trick someone □ His story didn't fool anyone. □ Don't be fooled by cheap copies.

foolish /ˈfuːlɪʃ/ ADJECTIVE silly or stupid □ *a foolish mistake* □ *He didn't want to appear foolish.*

foot /fʊt/ NOUN [*plural* **feet**]
1 one of the parts of your body that you stand on □ *He has a broken foot.* 🔁 *We got to our feet* (= stood up) *when she came in.* 🔁 *I've been on my feet* (= standing up) *all day.*
2 a unit for measuring length, equal to 30.48 centimetres. This is often written **ft**.
3 the foot of the bottom of something □ *We camped at the foot of the mountain.*
4 on foot if you travel on foot, you walk
♦ IDIOM put your feet up to rest and relax

footage /ˈfʊtɪdʒ/ NOUN, NO PLURAL a filmed record of an event □ *We bring you live footage of the ceremony.*

football /ˈfʊtbɔːl/ NOUN [*plural* **footballs**]
1 *no plural* a sport played by two teams who try to kick a ball into a goal 🔁 *The boys are playing football outside.* 🔁 *a football match* 🔁 *a game of football* 🔁 *a football team*
2 the ball used for playing football □ *Some kids were kicking a football about.*

footballer /ˈfʊtbɔːlə(r)/ NOUN [*plural* **footballers**] someone who plays football, especially as their job

footprint /ˈfʊtprɪnt/ NOUN [*plural* **footprints**] a mark that your foot leaves on the ground □ *footprints in the snow*

footstep /ˈfʊtstep/ NOUN [*plural* **footsteps**] the sound of someone walking □ *I could hear footsteps.*

for /fɔː(r)/ PREPOSITION
1 to be received or used by someone, or to help someone □ *There's a letter for you.* □ *She made a cake for her Mum.* □ *I did all the ironing for Peter.*
2 in order to do something or to get something □ *He asked me for money.* □ *Let's go for a walk.* □ *I went to the supermarket for some eggs.*
3 used to show a reason or what something is intended to do □ *What's this switch for?* □ *He was arrested for shoplifting.* □ *I gave her a necklace for her birthday.*
4 used to show an amount of time, distance, money, etc. □ *I've lived here for eight years.* □ *We walked for two miles.* □ *I got these trainers for £30.*
5 meaning something □ *What's the word for 'girl' in French?*
6 supporting or agreeing with someone or something □ *I voted for her.* □ *Are you for or against the new airport?*

> ➤ When you are explaining why someone does something, remember to use the infinitive **to** do something. Do not use **for**:
> ✓ *I went home to see my mother.*
> ✗ *I went home for seeing my mother.*

forbid /fəˈbɪd/ VERB [forbids, forbidding, forbade, forbidden] to tell someone that they must not do something □ *+ to do something They forbade their daughter to see Henry any more.* □ *+ from He is forbidden from discussing the case.* □ *The school rules forbid the use of mobile phones in class.*

forbidden /fəˈbɪdən/ ADJECTIVE not allowed □ *Smoking is forbidden throughout the hospital.* 🔁 *Alcohol is strictly forbidden.*

force¹ /fɔːs/ NOUN [*plural* **forces**]
1 *no plural* power or physical strength □ *The force of the explosion damaged many buildings.*
2 by force by violent physical action □ *They took the land by force.*
3 a group of people, such as police or soldiers, who are trained to work together 🔁 *the armed forces* □ *A defence force was sent into the region.*

force² /fɔːs/ VERB [forces, forcing, forced]
1 to make someone do something □ *+ to do something He forced me to give him money.* □ *often passive She was forced to move house.*
2 to make something move by using your strength □ *The police had to force the door open.*

forecast¹ /ˈfɔːkɑːst/ NOUN [*plural* **forecasts**] a statement about what you think will happen in the future, based on information 🔁 *a weather forecast* □ *+ of We had a forecast of heavy rain.*

forecast² /ˈfɔːkɑːst/ VERB [forecasts, forecasting, forecast] to make a forecast □ *Rain is forecast for the weekend.* □ *The company has forecast record profits.*

forehead /ˈfɔːhed/ NOUN [*plural* **foreheads**] the top part of your face above your eyes

foreign /ˈfɒrən/ ADJECTIVE from a country that is not your country 🔁 *a foreign language* □ *a group of foreign tourists*

> ➤ THESAURUS: Something or someone that is foreign is from a country that is not your country. Something that is international involves several countries. You might talk about an international conference, for example. An immigrant is someone who comes to live in a country that is not their own country.

foreigner /ˈfɒrənə(r)/ NOUN [*plural* **foreigners**] someone who comes from a country that is not your country

forest /ˈfɒrɪst/ NOUN [*plural* **forests**] a place where a lot of trees are growing together □ *We stayed at a camp deep in the forest.*

forever /fəˈrevə(r)/ ADVERB for all future time □ *You can't stay in your room forever.* □ *Their lives have been changed forever.*

forgave /fə'geɪv/ PAST TENSE OF **forgive**

forget /fə'get/ VERB [forgets, forgetting, forgot, forgotten]
1 to be unable to remember something □ *I've forgotten her name.* □ **+ that** *I forgot that you had been there before.* □ **+ about** *I had forgotten about the heat here.*
2 to not remember to do something or that something is happening □ **+ to do something** *I forgot to feed the dog.* □ **+ that** *He forgot that Milo was coming.* 🔁 *Don't forget to lock the door.* 🔁 *I completely forgot her birthday.*
3 to stop thinking or caring about something □ *Forget about your exams and come to the party.*

forgetful /fə'getful/ ADJECTIVE often forgetting things

forgive /fə'gɪv/ VERB [forgives, forgiving, forgave, forgiven] to stop being angry with someone for something they have done □ **+ for** *Have you forgiven him for breaking the window?* □ *His family can never forgive the killers.* □ *If anything happens to her, I'll never forgive myself.*

forgot /fə'gɒt/ PAST TENSE OF **forget**
forgotten /fə'gɒtən/ PAST PARTICIPLE OF **forget**

fork¹ /fɔːk/ NOUN [plural forks]
1 an object with a handle and points that you use for lifting food to your mouth 🔁 *a knife and fork*
2 a place where a road or river divides and goes in two different directions □ *We came to a fork in the road.*
3 a tool with a long handle and points that you use for digging

fork² /fɔːk/ VERB [forks, forking, forked] if a road or a river forks, it divides into two parts going in different directions □ *Just after the bridge, the road forks.*

form¹ /fɔːm/ NOUN [plural forms]
1 a type of something □ *What form of transport do you use?* □ *I have tried various forms of exercise.* □ *You need to use some form of wrist support.*
2 a document with questions and spaces to write your answers 🔁 *You have to fill in a form to get a passport.* □ *Can you sign this form, please?*
3 the shape of someone or something □ *I saw his lifeless form on the floor.*
4 a class at school □ *Which form are you in?*

> ➤ **THESAURUS:** A document is a general word for an official piece of paper. A form is a document with questions on it that you have to complete. For example, you have to fill in a form to get a passport. A questionnaire is a list of questions that several people answer in order to get information. A business might use a questionnaire to find out what customers think about their products.

form² /fɔːm/ VERB [forms, forming, formed]
1 to start to exist or to make something start to exist □ *How was the Earth formed?* □ *An idea formed in his mind.* □ *I formed a good impression of his work.* □ *His party is likely to form the next government.*
2 to be something or the thing that something is made of □ *This article could form the basis of a book.* □ *The area forms part of a safari park.*
3 to make a particular shape □ *The children held hands and formed a circle.*

formal /'fɔːməl/ ADJECTIVE
1 following rules about what is polite and correct, not friendly and relaxed □ *a formal dinner party* □ *The atmosphere was very formal.*
2 public or official, or following official rules or methods 🔁 *A formal announcement is expected tomorrow.* 🔁 *I wish to make a formal complaint.*

format /'fɔːmæt/ NOUN [plural formats] the way something is designed or arranged □ *Please send two photographs in digital format.* □ *There are plans to change the format of the competition.*

former¹ /'fɔːmə(r)/ ADJECTIVE existing or true in the past but not now □ *the former President* □ *In former times, people did not travel so much.*

former² /'fɔːmə(r)/ NOUN, NO PLURAL the former the first of two people or things you mention □ *We visited America and Canada but stayed longer in the former.*

formerly /'fɔːməlɪ/ ADVERB in the past but not now □ *Their house was formerly a shop.*

formula /'fɔːmjulə/ NOUN [plural formulas or formulae]
1 in mathematics or chemistry, a set of letters, numbers or symbols that represent a rule, structure, etc. □ *What's the formula for calculating the area of a circle?* 🔁 *a mathematical formula*
2 the combination of substances used to make something

fort /fɔːt/ NOUN [plural forts] a strong building used by soldiers to to defend a place from attack

forthcoming /ˌfɔːθ'kʌmɪŋ/ ADJECTIVE happening soon □ *forthcoming events* □ *They played some tracks from their forthcoming album.*

fortieth /'fɔːtɪɪθ/ NUMBER 40th written as a word

fortnight /'fɔːtnaɪt/ NOUN [plural fortnights] a period of two weeks □ *We're going to Greece for a fortnight.* □ *I've been very busy over the past fortnight.* □ *He visits her once a fortnight.*

fortunate /'fɔːtʃənət/ ADJECTIVE lucky □ *We were fortunate to catch our train, we were so late.* □ *It's extremely fortunate that no one was hurt.* □ *We should help people who are less fortunate than ourselves.*

fortunately /ˈfɔːtʃənətlɪ/ ADVERB used to say that something lucky has happened □ *Fortunately, nobody was injured.*

fortune /ˈfɔːtʃuːn/ NOUN [plural fortunes]
1 a very large amount of money □ *His uncle died and left him a fortune.* ⌻ *He made his fortune in the oil industry.* ⌻ *They spent a fortune on it.*
2 *no plural* good luck ⌻ *Sue had the good fortune to win first prize.*

forty /ˈfɔːtɪ/ NUMBER [plural forties] the number 40

forum /ˈfɔːrəm/ NOUN [plural forums] a place or situation in which people can discuss things and express their opinions □ *an online forum* □ *The programme is intended to be a forum for public debate.*

forward¹ /ˈfɔːwəd/ ADJECTIVE in the direction that is in front of you □ *a forward movement*

forward² /ˈfɔːwəd/ or **forwards** /ˈfɔːwədz/ ADVERB in the direction that is in front of you □ *The car moved slowly forwards.* □ *Amy leaned forward.* ⌻ *He rocked backwards and forwards.*

forward³ /ˈfɔːwəd/ VERB [forwards, forwarding, forwarded] to send a letter or e-mail you have received to someone else □ *He forwarded the e-mail to several colleagues.*

fossil /ˈfɒsəl/ NOUN [plural fossils] a dead animal or plant that has been kept in a piece of rock for thousands of years

fought /fɔːt/ PAST TENSE AND PAST PARTICIPLE OF **fight¹**

foul /faʊl/ ADJECTIVE [fouler, foulest]
1 very dirty or with a bad smell or taste □ *The tea tasted foul.*
2 very unpleasant ⌻ *foul weather* ⌻ *He's in a foul mood.*

found¹ /faʊnd/ VERB [founds, founding, founded] to start an organization □ *The college was founded in 1950.*

found² /faʊnd/ PAST TENSE AND PAST PARTICIPLE OF **find**

foundation /faʊnˈdeɪʃən/ NOUN [plural foundations]
1 foundations the part of a building that is under the ground and which supports it ⌻ *They have dug the foundations for our new home.*
2 when an organization, business or country is started □ *She has worked here since the company's foundation in 1997.*

fountain /ˈfaʊntɪn/ NOUN [plural fountains] a structure that pushes water up into the air for decoration in a garden or park

➤ **THESAURUS:** A fountain is a structure that pushes water up into the air for decoration. A spring is a place where water flows out of the ground. A well is a deep hole in the ground where you can get water, oil or gas. A reservoir is a large lake where water is collected and stored in order to be used by people.

four /fɔː(r)/ NUMBER [plural fours] the number 4

fourteen /ˌfɔːˈtiːn/ NUMBER the number 14
fourteenth /ˌfɔːˈtiːnθ/ NUMBER 14th written as a word

fourth /fɔːθ/ NUMBER 4th written as a word □ *You are fourth on the list.* □ *Mario finished fourth in the race.*

fox /fɒks/ NOUN [plural foxes] a wild animal that looks like a dog, with red fur and a thick tail

fraction /ˈfrækʃən/ NOUN [plural fractions] an amount, such as 1/2 or 3/8, that is part of a whole number

fracture¹ /ˈfræktʃə(r)/ VERB [fractures, fracturing, fractured] to crack or break something, especially a bone in your body □ *Emma's fractured her arm.*

fracture² /ˈfræktʃə(r)/ NOUN [plural fractures] a crack or break in something, especially a bone in your body

fragile /ˈfrædʒaɪl/ ADJECTIVE not very strong and can easily be broken, damaged or destroyed □ *The bones become fragile and more likely to break.* □ *a fragile peace*

fragment /ˈfrægmənt/ NOUN [plural fragments] a small piece that has broken off something □ *There were fragments of glass on the floor.*

➤ **THESAURUS:** A fragment is a small piece that has broken off something. A scrap is a small piece of amount of something. We often talk about a scrap of paper, a scrap of material or a scrap of food. A chip is a small piece which has broken off something hard, such as a plate.

fragrance /ˈfreɪɡrəns/ NOUN [plural fragrances] a pleasant smell □ *the sweet fragrance of jasmine flowers*

fragrant /ˈfreɪɡrənt/ ADJECTIVE smelling pleasant □ *fragrant flowers*

frail /freɪl/ ADJECTIVE [frailer, frailest] thin and weak □ *a frail old man*

frame¹ /freɪm/ NOUN [plural frames]
1 a structure that fits around the edge of something, for example a picture or a window
2 a structure that supports something, and around which the thing is built □ *My bike has a lightweight frame.*
3 frames the part that holds the glass parts in a pair of glasses

frame² /freɪm/ VERB [frames, framing, framed] to put something such as a picture in a frame □ *I'm going to get this photo framed.*

framework /ˈfreɪmwɜːk/ NOUN [plural frameworks] the basic ideas or principles that something is based on □ *This provides a framework for sustainable development.*

frank /fræŋk/ ADJECTIVE [franker, frankest] honest and saying what you think ⊞ *We had a fairly frank discussion.* ⊞ *To be quite frank, I don't think it'll work.*

fraud /frɔːd/ NOUN, NO PLURAL the crime of tricking people to get money □ *He was found guilty of credit card fraud.*

freak /friːk/ NOUN [plural freaks] a very strange person or a person who looks very strange

free¹ /friː/ ADJECTIVE

1 not costing any money □ *It's free to get into the museum.* □ *I've got two free tickets for the show.*
2 not controlled by people or laws □ *We were given free access to all the files.* □ *The country needs to hold free and fair elections.* □ **+ to do something** *You are free to leave whenever you wish.*
3 available to be used □ *Is this seat free?*
4 not busy □ *Are you free this evening?*
5 **free time** time when you are not busy and can do what you want
6 not a prisoner □ *He is once more a free man.* ⊞ *They broke into the prison and set the prisoners free.*

➤ **THESAURUS:** If something is free, it is available to be used. You might ask someone if a seat on a train is free if you want to sit there. Vacant has a similar meaning but is a more formal word. If something is spare, it is extra, and available to be used. You might have a spare bedroom in your house for guests to use. If something is empty, it contains nothing or no one. You might say that a room is empty if it contains no furniture, or no people.

free² /friː/ VERB [frees, freeing, freed] to allow a person or animal out of a prison or place where they were being kept □ *The hostages were freed this morning.*

free³ /friː/ ADVERB

1 without any payment □ *Children under 5 travel free.*
2 out of a place where a person or animal is being kept or tied up □ *They struggled to get free.* ⊞ *They managed to break free of their chains.*

freedom /ˈfriːdəm/ NOUN, NO PLURAL

1 the right to do what you want ⊞ *freedom of speech/movement*
2 the state of not being a prisoner

freely /ˈfriːli/ ADVERB without being limited or controlled ⊞ *The information is freely available.* □ *You can speak freely to me.*

freeway /ˈfriːweɪ/ NOUN [plural freeways] the US word for **motorway**

freeze /friːz/ VERB [freezes, freezing, froze, frozen]

1 to become very cold and hard, or to turn into ice □ *The lake freezes in winter.* □ **+ over** *The river froze over* (= became covered in ice).
2 to store food at a very cold temperature so it keeps for a long time □ *We'll eat some and freeze the rest.*

freezer /ˈfriːzə(r)/ NOUN [plural freezers] a machine for keeping food very cold

freezing /ˈfriːzɪŋ/ ADJECTIVE very cold □ *It's freezing in here!* ⊞ *It was freezing cold outside.*

French fries /ˌfrentʃ ˈfraɪz/ PLURAL NOUN long thin pieces of potato, fried in oil □ *a burger with French fries*

frenzy /ˈfrenzi/ NOUN, NO PLURAL a state or period of great excitement, activity and emotion ⊞ *a frenzy of activity* ⊞ *Their engagement has created a media frenzy.*

frequency /ˈfriːkwənsi/ NOUN, NO PLURAL how often something happens □ *Global warming may increase the frequency of severe hurricanes.*

frequent /ˈfriːkwənt/ ADJECTIVE happening often □ *Dave makes frequent visits to his grandmother.* □ *His e-mails are becoming more frequent.*

frequently /ˈfriːkwəntli/ ADVERB often □ *Lee is frequently late for work.* □ *She frequently appears in women's magazines.*

fresh /freʃ/ ADJECTIVE [fresher, freshest]

1 fresh food is not old, and has not been dried, frozen, etc. ⊞ *fresh fruit/vegetables* □ *This salad will stay fresh for a day or two.*
2 new and different ⊞ *They hope to make a fresh start in Australia.* □ *I'll put some fresh sheets on the bed.*
3 fresh air is clean air in outside areas ⊞ *I'm going for a walk to get some fresh air.*

➤ **THESAURUS:** If you describe food as fresh, it is not old, and has not been dried or frozen. Food which is raw is not cooked. Food which is natural has not been made by people or machines and has not had artificial things added to it.

Friday /ˈfraɪdi/ NOUN [plural Fridays] the day of the week after Thursday and before Saturday □ *It's my birthday on Friday.*

fridge /frɪdʒ/ NOUN [plural fridges] a machine that you store food or drink in to keep it cold and fresh □ *He opened the fridge to get some milk.* □ *There's some chocolate in the fridge.*

fried¹ /fraɪd/ PAST TENSE AND PAST PARTICIPLE OF **fry** □ *She fried the fish in butter.*

fried² /fraɪd/ ADJECTIVE cooked in hot oil or fat □ *a fried egg*

friend /frend/ NOUN [*plural* friends]
1 someone who you know well and like □ + *of* *She's a friend of mine.* 🖽 *Lindsay is my best friend.* 🖽 *They only told their family and close friends.*
2 make friends (with someone) to meet and become friends with someone □ *She soon made friends.* □ *I made friends with Alex at college.*

friendly /'frendlɪ/ ADJECTIVE [friendlier, friendliest] kind and pleasant towards someone □ + *to* *She's friendly to everyone.* □ *a friendly smile* □ *The staff are friendly and helpful.*

fright /fraɪt/ NOUN [*plural* frights] a sudden feeling of fear 🖽 *You gave me a fright, jumping out like that!* 🖽 *I got a fright when I saw it.*

frighten /'fraɪtən/ VERB [frightens, frightening, frightened] to make someone feel afraid or worried □ *A sudden noise frightened the horses.* □ *You'll frighten the baby!*

frightened /'fraɪtənd/ ADJECTIVE afraid or very worried □ + *of* *He's frightened of dogs.* □ + *to do* **something** *He was too frightened to tell his parents.* 🖽 *I felt very frightened.* □ *a frightened expression*

frightening /'fraɪtənɪŋ/ ADJECTIVE making you feel afraid or very worried □ *a frightening experience* □ *They look very frightening.* □ *That's a frightening thought!*

fringe /frɪndʒ/ NOUN [*plural* fringes]
1 hair that hangs down over the top part of your face
2 loose threads that hang down from the edge of something as decoration

frog /frɒg/ NOUN [*plural* frogs] a small brown or green animal that can jump and swim and lives near water

from /frɒm/ PREPOSITION
1 used to show where or when something started or where it was before □ *She's driving up from London.* □ *The shops are open from nine to five.* □ *He took a photograph from the drawer.* □ *You can get batteries from the shop over the road.* □ *He stole some money from his parents.*
2 used to show who gave or sent something □ *I had a lovely card from Julie.*
3 used to show where someone was born or lives □ *I'm from Taiwan.*
4 used to show how far something is □ *Do you live far from here?* □ *We are 15 miles from the nearest supermarket.*
5 used to show what something is made of or what has caused something □ *Yogurt is made from milk.* □ *He was shivering from the cold.*
6 from now on starting now and continuing into

the future □ *From now on I'll be much more careful about locking the house.*

front¹ /frʌnt/ NOUN [*plural* fronts]
1 the part of something that faces forwards, or the part that is furthest forwards □ *The house has a red front.* □ *The front of the car was badly damaged.*
2 in front of someone/something (a) next to the front part of something □ *Please don't park in front of the gates.* □ *He stood right in front of me.* □ *He jumped in front of the moving train.* (b) where someone can see or hear you □ *He hit the children in front of their parents.* □ *She loves performing in front of a large audience.*
3 in front further forward than someone or something □ *I was driving along when the car in front suddenly stopped.*

front² /frʌnt/ ADJECTIVE at the front of something 🖽 *I knocked on the front door.* 🖽 *We sat in the front row.*

frontier /'frʌntɪə(r)/ NOUN [*plural* frontiers] a dividing line between two countries □ *Pakistan's western frontier* □ + *of* *He extended the frontiers of his empire.* □ + *with* *The mountains mark Nepal's frontier with India.*

➤ **THESAURUS:** A frontier or a border is a line which separates two countries. You can also talk about a border between places where there is no passport check. For example, we talk about the border between Scotland and England. The outskirts are the outer parts of a town or city.

frost /frɒst/ NOUN [*plural* frosts] no plural a very thin layer of white ice that forms on surfaces outside when the weather is cold □ *There's frost on the ground.*

frosty /'frɒstɪ/ ADJECTIVE [frostier, frostiest] when it is frosty, everything is covered in frost (= a thin, white layer of ice) □ *a frosty morning*

frown /fraʊn/ VERB [frowns, frowning, frowned] to look as if you are angry, worried or thinking a lot by moving your eyebrows (= lines of hair above your eyes) down □ *She frowned when I suggested it.*

froze /frəʊz/ PAST TENSE OF freeze □ *The milk froze in the fridge.*

frozen¹ /'frəʊzən/ PAST PARTICIPLE OF freeze □ *It was so cold that the lake had frozen.*

frozen² /'frəʊzən/ ADJECTIVE frozen food is stored at a very cold temperature to make it last for a long time □ *a packet of frozen peas*

fruit /fruːt/ NOUN, NO PLURAL a food such as an apple which grows on a plant and contains the seeds of the plant 🖽 *fruit and vegetables* 🖽 *We eat plenty of fresh fruit.* 🖽 *I usually have a piece of fruit for breakfast.*

➤ Note that **fruit** is not usually used in the plural. Sometimes the plural **fruits** is used, meaning 'types of fruit' but it is not common:
✓ You should eat more fruit.
✗ You should eat more fruits.

fry /fraɪ/ VERB [fries, frying, fried] to cook something in hot oil or fat □ *Fry the onions in a little olive oil.*

frying pan /'fraɪɪŋ ˌpæn/ NOUN [plural frying pans] a flat pan with a long handle for frying food □ *Heat the oil in a large frying pan.*
◆ IDIOM out of the frying pan into the fire used for saying that someone has left one bad situation but is now in a different and much worse situation

ft /ˌef'tiː/ ABBREVIATION foot (= measurement) or feet

fuel /fjʊəl/ NOUN [plural fuels] a substance such as gas, wood or coal that burns to give heat, light or power □ *The trains run on diesel fuel.* ㊙ *fuel consumption*

fulfil /fʊl'fɪl/ VERB [fulfils, fulfilling, fulfilled] to do a particular job or something you are expected to do ㊙ *He fulfils an important role within the team.* ㊙ *He failed to fulfil his financial obligations.*
fulfill /fʊl'fɪl/ VERB [fulfills, fulfilling, fulfilled] the US spelling of **fulfil**

full /fʊl/ ADJECTIVE [fuller, fullest]
1 containing as much as possible □ *The train was full.* □ *He gave me a full bottle of milk.* □ *The jug was only half full.*
2 containing a lot of something □ *Your work is full of mistakes.* □ *My socks are full of holes.*
3 complete ㊙ *He told me the full story.* ㊙ *She made a full recovery.*
4 having eaten enough □ + **up** *No more cake for me, thanks – I'm full up.*
➔ go to **give full rein to something**

full stop /ˌfʊl 'stɒp/ NOUN [plural full stops] the mark (.) used for showing where a sentence ends

full-time /ˌfʊl-'taɪm/ ADJECTIVE, ADVERB working for all the hours of a normal job, not part of the time ㊙ *a full-time job* ㊙ *a full-time employee* ㊙ *We both work full-time.*

fun /fʌn/ NOUN, NO PLURAL
1 enjoyment and pleasure ㊙ *Skateboarding is really good fun.* ㊙ *It was great fun!* ㊙ *We had a lot of fun at the party.* □ *That sounds like fun.*
2 make fun of someone/something to make jokes about someone or something, in a way that is not kind □ *They're always making fun of my accent.*

function¹ /'fʌŋkʃən/ NOUN [plural functions] the purpose of someone or something ㊙ *Proteins*

perform different functions in the body. ㊙ *The operating system controls the basic functions of a computer.*
function² /'fʌŋkʃən/ VERB [functions, functioning, functioned] to work in the correct way ㊙ *In some patients these cells don't function properly.* □ *The system seems to be functioning normally.*

fund¹ /fʌnd/ NOUN [plural funds] an amount of money for a particular purpose □ *a pension fund* □ *We set up a fund for victims of the earthquake.*
fund² /fʌnd/ VERB [funds, funding, funded] to provide money for a particular purpose □ *The research was funded by the Medical Research Council.*

fundamental /ˌfʌndə'mentəl/ ADJECTIVE basic and important □ *the fundamental rules of management* □ *This raises some fundamental questions.*

funeral /'fjuːnərəl/ NOUN [plural funerals] a ceremony for a person who has recently died in which the body of the dead person is buried or burned ㊙ *I didn't go to her funeral.*

fungus /'fʌŋɡəs/ NOUN [plural fungi] a plant with no leaves or flowers, for example a mushroom (= plant that you can eat, with a stem and a flat or round top)

funny /'fʌnɪ/ ADJECTIVE [funnier, funniest]
1 making you laugh □ *a funny story* □ *I don't find him very funny.* □ *They looked so funny that she had to smile.* ㊙ *Luckily, he saw the funny side of the situation.*
2 strange, surprising or unusual □ *There was a funny noise coming from the engine.* ㊙ *The funny thing is, I was just about to call him when he called me.*

➤ Do not confuse the adjective **funny** with the noun **fun**. Something that is **funny** makes you laugh. Something that you describe as **fun** is very enjoyable although it may not make you laugh: □ *That was such a funny film – I laughed all the way through.* □ *Skating is fun.*

fur /fɜː(r)/ NOUN, NO PLURAL the soft hair on some animals □ *a rabbit with soft, brown fur*

furious /'fjʊərɪəs/ ADJECTIVE extremely angry □ *We're absolutely furious about this.* □ *I had a furious row with Charlotte.*
furnish /'fɜːnɪʃ/ VERB [furnishes, furnishing, furnished] to put furniture in a house or room □ *The six large rooms are furnished with antiques.*

furniture /'fɜːnɪtʃə(r)/ NOUN, NO PLURAL objects such as beds, tables and chairs that you put in a room ㊙ *A small bed and an old wardrobe were the only pieces of furniture in the room.*

➤ Remember that **furniture** is an uncountable noun:
✓ *We don't have any furniture.*
✗ *We don't have any furnitures.*

further¹ /'fɜ:ðə(r)/ ADJECTIVE, ADVERB
1 at or to a greater distance away □ **+ from** *Which is further from here, London or Aberdeen?* □ **+ up** *Santa Monica is a few miles further up the coast.* □ *I walked further than I needed.* □ *We travelled further north.*
2 more or extra 🖅 *If you need further information, please ask.* □ *He refused to comment further* (= say more). 🖅 *Prices may rise even further.*

further² /'fɜ:ðə(r)/ VERB [furthers, furthering, furthered] to help something be successful □ *These qualifications will help further your career.*

furthermore /ˌfɜ:ðə'mɔ:(r)/ ADVERB a formal word used when you are adding something to what you have already said □ *His plans will be very expensive. Furthermore, they will cause a lot of disruption.*

furthest /'fɜ:ðəst/ ADVERB, ADJECTIVE at or to the greatest distance or amount □ *Who can throw the ball the furthest?* □ **+ from** *They sat in the corner furthest from the door.* □ *We reached the furthest point south.*

fury /'fjʊərɪ/ NOUN, NO PLURAL a very strong feeling of anger □ *The announcement sparked fury from unions.*

fuss /fʌs/ NOUN, NO PLURAL
1 unnecessary worry, excitement or anger about something □ *I don't know what all the fuss is about.* 🖅 *I don't want to make a fuss about it.*
2 **make a fuss of someone** to give someone a lot of attention □ *He made a great fuss of her when she visited.*

fussy /'fʌsɪ/ ADJECTIVE [fussier, fussiest]
1 worrying too much about small details that are not important
2 only liking particular things □ *Children can be so fussy about food.* 🖅 *a fussy eater*

future¹ /'fju:tʃə(r)/ NOUN [plural futures]
1 **the future** the time to come after now □ *You can't know what will happen to you in the future.* 🖅 *We expect a decision in the near future.*
2 **in future** in the time from now on □ *In future, please be more careful.*

future² /'fju:tʃə(r)/ ADJECTIVE happening or existing in a time after now □ *future plans* □ *We need to preserve the planet for future generations.*

future tense /ˌfju:tʃə 'tens/ NOUN [plural future tenses] the form of a verb that you use when you are talking about what will happen in the future

Gg

G *or* **g** /dʒiː/ the seventh letter of the alphabet

g /dʒiː/ ABBREVIATION gram *or* grams

gadget /'gædʒɪt/ NOUN [*plural* **gadgets**] a tool or small piece of equipment □ *I've got a gadget to unblock the sink.*

gain /geɪn/ VERB [**gains, gaining, gained**]
1 to get or achieve something □ *You gain twenty extra points for that move.* ⊞ *We could not gain access (= get in) to the building.* ⊞ *Soldiers fought to gain control of the area.*
2 to increase in amount, speed, weight, etc. □ *I gained over 20 kilos when I was pregnant.*

galaxy /'gæləksɪ/ NOUN [*plural* **galaxies**] a very large group of stars in the universe □ *Our galaxy is the Milky Way.*

gale /geɪl/ NOUN [*plural* **gales**] a very strong wind □ *The old apple tree blew down in a gale.*

gallery /'gælərɪ/ NOUN [*plural* **galleries**] a large building or a shop where works of art are shown to the public

gallon /'gælən/ NOUN [*plural* **gallons**] a unit for measuring liquids, equal to about 4.5 litres

gallop /'gæləp/ VERB [**gallops, galloping, galloped**] a horse gallops when it runs at its fastest speed with all four feet off the ground at the same time

gamble¹ /'gæmbəl/ VERB [**gambles, gambling, gambled**] to risk money on the result of a game, race or competition □ *He enjoyed gambling on horse races.*
♦ PHRASAL VERB **gamble on something** to take a risk, hoping that something will happen □ *We've decided to gamble on the rain stopping before we have our barbecue.*

gamble² /'gæmbəl/ NOUN [*plural* **gambles**] something you decide to do that is a risk ⊞ *We took a gamble on the weather.* ⊞ *Their gamble paid off (= was successful).*

gambler /'gæmblə(r)/ NOUN [*plural* **gamblers**] someone who risks money on the result of a race or game

game /geɪm/ NOUN [*plural* **games**]
1 an activity that people do for enjoyment, that has rules, often needs skill, and is usually won or lost □ *a computer game* ⊞ *After dinner, we all played games.* □ *a game of tennis/chess*

2 *no plural* wild animals and birds that are hunted for their meat

gang /gæŋ/ NOUN [*plural* **gangs**]
1 a group of young people who spend time together and often cause trouble □ *Her son got involved in a gang.*
2 an organized group of criminals □ *Police have arrested a gang of bank robbers.*
3 an informal word meaning a group of friends who meet regularly □ *I'm meeting up with the gang tonight.*

➤ **THESAURUS:** A gang is a group of young people who spend time together and often cause trouble. We can also talk about a gang of criminals. A team is a group of people who work together, especially in sports. You can talk about a football or baseball team. You can also talk about a team of engineers or a team of managers. A crew is a group of people who work together on a ship, aeroplane or train.

gangster /'gæŋstə(r)/ NOUN [*plural* **gangsters**] a member of a group of criminals

gap /gæp/ NOUN [*plural* **gaps**]
1 an opening or space in the middle of something or between things □ *The fox got through a gap in the wall.* □ *He has a gap between his front teeth.*
2 a difference between two things □ *The gap between rich and poor is widening.* ⊞ *There's a big age gap between her two children.*
3 something missing □ *There's a gap in his memory around the time of the accident.*
4 a period of time when something stops □ *He's going back to university after a three-year gap.*

garage /'gærɑːʒ, 'gærɪdʒ/ NOUN [*plural* **garages**]
1 a small building that you keep your car in
2 a place where vehicles are repaired, or a shop selling petrol

garbage /'gɑːbɪdʒ/ NOUN, NO PLURAL the US word for rubbish

garden /'gɑːdən/ NOUN [*plural* **gardens**]
1 a piece of land next to a house where flowers, trees and vegetables are grown ⊞ *The front garden is mainly grass.*

2 gardens a large area of grass, trees, flowers, etc. for the public to use or around a big house
□ *I always like to visit gardens when I go on holidays.*

> ➤ THESAURUS: A garden is an area of land around a house where flowers, vegetables and grass grow. A park is an area of grass and trees in a town where people can go to relax. A field is an area of land used for growing crops or keeping animals, often as part of a farm.

gardener /ˈgɑːdnə(r)/ NOUN [plural gardeners] someone who works in a garden

gardening /ˈgɑːdnɪŋ/ NOUN, NO PLURAL the activity of working in and taking care of a garden

garlic /ˈgɑːlɪk/ NOUN, NO PLURAL a plant like a small onion with a strong taste and smell used in cooking to add flavour ▣ *Crush two cloves of garlic with the spices.*

garment /ˈgɑːmənt/ NOUN [plural garments] a formal word meaning a piece of clothing
□ *Garments, such as suits, may be hung up in special bags.*

gas /gæs/ NOUN [plural gases or gasses]
1 a substance that is not liquid or solid and that moves about like air □ *Oxygen and carbon dioxide are two of the gases that make up air.*
2 *no plural* a gas or mixture of gases that burns easily and is used for cooking or heating □ *a gas fire*
3 *no plural* the US word for **petrol**

gasp¹ /gɑːsp/ VERB [gasps, gasping, gasped]
1 to take a short sudden breath in through your open mouth because you are shocked or surprised □ *They all gasped in horror.*
2 to find it hard to breathe ▣ *He fell to the floor, gasping for breath.*

gasp² /gɑːsp/ NOUN [plural gasps] the sound of a sudden short breath

gate /geɪt/ NOUN [plural gates]
1 the part of a fence, wall etc. that opens and closes like a door □ *Please close the gate.*
2 the place where passengers get on or off a plane at an airport □ *Flight BA123 to Rome is now boarding at Gate 12.*

gather /ˈgæðə(r)/ VERB [gathers, gathering, gathered]
1 if people gather or are gathered, they come together or are brought together in a group ▣ *A crowd gathered at the airport.* □ *The teachers gathered all the children together in the dining hall.*
2 to collect things or bring them together □ *Police are gathering as much information as they can about*

the attacker. □ *The lecturer gathered together all her papers.*

gave /geɪv/ PAST TENSE OF give

gay /geɪ/ ADJECTIVE [gayer, gayest] homosexual or to do with homosexuals □ *a gay bar* □ *a gay marriage*

gaze¹ /geɪz/ VERB [gazes, gazing, gazed] to look at something or someone for a long time, especially because they are interesting or attractive □ *The children gazed at the toys in the window.*

> ➤ THESAURUS: To look at something means to turn your eyes in order to see something. Look is a general word. If you watch something, you look at it for a while. For example, we watch television. To gaze at something means to look at something or someone for a long time, especially because they are interesting or attractive. You might gaze at a beautiful painting or a nice view, for example. To stare at something means to look at it for a long time.

gaze² /geɪz/ NOUN, NO PLURAL a long look □ *Her gaze was fixed on a tree in the distance.*

GB /ˌdʒiːˈbiː/ ABBREVIATION Great Britain

GCSE /ˌdʒiːsiːesˈiː/ ABBREVIATION General Certificate of Secondary Education; an exam taken by students in England and Wales at around the age of 16 □ *He's doing GCSE maths.*

gear /gɪə(r)/ NOUN [plural gears]
1 the set of parts in a car or bicycle that controls how fast the wheels turn □ *Our new car has five gears.*
2 a particular position of the gears on a vehicle ▣ *She still finds it hard to change gear.* ▣ *Put the car into first gear and move off.*
3 *no plural* the clothes and equipment you use for a particular sport or job □ *tennis gear*

geese /giːs/ PLURAL OF goose

gel /dʒel/ NOUN [plural gels] a thick clear substance that is between a liquid and a solid ▣ *shower gel* ▣ *Do you use hair gel?*

gem /dʒem/ NOUN [plural gems] a valuable stone that is used in jewellery

gender /ˈdʒendə(r)/ NOUN [plural genders] the state of being male or female □ *The job application form asks you to say which gender you are.*

gene /dʒiːn/ NOUN [plural genes] a part of a living cell that is passed on from parents to children and that controls things like hair or skin colour. A biology word.

general¹ /ˈdʒenərəl/ ADJECTIVE
1 involving or affecting most people or things

□ *There was a general feeling of gloom.* 🔁 *Sales to the general public* (= ordinary people) *will begin on July 11.*

2 not detailed or exact, but giving the most important information □ *Can you give me a general idea of what it will cost?* 🔁 *I understand economics in general terms.* 🔁 *As a general rule* (= in most situations) *I use two eggs for every 125g flour.*

3 in general (a) considering the whole of something or someone □ *Schools are achieving better results in general.* □ *There is agreement among the population in general.* (b) in most situations □ *In general, I think it's better to travel by train.*

4 dealing with a lot of activities, subjects or parts of a subject □ *He does general household repairs.* □ *I'm looking for a general introduction to Western art.*

general² /ˈdʒenərəl/ NOUN [*plural* generals] an important army officer

general election /ˌdʒenərəl ɪˈlekʃən/ NOUN [*plural* general elections] an election in which all the people in a country vote to choose the people who will be in the next government

generally /ˈdʒenərəli/ ADVERB
1 by most people or in most cases □ *She's generally considered Britain's greatest actor.* □ *They were generally well dressed.*
2 usually □ *Children generally start school at about the age of five.*

general practitioner /ˌdʒenərəl prækˈtɪʃənə(r)/ NOUN [*plural* general practitioners] a doctor who looks after people from a particular area and treats them for a lot of different illnesses

➤ You will often see the abbreviation for general practitioner, which is **GP**.

generate /ˈdʒenəreɪt/ VERB [generates, generating, generated] to create or produce something □ *His work generated a lot of interest.* □ *The house uses solar power to generate electricity.*

generation /ˌdʒenəˈreɪʃən/ NOUN [*plural* generations] all the people in a family or society who were born at about the same time 🔁 *the younger generation* □ *There were four generations of the family at the wedding.*

generosity /ˌdʒenəˈrɒsəti/ NOUN, NO PLURAL the quality of being generous

generous /ˈdʒenərəs/ ADJECTIVE giving a lot of money, presents or time to others □ *The locals are kind and generous people.*

genetic /dʒɪˈnetɪk/ ADJECTIVE to do with the part of a living cell that is passed on from parents to their children and that controls things like hair or skin colour, or the scientific study of these cells. A biology word □ *a genetic defect*

genetics /dʒɪˈnetɪks/ NOUN, NO PLURAL the scientific study of how living things develop as a result of the qualities parents pass on to their children in part of their cells

genius /ˈdʒiːnjəs/ NOUN [*plural* geniuses] someone who is extremely clever or skilful

gentle /ˈdʒentəl/ ADJECTIVE [gentler, gentlest]
1 careful not to hurt or upset anyone or anything □ *He was a gentle man.* □ *She gave him a gentle tap on his shoulder.*
2 not strong, severe or violent □ *a gentle breeze*

➤ **THESAURUS:** If you are gentle, you are careful not to hurt or upset anyone or anything. If you are kind, you behave in a way that shows that you care about people and want to make them happy. Note that sympathetic does not mean the same as kind. If you are sympathetic, you show that you feel sorry for someone who is unhappy or suffering.

gentleman /ˈdʒentəlmən/ NOUN [*plural* gentlemen]
1 a word used to refer politely to a man □ *Good morning, gentlemen.* 🔁 *Ladies and gentlemen, welcome to the show.*
2 a man who is polite and treats people with respect □ *Her husband's a real gentleman.*

gently /ˈdʒentli/ ADVERB in a gentle way □ *He picked the injured bird up gently.*

genuine /ˈdʒenjuɪn/ ADJECTIVE real or true □ *a genuine work of art*

geography /dʒɪˈɒɡrəfi/ NOUN, NO PLURAL the study of the Earth's surface and the countries, weather and people of the world □ *human geography*

geology /dʒɪˈɒlədʒi/ NOUN, NO PLURAL the study of the Earth's rocks and soil

germ /dʒɜːm/ NOUN [*plural* germs] a very small living thing that can cause disease □ *This product kills most germs.*

gesture /ˈdʒestʃə(r)/ NOUN [*plural* gestures] a movement made with your hand, arm or head to express what you think or feel 🔁 *The driver made a rude gesture out of the car window.*

get /ɡet/ VERB [gets, getting, got]
1 to take, receive or buy something □ *Isabel got lots of birthday presents.* □ *Did you get my letter?* □ *I got a new dress today.*
2 to go somewhere and then bring something back □ *Could you get me a drink?* □ *I'll go and get the money.*
3 get away/in/out, etc. to move in a particular

direction □ *We managed to get over the wall.* □ *All the chickens have got out.* □ *Catch a bus, and get off near the cathedral.*
4 to become □ *The baby's getting bigger every day.* □ *I got wet in the rain.* □ *If I mention money, he always gets angry.* □ *The wine glasses got broken.*
5 if you get somewhere, you arrive there □ *We got to New York at 5 o'clock in the morning.* □ *What time will you get home?* □ *The train gets in at three thirty.*
6 if you get a bus, train, etc., that is how you travel. □ *I usually get the train to work.*
7 to become ill with a particular illness □ *They had an injection to stop them getting measles.*
♦ PHRASAL VERBS **get away with something** to avoid being punished or criticized □ *I'm hoping to miss the next meeting, if I can get away with it.* **get on**
1 to make progress □ **+ with** *I need to get on with my work.* □ *How are you getting on in your new job?* **2** to be friendly □ *Pierre and Alex don't really get on.* **get out of something** to avoid doing something □ *He'll do anything to get out of the washing up.* **get over something** to feel better after being ill or unhappy □ *He never really got over his wife's death.* **get round to doing something** to do something that you have been intending to do □ *I'd like to do more exercise, but I never seem to get round to it.* **get through** to manage to talk to someone on the telephone □ *I tried to ring her, but I couldn't get through.* **get through something** to reach the end of a difficult situation □ *It was a terrible illness, but his determination helped to get him through it.* **get (someone) up** to wake up and get out of bed □ *I always get up early.* □ *My Dad gets me up in the morning.*

ghost /gəʊst/ NOUN [plural ghosts] the spirit of a dead person which some people think they can see □ *Do you believe in ghosts?*
giant[1] /'dʒaɪənt/ NOUN [plural giants] in stories, a man who is extremely tall and strong
giant[2] /'dʒaɪənt/ ADJECTIVE much bigger than usual □ *a giant crane* □ *a giant tortoise*

gift /gɪft/ NOUN [plural gifts]
1 a present 🖭 *a wedding gift* 🖭 *Many children give gifts to their teacher at the end of term.* 🖭 *a gift shop* □ **+ from** *The necklace had been a gift from her boyfriend.*
2 a natural ability □ **+ for** *Adam has a gift for languages.*

gigantic /dʒaɪ'gæntɪk/ ADJECTIVE extremely big □ *a gigantic statue*
giggle[1] /'gɪgəl/ VERB [giggles, giggling, giggled] to laugh in a silly or nervous way
giggle[2] /'gɪgəl/ NOUN [plural giggles] a silly or nervous laugh
ginger[1] /'dʒɪndʒə(r)/ NOUN, NO PLURAL a root that has a spicy taste and is used in cooking
ginger[2] /'dʒɪndʒə(r)/ ADJECTIVE ginger hair is a red-brown colour

giraffe /dʒɪ'rɑːf/ NOUN [plural giraffes] an African animal with a very long neck and long legs

girl /gɜːl/ NOUN [plural girls] a female child or young woman □ *Police are searching for a missing 10-year-old girl.* 🖭 *a teenage girl* 🖭 *There were two little girls* (= very young girls) *playing in the garden.*

girlfriend /'gɜːlfrend/ NOUN [plural girlfriends]
1 a girl or woman that you are having a romantic relationship with □ *Dan has a new girlfriend.*
2 a female friend that a girl or woman has □ *I go out with my girlfriends once a week.*

give /gɪv/ VERB [gives, giving, gave, given]
1 to let someone have something □ *Give your bags to the porter.* □ *Make sure you give back all the books you borrowed.* □ *Let me give you some advice.* □ *This news gives us hope.* □ *He gave us permission to visit the temple.* □ *Could you give us some information about hotels?*
2 to make someone have something □ *They were given a severe punishment.* □ *Our boss gives us too much work.* □ *The sudden noise gave me a fright.*
3 give evidence/a performance/a speech, etc. to say something or to perform in public □ *She gave evidence at his trial.* □ *He gave a wonderful performance of Beethoven's Moonlight Sonata.*
4 to make a sound or a movement □ *He gave a shout of joy.* □ *She gave her brother a kick.*
♦ PHRASAL VERBS **give something away 1** to allow someone to have something without paying for it □ *I gave away all my old toys.* **2** to tell a secret □ *The party was meant to be a surprise, but Billy gave it away.* **give in** to agree to something you did not want to agree to □ *I kept asking for the new computer game, and eventually Dad gave in and bought it for me.* **give something out** to give something to a group of people □ *Can you give out the reading books please, Kazuo?* **give up (something) 1** if you give up a habit, you stop doing it □ *She's managed to give up smoking.* **2** to stop doing something before it is finished, because it is too difficult □ *I've given up trying to keep this room tidy.* □ *Don't give up – only another mile to go!*

> ► THESAURUS: If you **give** something to someone, you let them have it. If you **deliver** something, you take it to a place. For example, postmen deliver letters to people's homes. If you **hand** something **over** you give something to someone. Often, this is something that you do not want to give. For example, a bank worker might hand over money to a robber. If you **award** something to someone, you give the person a prize because they have done something good.

given[1] /'gɪvən/ ADJECTIVE decided or agreed □ *You have a given time to complete each question.* □ *On any given day, there are several accidents.*

given[2] /'gɪvən/ PAST PARTICIPLE OF **give**

given[3] /'gɪvən/ PREPOSITION considering the fact that □ *Given that they don't have much money, their offer is extremely generous.*

glacier /'glæsɪə(r)/ NOUN [*plural* glaciers] a large mass of ice that moves slowly down a mountain valley

glad /glæd/ ADJECTIVE [gladder, gladdest] pleased and happy because of something □ **+ that** *I'm just glad that the exams are over.* □ **+ to do something** *I'm so glad to see you.*

glamorous /'glæmərəs/ ADJECTIVE attractive, fashionable and exciting □ *She was looking very glamorous in a black dress.* □ *a glamorous lifestyle*

glamour /'glæmə(r)/ NOUN, NO PLURAL a special quality that makes someone or something seem attractive, fashionable and exciting □ *She will add some glamour to the show.*

glance[1] /glɑːns/ VERB [glances, glancing, glanced] to look at something or someone for a very short time □ **+ at** *Anselm glanced nervously at his watch.* □ **+ around** *He glanced around to see if anyone was looking.*

> ➤ **THESAURUS:** If you glance at something, you look at it for a very short time. You might glance at your watch. If you glimpse something, you see it for a very short time. You might glimpse a famous person in a big crowd.

glance[2] /glɑːns/ NOUN [*plural* glances] a quick look 🗎 *He cast a nervous glance at Yvonne.* 🗎 *Richard and I exchanged glances (= we looked at each other for a short time).*

glare[1] /gleə(r)/ VERB [glares, glaring, glared] to look at someone in a way that shows you are very angry □ *Mia glared at him.*

glare[2] /gleə(r)/ NOUN [*plural* glares]
1 *no plural* very strong bright light that makes your eyes hurt □ *He stood in the glare of the car's headlights.*
2 an angry look

glaring /'gleərɪŋ/ ADJECTIVE
1 very obvious 🗎 *a glaring mistake*
2 very bright, and making your eyes hurt □ *the glaring sun*

glass[1] /glɑːs/ NOUN [*plural* glasses]
1 *no plural* a hard transparent material, used for making bottles, windows, etc. 🗎 *There was broken glass all over the pavement.* 🗎 *She stepped on a piece of glass and cut her foot.*
2 a container made of glass, which you drink from □ *a tall glass* 🗎 *a wine glass* □ **+ of** *She drank three glasses of milk.* 🗎 *Betsy poured a glass of juice.*
3 glasses something you wear to help you see better, which consists of two pieces of plastic or

glass in a frame 🗎 *I need a new pair of glasses.* 🗎 *My Dad wears glasses.*

glass[2] /glɑːs/ ADJECTIVE made of glass □ *a glass bowl*

gleam /gliːm/ VERB [gleams, gleaming, gleamed] to shine □ *A light gleamed in the distance.*

glide /glaɪd/ VERB [glides, gliding, glided] to move in a smooth and quiet way □ *The waiters glide between the tables.*

glider /'glaɪdə(r)/ NOUN [*plural* gliders] an aeroplane with no engine which moves on air currents

glimpse /glɪmps/ NOUN [*plural* glimpses] when you see someone or something only for a very short time 🗎 *People climbed on fences, hoping to catch a glimpse of (= see) the princess.*

glitter /'glɪtə(r)/ VERB [glitters, glittering, glittered] to shine with small flashes of light □ *His eyes glittered in the light.*

global /'gləʊbəl/ ADJECTIVE to do with or involving the whole world □ *Global sales rose by 20%.* □ *global climate change*

global warming /ˌgləʊbəl 'wɔːmɪŋ/ NOUN, NO PLURAL the gradual increase in the Earth's temperature caused by pollution

globe /gləʊb/ NOUN [*plural* globes]
1 a large ball with a map of the Earth printed on it
2 the globe the world □ *The company has offices around the globe.*

glorious /'glɔːrɪəs/ ADJECTIVE
1 extremely beautiful or good □ *glorious sunshine* □ *The hotel is surrounded by glorious countryside.*
2 deserving or receiving praise □ *a glorious victory*

glory /'glɔːrɪ/ NOUN [*plural* glories] praise and admiration □ *His moment of glory came when he won the championship.*

glossy /'glɒsɪ/ ADJECTIVE [glossier, glossiest] smooth and shiny 🗎 *glossy hair* □ *a glossy surface*

glove /glʌv/ NOUN [*plural* gloves] something you wear to cover your hand 🗎 *a pair of gloves* 🗎 *I wear gloves in the winter.* 🗎 *It's a good idea to wear rubber gloves when you're cleaning.*

glow[1] /gləʊ/ NOUN, NO PLURAL
1 warm or soft light □ *the glow of the fire*
2 a glow of **satisfaction/pride** etc. a good feeling of being satisfied, proud, etc. □ *He felt a glow of satisfaction when he looked at his work.*

glow[2] /gləʊ/ VERB [glows, glowing, glowed]
1 to burn or shine with a soft light □ *A fire glowed in the corner of the room.*
2 glow with **pride/satisfaction/confidence**, etc. to show that you are very proud, satisfied, etc.
□ *She was glowing with pride as she watched her son accept the award.*

glue[1] /glu:/ NOUN [plural **glues**] a substance used for sticking things together □ *Use glue to stick the fabric onto the paper.*

glue[2] /glu:/ VERB [glues, gluing or glueing, glued] to stick something using glue □ *He glued the two pieces of wood together.*

go[1] /gəʊ/ VERB [goes, going, went, gone]
1 to travel or move somewhere □ *I'm going home now.* □ **+ to** *We're going to France for our holiday.* □ *He went into the other room.* □ *I wish she'd go away.* □ *He left home at 18 and never went back.*
2 to travel or move somewhere so that you can do something □ **+ to** *She goes to school in the next village.* □ **+ for** *Shall we go for a swim?* □ *We all went cycling.*
3 to leave or disappear □ *It's six o'clock, so I'll have to go soon.* □ *I'm sure I left my coat here, but it's gone.* □ *The food all went very quickly.*
4 if a road or path goes somewhere, it leads there □ *Does this road go to Edinburgh?*
5 the place where something goes is where it fits or is kept □ *That piece of the jigsaw goes at the top.* □ *The cups go on the top shelf.*
6 to become □ *Her face went pale.* □ *Your soup's gone cold.*
7 to happen in a particular way □ *The concert went well.* □ *How's your new job going?*
8 be going to do something (a) to intend to do something □ *I'm going to write to Molly.* □ *What were you going to say?* (b) to be expected to happen □ *I think it's going to rain.*
◆ PHRASAL VERBS **go by** if time goes by, it passes **go down** to become lower in level □ *His temperature has gone down a bit.* **go off** **1** if food goes off, it becomes rotten **2** to explode □ *A bomb has gone off in a busy London street.* **go off someone/ something** to stop liking someone or something □ *I've gone off spicy food.* **go on** **1** to continue for a period of time □ *His speech went on for hours.* **2** to continue doing something □ **+ ing** *He went on singing, despite the noise.*
□ **+ with** *Go on with your work.* **3** if something is going on, it is happening □ *What's going on?* **go out** to leave your house, especially for a social activity □ *Are you going out tonight?* **go round** to be enough for everyone □ *Is there enough bread to*

go round? **go through something** to experience something □ *She went through agony during the illness.* **go up** to become higher in level □ *Prices have gone up again.*

go[2] /gəʊ/ NOUN [plural **goes**]
1 an attempt ⊞ *It doesn't matter if you can't climb to the top – just have a go.*
2 when it is your turn to do something, especially in a game □ *Pick up a card, Adam – it's your go.*

goal /gəʊl/ NOUN [plural **goals**]
1 something that you want to achieve ⊞ *If she works hard, she should achieve her goal.* ⊞ *The government's long-term goal is to reduce the number of people in prison.*
2 a point scored when a ball goes into the net in a game such as football ⊞ *Cahill scored the first goal.* ⊞ *Giggs scored the winning goal.*
3 the area where the ball must go to score a point in a game such as football □ *He was standing in front of the goal.*

goalkeeper /ˈgəʊlˌkiːpə(r)/ NOUN [plural **goalkeepers**] the player who stands in front of the net in a game such as football and who tries to stop the ball going into the net

goat /gəʊt/ NOUN [plural **goats**] an animal with horns and long hair under its chin □ *The cheese is made from goat's milk.*

god /gɒd/ NOUN [plural **gods**]
1 God no plural the spirit that Christians, Muslims and Jews pray to ⊞ *Do you believe in God?*
2 a spirit that some people believe controls nature or represents a particular quality □ *Greek and Roman gods* □ **+ of** *Thor was the Viking god of thunder.*

goddess /ˈgɒdɪs/ NOUN [plural **goddesses**] a female god

goes /gəʊz/ VERB the present tense of the verb **go**[1] when it is used with 'he', 'she', or 'it' □ *He goes to work at eight o'clock.*

gold[1] /gəʊld/ NOUN [plural **golds**]
1 no plural a valuable pale yellow metal, used to make jewellery □ *bars of gold*
2 a gold medal (= prize for coming first in a competition or race) □ *He won gold in the long jump.*

gold[2] /gəʊld/ ADJECTIVE
1 made of gold □ *a gold ring*
2 having the colour of gold □ *a gold leather handbag*

golden /ˈgəʊldən/ ADJECTIVE
1 made of gold □ *a golden crown*
2 having the colour of gold □ *golden hair*

golf /gɒlf/ NOUN, NO PLURAL a game in which you have to hit a small ball into holes in the ground ⊞ *a golf ball* ⊞ *My Dad plays golf.* ⊞ *an 18-hole golf* *course* 🔊 *Professional golfers have someone to carry their golf clubs* (= sticks used for hitting the ball).

gone /gɒn/ PAST PARTICIPLE OF **go**

good¹ /gʊd/ ADJECTIVE [better, best]
1 suitable or of a high standard □ *That's a good idea.* □ *I've got some good news for you.* □ *She has been a good friend to me.* □ *I know a good way to cook rice.*
2 enjoyable or pleasant □ *Did you have a good holiday?* □ *We had a good time in Moscow.*
3 able to do something well □ *+ at* *Mark's very good at fixing cars.* □ *Ben's a pretty good cook.*
4 something you say to show you are pleased □ *Oh, good – Harry's arrived.*
5 good for you something that is good for you makes you healthy or makes your life better □ *Eat your vegetables – they're good for you.*
6 a good child or animal behaves well □ *The children have been very good.*

> ➤ Remember that **good** is an adjective and not an adverb. Use the adverb **well** to say that someone does something in a way that is good:
> ✓ *She is a good cook.*
> ✓ *She cooks very well.*
> ✗ *She cooks very* **good.**

good² /gʊd/ NOUN, NO PLURAL
1 something that produces an advantage
🔊 *Cleaning it with water won't do any good – you need soap.* 🔊 *I know this medicine tastes bad, but it's for your own good.*
2 no good/not any good not of good quality, or not helpful □ *These gloves are no good – they're too thin.* □ *It's no good phoning her – she never has her phone switched on.*
3 do someone good to make someone feel better or to make their life better □ *Have a day off work – it will do you good.*
4 what is morally right □ *We recognize the difference between good and evil.*
♦ IDIOM for good forever □ *I left home for good when I was 18.*

good afternoon /gʊd ˌɑːftə'nuːn/ EXCLAMATION something that you say when you meet someone in the afternoon

goodbye /gʊd'baɪ/ EXCLAMATION something you say when you are leaving or when other people are leaving □ *Goodbye, Anna. See you next week.* 🔊 *I felt sad when it was time to say goodbye.*

good evening /gʊd 'iːvnɪŋ/ EXCLAMATION a formal way of saying 'hello' when you see someone in the evening □ *Good evening ladies and gentlemen, and welcome to the show.*

good-looking /'gʊdlʊkɪŋ/ ADJECTIVE someone who is good-looking has an attractive face □ *Amy's new boyfriend is really good-looking.*

good morning /gʊd 'mɔːnɪŋ/ EXCLAMATION a formal way of saying 'hello' when you see someone in the morning □ *Good morning, everyone.*

goodness /'gʊdnɪs/ NOUN, NO PLURAL
1 being good and kind
2 things in food that will make you healthy when you eat it □ *Tomatoes are full of goodness.*
♦ IDIOMS for goodness' sake something you say when you are annoyed □ *For goodness sake, Dave, just open the door!* Goodness (me)! something you say when you are surprised □ *Goodness me, it's five o'clock already.*

good night /gʊd 'naɪt/ EXCLAMATION
1 something you say to someone just before you go to sleep at night □ *Good night, Mum.* 🔊 *He's upstairs saying good night to the children.*
2 a formal way of saying 'goodbye' to people late in the evening □ *Good night. Thanks for coming.*

goods /gʊdz/ PLURAL NOUN things that have been made to sell □ *electrical goods* □ *cars, jewellery and other luxury goods* 🔊 *Sales of household goods have fallen.*

goose /guːs/ NOUN [plural geese] a large white or grey bird

gorgeous /'gɔːdʒəs/ ADJECTIVE very beautiful or pleasant □ *The baby's absolutely gorgeous.* □ *gorgeous weather*

gorilla /gə'rɪlə/ NOUN [plural gorillas] an animal that looks like a very large monkey

gossip¹ /'gɒsɪp/ NOUN [plural gossips]
1 informal talk about other people, often about their private lives □ *She told me all the latest gossip.* □ *Tim loves a good gossip.*
2 someone who enjoys talking about other people's lives, in a way that you disapprove of

gossip² /'gɒsɪp/ VERB [gossips, gossiping, gossiped] to talk about other people, often about their private lives

got /gɒt/ PAST TENSE AND PAST PARTICIPLE OF **get**

> ➤ In North America the past participle of 'get' is **gotten** and not 'got'. □ *She'd gotten mad at him.*

govern /'gʌvən/ VERB [governs, governing, governed] to officially control a country or area □ *The country was governed by the Republicans.* □ *the governing party*

> ➤ THESAURUS: If a political party governs a country or area, it officially controls that place. Rule and reign have a similar meaning, but rule is also used to talk about kings and queens. Reign is only used to talk about kings and queens. If you lead a group of people, you control them. You can lead a team of workers or a political party, for example.

government /ˈɡʌvənmənt/ NOUN [plural governments] the group of people who control a country or area ⊞ The party will form the next government. ▢ The government has announced an increase in taxes. ⊞ a government department ⊞ He criticized government policies.

governor /ˈɡʌvənə(r)/ NOUN [plural governors] someone who is in charge of a place or organization ▢ the governor of Arkansas ▢ a school governor

gown /ɡaʊn/ NOUN [plural gowns]
1 a long formal dress that women wear on special occasions
2 a loose piece of clothing worn in hospital ▢ a hospital gown

GP /ˌdʒiːˈpiː/ ABBREVIATION general practitioner; a doctor who looks after people from a particular area and treats them for a lot of different illnesses

grab /ɡræb/ VERB [grabs, grabbing, grabbed] to take something suddenly or violently ▢ He grabbed my bag and ran away. ▢ She grabbed my arm as I fell.

grace /ɡreɪs/ NOUN, NO PLURAL
1 a smooth and attractive way of moving ▢ He kicks the ball with effortless grace.
2 a prayer that some people say before a meal ▢ Dad said grace.

graceful /ˈɡreɪsfʊl/ ADJECTIVE smooth and attractive in shape or in the way you move ▢ He watched her graceful movements. ▢ the graceful curve of the dome
• **gracefully** /ˈɡreɪsfʊlɪ/ ADVERB in a graceful way

gracious /ˈɡreɪʃəs/ ADJECTIVE polite and kind ▢ It was very gracious of you to apologize.

grade¹ /ɡreɪd/ NOUN [plural grades]
1 a number or letter that shows how good a student's work is ⊞ She got a grade A in her English exam. ⊞ He achieved top grades in his exams.
2 a level of quality or importance ▢ The jewellery is made from a lower grade of gold. ▢ He had been promoted to a higher grade at work.
3 the US word for **form¹** (= school class)

grade² /ɡreɪd/ VERB [grades, grading, graded] to separate things into groups of similar size or quality ▢ Hotels are graded according to the facilities they offer. ▢ a grading system

gradual /ˈɡrædʒʊəl/ ADJECTIVE happening slowly over a long period ▢ There has been a gradual improvement in his work. ▢ Recovery will be a very gradual process.

gradually /ˈɡrædʒʊəlɪ/ ADVERB slowly over a long period ▢ His health has gradually improved. ▢ Gradually, her life began to return to normal.

graduate¹ /ˈɡrædʒʊət/ NOUN [plural graduates] someone who has a degree (= qualification) from a university or college ▢ George is a graduate of Edinburgh University.

graduate² /ˈɡrædʒʊeɪt/ VERB [graduates, graduating, graduated] to get a degree (= qualification) from a university or college

graduation /ˌɡrædʒʊˈeɪʃən/ NOUN, NO PLURAL when you finish a university course and get a degree (= qualification) ▢ a graduation ceremony

grain /ɡreɪn/ NOUN [plural grains]
1 no plural the seeds of crops such as rice ▢ They export grain to Russia.
2 a seed from a crop such as rice ▢ + of a grain of wheat
3 one of the very small pieces of something such as sugar, salt, etc. ▢ + of grains of sand
4 the pattern of lines on the surface of wood

gram /ɡræm/ NOUN [plural grams] a unit for measuring weight. There are one thousand grams in a kilogram. Gram is often written g.

grammar /ˈɡræmə(r)/ NOUN no plural the rules of a particular language, for example how words are formed and how words are put together in a sentence ▢ French grammar

grammatical /ɡrəˈmætɪkəl/ ADJECTIVE
1 to do with grammar ▢ grammatical rules ▢ a grammatical error
2 correct according to the rules of grammar ▢ That sentence isn't grammatical, is it?

gramme /ɡræm/ NOUN [plural grammes] another spelling of **gram**

grand /ɡrænd/ ADJECTIVE [grander, grandest] very large, expensive or special, making you feel admiration ▢ The house was very grand.

grandad /ˈɡrændæd/ NOUN [plural grandads] an informal word for grandfather

grandchild /ˈɡræntʃaɪld/ NOUN [plural grandchildren] a child of your son or daughter ▢ We've got three grown-up children and five grandchildren.

granddaughter /ˈɡrændɔːtə(r)/ NOUN [plural granddaughters] the daughter of your son or daughter

grandfather /ˈɡrændfɑːðə(r)/ NOUN [plural grandfathers] the father of your mother or father ⊞ my paternal grandfather (= father's father) ⊞ my maternal grandfather (= mother's father) ▢ He recently became a grandfather.

grandma /ˈɡrænmɑː/ NOUN [plural grandmas] an informal word for grandmother ▢ At the weekend I usually visit my grandma.

grandmother /'grænmʌðə(r)/ NOUN [*plural* grandmothers] the mother of your mother or father
🔹 *my maternal grandmother* (= mother's mother)
🔹 *my paternal grandmother* (= father's mother)
▢ *We called in to see my grandmother.*

grandpa /'grænpɑ:/ NOUN [*plural* grandpas] an informal word for grandfather ▢ *My grandpa loved singing.*

grandparent /'grænpeərənt/ NOUN [*plural* grandparents] a parent of your father or your mother ▢ *I went to stay with my elderly grandparents.*

grandson /'grænsʌn/ NOUN [*plural* grandsons] the son of your son or daughter

granny /'græni/ NOUN [*plural* grannies] an informal word for grandmother

grant¹ /grɑ:nt/ VERB [grants, granting, granted]
1 to officially allow someone to have or to do something they have asked for 🔹 *The judge granted him permission to appeal.* ▢ *His request was granted.*
2 take something/someone for granted to expect something or someone to be there as usual and to forget that you are lucky to have them ▢ *We take our health for granted.*
3 take something for granted to expect something to happen without checking or thinking much about it ▢ *You can't take anything for granted.* 🔹 *She took it for granted that I would agree.*

grant² /grɑ:nt/ NOUN [*plural* grants] an amount of money that has been given to you for a special purpose 🔹 *The college received a grant of £20,000 to improve computer facilities.* ▢ *She applied for a research grant.*

grape /greɪp/ NOUN [*plural* grapes] a small, pale green or dark red fruit that grows in groups and is used to make wine 🔹 *a bunch of grapes*

graph /grɑ:f/ NOUN [*plural* graphs] a picture with lines drawn between different points, used to show how things compare to each other or how something changes

grasp /grɑ:sp/ VERB [grasps, grasping, grasped]
1 to take hold of something tightly ▢ *She saw the dog and grasped my hand.* ▢ *He grasped the rope and began to climb.*
2 to understand an idea ▢ *I still couldn't grasp what he was trying to tell me.* 🔹 *It might be difficult for children to grasp this concept.*

grass /grɑ:s/ NOUN, NO PLURAL a plant with very thin green leaves which covers gardens and fields ▢ *I cut the grass at the weekend.* 🔹 *a blade of grass* (= one leaf)
♦ IDIOM the grass is (always) greener on the other side the situation somewhere else or for someone else always seems better than your own

grate¹ /greɪt/ VERB [grates, grating, grated] to cut food into small, thin pieces by rubbing it against a grater (= kitchen tool) ▢ *grated cheese*

> ➤ **THESAURUS:** If you grate food such as cheese or carrots, you cut it into small thin pieces by rubbing it against a kitchen tool called a grater. If you grind something, you crush it into a powder. For example, we often grind black pepper and coffee. If you mince something, you cut it into very small pieces using a machine. We often mince meat such as beef before cooking it.

grate² /greɪt/ NOUN [*plural* grates] a frame of metal bars which holds the wood, coal, etc. in a fireplace (= space for a fire in the wall of a room)

grateful /'greɪtful/ ADJECTIVE pleased with someone and wanting to thank them because they have done something for you ▢ **+ for** *I'm very grateful for all your kindness.* ▢ **+ to** *I felt so grateful to him for stopping to help.* ▢ *She gave me a grateful smile.*

gratitude /'grætɪtjuːd/ NOUN, NO PLURAL a feeling of being grateful to someone ▢ *She expressed her gratitude to the hospital.*

grave¹ /greɪv/ NOUN [*plural* graves] a place where a dead body is buried

grave² /greɪv/ ADJECTIVE [graver, gravest] very serious ▢ *a grave mistake* 🔹 *You are in grave danger.* 🔹 *He expressed grave concern about the situation.*

gravity /'grævəti/ NOUN, NO PLURAL
1 the force that pulls things towards the earth and makes them fall to the ground
2 a formal word meaning how serious something is ▢ *We appreciate the gravity of the situation.*

gray /greɪ/ ADJECTIVE, NOUN [plural grays] the US spelling of **grey**

graze /greɪz/ VERB [grazes, grazing, grazed]
1 if animals graze, they move around eating grass and other plants
2 to hurt your skin by rubbing it against something hard and rough □ *I fell and grazed my knees.*

grease /griːs/ NOUN, NO PLURAL a substance such as fat or thick oil □ *a grease stain*

greasy /ˈgriːsɪ/ ADJECTIVE [greasier, greasiest] covered in or containing thick fat or oil □ *greasy food* □ *He wiped his greasy fingers on his jeans.*

great /greɪt/ ADJECTIVE [greater, greatest]
1 very good □ *This is a great opportunity for you to travel.* □ *Our builders have done a great job.* □ *Your hair looks great like that.* □ *I've had a great idea!* □ *We had a great time in Venice.*
2 very large in size, amount or level □ *The elephant lifted one of its great feet.* 🔁 *We had a great deal of* (= a lot of) *trouble getting the information we needed.* 🔁 *His dinner party was a great success.* □ *They were in great danger.*
3 important and powerful □ *great armies* □ *a great nation*
4 a slightly informal way of expressing pleasure or agreement □ *'We'll meet you at seven.' 'Great – see you then!'*

Great Britain /ˌgreɪt ˈbrɪtən/ NOUN England, Scotland and Wales

great-grand-daughter /ˌgreɪtˈgrændɔːtə(r)/ NOUN [plural great-grand-daughters] your grandchild's daughter

great-grandfather /ˌgreɪtˈgrændfɑːðə(r)/ NOUN [plural great-grandfathers] your grandmother's or grandfather's father

great-grandmother /ˌgreɪtˈgrænmʌðə(r)/ NOUN [plural great-grandmothers] your grandmother's or grandfather's mother

great-grandson /ˌgreɪtˈgrænsʌn/ NOUN [plural great-grandsons] your grandchild's son

greed /griːd/ NOUN, NO PLURAL when you want more of something than you need, especially food or money □ *Big businesses are often accused of greed and selfishness.*

greedy /ˈgriːdɪ/ ADJECTIVE [greedier, greediest] wanting more of something than you need □ *You greedy pig! You've eaten it all.*

➤ THESAURUS: If someone is greedy, they want more of something such as food or money than they need. If you are hungry, you have a feeling of wanting to eat. If you are starving you are ill because you do not have enough to eat.

green¹ /griːn/ ADJECTIVE
1 having the colour of leaves or grass □ *He's wearing a green coat.* □ *The curtains were dark green.*
2 to do with protecting the environment □ *She's*

involved in green politics. □ *We're trying to be green by cycling to work.*
3 green spaces places with grass and plants

green² /griːn/ NOUN [plural greens] the colour of leaves and grass

greengrocer /ˈgriːnˌgrəʊsə(r)/ NOUN [plural greengrocers]
1 someone who sells fruit and vegetables
2 greengrocer's a shop selling fruit and vegetables

greenhouse /ˈgriːnhaʊs/ NOUN [plural greenhouses] a building with glass walls and a glass roof that stays warm and is used for growing plants in

greenhouse gas /ˈgriːnhaʊs ˌgæs/ NOUN [plural greenhouse gases] a gas that stops heat from leaving the atmosphere, causing the temperature of Earth to increase □ *Greenhouse gases include carbon dioxide and methane.*

greet /griːt/ VERB [greets, greeting, greeted] to say something to someone when they arrive or when you meet them □ *She went outside to greet her visitors.* □ *He was greeted by a crowd of fans at the airport.*

greeting /ˈgriːtɪŋ/ NOUN [plural greetings] something polite or friendly that you say when you meet someone or send a message to someone □ *They exchanged friendly greetings.* □ *John sends his warmest greetings.*

grenade /grəˈneɪd/ NOUN [plural grenades] a small bomb that explodes a few seconds after someone throws it

grew /gruː/ PAST TENSE OF **grow**

grey¹ /greɪ/ ADJECTIVE having the colour you get when you mix black and white □ *The sheets were grey with dirt.*

grey² /greɪ/ NOUN [plural greys] the colour that you get when you mix black and white

grid /grɪd/ NOUN [plural grids] a pattern of lines that cross each other to form squares

grief /griːf/ NOUN, NO PLURAL a feeling of great sadness, especially when someone has died □ *He expressed his grief at his baby daughter's death.*
♦ IDIOM come to grief to fail or to have an accident □ *Drivers often come to grief on the mountain roads.*

grieve /griːv/ VERB [grieves, grieving, grieved] to feel very sad, especially because someone has died □ *She was still grieving for her dead son.*

grill¹ /grɪl/ VERB [grills, grilling, grilled] to cook food by putting it close to direct heat □ *Grill the fish for a couple of minutes on each side.*

grill² /grɪl/ NOUN [plural grills]
1 a piece of kitchen equipment which cooks food under a direct heat

2 metal bars which food can be cooked on over a fire

grim /grɪm/ ADJECTIVE [grimmer, grimmest]
1 very unpleasant, worrying or shocking □ *The situation looked pretty grim.* 🄱 *The pictures illustrate the grim reality of life in the refugee camps.*
2 serious and unfriendly □ *The men wore grim expressions.*

grin¹ /grɪn/ VERB [grins, grinning, grinned] to give a big smile □ *Ben was grinning broadly as he came out.*
♦ IDIOM grin and bear it to accept a difficult situation without complaining □ *You'll just have to grin and bear it.*

grin² /grɪn/ NOUN [plural grins] a big smile □ *His face broke into a broad grin.*

grind /graɪnd/ VERB [grinds, grinding, ground]
1 to crush something solid into a powder □ *ground pepper* □ *The rocks are ground into dust.*
2 to make something smooth or sharp by rubbing it against a hard surface

grip¹ /grɪp/ VERB [grips, gripping, gripped] to hold something tightly □ *Martha gripped his arm.* □ *I gripped the steering wheel tighter.*

grip² /grɪp/ NOUN [plural grips] when someone holds something tightly 🄱 *He tightened his grip on her shoulder.*

groan¹ /grəʊn/ VERB [groans, groaning, groaned] to make a long deep sound to express pain, unhappiness, etc. □ *He groaned in pain.*

groan² /grəʊn/ NOUN [plural groans] when you groan □ *She got slowly to her feet with a groan.*

grocer /ˈgrəʊsə(r)/ NOUN [plural grocers]
1 grocer's a shop selling food and things for the house
2 someone who runs a shop selling food and things for the house

groceries /ˈgrəʊsəriz/ PLURAL NOUN food and things for the house that you buy regularly □ *a bag of groceries* □ *More people now buy their groceries online.*

grocery /ˈgrəʊsəri/ ADJECTIVE to do with food and things for the house that you buy regularly or the shop where you buy these things □ *grocery shopping* □ *a grocery list*

groom /gruːm/ NOUN [plural grooms]
1 a bridegroom (= man who is getting married)
2 someone whose job is to look after horses

ground¹ /graʊnd/ NOUN [plural grounds]
1 the Earth's surface □ *The damaged satellite will fall to the ground next week.* □ *These plants grow best on higher ground.*
2 earth or soil □ *The ground is frozen.* □ *fertile ground*

3 an area where a particular sport is played □ *a football ground*

> **THESAURUS:** Ground, earth and soil all refer to the top layer of the land, where you can grow plants. Soil is the word that gardeners usually use for this, and ground and earth are more general. Dirt is any substance that is not clean or makes something become not clean. Dust is the layer of powder that you see on a surface that has not been cleaned for a long time.

ground² /graʊnd/ VERB [grounds, grounding, grounded] to stop an aircraft from leaving the ground

ground³ /graʊnd/ PAST TENSE AND PAST PARTICIPLE OF **grind**

ground floor /ˌgraʊnd ˈflɔː(r)/ NOUN, NO PLURAL the floor of a building at the level of the ground outside □ *The electrical department is on the ground floor.*

group¹ /gruːp/ NOUN [plural groups]
1 a number of people or things that are together or that belong together □ + of *There was a small group of people waiting outside.* □ *We split the samples into three different groups.*
□ *Environmental groups have opposed the plans.*
2 a number of people who perform music together 🄱 *a pop group*

group² /gruːp/ VERB [groups, grouping, grouped] to put people or things together in a group or groups □ *The children were grouped according to age.*

grouse¹ /graʊs/ NOUN [plural grouse] a type of fat bird that lives on open land and is hunted for sport

grouse² /graʊs/ VERB [grouses, grousing, groused] to complain about something □ *People always grouse about ticket prices.*

grouse³ /graʊs/ NOUN [plural grouses] a complaint

grow /grəʊ/ VERB [grows, growing, grew, grown]
1 if a person, animal or plant grows, it becomes bigger or taller □ *He's grown as tall as his father.* □ *The grass has grown a lot this week.*
2 if you grow plants, you put seeds in the ground and look after them □ *We grow vegetables in our garden.* □ *organically grown produce*
3 if your hair or nails grow, they become longer
4 to increase in amount or size □ *The world's population is growing rapidly.* □ *Since he changed schools, his confidence has grown.*
5 to become □ *It was growing dark.* □ *The sound grew louder.*
♦ PHRASAL VERBS grow out of something 1 if a child grows out of clothes, they become too big for them 2 to stop liking or doing something as you become older □ *I used to take a doll to bed, but I*

grew out of it in the end. **grow up** **1** to become older or to become an adult **2** to stop behaving like a child □ *I wish you'd grow up and take some responsibility!* **3** to develop □ *An unpleasant atmosphere grew up in the office.*

growl /graul/ VERB [growls, growling, growled] if an animal such as a dog growls, it makes a deep threatening noise in its throat □ *Two black guard dogs growled.*

grown /grəun/ PAST PARTICIPLE OF **grow**

grown-up[1] /'grəunʌp/ NOUN [plural grown-ups] an adult □ *The grown-ups enjoyed themselves as much as the children.*

grown-up[2] /'grəunʌp/ ADJECTIVE adult □ *We have three grown-up children.*

growth /grəuθ/ NOUN [plural growths]
1 *no plural* when something grows, develops or gets bigger □ **+ of** *the rapid growth of computer technology* □ **+ in** *The company reported a growth in sales.* □ *economic growth* □ *Warmth brings about growth in the garden.*
2 a lump that grows on the body □ *A growth developed on his hand.*

grumble /'grʌmbəl/ VERB [grumbles, grumbling, grumbled] to complain in an unhappy way, especially about small things □ *She was grumbling about the food.*

grunt /grʌnt/ VERB [grunts, grunting, grunted] to make a deep noise like a pig □ *He only grunted in response.*

guarantee[1] /ˌgærən'tiː/ NOUN [plural guarantees]
1 a promise that something will certainly be done or will happen ⊞ *I give a guarantee that we will do everything we can.* □ *Simply having talent is no guarantee of success.*
2 a promise that a product will be repaired or replaced if there is something wrong with it □ *a money-back guarantee* □ *The equipment has a one-year guarantee.*

guarantee[2] /ˌgærən'tiː/ VERB [guarantees, guaranteeing, guaranteed]
1 to make a promise that something will happen or be done □ *We couldn't guarantee his safety.*
2 to give a guarantee for a product that is sold

guard[1] /gɑːd/ NOUN [plural guards]
1 someone whose job is to protect a person or place, or to make sure that prisoners do not escape
2 under guard being protected or prevented from escaping □ *He was taken to the prison under armed guard.*
3 keep/stand guard to protect a person or place, or to make sure that prisoners do not escape □ *I stood guard over the money.*
4 on guard **(a)** responsible for protecting a person or place □ *There were no soldiers on guard that night.* **(b)** ready to deal with a difficult situation □ *You need to be on guard for suspicious phone calls.*

guard[2] /gɑːd/ VERB [guards, guarding, guarded]
1 to make sure that someone does not escape □ *You guard the back entrance.*
2 to protect someone or something □ *I guarded the children while he went for help.*

guardian /'gɑːdiən/ NOUN [plural guardians] someone who is legally responsible for a child when its parents have died

guerrilla /gə'rɪlə/ NOUN [plural guerrillas] a fighter who is a member of a small or unofficial army fighting for political reasons

guess[1] /ges/ VERB [guesses, guessing, guessed]
1 to give an answer or opinion without knowing all the facts □ **+ question word** *Guess how old she is.*
2 I guess a slightly informal phrase used to say that you think something is true □ *I guess we'll have to sell the car.*

guess[2] /ges/ NOUN [plural guesses] an answer or opinion made by guessing ⊞ *At a rough guess, I'd say he's forty.*

guest /gest/ NOUN [plural guests]
1 someone you invite to your house or to a party □ *a wedding guest* □ *She was one of 200 guests at the party.*
2 someone staying in a hotel □ *Hotel guests can use the gym for free.*

> ➤ THESAURUS: A guest is someone who is staying in a place that is not their home. A guest can stay in someone's house or at a hotel. A visitor is someone who comes to your house to see you for a short time. They may or may not sleep in your house. A lodger is a person who pays money to live in a room in someone else's house.

guesthouse /'gesthaus/ NOUN [plural guesthouses] a small hotel

guidance /'gaɪdəns/ NOUN, NO PLURAL advice about how you should do something □ *We provide guidance on environmental management.*

guide[1] /gaɪd/ NOUN [plural guides]
1 someone whose job is to show places to people who are visiting □ *A guide showed us around the cathedral.*
2 a book that gives information about a place or tells you how to do something

guide[2] /gaɪd/ VERB [guides, guiding, guided] to go with someone to show them where to go or tell them about a place

guidebook /'gaɪdbuk/ NOUN [plural guidebooks] a book which contains information for people visiting a particular place

guilt /gɪlt/ NOUN, NO PLURAL
1 an unpleasant feeling you get when you know you

have done something wrong □ *a sense of guilt*
□ *She felt no guilt at what she had done.*
2 the fact that you have done something wrong
□ *He admitted his guilt and accepted the
punishment.*

guilty /ˈgɪltɪ/ ADJECTIVE [guiltier, guiltiest]
1 ashamed because you have done something
wrong ⎈ *I felt guilty about lying to them.* □ *I had a
guilty conscience.*
2 having committed a crime □ **+ of** *They are guilty
of war crimes.* ⎈ *He pleaded guilty to theft.* ⎈ *He
was found guilty of drug smuggling.*

guitar /gɪˈtɑː(r)/ NOUN [*plural* guitars] an
instrument with strings that you play with your
fingers or a small piece of plastic ⎈ *an electric guitar*

gulf /gʌlf/ NOUN [*plural* gulfs] a large area of sea
almost surrounded by land □ *the Gulf of Taranto*

gum /gʌm/ NOUN [*plural* gums]
1 the hard pink part in your mouth that your teeth
grow from ⎈ *gum disease*
2 *no plural* a soft sweet substance that you chew
but do not swallow □ *a stick of gum*

gun /gʌn/ NOUN [*plural* guns] a weapon that fires
bullets from a metal tube ⎈ *The soldier quickly
loaded his gun.*

gunfire /ˈgʌnfaɪə(r)/ NOUN, NO PLURAL when guns
are fired or the sound that this makes □ *They
suddenly heard gunfire in the distance.*

gunman /ˈgʌnmən/ NOUN [*plural* gunmen] a man
who uses a gun to steal from people or kill them
□ *Two masked gunmen attacked him in his own
home.*

gush /gʌʃ/ VERB [gushes, gushing, gushed] if liquid
gushes, it flows out suddenly and in large
amounts □ *Blood was gushing from a wound on her
forehead.*

gust /gʌst/ NOUN [*plural* gusts] a sudden strong
wind □ *A gust of wind blew her hat off.*

gut /gʌt/ NOUN [*plural* guts]
1 the tube that takes food from your stomach to be
passed out of your body as waste
2 guts (a) courage and determination ⎈ *It took
guts to stand up to his father.* □ *He didn't have the
guts to tell me he was leaving.* (b) the organs inside
an animal's body

guy /gaɪ/ NOUN [*plural* guys] an informal word for a
man

gym /dʒɪm/ NOUN [*plural* gyms]
1 a room or building with equipment for doing
exercises □ *I go to the gym three times a
week.*
2 exercises that you do inside, especially at school
□ *We have gym on Wednesday.*

gymnast /ˈdʒɪmnæst/ NOUN [*plural* gymnasts]
someone trained to do a sport in which they use
their body to bend, jump, etc. in a beautiful
way

gymnastics /dʒɪmˈnæstɪks/ NOUN, NO PLURAL a
sport in which people use their bodies to bend, jump,
etc. in a beautiful way

H*h*

H *or* **h** /eɪtʃ/ the eighth letter of the alphabet

habit /'hæbɪt/ NOUN [*plural* habits] something that you do regularly, especially without thinking about It □ **+** *of* We want to get kids into the habit of regular exercise. ᴪ Tommy has a bad habit of biting his fingernails. ᴪ We asked people about their eating habits.

habitat /'hæbɪtæt/ NOUN [*plural* habitats] the place where an animal or a plant lives or grows ᴪ We wanted to study the lions in their natural habitat.

hack /hæk/ VERB [hacks, hacking, hacked]
1 to cut something roughly □ They hacked their way through the thick jungle. □ She hacked off chunks of hair.
2 to get into someone's computer illegally to look at information stored there. A computing word □ He hacked into military computer systems.

had /hæd/ PAST TENSE AND PAST PARTICIPLE OF have³

hadn't /'hædənt/ a short way to say and write had not □ Laura hadn't expected to win.

hail¹ /heɪl/ VERB [hails, hailing, hailed] If It halls, small white balls of frozen ice fall from the sky

hail² /heɪl/ NOUN, NO PLURAL small white balls of frozen ice that fall from the sky □ a hail storm

hair /heə(r)/ NOUN [*plural* hairs]
1 *no plural* all the thin threads that grow on your head ᴪ long/short hair ᴪ straight/curly hair ᴪ She's tall with shoulder-length blonde hair. ᴪ I need to get my hair cut.
2 one of the thin threads that grow on the surface of the skin of animals and humans □ It made the hairs on my arms stand up.

> ➤ Remember that 'hair' meaning 'all the hair on your head' is never used in the plural:
> ✓ She has short hair.
> ✗ She has short hairs.

♦ IDIOM **make someone's hair stand on end** to make someone very frightened or shocked □ The thought of finding a snake makes my hair stand on end.

hairbrush /'heəbrʌʃ/ NOUN [*plural* hairbrushes] a brush for brushing your hair

haircut /'heəkʌt/ NOUN [*plural* haircuts]
1 when someone cuts your hair □ You need a haircut.

2 the style in which your hair is cut □ She's got a new haircut.

hairdresser /'heədresə(r)/ NOUN [*plural* hairdressers]
1 someone whose job is to cut, arrange and colour people's hair
2 hairdresser's a place where a hairdresser works

hairdryer *or* **hairdrier** /'heədraɪə(r)/ NOUN [*plural* hairdryers *or* hairdriers] a piece of electrical equipment that dries your hair by blowing hot air over it

hairstyle /'heəstaɪl/ NOUN [*plural* hairstyles] the style in which your hair has been cut and arranged □ She showed off her new hairstyle.

hairy /'heərɪ/ ADJECTIVE [hairier, hairiest] covered with hair □ a hairy chest

half¹ /hɑːf/ NOUN, DETERMINER [*plural* halves]
1 1/2; one of two equal parts of something □ He ate half and I ate the other half. □ You have an hour and a half to play. ᴪ Meet us here in half an hour.
2 in half if you break, cut, etc. something in half, you divide it into two equal parts □ We cut the cake in half.
3 half past one/two, etc. 30 minutes after one o'clock/two o'clock, etc. □ He left at half past six.

half² /hɑːf/ ADVERB
1 to the amount of a half □ This glass is only half full. □ She is half Spanish (= one of her parents is Spanish).
2 partly, but not completely □ I was half asleep.

half-brother /'hɑːf,brʌðə(r)/ NOUN [*plural* half-brothers] a male relation with either the same father or the same mother as you

hall /hɔːl/ NOUN [*plural* halls]
1 an area just inside the entrance to a house that you go through to get to other rooms or to the stairs □ She checked her hair in the mirror in the hall. ᴪ The front door opens into a small entrance hall.
2 a large building or room where meetings, concerts and other events are held □ a concert hall □ a meeting at the village hall

hallo /hə'ləʊ/ EXCLAMATION another spelling of **hello**

halt¹ /hɔːlt/ VERB [halts, halting, halted]
1 to stop moving or to make something stop moving □ Traffic suddenly halted.

2 to stop happening or developing or to stop something happening or developing □ *The government is taking measures to halt the spread of the disease.* □ *These attacks should halt immediately.*

halt² /hɔːlt/ NOUN [*plural* halts]
1 when something stops moving 🔁 *The car came to a sudden halt.*
2 when something stops happening or developing 🔁 *He called a halt to the press conference and walked out.*

halve /hɑːv/ VERB [halves, halving, halved] to divide or cut something into two equal parts □ *Halve the mushrooms.*

ham /hæm/ NOUN, NO PLURAL meat from the leg of a pig which has been cooked using salt or smoke

hamburger /ˈhæmbɜːɡə(r)/ NOUN [*plural* hamburgers] a round flat shape made from very small pieces of meat that is fried and usually eaten between pieces of bread

hammer¹ /ˈhæmə(r)/ NOUN [*plural* hammers] a tool with a heavy metal or wooden part at the end of a handle, used for hitting nails, etc.

hammer² /ˈhæmə(r)/ VERB [hammers, hammering, hammered]
1 to hit something with a hammer □ *Hammer the nails in one by one.*
2 to hit something hard □ **+ on** *He was hammering on the door with his fists.* □ *The region was hammered by powerful storms.*

hamper¹ /ˈhæmpə(r)/ VERB [hampers, hampering, hampered] to make it difficult for someone or something to make progress □ *Rescue efforts were hampered by rain.*
hamper² /ˈhæmpə(r)/ NOUN [*plural* hampers] a large basket (= container made from very thin pieces of wood) with a lid, often used for carrying food

hand¹ /hænd/ NOUN [*plural* hands]
1 the part of your body at the end of your arm □ *I took her by the hand.* 🔁 *They walked hand in hand* (= with their hands joined together). 🔁 *Hold hands with me while we cross the road.* 🔁 *He refused to shake hands with my father.*
2 by hand (a) if something is made or done by hand, it is made or done by a person, not a machine (b) if a letter is delivered by hand, someone brings it to you without posting it
3 help 🔁 *Can I give you a hand with those bags?* 🔁 *Do you need a hand with the washing up?*
4 the part of a watch or clock that points to the time
♦ IDIOM **on the one hand ... on the other hand** used to compare the advantages and disadvantages of something □ *On the one hand, working at home*

saves me a lot of time, on the other hand it can be rather lonely.

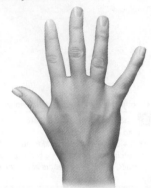

hand² /hænd/ VERB [hands, handing, handed] to give something to someone □ *Could you hand me a plate?*
♦ PHRASAL VERBS **hand something in** to give something to someone, for example a teacher □ *Have you handed in your homework?* **hand something out** to give something to everyone in a group □ *Can you hand out the textbooks?* **hand something over** to give something to someone □ *Hand over all your money.*

handbag /ˈhændbæɡ/ NOUN [*plural* handbags] a woman's bag for carrying things like money and keys □ *a black leather handbag*

handcuffs /ˈhændkʌfs/ PLURAL NOUN a pair of metal rings joined by a chain which police use to lock around a prisoner's wrists (= parts of the arms next to the hands)

handful /ˈhændful/ NOUN [*plural* handfuls]
1 an amount that you can hold in your hand □ *a handful of rice*
2 a handful of something a small number of something □ *Only a handful of people turned up.*
3 a handful an informal word for a child or an animal whose behaviour makes them difficult to deal with □ *Greta can be quite a handful.*

hand-held /ˈhænd,held/ ADJECTIVE small enough to hold in your hand during use □ *It was filmed using a hand-held video camera.*

handicap /ˈhændɪkæp/ NOUN [*plural* handicaps]
1 a disadvantage that prevents you doing something easily or as well as other people □ *Lack of qualifications can be a major handicap.*
2 an old-fashioned word for a physical or mental injury or disability that prevents someone from living normally □ *A school for children with mental and physical handicaps.*

handkerchief /'hæŋkətʃɪf/ NOUN [*plural* handkerchiefs] a small piece of cloth or thin, soft paper used for drying your nose or eyes

handle¹ /'hændəl/ NOUN [*plural* handles]
1 the part of an object that you use to pick it up and hold it □ *a brush with a long handle*
2 the part of a door that you hold when you open and close it 🈁 *a door handle*

handle² /'hændəl/ VERB [handles, handling, handled]
1 to deal with something □ *Mr Peters is handling all the arrangements for the trip.* 🈁 *I would have handled the situation differently.*
2 to touch something or to hold it with your hands □ *Try not to handle the fruit too much.*

handsome /'hænsəm/ ADJECTIVE [handsomer, handsomest] attractive, especially used about a man □ *a handsome young actor* □ *He looked so handsome in his uniform.*

handwriting /'hændraɪtɪŋ/ NOUN, NO PLURAL writing done with a pen or a pencil, not printed □ *The speech is written in a notebook in Dr King's own handwriting.*

handy /'hændɪ/ ADJECTIVE [handier, handiest]
1 useful and easy to use □ *It's a handy size for carrying in your pocket.*
2 near and easy to reach □ *The house is handy for the station.*
3 come in handy an informal phrase meaning to be useful □ *Bring the torch, it might come in handy.*

hang /hæŋ/ VERB [hangs, hanging, hung]
1 to attach something so that the top part is fixed and the lower part is able to move □ *Hang your jackets on the pegs.* □ *Joe was hanging upside down by his feet.* □ *The branches hung down to the ground.*
2 to kill someone by tying a rope around their neck and making them drop so that the rope is tight □ *He hanged himself in his prison cell.*

◆ PHRASAL VERBS **hang about/around** to stay in a place, doing nothing □ *There was a group of boys hanging round outside our house.* **hang on 1** to hold something tightly □ *Hang on tight and we'll pull you up.* **2** an informal word meaning to wait □ *Hang on a minute!* **hang something up** to put something such as clothing in a place where it can hang □ *We hung up our coats in the hall.*

happen /'hæpən/ VERB [happens, happening, happened]
1 if something happens, it takes place, usually without being planned □ *The accident happened last week.* □ *I pressed the button but nothing happened.* 🈁 *He'll be pleased, whatever happens.*
2 happen to do something to do something by chance □ *She just happened to be there and saw the whole thing.*

happily /'hæpɪlɪ/ ADVERB feeling, showing or expressing happiness □ *The girls were smiling happily.* 🈁 *They're happily married.*

happiness /'hæpɪnɪs/ NOUN, NO PLURAL the state of being happy 🈁 *He has finally found happiness in his personal life.* □ *My children are my greatest source of happiness.*

happy /'hæpɪ/ ADJECTIVE [happier, happiest]
1 pleased and feeling that a situation is good □ *It was the happiest day of her life.* □ *He looked really happy.* 🈁 *More money won't make her happy.*
2 making you feel happy □ *I had a very happy childhood.* □ *The story has a happy ending.*
3 Happy Birthday/Christmas, etc. used to say that you hope someone will be happy on a special day

➤ **THESAURUS:** If you are happy or cheerful, you are pleased, and feel that a situation is good. Delighted means very happy. If you are glad, you are happy because of something that has happened. Often you are glad because a bad or difficult situation has ended or because something bad has not happened. For example, you might be glad to be home after a long journey, or glad that your exams are finished.

harbor /'hɑːbə(r)/ NOUN [*plural* harbors] the US spelling of **harbour**

harbour /'hɑːbə(r)/ NOUN [*plural* harbours] a safe area of water near the coast, usually protected by big walls, where ships come so that people can go onto the land □ *The ship sailed into Sydney harbour.*

hard¹ /hɑːd/ ADJECTIVE [harder, hardest]
1 firm and solid and not easy to bend or break □ *This bread is a bit hard.* □ *The ball will only bounce on a hard surface.*
2 difficult to do □ + to do something *It was hard to concentrate with all the noise.* □ *The exam was really hard.*

3 unpleasant or full of problems 🔁 *They had a hard life.* 🔁 *He had a hard time in the army.*

hard² /hɑːd/ ADVERB [harder, hardest]
1 with a lot effort 🔁 *They always work hard.* 🔁 *You need to try harder.*
2 with a lot of force □ *It was raining hard when we got there.*

hard disk /ˌhɑːd ˈdɪsk/ or **hard drive** /ˈhɑːdˌdraɪv/ NOUN [plural hard disks or hard drives] a part inside a computer where information is stored. A computing word.

harden /ˈhɑːdən/ VERB [hardens, hardening, hardened] to become hard or solid □ *The mixture hardens into a solid gel.*

hardly /ˈhɑːdlɪ/ ADVERB only just or almost not □ *I hardly know him.* □ *He hardly spoke a word of English.* 🔁 *There were hardly any people there.* 🔁 *We hardly ever saw her.* □ *He'd hardly put the key in the door when down came the rain.*

> ➤ Notice that the word **hardly** does not mean 'with a lot of effort' or 'with a lot of force'. For these two meanings, use the word **hard**:
> ✓ *She works so hard.*
> ✗ *She works so hardly.*
> ✓ *It's raining hard.*
> ✗ *It's raining hardly.*

hardware /ˈhɑːdweə(r)/ NOUN, NO PLURAL the machines and equipment that make up a computer system. A computing word □ *We need to update our computer hardware and software.*

harm¹ /hɑːm/ VERB [harms, harming, harmed] to hurt, damage or cause problems for someone or something □ *You might harm your eyes if you sit too close to the TV.* □ *She believes that violent video games can harm children.* □ *We know that air travel harms the environment.*

harm² /hɑːm/ NOUN, NO PLURAL
1 damage, injury or problems 🔁 *The knife wasn't sharp enough to cause much harm.* 🔁 *If you stay with me, you won't come to any harm.* 🔁 *It wouldn't do any harm to ask for advice.*
2 there's no harm in doing something used to say that an action will not cause problems and may help a situation □ *I don't think you'll be able to persuade him to come, but there's no harm in trying.*

harmful /ˈhɑːmful/ ADJECTIVE causing damage, injury or problems □ *Use a cream to protect your skin from the sun's harmful rays.*

harmless /ˈhɑːmlɪs/ ADJECTIVE not causing any damage, injury or problems □ *This substance is harmless to animals.*

harmony /ˈhɑːmənɪ/ NOUN [plural harmonies]
1 when people live in a peaceful and friendly way □ *We live in harmony with our neighbours.*

2 a combination of musical notes that sound pleasant together □ *complex vocal harmonies*

harsh /hɑːʃ/ ADJECTIVE [harsher, harshest]
1 very cold, uncomfortable or difficult, etc. □ *a harsh climate* □ *a harsh winter* □ *The poor lived in very harsh conditions.*
2 cruel, severe and often unfair □ *a harsh punishment* 🔁 *harsh criticism* 🔁 *He had harsh words for his teammate.*

harvest¹ /ˈhɑːvɪst/ NOUN [plural harvests]
1 the activity of collecting crops □ *Heavy rains delayed the harvest.*
2 the amount of a crop that is collected □ *The price rise is due to poor wheat harvests.*

harvest² /ˈhɑːvɪst/ VERB [harvests, harvesting, harvested] to collect a crop □ *The apples are harvested in late summer.*

has /hæz/ VERB the present tense of the verb **have³** when it is used with **he**, **she** and **it** □ *He has brown eyes.*

hasn't /ˈhæzənt/ a short way to say and write has not □ *Anne hasn't arrived yet.*

hat /hæt/ NOUN [plural hats] a covering you wear on your head □ *a straw hat* □ *a fur hat*

hatch /hætʃ/ VERB [hatches, hatching, hatched] baby birds or reptiles hatch when they break out of their eggs □ *We watched the chicks hatch.*

hate¹ /heɪt/ VERB [hates, hating, hated] to dislike someone or something very much □ *+ ing I hate being late.* □ *I hate the idea of wasting all that money.*

> ➤ **THESAURUS:** If you dislike something or someone, you do not like it. Hate and loathe both mean that you dislike something or someone very much.

hate² /heɪt/ NOUN, NO PLURAL a very strong feeling that you do not like someone or something □ *There was a look of real hate in his eyes.*

hatred /'heɪtrɪd/ NOUN, NO PLURAL a very strong feeling that you do not like someone or something □ *I have a hatred of dogs.* ⊞ *He was accused of promoting racial hatred.*

haul /hɔːl/ VERB [hauls, hauling, hauled] to pull someone or something using a lot of effort □ *He managed to haul himself up on to the boat.*

haunt /hɔːnt/ VERB [haunts, haunting, haunted] if a ghost (= dead person's spirit) haunts a place, people think it appears there □ *People claim that the castle is haunted by the ghost of the young prince.*

haunted /'hɔːntɪd/ ADJECTIVE visited by ghosts (= spirits of dead people) ⊔ *Some people believe that this room is haunted.* □ *a haunted castle*

have¹ /hæv/ AUXILIARY VERB [has, having, had] used with the past participle of another verb to form the present perfect tense or the past perfect tense □ *I have bought a new car.* □ *Have you fed the rabbit?* □ *She has been feeling tired recently.* □ *They had opened a restaurant in Athens.*

have² /hæv/ MODAL VERB [has, having, had]
1 have to do something if you have to do something, you must do it □ *I have to go away for a few days.* □ *You'll have to give him the money.* ⊞ *I don't have to go to work tomorrow.*
2 used for telling someone how to do something □ *You have to press the green button.*

➤ Notice that when **have to** (sense 1) is negative, the negative form is usually made with **do**: □ *I don't have to go.* □ *He doesn't have to work.* The question form of **have to** is also made with **do**: □ *Do you have to tell him?* □ *Do we have to come?*

have³ /hæv/ VERB [has, having, had]
1 used for describing someone or something □ *He has got black hair.* □ *The room had patches of damp on the walls.* □ *The soup had a delicious flavour.*
2 to own something □ *He has a house in Spain.* □ *I have got three brothers.* □ *She has the determination to win.*
3 used for saying that someone has something with them □ *Do you have a towel I could use?* □ *He had a large dog with him.*
4 to have an illness is to suffer from it □ *She has cancer.* □ *I had a terrible headache.*
5 have a look/shower/walk, etc. to do a particular thing
6 to have food or drink is to eat it or drink it □ *You'll have lunch with us, won't you?* □ *I had a huge curry last night.*
7 to experience something □ *We've had a lot of problems.* □ *I hope you have a great time in Mexico.*
➡ go to **have your cake and eat it**

➤ Notice (*sense 2*) that **have** and **have got** are both used to mean 'to own something'. It is normal, especially in spoken English, to use the short forms of **have got** and **has got**: □ *I've got a dog.* (= I have got a dog). □ *She's got a dog.* (= She has got a dog).

haven't /'hævənt/ a short way to say and write have not □ *I haven't seen the film yet.*

hawk /hɔːk/ NOUN [plural hawks] a bird that can see very well and hunts small animals for food

hay /heɪ/ NOUN, NO PLURAL grass that has been cut and dried, used to feed animals

hazard /'hæzəd/ NOUN [plural hazards] something that could cause harm or damage ⊞ *Undercooked food is a potential health hazard.* ⊞ *a fire hazard*

➤ **THESAURUS:** A **hazard** is something that could cause harm or damage. For example, food that is not stored properly can be a health hazard. A **danger** is a situation where something may harm you. A **risk** is something that could cause problems in the future. For example, if the economic situation is bad, there is a risk that you will lose your job. An **accident** is a bad thing that happens that is not intended.

haze /heɪz/ NOUN [plural hazes] air that is difficult to see through because of heat, smoke, dust, etc.

he /hiː/ PRONOUN used to talk or write about a man, boy or male animal that has already been mentioned □ *Everyone likes Ted because he is so funny.* □ *Don't worry – he won't bite.*

head¹ /hed/ NOUN [plural heads]
1 the part of the body that contains the brain, eyes, mouth, etc. □ *She suffered serious head injuries.* □ *He turned his head to look at the clock.* ⊞ *nod/ shake your head* ⊞ *She was dressed in black from head to toe.*
2 your mind □ *The idea just popped into my head.*
3 the person who is in charge of an organization or a group of people □ *He is the former head of the prison service.*
4 the top or front of something □ *Put your name at the head of each page.* □ *I went straight to the head of the queue.*
◆ IDIOMS **be over someone's head** to be too difficult for someone to understand □ *The stuff about economics was right over my head* **go to someone's head** If success, praise, etc. goes to someone's head, they become too proud **head over heels 1** if you fall head over heels, you fall in a sudden and forceful way □ *He slipped on the ice and went head over heels.* **2** if you are head over heels in love, you love someone very much **keep your head** to stay calm □ *She kept her head in a crisis.*

➤ THESAURUS: The head of an organization or a group of people is the person who is in charge. Chief has a similar meaning. We often use chief to talk about the most important police officer in a group. A manager is someone who is in charge of other people at work. Boss is a more informal word for this. A principal is the person who is in charge of a school, college or university.

head² /hed/ VERB [heads, heading, headed]
1 to go towards a particular place □ *It's time for us to head home.* □ *We were heading north along the motorway.*
2 to be in charge of an organization or a group of people □ *She heads the development team.*
3 to hit a ball with your head

headache /'hedeɪk/ NOUN [plural headaches] a pain in your head 🖪 *I've got a splitting headache.* 🖪 *That noise is giving me a headache.*

headlight /'hedlaɪt/ NOUN [plural headlights] one of the two big lights at the front of a vehicle

headline /'hedlaɪn/ NOUN [plural headlines]
1 the words that are printed in large letters at the top of a newspaper article
2 headlines the most important news stories that are reported at the beginning of a news programme on the television or radio □ *Here is Charlotte Green with today's headlines.*

headquarters /'hed,kwɔːtəz/ PLURAL NOUN the central office from which a large business or organization is controlled □ *Our company headquarters are in London.*

headteacher /,hed'tiːtʃə(r)/ NOUN [plural headteachers] a teacher who is in charge of a school

heal /hiːl/ VERB [heals, healing, healed] to become healthy again, or to make a person or part of the body healthy again □ *The wound needs time to heal.* □ *The substance is used for healing cuts.* □ *With time, the body will heal itself.*

➤ THESAURUS: If something heals, it gets healthy again. For example, a wound heals. To cure means to make someone with an illness better again. Medicine can cure an illness. You can use the noun cure to talk about the thing that makes you better. A remedy is also something which treats an illness. We often use remedy to talk about things which are not medicine. For example, some people believe that drinking honey and lemon is a remedy for a cold.

health /helθ/ NOUN, NO PLURAL how well your body is □ *Her health has been very poor recently.* 🖪 *Too much red meat is bad for your health.* 🖪 *He* appeared to be *in good health.* 🖪 *She was forced to leave due to* ill health.

healthy /'helθɪ/ ADJECTIVE [healthier, healthiest]
1 physically well and not ill in any way □ *Exercise and a good diet can help you stay healthy.* □ *She seems perfectly healthy.*
2 having a good effect on your health 🖪 *healthy eating* 🖪 *She has a very healthy lifestyle.*

heap /hiːp/ NOUN [plural heaps] an untidy pile of things □ *I found a heap of dirty clothes at the top of the stairs.* 🖪 *His clothes were in a heap in the bottom of the wardrobe.*

hear /hɪə(r)/ VERB [hears, hearing, heard]
1 to be aware of sounds through your ears □ *Can you hear that clicking noise?* □ *I heard the sound of an explosion.* □ *She screamed, but nobody heard her.*
2 to be told something □ *+ that* I heard that she was unhappy in her job. □ *The court heard that the men both used false passports.* □ *+ about* Did you hear about Rob's accident?
3 have heard of someone/something to know that someone or something exists □ *I'd never heard of him before.*
◆ PHRASAL VERB **hear from someone** to receive a letter, email, telephone call, etc. from someone □ *Have you heard from Joss recently?*

➤ THESAURUS: If you hear something you are aware of sounds through your ears. If you listen to something, you pay attention to a sound so that you can hear it. If you overhear something, you hear something that someone says when they are not talking to you.

hearing /'hɪərɪŋ/ NOUN [plural hearings] your ability to hear □ *My hearing was affected by the constant noise.*

heart /hɑːt/ NOUN [plural hearts]
1 the organ that sends blood around your body 🖪 *My heart was beating very fast.* 🖪 *He suffers from heart disease.*
2 the centre of something □ *+ of* She lives in the heart of the city.
3 the most important part of something □ *+ of* Jealousy is at the heart of their problems. 🖪 *I really tried to get to the heart of what was upsetting her.*
4 someone's feelings or character □ *She captured the hearts of the audience.* □ *Ken has a kind heart.*
5 a shape (♥) that represents the human heart and human love
6 hearts one of the four types of playing card, which have the symbol (♥) printed on them
◆ IDIOMS **know/learn something (off) by heart** to know or learn something so well that you do not have to read it □ *I learned the whole poem off by heart.* **not have the heart to do something** to be too kind to do something □ *I didn't have the heart to tell him his story was rubbish.* **someone's heart**

sinks if someone's heart sinks, they are disappointed or expect that something bad will happen □ *My heart sank when I saw how dirty the holiday cottage was.*

➜ *go to* break[1] *someone's heart*

heart attack /'hɑːt ə,tæk/ NOUN [*plural* heart attacks] when someone's heart suddenly stops working □ *He died of a heart attack .*

heartbeat /'hɑːtbiːt/ NOUN [*plural* heartbeats] the regular sound or movement that your heart makes

heat[1] /hiːt/ NOUN [*plural* heats]
1 *no plural* the quality of being hot or how hot something is □ *The panels use heat from the sun.* □ *Turn up the heat until the soup is boiling.*
2 the heat very hot weather □ *I can't stand the heat in summer.*
3 a game or a race to decide who goes on to the next stage of a competition □ *Ian won his heat and went through to the semi-final.*

heat[2] /hiːt/ VERB [heats, heating, heated] to make something hot or hotter □ *We use solar energy to heat our water.* □ *Heat the oven to medium.*
◆ PHRASAL VERB **heat (something) up** to become hotter or to make something hotter □ *We heated up the soup over the fire.*

heater /'hiːtə(r)/ NOUN [*plural* heaters] a piece of equipment that heats water or a place □ *I'll turn this heater on.*

heaven /'hevən/ NOUN, NO PLURAL in some religions, the place where God lives and where good people go when they die

heavily /'hevɪli/ ADVERB
1 a lot or to a large degree □ *The soldiers were heavily armed.* □ *His wife is heavily pregnant.*
2 with a lot of force or weight □ *It was snowing heavily when we left.* □ *She fell heavily, twisting her ankle.*

heavy /'hevi/ ADJECTIVE [heavier, heaviest]
1 something that is heavy weighs a lot □ *The bags were too heavy for me to carry.*
2 if you say how heavy something is, you say how much it weighs □ *How heavy are these bricks?*
3 large in amount or degree 🖻 *heavy traffic* 🖻 *heavy rain/snow* 🖻 *There was heavy fighting in the region.*
4 a heavy smoker/drinker someone who smokes a lot/drinks a lot of alcohol

hectare /'hekteə(r)/ NOUN [*plural* hectares] a unit for measuring area equal to 10,000 square metres. This is often written **ha**.

he'd /hiːd/ a short way to say and write he had or he would □ *He'd never been there before.* □ *He'd do it for me if I asked him.*

hedge /hedʒ/ NOUN [*plural* hedges] a line of bushes or trees growing close together that separates one piece of land from another □ *A thick hedge surrounds the garden.*

heel /hiːl/ NOUN [*plural* heels]
1 the back part of your foot □ *She was getting a blister on her heel.*
2 the part of a shoe under the back of your foot 🖻 *She was wearing high heels.*

height /haɪt/ NOUN [*plural* heights]
1 how tall or high someone or something is □ *He's of average height.* □ *I'd say the wall's about four metres in height.*
2 how far above the ground something is □ *We are now flying at a height of 11,000 metres.*

heir /eə(r)/ NOUN [*plural* heirs] the person who has a legal right to someone's money or property when they die □ *He is the heir to a large fortune.*

held /held/ PAST TENSE AND PAST PARTICIPLE OF **hold[1]** □ *She held my hand* □ *We held the meeting in David's office.*

helicopter /'helɪkɒptə(r)/ NOUN [*plural* helicopters] a small aircraft without wings that is lifted into the air by long thin parts on top which turn round very fast

he'll /hiːl/ a short way to say and write he will □ *He'll be here soon.*

hell /hel/ NOUN, NO PLURAL
1 in some religions, the place where bad people go when they die
2 a very unpleasant experience □ *The last few months of the relationship were hell.*

hello /hə'ləʊ/ EXCLAMATION something you say when you meet someone or begin talking to someone on the telephone □ *Hello, Sophie. How are you?* □ *Hello, it's Mark.*

helmet /'helmɪt/ NOUN [*plural* helmets] a hard hat worn to protect your head □ *a cycling helmet* □ *a fireman's helmet*

help[1] /help/ VERB [helps, helping, helped]
1 to do something to make a situation or activity easier for someone □ *+ to do something I helped him to find somewhere to stay.* □ *I find a warm bath helps to relax me.* □ *+ with My Mum helped me with my homework.*
2 to make a situation better or easier □ *If you've got a cold, eating oranges might help. □ It helps if you put the heavier items at the bottom. □ I took some painkillers, but they didn't help much.*
3 can't help (doing) something if you can't help something, you cannot stop yourself from doing it or stop it happening □ *She couldn't help laughing when she saw his face.*

4 help yourself to take something without waiting for someone to give it to you □ *Help yourself to some food.*

help² /help/ EXCLAMATION **Help!** used to shout for help in a serious situation

help³ /help/ NOUN [*plural* helps]
1 *no plural* when someone does something to make a situation or an activity easier for someone 🖫 *He needs help with his garden.* 🖫 *I was in debt, but I didn't know where to get help.* 🖫 *These children get extra help with their reading.*
2 someone or something that helps someone 🖫 *Thanks for the advice. It was a great help.* □ *I couldn't work out how to use the system, and the instructions weren't much help.*

helpful /'helpful/ ADJECTIVE
1 useful □ *helpful advice*
2 willing to help □ *There was a lot of tidying up, but the children were very helpful.*

helpless /'helplɪs/ ADJECTIVE not able to do anything for yourself, or to help other people in trouble □ *How could anyone rob a helpless old man?*

hen /hen/ NOUN [*plural* hens] a female chicken

her¹ /hɜː(r)/ PRONOUN used as the object of a sentence to talk or write about a woman, girl or female animal that has already been mentioned □ *I'm looking for Mrs Peters. Have you seen her?* □ *I gave the letter to her.*

her² /hɜː(r)/ DETERMINER belonging to or to do with a woman, girl or female animal □ *Her hair is blonde.* □ *That's her problem, not mine.*

herb /hɜːb/ NOUN [*plural* herbs] a plant that is used for giving flavour to food and for making medicines □ *herbs and spices* □ *a herb garden*

herd /hɜːd/ NOUN [*plural* herds] a large group of animals of one type that live as a group □ *a herd of cattle*

here /hɪə(r)/ ADVERB
1 in or to this place □ *I like it here.* □ *Come here!* □ *You can leave your shoes here.* □ *He's American, but he's lived over here for years.*
2 used to say that someone or something has arrived or has been found □ *Here's Tom at last.* □ *Here's the house we are looking for.*
3 used when you give someone something □ *Here, put on this jacket.* □ *Here you are – we saved some food for you.*
4 here and there in a few different places □ *There were a few mistakes here and there.*

heritage /'herɪtɪdʒ/ NOUN, NO PLURAL the buildings, customs, culture, etc. of a country that is important because they have existed for a long time □ *Spain's cultural heritage*

hero /'hɪərəʊ/ NOUN [*plural* heroes]
1 someone who people admire because of the brave

or difficult things they have done □ *Nelson Mandela is a hero to many of us.*
2 the most important male character in a story or film □ *The hero of the book is a New York detective.*

heroine /'herəʊɪn/ NOUN [*plural* heroines]
1 a woman or girl who people admire because of the brave or difficult things she has done
2 the most important female character in a story or film

hers /hɜːz/ PRONOUN used to talk or write about things belonging to or to do with a woman or girl that has already been mentioned □ *I gave Sandra my phone number and she gave me hers.* □ *'Was it your idea, or Ann's?' 'It was hers.'*

➤ Notice that there is no apostrophe between the **r** and the **s** in **hers**.

herself /hɜː'self/ PRONOUN
1 the reflexive form of **her** □ *Did Barbara hurt herself when she fell down?* □ *She sang to herself as she worked.*
2 used to show that she does something without any help from other people □ *She always answers every fan letter herself.* 🖫 *She's only 3 but she can get dressed* all *by herself.*
3 used to emphasize the pronoun **she** □ *I wanted to speak to Gina herself.*
4 by herself not with or near other people □ *She always sits by herself.*

he's /hiːz/ a short way to say and write **he is** or **he has** □ *He's my brother.* □ *He's done all the work.*

hey /heɪ/ EXCLAMATION an word used to get someone's attention or show you are surprised □ *Hey, stop that!* □ *Hey, look at this!*

hi /haɪ/ EXCLAMATION hello □ *Hi, Charlotte!* □ *Hi, how are you?*

hide¹ /haɪd/ VERB [hides, hiding, hid, hidden]
1 to put or keep something or someone in a place where people cannot see or find them easily □ *I hid her presents under my bed.* □ *He kept his money hidden from his wife.*
2 to go to a place where people cannot see you □ *Eva was hiding and the other children were looking for her.* □ *He hid behind a tree.*
3 to not tell or show people your feelings or some information □ *Sarah didn't try to hide her disappointment at losing.* □ *I've got nothing to hide.*

➤ **THESAURUS:** If you **hide** something, you put or keep something in a place where people cannot find it easily. If you **bury** something, you put it in the ground and cover it up. If you **disguise** something or someone, you make them look like something else so that people will not recognize them. If you **cover** something, you put something over something else in order to hide it or protect it.

hide² /haɪd/ NOUN [*plural* hides] the skin of an animal

hiding /ˈhaɪdɪŋ/ NOUN, NO PLURAL when someone stays in a secret place or changes their appearance so that no one will find them 🔁 *The ex-spy is believed to be in hiding in London.* 🔁 *He knew he would be arrested so he went into hiding.*

high¹ /haɪ/ ADJECTIVE [higher, highest]
1 a large distance above the ground □ *The apples were too high to reach.* □ *It's best to keep medicines on a high shelf.*
2 a long distance from the bottom to the top □ *It is a very high building.* □ *They built a high wall around the house.*
3 having a particular height □ *The fence is 4 metres high.* □ *How high is Snowdon?*
4 large in amount or level 🔁 *The temperature was unusually high.* 🔁 *We drove at high speed through the town.* 🔁 *We were shocked at the high cost of housing.* 🔁 *They found high levels of pollution in the area.*
5 a high sound or musical note is near the top of the range of sounds □ *We could hear the children's high voices.*

➤ Remember that people who are big in height are described as **tall** and not **high**:
✓ *Her father is very tall.*
✗ *Her father is very high.*

high² /haɪ/ ADVERB [higher, highest]
1 at or to a large distance above the ground □ *She threw the ball high in the air.* □ *Dirty clothes were piled high in her bedroom.* □ *The village is located high above the sea.*
2 at or to a large amount or level □ *The temperature rose higher and higher.* □ *Prices remain high.*

highlight¹ /ˈhaɪlaɪt/ VERB [highlights, highlighting, highlighted] to emphasize something □ *These figures highlight a growing problem.*

highlight² /ˈhaɪlaɪt/ NOUN [*plural* highlights] the best part of an event or period of time □ *His singing was the highlight of the concert.*

highly /ˈhaɪli/ ADVERB very □ *highly qualified teachers* □ *This seems highly unlikely.*

high school /haɪ ˌskuːl/ NOUN [*plural* high schools] in the US, a school for children aged between 14 and 18

high street /haɪ ˌstriːt/ NOUN [*plural* high streets] the main street of a town, where the shops and banks are □ *Most of the high street banks will be raising their interest rates.*

high-tech /ˌhaɪˈtek/ ADJECTIVE using the most modern technology □ *high-tech security equipment* □ *high-tech computer graphics*

highway /ˈhaɪweɪ/ NOUN [*plural* highways] a US word for a road between towns and cities

hijack /ˈhaɪdʒæk/ VERB [hijacks, hijacking, hijacked] to take control of an aeroplane by force □ *Two students hijacked the plane in Thailand.*

hijacker /ˈhaɪdʒækə(r)/ NOUN [*plural* hijackers] someone who takes control of an aeroplane by force □ *The hijackers were arrested by Australian police.*

hike /haɪk/ NOUN [*plural* hikes] a long walk in the countryside

hill /hɪl/ NOUN [*plural* hills] a raised or high area of land, smaller than a mountain □ *We went walking in the Tuscan hills.*
♦ IDIOM **over the hill** if someone is over the hill, they are too old to do something

hilly /ˈhɪli/ ADJECTIVE [hillier, hilliest] a hilly area has a lot of hills

him /hɪm/ PRONOUN used as the object of a sentence to talk or write about a man, boy or male animal that has already been mentioned □ *I'm looking for Mr Peters. Have you seen him anywhere?* □ *She threw the book at him.*

himself /hɪmˈself/ PRONOUN
1 the reflexive form of *him* □ *He poked himself in the eye by mistake.* □ *The old man was muttering to himself.*
2 used to show that he does something without any help from other people □ *I was surprised he did all the cooking himself.* 🔁 *Jack can tie his shoelaces all by himself already.*
3 used to emphasize the pronoun *him* □ *He's never been to London himself.*
4 by himself not with or near other people □ *He stood by himself in a corner.*

Hindu¹ /ˈhɪnduː/ NOUN [*plural* Hindus] a person whose religion is Hinduism

Hindu² /ˈhɪnduː/ ADJECTIVE to do with Hinduism □ *The main Hindu gods are Brahma, Vishnu and Shiva.*

Hinduism /ˈhɪnduːɪzəm/ NOUN, NO PLURAL a religion of India and parts of South East Asia, which has many gods and teaches that after people die they will return to life in another body

hint¹ /hɪnt/ NOUN [*plural* hints]
1 a helpful piece of advice □ *Can you give me any hints on how to learn vocabulary?*
2 something that suggests what you think or want but not in a direct way 🔁 *She dropped a hint that something exciting was about to happen.* 🔁 *He kept yawning but no one took the hint and went home.*

➤ **THESAURUS:** A hint or a tip is a helpful piece of advice. A suggestion is a more general word for an idea that you mention. A clue is a piece of information that helps to solve a problem or a crime.

hint² /hɪnt/ VERB [hints, hinting, hinted] to suggest something in a way that is not clear or direct □ *Laura hinted that she might be leaving.*

hip /hɪp/ NOUN [plural hips] each of the two parts at the side of your body, below your waist and above your leg □ *Gran fell and broke her hip.*

hip-hop /'hɪphɒp/ NOUN, NO PLURAL a type of pop music in which the words are about social problems and are spoken not sung □ *hip-hop groups*

hippopotamus /ˌhɪpə'pɒtəməs/ NOUN [plural hippopotamuses or hippopotami] a large African animal with a heavy body, small ears and short legs, that lives near or in rivers

hire¹ /'haɪə(r)/ VERB [hires, hiring, hired]
1 to pay to use something for a period of time, especially a short period, and then return it □ *We hired bikes while we were on holiday.*
2 to begin to employ someone □ *I've decided to hire a cleaner.*

► Notice (*sense 1*) that in British English you **hire** things usually for a short time, only paying once to use them. You **rent**, usually for a longer period, a house or an office, etc., paying every month or many times. In American English you always **rent** things. The verb **hire** is not used.

hire² /'haɪə(r)/ NOUN, NO PLURAL when you pay to use something for a period of time □ *The holiday price includes the hire of a car.* ⊞ *There are boats for hire on the lake.*

his¹ /hɪz/ DETERMINER belonging to or to do with to him □ *Julian has left his coat behind.* □ *Blame Harry. It was his idea.*

his² /hɪz/ PRONOUN used to talk or write about things belonging to or to do with to a man, boy or male animal that has already been mentioned □ *I didn't have an umbrella so Grandad lent me his.*

hiss¹ /hɪs/ VERB [hisses, hissing, hissed] to make a noise like a long 's' sound □ *a hissing snake*

hiss² /hɪs/ NOUN [plural hisses] a sound like that made by a snake □ *We could hear the hiss of gas escaping from the pipe.*

historic /hɪ'stɒrɪk/ ADJECTIVE important in history □ *a historic victory*

historical /hɪ'stɒrɪkəl/ ADJECTIVE to do with history □ *historical records*

► Notice the difference between **historic** and **historical**. **Historic** means 'important in history'. **Historical** means 'to do with history': □ *This was a historic moment.* □ *She writes historical novels.*

history /'hɪstərɪ/ NOUN [plural histories] all the things that happened in the past, or the study of things that happened in the past □ *local history* □ *modern European history* □ *He studied history at university.* □ *history books*

hit¹ /hɪt/ VERB [hits, hitting, hit] to touch against someone or something with force □ *Stop hitting your brother!* □ *The plane hit the ground and burst into flames.* □ *I hit my head on the cupboard door.* □ *She hit him with a baseball bat.* □ *Storms hit the west coast last night.*

hit² /hɪt/ NOUN [plural hits]
1 something or someone that is very popular □ *The show was an instant hit.* □ *He's a big hit with the old ladies.*
2 when you touch against something with force □ *I got a hit on my arm.*

HIV /ˌeɪtʃaɪ'viː/ ABBREVIATION human immunodeficiency virus; the virus that causes the disease AIDS

hobby /'hɒbɪ/ NOUN [plural hobbies] something you like doing in your free time ⊞ *My Dad's favourite hobby is birdwatching.* ⊞ *It's my new hobby.* ⊞ *She didn't really have any hobbies.*

hockey /'hɒkɪ/ NOUN, NO PLURAL a game in which two teams use curved sticks to hit a ball into a net ⊞ *We play hockey at school.* ⊞ *a hockey stick* □ *a hockey team*

hold¹ /həʊld/ VERB [holds, holding, held]
1 to have something in your hand or hands □ *He was holding a big wooden box.* ⊞ *Hold tight – we're going over some rough ground.*
2 to support something or to stop something moving □ *The pieces of wood are held together with nails.* ⊞ *Use glue to hold the cardboard in place.*
3 to organize an event □ *We held the meeting in our office.* ⊞ *The general has promised to hold an election.*
4 to have space for something □ *The room holds 300 people.*
5 to contain something □ *This rack holds my wine collection.*
6 to have a particular job or position in an organization □ *She holds the post of director.*
7 hold your breath to deliberately not breathe
8 hold hands to curve your hand around someone else's hand
♦ PHRASAL VERBS **hold something/someone back** to stop someone or something making progress □ *A lack of formal education did not hold her back.* **hold on 1** to hold something tightly □ *Hold on tight! We're coming to get you.* **2** to wait □ *Hold on a minute – I just need to check my email.* **hold someone/something up** to make something or someone slow or late □ *We got held up by the*

traffic. □ *All these regulations are holding up progress.*

hold² /həʊld/ NOUN [plural **holds**]
1 when you hold something, or the way something is held 🔁 *I got hold of the handle and pulled it hard.* 🔁 *Try to catch hold of the rope.* 🔁 *My hands were so wet, I couldn't keep hold of the rail.*
2 get hold of something to manage to get something □ *Do you know where I can get hold of some cheap bricks?*
3 get hold of someone to manage to speak to someone □ *I've been trying to get hold of her all morning.*
4 the place in a ship or an aeroplane where goods or bags are stored

hole /həʊl/ NOUN [plural **holes**] a space in the surface of something □ **+ in** *He had a hole in his sock.* □ *She drilled a hole in the wall.*

➤ THESAURUS: Hole is a general word. A **tear** is a hole in something that has been pulled apart. We usually use **tear** to talk about thin things like paper or material. A **slot** is a small narrow hole in something, especially one where you put coins or bank cards. A **crack** is a narrow break in something. If a plate has a **crack** in it, it may still be in one piece, but it has a narrow break.

holiday /ˈhɒlɪdeɪ/ NOUN [plural **holidays**]
1 a time when you do not have to work or go to school 🔁 *What are you doing in the summer holidays?* 🔁 *The museum is very busy during school holidays.*
2 on holiday if you are on holiday, you are not working or not at school for a period □ *I'm on holiday next week.*
3 a period of time when you stay in a different place to enjoy yourself 🔁 *We're going on holiday next week.* □ *a skiing holiday* 🔁 *Spain is a popular holiday destination for British travellers.*

➤ The word **holiday** is used by British speakers of English. North American speakers of English use the word **vacation**.

hollow /ˈhɒləʊ/ ADJECTIVE [**hollower**, **hollowest**] having an empty space inside □ *hollow chocolate eggs* □ *a hollow tube*

holy /ˈhəʊli/ ADJECTIVE [**holier**, **holiest**]
1 to do with God or religion □ *The Koran is the Muslim holy book.* □ *The Golden Temple is a holy site in Punjab.*
2 having strong religious feelings □ *a holy man*

home¹ /həʊm/ NOUN [plural **homes**]
1 the place where you live or where you lived when you were a child □ *I left my watch at home.* 🔁 *He left home at the age of twenty.* 🔁 *Cambridge is my home town.*

2 a place where people or animals who need care live □ *a children's home* □ *an old people's home*
♦ IDIOM **be/feel at home** to be very relaxed and confident in a place

home² /həʊm/ ADVERB
1 to the place where you live 🔁 *It's time to go home.* 🔁 *Thousands of soldiers are returning home this week.* □ *I met Freddie on my way home.*
2 at the place where you live □ *Will you be home tomorrow?*

➤ Notice that you **go home** or **get home**. You do not 'go to home' or 'get to home':
✓ *I usually get home late.*
✗ *I usually get to home late.*

homeless¹ /ˈhəʊmlɪs/ ADJECTIVE having nowhere to live □ *Thousands of people have been made homeless by the earthquake.*
homeless² /ˈhəʊmlɪs/ NOUN **the homeless** people who have nowhere to live □ *The charity provides meals for the homeless.*
homemade /ˌhəʊmˈmeɪd/ ADJECTIVE made in someone's home and not in a factory □ *homemade cakes*

homework /ˈhəʊmwɜːk/ NOUN, NO PLURAL school work that you have to do at home 🔁 *Have you done your maths homework yet?* 🔁 *The teacher gives us too much homework.*

homicide /ˈhɒmɪsaɪd/ NOUN [plural **homicides**] a US or legal word for **murder** (= the crime of killing someone)

homosexual¹ /ˌhɒməˈsekʃuəl/ ADJECTIVE attracted to people of the same sex
homosexual² /ˌhɒməˈsekʃuəl/ NOUN [plural **homosexuals**] someone who is attracted to people of the same sex

honest /ˈɒnɪst/ ADJECTIVE
1 an honest person can be trusted and does not lie, cheat or steal □ *You can trust her – she's very honest.*
2 to be honest used before you say what you really think □ *To be honest, I don't really want to go.*

honestly /ˈɒnɪstli/ ADVERB
1 in an honest way □ *Martin told me honestly what he thought.* □ *He behaved very honestly and handed the money in to the police.*
2 used for emphasizing that what you are saying is true despite the fact that it is surprising □ *I honestly didn't realize you were all waiting for me.*
3 something you say to show that you are annoyed □ *Honestly, I wish you'd listen to what I tell you.*

honesty /ˈɒnɪsti/ NOUN, NO PLURAL being honest □ *Thanks for telling me. I appreciate your honesty.*

honey /'hʌnɪ/ NOUN, NO PLURAL a sweet food that bees make

honeymoon /'hʌnɪmuːn/ NOUN [plural honeymoons] a holiday that a man and woman go on just after their wedding □ Rob and Sarah went to Mexico for their honeymoon.

honor /'ɒnə(r)/ NOUN [plural honors] the US spelling of **honour**

honour /'ɒnə(r)/ NOUN [plural honours]
1 no plural the respect that people have for someone who has behaved well or achieved something that people admire □ I am fighting for my family's honour.
2 something that makes you proud □ It was an honour to meet him. □ It is a great honour to be here today.
3 in someone's honour/in honour of someone in order to show respect to someone □ I wrote the book in honour of my father.

hood /hʊd/ NOUN [plural hoods]
1 the part of a coat, etc. which you can pull up to cover the back of your head
2 the US word for **bonnet** (= part of a car)

hook¹ /hʊk/ NOUN [plural hooks]
1 a bent piece of metal or plastic that you hang things on □ Hang your coats on the hook.
2 a bent piece of metal used for catching fish
3 off the hook if a telephone is off the hook, the part you speak into has not been put back correctly, so nobody can call you

hook² /hʊk/ VERB [hooks, hooking, hooked] to hang or catch something using a hook

hoop /huːp/ NOUN [plural hoops] a ring of metal, plastic or wood

Hoover /'huːvə(r)/ NOUN [plural Hoovers] a machine that cleans floors by sucking up small bits. A trademark.

hoover /'huːvə(r)/ VERB [hoovers, hoovering, hoovered] to clean a floor using a machine that sucks up small bits □ He hoovered up the salt he'd spilt.

hop¹ /hɒp/ VERB [hops, hopping, hopped]
1 to jump on one leg
2 if a bird or animal hops, it moves by jumping □ A little bird hopped onto the arm of the chair.

hop² /hɒp/ NOUN [plural hops] a jump, especially on one leg

hope¹ /həʊp/ VERB [hopes, hoping, hoped] to think that something is possible and to wish for it to happen or be true □ + that I hope that David manages to get home for Christmas. □ + to do something I hope to start my own business next year. □ + for I'm hoping for a new bike for my birthday. ☐ 'Will the bank still be open?' 'I hope so!' ☐ 'Is he coming with us?' 'I hope not.'

hope² /həʊp/ NOUN [plural hopes]
1 no plural a feeling that the future will be good or that something good will happen ☐ The new centre offers hope to people with cancer. ☐ We knew it would be difficult to succeed, but we never lost hope.
2 something that you wish will happen or be true □ My hope is that he will agree to lend us the money. ☐ News of the president's interest really raised our hopes.
3 something that gives you a chance of success ☐ Going to court is our only hope of getting justice. ☐ There is little hope of finishing the work on time.
4 in the hope of something in order to try to get something or make something happen □ I left work early in the hope of meeting Tom.

hopeful /'həʊpfʊl/ ADJECTIVE feeling that the future will be good or that something good will happen □ I'm very hopeful that we can find a suitable house.
• **hopefully** /'həʊpfʊlɪ/ ADVERB
1 used to say that you hope something will happen □ Hopefully she'll have forgotten about our homework.
2 showing hope □ 'Is there any more?' she asked hopefully.

hopeless /'həʊplɪs/ ADJECTIVE
1 without any hope of succeeding □ We tried to put out the flames, but it was hopeless.
2 an informal word meaning very bad □ Chris was hopeless in goal.
• **hopelessly** /'həʊplɪslɪ/ ADVERB extremely ☐ We got hopelessly lost.

horizon /hə'raɪzən/ NOUN the horizon the line where the land and sky seem to meet

horizontal /ˌhɒrɪ'zɒntəl/ ADJECTIVE straight and parallel to the ground ☐ a horizontal line □ She was wearing a T-shirt with horizontal stripes.

hormone /'hɔːməʊn/ NOUN [plural hormones] a chemical that your body makes, which controls things such as how the body grows. A biology word.

horn /hɔːn/ NOUN [plural horns]
1 one of the two pointed things made of bone on the heads of some animals, such as a goat □ a bull's horns
2 a device in a vehicle that you press to make a loud noise ☐ He heard a car horn outside. ☐ Drivers sounded their horns as the men ran into the road.
3 a musical instrument made of metal that you blow into □ the French horn

horrible /'hɒrəbəl/ ADJECTIVE very unpleasant □ It was a horrible feeling to think I wouldn't see him again. □ a horrible situation □ Why are you being so horrible to everyone?

horrific /hɒˈrɪfɪk/ ADJECTIVE extremely bad, often involving death or injuries □ *a horrific car crash* □ *horrific scenes of violence*

horrified /ˈhɒrɪfaɪd/ ADJECTIVE extremely shocked and upset □ *He was horrified at the suggestion that he had cheated.*

horrify /ˈhɒrɪfaɪ/ VERB [horrifies, horrifying, horrified] to shock and upset someone □ *It's a story that will horrify any parent.*

horror[1] /ˈhɒrə(r)/ NOUN [*plural* horrors] a strong feeling of shock and upset □ *I watched in horror as the car burst into flames.*

horror[2] /ˈhɒrə(r)/ ADJECTIVE a horror film or story is very frightening and often unpleasant

horse /hɔːs/ NOUN [*plural* horses] a large animal which people ride or use for pulling things 🔁 *Have you ever ridden a horse?* 🔁 *The horse galloped (= ran) across the field.*

hose /həʊz/ NOUN [*plural* hoses] a long tube used for putting water on fires or gardens

hospital /ˈhɒspɪtəl/ NOUN [*plural* hospitals] a building where people go for medical treatment when they are ill or injured □ *Jane is in hospital having an operation.* 🔁 *She was taken to hospital after being stabbed.* 🔁 *He's recovered and is coming out of hospital tomorrow.* □ *a psychiatric hospital* 🔁 *Many hospital wards (= rooms where people stay) have been closed.*

➤ THESAURUS: A doctor is a person who treats people when they are ill. Doctors may work in a hospital or in a surgery. A nurse is a person who looks after people when they are ill, especially in a hospital. A surgeon is a doctor who does operations. A patient is someone who is being treated by a doctor or a nurse.

hospitality /ˌhɒspɪˈtælətɪ/ NOUN, NO PLURAL being friendly to visitors, liking to provide food and a pleasant place to stay □ *The hotel is known for its warm hospitality.*

host /həʊst/ NOUN [*plural* hosts] the person at a party or meal who has invited you and arranged everything

hostage /ˈhɒstɪdʒ/ NOUN [*plural* hostages] someone who is kept as a prisoner until the people holding them get what they want 🔁 *He was taken hostage by a group of militants.*

hostel /ˈhɒstəl/ NOUN [*plural* hostels] a cheap place for people to stay □ *a youth hostel* □ *He was staying in a hostel for homeless people.*

hostile /ˈhɒstaɪl/ ADJECTIVE unfriendly or showing strong dislike □ *a hostile reaction* □ *Hostile crowds booed at the Prime Minister.*

hot /hɒt/ ADJECTIVE [hotter, hottest]
1 having a high temperature □ *Don't touch the* oven. It's very hot. □ *Is there any hot water left?* □ *It was a very hot summer.* 🔁 *It was a boiling hot day.*
2 spicy □ *hot curries*

hotel /həʊˈtel/ NOUN [*plural* hotels] a building that you pay to stay in when you are travelling or on holiday 🔁 *We stayed in a five-star hotel.* 🔁 *Our hotel room didn't even have a television.* 🔁 *Hotel guests have free use of the swimming pool.*

hound /haʊnd/ NOUN [*plural* hounds] a dog used for hunting

hour /ˈaʊə(r)/ NOUN [*plural* hours]
1 a period of time that lasts 60 minutes. There are 24 hours in one day □ *Each lesson lasts an hour.* □ *An hour later, they had all gone.* □ *I do an hour's exercise every day.* 🔁 *I'll be about half an hour.*
2 the period of time when something happens □ *What hours do you work?* 🔁 *Our opening hours are 9–5.* 🔁 *Shall we meet up in the lunch hour?*
3 hours an informal word meaning a long time 🔁 *We spent hours talking on the phone.*

house /haʊs/ NOUN [*plural* houses] a building in which people, especially one family, live □ *Our house is the one with the yellow door.* 🔁 *We moved house last year.*

household /ˈhaʊshəʊld/ NOUN [*plural* households] all the people who live in the same house □ *Most UK households have access to the Internet.*

housewife /ˈhaʊswaɪf/ NOUN [*plural* housewives] a woman who stays at home to look after her family and house, and does not have a paid job □ *She tried to be the perfect housewife.*

housework /ˈhaʊswɜːk/ NOUN, NO PLURAL the work you do to keep your house clean and tidy 🔁 *She hated doing the housework.*

➤ Remember that **housework** is not used in the plural:
✓ *Who does most of the housework?*
✗ *Who does most of the houseworks?*

hover /ˈhɒvə(r)/ VERB [hovers, hovering, hovered] to stay still in the air □ *Police helicopters hovered overhead.*

hovercraft /ˈhɒvəkrɑːft/ NOUN [plural hovercrafts] a vehicle that travels across water or land, and has a cushion (= soft bag) of air under it

how /haʊ/ ADVERB
1 used for asking or talking about the way something is done □ *+ to do something* *I'll show you how to tie a knot.* □ *How will we get there?* □ *Do you know how to turn the oven on?*
2 used for asking or talking about size, amount, level or age □ *I don't know how old Maurice is exactly.* □ *How strong do you like your tea?* 🔁 *How much is that DVD player?* 🔁 *How many brothers and sisters have you got?*
3 used for asking or talking about what something is like or what form or condition it is in □ *How do you want this money – cash or cheque?* □ *How's work?* □ *How's the new extension going?*
4 used for asking or talking about someone's health 🔁 *Hello, how are you today?* □ *How's your leg now?*
5 How about ...? used for making a suggestion □ *How about asking the children to help?*
6 used to emphasize an adjective or an adverb □ *How odd that she didn't phone.* □ *He died? Oh, how sad.*

➤ Remember that **how** is not used with **like** to ask someone to describe someone or something. The correct phrase for this is **what is someone/something like?**:
✓ *What is your new teacher like?*
✗ *How is your new teacher like?*

however /haʊˈevə(r)/ CONJUNCTION, ADVERB
1 used for saying that something does not affect a situation □ *However hard he tried, he couldn't do it.* 🔁 *She wanted to travel to Australia however much it cost.* □ *Your donation, however small, will make an important difference.*
2 despite what has just been said □ *The business had been successful. Over the past few years, however, sales had started to fall.* □ *People were saying that the school was going to close. However, the school denied the rumours.*

howl¹ /haʊl/ VERB [howls, howling, howled]
1 if a dog howls, it makes a long, high noise
2 if the wind howls, it makes a lot of noise □ *The wind howled in off the sea.*
howl² /haʊl/ NOUN [plural howls] a long, loud sound made by a dog or similar animal

HQ /ˌeɪtʃˈkjuː/ ABBREVIATION **headquarters**
hug¹ /hʌɡ/ VERB [hugs, hugging, hugged] to put your arms around someone and hold them □ *My mother was always hugging and kissing us.* □ *Everyone was crying and hugging each other.*
hug² /hʌɡ/ NOUN [plural hugs] the action of putting your arms around someone and holding them 🔁 *I could see she was upset so I gave her a hug.*

huge /hjuːdʒ/ ADJECTIVE very big □ *The school has spent a huge amount of money on the project.* □ *The film was a huge success.* □ *I'm a huge fan of his music.* □ *The house was huge.*

hum /hʌm/ VERB [hums, humming, hummed]
1 to sing with your mouth closed □ *She hummed quietly to herself as she worked.*
2 to make a low continuous noise like someone humming □ *He turned the key and the engine hummed into life.*

human¹ /ˈhjuːmən/ ADJECTIVE to do with people and the way that people behave 🔁 *They appeared to have no respect for human life.* 🔁 *Everyone wants to win: it's human nature.* 🔁 *The human brain can process huge amounts of information.*

human² /ˈhjuːmən/ or **human being** /ˌhjuːmən ˈbiːɪŋ/ NOUN [plural humans or human beings] a person □ *Is there a vaccine to protect humans from the disease?* □ *Technology has enabled human beings to survive longer.*

humanity /hjuːˈmænəti/ NOUN, NO PLURAL all the people in the world □ *We must act now to save humanity.*

human rights /ˌhjuːmən ˈraɪts/ PLURAL NOUN basic rights such as freedom and fair treatment, especially by a government □ *The organization promotes human rights for all.*

humble /ˈhʌmbəl/ ADJECTIVE [humbler, humblest]
1 not believing that you are important
2 having a low social position □ *He comes from a humble background.*

humiliate /hjuːˈmɪlieɪt/ VERB [humiliates, humiliating, humiliated] to make someone feel stupid or ashamed □ *His wife accused him of humiliating her in public.*

humorous /ˈhjuːmərəs/ ADJECTIVE funny 🔁 *He told us a humorous story about a man on his wedding day.* 🔁 *The President made a humorous remark.*

humour /ˈhjuːmə(r)/ NOUN, NO PLURAL
1 the quality that makes something funny □ *She suddenly saw the humour in the situation and laughed loudly.*
2 the ability to know when something is funny, or to say things that make people laugh □ *He loved her for her humour and her quiet determination.* 🔁 *We share the same sense of humour.*

hundred /'hʌndrəd/ NUMBER [plural hundreds]
1 the number 100
2 hundreds a large number. An informal word □ **+ of** There were hundreds of people queuing for tickets.

hundredth[1] /'hʌndrədθ/ NUMBER 100th written as a word

hundredth[2] /'hʌndrədθ/ NOUN [plural hundredths] 1/100; one of a hundred equal parts of something □ He lost the race by two hundredths of a second.

hung /hʌŋ/ PAST TENSE AND PAST PARTICIPLE OF hang

hunger /'hʌŋgə(r)/ NOUN, NO PLURAL
1 a feeling that you want to eat □ It seemed that nothing would satisfy his hunger.
2 not having enough food □ These children are dying of hunger.

hungry /'hʌŋgrɪ/ ADJECTIVE [hungrier, hungriest] having a feeling of wanting to eat □ The children were starting to get hungry.

hunt /hʌnt/ VERB [hunts, hunting, hunted]
1 to chase and kill animals for food or for sport □ The men hunt seals and the women fish. □ **+ for** They were out hunting for rabbits.
2 to try to find someone or something □ **+ for** More than 40 officers are hunting for the killer. □ Investigators are hunting for more clues.

hunter /'hʌntə(r)/ NOUN [plural hunters] a person or animal that hunts

hurdle /'hɜ:dəl/ NOUN [plural hurdles] a problem that needs to be solved in order to make progress 🔁 Finding enough money was a major hurdle for our business. 🔁 He had to face many hurdles in his career.

hurricane /'hʌrɪkən/ NOUN [plural hurricanes] a storm with very strong winds

hurry[1] /'hʌrɪ/ VERB [hurries, hurrying, hurried]
1 to go somewhere quickly □ She turned and hurried back along the path. □ The streets were full of people hurrying home to their families.
2 to do something more quickly □ You'll have to hurry if you want to leave at six.
♦ PHRASAL VERB **hurry up** to start moving somewhere or doing something more quickly □ Hurry up! We're going to be late. □ I wish he'd hurry up in the bathroom.

hurry[2] /'hʌrɪ/ NOUN, NO PLURAL
1 in a hurry doing something or going somewhere quickly, because you do not have much time □ We had to finish the job in a hurry. □ I can't talk now – I'm in a hurry.
2 there's no hurry used for telling someone that they do not need to do something quickly because you have a lot of time □ Call me back when you're ready; there's no hurry.

hurt[1] /hɜ:t/ VERB [hurts, hurting, hurt]
1 to cause pain or injury to someone □ She fell and hurt her ankle. □ Will the injection hurt?
2 to be painful □ My shoulder hurts.
3 to make someone feel upset □ The truth can hurt sometimes. □ His criticism really hurt her.
♦ IDIOM **hurt someone's feelings** to make someone feel upset □ If you don't visit her, you'll hurt her feelings.

hurt[2] /hɜ:t/ ADJECTIVE
1 injured 🔁 Be careful – someone could get hurt.
2 upset 🔁 I was deeply hurt by his lack of appreciation.

husband /'hʌzbənd/ NOUN [plural husbands] the man that a woman is married to □ Her husband died five years ago.

husky[1] /'hʌskɪ/ ADJECTIVE [huskier, huskiest] a husky voice is deep and rough

husky[2] /'hʌskɪ/ NOUN [plural huskies] a type of large dog that is used to pull heavy things over snow

hut /hʌt/ NOUN [plural huts] a small, simple building made of wood, mud or metal

hydrofoil /'haɪdrəfɔɪl/ NOUN [plural hydrofoils] a type of boat that rises slightly above the surface of the water when it is moving fast

hydrogen /'haɪdrədʒən/ NOUN, NO PLURAL the lightest gas that exists, which combines with oxygen to make water. A chemistry word.

hygiene /'haɪdʒi:n/ NOUN, NO PLURAL keeping yourself and the things around you clean, so that you stay healthy □ The best way to avoid infection is to practise good hygiene. 🔁 Poor food hygiene can cause disease.

hymn /hɪm/ NOUN [plural hymns] a song sung by Christians to praise God

hyphen /'haɪfən/ NOUN [plural hyphens] the short line (-) used for joining two words together, or for showing that a word has been divided and part of it is on the next line

I *i*

I[1] *or* **i** /aɪ/ the ninth letter of the alphabet

I[2] /aɪ/ PRONOUN used to talk or write about yourself □ *I live near Edinburgh.* □ *I didn't forget your birthday, did I?*

ice /aɪs/ NOUN, NO PLURAL frozen water □ *The ice melted and the water began to rise.* 🕮 *Her hand felt like a block of ice.*

iceberg /ˈaɪsbɜːg/ NOUN [*plural* icebergs] a large mass of ice floating in the sea

ice cream /ˌaɪs ˈkriːm/ NOUN [*plural* ice creams]
1 *no plural* a sweet frozen food made from milk or cream □ *I'll have some strawberry ice cream, please.*
2 an amount of ice cream for one person □ *Would you like an ice cream?*

ice hockey /ˈaɪs ˌhɒkɪ/ NOUN, NO PLURAL a sport played on ice in which two teams use curved sticks to try to hit a small round object into a net

icon /ˈaɪkɒn/ NOUN [*plural* icons] a small symbol on a computer screen that represents a program or a file. A computing word □ *Click on the browser icon on your desktop.*

icy /ˈaɪsɪ/ ADJECTIVE [icier, iciest]
1 covered with ice □ *Drivers lost control of their cars on the icy roads.*
2 extremely cold □ *An icy wind was blowing.* □ *She threw off her jacket and jumped into the icy water.*

ID /ˌaɪˈdiː/ ABBREVIATION identification; an official document that proves who you are □ *We'll need some form of ID.*

I'd /aɪd/ a short way to say and write I would or I had □ *I'd like another drink, please.* □ *I'd just gone to bed when the phone rang.*

idea /aɪˈdɪə/ NOUN [*plural* ideas]
1 a thought or plan about something you could do 🕮 *It was a good/brilliant idea to look online.* 🕮 *Taking six children swimming was a bad idea.* 🕮 *I've had an idea about how to fix the fence.* □ + **to do something** *It was Kate's idea to buy a van.*
2 *no plural* knowledge about something 🕮 *I had no idea what was happening.* □ *Can you give us some idea of how many people are coming?* □ *Do you have any idea how to switch the heating on?*

ideal /aɪˈdɪəl/ ADJECTIVE exactly right for a particular purpose □ *It's an ideal house for a family.* 🕮 *The meeting was an ideal opportunity to make my announcement.*

identical /aɪˈdentɪkəl/ ADJECTIVE exactly the same 🕮 *She gave birth to identical twins.* □ *The room was identical to his own.*

identification /aɪˌdentɪfɪˈkeɪʃən/ NOUN, NO PLURAL an official document that gives details such as your name and your date of birth, sometimes with a photograph of you on it, to prove who you are □ *The men wore their uniforms and carried official identification.*

identify /aɪˈdentɪfaɪ/ VERB [identifies, identifying, identified] to recognize someone or something and to say who or what they are □ *She had to identify the body.* □ *Maps helped them identify the buildings.* □ *We were taught how to identify the signs of mental illness.*

identity /aɪˈdentətɪ/ NOUN [*plural* identities] who someone is □ *Police are trying to discover the identity of the thief.*

idiom /ˈɪdɪəm/ NOUN [*plural* idioms] a phrase that has a meaning that you cannot understand simply by knowing the meaning of the separate words □ *The idiom 'once in a blue moon' means 'very rarely'.*

idiot /ˈɪdɪət/ NOUN [*plural* idiots] a stupid person □ *I felt like a complete idiot.*

idle /ˈaɪdəl/ ADJECTIVE [idler, idlest]
1 if a machine is idle, it is not being used
2 lazy 🕮 *Those children are just bone idle* (= very lazy).

i.e. /ˌaɪˈiː/ ABBREVIATION used for giving more information to show what you mean □ *The whole trip, i.e. food, travel and hotel, cost £500.*

if /ɪf/ CONJUNCTION
1 used to say that something must happen before something else can happen or be true □ *If we leave now, we should catch the train.* □ *If you do your homework now, you can go out later.*
2 used to say that something will be the result of something that might happen or be true □ *He will have to go into hospital if his condition gets worse.* 🕮 *I hope the bricks will arrive tomorrow. If not, the builders won't be able to work.* 🕮 *Will you be at home tomorrow? If so* (= if you are)*, would you mind taking in a parcel for me?*

3 whether □ *I don't know if I can come on Thursday.* □ *He asked me if I minded him smoking.*
4 every time □ *I always call in at his house if I'm passing.*
5 if only used to talk about something you wish would happen or be true □ *If only he'd listen to your advice!*

ignite /ɪgˈnaɪt/ VERB [ignites, igniting, ignited] to start to burn or to make something start to burn □ *The fuel ignited, causing a massive fire.* □ *Lightning and high winds ignited the dry wood.*

ignorance /ˈɪgnərəns/ NOUN, NO PLURAL not knowing about a subject or a situation □ *The report suggests that there is widespread ignorance about the disease.*

ignorant /ˈɪgnərənt/ ADJECTIVE not knowing about something □ *Many people are ignorant of the dangers.*

ignore /ɪgˈnɔː(r)/ VERB [ignores, ignoring, ignored] to not pay attention to someone or something □ *He ignored all my advice.* □ *The sport has been generally ignored by the media.*

> ➤ THESAURUS: If you ignore someone or take no notice of them, you do not pay attention to them. If you neglect or reject someone, you do not give them enough love and attention.

I'll /aɪl/ a short way to say and write I will □ *I'll be back next week.* □ *I'll carry these things for you.*

ill /ɪl/ ADJECTIVE suffering from an illness ☐ *Do you feel ill?* ☐ *She fell ill after eating chicken that was not cooked properly.* ☐ *He is seriously ill with cancer.*

> ➤ Notice that you use **seriously ill** and not 'badly ill' to describe someone with a very bad illness.

> ➤ THESAURUS: If you are ill, you are suffering from an illness. Sick can have the same meaning, but in British English, it often also means that you feel as if you are going to vomit. If you are unhealthy, you do not have good health.

illegal /ɪˈliːgəl/ ADJECTIVE not allowed by the law □ *It is illegal to sell alcohol to children.* □ *They are involved in illegal activitites.*

> ➤ THESAURUS: If something is illegal, it is not allowed by law. It is illegal to drive a car without a licence. If something is forbidden, it is not allowed. For example a small child may be forbidden from playing with scissors.

illegally /ɪˈliːgəli/ ADVERB in an illegal way □ *Your car is parked illegally.* □ *He was found guilty of illegally possessing a firearm.*

illness /ˈɪlnɪs/ NOUN [plural illnesses]
1 a disease ☐ *He is suffering from a serious illness.* ☐ *Measles was once a common childhood illness.* □ *The illness is caused by a virus.*
2 no plural bad health □ *Illness prevented him from competing in the championship.*

illusion /ɪˈluːʒən/ NOUN [plural illusions]
1 a false idea or belief ☐ *He's under the illusion that it's easy to get a job.* ☐ *She had no illusions about her son's abilities.*
2 something that is not really what it seems to be ☐ *Try using mirrors to create an illusion of space.*

illustrate /ˈɪləstreɪt/ VERB [illustrates, illustrating, illustrated] to draw pictures to go in books, magazines, etc. □ *She illustrated several books for children.*

illustration /ˌɪləˈstreɪʃən/ NOUN [plural illustrations] a picture in a book, magazine, etc.

I'm /aɪm/ a short way to say and write I am □ *I'm hungry.* □ *I'm going to New York tomorrow.*

image /ˈɪmɪdʒ/ NOUN [plural images]
1 an idea or opinion that people have about someone or something ☐ *The agency is aiming to create an image of a dynamic, modern city.*
2 a picture, especially one on television, film or on a computer □ *We have new images of accident.* ☐ *A special camera was used to capture images of the child in its mother's womb.*
3 a picture that you have in your mind □ *Disturbing images filled his head.*

imaginary /ɪˈmædʒɪnəri/ ADJECTIVE existing in your mind but not real □ *It is perfectly normal for children to have imaginary friends.*

imagination /ɪˌmædʒɪˈneɪʃən/ NOUN, NO PLURAL your ability to think of new ideas or to form interesting pictures and stories in your mind. ☐ *Rory has a very vivid imagination.* ☐ *Reading encourages children to use their imagination.*

imagine /ɪˈmædʒɪn/ VERB [imagines, imagining, imagined]
1 to form a picture of someone or something in your mind □ **+ question word** *I tried to imagine what he would look like.* □ **+ that** *Imagine that you're the manager of a large company.* □ **+ ing** *Imagine having your own aeroplane!*
2 to think that something exists or is true when it does not or is not □ *I keep imagining I can hear voices.*

imitate /ˈɪmɪteɪt/ VERB [imitates, imitating, imitated]
1 to copy someone or something because you like

them or it □ *He tries to imitate the style of famous artists.*
2 to copy the way someone speaks or behaves as a joke □ *He's always imitating my friend's voice.*

immediate /ɪˈmiːdɪət/ ADJECTIVE happening now, and without delay ⌷ *I can't give you an immediate response.* □ *They demanded the immediate withdrawal of troops.*

immediately[1] /ɪˈmiːdɪətlɪ/ CONJUNCTION as soon as □ *Immediately I got the message, I ran to tell father.*

immediately[2] /ɪˈmiːdɪətlɪ/ ADVERB now or without delay □ *Come here immediately!* □ *I rang the doctor immediately.*

immense /ɪˈmens/ ADJECTIVE extremely large in size, amount or degree □ *Some children are under immense pressure to succeed.* □ *He used his immense wealth to help a lot of people.*

immigrant /ˈɪmɪɡrənt/ NOUN [plural immigrants] someone who has come to live in a country from another country

immigration /ˌɪmɪˈɡreɪʃən/ NOUN, NO PLURAL when people come to live in a foreign country □ *Immigration rose sharply in 2007.* ⌷ *The government has announced new immigration laws.*

imminent /ˈɪmɪnənt/ ADJECTIVE something that is imminent is going to happen very soon ⌷ *Her life is in imminent danger.* ⌷ *There is no imminent threat to health.*

immoral /ɪˈmɒrəl/ ADJECTIVE morally wrong □ *He accused her of immoral conduct.*

immune /ɪˈmjuːn/ ADJECTIVE unable to be infected by a particular disease. A biology word □ *Some people are naturally immune to the virus.*

immunity /ɪˈmjuːnətɪ/ NOUN, NO PLURAL your ability to avoid getting a particular disease. A biology word □ *Catching chickenpox gives lifelong immunity against the virus.*

impact[1] /ˈɪmpækt/ NOUN [plural impacts] the effect that something has □ *The changes will have a significant impact on schools.*

impact[2] /ɪmˈpækt/ VERB [impacts, impacting, impacted] to have an effect on something □ *A long journey could impact on the team's performance.*

imperative /ɪmˈperətɪv/ NOUN, NO PLURAL the imperative a verb form that you use to tell someone to do something

implant[1] /ɪmˈplɑːnt/ VERB [implants, implanting, implanted] to put something into someone's body to make it work or look better □ *A device is implanted in the heart which regulates the heartbeat.*

implant[2] /ˈɪmplɑːnt/ NOUN [plural implants] something that is put in someone's body to make it work or look better □ *dental implants*

imply /ɪmˈplaɪ/ VERB [implies, implying, implied] to suggest that something is true without saying it directly □ *Are you implying that he lied?*

import[1] /ɪmˈpɔːt/ VERB [imports, importing, imported]
1 to bring a product from another country into your country in order to sell it □ **+ into** *The cars had been imported into the UK.* □ **+ from** *Many electrical goods are imported from Japan.*
2 to copy computer information from another place. A computing word.
➜ go to **export**

import[2] /ˈɪmpɔːt/ NOUN [plural imports] a product that is brought from another country into your country in order to sell □ *The country is dependent on oil imports.*
➜ go to **export**[2]

importance /ɪmˈpɔːtəns/ NOUN, NO PLURAL when something is important □ **+ of** *This just shows the importance of education.* ⌷ *She stressed the importance of eating healthily.*

important /ɪmˈpɔːtənt/ ADJECTIVE
1 necessary or having a big effect on something □ *Books are an important part of our culture.* ▣ **+ to do something** *It's important to listen to what the teacher is saying.* □ **+ that** *It's important that people are given this information.* □ **+ to** *Amy's career is very important to her.* ⌷ *For me, the most important thing is to be happy.*
2 an important person has a lot of power or influence □ *The Prime Minister is the most important person in government.*

> ➤ Remember that something is **important to** someone and not **important for** someone:
> ✓ *My family is very important to me.*
> ✗ *My family is very important for me.*

importantly /ɪmˈpɔːtəntlɪ/ ADVERB more/most importantly used before saying something that is more important or the most important thing □ *I love it here in Hong Kong and more importantly, the children love it too.*

impossible /ɪmˈpɒsəbəl/ ADJECTIVE not possible ⌷ *an impossible task* □ **+ to do something** *It's impossible to explain.* ⌷ *Ink stains are almost impossible to get rid of.* ⌷ *Rain made it impossible for the game to continue.*

impress /ɪmˈpres/ VERB [impresses, impressing, impressed] to make someone feel admiration □ *He was trying to impress his friends in his new car.* □ *Her attitude impressed me.*

impression /ɪmˈpreʃən/ NOUN [plural impressions]
1 an idea or feeling that you get about someone or something ⌷ *I got the impression that he wasn't*

happy. 🖰 *She gives the impression of not really caring.*
2 the effect that someone or something has on you 🖰 *The film made a big impression on me*

impressive /ɪmˈpresɪv/ ADJECTIVE making you feel admiration □ *an impressive performance* □ *She's a very impressive woman.*

imprison /ɪmˈprɪzən/ VERB [imprisons, imprisoning, imprisoned] to put someone in prison or in a place they cannot escape from □ *He was imprisoned for fraud.*

improve /ɪmˈpruːv/ VERB [improves, improving, improved]
1 to become better □ *I hope the weather improves soon.* □ *The situation has slowly improved.*
2 to make something better □ *Exercise can improve your health.* □ *The new law is intended to improve road safety.* □ *This treatment will improve the quality of life for many cancer sufferers.*

➤ THESAURUS: If you improve something you make it better than it was before. If you **mend** something, you fix it when it is broken. If you **reform** something, you make changes to it in order to improve it. A government might reform the education system, for example. If you **correct** something, you make it right or show someone the mistakes in it. A teacher might **correct** the mistakes in an essay, for example.

---

improvement /ɪmˈpruːvmənt/ NOUN [plural improvements] the process of becoming better or of making something better 🖰 *His test results have shown a great improvement.* 🖰 *We have seen no improvement in the health service.* 🖰 *There has been a significant improvement in living standards.* □ *+in an improvement in behaviour*

improvise /ˈɪmprəvaɪz/ VERB [improvises, improvising, improvised] to decide what to say or do at the time when you are saying or doing it and not before □ *I had forgotten the notes for my talk so I had to improvise.*

impulse /ˈɪmpʌls/ NOUN [plural impulses]
1 a sudden feeling that makes you want to do something □ *He resisted the impulse to hit the man.*
2 on impulse without thinking first □ *On impulse, he put his arm around her.*

impulsive /ɪmˈpʌlsɪv/ ADJECTIVE doing things suddenly without thinking first □ *Jane is very impulsive.*

in¹ /ɪn/ PREPOSITION
1 inside something □ *He keeps his keys in the drawer.* □ *The books are in my bedroom.*
2 at a place □ *They live in Nottingham.*
3 being part of something □ *There's a hole in my trousers.* □ *There was a strange smell in the air.*
4 at a particular time □ *It's my birthday in May.*

5 after a period of time □ *I'll be back in a few minutes.*
6 wearing particular clothes □ *Who's the woman in the red dress?*
7 shown as part of something □ *I looked in the dictionary to find the spelling of 'weird'.*
8 using a particular thing □ *They were speaking in Japanese.* □ *The letter was written in purple ink.*

in² /ɪn/ ADVERB
1 into a place or towards the inside of something □ *Come in and sit down.* □ *Push the needle in.* □ *A wide belt will hold your tummy in.*
2 at your home or place of work □ *I'm sorry, Dad's not in. Can I take a message?* 🖰 *I usually get in at around eight.*

in³ /ɪn/ ABBREVIATION inch or inches

inappropriate /ˌɪnəˈprəʊprɪət/ ADJECTIVE not suitable for a particular situation or occasion □ *inappropriate behaviour*

inch /ɪntʃ/ NOUN [plural inches] a unit for measuring length, equal to about 2.5 centimetres □ *The ruler was 12 inches long.*

include /ɪnˈkluːd/ VERB [includes, including, included]
1 if one thing includes another thing, the second thing is part of the first thing □ *The price of the ticket includes dinner.* □ *The guest list included many famous people.* □ *Ryan's films include 'Sleepless in Seattle' and 'Against the Ropes'.*
2 to allow someone to be part of a group □ *+ in Students are included in making decisions.*

including /ɪnˈkluːdɪŋ/ PREPOSITION a word used to show that a person or thing is part of a larger group □ *We went to all the museums, including the new one.* □ *Seven people, including two young girls, died in the accident.*

income /ˈɪŋkʌm/ NOUN [plural incomes]
1 the amount of money you earn 🖰 *He had an annual income of £35,000.* 🖰 *The average household income has increased.* □ *+from She has had income from the sale of two houses.*
2 on a high/low income earning a lot/not much money □ *There aren't enough houses for people on low incomes.*

➤ THESAURUS: Your **pay** is how much money you earn from your job. A **wage** is the money that you are paid for doing your job, especially when you are paid every week. When you are paid every month, we usually use the word **salary**. We also use **salary** and **income** to talk about how much someone earns in a year. **Profit** is the money you make when you sell something for more than you paid for it.

---

income tax /ˈɪŋkʌm ˌtæks/ NOUN, NO PLURAL tax that you have to pay on the money you earn

inconvenience /ˌɪnkən'viːnjəns/ NOUN [plural inconveniences] problems that something or someone causes you □ We apologize for the delay and for any inconvenience caused.

inconvenient /ˌɪnkən'viːnjənt/ ADJECTIVE causing problems □ Have I called at an inconvenient time?

incorrect /ˌɪnkə'rekt/ ADJECTIVE wrong □ The answer to number three is incorrect. □ He'd been given incorrect information.

increase¹ /ɪn'kriːs/ VERB [increases, increasing, increased]
1 to become become bigger in size or amount ⊞ The number of students has increased dramatically over the last ten years. □ + in The house has increased in value. □ + by Their wages will increase by 4%.
2 to make something become bigger in size or amount ⊞ Being overweight increases the risk of heart disease. ⊞ The government plans to increase the number of police officers.

increase² /'ɪnkriːs/ NOUN [plural increases] a rise in amount or size □ price increases □ + in There's been a big increase in sales.

increasingly /ɪn'kriːsɪŋlɪ/ ADVERB more and more □ The need to reduce car use is becoming increasingly important.

incredible /ɪn'kredəbəl/ ADJECTIVE
1 extremely good or great □ To reach the finals is an incredible achievement. □ He showed incredible strength.
2 difficult to believe □ It's incredible that he didn't realize he was so ill.

indeed /ɪn'diːd/ ADVERB
1 used to emphasize what you are saying □ He was driving very fast indeed. □ It was indeed a mistake.
2 a formal word used to add something which supports what you have just said □ The Internet has become very popular. Indeed most people now have Internet access at home.

indefinite article /ɪnˌdefɪnɪt 'ɑːtɪkəl/ NOUN [plural indefinite articles] the word a or the word an

➤ There are two types of article in English grammar: a or an is the indefinite article and the is the definite article.

indefinitely /ɪn'defɪnɪtlɪ/ ADVERB for a period of time with no fixed limits □ The game was postponed indefinitely.

independence /ˌɪndɪ'pendəns/ NOUN, NO PLURAL
1 when a country is not controlled by another country ⊞ East Timor gained independence in 2002.
2 when someone does not depend on other people for help □ financial independence

independent /ˌɪndɪ'pendənt/ ADJECTIVE
1 not controlled by another government or organization □ independent companies □ + from Mozambique became independent from Portugal in 1975. □ + of The council will be independent of the government.
2 not depending on other people for help □ My great-grandmother's 90 but she's very independent. ⊞ Some students are financially independent.

index /'ɪndeks/ NOUN [plural indexes or indices] an alphabetical list in a book that tells you what page you can find information on □ Look up 'wild flowers' in the index.

indicate /'ɪndɪkeɪt/ VERB [indicates, indicating, indicated]
1 to show that something is true or that something exists □ The study indicates that 70% of road accidents happen on country roads.
2 to show someone what they should look at or where they should go □ There was an arrow indicating where to go.
3 to show which way you are going to turn in a vehicle □ Always indicate before turning.

indirect /ˌɪndɪ'rekt/ ADJECTIVE
1 not directly caused by something, or not directly related to something □ indirect effects
2 not going the shortest way □ an indirect route

indirect object /ˌɪndɪrekt 'ɒbdʒɪkt/ NOUN [plural indirect objects] in grammar, the person that something is given to, done to, etc. □ In the sentence 'I bought my mother a watch.', 'mother' is the indirect object.

indirect speech /ˌɪndɪrekt 'spiːtʃ/ NOUN, NO PLURAL reporting what someone said without repeating their exact words □ 'He said he would come with me' is an example of indirect speech.

individual¹ /ˌɪndɪ'vɪdʒuəl/ ADJECTIVE for or relating to one person only □ The choice you make depends on your individual circumstances.
• **individually** /ˌɪndɪ'vɪdʒuəlɪ/ ADVERB not with other things or people □ Wrap each glass individually. □ He talked to each student individually.

individual² /ˌɪndɪ'vɪdʒuəl/ NOUN [plural individuals] one person □ The medical study included 100 healthy individuals.

indoor /'ɪndɔː(r)/ ADJECTIVE inside a building □ an indoor swimming pool □ indoor activities □ indoor plants

indoors /ˌɪn'dɔːz/ ADVERB into or inside a building □ It was cooler indoors. ⊞ Police warned people to stay indoors. ⊞ We went indoors because it started to rain.

industrial /ɪn'dʌstrɪəl/ ADJECTIVE relating to industry and factories □ industrial laws □ Industrial *production fell last month.* □ *Pollution is caused by industrial processes.*

industry /'ɪndəstrɪ/ NOUN [plural industries]
1 no plural the production of goods, especially in a factory □ *The chemical is widely used in industry.* 🖢 *Heavy industry* (= production of large goods) *has almost disappeared from the area.*
2 all the companies involved in one particular type of trade or service □ *She had a successful career in the music industry.* □ *The violence has damaged the country's tourism industry.* □ *Electricity and gas industries are facing rising costs.*

inevitable /ɪn'evɪtəbəl/ ADJECTIVE certain to happen and not possible to avoid □ *Further conflict in the region is inevitable.*

infamous /'ɪnfəməs/ ADJECTIVE famous for doing something bad

infect /ɪn'fekt/ VERB [infects, infecting, infected]
1 to give someone an illness □ *+ with* Several patients were infected with the virus.
2 if a computer is infected with a virus (= harmful program), it is damaged because of it. A computing word.

> **THESAURUS:** If something such as a virus **infects** a person, it gives them an illness. To **pollute** means to make the air, land or water dirty and dangerous to live in because of harmful substances. To **poison** means to add a dangerous substance to something or kill or harm someone with a dangerous substance.

Infection /ɪn'fekʃən/ NOUN [plural infections] a disease that is caused by bacteria, a virus, etc. □ *an ear infection*

infectious /ɪn'fekʃəs/ ADJECTIVE an infectious disease can be passed from one person to another 🖢 *The virus is highly infectious.*

inferior /ɪn'fɪərɪə(r)/ ADJECTIVE not as good as someone or something else □ *Amy often felt inferior to the other women in the office.* □ *This cake was made with inferior ingredients.*

infinite /'ɪnfɪnət/ ADJECTIVE without any limits or end □ *The universe is infinite.*

infinitive /ɪn'fɪnətɪv/ NOUN [plural infinitives] the basic form of a verb that can be used to make all the other forms, for example *to play* or *to eat*

inflammation /ˌɪnflə'meɪʃən/ NOUN [plural inflammations] swelling, pain and sometimes red skin in part of your body □ *The drug will reduce the inflammation in your joints.*

inflate /ɪn'fleɪt/ VERB [inflates, inflating, inflated] to fill something with air □ *The tyres need to be inflated.*

inflict /ɪn'flɪkt/ VERB [inflicts, inflicting, inflicted] to make someone suffer something unpleasant or painful □ *The home team inflicted a heavy defeat on the visitors.*

influence¹ /'ɪnfluəns/ NOUN [plural influences]
1 the power to affect other people or things □ *+ over* He has considerable influence over his colleagues. □ *+ on* Exchange rates have a big influence on our business.
2 someone or something that has an effect on other people or things □ *Ann is a good influence on you.* □ *Her films reflect her many cultural influences.*

influence² /'ɪnfluəns/ VERB [influences, influencing, influenced] to have an effect on someone or something □ *His advice influenced my decision.* □ *My early work was influenced by Samuel Beckett.*

influential /ˌɪnflu'enʃəl/ ADJECTIVE having a lot of influence 🖢 *He was one of the most influential figures in Hollywood at that time.*

influenza /ˌɪnflu'enzə/ NOUN, NO PLURAL a formal word for **flu** (= illness like a very bad cold)

inform /ɪn'fɔːm/ VERB [informs, informing, informed] to tell someone about something, especially officially □ *If you come here again I'll inform the police.* □ *+ that* We were informed that our luggage had been lost. □ *+ of* I'll inform you of my decision. 🖢 *Please keep me informed of your plans.*

informal /ɪn'fɔːməl/ ADJECTIVE relaxed and friendly, or suitable for relaxed occasions □ *The meeting was informal.* □ *We can wear informal clothes to the office at weekends.*

information /ˌɪnfə'meɪʃən/ NOUN, NO PLURAL facts about someone or something □ *+ on* Have you got any information on things to do in the area? □ *+ about* I gave him some information about our services. 🖢 *The report provides a lot of information about medical errors.* 🖢 *For further information visit our website.* 🖢 *That is a very interesting piece of information.*

> Remember that **information** cannot be used in the plural:
> ✓ I got some **information** off the Internet.
> ✗ I got some informations off the Internet. To talk about one fact about a subject and not many facts, use the phrase **piece of information**: □ Here's a useful **piece of information**.

information technology /ˌɪnfəˌmeɪʃən tek'nɒlədʒɪ/ NOUN, NO PLURAL the study or use of computers to store, send or use information

> You will often see the abbreviation for information technology, which is **IT**.

infrared /ˌɪnfrəˈred/ ADJECTIVE infrared light cannot be seen but gives out heat

ingredient /ɪnˈgriːdɪənt/ NOUN [plural ingredients]
1 one of the things you use to make a particular food □ Mix the dry ingredients in a bowl.
2 one of the qualities something needs to be successful □ Music is an essential ingredient of most teenagers' lives.

inhabit /ɪnˈhæbɪt/ VERB [inhabits, inhabiting, inhabited] to live in a particular place □ The series looks at the creatures that inhabit our planet.

inhabitant /ɪnˈhæbɪtənt/ NOUN [plural inhabitants] someone who lives in a place □ There are differences between the inhabitants of the two islands.

➤ **THESAURUS:** An inhabitant is someone who lives in a place. You can talk about the inhabitants of a town or a country. A native is someone who was born in a particular place. You can be a native of a town or a region or a country. A citizen is someone who has the right to live in a particular country permanently. You may become a citizen of a country where you were not born.

inhale /ɪnˈheɪl/ VERB [inhales, inhaling, inhaled] to breathe air, smoke, etc. into your lungs □ She inhaled deeply.

inherit /ɪnˈherɪt/ VERB [inherits, inheriting, inherited] to receive money or other possessions from someone who has died □ Imogen inherited the house from her father.

inheritance /ɪnˈherɪtəns/ NOUN [plural inheritances] money or possessions that you receive from someone who has died □ She lived on a small inheritance from her grandmother.

initial¹ /ɪˈnɪʃəl/ ADJECTIVE at the beginning
🕮 Initial reports suggest the crash was caused by engine failure. 🕮 My initial reaction was horror.
• **initially** /ɪˈnɪʃəlɪ/ ADVERB in the beginning □ Initially, things were very difficult.

initial² /ɪˈnɪʃəl/ NOUN [plural initials] the first letter of a word, especially someone's name □ His initials are J.C.

inject /ɪnˈdʒekt/ VERB [injects, injecting, injected] to put a substance into someone's body using a needle □ She has to inject herself with insulin every day.

injection /ɪnˈdʒekʃən/ NOUN [plural injections] when a substance is put into someone's body using a needle □ insulin injections

injure /ˈɪndʒə(r)/ VERB [injures, injuring, injured] to hurt someone or something □ Matt injured his knee in a skiing accident.

injured /ˈɪndʒəd/ ADJECTIVE hurt □ Fiona was badly injured in a road accident.

injury /ˈɪndʒərɪ/ NOUN [plural injuries] damage to part of your body 🕮 a serious head injury 🕮 He was lucky to suffer only minor injuries in the crash.

➤ **THESAURUS:** An injury is damage to a part of your body. Injuries can be on the outside or the inside of your body. A wound or a cut is an injury where your skin is broken. A wound is often more serious than a cut. A fracture is a break, especially to a bone in your body.

injustice /ɪnˈdʒʌstɪs/ NOUN [plural injustices] when people are treated unfairly or an action that is unfair □ I was hurt by the injustice of her criticism.

ink /ɪŋk/ NOUN [plural inks] a coloured liquid used for writing or printing

inn /ɪn/ NOUN [plural inns] a small hotel or pub, especially in the countryside

inner /ˈɪnə(r)/ ADJECTIVE on the inside or close to the centre of something □ She kept her purse in the inner pocket of her bag. □ inner London

innocence /ˈɪnəsəns/ NOUN, NO PLURAL when someone is not guilty of a crime □ New evidence proved his innocence.

innocent /ˈɪnəsənt/ ADJECTIVE not guilty of a crime □ An innocent man had been hanged. □ She claims she is innocent of the crime.

innovation /ˌɪnəˈveɪʃən/ NOUN [plural innovations] something completely new, especially a new method of doing something □ He keeps up with all the latest innovations in medicine.

inquire /ɪnˈkwaɪə(r)/ VERB [inquires, inquiring, inquired] to ask for information about something □ He inquired how to get to the library. □ I'm inquiring about the job advertised in the paper.

inquiry /ɪnˈkwaɪərɪ/ NOUN [plural inquiries] a question you ask in order to get information □ We've had a number of inquiries about new cars.

insane /ɪnˈseɪn/ ADJECTIVE
1 having a serious mental illness
2 very silly □ Her work schedule is just insane.

insect /ˈɪnsekt/ NOUN [plural insects] a small creature with six legs and often wings, for example a bee or a fly

insert /ɪnˈsɜːt/ VERB [inserts, inserting, inserted] to put something into something else □ He inserted some coins into the meter. □ You need to insert a few more examples.

inside¹ /ɪnˈsaɪd/ PREPOSITION in or into a building, container or area □ She put the book inside her bag. □ Draw a cross inside the box.

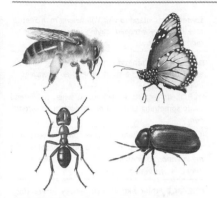

inside² /ɪn'saɪd/ NOUN [plural insides]
1 the inside the part that is in the middle and not on the outside □ The inside of his jacket was torn.
2 Inside out if clothes are inside out, the part that should be on the inside is on the outside □ You've got your socks on inside out.

> **THESAURUS:** The inside of something is the part that is in the middle and not on the outside. Inside is a general word. The interior of something is the inside, especially of a room or a building. The contents are what is inside something. We often talk about the contents of a book or a bag. The core of something is the central part. For example, the core of an apple is the hard part with seeds.

inside³ /'ɪnsaɪd/ ADJECTIVE in or facing the middle of something □ Keep it in an inside pocket.

inside⁴ /ɪn'saɪd/ ADVERB
1 in or into a building □ Come inside – you'll get cold.
2 in or into a container or an area □ Has that tin got anything inside?

insist /ɪn'sɪst/ VERB [insists, insisting, insisted]
1 to say firmly that something must happen or be done □ + on I always insist on a single room.
□ + on Fay insisted on paying. □ + that The school insists that all students must wear full uniform.
2 to keep saying firmly that something is true
□ + that Mark insists that he hasn't done anything wrong.

inspect /ɪn'spekt/ VERB [inspects, inspecting, inspected] to look very carefully at someone or something □ He inspected our documents closely.
inspection /ɪn'spekʃən/ NOUN [plural inspections]
1 when you look very carefully at someone or something ⊞ On close inspection, I realized the note wasn't in Josh's handwriting.
2 an official visit to a place to check that it is

working properly ⊞ Public health officers carry out regular inspections of restaurants.

inspector /ɪn'spektə(r)/ NOUN [plural inspectors]
1 someone whose job is to look very carefully at a place such as a school or restaurant
2 a police officer with quite a high rank

inspire /ɪn'spaɪə(r)/ VERB [inspires, inspiring, inspired] to give someone ideas and enthusiasm
□ My mother inspired me to write stories.

install or **instal** /ɪn'stɔːl/ VERB [installs or instals, installing, installed]
1 to put a piece of equipment in place and make it ready to use □ We have installed central heating.
2 to put software on to a computer to be used. A computing word □ I installed the software and began the work.

instance /'ɪnstəns/ NOUN [plural instances] for instance for example □ Some birds, penguins for instance, cannot fly at all.

instant¹ /'ɪnstənt/ ADJECTIVE
1 happening immediately □ The film was an instant success.
2 able to be prepared very quickly □ instant coffee

instant² /'ɪnstənt/ NOUN [plural instants]
1 a very short time □ The doctor will be with you in an instant.
2 a particular moment in time □ At that very instant, the phone rang.

instantly /'ɪnstəntlɪ/ ADVERB immediately □ I recognized him instantly.

instead /ɪn'sted/ ADVERB in place of someone or something else □ Bob was ill so Joe went instead.
□ + of You could use a pencil instead of a pen.
□ Instead of moaning you could actually help.

> Notice that when you put a verb after instead, you need the preposition of before the verb. Also, the verb must be in the -ing form:
> □ **Instead of** lying in bed all day, you could work.

instinct /'ɪnstɪŋkt/ NOUN [plural instincts] the natural way you react or behave without thinking or being taught □ These animals have a strong survival instinct. □ My first instinct was to run away.

institute /'ɪnstɪtjuːt/ NOUN [plural institutes] an organization where people study a particular subject □ We have a training institute in Florida.

institution /ˌɪnstɪ'tjuːʃən/ NOUN [plural institutions] a large organization □ I have worked for several banks and other financial institutions.

instruct /ɪn'strʌkt/ VERB [instructs, instructing, instructed]
1 to tell someone to do something □ I instructed her to go straight home.
2 to teach someone □ Staff will be instructed in the correct use of the machinery.

instruction /ɪnˈstrʌkʃən/ NOUN [plural instructions] instructions printed information about how to do something □ Read the instructions before you begin. 🔊 Make sure you follow the instructions.

instructor /ɪnˈstrʌktə(r)/ NOUN [plural instructors] someone who teaches a sport or a skill □ a driving instructor

instrument /ˈɪnstrəmənt/ NOUN [plural instruments]
1 something used for making music, for example a guitar or a piano 🔊 She plays several musical instruments.
2 a tool for doing a particular task □ surgical instruments

insufficient /ˌɪnsəˈfɪʃənt/ ADJECTIVE not enough □ There was insufficient evidence to make an arrest.

insult¹ /ɪnˈsʌlt/ VERB [insults, insulting, insulted] to say or do something rude that offends someone □ He was fired for insulting his manager.

insult² /ˈɪnsʌlt/ NOUN [plural insults] a remark or action that is rude and offends someone □ The crowd were hurling insults at the referee. □ To sell the jewellery is an insult to her memory.

insurance /ɪnˈʃɔːrəns/ NOUN, NO PLURAL an arrangement in which you pay a company money and they pay the costs if you have an accident or are ill, or if something you own is damaged or stolen □ car insurance 🔊 I've taken out health insurance.

insure /ɪnˈʃɔː(r)/ VERB [insures, insuring, insured] to pay money to a company who will pay the costs if you have an accident or are ill, or if something you own is damaged or stolen □ + for She insured her jewellery for £50,000. □ + against Are you insured against loss of earnings?

intact /ɪnˈtækt/ ADJECTIVE not broken or damaged □ One of the mosaic floors has been preserved intact.

integrity /ɪnˈtegrətɪ/ NOUN, NO PLURAL the quality of being honest and having high moral standards □ Colleagues praised his integrity.

intelligence /ɪnˈtelɪdʒəns/ NOUN, NO PLURAL your ability to learn and understand things □ No one is questioning your son's intelligence.

intelligent /ɪnˈtelɪdʒənt/ ADJECTIVE clever and able to understand things quickly 🔊 These students are highly intelligent.

intelligently /ɪnˈtelɪdʒəntlɪ/ ADVERB in an intelligent way □ He spoke intelligently about politics.

intend /ɪnˈtend/ VERB [intends, intending, intended] to plan to do something □ + to do

something I intend to visit Will when I'm in Seattle. □ + ing They intended staying longer but their money ran out.

intensive /ɪnˈtensɪv/ ADJECTIVE involving a lot of effort or activity in a short time □ an intensive language course

intent /ɪnˈtent/ NOUN, NO PLURAL when you intend to do something □ It was not my intent to offend him.

intention /ɪnˈtenʃən/ NOUN [plural intentions] the thing you plan to do □ + to do something It is my intention to finish before 5 o'clock. 🔊 He had no intention of obeying his father.

interact /ˌɪntərˈækt/ VERB [interacts, interacting, interacted] to talk to other people and do things with them □ Joe always interacted well with other children.

interest¹ /ˈɪntrəst/ NOUN [plural interests]
1 no plural the feeling of wanting to know about something or give your attention to something □ + in I have no interest in cricket. 🔊 I try to take an interest in my husband's work. 🔊 In the end, I lost interest in my studies.
2 something that you enjoy doing or learning about □ My main interests are sport and reading.
3 no plural extra money that you have to pay back when you have borrowed money, or that a bank pays you for having your money □ + on The interest on the car payments was huge. 🔊 I had to pay interest on the loan. 🔊 They charge 10% interest.

interest² /ˈɪntrəst/ VERB [interests, interesting, interested] to make someone want to know about something or do an activity □ + in I'm trying to interest him in Chinese music. □ Can I interest you in a boat ride?

interested /ˈɪntrestɪd/ ADJECTIVE
1 having or showing interest □ + in Dan is very interested in old cars. □ + to do something I'd be interested to hear her side of the story.
2 wanting to do something □ + in I'm not interested in making money. □ I'm interested in buying a bike.

interesting /ˈɪntrəstɪŋ/ ADJECTIVE making you feel interested □ It was a very interesting story. □ It is interesting to note that he had never been to Egypt.

➤ Remember the difference between the words **interesting** and **interested**. **Interesting** means 'making you feel interested'. **Interested** is how you feel when something is interesting: □ It's a very interesting subject. □ I'm very interested in the subject.

interest rate /ˈɪntrəst ˌreɪt/ NOUN [plural interest rates] the amount of extra money that you have to pay back when you borrow money, or that a bank pays you for having your money 🕮 *Interest rates rose by 1.5% last month.* □ *Banks announced a cut in interest rates.*

interfere /ˌɪntəˈfɪə(r)/ VERB [interferes, interfering, interfered] to get involved in a situation where you are not wanted □ *Many teenagers feel their parents interfere too much in their lives.*

♦ PHRASAL VERB **interfere with something** to affect something in a bad way □ *The illness doesn't interfere with my ability to do the job.*

interior¹ /ɪnˈtɪərɪə(r)/ NOUN [plural interiors] the inside of something □ *The interior of the house was beautifully decorated.*

interior² /ɪnˈtɪərɪə(r)/ ADJECTIVE on or for the inside of something □ *an interior wall*
➔ go to **exterior**

intermediate /ˌɪntəˈmiːdiət/ ADJECTIVE between a basic and advanced level in a subject □ *an intermediate English course* 🕮 *The book is for students studying maths at an intermediate level.*

internal /ɪnˈtɜːnəl/ ADJECTIVE
1 inside your body □ *internal injuries* □ *internal organs*
2 within an organization or country □ *an internal investigation* □ *internal flights*

international /ˌɪntəˈnæʃənəl/ ADJECTIVE involving several countries □ *international law* □ *an international conference* □ *international trade*

▸ THESAURUS. Something that is international involves several countries. Something that is global or universal affects or involves the whole world.

Internet¹ /ˈɪntənet/ NOUN, NO PLURAL the Internet a computer system that allows people around the world to share information □ *I found this hotel on the Internet.*

Internet² /ˈɪntənet/ ADJECTIVE to do with the Internet 🕮 *Most homes now have Internet access.* 🕮 *Internet users*

interpret /ɪnˈtɜːprɪt/ VERB [interprets, interpreting, interpreted] to change what someone has said into a different language □ *If you don't speak French, we can provide someone to interpret for you.*

interpreter /ɪnˈtɜːprɪtə(r)/ NOUN [plural interpreters] someone whose job is to change what someone says into a different language

interrupt /ˌɪntəˈrʌpt/ VERB [interrupts, interrupting, interrupted] to stop someone when they are in the middle of saying or doing something □ *I'm sorry to interrupt, but what time do we have to leave?* □ *Could I just interrupt you for a moment?*

interruption /ˌɪntəˈrʌpʃən/ NOUN [plural interruptions] something that stops you doing or saying something □ *I can't work with all these interruptions.*

interval /ˈɪntəvəl/ NOUN [plural intervals]
1 a period of time between two things □ *Her husband died in 1990, and after a decent interval, she married again.* 🕮 *After a short interval the police arrived.* 🕮 *+ of an interval of two weeks*
2 at weekly/monthly etc. intervals used for saying how often something happens □ *Meetings are held at regular intervals.* □ *You should have a dental check-up at six-month intervals.*

interview¹ /ˈɪntəvjuː/ NOUN [plural interviews]
1 a meeting in which someone asks you a lot of questions to find out if you are suitable for a job or a place on a course 🕮 *I have got an interview this afternoon.* 🕮 *I wear this suit for job interviews.* □ *+ for I didn't even get an interview for the job.*
2 a meeting in which someone asks a famous person questions 🕮 *Most reporters are nervous if they do an interview with the Queen.* 🕮 *The singer doesn't give interviews very often.* 🕮 *In an exclusive interview with this paper, she talks openly about her marriage.*

interview² /ˈɪntəvjuː/ VERB [interviews, interviewing, interviewed] to ask someone questions at an interview □ *The driver was interviewed by police.*

intimidate /ɪnˈtɪmɪdeɪt/ VERB [intimidates, intimidating, intimidated] to frighten someone, especially by threatening them □ *He won't let his attackers intimidate him into moving away from the area.*

into /ˈɪntu/ PREPOSITION
1 towards the inside of a room, container, area, etc. □ *We went into the house.* □ *I got into bed.* □ *He put earth into the hole.*
2 towards the lower part of a substance □ *Our feet sank into the soft sand.* □ *He fell into the water.*
3 hitting against something □ *I drove into a wall.*
4 used for saying how something or someone changes □ *She cut the pizza into four pieces.* □ *The caterpillar changed into a butterfly.*
5 towards a particular thing □ *He looked into my eyes.* □ *She gazed into the mirror.*
6 to do with a particular subject or situation □ *How did we get into this mess?* □ *We are holding an investigation into child poverty.*
7 used when talking about dividing one number by another □ *2 into 4 goes twice.*

introduce /ˌɪntrəˈdjuːs/ VERB [introduces, introducing, introduced]
1 if you introduce two people who do not know each other, you tell each of them the other person's

name □ **+ to** *He introduced me to his sister.* □ *Have you two been introduced?*
2 to make something start to happen or be used □ *The new law was introduced in 1999.*

► **THESAURUS:** If you **introduce** something, you make it start to happen or be used. If you **launch** a new product, you start to sell it. If you **establish** a business or organization, you start it. **Start** and **begin** are more general words to describe these actions.

---

introduction /ˌɪntrəˈdʌkʃən/ NOUN [*plural* introductions]
1 *no plural* when something is started or begins to be used □ *They opposed the introduction of identity cards.*
2 the first part of a book, speech or piece of music

invade /ɪnˈveɪd/ VERB [invades, invading, invaded] to enter a country with an army, and try to take control of it □ *7000 troops invaded the country.*

invalid[1] /ɪnˈvælɪd/ ADJECTIVE not acceptable because of a law or rule □ *an invalid bus pass*
invalid[2] /ˈɪnvəlɪd/ NOUN [*plural* invalids] someone who is ill or unable to look after themselves

invasion /ɪnˈveɪʒən/ NOUN [*plural* invasions] an attack on a country by an army entering it □ **+ of** *The government decided to launch an invasion of the country.*

invent /ɪnˈvent/ VERB [invents, inventing, invented] to design or create a new type of thing □ *Thomas Edison invented the electric light bulb.* □ *There was a lot of argument about who had invented the word.*

invention /ɪnˈvenʃən/ NOUN [*plural* inventions]
1 a new type of thing which someone has designed or created □ *The washing machine was a brilliant invention.*
2 *no plural* when someone designs or creates a new type of thing □ **+ of** *The invention of the computer would change the world forever.*

inventor /ɪnˈventə(r)/ NOUN [*plural* inventors] someone who has invented something new
invest /ɪnˈvest/ VERB [invests, investing, invested] to put money in a bank or business in order to make more money □ *My Dad has invested some money in the business.*
investigate /ɪnˈvestɪgeɪt/ VERB [investigates, investigating, investigated] to try to find out about something such as an accident or crime □ *Police are investigating his death.*
investigation /ɪnˌvestɪˈgeɪʃən/ NOUN [*plural* investigations] an attempt to find out about something such as an accident or a crime

🖫 *Officials have launched an investigation into what happened.*
invisible /ɪnˈvɪzəbəl/ ADJECTIVE impossible to see □ *The star is almost invisible.*

invitation /ˌɪnvɪˈteɪʃən/ NOUN [*plural* invitations] when someone asks you if you would like to go somewhere or do something □ **+ to** *We've had an invitation to William and Charlotte's wedding.* □ **+ to do something** *He accepted an invitation to meet the President.*

invite /ɪnˈvaɪt/ VERB [invites, inviting, invited] to ask someone if they would like to do something or go somewhere □ **+ for** *We've invited some friends round for dinner.* □ **+ to** *Raj has invited me to his birthday party.* □ **+ to do something** *Beth was invited to speak at the conference.*
♦ PHRASAL VERB **invite someone over/round** to ask someone to come to your house, for example to have a meal with you □ *I've invited Ann round tonight.*

involve /ɪnˈvɒlv/ VERB [involves, involving, involved]
1 if an activity or situation involves something, that thing is a part of it □ *The treatment involves a slight risk.* □ **+ ing** *The job involves selling Internet space to companies.*
2 to affect someone or something □ *Crimes involving children are very rare.* □ *Five vehicles were involved in the accident.*
3 to allow someone to take part in something □ **+ in** *The school tries to involve students in decision-making.*

Irish[1] /ˈaɪrɪʃ/ ADJECTIVE belonging to or from Ireland
Irish[2] /ˈaɪrɪʃ/ NOUN the Irish people from Ireland

iron[1] /ˈaɪən/ NOUN [*plural* irons]
1 *no plural* a hard strong metal that is also found in small amounts in your blood and some food □ *The railings were made from iron.* □ *Spinach contains vitamin C and iron.*
2 a piece of electrical equipment that you press on clothes to make them smooth □ *Have you switched the iron off?*

iron[2] /ˈaɪən/ VERB [irons, ironing, ironed] to make clothes smooth using an iron □ *Ben was ironing some shirts.*

iron[3] /ˈaɪən/ ADJECTIVE made from iron □ *iron gates*

ironic /aɪˈrɒnɪk/ ADJECTIVE an ironic situation is surprising, often because it is the opposite of what you expected □ *It's ironic that a man who spent his life treating heart disease should die of a heart attack.*
irony /ˈaɪrəni/ NOUN [*plural* ironies] a situation that is surprising because it is the opposite of what

you expected ▣ *The irony is that the man who cooks all this marvellous food can no longer taste it.*

irregular /ɪˈregjʊlə(r)/ ADJECTIVE
1 having a different amount of time or space between separate things ▣ *an irregular heartbeat* □ *The trees had been planted at irregular intervals.*
2 not smooth or even □ *irregular shapes*
3 not following the usual rules of grammar □ *irregular verbs*

irritate /ˈɪrɪteɪt/ VERB [irritates, irritating, irritated]
1 to make someone feel annoyed □ *It irritates me that he never helps with the washing up.*
2 to make something such as your skin or eyes sore □ *Some sun creams can irritate your skin.*

is /ɪz/ VERB the present tense of the verb *be* when it is used with *he*, *she*, or *it* □ *He is tall.* □ *It is too hot.*

➤ Note that instead of *he is*, *she is* and *it is*, people often say and write the short forms, *he's*, *she's* and *it's*: □ *He's here.* □ *She's tall.* □ *It's great.*

-ish /ɪʃ/ SUFFIX -ish is added to the end of words to mean 'slightly' □ *reddish* (= slightly red)

Islam /ˈɪzlɑːm/ NOUN, NO PLURAL the Muslim religion that was started by Mohammed

Islamic /ɪzˈlæmɪk/ ADJECTIVE to do with Islam □ *Islamic law* □ *the Islamic faith*

island /ˈaɪlənd/ NOUN [*plural* islands] an area of land surrounded by sea □ *There are lots of unusual plants on the island.* □ *the Caribbean island of Trinidad* ▣ *a remote island in the Pacific Ocean* □ *the Channel Islands*

isn't /ˈɪzənt/ a short way to say and write is not □ *It isn't fair.*

isolate /ˈaɪsəleɪt/ VERB [isolates, isolating, isolated] to separate someone or something from other people or things □ *The infected animals were isolated in a field.*
• **isolated** /ˈaɪsəleɪtɪd/ ADJECTIVE
1 feeling alone and sad that you do not meet other people □ *Old people often feel isolated.*
2 far away from other places □ *an isolated farmhouse*

issue¹ /ˈɪʃuː/ NOUN [*plural* issues]
1 a subject that people discuss or that causes problems □ + *of* We discuss the issue of money. ▣ *Nelly raised the issue of transport.* ▣ *The environment is a key issue in this election campaign.* ▣ *The issue arose because one of the children made a complaint.*
2 a newspaper or magazine that is one of a number printed and sold at the same time □ *Have you seen this week's issue of the magazine?*

issue² /ˈɪʃuː/ VERB [issues, issuing, issued]
1 to say something to the public in an official way ▣ *issue a statement/warning*
2 to supply someone with something □ + *with* We were all issued with pens.

IT /ˌaɪˈtiː/ ABBREVIATION **information technology**

it /ɪt/ PRONOUN
1 used to talk or write about something that has already been mentioned □ *I've lost my book. Have you seen it?* □ *It was a great day.*
2 used to talk about a fact or opinion □ *It's expensive to travel by train.* □ *It's very quiet here, isn't it?* □ *What's it like in Spain?*
3 used to talk about the weather, time and dates □ *It rained yesterday.* □ *What time is it?* □ *It's 3 o'clock.*
4 used to talk about distance □ *It's a long way to the coast.* □ *How far is it to your house?*
5 used to tell someone who is there, on the telephone, etc. □ *Hello, it's Pat here.* □ *It's your brother at the door.*

itch /ɪtʃ/ VERB [itches, itching, itched] if part of your body itches, it feels uncomfortable and makes you want to scratch it
♦ IDIOM **be itching to do something** an informal phrase meaning to want to do something very much □ *I was itching to play football again.*

itchy /ˈɪtʃi/ ADJECTIVE an itchy part of your body feels uncomfortable and makes you want to scratch it

it'd /ˈɪtəd/ a short way to say and write it would or it had □ *It'd be good if you could come.* □ *It'd been raining all day.*

item /ˈaɪtəm/ NOUN [*plural* items] one thing which is part of a group or is on a list □ *There were several items on the list.* ▣ *He left his mobile phone and other personal items in the car.* ▣ *She had some very expensive items of clothing in her wardrobe.*

it'll /ˈɪtəl/ a short way to say and write it will □ *It'll be nice to see you.*

it's /ɪts/ a short way to say and write it is or it has □ *It's snowing.* □ *It's been a long time since I saw you.*

➤ Try not to confuse the spellings of *its* and *it's*. *Its* is the possessive form of *it*, and tells you something belongs to it: *The bird built its nest.* *It's* is a short form of two words put together: *I think it's going to rain.*

its /ɪts/ ADJECTIVE belonging to or to do with it □ *Keep the hat in its box.* ▣ *The school has its own tennis courts.*

itself /ɪtˈself/ PRONOUN
1 the reflexive form of *it* □ *The school has transformed itself.* □ *Australia has found itself in a difficult position.*

2 used to show that a thing or animal does something without any help from anyone or anything else □ *The cut soon healed itself.* ⧉ *The dog managed to get free all by itself.*
3 used to emphasize the pronoun *it* □ *I don't dislike the building itself.*

4 by itself not with or near other things □ *The cottage stood by itself on a hillside.* □ *Talent by itself is not enough to make you successful.*

I've /aɪv/ a short way to say and write I have □ *I've finished my homework.* □ *I've got six cats.*

J j

J or **j** /dʒeɪ/ the tenth letter of the alphabet

jab /dʒæb/ NOUN [plural jabs] when you quickly push something sharp into or towards something □ She gave him a jab in the ribs with her elbow.

jacket /'dʒækɪt/ NOUN [plural jackets] a short coat, usually with long sleeves □ a leather jacket □ a denim jacket

jail /dʒeɪl/ NOUN [plural jails] a building where criminals are kept □ She was sentenced to 12 months in jail. 🔄 He's just been released from jail.

jam¹ /dʒæm/ NOUN [plural jams]
1 a sweet, sticky food made of fruit and sugar that you spread on bread □ strawberry jam
2 a line of vehicles that are not moving or are moving very slowly 🔄 I got stuck in a traffic jam.

jam² /dʒæm/ VERB [jams, jamming, jammed]
1 to push something into a space so that it fits very tightly □ She jammed the clothes into her suitcase.
2 to become or to make something become unable to move or work □ I tried to open the door but it was jammed.
3 to fill a place completely with people or things □ **+ with** The M6 was jammed with traffic after an accident. 🔄 All the cupboards were jammed full of clothes.

January /'dʒænjuəri/ NOUN [plural Januarys] the first month of the year, after December and before February □ My birthday is in January.

jar /dʒɑː(r)/ NOUN [plural jars] a glass container with a wide neck and a lid, used for storing food □ a jam jar □ a jar of coffee

> ➤ **THESAURUS:** A jar is a glass container with a wide neck and a lid. It is used for storing food. For example, we keep jam in a jar. A pot is a round container with or without a lid, used for storing things in, for cooking or for growing plants in. A jug is a container with a handle used for pouring liquids. A vase is a container for flowers.

jaw /dʒɔː/ NOUN [plural jaws] the lower part of your face made up of two bones that your teeth grow in
♦ IDIOM someone's jaw drops if someone's jaw drops, they show with their face that they are extremely surprised □ She told us what she earned and our jaws dropped.

jazz /dʒæz/ NOUN, NO PLURAL a type of music with a strong beat that is often changed or added to as it is played □ modern jazz

jealous /'dʒeləs/ ADJECTIVE
1 feeling angry and unhappy because someone has something you want or because you want to be like someone else □ **+ of** He's jealous of his brother's success. 🔄 She made me jealous by going out with her other friends.
2 feeling upset and angry because you think someone you love is in love with someone else □ a jealous wife

jealousy /'dʒeləsi/ NOUN, NO PLURAL jealous feelings

jeans /dʒiːnz/ PLURAL NOUN trousers made of denim (= thick, usually blue, cotton)

jelly /'dʒeli/ NOUN [plural jellies]
1 a soft, sweet food with a fruit flavour that shakes when you move it and is eaten cold □ a bowl of jelly and ice cream
2 a US word for **jam¹**

jellyfish /'dʒelifɪʃ/ NOUN [plural jellyfish or jellyfishes] a sea animal with a soft transparent body that can sting you (= hurt you by putting poison into your skin)

jerk /dʒɜːk/ VERB [jerks, jerking, jerked]
1 to make a short sudden movement □ *The driver started the engine and the old bus jerked forward.*
2 to pull something with a sudden rough movement □ *He jerked his hand away.*

jersey /'dʒɜːzɪ/ NOUN [*plural* jerseys] a warm piece of clothing with sleeves that you pull on over your head and wear on the top half of your body

Jesus /'dʒiːzəs/ or **Jesus Christ** /,dʒiːzəs 'kraɪst/ NOUN the man who Christians believe to be the son of God and on whose teaching Christianity is based

jet /dʒet/ NOUN [*plural* jets]
1 a fast plane with powerful engines □ *a passenger jet*
2 a strong fast flow of liquid or gas forced through a small hole □ *The printer releases jets of coloured ink.*

Jew /dʒuː/ NOUN [*plural* Jews] someone whose religion is Judaism or whose family originally came from the ancient Hebrew people of Israel

jewel /'dʒuːəl/ NOUN [*plural* jewels] a valuable stone, used to make jewellery □ *a ring set with precious jewels*

jewellery /'dʒuːəlrɪ/ NOUN, NO PLURAL things that you wear to decorate your body and clothes, often made of metal and valuable stones □ *She wears a lot of gold jewellery.* 🔹 *a beautiful piece of jewellery*

jewelry /'dʒuːəlrɪ/ NOUN, NO PLURAL the US spelling of **jewellery**

Jewish /'dʒuːɪʃ/ ADJECTIVE to do with Jews or Judaism □ *a Jewish religious festival* □ *Jewish history*

job /dʒɒb/ NOUN [*plural* jobs]
1 the work someone does regularly for money 🔹 *He needs to get a job.* 🔹 *They offered me a job in the shop.* 🔹 *He lost his job because of the illness.* □ *+ as* *She got a job as a chef.* 🔹 *a part-time/full-time job*
2 a piece of work □ *There are plenty of jobs to do about the house.*
3 a good/bad, etc. job the standard of work someone has done □ *You've made a good job of that painting.* □ *The builders did a great job.*

> ➤ If you want to ask someone what type of job they do, the usual question is **What do you do?** or **What do you do for a living?**. People do not usually ask 'What is your job?'.

jobless /'dʒɒblɪs/ PLURAL NOUN the jobless people who do not have a job

jockey /'dʒɒkɪ/ NOUN [*plural* jockeys] someone who rides a horse in races □ *a champion jockey*

jog¹ /dʒɒg/ VERB [jogs, jogging, jogged] to run slowly, especially for exercise □ *She jogs around the park every morning.*

jog² /dʒɒg/ NOUN [*plural* jogs] a slow run for exercise □ *They've gone for a jog along the beach.*

join /dʒɔɪn/ VERB [joins, joining, joined]
1 to become a member of a group or organization □ *I've joined a rowing club.* □ *He joined the army last year.* □ *I joined the company in 1999.*
2 to connect things together □ *+ to* *You have to join the metal part to the wood.*
3 to come together at a particular point □ *The track joins the main road just around this corner.*
4 to come together with other people □ *Please welcome Jill Smith, who joins us from London.* □ *Would you like to join us for lunch?*
5 join hands to hold someone's hand with your hand
♦ PHRASAL VERB **join in** to take part in an activity with other people □ *He didn't join in with the singing.*

joint¹ /dʒɔɪnt/ NOUN [*plural* joints]
1 a place in your body where two bones meet □ *painful hip joints*
2 a large piece of meat that is cooked whole □ *a joint of beef*
3 a place where two or more things join □ *Water was leaking from a joint in the pipe.*

joint² /dʒɔɪnt/ ADJECTIVE done or owned together 🔹 *The project was a joint effort between Tom and Sue.* 🔹 *Some married couples have a joint account.*

joke¹ /dʒəʊk/ NOUN [*plural* jokes] something that someone says or does to make people laugh 🔹 *Matt is always telling jokes.*

joke² /dʒəʊk/ VERB [jokes, joking, joked]
1 to make a joke □ *The kids were laughing and joking about him missing the goal.*
2 Just/Only joking! something you say meaning that what you have just said is not true and was intended to be funny □ *There's a big rip in your trousers. Only joking!*
3 You're joking! something you say when someone says something extremely surprising □ *'She's only twenty.' 'You're joking! I thought she was nearer forty!'*

jolly /'dʒɒlɪ/ ADJECTIVE [jollier, jolliest] happy □ *a man with a jolly face*

journal /'dʒɜːnəl/ NOUN [*plural* journals]
1 a magazine about a particular subject □ *He subscribes to several political journals.*
2 a book in which someone writes what they have done each day

➤ **THESAURUS:** Publication is a general word for something that is printed and sold. A magazine is a thin book with pictures in it which is published every week or every month. There are lots of different kinds of magazines, for example fashion magazines and gardening magazines. A journal is a magazine about a particular subject, for professional people or people who study a particular subject. If you are a doctor, you might read a medical journal. A newspaper is a publication with reports and pictures about recent events. Newspapers are sold every day or every week.

journalism /'dʒɜːnəlɪzəm/ NOUN, NO PLURAL
the work of writing articles for newspapers, magazines, television or radio □ *a career in journalism*

journalist /'dʒɜːnəlɪst/ NOUN [*plural* journalists] someone whose job is to write articles for newspapers, magazines, television or radio

journey /'dʒɜːnɪ/ NOUN [*plural* journeys] when you travel from one place to another, especially a long distance □ *He has a two-hour journey to work each day.* □ *The train journey was very pleasant.*

➤ **THESAURUS:** A journey is when you travel from one place to another, especially a long distance. A drive is a journey in a car. The words outing and trip describe going somewhere, doing something, and then coming back. An outing is for pleasure, and is usually quite short. A trip can be for work or for pleasure, and may be longer than an outing. For example you might go on an outing or a trip to the beach. You might go on a business trip to a foreign country. Travel is a more general word to describe the activity of going from one place to another. Note that the word travel is not usually used in the plural.

joy /dʒɔɪ/ NOUN [*plural* joys]
1 a feeling of being very happy □ *She finally experienced the joy of holding her child.*
2 something that makes you very happy □ *The new model is a joy to drive.*

Judaism /'dʒuːdeɪˌɪzəm/ NOUN, NO PLURAL the Jewish religion which is based on the Old Testament of the Bible

judge[1] /dʒʌdʒ/ VERB [judges, judging, judged]
1 to form an opinion about someone or something □ **+ on** *I tend to judge books on their story rather than their use of language.* □ **+ by** *It's wrong to judge people by what clothes they wear.* □ *The event was judged a success.*
2 to decide who or what is the winner of a competition □ *I was asked to judge the competition.*

judge[2] /dʒʌdʒ/ NOUN [*plural* judges]
1 someone who is in charge of a trial in court and decides what punishments should be given
2 someone who judges a competition

judgement *or* **judgment** /'dʒʌdʒmənt/ NOUN [*plural* judgements *or* judgments]
1 the ability to make good decisions or form correct opinions ▣ *When it comes to education, I trust her judgement.* ▣ *I can't tell you exactly how much salt to add – just use your judgement.*
2 an opinion about someone or something ▣ *In my judgement, it wouldn't be a very sensible thing to do.* ▣ *You will have to make a judgement about whether or not to trust her.*
3 the decision made by a judge in a court ▣ *He is due to pass judgment on Wednesday.*

jug /dʒʌg/ NOUN [*plural* jugs] a container with a handle used for pouring liquids □ *a milk jug* □ *a jug of cream*

juggle /'dʒʌgəl/ VERB [juggles, juggling, juggled] to keep several balls, etc. in the air by repeatedly throwing them up and catching them

juice /dʒuːs/ NOUN [*plural* juices] the liquid in fruit or vegetables, often used as a drink □ *a glass of orange juice*

juicy /'dʒuːsɪ/ ADJECTIVE [juicier, juiciest] full of juice □ *a nice juicy peach*

July /dʒuːˈlaɪ/ NOUN [*plural* Julys] the seventh month of the year, after June and before August □ *Clara will be 11 in July.*

jump[1] /dʒʌmp/ VERB [jumps, jumping, jumped]
1 to push yourself off the ground or other surface with your legs □ *We jumped up and down in excitement.* □ **+ over** *The dog jumped over the wall.* □ *He jumped down from the tree.*
2 to go over something by pushing yourself into the air with your legs □ *The horse jumped the fence.*
3 to move or go somewhere quickly □ *As soon as I heard the news, I jumped on a train to Scotland.*

□ *He jumped to his feet when she came in.*
4 to make a movement because you are suddenly afraid ▣ *The noise of the bell made me jump.*
◆ PHRASAL VERB **jump at something** to accept an opportunity in a very eager way ▣ *He jumped at the chance to work in Africa.*

jump² /dʒʌmp/ NOUN [*plural* jumps] when you push yourself off the ground with your legs □ *Do three more jumps.*

jumper /ˈdʒʌmpə(r)/ NOUN [*plural* jumpers] a warm piece of clothing with sleeves that you pull on over your head and wear on the top half of your body

junction /ˈdʒʌŋkʃən/ NOUN [*plural* junctions] a place where roads or railway lines meet and cross □ *Turn right at the junction ahead.*

June /dʒuːn/ NOUN [*plural* Junes] the sixth month of the year, after May and before July □ *We're moving house in June.*

jungle /ˈdʒʌŋgəl/ NOUN [*plural* jungles] a thick forest in a hot country □ *the Peruvian jungle*

junior /ˈdʒuːnjə(r)/ ADJECTIVE
1 having a lower position in an organization □ *junior staff* □ *She's a junior minister at the Foreign Office.*
2 of or for younger people □ *junior members of the tennis club* □ *junior classes*

junk /dʒʌŋk/ NOUN, NO PLURAL old things with little use or value □ *Most of this is junk and we can just get rid of it.*

junk food /ˈdʒʌŋk ˌfuːd/ NOUN, NO PLURAL food that is not good for your health but that you can eat or prepare quickly

juror /ˈdʒʊərə(r)/ NOUN [*plural* jurors] one of the people in a court of law who listen to the facts and decide if someone is guilty of a crime or not

jury /ˈdʒʊərɪ/ NOUN [*plural* juries] a group of people in a court of law who listen to the facts and decide if someone is guilty of a crime or not

just¹ /dʒʌst/ ADVERB
1 at this time, or at a particular time in the past □ *I'm just getting dressed.* □ *We were just sitting down to dinner.* ▣ *Just then, a man came in.* ▣ *I can't talk to you just now.*
2 a very short time ago □ *I've just finished work.* □ *The clock's just struck five.*
3 only □ *I'll just have a sandwich.* □ *It was just a joke.* □ *I just want to go home.*
4 almost not ▣ *I could only just see him.* □ *We just managed to swim to the shore.* □ *She was just ahead of me.*
5 used to emphasize what you are saying □ *I was just devastated by the news.* □ *A cold drink was just what I needed.*
6 just about almost □ *I've just about finished here.*
7 be just about to do something to be going to do something very soon □ *I was just about to phone you.*
8 just as at the same time as □ *Just as we got there, the fire alarm went off.*

just² /dʒʌst/ ADJECTIVE fair □ *a just decision*

justice /ˈdʒʌstɪs/ NOUN, NO PLURAL
1 fair treatment of people by the law □ *The group is fighting for justice for all.*
2 the system of laws which judges and punishes people □ *the criminal justice system*

K*k*

K¹ *or* **k** /keɪ/ the 11th letter of the alphabet

K² /keɪ/ ABBREVIATION one thousand □ *She earns £30K a year.*

kangaroo /ˌkæŋɡəˈruː/ NOUN [*plural* kangaroos] an Australian animal that moves by jumping, and carries its baby in a pouch (= a pocket at the front of its body)

keen /kiːn/ ADJECTIVE [keener, keenest]
1 interested in or enjoying a particular activity very much □ *Jim's a keen swimmer.* □ *+ on She's very keen on riding.* 🔁 *She has a keen interest in art.*
2 wanting to do something □ *+ to do something Everyone seemed very keen to help.*

keep /kiːp/ VERB [keeps, keeping, kept]
1 to make someone or something stay in a particular state □ *Keep the door closed.* □ *The noise kept me awake.* □ *Keep still!* □ *Keep your mouth shut!*
2 to prevent someone or something going to a particular place □ *Keep the children away from the fire.* □ *I tried to keep the sun off my face.* □ *A high fence kept out strangers.*
3 keep doing something to continue to do something, or to do something repeatedly □ *It's hard to keep going when you're so tired.* □ *I keep forgetting to lock the door.*
4 to continue to have or own something □ *You can keep the book.* □ *The company has promised that they will keep their jobs.*
5 to put something in a particular place when you are not using it □ *I keep my diary in a drawer.* 🔁 *This ring is valuable – make sure you keep it in a safe place.*
6 to make someone stay in a particular place □ *They're keeping him in hospital for a few more days.* □ *She was kept in after school.*
7 keep a promise to do what you have promised to do
8 keep a secret to not tell anyone a secret
➡ go to **keep an eye on someone/something**
◆ PHRASAL VERBS **keep on doing something** to continue to do something, or to do something repeatedly □ *He ignored the cries and kept on walking.* □ *They keep on waking me up.* **keep up**
1 to move at the same speed as someone else □ *She walks so fast I can hardly keep up.* **2** to make the same amount of progress as someone or something else □ *Their rivals invested in new technology, and they failed to keep up.* **keep up something** to continue

to do something □ *I've been keeping up my exercise programme.*

➤ **THESAURUS:** If you **keep** something, you put something in a particular place when you are not using it. You might keep your keys in a bag. If you **preserve** something, you keep it the same and stop it from being lost or destroyed. For example, you can preserve things in a museum. If you **collect** something, you get things from different places and put them together. Some people collect stamps. If you **store** something, you keep it somewhere, For example, you can store information on a computer and you can store food in a cupboard.

kept /kept/ PAST TENSE AND PAST PARTICIPLE OF **keep**

kettle /ˈketəl/ NOUN [*plural* kettles] a container with a lid and a handle, used for boiling water 🔁 *I've put the kettle on (= I am heating water in a kettle) for a cup of tea*

key /kiː/ NOUN [*plural* keys]
1 a small metal object used for locking something such as a door or window, or for starting the engine of a vehicle 🔁 *I switched the light off and turned the key in the lock.* 🔁 *Have you seen my car keys?* 🔁 *a bunch of keys*
2 a button on a computer keyboard or a telephone 🔁 *Use the arrow keys to move from one image to the next.* □ *Press any key to continue.*
3 the main thing that helps you to achieve something □ *+ to Confidence is the key to success in this business.*
4 one of the white or black parts you press on a piano or a similar instrument to make a sound
5 a list of answers to questions in an exercise or test

keyboard /ˈkiːbɔːd/ NOUN [*plural* keyboards]
1 a piece of computer equipment with keys (= buttons) on it that you press to put information into the computer
2 the set of keys on a musical instrument such as a piano □ *a piano keyboard*

kg /ˌkeɪˈdʒiː/ ABBREVIATION kilogram or kilograms

kick¹ /kɪk/ VERB [kicks, kicking, kicked]
1 to hit someone or something with your foot □ *Jane kicked the ball over the fence.* □ *He kicked me in the leg.*

2 to move your legs quickly and with force □ *She was carried, kicking and screaming, to the car.*
◆ PHRASAL VERBS **kick (something) off** to start something □ *We kicked off the meeting with a discussion about love.* **kick someone out** to make someone leave a place □ *He was kicked out of the army for laziness.*

kick² /kɪk/ NOUN [*plural* **kicks**]
1 when you kick, or kick something □ *I gave him a kick in the leg.*
2 an informal word meaning a feeling of pleasure or excitement ⊞ *He gets a kick out of driving fast.*

kick-off /'kɪkɒf/ NOUN [*plural* **kick-offs**] the start of a football game

kid /kɪd/ NOUN [*plural* **kids**]
1 an informal word meaning child □ *Have they got any kids?* □ *You can't expect him to look after the baby – he's just a kid.*
2 a young goat

kidnap /'kɪdnæp/ VERB [**kidnaps, kidnapping, kidnapped**] to take someone away using force, and to ask their family or the government for something such as money in exchange for their safe return □ *The journalist was kidnapped three weeks ago.*

► THESAURUS: If you **kidnap** someone, you take them away using force and ask for money from their family or a government in exchange for their safe return. If you **hijack** a plane, you take control of it by force. If you **capture** someone or something, you catch them and do not allow them to escape.

kidnapper /'kɪdnæpə(r)/ NOUN [*plural* **kidnappers**] a person who takes someone away using force, and asks for money in exchange for their safe return □ *The kidnappers have demanded a ransom of £2 million.*

kidney /'kɪdnɪ/ NOUN [*plural* **kidneys**] one of the two organs in your body that clean your blood and remove waste from it. A biology word.

kill /kɪl/ VERB [**kills, killing, killed**] to make a person or animal die □ *Two people were killed in the crash.* □ *The explosion killed six people.* □ *He tried to kill himself.*

► THESAURUS: If someone **kills** a person or an animal, they make it die. If a person **murders** someone, they kill that person deliberately. To **execute** someone means to kill someone as an official punishment. To **assassinate** someone means to kill a famous person, often a politician. President Abraham Lincoln was **assassinated**, for example.

killer /'kɪlə(r)/ NOUN [*plural* **killers**] a person who kills someone □ *Police have appealed for more information to help catch the killer.*
◆ IDIOM **make a killing** to make a lot of money
kilo /'kiːləʊ/ NOUN [*plural* **kilos**] a short way to say and write **kilogram**

kilogram *or* **kilogramme** /'kɪlə,ɡræm/ NOUN [*plural* **kilograms** *or* **kilogrammes**] a unit for measuring weight, equal to 1000 grams. This is often written **kg**. □ *Katherine weighs 60 kilograms.*

kilometre /'kɪləmiːtə(r), kɪ'lɒmɪtə(r)/ NOUN [*plural* **kilometres**] a unit for measuring distance, equal to 1000 metres. This is often written **km**. □ *We live 20 kilometres from the coast.*

kind¹ /kaɪnd/ NOUN [*plural* **kinds**]
1 a type of person or thing □ *+ of* *What kind of dog have you got?* ⊞ *Encourage children to try different kinds of fruit.* ⊞ *There are all kinds of styles to choose from.*
2 kind of an informal phrase that means slightly □ *It's kind of like Sara's dress.*

kind² /kaɪnd/ ADJECTIVE [**kinder, kindest**] behaving in a way that shows you care about people and want to make them happy □ *She's the kindest person I know.* □ *+ to* *You've all been very kind to me.* □ *+ of* *It was kind of you to help us.* □ *Thank you for your kind offer.*

kindergarten /'kɪndəɡɑːtən/ NOUN [*plural* **kindergartens**]
1 in the UK, a school for children under five
2 in the US, the first year of school education for children aged five or six

kindness /'kaɪndnɪs/ NOUN, NO PLURAL when someone is kind □ *What I like most about him is his kindness.*

king /kɪŋ/ NOUN [*plural* **kings**] a man who rules a country, being the most important male member of its royal family □ *He's the future king of Great Britain.*

kingdom /'kɪŋdəm/ NOUN [*plural* **kingdoms**] a country ruled by a king or queen □ *the United Kingdom* □ *the kingdom of Denmark*

kiosk /'kiːɒsk/ NOUN [*plural* **kiosks**] a small shop that sells things such as newspapers, drinks and sweets

kiss¹ /kɪs/ VERB [**kisses, kissing, kissed**] to touch someone with your lips, especially on their mouth or face, to show that you feel love or affection for them ⊞ *He kissed her goodbye and got into the car.* □ *She leaned towards him and kissed his cheek.*

kiss² /kɪs/ NOUN [plural kisses] when you kiss someone 🖲He gave her a kiss. □ **+ on** a kiss on the lips

kit /kɪt/ NOUN [plural kits]
1 the clothes that you need for a particular activity 🖲I brought my football kit home for washing.
2 a set of tools or equipment that you need for a particular activity □ a first aid kit □ a bicycle repair kit
3 a set of parts that you can put together to make something □ I got a model boat kit for my birthday.

kitchen /ˈkɪtʃɪn/ NOUN [plural kitchens] a room where you prepare and cook food, and sometimes eat food □ John is in the kitchen. 🖲I sat at the kitchen table and drank my coffee.

kitten /ˈkɪtən/ NOUN [plural kittens] a young cat

km ABBREVIATION kilometre or kilometre

knee /niː/ NOUN [plural knees] the part in the middle of your leg where the leg bends □ a knee injury

kneel /niːl/ VERB [kneels, kneeling, knelt] to move into a position in which your knees and lower legs are on the ground, or to be in this position □ **+ down** She knelt down beside me and stroked my hair. □ He was kneeling by the bed, praying.

knelt /nelt/ PAST TENSE AND PAST PARTICIPLE OF kneel
knew /njuː/ PAST TENSE OF know
knickers /ˈnɪkəz/ PLURAL NOUN a piece of underwear for women or girls, which covers the bottom

knife /naɪf/ NOUN [plural knives] a tool with a blade and a handle, used especially for cutting food 🖲Have we got enough knives and forks? 🖲a sharp knife

knight /naɪt/ NOUN [plural knights]
1 in the past, a soldier of a high social class who rode a horse
2 a man who has been given an honour by a British king or queen that allows him to use the title 'Sir'

knit /nɪt/ VERB [knits, knitting, knitted] to make something, for example a piece of clothing, using two long knitting needles (= pointed metal or wooden sticks) and wool □ I'm knitting a scarf.

knives /naɪvz/ PLURAL OF knife

knock¹ /nɒk/ VERB [knocks, knocking, knocked]
1 to hit someone or something so that it moves or falls □ **+ over** The cat knocked over the vase. □ The blast knocked us off our feet. □ I fell and knocked my tooth out.
2 to hit a hard surface, especially a door, with your hand in order to get attention □ Knock before you come in. □ **+ on** I knocked on the door but nobody answered.
♦ PHRASAL VERB knock someone out **1** to make someone become unconscious **2** to defeat a person or a team in a competition □ **+ of** Liverpool have been knocked out of the competition.

knock² /nɒk/ NOUN [plural knocks] the sound of someone or something knocking on a hard surface □ There was a knock at the door.

knot¹ /nɒt/ NOUN [plural knots]
1 a join made by tying two ends of string, rope or cloth together 🖲to tie a knot
2 a mass of untidy, twisted threads of hair, string, etc. that are difficult to separate □ Let's comb these knots out of your hair.
3 a unit for measuring how fast a ship is travelling

knot² /nɒt/ VERB [knots, knotting, knotted] to tie something with a knot □ A scarf was knotted around his neck.

➤ THESAURUS: To tie two things means to join them together using string, rope etc. To knot something means to tie two ends of string, rope etc together. To knit means to make something, for example clothing, using wool and special long needles. To weave means to make cloth by passing threads over and under each other on a special frame called a loom.

know /nəʊ/ VERB [knows, knowing, knew, known]
1 to have information or knowledge about something □ I didn't know the answer to her questions. 🖲'What's the capital of Hungary?' 'I don't know.' □ **+ question word** Do you know where he lives? □ She knows how to make me happy. □ **+ about** I didn't know about the course.
2 to be familiar with a person □ I didn't know anyone at the party. 🖲I got to know her when I was a student. 🖲I don't know him very well.
3 to be familiar with a place or a thing because you have been there, seen it, used it, etc. □ Do you know Berlin well? □ I know his work.
4 let someone know to tell someone something □ I'm going to be late – could you let John know, please?

(= everyone knows) *that he has health problems.*
□ *+ of* *She has a good knowledge of sport.*

> ► Remember that to **know** something means to *have* knowledge about something. To **find out** something is to *get* knowledge about something:
> ✓ *I called Annie to find out when she was leaving.*
> ✗ *I called Annie to know when she was leaving.*

knowledge /ˈnɒlɪdʒ/ NOUN, NO PLURAL the information that you know about something
🕮 *Candidates need to show that they have a basic knowledge of English.* 🕮 *It's common knowledge*

known[1] /nəʊn/ PAST PARTICIPLE OF **know**
known[2] /nəʊn/ ADJECTIVE
1 that people know about □ *There is no known cure for the disease.*
2 famous □ *She is known for her performance in the film 'The Red Shoes'.*

Koran /kəˈrɑːn/ NOUN the Koran the holy book of the Islamic religion

L *or* **l** /eɪ/ the 12th letter of the alphabet

lab /læb/ NOUN [*plural* labs] a short way to say and write **laboratory**

label[1] /ˈleɪbəl/ NOUN [*plural* labels] a small piece of paper or cloth that is fixed to something and gives information about it □ *The washing instructions are on the label.* □ *I looked at the ingredients on the label.*

> ➤ THESAURUS: A label or a tag is a small piece of paper or cloth that is fixed to something and gives information about it. Goods in shops usually have a price tag on them, and clothes usually have a label inside to tell you how to clean them. A ticket is a small piece of paper that shows that you have paid to do something. You might have a train ticket or a theatre ticket, for example.

label[2] /ˈleɪbəl/ VERB [labels, labelling/US labeling, labelled/US labeled] to fix a label to something □ *All the boxes have been carefully labelled.* □ *Manufacturers should label their products more clearly.*

laboratory /ləˈbɒrətəri/ NOUN [*plural* laboratories] a room containing equipment for scientific work □ *a laboratory experiment* □ *Tests were carried out at a laboratory.*

labour /ˈleɪbə(r)/ NOUN, NO PLURAL
1 workers, especially in a particular country or type of work 🔄 *There is a shortage of skilled labour.* □ *the rising cost of labour* 🔄 *the labour market*
2 work, especially hard, physical work 🔄 *He was used to hard, manual labour.*

labourer /ˈleɪbərə(r)/ NOUN [*plural* labourers] a person who does hard physical work □ *a farm labourer*

Labour Party /ˈleɪbər ˌpɑːti/ NOUN, NO PLURAL in the UK, one of the main political parties

lace /leɪs/ NOUN [*plural* laces]
1 a decorative cloth with delicate patterns of many holes □ *a collar trimmed with lace*
2 a piece of string for tying up shoes or other clothing 🔄 *He bent down to tie his shoe laces.*

lack[1] /læk/ VERB [lacks, lacking, lacked] to be without something or not to not have enough of something □ *Audrey lacks a sense of humour.* □ *We lack the resources to deal with all the requests.*

lack[2] /læk/ NOUN, NO PLURAL when you do not have something, or you do not have enough of something □ **+ of** *He was suffering from lack of sleep.* 🔄 *He shows a complete lack of understanding.*

ladder /ˈlædə(r)/ NOUN [*plural* ladders] a set of steps that you use for climbing up to high places and can move around to different places □ *He had to climb a ladder to reach the top cupboard.*

ladies /ˈleɪdɪz/ PLURAL NOUN a public toilet for women and girls □ *Where is the ladies, please?*

lady /ˈleɪdɪ/ NOUN [*plural* ladies]
1 a polite word for a woman □ *Ask that lady if the seat by her is free.* 🔄 *Good evening ladies and gentlemen.*
2 in the UK, a title for a woman with a high social rank

laid /leɪd/ PAST TENSE AND PAST PARTICIPLE OF **lay**[1] □ *She laid the baby on the blanket.*

lain /leɪn/ PAST PARTICIPLE OF **lie**[3] (= put your body in a flat position) □ *I had lain down for a moment and fallen fast asleep.*

lake /leɪk/ NOUN [*plural* lakes] a large area of water with land all around it □ *Lake Como*

> ➤ THESAURUS: A lake is a large area of water with land all around it. Lakes can be natural or created by people. A reservoir is a large lake where water is collected and stored in order to be used by people. A pond is a small area of water, smaller than a lake. Some people have a pond in their garden.

lamb /læm/ NOUN [*plural* lambs]
1 a young sheep
2 *no plural* meat from a young sheep □ *roast lamb* □ *lamb chops*

lame /leɪm/ ADJECTIVE [lamer, lamest] not able to walk well because of an injury □ *a lame horse*

lamp /læmp/ NOUN [*plural* lamps] a light, especially one which stands on a table □ *a table lamp* □ *a bedside lamp* □ *an old oil lamp*

land[1] /lænd/ NOUN [*plural* lands]
1 *no plural* an area of ground □ *an acre of land* 🔄 *agricultural land*

2 *no plural* the part of the Earth not covered by water ☐ *It's good to be back on dry land.*
3 a word for a country used especially in stories ☐ *He talked of his adventures in foreign lands.*

land² /lænd/ VERB [lands, landing, landed]
1 when an aircraft lands, it arrives on the ground after a flight ☐ *The plane landed around 3pm.* ☐ *The flight landed safely at Glasgow airport.*
2 to stop somewhere after flying or falling ☐ *The bird landed on a branch.* ☐ *The book fell off the table and landed on the floor.* ☐ *I slipped but managed to land on my feet.*

landing /'lændɪŋ/ NOUN [plural landings]
1 the process of moving a plane down to the ground ☐ *The helicopter made an emergency landing.*
2 the floor at the top of some stairs or the floor between two sets of stairs ☐ *She reached the second-floor landing.*

landlady /'lændleɪdɪ/ NOUN [plural landladies] a woman who owns a house that someone else pays to live in

landlord /'lændlɔːd/ NOUN [plural landlords] a man who owns a house that someone else pays to live in ☐ *Her landlord raised the rent.*

landmark /'lændmɑːk/ NOUN [plural landmarks] a place, especially a building, that helps you know where you are because you can easily recognize it ☐ *The tower is one of the city's most famous landmarks.* ☐ *He spotted a familiar landmark.*

landscape /'lændskeɪp/ NOUN [plural landscapes] a view of a large area of land ☐ *He looked out at the beautiful landscape.* ☐ *a snowy landscape*

lane /leɪn/ NOUN [plural lanes]
1 a narrow road ☐ *We drove along narrow country lanes.*
2 a strip of a road separated by painted lines ☐ *She pulled out into the fast lane.* ☐ *The northbound lane of the motorway was closed after an accident.*

language /'læŋgwɪdʒ/ NOUN [plural languages]
1 *no plural* communication using speech and writing ☐ *formal language* ☐ *He used some interesting language to describe the scene.* ☐ *+ of the language of diplomacy*
2 the words used by a particular group, especially the people that live in one country ☐ *the English language* ☐ *All children should learn a foreign language.* ☐ *Do you speak any other languages?*

> ► **THESAURUS:** Language refers to communication using speech and writing. Speech refers to the ability to speak or the way that someone speaks. Your accent is the way that you say words, according to where you come from.

lap /læp/ NOUN [plural laps]
1 the top part of a person's legs when they are in a sitting position ☐ *Jessie sat on her mother's lap.*
2 one complete journey around a race track ☐ *He crashed on the first lap of the race.*

laptop /'læptop/ NOUN [plural laptops] a small computer that can be carried easily. A computing word.

large /lɑːdʒ/ ADJECTIVE [larger, largest] big or bigger than normal in size or amount ☐ *a large house* ☐ *A large number of people were waiting.* ☐ *Large parts of the country are without power.*

laser /'leɪzə(r)/ NOUN [plural lasers] a very narrow, powerful beam of light ☐ *a laser beam* ☐ *The surgery uses lasers.*

last¹ /lɑːst/ ADJECTIVE, DETERMINER
1 most recent ☐ *We moved house last October.* ☐ *In the last few months we have been very busy.* ☐ *On my last birthday, he gave me a necklace.* ☐ *The last time I ate fish, I was ill.* ☐ *Their last album was a huge success.*
2 coming after all the others ☐ *We caught the last train to Cambridge.* ☐ *This is the last time I will ever help you.* ☐ *That was her last public appearance.*
3 the last moment/minute the latest possible time before something ☐ *Our flight was cancelled at the last moment.* ☐ *Don't leave it to the last minute to book a hotel.*
4 the final one remaining ☐ *She ate my last toffee.*

last² /lɑːst/ VERB [lasts, lasting, lasted]
1 to continue for a period of time ☐ *The lesson seemed to last for ever.* ☐ *The film lasted over three hours.*
2 to remain in good condition ☐ *These boots have lasted well.*
3 to be enough ☐ *The food lasted for three days.*

last³ /lɑːst/ ADVERB
1 after all the others ☐ *She arrived last.* ☐ *Make sure you add the sugar last.* ☐ *I came last in the swimming race.*
2 most recently ☐ *When did you last see Anna?*

lasting /'lɑːstɪŋ/ ADJECTIVE continuing to exist for a long time ☐ *They hope to achieve a lasting peace.* ☐ *His book made a lasting impression on me.*

lastly /'lɑːstlɪ/ ADVERB after all other people or things ☐ *Lastly, I just want to thank my wife.*

late /leɪt/ ADJECTIVE, ADVERB [later, latest]
1 after the time that is expected or necessary ☐ *The bus was late.* ☐ *+ for If you don't hurry, you'll be late for work.* ☐ *I was too late to help him.* ☐ *I'm coming to the meeting, but I might be a bit late.*
2 near the end of the day ☐ *The children stayed up late to watch a movie.* ☐ *Will the party go on late?* ☐ *It's getting late – we should leave.*
3 near the end of a period of time ☐ *the late 18th*

century □ *It was late afternoon by the time we arrived.*

lately /ˈleɪtlɪ/ ADVERB recently □ *I haven't been to many parties lately.*

later /ˈleɪtə(r)/ ADJECTIVE, ADVERB after the time you have been talking about □ *Later, he married an artist.* □ *She rang me later to apologize.* □ *Two years later I received a letter from him.* □ *Is there a later train?*

latest /ˈleɪtɪst/ ADJECTIVE most recent □ *I regularly check the Internet for the latest news.* □ *We stock all the latest fashions.*

Latin /ˈlætɪn/ NOUN, NO PLURAL the language of the ancient Romans

latitude /ˈlætɪtjuːd/ NOUN [*plural* latitudes] the position of a place along imaginary lines around the Earth north and south of the equator (= line around the middle of the Earth). It is measured in degrees north and south.

latter /ˈlætə(r)/ ADJECTIVE nearer the end of a period of time than the beginning 🕀 *the latter part of the 19th century*

laugh¹ /lɑːf/ VERB [laughs, laughing, laughed] to make a sound of enjoyment when you think something is funny □ **+ at** *She laughed at my jokes.* □ **+ about** *We can laugh about the whole thing now.* 🕀 *It really made me laugh.* 🕀 *They burst out laughing* (= suddenly laughed loudly).

◆ PHRASAL VERB **laugh at someone/something** to laugh or say something rude because you think someone or something is stupid □ *Wallis just laughed at the suggestion.*

laugh² /lɑːf/ NOUN [*plural* laughs]
1 when you laugh, or the sound that you make when you laugh 🕀 *He gave a nervous laugh.* □ *He has a very loud laugh.*
2 **have a laugh** an informal phrase that means to have fun and enjoy yourself □ *We all have such a laugh together.*

laughter /ˈlɑːftə(r)/ NOUN, NO PLURAL when someone laughs or the sound that they make when they laugh □ *I could hear laughter in the next room.*

launch /lɔːntʃ/ VERB [launches, launching, launched]
1 to put a boat or ship in the water for the first time
2 to send a spacecraft into the sky □ *The first Sputnik satellite was launched into space in 1957.*
3 to start to sell a new product □ *The latest model will be launched next month.*

laundry /ˈlɔːndrɪ/ NOUN, NO PLURAL clothes that are going to be washed, or have just been washed □ *a pile of dirty laundry* □ *a laundry basket* 🕀 *I've done the laundry.*

lava /ˈlɑːvə/ NOUN, NO PLURAL the hot liquid rock that comes out of a volcano (= mountain that

explodes) and becomes solid as it cools down. A geography word.

lavatory /ˈlævətərɪ/ NOUN [*plural* lavatories] a formal word for toilet □ *a public lavatory*

law /lɔː/ NOUN [*plural* laws]
1 an official rule in a country or state that everyone must obey □ **+ against** *laws against discrimination*
2 **the law** an official set of rules that everyone in a country or state must obey 🕀 *They have broken the law.*
3 **by law** if you have to do something by law, there is an official rule which says that you must do it □ *You are required by law to provide this information.*
4 **be against the law** to not be allowed by law □ *Driving at the age of 13 is against the law.*

➤ **THESAURUS:** A rule is an instruction about what is allowed or what is not allowed. Games have rules, and schools have rules about how students must behave. A law is an official set of rules that everyone in a country must obey. An order is an instruction to do something. Soldiers give orders to other soldiers.

lawn /lɔːn/ NOUN [*plural* lawns] an area of short grass in a garden 🕀 *I need to mow the lawn* (= cut the grass with a machine).

lawyer /ˈlɔːjə(r)/ NOUN [*plural* lawyers] someone whose job is to advise people about the law and to act for other people in legal situations 🕀 *a defence lawyer* □ *His lawyer said he would appeal against the sentence.*

lay¹ /leɪ/ VERB [lays, laying, laid]
1 to put something down carefully □ **+ on** *She laid the book on the table.* □ **+ down** *Slowly, he laid down the gun.* □ *I went to lay flowers on his grave.*
2 **lay the table** to put knives, forks, etc. on a table to prepare for a meal
3 if a bird lays an egg, it produces it

➤ Try not to confuse the verbs **lay** and **lie**. To **lay** something somewhere is to put something down. To **lie** somewhere is to be in a flat position: □ *She looked for a place to lay the baby.* □ *Why don't you lie on the sofa and watch TV?*

lay² /leɪ/ PAST TENSE OF lie³

layer /ˈleɪə(r)/ NOUN [*plural* layers] an amount of a substance that covers something or is between other things □ **+ of** *The grass was covered with a layer of snow.* 🕀 *Remove the outer layers of the onion.* □ *Wear several layers of clothing.* □ *Dust had settled in a thin layer over everything.*

lead¹ /liːd/ VERB [leads, leading, led]
1 to show someone where to go by going first or

going with them □ *You lead and I'll follow on my bike.* □ *She led me into a large room.*

2 if a road, path, etc. leads somewhere, that is where it goes □ **+ to** *This road leads to London.*

3 to be winning in a race or competition, or to be the most successful at something □ *Liverpool were leading 2-0 at the end of the first half.* □ **+ by** *They are leading by three goals to one.* 🔁 *Our company leads the world in computer technology.*

4 to direct or control an activity or a group of people □ *The team should be led by someone with a lot of experience.* □ *A new officer is leading the investigation.*

5 lead a comfortable/full/normal, etc. life to live in a particular way

6 lead the way to be the first to do something □ *This university led the way in introducing schemes to attract poorer students.*

♦ PHRASAL VERB **lead to something** to cause something to happen or exist □ *Long hours at work led to the breakdown of his marriage.* □ *Using the mouse too much can lead to wrist problems.*

lead² /liːd/ NOUN [*plural* leads]

1 the position in a race or competition where you are winning □ *Jenkins has been in the lead for most of the race.* 🔁 *Juventus took the lead after 23 minutes.*

2 a long, narrow piece of leather attached to a dog's collar in order to hold it. 🔁 *All dogs must be kept on a lead.*

3 a wire that connects a piece of electrical equipment to an electricity supply

lead³ /led/ NOUN [*plural* leads]

1 a soft, dark grey metal

2 the dark grey inside part of a pencil

leader /ˈliːdə(r)/ NOUN [*plural* leaders] a person who is in charge of a group of people □ **+ of** *the leader of the expedition* 🔁 *a religious leader* 🔁 *the country's political leaders* □ *the Republican Party leader*

leading /ˈliːdɪŋ/ ADJECTIVE most important or most successful □ *He is one of Scotland's leading playwrights.* □ *the team's leading scorer*

leaf /liːf/ NOUN [*plural* leaves] a flat green part of a plant or tree that grows out from a stem or a branch □ *The sun shone through the leaves.* □ *a plate of salad leaves*

leaflet /ˈliːflɪt/ NOUN [*plural* leaflets] a piece of paper that gives printed information about something □ *a leaflet about recycling*

league /liːg/ NOUN [*plural* leagues]

1 a group of teams that play sports matches against each other □ *the professional basketball league* 🔁 *I'm still hoping we can win the league this season.* 🔁 *They're top of the league table.*

2 a group of people or countries who agree to work together

leak¹ /liːk/ NOUN [*plural* leaks] a hole that liquid or gas can escape or enter through, or the gas or liquid that escapes □ *There could be a leak in the pipe.* 🔁 *a gas leak*

leak² /liːk/ VERB [leaks, leaking, leaked] if gas or liquid leaks, it escapes from or enters something and if an object leaks, gas or liquid escapes from or enters it through a hole □ *Gas was leaking from somewhere under the floor.* □ *My boots leak.*

leaky /ˈliːkɪ/ ADJECTIVE [leakier, leakiest] having small holes or cracks which a gas or liquid can escape from □ *a leaky roof*

lean¹ /liːn/ VERB [leans, leaning, leant *or* leaned]

1 to move your body in a particular direction by bending at the waist □ **+ forward** *He leaned forward to kiss her.* □ **+ back** *She leaned back in her chair.* □ **+ over** *Could you lean over and get the salt for me?* □ **+ out** *She leaned out of the window.*

2 to put something against something so that it is supported by it, or to be in this position □ **+ on** *She leaned her head on his shoulder.* □ **+ against** *A bike was leaning against the wall.*

lean² /liːn/ ADJECTIVE [leaner, leanest] with no fat or little fat □ *I only buy lean meat.*

➤ **THESAURUS:** We usually use **lean** to talk about meat, although it is sometimes used to talk about people. If you want to say that a person has little fat, the word is **thin**. If someone is thin in an attractive way, you can use the words **slim** or **slender**, especially for women. **Skinny** means very thin, often in an unattractive way. **Skinny** is an informal word.

leap¹ /liːp/ VERB [leaps, leaping, leapt *or* leaped]

1 to move suddenly and quickly □ *She leapt up and ran to the door.* □ *I leapt out of bed.*

2 to jump high or a long distance □ *We saw dolphins leaping out of the water.* □ *The dancer leapt into the air.*

leap² /liːp/ NOUN [*plural* leaps] a big jump □ *He took an impressive leap over the fence.*

leap year /liːp jɪə(r)/ NOUN [*plural* leap years] a year that happens every four years and has 366 days. The extra day is February 29.

learn /lɜːn/ VERB [learns, learning, learnt *or* learned]

1 to get to know about something or get to know how to do something □ **+ to do something** *He's learning to drive.* □ *She wanted to learn English.* □ **+ question word** *I learned how to cook from my mother.* □ **+ about** *We learnt about the local culture.* □ **+ from** *I've learnt from my mistakes.*

2 to find out some news or information □ **+ that** *I was surprised to learn that she'd already left.* □ **+**

whether *Today he will learn whether he needs surgery.*

learner /ˈlɜːnə(r)/ NOUN [*plural* **learners**] a person who is learning something □ *It's a book for young language learners.* 🔊 *He was a quick learner.*

lease /liːs/ VERB [**leases, leasing, leased**] to rent something to someone □ *They lease the land from the local council.*

least¹ /liːst/ ADVERB

1 less than anyone or anything else in size, amount or degree □ *She chose the least expensive trousers.* □ *He always turns up when you least expect him.* □ *These price rises will affect those who are least able to afford them.*
2 at least (a) not less than □ *She must be at least 50.* □ *It will take at least two hours to get there.* (b) used before you add a positive statement after talking about something bad □ *She was very late, but at least she phoned to let us know.* (c) used to correct what you have just said or to make it less certain □ *I saw her in the library – at least, I think it was her.*

least² /liːst/ DETERMINER, PRONOUN

1 the smallest amount, size or degree □ *The person who had the least difficulty was the tallest.* □ *Of everyone here, I know least about the subject.* □ *He is the richest, but he gave the least.*
2 not in the least (bit)/not the least bit not at all □ *He wasn't the least bit sorry for all the trouble he caused.*

leather /ˈleðə(r)/ NOUN, NO PLURAL a strong material for making shoes, bags and clothes that is made from the skin of an animal □ *a leather jacket* □ *a pair of black leather boots*

leave¹ /liːv/ VERB [**leaves, leaving, left**]

1 to go away from a place □ *I left the office early.* □ *The train leaves at two.* □ *I left work at four thirty.* 🔊 *I left home when I was 18.*
2 to not take something with you when you go away □ *Maria left her umbrella on the bus.* □ *+ behind I left all my books behind.*
3 to put something or someone somewhere □ *Leave your shoes by the door.* □ *I left the children with a neighbour.*
4 to allow something to be in a particular position or state □ *Leave the conditioner in your hair for five minutes.* □ *She left the door unlocked.*
5 to not use all of something □ *Is there any milk left?*
6 to not do something but do it later or let someone else do it □ *I'll leave the washing up and do it in the morning.* □ *+ to I left all the driving to her.*
7 to give something to someone after your death □ *Her grandmother left Joy all her jewellery.*
8 leave someone/something alone to stop touching something or talking to someone

□ *Journalists wouldn't leave her alone.* □ *Leave my clothes alone.*

♦ PHRASAL VERBS **leave someone/something out** to not include someone or something □ *I told him what she said, but I left out the rude bits.* 🔊 *Some of our members felt left out because they could not do the activities.* **leave something over** if something is left over, it is what remains when the rest of something has been used □ *There was a lot of food left over from the party.*

> ➤ **THESAURUS:** To leave means to go away from a place. The words depart and set off have a similar meaning, but are especially used to describe the start of a journey. For example we can ssay that a train departs at a particular time. Depart is a more formal word than set off.

leave² /liːv/ NOUN, NO PLURAL a period of holiday from work □ *I had a week's leave.* □ *He committed the crime while he was on leave from the army.*

leaves /liːvz/ PLURAL OF **leaf**

lecture¹ /ˈlektʃə(r)/ NOUN [*plural* **lectures**] a talk by someone to a group of people to teach them about something □ *+ on a lecture on economics* 🔊 *He was due to give a lecture at Leeds University.* 🔊 *He attended a lecture by Carl Jung.*

lecture² /ˈlektʃə(r)/ VERB [**lectures, lecturing, lectured**] to give a lecture or lectures about a particular subject □ *He lectured on history at Cambridge University.*

led /led/ PAST TENSE AND PAST PARTICIPLE OF **lead**¹ □ *Connor led a wild life for many years.* □ *Where have you led us?*

left¹ /left/ ADJECTIVE, ADVERB on or towards the side of your body that is to the west if you are facing north 🔊 *Can you write with your left hand?* 🔊 *You stand on the left side of him.* 🔊 *Now turn left.* □ *Click on the link in the top left corner of the screen.*

left² /left/ NOUN, NO PLURAL the left side or direction □ *Stop just here on the left.* □ *Diana is standing to the left of Robert.*

left³ /left/ PAST TENSE AND PAST PARTICIPLE OF **leave**¹ □ *She left early.* □ *I've left my book at home.*

left-handed /ˌleft'hændɪd/ ADJECTIVE using your left hand to do things, especially to write □ *Are you left-handed?* □ *a left-handed batsman*

leg /leg/ NOUN [*plural* **legs**]

1 one of the parts of the body that animals and humans stand and walk on □ *I broke my leg skiing.* □ *How many legs do spiders have?* □ *Try standing on one leg.*
2 the part of a pair of trousers that covers one leg
3 one of the pieces that supports a table, chair, etc.

legal /ˈliːɡəl/ ADJECTIVE allowed by the law □ *Is it legal to ride your bike on the pavement?*

legend /ˈledʒənd/ NOUN [*plural* **legends**]
1 an old traditional story that is usually not true □ *the legend of St George and the dragon*
2 a very famous person □ *Formula One legend, Ayrton Senna*

leisure /ˈleʒə(r)/ NOUN, NO PLURAL time when you do not have to work □ *Families are spending more on leisure.* 🔊 *What do you do in your leisure time?*
♦ IDIOM **at your leisure** when you have time □ *Take the brochure home and read it at your leisure.*

lemon /ˈlemən/ NOUN [*plural* **lemons**] an oval fruit with a hard, yellow skin and very sour juice □ *tea with a slice of lemon* □ *Add the juice of a lemon.*

lemonade /ˌleməˈneɪd/ NOUN [*plural* **lemonades**] a cold drink with a lemon flavour and a lot of bubbles □ *a bottle of lemonade*

lend /lend/ VERB [**lends, lending, lent**] to allow someone to use something or have some money for a short time □ *Could you lend me £5, Mum?* □ **+ to** *Adam has lent his MP3 player to Andy.* □ *The bank no longer lends to first-time buyers.*
♦ IDIOM **lend a hand** to help someone

> ► Remember that when you **lend** something, you give something to someone else to use. When you use something that belongs to someone else, the verb is **borrow** □ *Dan lent me his mobile* □ *I borrowed Dan's mobile.*

length /leŋθ/ NOUN [*plural* **lengths**]
1 how long something is from one end to the other end □ *Measure the table's length.* □ *The pieces of wood were all different lengths.*
2 at length if you talk at length, you talk for a long time □ *The doctor explained the different treatments at length.*

lengthen /ˈleŋθən/ VERB [**lengthens, lengthening, lengthened**] to become longer or to make something longer □ *I think you should lengthen that skirt.* □ *Shadows lengthened as the sun went down.*

lengthy /ˈleŋθɪ/ ADJECTIVE [**lengthier, lengthiest**] taking a long time □ *Getting a passport was a lengthy process.*

lens /lenz/ NOUN [*plural* **lenses**] a curved piece of glass that you look through in glasses, cameras and scientific instruments □ *a zoom lens* □ *Adjust the lens in the telescope.*

lent /lent/ PAST TENSE AND PAST PARTICIPLE OF **lend** □ *I lent him a book.* □ *I've lent her some money.*

lentil /ˈlentɪl/ NOUN [*plural* **lentils**] a small orange, brown or green seed that is dried and cooked □ *lentil soup*

leopard /ˈlepəd/ NOUN [*plural* **leopards**] a large animal of the cat family with yellow fur and dark spots

less[1] /les/ DETERMINER, PRONOUN a smaller amount of □ *We'll have to spend less money.* □ *I have less time than Patrick.* □ *I had less on my plate than you.* □ **+ of** *He spends less of his time with his children.*

> ► Notice that **less** is used with uncountable nouns, for example *time* and *money*. With the plural form of countable nouns, for example *cars* and *people* use **fewer**: □ *I have* **less** *money than I used to.* □ *I have* **fewer** *problems than I used to.*

less[2] /les/ PREPOSITION taking away a particular amount □ *The cost will be £100 less the discount.*

less[3] /les/ ADVERB
1 used to make comparative forms of adjectives and adverbs, with the meaning 'not as much' □ *My clothes are less expensive.* 🔊 *I'm less patient than you.* 🔊 *These instructions are a lot less complicated.* 🔊 *I'm less and less interested in TV.*
2 to a smaller degree □ *I exercise less these days.* 🔊 *I eat less than I used to.* 🔊 *I see her less and less.*

-less /lɪs/ SUFFIX -less is added to the end of words to mean 'without' □ *hopeless* □ *thoughtless*

lessen /ˈlesən/ VERB [**lessens, lessening, lessened**] to become less or to make something less □ *The drugs should lessen the pain.*

lesson /ˈlesən/ NOUN [*plural* **lessons**] a period of time in which you learn something or teach someone something □ *When's your next lesson?* □ *a driving lesson* 🔊 *I'm taking swimming lessons.*

let /let/ VERB [**lets, letting, let**]
1 to allow someone to do something or something to happen □ *He won't let anyone use his tools.* □ *This card lets me travel free.*
2 to allow someone or something to go somewhere □ **+ in** *They won't let him in the building.* □ *She won't let the children out of her sight.* □ *These windows let in the rain.*
3 let's used to make a suggestion about what to do □ *Let's go swimming.* □ *Let's get out of here.*
4 let go to stop holding something □ *He grasped my hand and wouldn't let go.* □ *Now you can let go of the rope.*
5 let someone know to tell someone something □ *Could you let Mick know I'll be late?* □ *I want to let everyone know why I acted the way I did.*
6 to rent a room, building, etc. to someone
♦ PHRASAL VERBS **let someone down** to upset someone by behaving badly or not doing something

they expected you to do □ *Our suppliers have let us down.* □ *You've let yourself down and you've let your family down.* **let someone off** to not punish someone for something bad they have done

lethal /'li:θəl/ ADJECTIVE causing or able to cause death □ *a lethal weapon* □ *a lethal dose of the drug*

letter /'letə(r)/ NOUN [plural **letters**]
1 a message that you write and send by post to another person 🔁 *Why don't you write a letter?* 🔁 *I got a letter from Laura this morning.*
2 one of the written shapes that you combine to write words, like *a*, *b* or *c* □ *the letters of the alphabet*

> ➤ THESAURUS: A message is a piece of written or spoken information sent from one person to another. A letter is a message that you write and send by post to another person. A note is a short informal letter, or a piece of writing to help you to remember something. For example, you might write a note to remind you to phone someone. A memo is a short note that you write to someone who works in the same company as you.

lettuce /'letɪs/ NOUN [plural **lettuces**] a vegetable with large green leaves that are used in salads

level[1] /'levəl/ ADJECTIVE
1 flat or horizontal □ *a piece of level ground* □ *Add a level tablespoonful of flour.*
2 at the same height as something else □ **+ with** *The picture needs to be level with the mirror next to it.*

level[2] /'levəl/ VERB [**levels**, **levelling**/US **leveling**, **levelled**/US **leveled**] to make something flat, smooth or horizontal □ *The ground will have to be levelled before they can build on it.*

level[3] /'levəl/ NOUN [plural **levels**]
1 the amount, size or number of something 🔁 *Sudoku puzzles need a high level of concentration.* 🔁 *Low levels of pollution were recorded.* □ *Unemployment has stayed at the same level for over three years.*
2 a particular height or distance above or below the ground □ *She hung the pictures at eye level.* □ *The water level was rising.*
3 the particular ability or standard of someone or something □ *It's best to start at beginners' level.* □ *He played squash at international level.*

lever /'li:və(r)/ NOUN [plural **levers**]
1 a handle that operates a machine or engine □ *Push the lever up to start the engine.* □ *a gear lever*
2 a strong bar that you press on in order to move something heavy

liable /'laɪəbəl/ ADJECTIVE **liable to do something** often doing something, especially something bad □ *She's liable to lose her temper.*

liar /'laɪə(r)/ NOUN [plural **liars**] someone who tells lies

liberal /'lɪbərəl/ ADJECTIVE accepting different ideas and types of behaviour □ *It's a very liberal society.*

liberty /'lɪbətɪ/ NOUN, NO PLURAL freedom to do, or go where you want or say what you want □ *Prisoners are deprived of their liberty.*

librarian /laɪ'breərɪən/ NOUN [plural **librarians**] someone who works in a library □ *the school librarian*

library /'laɪbrərɪ/ NOUN [plural **libraries**] a building or room that has a lot of books, CDs or DVDs that you can borrow 🔁 *library books*

licence /'laɪsəns/ NOUN [plural **licences**] an official document that gives someone permission to do or have something □ *a driving licence* □ *a licence to sell alcohol*

license[1] /'laɪsəns/ VERB [**licenses**, **licensing**, **licensed**] to give someone official permission to do something □ *The restaurant is licensed to serve alcohol.*

license[2] /'laɪsəns/ NOUN [plural **licenses**] the US spelling of **licence**

lick /lɪk/ VERB [**licks**, **licking**, **licked**] to move your tongue over something □ *The cat was licking its paws.* □ *She licked her lips nervously.*

lid /lɪd/ NOUN [plural **lids**] a cover that fits the top of a container □ *Can you get the lid off this jar?*

lie[1] /laɪ/ VERB [**lies**, **lying**, **lied**] to say something that you know is not true □ **+ about** *He lied about his age.* □ **+ to** *Did you lie to me?*

lie[2] /laɪ/ NOUN [plural **lies**] something that you say that is not true when you know that it is not true 🔁 *He's always telling lies.*

> ➤ Notice that people **tell lies**. They do not 'say lies':
> ✓ *Don't tell lies, Oliver.*
> ✗ *Don't say lies, Oliver.*

lie[3] /laɪ/ VERB [**lies**, **lying**, **lay**, **lain**]
1 to be in a flat position, for example on the floor or on a bed, or to put your body into this position □ *She's been lying on a beach all day.* □ *Lie flat on your back.* □ *Go and lie on the couch.*
2 to be in a particular position □ *The town lies to the east of Geneva.* □ *There were clothes lying all over the floor.* □ *Snow lay on the hills.*
♦ PHRASAL VERB **lie down** to put your body into a flat position, especially to rest □ *I don't feel well – I'm going to lie down for a while.*

► Notice that the past tense of **lie** when it means 'to say something that you know is not true' is **lied**. The past tense of **lie** when it means 'to be in a flat position' is **lay**.

lieutenant /lefˈtenənt/ NOUN [plural lieutenants] an officer in the army or navy

life /laɪf/ NOUN [plural lives]
1 the time between being born and dying 🔲 He spent his life helping others. 🔲 I've had these problems my whole life. 🔲 He lived in Glasgow all his life. □ Our lives have been ruined by this disease.
2 the way someone lives 🔲 They live a simple life. 🔲 We lead a quiet life. 🔲 This course will change your life.
3 the existence of a person 🔲 I'm not prepared to risk my life to save your dog. 🔲 He saved my life. 🔲 Hundreds of soldiers have lost their lives in this war.
4 no plural living things □ Is there human life anywhere else in the universe? □ plant life
5 energy and enthusiasm □ Try to put a bit more life into your singing. 🔲 He's always full of life.

lifeboat /ˈlaɪfbəʊt/ NOUN [plural lifeboats] a boat used for saving people from dangerous situations at sea □ the lifeboat crew

lifestyle /ˈlaɪfstaɪl/ NOUN [plural lifestyles] the way that someone lives □ We try to have a healthy lifestyle.

lifetime /ˈlaɪftaɪm/ NOUN [plural lifetimes] the length of time that a particular person is alive □ These children will see such technological advances in their lifetime.

lift¹ /lɪft/ VERB [lifts, lifting, lifted] to move something upwards or raise it □ She lifted the baby out of his cot. □ He was so weak that he couldn't lift his head.

lift² /lɪft/ NOUN [plural lifts]
1 a machine like a large box that carries people or things between floors in a tall building 🔲 Take the lift to the sixth floor.
2 a ride in someone's car 🔲 Could you give me a lift home?

light¹ /laɪt/ NOUN [plural lights]
1 no plural the energy from something such as the sun or a piece of electrical equipment that allows us to see □ There isn't enough light to read. 🔲 A ray of light shone through the curtains. 🔲 The room was filled with bright light.
2 a piece of equipment that produces light 🔲 Don't forget to switch off the light. 🔲 I turned on the light. 🔲 Where is the light switch?
3 set light to something to make something burn

light² /laɪt/ VERB [lights, lighting, lit]
1 to make something start to burn 🔲 Let's light the fire.

2 to start burning □ Why won't the cooker light?
3 to light a place is to make it brighter □ The room was lit with candles.

► **THESAURUS**: If you burn something, you destroy it with fire. When you light a fire, you make it start to burn. You can also say that you set fire to something. Note that you light a fire, but set fire to the wood or coal that you want to burn. If you make a light work, you turn it on or switch it on.

light³ /laɪt/ ADJECTIVE [lighter, lightest]
1 bright or not dark □ It's still light enough to read. 🔲 Mike got up as soon as it began to get light.
2 pale in colour □ light blue □ You can make colours lighter by adding white to them.
3 not heavy □ My bike has a very light frame. □ This bag feels light.
4 not strong or in large amounts 🔲 Light winds reduced the temperature. 🔲 Traffic is light around London tonight. □ I felt a light touch on my arm.

light bulb /ˈlaɪt ˌbʌlb/ NOUN [plural light bulbs] a hollow glass object that contains a wire which produces light when electricity passes through it □ energy-saving light bulbs

lighter /ˈlaɪtə(r)/ NOUN [plural lighters] a small object that produces a flame to make a cigarette start burning □ Do you have a lighter I could use?

lighting /ˈlaɪtɪŋ/ NOUN, NO PLURAL the lights used in a room □ soft lighting

lightly /ˈlaɪtlɪ/ ADVERB
1 gently □ She touched me lightly on the arm and smiled.
2 not much □ a lightly boiled egg □ She was lightly tanned.

lightning /ˈlaɪtnɪŋ/ NOUN, NO PLURAL a bright flash of electricity in the sky that sometimes happens in a storm □ a flash of lightning 🔲 thunder and lightning 🔲 The church was struck by lightning in the storm.

like¹ /laɪk/ PREPOSITION
1 similar to □ Geraldine looks just like her mother.
2 in a similar way to □ She dances like a professional.
3 if you ask what someone or something is like, you want someone to describe them □ What's your new teacher like?
4 used to give examples □ I love sports like tennis and badminton.

like² /laɪk/ CONJUNCTION
1 as if □ You look like you've seen a ghost.
2 in the same way as. An informal word □ Tie the knot like I showed you.

like³ /laɪk/ VERB [likes, liking, liked]

1 to think that something or someone is pleasant or enjoyable □ *I like pizza.* □ *I don't like football.* 卧 *I like this house better than our old house.* 卧 *I don't like the idea of eating raw fish.* 卧 *He liked the way she talked.* □ **+ ing** *I don't like coming home after dark.* □ **+ to do something** *I like to get up early.*

2 Would you like ...? used to offer someone something □ *Would you like a biscuit?* □ *Would you like to come with us?*

3 would like if you would like something, you want it □ *I'd like a cup of tea.*

4 would like to do something if you would like to do something, you want to do it □ *I'd like to go home now.*

5 if you like (a) used when you make an offer □ *I'll come with you if you like.* (b) used to say yes when someone suggests doing something □ *'Shall I bring some food?' 'Yes, if you like.'*

➤ Notice that **would like** meaning 'want to do something' *(sense 4)* is followed by the verb form **to do something**:
✓ I would like to go home.
✗ I would like that I go home.

likelihood /'laɪklɪhʊd/ NOUN, NO PLURAL the possibility that something will happen □ *There's a strong likelihood of rain today.*

likely /'laɪklɪ/ ADJECTIVE

1 expected to happen □ **+ to do something** *People are more likely to come if the weather is good.* □ **+ that** *It's very likely that nobody will come.*

2 probably true □ *That seems the most likely explanation.*

limb /lɪm/ NOUN [plural limbs] a leg or an arm

lime¹ /laɪm/ NOUN [plural limes]

1 a small, sour fruit that looks like a green lemon □ *Add the juice of two limes.*

2 no plural a white substance that is used to help plants grow and to make cement (= substance used in building)

lime² /laɪm/ ADJECTIVE having a bright green colour □ *a lime green shirt*

limit¹ /'lɪmɪt/ NOUN [plural limits]

1 the largest or smallest amount or level that is allowed or possible 卧 *There's a time limit for this test* 卧 *She had above the legal limit of alcohol in her blood.* 卧 *Each person is allowed 10kg of luggage, and you are over the limit.* □ **+ to** *There's a limit to how much I can help her.*

2 the outside edge of an area □ *the city limits*

limit² /'lɪmɪt/ VERB [limits, limiting, limited] to keep someone or something below a particular amount or level □ *Places on the course are limited, so book early.* □ *People covered their windows to limit damage from the storm.* □ **+ to** *I shall have to limit you to one cake each.*

limp¹ /lɪmp/ VERB [limps, limping, limped] to walk with difficulty because your leg or foot hurts □ *Beckham limped off the pitch.*

limp² /lɪmp/ NOUN, NO PLURAL a way of walking that is not even and shows that someone's leg or foot hurts □ *He walked with a limp.*

line¹ /laɪn/ NOUN [plural lines]

1 a long thin mark □ *There are white lines in the middle of the road.* 卧 *Draw a straight line from A to B.* 卧 *Sign on the dotted line.* 卧 *The first runners have already crossed the finishing line.*

2 a row of things or people □ *The children formed a line.* □ *There is a line of old oak trees by the road.*

3 a row of words on a page □ *Look at the first line of the poem.*

4 a piece of rope, wire, etc. used for a particular purpose □ *I was hanging the washing on the line.*

5 the US word for **queue**

line² /laɪn/ VERB [lines, lining, lined]

1 to be in a row along the sides of something □ *Police officers will line the route of the procession.*

2 to cover the inside of a piece of clothing or a container with something □ *The coat is lined with fur.*

linen /'lɪnɪn/ NOUN, NO PLURAL

1 a type of cloth like a heavy, slightly rough, cotton that is made from a plant □ *a linen jacket*

2 things made of cloth used to cover beds or tables □ *table linen*

linger /'lɪŋgə(r)/ VERB [lingers, lingering, lingered] to stay somewhere for a long time □ *Fans were still lingering at the stage door.* □ *The smell of fish seemed to linger for days.*

lining /'laɪnɪŋ/ NOUN [plural linings] a covering on the inside of a piece of clothing or container □ *a jacket lining* □ *a silver box with a velvet lining*

link¹ /lɪŋk/ NOUN [plural links]

1 a relationship between two people or things □ **+ between** *Research soon proved the link between smoking and lung cancer.* □ **+ with** *It is thought that the group has links with terrorist organizations.*

2 a connection between two files, especially on a website. A computing word. □ *Click on the link to reserve your tickets.*

3 one of the rings of a chain

link² /lɪŋk/ VERB [links, linking, linked] if two people or things are linked, they are connected to each other in some way □ *Were these two events linked in any way?* 卧 *Diet and health are closely linked.* □ *A bridge links the two buildings.*

lion /'laɪən/ NOUN [plural lions] a large, wild animal of the cat family, the male of which has thick hair around its head

lip /lɪp/ NOUN [plural lips] either the upper or the lower outside edge of your mouth □ *He kissed her lightly on the lips.*

lipstick /ˈlɪpstɪk/ NOUN [plural lipsticks] make-up that women put on their lips to make the lips a different colour □ *She was wearing bright red lipstick.*

liquid¹ /ˈlɪkwɪd/ NOUN [plural liquids] a substance that can flow, such as water or oil □ *In hot weather make sure you drink plenty of liquids.*

liquid² /ˈlɪkwɪd/ ADJECTIVE in the form of a liquid □ *a liquid soap*

list¹ /lɪst/ NOUN [plural lists] a group of things such as names, numbers or prices, written one below the other □ *His name is on the list.* 🗫 *a shopping list* 🗫 *I've added your name to the list.* 🗫 *You should make a list of things to do.*

> ➤ Notice the preposition. Something is **on** a list and not 'in' a list:
> ✓ *I'll put your name on the list.*
> ✗ *I'll put your name in the list.*

list² /lɪst/ VERB [lists, listing, listed] to write a list, or to give information in the form of a list □ *The players are listed alphabetically.*

listen /ˈlɪsən/ VERB [listens, listening, listened]
1 to pay attention to a sound so that you can hear it □ + **to** *Listen to me when I'm talking!* □ *Do you ever listen to classical music?* □ *I often listen to the radio.*
2 to pay attention to someone's advice and do what they suggest □ *I told you to wear a coat but you wouldn't listen!*

lit /lɪt/ PAST TENSE AND PAST PARTICIPLE OF **light²** □ *She lit the fire.* □ *I haven't lit the candles yet.*

literary /ˈlɪtərəri/ ADJECTIVE to do with books, writers and literature 🗫 *a literary critic* □ *a literary magazine*

literature /ˈlɪtrətʃə(r)/ NOUN, NO PLURAL stories, poetry and plays □ *He's studying English literature.* □ *20th-century children's literature*

litre /ˈliːtə(r)/ NOUN [plural litres] a unit for measuring liquid □ + **of** *a litre of water* □ *Petrol now costs more than £1 per litre.*

litter /ˈlɪtə(r)/ NOUN, NO PLURAL paper and other rubbish that people have thrown on the ground in a public place 🗫 *You can be fined for dropping litter.*

little¹ /ˈlɪtəl/ DETERMINER, PRONOUN, ADVERB [less, least]
1 not much □ *There is little hope of finding them alive.* □ *She cares so little for other people's opinions.* □ *It costs very little to go on a camping holiday.* □ + **of** *I remember very little of what he said.*
2 a little a small amount or to a small degree □ *I added a little salt.* □ *'Would you like milk?' 'Just a little, please.'* □ *Jump up and down a little to keep warm.* □ *I'm feeling a little cold.*

little² /ˈlɪtəl/ ADJECTIVE [littler, littlest]
1 small □ *They stuck little pieces of cardboard all over it.* □ *He's got his own little bicycle.* 🗫 *Can I have a little bit of butter?*
2 short in time or distance 🗫 *It's only a little way to the hotel.* 🗫 *He'll be here in a little while.*
3 young 🗫 *a little boy/girl* 🗫 *my little brother/sister*

live¹ /lɪv/ VERB [lives, living, lived]
1 to be alive □ *Cats don't usually live for much more than twenty years.* □ *People are living longer these days.*
2 to have your home in a certain place □ *How long have you lived in Madrid?* □ *I live next door to Sam.*
3 to pass your life in a certain way □ *She's used to living alone.*
♦ PHRASAL VERB **live on something 1** to eat a particular type of food □ *They live on nuts and insects.* **2** money you live on is money you use for the things you need □ *We managed to live on our savings for two years.*

live² /laɪv/ ADJECTIVE
1 not dead □ *We bought some live oysters.*
2 a live broadcast is happening as you watch or hear it

live³ /laɪv/ ADVERB if something is broadcast live, it is happening as you watch or hear it □ *We are going live to our correspondent in Berlin.*

lively /ˈlaɪvli/ ADJECTIVE [livelier, liveliest] full of activity, interest or energy □ *a group of lively children* 🗫 *There was a lively debate on the issue.* □ *The café has great food and a lively atmosphere.*

liver /ˈlɪvə(r)/ NOUN [plural livers] a large organ in your body that is very important for cleaning your blood. A biology word.

living¹ /ˈlɪvɪŋ/ NOUN [plural livings] the money you earn from working and that you live on 🗫 *I make my living as a professional actor.* 🗫 *He earns a living by teaching the piano.* 🗫 *I make a decent living (= enough money).* 🗫 *What do you do for a living? (= What is your job?)*

living² /ˈlɪvɪŋ/ ADJECTIVE alive □ *a living organism* □ *She has no living relatives.*

living room /ˈlɪvɪŋ ˌruːm/ NOUN [plural living rooms] a room in a house for sitting and relaxing in □ *I was in the living room, watching television.*

lizard /ˈlɪzəd/ NOUN [plural lizards] a reptile with four legs, a long body and a tail

load¹ /ləʊd/ VERB [loads, loading, loaded]
1 to put something into a vehicle, especially a ship or a truck □ **+ up** *We loaded up the van with furniture.* □ **+ onto** *The boxes are loaded onto a truck.* □ **+ with** *A tanker loaded with oil has sunk off the coast.*
2 to put something into a machine or piece of equipment □ *Have you loaded the dishwasher?*
3 to put a program into a computer's memory so you can use it □ *The computer is loaded with anti-virus software.*
4 to put bullets in a gun

load² /ləʊd/ NOUN [plural loads]
1 the things that a vehicle or person is carrying or can carry 🔲 *The ship was carrying a load of new cars.* □ *There were two lorry loads of rubbish.* □ *Take another load upstairs.*
2 loads/a load an informal word meaning a large amount □ *We have loads to talk about.* □ **+ of** *He brought a load of food with him.*

loaf /ləʊf/ NOUN [plural loaves] a large piece of bread for cutting into smaller pieces □ **+ of** *a loaf of bread* □ *a brown sliced loaf*

loan¹ /ləʊn/ NOUN [plural loans] money that you borrow 🔲 *He wasn't able to repay the loan.* 🔲 *They took out a loan (= arranged to borrow money) to extend the house.* 🔲 *a bank loan*

loan² /ləʊn/ VERB [loans, loaning, loaned] to lend something to someone □ *My brother loaned me the money to buy a new car.*

loathe /ləʊð/ VERB [loathes, loathing, loathed] to hate someone or something □ *I loathe shopping.*
loaves /ləʊvz/ PLURAL OF **loaf**
lobster /ˈlɒbstə(r)/ NOUN [plural lobsters] a sea animal with a hard shell, two large claws (= hard curved parts) and eight legs

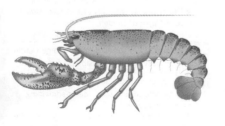

local /ˈləʊkəl/ ADJECTIVE to do with the area near to you □ *our local library* □ *a local newspaper*

🔲 *local government* 🔲 *Local residents are unhappy about the plans.*

locally /ˈləʊkəli/ ADVERB in or from the area near to you □ *Most of our vegetables are grown locally.* □ *The hill is known locally as Old Misty.*

locate /ləʊˈkeɪt/ VERB [locates, locating, located] be located by/in/near, etc. to be in a particular place □ *Their headquarters are located in Paris.* □ *The camps are mostly located near the border.*

location /ləʊˈkeɪʃən/ NOUN [plural locations] a place or position □ **+ of** *Nobody knows the exact location of the meeting.* □ *We have over 200 staff at 40 locations across the country.*

lock¹ /lɒk/ NOUN [plural locks] a device that fastens things such as doors and drawers, usually opened and closed using a key □ *There was no lock on the door.* □ *We had to change the lock on the front door.*

lock² /lɒk/ VERB [locks, locking, locked]
1 to fasten something such as a door with a key, or to be fastened this way 🔲 *Lock the door when you leave.* □ *This door doesn't lock.*
2 to put something or someone in a place that is locked □ **+ up** *He's a dangerous criminal who should be locked up.* □ **+ away** *I locked all my jewellery away in a box.* □ **+ in** *The medicines are locked in a cupboard.*

locker /ˈlɒkə(r)/ NOUN [plural lockers] a small cupboard, especially one that can be locked □ *I left my suitcase in a luggage locker at the station.*

lodge /lɒdʒ/ VERB [lodges, lodging, lodged] to live in a room in someone else's house and pay them rent

loft /lɒft/ NOUN [plural lofts] the space between the roof of a house and the rooms □ *Our suitcases are stored in the loft.*

log¹ /lɒg/ NOUN [plural logs] a part of a branch or tree that has been cut up

log² /lɒg/ VERB [logs, logging, logged] to make an official written record of something
♦ PHRASAL VERBS **log in/on** to start using a computer, website, etc. by typing in a word or code (= series of letters or numbers) **log off/out** to stop using a computer, website, etc. by clicking on something on the screen

logic /ˈlɒdʒɪk/ NOUN, NO PLURAL a way of thinking using facts and reason □ *I could see the logic of his argument.*

logo /ˈləʊgəʊ/ NOUN [plural logos] a design that is the symbol of a company or a product □ *The company has launched a new logo.*

lone /ləʊn/ ADJECTIVE alone, single or only □ *He was killed by a lone gunman.* 🔲 *She's a lone parent with two young children.*

loneliness /'ləʊnlɪnɪs/ NOUN, NO PLURAL when you are unhappy because you are alone □ *He felt a growing sense of loneliness.*

lonely /'ləʊnlɪ/ ADJECTIVE [lonelier, loneliest] unhappy because you are alone, with no friends around you 🗅 *She suddenly felt very lonely.* 🗅 *I get lonely at the weekends.*

long¹ /lɒŋ/ ADJECTIVE [longer, longest]
1 lasting a lot of time 🗅 *It took a long time to persuade her to come.* □ *There were long delays on the trains.*
2 measuring a long distance from one end to the other □ *She has very long hair.* □ *We went on a long journey.* □ *How long is the rope?* 🗅 *It's a long way home from here.*
3 having a certain length □ *The garden is 50m long.* □ *The film was three hours long.*

long² /lɒŋ/ ADVERB [longer, longest]
1 for a long time □ *Have you been waiting long?* □ *It won't be long till she starts school.* □ *The concert didn't last long.*
2 much earlier or later than the time you are talking about 🗅 *The house was knocked down long ago.* 🗅 *He was a vegetarian long before I met him.*
3 as long as used for saying that something must happen or be true before something else can happen or be true □ *You can borrow my jacket as long as you bring it back tomorrow.*

long³ /lɒŋ/ VERB [longs, longing, longed] to want something very much □ *I was longing to sit down.* □ *They were longing for a chance to rest.*

look¹ /lʊk/ VERB [looks, looking, looked]
1 to turn your eyes to see something □ **+ at** *She was looking at the view.* □ *Look behind you.* □ *Oh look, there's a deer over there!* □ *Look where you're going!*
2 to try to find something or someone □ **+ for** *I'm looking for my passport.*
3 to have a particular appearance □ *You look a bit tired.* □ *Kate looked fine when I saw her yesterday.*
4 to seem □ *It looks as if Joe won't be coming.* □ *His job prospects are looking good.*

> ➤ Notice the prepositions that are used with **look**. When you turn your eyes to see something (*sense 1*), you look **at** something:
> ✓ I looked **at** the clock.
> ✗ I looked the clock.

♦ PHRASAL VERBS **look after someone** to take care of someone or something □ *Her husband looks after the baby during the day.* **look forward to something** to feel pleased and excited about something that is going to happen □ *I'm really looking forward to meeting his family.*

> ➤ When *look forward to* is followed by a verb, the verb is in the *-ing* form:
> ✓ We're looking forward to seeing you!
> ✗ We're looking forward to see you.

look out to be careful because something might be dangerous □ *Look out! The path is very slippery.*
look something up to look in a book, on a computer, etc. to find information about something □ *I looked up the word 'digest' in the dictionary.*

look² /lʊk/ NOUN [plural looks]
1 when you look at something or someone 🗅 *May I have a look at your watch?* 🗅 *Take a look at these documents.* 🗅 *I had a good look round their house.*
2 when you try to find something or someone 🗅 *I had a look outside, but I couldn't see her.*
3 an expression on someone's face □ *She gave me a warning look.* □ *There was a look of fear on his face.*
4 the appearance of someone or something 🗅 *I don't like the look of those black clouds.*
5 someone's looks how attractive someone is □ *She is worried that she is losing her looks.*

loom /luːm/ NOUN [plural looms] a machine for making cloth

loop /luːp/ NOUN [plural loops] a circle of something such as a thread, a piece of string or a narrow piece of cloth □ *Make a loop and pull one end through it.*

loose /luːs/ ADJECTIVE [looser, loosest]
1 not tight or firmly fixed □ *a loose knot* □ *Wear loose, comfortable clothing.* 🗅 *One of the screws had come loose.*
2 not tied up or shut in □ *Her hair was hanging loose.* □ *Let the dogs run around loose.*

loosen /'luːsən/ VERB [loosens, loosening, loosened] to make something less firm, fixed or tight □ *I had to loosen my belt.* □ *She loosened her grip on Frank's arm.*

lord /lɔːd/ NOUN [plural lords]
1 used as the title of a man with a high social rank in the UK, or a man with this title □ *Lord Asquith* □ *the Lord Mayor of London*
2 Lord used in prayers as a way of addressing God

lorry /'lɒrɪ/ NOUN [plural lorries] a large vehicle for carrying heavy goods by road 🗅 *a lorry driver*

lose /luːz/ VERB [loses, losing, lost]
1 to not be able to find someone or something □ *I've lost my keys.*
2 to have something taken away from you 🗅 *Fifty people have lost their jobs.* 🗅 *He was willing to lose his life for his beliefs.*
3 to have less of something than you had before 🗅 *She has lost weight recently.* 🗅 *The children soon lost interest in the animals.* 🗅 *The business is losing money.*

4 to not have something you had before 🗫 *I was so angry, I lost control and started shouting.* 🗫 *I would hate to lose contact with my friends.* 🗫 *I lost sight* (= stopped being able to see) *of the train.*

5 to be beaten in a competition, election, etc. □ **+ by** *I lost by 4 games to 6.* 🗫 *We narrowly lost* (= only just lost) *the match.*

loss /lɒs/ NOUN [*plural* losses]

1 when you lose something □ *She was sacked over the loss of confidential documents.* □ **+ of** *He spoke about the loss of his home in a fire.* 🗫 *There will be some job losses.*

2 when a business spends more money than it earns, or this amount of money □ **+ of** *The company announced a pre-tax loss of £2 million.*

lost[1] /lɒst/ ADJECTIVE

1 if something is lost, nobody knows where it is □ *The painting has been lost for centuries.*

2 someone who is lost does not know where they are 🗫 *How did you get lost when you had a map?* 🗫 *We were hopelessly lost.*

lost[2] /lɒst/ PAST TENSE OF **lose**

lot /lɒt/ NOUN [*plural* lots]

1 a lot/lots a large number or amount □ **+ of** *There were a lot of people there.* □ *I bought lots of food.* □ *She doesn't eat a lot.* □ *We've got a lot to talk about.*

2 a lot better/happier/quicker, etc. much better/happier/quicker, etc. □ *You'd keep a lot warmer if you wore a hat.*

➤ Notice (*sense 1*) that **a** only goes before **lot** and not before **lots** □ *She has a lot of friends.* □ *She has lots of friends.*

lottery /ˈlɒtəri/ NOUN [*plural* lotteries] a game where people win money or prizes when their number or ticket is chosen by chance from many others 🗫 *He looked like he'd won the lottery.*

loud[1] /laʊd/ ADJECTIVE [louder, loudest] making a lot of sound 🗫 *a loud noise* 🗫 *She asked again in a louder voice.* ⊔ *The music was too loud for me.*

loud[2] /laʊd/ ADVERB [louder, loudest]

1 making a lot of sound □ *Could you speak a little louder please?* □ *I screamed as loud as I could.*

2 out loud so that other people can hear you □ *I read the letter out loud.* □ *She laughed out loud.*

loudly /ˈlaʊdli/ ADVERB making a lot of sound ⊔ *The crowds cheered loudly.* □ *I knocked again more loudly.*

lounge /laʊndʒ/ NOUN [*plural* lounges]

1 a room in a house where you sit and relax □ *I was watching TV in the lounge.*

2 a room in a public building where people can sit to relax or to wait □ *a hotel lounge* 🗫 *an airport lounge*

love[1] /lʌv/ VERB [loves, loving, loved]

1 to have a strong romantic feeling for someone □ *I love you.*

2 to have a strong emotional feeling for a friend or family member who you like and care about □ *I loved my mother very much.*

3 to like or enjoy something very much □ *I love Chinese food.* □ **+ ing** *He loves playing with the children.* □ **+ to do something** *I'd love to be able to play the piano.*

➤ **THESAURUS:** If you **like** someone, you think that they are pleasant. If you **love** or **adore** someone, you like them very much. If you **admire** someone, you like and respect them very much. Note that you can use all of these words to talk about things as well as people.

love[2] /lʌv/ NOUN [*plural* loves]

1 *no plural* a strong romantic feeling for someone 🗫 *She fell in love with him at university.* 🗫 *Within days, they were madly in love* (= loved each other very much). □ **+ for** *My love for him did not survive.*

2 *no plural* a strong emotional feeling for a friend or family member who you like and care about □ **+ for** *Her love for her children kept her going.*

3 *no plural* a feeling of liking or enjoying something very much □ **+ of** *I did not share her love of opera.*

4 *no plural* used at the end of a letter □ *Hope to see you soon. Love, Emma.* □ *Have a great birthday. Lots of love, Mum.*

lovely /ˈlʌvli/ ADJECTIVE [lovelier, loveliest]

1 beautiful or attractive □ *She has lovely eyes.* 🗫 *You look lovely in that dress.*

2 enjoyable or pleasant □ *It was lovely to see you again.* □ *It was a lovely evening.*

3 kind and friendly □ *She's a really lovely woman.*

lover /ˈlʌvə(r)/ NOUN [*plural* lovers]

1 a person who is having a romantic relationship with someone else

2 someone who is very interested in or enthusiastic about something □ *an art lover* □ *a music lover* □ *I've always been an animal lover.*

loving /ˈlʌvɪŋ/ ADJECTIVE

1 showing or expressing love □ *a loving look* □ *She has a very loving family.*

2 in loving memory used to remember someone who has died ⊔ *in loving memory of my father, John.*

low[1] /ləʊ/ ADJECTIVE [lower, lowest]

1 near to the ground or short in height □ *a low hedge* □ *I can reach the lowest branches.*

2 less than usual in amount or level □ *We are experiencing very low temperatures.* □ *I try to look*

for the lowest prices. □ *The risk of frost is very low now.* □ + **in** *Skimmed milk is low in fat.*
3 a low sound or musical note is near the bottom of the range of sounds
4 quiet □ *He spoke in a low voice.*

low² /ləʊ/ ADVERB [lower, lowest] in or to a low position or level □ *Their supplies began to run low.* □ *They flew low over the desert.*

lower /'ləʊə(r)/ VERB [lowers, lowering, lowered]
1 to reduce something in amount or degree □ *They have lowered their prices.* 🔂 *A good diet can lower your risk of heart disease.* 🔂 *She lowered her voice to a whisper.*
2 to move something to a position nearer the bottom of something or nearer the ground □ + **into** *They lowered the boat into the water.* □ *She lowered her head slightly.*

loyal /'lɔɪəl/ ADJECTIVE always supporting or being a friend to someone 🔂 *a loyal fan* 🔂 *We want to reward loyal customers.* 🔂 *He remained loyal to the king.*

loyalty /'lɔɪəltɪ/ NOUN, NO PLURAL being loyal to someone 🔂 *You always have a sense of loyalty to your home town.* □ + **to** *The fans have demonstrated their loyalty to the team.*

Ltd ABBREVIATION Limited; used in the names of companies □ *Joe Bloggs Shoes Ltd*

luck /lʌk/ NOUN, NO PLURAL
1 when something good happens by chance 🔂 *With a bit of luck, we'll be there by lunch time.* 🔂 *Meeting Tim was a real piece of luck.* 🔂 *I wished him luck with his exam.*
2 the way things happen by chance 🔂 *bad/good luck* □ *Whether or not you'll get on the course depends on your luck.*
3 when you are successful at something 🔂 *Have you had any luck selling your house?* □ *I've been trying to buy a wedding dress, but without any luck so far.*
4 **Good luck!** used to tell someone that you hope they will succeed □ *Good luck with your exams.*

lucky /'lʌkɪ/ ADJECTIVE [luckier, luckiest]
1 a lucky person has good luck □ + **to do something** *You're lucky to live so near the school.* □ + **that** *It's lucky that they didn't discover the truth.*
2 bringing good luck □ *a lucky charm*

luggage /'lʌgɪdʒ/ NOUN, NO PLURAL a traveller's bags and cases 🔂 *I was only travelling with hand*

luggage. 🔂 *Each passenger can check in two pieces of luggage.* 🔂 *a luggage rack*

> ➤ Remember that the noun **luggage** is not used in the plural:
> ✓ *I had so much luggage .*
> ✗ *I had so many luggages.*

lump /lʌmp/ NOUN [plural lumps]
1 a small piece of something without a clear shape □ + **of** *a lump of coal* □ *a bowl of sugar lumps*
2 a hard piece of tissue growing on or in your body □ *She found a lump in her breast.*

lunch /lʌntʃ/ NOUN [plural lunches] the meal that you eat in the middle of the day 🔂 *I had a sandwich for lunch.* 🔂 *I had lunch with a friend.* 🔂 *We ate lunch in a small café.* 🔂 *I'll call you during my lunch break.*

lunchtime /'lʌntʃtaɪm/ NOUN [plural lunchtimes] the time in the middle of the day when you have a meal □ *I'll meet you at lunchtime.* □ *They arrived yesterday lunchtime.*

lung /lʌŋ/ NOUN [plural lungs] one of the two organs inside your chest like bags that you use for breathing. A biology word.

lure /ljʊə(r)/ VERB [lures, luring, lured] to persuade a person or an animal to do something using a reward □ *Scraps of food are used to lure the animals.* □ *They're offering special deals to lure customers back.*

lurk /lɜːk/ VERB [lurks, lurking, lurked] to wait secretly where you cannot be seen, especially because you are going to do something bad □ *Someone was lurking in the bushes.*

luxurious /lʌg'ʒʊərɪəs/ ADJECTIVE very comfortable and expensive □ *The hotel room was very luxurious.* □ *She enjoyed a luxurious lifestyle.*

luxury /'lʌkʃərɪ/ NOUN [plural luxuries]
1 a situation in which you are very comfortable, with expensive or beautiful things □ *They live in luxury.* □ *We stayed in five-star luxury.* □ *a luxury hotel* □ *luxury goods*
2 something that is pleasant, and often expensive, but not necessary □ *We couldn't afford luxuries such as chocolate.*

lyrics /'lɪrɪks/ PLURAL NOUN the words of a song □ *He wrote the lyrics for most of their songs.*

M*m*

M or **m** /em/ the 13th letter of the alphabet

m /em/ ABBREVIATION **metre** or **metres**, or **million**

machine /mə'ʃiːn/ NOUN [*plural* machines] a piece of equipment that uses power to do a particular job □ *a washing machine* □ *a coffee machine* ⬚ *He used a fax machine in the office.* □ *Cows are usually milked by machine.*

> ➤ THESAURUS: A machine is a piece of equipment that uses power to do a particular job. An engine is part of a machine that uses energy to produce movement. For example, a car is a machine which has an engine to make it move. A motor is a smaller type of engine. For example, a car's engine contains motors to make the various parts work.

machine gun /mə'ʃiːn ˌɡʌn/ NOUN [*plural* machine guns] an automatic gun that fires a lot of bullets very quickly

machinery /mə'ʃiːnəri/ NOUN, NO PLURAL big machines □ *farm machinery* ⬚ *Cranes and other heavy machinery were used to remove the rocks.*

mad /mæd/ ADJECTIVE [madder, maddest]
1 an informal word meaning stupid □ *Swimming where you know there are sharks is a mad thing to do.* □ *I thought he was mad wanting to climb Everest.*
2 mentally ill ⬚ *The poor woman went mad with grief.*
3 a mainly US word meaning very angry □ *I got mad at him for lying to me.*
4 go mad an informal phrase meaning to become very angry or behave in a way that is not controlled □ *She'll go mad if she finds out you tricked her.*
5 be mad about/on someone/something to like someone or something very much □ *He's mad about football.*
6 like mad (a) as quickly as possible and using a lot of energy □ *She was running like mad to keep up with the others.* (b) a lot □ *My arms were hurting like mad.*

madam /'mædəm/ NOUN [*plural* madams]
1 a formal and polite word used for talking to a woman, for example when serving her in a shop or restaurant □ *Can I help you, madam?*

2 Dear Madam a way of beginning a formal letter to a woman when you do not know her name □ *Dear Madam, I'm writing to enquire about the job which was advertised in the newspaper.*

made /meɪd/ PAST TENSE AND PAST PARTICIPLE OF **make**

madness /'mædnɪs/ NOUN, NO PLURAL stupid or dangerous behaviour ⬚ *In a moment of madness he hit the other man.*

magazine /ˌmæɡə'ziːn/ NOUN [*plural* magazines] a thin book with pictures in it which is usually published every week or every month ⬚ *Amy was reading a magazine.* □ *a fashion magazine* □ *a magazine article*

magic[1] /'mædʒɪk/ NOUN, NO PLURAL
1 a strange power that some people believe exists, causing strange things to happen that you cannot explain ⬚ *Wizards use magic.*
2 tricks, such as making things disappear, which are done to entertain people □ *Children love watching magic.*

magic[2] /'mædʒɪk/ ADJECTIVE
1 involving tricks such as making things disappear ⬚ *magic tricks* □ *a magic show*
2 able to make impossible things happen ⬚ *a magic wand* □ *a magic potion*

magical /'mædʒɪkəl/ ADJECTIVE
1 special and exciting or attractive □ *a magical atmosphere* □ *a magical place*
2 done using magic, or having magic powers □ *magical powers* □ *magical healing*
• **magically** /'mædʒɪkəli/ ADVERB using magic, or in a way that seems to be magic □ *The next morning, the missing books had magically reappeared on the shelf.*

magician /mə'dʒɪʃən/ NOUN [*plural* magicians]
1 someone who does magic tricks to entertain people
2 someone who has magic powers, especially in stories

magistrate /'mædʒɪstreɪt/ NOUN [*plural* magistrates] a judge who deals with crimes which are not of the most serious type

magnet /'mægnɪt/ NOUN [*plural* magnets] a piece of iron which makes other metal objects move towards it

magnetic /mæg'netɪk/ ADJECTIVE having the power to attract metal objects □ *Iron has magnetic properties.* □ *The satellite will measure the sun's magnetic field.*

maid /meɪd/ NOUN [*plural* maids] a woman whose job is to keep the rooms clean and tidy in a hotel or house

mail¹ /meɪl/ NOUN, NO PLURAL
1 letters and packages which are sent by post □ *My mail was delivered to the wrong address.*
2 the system of sending and delivering letters and packages □ *His passport was sent in the mail.*

➤ Remember that the noun **mail** is not used in the plural:
✓ *We get a lot of mail.*
✗ *We get a lot of mails.*

➤ **THESAURUS:** A letter is a message that you write and send to another person. A parcel is something wrapped in paper and sent somewhere. Correspondence is letters that people write to each other, or the activity of writing letters. The mail or the post is the service that collects and delivers letters and parcels, or the letters and parcels which are sent.

mail² /meɪl/ VERB [mails, mailing, mailed]
1 to send a letter or package in the post
2 to e-mail someone □ *I'll mail you some photos.*

main /meɪn/ ADJECTIVE biggest or most important
□ *The main reason I do sport is to improve my health.* □ *a main road* □ *Police guarded the main entrance of the building.*

mainly /'meɪnlɪ/ ADVERB mostly or in most cases
□ *Her job mainly involves organizing conferences.*

□ *We chose Spain mainly because of the weather.*
□ *The spice is used mainly in Indian cooking.*

maintain /meɪn'teɪn/ VERB [maintains, maintaining, maintained]
1 to make something continue at the same level or in the same way as before □ *Players need to maintain their fitness levels.* □ *The Republican Party has maintained control of the country.*
2 to keep a house or piece of equipment in good condition □ *The car wasn't maintained properly.*

maintenance /'meɪntənəns/ NOUN, NO PLURAL regular cleaning or repairs done to keep something in good condition 🔁 *The bridge has been closed for maintenance work.*

majesty /'mædʒəstɪ/ NOUN [*plural* majesties]
His/Her/Your Majesty a title used when speaking to or about a king or queen □ *Her Majesty will be attending a Thanksgiving service next week.*

major¹ /'meɪdʒə(r)/ ADJECTIVE very big, serious or important □ *a major problem* □ *major changes* □ *The company has offices in all major cities.*

major² /'meɪdʒə(r)/ NOUN [*plural* majors] an army officer above the rank of captain

majority /mə'dʒɒrətɪ/ NOUN [*plural* majorities]
no plural most of the people or things in a group
□ **+ of** *The study showed that a majority of people have access to the Internet.* □ *The illness is linked to diet in the majority of cases.* 🔁 *The vast majority of students agreed with the proposal.*

make /meɪk/ VERB [makes, making, made]
1 to create or produce something □ *I'll make dinner.* □ *She makes all the children's clothes.* □ *They've made a film of the book.* □ *The children were making so much noise.*
2 to cause someone to feel a particular emotion □ *It made me so angry.* □ *That film makes me cry.*
3 to force someone to do something □ *My parents made me do my homework.* □ *No one is going to make you go if you don't want to.*
4 used with some nouns to do with speech □ *May I make a suggestion?* □ *He made a very strange comment.* □ *I've made a complaint.* □ *He made an interesting point.*
5 make a **decision** to decide something □ *Have you made a decision yet?*
6 make a **mistake** to do something wrong □ *Everyone makes mistakes.*
7 to earn money □ *He makes about $90,000 a year.* □ *You can make a lot of money in banking.*
8 to be the total amount of two or more numbers added together □ *Six and six makes twelve.*
9 make do to accept or use something although it is not exactly what you wanted □ *If we can't borrow Andrew's van we'll have to make do with the car.*
10 make it to manage to go somewhere or manage to arrive somewhere in time to do something □ *If we run we might just make it before the train leaves.*
◆ PHRASAL VERBS **make something into**

something to change something so that it becomes something else □ *We've made the spare room into an office.* make something/someone out to be able to see or hear something or someone although with difficulty □ *His voice was very low but I could just make out what he said.* make up to become friendly again after an argument make up something to give an explanation that is not true □ *He made up some excuse about the train being late.*

> ► THESAURUS: Make is a general word. To manufacture something means to make it in a factory. If you construct or build something, you make it by putting materials or parts together. Produce is also a general word for making or creating things. When we talk about growing things such as crops, we usually use the word produce. A tree produces fruit, for example.

make-up /ˈmeɪkʌp/ NOUN, NO PLURAL coloured substances that you put on your face to improve or change your appearance 🕮 *A lot of women wear make-up.* 🕮 *She was putting on her make-up.*

malaria /məˈleərɪə/ NOUN, NO PLURAL a serious tropical disease which people can get if they are bitten by a mosquito (= type of insect)

male[1] /meɪl/ ADJECTIVE belonging to the sex that does not have babies □ *male students* □ *a male swan* □ *The group's members are mostly male.*

male[2] /meɪl/ NOUN [plural males] a male person or animal □ *Thirty thousand adult males disappear every year.*

mall /mɔːl, mæl/ NOUN [plural malls] a shopping centre that is indoors

mammal /ˈmæməl/ NOUN [plural mammals] an animal that feeds its babies on milk from its own body □ *Humans, cows and dogs are mammals.*

man /mæn/ NOUN [plural men]
1 an adult male human □ *a young man* □ *an old man* □ *a married man* □ *I work mainly with men.*
2 no plural humans considered as a group □ *Man is closely related to the ape.*

manage /ˈmænɪdʒ/ VERB [manages, managing, managed]
1 to succeed in doing something □ + to do something *The prisoners managed to escape.* □ *We couldn't manage without your help.* □ *Emma managed a smile even though she didn't feel very happy.*
2 to be in charge of a business, team, etc. □ *Who manages the business for you?* □ *Alan is managing the new project.*

management /ˈmænɪdʒmənt/ NOUN, NO PLURAL
1 the job of controlling a business or activity □ *a job in management* 🕮 *management skills*
2 the people who control a company □ *The management has agreed to further talks.* □ *The restaurant is under new management.* 🕮 *senior management*
3 the way that something is controlled □ + of *The government's successful management of the economy continues.*

manager /ˈmænɪdʒə(r)/ NOUN [plural managers] someone who is in charge of a company, team, etc. □ *a project manager* □ *a football manager* 🕮 *She's a senior manager for a law firm.* □ + of *Can I speak to the manager of the hotel, please?*
• **manageress** /ˌmænɪdʒəˈres/ NOUN [plural manageresses] a woman who is in charge of a restaurant, shop, etc.

manipulate /məˈnɪpjuleɪt/ VERB [manipulates, manipulating, manipulated] to control someone or something so that they do what you want, often in a dishonest way □ *He knew how to manipulate the media.*

mankind /ˌmænˈkaɪnd/ NOUN, NO PLURAL all humans □ *This is one of the most terrible diseases in the history of mankind.*

man-made /ˌmænˈmeɪd/ ADJECTIVE made or caused by people and not natural □ *a man-made lake* □ *man-made disasters*

manner /ˈmænə(r)/ NOUN [plural manners]
1 the way in which something happens or is done □ *The boys behaved in a very responsible manner.* □ + of *The manner of his death was extremely shocking.*
2 manners polite ways of behaving in a social situation 🕮 *His parents taught him good manners.* 🕮 *It's bad manners* (= it is not polite) *to talk when your mouth is full of food.* 🕮 *She needs to learn some manners.*

mansion /ˈmænʃən/ NOUN [plural mansions] a very large, expensive house

manslaughter /ˈmænslɔːtə(r)/ NOUN, NO PLURAL the crime of killing someone but not intentionally

manual[1] /ˈmænjuəl/ ADJECTIVE involving your hands or physical strength 🕮 *manual work* 🕮 *manual labour*

manual[2] /ˈmænjuəl/ NOUN [plural manuals] a book that tells you how to do something such as use a machine

manufacture /ˌmænjuˈfæktʃə(r)/ VERB [manufactures, manufacturing, manufactured] to make something in a factory □ *The company manufactures car parts*

manufacturer /ˌmænjuˈfæktʃərə(r)/ NOUN [plural manufacturers] a company that makes something in a factory □ *food manufacturers*

many /'menɪ/ DETERMINER, PRONOUN [plural more, most]

1 a lot or a large number □ *Were there many people at the party?* □ *We've had so many problems.* □ *There are too many people here.* □ *She doesn't have many friends.*

2 how many used to ask about the number of something □ *How many chairs will you need?*

> ➤ Remember that **many** is used with the plural forms of *countable* nouns. It is not used with *uncountable* nouns:
> ✓ How **many** plates do we need?
> ✗ How many food do we need?
> With uncountable nouns, the word **much** is used: □ How much food do we need?

map /mæp/ NOUN [plural maps] a drawing of an area which shows things such as roads, rivers and hills □ *Where's Tokyo on this map?* 🔁 *Emma stopped the car and looked at the map.* 🔁 *She drew a little map to show where her house was.* 🔁 *a road map* □ **+ of** *Have you got a map of France?*

marathon /'mærəθən/ NOUN [plural marathons] a race in which people run approximately 26 miles or 42 kilometres 🔁 *She ran her first marathon last year.*

marble /'maːbəl/ NOUN [plural marbles]

1 *no plural* a type of smooth stone used for making things □ *a marble statue*

2 a small glass ball that children play with

March /maːtʃ/ NOUN [plural Marches] the third month of the year, after February and before April □ *I'm going to Chile in March.*

march¹ /maːtʃ/ VERB [marches, marching, marched]

1 if soldiers march, they walk together with the same, regular steps

2 to walk somewhere quickly in an angry, confident or determined way □ **+ into/out of** *He marched into the office and demanded to speak to the manager.*

3 to walk with many other people in order to protest (= show that you disagree) about something □ **+ through** *Anti-war protesters marched through the streets.*

march² /maːtʃ/ NOUN [plural marches]

1 an event in which a large group of people walk somewhere to protest (= show that they disagree) about something □ **+ against** *2,000 people took part in a march against the new employment laws.*

2 a walk with regular steps done by soldiers □ *a slow march*

margin /'maːdʒɪn/ NOUN [plural margins] the empty space at the side of a page □ *The teacher had written some comments in the margin.*

marine¹ /məˈriːn/ ADJECTIVE to do with the sea and the animals that live there □ *marine animals* □ *the marine environment*

marine² /məˈriːn/ NOUN [plural marines] a soldier who fights on land and at sea

mark¹ /maːk/ NOUN [plural marks]

1 an area of something that is a different colour from the thing it is on □ *There's a dirty mark on the sofa.* □ *The rabbit's fur is brown, with black marks.* □ *The bite marks have gone now.*

2 a number or letter that says how well you have done a piece of school work, exam, etc. 🔁 *a high/low mark* 🔁 *He got top marks* (= the best possible marks) *in all his exams.*

> ➤ **THESAURUS:** A mark is an area of something that is a different colour from the thing it is on. A spot is a round shape that is often part of a pattern. A stain is a dirty mark on something that is difficult to remove. A scratch is a mark left on a surface by something sharp.

mark² /maːk/ VERB [marks, marking, marked]

1 to judge the quality of and correct a student's work, exam, etc.

2 to make a mark on the surface of something □ *Shoes with black soles may mark this floor.*

3 to write words or a symbol on something □ *I've marked on the list the people I want to see.* □ *Go along the path marked 'exit'.*

market /'maːkɪt/ NOUN [plural markets]

1 a building or outside area where people sell things □ *a street market* □ *an outdoor market* □ *a fish market* 🔁 *a market stall*

2 the people who want to buy something □ *There is a huge market for mobile phones.* □ *Our main market is in Europe.* □ *The magazine is aimed at the teenage market.*

3 on the market available for people to buy □ *The house has been on the market for six months.*

marriage /'mærɪdʒ/ NOUN [plural marriages]

1 the legal relationship of being husband and wife □ *My parents had a long and happy marriage.*

2 the ceremony in which a man and woman become husband and wife □ *The marriage took place in St Paul's Cathedral.*

> ➤ Notice that a **marriage** is a ceremony in which a man and woman become husband and wife. The occasion when two people become husband and wife, when friends and family dance and eat, etc. is called a **wedding**:
> ✓ I was invited to the wedding.
> ✗ I was invited to the marriage.

married /ˈmærɪd/ ADJECTIVE
1 having a husband or wife □ *a married man* □ *a married couple* □ **+ to** *Miranda is married to John.* 🔊 *They are getting married in June.*
2 to do with marriage □ *married life*

marry /ˈmærɪ/ VERB [marries, marrying, married]
1 to make someone your husband or wife in a special ceremony □ *Andrew has asked me to marry him.* □ *Her brother never married.*
2 to officially perform the ceremony that makes two people become husband and wife □ *They were married by the bishop.*

marsh /mɑːʃ/ NOUN [plural marshes] an area of land that is soft and wet all the time

marvellous /ˈmɑːvələs/ ADJECTIVE extremely good □ *That's marvellous news!*

masculine /ˈmæskjʊlɪn/ ADJECTIVE
1 to do with men, or having qualities that are typical of a man □ *a deep, masculine voice*
2 in English grammar, masculine forms of words refer to males. For example, *he* is a masculine pronoun.

mask[1] /mɑːsk/ NOUN [plural masks] something that you wear over your face in order to protect it, to hide or for decoration □ *a carnival mask* □ *The surgeon removed his mask to speak to her.*

mask[2] /mɑːsk/ VERB [masks, masking, masked] to prevent something such as a feeling or smell from being noticed □ *She sprayed air freshener to mask the cooking smells.*

mass /mæs/ NOUN [plural masses]
1 a large lump or quantity of something with no clear shape □ **+ of** *After the crash, the car was a mass of tangled metal.* □ *The little girl had a mass of blonde curls.*
2 masses a lot of something. An informal word. □ *He's got masses of toys.*
3 Mass a ceremony in some Christian churches in which people eat bread and drink wine

massacre /ˈmæsəkə(r)/ NOUN [plural massacres] the killing of a large number of people

massage[1] /ˈmæsɑːʒ/ VERB [massages, massaging, massaged] to rub parts of a person's body in order to make them relax or to make the muscles less painful □ *Could you massage my shoulders?*

massage[2] /ˈmæsɑːʒ/ NOUN [plural massages] when someone rubs parts of a person's body in order to make them relax or to make the muscles less painful 🔊 *I gave her a foot massage.*

massive /ˈmæsɪv/ ADJECTIVE very big □ *She earns a massive amount of money.*

mast /mɑːst/ NOUN [plural masts]
1 a tall pole used for sending out radio, television or mobile phone signals
2 a tall pole for holding the sails of a boat or ship

master[1] /ˈmɑːstə(r)/ NOUN [plural masters]
1 a man who has control over something □ *a dog and its master*
2 someone who is very good at a particular activity □ *a master of disguise*

master[2] /ˈmɑːstə(r)/ VERB [masters, mastering, mastered] to learn how to do something well □ *Juggling needs quite a lot of practice before you master it.*

mat /mæt/ NOUN [plural mats]
1 a flat piece of material for covering or protecting part of a floor □ *a door mat*
2 a small piece of material for putting under something to protect a table's surface □ *a table mat*

match[1] /mætʃ/ NOUN [plural matches]
1 a sports competition between two players or two teams 🔊 *a football match* 🔊 *Who won the match?*
2 a short, thin piece of wood with a substance on the end that produces fire when it is rubbed on a rough surface 🔊 *He struck a match to light a candle.*
3 something that is similar to another thing or suitable to be with another thing, especially in its colour or pattern □ *This isn't the same make of paint but it's a very good match.*

match[2] /mætʃ/ VERB [matches, matching, matched]
1 to be the same colour or style □ *Her handbag matched her shoes.* □ *His handwriting matched that on the letter.*
2 to put two people or things together because they are suitable for each other □ **+ to** *Match the word on the left to its meaning on the right.*

mate[1] /meɪt/ NOUN [plural mates]
1 an informal word for a friend □ *He's a good mate of mine.* 🔊 *She's my best mate.*
2 the male or female that an animal breeds with

mate[2] /meɪt/ VERB [mates, mating, mated] animals and birds mate when they have sex to produce babies □ *Swans mate for life.*

material /mə'tɪərɪəl/ NOUN [plural materials]
1 cloth □ The jacket was made of a very thick material.
2 a substance used for making something else □ building materials □ raw materials for the steel industry

maternal /mə'tɜ:nəl/ ADJECTIVE
1 to do with, or typical of, a mother □ maternal feelings 🖪 a maternal instinct
2 related through your mother's side of your family □ your maternal grandmother

math /mæθ/ NOUN, NO PLURAL the US word for **maths**

mathematical /,mæθə'mætɪkəl/ ADJECTIVE to do with or using mathematics □ a mathematical genius □ a mathematical calculation

mathematics /,mæθə'mætɪks/ NOUN, NO PLURAL the study of measurements, numbers, quantities and shapes. A formal word.

maths /mæθs/ NOUN, NO PLURAL a short way to say and write **mathematics**

matinée /'mætɪneɪ/ NOUN [plural matinées] a performance at a theatre or cinema in the afternoon

matter¹ /'mætə(r)/ NOUN [plural matters]
1 a subject or situation □ He wants to see you to discuss a personal matter. □ We need to think about all the practical matters. □ + for This is a matter for the police.
2 the matter used to talk about something that is wrong with something or causing a problem
🖪 What's the matter with Rachel? She's very quiet.
🖪 I know something's the matter with Eve. □ What's the matter with these tomatoes? They look brown.
3 no plural any substance that takes up space and is part of the physical universe
4 as a matter of fact used to add information or to say that something that has just been said is wrong □ As a matter of fact, he's one of the richest men in the country.

matter² /'mætə(r)/ VERB [matters, mattering, mattered] to be important 🖪 It doesn't matter if you're late – we can save you some food. □ Does it matter if the door isn't completely closed? □ Winning matters to him more than it should.

mattress /'mætrɪs/ NOUN [plural mattresses] the thick, soft part of a bed, that you lie on

mature¹ /mə'tjʊə(r)/ ADJECTIVE
1 completely grown or developed □ a mature male elephant □ mature trees
2 behaving in a sensible way, like an adult □ He's a very mature 13-year-old.

mature² /mə'tjʊə(r)/ VERB [matures, maturing, matured]

1 to become completely grown or developed
2 to start to behave in a sensible way, like an adult

maximum¹ /'mæksɪməm/ NOUN, NO PLURAL the greatest amount or degree that is possible or allowed □ The maximum I'm prepared to pay is £200. □ The car will hold a maximum of five people.

maximum² /'mæksɪməm/ ADJECTIVE being the greatest amount or degree that is possible or allowed □ The maximum speed limit is 40 mph on this road. □ The crime carries a maximum penalty of five years' imprisonment.

May /meɪ/ NOUN [plural Mays] the fifth month of the year, after April and before June □ The weather was awful in May.

may /meɪ/ MODAL VERB
1 used to talk about the possibility that something is true or something will happen □ I may apply for the job, but I'm not sure yet. □ He thinks she may be lying.
2 a formal word used for asking for or giving permission □ May I ask what you're doing in my room? □ You may leave the table now.

maybe /'meɪbi:/ ADVERB possibly □ Maybe she called earlier. □ Maybe they're not coming. □ It'll take two, maybe three, days to paint the room.

mayor /meə(r)/ NOUN [plural mayors] a man or woman elected as the official leader of a town or city

me /mi:/ PRONOUN used as the object in a sentence to talk or write about yourself □ Would you make me a cup of tea, please? □ Are there any letters for me? □ Hi, it's me. Sorry, but I'm going to be late.

➤ Remember that **me** is used after a verb or preposition. In a sentence in which you are doing the action, use **I** before the verb: □ I gave her some flowers. □ He gave **me** some flowers.

meal /mi:l/ NOUN [plural meals] food that you eat at one time, for example breakfast 🖪 We're going out for a meal on Saturday night. 🖪 I have my main meal in the evening.

➤ THESAURUS: Meal is a general word for food that you eat at a particular time. The first meal that you eat in the morning is called breakfast. The meal that you eat in the middle of the day is usually called lunch. This meal is also sometimes called dinner. Usually, dinner is the main meal in the evening. Some people call this meal tea. A lighter meal in the evening or in the afternoon is also called tea. A snack is a small amount of food that you eat between meals.

mean¹ /mi:n/ VERB [means, meaning, meant]
1 to have a particular meaning □ What does 'intrepid' mean? □ Her name means 'lucky' in Arabic.
2 to try to express an opinion or a fact □ I didn't know

what she meant when she told me to speak like a lady. □ *What did she mean by 'too academic'?* 🔁 *I see what you mean about his bad temper.*
3 to intend to do something □ **+ to do something** *I'm sorry. I didn't mean to upset you.* □ *Did you mean to take this turning?*
4 to be a sign that something will happen, or to have a particular result □ **+ that** *Higher wages meant that more people could afford cars.* □ *Dark clouds usually mean rain.*
5 be meant to do something if you are meant to do something, someone has said that you must do it □ *I'm meant to do my homework before I watch TV.*

mean² /miːn/ ADJECTIVE [meaner, meanest]
1 a mean person does not like spending money or giving things to other people □ *She's too mean to pay to have her hair cut.*
2 unkind □ *Mum, Adam's being mean to me!*

mean³ /miːn/ NOUN [plural means] the average. A mathematics word.
➡ go to **means**

meaning /ˈmiːnɪŋ/ NOUN [plural meanings]
1 what a word or action expresses □ *The music conveys the meaning of the text.* □ *I didn't understand the meaning of his words.* □ *We searched for a hidden meaning in his letter.*
2 importance or purpose □ *We all want to understand the meaning of life.* □ *He helped me understand the meaning of these events.*

means /miːnz/ NOUN [plural means]
1 a way or method of doing something □ *a means of transport* □ *a means of payment*
2 money □ *Does he have the means to buy a car?*
3 by all means used to politely give someone permission to do something □ *'Can I have a look at your magazine?' 'By all means.'*
4 by no means not at all or in no way □ *It was by no means the worst talk I'd heard.*

meant /ment/ PAST TENSE AND PAST PARTICIPLE OF **mean**¹ □ *I meant every word I said.* □ *She had meant to tell him but forgot.*

meantime /ˈmiːntaɪm/ NOUN, NO PLURAL in the meantime in the time before something happens □ *We're having the car repaired but in the meantime we're borrowing my sister's.*

meanwhile /ˈmiːnwaɪl/ ADVERB
1 in the time before something happens □ *I'll start the report once the sales figures are in. Meanwhile I've got plenty of work to do.*
2 at the same time □ *Tom was enjoying himself with his friends. Meanwhile, I was working like crazy back here.*

measles /ˈmiːzəlz/ NOUN, NO PLURAL an infectious disease, especially among children, in which you feel very hot and your skin is covered in red spots

measure¹ /ˈmeʒə(r)/ VERB [measures, measuring, measured]
1 to find how tall, long, wide, fast, etc. something is □ *She was measuring the window for some new curtains.*
2 to be a particular size □ *The room measures 3.5 metres from the door to the window.*

measure² /ˈmeʒə(r)/ NOUN [plural measures]
1 an official action done to achieve something or deal with something 🔁 *The school is being closed as a temporary measure.* 🔁 *The government is introducing new measures to fight crime.*
2 a unit used in measuring □ *A kilogram is a measure of weight, while a kilometre is a measure of distance or length.*

measurement /ˈmeʒəmənt/ NOUN [plural measurements] a size or amount found by measuring □ *Can you write down the exact measurements of the floor?*

➤ **THESAURUS:** A measurement is a size or amount found by measuring. A thing's size is how big, small, long, wide etc. it is. Length is how long something is from one end to the other end. Height is how tall or high someone or something is. Note that we only use height to talk about people, not length. Width is how much a thing measures from side to side. Depth is the distance from the top to the bottom of something.

meat /miːt/ NOUN [plural meats] the flesh of animals eaten as food 🔁 *red meat such as beef* 🔁 *white meat such as chicken*

➤ **THESAURUS:** Meat is a general word for the flesh of animals eaten as food. The meat that we get from a cow is called beef. The meat that we get from a pig is called pork. Thin slices of salty meat from a pig are called bacon. Thin slices of cooked meat from the leg of a pig are called ham. The meat we get from a sheep is usually called lamb.

mechanic /mɪˈkænɪk/ NOUN [plural mechanics] someone whose job is to repair vehicles and machines 🔁 *a car mechanic*

mechanical /mɪˈkænɪkəl/ ADJECTIVE to do with machines □ *There must have been a mechanical failure.* □ *a mechanical device*

mechanism /ˈmekənɪzəm/ NOUN [plural mechanisms] a working part of a machine, or its system of working parts □ *The springs are part of the clock's mechanism.*

medal /ˈmedəl/ NOUN [plural medals] a metal disk given as a prize in a competition or for brave actions 🔁 *an Olympic medal* 🔁 *a gold/silver/bronze medal* 🔁 *He was awarded a medal for bravery.*

media /'miːdɪə/ PLURAL NOUN the media
newspapers, television and radio or other
means of communicating information to the public
□ *There was nothing in the media about his speech.*
median /'miːdɪən/ ADJECTIVE being the median. A
mathematics word □ *the median price/age*

medical /'medɪkəl/ ADJECTIVE to do with
medicine or doctors and their work 🔁 *He did not
need any medical treatment.* 🔁 *She's receiving the
best medical care.* 🔁 *the medical staff* 🔁 *a serious
medical condition*

medicine /'medɪsɪn/ NOUN [*plural* medicines]
1 a substance used to treat or prevent illnesses
□ *cough medicine* 🔁 *Have you taken your medicine?*
2 *no plural* the science of treating and preventing
illnesses 🔁 *He studied medicine at the University of
Melbourne.* □ *traditional Chinese medicine*

medieval /ˌmedɪˈiːvəl/ ADJECTIVE to do with the
period of history from about 1000 to 1500 □ *a
medieval castle*

medium /'miːdɪəm/ ADJECTIVE in the middle of a
group of amounts or sizes □ *He is dark and of medium
height.* □ *Heat a large pan over a medium heat.*
🔁 *Small and medium sized businesses will be affected.*

meet /miːt/ VERB [meets, meeting, met]
1 to come to the same place as someone else by
chance □ *Guess who I met in town?*
2 to come to the same place as someone else because
you have arranged to see them □ *Let's meet for a
coffee next week.* □ *Is there anywhere we can meet
privately?* □ *The committee meets once a month.*
3 to wait for someone at a particular place
where they will arrive □ *We'll meet her at the airport.*
4 to be with and speak to someone for the first time
□ *Have you met my big sister, Jane?* 🔁 *I'm very
pleased to meet you at last.*

♦ PHRASAL VERB **meet up** to come together with other
people in order to do something □ *We meet up about
once a week for a chat.*

meeting /'miːtɪŋ/ NOUN [*plural* meetings] a time
when people come together, especially to discuss
something □ *We need to arrange a meeting to discuss
this matter.* □ *Anne's in a meeting at the moment.*

melody /'melədɪ/ NOUN [*plural* melodies] a tune,
especially one that is pleasant to listen to □ *The
song had a lovely melody.*
melon /'melən/ NOUN [*plural* melons] a large
round fruit with a thick green or yellow skin and
sweet, yellow or orange flesh

melt /melt/ VERB [melts, melting, melted] to
become soft or liquid when heated □ *By afternoon
the snow had melted.* □ *Salt is used to melt ice on
roads.* □ *Stir in the melted butter.*

member /'membə(r)/ NOUN [*plural* members] a
person who belongs to a group or organization □ **+
of** *He's the youngest member of the team.* 🔁 *They
celebrated with friends and family members.* 🔁 *It
was reported by a member of the public.* 🔁 *The
restaurant is open to members of staff.*

membership /'membəʃɪp/ NOUN [*plural*
memberships]
1 *no plural* being a member □ **+ of** *Membership of
the gym costs £600 a year.*
2 all the people who are members of a group or
organization □ *The union membership voted to
reject the offer.*

memo /'meməʊ/ NOUN [*plural* memos] a short
note that you send to someone who works in the
same company or organization as you
memorable /'memərəbəl/ ADJECTIVE a
memorable event is one that you remember
because it is special or important □ *Their kiss was
the most memorable moment of the film.*

memory /'memərɪ/ NOUN [*plural* memories]
1 the ability to remember things □ *There are several
ways to improve your memory.* □ **+ for** *I've got an
awful memory for names (= I don't remember them).*
2 something that you remember □ **+ of** *He has happy
memories of his school days.* 🔁 *The pictures brought
back painful memories.*
3 *no plural* the part of a computer where information
is stored. A computing word □ *6GB of memory*

> ► **THESAURUS:** A memory is a thing that you
> remember. A souvenir is a thing that you buy to
> help you remember a particular place or an
> occasion. For example, many people buy
> souvenirs when they go on holiday. If you
> write something down to help you to remember
> it, you can call this piece of paper a note.

men /men/ PLURAL OF man
menace /'menəs/ NOUN [*plural* menaces]
something that causes or might cause trouble or
danger □ *These biting flies are a real menace.*

mend /mend/ VERB [mends, mending, mended]
to repair something that is broken or damaged
□ *We need to mend the hole in the tent.* □ *I took my watch to be mended.*

mental /'mentəl/ ADJECTIVE to do with the mind or thinking □ *mental arithmetic* □ *Does she have the mental strength to be a top player?* 🔁 *mental illness* 🔁 *mental health services*

mention /'menʃən/ VERB [mentions, mentioning, mentioned]
1 to talk or to write about something, but not in detail □ *Nobody mentioned it before.* □ *+ in His name was mentioned in the report.* □ *+ to Don't mention it to Jonathan.* □ *+ that You mentioned that he's got a new car.* 🔁 *As I mentioned earlier, I hadn't met him before.*
2 don't mention it something you say to be polite when someone thanks you for something

> **THESAURUS:** If you mention something, you talk or write about something, but not in detail. If you hint, you suggest something in a way that is not clear or direct. If you reveal something, you tell someone something that is secret or surprising. If you claim something, you say that it is true, although there is no clear proof.

menu /'menjuː/ NOUN [plural menus]
1 a list of the food available in a restaurant □ *Would you like to look at the menu?* □ *We have a three-course set menu.*
2 on a computer, a list of choices on the screen that you can choose from. A computing word. 🔁 *a drop-down menu*

merchant /'mɜːtʃənt/ NOUN [plural merchants]
someone who has a business buying and selling goods □ *a wine merchant*

mercy /'mɜːsɪ/ NOUN, NO PLURAL the quality of being kind and willing to forgive someone, especially someone you have power over 🔁 *The judge showed no mercy to the killers.* □ *He ignored their pleas for mercy.*

merge /mɜːdʒ/ VERB [merges, merging, merged] if two things or organizations merge, they combine or join with each other □ *Her work life seemed to be increasingly merging with her home life.* □ *The two companies merged in 1999.*

merit /'merɪt/ NOUN [plural merits] a quality that makes something or someone valuable or important □ *The film lacks artistic merit.* □ *Players are picked for the team on merit.*

mermaid /'mɜːmeɪd/ NOUN [plural mermaids] in stories, a beautiful creature who lives in the sea and is half a woman and half a fish

merry /'merɪ/ ADJECTIVE [merrier, merriest]
happy and showing that you are enjoying yourself □ *He whistled a merry tune.*

mess /mes/ NOUN [plural messes]
1 an untidy or dirty state □ *The kitchen's in a mess.*
2 someone or something that is dirty or untidy □ *I'd been gardening and I looked a right mess.* □ *Your room's a complete mess.*
3 something that is in a confused state or that involves a lot of problems □ *His whole life was in a mess.* 🔁 *He made a complete mess of the accounts.*
♦ PHRASAL VERBS [messes, messing, messed] **mess about/around** to waste time with silly behaviour □ *Stop messing about and get on with your work!* **mess something up 1** to do something badly or to spoil something □ *I messed up my French exam.* **2** to make something untidy □ *She messed up all my carefully arranged papers.*

message /'mesɪdʒ/ NOUN [plural messages] a piece of written or spoken information sent from one person to another 🔁 *I sent a message wishing him luck.* 🔁 *I left a message on her phone.* 🔁 *a text message* □ *+ from She's received thousands of messages from her fans.* □ *+ of messages of support*

messenger /'mesɪndʒə(r)/ NOUN [plural messengers] someone who carries messages from one person to another

messy /'mesɪ/ ADJECTIVE [messier, messiest]
1 untidy or dirty □ *a messy room* □ *He had long, messy hair.*
2 complicated and unpleasant to deal with □ *a messy divorce*

met /met/ PAST TENSE AND PAST PARTICIPLE OF **meet**

metal /'metəl/ NOUN [plural metals] a hard shiny material such as iron, gold or silver □ *The car was now a heap of twisted metal.* 🔁 *precious metals*

metaphor /'metəfə(r)/ NOUN [plural metaphors] a way of describing something by comparing it to something else □ *To use a boxing metaphor, the minister got knocked out in the first round.*

meter /'miːtə(r)/ NOUN [plural meters]
1 a device that measures and records the amount of something 🔁 *a gas meter* □ *Take a meter reading on the day you move in.*
2 the US spelling of **metre**

method /'meθəd/ NOUN [plural methods] a way of doing something, especially a planned or organized way □ *+ of methods of disease prevention* □ *+ for We need to develop new methods for dealing with the problem.* 🔁 *Artists here use traditional methods.* □ *teaching methods* □ *farming methods*

metre /'miːtə(r)/ NOUN [plural metres] a unit for measuring length, equal to 100 centimetres. □ *+ of Almost two metres of snow had fallen.* □ *It's suitable for boats up to three metres in length.* □ *He fell just ten metres from the finish line.* □ *a 400 metre runner* 🔁 *2500 square metres of office space*

metric /'metrɪk/ ADJECTIVE to do with a system of measuring that uses units such as litres and grams, based on tens

mg /ˌem 'dʒiː/ ABBREVIATION **milligram**

miaow[1] /miːˈaʊ/ NOUN [plural miaows] the sound that a cat makes

miaow[2] /miːˈaʊ/ VERB [miaows, miaowing, miaowed] a cat miaows when it makes this sound

mice /maɪs/ PLURAL OF **mouse**

microphone /'maɪkrəfəʊn/ NOUN [plural microphones] an electronic device used for recording sound or making sound louder □ Speak into the microphone. □ She took the microphone to address the crowd.

microscope /'maɪkrəskəʊp/ NOUN [plural microscopes] a piece of equipment with lenses (= curved pieces of glass) that makes very small objects look much larger so that you can study them closely

microwave /'maɪkrəweɪv/ NOUN [plural microwaves] a **microwave oven**

microwave oven /ˌmaɪkrəweɪv 'ʌvən/ NOUN [plural microwave ovens] an oven that cooks food very quickly using electrical and magnetic waves instead of heat

midday /ˌmɪdˈdeɪ/ NOUN, NO PLURAL twelve o'clock in the middle of the day, or around this time

□ She arrived at midday yesterday. 🕭 We waited in the hot midday sun. 🕭 They had bread and cheese for their midday meal.

middle[1] /'mɪdəl/ NOUN [plural middles]
1 the middle the point, position or part furthest from the sides or edges of something □ Let me sit in the middle. □ **+ of** They live on an island in the middle of the ocean.
2 the point in a period of time that is half way through that period of time □ **+ of** I woke up in the middle of the night. □ He stood up and asked a question in the middle of the meeting.
3 be in the middle of doing something to be busy doing something □ I can't come to the phone – I'm in the middle of bathing the children.

middle[2] /'mɪdəl/ ADJECTIVE in the central point or position of something □ I liked the middle section of the book. □ I was driving in the middle lane. □ He's the middle child of a family of five boys.

middle-aged /ˌmɪdəlˈeɪdʒd/ ADJECTIVE approximately between the ages of 45 and 60 □ a middle-aged man

middle class[1] /ˌmɪdəl 'klɑːs/ NOUN [plural middle classes] the social class that consists mainly of educated people who have a good standard of living

middle class[2] /ˌmɪdəl 'klɑːs/ ADJECTIVE to do with the middle class □ a middle class family

midnight /'mɪdnaɪt/ NOUN, NO PLURAL twelve o'clock at night □ The competition closes at midnight tonight. □ It was past midnight when we finally got home.

might[1] /maɪt/ MODAL VERB
1 used to talk about the possibility that something is true or something will happen □ He might stay. □ It might rain.
2 you might like/want to do something used to make polite suggestions □ You might want to take some extra food with you.
3 might as well used to say that you should probably do something because there is nothing better to do □ If you can't be bothered to practise, you might as well give up the piano.

might[2] /maɪt/ NOUN, NO PLURAL a formal word meaning power or strength 🕭 He pulled with all his might.

mighty /'maɪti/ ADJECTIVE [mightier, mightiest] a formal word meaning big and powerful □ the mighty Mississippi River

migrate /maɪˈɡreɪt/ VERB [migrates, migrating, migrated]
1 if birds or animals migrate, they travel to a different part of the world at the same time

each year □ *The birds migrate northwards in spring.*
2 to move to a different country to find work □ *His family migrated to Australia in 1918.*

migration /maɪˈɡreɪʃən/ NOUN, NO PLURAL when birds, animals or people travel to a different part of the world at the same time each year

mild /maɪld/ ADJECTIVE [milder, mildest]
1 mild weather is quite warm □ *The weather was unusually mild for November.* 🕮 *The mild winter had prevented ice from forming on the lake.*
2 not severe or not serious □ *The virus causes a relatively mild illness.* □ *She looked at him with mild annoyance.*
3 having a flavour that is not strong □ *mild cheese* □ *Chicken has a mild flavour.*

mile /maɪl/ NOUN [plural miles] a unit for measuring distance, equal to 1.6 kilometres □ *The ship was 20 miles off the coast.* 🕮 *His car was travelling at a speed of 110 miles per hour.* 🕮 *The traffic jam was six miles long.*

milestone /ˈmaɪlstəʊn/ NOUN [plural milestones] an important event in someone's life or in the development of something □ *The game was a milestone in British sporting history.*

military /ˈmɪlɪtəri/ ADJECTIVE to do with the army, navy or air force 🕮 *Military forces invaded the country.* 🕮 *Many soldiers were injured in military operations.* 🕮 *a military base* □ *a military commander*

milk[1] /mɪlk/ NOUN, NO PLURAL a white liquid produced by female animals, which people drink or which is used to feed babies □ *Would you like a glass of milk?* □ *Breast milk contains important nutrients for babies.*

milk[2] /mɪlk/ VERB [milks, milking, milked] to take milk from a cow or goat □ *The cows are milked by machine.*

mill /mɪl/ NOUN [plural mills]
1 a building with machinery for crushing grain □ *The wheat for our bread comes from a traditional mill*
2 a factory that produces a particular material such as cotton, paper or wool □ *a paper mill*

millennium /mɪˈlenɪəm/ NOUN [plural millennia] a period of a thousand years

milligram *or* **milligramme** /ˈmɪlɪgræm/ NOUN [plural milligrams *or* milligrammes] a unit for measuring weight, equal to 1/1000 of a gram. This is often written **mg**

milliliter /ˈmɪlɪliːtə(r)/ NOUN [plural milliliters] the US spelling of **millilitre**

millilitre /ˈmɪlɪliːtə(r)/ NOUN [plural millilitres] a unit for measuring liquid, equal to 1/1000 of a litre. This is often written **ml**

millimeter /ˈmɪlɪmiːtə(r)/ NOUN [plural millimeters] the US spelling of **millimetre**

millimetre /ˈmɪlɪmiːtə(r)/ NOUN [plural millimetres] a unit for measuring length, equal to 1/1000 of a metre. This is often written **mm**

million /ˈmɪljən/ NUMBER [plural millions *or* million]
1 the number 1,000,000
2 millions a very large number. An informal word □ **+ of** *There were millions of flies crawling on the food.*

millionaire /ˌmɪljəˈneə(r)/ NOUN [plural millionaires] someone who has £1,000,000 or $1,000,000 or more

millionth[1] /ˈmɪljənθ/ NUMBER 1,000,000th written as a word

millionth[2] /ˈmɪljənθ/ NOUN [plural millionths] 1/1,000,000; one of a million equal parts of something

mimic /ˈmɪmɪk/ VERB [mimics, mimicking, mimicked] to copy the way someone speaks or behaves as a joke

min /mɪn/ ABBREVIATION
1 minute[1]; used in writing
2 minimum[1] and [3]; used in writing

mince /mɪns/ VERB [minces, mincing, minced] to cut food into very small pieces using a machine □ *minced beef*

mind[1] /maɪnd/ NOUN [plural minds]
1 your brain, or your ability to think, understand, remember, etc. □ *All sorts of thoughts went through my mind.*
2 make up your mind to decide □ *I couldn't make up my mind whether to go to Paris or not.*
3 on your mind if something is on your mind, you are thinking about it a lot and usually worrying about it □ *I've got a lot on my mind at the moment.*
4 have someone/something in mind to be thinking of a particular person or thing □ *Do you have any particular colour in mind for the curtains?*
♦ IDIOMS be/go out of your mind to become extremely worried or upset □ *We were out of our minds with worry for them.* take your mind off something to stop you thinking about something bad by making you think about something else □ *I'm in a lot of pain, but going dancing takes my mind off it.*

mind[2] /maɪnd/ VERB [minds, minding, minded]
1 to be upset or annoyed by something □ *Do you mind if I smoke?* □ *I'm sure Sue wouldn't mind you borrowing her car.*

2 would you mind doing something used to ask someone politely to do something □ *Would you mind opening the window?*
3 used to tell someone to be careful not to get hurt □ *Mind your head on that branch.*
4 never mind used to say that something is not important □ *'I haven't finished my homework.'* *'Never mind, you can hand it in tomorrow.'*
♦ PHRASAL VERB **mind out** used to tell someone to be careful not to get hurt □ *Mind out – there's a car coming!*

mine¹ /maɪn/ PRONOUN used to talk or write about things belonging to or to do with you □ *Is this book yours or mine?* □ *Jan is a friend of mine.*

mine² /maɪn/ NOUN [*plural* mines]
1 a place where people dig something such as coal or gold from the ground □ *a coal mine*
2 a bomb that is hidden in the ground or in water, which explodes when someone touches it
mine³ /maɪn/ VERB [mines, mining, mined]
1 to dig into the ground in order to get something such as coal or gold □ *Diamonds are mined from the rocks.*
2 to put bombs under the ground or in water
miner /ˈmaɪnə(r)/ NOUN [*plural* miners] someone who works in a mine

mineral /ˈmɪnərəl/ NOUN [*plural* minerals]
1 a natural substance in the earth, such as coal, salt or gold □ *Our mineral resources are not great.*
2 a natural substance such as iron that your body needs to stay healthy 🔁 *Some vegetables contain a lot of vitamins and minerals.*

mineral water /ˈmɪnərəl ˌwɔːtə(r/ NOUN [*plural* mineral waters] water that you buy in bottles, which comes from under the ground □ *a bottle of mineral water*

miniature /ˈmɪnətʃə(r)/ ADJECTIVE very much smaller than normal □ *a miniature camera*
minibus /ˈmɪnɪbʌs/ NOUN [*plural* minibuses] a small bus for about 12 people
minimal /ˈmɪnɪməl/ ADJECTIVE very small in amount or degree □ *The fire caused minimal damage.*

minimum¹ /ˈmɪnɪməm/ ADJECTIVE being the smallest amount or degree that is possible or allowed 🔁 *The minimum age for driving in the UK is 17.* □ *£250 was the minimum amount needed to open a bank account.*

minimum² /ˈmɪnɪməm/ NOUN, NO PLURAL the smallest amount or degree that is possible or allowed 🔁 *We need to keep costs to a minimum.* □ **+ of** *He did his duties with the minimum of fuss.* □ *The hotel costs a minimum of £200 a night.*

mining /ˈmaɪnɪŋ/ NOUN, NO PLURAL the job of digging something such as coal or gold from the ground □ *the mining industry*

minister /ˈmɪnɪstə(r)/ NOUN [*plural* ministers]
1 a politician who is in charge of a government department 🔁 *Government ministers will visit China next week.* □ **+ of/for** *the Minister for Education*
2 a priest in some Christian churches □ *a Methodist minister*

ministry /ˈmɪnɪstri/ NOUN [*plural* ministries] a government department □ *the Ministry of Defence* □ *ministry officials*

minor¹ /ˈmaɪnə(r)/ ADJECTIVE not serious or important 🔁 *He suffered minor injuries in the accident.* □ *I've made a few minor changes to the report.* 🔁 *The problems were relatively minor.*

minor² /ˈmaɪnə(r)/ NOUN [*plural* minors] someone who is legally a child

minority /maɪˈnɒrəti/ NOUN [*plural* minorities] a small group of people which is part of a much larger group 🔁 *A small minority of our students are from Africa.*

mint /mɪnt/ NOUN [*plural* mints]
1 a plant with strong-smelling leaves, used in cooking
2 a type of sweet with a strong flavour

minus /ˈmaɪnəs/ ADJECTIVE less than zero □ *minus ten degrees*

minute¹ /ˈmɪnɪt/ NOUN [*plural* minutes]
1 a period of 60 seconds □ *The journey only lasted a few minutes.* □ *I loved every minute of my visit.* □ *Rendell scored in the eighth minute.*
2 a short time □ *Wait a minute while I look for my keys.* □ *Just a minute – I need to phone Clara.*
3 the exact time □ *I knew something was wrong the minute I saw him.* □ *At that very minute there was a loud explosion.*
4 any minute very soon □ *Paul will be here any minute now.* □ *The bomb could explode at any minute.*
5 this minute immediately □ *Come here this minute!*
➜ *go to* **minutes**

minute² /maɪˈnjuːt/ ADJECTIVE extremely small □ *Minute traces of blood were found on his clothes.*

minutes /ˈmɪnɪts/ PLURAL NOUN a written record of a meeting 🔁 *Who is going to take the minutes?*

miracle /ˈmɪrəkəl/ NOUN [*plural* miracles]
1 something extremely lucky that happens and that no one would expect □ *It's a miracle that no one was killed in the accident.* □ *a miracle cure*
2 something that happens which seems impossible and that people think God has done

miraculous /mɪˈrækjʊləs/ ADJECTIVE extremely lucky and not expected 🖫 *He made a miraculous recovery.*

mirror /ˈmɪrə(r)/ NOUN [*plural* mirrors] a piece of special glass that you look at to see an image of yourself □ *Ben was looking at himself in the mirror.*

miserable /ˈmɪzərəbəl/ ADJECTIVE
1 very unhappy □ *She's miserable because all her friends are away.* □ *Dan looked pretty miserable.*
2 making you feel unhappy □ *What miserable weather!* □ *She'd had a miserable childhood.*

misery /ˈmɪzəri/ NOUN, NO PLURAL great unhappiness or suffering □ *Bad weather has caused misery for thousands of travellers.*

mislead /ˌmɪsˈliːd/ VERB [misleads, misleading, misled] to make someone believe something that is not true □ *The government deliberately misled the public about the state of the economy.*

Miss /mɪs/ NOUN [*plural* Misses] a word used before the name of a girl or a woman who is not married □ *Miss Smith* □ *Miss Zoe Arnison*

miss¹ /mɪs/ VERB [misses, missing, missed]
1 to fail to hit or catch something you are aiming at 🖫 *A bullet narrowly missed* (= only just missed) *his spine.* □ *He missed the penalty.*
2 to not go to something or experience something □ *I had to miss my daughter's school concert.* □ *Don't miss their new show!*
3 to miss a train, bus, plane, etc. is to not arrive in time to catch it
4 to feel sad because of someone you can no longer be with or something you can no longer have or do 🖫 *I missed my family terribly when I lived abroad.* □ *+ ing I miss being able to walk on the beach.*
♦ PHRASAL VERB **miss someone/something out** to not include someone or something □ *He read us the book, but he missed out all the rude words.*

➤ THESAURUS: If you **miss** something, you do not go to it or experience it. We often use this word for things or experiences that we want to go to or experience, but cannot. If you **avoid** doing something, you stay away from it. If you **prevent** something, you stop it from happening, or stop someone from doing something. If you **skip** something, you do not do something that you should do, or something that you usually do. For example, you might **skip** a meal if you feel unwell.

miss² /mɪs/ NOUN [*plural* misses] when you do not hit something you are aiming at □ *His miss cost his team the match.*
♦ IDIOM **give something a miss** to decide not to do something □ *I was feeling tired, so I decided to give the party a miss.*

missile /ˈmɪsaɪl/ NOUN [*plural* missiles]
1 a weapon that travels long distances and explodes when it hits something □ *long-range missiles*
2 an object that someone throws to hit someone or something □ *Police were hit by bottles, stones and other missiles.*

missing /ˈmɪsɪŋ/ ADJECTIVE if someone or something is missing, they are not where you expect them to be and you do not know where they are 🖫 *Some important documents had gone missing.* □ *Rescue teams are looking for three missing climbers.*

mist /mɪst/ NOUN [*plural* mists] very small drops of water in the air that make it difficult for you to see 🖫 *A fine mist hung over the city.* 🖫 *The morning mist had lifted.*

mistake¹ /mɪˈsteɪk/ NOUN [*plural* mistakes]
1 something wrong that you do 🖫 *We've all made mistakes.* 🖫 *She knew that inviting him would be a big mistake.* 🖫 *There were lots of spelling mistakes in his writing.* □ *+ to do something It was a mistake to come here.*
2 **by mistake** by accident □ *He deleted the file by mistake.* □ *The letter was delivered to the wrong house by mistake.*

➤ THESAURUS: A **mistake** is something wrong that you do. If something bad or wrong is your fault, you are **responsible** for it. If you take the **blame** for something bad that happens, you accept responsibility for it.

mistake² /mɪˈsteɪk/ VERB [mistakes, mistaking, mistook, mistaken] to understand something in the wrong way □ *No one could mistake his meaning.*
♦ PHRASAL VERB **mistake someone/something for someone/something** to think wrongly that a person or thing is someone or something else □ *People often mistake Clare for her sister.*

mistook /mɪˈstʊk/ PAST TENSE OF **mistake²**

mix /mɪks/ VERB [mixes, mixing, mixed]
1 to combine two or more substances □ *If you mix black paint and white paint, you get grey.* 🖫 *In a small bowl, mix together the garlic and butter.* □ *+ with Mix the powder with water.*
2 to combine □ *Oil and water don't mix.*
3 to talk to people and spend time with them socially □ *Marija was very shy and found it difficult to mix.* □ *+ with My Mum doesn't like the people I mix with.*
♦ PHRASAL VERBS **mix someone/something up** to think that a person or thing is someone or something else □ *The twins are very alike and the teacher often mixes them up.* **mix something up** to put a group of things in the wrong order □ *Somehow the pages have all got mixed up.*

mixture /ˈmɪkstʃə(r)/ NOUN [*plural* mixtures] a combination of different things 🖫 *The city is a* *strange mixture of old and new buildings.* □ *+ of I felt a mixture of anger and sadness.* □ *Stir the mixture until the sugar dissolves.*

mm /ˌem ˈem/ ABBREVIATION **millimetre**

moan /məʊn/ VERB [moans, moaning, moaned]
1 to complain about something, often in a way that annoys other people □ *Oh stop moaning!* □ *Tim was moaning about the weather.*
2 to make a long, low sound, usually because you are in pain □ *I could hear the injured passengers moaning in pain.*

mobile¹ /ˈməʊbaɪl/ ADJECTIVE able to move or be moved □ *He was older and less mobile than his wife.* □ *a mobile home*

mobile² /ˈməʊbaɪl/ NOUN [plural mobiles] a telephone that you carry with you □ *Is your mobile switched on?* 🕮 *Have you got my mobile number?*

mobile phone /ˌməʊbaɪl ˈfəʊn/ NOUN [plural mobile phones] a telephone that you carry with you

mock /mɒk/ VERB [mocks, mocking, mocked] to be unkind to someone by making jokes about them or by copying what they say or do □ *Other people might mock David's voice, but I love it.*

modal verb /ˌməʊdəl ˈvɜːb/ NOUN [plural modal verbs] a verb such as 'ought' or 'might' that is used to show ideas such as being possible, necessary, certain, etc.

model¹ /ˈmɒdəl/ NOUN [plural models]
1 a small copy of something bigger □ *+ of On display was a model of the ship.* 🕮 *He enjoys making models of aeroplanes.*
2 a person whose job is to wear clothes at fashion shows and for magazine photographs 🕮 *a fashion model* □ *a male model*

model² /ˈmɒdəl/ ADJECTIVE a model car, building, etc. is a small copy of a real one □ *He enjoys making model planes.*

model³ /ˈmɒdəl/ VERB [models, modelling/US modeling, modelled/US modeled] to work as a model, wearing clothes at fashion shows and for magazine photographs

moderate /ˈmɒdərət/ ADJECTIVE not extreme □ *moderate heat* □ *The doctor told him to take moderate exercise.*

modern /ˈmɒdən/ ADJECTIVE to do with the present time and not the past 🕮 *In the modern world, most women go out to work.* 🕮 *Modern life is very busy.* 🕮 *modern art*

► THESAURUS: Modern means to do with the present time and not the past. Something that is recent happened only a short time ago. Something that is current exists or is happening now.

modest /ˈmɒdɪst/ ADJECTIVE not talking about your skills and achievements even when you have been successful □ *Paul is very modest.*

► THESAURUS: Someone who is modest does not talk about their skills and achievements even when they have been successful. Someone who is humble does not believe that they are important. Someone who is shy is nervous, and not confident when meeting and speaking to people.

Mohammed /məˈhæmɪd/ NOUN the holy man on whose ideas the religion of Islam is based

moist /mɔɪst/ ADJECTIVE [moister, moistest] slightly wet □ *moist air*

moisture /ˈmɔɪstʃə(r)/ NOUN, NO PLURAL a small amount of liquid in or on something □ *This helps keep the moisture in the soil.*

moisturizer or **moisturiser** /ˈmɔɪstʃəraɪzə(r)/ NOUN [plural moisturizers] a cream you put on your skin to make it soft and not dry

mole /məʊl/ NOUN [plural moles]
1 a small brown spot on your skin which is permanent
2 a small animal which lives underground and is almost blind

molecule /ˈmɒlɪkjuːl/ NOUN [plural molecules] the smallest unit that a chemical element or compound (= substance formed from two or more parts or substances) can be divided into. Molecules are made up of two or more atoms. A chemistry or physics word.

mom /mɒm/ NOUN [plural moms] the US word for **mum**

moment /ˈməʊmənt/ NOUN [plural moments]
1 a short period of time □ *Stop what you're doing for a moment.* 🕮 *Wait a moment – I'm not ready.* 🕮 *Please take a moment (= use a short period of time) to read this information.*
2 a particular point in time □ *Just at that moment, she heard a door slam.* □ *Winning this competition has been the proudest moment in my athletics career.*
3 at the moment now □ *The house is empty at the moment.*
4 at any moment at any time soon □ *Doctors have said he could die at any moment.*
5 in a moment very soon □ *I'll explain what I mean in a moment.* □ *I'll be back in a moment.*

monarch /ˈmɒnək/ NOUN [plural monarchs] a king or queen

monarchy /ˈmɒnəkɪ/ NOUN [plural monarchies] a country that has a king or queen □ *Britain is a monarchy.*

monastery /ˈmɒnəstərɪ/ NOUN [plural monasteries] a building where monks (= religious men) live

Monday /ˈmʌndɪ/ NOUN [plural Mondays] the day of the week after Sunday and before Tuesday □ *On Monday, I went to London.* □ *See you next Monday.*

money /'mʌnɪ/ NOUN, NO PLURAL
1 coins and paper notes that you use for buying things □ *We don't have the money for a new car.* 🔊 *Dan spends most of his money on computer games.* 🔊 *I'm trying to save some money.* 🔊 *She earns a lot of money.*
2 make money to earn money or to make a profit □ *He had never made much money from writing.* □ *She made a lot of money from the sale of the house.*

monitor[1] /'mɒnɪtə(r)/ VERB [monitors, monitoring, monitored] to check something regularly to see how it changes □ *The school monitors the progress of all its students.*

monitor[2] /'mɒnɪtə(r)/ NOUN [plural monitors] a screen that is attached to a computer. A computing word □ *a computer monitor*

monk /mʌŋk/ NOUN [plural monks] one of a group of religious men who live together

monkey /'mʌŋkɪ/ NOUN [plural monkeys] an animal with a long tail that lives in trees in hot countries □ *The monkeys were trained to perform simple tasks.*

monster /'mɒnstə(r)/ NOUN [plural monsters] in stories, a very big and frightening creature □ *My little boy thinks there are monsters under his bed.*

month /mʌnθ/ NOUN [plural months] one of twelve periods that a year is divided into □ *the month of May* □ *the winter months* 🔊 *I went to France last month.* 🔊 *It's my birthday next month.*

monthly /'mʌnθlɪ/ ADJECTIVE, ADVERB happening once a month □ *a monthly meeting* □ *He is paid monthly.*

monument /'mɒnjumənt/ NOUN [plural monuments] something that has been built in memory of a person or event □ *They built a monument to Sir Walter Scott.*

moo /mu:/ VERB [moos, mooing, mooed] a cow moos when it makes a long low sound

mood /mu:d/ NOUN [plural moods] someone's feelings at a particular time 🔊 *I woke up in a bad mood this morning.* 🔊 *You're in a good mood today!*

moody /'mu:dɪ/ ADJECTIVE [moodier, moodiest] often becoming angry or unhappy □ *moody teenagers*

moon /mu:n/ NOUN [plural moons] the moon the round object that you see in the sky at night and which moves around the Earth 🔊 *The moon shone brightly.* 🔊 *Neil Armstrong made the first moon landing.*

moonlight /'mu:nlaɪt/ NOUN, NO PLURAL light that comes from the moon □ *His eyes shone in the moonlight.*

moor[1] /mɔ:(r)/ NOUN [plural moors] a large high area of land that is covered with grass and bushes. A geography word.

moor[2] /mɔ:(r)/ VERB [moors, mooring, moored] to fasten a boat to something

moral[1] /'mɒrəl/ ADJECTIVE to do with right and wrong and the way people should behave 🔊 *She had high moral standards.* □ *He objected to the war for moral reasons.*

moral[2] /'mɒrəl/ NOUN [plural morals] something that a story or experience teaches you about how to behave 🔊 *The moral of the story is never give up.*
➜ go to **morals**

morale /mə'rɑ:l/ NOUN, NO PLURAL how confident or happy a person or group of people feel □ *Morale in the office is fairly low.* 🔊 *Pay rises usually improve morale.*

morally /'mɒrəlɪ/ ADVERB to do with what is right or wrong behaviour □ *Not paying your taxes is morally wrong.*

morals /'mɒrəlz/ PLURAL NOUN the beliefs someone has about what is right and wrong behaviour □ *His remarks have started a public debate on the nation's morals.*

more[1] /mɔ:(r)/ DETERMINER, PRONOUN
1 a larger number or amount □ *He has more friends than anyone else I know.* 🔊 *The bill was more than £10,000.* □ *He knows more about elephants than anyone else in the UK.* 🔊 *More and more people are buying organic food.*
2 something in addition to what you have, what is there, or what you have talked about 🔊 *Is there any more cake?* 🔊 *Would you like some more coffee?* □ *You need to do more to help.* □ *8 people died, and at least twenty more were injured.*

more[2] /mɔ:(r)/ ADVERB
1 used to make comparative forms of adjectives and adverbs, especially ones with 2 or more syllables 🔊 *He's more patient than I am.* □ *More recently, I have begun to enjoy crime novels.* 🔊 *Harry's a lot more emotional than his sister.*
2 to a greater degree 🔊 *I exercise more than I used to.* 🔊 *I like her more and more.*
3 more or less almost, but not exactly □ *We've more or less finished decorating the kitchen.* □ *She more or less said she didn't trust us.*
4 the more ... the more/less used to say that if one thing increases, another thing will increase or decrease □ *The more I read about Cuba, the more I want to go there.* □ *The more I see her, the less I like her.*

moreover /mɔ:'rəʊvə(r)/ ADVERB a formal word for **also** □ *We do not have the facilities for this project. Moreover, we do not have enough staff.*

morning /'mɔːnɪŋ/ NOUN [plural mornings]
1 the early part of the day from when the sun rises to the middle of the day □ He takes the dog for a walk every morning. ⚕ He was late this morning.
2 in the morning (a) in the early part of the day □ I'm usually quite tired in the morning. (b) tomorrow morning □ See you in the morning.
3 Good morning! used to say 'hello' when you meet someone in the morning

mortgage /'mɔːgɪdʒ/ NOUN [plural mortgages] money that you borrow from a bank or financial organization in order to buy a house or land ⚕ They've taken out a huge mortgage on the flat.

mosque /mɒsk/ NOUN [plural mosques] a place where Muslims meet and pray

mosquito /məˈskiːtəʊ/ NOUN [plural mosquitoes or mosquitos] an insect which feeds by biting people or animals and sucking their blood

most¹ /məʊst/ DETERMINER, PRONOUN
1 the largest number or amount □ Most people support the policy. □ Which club has spent most money on new players this season? □ All three children eat a lot but Tom eats the most.
2 almost all □ Most of my friends are people I know from work. □ I like most types of fruit.
3 at the most and not more □ The trip should cost £500 at the most.
4 make the most of something to get as much advantage as possible from something that may not continue □ Make the most of the good weather while it lasts.

most² /məʊst/ ADVERB
1 used to make superlative forms of adjectives and adverbs, especially ones with two or more syllables □ Paul was the most intelligent boy in the class. □ Most importantly, he has learned to pay more attention in class.
2 more than anyone or anything else □ What kind of music do you like most?

mostly /'məʊstlɪ/ ADVERB in most cases or most of the time □ They mostly play indoors. □ The band plays mostly '70s music.

motel /məʊˈtel/ NOUN [plural motels] a hotel near a main road for people who are travelling by car

moth /mɒθ/ NOUN [plural moths] an insect with large wings that flies at night

mother /'mʌðə(r)/ NOUN [plural mothers] the female parent of a person or animal □ My mother was very tall. □ The animals learn to hunt from their mother.

mother-in-law /'mʌðərɪnˌlɔː/ NOUN [plural mothers-in-law] the mother of your husband or wife

motion /'məʊʃən/ NOUN [plural motions] movement or how something moves □ The motion of the waves made him sleepy. ⚕ Do not attempt to get off while the ride is in motion.

motive /'məʊtɪv/ NOUN [plural motives] the reason someone has for doing something □ There seemed to be no motive for the attack.

➤ THESAURUS: The reason for something is why it happened, exists or is true. A motive is the reason that someone has for doing something. We often talk about the motive for committing a crime. A cause is what makes something happen. Your purpose is what you intend to achieve when you do something. Your intention is the thing that you plan to do.

motor /'məʊtə(r)/ NOUN [plural motors] the part of a machine that uses petrol, electricity, etc. to produce movement and make the machine work □ an electric motor

motorbike /'məʊtəbaɪk/ NOUN [plural motorbikes] a vehicle with two wheels and an engine. You sit on it like a bicycle.

motorcycle /'məʊtəsaɪkəl/ NOUN [plural motorcycles] a motorbike or moped

motorist /'məʊtərɪst/ NOUN [plural motorists] someone who drives a car □ The motorist was driving above the speed limit.

motor racing /'məʊtə ˌreɪsɪŋ/ NOUN, NO PLURAL the sport of driving cars very fast around a track

motorway /'məʊtəweɪ/ NOUN [plural motorways] a wide road for vehicles travelling fast over long distances

mould /məʊld/ NOUN [plural moulds]
1 a hollow container which a liquid is poured into so that the liquid has the same shape as the container when it is cool and firm □ a jelly mould
2 a soft green or black substance that grows on old food or in wet conditions □ The bathroom ceiling was covered in mould.

mouldy /ˈməʊldɪ/ ADJECTIVE [mouldier, mouldiest] covered with a soft green or black substance that grows on old food or in wet conditions □ *The bread has gone mouldy.*

► THESAURUS: Food that is mouldy is covered in the soft green or black substance that grows on old food. Food that is stale is not fresh. Food that is rotten is decaying or decayed. Food that is bad does not taste or smell good because it is old.

mound /maʊnd/ NOUN [plural mounds] **1** a small hill or pile of earth or stones □ *a burial mound* **2** a pile or large amount of something □ *a mound of ironing*

Mount /maʊnt/ NOUN, NO PLURAL used before the names of mountains □ *the top of Mount Everest*

mount /maʊnt/ VERB [mounts, mounting, mounted] **1** if a feeling among a group of people mounts, it increases in level □ *Fears are mounting for the safety of the young climbers.* **2** to get on a horse or bicycle ♦ PHRASAL VERB **mount up** to gradually increase □ *The cost soon mounts up.*

mountain /ˈmaʊntɪn/ NOUN [plural mountains] a very high hill □ *the Rocky Mountains* □ *We spent our holiday walking in the mountains.* □ *a mountain range*

mourn /mɔːn/ VERB [mourns, mourning, mourned] to be very sad because someone you love has died □ *She was still mourning for her husband.*

mouse /maʊs/ NOUN [plural mice] **1** a small animal with grey or brown fur and a long tail **2** a small device that you move with your hand in order to make a computer do things. A computing word.

moustache /məˈstɑːʃ/ NOUN [plural moustaches] a line of hair that some men grow above their top lip

mouth /maʊθ/ NOUN [plural mouths] **1** the part of your face that you use for speaking and eating and which contains your tongue and teeth **2** the place where a river flows into the sea

mouthful /ˈmaʊθfʊl/ NOUN [plural mouthfuls] an amount of food or drink that you put in your mouth at one time □ *She ate a few mouthfuls of soup.*

move¹ /muːv/ VERB [moves, moving, moved] **1** to change position, or to change the position of something □ *Please move your bag off the kitchen table.* □ *He moved forwards to kick the ball.* ⊔ *Nobody moved as the clock struck.* ⊔ *I'm sure I saw the curtain move.* **2** if a person or an organization moves, they go to live or work in a different place □ **+ to** *We moved to London in 2003.* 🕮 *We moved house over ten times while I was a child.* □ *Our office is moving to Bristol.* ♦ PHRASAL VERBS **move in** to begin to live in a new home or work in a new place □ *We moved in last year.* **move out** to leave the place where you have been living or working □ *I moved out of my parents' house when I was 18.*

move² /muːv/ NOUN [plural moves] **1** an action that achieves something 🕮 *Buying a house turned out to be a good move.* 🕮 *They made no move to help her.* 🕮 *I've given him my phone number – it's up to him to make the next move.* **2** when you go to live or work in another place □ *I've packed all my files ready for the office move.* ⊓ *They split up after her move to London.* **3** a change of position □ *The slightest move was painful.* ♦ IDIOM **get a move on** an informal phrase meaning to hurry □ *Get a move on – we're going to be late!*

movement /ˈmuːvmənt/ NOUN [plural movements] **1** a change of position or place □ *I saw a slight movement of the curtain.* □ *Try to make slow, graceful movements of the arms.* □ *The police tracked the movements of all the suspects.* **2** a group of people with the same interests or aims □ *the anti-war movement*

movie /ˈmuːvɪ/ NOUN [plural movies] **1** a film □ *Do you have a favourite movie?* □ *a movie star* □ *a horror movie* **2** the movies a cinema □ *Let's go to the movies.*

MP /ˌemˈpiː/ ABBREVIATION Member of Parliament; someone who has been elected to the British parliament

MP3 /ˌempiːˈθriː/ NOUN [plural MP3s] a computer file that stores music and recorded speech

MP3 player /ˌem piː ˈθriː ˌpleɪə(r)/ NOUN [plural MP3 players] a small piece of computer equipment for storing and playing music and recorded speech

mph /ˌempiːˈeɪtʃ/ ABBREVIATION miles per hour; a unit for measuring speed □ *The maximum speed on this road is 30 mph.*

Mr /ˈmɪstə(r)/ NOUN a title used before a man's name □ *My art teacher is called Mr Jackson.* □ *Hello, Mr Rose.*

Mrs /ˈmɪsɪz/ NOUN a title used before a married woman's name □ *That's my neighbour, Mrs Baker.* □ *Good morning, Mrs Clarke.*

Ms /mɪz, məz/ NOUN a title sometimes used before a woman's name. It does not tell you if she is married or not. □ *Ms Duggan*

much¹ /mʌtʃ/ DETERMINER, PRONOUN

1 how much used in questions about amounts □ *How much fruit do you eat each day?* □ *The pay depends on how much responsibility you take on.* □ *How much are (= what is the price of) these apples?*
2 used in negative sentences to say that there is not a large amount of something □ *A few more days won't make much difference.* □ *She doesn't say much.* □ *There isn't much to laugh about.* □ *'Do you have any money?' 'Not much.'*
3 too much more than is wanted, needed or acceptable □ *We bought far too much food.* □ *We've got too much work.*
4 so much used to emphasize the large amount of something □ *I have so much work to do.* □ *Why did you give me so much food?*
5 as much used to talk about amounts that are as large as something else □ *I hope I can give you as much support as you've given me.*

► Remember that **much** is only used with uncountable nouns:
✓ *I've eaten too much food.*
✗ *There are too much cars on the road.*
With countable nouns that are in the plural, the word **many** is used: □ *How many dogs do they have?*

---

much² /mʌtʃ/ ADVERB

1 often or a lot □ *Do you miss your old school much?* 🔁 *Thanks very much – you've been a great help.* 🔁 *He doesn't love her as much as she loves him.* 🔁 *I had to work away from home too much in my last job.*
2 used to emphasize comparative adjectives □ *He's much taller than his brother.* □ *She's much more beautiful now she's older.*

mud /mʌd/ NOUN, NO PLURAL soft wet soil □ *His football boots were covered in mud.*

muddy /ˈmʌdɪ/ ADJECTIVE [muddier, muddiest] covered or filled with mud □ *The track through the woods was very muddy.* □ *Take off your muddy boots.*

mug /mʌg/ NOUN [plural mugs] a cup with straight sides and a handle □ *a mug of hot chocolate*

multiple /ˈmʌltɪpəl/ ADJECTIVE many □ *She suffered multiple injuries in the crash.*

multiply /ˈmʌltɪplaɪ/ VERB [multiplies, multiplying, multiplied] to increase a number by adding it to itself a particular number of times. A mathematics word □ *13 multiplied by 3 is 39.*

mum /mʌm/ NOUN [plural mums] an informal word for mother □ *Can I have another cake, Mum?* □ *How's your mum?*

mumble /ˈmʌmbəl/ VERB [mumbles, mumbling, mumbled] to speak quietly or without opening your mouth enough, so that people cannot understand you □ *He mumbled something about not having enough money.*

mummy /ˈmʌmɪ/ NOUN [plural mummies] a child's word for mother □ *Mummy, can we go now?* □ *Where's your mummy, Jake?*

murder¹ /ˈmɜːdə(r)/ NOUN [plural murders] the crime of killing someone deliberately 🔁 *He admitted committing the murder.* 🔁 *He was charged with attempted murder (= trying to kill someone).*

murder² /ˈmɜːdə(r)/ VERB [murders, murdering, murdered] to kill someone deliberately □ *She denies murdering her husband.*

murderer /ˈmɜːdərə(r)/ NOUN [plural murderers] someone who has murdered another person

murmur /ˈmɜːmə(r)/ VERB [murmurs, murmuring, murmured] to speak very quietly □ *He murmured something in her ear.*

► **THESAURUS:** To murmur means to speak very quietly. To mutter also means to speak quietly, but usually because you are angry or complaining about something. If you whisper, you talk very quietly to someone, so that other people cannot hear. If you mumble, you speak quietly or without opening your mouth enough so that people cannot understand you.

---

muscle /ˈmʌsəl/ NOUN [plural muscles] one of the parts in the body that are connected to bones and that cause the body to move by becoming shorter or longer □ *stomach muscles* 🔁 *Joe has pulled a muscle (= injured the muscle) in his leg.*

museum /mjuːˈziːəm/ NOUN [plural museums] a building where collections of interesting things are arranged for people to see □ *the Natural History Museum*

mushroom /ˈmʌʃrʊm/ NOUN [plural mushrooms] a type of fungus (= plant with no leaves or flowers) that you can eat, with a stem and a flat or round top □ *mushroom risotto*

music /'mjuːzɪk/ NOUN, NO PLURAL
1 sounds arranged in patterns, sung or played by instruments ⊞ *Do you like classical music?* ⊞ *I've been listening to a lot of dance music recently.* □ *a music teacher*
2 the written sounds that represent a piece of music ⊞ *I wish I could read music.*

➤ Remember that the noun **music** is not used in the plural:
✓ *He listens to a lot of music.*
✗ *He listens to a lot of musics.*

musical[1] /'mjuːzɪkəl/ ADJECTIVE
1 to do with music □ *She has no musical training.* ⊞ *Do you play a musical instrument?*
2 good at playing or singing music □ *The whole family is very musical.*

musical[2] /'mjuːzɪkəl/ NOUN [*plural* musicals] a play or film in which there is a lot of singing and dancing □ *He loves all the old Hollywood musicals.*

musician /mjuː'zɪʃən/ NOUN [*plural* musicians] someone who plays a musical instrument □ *She's one of our most talented young musicians.*

Muslim[1] /'mʊzlɪm/ or **Moslem** /'mɒzləm/ NOUN [*plural* Muslims or Moslems] someone who believes in Islam

Muslim[2] /'mʊzlɪm/ or **Moslem** /'mɒzləm/ ADJECTIVE to do with Islam □ *Friday is the Muslim holy day.*

must /məs, məst, *stressed* mʌst/ MODAL VERB
1 used to say that something is necessary □ *You must arrive for your interview on time.*
2 used to say that you think something is true □ *You must be very tired after such a long journey.* □ *They must have known about the money.*
3 used to make an offer or a suggestion □ *You must come over for dinner.* □ *We must meet up soon.*

mustache /mʌ'stæʃ/ NOUN [*plural* mustaches] a US spelling of **moustache**

mustard /'mʌstəd/ NOUN, NO PLURAL a cold yellow or brown sauce used to give food a hot taste

mustn't /'mʌsənt/ a short way to say and write must not □ *I mustn't forget.*

➤ Note that **mustn't** means it is *necessary not to do something*. To say that it is *not necessary to do something*, use **don't need/have to**:
✓ *You mustn't walk on the railway line. It's dangerous.*
✓ *Come if you like but you don't need to.*
✗ *Come if you like but you mustn't to.*

mutter /'mʌtə(r)/ VERB [mutters, muttering, muttered] to speak quietly, often when you are complaining □ *He muttered something about people never listening to him.*

my /maɪ/ DETERMINER belonging to or to do with me □ *There's my son.* □ *Have you seen my boots anywhere?*

myself /maɪ'self/ PRONOUN
1 the reflexive form of *I* □ *I was washing myself.* □ *I cut myself on the glass.* □ *I felt really proud of myself.*
2 used to show that you do something without any help from other people □ *I suppose I'll have to do it myself if no one else can be bothered.* ⊞ *I can't take care of him all by myself.*
3 used to emphasize the pronoun *I* □ *I have not seen the film myself.*
4 by myself not with or near other people □ *I live by myself.*

mysterious /mɪ'stɪərɪəs/ ADJECTIVE strange and difficult to understand or explain ⊞ *He died in mysterious circumstances.* □ *No one knows why she left – it's very mysterious.*

mystery /'mɪstəri/ NOUN [*plural* mysteries] something strange which you do not understand and which cannot be explained ⊞ *She set out to solve the mystery of his disappearance.*

➤ THESAURUS: A mystery is a strange thing that you do not understand and which cannot be explained. A secret is a piece of information that must not be told to other people. A puzzle is something that is difficult to understand.

myth /mɪθ/ NOUN [*plural* myths]
1 a story about ancient gods, heroes (= brave people) and monsters (= frightening creatures) □ *Greek and Roman myths*
2 something that many people believe, but which is not true □ *It's a myth that eating late at night makes you fat.*

mythology /mɪ'θɒlədʒɪ/ NOUN, NO PLURAL stories about ancient gods and heroes (= brave people)

N*n*

N[1] *or* **n** /en/ the 14th letter of the alphabet

N[2] /en/ ABBREVIATION **north**[2]

nail[1] /neɪl/ NOUN [*plural* **nails**]
1 the hard covering on top of the ends of your fingers and toes ⊞ *You need to cut your nails.* ⊞ *a pair of nail scissors*
2 a thin pointed piece of metal, used to join things together, especially pieces of wood

nail[2] /neɪl/ VERB [**nails, nailing, nailed**] to attach or join something with a nail or nails □ *Nail the number on the door.*

naked /'neɪkɪd/ ADJECTIVE not wearing any clothes □ *He stripped naked to the waist to cut the grass.* ⊞ *The children were running around stark naked in the sun.*

name[1] /neɪm/ NOUN [*plural* **names**] the word or words that you use to refer to a person, animal, place or thing □ *What's your name?* ⊞ *Write your name and address here.* □ *I can't remember the name of the street.* □ *She changed her name when she got married.*

> ➤ **THESAURUS:** Name is a general word for the word or words that you use to refer to a person, animal, place or thing. Your **surname** is your last name or family name. You **first name** is the name that comes before your surname. Your parents usually choose your first name. A **nickname** is a name that you use for someone that is not their real name.

name[2] /neɪm/ VERB [**names, naming, named**]
1 to give someone or something a name □ *They've named their son Samuel.* □ *The ship has not been named yet.*
2 to say what the name of someone or something is □ *The dead men will not be named until their families have been informed.*

> ➤ Note that to **name** someone is to give someone, (often a baby), or something a name. To say the name of someone or something, use **be called**:
> ✓ *She is called Justina.*
> ✗ *She is named Justina.*

nanny /'nænɪ/ NOUN [*plural* **nannies**] a person whose job is to look after someone's child or children, usually in their own home

nappy /'næpɪ/ NOUN [*plural* **nappies**] a thick piece of soft cloth or paper that you fasten around a baby's bottom ⊞ *Could you change the baby's nappy?*

narrow /'nærəʊ/ ADJECTIVE [**narrower, narrowest**]
1 not very wide □ *She found a narrow door in the garden wall.* □ *The road was too narrow for overtaking.*
2 only just achieved ⊞ *We had a narrow escape when our car went off the road.*

nasty /'nɑːstɪ/ ADJECTIVE [**nastier, nastiest**] very unpleasant or unkind □ *The drug left a nasty taste in my mouth.* □ *He's always saying nasty things about everybody.*

nation /'neɪʃən/ NOUN [*plural* **nations**]
1 a country with its own government □ *the African nations*
2 the people of a country □ *Today the nation is voting for a new government.*

national /'næʃənəl/ ADJECTIVE
1 to do with the whole of a country □ *They report local, national and international news.* ⊞ *House prices in the south-east are well above the national average.*
2 typical of a particular country □ *Paella is the national dish of Spain.* □ *Dancers in national costume greeted the president.*

nationality /ˌnæʃə'nælətɪ/ NOUN [*plural* **nationalities**] the state of being a legal member of a particular country □ *Omar has British nationality.* ⊞ *Louis has dual nationality because his mother is French and his father is American.*

native[1] /'neɪtɪv/ ADJECTIVE to do with the place you were born in □ *His native language is French.* □ *In 1965 he left his native Austria.*

native[2] /'neɪtɪv/ NOUN [*plural* **natives**] someone who was born in a particular place □ *She's a native of New South Wales.*

natural /'nætʃərəl/ ADJECTIVE
1 to do with or made by nature, not by people or machines □ *the natural world* □ *an area of great natural beauty* 🔂 *An earthquake is an example of a natural disaster.* 🔂 *The old man had died of natural causes.*
2 normal or to be expected □ *It's only natural to be a little nervous before a test.*

naturally /'nætʃərəlɪ/ ADVERB
1 as would be expected □ *Naturally, we were annoyed not to win.*
2 in a way that is normal □ *Joe began to relax and act a bit more naturally.*
3 without help from anything artificial □ *Let the skin heal naturally.*

nature /'neɪtʃə(r)/ NOUN [plural natures]
1 no plural everything in the world that was not made or changed by people, such as animals, trees, the sea, etc. □ *I love watching programmes about nature.* □ *the forces of nature*
2 a person's character or qualities 🔂 *It's human nature to protect one's family.* 🔂 *It's not in her nature to be unkind.*

➤ Note that **nature** (sense 1) is never used with **the**:
✓ *I've always loved nature.*
✗ *I've always loved the nature.*

naughty /'nɔːtɪ/ ADJECTIVE [naughtier, naughtiest] behaving badly or not doing what you are told to do □ *You've been a very naughty little boy.*

naval /'neɪvəl/ ADJECTIVE to do with the navy □ *an important naval base*

navigate /'nævɪgeɪt/ VERB [navigates, navigating, navigated] to use a map or other equipment to find your way somewhere in a vehicle □ *My mother always drove and my father had to navigate.*

navigation /,nævɪ'geɪʃən/ NOUN, NO PLURAL the process of using maps or other equipment to find your way somewhere

navigator /'nævɪgeɪtə(r)/ NOUN [plural navigators] someone who uses a map or other equipment to find the way somewhere in a vehicle

navy¹ /'neɪvɪ/ NOUN [plural navies]
1 the navy military ships and the soldiers that work on them 🔂 *Matt is hoping to join the navy.*
2 a very dark blue colour

navy² /'neɪvɪ/ ADJECTIVE of a very dark blue colour □ *a navy jacket*

near¹ /nɪə(r)/ PREPOSITION, ADVERB [nearer, nearest]
1 a short distance away □ *I live quite near Tom.* □ **+ to** *We rented a house near to the beach.* □ *Stand a little nearer and you'll be able to see better.* □ *They took him to the nearest hospital.*
2 a short time in the future □ *I don't want to take on extra work so near my exams.* 🔂 *It's a bit early to plan the food – let's talk about it nearer the time.*

near² /nɪə(r)/ ADJECTIVE [nearer, nearest] not far away in distance or time 🔂 *Will you be seeing Kate in the near future?* □ *He is a near neighbour of mine.*

nearby /'nɪəbaɪ/ ADJECTIVE, ADVERB quite close to where you are or the place you are talking about □ *We went to a nearby restaurant for dinner.* □ *Is there a bank nearby?*

➤ Note that **nearby** is not a preposition. The preposition with the same meaning is **near**:
✓ *Their apartment is very near the office.*
✗ *Their apartment is very nearby the office.*

nearly /'nɪəlɪ/ ADVERB almost but not completely □ *We're nearly there.* □ *Nearly everyone had a good time.* □ *They've lived there for nearly three years.*

neat /niːt/ ADJECTIVE [neater, neatest] tidy and arranged carefully □ *Your handwriting's very neat.* 🔂 *Anna always keeps her room neat and tidy.*

necessarily /,nesə'serɪlɪ/ ADVERB not necessarily not in every case □ *Men aren't necessarily stronger than women.*

necessary /'nesəserɪ/ ADJECTIVE needed in order to do something, get something or make something happen □ *The website lists the necessary skills for each job.* 🔂 *I can work late if necessary.* □ **+ to do something** *Is it necessary to come early?* □ **+ for** *Good English is necessary for this job.*

necessity /nɪ'sesətɪ/ NOUN [plural necessities] something that is needed □ *A warm coat is a necessity in this weather.*

neck /nek/ NOUN [plural necks]
1 the part of your body between your head and your shoulders □ *She had her headphones around her neck.*
2 the opening in a piece of clothing that you put your head through ▪ *This T-shirt is too baggy around the neck.*
3 the narrow part of a bottle near its opening

necklace /'neklɪs/ NOUN [plural necklaces] a piece of jewellery you wear around your neck □ *a diamond necklace*

need¹ /niːd/ VERB [needs, needing, needed]
1 if you need something, you must have it in order to exist or to do something □ *I need a sharp knife.* □ *I need your advice.* □ *Do you need any help?* □ *This provides the energy needed to heat the building.*
2 if you need to do something, you must do it, and if you need to have a particular quality, you must have it □ **+ to do something** *We all need to eat and drink.* □ *You need to make more effort with your studies.* □ *You need to be tough to be a doctor.*
3 someone **doesn't need to do something/needn't do something** it is not necessary for someone to do something □ *She doesn't need to pay me.*

need² /niːd/ NOUN [plural needs]
1 something that it is necessary to have □ **+ for** *There is an urgent need for more nurses.*
2 something that it is necessary to do □ **+ to do something** *He recognizes the need to invest more money.* 🔁 *There is no need to wait for me.*
3 **be in need of something** to need something □ *This house is in need of a thorough clean.*

➤ Remember that the noun **need** takes the preposition **for**:
✓ *There is a need for more housing.*
✗ *There is a need of more housing.*

---

needle /ˈniːdəl/ NOUN [plural needles]
1 a small, pointed piece of metal used for sewing 🔁 *a needle and thread* 🔁 *Can you thread this needle for me?*
2 a long thin piece of wood, metal or plastic that is used for knitting (= making something with wool and two long sticks) 🔁 *a pair of knitting needles*
3 the thin, sharp metal part of a medical instrument for putting a drug into someone's body or taking blood out

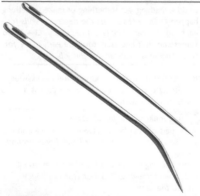

needn't /ˈniːdənt/ a short way to say and write **need not**

negative¹ /ˈnegətɪv/ ADJECTIVE
1 not feeling hope or enthusiasm □ *Since his illness* he's been feeling very negative. 🔁 *You'll never win until you lose that negative attitude.*
2 bad or harmful □ *The drug has a number of negative effects.*
3 a negative word or phrase expresses the meaning 'not' or 'no' □ *a negative sentence* □ *We got a negative reply to our request.*
4 a negative number is less than zero, for example −5. A mathematics word.

negative² /ˈnegətɪv/ NOUN [plural negatives] a film before it is printed, where light objects appear dark and dark objects appear light

neglect¹ /nɪˈglekt/ VERB [neglects, neglecting, neglected] to not give someone or something enough care and attention □ *I've been neglecting the housework because I've been so busy.* □ *The couple are accused of neglecting their children.*

neglect² /nɪˈglekt/ NOUN, NO PLURAL when someone or something does not get enough care or attention □ *The garden has suffered years of neglect.*

negotiate /nɪˈgəʊʃɪeɪt/ VERB [negotiates, negotiating, negotiated] to try to make an agreement with someone by having discussions with them □ *Employees are currently negotiating with managers over a pay rise.* □ *The two parties are hoping to negotiate a settlement to the conflict.*

neighbor /ˈneɪbə(r)/ NOUN [plural neighbors] the US spelling of **neighbour**

● **neighborhood** /ˈneɪbəhʊd/ NOUN [plural neighborhoods] the US spelling of **neighbourhood**

neighbour /ˈneɪbə(r)/ NOUN [plural neighbours] someone who lives near you or in the next house to you □ *We asked a neighbour to feed the cat.* 🔁 *Cecilia was our next-door neighbour for twelve years.*

neighbourhood /ˈneɪbəhʊd/ NOUN [plural neighbourhoods] an area of a town or city □ *This is a pretty neighbourhood with a lot of trees and parks.*

neither¹ /ˈnaɪðə(r)/ DETERMINER, PRONOUN not either of two people or things □ *Neither woman seemed to understand English.* □ *Neither of us can go.*

neither² /ˈnaɪðə(r)/ ADVERB used to say that a negative statement is also true about someone or something else □ *I can't go and neither can Fay.* □ *'I don't like garlic.' 'Neither does Richard.'* 🔁 *'I'm not working today.' 'Me neither, let's go out.'*

neither³ /ˈnaɪðə(r)/ CONJUNCTION **neither ... nor** used when something negative is true of two people or things □ *Neither Peter nor Michael turned up.* □ *I neither know, nor care, where he is.*

nephew /ˈnefjuː/ NOUN [plural nephews] the son of your brother or sister, or the son of your wife's or husband's brother or sister

nerve /nɜːv/ NOUN [plural **nerves**]
1 one of the connections like threads that carry messages between your brain and other parts of your body. A biology word □ *the optic nerve* □ *nerve endings*
2 the courage you need to do something difficult or dangerous □ + *to do something I didn't have the nerve to jump.*
3 nerves nervous feelings ⊞ *She went for a walk to calm her nerves.*
♦ IDIOM **get on someone's nerves** to annoy someone, especially by doing the same thing many times □ *His constant complaints were getting on my nerves.*

nervous /ˈnɜːvəs/ ADJECTIVE
1 worried or frightened □ *I get terribly nervous just before I go on stage.* □ *a nervous laugh* □ + *about She was very nervous about her interview.*
2 to do with the nerves in your body. A biology word □ *nervous disorders*

nervously /ˈnɜːvəslɪ/ ADVERB in a worried, slightly frightened, way □ *She giggled nervously.*

nervousness /ˈnɜːvəsnɪs/ NOUN, NO PLURAL a worried, slightly frightened feeling □ *He struggled to hide his nervousness.*

nervous system /ˈnɜːvəs ˌsɪstəm/ NOUN [plural **nervous systems**] all the nerves in your body and the way they connect to your brain to send messages about feeling and movement. A biology word.

nest /nest/ NOUN [plural **nests**] a place where birds or some kinds of insects and animals live and have their babies □ *We found a bird's nest in a tree.*

net /net/ NOUN [plural **nets**]
1 a material made of crossed string or rope with holes between, or something made from this and used for a particular purpose ⊞ *a fishing net* ⊞ *a mosquito net* ⊞ *The acrobats performed without a safety net.*
2 a thin material made of crossed threads with holes between □ *net curtains*
3 the Net the Internet ⊞ *She spends hours surfing the Net.*

network /ˈnetwɜːk/ NOUN [plural **networks**]
1 a system of roads, railways lines, etc. that cross

and connect with one another □ *A strike has shut down the railway network.*
2 a group of people or companies that work together or help each other □ *She is lucky to have the support of a wide network of friends.* □ *The company has a network of dealers throughout the country.*
3 a system of computers that are all connected together so that they can share information

neutral /ˈnjuːtrəl/ ADJECTIVE
1 not supporting either side in an argument, war or competition □ *The referee must remain neutral.*
2 a neutral colour is not strong or bright

never /ˈnevə(r)/ ADVERB not ever □ *I've never been abroad.* □ *It's never too late to learn.* □ *I promise never to say that again.* □ *I would never do anything to hurt you.*

➤ Note that **never** usually goes before a 'to infinitive'. It does not go between 'to' and the verb:
✓ *I promise never to do it again.*
✗ *I promise to never do it again.*

nevertheless /ˌnevəðəˈles/ ADVERB despite that □ *The car isn't perfect, but it's very good nevertheless.*

new /njuː/ ADJECTIVE [**newer, newest**]
1 not existing before, or only recently made, bought, invented, etc. □ *A new hospital is being built in the city.* □ *We are creating new online materials.* ⊞ *New technology has improved international communications.* □ *He bought a new jacket.* □ *I got a new bike for my birthday.*
2 different □ *I met my new boss today.* □ *He showed me a new way to make cheese sauce.*
3 not familiar □ *Working in a team is a new experience for me.* □ + *to The business world is still new to her.*
4 new to something if you are new to an area or an activity, you have only recently come there or started to do it □ *She's still quite new to the job.*

➤ THESAURUS: Something which is new did not exist before, or has recently been made, bought, invented etc. Something which is fresh is new and different, in a good way. For example, you might talk about putting fresh sheets on the bed. Food which is fresh is not old and has not been dried or frozen. Something which is unused has never been used.

newborn /ˈnjuːbɔːn/ ADJECTIVE a newborn baby has just been born
newly /ˈnjuːlɪ/ ADVERB recently □ *the newly appointed London Mayor*

news /nju:z/ NOUN, NO PLURAL
1 new information □ **+ about** *Have you heard the news about Raj?* □ **+ of** *News of her safe return was greeted with joy.* □ **+ on** *Is there any news on the wedding date yet?* ☖ *We've had some good news; Beth is pregnant.* ☖ *I'm afraid I've got some bad news.*
2 the news information about important events on the radio or television, or in newspapers, etc. ☖ *the local/national news* □ *They always watch the news at 10 o'clock.*

> ➤ Remember that **news** is used with a singular verb:
> ✔ *The news is so bad at the moment.*
> ✗ *The news are so bad at the moment.*

newsagent /'nju:zeɪdʒənt/ NOUN [plural newsagents]
1 someone who sells newspapers and magazines
2 newsagent's a shop that sells newspapers and magazines and usually other things like sweets and cigarettes

newspaper /'nju:zpeɪpə(r)/ NOUN [plural newspapers] large folded pieces of paper printed with reports and pictures about recent events and sold every day or every week □ *I saw your picture in the newspaper.* ☖ *He started his career working on the local newspaper.*

New Year /ˌnju: 'jɪə(r)/ NOUN, NO PLURAL the first few days of January, when people often celebrate □ *They're having a New Year's party.* □ *Happy New Year!*
New Year's Day /ˌnju: jɪəz 'deɪ/ NOUN [plural New Year's Days] 1 January, the first day of the year
New Year's Eve /ˌnju: jɪəz ' i:v/ NOUN [plural New Year's Eves] 31 December, the last day of the year

next¹ /nekst/ ADJECTIVE
1 following or happening immediately after □ *What's the next name on the list?* □ *I need to phone him in the next hour.* □ *The next morning he felt much better.* □ *Next time I see Sally, I'll ask her.*
2 next week/Saturday/year, etc. the week/Saturday/year, etc. after this one □ *Do you want to come round next weekend?*
3 nearest to the place where you are now □ *Take the next left.* □ *The next town is five miles away.*

next² /nekst/ PRONOUN
1 the person or thing that follows or happens immediately after someone or something else □ *Who's next to see the doctor?*
2 the week/Saturday/year, etc. after next two

weeks/Saturdays/years, etc. from the present □ *I'm going to New York the week after next.*

next³ /nekst/ PREPOSITION
1 next to in a position at the side of someone or something □ *I put the book down next to her.* ☖ *Nobody wants to live right next to a motorway.*
2 next to nothing almost nothing □ *I earn next to nothing from my writing.*

next⁴ /nekst/ ADVERB immediately after something else □ *What will happen next?* □ *Next we need to paint the walls.*

next door /ˌnekst 'dɔ:(r)/ ADJECTIVE, ADVERB in the next house, building or room ☖ *We have very nice next door neighbours.* □ *Our office is next door to the station.* □ *We get on well with the people next door.*
NHS /ˌen eɪtʃ'es/ ABBREVIATION **the NHS** the National Health Service; the system which provides free medical treatment for people in the UK □ *He had the operation done on the NHS.*

nice /naɪs/ ADJECTIVE [nicer, nicest]
1 pleasant, good or attractive □ *If the weather's nice, we can go for a walk.* □ *She took me to a really nice restaurant.* ☖ *Have a nice time in Germany!*
2 kind or friendly □ *That wasn't a very nice thing to do.* □ **+ to** *She's always nice to the children.* □ **+ of** *It was very nice of Rob to give me a lift.* □ **+ about** *My tutor was really nice about my work.*

> ➤ THESAURUS: Nice is a general word. If something or someone is nice to look at, you can say they are attractive. If an experience is nice, you can say that it is pleasant or enjoyable. If an experience is very nice, you can say that it is great or fantastic. If a person is nice because they are kind and pleasant, you can say that they are friendly.

nickname¹ /'nɪkneɪm/ NOUN [plural nicknames] a name that you use for someone that is not their real name □ *His nickname at school was 'President' because his real name's Kennedy.*
nickname² /'nɪkneɪm/ VERB [nicknames, nicknaming, nicknamed] to call someone by a nickname □ *They nicknamed him 'Scottie'.*

niece /ni:s/ NOUN [plural nieces] the daughter of your brother or sister, or the daughter of your wife's or husband's brother or sister

night /naɪt/ NOUN [plural nights]
1 the time when it is dark and when people usually sleep ☖ *I hardly slept last night.* ☖ *I spent the night at my sister's.* ☖ *The dog woke me up in the middle of the night.* ☖ *He's been having sleepless nights worrying about work.*
2 at night during the time when it is dark □ *I don't walk the streets on my own at night.*
3 the part of the evening before you go to bed ☖ *I*

went out with David last night. □ *Are you doing anything on Saturday night?* □ *I'm having a night out with my friends on Friday.*

4 Good night. something you say when you leave someone in the evening, or when you or they go to bed

➤ Notice that we usually say **at night** to mean 'during the time when it is dark':
✓ *I never drive at night.*
✗ *I never drive in the night.*

nightclub /'naɪtklʌb/ NOUN [plural **nightclubs**] a place where people can dance and drink late at night

nightmare /'naɪtmeə(r)/ NOUN [plural nightmares]
1 a frightening dream □ *Older children often have nightmares.*
2 a very unpleasant experience □ *The drive home was a complete nightmare.*

nine /naɪn/ NUMBER [plural **nines**] the number 9

nineteen /ˌnaɪn'tiːn/ NUMBER [plural **nineteens**] the number 19

nineteenth /ˌnaɪn'tiːnθ/ NUMBER 19th written as a word

ninetieth /'naɪntɪəθ/ NUMBER 90th written as a word

ninety /'naɪntɪ/ NUMBER [plural **nineties**]
1 the number 90
2 the nineties the years between 1990 and 1999

ninth[1] /naɪnθ/ NUMBER 9th written as a word

ninth[2] /naɪnθ/ NOUN [plural **ninths**] 1/9; one of nine equal parts of something

No. *or* **no.** /nəʊ/ ABBREVIATION **number**[1]

no[1] /nəʊ/ EXCLAMATION
1 used to refuse, disagree or give a negative answer □ *'Can you give me a lift to the station?' 'No, sorry, I need to get straight home.'* □ *'Tim's really stupid.' 'No he isn't!'* □ *'Can I have some more cake?' 'No, you've had enough already.'* □ *'Are you all right?' 'No, I've got my foot stuck.'*
2 used to agree with a negative statement □ *'The weather's not very good today.' 'No, it's a bit cold.'*
3 used to express shock or surprise 🔁 *Oh no! I've left my passport at home!* □ *'Chris and Alice are getting married.' 'No! They've only known each other a few weeks!'*

no[2] /nəʊ/ ADVERB not any □ *She's no better this morning.* 🔁 *No fewer than four players were sent off during the match.* □ *Payment is due no later than the 15th.*

no[3] /nəʊ/ DETERMINER
1 not any □ *They have no money.* □ *There is no need to bring a coat.* □ *No decisions have been taken yet.*

2 used to say that something is not allowed □ *No smoking.*

noble /'nəʊbəl/ ADJECTIVE [**nobler**, **noblest**]
1 brave and honest, or helping other people in a way that people admire □ *We are doing important work for a noble cause.*
2 belonging to a high social class □ *He comes from a noble family.*

nobody /'nəʊbədɪ/ PRONOUN not any person □ *Nobody tells me what to do!* □ *There was nobody at home.* 🔁 *Nobody else noticed it.*

➤ Note that **nobody** is always followed by a singular verb:
✓ Nobody has said anything.
✗ Nobody have said anything.

nod[1] /nɒd/ VERB [**nods**, **nodding**, **nodded**] to move your head up and down, especially to agree or to say 'yes' 🔁 *He nodded his head enthusiastically.* 🔁 *His wife nodded in agreement.*

nod[2] /nɒd/ NOUN [plural **nods**] when you nod your head 🔁 *He gave a small nod.*

noise /nɔɪz/ NOUN [plural **noises**]
1 a sound 🔁 *Did you hear a noise outside?* 🔁 *The bird was making screeching noises.* 🔁 *There was a sudden, loud noise.*
2 *no plural* sound that is loud or unpleasant □ *+ of* *He shouted over the noise of the engine.* 🔁 *Could you please make a little less noise?* 🔁 *The background noise made it difficult to hear.*

noisy /'nɔɪzɪ/ ADJECTIVE [**noisier**, **noisiest**] making a lot of noise □ *a noisy party* □ *Some people complain about noisy neighbours.* □ *The fridge seems very noisy – is there something wrong with it?*

nominate /'nɒmɪneɪt/ VERB [**nominates**, **nominating**, **nominated**] to suggest someone for a job, position or prize □ *Charles nominated Peter as leader of the group.* □ *She was nominated for an Oscar.*

non- /nɒn/ PREFIX non- is added to the beginning of words to mean 'not' □ *a non-smoker* (= someone who does not smoke)

none /nʌn/ PRONOUN not any □ *+ of* *None of them are going to admit to being wrong.* □ *We looked for more biscuits but there were none left.* 🔁 *Most people there ate little food, or none at all.*

nonetheless /ˌnʌnðə'les/ ADVERB despite that □ *It was not easy; nonetheless, he tried his best.* □ *There have been one or two delays; the road will open on time, nonetheless.*

nonsense /'nɒnsəns/ NOUN, NO PLURAL something that is not true or sensible 🔁 *His theory is a load of nonsense.* 🔁 *You're talking nonsense.* 🔁 *These reports are absolute nonsense.*

noodle /ˈnuːdəl/ NOUN [*plural* **noodles**] a long thin piece of pasta

noon /nuːn/ NOUN, NO PLURAL twelve o'clock in the middle of the day □ *We'll have our lunch at noon.* □ *It was a few minutes past noon.*

no one *or* **no-one** /ˈnəʊwʌn/ PRONOUN not any person □ *No one's in at the moment.* □ *No one knows what happened.* □ *There was no one to ask.* ⌨ *There was no one else in the building.*

> ➤ Note that **no one** is always followed by a singular verb:
> ✓ *No one tells me anything.*
> ✗ No one tell me anything.

nor /nɔː(r)/ CONJUNCTION
1 **neither ... nor** used when something negative is true of two people or things □ *Neither Jack nor Jenny is at home.* □ *Neither the teachers nor the parents are happy with the situation.*
2 used after a negative statement to say that the same is true for someone else □ *He didn't see anything unusual, and nor did any of his friends.* □ *I'm sure Jack wouldn't like that and nor would I.*

normal /ˈnɔːməl/ ADJECTIVE usual and expected
□ **+ to do something** *It's normal to feel hungry at lunchtime.* □ **+ for** *This temperature is normal for August.* ⌨ *He just wants to live a normal life.* ⌨ *There's been a lot of building work, but we should be back to normal soon.*

> ➤ THESAURUS: Something that is normal is usual and expected. Something that is common exists or happens often and in many places. For example, you can say that traffic jams are common in large cities. If something is typical, it has the usual qualities of a particular person or thing. You can talk about the typical food of a particular region, for example. If something is ordinary, it is not unusual or different.

normally /ˈnɔːməlɪ/ ADVERB
1 usually □ *We normally go to bed pretty early.* □ *Normally, I drive to work.* □ *I don't normally do this kind of thing.*
2 in the usual and expected way □ *This plant has developed normally, but the other one is diseased.*

north[1] /nɔːθ/ NOUN, NO PLURAL the direction that is to your left when you are facing the rising sun

north[2] /nɔːθ/ ADJECTIVE, ADVERB in or towards the north □ *the cold north wind* □ *We were travelling north on the motorway.*

north-east[1] /ˌnɔːθˈiːst/ NOUN, NO PLURAL the direction between north and east

north-east[2] /ˌnɔːθˈiːst/ ADJECTIVE, ADVERB in or towards the north-east □ *The north-east region of Spain.*

northern /ˈnɔːðən/ ADJECTIVE in or from the north □ *the cold northern climate* □ *Northern districts will have some rain.*

North Pole /ˌnɔːθ ˈpəʊl/ NOUN **the North Pole** the point on the Earth that is furthest north

north-west[1] /ˌnɔːθˈwest/ NOUN, NO PLURAL the direction between north and west

north-west[2] /ˌnɔːθˈwest/ ADJECTIVE, ADVERB in or towards the north-west

nose /nəʊz/ NOUN [*plural* **noses**]
1 the part of your face that you breathe and smell through ⌨ *I need to blow my nose.* ⌨ *I had sore eyes and a runny nose.*
2 the front part of something that sticks out, for example, the front of an aircraft
◆ IDIOMS **turn your nose up at something** to refuse to accept something because you do not think it is good enough for you □ *She turned her nose up at my soup.* **under someone's nose** if something happens under someone's nose, they are there when it happens, but they do not notice □ *He was rescued from under the noses of his guards.*

nostril /ˈnɒstrɪl/ NOUN [*plural* **nostrils**] one of the two openings in your nose that you breathe and smell through

not /nɒt/ ADVERB
1 used after verbs like *be* and *do* and modal verbs to make negative sentences. It often becomes **n't** when it is added to verbs □ *I'm not going.* □ *They have not made a decision yet.* □ *It isn't fair.* □ *I can't hear you.*
2 used to give the next words or phrase a negative meaning □ *I told her not to look.* □ *Not everyone was happy with the decision.* □ *'Are you ready?' 'Not yet.'* □ *'Did it upset you?' 'Not at all.'* □ *Let's not go there again.*
3 used with verbs like *hope* and *suspect* or adverbs like *certainly* or *definitely* to make a negative reply □ *'Will you be much longer?' 'I hope not.'* □ *'Can I borrow £5?' 'Certainly not.'*
4 **or not** used to express a negative possibility □ *I don't know if he'll be there or not.*

> ➤ Note that **not** usually goes before a 'to infinitive'. It does not go between 'to' and the verb:
> ✓ *He told me* **not to** *be late*
> ✗ He told me to not be late.

notable /ˈnəʊtəbəl/ ADJECTIVE important and worth remembering □ *The most notable part of the evening was the music.* ⌨ *The whole family were there, with one notable exception.*

note¹ /nəʊt/ NOUN [plural notes]
1 a short piece of writing to help you remember something 🖹 *I made a note of his phone number.* □ *I've got a note of all their names.*
2 a short letter 🖹 *I wrote her a note to say how sorry I was.*
3 notes information that you write down when you are reading a book, in a lesson, etc. 🖹 *There is a handout, so you don't need to take notes.*
4 a piece of paper money □ *a five pound note*
5 a single musical sound or the written sign for it □ *I can't reach the high notes.*

note² /nəʊt/ VERB [notes, noting, noted] to notice something or to pay attention to something □ + *that* *I noted that she always wore red, and wondered why.* □ *We noted the absence of the prince.*
♦ PHRASAL VERB **note something down** to write something down so that you will not forget it □ *I noted down the train times.*

notebook /'nəʊtbʊk/ NOUN [plural notebooks]
1 a small book that you use to write things down in
2 a very small computer that you can carry around. Λ computing word.

notepaper /'nəʊtpeɪpə(r)/ NOUN, NO PLURAL plain paper that you use for writing letters on □ *a sheet of headed notepaper*

nothing /'nʌθɪŋ/ PRONOUN
1 not anything □ *There's nothing to eat.* □ *There's nothing wrong with me.* □ *He carried on as if nothing had happened.* 🖹 *There was nothing else we could do.* 🖹 *I've heard nothing but (= only) praise for her work.*
2 for nothing (a) without being paid □ *He mended my car for nothing.* (b) with no successful result □ *You mean we did all that work for nothing?*
3 nothing like not at all similar □ *He's nothing like his brother.*

> ► Remember that **nothing** is not used with other negative words, such as 'not' and 'never':
> ✓ *She said nothing.*
> ✗ *She didn't say nothing.* □ *She didn't say anything.*

notice¹ /'nəʊtɪs/ VERB [notices, noticing, noticed] to become aware of something because you see, hear, feel, smell or taste it □ *I noticed a funny smell in the hall.* □ *Did you notice the way George was looking at Emily?* □ + *that* *I noticed that the kitchen window was open.* □ + *question word* *He noticed how she kept checking her mobile.*

> ► Note that the verb **notice** is *not* used with the verbs 'can' and 'could':
> ✓ *I noticed that she was thinner.*
> ✗ *I could notice that she was thinner.*

notice² /'nəʊtɪs/ NOUN [plural notices]
1 a written sign □ *a notice pinned on the board* □ *A notice on the door said 'Closed'.* □ *The council has put up warning notices near to the river.*
2 no plural attention 🖹 *No one took any notice of* (= paid attention to) *her.*

noticeable /'nəʊtɪsəbəl/ ADJECTIVE obvious or easy to see □ *There was a noticeable difference in his appearance.* □ *The most noticeable feature was the smell.*

notify /'nəʊtɪfaɪ/ VERB [notifies, notifying, notified] to officially tell someone about something □ *You will be notified of the date.*

notion /'nəʊʃən/ NOUN [plural notions] an idea or a belief □ *This goes against the whole notion of free speech.*

notorious /nəʊ'tɔ:rɪəs/ ADJECTIVE famous for something bad □ *a notorious criminal*

noun /naʊn/ NOUN [plural nouns] a word that refers to a person, a thing, or a quality. For example, *tree*, *Sue*, *air* and *happiness* are nouns.

novel /'nɒvəl/ NOUN [plural novels] a book that tells an invented story □ *a historical/romantic novel*

> ► THESAURUS: Book is a general word for pages joined together inside a cover. A story or a tale is a description of events, which can be real or invented. Stories and tales can be spoken or written. For example, 'Cinderella' is a story. A novel is a book that tells an invented story. For example, 'War and Peace' is a novel.

novelist /'nɒvəlɪst/ NOUN [plural novelists] a person who writes books that tell an invented story
November /nəʊ'vembə(r)/ NOUN [plural Novembers] the eleventh month of the year, after October and before December □ *What's the weather like in November?*

now /naʊ/ ADVERB
1 at the present time □ *It is now five o'clock.* □ *I'm working as a teacher now.* 🖹 *He has refused to speak until now.*
2 from this moment □ *Now I can see him.* □ *You can look at the answers now.* 🖹 *From now on, I'll be giving you homework every day.* □ *Now I can afford to go on holiday.*
3 immediately □ *I'll do it now.* 🖹 *I want to see you in my office right now!*
4 used to start a sentence □ *Now, can anyone tell me the last two kings of England?*
5 (every) now and then sometimes, but not often □ *Every now and then I treat myself to a really hot curry.*

6 just now a very short time ago □ *I saw Jim outside just now.*

nowadays /'nauə,deɪz/ ADVERB at the present time, usually when compared to the past □ *Nowadays, women usually have their babies in hospital.* □ *There's much more for youngsters to do nowadays than there was 20 years ago.*

nowhere /'nəuweə(r)/ ADVERB
1 not anywhere □ *We've got nowhere to go.* ⊞ *These birds are found nowhere else in the world.*
2 nowhere near not at all close in distance, time or a quality □ *Paris is nowhere near Marseilles.* □ *The stadium was nowhere near full.*

nuclear /'nju:klɪə(r)/ ADJECTIVE to do with the reaction that happens when atoms are divided or forced together ⊞ *nuclear power* ⊞ *a nuclear bomb*

nucleus /'nju:klɪəs/ NOUN [*plural* nuclei] the central or most important part of something □ *The nucleus of the cell performs several important functions.* □ *The nucleus of the team hasn't changed.*

nude /nju:d/ ADJECTIVE not wearing any clothes □ *a nude woman*

nuisance /'nju:səns/ NOUN [*plural* nuisances] a person, thing or situation that annoys you or causes problems for you □ *The rabbits have become a nuisance to local gardeners.* ⊞ *'I've locked myself out.' 'Oh, what a nuisance!'*

numb /nʌm/ ADJECTIVE [number, numbest] if a part of your body is numb, you cannot feel it ⊞ *I was so cold my hands had gone completely numb.*

number¹ /'nʌmbə(r)/ NOUN [*plural* numbers]
1 a word or a symbol showing how many of something there are or in what position something is in a series □ *the number four* □ *Please write down any three figure number.* □ *I was number eight on the list.*
2 a quantity of things or people □ *+ of* We hope to increase the number of customers. ⊞ *He keeps a large number of animals.* □ *A number of* (= several) *people have complained.*
3 a number that represents something or someone, for example to show what they are or who they belong to □ *a membership number* □ *What is your account number?*
4 a telephone number □ *I'll give you my number.* ⊞ *I must have dialled the wrong number.*

► THESAURUS: Number is a general word for a word or a symbol showing how many of something there are or in what position something is in a series. Figure is often used to refer to a number that tells you an amount, especially in official documents. For example, you can talk about unemployment figures (how many people are unemployed). A unit is a measure used to show an amount or level. For example, you can say that a centimetre is a unit of length.

number² /'nʌmbə(r)/ VERB [numbers, numbering, numbered] to give a thing or a person a number as part of a series □ *The boxes are all clearly numbered.* □ *Have you numbered the pages?*

numerous /'nju:mərəs/ ADJECTIVE many
□ *Numerous people have had the same experience.*
⊞ *I've met him on numerous occasions.*

nun /nʌn/ NOUN [*plural* nuns] a member of a religious group of women who live away from other people

nurse¹ /nɜ:s/ NOUN [*plural* nurses] a person whose job is to look after people when they are ill or injured, especially in a hospital □ *She works as a nurse at the hospital.*

nurse² /nɜ:s/ VERB [nurses, nursing, nursed] to look after someone when they are ill or injured □ *He had nursed her back to health over several weeks.*

nursery /'nɜ:sərɪ/ NOUN [*plural* nurseries]
1 a place where babies and young children are looked after while their parents are at work □ *Lizzie goes to a local nursery three days a week.*
2 a place where plants are grown and sold

nursing /'nɜ:sɪŋ/ NOUN, NO PLURAL the job of being a nurse

nut /nʌt/ NOUN [*plural* nuts]
1 the fruit of some trees that has a hard shell and an inside part that can often be eaten □ *a cashew nut* □ *a bag of mixed nuts*
2 a small piece of metal with a hole in the middle which fits onto the end of a bolt (= thin piece of metal) to hold things together □ *a wheel nut*

nutrient /'nju:trɪənt/ NOUN [*plural* nutrients] any substance in food that gives you energy and makes you healthy □ *Iron is an essential nutrient for many animals.*

nutrition /nju:'trɪʃən/ NOUN, NO PLURAL food and the way it affects your health □ *Good nutrition is necessary for a quick recovery.* □ *information about nutrition*

Oo

O or **O** /əʊ/ the 15th letter of the alphabet

oak /əʊk/ NOUN [*plural* oaks] a large tree with hard wood, or the wood from this tree

oasis /əʊ'eɪsɪs/ NOUN [*plural* oases] a place in a desert where there are plants and water

oath /əʊθ/ NOUN [*plural* oaths] a formal promise 🐟 *Members swear an oath of secrecy about the group.*

obese /əʊ'biːs/ ADJECTIVE extremely fat

obey /ə'beɪ/ VERB [obeys, obeying, obeyed] to do what a person or rule tells you to do □ *He was taught to obey his parents.* 🐟 *Drivers must obey the law.* 🐟 *He refused to obey a court order.*

object¹ /'ɒbdʒɪkt/ NOUN [*plural* objects]
1 a thing that you can see or touch but not a person or animal □ *There were various objects on the table.* □ *Keep sharp objects away from children.*
2 an aim or purpose □ *His main object in life was to become rich.* □ **+ of** *The object of the exercise is to improve teaching standards.*
3 in grammar, the person or thing that a verb affects □ *In the sentence 'I ate the apple', 'apple' is the object.*

object² /əb'dʒekt/ VERB [objects, objecting, objected] to say that you do not want something to happen □ *Nobody objected to the original proposal.*

objection /əb'dʒekʃən/ NOUN [*plural* objections] a reason you do not want something to happen □ *My only objection is that he is too young.* 🐟 *I have no objections to the changes.*

obligation /,ɒblɪ'ɡeɪʃən/ NOUN [*plural* obligations] a duty to do something 🐟 *Schools have a legal obligation to take good care of students.*

observation /,ɒbzə'veɪʃən/ NOUN [*plural* observations] when you watch someone or something very carefully □ *He has been kept in hospital for observation.*

observe /əb'zɜːv/ VERB [observes, observing, observed] to watch someone or something very carefully □ *Police continued to observe his actions with interest.*

obstacle /'ɒbstəkəl/ NOUN [*plural* obstacles]
1 something that stops you from doing what you want to do □ *He had overcome a lot of obstacles in his life.*
2 an object that is in front of you and that you must move or go around in order to go forward

obstruct /əb'strʌkt/ VERB [obstructs, obstructing, obstructed]
1 to block somewhere such as a road, door or path, so that people cannot move along or through it □ *The road was obstructed by a fallen tree.*
2 to try to prevent something from happening □ *He was arrested for obstructing the police investigation.*

obtain /əb'teɪn/ VERB [obtains, obtaining, obtained] a formal word meaning to get something □ *Clients can obtain information from our website.*

➤ Note that the word **obtain** is used mainly in formal situations and is not common. The usual word is **get**:
  ✓ *Where did you get your jacket?*
  ✗ *Where did you obtain your jacket?*

obvious /'ɒbvɪəs/ ADJECTIVE easy to see or understand □ **+ that** *It was obvious that she was unhappy.* 🐟 *He started crying for no obvious reason.* □ **+ to** *It was obvious to anyone in the room that he was lying.*

obviously /'ɒbvɪəslɪ/ ADVERB used for giving information that you expect other people will already know or will agree with □ *Obviously, I'll need some help.* □ *Obviously we're not happy with this situation.*

occasion /ə'keɪʒən/ NOUN [*plural* occasions]
1 a particular time when something happens □ *I've met him on several occasions.* 🐟 *He has run in the race on three previous occasions.*
2 an important event 🐟 *She only wore the shoes for special occasions.*

occasional /ə'keɪʒənəl/ ADJECTIVE happening sometimes but not often □ *They made occasional visits to Scotland.* 🐟 *Eating the occasional ice cream won't make you fat.*
• **occasionally** /ə'keɪʒənəlɪ/ ADVERB sometimes but not often □ *I occasionally go to the theatre.*

occupation /,ɒkju'peɪʃən/ NOUN [*plural* occupations]
1 a formal word meaning job □ *Firefighting is a dangerous occupation.* □ *professional occupations*
2 a formal word meaning something you like doing in your free time □ *Reading is his favourite occupation.*
3 *no plural* when an army enters a country or area

and takes control of it □ **+ of** *the Roman occupation of Britain*

occupy /ˈɒkjupaɪ/ VERB [occupies, occupying, occupied]

1 to occupy a space is to fill it □ *A table occupied the centre of the room.*
2 if someone occupies a building, they live or work there □ *The building is occupied by several small companies.*
3 to keep someone busy □ *She has more than enough to occupy her.* □ *He occupied himself with the garden.*
4 to enter a country or area and take control of it with an army □ *Soldiers were occupying the town.*

occur /əˈkɜː(r)/ VERB [occurs, occurring, occurred] a formal word meaning to happen □ *The accident occurred last night.*

♦ PHRASAL VERB **occur to someone** if something occurs to you, you suddenly think it □ *It never occurred to me that I should see a doctor about it.*

ocean /ˈəʊʃən/ NOUN [plural oceans] one of the 5 large areas of sea in the world □ *the Atlantic Ocean*

➤ **THESAURUS:** Sea is the salt water that covers most of the Earth's surface. A sea is a large area of salt water. An ocean is one of the 5 large areas of sea in the world. A lake is a large area of fresh water with land all around it. A wave is a raised line of water that moves across the sea or other area of water. The tide is the regular rise and fall of the level of the sea.

o'clock /əˈklɒk/ ADVERB used after the numbers one to twelve to say what time of day it is □ *School starts at nine o'clock.* □ *'What time is it?' 'It's nearly 12 o'clock.'*

October /ɒkˈtəʊbə(r)/ NOUN [plural Octobers] the tenth month of the year, after September and before November □ *He retired in October.*

odd /ɒd/ ADJECTIVE [odder, oddest]
1 strange □ *It seems an odd choice.* □ *He's very odd.*
2 without the other one of a pair □ *an odd shoe*
3 an odd number is a number that you cannot divide exactly by two □ *5 and 7 are odd numbers.*

of /ɒv/ PREPOSITION
1 used to show an amount or measurement □ *hundreds of people* □ *a pint of milk* □ *an increase of 13%* □ *I'm part of a team.* □ *I left home at the age of 16.*
2 used to show which members of a group are affected or being talked about □ *I have some bananas, but none of them are ripe.* □ *Many of our members are over 60.* □ *All of the children will receive a present.*
3 used to talk about the characteristics or qualities

that someone or something has □ *Did you notice the size of their offices?*
4 used after a noun to show a particular example of that thing □ *There have been several cases of cholera.* □ *I grew up in the town of Aylesbury.* □ *We worked together for a short period of time.*
5 made from or caused by something □ *They constructed a building of ice.* □ *There was a large pile of newspapers in the corner.* □ *The whole house smelled of garlic.* □ *We could hear their shouts of joy.* □ *He died of hunger.*
6 about something, showing something or to do with something □ *He told us stories of his adventures in India.* □ *I need a map of Berlin.* □ *I always carry a photograph of my children.* □ *You remind me of my sister.* □ *He was frightened of bees.*
7 containing something □ *I gave her a box of chocolates.* □ *Would you like a glass of water?* □ *I read a book of his poems.*
8 belonging to or experienced by someone or something □ *The furniture is the property of the school.* □ *I lost the lid of the box.* □ *We must consider the needs of the patients.*
9 used to show the position of something or someone □ *We live just south of Edinburgh.* □ *I sat at the side of the bed.* □ *There is a large garden to the rear of the property.*

off¹ /ɒf/ ADVERB, PREPOSITION
1 away from the top or surface of something □ *I took the book off the shelf.* □ *Keep off the grass.* □ *I'm trying to get the mud off my shoes.* □ *Make sure you don't fall off!*
2 no longer attached to something □ *The petals have all dropped off.* □ *Some tiles have come off the roof.*
3 away in distance, in time or from a place □ *We were drifting a few miles off the coast.* □ *The holiday seems a long way off.* □ *He walked off and left me.*
4 if you take clothes off, you stop wearing them □ *I took off my jacket.* □ *He had his shoes off.*
5 out of a public vehicle □ *I got off the train in Padua.* □ *Take the number 7 bus and get off at the station.*
6 not operating □ *I switched the heating off.* □ *Make sure your phones are off.*
7 if a price has a particular amount off, it is reduced by that amount □ *All computer games are 20% off this week.*
8 not at work or at school □ *Why don't you take the day off?* □ *She's off work today.*
9 near to something, and usually connected to it □ *My office is off the main corridor.* □ *Our road is just off the main road.*

off² /ɒf/ ADJECTIVE if food is off, it is rotten and cannot be eaten □ *This milk is off.*

offence /əˈfens/ NOUN [plural offences]
1 a crime □ *The police charged him with three offences.* 🔁 *He has committed several violent offences.* 🔁 *Burning the flag is a criminal offence in some countries.*

2 *no plural* when you upset someone by saying or doing something 🔾 *His comments certainly caused offence.* 🔾 *Philip took offence (= felt offended) at the suggestion.*

offend /ə'fend/ VERB [offends, offending, offended] to make someone feel upset or angry by something you say or do □ *I hope I didn't offend anyone.*

offense /ə'fens/ NOUN [plural offenses] the US spelling of **offence**

offensive /ə'fensɪv/ ADJECTIVE rude and insulting □ *offensive remarks* 🔾 *He found the question deeply offensive.*

offer¹ /'ɒfə(r)/ VERB [offers, offering, offered]
1 to ask someone if they want something □ *She offered me another drink.* □ **+ to** *He offered the sweets to all the children in the class.*
2 to say that you will do something for someone □ **+ to do something** *She offered to carry my bag for me.*

offer² /'ɒfə(r)/ NOUN [plural offers]
1 when you ask someone if they want something or if you can do something for them 🔾 *It was a very generous offer.* 🔾 *I've had several job offers.* 🔾 *She accepted his offer to drive her home.* □ **+ of** *an offer of help*
2 an amount of money offered 🔾 *They made an offer of £300,000 for the house.*
3 **on offer** being sold at a lower price than usual □ *These chocolates were on offer.*

office /'ɒfɪs/ NOUN [plural offices]
1 a building where people work for a company 🔾 *Our head office (= main office) is in London.* 🔾 *an office building* 🔾 *office workers*
2 a room or building used for a particular purpose □ *the tourist information office* □ *The ticket office opens at 8 o'clock.* □ *The manager is in her office.*

officer /'ɒfɪsə(r)/ NOUN [plural officers]
1 a person in the army, navy or air force who is in charge of ordinary soldiers □ *senior army officers*
2 someone who has a particular job in a government or organization □ *a prison officer* □ *immigration officers* □ *He's the chief executive officer of the company.*

official¹ /ə'fɪʃəl/ ADJECTIVE done or approved by a government or someone in authority □ *an official announcement* □ *Canada has two official languages.* □ *Official figures show that crime has risen by 10%.*

➤ **THESAURUS:** Something which is **official** has been done or approved by a government or someone in authority. Something that is **proper** is correct and suitable. For example, you can talk about the **proper** equipment for a job. Something that is **legal** is permitted by law.

official² /ə'fɪʃəl/ NOUN [plural officials] someone who has an important job in an organization, especially a government 🔾 *government officials*

officially /ə'fɪʃəli/ ADVERB publicly and formally □ *The new library is now officially open.* □ *He will officially retire next week.*

often /'ɒfən, 'ɒftən/ ADVERB
1 many times □ *I often go to the cinema.* □ *I don't play tennis very often now.* 🔾 *How often do you see Jess?* 🔾 *I wish I could travel more often.* 🔾 *He visits the area quite often.*
2 in many situations or cases □ *Jokes are often difficult to translate.* □ *Often, schools are unable to deal with problem students.*

oh /əʊ/ EXCLAMATION
1 used when you have just understood something □ *Oh, I see.* □ *Oh, so that's why she isn't here.*
2 used when you are disappointed or annoyed □ *Oh, that's a shame!* □ *Oh no, the computer has just crashed!*
3 used when you are very pleased or surprised □ *Oh, that's very kind!* □ *Oh, that's fantastic!*

oil¹ /ɔɪl/ NOUN, NO PLURAL
1 a thick, dark liquid under the ground that is used for making petrol □ *Oil prices have increased.* □ *the oil industry* □ *US oil production*
2 a thick liquid from plants or animals, used in cooking □ *olive oil* □ *vegetable oil* □ *Heat the oil in a pan and fry the onions until soft.*

oil² /ɔɪl/ VERB [oils, oiling, oiled] to put oil on something

oily /'ɔɪli/ ADJECTIVE [oilier, oiliest] like oil, or covered with oil □ *an oily liquid* □ *an oily cloth*

OK¹ *or* **okay** /əʊ'keɪ/ EXCLAMATION
1 an informal way of agreeing or asking someone if they agree □ *'I'll come over after work.' 'OK'.* □ *OK! I'll do it!* □ *You need to do your homework before Friday, OK?*
2 used before you start talking, especially to many people □ *OK, first of all I'd like to welcome you all to the school.*

OK² *or* **okay** /əʊ'keɪ/ ADJECTIVE, ADVERB
1 an informal word meaning allowed or acceptable 🔾 *Is it OK if I get there a bit later?* 🔾 *'I'm really sorry I forgot your birthday.' 'That's OK.'* □ **+ to do something** *Is it OK to open the window?*
2 an informal word meaning healthy and happy □ *'How are you?' 'I'm OK, thanks.'* □ *Are you feeling OK now?*
3 an informal word meaning good enough □ *Do I look OK in this dress?* □ *I think I did OK in the exam.*

old /əʊld/ ADJECTIVE [older, oldest]
1 used to talk about someone's age 🔾 *How old are you?* □ *He's nine years old.*

2 having lived or existed for a long time 🪶 *an old man/woman* □ *an old church* □ *She's not old enough to vote.* □ *I'm too old to go out all night.* □ *My older brother (= older than me) is a builder.*
3 having been owned or used for a long time □ *I wore a pair of old shoes.*
4 used to talk about something or someone from a time before now □ *My old car didn't have air conditioning.* □ *The old road went through the town centre.* □ *I saw one of my old teachers yesterday.*
5 an old friend someone who has been your friend for a long time

old age /ˌəʊld ˈeɪdʒ/ NOUN, NO PLURAL the time when someone is old □ *He wrote poems in his old age.*

old-fashioned /ˌəʊld-ˈfæʃənd/ ADJECTIVE not modern or fashionable □ *old-fashioned clothes* □ *His ideas are very old-fashioned.* □ *He contacted her in the old-fashioned way, by writing a letter.*

olive /ˈɒlɪv/ NOUN [*plural* olives] a small black or green fruit that is not sweet. It is eaten and is used to make oil for cooking.

Olympic Games /əˌlɪmpɪk ˈɡeɪmz/ or **Olympics** /əˈlɪmpɪks/ PLURAL NOUN the Olympic Games/the Olympics the international sports competition that takes place every four years in a different country

omelet /ˈɒmlɪt/ NOUN [*plural* omelets] the US spelling of **omelette**

omelette /ˈɒmlɪt/ NOUN [*plural* omelettes] a food made by mixing eggs and frying them, often with other food inside □ *a cheese omelette*

omit /əˈmɪt/ VERB [omits, omitting, omitted] to not include something □ *This detail was omitted from the documents.*

on¹ /ɒn/ PREPOSITION
1 touching or supported by the top surface of something □ *The books are on the table.* □ *We built our house on a hill.* □ *I was standing on one leg.*
2 onto something □ *Rain was falling on the crowd.* □ *I jumped on the bike.*
3 sticking to or hanging from something □ *There were lots of pictures on the walls.* □ *Put your coat on the peg.*
4 used to say what day or date something happens □ *He's coming to see us on Friday.*
5 about □ *He gave me a book on Scottish history.* □ *I can't comment on her views.*
6 using a particular form of transport □ *I came on the bus.*
7 being performed or broadcast □ *The programme will be on TV next week.*
8 used to say how much time or money you use for a particular thing □ *We spent £300 on flowers.*
9 as a result of touching or hitting something □ *I tripped on a loose stone.* □ *She hit her head on the shelf.*
10 using a particular machine or piece of equipment

□ *He's on the phone at the moment.* □ *The letter was written on a typewriter.*

on² /ɒn/ ADVERB
1 if you have a piece of clothing on, you are wearing it □ *Put your coat on.*
2 if a machine or a piece of equipment is on, it is working or being used □ *Switch the light on.* □ *Shall we have the heating on?*
3 used to show that an action continues □ *We worked on into the night.* □ *We all became bored as he droned on about football.*
4 onto a vehicle □ *I got on at Cambridge station.*
5 being performed or broadcast □ *What's on at the cinema?*
6 going to take place □ *Is the party still on?*
7 forward □ *They moved on.* □ *We went on until we came to a river.*
8 on and on continuing for a long time □ *The speeches went on and on.*

once¹ /wʌns/ ADVERB
1 one time only □ *He only did it once.* □ *It's the kind of opportunity you get once in your life.* □ *I only met him once.*
2 once a/every one time in every period of time □ *I wash my car once a week.* □ *We meet about once every four or five months.*
3 at a time in the past □ *People once lived in caves.* □ *They once owned the whole town.* □ *I was a communist once.*
4 once again/more again, or one more time □ *I found myself alone once more.* □ *He is once again in prison.* □ *Basic errors have once again cost lives.*
5 at once (a) immediately □ *Miss Peters wants to see you at once.* (b) at the same time □ *I can't do two things at once.*
6 once or twice a few times □ *I've met him once or twice.*

once² /wʌns/ CONJUNCTION as soon as □ *Once you've finished, you can go.* □ *Once I started getting into debt, I was always anxious.*

one¹ /wʌn/ NUMBER [*plural* ones] the number 1

one² /wʌn/ DETERMINER
1 used to talk about one particular person or thing □ *We've only had one reply.* □ **+ of** *One of my friends came round.* 🪶 *One or two of the apples were rotten.*
2 one day/evening, etc. on a day/evening, etc. in the future that has not been decided □ *We must meet up for lunch one day.*

one³ /wʌn/ PRONOUN [*plural* ones]
1 used to avoid repeating a word □ *These plums are delicious – would you like one?* □ *My fridge broke and I had to buy a new one.* □ *Our house is one of the ones with a yellow door.*
2 a formal word meaning anyone or you □ *One can see the sea from here.*

3 one another each other □ *They embraced one another.* □ *They have great respect for one another.*

4 one by one one after the other □ *One by one, people began to get up and leave.*

oneself /wʌn'self/ PRONOUN the reflexive form of 'one' used for talking about yourself or people in general. A formal word □ *One can lie to oneself as well as to other people.*

one-way /ˌwʌn'weɪ/ ADJECTIVE

1 allowing cars to travel in one direction only 🔁 *It was a narrow one-way street.* 🔁 *The town had a very complicated one-way system.*

2 a one-way ticket, price, etc. is for travelling to a place but not coming back □ *The airline is offering one-way fares to Paris for £25.*

onion /'ʌnjən/ NOUN [plural onions] a round vegetable with many layers that makes your eyes hurt when you cut it □ *Fry the onions until they are soft.* □ *onion soup*

online /ˌɒn'laɪn/ ADJECTIVE, ADVERB using the Internet □ *online advertising* □ *online videos* 🔁 *Younger people are more likely to go online for the news.* 🔁 *Many people now shop online.*

only¹ /'əʊnlɪ/ ADVERB

1 used to emphasize how small an amount, number, etc. is □ *There are only two weeks left.* □ *Only one of us can win.* □ *She left the job after only a week.* □ *This is only the beginning.*

2 nobody or nothing else □ *Only you can do it.* □ *I only use the best quality ingredients.* □ *She would only say that she was disappointed.*

3 used to say that something is not important or not intended to be harmful □ *'What's that noise?' 'Oh, it's only the children.'* □ *I was only trying to help.*

4 only just (a) a very short time ago □ *I've only just finished my essay.* (b) by a very small amount □ *He only just beat me.*

only² /'əʊnlɪ/ CONJUNCTION used to say that something cannot happen or is not true □ *I'd like to come, only I have to work.*

only³ /'əʊnlɪ/ ADJECTIVE without any others of the same type □ *It was the only book on keeping goats that I could find.* □ *His only son was killed in the war.* 🔁 *She was an only child* (= had no brothers or sisters).

onto /'ɒntuː/ PREPOSITION used for showing movement into a position in or on something □ *I climbed onto the roof.* □ *Jim got onto the bus.* □ *The dog rolled onto its side.*

open¹ /'əʊpən/ ADJECTIVE

1 not shut or fastened 🔁 *The window was wide open.* □ *An open book lay on the table.* □ *The door* burst open and Ella ran in. □ *His eyes were open and he was still breathing.*

2 available to be visited or used □ *We are open from 9–5.* □ *Is the restaurant open on Mondays?* □ *The new road will be open in June.*

3 not covered, surrounded or blocked 🔁 *She had a love of open spaces.* □ *He had an open wound on his leg.* □ *The Oxford road is open again.*

4 if a computer program or document is open, it is ready to use. A computing word.

5 honest and not keeping secrets □ *He was very open with me about his work.* □ *We would like to see a more open style of government.*

➤ **THESAURUS:** Open is a general word. If you open something that is locked, for example a door, you can use the word unlock. If you open something that is fastened, you can use the words undo or unfasten. For example, you can undo a coat. If you open something that was folded, you can use the word unfold. For example, you can unfold a map or a T-shirt.

open² /'əʊpən/ ADJECTIVE

1 to move to a position that is not shut or fastened, or to make something do this □ *He opened the door.* □ *I opened my eyes.* □ *Open your books on page 34.*

2 to remove the cover from a package, letter, etc. □ *I opened my birthday presents this morning.* □ *Have you opened the letter from the bank yet?*

3 to become available to be visited or used, or to make something available to be visited or used □ *The new supermarket opened last week.* □ *They will be opening the new road in December.* □ *What time does the surgery open?* □ *We don't open on Sundays.*

4 to make a computer program or document ready to use. A computing word □ *Open the spreadsheet and click at the top of the column.*

5 to begin something □ *He opened the meeting with a speech of welcome.* □ *Police have opened an enquiry into the shooting.*

6 if you open a bank account, you make an arrangement with a bank to keep your money there

opener /'əʊpənə(r)/ NOUN [plural openers] something that opens a container such as a bottle or a can □ *a tin opener*

opening¹ /'əʊpənɪŋ/ NOUN [plural openings]

1 a hole or space □ *There was an opening in the fence.*

2 an event to mark the start of a place, building, etc. being available to visit or use □ *We all went to the opening of the new museum.*

opening² /'əʊpənɪŋ/ ADJECTIVE happening at the beginning of something 🔁 *I'd like to make a few* *opening remarks.* □ *The opening chapter is rather technical.*

opera /ˈɒpərə/ NOUN [plural operas] a musical play in which the words are sung □ *an opera singer*

operate /ˈɒpəreɪt/ VERB [operates, operating, operated]
1 if machinery or equipment operates, it works, and if you operate it, you make it work □ *The radio operates on batteries.* □ *My job was to operate the switchboard.*
2 to cut into someone's body to repair or remove a part when someone is ill □ + **on** *They operated on the boy to save his sight.*

operation /ˌɒpəˈreɪʃən/ NOUN [plural operations]
1 when a doctor cuts into someone's body in order to repair or remove part of it 🔁 *He has to have an operation on his heart.* 🔁 *a minor operation*
2 a carefully planned and organized action □ *a rescue operation* □ *It was a joint operation between British and Spanish troops.*

operator /ˈɒpəreɪtə(r)/ NOUN [plural operators]
1 someone whose job is to work a machine □ *a lift operator*
2 someone whose job is to connect telephone calls □ *Ask the operator to put you through to his extension.*
3 a person or company that does a particular type of business □ *a tour operator*

opinion /əˈpɪnjən/ NOUN [plural opinions] what you think or believe □ + **of** *What's your opinion of the new arts centre?* □ + **about** *My opinions about education have changed.* 🔁 *She has strong opinions about the war.* 🔁 *In my opinion, you did the right thing.* 🔁 *She didn't give* (= say) *her opinion of the film.* 🔁 *I have a very high/low* (= good/bad) *opinion of most of my colleagues.*

> ➤ Note that you **give** (or **express**) an opinion. You do not 'say' an opinion:
> ✓ *Did she give her opinion of Claudia's work?*
> ✗ *Did she say her opinion of Claudia's work?*

opponent /əˈpəʊnənt/ NOUN [plural opponents] someone you compete against in a game or a competition □ *He beat his opponent by four points.*

opportunity /ˌɒpəˈtjuːnəti/ NOUN [plural opportunities] a chance to do something or a situation when you can do something □ *She saw the trip as the opportunity of a lifetime.* □ + **for** *There will be an opportunity for questions later.* □ + **to do something** *I had the opportunity to travel a lot in Europe.* 🔁 *I took the opportunity to speak to the senator in private.*

> ➤ THESAURUS: Chance is a general word to talk about things that might happen or when it is possible for you to do something that you want to do. An opportunity is a chance to do something or a situation when you can do something. You can say that you have a chance or an opportunity to go to America. A possibility is the chance that something might happen. For example, you can say that there is a chance or a possibility that it will rain.

oppose /əˈpəʊz/ VERB [opposes, opposing, opposed] to disagree with someone's ideas, plans or actions and try to change or stop them □ *Local people opposed the plan to expand the airport.*

opposite¹ /ˈɒpəzɪt/ ADJECTIVE
1 facing something or on the other side of something □ *The answers are on the opposite page.* □ *She lives on the opposite side of town.*
2 completely different □ *Her remarks had the opposite effect to what she intended.* □ *They walked off in opposite directions.*

opposite² /ˈɒpəzɪt/ NOUN [plural opposites] someone or something that is completely different from someone or something else □ *Hot is the opposite of cold.* □ *My sister and I are complete opposites.*

optical /ˈɒptɪkəl/ ADJECTIVE to do with the eyes, sight or light □ *an optical instrument*

optimism /ˈɒptɪmɪzəm/ NOUN, NO PLURAL when you believe that good things will happen □ *She was full of optimism about her new job.*

optimistic /ˌɒptɪˈmɪstɪk/ ADJECTIVE hoping or believing that good things will happen □ *I'm not feeling very optimistic about this exam.*

option /ˈɒpʃən/ NOUN [plural options] something that you can choose or decide to do □ *There are several options open to me.* □ *Is there a vegetarian option on the menu?* □ *Our only option was to accept his offer.* □ + **of doing something** *We have the option of buying or leasing a car.*

> ➤ THESAURUS: An option or a choice is something that you can choose or decide to do. An alternative is another possibility or choice. For example, if you usually go to work by car, you need to find an alternative if your car breaks down. A preference is when you prefer one thing to another or the thing that you like or prefer.

optional /ˈɒpʃənəl/ ADJECTIVE if something is optional, you can have it or do it if you want to, but you do not have to □ *Music was an optional subject at my school.* 🔁 *The car has a lot of optional extras.*
-or /-ə(r)/ SUFFIX another way of spelling **-er**

or /ɔː(r)/ CONJUNCTION
1 used to show possibilities or choices □ *Would you prefer tea or coffee?* □ *We could see a film or go for a walk.* □ *Their little girl must be seven or eight.* □ *Shall we have pizza, pasta or risotto?*
2 used after a negative verb to say not any of a list of things or people □ *I don't like him or his sister.*
3 used for saying what will happen if something is not done □ *I'd better go or I'll miss the last bus.*

oral /ˈɔːrəl/ ADJECTIVE spoken, not written □ *an oral examination*

orange[1] /ˈɒrɪndʒ/ ADJECTIVE having the colour you get if you mix red and yellow □ *This bush has tiny orange flowers in summer.*

orange[2] /ˈɒrɪndʒ/ NOUN [*plural* oranges]
1 a round fruit with orange skin and a lot of juice □ *orange juice*
2 the colour you get if you mix red and yellow

orbit[1] /ˈɔːbɪt/ NOUN [*plural* orbits] the circular path along which something moves around a sun, moon or planet □ *The spaceship is in orbit round the moon.*

> ─► THESAURUS: A circle is a flat shape whose outside edge is a continuous curved line which is always the same distance away from a central point. An orbit is the circular path along which something moves around a sun, moon or planet. A circuit is a path, route or track that forms a circle. A cycle is a series of things that happen one after the other and then start again.

orbit[2] /ˈɔːbɪt/ VERB [*orbits, orbiting, orbited*] to go round a sun, moon or planet □ *The spacecraft is orbiting Earth.*

orchard /ˈɔːtʃəd/ NOUN [*plural* orchards] an area of land where fruit trees are grown □ *a cherry orchard*

orchestra /ˈɔːkɪstrə/ NOUN [*plural* orchestras] a large group of musicians playing together □ *a symphony orchestra*

ordeal /ɔːˈdiːl/ NOUN [*plural* ordeals] a very unpleasant experience □ *He spent ten years in prison, but survived the ordeal with great courage.*

order[1] /ˈɔːdə(r)/ NOUN [*plural* orders]
1 an instruction to do something ⮹ *The soldier was given the order to shoot.* ⮹ *I refuse to take orders from that man.* ⮹ *They obeyed the order to retreat.*
2 when you ask for food or goods that you will pay for. ⮹ *The waiter came to take our order.*
3 the way things are arranged ⮹ *The books are in alphabetical order of their authors.* □ *List the options in your order of preference.*
4 a state where everything is tidy or in its correct state □ *I need to get my accounts in order.*

5 in order to do something so that something can happen or be done □ *She took the money in order to buy food.* □ *I phoned him in order to arrange a meeting.*
6 out of order not working correctly □ *The toilets are out of order today.*

order[2] /ˈɔːdə(r)/ VERB [*orders, ordering, ordered*]
1 to tell someone to do something □ **+ to do something** *The doctor ordered her to rest for a few days.* □ *The government has ordered an enquiry into the accident.*
2 to ask for food or goods that you will pay for □ *I ordered some magazines from the newsagent.* □ *I ordered the pizza.*
3 to arrange things in a particular way □ *I ordered the CDs according to the type of music.*

ordinary /ˈɔːdənrɪ/ ADJECTIVE
1 normal and not unusual or different □ *It was just an ordinary Monday morning.* □ *Ordinary people don't buy designer clothes.*
2 out of the ordinary unusual or different from normal □ *Your tests show nothing out of the ordinary.*

organ /ˈɔːgən/ NOUN [*plural* organs]
1 a part of your body that has a special purpose □ *an organ donor* (= someone who lets their organs be used after they die)
2 a large musical instrument with keys like a piano and several long pipes that air is pushed through, often found in churches □ *She played the organ at our wedding.*

organic /ɔːˈgænɪk/ ADJECTIVE
1 organic food is produced without using chemicals □ *I only buy organic vegetables.*
2 found in or made by living things □ *organic fertilizers*

organism /ˈɔːgənɪzəm/ NOUN [*plural* organisms] any living thing, especially one that is very small. A biology word □ *Samples of marine organisms were collected from the sea bed.*

organization *or* **organisation** /ˌɔːgənaɪˈzeɪʃən/ NOUN [*plural* organizations]
1 a group of people who work together for a purpose □ *He's working for a voluntary organization that helps ex-prisoners.*
2 the activity of arranging or preparing for an event or an activity □ *The festival took months of organization.*
3 the way in which something is arranged or organized □ *Paul's essays show a lack of organization.*

organize *or* **organise** /ˈɔːgənaɪz/ VERB [*organizes, organizing, organized*]
1 to arrange and prepare an event or an activity □ *We've organized a surprise party for his birthday.*
2 to make something tidy or to put something in order □ *He organized all the papers into neat piles.*

organized or **organised** /ˈɔːgənaɪzd/ ADJECTIVE

1 involving a group of people who plan and do something together □ We went on an organized tour of the city.
2 an organized person is good at planning and arranging things □ I'm just not very organized.

organizer or **organiser** /ˈɔːgənaɪzə(r)/ NOUN [plural organizers] someone who organizes an event or an activity □ a conference organizer

origin /ˈɒrɪdʒɪn/ NOUN [plural origins]

1 the cause of something or place where something starts □ There are many theories about the origin of our solar system. □ The English language contains many words of Anglo-Saxon origin.
2 the country, race, class etc. that someone comes from □ Her family are Italian in origin. ✏ Please state your ethnic origin on the form.

original /əˈrɪdʒɪnəl/ ADJECTIVE

1 existing from the beginning, or not having been changed □ The original story had been changed over the centuries. □ Our house still has the original fireplaces.
2 new and interesting, and not like others of its type □ a novel full of original ideas ✏ Her paintings are highly original.
3 done by the artist himself or herself □ He owns an original drawing by Picasso.

> ► **THESAURUS:** If something such as a painting is done by the artist himself or herself, you can say that it is original. If you say that a painting is authentic or genuine, you are emphasizing that it is real or true and not a copy.

originally /əˈrɪdʒɪnəlɪ/ ADVERB in the beginning □ His family comes from Scotland originally. □ The building was originally used as a store.

orphan /ˈɔːfən/ NOUN [plural orphans] a child whose parents are both dead

orphanage /ˈɔːfənɪdʒ/ NOUN [plural orphanages] a home for children whose parents are both dead

other¹ /ˈʌðə(r)/ ADJECTIVE

1 used to talk about something or someone else of a similar type □ Do you have any other news to tell me? □ I have lots of other questions. ✏ I prefer living with other people. ✏ There were lots of other things to do.
2 different from the thing or person you have been talking about □ There must be some other reason. □ Does this dress come in any other colours? ✏ I thought Kate would be taller than Jo, but it was the other way round (= the opposite).
3 used to talk about the second of two things or people, when the first has already been mentioned □ Where is my other glove? □ I live on the other side

of town. ✏ This vase is Chinese, and the other one is Japanese.
4 used to talk about the remaining people or things □ The other team members will arrive tomorrow.
5 the other day/week, etc. a few days/weeks, etc. ago □ I saw Adam the other day.

other² /ˈʌðə(r)/ PRONOUN

1 the second of two □ Here's one sock, but where is the other?
2 others things or people of a similar type □ I really enjoyed that book. Do you have any others by her?
3 the others the remaining people or things □ I've found some of her letters, but where are the others? □ Wait for the others to arrive.

otherwise /ˈʌðəwaɪz/ ADVERB

1 used to say what will happen if something is not done or is not true □ You need to get up, otherwise you'll be late. □ I hope it won't be cold. Otherwise we'll need to take coats.
2 if the thing that has just been mentioned is not true □ He must have seen the letter, otherwise how could he have known the truth?
3 except for the thing that has just been mentioned □ I've got a cold, but I'm fine otherwise. □ One person raised his hand. Otherwise, nobody moved.
4 different to what has been said □ Unless I hear otherwise, I'll be there at ten. □ I thought the food was fine, but Des thought otherwise.

ought /ɔːt/ MODAL VERB ought to do something (a) used to say what is the best or right thing to do □ I think we ought to call the police. □ He ought to wear glasses. (b) used to say that you expect something to be true □ They ought to reach Berlin by tomorrow. □ Three loaves ought to be enough.

oughtn't /ˈɔːtənt/ a short way to say and write ought not □ You really oughtn't to see him again.

ounce /aʊns/ NOUN [plural ounces] a unit for measuring weight, equal to equal to 28.35 grams. This is often written oz.

our /ˈaʊə(r)/ ADJECTIVE belonging to or to do with us □ That is our car.

ours /ˈaʊəz/ PRONOUN used to talk or write about things belonging to or to do with us □ That car is ours. □ These books are ours.

ourselves /aʊəˈselvz/ PRONOUN

1 the reflexive form of we □ We saw ourselves in the mirror. □ We should keep some of the money for ourselves.
2 used to show that we do something without any help from other people □ We painted the room ourselves. ✏ We built the house all by ourselves.
3 used to emphasize the pronoun we □ We ourselves played no part in this.
4 by ourselves not with or near other people □ They left us by ourselves in a cold room.

out /aʊt/ ADVERB, PREPOSITION

1 from inside a container, hole, vehicle, etc. □ *She opened her bag and took out an umbrella.* □ *+ of He got out of the car.* 🔁 *I opened the cupboard and a bag of rice fell out.*

2 away from your home or work for a social activity

3 away from your home or work □ *I phoned, but you were out.* 🔁 *Are you going out tonight?* □ *I was out with Gerry last night.*

4 away from a building or place □ *I stood out in the garden.* □ *+ of She was dragged out of the room by armed guards.* □ *He is not allowed to go out of the country.*

5 if a fire or light is out, it is not shining □ *When we reached the house, all the lights were out.*

6 out of used to say what something is made from □ *The shelter was made out of sticks.*

7 two/six, etc. out of ten/a hundred, etc. used to say how many people or things in a group are involved in or affected by something

outbreak /ˈaʊtbreɪk/ NOUN [plural outbreaks] when something such as war or a disease starts □ *There's been a fresh outbreak of measles in the area.*

outburst /ˈaʊtbɜ:st/ NOUN [plural outbursts] when someone suddenly says something that shows strong emotion, especially anger □ *Her outburst shocked her colleagues.*

outcome /ˈaʊtkʌm/ NOUN [plural outcomes] the final result of something □ *What was the outcome of your discussion?*

> ➤ **THESAURUS:** Result is a general word for what happens because of something else. An outcome is the final result of something. A conclusion is a decision that you make after thinking carefully about something, or the last part of something. For example, you can talk about the conclusion of an essay. An effect is what happens as a result of something else. For example, the effect of eating too much junk food is that you may become overweight or ill.

outdoor /ˈaʊtdɔ:(r)/ ADJECTIVE happening or done outside or for use outside □ *an outdoor swimming pool* □ *outdoor shoes*

outdoors /ˌaʊtˈdɔ:z/ ADVERB outside □ *She sat outdoors in the sun.* □ *Don't go outdoors if it's raining.*

outer /ˈaʊtə(r)/ ADJECTIVE

1 on or near the outside of something □ *Peel off the outer layers of the onion.*

2 furthest away from the centre □ *the outer suburbs of Paris*

outfit /ˈaʊtfɪt/ NOUN [plural outfits] a set of clothes that are worn together □ *I've bought myself*

a new outfit for the wedding. □ *Jake got a cowboy outfit for his birthday.*

outgoing /ˈaʊtɡəʊɪŋ/ ADJECTIVE friendly and liking to talk to other people □ *Sally's quite a confident, outgoing girl.*

outing /ˈaʊtɪŋ/ NOUN [plural outings] a short journey made for pleasure □ *I took the kids on an outing to the seaside.*

outline /ˈaʊtlaɪn/ NOUN [plural outlines] a line that shows the shape of something □ *First he drew the outline of a church seen against the sky.*

outlook /ˈaʊtlʊk/ NOUN [plural outlooks] what experts think may happen in the future □ *The outlook for the economy is poor.*

outrage /ˈaʊtreɪdʒ/ VERB [outrages, outraging, outraged] to make someone feel shocked and angry □ *Fay was outraged by his behaviour.*

outrageous /aʊtˈreɪdʒəs/ ADJECTIVE shocking or very unreasonable □ *His behaviour was absolutely outrageous.* □ *This restaurant charges outrageous prices.*

outside¹ /aʊtˈsaɪd/ ADVERB not inside a building □ *Let's eat outside.* □ *He went outside for a cigarette.*

outside² /aʊtˈsaɪd, ˈaʊtsaɪd/ NOUN the outside the outer surface or part of something □ *The outside of the house was painted white.* □ *The cake was burnt on the outside.*

outside³ /aʊtˈsaɪd/ PREPOSITION not inside a building, room or area, but near it □ *He was standing outside our house.* □ *I come from a small village just outside York.*

outskirts /ˈaʊtskɜ:ts/ PLURAL NOUN the outskirts the outer parts of a town or city □ *He lives on the outskirts of Edinburgh.*

outspoken /ˌaʊtˈspəʊkən/ ADJECTIVE saying exactly what you mean, even if it upsets people □ *She is an outspoken critic of the government.*

outstanding /ˌaʊtˈstændɪŋ/ ADJECTIVE excellent □ *an outstanding student*

oval¹ /ˈəʊvəl/ ADJECTIVE shaped like a circle with the edges pressed slightly together □ *an oval table*

oval² /ˈəʊvəl/ NOUN [plural ovals] an oval shape □ *He drew an oval.*

oven /ˈʌvən/ NOUN [plural ovens] the part of a cooker that is shaped like a box with a door and is used for cooking and heating food □ *Bake the cake in the centre of the oven for 30 minutes.*

over¹ /ˈəʊvə(r)/ PREPOSITION

1 above someone or something, or moving across the place above someone or something □ *His photograph hung over the fireplace.* □ *An eagle flew right over our heads.*

2 more than □ *He's over 90 years old.* □ *She left school just over three years ago.*

3 across □ *We ran over the bridge.*
4 covering something or someone □ *I put a blanket over her legs.* □ *There was snow over the hills.*
🖢 *You've got mud all over your clothes.*
5 on the other side of something □ *There is a house just over that hill.* □ *The sun set over the horizon.*
□ *My house is just over the road.*

over² /ˈəʊvə(r)/ ADVERB
1 moving across the place above someone or something □ *An aeroplane flew over.*
2 from one side to the other □ *That bridge isn't safe – I'm not going over.*
3 higher in number or amount □ *Children aged seven and over may swim alone.*
4 onto the other side □ *The dog rolled over in the mud.* □ *Turn your papers over.*
5 to a particular place □ *He walked over to speak to them.* □ *Would you like to come over for lunch?*
6 towards the side □ *Could you stand a bit further over to the right?* □ *I moved over to make room for him.*
7 remaining □ *There were two cakes left over.*
8 all over again again, from the beginning □ *My computer crashed, and I had to do my essay all over again.*
9 over and over again and again □ *I told her over and over again not to talk to strangers.*

overall¹ /ˌəʊvərˈɔːl/ ADVERB considering or including everything or everyone □ *Overall, I'm very pleased with the film.*

overall² /ˈəʊvərɔːl/ NOUN [*plural* **overalls**]
1 a piece of clothing like a thin coat worn over ordinary clothes to protect them □ *She wears an overall when cleaning the house.*
2 overalls a piece of clothing that covers the legs and body, worn to protect clothing during dirty work

overboard /ˈəʊvəbɔːd/ ADVERB over the side of a ship or boat and into the water □ *He jumped overboard to save the drowning man.* □ *Man overboard!*
♦ IDIOM go overboard to do something too much, often because you are excited about something □ *I think you've gone a bit overboard with the decorations.*

overcame /ˌəʊvəˈkeɪm/ PAST TENSE OF **overcome**

overcome /ˌəʊvəˈkʌm/ VERB [**overcomes**, overcoming, overcame, overcome] to manage to deal successfully with a problem □ *She has struggled to overcome her depression.*

overdose /ˈəʊvədəʊs/ NOUN [*plural* **overdoses**] more of a drug or medicine than is safe □ *an overdose of sleeping pills*

overdue /ˌəʊvəˈdjuː/ ADJECTIVE if something is overdue, it should have happened, been done, been paid, etc. before now □ *Our library books are overdue.*

overhead /ˌəʊvəˈhed/ ADVERB, ADJECTIVE above your head or high above the ground □ *A plane was flying overhead.* □ *overhead cables*

overhear /ˌəʊvəˈhɪə(r)/ VERB [**overhears**, overhearing, overheard] to hear what someone says when they are not talking to you □ *I overheard them talking about me.*

overlook /ˌəʊvəˈlʊk/ VERB [**overlooks**, overlooking, overlooked]
1 to fail to notice or consider something □ *You have overlooked one important detail.*
2 to have a view over a place □ *The house overlooks the river.*

overnight /ˈəʊvənaɪt/ ADJECTIVE, ADVERB for or during the night □ *an overnight train* □ *The centre provides overnight accommodation.* 🖢 *We stayed overnight in London.*

overtake /ˌəʊvəˈteɪk/ VERB [**overtakes**, overtaking, overtook, overtaken] to move past a vehicle that is travelling in the same direction □ *He overtook a police car.*

overthrow /ˌəʊvəˈθrəʊ/ VERB [**overthrows**, overthrowing, overthrew, overthrown] to take power away from a leader or a government by force □ *They are plotting to overthrow the current regime.*

overtime /ˈəʊvətaɪm/ NOUN, NO PLURAL extra time spent working in addition to your normal working hours 🖢 *We had to work overtime to get everything finished.*

overturn /ˌəʊvəˈtɜːn/ VERB [**overturns**, overturning, overturned] to turn something upside down or to turn upside down □ *Chairs were overturned and glasses were broken.* □ *The bus overturned in wet conditions.*

overweight /ˌəʊvəˈweɪt/ ADJECTIVE an overweight person is too heavy □ *I'm about four kilos overweight.*

overwhelm /ˌəʊvəˈwelm/ VERB [**overwhelms**, overwhelming, overwhelmed] to have a very strong and sudden effect on someone □ *We were overwhelmed with joy.*

overwhelming /ˌəʊvəˈwelmɪŋ/ ADJECTIVE
1 very large or important □ *They won an overwhelming victory over their rivals.* 🖢 *An overwhelming majority of workers voted to strike.*
2 overwhelming emotions and feelings are very strong □ *There's an overwhelming feeling of relief.*
□ *The temptation was almost overwhelming.*

owe /əʊ/ VERB [**owes**, owing, owed]
1 to have to pay money to someone □ *I owe Val £10.* □ *+ to He owes money to suppliers.*
2 to have something only because of someone or something □ *+ to He owes his success to his family.*

owing to /ˈəʊɪŋ tə/ PREPOSITION because of □ *He withdrew from the competition owing to a back injury.*
□ *The club closed down owing to lack of funding.*

owl /aʊl/ NOUN [*plural* **owls**] a large bird that hunts at night

own[1] /əʊn/ ADJECTIVE belonging to or done by the person mentioned □ *I need to spend more time with my own family.* □ *The rules are for your own safety.* □ *Is this all your own work?* 🖥 *I'd love to have a horse of my very own.*

own[2] /əʊn/ PRONOUN

1 used to show that something belongs to someone or something □ *I lent him a pencil, because he forgot to bring his own.* □ *There are plenty of showers – each bedroom has its own.*

2 on your own (a) without help from anyone else □ *He managed to finish the work on his own.* □ *Did you do this all on your own?* (b) alone □ *I live on my own in a small flat.*

3 of your own if someone or something has something of its own, it belongs only to them □ *I'd love a bedroom of my own.* □ *Each apartment has a small garden of its own.*

♦ IDIOM **get your own back** to do something unpleasant to someone who has done something unpleasant to you

own[3] /əʊn/ VERB [owns, owning, owned] you own something if it belongs to you, especially if you have bought it □ *I own a car.* □ *He doesn't own a single book.*

♦ PHRASAL VERB **own up** to admit that you did something wrong □ *Nobody owned up to breaking the chair.*

owner /ˈəʊnə(r)/ NOUN [*plural* owners] a person who owns something

ownership /ˈəʊnəʃɪp/ NOUN, NO PLURAL when someone owns something 🖥 *Home ownership has risen.*

oxygen /ˈɒksɪdʒən/ NOUN, NO PLURAL a gas that has no taste, colour or smell, and forms part of the air. A chemistry word.

oyster /ˈɔɪstə(r)/ NOUN [*plural* oysters] a type of sea creature in a shell that can be eaten

ozone /ˈəʊzəʊn/ NOUN, NO PLURAL a form of oxygen with a strong smell. A chemistry word.

Pp

P or **p** /piː/ the 16th letter of the alphabet

p /piː/ ABBREVIATION **page** or **pence**

pace /peɪs/ NOUN [*plural* **paces**] the speed at which something happens or at which someone does something □ *the pace of change* □ *He was walking at a very slow pace.*

pack¹ /pæk/ VERB [**packs, packing, packed**]
1 to put things in a bag or case ready for a journey □ *She packed hurriedly and caught the next train.* □ *Ben packed his bag for the holiday.* □ *Make sure you pack your swimming costume.*
2 to put something into a box so it can be moved, sold or stored □ *She has a job packing chocolates in a factory.* □ **+ in** *The food was packed in brown paper bags.* □ **+ up** *They packed up all their furniture ready for the house move.*
3 if people pack a place, a lot of them go there and fill it □ *Reporters packed the courtroom.* □ **+ into** *More then 15,000 fans packed into the sports stadium.*
◆ PHRASAL VERB **pack (something) up** to put things into bags or boxes so that they can be moved □ *He packed up his belongings and left.* □ *We decided to pack up and go home.*

pack² /pæk/ NOUN [*plural* **packs**]
1 a set of documents that have been put together 🖭 *All new students will receive an information pack.* □ *If you are interested in the job, you can download an application pack.*
2 a set of products that are sold together □ **+ of** *I bought a pack of 6 cakes.* □ *a pack of chewing gum*
3 a set of 52 cards that you play games with □ **+ of** *a pack of cards*
4 a group of animals that live and hunt together □ **+ of** *a pack of wolves*
5 a group of similar people, especially people you do not like □ **+ of** *There was a pack of kids standing outside the shop.*

package /ˈpækɪdʒ/ NOUN [*plural* **packages**] something that has been wrapped in paper or put in a box, especially so it can be sent by post □ *He sent the package to his brother.* □ *Police will destroy any suspicious packages.*

packed /pækt/ ADJECTIVE very crowded □ *The train was packed.*

packet /ˈpækɪt/ NOUN [*plural* **packets**] a box or bag containing several of the same things □ *There were a lot of seeds in the packet.* 🖭 *He opened the packet and offered me some peanuts.* □ **+ of** *a packet of biscuits* □ *a packet of crisps*

pact /pækt/ NOUN [*plural* **pacts**] an agreement between two people, groups or countries 🖭 *We made a pact never to tell anyone what happened.*

pad¹ /pæd/ NOUN [*plural* **pads**]
1 a thick piece of soft material, used for protecting something or for making it more comfortable □ *I always wear knee pads and elbow pads when I'm roller skating.*
2 a book of pieces of paper, used for writing or drawing on □ *a sketch pad*

pad² /pæd/ VERB [**pads, padding, padded**] to fill or wrap something with a soft material □ *The horses' hooves had been padded with cloth to muffle the sound.*

paddle /ˈpædəl/ NOUN [*plural* **paddles**] a short piece of wood with a flat end, used for rowing a boat

page /peɪdʒ/ NOUN [*plural* **pages**]
1 a piece of paper in a book, newspaper or magazine, or one side of it □ *The information can be found on page 135.* 🖭 *His picture was on the front page of the newspaper.* 🖭 *She turned the pages very slowly.*
2 the writing or pictures that you see on a computer screen, especially as part of a website □ *You need to refresh the page to see the information.* 🖭 *Visit our information page to find out more.*

paid /peɪd/ PAST TENSE AND PAST PARTICIPLE OF **pay**¹

pain /peɪn/ NOUN [*plural* **pains**]
1 the unpleasant feeling you have when part of your body hurts □ *stomach pains* 🖭 *He felt a stinging pain.* 🖭 *Aspirin is used to relieve pain* (= make pain less bad)*.* 🖭 *Ann felt a sharp pain in her leg.* □ **+ in** *He had pains in his chest.*
2 be in pain to have an unpleasant feeling because part of your body hurts □ *Amy was in constant pain from a broken shoulder.* □ *He was obviously in great pain.*

3 *no plural* sadness ⌾ *She felt that seeing him would cause her too much pain.* ⌾ *Nothing I can say will ease the pain* (= make it less bad). □ *+ of The pain of leaving his wife behind was almost too much to bear.*
4 an informal word meaning someone or something that is annoying □ *Sometimes she can be a real pain.*

painful /'peɪnfʊl/ ADJECTIVE causing pain □ *Is your knee still painful?* □ *She had a painful lump on her arm.*

painkiller /'peɪnkɪlə(r)/ NOUN [*plural* painkillers] a drug that reduces pain

paint¹ /peɪnt/ NOUN [*plural* paints] a coloured substance that you put on a surface to change its colour or to make a picture □ *a tin of red paint* ⌾ *The ceiling needs a new coat of paint.* □ *a box of oil paints*

paint² /peɪnt/ VERB [paints, painting, painted]
1 to put paint on a surface □ *Dan was painting the front door.* □ *The dining room was painted red.*
2 to make a picture using paint □ *He painted a portrait of the queen.*

painter /'peɪntə(r)/ NOUN [*plural* painters]
1 an artist who makes pictures using paint
2 someone whose job is to paint buildings and rooms ⌾ *My Dad is a painter and decorator.*

painting /'peɪntɪŋ/ NOUN [*plural* paintings]
1 a picture that someone has made using paint □ *They sold a painting by Monet.*
2 *no plural* the activity of painting walls or pictures □ *I enjoy painting.*

pair /peə(r)/ NOUN [*plural* pairs]
1 two things of the same kind that you use or keep together □ *+ of a pair of socks* □ *a pair of shoes* □ *a pair of china dogs*
2 a single thing made up of two parts □ *I bought a pair of jeans.* □ *a pair of glasses* □ *a pair of scissors*
3 two people who do something together, or who are friends □ *The Australian pair won the game.* □ *The teacher asked us to work in pairs.*

palace /'pælɪs/ NOUN [*plural* palaces] a big, grand house where a king or queen lives □ *the presidential palace* □ *Crowds of people stood outside the palace gates.*

pale /peɪl/ ADJECTIVE [paler, palest]
1 light in colour □ *She was wearing a pale blue T-shirt.* □ *the pale light of dawn*
2 having very white skin, especially because

you are ill or because you have had a shock □ *She looked very pale and thin.* ⌾ *He suddenly went very pale.*

palm /pɑːm/ NOUN [*plural* palms]
1 the inside surface of your hand ⌾ *She kept wiping the palms of her hands on her skirt.*
2 a tree that grows in hot, dry places

pamphlet /'pæmflɪt/ NOUN [*plural* pamphlets] a thin book with a paper cover, which has information in it

pan /pæn/ NOUN [*plural* pans] a metal container with a handle, used for cooking food □ *Cover the pan with a lid.*

> ➤ THESAURUS: Pan is a general word for a metal container with a handle, used for cooking food. A round pan with a handle, and often a lid, is called a saucepan. You might use a saucepan for cooking sauce, but also for boiling vegetables or pasta, for example. A frying pan is a flat pan with a long handle, used for frying food.

pancake /'pæŋkeɪk/ NOUN [*plural* pancakes] a thin food made by frying a mixture of milk, flour and eggs

panda /'pændə/ NOUN [*plural* pandas] a large animal from China which is black and white, and looks like a bear

pane /peɪn/ NOUN [*plural* panes] a piece of glass used in a window or door □ *a pane of glass*

panel /'pænəl/ NOUN [*plural* panels]
1 a usually rectangular piece of wood, glass, etc. that is part of a door, wall, etc.
2 a group of people who are chosen to discuss or judge something, or to answer questions □ *A panel of judges will decide on the winner.*

panic¹ /'pænɪk/ NOUN, NO PLURAL a sudden strong feeling of fear or worry that makes you unable to think calmly ⌾ *The fire caused panic.* □ *People ran into the streets in panic when the earthquake struck.*

panic² /'pænɪk/ VERB [panics, panicking, panicked] to be so frightened or worried that you cannot think calmly □ *There's no need to panic. We've got plenty of time.*

pant /pænt/ VERB [pants, panting, panted] to breathe quickly and noisily, especially because you have been using a lot of physical effort □ *He was sweating and panting.*

pants /pænts/ PLURAL NOUN
1 a piece of underwear that covers your bottom ⌾ *a clean pair of pants*
2 the US word for **trousers**

paper¹ /'peɪpə(r)/ NOUN [*plural* papers]

1 *no plural* the thin material that you write on or draw on, or that you wrap things in 🔁 *I wrote his address on a piece of paper.* □ *The present was wrapped in pretty pink paper.*

2 a newspaper 🔁 *Have you read today's paper?* 🔁 *I saw the article in the local paper.*

3 an exam □ *an exam paper* □ *He showed me last year's maths paper.*

➔ *go to* **papers**

paper² /'peɪpə(r)/ ADJECTIVE made from paper or cardboard □ *a paper bag* □ *paper cups*

papers /'peɪpəz/ PLURAL NOUN official documents □ *legal papers* □ *He's signed the divorce papers.*

parachute /'pærəʃuːt/ NOUN [*plural* parachutes] a large piece of cloth attached to a person's body by strings that they use to help them fall safely if they jump from an aircraft

parade¹ /pə'reɪd/ NOUN [*plural* parades] an event in which people or vehicles move through an area to celebrate something, often with music, decorations, etc. □ *Hundreds of people took part in the carnival parade.*

parade² /pə'reɪd/ VERB [parades, parading, paraded] to walk with a lot of other people in order to celebrate something or to complain about something □ *Demonstrators paraded through the streets of the city.*

paradise /'pærədaɪs/ NOUN, NO PLURAL

1 in some religions, the place good people go when they die

2 a perfect place or situation □ *The island is a paradise for birdwatchers.*

paragraph /'pærəgrɑːf/ NOUN [*plural* paragraphs] a part of a piece of writing that starts on a new line and contains one or more sentences □ *I read the first paragraph of the article.*

parallel /'pærəlel/ ADJECTIVE parallel lines have the same distance between them all the way along 🔁 *She drew two parallel lines.* 🔁 *Lockwood Road runs parallel to Hollies Road.*

paralyse /'pærəlaɪz/ VERB [paralyses, paralysing, paralysed] if someone is paralysed by something, they are unable to move their body, or are unable to move part of their body □ *He was paralysed by a skiing accident in which he broke his neck.*

paralyze /'pærəlaɪz/ VERB [paralyzes, paralyzing, paralyzed] the US spelling of **paralyse**

paramedic /ˌpærə'medɪk/ NOUN [*plural* paramedics] someone who works in an ambulance (= medical emergency vehicle) and is trained to help ill or injured people

parcel /'pɑːsəl/ NOUN [*plural* parcels] something wrapped in paper and sent somewhere □ *A parcel arrived for you this morning.* 🔁 *She opened the parcel and there were three books inside.*

pardon /'pɑːdən/ EXCLAMATION

1 used to ask someone to repeat what they have just said because you did not hear it □ *'We're going to be late.' 'Pardon?' 'I said, we're going to be late.'*

2 pardon me used when you have just made a rude noise with your body

parent /'peərənt/ NOUN [*plural* parents] your mother or father □ *My parents divorced last year.* □ *Her proud parents watched as she received the award.*

parish /'pærɪʃ/ NOUN [*plural* parishes] an area that has its own church □ *a parish priest*

park¹ /pɑːk/ NOUN [*plural* parks] an area of grass and trees in a town where people can go to relax □ *I went for a walk in the park.* 🔁 *They were sitting on a park bench.*

park² /pɑːk/ VERB [parks, parking, parked] to leave a vehicle in a place, for example by the side of the road or in a car park 🔁 *She parked the car outside the house.* □ *Dad drove into town but couldn't find anywhere to park.*

parking /'pɑːkɪŋ/ NOUN, NO PLURAL

1 space where you can park your vehicle □ *There is free parking for museum visitors.* 🔁 *She drove round, looking for a parking space.*

2 the process of putting a vehicle into a space and leaving it there □ *Many learner drivers find parking very difficult.*

parking lot /'pɑːkɪŋ ˌlɒt/ NOUN [*plural* parking lots] the US word for **car park**

parliament /'pɑːləmənt/ NOUN [*plural* parliaments] a group of people who make the laws for a country □ *the Scottish parliament* 🔁 *He entered parliament (= was elected to a parliament) in 1981.*

> ➤ THESAURUS: A parliament is a group of people who make the laws for a country. A government is a group of people who control a country or area. A party is an organized group of people who share the same political beliefs and try to get elected to the government. The members of one party may form a government, but the members of other political parties may also be part of the parliament.

parole /pə'rəʊl/ NOUN, NO PLURAL an arrangement in which someone is allowed to leave prison early but must go back to prison if they do not behave well 🔁 *Roberts was released on parole in 2005.*

parrot /'pærət/ NOUN [*plural* parrots] a tropical bird with brightly coloured feathers that can copy what people say

part¹ /pɑːt/ NOUN [*plural* parts]

1 one of the pieces, areas, amounts, etc. that

together make something □ *The pizza is cut into six equal parts.* □ *She lives in a remote part of Scotland.* □ *I spent part of the day working in the garden.* □ *They made me feel part of the family.*
2 take part to be involved in an activity with other people □ *Everyone can take part in the competition.* □ *She took part in a run for charity.*
3 some, but not all of something □ **+ of** *Part of the problem is that he works such long hours.* □ *Part of me thinks that we should just forget about her.*
4 a character in a play, film, etc. or the words or actions that the character has to say or do 🕮 *He's playing the part of Othello.* □ *I need to learn my part.*
5 a piece of a machine or a piece of equipment 🕮 *We took plenty of spare parts for the van.*

▶ **THESAURUS:** A part is one of the pieces, areas, amounts, etc. that together make something. Part, piece and section are very similar in meaning. Part is the most general of these words. You can talk about a part of a car, a part of your life or a part of a place, for example. A section is one of the parts that together make up something. For example, you can talk about a section of a newspaper. A piece is one of the parts that join together to make a particular thing. For example, you can talk about a piece of a car. A portion is a part of a total amount. We often use portion to talk about food. For example, you can talk about a portion of cake.

part² /pɑːt/ VERB [parts, parting, parted]
1 when people part, they go away from each other □ *We parted at the end of the street.* 🕮 *They parted company in Toronto.* □ *After ten years of marriage, they agreed to part.*
2 when two things part, they move away from each other to leave a space, and if you part two things, you make a space between them □ *Suddenly, the clouds parted and we had a wonderful view.* □ *We parted the curtains slightly.*
♦ PHRASAL VERB **part with something** to give something away, often when you do not want to □ *I couldn't bear to part with my books.*

partial /ˈpɑːʃəl/ ADJECTIVE not complete □ *a partial success*

partially /ˈpɑːʃəlɪ/ ADVERB not completely □ *a partially eaten biscuit*

participant /pɑːˈtɪsɪpənt/ NOUN [plural participants] someone who takes part in an event or activity with other people □ *She was an active participant in the debate.*

participate /pɑːˈtɪsɪpeɪt/ VERB [participates, participating, participated] to take part in an event or activity □ *The programme aims to encourage more children to participate in sport.*

participle /ˈpɑːtɪsɪpəl/ NOUN [plural participles] a word formed from a verb and used as an adjective, or to form different tenses of the verb. The present participle usually ends in '-ing' and the past participle usually ends in '-ed'.

particle /ˈpɑːtɪkəl/ NOUN [plural particles] a very small piece of something □ *a particle of dust* □ *tiny carbon particles*

particular /pəˈtɪkjʊlə(r)/ ADJECTIVE
1 used to show that you are talking about one person or thing and not others □ *On that particular day I was early.* □ *Is there a particular person I should speak to about this?*
2 especially great □ *He took particular care when writing the letter.* □ *Aircraft safety is an area of particular concern.*

particularly /pəˈtɪkjʊləlɪ/ ADVERB
1 very, or more than usual □ *The noise was particularly loud.* □ *Young babies are particularly vulnerable.* 🕮 *They were not particularly helpful.*
2 used to show that something is true for one person or thing more than others □ *Temperatures were very high this summer, particularly in July.* □ *The changes will affect those on low incomes, particularly the elderly.*

partly /ˈpɑːtlɪ/ ADVERB in some ways or to some degree, but not completely □ *I was partly to blame for the mix-up.* □ *He had to leave his job, partly because of his health.* □ *That's only partly true.*

partner /ˈpɑːtnə(r)/ NOUN [plural partners]
1 one of two people who do something together, such as dancing or playing a game 🕮 *a dance partner* □ *a tennis partner*
2 one of two or more people who own a business together 🕮 *She's a senior partner in a law firm.* 🕮 *his former business partner*
3 someone you are married to or have a sexual relationship with □ *She lives with her long-term partner and their two children.*

part of speech /ˌpɑːt əv ˈspiːtʃ/ NOUN [plural parts of speech] in grammar, one of the groups that words belong to according to the job they do, such as noun, verb, adjective or adverb

part-time /ˌpɑːtˈtaɪm/ ADJECTIVE, ADVERB working for only part of a full working day or week 🕮 *a part-time job* 🕮 *She works part-time for the local newspaper.*

party /ˈpɑːtɪ/ NOUN [plural parties]
1 an event where people celebrate something or enjoy themselves together eating, drinking, dancing, etc. 🕮 *a birthday party* 🕮 *We're having a party next week.* 🕮 *He threw a huge party to celebrate.*
2 an organized group of people who share the same political beliefs and try to get elected to the

government 🔁 *a political party* 🔁 *the party leader* □ *He joined the Labour Party in 1936.*
3 a group of people travelling or doing something together □ + *of The museum was busy with several parties of schoolchildren.*

> ➤ Note that you **have** or **throw** a party (*sense 1*): You do not 'make' a party:
> ✓ *We're having a party for Celia's 21st birthday.*
> ✗ *We're making a party for Celia's 21st birthday.*

pass¹ /pɑːs/ VERB [passes, passing, passed]
1 to go past something □ *The lorry passed us on a bend.* □ *I pass her house every morning.*
2 to move in a particular direction or to a particular place □ *The procession passed in front of the town hall.* □ *The road passes through a forest.*
3 to be successful in an exam □ *She passed her entrance exams.* □ *I've got my driving test tomorrow, but I don't think I'll pass.*
4 to give someone something with your hand □ *Pass me the butter, please.* □ + *to He passed a note to his colleague.*
5 if time passes, it goes by □ *A whole year passed and she did not receive a letter from him.* □ *The morning passed slowly.*
6 pass the time to do something to use a period of time □ *I passed the time reading a book.*
7 to kick, hit or throw the ball to someone else on your team in a sport □ *He passed the ball to Edwards.*

> ➤ Remember that you **spend** a period of time somewhere. You do not 'pass' a period of time: □ *I spent the summer in Barcelona.* □ *I've spent all morning cleaning.* □ *We spent the holidays at my grandparents'.*

◆ PHRASAL VERBS **pass something around/round** to offer something to everyone in a group □ *She passed round the biscuits.* **pass away/on** to die **pass something on** to give someone something that has been given to you □ *Can you pass on a message for me?* □ *When you've finished with the book, could you pass it on to Paola?* **pass out** to become unconscious □ *When I saw the blood, I passed out.*

pass² /pɑːs/ NOUN [plural passes]
1 a successful result in an exam or on a course
2 a ticket or document that allows you to go into a place or to travel on a vehicle 🔁 *Have you got your bus pass?*
3 when you kick, hit or throw the ball to someone else on your team in a sport
4 a narrow path between mountains

passage /ˈpæsɪdʒ/ NOUN [plural passages]
1 a long narrow room or area that connects rooms or places □ *He ran down a narrow passage between buildings.* □ *a secret underground passage*

2 a part of a piece of writing or music □ *Read the next passage aloud.* □ + *from He quoted a passage from the Bible.*

passenger /ˈpæsɪndʒə(r)/ NOUN [plural passengers] someone travelling in a vehicle who is not the driver or someone who works on it 🔁 *an airline passenger* 🔁 *I sat in the passenger seat.*

passion /ˈpæʃən/ NOUN [plural passions]
1 very strong beliefs and opinions about something □ *He spoke with real passion.* 🔁 *Passions are running high* (= people are very angry and upset) *in the city.*
2 a very strong feeling of love □ *He kissed her in a moment of passion.*

passionate /ˈpæʃənɪt/ ADJECTIVE
1 showing strong emotions or beliefs □ *She's a passionate advocate of animal rights.* □ *I feel very passionate about this issue.*
2 having a strong feeling of love □ *They had a very passionate relationship.*

passive /ˈpæsɪv/ ADJECTIVE a passive verb is used when the person or thing that is the subject of the verb does not do the action but has something done to them, for example in the sentence *The leaves are being eaten by caterpillars.*

passport /ˈpɑːspɔːt/ NOUN [plural passports] an official document with your photograph and personal details that you carry when you travel to a foreign country □ *a British passport* 🔁 *You have to show your passport.* □ *passport control*

password /ˈpɑːswɜːd/ NOUN [plural passwords] a secret word that you have to know before you are allowed into a place, or before you can use a computer or system 🔁 *Please enter your password.*

past¹ /pɑːst/ PREPOSITION, ADVERB
1 up to and further than □ *She dashed past me, gasping as she ran.* □ *He just walked past without saying hello.* □ *Bullets flew past my head.* □ *Follow the road past a cottage.*
2 further than □ *Turn right just past the bridge.* □ *A few miles past the farm, we came to a turning.*
3 used for saying the time up to 30 minutes after an hour □ *It's ten past three.* □ *I'll meet you at half past ten.*

past² /pɑːst/ ADJECTIVE
1 having happened or existed in the time before the present □ *I have admitted my past mistakes.*
2 used to talk about a period of time just before the present □ *The past few days have been very difficult for all of us.*

past³ /pɑːst/ NOUN, NO PLURAL
1 the past the time before the present □ *I have met him a few times in the past.* □ *When we meet, we never talk about the past.*
2 someone's past is their life and experiences until

now, and a country's past is what has happened there and what its people have done □ *I don't know much about her past.* □ *The country is trying to forget its military past.*
3 the past the form of a verb that is used for talking about things that happened before the present

pasta /ˈpæstə/ NOUN, NO PLURAL a food made from flour, water and eggs and formed into different shapes □ *pasta with tomato sauce*

past participle /ˌpɑːst ˈpɑːtɪsɪpəl/ NOUN [*plural* past participles] the form of a verb that usually ends with '-ed' and is used to form the perfect tense, passive forms and sometimes adjectives

pastry /ˈpeɪstri/ NOUN [*plural* pastries]
1 *no plural* a mixture of flour and fat made into a flat piece and baked with food inside
2 a cake made with pastry

past tense /ˌpɑːst ˈtens/ NOUN [*plural* past tenses] a form of a verb that you use when you are talking about what has happened in the past. For example, *relaxed* in *I relaxed after the race* is a past tense.

pasty[1] /ˈpeɪsti/ ADJECTIVE [pastier, pastiest] having skin that is pale and looks unhealthy

pasty[2] /ˈpæsti/ NOUN [*plural* pasties] a piece of pastry folded around food such as meat and vegetables

pat[1] /pæt/ VERB [pats, patting, patted] to touch or to hit someone or something gently with your flat hand in a friendly way □ *Celia patted his shoulder kindly.* □ *He patted the horse's neck.*
♦ IDIOM pat someone on the back to praise someone for something they have done □ *I patted myself on the back for a job well done.*

> ► THESAURUS: To pat someone or something means to touch or to hit someone or something gently with your flat hand in a friendly way. You might pat a dog. To stroke something means to rub it gently with your hand. For example, you might stroke a cat. To tap means to knock gently or hit your fingers or feet gently against something. You might tap someone on the arm to get their attention. To slap means to hit something or someone with the flat part of your hand.

pat[2] /pæt/ NOUN [*plural* pats] when you pat someone or something □ *He gave the dog a pat on the head.*
♦ IDIOM a pat on the back praise for doing something □ *She deserves a pat on the back.*

patch[1] /pætʃ/ NOUN [*plural* patches]
1 a small area of something, especially that is different from what is around it □ *a patch of grass* □ *a vegetable patch* (= area of ground where you grow vegetables) □ *There's a damp patch on the wall.*

2 a piece of material used to cover a hole □ *a jacket with patches on the elbows*

patch[2] /pætʃ/ VERB [patches, patching, patched] to repair a hole using a patch □ *We patched the hole in the roof.*

patent /ˈpeɪtənt/ NOUN [*plural* patents] an official document that gives one person or company the right to make and sell a product and stops others from copying it

path /pɑːθ/ NOUN [*plural* paths] a narrow route across a piece of ground that people walk or ride a bicycle along □ *We walked along a narrow path through the woods.* □ *Dad was coming up the garden path.* 🖥 *There's a cycle path beside the canal.*

pathetic /pəˈθetɪk/ ADJECTIVE an informal word meaning not at all useful, skilful or effective □ *This knife is pathetic. It won't cut anything!* 🖥 *She made a pathetic attempt to deny it.*

patience /ˈpeɪʃəns/ NOUN, NO PLURAL the ability to stay calm, especially when waiting for something, doing something for a long time or dealing with something or someone annoying □ *You need to have a lot of patience when dealing with young children.* 🖥 *I'm losing my patience with her silly behaviour.*

patient[1] /ˈpeɪʃənt/ ADJECTIVE showing patience □ **+ with** *I'm a slow learner and he's been very patient with me.* □ *I'm not a very patient person.*

patient[2] /ˈpeɪʃənt/ NOUN [*plural* patients] someone who is being treated by a doctor or a nurse 🖥 *The clinic treats patients with eye problems.* □ *Every patient receives advice about healthy eating.*

patrol[1] /pəˈtrəʊl/ VERB [patrols, patrolling/*US* patroling, patrolled/*US* patroled] to go around an area or building watching for any trouble or problems □ *Troops patrol the border.*

patrol[2] /pəˈtrəʊl/ NOUN [*plural* patrols]
1 a group of soldiers or police officers who patrol an area 🖥 *a police patrol*
2 when someone patrols an area 🖥 *The soldiers were on a routine patrol when they were attacked.*

pattern /ˈpætən/ NOUN [*plural* patterns]
1 the way in which something normally happens or is organized □ **+ of** *the pattern of the seasons* 🖥 *When we analyzed the data, a clear pattern emerged.* 🖥 *annual weather patterns*
2 a design of shapes, colours, etc. repeated on a surface □ *The room was decorated in floral patterns.* □ *The boxes are carved with intricate patterns.*
3 a set of instructions and shapes used for making something □ *a sewing pattern*

pause[1] /pɔːz/ VERB [pauses, pausing, paused] to stop what you are doing for a short time □ **+ to do**

something The actor paused to speak to fans. □ He paused for a moment before replying.

pause² /pɔːz/ NOUN [*plural* pauses] a short stop or rest 🔁 There was a long pause before anyone spoke. □ + *for* He kept going with hardly a pause for breath.

pave /peɪv/ VERB [paves, paving, paved] to make a layer of stones, bricks etc. on an area of ground □ The courtyard is paved with local stone.
♦ IDIOM **pave the way for something** to do something that makes it possible for something else to happen □ This decision could pave the way for other legal cases.

pavement /ˈpeɪvmənt/ NOUN [*plural* pavements] a path next to a road which people walk along □ He waited on the pavement in front of the shop.

paw /pɔː/ NOUN [*plural* paws] the foot of some animals, such as cats and dogs

pay¹ /peɪ/ VERB [pays, paying, paid]
1 to give money in order to buy something or because you owe someone □ + *for* I'll pay for the meal. 🔁 He offered to pay the bill. □ I don't pay tax in this country. □ + *by* Can I pay by credit card?
2 to give someone money for work that they do □ I need the money to pay the builder. □ I get paid on the 15th of each month.
3 pay attention to concentrate on something □ She paid great attention to his words.
4 pay someone a compliment to say something nice about someone
5 pay someone/something a visit to visit someone or something
♦ PHRASAL VERB **pay someone back** to do something bad to someone because of something bad they have done to you

➤ Note that you pay **for** the thing that you are buying:
✓ Camille paid for the watch.
✓ Camille paid £120 for the watch.
✗ Camille paid the watch.

➤ THESAURUS: To pay means to give money in order to buy something or because you owe someone, or to give someone money for work that they do. To earn means to get money for work that you do. To win means to get something because you have been successful in a game, competition etc. To spend means to use money to buy things.

pay² /peɪ/ NOUN, NO PLURAL someone's pay is the amount of money they are paid by their employer □ The job's boring, but the pay's good. 🔁 I asked

him for a pay rise. 🔁 Many workers are facing pay cuts.

payment /ˈpeɪmənt/ NOUN [*plural* payments]
1 money paid for something 🔁 We make monthly payments. □ All payments will be made to your bank account. 🔁 He received a cash payment of £200.
2 *no plural* when you pay for something □ + *of* He was involved with the payment of bribes.

PC /ˌpiːˈsiː/ ABBREVIATION
1 personal computer
2 police constable; used before a police officer's name □ PC Evans

pea /piː/ NOUN [*plural* peas] a small round green vegetable

peace /piːs/ NOUN, NO PLURAL
1 a situation in which there is no war or violence □ The two countries have been at peace for 50 years. 🔁 We are seeking to bring peace to the region. 🔁 The police were at the demonstration to keep the peace. 🔁 peace talks 🔁 a peace deal
2 a situation which is quiet and calm □ I want a little peace to get on with my homework. 🔁 She goes to the library for a bit of peace and quiet.

peaceful /ˈpiːsfʊl/ ADJECTIVE
1 not involving war or violence □ a peaceful protest 🔁 It says its nuclear programme is for peaceful purposes.
2 quiet and calm □ She felt more peaceful than she had all day. □ a peaceful seaside town

peach /piːtʃ/ NOUN [*plural* peaches] a round fruit with a soft skin, pale orange flesh and a large stone inside

peak /piːk/ NOUN [*plural* peaks]
1 the highest, greatest or most successful level □ the peak of the holiday season 🔁 She reached the peak of her career in the 1990s. 🔁 The trains are very crowded at peak times.
2 the pointed top of a mountain or hill 🔁 snow-covered mountain peaks
3 the flat part at the front of a cap (= soft hat) that sticks out

peanut /ˈpiːnʌt/ NOUN [*plural* peanuts] a type of nut that grows underground in a shell and can be eaten

pear /peə(r)/ NOUN [*plural* pears] a fruit with green, yellow or brown skin and white flesh which is round at the bottom and narrower at the top

pearl /pɜːl/ NOUN [*plural* pearls] a round, white object, formed inside the shell of an oyster (= sea creature), and used for making jewellery □ a pearl necklace

peasant /'pezənt/ NOUN [plural peasants] a poor person who works on the land in a poor country □ a peasant farmer

peck /pek/ VERB [pecks, pecking, pecked] if a bird pecks, it hits something or picks something up with its beak □ Birds pecked at the crumbs.

peculiar /pɪ'kju:lɪə(r)/ ADJECTIVE strange or not expected, sometimes in an unpleasant way □ a very peculiar smell □ It seems peculiar that no one noticed. □ That would explain his peculiar behaviour recently.

pedal /'pedəl/ NOUN [plural pedals] a part that you push with your foot, such as on a bicycle, in a car or on a machine ⌷ the brake pedal

pedestrian /pɪ'destrɪən/ NOUN [plural pedestrians] someone who is walking and not travelling in a vehicle □ Pedestrians and cyclists are given priority in the city centre.

peel¹ /pi:l/ VERB [peels, peeling, peeled]
1 to remove the skin of a vegetable or a piece of fruit □ She was peeling potatoes. □ + off Let the peppers cool then peel off the skin.
2 if paint or skin peels, it comes off in small pieces □ The paint was peeling off the walls.

peel² /pi:l/ NOUN, NO PLURAL the skin of some fruit and vegetables □ orange peel

peer /pɪə(r)/ VERB [peers, peering, peered] to look at something carefully, usually because it is difficult to see □ He peered through a downstairs window.

pen /pen/ NOUN [plural pens]
1 an object used for writing with ink ⌷ a ballpoint pen □ Have you got a pen and paper?
2 a small area surrounded by a fence and used for keeping animals in

pence /pens/ PLURAL OF **penny** □ a ten pence coin

pencil /'pensəl/ NOUN [plural pencils] a long thin wooden object for writing or drawing, with a black or coloured substance in the centre □ coloured pencils □ a pencil drawing

penetrate /'penɪtreɪt/ VERB [penetrates, penetrating, penetrated] to get into or through something □ Rain could not penetrate those thick trees. □ The knife penetrated his heart.

pen friend /'pen ,frend/ NOUN [plural pen friends] a friend you write letters to, but do not meet

penguin /'peŋgwɪn/ NOUN [plural penguins] a black and white bird that cannot fly but uses its wings to swim under water

penis /'pi:nɪs/ NOUN [plural penises] the male organ for urinating and producing babies. A biology word.

penknife /'pennaɪf/ NOUN [plural penknives] a small knife with blades that fold into the handle

penny /'penɪ/ NOUN [plural pence or pennies or p] a small British coin worth one hundredth of £1 □ Crisps cost 40 pence.

> ➤ Note that when you are saying how much something costs, the plural **pence** is used. When you are talking about the coins themselves, use the plural **pennies**: □ It cost me fifty pence. □ I only had a few pennies left in my purse.

pension /'penʃən/ NOUN [plural pensions] an amount of money that a government or company regularly gives someone when they are too old to work ⌷ My grandma gets a state pension (= a pension that a government gives people). ⌷ a company pension (= a pension that a company gives to former employees) ⌷ The company has a good pension scheme.

pensioner /'penʃənə(r)/ NOUN [plural pensioners] someone who gets a pension

people /'pi:pəl/ PLURAL NOUN men, women and children □ young people □ How many people have you invited to your party? □ People don't like being criticized.

> ➤ Remember that the noun **people** always takes a plural verb: □ People are generally happy with the government.

> ➤ Remember also that you do not say 'all people' or 'every people'. Instead you say **everyone** or **everybody**:
> ✓ Everyone feels sad sometimes.
> ✗ All people feel sad sometimes.

pepper /'pepə(r)/ NOUN [plural peppers]
1 no plural a powder with a strong taste which is added to food ⌷ He sprinkled salt and pepper on his food. ⌷ freshly ground black pepper
2 a hollow red, green or yellow vegetable which is eaten raw or cooked □ a sliced red pepper

per /pɜ:(r)/ PREPOSITION for each □ The meal will cost £20 per person. □ He was driving at 65 miles per hour when the crash happened. □ How much are the apples per kilo?

percent or **per cent** /pə'sent/ ADVERB, ADJECTIVE, NOUN, NO PLURAL in or for every 100, shown by the symbol % □ Sales have increased by ten percent. □ There has been five percent fall in the number of people who are unemployed. □ Sixty percent of schoolchildren felt that they got too much homework.

percentage /pə'sentɪdʒ/ NOUN [plural percentages] a number that is expressed as a number in 100 ⌷ A high percentage of students got top grades. □ What percentage of children have a television in their bedrooms?

perch /pɜːtʃ/ VERB [perches, perching, perched]
1 if something is perched somewhere, it is on the top or edge of something □ The house is perched on a hillside next to the lake.
2 to sit on the edge of something □ She perched on a stool next to me.

perfect¹ /ˈpɜːfɪkt/ ADJECTIVE
1 without any mistakes or faults □ Emma has perfect teeth. □ Your English is perfect. □ This building is a perfect example of 1930s architecture.
2 exactly right for something □ Jones was the perfect choice for the role. □ South Beach is the perfect place for a holiday.

> **THESAURUS:** Something that is perfect has no mistakes or faults. Something that is pure is not mixed with anything else. You can talk about pure gold or pure water. Something that is excellent is extremely good or of a very high quality.

perfect² /ˈpɜːfɪkt/ NOUN, NO PLURAL the perfect the tense of a verb that in English is formed with has/have/had and the past participle □ 'He has played tennis for years' is in the perfect.

perfect³ /pəˈfekt/ VERB [perfects, perfecting, perfected] to make something perfect □ The hills are ideal for skiers determined to perfect their technique.

perfection /pəˈfekʃən/ NOUN, NO PLURAL the state of being perfect □ Some people try to achieve physical perfection. □ The meat was cooked to perfection (= it was cooked perfectly).

perfectly /ˈpɜːfɪktli/ ADVERB
1 in an extremely good way □ The children behaved perfectly. □ His arrival was perfectly timed because the meal was just ready.
2 completely □ It was perfectly obvious that he was lying. □ The equipment is old but it's perfectly safe.

perform /pəˈfɔːm/ VERB [performs, performing, performed]
1 to do a task □ Surgeons perform operations. □ He found it difficult to perform simple tasks after the accident.
2 to act in a play, sing a song, etc. with people watching you □ It was the first time we'd performed the song. □ I love performing in front of a live audience.
3 perform well/poorly/badly etc. to do something well or badly □ His team performed poorly in both games. □ The business has performed well (= it has been successful) in difficult circumstances.

performance /pəˈfɔːməns/ NOUN [plural performances]
1 an occasion when someone acts in a play, sings a song, etc. with people watching them ⊞ The show included a live performance by several bands.
⊞ Kylie gave a great performance. □ + of We went to a performance of Mozart's 'Magic Flute'.
2 the level of success that someone or something has ⊞ The team needs to improve its performance.
⊞ Her poor performance in the exams was very disappointing.

performer /pəˈfɔːmə(r)/ NOUN [plural performers] a singer, actor, etc. who performs □ She's a great performer. □ a circus performer

perfume /ˈpɜːfjuːm/ NOUN [plural perfumes] a liquid that women put on their skin to make them smell nice ⊞ She always wears perfume. □ I could smell her perfume.

perhaps /pəˈhæps/ ADVERB possibly □ I can't find Leo. Perhaps he's left. □ Perhaps I shouldn't have told him.

period /ˈpɪərɪəd/ NOUN [plural periods]
1 an amount of time □ The work was done over a two-year period. ⊞ Rachel has learned a lot in a short period of time. ⊞ He had spent long periods in prison. □ + of He lived there for a period of several years.
2 a time in history □ the Victorian period □ one of the earliest geological periods

perish /ˈperɪʃ/ VERB [perishes, perishing, perished] a formal word meaning to die □ Four children perished in the fire.

permanent /ˈpɜːmənənt/ ADJECTIVE lasting forever or for a very long time □ The accident left him with permanent brain damage. □ Ella has been offered a permanent job. □ We need a permanent solution to the problem.

> **THESAURUS:** Something that is permanent lasts forever or for a long time. You might have a permanent job or a permanent home, for example. Something that is constant never stops. For example you might talk about constant pain or constant noise. Something that is stable does not change over a period of time. For example, the price of something such as oil or gold might be stable.

permanently /ˈpɜːmənəntli/ ADVERB in a way that lasts forever or for a very long time □ Her sight had been permanently damaged. □ Many new mothers feel permanently tired.

permission /pəˈmɪʃən/ NOUN, NO PLURAL if you have permission to do something, someone says you can do it ⊞ A doctor can't operate on you unless you give permission. ⊞ You need to get permission from your teacher if you want to leave the class early. ⊞ Rob had taken his Dad's car *without permission.* □ *+ to do something* I asked her permission to use the phone.

> ➤ Remember that you **get permission** or **give permission** to do something. You do not 'get/ give a permission':
> ✓ I **got permission** from my teacher to leave early.
> ✗ I got a permission from my teacher to leave early.

---

permit¹ /pə'mɪt/ VERB [permits, permitting, permitted] a formal word meaning to allow something □ *Smoking is not permitted anywhere in the building.*

permit² /'pɜːmɪt/ NOUN [plural permits] an official document that allows you to do something □ *a work permit*

persist /pə'sɪst/ VERB [persists, persisting, persisted] if something bad persists, it continues □ *If the problem persists, talk to your doctor.*

persistent /pə'sɪstənt/ ADJECTIVE
1 continuing to do something even when it is difficult or when someone tells you to stop □ *I said I wasn't interested but the salesman was quite persistent.*
2 if something unpleasant is persistent, it continues for a long time □ *persistent rain*

person /'pɜːsən/ NOUN [plural people] a man, woman or child □ *Heather's a really nice person.* □ *Tatsuya was the first person in his family to go to university.* □ *How many people were at the party?* 🔁 *Jeremy is the kind of person who knows everything.*

> ➤ Note that the plural of person is usually **people**. The plural 'persons' is sometimes used in formal writing but it is not used generally:
> ✓ Most **people** here own a car.
> ✗ Most persons here own a car.

---

personal /'pɜːsənəl/ ADJECTIVE
1 belonging to, or to do with one particular person □ *a personal opinion* □ *personal belongings* 🔁 *I know from personal experience that the exam is very difficult.*
2 private and to do with your health, relationships, etc. 🔁 *The singer's personal life has been quite troubled.* □ *Never give out personal information to a company on the phone.*

personal computer /ˌpɜːsənəl kəm'pjuːtə(r)/ NOUN [plural personal computers] a small computer that is designed to be used by one person

personality /ˌpɜːsə'nælətɪ/ NOUN [plural personalities]
1 someone's character and the qualities they have 🔁 *Artie has a very outgoing personality.* □ *The accident had changed his personality.*
2 a famous person 🔁 *He's one of America's best-known TV personalities.*

personally /'pɜːsnəlɪ/ ADVERB
1 used when stating your own opinion □ *Personally, I don't like him.*
2 done by you and not by anyone else □ *He wrote to everyone personally.*

personnel /ˌpɜːsə'nel/ NOUN, NO PLURAL the people who work for a particular company or organization □ *army personnel*

persuade /pə'sweɪd/ VERB [persuades, persuading, persuaded] to make someone agree to do something by telling them why they should do it □ *+ to do something* I tried to persuade Tanya to come with us.

persuasion /pə'sweɪʒən/ NOUN, NO PLURAL when you persuade someone 🔁 *After a little gentle persuasion, he agreed to come with us.*

pest /pest/ NOUN [plural pests]
1 an animal or insect that destroys crops
2 an informal word for an annoying person, often a child

pesticide /'pestɪsaɪd/ NOUN [plural pesticides] a chemical used for killing insects which destroy crops

pet /pet/ NOUN [plural pets] an animal that you keep in your home 🔁 *Do you have any pets?* □ *Dogs and cats are very popular pets.* □ *Adam has a pet rabbit.*

petal /'petəl/ NOUN [plural petals] one of the coloured parts of a flower □ *rose petals*

petition /pɪ'tɪʃən/ NOUN [plural petitions] a piece of paper that a lot of people sign to try to get a government or someone in authority to do something 🔁 *We signed a petition against the closure of the post office.*

petrol /'petrəl/ NOUN, NO PLURAL a fuel for cars, made from oil □ *I've just filled the car up with petrol.* □ *petrol prices*

> ➤ THESAURUS: Oil is a thick, dark liquid from under the ground. Fuel is a general word for a substance that burns to give heat, light or power. Petrol is a fuel for cars, made from oil. Diesel is a heavy type of oil that is used as a fuel. Buses and lorries usually use diesel. Gas is a substance that is not liquid or solid and moves about in the air. We often use gas for cooking or heating. Gas is also the American word for petrol.

---

petrol station /'petrəl ˌsteɪʃən/ NOUN [plural petrol stations] a place where you buy petrol for a car

pharmacist /'fɑːməsɪst/ NOUN [plural pharmacists] someone who prepares and sells medicines

pharmacy /ˈfɑːməsɪ/ NOUN [plural pharmacies] a shop where medicines are prepared and sold □ You can get most medicines at your local pharmacy.

phase /feɪz/ NOUN [plural phases] a stage in the development of a thing or person □ The first phase of the project was to interview 100 students. □ Children go through so many phases.

PhD /ˌpiː.eɪtʃˈdiː/ ABBREVIATION Doctor of Philosophy; the highest university degree □ He's doing a PhD in applied mathematics.

philosopher /fɪˈlɒsəfə(r)/ NOUN [plural philosophers] someone who studies ideas about life

philosophy /fɪˈlɒsəfɪ/ NOUN, NO PLURAL the study of ideas about life □ She did philosophy at university.

phone[1] /fəʊn/ NOUN [plural phones]
1 a telephone 🖫 Here's my phone number. 🖫 The phone was ringing. 🖫 Can you answer the phone please? □ You can order a pizza by phone.
2 on the phone using the telephone □ Mum's on the phone at the moment. □ I talk to my cousins on the phone every week.

phone[2] /fəʊn/ VERB [phones, phoning, phoned] to speak to someone using a telephone □ I phoned my grandma last night. □ + up I'll phone up and find out when the library opens.

➤ Note that you **phone** a person or place. You do not 'phone to' a person or place:
✓ I'll phone Javier.
✗ I'll phone to Javier.
✓ I'll phone the hospital.
✗ I'll phone to the hospital.

♦ PHRASAL VERB **phone (someone) back** to call someone again using a telephone, because you could not talk to them the first time □ I'm busy just now. I'll phone you back later.

phone call /fəʊn ˌkɔːl/ NOUN [plural phone calls] when you speak to someone using a telephone 🖫 I'm just going to make a quick phone call.

phone number /fəʊn ˌnʌmbə(r)/ NOUN [plural phone numbers] the series of numbers that you use to call a particular telephone □ What's your phone number?

photo /ˈfəʊtəʊ/ NOUN [plural photos] a photograph □ digital photos □ Who's that woman in the photo? 🖫 She took a photo of Clare and me on the beach. 🖫 They showed us their wedding photos. □ + of There were photos of the children all over the house.

photocopy /ˈfəʊtəʊkɒpɪ/ NOUN [plural photocopies] a copy of a document that you make using a photocopier (= a machine that copies a document by taking a photograph of it) 🖫 He made a photocopy of the instructions.

photograph[1] /ˈfəʊtəɡrɑːf/ NOUN [plural photographs] a picture made with a camera 🖫 I took a photograph using my new camera. □ + of a photograph of Lake Geneva

photograph[2] /ˈfəʊtəɡrɑːf/ VERB [photographs, photographing, photographed] to make a picture of something using a camera □ She photographed me in the school play.

photographer /fəˈtɒɡrəfə(r)/ NOUN [plural photographers] someone who takes photographs, especially as their job □ He's a professional photographer. □ a press photographer (= photographer for a newspaper) □ a fashion photographer

photography /fəˈtɒɡrəfɪ/ NOUN, NO PLURAL the art of taking photographs 🖫 digital photography □ John teaches photography at the college.

phrasal verb /ˌfreɪzəl ˈvɜːb/ NOUN [plural phrasal verbs] a verb that you use with an adverb or preposition, which has a different meaning from the verb used alone □ 'Give up' and 'get on' are examples of phrasal verbs.

phrase /freɪz/ NOUN [plural phrases] a group of words that have a particular meaning 🖫 She used the phrase 'unwelcome attention' several times.

➤ THESAURUS: A phrase is a group of words that have a particular meaning. A sentence is a group of words that usually includes a verb and expresses a statement or question. An expression is a word or phrase. An idiom is a phrase that has a meaning that you cannot understand simply by knowing the meaning of the separate words. A saying is a phrase or sentence that people often use, giving advice or saying something that many people believe is true.

physical /ˈfɪzɪkəl/ ADJECTIVE
1 to do with the body □ These children have low levels of physical activity.
2 to do with real things that you can see or touch, and not things that exist only in your mind □ There was no physical evidence to link him to the crime.

physicist /ˈfɪzɪsɪst/ NOUN [plural physicists] someone who studies physics, usually as their job

physics /ˈfɪzɪks/ NOUN, NO PLURAL the scientific study of natural forces, for example, heat, light, sound and electricity

pianist /ˈpɪənɪst/ NOUN [plural pianists] someone who plays the piano □ a concert pianist

piano /prˈænəʊ/ NOUN [plural pianos] a musical instrument that you play by pressing the black and white keys on a long keyboard

pick¹ /pɪk/ VERB [picks, picking, picked]
1 to choose a person or thing from a group □ *Jones has been picked for the England team.* □ *Pick any card from the pack.*
2 to take fruit, flowers or vegetables from the plant or tree they are growing on □ *The children picked a bunch of wild flowers for their mum.* □ *I picked a few strawberries for tea.*
♦ PHRASAL VERBS **pick on someone** to treat one particular person unkindly or unfairly □ *Please stop picking on your brother.* **pick someone/ something up** to go and collect someone or something from somewhere □ *Could you pick me up at the airport tomorrow?* □ *I need to pick up my dry cleaning.* **pick something up 1** to lift something □ *She picked up the phone and started to dial.* □ *They asked us to pick up the litter.* **2** to learn something by watching or listening instead of having lessons □ *I just picked the language up while I was living in Mexico.*

pick² /pɪk/ NOUN, NO PLURAL have/take your pick to choose what you want from a group □ *You can take your pick from a wide range of cheeses.*

picnic¹ /ˈpɪknɪk/ NOUN [plural picnics] a meal that you take with you to eat outdoors 🖫 *We had a picnic on the beach.* 🖫 *There's a beautiful picnic area in the forest.*

➤ Note that you have a picnic. You do not 'make' a picnic:
✓ We had a picnic in the park.
✗ We made a picnic in the park.

picnic² /ˈpɪknɪk/ VERB [picnics, picnicking, picnicked] to have a picnic

picture¹ /ˈpɪktʃə(r)/ NOUN [plural pictures] a painting, drawing or photograph □ *The walls were covered with pictures of her family.* 🖫 *Draw a picture of your house.* 🖫 *Can I take a picture (= take a photograph) of your garden?*

➤ THESAURUS: Picture is a general word. A painting is a picture that someone has made using paint. A drawing is a picture done with a pencil or pen. A sketch is a drawing that is done quickly. An illustration is a picture in a book, magazine etc.

picture² /ˈpɪktʃə(r)/ VERB [pictures, picturing, pictured] to form an image of something in your mind □ *I just couldn't picture my mother as a young girl.*

pie /paɪ/ NOUN [plural pies] food such as meat, vegetables or fruit, baked in a covering of pastry

□ *apple pie and custard* □ *chicken and mushroom pie*

piece /piːs/ NOUN [plural pieces]
1 an amount or example of something of a particular type □ *a piece of wood* □ *Use a fresh piece of paper for each answer.* □ *Let me give you a piece of advice.*
2 one of the parts that join together to make a particular thing □ *a jigsaw with 300 pieces* □ *Cut the pizza into eight pieces.* 🖫 *He took the clock to pieces to repair it.* 🖫 *I just touched the stool and it fell to pieces.*
3 a coin of a particular value □ *a 50p piece*

pier /pɪə(r)/ NOUN [plural piers] a long wooden or metal structure built out over the sea that people can walk along

pierce /pɪəs/ VERB [pierces, piercing, pierced] if a sharp object pierces something, it makes a hole in it 🖫 *I've just had my ears pierced.*

pig /pɪg/ NOUN [plural pigs] a farm animal with a fat body, small eyes and a curly tail, kept for meat

pigeon /ˈpɪdʒɪn/ NOUN [plural pigeons] a grey bird that is often seen in towns or kept for racing

pile¹ /paɪl/ NOUN [plural piles] a number of things one on top of the other □ *a pile of leaves* □ *Dirty dishes were stacked in piles around the room.*

➤ THESAURUS: A pile or a stack is a number of things one on top of the other. A heap is an untidy pile of things. A mound is a small hill or pile of earth or stones.

pile² /paɪl/ VERB [piles, piling, piled] to put things on top of each other in a pile □ *They piled all the chairs against the wall.*

pilgrim /ˈpɪlgrɪm/ NOUN [plural pilgrims] a person who is travelling to a holy place
pilgrimage /ˈpɪlgrɪmɪdʒ/ NOUN [plural pilgrimages] a journey to a holy place □ *They went on a pilgrimage to Mecca.*

pill /pɪl/ NOUN [plural pills] a small piece of solid medicine that you swallow □ *antihistamine pills*

pillar /ˈpɪlə(r)/ NOUN [plural pillars] a tall, strong structure, usually made of stone, used to support something □ *The statue is on top of a stone pillar.*

pillow /ˈpɪləʊ/ NOUN [plural pillows] a bag full of feathers or other soft material that you rest your head on when you are in bed

pilot /ˈpaɪlət/ NOUN [plural pilots] someone who flies a plane or other aircraft □ *an airline pilot* □ *a pilot's licence*

➤ THESAURUS: Someone who flies a plane or other aircraft is called a pilot. Someone who drives a car or other motor vehicle is called a driver. Someone who sits on and controls a bicycle, motorbike or horse is called a rider. Someone who is walking and not using a vehicle is called a pedestrian.

pin¹ /pɪn/ NOUN [plural pins]
1 a very thin, pointed piece of metal used for holding together pieces of cloth when you are sewing
2 a thin piece of metal or wood, used for holding things together □ He's had a pin in his leg since the accident.

➤ THESAURUS: A pin is a very thin, pointed piece of metal used for holding together pieces of cloth when you are sewing. A needle is a small, pointed piece of metal used for sewing. A nail is a thin, pointed piece of metal used to join things together, especially pieces of wood. A screw is a small, pointed metal object used to fix things together by turning it around into a hole. A clip is a small object that fastens something together or to something else. For example, you might wear a hair clip to keep your hair tidy and a paper clip holds paper together.

pin² /pɪn/ VERB [pins, pinning, pinned]
1 to fasten something in place with a pin □ She pinned the flower to her dress.
2 to hold someone somewhere firmly so that they cannot move □ The policemen pinned him against the wall.

pinch¹ /pɪntʃ/ VERB [pinches, pinching, pinched]
1 to press someone's skin or flesh tightly between your thumb and finger, especially in order to hurt them □ Tom pinched me, Mum!
2 an informal word that means to steal something □ Have you pinched my magazine?
pinch² /pɪntʃ/ NOUN [plural pinches]
1 a small amount of something that you pick up between your finger and thumb ℗ Add a pinch of salt.
2 when you pinch someone □ She gave him a pinch on the arm.
pine¹ /paɪn/ NOUN [plural pines] a tall tree with needles (= thin pointed leaves)
pine² /paɪn/ VERB [pines, pining, pined] to feel sad, usually because you are not with a person that you love
pineapple /ˈpaɪnæpəl/ NOUN [plural pineapples] a large fruit with sweet yellow flesh and a thick brown skin with sharp points on it □ pineapple juice

pink¹ /pɪŋk/ ADJECTIVE having the colour you get if you mix red and white □ She wore a pink dress. □ His cheeks were pink from running.

pink² /pɪŋk/ NOUN, NO PLURAL the colour you get if you mix red and white

pint /paɪnt/ NOUN [plural pints] a unit for measuring liquid, equal to 0.57 litres ℗ a pint of milk/beer
pioneer¹ /ˌpaɪəˈnɪə(r)/ NOUN [plural pioneers]
1 one of the first people to develop a new idea, skill or method □ Charles Babbage was one of the pioneers of computer technology.
2 one of the first people to go to a new country to live and work there □ the American pioneers
pioneer² /ˌpaɪəˈnɪə(r)/ VERB [pioneers, pioneering, pioneered] to be one of the first people to do or make something □ The hospital is pioneering new surgical techniques.
pip /pɪp/ NOUN [plural pips] a small seed in a fruit such as an apple or lemon

➤ THESAURUS: A seed is the thing that a plant produces and that new plants grow from. A pip is a small seed in a fruit such as an apple or a lemon. The hard piece in the middle of fruits such as cherries or peaches is called a stone.

pipe /paɪp/ NOUN [plural pipes]
1 a metal or plastic tube through which water or gas can flow ℗ A pipe had burst and there was water everywhere.
2 a tube with a hollow bowl at one end used for smoking tobacco ℗ Grandpa used to smoke a pipe.

pipeline /ˈpaɪplaɪn/ NOUN [plural pipelines] a long pipe that crosses the land or sea and carries oil or gas
♦ IDIOM in the pipeline being planned or organized, or about to happen □ Further job losses are in the pipeline.

pirate /ˈpaɪrət/ NOUN [plural pirates] someone who steals things from ships while they are at sea □ As a boy, he loved stories about pirates.

pistol /ˈpɪstəl/ NOUN [plural pistols] a small gun that is held in one hand

pit /pɪt/ NOUN [plural pits]
1 a large, deep hole dug in the ground □ The dead animals were buried in a pit.
2 a deep mine, especially a coal mine □ His father and grandfather had both worked at the pit.

pitch¹ /pɪtʃ/ NOUN [plural pitches]
1 an area of ground, often with lines marked on it, where people play games like football or cricket □ a football pitch
2 how high or low a sound is

> ➤ **THESAURUS:** A pitch is an area of ground where people play games such as football, rugby, or cricket. A course is a piece of land that a race is run over or where a game of golf is played. A court is an area where you play a sport such as tennis or basketball. A ground is an area where a sport is played, but includes the seats as well as the pitch.

pitch² /pɪtʃ/ VERB [pitches, pitching, pitched] pitch a tent to put up a tent so that it is ready to use

pity¹ /ˈpɪti/ NOUN, NO PLURAL
1 sadness you feel for other people who are suffering or in trouble □ She felt a wave of pity for the poor old man, abandoned by his family.
2 it's a pity... used for saying that you feel sorry or disappointed about a situation □ It's a pity that John couldn't come.
3 take pity on someone to feel so sorry for someone that you help them □ Mark took pity on me and gave me a lift home.

pity² /ˈpɪti/ VERB [pities, pitying, pitied] to feel pity for someone □ I really pity her, having a mother like that.

pizza /ˈpiːtsə/ NOUN [plural pizzas] a flat round piece of bread with cheese, vegetables or meat on top that is baked in an oven □ a mushroom pizza
🔁 Would you like another slice of pizza?

place¹ /pleɪs/ NOUN [plural places]
1 a particular area, position, town, building, etc. □ We rented a place by the sea. □ I imagine Beijing is a very interesting place. □ She broke her arm in three places. 🔁 Make sure you keep the money in a safe place. 🔁 Smoking is not allowed in public places.
2 the position where something should be, or where something or someone usually is □ Put the books back in their proper place on the shelf.
3 take place to happen □ The election is due to take place next month. □ The wedding took place in secret.
4 a seat on a public vehicle or in a public building □ Please go back to your places and sit down.
🔁 Would you save my place while I get a coffee?

5 a position in a queue (= line of people waiting)
🔁 Now I've lost my place in the queue.
6 in first/third/last, etc. place used to show someone's position at the end of a race or competition
7 in place in the correct position □ Make sure the safety harness is in place.
8 in place of someone/something instead of someone/something □ Pat is here today, in place of Marc, who is ill.

> ➤ **THESAURUS:** A place is a particular position, or the position where something should be, or where something or someone usually is. A site is a place where something happens or happened, or a place used for a certain purpose. For example, you can talk about the site where a battle took place or the site of a new hospital (where it will be built). A spot or a location is a place or position. Spot is a more informal word. You might talk about a nice spot for a picnic, or the location where a film is made.

place² /pleɪs/ VERB [places, placing, placed]
1 to put something somewhere, usually with care □ He placed his hand on her shoulder. □ She placed a flower on the grave.
2 to cause someone or something to be in a particular situation or state □ He had placed me in a very difficult situation by promising that I would go to the party. □ Money worries placed a great strain on their marriage. □ The government has placed restrictions on public pay rises.

plain¹ /pleɪn/ ADJECTIVE [plainer, plainest]
1 obvious 🔁 She made it quite plain that she didn't like me.
2 in one colour or without any decoration or pattern □ a plain white tablecloth
3 simple or ordinary □ He likes fairly plain cooking.
4 a plain person is not attractive

plain² /pleɪn/ NOUN [plural plains] a large flat area of land

plan¹ /plæn/ VERB [plans, planning, planned]
1 to decide what you are going to do and how you are going to do it □ We spent months planning the wedding. □ Always plan your essay before you start writing. □ We got a designer in to plan the garden.
2 to hope and expect to do something in the future □ + to do something Natasha is planning to go to university next year. □ + on doing something They're planning on taking a year off to travel.

plan² /plæn/ NOUN [plural plans]
1 an idea or arrangement for something you hope to do in the future □ What are your plans for the future? □ + to do something We have no plans to move house at the moment. 🔁 There's been a change of plan. We're going out on Friday instead.

2 a drawing that shows how a building, town, machine, etc. will be built □ *The council is showing its plans to develop the city centre.*

plane /pleɪn/ NOUN [*plural* **planes**] an aeroplane

planet /'plænɪt/ NOUN [*plural* **planets**] any of the large objects in space that move around a sun or star □ *the planet Venus*

plank /plæŋk/ NOUN [*plural* **planks**] a long flat piece of wood

plant¹ /plɑ:nt/ NOUN [*plural* **plants**] any living thing that grows from the ground and has a stem, roots and leaves □ *Young plants must be protected from frost.* □ *a tobacco plant*

plant² /plɑ:nt/ VERB [**plants, planting, planted**] to put seeds or plants in soil so that they grow □ *They're planting trees along the roadside.*

plaster¹ /'plɑ:stə(r)/ NOUN [*plural* **plasters**]
1 a piece of soft sticky cloth that you put over a cut to keep it clean
2 *no plural* a substance that is put on walls and dries to form a hard, smooth surface
3 in plaster if your arm, leg etc. is in plaster, it has a hard cover around it to protect a broken bone
plaster² /'plɑ:stə(r)/ VERB [**plasters, plastering, plastered**] to put plaster on walls

plastic¹ /'plæstɪk/ NOUN [*plural* **plastics**] a light strong substance made from chemicals and used to make many different things □ *toys made of plastic*

plastic² /'plæstɪk/ ADJECTIVE made of plastic □ *plastic bags*

plate /pleɪt/ NOUN [*plural* **plates**] a flat dish for eating or serving food from □ *a paper/plastic plate* □ *Pass your plates.*

platform /'plætfɔ:m/ NOUN [*plural* **platforms**]
1 the area next to the tracks at a railway station, where passengers get on and off trains □ *The 9:45 service to Leeds will leave from platform 4.*
2 a raised area of floor where performers and speakers stand so that the audience can see them

platinum /'plætɪnəm/ NOUN, NO PLURAL a very valuable silver metal that is used to make jewellery

play¹ /pleɪ/ VERB [**plays, playing, played**]
1 to spend time enjoying yourself with games or toys □ *The children were playing in the garden.*
2 to take part in a sport or game □ *He plays cricket*

on Saturdays. □ *Luke played well in the last match.* □ + *for* *He used to play for the national team.*
3 to make music with a musical instrument, or to perform a piece of music □ *Do you play the piano?* □ *He played all the Beethoven sonatas.*
4 if you play a CD, DVD, etc., you put it in a machine to make it produce sound or images
5 to act as a character in a film, play, etc. 🎭 *She plays the part of Harry's daughter.*

play² /pleɪ/ NOUN [*plural* **plays**]
1 a story that is performed by actors in a theatre 🎭 *Our school is putting on a play.*
2 *no plural* the activity of enjoying yourself with games and toys □ *Young children learn best through play.*

player /'pleɪə(r)/ NOUN [*plural* **players**]
1 someone who plays a sport or game
2 someone who plays a musical instrument
3 a machine for playing DVDs, CDs, etc.

playground /'pleɪɡraʊnd/ NOUN [*plural* **playgrounds**] an area, often next to a school or in a public park, where children play □ *Harry fell and hurt his knee in the playground.*

playing card /'pleɪɪŋ ˌkɑ:d/ NOUN [*plural* **playing cards**] one of a set of 52 rectangular pieces of card used for playing games

playing field /'pleɪɪŋ ˌfi:ld/ NOUN [*plural* **playing fields**] an area of land used for playing sports such as football □ *the school playing fields*

plea /pli:/ NOUN [*plural* **pleas**] when someone asks for something in a serious and emotional way □ *I couldn't ignore this plea for help.*

pleasant /ˈplezənt/ ADJECTIVE nice or enjoyable □ *We had a very pleasant evening at Sarah's.* □ *It was very pleasant, sitting out in the garden.* □ *Our new neighbours seem very pleasant.*

pleasantly /ˈplezəntlɪ/ ADVERB in a pleasant way □ *She smiled very pleasantly at us.* ▣ *I was pleasantly surprised by his attitude.*

please¹ /pliːz/ EXCLAMATION
1 used as a polite way of asking for something □ *Could I have a glass of water, please?* □ *Please could you turn the music down?* □ *Would you please leave?*
2 yes, please used as a polite way of accepting an offer □ *'Would you like another biscuit?' 'Yes, please.'*

please² /pliːz/ VERB [pleases, pleasing, pleased] to make someone happy by doing what they want □ *You can't please everyone.* □ *My mother is quite hard to please.*

pleased /pliːzd/ ADJECTIVE happy or satisfied with something □ **+ with** *He was pleased with the way the garden looked.* □ **+ at** *We were all pleased at the result.* □ **+ to do something** *She looked pleased to see him.* □ *She wasn't pleased when he told her he'd lost the tickets.*

pleasure /ˈpleʒə(r)/ NOUN [*plural* pleasures]
1 *no plural* a feeling of enjoyment or satisfaction ▣ *She took pleasure in cooking.* ▣ *It gives me great pleasure to be here today.*
2 something that you enjoy □ *He enjoys the simple pleasures of life.* ▣ *It's a great pleasure to welcome you back.*

pledge /pledʒ/ NOUN [*plural* pledges] a serious promise ▣ *The government has made a pledge to improve school food.* □ *He has received pledges of support from all over the world.*

plenty /ˈplentɪ/ PRONOUN, ADVERB a lot of something, as much as you need or more than you need □ **+ of** *You'll have plenty of time to complete the test.* □ *Remember to drink plenty of water.* ▣ *There's plenty more bread in the freezer if we run out.*

plot¹ /plɒt/ NOUN [*plural* plots]
1 the story of a play, book or film □ *the plot of a novel* □ *The film's plot is based on a true story.*
2 a secret plan, especially to do something bad □ *They discovered a plot to kidnap a soldier*
3 a piece of land to be used for a particular purpose

□ *a vegetable plot* □ *a plot of land*
➜ go to **lose the plot**

plot² /plɒt/ VERB [plots, plotting, plotted] to plan to do something bad or illegal □ *The group may be plotting more attacks.*

plough /plaʊ/ VERB [ploughs, ploughing, ploughed] to turn over soil with a plough

plug¹ /plʌg/ NOUN [*plural* plugs]
1 an object attached to a piece of electrical equipment by a wire which connects it to an electricity supply
2 an object that you use for blocking a hole, especially in a bath or sink □ *a bath plug*

plug² /plʌg/ VERB [plugs, plugging, plugged] to push something into a hole to block it □ *We need to plug the leak in the boat.*

◆ PHRASAL VERBS **plug something in** to connect a piece of electrical equipment to the electricity supply □ *I plugged in my laptop.* **plug something into something 1** to connect one piece of electrical equipment to another □ *Plug the camera into your computer to download pictures.* **2** to connect a piece of electrical equipment to the electricity supply □ *Don't leave your phone charger plugged into a socket when you're not using it.*

plum /plʌm/ NOUN [*plural* plums] a soft red, purple or yellow fruit with a smooth skin and a large seed in the middle

plunge /plʌndʒ/ VERB [plunges, plunging, plunged]
1 to fall suddenly and with force □ *The bus plunged off a mountain road.*
2 to jump, especially into water □ *They plunged into the cool water.*
3 to push something violently into something □ *He plunged a knife into her stomach.*

pluperfect /ˌpluːˈpɜːfɪkt/ NOUN, NO PLURAL the tense of a verb that shows that an action finished before a particular time or event in the past, formed using *had* and a past participle

plural¹ /ˈplʊərəl/ NOUN [*plural* plurals] the form of a noun, pronoun or verb that you use when there is more than one of something

plural² /ˈplʊərəl/ ADJECTIVE in the plural form □ *a plural noun*

plus¹ /plʌs/ PREPOSITION
1 added to □ *8 plus 2 is 10.* □ *He charges $50 an hour, plus travel expenses.*
2 as well as □ *There are six children, plus two adults.*

plus² /plʌs/ NOUN [*plural* pluses] a mathematical symbol (+) showing that a number is to be added to another

PM /ˌpiːˈem/ ABBREVIATION **prime minister**

pm or **p.m.** /ˌpiːˈem/ ABBREVIATION added after the time to show that it is in the afternoon or the evening

pocket /ˈpɒkɪt/ NOUN [plural **pockets**] an extra piece of cloth sewn into a piece of clothing or a bag, used for keeping small things in □ *It was in my jeans pocket.* □ *He pulled his wallet from his back pocket.*

pocket money /ˈpɒkɪt ˌmʌni/ NOUN, NO PLURAL money that parents regularly give their children to buy small things □ *They spent all their pocket money on sweets.*

podcast /ˈpɒdkɑːst/ NOUN [plural **podcasts**] a recording that you get from a website and then listen to on a computer or MP3 player (= small piece of computer equipment)

poem /ˈpəʊɪm/ NOUN [plural **poems**] a piece of writing using interesting language, arranged in short lines, often using words with the same sounds □ *a love poem* ☐ *He wrote a poem for her.*

poet /ˈpəʊɪt/ NOUN [plural **poets**] someone who writes poems □ *He was a poet and novelist.*

poetry /ˈpəʊɪtri/ NOUN, NO PLURAL poems in general □ *a book of poetry*

point¹ /pɔɪnt/ NOUN [plural **points**]
1 an idea, opinion, or thing you want to say ☐ *He made the point that some people wouldn't be able to afford the service.* ☐ *I do take your point* (= understand your opinion) *about the high fence.* ☐ *'Meg says it's not fair for the girls to do all the work.' 'Well, she does have a point* (= her opinion is worth considering)'*.
2 the reason for something or the purpose of something ☐ *What's the point of going home if you just have to go straight back out again?* ☐ *I can't really see the point of exercising.* ☐ *There's no point in asking her – she won't come.*
3 the most important thing about what has been said ☐ *The point is, we can't afford a holiday.* ☐ *She talked for so long, I thought she'd never get to the point.*
4 a particular time in an event or process ☐ *At that point, we decided to leave.* ☐ *I've reached the point with my studies where I'd like to specialize more.* ☐ *At some point today, I need to phone Miriam.*
5 a particular place □ *Drinks are available at several points along the route.* □ *This is the highest point in England.*
6 a feature or characteristic ☐ *I know you don't like Mike, but he does have some good points.*
7 the sharp end of something □ *Make a small hole with the point of a needle.*

8 the mark '.' that is used in numbers that have a part less than one, e.g. 5.34
9 a unit for showing the score in a game or a competition □ *Who got the highest number of points?* ☐ *You score 2 points for each correct answer.*
10 be at the point of doing something to be going to do something very soon □ *We were at the point of signing the contract when the buyers pulled out.*

point² /pɔɪnt/ VERB [points, pointing, pointed]
1 to show someone something by holding your finger or a thin object towards it □ + *at* *He pointed at a man in black.* □ *She pointed towards the door with her umbrella.*
2 to face in a particular direction, or to make something face a particular direction □ + *at* *He pointed the gun at the target.* □ *The sign points north.* □ *What time is it when the little hand points to the three?*
♦ PHRASAL VERB **point something out** to make someone aware of a fact □ *He pointed out that he had been waiting for over an hour.*

pointed /ˈpɔɪntɪd/ ADJECTIVE with a sharp end □ *a pointed stick*

pointless /ˈpɔɪntlɪs/ ADJECTIVE having no purpose or meaning □ *a pointless argument* □ *It's pointless asking him – he'll never come.*

point of view /ˌpɔɪnt əv ˈvjuː/ NOUN [plural points of view]
1 a way of considering or judging a situation □ *From a practical point of view, I see nothing wrong.*
2 an opinion about something □ *They have different points of view.*

poison¹ /ˌpɔɪzən/ NOUN [plural poisons] a substance that causes death or illness when you eat, drink or breathe it □ *a deadly poison* □ *rat poison*

poison² /ˈpɔɪzən/ VERB [poisons, poisoning, poisoned] to kill or harm someone with poison □ *They were poisoned by carbon monoxide fumes.*

poisonous /ˈpɔɪzənəs/ ADJECTIVE containing poison □ *This cleaning liquid is poisonous.*

poke /pəʊk/ VERB [pokes, poking, poked]
1 to quickly push something or someone with your finger or with something sharp □ *He poked me in the stomach.*
2 to appear through a hole or from behind something □ *She poked her head through the curtains.* □ *His hair was poking out from under his hat.*

poker /ˈpəʊkə(r)/ NOUN [plural pokers] a card game played for money

polar /'pəʊlə(r)/ ADJECTIVE to do with the north or south pole (= areas at the top and bottom of the Earth) □ *a polar region* □ *polar ice*

polar bear /'pəʊlə ˌbeə(r)/ NOUN [plural polar bears] a large white bear that lives near the North Pole

pole /pəʊl/ NOUN [plural poles]
1 a long thin stick made of metal or wood, often used for supporting something □ *an aluminium tent pole*
2 one of the two areas at the most northern and southern points of the Earth

police /pə'li:s/ NOUN, NO PLURAL the people whose job is to make people obey the law and to catch people who break the law ℗ *One of his neighbours called the police.* □ *Last night police were questioning four men.* ℗ *the police force* ℗ *a police investigation*

policeman /pə'li:smən/ NOUN [plural policemen] a male police officer

police officer /pə'li:s ˌɒfɪsə(r)/ NOUN [plural police officers] a member of the police □ *an armed police officer*

police station /pə'li:s ˌsteɪʃən/ NOUN [plural police stations] a building where the police have their offices

policewoman /pə'li:swʊmən/ NOUN [plural policewomen] a female police officer

policy /'pɒləsɪ/ NOUN [plural policies] a plan about how to deal with something by a government, political party, business, etc. □ *government policies* ℗ *US foreign policy* □ *the party's policy on immigration*

polish[1] /'pɒlɪʃ/ VERB [polishes, polishing, polished] to rub something until it shines □ *Remember to polish your shoes.*

polish[2] /'pɒlɪʃ/ NOUN [plural polishes] a substance used to polish something ℗ *shoe polish* □ *furniture polish*

polite /pə'laɪt/ ADJECTIVE [politer, politest] behaving in a pleasant way towards other people, for example, saying 'thank you' and 'please' □ *Her children are very polite.* □ *+ to* *She was polite to hospital staff.* □ *+ to do something* *He was too polite to interrupt.*

politely /pə'laɪtlɪ/ ADVERB in a polite way □ *'Would you like a seat?' he asked her politely.* □ *She politely declined the invitation.*

political /pə'lɪtɪkəl/ ADJECTIVE to do with politics, politicians or government ℗ *a political party* ℗ *a political leader* □ *a political and economic crisis*

politician /ˌpɒlɪ'tɪʃən/ NOUN [plural politicians] someone whose job is politics, especially someone who has been elected to a parliament □ *People don't seem to trust politicians.*

politics /'pɒlɪtɪks/ NOUN, NO PLURAL
1 ideas or activities to do with governing a country □ *He's very interested in politics.*
2 the job of being a politician ℗ *He entered politics after leaving university.*

poll /pəʊl/ NOUN [plural polls]
1 when a number of people are asked their opinion on a particular subject ℗ *The poll showed that about 55% of people are against the war.* ℗ *The poll was conducted for a local newspaper.*
2 a political election in which people vote ℗ *Voters go to the polls* (= vote) *on 24 November.*

pollute /pə'lu:t/ VERB [pollutes, polluting, polluted] to allow harmful substances to go into the air, soil or water □ *We need to find energy sources which don't pollute the environment.*

pollution /pə'lu:ʃən/ NOUN, NO PLURAL
1 harmful substances in the air, soil or water ℗ *the health effects of air pollution* ℗ *a major source of pollution* □ *+ from* *We need to reduce pollution from traffic.*
2 when harmful substances are allowed into the air, soil or water □ *+ of* *We need to take action against the pollution of the oceans.*

pond /pɒnd/ NOUN [plural ponds] a small area of water, smaller than a lake □ *a garden pond* □ *a fish pond*

pony /'pəʊnɪ/ NOUN [plural ponies] a small horse

pool /pu:l/ NOUN [plural pools]
1 an area of water made for swimming in □ *The hotel has an indoor pool.* □ *a heated pool*
2 a small area of liquid □ *There was a small pool of blood on the floor.*

poor /pʊə(r)/ ADJECTIVE [poorer, poorest]
1 having little money and owning few things □ *a poor country* □ *His family were very poor.*
2 of a low standard ℗ *The paper was of poor quality.* ℗ *He's in very poor health.* □ *It was a poor performance by the team generally.*
3 used to show that someone or something deserves sympathy □ *Poor you! You sound so ill.* □ *The poor little thing is all wet.*

• **poorly** /'pʊəlɪ/ ADVERB badly or not well enough □ *a poorly paid job* □ *He performed fairly poorly in both matches.*

pop[1] /pɒp/ NOUN [plural pops]
1 *no plural* modern music with short, simple songs and a strong beat ℗ *pop music* ℗ *a pop star* ℗ *a pop song*
2 a short sound like something exploding □ *They heard a loud pop.* □ *The bottle opened with a pop.*

pop[2] /pɒp/ VERB [pops, popping, popped]
1 to go somewhere quickly, for a short time
□ **+ out** *I just popped out for a few minutes.*
□ **+ into** *I need to pop into the office.*
2 to put something somewhere quickly □ *I'll just pop the pizza in the oven.* □ *Karen popped her head around the door.*
3 to make a short sound like something exploding
□ *The fire crackled and popped.* 🔊 *I could hear balloons popping in the background.*
♦ PHRASAL VERB **pop up** to suddenly appear □ *Bars and cafés are popping up all over the place.*

Pope /pəʊp/ NOUN [plural Popes] the leader of the Catholic Church

poppy /'pɒpɪ/ NOUN [plural poppies] a tall, red flower that grows in fields

popular /'pɒpjʊlə(r)/ ADJECTIVE liked by a lot of people □ *a popular tourist destination* □ *She was a very popular student.* □ **+ with** *The beach is popular with tourists.* 🔊 *Podcasts are becoming increasingly popular.*

population /ˌpɒpjʊ'leɪʃən/ NOUN [plural populations]
1 all the people who live in an area, country, etc.
🔊 *The troops are there to protect the local population.* □ *More than half the world's population live in cities.*
2 the number of people who live in an area, country, etc. □ **+ of** *The city has a population of around two million.*

> ► THESAURUS: Population means all the people who live in an area, country, etc. Society is all the people who live in a group or in a particular country or area. We often use society to talk about the opinions and beliefs of the people in an area. The public means people generally. A citizen is someone who has the right to live in a country permanently.

pore /pɔ:(r)/ NOUN [plural pores] one of the very small holes in your skin that sweat comes out of. A biology word.

pork /pɔ:k/ NOUN, NO PLURAL meat from a pig
□ *roast pork*

port /pɔ:t/ NOUN [plural ports] a place where ships can stop on the coast, and the town or city around it
□ *the Israeli port of Haifa* □ *a major shipping port*
□ *It's a small fishing port on the south coast.*

portable /'pɔ:təbəl/ ADJECTIVE small enough to be carried easily □ *a portable television* □ *a portable DVD player*

porter /'pɔ:tə(r)/ NOUN [plural porters]
1 someone whose job is to carry bags for people at a station, hotel, etc. □ *The porter will take your bags up to your room.*

2 someone whose job is to look after a building
□ *the night porter at the hotel*

portion /'pɔ:ʃən/ NOUN [plural portions] a part of a total amount □ *She spends a large portion of her income on clothes.*

portrait /'pɔ:treɪt/ NOUN [plural portraits] a painting or photograph of a person, especially of their face □ *a portrait of the prince* 🔊 *a portrait painter*

posh /pɒʃ/ ADJECTIVE [posher, poshest]
1 an informal word meaning expensive and comfortable □ *a posh hotel* □ *a posh London restaurant*
2 an informal word meaning from a high social class
□ *a posh accent*

position /pə'zɪʃən/ NOUN [plural positions]
1 a way of standing, sitting or lying □ *I must have been sleeping in an awkward position.*
2 the place where something is, or the way in which it has been put there □ *His pipe was in its usual position, beside his chair.* □ *Push the lever to the 'on' position.*
3 the situation that someone is in 🔊 *Our team is in a strong position to win the championship.* 🔊 *Her demands put me in a very difficult position.*
□ *Unfortunately, I am not in a position (= I am not able) to help you.* □ *In her position, I'd hire a really good lawyer.*
4 a job or post □ *He applied for a teaching position.* 🔊 *Our marketing manager left, and we have not yet filled his position.*

positive /'pɒzɪtɪv/ ADJECTIVE
1 completely certain □ **+ that** *Are you absolutely positive that he's German?* □ **+ about** *Jack has seen the letter. I'm positive about that.*
2 feeling happy about a situation and believing that the future will be good 🔊 *He has a very positive attitude to life.* 🔊 *It can be difficult to remain positive when you have so many problems.*

possess /pə'zes/ VERB [possesses, possessing, possessed] a formal word meaning to have something □ *He was charged with possessing an illegal weapon.* □ *Candidates should possess strong communication skills.*

possession /pə'zeʃən/ NOUN [plural possessions] something you own or have 🔊 *They packed up their personal possessions.*

possessive[1] /pə'zesɪv/ ADJECTIVE
1 not wanting to share your things with other people □ *Children are very possessive with their toys.*
2 in grammar, showing who or what a person or thing belongs to □ *a possessive pronoun such as 'mine'*

possessive² /pə'zesɪv/ NOUN [plural possessives] in grammar, a word that shows who or what a person or thing belongs to

possibility /ˌpɒsə'bɪlətɪ/ NOUN [plural possibilities]
1 the chance that something might happen □ + of We were warned about the possibility of flooding. □ + that There's a strong possibility that the tour will be cancelled.
2 something that might happen ⊞ Civil war is now a real possibility.

possible /'pɒsəbəl/ ADJECTIVE
1 something that is possible can happen or be done □ + to do something It isn't possible to see the doctor today. ⊞ Try to avoid the area if possible.
2 something that is possible may be true □ + that It's possible that I made a mistake. □ That doesn't seem possible. ⊞ There are several possible explanations.
3 as soon/quickly, etc. as possible as soon, quickly, etc. as you can □ We need the work done as quickly as possible.

possibly /'pɒsəblɪ/ ADVERB perhaps □ It could take about 5 days, possibly longer.

post¹ /pəust/ NOUN [plural posts]
1 the service which collects and delivers letters and packages, or the letters and packages sent □ I sent it by post. □ Has the post arrived yet?
2 a job □ the post of finance director □ a teaching post ⊞ He held a senior post at the bank.
3 a long piece of wood fixed into the ground ⊞ a fence post ⊞ a goal post
4 a message which has been put on a website. A computing word □ a blog post □ She announced the tour in a post on her website.

post² /pəust/ VERB [posts, posting, posted]
1 to send a letter or package by post ⊞ I posted the letter yesterday.
2 to put a message, video, picture, etc. on a website. A computing word □ He posted a message to fans on his website. □ A video of the interview was posted on the Internet.

postbox /'pəustbɒks/ NOUN [plural postboxes] a container in a public place where letters can be posted

postcard /'pəustkɑːd/ NOUN [plural postcards] a card with a picture on one side. You write on the other side and send the card by post without an envelope □ a picture postcard □ I'll send you a postcard from Tokyo.

post code /'pəustkəud/ NOUN [plural post codes] a series of letters and numbers at the end of an address

poster /'pəustə(r)/ NOUN [plural posters] a large notice or picture used for advertising, for decorating a wall, or for giving information □ She has posters of movie stars all over her bedroom walls.

postman /'pəustmən/ NOUN [plural postmen] someone whose job is to deliver letters and packages to houses or offices □ Has the postman been yet?

post office /'pəust ˌɒfɪs/ NOUN [plural post offices] a shop where you can post letters and packages, and buy stamps

postpone /pəust'pəun/ VERB [postpones, postponing, postponed] to decide to do something at a later time than planned □ We had to postpone our trip to Paris.

pot /pɒt/ NOUN [plural pots] a round container used for cooking, for storing things in, or for growing plants in □ + of a pot of paint ⊞ a pile of dirty pots and pans (= containers used for cooking) ⊞ a flower pot (= container for growing plants)

potato /pə'teɪtəu/ NOUN [plural potatoes] a very common white, round vegetable that grows underground with a brown or yellow skin □ mashed potato □ roast potatoes

pottery /'pɒtərɪ/ NOUN, NO PLURAL
1 objects such as bowls and cups made from clay
2 the job or activity of making things from clay

poultry /'pəultrɪ/ NOUN, NO PLURAL
1 birds such as chickens that are kept for people to eat
2 the meat from these birds

pounce /pauns/ VERB [pounces, pouncing, pounced] to jump or move forward suddenly to attack or catch someone or something □ The cat pounced on the mouse.

pound¹ /paund/ NOUN [plural pounds]
1 the main unit of money in Britain. The written symbol is £. □ They cost just a few pounds each. □ a multi-million pound contract

2 a coin worth one pound
3 a unit for measuring weight, equal to 0.454 kilograms. This is often written **lb**.

pound² /paʊnd/ VERB [pounds, pounding, pounded] to hit something hard repeatedly □ *Someone was pounding at the door, trying to get in.*

pour /pɔː(r)/ VERB [pours, pouring, poured]
1 to make a liquid flow out of a container □ **+ into** *She poured the orange juice into a glass.* □ **+ out** *She poured out the tea.* □ **+ over** *Pour the sauce over the chicken.*
2 to rain very hard ⚏ *It's pouring with rain outside.* □ *The rain was pouring down.*
3 to flow out of something fast and in large quantities □ *Water was pouring through the ceiling.* □ *The sweat poured down his face.*

poverty /ˈpɒvəti/ NOUN, NO PLURAL the state of being poor □ *Many families are living in poverty.* □ *a campaign to reduce global poverty*

powder /ˈpaʊdə(r)/ NOUN [plural powders] a substance in the form of very small dry pieces, like dust □ *chilli powder* □ *washing powder* □ *She sprinkled some cocoa powder on the top.*

power /ˈpaʊə(r)/ NOUN [plural powers]
1 the ability to control or influence people or things □ *economic/military power* □ **+ over** *The big factory owners had a lot of power over local people.* □ *They really understand the power of the media.*
2 energy used for working machines, or the supply of this energy ⚏ *nuclear power* ⚏ *We are looking at new ways to generate power.* ⚏ *Electricity companies are working day and night to restore power to the area.*
3 a country with a lot of influence in the world □ *He says that Western powers are failing to deal with climate change.*
4 strength or force □ *The power of the blast knocked me over.*
5 the official right to do something □ **+ to do something** *We don't have the power to issue visas.* □ *The committee's powers are limited.*

powerful /ˈpaʊəful/ ADJECTIVE
1 having the ability to control or influence people or things □ *a powerful politician* □ *a powerful nation*
2 having a lot of physical force □ *a powerful earthquake*
3 very effective, being able to do a lot □ *Computers have become more powerful.*

practical¹ /ˈpræktɪkəl/ ADJECTIVE
1 to do with real situations, not ideas ⚏ *They provide practical advice.*
2 useful and suitable ⚏ *It's the most practical solution to the problem.* □ *It's not practical to cycle in a long skirt.*

3 good at repairing things and doing things with your hands □ *He's not a very practical person.*
4 able to make sensible decisions □ *She's much more practical than her sister.*

practical² /ˈpræktɪkəl/ NOUN [plural practicals] a lesson or an exam in which students learn or use practical skills

practically /ˈpræktɪkəli/ ADVERB almost □ *It was practically full.* □ *Practically everything was destroyed.*

practice¹ /ˈpræktɪs/ NOUN [plural practices]
1 when you do something often so that you get better at it □ *He'll soon learn to play the violin with a bit more practice.* □ *He goes to choir practice on Mondays.*
2 an activity, especially one that people have been doing for a long time □ *They campaigned to end the practice of torture.* □ *She studied their religious practices.*
3 be out of practice to not have done something for a long time □ *I'd love to play in your hockey team, but I'm a bit out of practice.*

practice² /ˈpræktɪs/ VERB [practices, practicing, practiced] the US spelling of **practise**

practise /ˈpræktɪs/ VERB [practises, practising, practised] to do something again and again so that you get better at it □ **+ ing** *Practise breathing through your nose.* □ *To become a good musician, you must practise regularly.*

➤ Remember that in British English, **practise** with an s is a verb. **Practice** with a c is a noun: □ *This gave me a chance to practise my language skills.* □ *I have football practice tonight.*

praise¹ /preɪz/ VERB [praises, praising, praised] to say how well someone has done and how you admire them □ **+ for** *He was widely praised for his work.* □ *The prime minister praised the rescue effort.*

praise² /preɪz/ NOUN, NO PLURAL when you praise someone □ **+ for** *She received praise for her handling of the incident.* ⚏ *He won praise from the team coach.*

pray /preɪ/ VERB [prays, praying, prayed] to speak to a god □ **+ for** *She knelt down and prayed for forgiveness.* □ **+ to** *He prayed to Allah.*

prayer /preə(r)/ NOUN [plural prayers]
1 the words that you use when you pray to a god □ *the Lord's prayer* ⚏ *He said a prayer of thanks.* □ *They went to the mosque for Friday prayers.*
2 no plural when you pray to a god □ *They knelt in prayer.*

preach /priːtʃ/ VERB [preaches, preaching, preached] to talk to a group of people about a religious subject, usually as part of a church service 🔄 *Father Andrew will preach the sermon.*

preacher /'priːtʃə(r)/ NOUN [plural preachers] someone who talks to people about a religious subject at a church service

precaution /prɪ'kɔːʃən/ NOUN [plural precautions] something you do to avoid an accident or a problem happening 🔄 *We're taking all necessary precautions.* 🔄 *They stopped work on the site as a safety precaution.*

precious /'preʃəs/ ADJECTIVE
1 very valuable and rare □ *precious stones* □ *In many parts of the world, water is a precious resource.*
2 very important to someone □ *His books are very precious to him.*

precise /prɪ'saɪs/ ADJECTIVE
1 exact □ *the precise location* □ *He didn't give any precise details.* 🔄 *At that precise moment, the bell rang.*
2 careful and accurate □ *Her work is very precise.*

precisely /prɪ'saɪslɪ/ ADVERB
1 exactly or accurately □ *We need to find out precisely what happened.* □ *It arrived at precisely 12.34.*
2 used to strongly agree with someone's opinion

predator /'predətə(r)/ NOUN [plural predators] an animal that hunts and eats other animals

predict /prɪ'dɪkt/ VERB [predicts, predicting, predicted] to say that you think something will happen in the future □ *They're predicting snow for next week.*

prediction /prɪ'dɪkʃən/ NOUN [plural predictions] when you say that you think something will happen in the future, or what you think will happen 🔄 *I don't want to make any predictions yet.*

prefer /prɪ'fɜː(r)/ VERB [prefers, preferring, preferred] to like or to want one thing more than something else □ *I prefer the red dress to the black one.* □ **+ to do something** *We'd prefer to stay near the beach.* □ *He prefers not to talk about his family in public.* □ **+ ing** *I prefer working from home.* □ *You can bring you own food if you prefer.*

preference /'prefərəns/ NOUN [plural preferences] when you prefer one thing to another, or something that you like or prefer □ *The children showed a preference for sweet foods.*

pregnancy /'pregnənsɪ/ NOUN [plural pregnancies] the period when a woman or a female animal carries a developing baby inside her □ *Smoking during pregnancy can harm the baby.*

pregnant /'pregnənt/ ADJECTIVE if a woman or a female animal is pregnant, she is carrying a developing baby inside her 🔄 *a pregnant woman*

□ **+ with** *She was pregnant with twins.* 🔄 *She got pregnant again quite quickly.*

prehistoric /ˌpriːhɪ'stɒrɪk/ ADJECTIVE to do with the time in the past before history was written down □ *prehistoric times* □ *prehistoric animals*

prejudice /'predʒudɪs/ NOUN [plural prejudices] when someone has an unfair opinion or dislike of someone or something without knowing or understanding them 🔄 *racial prejudice* □ *There is still prejudice against people with mental disabilities.*

premature /'premətjuə(r)/ ADJECTIVE a premature baby is born before the time it should have been born

premier /'premjə(r)/ ADJECTIVE best, most successful or most important □ *France's premier resort* □ *one of the world's premier sports events*

premiere /'premieə(r)/ NOUN [plural premieres] the first public showing or performance of a film, play, etc. 🔄 *the world premiere of the new James Bond film*

preparation /ˌprepə'reɪʃən/ NOUN [plural preparations]
1 no plural when you get ready for something □ **+ for** *This is ideal preparation for next week's game.* 🔄 *We did some shopping in preparation for the trip.* □ *Make sure the food preparation area is clean.*
2 something you do to get ready for something □ *How are the wedding preparations going?* 🔄 *We're making the final preparations for the show.*

prepare /prɪ'peə(r)/ VERB [prepares, preparing, prepared] to get ready for something or to make something ready □ **+ for** *We need to prepare for the long journey.* □ **+ to do something** *They are preparing to open a new shop.* □ *He prepared a report on the company.* □ *We have to prepare students for working life.* 🔄 *Prepare yourself for a shock when you see him.*

preposition /ˌprepə'zɪʃən/ NOUN [plural prepositions] a word or phrase used before a noun or a pronoun to show things like position, time or method. For example, *in*, *by* and *out of* are prepositions.

prescribe /prɪ'skraɪb/ VERB [prescribes, prescribing, prescribed] to tell a patient to take a particular medicine □ *Doctors often prescribe antibiotics for infections.*

prescription /prɪ'skrɪpʃən/ NOUN [plural prescriptions] a written instruction from a doctor saying that someone needs a particular medicine □ **+ for** *a prescription for sleeping pills* 🔄 *a prescription drug* (= medicine that must be prescribed by a doctor)

presence /'prezəns/ NOUN, NO PLURAL the fact of someone or something being somewhere □ *Tests* indicated the presence of the disease. 🔁 *He was questioned in the presence of a lawyer.*

present[1] /'prezənt/ NOUN [*plural* presents]
1 something you give to someone, for example for their birthday □ *I've got a present for you.* 🔁 *a birthday present* 🔁 *The children opened their Christmas presents.*
2 the present the time now
3 at present now □ *He doesn't have a job at present.*

present[2] /'prezənt/ ADJECTIVE
1 being in a particular place □ *Both men were present at the meeting.* □ *Vitamin D is present in small quantities in food.*
2 to do with the time now □ *The present system isn't working.* 🔁 *We'll look at fashion from the 50s to the present day.*

present[3] /prɪ'zent/ VERB [presents, presenting, presented]
1 to give something to someone formally, often at a ceremony □ *She presented the best actor award.* □ *The captain was presented with the trophy.*
2 to introduce a radio or television show □ *She presents the news on the BBC.*

presentation /ˌprezən'teɪʃən/ NOUN [*plural* presentations]
1 a talk to a group of people explaining or describing something 🔁 *She gave a presentation on her research.*
2 when something, such as a prize, is formally given to someone □ *a presentation ceremony*

presenter /prɪ'zentə(r)/ NOUN [*plural* presenters]
someone who introduces the parts of a radio or television programme □ *the presenter of Radio 4's Today Programme*

present participle /ˌprezənt 'pɑːtɪsɪpəl/ NOUN [*plural* present participles] the form of a verb ending in *-ing*, usually used after the verb *be*. For example, *going* in *I was going.*

present tense /ˌprezənt 'tens/ NOUN [*plural* present tenses] a form of a verb used to show that the action is happening now

preserve /prɪ'zɜːv/ VERB [preserves, preserving, preserved] to keep something the same, stopping it from being lost or destroyed □ *We try to preserve our traditions and culture.* □ *ancient fossils preserved in rocks*

president /'prezɪdənt/ NOUN [*plural* presidents]
1 the elected leader of a country that has no king or queen □ *the Russian president* □ + *of* *the president of Pakistan* □ *President Bush*
2 the person with the highest position in a company or an organization □ + *of* *He became president of General Motors in 1920.*

press[1] /pres/ VERB [presses, pressing, pressed]
1 to push something, or to push something firmly against something else □ *Press the red button.*

□ *Orla pressed her lips together.* □ *Nothing's happening – try pressing harder.*
2 to make clothes flat by ironing them

press[2] /pres/ NOUN [*plural* presses]
1 the press newspapers and magazines, and the people who write for them □ *He issued a statement to the press.* □ *Press reports suggested that he was sacked from the post.* □ *She was mocked in the press.*
2 a push against something □ *I gave the button a press and a bell rang.*
3 a machine that prints books, newspapers, etc.

press conference /'pres ˌkɒnfərəns/ NOUN [*plural* press conferences] an official meeting at which someone gives information to people who work in television and on newspapers and answers their questions 🔁 *The police are holding a press conference this afternoon.*

pressure /'preʃə(r)/ NOUN [*plural* pressures]
1 *no plural* when someone tries to persuade or force someone to do something □ + *to do something* *The government are under pressure to change the law.* 🔁 *Her father put pressure on her to study medicine.* 🔁 *I don't want to put you under pressure.*
2 *no plural* the force on or against a surface from something pressing on it □ *Applying pressure to the wound will stop the bleeding.*
3 *no plural* the force that a liquid or gas has when it is inside something □ *air pressure* □ *high blood pressure*
4 difficulties and problems that cause you to worry □ *the pressures of work*

presumably /prɪ'zjuːməblɪ/ ADVERB used for saying something that you think is probably true □ *Presumably the picnic will be cancelled if it rains.*

pretend /prɪ'tend/ VERB [pretends, pretending, pretended]
1 to try to make someone believe something that is not true □ + *that* *She closed her eyes and pretended that she was asleep.* □ + *to do something* *Chris was sitting at the table, pretending to do his homework.*
2 to imagine that something is true as part of a game □ + *to do something* *The children were pretending to be robots.*

pretty[1] /'prɪtɪ/ ADJECTIVE [prettier, prettiest]
people and things that are pretty are attractive, often in a delicate way □ *His girlfriend is very pretty.* □ *She was wearing a pretty white dress.* □ *What pretty flowers!*

pretty[2] /'prɪtɪ/ ADVERB
1 quite □ *Eight out of ten is a pretty good mark.*
2 very 🔁 *That's a pretty good salary, if you ask me!*

prevent /prɪ'vent/ VERB [prevents, preventing, prevented] to stop something happening or someone doing something □ *Police are working* hard to prevent gun crime. □ **+ from** *They were prevented from leaving the building.*

prevention /prɪˈvenʃən/ NOUN, NO PLURAL when you prevent something ⊞ *crime prevention* □ *the prevention of infection*

preview /ˈpriːvjuː/ NOUN [plural previews]
1 a showing or performance of a film, play, etc. to a small group of people before it is shown to everyone □ *Previews of the musical start this week.*
2 a short piece of a film, programme, etc. used to advertise it

previous /ˈpriːvɪəs/ ADJECTIVE happening or existing before □ *Please write down your previous address.* □ *I have some previous experience of working with children.*

previously /ˈpriːvɪəslɪ/ ADVERB before □ *I'd met Sven a few months previously.* □ *He previously worked in a bank.*

prey /preɪ/ NOUN, NO PLURAL an animal or bird that another animal hunts, kills and eats

price /praɪs/ NOUN [plural prices] the amount of money that something costs ⊞ *Food prices continue to rise.* ⊞ *House prices are falling.*

priceless /ˈpraɪsləs/ ADJECTIVE extremely valuable □ *priceless works of art*

pride /praɪd/ NOUN, NO PLURAL
1 a feeling of pleasure because you have achieved something or because someone such as your child has achieved something □ *There was such pride in his face as he looked at his baby daughter.*
2 respect for yourself ⊞ *Jenny always took pride in her appearance.*

priest /priːst/ NOUN [plural priests] someone who performs religious services in some religions □ *a Roman Catholic priest*

primary /ˈpraɪmərɪ/ ADJECTIVE main □ *Heart disease is still one of the primary causes of early death.*

primary school /ˈpraɪmərɪ ˌskuːl/ NOUN [plural primary schools] a school for children between the ages of four and eleven

prime minister /ˌpraɪm ˈmɪnɪstə(r)/ NOUN [plural prime ministers] the leader of the government in Britain and in many other countries of the world □ *the Irish prime minister*

primitive /ˈprɪmɪtɪv/ ADJECTIVE belonging to the earliest stages of development □ *primitive man* □ *a primitive computer*

prince /prɪns/ NOUN [plural princes] the son or male grandchild of a king or queen, or the male ruler of a small state or country □ *Prince Charles*

princess /prɪnˈses/ NOUN [plural princesses] the daughter or female grandchild of a king or queen, or the wife of a prince □ *Princess Caroline of Monaco*

principal¹ /ˈprɪnsɪpəl/ ADJECTIVE main □ *Steel-making was the principal industry in the area.*

principal² /ˈprɪnsɪpəl/ NOUN [plural principals] the person in charge of a school, college or university

principle /ˈprɪnsɪpəl/ NOUN [plural principles]
1 a general rule or idea about how something is done □ *The government has drawn up principles of good practice for landlords.*
2 a general rule that you base your behaviour on because you think it is morally right ⊞ *It was against his principles to borrow money.*

print¹ /prɪnt/ VERB [prints, printing, printed]
1 to produce words, pictures, etc. on paper or another surface using a machine □ *We printed 500 copies of the letter.* □ *Cooking instructions are printed on the back of the label.* □ *All our reference books are printed in Italy.* □ *Is this document ready to print?*
2 to write words without joining the letters together □ *Print your name at the top of the form.*
♦ PHRASAL VERB **print something out** to make a printed copy of a document or image from a computer □ *I printed out the map.*

print² /prɪnt/ NOUN [plural prints]
1 words, pictures, etc. that are produced on paper or another surface using a machine □ *She can only read books with large print.* □ *I was so excited to see my name in print.*
2 a mark that is left when something has pressed on a surface □ *Prints from his boots could still be seen in the mud.*
3 a fingerprint (= mark left when someone has touched something)

printer /ˈprɪntə(r)/ NOUN [plural printers]
1 a machine that prints words and pictures from a computer
2 a person or company whose business is printing books, newspapers, etc.

prison /ˈprɪzən/ NOUN [plural prisons] a building where criminals are kept □ *Her father is in prison.* ⊞ *If he commits another crime he will be sent to prison.* ⊞ *He was released from prison last month.*

prisoner /ˈprɪzənə(r)/ NOUN [plural prisoners]
1 someone who is kept in prison as a punishment □ *Four prisoners share each cell.*
2 someone who is kept in a place and cannot get out ⊞ *Her father kept her prisoner in the cellar for over 20 years.*

> ➤ THESAURUS: A prisoner is someone who is kept in prison as a punishment. Convict has a similar meaning. A captive is someone who is a prisoner, but a captive may or may not be in a prison. A hostage is someone who is kept as a prisoner until the people holding them get what they want. For example, someone who has been kidnapped or in a hijack might be a hostage.

privacy /'prɪvəsɪ, 'praɪvəsɪ/ NOUN, NO PLURAL
being alone where people cannot see or hear you □ A higher fence will give us a bit more privacy.

private¹ /'praɪvɪt/ ADJECTIVE
1 belonging to or used by only one person, or a small group of people □ a private beach □ The prince flew in on his private plane.
2 where other people cannot see or hear you □ Can we find somewhere more private?
3 to do with relationships, family and the things that people do when they are not working 🐾 He never discusses his private life in interviews □ I never make private calls from the office.
4 owned and managed by people or companies, not by the government □ private industry □ a private hospital

private² /'praɪvɪt/ NOUN, NO PLURAL in private
with no one else present □ Could I speak to you in private for a moment?

privately /'praɪvɪtlɪ/ ADVERB
1 away from other people □ Can we talk privately?
2 a privately owned company is owned by a person or business and not by the government

private school /ˌpraɪvɪt 'skuːl/ NOUN [plural private schools] a school which parents must pay to send their children to

privilege /'prɪvɪlɪdʒ/ NOUN [plural privileges] a special right or advantage given to only one person, or to only a few people □ The directors have special privileges such as their own dining room.

prize /praɪz/ NOUN [plural prizes] something won in a competition or given as a reward for good work 🐾 The first prize was a trip to France. 🐾 Adam won a prize in the competition.

probable /'prɒbəbəl/ ADJECTIVE something that is probable is probably true or will probably happen □ A cigarette was the probable cause of the fire. □ It now seems probable that we will go to war.

probably /'prɒbəblɪ/ ADVERB used for saying that something will almost certainly happen or is almost certainly true □ I'll probably be late. □ He'll probably lose it anyway.

problem /'prɒbləm/ NOUN [plural problems]
1 a situation that is causing difficulties □ financial problems □ + with There's a problem with the car. 🐾 He's having problems with someone at work. 🐾 I don't want to cause any problems for you. □ We had problems finding a hotel.
2 no problem (a) used for agreeing to do something for someone □ 'Could you get some milk on the way home, please?' 'Sure, no problem.' (b) used when someone thanks you for something □ 'Thanks for lending me your bike.' 'No problem.'
3 a question that you have to answer or solve □ maths problems

> ➤ Note that you 'have problems **doing** something'. You do not have problems 'to do something':
> ✓ We had problems finding the house.
> ✗ We had problems to find the house.

> ➤ A very bad problem is a **serious** problem and not an 'important' problem:
> ✓ Debt is a very serious problem.
> ✗ Debt is a very important problem.

proceed /prə'siːd/ VERB [proceeds, proceeding, proceeded]
1 to continue something. A formal word. □ She has decided not to proceed with her application.
2 proceed to do something to do something next, especially something annoying □ He said he wasn't hungry and proceeded to eat two slices of cake.

process /'prəʊses/ NOUN [plural processes]
1 a series of actions or events that have a particular result □ the production process □ Getting a visa is a lengthy process.
2 a series of changes □ the ageing process

procession /prə'seʃən/ NOUN [plural processions] a line of people or vehicles moving along slowly, one behind the other □ a funeral procession

proclaim /prə'kleɪm/ VERB [proclaims, proclaiming, proclaimed] to state something publicly or officially □ He proclaimed his innocence.

produce¹ /prə'djuːs/ VERB [produces, producing, produced]
1 to make, grow or create something □ The new factory will produce goods for export. □ The plum tree didn't produce much fruit last year. □ The sun produces both light and heat.
2 to have a particular effect □ This style of teaching produces better results.
3 to organize the actors, equipment and money, etc. that are needed for a film, programme, play or musical recording □ a film produced by George Lucas
4 to show something so that people can see it □ The conjuror produced a rabbit from a hat. □ The diary was produced as evidence at the trial.

produce² /'prɒdjuːs/ NOUN, NO PLURAL things that are grown or produced on farms, especially food ☝ *The village shop sells local produce.*

producer /prə'djuːsə(r)/ NOUN [*plural* producers] someone who organizes the actors, equipment and money, etc. that are needed for a film, programme or musical recording □ *an independent producer*

product /'prɒdʌkt/ NOUN [*plural* products] something that is produced in large numbers for selling ☝ *dairy products* □ *household cleaning products*

production /prə'dʌkʃən/ NOUN [*plural* productions]
1 *no plural* making, growing or producing something, or the amount that is produced □ *the production of organic food* □ *We now have this type of car in production.* □ *We have increased production by 30%.*
2 a performance or number of performances of a play or show □ *He played the lead in the school production of 'Grease'.*

profession /prə'feʃən/ NOUN [*plural* professions] a type of job that needs special qualifications and training, for example, medicine, law and teaching □ *He is considering going into the legal profession.*

professional /prə'feʃənəl/ ADJECTIVE
1 to do with a type of job that needs special qualifications and training □ *professional training*
2 doing something for money instead of as a hobby or for pleasure □ *a professional footballer*

professor /prə'fesə(r)/ NOUN [*plural* professors]
1 in the UK, the most important teacher in a university department
2 in the US, a teacher in a university or college

profit /'prɒfɪt/ NOUN [*plural* profits] money you make by selling something for more than you paid for it □ *The company is looking for ways to increase its profits.* ☝ *We made a profit when we sold the house.*

➤ Note that you **make** a profit. You do not 'gain' a profit:
✓ *We made a big profit on the sale.*
✗ *We gained a big profit on the sale.*

program¹ /'prəʊgræm/ NOUN [*plural* programs]
1 a set of instructions put into a computer to make it perform a task. A computing word. □ *a word-processing program*
2 the US spelling of **programme**

program² /'prəʊgræm/ VERB [programs, programming, programmed] **1** to put a set of instructions into a computer or piece of electronic

equipment to make it do something. A computing word.

programme /'prəʊgræm/ NOUN [*plural* programmes]
1 a television or radio show □ *an arts programme*
2 a thin book that gives information about an event or performance

progress¹ /'prəʊgres/ NOUN, NO PLURAL
1 improvement of skills or knowledge ☝ *Freya has made a lot of progress in the last year.*
2 in progress happening or being done now □ *Work is now in progress to develop the site.*
3 movement forwards or towards something □ *The bus made very slow progress through the crowds.*

progress² /prə'gres/ VERB [progresses, progressing, progressed]
1 to develop □ *The work is progressing well.* □ *As the disease progresses, the patient requires more care.*
2 if a period of time progresses, it continues □ *As the evening progressed, I felt more and more tired.*
3 to go forward □ *They progressed slowly up the icy ridge.*

prohibit /prə'hɪbɪt/ VERB [prohibits, prohibiting, prohibited] to not allow people officially to do something □ *Smoking is prohibited in most public places.*

project /'prɒdʒekt/ NOUN [*plural* projects]
1 a piece of work that is planned with a particular aim □ *a research project* □ *a major construction project*
2 a piece of work done by a student, often involving collecting information on a subject and writing about it ☝ *Hannah's doing a project on Henry VIII.*

prominent /'prɒmɪnənt/ ADJECTIVE
1 important and known by a lot of people □ *a prominent member of the government*
2 sticking out or easily seen □ *a prominent landmark*

promise¹ /'prɒmɪs/ VERB [promises, promising, promised] to tell someone that you will certainly do something □ **+ to do something** *I've promised to help Rebecca with the food.* □ **+ that** *I promise that I'll pay you back.* □ *But you promised me you'd come!*

➤ **THESAURUS:** If you promise something, you tell someone that you will certainly do something. If you guarantee something, you make a promise that something will happen or be done. If you assure someone, you tell them that something is certainly true or will certainly happen. If you swear something, you make a promise.

promise² /'prɒmɪs/ NOUN [plural promises]
something that someone promises to do 🕮 *I'm not
making any promises.* 🕮 *I try to keep my promises*
(= do what I have said I will do). 🕮 *The unions
accused the government of breaking its promise to
them* (= not doing what it said it would).

promote /prə'məʊt/ VERB [promotes, promoting,
promoted]
1 to give someone a more important job or a job
that earns more money in the same organization
□ *Jack's been promoted to store manager.*
2 to tell people about something in order to
persuade them to buy it or use it □ *The book stores
are all promoting her latest novel.*

promotion /prə'məʊʃən/ NOUN [plural
promotions]
1 a move to a more important job or a job that
earns more money in the same organization 🕮 *Let's
hope she gets her promotion.*
2 *no plural* activities and materials which tell
people about something in order to persuade them
to buy it or use it

prompt /prɒmpt/ ADJECTIVE doing something or
happening without delay or at exactly the right time
□ *Thank you for your prompt reply to my letter.*

prone /prəʊn/ ADJECTIVE often suffering from
something □ *He's always been prone to headaches.*
□ *an injury-prone football player*

pronoun /'prəʊnaʊn/ NOUN [plural pronouns] a
word that can be used in place of a noun. For
example, in the sentence *Sara ate the ice cream*,
Sara and *the ice cream* could be changed to
pronouns and the sentence would be *She ate it.*

pronounce /prə'naʊns/ VERB [pronounces,
pronouncing, pronounced] to say the sound of a
word or letter □ *The two 'z's in pizza are
pronounced 'tz'.* □ *How do you pronounce your
surname?*

pronunciation /prəˌnʌnsɪ'eɪʃən/ NOUN [plural
pronunciations] the way that a word is pronounced
□ *The pronunciation of some Arabic words is very
difficult for English speakers.*

proof /pruːf/ NOUN, NO PLURAL facts or objects
which prove that something is true □ *+ that Do we
have any proof that she was actually there?* 🕮 *I was
asked to provide proof of identity.*

propaganda /ˌprɒpə'gændə/ NOUN, NO PLURAL
ideas, information or opinions that are spread by a
political group or by one side in a war, in order to
influence people

proper /'prɒpə(r)/ ADJECTIVE
1 correct and suitable □ *The staff hadn't received
proper training.* □ *The proper procedures were
followed.*

2 real or good enough □ *This is my first proper meal
for days.*

properly /'prɒpəli/ ADVERB correctly or well
□ *You're not properly dressed for the cold.* □ *Come
on, children, sit up properly.*

property /'prɒpəti/ NOUN [plural properties]
1 a house and the land it is on 🕮 *Private property –
keep off!* □ *property prices*
2 *no plural* the things that belong to you
🕮 *Customers must look after their personal property.*

➤ Remember that **property** meaning 'the things
that belong to you' is not used in the plural:
✓ *Stolen* **property** *is returned to the rightful
owners.*
✗ *Stolen* **properties** *are returned to the rightful
owners.*

prophet /'prɒfɪt/ NOUN [plural prophets] in some
religions, a man chosen by God to teach people and
give them his messages □ *the Prophet Isaiah*

proportion /prə'pɔːʃən/ NOUN [plural
proportions]
1 a part of a whole amount or total □ *A small
proportion of old people live in care homes.*
2 the number or amount of two groups or things
when compared with each other □ *The proportion
of women to men in the company has risen.*

proposal /prə'pəʊzəl/ NOUN [plural proposals]
1 a plan or suggestion □ *The council has a new
proposal to ease traffic congestion.*
2 when someone asks another person to marry them

propose /prə'pəʊz/ VERB [proposes, proposing,
proposed]
1 to suggest a plan or idea □ *I propose that we hold
the meeting at a later date.*
2 to ask someone to marry you

➤ Note that **propose** meaning 'to suggest a plan
or idea' is followed by **that** and not 'to do
something':
✓ *I propose* **that** *we discuss this with Maria
tomorrow.*
✗ *I propose to discuss this with Maria tomorrow.*

prosecute /'prɒsɪkjuːt/ VERB [prosecutes,
prosecuting, prosecuted] to accuse someone of a
crime and take them to court □ *She is being
prosecuted for fraud.*

prosper /'prɒspə(r)/ VERB [prospers, prospering,
prospered] to succeed, especially by making a lot of
money

prosperity /prɒs'perəti/ NOUN, NO PLURAL
success, especially having a lot of money

protect /prə'tekt/ VERB [protects, protecting,
protected] to keep someone or something safe
from harm or danger □ *A mother will always protect
her children.* □ *+ from Protect the young plants
from frost.*

protection /prə'tekʃən/ NOUN, NO PLURAL when someone or something is protected □ **+ against** A good diet provides protection against some diseases.

protein /'prəuti:n/ NOUN [plural proteins] a substance in foods such as eggs, meat and milk that is necessary for strength and growth

protest[1] /prə'test/ VERB [protests, protesting, protested] to march or stand with a group of other people to show that you disagree with something □ Thousands marched to protest about the war.

protest[2] /'prəutest/ NOUN [plural protests] a strong statement saying that something is wrong, or an organized action against something □ Several MPs resigned in protest at the cuts. □ Students organized a peaceful protest against the regime.

> ➤ THESAURUS: A protest, demonstration or march is an event where a group of people march together to show that they support or disagree with something. A riot is a time when a large crowd of people behave wildly in a public place. A strike is a period of time when workers refuse to work because of an argument with their employer.

Protestant /'prɒtɪstənt/ ADJECTIVE to do with Protestants or their church

protester /prə'testə(r)/ NOUN [plural protester] someone who does something to show that they do not agree with something □ Anti-airport protesters blocked the roads.

proud /praud/ ADJECTIVE [prouder, proudest]
1 feeling pleased about your achievements or about the achievements of someone such as your child □ She felt very proud when her son got the award. ᵻ Holding the winner's trophy was a really proud moment for me. □ **+ of** I'm proud of the fact that I carried on and didn't give up. □ **+ to do something** He was very proud to play for the national team.
2 thinking that you are better than other people, in a way that annoys people

prove /pru:v/ VERB [proves, proving, proved] to show that something is true ᵻ Carter was determined to prove his innocence. □ **+ that** DNA tests proved that he was guilty.

provide /prə'vaɪd/ VERB [provides, providing, provided] to give or supply something □ The hospital provides information on the treatments available. □ School provides an opportunity for children to learn and develop. □ **+ with** The refugees were provided with food and shelter.

provided /prə'vaɪdɪd/ or **providing** /prə'vaɪdɪŋ/ CONJUNCTION used when saying that one thing will happen only if another thing happens □ You'll do well in the test, provided that you work hard. □ Providing you have no objection, I'd like you to work next Sunday.

province /'prɒvɪns/ NOUN [plural provinces] one of the parts that some countries are divided into □ Sichuan province in China

provoke /prə'vəuk/ VERB [provokes, provoking, provoked] to cause a particular reaction or feeling, often an angry one □ His remarks have provoked a lot of criticism.

PS /ˌpi:'es/ ABBREVIATION postscript; you write PS when you want to add something to the end of a letter □ PS Say hi to David from me.

PTO /ˌpi:ti:'əu/ ABBREVIATION please turn over; written at the bottom of a page to show that someone should turn the page and read the other side

pub /pʌb/ NOUN [plural pubs] a place where people buy and drink alcoholic drinks, especially in the UK

> ➤ THESAURUS: A pub is a place where people buy and drink alcoholic drinks, especially in the UK. A bar is also a place that sells alcoholic drinks, especially in a city or town. A restaurant is a place where you can buy and eat a meal. A café is a small restaurant that serves drinks and things to eat, but not usually alcoholic drinks. A cafeteria is a restaurant where the customers buy food and drink and take it to a table to eat it. Companies and schools often have a cafeteria.

public[1] /'pʌblɪk/ ADJECTIVE
1 to do with the people generally of a country ᵻ There has been a change in public opinion on this issue. ᵻ There is a lot of public support for the idea.
2 available for everyone □ a public park □ public libraries □ public events

public[2] /'pʌblɪk/ NOUN, NO PLURAL
1 the public people generally ᵻ A member of the public called the police ᵻ The product will go on sale to the general public tomorrow.
2 in public in a place where anyone can see □ He was embarrassed when his parents kissed in public.

publication /ˌpʌblɪ'keɪʃən/ NOUN [plural publications]
1 no plural the process of printing and selling a book, magazine, etc. □ The publication of the images provoked a strong reaction.
2 something such as a magazine or newspaper that is printed and sold

publicity /pʌb'lɪsəti/ NOUN, NO PLURAL attention that something gets from newspapers, television, etc. ᵻ The affair attracted a lot of publicity.

public school /ˌpʌblɪk 'sku:l/ NOUN [plural public schools]
1 in the UK, a school that you pay to go to, often where you stay as well as study
2 in the US, a school that the government pays for

public transport /ˌpʌblɪk 'trænspɔ:t/ NOUN, NO PLURAL trains and buses that people can use □ We *need to encourage more people to use public transport.*

publish /'pʌblɪʃ/ VERB [publishes, publishing, published]
1 to print a book, magazine, etc. so that people can buy it □ *The book was published in September.*
2 to make information available to people generally □ *The company does not publish sales information.*

publisher /'pʌblɪʃə(r)/ NOUN [plural publishers] a person or company that publishes books, newspapers or magazines

pudding /'pʊdɪŋ/ NOUN [plural puddings] sweet food eaten at the end of a meal □ *We've got ice cream for pudding.*

puddle /'pʌdəl/ NOUN [plural puddles] a small pool of rain on the ground □ *Young children love splashing in puddles.*

puff[1] /pʌf/ VERB [puffs, puffing, puffed] to breathe quickly because you have been exercising 🔁 *John was puffing and panting as he came up the hill.*

puff[2] /pʌf/ NOUN [plural puffs] a small amount of breath, wind, air or smoke □ *a puff of air*

pull[1] /pʊl/ VERB [pulls, pulling, pulled]
1 to hold something and move it towards you □ *He pulled the door open.* 🔁 *Stop pulling my hair!* □ **+ at** *He kept pulling at my sleeve.*
2 if a machine, vehicle, etc. pulls something, it is attached to it and moves it □ *We had to get a tractor to pull our car out of the mud.*
3 to separate the pieces of something or to damage something □ **+ apart** *We pulled apart the curtains and looked inside.* □ **+ down** *The old houses will be pulled down.* □ **+ off** *He pulled off the insect's wings.*
➡ go to **pull your socks up**
◆ PHRASAL VERBS **pull over** if a vehicle pulls over, it moves to the side of the road and often stops □ *Pull over at the lights and I'll get out there.* **pull up** if a vehicle pulls up, it stops

pull[2] /pʊl/ NOUN [plural pulls] when you hold something and move it towards you □ *give the handle a pull*

pulse /pʌls/ NOUN [plural pulses] your pulse is the regular movement that you feel on your lower arm or neck, caused by your heart pushing blood through your body 🔁 *The nurse took my pulse (= counted the number of movements in one minute).*

pump[1] /pʌmp/ NOUN [plural pumps] a piece of equipment that makes a gas or liquid move into or out of something □ *She got a bicycle pump and put some air in the tyres.* 🔁 *a petrol pump (= for putting petrol into a car)* □ *a water pump*

pump[2] /pʌmp/ VERB [pumps, pumping, pumped] to force liquid or gas to move somewhere □ *Your heart pumps blood around your body.* □ *Water is pumped from the well.*

◆ PHRASAL VERB **pump something up** to put air into something using a pump □ *Ellie was pumping her bike tyres up.*

pumpkin /'pʌmpkɪn/ NOUN [plural pumpkins] a large, round, orange vegetable with a thick skin

punch[1] /pʌntʃ/ VERB [punches, punching, punched]
1 to hit someone or something with your closed hand □ *He punched the man in the face.*
2 to make a small hole in something using a special tool 🔁 *The tool is used for punching holes in metal.*

punch[2] /pʌntʃ/ NOUN [plural punches] a hit using your closed hand

punctual /'pʌŋktʃuəl/ ADJECTIVE arriving at exactly the arranged time and not late □ *Robert was always very punctual.* □ *Switzerland has punctual and reliable trains.*

punctuation mark /,pʌŋktʃu'eɪʃən ,maːk/ NOUN [plural punctuation marks] one of the marks such as , . ! which are used in writing

punish /'pʌnɪʃ/ VERB [punishes, punishing, punished] to make someone suffer because they have done something wrong □ **+ for** *He was punished for his crimes.* □ **+ by/with** *People who drop litter will be punished with fines.*

punishment /'pʌnɪʃmənt/ NOUN [plural punishments] something that is done to punish someone 🔁 *He had to stay behind after school as a punishment.* □ **+ for** *The maximum punishment for murder was life in prison.* 🔁 *The old man escaped punishment after promising never to drive again.*

pupil /'pjuːpəl/ NOUN [plural pupils]
1 a student in a school □ *primary school pupils* □ *former pupils of the school*
2 the small black circle in the middle of your eye 🔁 *Pupils dilate to let in more light.*

puppet /'pʌpɪt/ NOUN [plural puppets] a toy in the shape of an animal or person that you move by pulling strings or by putting it on your hand □ *The children enjoyed the puppet show.*

puppy /'pʌpɪ/ NOUN [plural puppies] a young dog

purchase[1] /'pɜːtʃəs/ VERB [purchases, purchasing, purchased] a formal word meaning to buy something □ *Tickets may be purchased in advance.*

purchase[2] /'pɜːtʃəs/ NOUN [plural purchases]
1 a formal word meaning something you have bought □ *I was admiring your purchases.*
2 no plural a formal word meaning the act of buying something □ *There has been an increase in the purchase of household goods.*

pure /pjʊə(r)/ ADJECTIVE [purer, purest]
1 not mixed with anything else □ *pure gold* □ *pure oxygen*
2 clean □ *pure water*

purely /ˈpjʊəlɪ/ ADVERB only or simply □ *She is criticized purely because of her appearance.*

purple[1] /ˈpɜːpəl/ ADJECTIVE having the colour you get if you mix red and blue □ *The carpet was dark purple.* □ *His face was purple with rage.*

purple[2] /ˈpɜːpəl/ NOUN, NO PLURAL the colour you get if you mix red and blue

purpose /ˈpɜːpəs/ NOUN [plural purposes]
1 what you intend to achieve when you do something □ **+ of** *The main purpose of the trip was to improve students' French.* □ *The website can be used for educational purposes too.*
2 on purpose deliberately □ *He broke the vase on purpose to annoy me.*

purse /pɜːs/ NOUN [plural purses]
1 a small container that women carry money in □ *She had a lot of money in her purse.* □ *Mary opened her purse and got out some coins.*
2 the US word for **handbag**

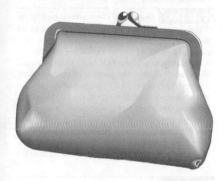

pursue /pəˈsjuː/ VERB [pursues, pursuing, pursued] to chase someone or something in order to catch them □ *Should the police pursue stolen cars at high speed?*

push[1] /pʊʃ/ VERB [pushes, pushing, pushed] to press against someone or something with your hands or body, so that they move □ *I had to push him up the hill in his wheelchair.* □ *The new tooth is pushing the old one out.* □ *She pushed the door open.* □ *He pushed back his chair.*
♦ PHRASAL VERB push someone/something over to push someone or something so that they fall □ *He pushed his friend over in the playground.*

push[2] /pʊʃ/ NOUN [plural pushes] when you press against someone or something with your hands or body, so that it moves □ *The door's a bit stiff – give it a good push.*

put /pʊt/ VERB [puts, putting, put]
1 to move something to a place or position □ *Put the shopping on the table.* □ *He put his hands in the air.* □ *She put her arms around me.*
2 to write something □ *Where do I put my address?* □ *I need to leave her a message, but I'm not sure what to put.*
➡ go to **put your feet up**
♦ PHRASAL VERBS put something away to put something in the place where it is kept □ *He never puts his clothes away.* put something back to put something in the place where it came from □ *Could you put the milk back in the fridge?* put someone/something down to put someone or something onto a surface □ *He put down the gun.* put off something to delay doing something □ *I know I'll need an operation on my shoulder, but I'm trying to put it off as long as possible.* put something on **1** to start wearing something □ *You'd better put on a coat.* **2** to make a machine or piece of equipment start working □ *Shall we put the heating on?* put something out **1** to make a fire stop burning □ *Firefighters were called to put out the blaze.* **2** to turn a light off put someone through to connect someone to the person they want to speak to on the telephone □ *Just a moment, I'll put you through to the accounts department.* put up with someone/something to accept a situation or someone's behaviour although you do not like it □ *I can't put up with his laziness any longer!*

puzzle[1] /ˈpʌzəl/ NOUN [plural puzzles]
1 a game or toy that gives you a problem to solve 🔲 *Ben was doing a jigsaw puzzle.*
2 something that is difficult to understand 🔲 *Researchers hope to solve the puzzle of why some children develop the disease.*

puzzle[2] /ˈpʌzəl/ VERB [puzzles, puzzling, puzzled] if something puzzles you, you feel confused because you do not understand it □ *Their unexplained deaths puzzled police for years.*

pyjamas /pəˈdʒɑːməz/ PLURAL NOUN loose trousers and a shirt that you wear in bed 🔲 *He was wearing a pair of pyjamas.* □ *silk pyjamas*

pyramid /ˈpɪrəmɪd/ NOUN [plural pyramids] a solid shape with a square base and triangular sides which form a point at the top

Qq

Q or q /kju:/ the 17th letter of the alphabet

quack /kwæk/ VERB [quacks, quacking, quacked]
to make the sound of a duck (= a water bird with
short legs and a wide, flat beak)

qualification /ˌkwɒlɪfɪˈkeɪʃən/ NOUN [plural
qualifications] an exam you have passed or a course
you have completed 🔁 He has no formal academic
qualifications. 🔁 She gained her teaching
qualification at Leeds University.

qualify /ˈkwɒlɪfaɪ/ VERB [qualifies, qualifying,
qualified] to pass an exam or to complete a course
needed to do a job □ + as He qualified as a lawyer.
□ + in She qualified in medicine in London.

quality /ˈkwɒlətɪ/ NOUN [plural qualities]
1 no plural how good or bad something is 🔁 All
our courses are of a very high quality. □ + of The
quality of her work is much better now. 🔁 Your
health affects your quality of life. 🔁 We are taking
measures to improve air quality.
2 a part of someone's character □ Her best qualities
are her kindness and honesty.

quantity /ˈkwɒntətɪ/ NOUN [plural quantities]
the amount or number of something □ + of We
only need a small quantity of paper. □ People throw
away huge quantities of food. 🔁 It can be produced
cheaply and in large quantities. 🔁 We need to
improve both the quantity and quality of facilities.

quarry /ˈkwɒrɪ/ NOUN [plural quarries] a place
where stone is dug out of the ground □ a limestone
quarry

quarter /ˈkwɔːtə(r)/ NOUN [plural quarters]
1 1/4; one of four equal parts of something □ We
cut the cake into quarters.
2 quarter past/to 15 minutes after/before the
hour □ He arrived at quarter past three.
3 quarter after/of the US phrase for 15 minutes
after/before the hour

quarter-final /ˌkwɔːtəˈfaɪnəl/ NOUN [plural
quarter-finals] the part of a competition involving
the last eight teams or players □ She reached the
quarter-finals of Wimbledon.

quay /kiː/ NOUN [plural quays] a hard area built
next to the water where things are put onto and
taken off ships

queen /kwiːn/ NOUN [plural queens]
1 a woman who rules a country which has a royal
family □ Queen Elizabeth II □ + of the Queen of
Denmark
2 the wife of a king

query /ˈkwɪərɪ/ NOUN [plural queries] a question
□ Please phone me if you have any queries.

quest /kwest/ NOUN [plural quests] a search for
something or an attempt to do something,
especially a long and difficult one □ He vowed to
continue his quest for justice.

question¹ /ˈkwestʃən/ NOUN [plural questions]
1 the words you say or write when you want to ask
something 🔁 After the talk, some people asked
questions. 🔁 He refused to answer my question.
2 a situation or problem that needs to be discussed
or solved □ There is the question of how much to
pay him. 🔁 Toni raised the question of transport.
3 be a question of something used to talk about
the most important fact in a situation □ It's a
question of cost.
4 out of the question if you say that something is
out of the question, you are emphasizing that it is
not possible □ A pay rise is out of the question at the
moment.

question² /ˈkwestʃən/ VERB [questions,
questioning, questioned]
1 to ask someone questions, often officially □ She
was questioned by the police. □ He questioned me
about where I had found the jewels. □ He
questioned why I had decided to leave my job.
2 to express doubts about something □ They
questioned the truth of his statement.

question mark /ˌkwestʃən ˈmɑːk/ NOUN [plural
question marks] the mark (?) that you write after a
sentence which is a question

questionnaire /ˌkwestʃəˈneə(r)/ NOUN [plural
questionnaires] a list of questions to be answered
by several people to get information 🔁 The students
were asked to complete a short questionnaire.

queue¹ /kjuː/ NOUN [plural queues] a line of
people waiting for something □ + of There was a
long queue of people waiting for taxis. 🔁 We joined
the queue for tickets.

queue[2] /kju:/ VERB [queues, queuing, queued] to stand in a queue □ We had to queue for three hours to get the tickets.

quick /kwɪk/ ADJECTIVE [quicker, quickest] taking a short time □ Can we take a quick break? □ I had a quick look at the website.

➤ THESAURUS: Quick and fast are general words to describe something that takes a short time. Rapid is similar in meaning, but is often used to talk about changes or movements that happen quickly. For example, you might talk about a rapid change in the economy. We also use the word swift to talk about movements. Swift is also used to talk about a process or an event that happens quickly. Something that is brief is short. For example, you can say that a meeting is brief if it does not take much time.

quickly /'kwɪkli/ ADVERB
1 in a short time or immediately □ I get bored quickly. □ He quickly realized his mistake. ☜ I need to sort this out as quickly as possible.
2 fast □ He had to move quickly. □ The fire quickly spread.

quiet[1] /'kwaɪət/ ADJECTIVE [quieter, quietest]
1 making little noise or no noise □ a quiet voice ☜ He asked everyone to be quiet. ☜ He kept quiet, not wanting to disturb her. □ He was quite quiet and shy.
2 calm and without much activity □ It was a quiet street with little traffic. □ It had been a very quiet week.

➤ THESAURUS: Something or someone that is quiet is making little or no noise. A soft sound is not loud. For example, you can talk about a soft voice or soft music. A low sound is near the bottom of the range of sounds. A low voice is quiet.

quiet[2] /'kwaɪət/ NOUN, NO PLURAL a quiet situation or time □ She returned to the quiet of her room. ☜ All he wanted was a bit of peace and quiet.

quietly /'kwaɪətli/ ADVERB with little or no noise □ She slipped quietly from the room. □ 'It's okay,' she said quietly.

quit /kwɪt/ VERB [quits, quitting, quit]
1 to leave a job, school, etc. □ He's quit his job. □ She quit university to become a singer.
2 to stop doing something □ I'm going to quit smoking.

quite /kwaɪt/ ADVERB
1 to some degree but not very or completely □ I'm quite hungry but I don't mind waiting. □ I'm quite nervous about it. □ They're quite likely to win.
2 completely □ I'm afraid I'm not quite ready. □ She made her opinion quite clear. □ It had quite the opposite effect.
3 quite a bit/a few/a while, etc. a large amount, a long time, etc. compared to what is normal or expected □ He lost quite a bit of money. □ It took us quite a while.

quiz /kwɪz/ NOUN [plural quizzes] a competition in which you have to answer questions □ a general knowledge quiz

quota /'kwəʊtə/ NOUN [plural quotas] an amount that someone is allowed to have or has to do □ EU fishing quotas □ We all have to achieve our quota of sales.

quotation /kwəʊ'teɪʃən/ NOUN [plural quotations] a set of words taken from a speech or piece of writing □ a quotation from Shakespeare

quotation marks /kwəʊ'teɪʃən 'mɑːks/ PLURAL NOUN the symbols ' ' or " " used in writing to show that someone's words are being repeated exactly

quote[1] /kwəʊt/ VERB [quotes, quoting, quoted] to repeat someone's words exactly as they said or wrote them □ He quoted a passage from the Bible. □ One newspaper quoted him as saying: 'People are only interested in price.'

➤ THESAURUS: If you repeat something, you say it again. If you quote someone, you repeat their words exactly as they said or wrote them. If you copy something, you write down words or information that you have found somewhere. If you dictate something, you say words for someone to write down.

quote[2] /kwəʊt/ NOUN [plural quotes] someone's words which are repeated exactly as they said or wrote them □ a famous quote from Adam Smith

R *or* r /ɑ:(r)/ the 18th letter of the alphabet

rabbit /'ræbɪt/ NOUN [*plural* rabbits] a small animal with long ears and soft fur, which people keep as a pet, or which lives in holes in the ground □ *She let me stroke her pet rabbit.*

race¹ /reɪs/ NOUN [*plural* races]
1 a competition to see who can get somewhere fastest or do something fastest □ *I'm running in a race this weekend.* 🔁 *Lewis won the race.*
2 one of the groups that people can be divided into according to their skin colour and physical characteristics □ *It's our hope that people of all races can live together in peace.*

race² /reɪs/ VERB [races, racing, raced]
1 to compete against someone in a race □ *I'll race you to the postbox.* □ **+ against** *His horse will be racing against some of the best horses in the country.*
2 to go somewhere very quickly, or to move someone or something very quickly □ **+ to** *Ambulances raced to the scene of the accident.* □ *Emma raced down the stairs to answer the door.* □ *He was raced to hospital with a suspected heart attack.*

> **THESAURUS:** If you race somewhere, you go there very quickly, or move someone or something very quickly. There are several other words with a similar meaning. You can also say that you **rush**, **hurry** or **speed** somewhere, or **rush** someone somewhere.

racial /'reɪʃəl/ ADJECTIVE to do with a person's race □ *racial discrimination*

racing /'reɪsɪŋ/ NOUN, NO PLURAL the sport of racing animals or vehicles 🔁 *Dad watches horse racing on the television.* 🔁 *He's one of the most famous people in motor racing.* 🔁 *a racing driver*

racism /'reɪsɪzəm/ NOUN, NO PLURAL unfair treatment of someone or dislike of someone because they belong to a different race □ *The scheme aims to tackle racism in schools.* □ *He was a victim of racism.*

racist¹ /'reɪsɪst/ NOUN [*plural* racists] someone who dislikes people or treats them unfairly because they belong to a different race

racist² /'reɪsɪst/ ADJECTIVE to do with unfair treatment of someone or dislike of someone because they belong to a different race □ *racist remarks*

rack /ræk/ NOUN [*plural* racks] a place where things are kept, usually made of narrow pieces of wood or metal □ *I put my bag in the luggage rack.*

racket /'rækɪt/ NOUN [*plural* rackets] a piece of equipment that you use for hitting the ball in games such as tennis □ *a tennis racket*

radar /'reɪdɑ:(r)/ NOUN [*plural* radars] a system or piece of equipment that uses radio waves to find the position of aeroplanes, ships, etc.

radical /'rædɪkəl/ ADJECTIVE
1 believing that there should be big political and social changes □ *radical views*
2 big and important □ *radical changes*

radio /'reɪdɪəʊ/ NOUN [*plural* radios]
1 a piece of equipment that you use for listening to programmes which are broadcast 🔁 *Raj switched the radio on to hear the news.* □ *He bought a digital radio.*
2 *no plural* programmes that you listen to using a radio 🔁 *I enjoy listening to the radio.* 🔁 *The local radio station broadcasts travel news.* 🔁 *a radio show* □ *James is a radio presenter.*
3 *no plural* a system of broadcasting that uses sound waves instead of wires to send messages □ *He gave*

orders by radio. 🕮 They lost radio contact with the crew.

radioactive /ˌreɪdɪəʊˈæktɪv/ ADJECTIVE sending out harmful radiation (= energy from a nuclear reaction). A physics word □ radioactive substances

raft /rɑːft/ NOUN [plural rafts] a flat boat made from long pieces of wood tied together

rag /ræg/ NOUN [plural rags] an old piece of cloth □ an oily rag

rage /reɪdʒ/ NOUN, NO PLURAL extreme anger that you cannot control □ He killed his wife in a fit of jealous rage. 🕮 I've never seen him fly into a rage (= become extremely angry) like that before.

raid¹ /reɪd/ NOUN [plural raids]
1 a sudden military attack □ a bombing raid
2 a sudden unexpected visit from the police, who enter a building and search it □ Guns were found during a police raid on the house.
3 a violent attack on a bank, shop, etc. to steal things □ He was arrested for a £250,000 raid on a jeweller's shop.

raid² /reɪd/ VERB [raids, raiding, raided]
1 to attack a place using weapons □ Troops raided villages. □ Armed robbers raided her home.
2 to use force to enter a place in order to search it □ Police raided the factory and questioned staff.

rail /reɪl/ NOUN [plural rails]
1 no plural the railway system □ Travelling by rail is more relaxing than driving. 🕮 Rail fares have increased again.
2 a bar for hanging things on 🕮 a towel rail
3 one of the two long metal bars that form a track for trains

railing /ˈreɪlɪŋ/ NOUN [plural railings] a fence made of vertical metal bars, or the bar that goes along the top of a fence like this □ He was leaning on the railings.

railway¹ /ˈreɪlweɪ/ NOUN [plural railways]
1 a track for trains to travel on □ Glasgow has Scotland's only underground railway.
2 the railway the system and organizations to do with trains □ We need to encourage more people to use the railway.

railway² /ˈreɪlweɪ/ ADJECTIVE to do with trains and the tracks they use 🕮 I'll meet you at the railway station. 🕮 Children should be told about the danger of playing on railway lines. □ a railway bridge

rain¹ /reɪn/ NOUN, NO PLURAL water that falls from the sky □ The children didn't want to go out in the rain. 🕮 Heavy rain (= a large amount of rain) has caused flooding in the area. 🕮 500mm of rain fell

last month. 🕮 It was pouring with rain (= a lot of rain was falling) outside.

➤ THESAURUS: Water that falls from the sky is called rain. A mixture of snow and rain is called sleet. Small white balls of frozen ice that fall from the sky are called hail. A short period of rain is called a shower. A time when there is suddenly a lot of rain and wind is called a storm. One piece of rain is called a drop of rain.

rain² /reɪn/ VERB [rains, raining, rained] when it rains, water falls from the sky 🕮 It's raining so take an umbrella. 🕮 It rained heavily (= a lot of rain fell) all night.

rainbow /ˈreɪnbəʊ/ NOUN [plural rainbows] a curved line of colours that you see in the sky when it is raining and sunny at the same time

raincoat /ˈreɪnkəʊt/ NOUN [plural raincoats] a light coat that you wear when it rains □ She was wearing a blue raincoat.

rainfall /ˈreɪnfɔːl/ NOUN, NO PLURAL the amount of rain that falls in a particular place over a particular period of time 🕮 Heavy rainfall lead to widespread flooding.

rainforest /ˈreɪnfɒrɪst/ NOUN [plural rainforests] a tropical forest with very tall trees which are close together, in an area where it rains a lot. A geography word □ the Amazon rainforest

rainy /ˈreɪnɪ/ ADJECTIVE [rainier, rainiest] raining a lot □ a rainy day

raise /reɪz/ VERB [raises, raising, raised]
1 to lift something to a higher position □ Raise your hand if you know the answer. □ The wreck was slowly raised from the sea bed. □ She raised her eyebrows in surprise.
2 to increase the amount or level of something □ They've raised the rent again. □ We are trying to raise standards in the school. □ This case has raised awareness of the disease.
3 to collect money for a particular purpose □ We're raising money for charity.
4 if you raise children, you look after them until they are adults □ My wages are not enough to raise a family.

➤ Note that **raise** is always followed by an object:
□ She raised her hand. □ They have raised taxes. The verb **rise** has the same meaning but is used without an object:
✓ Taxes have risen.
✗ Taxes have raised.

raisin /ˈreɪzən/ NOUN [plural raisins] a dried grape (= small round fruit)

rake /reɪk/ VERB [rakes, raking, raked] to use a rake to collect dead leaves or to make soil smooth

rally /ˈrælɪ/ NOUN [plural rallies]
1 a large public meeting to support something or to complain about something □ *Over 1000 people attended an anti-war rally.*
2 a car race on public roads □ *a rally driver*

Ramadan /ˌræmə'dæn/ NOUN, NO PLURAL the ninth month of the Islamic year, when Muslims do not eat anything during the day

ramp /ræmp/ NOUN [plural ramps] a sloping surface that joins two places that are at different levels □ *We should be able to get the wheelchair up the ramp quite easily.*

ran /ræn/ PAST TENSE OF run¹

ranch /rɑːntʃ/ NOUN [plural ranches] a large farm where cows or horses are kept

random /ˈrændəm/ ADJECTIVE
1 done without a plan or a system □ *a random selection*
2 at random without a plan or system □ *The killer chose his victims at random.*

rang /ræŋ/ PAST TENSE OF ring²

range¹ /reɪndʒ/ NOUN [plural ranges]
1 a group of things of a similar type □ **+ of** *The shop stocks a huge range of toys and games.* ⊞ *There is a wide range of courses to choose from.*
2 all the ages, numbers, etc. that are included within fixed limits ⊞ *Most of the sofas we sell are in the £500–£1,000 price range.* ⊞ *The programme is aimed at children in the 10–13 age range.*
3 the distance from which something can be seen, heard or reached ⊞ *Spectators have to stand well out of range of the arrows.* ⊞ *He shot the man at close range* (= from a position that is very close).
4 a group of hills or mountains ⊞ *a mountain range*

range² /reɪndʒ/ VERB [ranges, ranging, ranged] to include both things that are mentioned, and other things between them □ **+ from** *The company has accommodation ranging from hostels to luxury hotels.*

□ *Prices range from £70–£150 per night.* □ **+ between** *The dancers' ages ranged between 16 and 40.*

rank¹ /ræŋk/ NOUN [plural ranks] someone's level in an organization or in society ⊞ *A private is the lowest rank in the British army.* ⊞ *A duchess has a very high social rank.* □ **+ of** *He held the rank of colonel.* □ *There are now more women in the senior ranks of the profession.*

rank² /ræŋk/ VERB [ranks, ranking, ranked] to have a certain position that shows how good, bad, important, etc someone or something is □ **+ as** *He ranks as one of the world's best actors.* □ **+ among** *The country ranks among the world's poorest.*

ransom /ˈrænsəm/ NOUN [plural ransoms] an amount of money that is paid to a criminal so that they will give back a person they have taken as a prisoner ⊞ *They paid a ransom of over $1million.*

rap /ræp/ NOUN [plural raps]
1 a quick hard hit □ *There was a rap on the window.*
2 a type of pop music with words that are spoken in rhythm

rapid /ˈræpɪd/ ADJECTIVE done, happening or moving quickly □ *There has been a rapid growth in air travel.*

rare /reə(r)/ ADJECTIVE [rarer, rarest] not happening or existing often □ *This type of attack is extremely rare.* □ *This is a rare example of a blue diamond.* □ *On rare occasions, errors are made.* □ **+ to do something** *It's rare to find a vase like this in perfect condition.*

rarely /ˈreəlɪ/ ADVERB not often □ *I rarely see him.* □ *He's a keen football fan and rarely misses a game.*

rash /ræʃ/ NOUN [plural rashes] an area of red spots on your skin, often caused by an illness ⊞ *I came out in a rash* (= developed a rash).

raspberry /ˈrɑːzbərɪ/ NOUN [plural raspberries] a small soft red fruit that grows on bushes

rat /ræt/ NOUN [plural rats] an animal that looks like a large mouse with a long tail

rate /reɪt/ NOUN [plural rates]
1 how often something happens, or the number of people or things it happens to □ *Unemployment rates have fallen.* □ *We need to lower crime rates.* □ *The birth rate has risen.*
2 the speed at which something happens □ *The rate of progress has been very slow.* □ *The disease is spreading at a tremendous rate.* ⊞ *At this rate, we'll have eaten all the food before lunch time.*
3 an amount of money that is paid for something □ *They charge very high rates for their services.* □ *Rates of pay have risen.* □ *The exchange rate is in our favour at the moment.* □ *The banks have raised interest rates.*
4 at any rate used to say that at least one part of what you have said is certain □ *He's gone to see his cousin or someone – a relative at any rate.*

rather /ˈrɑːðə(r)/ ADVERB
1 slightly □ *It's rather cold in here, isn't it?* □ *He felt rather tired after such a long journey.*
2 rather than instead of □ *Many people choose to rent rather than buy houses.* □ *Rather than punishment, some children need support to improve their behaviour.*
3 would rather used when saying what you would prefer to do □ *I would rather talk about this later if you don't mind.* □ *I'd rather go swimming.*

ratio /ˈreɪʃɪəʊ/ NOUN [*plural* ratios] the relationship between two numbers or amounts that shows how much bigger one is than the other □ *Our nursery has a ratio of one member of staff to three children.*
rational /ˈræʃənəl/ ADJECTIVE reasonable and sensible □ *a rational decision*
rattle¹ /ˈrætəl/ VERB [rattles, rattling, rattled]
1 if something rattles, it makes a noise by hitting against something else repeatedly □ *The windows were rattling in the wind.*
2 to shake something so that it makes a noise □ *She rattled the door but it was locked.*
rattle² /ˈrætəl/ NOUN [*plural* rattles]
1 a baby's toy that makes a noise when you shake it
2 the noise that something hard and loose makes when it is shaken □ *There's a bad rattle coming from the engine.*

raw /rɔː/ ADJECTIVE [rawer, rawest]
1 raw food is not cooked □ *raw vegetables* □ *raw meat*
2 a raw substance is still in its natural state 🔁 *raw materials* 🔁 *Raw sewage had been pumped into the river.*

ray /reɪ/ NOUN [*plural* rays] a beam of light □ *a ray of sunlight*

razor /ˈreɪzə(r)/ NOUN [*plural* razors] a sharp tool that you use for shaving hair from your face and body □ *He uses an electric razor.* 🔁 *a razor blade*

re- /riː/ PREFIX re- is added to the beginning of words to mean 'again' □ *reappear* □ *rearrange*

reach¹ /riːtʃ/ VERB [reaches, reaching, reached]
1 to arrive somewhere □ *We didn't reach the cottage until after dark.* □ *The train reached London at 10.34.* □ *My letter never reached him.*
2 to be able to touch or hold something □ *I can't reach the top shelf.*
3 to stretch out your arm to touch or hold something □ *He reached over me to get some bread.* □ *+ for As I reached for the fruit, I fell off the ladder.*

> ► Note that reach meaning 'to arrive somewhere' is never followed by 'to':
> ✓ *It was midnight by the time we reached London.*
> ✗ *It was midnight by the time we reached to London.*

reach² /riːtʃ/ NOUN, NO PLURAL
1 beyond/out of (someone's) reach (a) too far away to touch or hold □ *Keep all medicines out of reach.* (b) not possible for someone to have or achieve □ *They feel that a university education is beyond their reach.*
2 within (someone's) reach (a) close enough for someone to touch or hold □ *I made sure all his equipment was within reach.* (b) possible for someone to get or achieve □ *Suddenly, the gold medal seems within her reach.*

react /rɪˈækt/ VERB [reacts, reacting, reacted] to behave or feel a particular way because of something that has happened or something someone has said □ *How did Helen react when she heard the news?* □ *+ to He reacted angrily to their criticism.* □ *+ by He reacted by sacking 10 workers.*

reaction /rɪˈækʃən/ NOUN [*plural* reactions] behaviour or feelings that are a result of something that has happened or something someone has said □ *Did you see his reaction when he found out?* □ *+ to There has been a huge reaction to his death.*

read /riːd/ VERB [reads, reading, read]
1 to look at words and understand them □ *He was reading a novel.* □ *+ about I read about the court case in the papers.* □ *+ that I read that they were going to open a new store.*
2 to look at words and say them aloud □ *I always read a story to the children at bedtime.*
♦ PHRASAL VERBS read something out to read something aloud □ *He read out the list of names.*
read something through to read the whole of something, often to check for mistakes □ *Make sure you read through your essay and correct your spelling.*

> ► THESAURUS: Read is a general word. If you read something very quickly, you can say that you scan it. For example, you might scan a telephone directory to find a number. If you read something slowly and carefully, you can say that you study it. For example, you might study a timetable to find out which train you need to catch.

reader /ˈriːdə(r)/ NOUN [*plural* readers] a person who reads □ *Regular readers will recognize this name.*

reading /ˈriːdɪŋ/ NOUN, NO PLURAL the activity of looking at and understanding written words □ *How does the school teach reading?* □ *The course will help you improve your reading skills.*

ready /ˈredɪ/ ADJECTIVE
1 prepared for something 🔁 *He was getting ready to leave.* □ *+ for Are the children ready for bed?*
2 prepared and available to use, eat, etc. □ *Dinner's ready.* □ *The report should be ready by the end of the year.*

3 willing □ **+ to do something** *He was always ready to help.*

real /rɪəl/ ADJECTIVE
1 existing, and not invented or imaginary 🔁 *In real life the actor is a quiet family man.* □ *The story is based on real events.*
2 true and not pretended □ *Everyone calls her 'Sunny' but her real name is Barbara.* □ *The real reason he missed the class was that he had forgotten to bring his homework.*
3 not artificial □ *The seats are made of real leather.* □ *The diamond looked real.*

realistic /ˌrɪəˈlɪstɪk/ ADJECTIVE accepting or based on the true facts of a situation 🔁 *The team has a realistic chance of winning the competition.* □ **+ about** *Navarez seems realistic about his future.*

reality /rɪˈæləti/ NOUN [plural realities]
1 the true facts of a situation □ *We must face reality.*
2 in reality used when saying what the true situation is, especially when it seems different □ *Everyone thought she was very successful, but in reality she was almost bankrupt.*

realize or **realise** /ˈrɪəlaɪz/ VERB [realizes, realizing, realized] to know and understand something that you did not know or understand before 🔁 *I suddenly realized that he wasn't joking.* □ *I didn't realize he was so ill.*

really /ˈrɪəli/ ADVERB
1 very or very much □ *I really like Dan.* □ *I'm really excited about the holiday.* □ *I don't really like fish.*
2 used for saying what the true situation is □ *Did you really mean what you said?* □ *He doesn't really have much choice.*
3 not really no or not completely □ *'Are you ready for your trip?' 'Not really, there are still a lot of things I need to do.'*
4 Really? used when you are surprised or interested by what someone has just said □ *'Mrs Robinson is leaving the school in July.' 'Really?'*

reap /riːp/ VERB [reaps, reaping, reaped] to cut and collect a crop

rear[1] /rɪə(r)/ NOUN, NO PLURAL the rear the back part of something □ *They were sitting at the rear of the plane.*

rear[2] /rɪə(r)/ VERB [rears, rearing, reared] if you rear children or animals, you look after them as they grow

rear[3] /rɪə(r)/ ADJECTIVE at the back of something □ *The rear wheels of the car were stuck in mud.*

reason /ˈriːzən/ NOUN [plural reasons]
1 the reason for something is why it happened, exists or is true □ **+ for** *No one knows the reason for his disappearance.* □ **+ that** *The reason that I phoned was to see if you want to meet for lunch.* 🔁 *There are many good reasons for taking up a sport.* 🔁 *He did not give any reason for his lateness.* 🔁 *That is the reason why I moved to Paris.*
2 no plural a good cause for something □ **+ to do something** *We have reason to suspect he is guilty.* 🔁 *There is no reason to be afraid.* 🔁 *She could see no reason to apologize.*

reasonable /ˈriːzənəbəl/ ADJECTIVE
1 sensible and fair □ *I suppose it's a reasonable decision.* □ *Any reasonable person would agree with that.*
2 if something is reasonable, there are good reasons why you think it is true or correct □ *They made the reasonable assumption that we would be late.* □ *These figures seem reasonable to me.*
3 not very expensive □ *Their clothes are very reasonable.*

reassure /ˌriːəˈʃɔː(r)/ VERB [reassures, reassuring, reassured] to say or do something to make someone feel less worried □ *He tried to reassure me that everything would be all right.*

rebel /ˈrebəl/ NOUN [plural rebels]
1 someone who fights against a government □ *Rebels have clashed with government troops.*
2 someone who refuses to obey rules or people in authority □ *He was always a bit of a rebel at school.*

rebellion /rɪˈbeljən/ NOUN [plural rebellions] the use of violence to try to change a government □ *The government tried to crush the rebellion.*

receipt /rɪˈsiːt/ NOUN [plural receipts] a piece of paper you get when you buy something or when you have paid money to someone □ *Make sure you keep the receipt.* □ *a credit card receipt* □ **+ for** *The receipt for the clothes was still in the bag.*

receive /rɪˈsiːv/ VERB [receives, receiving, received] to get or be given something □ **+ from** *She received a letter from her aunt.* □ *She has been receiving treatment for cancer.* □ *The story received a lot of attention.* □ *He received an award for his work.*

receiver /rɪˈsiːvə(r)/ NOUN [plural receivers] the part of a telephone that you hear and speak through □ *'Goodbye,' he said, and replaced the receiver.*

recent /ˈriːsənt/ ADJECTIVE happening only a short time ago □ *recent events* □ *The most recent figures show that violent crimes are increasing.* □ *These changes are relatively recent.*

recently /ˈriːsəntli/ ADVERB a short time ago □ *I saw Ann quite recently.* □ *He recently bought a new car.* □ *Recently, the situation has become worse.*

reception /rɪˈsepʃən/ NOUN [plural receptions]
1 a big, formal party 🔁 *The wedding reception was at a hotel.* 🔁 *Government leaders will attend a reception hosted by the Queen.* □ **+ for** *a reception for the French president*
2 no plural the place where people go when they arrive at a hotel, office building, etc. □ *He was checking*

in at reception. 🔊 *She walked up to the reception desk.* 🔊 *The hotel has a large reception area.*

recession /rɪ'seʃən/ NOUN [*plural* recessions] a time when a country's economy is not successful □ *The rise in oil prices could cause a recession.*

recipe /'resɪpɪ/ NOUN [*plural* recipes] a set of instructions for how to cook something 🔊 *a recipe book* □ **+ for** *This is a delicious recipe for chocolate cake.*

reckless /'rekləs/ ADJECTIVE doing something without caring or thinking about the results of your actions □ *reckless driving*

reckon /'rɒkən/ VERB [reckons, reckoning, reckoned]
1 to think that something is true □ *I reckon we'll win.*
2 to calculate □ *The cost of restoring the painting is reckoned at £8,000.*

recognition /,rekəg'nɪʃən/ NOUN, NO PLURAL
1 the fact of knowing someone or something because you have seen them before □ *a smile of recognition*
2 agreement that something is true or important □ *There is a growing recognition that play is important in children's development.*

recognize *or* **recognise** /'rekəgnaɪz/ VERB [recognizes, recognizing, recognized]
1 to know who or what someone or something is because you have seen them before □ *I recognized his face but couldn't remember his name* □ *Emma hadn't seen him for 50 years, but recognized him immediately.*
2 to accept that something is true □ *We recognize the importance of research.* □ **+ that** *Most people recognize that there is no easy solution to the problem of global warming.*

recommend /,rekə'mend/ VERB [recommends, recommending, recommended]
1 to advise someone to do something □ **+ that** *Health experts recommend that you eat at least five portions of fruit or vegetables every day.* □ *We don't recommend the use of this drug.*
2 to suggest to someone that they would like something □ **+ to** *My sister recommended this book to me.*

➤ Note that **recommend**, meaning 'to advise' is followed by a noun or is followed by **that**.... It is not followed by 'to do something':
✓ *She recommended new glasses.*
✓ *She recommended that I buy new glasses.*
✗ *She recommended me to buy new glasses.*

recommendation /,rekəmen'deɪʃən/ NOUN [*plural* recommendations]
1 something that someone advises you to do □ *The school will consider the inspector's recommendations.*

2 something that a person suggests you would like □ *I bought the game on my friend's recommendation.*

record¹ /'rekɔːd/ NOUN [*plural* records]
1 a piece of information that has been stored in a document or on a computer 🔊 *They keep records of all sales.* 🔊 *Records show that crime has risen.* 🔊 *medical/dental records* 🔊 *She now has a criminal record .*
2 the best achievement ever in a particular activity, especially a sport 🔊 *He holds the record for the high jump.* 🔊 *She broke the previous record by 2 seconds.* 🔊 *He has set a new record for sailing the Atlantic.*
3 a round flat piece of plastic that music and speech can be stored on □ *I found a pile of old jazz records.*

record² /'rekɔːd/ ADJECTIVE bigger, better, faster, etc. than has ever happened or existed before □ *Record temperatures have led to water shortages.* 🔊 *He finished the race in record time.*

record³ /rɪ'kɔːd/ VERB [records, recording, recorded]
1 to put sounds or images on a CD, video, etc. 🔊 *I phoned her, but all I got was a recorded message.* □ *The band recorded their first album in 1982.*
2 to keep information about something in a document or on a computer □ *All their addresses are recorded in a central database.*

recorder /rɪ'kɔːdə(r)/ NOUN [*plural* recorders] a simple musical instrument made from a wooden pipe with holes that you cover with your fingers as you blow

recording /rɪ'kɔːdɪŋ/ NOUN [*plural* recordings] sounds or images that have been recorded □ *I have a recording of the poet's own voice.*

recover /rɪ'kʌvə(r)/ VERB [recovers, recovering, recovered]
1 to get better after being ill, injured or upset □ *The doctor says I am recovering very well.* □ **+ from** *He is recovering from a serious illness.* □ *Most parents never recover from the death of a child.*
2 to return to a normal condition after problems or damage □ *The sea can take years to recover after an oil spillage.* □ *There are signs that the economy is recovering.*

recovery /rɪ'kʌvərɪ/ NOUN [*plural* recoveries]
1 the process of getting better after being ill, injured or upset 🔊 *He made a miraculous recovery.* 🔊 *She is expected to make a full recovery from her injuries.*
2 the process of returning to a normal condition after problems or damage □ *economic recovery*

recreation /,rekrɪ'eɪʃən/ NOUN, NO PLURAL a formal word meaning enjoyable things that you do in your free time □ *outdoor recreation*

recruit¹ /rɪ'kruːt/ VERB [recruits, recruiting, recruited] to find new people to work for a company or join an organization □ *The company recruits a few school-leavers each year.*

recruit² /rɪˈkruːt/ NOUN [*plural* recruits] someone who has recently joined a company or organization 🖻 *New recruits are given a tour of the building.*

rectangle /ˈrektæŋgəl/ NOUN [*plural* rectangles] a shape with four straight sides and four angles of 90 degrees. The opposite sides are of the same length, but two sides are longer than the other two.

rectangular /rekˈtæŋgjʊlə(r)/ ADJECTIVE having the shape of a rectangle □ *a rectangular table*

recycle /riːˈsaɪkəl/ VERB [recycles, recycling, recycled] to save something so that it can be used again or to do something to a substance so that it can be used again □ *I keep the bags in this drawer and recycle them.* □ *Most plastics can be recycled.*

recycling /riːˈsaɪklɪŋ/ NOUN, NO PLURAL the process of dealing with things which have been used so that they can be used again □ *We need to encourage recycling.*

red¹ /red/ ADJECTIVE
1 having the colour of blood □ *She drives a red car.* 🖻 *He was wearing a bright red shirt.* 🖻 *The carpet was dark red.*
2 red hair is an orange colour

red² /red/ NOUN [*plural* reds] the colour of blood □ *The walls were painted a deep red.*

reduce /rɪˈdjuːs/ VERB [reduces, reducing, reduced] to make something smaller or less □ *Eating a healthy diet significantly reduces your risk of heart disease.* □ *We need to reduce pollution.* □ **+ to** *We have reduced the number of classes from six to four.*

> ► **THESAURUS:** If you reduce, cut or decrease something, you make it smaller or less. You can also say that something decreases if it becomes smaller or less. For example, you can say that the risk of disease decreases if you stop smoking. Cut is a slightly more informal word. If you lower something, you make it smaller in amount or degree. For example, a shop might cut, lower, reduce or decrease its prices. You might lower your voice to make it quieter.

reduction /rɪˈdʌkʃən/ NOUN [*plural* reductions] a decrease in the size, number, or amount of something 🖻 *We're offering huge price reductions.* □ **+ in** *There has been a significant reduction in the number of deaths on our roads.*

reef /riːf/ NOUN [*plural* reefs] a line of rocks, sand or coral (= hard substance made from small sea creatures) near the surface of the sea. A geography word.

refer /rɪˈfɜː(r)/
♦ PHRASAL VERBS [refers, referring, referred] **refer to someone/something** to mention someone or something □ *She referred to the wedding several times.* □ **+ as** *He referred to the man as 'Robert'.*
refer to something 1 a formal word meaning to look at something in order to get information □ *Please refer to the catalogue for more details.*
2 to be about something □ *The figures refer to the period between 1990 and 2000.*

referee¹ /ˌrefəˈriː/ NOUN [*plural* referees] the person in a game such as football, who makes sure the players obey the rules □ *The referee blew his whistle to end the game.*

referee² /ˌrefəˈriː/ VERB [referees, refereeing, refereed] to be a referee during a game □ *Dixon refereed the match.*

reference /ˈrefrəns/ NOUN [*plural* references]
1 a remark that mentions someone or something 🖻 *She made no reference to what had happened the day before.*
2 *no plural* the process of looking at something to get information, or the thing you look at 🖻 *He filed the documents away for future reference.*
3 a written report on your character that someone reads before offering you a job □ *You'll need a reference from your previous employer.*

referendum /ˌrefəˈrendəm/ NOUN [*plural* referenda *or* referendums] when the people of a country vote on a political question 🖻 *We promise to hold a referendum on the issue.*

reflect /rɪˈflekt/ VERB [reflects, reflecting, reflected]
1 if something is reflected, you can see an image of it in a surface like a mirror □ **+ in** *She caught sight of herself reflected in a shop window.*
2 to be a sign of something □ **+ question word** *Her face reflected how she felt inside.* 🖻 *The price reflects the fact that the house is in a very popular area.*
3 to think carefully about something, especially something that has happened □ **+ on** *I need time to reflect on my experiences.*

reflexive /rɪˈfleksɪv/ ADJECTIVE to do with words that show that the subject of a verb is the same as its object □ *'Hurt yourself' is a reflexive verb.* □ *'Himself' is a reflexive pronoun.*

reform¹ /rɪˈfɔːm/ VERB [reforms, reforming, reformed] to make changes to something in order to improve it □ *There are plans to reform the exams system.*

reform² /rɪˈfɔːm/ NOUN [*plural* reforms] changes that are made to improve something, or the process of making these changes □ *There were calls for reform of the tax system.*

refresh /rɪ'freʃ/ VERB [refreshes, refreshing, refreshed]
1 to make you feel cooler or less tired □ *The cool air refreshed him a bit.* □ *She woke up feeling refreshed and rested.*
2 to change what is on a computer screen so that you can see the latest information. A computing word.

refreshing /rɪ'freʃɪŋ/ ADJECTIVE making you feel cooler or less tired □ *a refreshing drink*

refreshments /rɪ'freʃmənts/ PLURAL NOUN food and drink □ *Are refreshments available inside the park?* ⊞ *Light refreshments will be provided.*

refrigerator /rɪ'frɪdʒəreɪtə(r)/ NOUN [plural refrigerators] a machine that you can store food or drink in to keep it cold and fresh

refuge /'refjuːdʒ/ NOUN [plural refuges] protection from danger ⊞ *The family took refuge from the fighting in a church*

refugee /ˌrefjuˈdʒiː/ NOUN [plural refugees] a person who goes to another country because they are not safe in their own country ⊞ *a refugee camp*

refund¹ /rɪ'fʌnd/ VERB [refunds, refunding, refunded] to give someone back some money that they have paid ⊞ *We'll refund your money if you're not completely satisfied.*

refund² /'riːfʌnd/ NOUN [plural refunds] money you have paid that is given back to you ⊞ *He got a refund from the airline.*

refusal /rɪ'fjuːzəl/ NOUN [plural refusals] when you refuse to accept or to do something □ *His refusal to discuss the problem led to more bad feeling.*

refuse¹ /rɪ'fjuːz/ VERB [refuses, refusing, refused]
1 to say that you will not do something □ *He refused to help me.* □ *She refused a request for an interview.*
2 to say that you will not accept something you are offered □ *Gerry refused a cup of tea but took a glass of water.*

refuse² /'refjuːs/ NOUN, NO PLURAL a formal word for rubbish that people throw away □ *household refuse*

regard¹ /rɪ'gɑːd/ VERB [regards, regarding, regarded] to think about someone or something in a particular way □ *My mother still regards me as a child.* □ *He was regarded with suspicion by many.*

regard² /rɪ'gɑːd/ NOUN, NO PLURAL respect or care for someone or something ⊞ *They went ahead without regard for our opinion.*

regarding /rɪ'gɑːdɪŋ/ PREPOSITION about □ *I'd like to talk to you regarding next weekend.* □ *Police have appealed for information regarding the incident.*

regardless /rɪ'gɑːdlɪs/ ADVERB without paying any attention to something □ *Regardless of the cost, I'm determined to take this holiday.* □ *We warned them, but they carried on regardless.*

regards /rɪ'gɑːdz/ PLURAL NOUN
1 used when sending good wishes to someone ⊞ *Give my regards to Fiona when you see her.*
2 used at the end of a friendly but polite letter or e-mail

regiment /'redʒɪmənt/ NOUN [plural regiments] a large group of soldiers in an army

region /'riːdʒən/ NOUN [plural regions] a large area of land such as a part of a country with a particular characteristic □ *We visited some of the wine-making regions of Spain.* □ *The region's economy is growing steadily.*

> ➤ THESAURUS: Area is a general word for a part of a place. A region is a large area of land such as a part of a country with a particular characteristic. A district is a part of a country or a city. District is often used to talk about areas where people work, for example, a business district, or where a particular thing is done, for example a mining district. A neighbourhood is an area of a town or city, especially one where people live.

register¹ /'redʒɪstə(r)/ VERB [registers, registering, registered]
1 to put your name on an official list □ **+ for** *We registered for the swimming class.* □ **+ with** *Make sure you register with the embassy.* □ *You must register your son's birth in the next week.*
2 if a device registers a measurement, it shows it □ *The earthquake registered 8.6 on the Richter scale.*

register² /'redʒɪstə(r)/ NOUN [plural registers] an official list of names □ *Our teacher takes the register every morning.* □ *a register of births and deaths*

registration /ˌredʒɪˈstreɪʃən/ NOUN [plural registrations] when you put your name on an official list □ **+ for** *Registration for next term's classes starts on the 20th.* ⊞ *a registration fee* ⊞ *You need to complete a registration form.*

regret¹ /rɪ'gret/ VERB [regrets, regretting, regretted] to wish that something had not happened and to feel sorry about it □ *He regretted his decision.* □ **+ ing** *Yes I'm sorry, I regret saying that.* □ *I regret not working harder at school.* □ **+ that** *I'm now regrets that he didn't do more.*

regret² /rɪ'gret/ NOUN [plural regrets] a sad feeling about something that has happened ⊞ *Marion had no regrets about leaving home.* ⊞ *He expressed regret for his actions.* ⊞ *It is with great regret that I am leaving the club.*

regular /ˈreɡjʊlə(r)/ ADJECTIVE
1 happening often or doing something often ⊞ *We all know the benefits of regular exercise.* ⊞ *I keep in regular contact with my family.* ⊞ *He writes to me on a regular basis.* ☐ *She was a regular visitor to the museum.*
2 having the same amount of time or space between each thing ☐ *He has a regular heartbeat.* ⊞ *I still see the doctor at regular intervals.*
3 following the usual rules of grammar ☐ *'Cat' has a regular plural.* ⊞ *'Pick' is a regular verb.*
4 a US word meaning usual ☐ *My regular doctor was away.*

regularly /ˈreɡjʊləlɪ/ ADVERB
1 often ☐ *We regularly have to call the police on a Saturday night.* ☐ *Patients are regularly denied medical care.*
2 with the same amount of time or space between each thing ☐ *The flowers were planted regularly along the border.* ☐ *All the equipment is regularly checked.*

rehearsal /rɪˈhɜːsəl/ NOUN [plural rehearsals] a practice for a performance ☐ *We are starting rehearsals for the new show.*
rehearse /rɪˈhɜːs/ VERB [rehearses, rehearsing, rehearsed] to practise performing something ☐ *Can we rehearse that last bit again?*
reign¹ /reɪn/ VERB [reigns, reigning, reigned] to rule over a country as a king or queen ☐ *Queen Victoria reigned for over sixty years.*
reign² /reɪn/ NOUN [plural reigns] the time when someone is the king or queen of a country ☐ *in the reign of King John*
rein /reɪn/ NOUN [plural reins] a long piece of leather which goes around a horse's neck and is used to control it ☐ *He held the horse's reins tightly.*
reinforce /ˌriːɪnˈfɔːs/ VERB [reinforces, reinforcing, reinforced] to make something stronger ☐ *reinforced glass* ☐ *The concrete walls have been reinforced with steel.*
reject /rɪˈdʒekt/ VERB [rejects, rejecting, rejected]
1 to refuse to accept something ☐ *The machine rejected my coin.* ☐ *Unions rejected the offer.*
2 to decide not to accept someone for a job, a course, etc. ☐ *He was rejected for the job.* ☐ *Her application was rejected.*
3 to not give someone enough love or attention ☐ *He felt rejected by his family.*
relate /rɪˈleɪt/ VERB [relates, relating, related]
1 to show a connection between two things ☐ *The study attempted to relate mobile phone use to headaches.*
2 to tell a story or to say what happened ☐ *They related their strange experience to their friends.*
♦ PHRASAL VERB **relate to someone/something** to be connected with someone or something ☐ *The charges relate to the death of a man last November.* ☐ *The figures relate to the period 2004–2005.*

➤ Remember that one thing is **related to** another thing. It is not 'related with' another thing:
✓ *Health is very much related to diet.*
✗ *Health is very much related with diet.*

relation /rɪˈleɪʃən/ NOUN [plural relations]
1 a connection between things ☐ + **between** *Scientists established the relation between smoking and lung cancer.* ⊞ *Most movies bear no relation to* (= are nothing like) *reality.*
2 someone in your family ⊞ *All our friends and relations were there.* ☐ + **of** *He's a distant relation of Tolstoy.*

relationship /rɪˈleɪʃənʃɪp/ NOUN [plural relationships] the way people or groups feel about each other and deal with each other ☐ + **with** *Anne felt she had a good relationship with her brother.* ☐ + **between** *There's a close relationship between our two countries.* ⊞ *They had a father-son relationship.*

relative¹ /ˈrelətɪv/ NOUN [plural relatives] a member of your family ⊞ *We invited all our friends and relatives.* ⊞ *She has no close relatives.* ⊞ *He's a distant relative of the prime minister.*

relative² /ˈrelətɪv/ ADJECTIVE compared with similar people or things ☐ *We are in a period of relative calm.* ☐ *It compares the relative merits of the two education systems.*

relatively /ˈrelətɪvlɪ/ ADVERB quite, compared with similar people or things ☐ *It's a relatively easy journey.*

relax /rɪˈlæks/ VERB [relaxes, relaxing, relaxed] to rest and become calmer and less worried ☐ *We spent the afternoon relaxing by the pool* ☐ *Relax – the children are quite safe.* ☐ *A holiday will help to relax you.*

relaxation /ˌriːlækˈseɪʃən/ NOUN, NO PLURAL when you relax or relax a part of your body ☐ *We practised relaxation techniques.* ⊞ *I need a little rest and relaxation.*

relaxed /rɪˈlækst/ ADJECTIVE feeling calm, comfortable and not worried ☐ *People are relaxed and enjoying themselves.* ☐ *a relaxed atmosphere*
relaxing /rɪˈlæksɪŋ/ ADJECTIVE making you feel relaxed ☐ *We had a relaxing break in the country.* ☐ *a relaxing massage*

release¹ /rɪˈliːs/ VERB [releases, releasing, released] to allow a person or an animal to go free ☐ *Three more prisoners have been released.* ☐ + **from** *He was released from prison in 2004.*

release² /rɪˈliːs/ NOUN [plural releases] when someone or something is allowed to go free ☐ + **of** *The government demanded the release of the* hostages. □ + *from* *I met him just after his release from prison.*

relevant /'reləvənt/ ADJECTIVE connected to or important for a subject, situation, etc. □ *Is this answer relevant to the question?* 🖥 *They sent us all the relevant information.*

reliable /rɪ'laɪəbəl/ ADJECTIVE
1 a reliable person can be trusted to do what they say they will do or to do something well □ *We need to find a reliable supplier of spare parts.* □ *He's one of the team's most reliable players.*
2 a reliable system, piece of equipment, vehicle, etc. works well and does not often stop working □ *I need a reliable car to get me to work.* □ *The trains aren't very reliable.*

relief /rɪ'li:f/ NOUN, NO PLURAL a good feeling because something bad or unpleasant stops or does not happen 🖥 *He gave a sigh of relief.* □ *It was a relief to be outside in the fresh air again.* □ *To my relief, no one was hurt.*

relieve /rɪ'li:v/ VERB [relieves, relieving, relieved] to stop pain, suffering or a problem or to make it less □ *The drug is used to relieve pain.* □ *The new clinic will relieve pressure on the hospital.* □ *He read magazines to relieve the boredom.*

relieved /rɪ'li:vd/ ADJECTIVE feeling good because something bad or unpleasant stops or does not happen □ *I'm so relieved that you're home safely.* □ *She looked relieved.*

religion /rɪ'lɪdʒən/ NOUN [plural religions] belief in a god or gods, and the activities and traditions to do with this belief □ *What is the role of religion in our society?* □ *We teach respect for different religions and cultures.*

religious /rɪ'lɪdʒəs/ ADJECTIVE
1 to do with religion □ *a religious service* 🖥 *a religious leader* 🖥 *religious beliefs*
2 having strong beliefs about a god or gods 🖥 *He was a deeply religious man.* □ *I'm not particularly religious.*

rely /rɪ'laɪ/
♦ PHRASAL VERB [relies, relying, relied] **rely on someone/something** 1 to need someone or something in order to exist or be successful □ *We rely on the help of parents and friends.* 🖥 *The system relies heavily on computer technology.* 2 to trust someone or something to do what they say they will do or what they should do □ *You can rely on our support.* □ *We can rely on Alan to sort it out.* □ *You can't rely on the trains in this country.*

remain /rɪ'meɪn/ VERB [remains, remaining, remained]
1 to continue to be in the same state or condition □ *He remained silent on the issue.* □ *His location*

remains a mystery. □ *I won't vote for them while he remains leader.*
2 to be left when everything or everyone else has gone □ *All that remains in the fireplace is a pile of ash.* □ *The chemotherapy kills the cancer cells that remain after surgery.*

remainder /rɪ'meɪndə(r)/ NOUN, NO PLURAL the remainder what is left of something after some of it has gone □ *He spent the remainder of his life in London.* □ *I tipped the remainder of the liquid away.*

remaining /rɪ'meɪnɪŋ/ ADJECTIVE continuing to be there after other people or things have gone, been used, etc. □ *The remaining contestants will perform tonight.* □ *We can use the remaining time to tidy up.*

remains /rɪ'meɪnz/ PLURAL NOUN parts of something that are left after the main part has gone □ *People returned to the remains of their burnt homes.* □ *the remains of a Roman temple*

remark¹ /rɪ'mɑːk/ VERB [remarks, remarking, remarked] to express an opinion or a thought □ + *that* *Tim remarked that he liked Di's hat.* □ + *on* *She didn't remark on the new painting.*

remark² /rɪ'mɑːk/ NOUN [plural remarks] something you say when expressing an opinion or a thought □ + *about* *He made a nasty remark about my writing.* □ + *on* *The President's remarks on immigration caused controversy.* 🖥 *He made a racist remark.*

remarkable /rɪ'mɑːkəbəl/ ADJECTIVE surprising or noticeable, usually in a way that you admire □ *It's a remarkable story.* □ *It's remarkable how quickly she recovered.*

remarkably /rɪ'mɑːkəblɪ/ ADVERB in a very surprising or noticeable way □ *Remarkably, there were no injuries.* □ *They looked remarkably similar.*

remedy /'remədɪ/ NOUN [plural remedies]
1 something that treats an illness 🖥 *a herbal remedy* □ *This is a traditional remedy for toothache.*
2 something that solves a problem □ *Their policies are seen as a remedy for the country's economic crisis.*

remember /rɪ'membə(r)/ VERB [remembers, remembering, remembered]
1 to have something from the past in your mind or to bring something back to your mind □ *I couldn't remember her name.* □ + *question word* *I don't remember why we chose it.* □ + *that* *She suddenly remembered that she'd left the window open.* □ + *ing* *He remembered seeing a young girl outside.* □ + *as* *He will be remembered as a great player.*
2 not to forget to do something □ + *to do something* *Remember to take your key with you.*

➤ **THESAURUS:** If you remember something, you don't forget to do it. If you make someone else remember to do something, you remind them to do it. If you remember who or what someone or something is because you have seen them before, you can say that you recognize the person or thing. If you remember how to do something because you have studied it carefully, you can say that you learn it. For example, you must learn the rules of English grammar.

remind /rɪˈmaɪnd/ VERB [reminds, reminding, reminded] to make someone remember something □ **+ to do something** *Remind me to close the window before I go out.* □ *She reminded herself why she was there.* □ **+ that** *I want to remind everybody that the bus will leave at four o'clock.* □ **+ of** *She sent an email reminding students of the new timetable.*

◆ PHRASAL VERB **remind someone of someone/ something 1** to make you think about someone or something from the past □ *That picture reminds me of our holiday last year.* **2** to make you think about someone or something because of being similar to them □ *Thomas reminded her of her father.*

➤ Note that if someone or something makes you think about someone or something from the past, they **remind** you **of** them. **Remind** in this sense is always followed by **to**:
✓ She **reminds** me **of** my sister.
✗ She reminds me my sister.

remote /rɪˈməʊt/ ADJECTIVE [remoter, remotest] a remote place is very far away from other places □ *a remote village*

removal /rɪˈmuːvəl/ NOUN [plural removals] when something is removed □ *He called for the removal of foreign troops.* □ *Doctors advised the removal of the tumour.*

remove /rɪˈmuːv/ VERB [removes, removing, removed] to take something away or to get rid of something □ *The police have removed the car.* □ *Doctors removed the tumour.* □ **+ from** *Remove the pan from the heat and stir in the cream.*

renew /rɪˈnjuː/ VERB [renews, renewing, renewed] **1** to start doing something again after a break, often with more energy □ *We'll renew our attempt to get the rules changed.* **2** to make or to pay for something to continue for another period of time □ *You can renew your bus pass at the office.*

renewable /rɪˈnjuːəbəl/ ADJECTIVE describes a type of natural energy such as power from the sun which can be replaced quickly and which will not end

rent¹ /rent/ VERB [rents, renting, rented] **1** to pay someone money so that you can use a house or other building □ *We rented a villa near the beach.* **2** to allow other people to pay to use something you own □ **+ out** *They rent out the building for weddings.* □ **+ to** *We'll rent the house to students while we're away.* **3** a mainly US word meaning to pay someone money to use something such as a car or tools for a short time □ *She rented a car for the week.*

➤ Note that in British English, **rent** is mainly used for houses and other buildings. The verb **hire** means 'to pay someone money to use something such as a car or tools for a short time'.

rent² /rent/ NOUN [plural rents] money you pay to the owner of a house or other building to use it ▣ *He's struggling to pay the rent.*

repaid /ˌriːˈpeɪd/ PAST TENSE AND PAST PARTICIPLE OF **repay**

repair¹ /rɪˈpeə(r)/ VERB [repairs, repairing, repaired] to fix something that is damaged or not working □ *Can the washing machine be repaired?* ▣ *It will cost millions to repair the damage done by the storms.*

repair² /rɪˈpeə(r)/ NOUN [plural repairs] something you do to repair something □ *The ship needed extensive repairs.*

repay /ˌriːˈpeɪ/ VERB [repays, repaying, repaid] to pay back money that you have borrowed □ *They are struggling to repay the loans.*

repeat /rɪˈpiːt/ VERB [repeats, repeating, repeated]
1 to say something again □ *Could you repeat your name please?* □ *She repeated her request.* □ *I don't want to repeat myself* (= say the same thing again). **2** to do something again or to happen again □ *I hope this mistake will never be repeated.* □ *The programme is repeated on Friday at 10pm.*

repeated /rɪˈpiːtɪd/ ADJECTIVE done or happening several times □ *After repeated attempts to phone him, I finally went round to his office.*

repeatedly /rɪˈpiːtɪdlɪ/ ADVERB again and again □ *The victim had been stabbed repeatedly.*

replace /rɪˈpleɪs/ VERB [replaces, replacing, replaced]
1 to take the place of another thing or person □ *The company bought new computers to replace the old ones.* □ *The cinema was demolished and replaced by a supermarket.* □ **+ with** *The phone has been replaced with a newer version.* □ **+ as** *He was replaced as chairman last year.*

2 to put something back where it was before or in its correct position □ *Make sure you replace the books in exactly the right order.*

replacement /rɪ'pleɪsmənt/ NOUN [plural replacements] a person or thing that replaces another one □ *This is broken so I'd like a replacement, please.* ✍ *They will have to find a replacement for the injured goalkeeper.*

replay /'ri:pleɪ/ NOUN [plural replays] a sports match that is played again because nobody won the first time □ *He scored in the second-round replay.*

reply¹ /rɪ'plaɪ/ VERB [replies, replying, replied] to answer □ *'No, I don't!' he replied angrily.* □ *+ that He replied that he was planning to stay another week.* □ *+ to You haven't replied to my question yet.*

reply² /rɪ'plaɪ/ NOUN [plural replies] an answer □ *+ to We've had a number of replies to our advertisement.* □ *In reply, Phoebe gave a nod.* ✍ *He received no reply to his letters.*

report¹ /rɪ'pɔ:t/ NOUN [plural reports]
1 a description of something that has happened □ *+ of Reports of an accident are just coming in.* ✍ *a television news report*
2 a teacher's written description of a student's progress ✍ *a school report*

report² /rɪ'pɔ:t/ VERB [reports, reporting, reported]
1 to tell people about an event or situation on television, on radio, in newspapers, etc. □ *The whole story was reported in the papers.* □ *+ on Tonight we'll be reporting on religious education.*
2 to tell someone officially that something has happened □ *+ to Did you report the incident to the police?*

reported speech /rɪ,pɔ:tɪd 'spi:tʃ/ NOUN, NO PLURAL the words you use when you say what someone has said without using their exact words

reporter /rɪ'pɔ:tə(r)/ NOUN [plural reporters] a person whose job is to describe events for newspapers, television or radio news programmes, etc. ✍ *a newspaper reporter*

represent /,reprɪ'zent/ VERB [represents, representing, represented]
1 to speak or to act officially for someone else □ *Our MPs represent us in the government.* □ *He was represented by a lawyer.*
2 to be a symbol or an example of something □ *The crown represents the king or queen.* □ *The black lines on the map represent railways.*

representative¹ /,reprɪ'zentətɪv/ NOUN [plural representatives] someone who represents someone else □ *a union representative* □ *There were representatives of several international organizations at the meeting.*

representative² /,reprɪ'zentətɪv/ ADJECTIVE typical of a group of people or things □ *a representative sample* □ *These statistics are representative of the overall population.*

reproduce /,ri:prə'dju:s/ VERB [reproduces, reproducing, reproduced]
1 to make something again or to copy something □ *The child had reproduced his father's signature.* □ *Other scientists failed to reproduce the same results.*
2 to produce babies, young animals or plants. A biology word. □ *The virus reproduces quickly.*

reproduction /,ri:prə'dʌkʃən/ NOUN [plural reproductions]
1 a copy of something □ *a reproduction of the painting*
2 the process of producing babies or young animals or plants. A biology word. □ *human reproduction*

reptile /'reptaɪl/ NOUN [plural reptiles] an animal with cold blood that produces eggs, such as a snake. A biology word.

republic /rɪ'pʌblɪk/ NOUN [plural republics] a country with no king or queen, but with an elected government and usually a president (= elected leader)

reputation /,repju'teɪʃən/ NOUN [plural reputations] the opinion that most people have of someone or something based on experience □ *The restaurant has a very good reputation* □ *+ for He has a reputation for being a very tough player.* □ *+ as The country has built a reputation as a tourist destination*

request¹ /rɪ'kwest/ NOUN [plural requests] when someone politely asks for something ✍ *I've got a request to make.* □ *+ for There were hundreds of requests for information.* □ *+ to do something The man refused repeated requests to leave.*

request² /rɪ'kwest/ VERB [requests, requesting, requested] to ask politely for something □ *The committee requested additional information.* □ *The pilot requested permission to land.*

► Note that you **request** something. You do not 'request for' something:
✓ *He requested an invitation.*
✗ *He requested for an invitation.*

require /rɪ'kwaɪə(r)/ VERB [requires, requiring, required] to need something □ *Do you require any further information?* □ *He required treatment for an ankle injury.*

requirement /rɪ'kwaɪəmənt/ NOUN [plural requirements] something that you need or want ✍ *Each kitchen is designed to meet customer requirements.*

rescue¹ /ˈreskjuː/ VERB [rescues, rescuing, rescued] to save someone from danger □ + *from* *Firefighters rescued the people from the burning house.*

rescue² /ˈreskjuː/ NOUN [plural rescues] when someone is saved from danger □ *They were lost with no hope of rescue.* 🔁 *Fire fighters made several rescue attempts.* 🔁 *A passing driver came to her rescue.*

research¹ /rɪˈsɜːtʃ, ˈriːsɜːtʃ/ NOUN [plural researches] when you study a subject carefully to find new information □ + *into* *They fund research into causes of cancer.* 🔁 *The research was carried out in 2005.* 🔁 *The research shows little educational benefit to homework.*

research² /rɪˈsɜːtʃ, ˈriːsɜːtʃ/ VERB [researches, researching, researched] to study a subject carefully to find new information □ *She is researching her family history.* □ *I was researching a book about Einstein.*

• **researcher** /rɪˈsɜːtʃə(r)/ NOUN [plural researchers] a person who researches something

resemblance /rɪˈzembləns/ NOUN [plural resemblances] when things or people look or seem similar in some way □ *Can you see the resemblance between the brothers?* 🔁 *The film bears little resemblance to* (= is quite different from) *the original book.*

resemble /rɪˈzembəl/ VERB [resembles, resembling, resembled] to look similar or to seem similar in some way □ *Tom resembles his father.* □ *The website resembles the front page of a newspaper.*

resent /rɪˈzent/ VERB [resents, resenting, resented] to feel angry or unhappy about something you think is unfair □ *She resented being interrupted.* □ *He resented his sister because of the attention she received.*

reservation /ˌrezəˈveɪʃən/ NOUN [plural reservations] an arrangement to keep a place for you in a restaurant, hotel, plane, etc. □ + *for* *We have a reservation for dinner.* 🔁 *I'd like to make a reservation for two double rooms, please.*

reserve¹ /rɪˈzɜːv/ VERB [reserves, reserving, reserved]
1 to ask a hotel, restaurant, etc. to keep a place for you □ *I'd like to reserve a table for dinner tonight, please.* □ *We reserved seats in a no-smoking section.*
2 to keep something for a particular use or person □ + *for* *Some seats are reserved for elderly or disabled passengers.* □ *Mix in half the sugar, reserving the rest for the icing.*

reserve² /rɪˈzɜːv/ NOUN [plural reserves]
1 an amount of something you have available to use in the future □ *the world's oil reserves* □ *She seems to have amazing reserves of energy and patience.*

2 someone or something available to be used if another person or thing is not available □ *He was a reserve in the England team.* □ *He managed to open his reserve parachute.*
3 an area of land where plants or animals are protected 🔁 *a nature reserve*

reservoir /ˈrezəvwɑː(r)/ NOUN [plural reservoirs] a large lake where water is collected and stored in order to be used by people in an area

resign /rɪˈzaɪn/ VERB [resigns, resigning, resigned] to officially say that you are leaving your job □ *She resigned from her post as finance director.*
♦ PHRASAL VERB **resign yourself to something** to accept something unpleasant that you cannot change □ *He had resigned himself to defeat.* □ *They're resigned to losing the house.*

resignation /ˌrezɪɡˈneɪʃən/ NOUN [plural resignations]
1 when you officially say that you are leaving your job □ *a letter of resignation* □ *There have been calls for the minister's resignation.* 🔁 *He's handed in his resignation.*
2 no plural a feeling of accepting something unpleasant that you cannot change □ *a look of resignation*

resist /rɪˈzɪst/ VERB [resists, resisting, resisted]
1 to try to stop something from happening or to refuse to accept something □ *The bank resisted pressure to cut interest rates.*
2 to stop yourself from doing or having something you want 🔁 *She resisted the temptation to take a look.* □ *The opportunity was too good to resist.*
3 to fight against someone or something, especially when they are attacking you. □ *They couldn't resist the attackers.* 🔁 *He resisted arrest.*

resistance /rɪˈzɪstəns/ NOUN, NO PLURAL
1 when you refuse to accept something 🔁 *The plans have met stiff resistance.*
2 when you fight against someone or something □ *armed resistance*

resort /rɪˈzɔːt/ NOUN [plural resorts]
1 a place where people go on holiday □ *a popular seaside resort* □ *a ski resort*
2 a last resort something you do only when everything else has failed □ *I suppose we could borrow the money as a last resort.*
♦ PHRASAL VERB [resorts, resorting, resorted] **resort to something** to do something you do not want to do in order to solve a problem □ *The worst thing would be to resort to violence.*

resource /rɪˈzɔːs/ NOUN [plural resources] something that you have and are able to use 🔁 *the country's natural resources* □ *He blamed a lack of resources for the delays.*

respect¹ /rɪˈspekt/ NOUN [plural respects]
1 the feeling of admiring someone or something because of their behaviour or their achievements □ + *of* *She earned the respect of her colleagues.*

2 polite behaviour towards someone □ **+ for** *Their behaviour shows a lack of respect for others.* ⬒ *He treats everyone with respect.*
3 a part of something or a way of thinking about it □ *In many respects, the two boys are very similar.* □ *The plan was good in every respect.*

respect² /rɪ'spekt/ VERB [respects, respecting, respected] to admire someone or something because of their behaviour or achievements □ *I respect her enormously.* ⬒ *He was highly respected in the local community.*

respectable /rɪ'spektəbəl/ ADJECTIVE
1 accepted by society as good, correct, honest, etc. ⬓ *Simon comes from a respectable family.*
2 quite good □ *a perfectly respectable score*
• **respectably** /rɪ'spektəblɪ/ ADVERB in a socially acceptable way □ *She was respectably dressed.*

respond /rɪ'spɒnd/ VERB [responds, responding, responded] to answer or to react □ *If someone hits you, you tend to respond by hitting back.* □ *'That's not my problem,' Gina responded.* □ *Police responded quickly to the call.*

response /rɪ'spɒns/ NOUN [plural responses] an answer or a reaction □ *His response was a shake of his head.* □ *What was the response of his colleagues to his announcement?*

responsibility /rɪ,spɒnsə'bɪlətɪ/ NOUN [plural responsibilities]
1 something that you must do or deal with □ **+ for** *The manager has responsibility for all the business.* □ **+ of** *The first responsibility of a government is to protect its citizens.* □ **+ to do something** *It's my responsibility to make sure all the doors are locked.* □ *They share the childcare responsibilities.*
2 blame for doing something, usually something bad ⬒ *I take full responsibility for the mistake.*

responsible /rɪ'spɒnsəbəl/ ADJECTIVE
1 if you are responsible for something, you are the person who must do it or deal with it □ **+ for** *Who is responsible for keeping the money?* □ *the minister responsible for transport*
2 if you are responsible for something which happens, you are to blame for it □ **+ for** *Is human activity responsible for global warming?* ⬒ *He felt partly responsible for the mess.*

rest¹ /rest/ NOUN [plural rests]
1 the rest the part of something that is left, or the people or things that are left □ *I don't want to spend the rest of my life here.* □ *The rest of the country will have showers.* □ *I want half of you in this room and the rest outside.*
2 a time when you relax or sleep ⬒ *Why don't you have a rest before dinner?*

rest² /rest/ VERB [rests, resting, rested]
1 to relax or sleep after an activity □ *You should*

rest every few minutes when you're lifting such heavy weights.
2 to be supported by something, or to put something on something else for support □ *He left his spade resting against a wall.* □ *Mo rested her hands on the piano keys for a moment.*

restart /,ri:'stɑ:t/ VERB [restarts, restarting, restarted] to turn a computer off and then on again □ *Have you tried restarting your computer?*

restaurant /'restrɒnt/ NOUN [plural restaurants] a place where you can buy and eat a meal □ *a Chinese restaurant*

restless /'restlɪs/ ADJECTIVE not able to stay still or quiet because you are nervous, worried or bored □ *The audience began to get restless after about an hour.*

restrain /rɪ'streɪn/ VERB [restrains, restraining, restrained]
1 to stop someone from doing something, often using force □ *He attacked the man as friends tried to restrain him.*
2 to control your emotions or behaviour □ *We had to restrain ourselves from laughing.*

restrict /rɪ'strɪkt/ VERB [restricts, restricting, restricted] to limit something □ *We are restricting people to one ticket each.* □ *Parents can restrict children's access to certain websites.*

restriction /rɪ'strɪkʃən/ NOUN [plural restrictions] a limit on something □ *Are there any parking restrictions on this road?* ⬒ *Airlines imposed restrictions on hand luggage.*

result¹ /rɪ'zʌlt/ NOUN [plural results]
1 what happens because of something else □ **+ of** *This could be another result of global warming.* ⬒ *He died as a result of the accident.* ⬒ *He tried to play again too quickly, with the result that he made the injury worse.*
2 the score or the winner at the end of a competition, an election, an exam etc. □ *the election result* □ **+ of** *Do you know the result of yesterday's match?* ⬒ *She got good exam results.*

result² /rɪ'zʌlt/ VERB [results, resulting, resulted] to happen because of something else □ *The fire apparently resulted from a dropped cigarette.*
♦ PHRASAL VERB **result in something** to cause something □ *The changes will result in the loss of 300 jobs.*

resume /rɪ'zju:m/ VERB [resumes, resuming, resumed] a formal word meaning to start again ⬓ *Normal train services will resume next week.*

retire /rɪ'taɪə(r)/ VERB [retires, retiring, retired] to stop working because you are old □ *Many people retire at 65.* □ **+ from** *She has just retired from a career in nursing.* □ **+ as** *He retired as director in 2005.*

► THESAURUS: If you retire, you stop working because you are old. If you resign, you officially say that you are leaving your job, perhaps because you have a new job to go to. You can also say that you quit your job or leave your job. If you lose your job because you have done something wrong, you get the sack.

retired /rɪˈtaɪəd/ ADJECTIVE no longer working because you are old □ *a retired teacher*

retirement¹ /rɪˈtaɪəmənt/ NOUN [*plural* retirements] the period of time after you stop working because you are old □ *I hope you enjoy your retirement.*

retirement² /rɪˈtaɪəmənt/ ADJECTIVE to do with the time when you stop working because you are old ⊞ *He is close to retirement age.* □ *a retirement party*

retreat¹ /rɪˈtriːt/ NOUN [*plural* retreats] when an army moves back because it does not want to fight □ *a strategic retreat*

retreat² /rɪˈtriːt/ VERB [retreats, retreating, retreated] if an army retreats, it moves back because it does not want to fight

return¹ /rɪˈtɜːn/ VERB [returns, returning, returned]
1 to go or come back to a place □ *We fly out on Friday and return the following Wednesday.* □ **+ to** *We all returned to our classrooms.* □ **+ from** *He returned from his skiing holiday with a broken leg.* ⊞ *All the air crew have returned safely.*
2 to take, put or send something back □ *Please return your books by Friday.* □ **+ to** *All sports equipment should be returned to the gym.*

return² /rɪˈtɜːn/ NOUN [*plural* returns]
1 when someone comes or goes back to a place □ **+ to** *On my return to the house, I found the door wide open.* □ **+ from** *After his return from Africa, he settled in London.* ⊞ *They celebrated the safe return of the climbers.*
2 when something is taken, put or sent back □ **+ of** *We are delighted at the safe return of the stolen paintings.*
3 a ticket that allows you to travel to a place and back again □ *I'd like a return to Glasgow, please.*

reunion /ˌriːˈjuːnjən/ NOUN [*plural* reunions] a meeting of people such as friends or family members who have not seen each other for a long time □ *a family reunion*

reveal /rɪˈviːl/ VERB [reveals, revealing, revealed]
1 to tell someone something that is secret or surprising □ *He refused to reveal details of the project.*
2 to show something that you could not see before □ *The mobile phone has a screen which slides back to reveal the keyboard.*

revenge /rɪˈvendʒ/ NOUN, NO PLURAL when you hurt or upset someone because they have hurt or upset you or someone that you love ⊞ *Ben had ruined her life and she was determined to get revenge.* ⊞ *a revenge attack*

reverse /rɪˈvɜːs/ VERB [reverses, reversing, reversed]
1 if a vehicle reverses, it moves backwards □ *A car was reversing.*
2 to make a vehicle move backwards □ *She reversed the car into the parking space.*
3 to change something so that it is the opposite of what it was before ⊞ *The government has reversed its decision.*

review¹ /rɪˈvjuː/ VERB [reviews, reviewing, reviewed]
1 to examine something again, often in order to decide if changes should be made □ *The company is reviewing its safety procedures following the accident.* □ *Lawyers are reviewing the case.*
2 to write your opinion of a new book, play, etc. □ *She reviewed the book for the New York Times.*

review² /rɪˈvjuː/ NOUN [*plural* reviews]
1 when something is examined again, often in order to decide if changes need to be made □ **+ of** *The government is conducting a review of the policy.*
2 an article which gives someone's opinion of a new book, play, etc. □ *a film review* ⊞ *The play got some good reviews.* □ **+ of** *He wrote a review of the book.*

revise /rɪˈvaɪz/ VERB [revises, revising, revised]
1 to study for an exam by looking again at the work you have done □ **+ for** *Guy was busy revising for his Chinese exam.*
2 to change something, often in order to improve it □ *The revised edition of the dictionary has hundreds of new words in it.* □ *We've had to revise our plans.*

revision /rɪˈvɪʒən/ NOUN [*plural* revisions] work that you do before an exam, by looking at work you have already done ⊞ *I need to do some revision for my history test.*

revive /rɪˈvaɪv/ VERB [revives, reviving, revived] to make someone conscious again □ *Doctors were unable to revive him.*

revolt /rɪˈvəʊlt/ NOUN [*plural* revolts]
1 when a group of people use violence in order to change a government
2 when people refuse to accept the authority of a leader □ *The leader is facing a revolt by members of his party.*

revolting /rɪˈvəʊltɪŋ/ ADJECTIVE extremely unpleasant □ *a revolting smell*

revolution /ˌrevəˈluːʃən/ NOUN [*plural* revolutions]
1 a time when people use violence to change a government □ *the French Revolution of 1789*
2 a complete change in something such as an

industry or society □ *Computers have led to a revolution in the way we work.* □ *the Industrial Revolution*

revolutionary¹ /ˌrevəˈluːʃənərɪ/ ADJECTIVE
1 completely new and different □ *revolutionary technology*
2 to do with a time when people use violence to change a government □ *Castro's revolutionary movement*

revolutionary² /ˌrevəˈluːʃənərɪ/ NOUN [*plural* revolutionaries] someone who is involved in using violence to change a government

revolve /rɪˈvɒlv/ VERB [revolves, revolving, revolved] to move in a circle around something □ *The Earth revolves around the sun.*

revolver /rɪˈvɒlvə(r)/ NOUN [*plural* revolvers] a type of small gun

reward¹ /rɪˈwɔːd/ NOUN [*plural* rewards] something you get for doing something good or useful □ *financial rewards* □ **+ for** *The victim's family are offering a £5,000 reward for any information that helps catch the killer.* □ *He got his reward for all his hard work when the team scored a goal.*

reward² /rɪˈwɔːd/ VERB [rewards, rewarding, rewarded] to give someone something good for something they have done □ **+ for** *He was rewarded for all his hard work.* □ **+ with** *The baby rewarded me with a smile as I picked her up.*

rhino /ˈraɪnəʊ/ NOUN [*plural* rhinos] an informal word for **rhinoceros**

rhinoceros /raɪˈnɒsərəs/ NOUN [*plural* rhinoceroses] a large, grey animal from Africa and Asia that has thick skin and a horn on its nose

rhyme¹ /raɪm/ VERB [rhymes, rhyming, rhymed] if words rhyme, they end with the same sound □ *'Ghost' rhymes with 'toast'.*

rhyme² /raɪm/ NOUN [*plural* rhymes]
1 a word that sounds like another, or a pair of words that have a similar sound □ *I don't think there is a rhyme for 'orange'.*
2 a short poem or song using words which rhyme □ *a book of children's rhymes*

rhythm /ˈrɪðəm/ NOUN [*plural* rhythms] a repeated pattern of sounds or movements □ *He had an irregular heart rhythm.* □ **+ of** *Amy's foot was tapping to the rhythm of the music.* 🔊 *She has a good sense of rhythm.*

rib /rɪb/ NOUN [*plural* ribs] one of the curved bones in your chest, around your heart and lungs

ribbon /ˈrɪbən/ NOUN [*plural* ribbons] a long, narrow piece of cloth, used for example to tie your hair up, or as a decoration on a present

rice /raɪs/ NOUN, NO PLURAL brown or white grains that you cook and eat as food □ *boiled rice* 🔊 *a grain of rice* □ *brown rice* □ *rice fields*

rich¹ /rɪtʃ/ ADJECTIVE [richer, richest]
1 having a lot of money □ *Her Dad's very rich.* □ *rich countries* 🔊 *He was looking for ways to get rich* (= become rich).
2 full of something good 🔊 *Nuts and seeds are a rich source of iron.* □ **+ in** *Oranges are rich in vitamin C.*
3 rich food contains a lot of butter or cream □ *The cake was very rich so I only ate a small piece.*

rich² /rɪtʃ/ NOUN, NO PLURAL the rich people who have a lot of money □ *She enjoyed reading about the lifestyles of the rich and famous.*

riches /ˈrɪtʃɪz/ PLURAL NOUN a word used in stories meaning a lot of money and expensive things

> ► **THESAURUS:** Money is a general word for coins and paper notes that you use for buying things. Riches is a literary word meaning a lot of money and expensive things. For example, you might talk about a king's riches in a story. Someone's wealth is all the money and expensive things that they have. A fortune is a very large amount of money.

rid /rɪd/ ADJECTIVE
1 get rid of something (a) to throw something away or give it to someone else □ *My parents got rid of the old sofa and bought a new one.* (b) to make something go away that you do not want □ *I opened the window to get rid of the smell.* □ *I can't seem to get rid of this cold.*
2 get rid of someone to make someone go away □ *He arrived at 7 o'clock and we couldn't get rid of him.*

ridden /ˈrɪdən/ PAST PARTICIPLE OF **ride**¹

ride¹ /raɪd/ VERB [rides, riding, rode, ridden]
1 to travel on a bicycle, motorcycle or horse □ *I learned to ride a bike when I was six.* □ *Do you ride* (= ride a horse)? □ *He turned and rode off.*
2 to travel in or on a vehicle □ *She had been riding around in the car all day.*

ride[2] /raɪd/ NOUN [plural rides] a journey in or on a vehicle □ It was a short bus ride from the airport to the hotel. 🔁 We went for a bike ride. □ + in I had a ride in her new car. □ + on Can I have a ride on your bike?

rider /'raɪdə(r)/ NOUN [plural riders] someone sitting on and controlling a bicycle, motorcycle or horse □ horse riders

ridge /rɪdʒ/ NOUN [plural ridges] a long narrow piece of high land □ mountain ridges

ridiculous /rɪ'dɪkjʊləs/ ADJECTIVE very silly □ It's a ridiculous idea!

rifle /'raɪfəl/ NOUN [plural rifles] a type of long gun

right[1] /raɪt/ ADJECTIVE
1 correct □ + about He was right about the train being late. □ Make sure you sign in the right place. □ Are we going in the right direction? 🔁 I got most of the answers right. 🔁 'I hear you're leaving.' 'That's right, I've got a new job.'
2 suitable or in the condition that you want or expect □ + for He is not the right person for the job. □ We didn't have the right clothes for the weather. 🔁 I need a new table, and this one looks just right. □ As soon as I saw her, I knew that something wasn't right.
3 fair or acceptable □ It doesn't seem right that so many people in the world are hungry. □ + to do something It's not right to tax the poor.
4 on or to the side that is towards the east when you are facing north □ I write with my right hand. □ We sat on the right side of the church.

right[2] /raɪt/ NOUN [plural rights]
1 something that you are allowed to do or have, either officially or because it is acceptable □ + to Everyone has a right to a decent education. □ These laws protect their religious rights. 🔁 You have no right to speak to me like that.
2 the side or direction that is on or towards the right side of your body □ There's a chemist over there on the right.
3 behaviour that is morally good □ These children do not know right from wrong.

➤ Note (noun, sense 1) that you have a **right to** something or the **right to do** something. You do not have the 'right of' something:
✓ Everybody has a right to healthcare.
✗ Everybody has a right of healthcare.

right[3] /raɪt/ ADVERB
1 towards the direction that is to the east when you are facing north □ Now turn right.
2 exactly □ Don't move – stay right there. □ We were right in the middle of dinner. □ Stay right behind me.
3 immediately □ I'll come right after lunch. 🔁 I want the work done right now.
4 all the way □ This road goes right round the

outside of the park. □ I watched the film right to the end.
5 correctly □ Can't you do anything right?
6 used to get someone's attention before you speak or start to do something □ Right, shall we go outside?

right-handed /ˌraɪt'hændɪd/ ADJECTIVE using your right hand to do things, especially to write □ Are you right-handed? □ a right-handed tennis player

rigid /'rɪdʒɪd/ ADJECTIVE
1 unwilling to change or impossible for someone to change □ a rigid schedule □ The rules are very rigid.
2 stiff and impossible to bend □ a rigid frame

rim /rɪm/ NOUN [plural rims] the edge of something round, such as a cup, bowl or wheel

ring[1] /rɪŋ/ NOUN [plural rings]
1 a round piece of jewellery that you wear on your finger 🔁 a wedding ring □ I was wearing a diamond ring.
2 something in the shape of a circle □ The children sat in a ring around the story-teller. □ The house was surrounded by a ring of fire.
3 give someone a ring to telephone someone □ I'll give you a ring tomorrow.
4 the sound a bell makes □ Did I hear a ring at the door?

ring[2] /rɪŋ/ VERB [rings, ringing, rang, rung]
1 if a bell rings, it produces a sound, and if you ring a bell, you make it produce a sound □ I think I heard the doorbell ring.
2 to telephone someone □ I'm ringing about the car you have for sale.

➤ Note that you **ring** (= telephone) a person or place. You do not 'ring to' a person or place:
✓ I'll just ring my sister.
✗ I'll just ring to my sister.

◆ PHRASAL VERBS **ring (someone) back** to telephone someone after they have telephoned you □ I'm a bit busy – can I ring you back later? **ring someone up** to telephone someone □ She rang me up in the middle of the night.

rinse /rɪns/ VERB [rinses, rinsing, rinsed] to remove dirt or soap from something by putting it in clean water □ Rinse your hair well after shampooing it.

riot /'raɪət/ NOUN [plural riots] a time when a large crowd of people behave violently in a public place □ His election caused riots in the capital. 🔁 Riot police were brought in to control the crowd.

rip[1] /rɪp/ VERB [rips, ripping, ripped]
1 to tear something roughly □ She ripped sheets into strips and used them as bandages. □ Steve ripped his trousers on the barbed wire.
2 to remove something quickly and forcefully □ The storm ripped the roof off their house.
◆ PHRASAL VERB **rip something up** to tear something into small pieces □ I ripped the letter up and put it in the bin.

rip² /rɪp/ NOUN [*plural* rips] a rough tear □ *There was a rip in my sleeve where the handle had caught it.*

ripe /raɪp/ ADJECTIVE [riper, ripest] ripe fruit is ready to be picked or eaten □ *The plums were ripe and juicy.* □ *ripe tomatoes*

ripple /ˈrɪpəl/ NOUN [*plural* ripples] a small movement on the surface of water □ *Tiny fish were causing ripples in the water.*

rise¹ /raɪz/ VERB [rises, rising, rose, risen]
1 to go up □ *A column of smoke rose above the village.* □ *+ up* *The balloon rose up into the air.* □ *The sun rises in the east.* □ *Ahead, the ground rose steeply.*
2 to increase in level □ *Prices have risen this year.* ⓖ *Profits rose sharply in the second half of the year.* □ *The government has tried to calm rising panic about fuel costs.*
3 to stand up □ *We all rose when the judge entered.*

➤ Note that **rise** has no object after it. If you want to say 'to make something go up' or 'to make something increase in level', use the verb **raise**. Raise is always followed by an object:
✓ She raised her hand.
✗ She rose her hand.
✓ They raised prices.
✗ They rose prices.

rise² /raɪz/ NOUN [*plural* rises] an increase in level □ *There has been a rise in the number of homeless people.*

risk¹ /rɪsk/ NOUN [*plural* risks]
1 a possibility that something bad will happen □ *+ of* *We face the risk of losing our homes.* □ *+ that* *There's a risk that the whole project might be called off.* ⓖ *If you give up your job, you will be taking a big risk.*
2 at risk in a situation where something bad might happen □ *Their traditional way of life is at risk.* □ *These children are at risk of violence.*

risk² /rɪsk/ VERB [risks, risking, risked]
1 to put yourself in a situation where something bad could happen to you □ *He risked punishment by entering the room.* □ *+ ing* *She risked failing her exams.*
2 to take the chance of damaging or losing something ⓖ *Soldiers are risking their lives every day.* □ *We have risked a lot of money on this business.*
3 to do something although you know there is a possibility that something bad will happen □ *I risked a glance at the document.* □ *+ ing* *She couldn't risk phoning him.*

➤ Note that the verb **risk** is followed by **doing something** and never by 'to do something':
✓ I wouldn't risk telling him.
✗ I wouldn't risk to tell him.

rival¹ /ˈraɪvəl/ NOUN [*plural* rivals] a person or organization that competes against another □ *The two teams are bitter rivals.*

rival² /ˈraɪvəl/ ADJECTIVE competing against each other □ *rival gangs* □ *rival political parties*

rivalry /ˈraɪvəlrɪ/ NOUN, NO PLURAL when people or organizations compete against each other □ *There's a lot of rivalry between the twins.*

river /ˈrɪvə(r)/ NOUN [*plural* rivers] a large stream of water that flows across land □ *There were several boats on the river.* ⓖ *He crossed the river using the main bridge.* □ *the River Nile*

➤ **THESAURUS:** A river is a long line of water that flows across land to the sea. A stream is a very narrow river. A canal is a long passage filled with water, for boats to travel along. Canals are made by man. A channel is a narrow piece of sea. For example, the English Channel is the narrow piece of sea between Britain and France.

road /rəʊd/ NOUN [*plural* roads]
1 a hard, level surface for vehicles to travel along □ *There were a lot of cars parked in the road.* ⓖ *Children need to learn how to cross the road safely.* ⓖ *The accident happened on the main road between Pula and Porec.* ⓖ *We live on a very busy road.* ⓖ *He died in a road accident.*
2 by road in a vehicle that travels on the road □ *The journey to London is three hours by road.*
3 over/across the road on the opposite side of a road □ *Mark and Carrie live across the road from us.*
4 down/along the road further on the same road □ *My school is just down the road.*

roam /rəʊm/ VERB [roams, roaming, roamed] to walk or travel around a place without a particular aim □ *You see youths roaming the streets at night.*

roar¹ /rɔ:(r)/ VERB [roars, roaring, roared]
1 when a lion roars, it makes a loud sound
2 to make a continuous loud sound □ *Planes roared overhead.*

➤ **THESAURUS:** When a lion roars, it makes a loud sound. When a dog makes a loud sound, you can use the word bark. When a dog or a wolf makes a long, high noise, we say that it howls. When an animal such as a dog or a bear makes a deep, threatening noise in its throat, we say that it growls. When an animal such as a dog makes an angry sound and shows its teeth, we say that it snarls.

roar² /rɔ:(r)/ NOUN [*plural* roars]
1 the call or sound that a lion makes
2 a loud deep sound □ *the roar of the engine*

roast¹ /rəʊst/ VERB [roasts, roasting, roasted]
1 to cook meat or vegetables in an oven or over a fire □ *Roast the potatoes at the same time as the turkey.*

2 meat or vegetables roast when they cook in an oven or over a fire □ *The sauce can be made while the vegetables are roasting.*

roast² /rəʊst/ NOUN [plural roasts] a piece of meat that has been cooked in the oven □ *We're having a roast tonight.*

roast³ /rəʊst/ ADJECTIVE cooked in the oven □ *roast potatoes* □ *roast beef*

rob /rɒb/ VERB [robs, robbing, robbed] to steal something from a place or person ⭓ *They robbed a bank.* □ **+ of** *The family were robbed of jewellery worth at least £1 million.*

➤ Remember that thieves **rob** people and places. They **steal** money and objects: □ *My parents were robbed in the street.* □ *They had robbed a bank.* □ *They stole my father's wallet.* □ *They stole five hundred pounds from her.*

robber /'rɒbə(r)/ NOUN [plural robbers] a person who steals ⭓ *Armed robbers broke into his house.* ⭓ *a bank robber*

robbery /'rɒbərɪ/ NOUN [plural robberies] the crime of stealing something from a person or place ⭓ *He committed several robberies.* ⭓ *a bank robbery* ⭓ *He was in prison for armed robbery.*

➤ THESAURUS: Theft is a general word for the crime of stealing something. Robbery is the crime of stealing something from a person or a place. Robbery often involves violence or threats. For example, if someone goes into a bank with a gun and demands money, this is called a bank robbery. Burglary is the crime of going into a building and stealing things. For example, if someone comes into your house at night and steals things, this is called a burglary.

robe /rəʊb/ NOUN [plural robes] a long loose piece of clothing □ *a priest's robes*

robin /'rɒbɪn/ NOUN [plural robins] a small brown bird with a red chest

robot /'rəʊbɒt/ NOUN [plural robots] a machine that can do things like a person

robust /rəʊ'bʌst/ ADJECTIVE strong □ *a robust economy* □ *He was in robust health.*

rock¹ /rɒk/ NOUN [plural rocks]
1 *no plural* the hard stone substance that the Earth is made of □ *volcanic rock* □ *The team were digging a tunnel through solid rock.*
2 a large stone □ *Protesters threw rocks at the police.*
3 a type of music with a strong beat that is played on electric guitars and drums □ *He played in a rock band.*

➤ THESAURUS: Rock is the hard substance that the Earth is made of. Caves are made of rock. A large piece of this substance is also called a rock. A smaller piece of rock is called a stone. Children often enjoy throwing stones into water. We also use the word stone to talk about the substance that rock is made of. For example, you might live in a house made of stone. A very large rock is called a boulder.

rock² /rɒk/ VERB [rocks, rocking, rocked] to move or move something gently backwards and forwards or from side to side □ *She was rocking the baby in her arms.* □ *The boats rocked gently in the harbour.*

rocket /'rɒkɪt/ NOUN [plural rockets]
1 a long thin spacecraft □ *The Ariane rocket was launched from the EU space centre.*
2 a long thin weapon with a bomb in it which is fired from a plane or ship □ *Rockets were fired across the border.* □ *a rocket attack*
3 something which explodes high in the sky and makes bright lights for entertainment

rock music /'rɒk ˌmjuːzɪk/ NOUN, NO PLURAL a type of music with a strong beat that is played on electric guitars and drums

rocky /'rɒkɪ/ ADJECTIVE [rockier, rockiest] made of rock, or covered with rocks □ *the rocky slopes of the mountains*

rod /rɒd/ NOUN [plural rods] a long thin pole ⭓ *a fishing rod*

rode /rəʊd/ PAST TENSE OF **ride¹**

rogue /rəʊg/ NOUN [plural rogues] a dishonest or badly behaved man or boy ⭓ *He's a lovable rogue* (= someone who behaves badly but you still like them).

role /rəʊl/ NOUN [plural roles]
1 the character that an actor is in a play or film ⭓ *Daniel Radcliffe played the role of Harry Potter in the film.* ⭓ *It was his first starring role* (= important role) *in a Hollywood movie.*
2 the job or purpose that someone or something has ⭓ *Diet plays an important role in good health.* □ **+ of** *The role of women has changed greatly over the last century.*

roll¹ /rəʊl/ VERB [rolls, rolling, rolled]
1 to move along like a ball, or to make something move in this way □ **+ down/along, etc.** *Rocks sometimes rolled down the hills.* □ *She rolled the ball along the ground.*
2 to move on wheels, or to make something on wheels move □ *Take the brake off and let the car roll forwards.* □ **+ into** *The train rolled into the station.* □ *I rolled the bike into the garage.*
3 to turn your body when you are lying down, or to turn someone else's body when they are lying down □ **+ over** *My back hurts every time I roll over in bed.* □ *She rolled the baby onto his tummy.*

4 to fold something so that it forms the shape of a ball or a tube □ *She rolled her clothes in tissue paper before packing them.* □ *+ up Roll the sleeping bag up tightly and tie the string around it.*

♦ PHRASAL VERB **roll something up 1** to make a piece of clothing shorter by folding it □ *She rolled her sleeves up so they didn't get wet.* **2** to fold something so that it forms the shape of a ball or tube □ *The carpet had been rolled up.*

> THESAURUS: If something rolls, or if you roll it, it moves along like a ball, or you make it move in this way. If something revolves, it moves in a circle around something. For example, the Earth revolves around the sun. If something spins, or if you spin it, it turns round and round very quickly, or you make it do this. For example, dancers sometimes spin. If something rotates, or if you rotate it, it moves around like a wheel.

roll² /rəʊl/ NOUN [*plural* rolls]
1 a small round piece of bread for one person, often with something such as meat or cheese in it □ *I had a cheese roll for lunch.*
2 something that has been rolled into the shape of a tube □ *+ of a roll of toilet paper* □ *We'll need 12 rolls of wallpaper for this room.*

roller skate /ˈrəʊlə ˌskeɪt/ NOUN [*plural* roller skates] a boot with two pairs of wheels on the bottom, used for skating

Roman Catholic¹ /ˌrəʊmən ˈkæθlɪk/ NOUN [*plural* Roman Catholics] a member of the part of the Christian church that has the Pope for a leader

Roman Catholic² /ˌrəʊmən ˈkæθlɪk/ ADJECTIVE to do with, or belonging to, the Roman Catholic Church

romance /rəʊˈmæns/ NOUN [*plural* romances]
1 *no plural* the feelings connected with being in love □ *They met at college and romance soon blossomed*
2 a short relationship between people who are in love 🔒 *The couple had a whirlwind romance* (= short and exciting relationship).
3 a love story □ *She read mainly romances.*

romantic /rəʊˈmæntɪk/ ADJECTIVE to do with feelings of love 🔒 *a romantic relationship* 🔒 *His latest film is a romantic comedy.* □ *a romantic dinner for two*

roof /ruːf/ NOUN [*plural* roofs] the part that covers the top of a building or vehicle □ *The house has a red tiled roof.* □ *+ of He climbed onto the roof of the building.*

room /ruːm, rʊm/ NOUN [*plural* rooms]
1 one of the areas a building is divided into inside □ *We have three rooms downstairs and four upstairs.*

□ *She got up and left the room.* 🔒 *He went back to his hotel room.*
2 *no plural* space for something □ *+ for Is there room for another chair?* □ *There wasn't enough room in the car for everyone.* □ *+ to do something They had no room to move.*

root /ruːt/ NOUN [*plural* roots] the part of a plant that grows underground □ *+ of the roots of the tree*

rope /rəʊp/ NOUN [*plural* ropes] very thick strong string

> THESAURUS: Thread is a long, thin piece of cotton, wool, etc. used for sewing. String is strong thread, used for tying things. Rope is very thick strong string, which is also used for tying things. Strong rope made of metal is called cable. Metal made into long, thin pieces, used for fastening things together, or to make fences, etc. is called wire.

rose¹ /rəʊz/ NOUN [*plural* roses] a garden plant with sharp points on the stems and flowers that smell sweet

rose² /rəʊz/ PAST TENSE OF **rise¹** □ *The temperature rose steadily as the day wore on.*

rot /rɒt/ VERB [rots, rotting, rotted] to decay or to make something decay □ *The leaves fall on the forest floor and gradually rot into the soil.* □ *Sugar rots the teeth.*

rotate /rəʊˈteɪt/ VERB [rotates, rotating, rotated] to turn around like a wheel, or to make something turn around like a wheel □ *Each wheel rotates on its own axle.*

rotten /ˈrɒtən/ ADJECTIVE
1 decayed or decaying □ *rotten eggs* □ *a rotten floorboard*
2 an informal word meaning very bad or unpleasant □ *We had a rotten meal there.* □ *I felt rotten when I woke up.*

rough /rʌf/ ADJECTIVE [rougher, roughest]
1 not smooth □ *We drove along a rough track.* □ *I get very rough skin on my feet.*
2 not gentle □ *Rugby is a rough game.*
3 not exact □ *a rough guess/estimate*

roughly /ˈrʌflɪ/ ADVERB
1 approximately □ *There were roughly ten thousand people in the stadium.* 🔒 *They're roughly the same size.* □ *Her name roughly translates as 'white flower'.*
2 in a quick way, without being careful or gentle □ *If you handle the flowers roughly, you'll damage them.* □ *roughly chopped onions*

round¹ /raʊnd/ ADVERB, PREPOSITION
1 on all sides □ *We sat round the table.* □ *We tied a rope round the tree.*
2 moving in a circle or along the edges of something

□ *The Moon goes round the Earth.* 🔊 *We drove round and round in circles.*

3 to face the opposite direction □ *If you look round, you can see the clock.* 🔊 *He turned round and waved.*

4 to the other side of something □ *We were allowed to go round the back of the theatre.* 🔊 *I saw Jo coming round the corner.*

5 in or to different parts of a place □ *We travelled all round Spain.*

6 to someone's home 🔊 *Why don't you come round for supper?* 🔊 *I'm going round to Fred's after school.*

7 from one person or place to another □ *The news got round pretty quickly.* □ *Please pass the books round to everyone.*

round² /raʊnd/ ADJECTIVE [rounder, roundest] having the shape of a circle or a ball □ *a round table* □ *The Earth is round.*

roundabout /ˈraʊndəbaʊt/ NOUN [plural roundabouts]

1 a place where several roads meet and the traffic must go around a circle in the same direction before turning onto the next road □ *Turn left at the roundabout.*

2 a round structure that children sit on while it turns round

route /ruːt/ NOUN [plural routes] a way of getting from one place to another 🔊 *Which route do you take to work?* □ *a bus route* □ **+ of** *There were police all along the route of the march.* □ *It's the main route between London and Bristol.*

routine¹ /ruːˈtiːn/ NOUN [plural routines] the usual things that you do and they way you do them 🔊 *Exercise should be part of your daily routine.* □ *They settled into a routine of family life.*

routine² /ruːˈtiːn/ ADJECTIVE normal and done regularly □ *a routine inspection*

row¹ /rəʊ/ NOUN [plural rows] a number of people or things arranged next to each other in a line □ *the front row of seats* □ *Sow the seeds in a straight row.* □ *a row of figures*

➤ **THESAURUS:** A row or a line is a number of things or people arranged next to each other. A queue is a line of people who are waiting for something. In American English, the word line is also used with this meaning.

row² /rəʊ/ VERB [rows, rowing, rowed] to pull a boat through water using oars (= long wooden poles)

row³ /raʊ/ NOUN [plural rows] a noisy argument or strong disagreement 🔊 *Tom had a row with his girlfriend.* □ *The incident caused a political row.* □ *They went on strike in a row over pay.*

row⁴ /raʊ/ VERB [rows, rowing, rowed] to argue noisily □ *They were always rowing and falling out.*

➤ Notice the different pronunciations. **row**¹ and **row**² are pronounced the same and rhyme with **low**. **row**³ and **row**⁴ are pronounced differently and they rhyme with **how**.

royal /ˈrɔɪəl/ ADJECTIVE to do with a king or queen or their family 🔊 *the Danish royal family* □ *a royal wedding*

royalty /ˈrɔɪəlti/ NOUN, NO PLURAL all the members of the king or queen's family

rub /rʌb/ VERB [rubs, rubbing, rubbed] to move your hand or an object backwards and forwards over a surface □ *He was rubbing his eyes.* □ *She rubbed her cheek against the velvet.*

♦ PHRASAL VERB **rub something out** to remove words or pictures by rubbing them with a piece of rubber or a cloth □ *Copy these words off the board before I rub them out.*

rubber /ˈrʌbə(r)/ NOUN [plural rubbers]

1 *no plural* a strong substance that stretches and bends easily, made from tree juices □ *shoes with rubber soles* □ *a pair of rubber gloves*

2 a small block that you rub on paper in order to remove pencil marks

rubbish /ˈrʌbɪʃ/ NOUN, NO PLURAL

1 things that have been thrown away because they are no longer wanted □ *Put the rubbish in the bin.* □ *More household rubbish could be recycled.* 🔊 *a rubbish bin*

2 an informal word for something someone says that is not true or is stupid 🔊 *He's talking rubbish.*

3 an informal word for something of very bad quality □ *Her new chat show is absolute rubbish.*

➤ **THESAURUS:** Rubbish is things that have been thrown away because they are no longer wanted. Litter is paper and other rubbish that people have thrown on the ground in a public place. Waste is rubbish or other material that cannot be used for anything. You can talk about industrial waste, for example, which might include chemicals. Junk is old things with little use or value.

rubble /ˈrʌbəl/ NOUN, NO PLURAL the broken pieces that are left when a building falls down □ *a pile of rubble*

rude /ruːd/ ADJECTIVE [ruder, rudest]

1 insulting and not polite □ **+ to** *She was very rude to hotel staff.* □ *I don't mean to be rude, but isn't it a bit old?* □ **+ to do something** *It would be rude to ignore them.*

2 embarrassing or offensive and not acceptable in a polite situation □ *rude jokes* □ *a rude word*

➤ Note that someone is **rude to** someone else and not 'rude with' someone else:
✓ He was very rude to my mother.
✗ He was very rude with my mother.

rug /rʌg/ NOUN [*plural* rugs] a cover for the floor which is not fixed □ *a sheepskin rug*

rugby /ˈrʌgbɪ/ NOUN, NO PLURAL a sport played by two teams in which the players throw and run with an oval ball 🔁 *a rugby player* 🔁 *He plays rugby.*

rugged /ˈrʌgɪd/ ADJECTIVE rough with a lot of rocks □ *a rugged coastline*

ruin¹ /ˈruːɪn/ VERB [ruins, ruining, ruined] to spoil something completely □ *The rain ruined my hairstyle.* □ *The injury threatens to ruin her athletics career.*

ruin² /ˈruːɪn/ NOUN [*plural* ruins]
1 something such as an old building that has fallen down □ *a Roman ruin* □ *the ancient Inca ruins of Machu Picchu*
2 **in ruins** destroyed or completely spoilt □ *The city was in ruins after the earthquake.*

rule¹ /ruːl/ NOUN [*plural* rules]
1 an instruction about what is allowed or what is not allowed □ *It's against the rules to move your feet when you're holding the ball.* 🔁 *She was disqualified from the competition for* breaking the rules. 🔁 *You must* follow (= obey) *all the* rules carefully. 🔁 *There are* strict rules about employing staff.
2 the person or group that controls a country or an area 🔁 *The country is under* military rule.

rule² /ruːl/ VERB [rules, ruling, ruled] to control a country or an area □ *He ruled France in the 18th century.* □ *She is a minister in the ruling socialist party.*

ruler /ˈruːlə(r)/ NOUN [*plural* rulers]
1 a person who controls a country or an area □ *Gandhi never became ruler of India.*
2 a flat strip of wood, plastic or metal, used to draw straight lines or for measuring short lengths

rumble /ˈrʌmbəl/ VERB [rumbles, rumbling, rumbled] to make a low continuous sound □ *Thunder rumbled in the distance.*

rumor /ˈruːmə(r)/ NOUN [*plural* rumors] the US spelling of **rumour**

rumour /ˈruːmə(r)/ NOUN [*plural* rumours] information that people tell each other, although it may not be true □ *I heard a rumour that Jen was leaving.* 🔁 *Someone has been* spreading rumours.

run¹ /rʌn/ VERB [runs, running, ran, run]
1 to move with very fast steps □ *We had to run for the bus.* □ *They ran down the street screaming.*
2 to run in a race or as a sport □ *I'm hoping to run a marathon.* □ *He runs every morning.*

3 to control or organize an organization, event or activity □ *She runs a successful transport business.* □ *The college runs part-time courses.* □ *The party is not ready to run the country.*
4 if a machine or a piece of equipment is running, it is being used □ *I left the engine running while I ran into the house.* □ **+ on** *The heating runs on solar energy.*
5 if a liquid runs somewhere, it flows in that direction □ *I had tears running down my face.* □ *Water ran over the side of the bath.*
6 if buses and trains are running, they are travelling and people can use them □ *The number 5 bus runs every 10 minutes.* 🔁 *The trains never run on time.*
7 if something runs in a particular direction or position, that is where it is □ *A path ran behind the house.* □ *Wires ran overhead.*
♦ PHRASAL VERBS **run away** to leave a place secretly 🔁 *I ran away from home several times.* **run someone/something down** to knock someone or something over with a vehicle □ *The lorry driver simply ran him down.* **run into someone** to meet someone by chance □ *I ran into Jake at the supermarket.* **run into something** to drive a vehicle into an object □ *I lost control and ran into a wall.* **run out** 1 to use the whole amount of something □ *We have run out of money.* 2 to be completely used □ *The milk has run out.* **run someone/something over** to drive over someone or something in a vehicle □ *I reversed and ran over his bike.*

run² /rʌn/ NOUN [*plural* runs]
1 when you run in a race or as a sport 🔁 *I always go for a run before breakfast.* □ *That run was fast enough to give him a place in the Olympic team.*
2 when you move with very fast steps 🔁 *When she saw Terry, she* broke into a run (= started running).
3 a point that a player wins in a game like cricket or baseball 🔁 *He scored 58 runs.*

rung¹ /rʌŋ/ NOUN [*plural* rungs] a step on a ladder (= a piece of equipment with steps you climb up to reach a high place)

rung² /rʌŋ/ PAST PARTICIPLE OF **ring²** □ *Have you rung your mother?*

runner /ˈrʌnə(r)/ NOUN [*plural* runners] a person or animal that runs □ *He's a very fast runner.* □ *a marathon runner*

runner-up /ˌrʌnərˈʌp/ NOUN [*plural* runners-up] the person who finishes in second place in a competition 🔁 *She finished runner-up in last year's race.*

running /ˈrʌnɪŋ/ ADJECTIVE
1 used to say that something happens a number of times, one directly after another □ *The album is at number one for the third week running.*

2 running water water which comes through pipes from a water supply □ *The cottage has no running water or electricity.*

---

runway /ˈrʌnweɪ/ NOUN [*plural* runways] the long, wide road at an airport that aeroplanes take off from and land on

rural /ˈrʊərəl/ ADJECTIVE to do with the countryside 🔊 *She grew up in a rural area.* □ *a rural community*

rush¹ /rʌʃ/ NOUN [*plural* rushes]
1 a sudden, strong movement or feeling □ *a rush of cold air* 🔊 *She felt a rush of excitement.*
2 a hurry □ *It was a bit of a rush but we got there in time.*
3 be in a rush to be hurrying □ *I was in a rush to get to the airport on time.*

rush² /rʌʃ/ VERB [rushes, rushing, rushed]
1 to move or to do something quickly and suddenly □ *Firefighters rushed to the scene.* □ *Several colleagues rushed to help the woman.*

2 to take someone or something somewhere very quickly 🔊 *He was rushed to hospital in an ambulance.*
3 to do something too quickly and without enough care □ *I don't want to rush things.*

rush hour /rʌʃ ˌaʊə(r)/ NOUN [*plural* rush hours] the time when there is most traffic because people are travelling to or from work 🔊 *the morning rush hour* 🔊 *Trains are packed during the evening rush hour.*

rust¹ /rʌst/ NOUN, NO PLURAL a brown substance that forms on iron and other metals if they are in air and water

rust² /rʌst/ VERB [rusts, rusting, rusted] to become covered in rust □ *The equipment was just left to rust.*

rusty /ˈrʌsti/ ADJECTIVE [rustier, rustiest] covered in rust (= a reddish-brown substance that forms on metal) □ *rusty nails*

ruthless /ˈruːθlɪs/ ADJECTIVE cruel and trying to achieve what you want without caring how your behaviour affects others □ *a ruthless dictator*

Ss

S¹ or **S** /es/ the 19th letter of the alphabet

S² /es/ ABBREVIATION **south²**

sack /sæk/ NOUN [*plural* sacks]
1 a large bag made of strong material used for carrying or storing things □ *a sack of potatoes*
2 the sack when you lose your job ⌨ *He got the sack for being late all the time.* ⌨ *They'll give her the sack if she doesn't work harder.*

sacred /'seɪkrɪd/ ADJECTIVE
1 holy, or to do with God □ *a sacred shrine*
2 to do with religion □ *sacred music*

sacrifice¹ /'sækrɪfaɪs/ NOUN [*plural* sacrifices]
1 giving up something important to you in order to achieve something that is more important, or the thing that you give up in this way ⌨ *We had to make sacrifices in order to be able to buy a house.*
2 the act of killing someone or something and offering them to a god, or the person or animal that is killed in this way

sacrifice² /'sækrɪfaɪs/ VERB [sacrifices, sacrificing, sacrificed]
1 to give up something that is important to you in order to achieve something that is more important □ *He sacrificed his life to save his fellow soldiers.*
2 to kill someone or something and offer them to a god

sad /sæd/ ADJECTIVE [sadder, saddest]
1 unhappy ⌨ *I felt sad saying goodbye to them.* □ **+ to do something** *I'll be sad to leave the company after so many years.*
2 making you feel unhappy □ *a sad film* □ *a sad story*

saddle /'sædəl/ NOUN [*plural* saddles]
1 a leather seat for putting on a horse's back
2 a seat on a bicycle or motorcycle

sadness /'sædnɪs/ NOUN, NO PLURAL a feeling of unhappiness □ *It is with great sadness that we announce the death of our mother, Nancy.*

safe¹ /seɪf/ ADJECTIVE [safer, safest]
1 unlikely to cause harm or damage □ *That ladder doesn't look very safe.* □ **+ to do something** *Is it safe to drink the water?* ⌨ *We need a safe place to rest.*
2 not in danger of being harmed, damaged, lost, etc. □ *You must keep these documents safe.* □ **+ from** *Nobody is safe from the disease.*

3 not damaged, harmed, stolen, etc □ *Thank goodness you're safe!*

safe² /seɪf/ NOUN [*plural* safes] a strong box with a lock, where money or valuable objects are kept

safely /'seɪflɪ/ ADVERB without risk or danger □ *Drive safely.* □ *We got everyone home safely.*

safety /'seɪftɪ/ NOUN, NO PLURAL being safe, not being in danger or dangerous □ *The safety of passengers is our first concern.* □ *Tests will ensure the safety of the drugs.*

sag /sæg/ VERB [sags, sagging, sagged] to hang down or not be firm □ *The mattress has begun to sag in the middle.*

saga /'sɑːgə/ NOUN [*plural* sagas] a long story, especially one about a group of people over many years □ *a family saga*

said /sed/ PAST TENSE AND PAST PARTICIPLE OF **say**
□ *She said she was coming.* □ *They have said I can come back any time.*

sail¹ /seɪl/ VERB [sails, sailing, sailed]
1 to travel somewhere in a ship or a boat □ *They're sailing off the coast of Sweden.*
2 to start a journey in a ship □ *The ferry sails at noon.*

sail² /seɪl/ NOUN [*plural* sails] a sheet of strong cloth attached to a boat, which catches the wind and carries the boat along

sailor /'seɪlə(r)/ NOUN [*plural* sailors]
1 someone who works on a ship □ *a merchant sailor*
2 someone who goes sailing □ *Joe's a keen sailor.*

saint /seɪnt/ NOUN [*plural* saints] a dead person that the Christian church believes was especially holy □ *Saint Francis*

sake /seɪk/ NOUN [*plural* sakes]
1 for someone's sake in order to help someone □ *For his mother's sake, he wanted to be there.* □ *Please don't go to any trouble just for my sake.*
2 for the sake of something in order to get or achieve something □ *I gave in for the sake of peace.*

salad /'sæləd/ NOUN [*plural* salads] a mixture of usually raw vegetables that sometimes includes other food, such as fish or cheese □ *a mixed salad* □ *rice salad*

salary /'sælərɪ/ NOUN [plural salaries] an amount of money that a person is paid for doing their job each month or year □ The job offers an annual salary of £35,000.

sale /seɪl/ NOUN [plural sales]
1 no plural the process of selling things for money □ the sale of houses
2 a time when goods are sold at cheaper prices than usual □ the January sales
3 for sale available for someone to buy □ Are these paintings for sale? 🔁 They've just put their house up for sale.
4 on sale offered for sale □ The DVD is on sale now.

salesman /'seɪlzmən/ NOUN [plural salesmen] a man whose job is to sell goods or services to customers
saleswoman /'seɪlzwumən/ NOUN [plural saleswomen] a woman whose job is to sell goods or services to customers
salmon /'sæmən/ NOUN [plural salmon]
1 a large silver fish that swims up rivers to produce its eggs
2 the orange-pink flesh from this fish eaten as food

salt /sɔːlt/ NOUN, NO PLURAL a white substance that comes from the ground or the sea and is used often for giving flavour to food 🔁 salt and pepper 🔁 Add a pinch of salt.

salty /'sɔːltɪ/ ADJECTIVE [saltier, saltiest] containing salt or tasting very strongly of salt □ I thought the soup was too salty.

salute /sə'luːt/ NOUN [plural salutes] a movement that shows respect to someone you meet, especially a military officer □ The Queen returned the salute.

same¹ /seɪm/ ADJECTIVE, PRONOUN
1 the same (a) the person or thing mentioned, not a different one □ He won the lottery and left his job on the same day. 🔁 We both started speaking at the same time. (b) exactly like someone or something else 🔁 I was wearing the same jacket as Barbara. 🔁 He broke his own mobile phone and now he's done the same thing to mine! □ You know I'd do the same for you. (c) not changed □ I thought she might have grown up a bit since leaving home, but she's just the same.
2 at the same time used to say that another thing is also true □ He needs to keep active, but at the same time he should be careful of his knees.

same² /seɪm/ ADVERB in the same way □ We tend to dress the same. □ We treat all our children the same.

sample /'sɑːmpəl/ NOUN [plural samples] a small amount or number of something that shows what the rest is like 🔁 The magazine came with a free

sample of chocolate. 🔁 This was a random sample of consumers.

sand /sænd/ NOUN, NO PLURAL very small grains of rock that are found on beaches and in deserts

sandal /'sændəl/ NOUN [plural sandals] a light open shoe for wearing when the weather is warm

sandwich /'sænwɪdʒ/ NOUN [plural sandwiches] two pieces of bread with food between them □ a ham sandwich □ a toasted sandwich

sandy /'sændɪ/ ADJECTIVE [sandier, sandiest] covered with sand, or with sand inside □ a sandy beach □ sandy shoes

sane /seɪn/ ADJECTIVE [saner, sanest] not mentally ill □ The judge was told that Foster was sane at the time of the murder.

sang /sæŋ/ PAST TENSE OF sing

sank /sæŋk/ PAST TENSE OF sink¹ □ The ship sank in rough waters.

Santa Claus /ˌsæntə 'klɔːz/ or **Santa** /'sæntə/ NOUN an imaginary old man with a white beard in a red coat who children believe brings presents on Christmas Eve □ What did Santa bring you?

sat /sæt/ PAST TENSE AND PAST PARTICIPLE OF sit □ He sat down. □ I've sat here for an hour waiting for you!

satellite /'sætəlaɪt/ NOUN [plural satellites] a piece of equipment that is put in space to travel around the Earth in order to send and receive information □ a satellite link □ a weather/communications satellite

satisfaction /ˌsætɪs'fækʃən/ NOUN, NO PLURAL a feeling of pleasure at having achieved something or got something good □ She looked at the finished work with satisfaction. □ + from doing something I get a lot of satisfaction from cooking. 🔁 Job satisfaction is extremely important.

satisfactory /ˌsætɪs'fæktərɪ/ ADJECTIVE of a good enough standard □ Her progress in maths was described as satisfactory. □ We are still waiting for a satisfactory outcome to the situation.

satisfied /'sætɪsfaɪd/ ADJECTIVE pleased because you have achieved something or got something good □ + with Are you satisfied with the progress on the project? □ You're never satisfied – that's your problem. □ a satisfied customer

satisfy /'sætɪsfaɪ/ VERB [satisfies, satisfying, satisfied] to make someone pleased by giving them what they want or need □ The resort should satisfy even the most experienced skiers. □ This proposal is unlikely to satisfy campaigners.

Saturday /'sætədɪ/ NOUN [plural Saturdays] the day of the week after Friday and before Sunday □ On Saturday, we went shopping. □ What are you doing next Saturday?

sauce /sɔːs/ NOUN [plural sauces] a liquid food with a particular flavour that you put on other food □ *She had spaghetti with tomato sauce.* □ *ice cream with chocolate sauce*

saucepan /'sɔːspən/ NOUN [plural saucepans] a round metal container with a handle, used for cooking food on top of an oven

saucer /'sɔːsə(r)/ NOUN [plural saucers] a small plate that goes under a cup □ *a cup and saucer*

sausage /'sɒsɪdʒ/ NOUN [plural sausages] a long tube of meat mixed with spices

savage /'sævɪdʒ/ ADJECTIVE very violent and cruel □ *savage beatings*

save /seɪv/ VERB [saves, saving, saved]
1 to stop someone or something being harmed, killed or destroyed □ *The firefighters saved everyone in the building.* □ *Switch off lights and help save the planet.* □ + *from* *A shelter of branches and leaves saved them from freezing.* ⊞ *The correct equipment could save your life.*
2 to avoid using something, or to use less of it than usual □ *You can save 40 minutes by taking the motorway.*
3 to keep something so that you can use it later □ *Save any food that's left over and heat it up later.* □ *We're saving our energy for tomorrow's walk.*
4 to keep money, usually in a bank, so that you can use it later □ *We have saved regularly all our lives.*
5 to make a computer store information. A computing word □ *Make sure you save your work regularly.*
6 to not allow the ball to go in the net in sports such as football □ *He saved a penalty.*
♦ PHRASAL VERB **save up** to keep money so that you can use it in the future □ + *for* *I'm saving up for a new car.*

savings /'seɪvɪŋz/ PLURAL NOUN money that you have saved in a bank □ *Joe's going to spend all his savings on a drum kit.*

saw¹ /sɔː/ NOUN [plural saws] a tool with a thin blade used for cutting through wood or metal

> ➤ THESAURUS: A blade is the sharp part of a tool which cuts. We often use a saw to cut through wood or metal, for example if we are building something. If you are cutting wood for a fire, you might use an axe. A knife is a smaller tool with a blade and a handle, used especially for cutting food.

saw² /sɔː/ VERB [saws, sawing, sawed, sawn] to cut through wood or metal using a saw
saw³ /sɔː/ PAST TENSE OF see □ *I saw Paolo last week.*

say /seɪ/ VERB [says, saying, said]
1 to express something in words □ *I asked her about the rumours, but she wouldn't say anything.* □ *I asked for more money, but my boss said no.* □ + *that* *Officials say that the death toll has reached 30.* □ + *about* *Did she say anything about the wedding?*
2 to give information in words or signs □ *What does the notice say?* □ *My watch said six.*

> ➤ Remember that you **say** something but you do not 'say someone something':
> ✓ She said she was leaving.
> ✗ She said me she was leaving.

> ➤ THESAURUS: If you say something, you express it in words. If you tell someone something, you give them information by speaking. If you speak or talk, you say words in order to communicate. When more than one person is having a conversation, we usually use the word talk, not speak.

saying /'seɪɪŋ/ NOUN [plural sayings] a phrase or sentence that people often use, giving advice or saying something that many people believe is true □ *Gran's favourite saying was 'an apple a day keeps the doctor away'.*

scale /skeɪl/ NOUN [plural scales]
1 the general size or level of something □ *The hurricane has caused destruction on a huge scale.* □ *Experts warn that the scale of the problem is increasing.*
2 a series of numbers or marks used for measuring the level of something □ *The earthquake measured 3.2 on the Richter scale.* □ *Patients are asked to grade the pain they feel on a scale of one to ten.*
3 the size of something such as a model or a map, compared to the real size of the thing it represents □ *What's the scale of the map?*
4 scales an instrument for weighing things ⊞ *a set of kitchen scales* ⊞ *I weighed myself on the bathroom scales.*
5 a series of musical notes that goes up in order □ *the scale of G major* ⊞ *I try to practise my scales each day.*

6 one of the small thin pieces covering the skin of a fish or snake

scalp /skælp/ NOUN [*plural* scalps] the skin on the part of the head where the hair grows

scan¹ /skæn/ VERB [scans, scanning, scanned]
1 to use a piece of equipment to copy a picture of something onto a computer □ *Scan the photo and then e-mail it to me.*
2 to read something very quickly □ *Lou scanned the jobs section of the paper, looking for anything suitable.*

scan² /skæn/ NOUN [*plural* scans] a medical process in which a special machine produces an image of the inside of your body □ *a brain scan*

scandal /'skændəl/ NOUN [*plural* scandals]
1 a situation in which important people behave in a way that is morally very wrong □ *a political/ financial scandal*
2 talk or writing in the newspapers, etc. about behaviour that shocks people

scanner /'skænə(r)/ NOUN [*plural* scanners] a machine that copies a picture or document into a computer. A computing word.

scar¹ /skɑ:(r)/ NOUN [*plural* scars] a mark that is left on skin from an injury 🖾 *The surgery left a small scar.*

scar² /skɑ:(r)/ VERB [scars, scarring, scarred] to cause a scar □ *He was badly scarred by the fire.*

scarcely /'skeəslɪ/ ADVERB almost not at all □ *The place had scarcely changed.* □ *I could scarcely believe it.*

scare¹ /skeə(r)/ VERB [scares, scaring, scared] to frighten or to worry someone □ *We don't want to scare people.* □ *The reports are intended to scare us into driving more carefully.*

scare² /skeə(r)/ NOUN [*plural* scares]
1 a situation in which a lot of people are frightened or worried about something □ *a public health scare* 🖾 *There was a bomb scare at the airport.*
2 when something frightens or worries you for a short time 🖾 *It gave us all a scare when Maria fainted.*

scared /skeəd/ ADJECTIVE frightened □ *I'm scared of spiders.* □ *She's scared of her teacher.* □ *She lay in bed, too scared to move.* 🖾 *I'm scared stiff*

(= very frightened) *of heights.* 🖾 *I was scared to death* (= very frightened) *of messing it up.*

> ➤ **THESAURUS:** If you are worried or anxious, you are thinking a lot about problems or bad things that could happen. If you are scared, frightened or afraid, you are very worried about something.

scarf /skɑ:f/ NOUN [*plural* scarves] a piece of cloth that you wear around your neck or head to keep warm or to look attractive □ *a silk scarf* □ *a thick woollen scarf*

scatter /'skætə(r)/ VERB [scatters, scattering, scattered] to spread something in a lot of places over a wide area □ *Scatter the seeds evenly over the prepared soil.*

scene /si:n/ NOUN [*plural* scenes]
1 the place where an event happens □ + *of the scene of the accident* 🖾 *a crime scene* □ *An ambulance was very quickly on the scene.*
2 part of a play, a book or a film that happens in one place □ *We'll have to film the scene on the beach next.* □ + *from It was like a scene from a Hollywood movie.*
3 a place or situation as someone sees it □ + *of Before me was a scene of celebration.* □ *Rescuers described a scene of utter devastation.*

scenery /'si:nərɪ/ NOUN, NO PLURAL
1 what you see around you, especially the countryside □ *You get to see some wonderful scenery from the train.* □ *We stopped to take in the stunning scenery.* 🖾 *He needed a change of scenery* (= to go somewhere different).
2 the large pictures used in the theatre behind the actors

scent /sent/ NOUN [*plural* scents]
1 a good smell □ *The scent of lilies can fill a whole room.*
2 the smell of an animal that other animals can follow

schedule¹ /'ʃedju:l/ NOUN [*plural* schedules] a plan that shows when things should happen or be done □ *a flight schedule* □ *He has a very busy work schedule.* □ *The building work finished on schedule* (= when planned). □ *The project is already six months behind schedule.*

schedule² /'ʃedju:l/ VERB [schedules, scheduling, scheduled] to plan that something will happen at a particular time □ *The meeting has been scheduled for next Wednesday.*

scheme /ski:m/ NOUN [*plural* schemes] a plan or system for doing something □ *a national training scheme* □ *a pension scheme*

school /sku:l/ NOUN [*plural* schools]
1 a place where children go to learn 🖾 *You'll go to school when you're five years old.* □ *We walked home from school together.*

2 *no plural* the time when you are at school □ *He plays football after school on a Wednesday.* 🔊 *She left school at sixteen.*

3 a place where people go to learn a particular skill 🔊 *a language school*

4 in the US, a college or university □ *Where did you go to school?*

➤ **THESAURUS:** A place where children go to learn is called a **school**. A school for children under five is called a **kindergarten**. A **nursery** is a place where babies and small children are looked after while their parents are at work. A **college** is a place where people go to learn after they have left school. Often people learn a skill or how to do a particular job at college. A **university** is a place where you go to study at the highest level after leaving school.

schoolgirl /ˈskuːlɡɜːl/ NOUN [*plural* schoolgirls] a girl who goes to school

science /ˈsaɪəns/ NOUN, NO PLURAL the study and knowledge of the physical world and the way things happen in it 🔊 *He studied science and mathematics.* □ *Few now question the science behind climate change.*

science fiction /ˌsaɪəns ˈfɪkʃən/ NOUN, NO PLURAL stories and films that take place in an imagined future or in other parts of the universe □ *a science fiction novel*

scientific /ˌsaɪənˈtɪfɪk/ ADJECTIVE to do with science 🔊 *scientific research* 🔊 *a paper in a scientific journal*

scientist /ˈsaɪəntɪst/ NOUN [*plural* scientists] someone who studies science or who works in science □ *Scientists believe the condition is genetic.* □ *a team of forensic scientists*

scissors /ˈsɪzəz/ PLURAL NOUN a cutting tool that you hold in one hand that has two blades joined in the middle 🔊 *a pair of scissors* □ *She cut them up using kitchen scissors.*

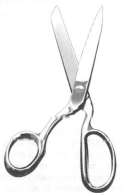

➤ Remember that **scissors** is a plural noun:
   ✓ You'll need *some* scissors.
   ✗ You'll need *a* scissors.

scoop /skuːp/ VERB [scoops, scooping, scooped] to lift or to remove something in your curved hands or with a large spoon or similar tool □ *She scooped up a handful of water.* □ *Scoop out the seeds with a teaspoon.*

scooter /ˈskuːtə(r)/ NOUN [*plural* scooters]
1 a smaller and less powerful motorcycle 🔊 *Young men ride by on motor scooters.*
2 a child's toy with two wheels at either end of a board and a tall handle, which you stand on and push yourself along

score[1] /skɔː(r)/ VERB [scores, scoring, scored] to get a point in a game, test or competition 🔊 *Ronaldo scored the winning goal.* 🔊 *Racing drivers score 10 points for a win.* □ **+ for** *Hamilton has scored again for the Rovers.* □ **+ against** *He scored against Brazil in the World Cup.*

score[2] /skɔː(r)/ NOUN [*plural* scores] the number of points that you get in a game, test or competition 🔊 *What was the final score?* 🔊 *What's the highest score you can get?* 🔊 *Katie's test scores weren't very good.*

scout /skaʊt/ NOUN [*plural* scouts]
1 the Scouts an organization for young people that encourages activities outdoors and practical skills
2 a member of the Scouts 🔊 *a boy scout*

scramble /ˈskræmbəl/ VERB [scrambles, scrambling, scrambled] to climb or move using your hands and feet, especially with difficulty □ *We scrambled up the side of the hill.*

scrap /skræp/ NOUN [*plural* scraps] a small piece or amount of something 🔊 *I have his address written on a scrap of paper.* □ *There isn't a scrap of evidence against us.*

scrape /skreɪp/ VERB [scrapes, scraping, scraped] to get something off a surface by using something sharp or rough □ *Scrape the mud off your shoes before you come in.*

scratch[1] /skrætʃ/ VERB [scratches, scratching, scratched]
1 to make a mark on a surface with something sharp or pointed □ *The car was quite badly scratched.* □ *Students had scratched their names on the desks.*
2 to rub your nails on your skin, usually because it feels uncomfortable □ *She scratched her nose.* □ *Try not to scratch the spots.*

scratch[2] /skrætʃ/ NOUN [*plural* scratches]
1 a mark left on a surface or your skin by something

sharp □ *He looked for scratches on the car.* □ *They escaped with minor scratches.*
2 from scratch from the beginning □ *They learn to cook simple, healthy meals from scratch.*

scream[1] /skri:m/ VERB [screams, screaming, screamed] to make a high, loud sound because you are frightened, excited or in pain □ **+ out** *The woman screamed out and the man ran off.* □ **+ in** *The children screamed in terror.* □ **+ with** *He was screaming with pain.* 🔁 *She screamed at the top of her voice.*

scream[2] /skri:m/ NOUN [plural screams] a loud, high noise or shout □ **+ of** *a scream of agony* □ *She let out a high-pitched scream.*
♦ IDIOM be a scream to be very funny. An informal phrase.

screen /skri:n/ NOUN [plural screens]
1 the part of a computer, television or cinema that you watch images on 🔁 *a computer screen* □ *a 17-inch screen* 🔁 *Fans watched on giant TV screens.*
2 a piece of wood, cloth, metal, etc. that divides one area from another or prevents something from being seen □ *We were separated by a glass screen.*

screw[1] /skru:/ NOUN [plural screws] a small, pointed, metal object used to fix things together by turning it around into a hole
screw[2] /skru:/ VERB [screws, screwing, screwed]
1 to fix a screw into something □ *Screw the bits of wood together.*
2 to attach or to fasten something with a turning movement □ *Screw the lid on tightly.*
♦ PHRASAL VERB screw something up to crush something, especially paper □ *He screwed up her letter and dropped it in the bin.*

scribble /'skrɪbəl/ VERB [scribbles, scribbling, scribbled]
1 to write very quickly and in an untidy way □ *I scribbled his name down before I forgot it.*
2 to draw untidy lines and shapes □ *The baby had a pen and was scribbling on the wall.*

script /skrɪpt/ NOUN [plural scripts] the words of a film, play, speech, etc. 🔁 *a film script* □ *She writes scripts for TV series.*

scrub /skrʌb/ VERB [scrubs, scrubbing, scrubbed] to rub something hard to get it clean □ *We'll need to scrub these stains off the floor.*

sculpture /'skʌlptʃə(r)/ NOUN [plural sculptures]
1 an object that an artist makes using a material like clay, stone or wood □ *'The Kiss' is a famous sculpture by Rodin.*
2 no plural the art of making objects using materials like clay, stone or wood

sea /si:/ NOUN [plural seas]
1 no plural the salt water that covers most of the Earth's surface □ *They live by the sea.* □ *I love*

swimming in the sea. □ *Australia is completely surrounded by sea.*
2 a large area of salt water □ *the Dead Sea*

seafood /'si:fu:d/ NOUN, NO PLURAL fish and sea animals that you can eat, especially animals in shells

seal[1] /si:l/ NOUN [plural seals] a large animal with shiny fur that spends its time both in the sea and on land

seal[2] /si:l/ VERB [seals, sealing, sealed]
1 to stick the top part of an envelope down so that it is closed
2 to close a container or an area by covering it completely with something so that air or liquid cannot get into it or get out of it

sea level /'si: ˌlevəl/ NOUN, NO PLURAL the average level of the sea's surface, used as the point from which the height of land is measured □ *The summit is 4000 feet above sea level.*

seam /si:m/ NOUN [plural seams] a line of sewing that joins two pieces of cloth □ *The seam has split.*

search[1] /sɜ:tʃ/ VERB [searches, searching, searched] to look carefully for something or someone □ **+ for** *I'm still searching for my keys.* □ **+ through** *Firefighters searched through the wreckage for survivors.*

search[2] /sɜ:tʃ/ NOUN [plural searches]
1 an attempt to find someone or something 🔁 *The police made a thorough search for the missing child.* □ **+ for** *We will not stop in our search for her.*
2 in search of in order to find □ *They went off in search of somewhere to eat.*
3 an attempt to find information on the Internet. A computing word 🔁 *Have you done a search on his name?*

search engine /'sɜ:tʃ ˌendʒɪn/ NOUN [plural search engines] a computer program that helps you to search for something on the Internet. A computing word.

seaside /'si:saɪd/ NOUN, NO PLURAL a place near the sea where people go on holiday □ *Let's have a day at the seaside.* 🔁 *a seaside resort*

season /'si:zən/ NOUN [plural seasons]
1 one of the four main periods that the year is divided into, each having different weather □ *Spring is my favourite season.*
2 a period of the year when a particular thing happens □ *the football season* □ *This hotel will be packed in the holiday season.*

seat /si:t/ NOUN [plural seats]
1 a piece of furniture for sitting on □ *a garden seat* □ *He was in the passenger seat of the car.*
2 a chair that you pay to sit on in a vehicle or in a theatre □ *I've booked three seats for the theatre.* □ *I prefer window seats in aeroplanes.*

seat belt /ˈsiːt ˌbelt/ NOUN [plural seat belts] a strong belt in a car or plane that goes across your body □ Please fasten your seat belts now.

second[1] /ˈsekənd/ NUMBER 2nd written as a word □ Julia is their second daughter. □ Marta came second in the race. □ This programme is the second in a series of three.

second[2] /ˈsekənd/ NOUN [plural seconds]
1 one of 60 parts that a minute is divided into □ He ran the race in 57 seconds.
2 a very short time □ Just wait a second.

secondary /ˈsekəndərɪ/ ADJECTIVE secondary education is for students between the age of 11 and 18

secondary school /ˈsekəndərɪ ˌskuːl/ NOUN [plural secondary schools] a school for students between the ages of 11 and 18

second-class[1] /ˌsekənd ˈklɑːs/ ADJECTIVE describes the less expensive way of travelling that most people choose and the less expensive way of sending post that is slower □ a second-class compartment □ a second-class stamp

second-class[2] /ˌsekənd ˈklɑːs/ ADVERB using the cheapest type □ I sent the letter second-class.

second-hand /ˌsekənd ˈhænd/ ADJECTIVE, ADVERB used for describing things which someone else has owned before you □ a second-hand car □ Kathryn buys all her clothes second-hand.

secret[1] /ˈsiːkrɪt/ NOUN [plural secrets]
1 a piece of information that must not be told to other people 🔁 I'll tell you a little secret. 🔁 She can't keep a secret (= not tell someone a secret)
2 in secret without other people knowing □ They began to meet in secret.

secret[2] /ˈsiːkrɪt/ ADJECTIVE not told or shown to other people □ secret information 🔁 The facts of the case were kept secret. □ The talks were held at a secret location.

secretary /ˈsekrətərɪ/ NOUN [plural secretaries]
1 someone whose job is to type letters, arrange meetings and take notes at business meetings, etc. □ Please leave a message with my secretary if I'm out.
2 someone who is in charge of a government department □ the education secretary □ He's the former British foreign secretary.

sect /sekt/ NOUN [plural sects] a group of people who have different beliefs from a larger group, especially in a religion

section /ˈsekʃən/ NOUN [plural sections] one of the parts that together make up something □ The table has three sections that fit together. □ the fiction section of the library □ the arts section of the newspaper

secure /sɪˈkjʊə(r)/ ADJECTIVE
1 unlikely to fail or change □ a secure job □ They are financially secure.
2 safe, confident and not worried □ Children need to feel secure.
3 safe against attack or harm □ You can make your home more secure by installing a burglar alarm.
4 a secure place is guarded so that only particular people can go into it or leave it □ Police have taken the family to a secure location. □ a secure area of the airport
5 firmly fixed or fastened □ Check that the ropes are secure.

security /sɪˈkjʊərətɪ/ NOUN, NO PLURAL
1 safety from danger or crime and the things that are done to achieve this 🔁 We need to tighten airport security. 🔁 The policy was a threat to national security.
2 a feeling of safety and confidence or a situation that provides this 🔁 A stable family background can give children a sense of security.
3 the situation when something is unlikely to fail or change 🔁 Job security is very important for most people. 🔁 A lot of people are worried about financial security.

see /siː/ VERB [sees, seeing, saw, seen]
1 to look at someone or something and notice them □ The dog goes mad whenever he sees a cat. □ I saw you coming. □ Can you see where the switch is?
2 to meet someone or spend time with them □ Have you seen Peter much lately? □ I'm seeing Billie at the weekend.
3 to watch a film, television programme, etc. □ Did you see 'Pride and Prejudice'?
4 to understand something 🔁 Now I see what you mean. 🔁 I don't see why I should tidy up your mess. 🔁 'He couldn't come because he didn't have a ticket.' 'Oh, I see.'
5 to find out something by waiting for something to happen □ I'll see what she says. □ Let's see how today's lesson goes. □ See if you can arrange a taxi.
6 to find out information about something □ Can you see what time the bank opens? □ As we have seen, Cromwell was hated by the Irish.
7 I'll see/We'll see used to say that you will consider agreeing to what someone has asked, but will not decide immediately □ 'Can I have a new bike for my birthday?' 'We'll see.'
8 let me see used when you are trying to remember something □ It must have been – let me see – at least fifteen years ago.
9 See you. an informal way of saying goodbye
➜ go to not see eye to eye
◆ PHRASAL VERBS see someone off to go with someone to say goodbye to them see to something to deal with something □ Don't worry about the travel arrangements – I'll see to all that.

➤ THESAURUS: If you see something, you use your eyes and notice it. If you look at something, you turn your eyes to see it. If you watch something, you look at it for a while. For example, we watch television.

seed /siːd/ NOUN [*plural* seeds] a thing that a plant produces and that new plants grow from ⊞ *Sow the seeds about two centimetres deep in the soil.* □ *sunflower seeds*

seek /siːk/ VERB [seeks, seeking, sought] a formal word meaning to try to find or achieve something □ *They were seeking a long-term solution.*

➤ Note that **seek**, meaning 'to try to find' is only used in formal English. The usual phrase for this meaning is **look for**:
✓ *I'm looking for a good hairdresser.*
✗ I'm seeking a good hairdresser.

seem /siːm/ VERB [seems, seeming, seemed] to appear to be something □ *He seemed very pleased to see you.* ⊞ *She seemed like a very nice young woman.* ⊞ *It seems likely that he will be in hospital for several weeks.* □ *It seems strange we haven't heard from him.* □ **+ to do something** *Nothing seems to worry him.*

➤ THESAURUS: If something seems to be true, or appears to be true, you think that it is probably true, although you cannot be sure. If something sounds or looks good, bad, etc., it seems that way from what you have heard or read.

seen /siːn/ PAST PARTICIPLE OF **see**

seize /siːz/ VERB [seizes, seizing, seized] to take something into your hand quickly and firmly □ *Joel seized my hand and shook it.*

seldom /ˈseldəm/ ADVERB not often □ *He seldom travelled abroad.* □ *A teacher's job is seldom an easy one.*

select /sɪˈlekt/ VERB [selects, selecting, selected] to choose someone or something □ *She selected some items and went to pay for them.* □ **+ for** *Hawthorne has been selected for the Olympic hockey team.*

selection /sɪˈlekʃən/ NOUN [*plural* selections] a range of things that you can choose from ⊞ *The shop has a wide selection of boots and shoes.*

self /self/ NOUN [*plural* selves] your character ⊞ *He was worried about revealing his true self to her.*

self-confidence /ˌselfˈkɒnfɪdəns/ NOUN, NO PLURAL being sure of yourself and your own abilities

self-confident /ˌselfˈkɒnfɪdənt/ ADJECTIVE sure of yourself and your own abilities

selfish /ˈselfɪʃ/ ADJECTIVE thinking only about yourself and not about what other people might want or need □ *He's a very selfish person.* □ *I decided to stay for purely selfish reasons.*

self-service /ˌselfˈsɜːvɪs/ ADJECTIVE involving customers getting or doing something themselves □ *a self-service restaurant* □ *The airline provides a self-service check-in.*

sell /sel/ VERB [sells, selling, sold]
1 to give someone something in exchange for money □ **+ for** *They sold the house for £450,000.* □ **+ to** *She sold the business to a Chinese company.* □ *He sold me his bike.*
2 to have something available for people to buy □ *The shop sells handmade chocolates.* □ *Do you sell batteries?*
◆ PHRASAL VERB **sell out** **1** if a shop sells out of something, there is none of it left for people to buy □ *I'm sorry, we've sold out of milk.* **2** if something sells out, there is none left for people to buy □ *When I got there, all the tickets had sold out.*

seller /ˈselə(r)/ NOUN [*plural* sellers] someone who is selling something □ *ticket sellers*

semicircle /ˈsemɪsɜːkəl/ NOUN [*plural* semicircles] half a circle

semicolon /ˌsemɪˈkəʊlən/ NOUN [*plural* semicolons] a mark (;) used to separate different parts of a sentence or list

semi-final /ˌsemɪˈfaɪnəl/ NOUN [*plural* semi-finals] one of the two games in a competition which are played just before the last game ⊞ *Sweden reached the semi-final of the 1994 World Cup.*

send /send/ VERB [sends, sending, sent]
1 to arrange for something to go somewhere □ *He sent me an e-mail.* □ *Sophia sent him a birthday card.* □ **+ to** *I sent a text message to my Dad.*
2 to make someone go somewhere ⊞ *He was sent home from school because he was sick.* □ **+ to** *The doctor took one look and sent me straight to hospital.* □ *The government sent a team of rescue workers to the area.*
◆ PHRASAL VERBS **send for someone** to ask for someone to come to you □ *They sent for a doctor.*
send off for something to write to an organization and ask them to send you something □ *I sent off for a catalogue.*

senior[1] /ˈsiːnɪə(r)/ ADJECTIVE
1 having a higher position in an organization □ *senior government officials* □ *She has a very senior position in the company.*
2 older □ *senior members of the family* □ *senior players*

senior[2] /ˈsiːnɪə(r)/ NOUN [*plural* seniors] **be 5/10 etc. years someone's senior** to be 5/10 etc. years older than someone □ *My brother is six years my senior.*

sensation /sen'seɪʃən/ NOUN [plural sensations]
1 a physical feeling, or the ability to have physical feelings □ *He had a burning sensation in his chest.* 🔁 *She lost all sensation in the right side of her face.*
2 a state of excitement or shock □ *The announcement caused quite a sensation.*

sense¹ /sens/ NOUN [plural senses]
1 no plural a feeling or belief about someone or something □ *People need work that gives them a sense of achievement.* □ *They have created a sense of calm in the building.* □ *I got the sense that he was worried about something.*
2 one of the 5 abilities of sight, touch, taste, hearing and smell □ *Janet lost her sense of smell after an illness.*
3 no plural a natural quality 🔁 *I don't think he has much of a sense of humour.* □ *She has a great sense of style.*
4 no plural the ability to understand things and make sensible decisions 🔁 *Someone had the sense to call an ambulance.* 🔁 *We were grateful for her good sense.*
5 the meaning of a word or of speech or writing □ *A single English word can have lots of different senses.* □ *You only have to understand the general sense of the passage.*
6 make sense to have a clear meaning □ *Her explanations didn't make sense.*

sense² /sens/ VERB [senses, sensing, sensed] to become aware of something without being told □ + **that** *I sensed that not many people agreed with what I was saying.*

sense of humour /ˌsens əv 'hjuːmə(r)/ NOUN, NO PLURAL your ability to understand things that are funny and to say funny things yourself □ *She's got a good sense of humour.*

sensible /'sensɪbəl/ ADJECTIVE showing good judgment and the ability to make good decisions □ *Lizzie's a very sensible girl.* 🔁 *a sensible decision* 🔁 *It's sensible to have insurance when you travel.*

➤ Note that **sensible** does not mean 'very easily offended or upset'. For this, use the word **sensitive**.

sensitive /'sensɪtɪv/ ADJECTIVE
1 being aware of other people's feelings and careful not to upset them □ *He's a very sensitive, caring young man.*
2 a sensitive situation or subject needs to be dealt with or spoken about carefully in order to avoid offending people □ *Mental health is a sensitive issue.*
3 very easily offended or upset □ *Jamie's very sensitive about being bald.* □ *She was very sensitive to criticism.*
4 very quickly and easily affected by something □ *Fair skin is usually very sensitive to the sun.*

sensor /'sensə(r)/ NOUN [plural sensors] a device that notices things such as heat, light or movement □ *A sensor on the front of the camera measures how much light is available.*

sent /sent/ PAST TENSE AND PAST PARTICIPLE OF **send**

sentence /'sentəns/ NOUN [plural sentences]
1 a group of words that usually includes a verb and expresses a statement or question □ *He hadn't finished his sentence before she interrupted him.*
2 the punishment that a judge gives to someone who has committed a crime 🔁 *Floyd received a five year prison sentence.* 🔁 *He is serving a life sentence* (= in prison for the rest of his life) *for killing a police officer.* 🔁 *Two of the killers were given a death sentence* (= a punishment of death).

separate¹ /'sepərət/ ADJECTIVE
1 different and not the same 🔁 *This is a completely separate matter.* □ *The children have separate bedrooms.*
2 not touching something else or not joined to it □ + **from** *Cycle paths keep bikes separate from traffic.*
• **separately** /'sepərətlɪ/ ADVERB not together □ *Each of the suspects was interviewed separately by the police.*

separate² /'sepəreɪt/ VERB [separates, separating, separated]
1 to divide something into different parts □ + **into** *The class was separated into two teams.* □ + **from** *This article about his life separates fact from fiction.*
2 to be between two things so that they do not touch each other □ *The north and the south are separated by a range of high mountains.* □ + **from** *Only a thin camping mat separated me from the hard ground.*
3 to keep people apart from each other □ *A teacher had to separate the boys who were fighting.*

September /sep'tembə(r)/ NOUN [plural Septembers] the ninth month of the year, after August and before October □ *School starts again in September.*

sequel /'siːkwəl/ NOUN [plural sequels] a book, play or film that continues an earlier story

sequence /'siːkwəns/ NOUN [plural sequences] a series of things that happen one after the other 🔁 *It was a remarkable sequence of events.*

sergeant /'sɑːdʒənt/ NOUN [plural sergeants]
1 an officer of middle rank in the police □ *Sergeant Adam Cragg was the officer in charge.*
2 an officer of middle rank in the army

series /'sɪəriːz/ NOUN [plural series]
1 a series of something several similar things that happen or are done one after the other □ *a series of accidents* □ *They held a series of meetings.*
2 a set of television or radio programmes with the same subject or the same characters 🔁 *They're*

filming a new TV series. □ *a comedy series* □ *+ of an old series of 'Cheers'*

serious /'sɪərɪəs/ ADJECTIVE

1 very bad ⏧ *a serious accident* ⏧ *serious injuries* ⏧ *Noy was involved in several killings and other serious crimes.*

2 important and needing attention ⏧ *The report raises serious questions about the quality of education.* ⏧ *Obesity is becoming a serious health issue.*

3 meaning what you are saying and not joking or pretending □ *I can never tell when he's joking and when he's being serious.* □ *+ about Are you serious about becoming a teacher?*

4 a serious person is sensible, quiet, and does not laugh much □ *William was a very serious little boy.*

seriously /'sɪərɪəslɪ/ ADVERB

1 very badly ⏧ *Her father is seriously ill.* ⏧ *Jan was seriously injured in the accident.*

2 in a way that shows you think something is important ⏧ *We're taking these threats very seriously.*

sermon /'sɜːmən/ NOUN [*plural* sermons] a speech that a priest makes in a church

servant /'sɜːvənt/ NOUN [*plural* servants] someone who works in a big house and does jobs such as cooking and cleaning for the person who owns the house

serve /sɜːv/ VERB [serves, serving, served]

1 to give someone food or drink □ *I'll serve the soup and you can give out the spoons.* □ *Serve the cheese with crusty bread.*

2 to sell things to customers in a shop □ *Are you being served?*

3 to work for a person or an organization □ *Brown had served the family for fifty years.* □ *As a soldier, he served in Egypt.* □ *+ as He served as treasurer for three years.*

4 to provide something for people or an area □ *This hospital serves nearly a million local people.* □ *There is no bus network serving these villages.*

5 serve someone right if a bad situation or result serves you right, you deserve it □ *If you're sick, it serves you right for eating too much chocolate.*

service /'sɜːvɪs/ NOUN [*plural* services]

1 a system to provide something that people need, or an organization that provides it □ *There have been cuts in mental health services.* □ *The firm has promised to improve the bus service.* ⏧ *The charity provides basic services to homeless people.* ⏧ *We are offering a free e-mail service.*

2 *no plural* the help that someone gives you in a place such as a hotel or shop □ *I love the things they sell, but the service is awful.*

3 *no plural* the period of time that you work for a business or organization □ *She resigned after 25 years' service in the company.* ⏧ *He has 30 years of military service.*

4 a religious ceremony ⏧ *The queen attended a service to remember the dead.*

5 the services a country's military organizations

session /'seʃən/ NOUN [*plural* sessions] a period of time that is used for doing something □ *He missed last night's training session.*

set¹ /set/ VERB [sets, setting, set]

1 to put something somewhere □ *Set the tray down on the table.*

2 to decide the time or date of something ⏧ *Have they set a date for the meeting?* □ *The government has set a timetable for change.*

3 to decide on a level for something □ *Prices were set too high.* ⏧ *We need to set a limit on what we will spend.* ⏧ *The company has set new targets for growth.*

4 if a book, film, etc. is set somewhere, that is where the story happens □ *Her first novel is set in Berlin.*

5 to make a piece of equipment ready to work at a particular time □ *Don't forget to set the DVD to record.* ⏧ *Did you set the alarm?*

6 the sun sets when it goes down

7 if a teacher sets work or sets an exam, they tell the students to do it □ *The teacher doesn't set my children enough homework.*

8 set an example to behave in a way that other people may copy □ *I try to set the children a good example by wearing my cycle helmet.*

9 set someone/something free to allow a person or an animal to leave of the place where they are being kept

10 if a substance sets, it becomes solid □ *Wait an hour or so for the jelly to set.*

◆ PHRASAL VERBS **set off** to start a journey □ *We need to set off early tomorrow.* **set out** to start a journey □ *We set out after breakfast.* **set something up** to start a business, organization or group □ *A tribunal was set up to hear the case.* □ *He set up his firm in 2003.*

set² /set/ NOUN [*plural* sets]

1 a group of people or things that belong together or are used together □ *a set of chairs* □ *a chess set*

2 a radio or television □ *We have a technical problem; please do not adjust your set.*

3 the place where actors perform in a play, film, etc. □ *He had to wear the wig all the time on set.*

setback /'setbæk/ NOUN [*plural* setbacks] a problem that stops you making progress ⏧ *The project suffered a major setback when the manager resigned.*

setting /'setɪŋ/ NOUN [*plural* settings] the place where something is or where something happens □ *The hotel is the perfect setting for a wedding reception.*

settle /'setəl/ VERB [settles, settling, settled]

1 if you settle an argument, you end it by agreeing something □ *I wish they would settle their differences.* □ *The case was settled out of court.*

2 to decide on something or to arrange something

🔯 *That settles it – I'm leaving!* 🔯 *That's settled – we'll all meet next Tuesday.*

3 to become relaxed and comfortable in a situation □ *Harry settled into his armchair and fell asleep.* □ *Settle back and enjoy the show!*

4 to go somewhere and make your home there □ *The family settled in New South Wales.* □ *They may not settle permanently in the UK.*

5 to pay money that you owe □ *The bill can be settled in cash or with a cheque.* 🔯 *This money helped us settle our debts.*

◆ PHRASAL VERBS **settle down** to start to live a life with less change, for example by staying somewhere for a long time or staying in a relationship □ *I'm not ready to settle down and have kids yet.* **settle (someone) down** to become calm or make someone calm after being nervous or excited □ *Settle down now, it's time to do some work.* **settle in** to start to feel happy and confident in a new situation □ *She's finding it difficult to settle in at her new school.*

settlement /'setəlmənt/ NOUN [*plural* settlements]

1 an agreement that ends an argument 🔯 *The two sides have failed to reach a settlement.* 🔯 *a divorce settlement*

2 a place where people have come and built homes □ *New settlements have grown up in the desert.*

seven /'sevən/ NUMBER [*plural* sevens] the number 7

seventeen /ˌsevən'tiːn/ NUMBER the number 17
seventeenth /ˌsevən'tiːnθ/ NUMBER 17th written as a word

seventh[1] /'sevənθ/ NUMBER 7th written as a word □ *the seventh day of the week*

seventh[2] /'sevənθ/ NOUN [*plural* sevenths] 1/7; one of seven equal parts of something

seventieth /'sevəntɪəθ/ NUMBER 70th written as a word
seventy /'sevəntɪ/ NUMBER [*plural* seventies]
1 the number 70
2 the seventies the years between 1970 and 1979

several /'sevərəl/ DETERMINER, PRONOUN more than a few but not a lot □ *I met him several years ago.* □ *Several people admired her dress.* □ *+ of Several of my friends have dogs.* □ *Would you like one of these leaflets? I've got several.*

➤ If you want to say 'a very small number' do not use the word **several**. Instead, use the phrase **a few**:
✓ *I've got a lot of friends but only a few close friends.*
✗ *I've got a lot of friends but only several close friends.*

severe /sɪ'vɪə(r)/ ADJECTIVE
1 very bad □ *severe weather conditions* □ *He suffered severe head injuries in the accident.* □ *She has severe health problems.*
2 extreme □ *severe punishments* □ *severe criticism*
3 not friendly or kind □ *a severe expression*

➤ THESAURUS: A severe person is not friendly or kind. A strict person expects people to obey their rules. A teacher might be strict with pupils, for example. A tough person is physically or mentally strong. A difficult person is not friendly or easy to please.

sew /səʊ/ VERB [sews, sewing, sewed, sewn] to use a needle and thread to join things together □ *He sewed the button back on his shirt.*

sex /seks/ NOUN [*plural* sexes]
1 *no plural* the act in which a man puts his penis into a woman's vagina □ *sex education*
2 the fact of being male or female □ *It is now technically possible for couples to choose the sex of their baby.* □ *There are laws against sex discrimination.*

sexual /'sekʃuəl/ ADJECTIVE
1 to do with or involving the activity of sex □ *a sexual relationship* □ *sexual behaviour*
2 to do with the differences between men and women □ *sexual equality*

shade[1] /ʃeɪd/ NOUN [*plural* shades]
1 *no plural* an area which is cooler and darker because there is no light from the sun □ *He was lying in the shade of a tree.* □ *On hot days I prefer sitting in the shade.* □ *This plant prefers shade.*
2 an object that goes around a light and prevents the light being too bright □ *a lamp with a purple shade*
3 a particular type of a colour □ *+ of The wall was painted in a deep shade of green.*

shade[2] /ʃeɪd/ VERB [shades, shading, shaded] to protect something from the sun □ *A row of trees shaded the path.*

shadow /'ʃædəʊ/ NOUN [*plural* shadows] a dark shape on a surface caused when an object is between the surface and a bright light □ *There was a shadow on the wall.* 🔯 *The candle cast shadows around the room.*

➤ THESAURUS: A shadow is a dark shape on a surface caused when an object is between the surface and a bright light. Shade is an area which is cooler and darker because there is no light from the sun. For example, you might sit in the shade on a very hot day. A shelter is a building or other structure that provides protection from harm or bad weather. For example you might sit in a shelter while you are waiting for a bus.

shady /ˈʃeɪdɪ/ ADJECTIVE [shadier, shadiest] a shady place has little light because it is covered by something □ *The plant will grow best in a shady spot.*

shake¹ /ʃeɪk/ VERB [shakes, shaking, shook, shaken]
1 to make many quick small movements from side to side or up and down □ *The whole area shook when the bomb landed.* □ *Mina was shaking with fear.* □ *His hands were shaking as he tried to sign his name.*
2 to make something move quickly from side to side or up and down several times □ *The wind was shaking the trees and rattling the windows.* □ *A huge explosion shook the building.* □ *Shake the bottle before opening.*
3 shake your head to move your head from side to side as a way of saying 'no' □ *I asked if she was coming and he just shook his head.*
4 shake hands to hold someone's hand and move it up and down when you meet them for the first time or when making an agreement □ *He shook hands with the Prime Minister.* □ *We shook hands and the deal was done.*

> ► **THESAURUS:** If something or someone shakes, they make many quick small movements from side to side or up and down. If someone shivers or trembles, they shake slightly because they are frightened. You can also shiver if you are cold or ill. If something sways it moves slowly from side to side. Trees sway in the wind.

shake² /ʃeɪk/ NOUN [plural shakes] a quick movement from side to side or backwards and forwards ⊞ *Give the bottle a quick shake.*

shall /ʃæl/ MODAL VERB
1 used to make a suggestion or an offer □ *Shall we play chess?* □ *Shall I open the window?*
2 how/what/when, etc. shall used to ask someone what to do □ *What shall I cook for dinner?* □ *When shall we phone him?*
3 used as a formal way of saying what you will do in the future □ *I shall make an official complaint.* □ *I shall never forget this moment.*

shallow /ˈʃæləʊ/ ADJECTIVE [shallower, shallowest] not deep ⊞ *shallow water* ⊞ *The children were playing in the shallow end of the pool.* □ *The lake was quite shallow.* □ *a shallow dish*

shame /ʃeɪm/ NOUN, NO PLURAL
1 it's/what a shame used when saying that you are disappointed about something □ *What a shame that you can't come to the party.* □ *It's a shame we can't stay longer.* □ *It would be a great shame if you had to give up playing the violin.*
2 the embarrassing feeling you have when you know you have done something wrong ⊞ *Emma felt a sense of shame about the things she had done.*

□ **+ of** *He had suffered the shame of being arrested in front of his friends.*

shampoo /ʃæmˈpuː/ NOUN [plural shampoos] liquid soap used especially for washing your hair □ *a bottle of shampoo*

shan't /ʃɑːnt/ a short way to say and write shall not □ *I shan't be late.*

shape¹ /ʃeɪp/ NOUN [plural shapes]
1 the form that is made by the outer edge of something □ *She made a cake in the shape of a piano.* □ *His body has changed shape dramatically.* □ *The children stuck coloured shapes onto the card.* □ *What shape is the window?*
2 the health or condition of someone or something ⊞ *The team is in good shape for Saturday's match.* ⊞ *He leaves the company in better shape than he found it.* ⊞ *I'm getting a bit out of shape* (= not strong and healthy). ⊞ *He runs every day to keep in shape* (= stay strong and healthy).

shape² /ʃeɪp/ VERB [shapes, shaping, shaped] to make something a particular shape □ *He shapes the clay pots on the potter's wheel.*

share¹ /ʃeə(r)/ VERB [shares, sharing, shared]
1 to divide something between two or more people □ **+ between** *We had two pizzas to share between 7 people.* □ **+ among** *I shared the sweets among the children.*
2 to have or use something at the same time as someone else □ *There aren't enough books to go round so some of you will have to share.* □ *She shares a home with her elderly mother.* □ *We must all share the blame for the accident.*
3 to allow someone to have part of something that is yours or to use something that is yours □ *She kindly shared her lunch with me.* □ *William wouldn't share his toys.*
♦ PHRASAL VERB **share something out** to divide something between each person in a group □ *We shared out the food between us.*

share² /ʃeə(r)/ NOUN [plural shares]
1 a part of a total number or amount of something that is divided between people □ *I took my share of the cake.* ⊞ *We hope to increase our share of the market.* ⊞ *She wants a larger share of the profits.*
2 one of the equal parts of the value of a company that you can buy or sell □ **+ in** *She has shares in the bank.* ⊞ *I bought shares in his business.* ⊞ *Shares rose/fell* (= increased/lost value) *at the news.*

shareholder /ˈʃeəhəʊldə(r)/ NOUN [plural shareholders] someone who owns shares in a company

shark /ʃɑːk/ NOUN [plural sharks] a large sea fish with very sharp teeth

sharp¹ /ʃɑːp/ ADJECTIVE [sharper, sharpest]
1 having a thin edge or a pointed end that can cut things easily □ *a sharp knife* □ *sharp teeth*

2 a sharp decrease or increase is sudden and large ⊞ *There has been a sharp rise in crime.*
3 a sharp bend or turn is one that changes direction suddenly
4 a sharp pain is sudden, short and painful
5 a sharp image is clear □ *I can get a really sharp focus with this camera.*
6 clever and quick to notice things
7 if your hearing or eyesight (= how well you can see) is sharp, you can hear or see very well
8 showing anger □ *She received a sharp answer from her mother.*

sharp² /ʃɑːp/ NOUN [plural sharps] in written music, a sign (♯) that makes a note higher by half a note

sharp³ /ʃɑːp/ ADVERB
1 5 o'clock, 6.15, etc. sharp at exactly 5 o'clock, 6.15, etc.
2 with a sudden change of direction □ *Turn sharp left at the next set of traffic lights.*

sharpen /ˈʃɑːpən/ VERB [sharpens, sharpening, sharpened] to make something sharp or sharper □ *The lion was sharpening its claws on a tree.* □ *I need to sharpen this pencil.*

sharpener /ˈʃɑːpənə(r)/ NOUN [plural sharpeners] a device that you use to make pencils or knives sharp

sharply /ˈʃɑːplɪ/ ADVERB
1 suddenly and by a large amount ⊞ *Temperatures fall sharply at night.*
2 in a strong and angry way □ *The report sharply criticized his behaviour.*

shatter /ˈʃætə(r)/ VERB [shatters, shattering, shattered] to break into lots of very small pieces or to break something into lots of very small pieces □ *He dropped the glass and it shattered.* □ *The explosion shattered windows.*

shave¹ /ʃeɪv/ VERB [shaves, shaving, shaved] to use a razor (= thin, sharp piece of metal) to cut away hair that is growing on your face or body □ *He shaved and showered, then got dressed.* □ **+ off** *He shaved off his beard.*

shave² /ʃeɪv/ NOUN [plural shaves] when you shave □ *You need a shave and a haircut.*

shaver /ˈʃeɪvə(r)/ NOUN [plural shavers] an electrical tool for shaving hair

she /ʃiː/ PRONOUN used to talk or write about a woman, girl or female animal that has already been mentioned □ *Madeleine is funny. She really makes me laugh.*

shed¹ /ʃed/ NOUN [plural sheds] a simple wooden or metal building used for working in or for storing things ⊞ *a garden shed*
shed² /ʃed/ VERB [sheds, shedding, shed] to make or allow clothes, skin, leaves etc. to fall or drop off □ *Snakes shed their skin.*

she'd /ʃiːd/ a short way to say and write she had or she would □ *She'd forgotten her umbrella.* □ *She'd rather not say.*

sheep /ʃiːp/ NOUN [plural sheep] a farm animal with a thick wool coat ⊞ *a flock of sheep*

➤ Remember that the plural form of **sheep** is the same as the singular form: □ *He has a lot of sheep.*

sheer /ʃɪə(r)/ ADJECTIVE
1 used to emphasize the degree, size, strength, etc. of something □ *The sheer scale of the building is breathtaking.* □ *The first problem is the sheer size of the city.*
2 complete or only □ *It was sheer luck that no one was hurt.* □ *He ate four bags of crisps. It was just sheer greed.*
3 very steep or vertical ⊔ *There were sheer cliffs on either side of the beach.*

sheet /ʃiːt/ NOUN [plural sheets]
1 a large, flat piece of cloth used to cover a bed □ *I'll just change the sheets on your bed.*
2 a single piece of paper or a document on a single piece of paper □ **+ of** *an A4 sheet of paper* □ *She gave him a fact sheet about diabetes.*
3 a large thin flat piece of metal, plastic, glass, etc. □ **+ of** *a sheet of aluminium foil* □ *They covered it with a plastic sheet.*

shelf /ʃelf/ NOUN [plural shelves] a flat piece of wood, metal, etc. fixed horizontally to a wall or as part of a cupboard, used for putting things on □ *She stood on a chair to reach the top shelf of the kitchen cupboard.* ⊞ *He got a job stacking supermarket shelves.*

shell /ʃel/ NOUN [plural shells]
1 a hard covering on an egg or a nut □ *Remove the hard outer shell of the nut.*
2 a hard covering that protects the body of some sea creatures or other animals □ *a snail shell*

she'll /ʃiːl/ a short way to say and write she will □ She'll be back in a minute.

shelter[1] /ˈʃeltə(r)/ NOUN [plural shelters]
1 a building or other structure that provides protection from harm or bad weather □ an underground bomb shelter □ Earthquake victims are living in temporary shelters.
2 no plural protection from danger or bad weather ⊞ It was pouring with rain, so we took shelter in a shop doorway. □ The explosion sent people running for shelter.

shelter[2] /ˈʃeltə(r)/ VERB [shelters, sheltering, sheltered]
1 to stay in a place where you are protected from harm or bad weather □ We sheltered from the rain under a tree. □ Thirty people sheltered in the basement.
2 to protect someone from harm □ The family were accused of sheltering criminals.

shelves /ʃelvz/ PLURAL OF shelf
shepherd /ˈʃepəd/ NOUN [plural shepherds] someone whose job is to look after sheep
she's /ʃiːz/ a short way to say and write she is or she has □ She's my friend. □ She's always been my friend.
shield[1] /ʃiːld/ NOUN [plural shields] a large, flat object that is carried to protect someone's body from an attack □ They were faced by police carrying riot shields.
shield[2] /ʃiːld/ VERB [shields, shielding, shielded] to protect someone or something from harm or danger □ He had his hand over his eyes, shielding them from the strong sun.
shift[1] /ʃɪft/ VERB [shifts, shifting, shifted] to move something or to change position □ Tom shifted uncomfortably in his seat. □ She shifted her weight from foot to foot.
shift[2] /ʃɪft/ NOUN [plural shifts]
1 a change from one thing to another □ This represents a major shift in policy.
2 the period of time when one group of people works ⊞ The miners worked 12-hour shifts. ⊞ Who's on the night shift this week?
shift key /ˈʃɪft ˌkiː/ NOUN [plural shift keys] the key on a computer that allows you to write capital letters (= large letters, for example at the beginning of sentences). A computing word.

shine /ʃaɪn/ VERB [shines, shining, shone]
1 to send out or reflect light ⊞ The sun's shining – let's eat outside. □ We could see the lights of the city shining below us.
2 to point a light on something □ Don't shine your torch in my face.

3 to be bright and shiny □ She polished the pans until they shone.

shining /ˈʃaɪnɪŋ/ ADJECTIVE a shining example of something someone or something that is very good at something □ She's a shining example of growing old gracefully.

shiny /ˈʃaɪni/ ADJECTIVE [shinier, shiniest] with a smooth surface that reflects light □ shiny hair □ a shiny new bicycle

ship /ʃɪp/ NOUN [plural ships] a large boat that carries passengers or goods on sea journeys □ Her ship sails from Southampton tomorrow. □ They travelled from South Africa by ship.

shirt /ʃɜːt/ NOUN [plural shirts] a piece of clothing for the top half of your body, often made from cotton, with long or short sleeves, a collar, and buttons down the front

> ▶ THESAURUS: Both men and women wear shirts. A blouse is a woman's shirt. A T-shirt is a piece of clothing made from soft cotton which you wear on the top part of your body. A T-shirt can have long or short sleeves, but does not usually have buttons down the front.

shiver /ˈʃɪvə(r)/ VERB [shivers, shivering, shivered] to shake slightly because you are cold or frightened □ She shivered in her thin cotton dress.

shock[1] /ʃɒk/ NOUN [plural shocks]
1 no plural a strong and unpleasant reaction you have when something bad happens that you do not expect □ The whole town is in shock at the news of the closures. ⊞ You gave me such a shock bursting in like that! ⊞ I got quite a shock when I saw the bill.
2 something that happens and makes you very surprised or upset □ The news of his arrest was a terrible shock to his family.
3 a current of electricity that passes through your body ⊞ I got an electric shock when I unplugged the iron.

shock[2] /ʃɒk/ VERB [shocks, shocking, shocked] to surprise and upset someone very much □ I was shocked to see how ill he looked.

shocking /ˈʃɒkɪŋ/ ADJECTIVE making you feel surprised and upset □ The news report contained some shocking scenes of the war.

shoe /ʃuː/ NOUN [plural shoes] something made of leather or a similar material that you wear on your foot □ high-heeled shoes 🔁 a pair of shoes □ a shoe shop

shone /ʃɒn/ PAST TENSE AND PAST PARTICIPLE OF **shine**
shook /ʃuk/ PAST TENSE OF **shake**[1]

shoot[1] /ʃuːt/ VERB [shoots, shooting, shot]
1 to fire a gun or other weapon □ I shot an arrow in the air. □ Stop or I'll shoot!
2 to kill or injure a person or animal with a gun □ He had been shot three times in the chest. 🔁 A passer-by was shot dead in the incident.
3 to go somewhere very quickly □ The rocket shot up into the air. □ Pain shot through his body.
4 to make a film or video, or take a photograph □ They're shooting some scenes at Alnwick Castle.

shoot[2] /ʃuːt/ NOUN [plural shoots] a new part of a plant or a very young plant □ bamboo shoots

shop[1] /ʃɒp/ NOUN [plural shops] a place where goods are sold or a particular service is provided □ a flower shop □ We spent the afternoon going around the shops at the mall.

➤ **THESAURUS:** Shop is a general word for a place where goods are sold or a particular service is provided. A store is the same as a shop. The word store is more common in American English. A department store is a large shop that has different departments which sell different types of product. A supermarket is a large shop that sells food and other goods.

shop[2] /ʃɒp/ VERB [shops, shopping, shopped] to buy things in shops □ I hate shopping for clothes.

shop assistant /ʃɒp əˌsɪstənt/ NOUN [plural shop assistants] someone who sells things and looks after customers in a shop

shopkeeper /ˈʃɒpkiːpə(r)/ NOUN [plural shopkeepers] someone who owns or manages a shop

shopping /ˈʃɒpɪŋ/ NOUN, NO PLURAL
1 the activity of going around shops to buy things 🔁 Let's go shopping tomorrow.
2 the things you buy at the shops □ Can you get the shopping out of the boot?

shopping centre /ˈʃɒpɪŋ ˌsentə(r)/ NOUN [plural shopping centres] an area or large building with a lot of different shops

shore /ʃɔː(r)/ NOUN [plural shores] the area of land next to the sea or next to a lake

short /ʃɔːt/ ADJECTIVE [shorter, shortest]
1 small in height, length or distance □ a short skirt □ The school is a short walk from here. □ She has short hair. □ My brother is very short
2 continuing for a small period of time □ We watched a short film about whales. □ We'll take a short break now.
3 not having many words or pages □ Can you give us a short description of the house? □ It's quite a short book.
4 not having enough of something □ + of The troops are short of equipment. 🔁 Water was in short supply.
5 be short for something to be a shorter way of saying or writing something □ 'Jon' is short for 'Jonathan'.

shortage /ˈʃɔːtɪdʒ/ NOUN [plural shortages] when there is not enough of something □ People in the region face severe food shortages.
shorten /ˈʃɔːtən/ VERB [shortens, shortening, shortened] to make something shorter or to become shorter □ We're working hard to shorten the waiting list for the operation. □ The days are shortening.
shortly /ˈʃɔːtlɪ/ ADVERB
1 soon □ We'll shortly be arriving at Waverley Station.
2 shortly before/after within a short period of time before or after something □ The bomb exploded shortly before midday.

shorts /ʃɔːts/ PLURAL NOUN
1 short trousers that stop above your knees □ a pair of shorts
2 a mainly US word for underwear for men

shot[1] /ʃɒt/ NOUN [plural shots]
1 the act of firing a gun or the sound of it being fired □ I heard a shot out in the street. 🔁 Someone took a shot at me!
2 a kick, hit or throw of the ball to try to score a point or points □ It was an excellent shot that just missed the goal.

3 a photograph or an image in a film □ *I managed to get some good shots of the mountains.*

shot[2] /ʃɒt/ PAST TENSE AND PAST PARTICIPLE OF **shoot**[1]

should /ʃʊd/ MODAL VERB
1 used to say what is the best or right thing to do □ *He said that we should all go home.* □ *Should I write her a letter?* □ *You shouldn't eat too much chocolate.*
2 used to say that you expect something to be true □ *The train should be arriving in a couple of minutes.* □ *The children should be asleep by eight.*
3 should have used to say what would have been the right thing to do when you have done something different □ *I should have helped him.* □ *I'm late – I should have taken a taxi.*

shoulder /'ʃəʊldə(r)/ NOUN [plural shoulders]
one of the two parts of your body between your neck and your arms

shouldn't /'ʃʊdənt/ a short way to say and write should not □ *You shouldn't wait out in the rain.*
should've /'ʃʊdəv/ a short way to say and write should have □ *You should've seen him!*

shout[1] /ʃaʊt/ VERB [shouts, shouting, shouted] to say something very loudly or to make a loud noise with your voice □ *Someone was shouting my name.* □ *There's no need to shout.* □ *+ at* *She's always shouting at the children.*

shout[2] /ʃaʊt/ NOUN [plural shouts] a loud cry or call □ *There were shouts of approval from the crowd.*

shove /ʃʌv/ VERB [shoves, shoving, shoved] to push someone or something hard or roughly □ *Someone shoved me in the back.*
shovel /'ʃʌvəl/ NOUN [plural shovels] a tool for digging or moving earth, sand, snow, etc. □ *a garden shovel*

show[1] /ʃəʊ/ VERB [shows, showing, showed, shown]
1 to prove that something exists or is true □ *+ that* *The evidence shows that he could not have committed the crime.* □ *Polls show an increase in support for the president.* 🔁 *This incident shows why it is important to follow safety regulations.*
2 to allow someone to see something or to cause them to see it □ *Show me your new bike.* □ *Young people were shown images of knife wounds.* □ *His website shows pictures of him with his family.*
3 to express your feelings □ *I try to show an interest in his work.* □ *The man showed no emotion as the judge read his sentence.*
4 to tell someone where to go or where someone is, by explaining, pointing or taking them there □ *I*

showed her where to put her coat. □ *+ to* *I'll show you to your room.*
5 to allow someone to watch you doing something so that they learn how to do it □ *Can you show me how to work the DVD player?*
6 to be able to be noticed □ *The scar hardly shows.* □ *I tried not to let my disappointment show.*
♦ PHRASAL VERBS **show off** to behave in a way that makes people notice you, or to talk a lot about something that you own, because you want people to admire you □ *He's always showing off about his cars.*
show up to arrive □ *She showed up an hour late.*

show[2] /ʃəʊ/ NOUN [plural shows]
1 a performance in the theatre or on radio or television □ *He is starring in a new comedy show on the BBC.*
2 an event where people or businesses can show things to the public □ *We went to a boat show.* □ *a fashion show*
3 on show able to be seen □ *Some of her statues are on show in New York.*

shower /'ʃaʊə(r)/ NOUN [plural showers]
1 a piece of bathroom equipment that produces a flow of water that you stand under to wash yourself □ *Adam's in the shower.*
2 an act of washing yourself under a shower 🔁 *I had a shower to cool off.*
3 a short period of rain □ *We got caught in a shower.*

shown /ʃəʊn/ PAST PARTICIPLE OF **show**[1]
shrank /ʃræŋk/ PAST TENSE OF **shrink**
shriek /ʃriːk/ VERB [shrieks, shrieking, shrieked] to make a loud high noise or speak in a loud high voice because you are afraid, excited, etc. □ *She shrieked when she saw the mouse.* □ *'Watch out!' he shrieked.*
shrine /ʃraɪn/ NOUN [plural shrines] a religious place where people go to pray, often because it has something to do with a holy person □ *a shrine to the Virgin Mary*
shrink /ʃrɪŋk/ VERB [shrinks, shrinking, shrank, shrunk] to get smaller or to make something smaller in size, amount or value □ *My sweater shrank in the wash.* □ *The number of honey bees has shrunk dramatically.*
shrug /ʃrʌg/ VERB [shrugs, shrugging, shrugged] to raise and lower your shoulders in a movement that shows you do not know something or that you do not care about it 🔁 *She shrugged her shoulders and said 'I don't mind.'*

> ► **THESAURUS:** If you shrug your shoulders, you raise and lower your shoulders in a movement that shows you do not know something or that you do not care about it. If you nod your head, you move it up and down, especially to agree or to say 'yes'. If you shake your head, you move it from side to side as a way of saying 'no'.

shrunk /ʃrʌŋk/ PAST PARTICIPLE OF **shrink**

shudder /'ʃʌdə(r)/ VERB [shudders, shuddering, shuddered] to shake suddenly, usually because of shock or disgust □ *She shuddered when she thought of his injuries.*

shuffle /'ʃʌfəl/ VERB [shuffles, shuffling, shuffled]
1 to walk slowly, sliding your feet along the ground without lifting them □ *The old woman shuffled slowly into the hall.*
2 to mix up a set of playing cards before playing a game □ *Whose turn is it to shuffle?*

shut¹ /ʃʌt/ VERB [shuts, shutting, shut]
1 to close something or to become closed □ *Could you please shut the window? □ I heard the door shut as he left. □ She shut her eyes and tried to remember his face.*
2 to close a business for the day or for a short period of time □ *The shop shuts at 6 every evening*
♦ PHRASAL VERBS **shut (something) down** if a business, factory, shop etc. shuts down, or if someone shuts it down, it closes □ *The factory shut down several years ago.* **shut (someone) up** an informal word meaning to stop talking or make someone stop talking □ *I wish he'd shut up for once. □ Once she gets on to the old days, nothing will shut her up.*

shut² /ʃʌt/ ADJECTIVE
1 closed □ *All the windows were shut.*
2 if a business is shut, it has closed for the day or for a short period of time □ *The swimming pool is shut for repairs.*

shuttle /'ʃʌtəl/ NOUN [plural shuttles] an air, train or other transport service that goes backwards and forwards between two places □ *There's a shuttle bus to the airport.*

shy /ʃaɪ/ ADJECTIVE [shyer, shyest] nervous and not confident when meeting and speaking to people ⮥ *My brother is painfully shy (= very shy).*

sibling /'sɪblɪŋ/ NOUN [plural siblings] a brother or sister □ *Most younger children tend to copy their older siblings.*

sick /sɪk/ ADJECTIVE [sicker, sickest]
1 sick people or animals are ill □ *He looks after his sick mother.* ⮥ *I got sick on holiday.*
2 feel sick to feel as if you are going to vomit □ *The smell made me feel physically sick.*
3 be sick to vomit ⮥ *He was violently sick.*
4 off sick not at work because you are ill
5 sick of something/someone an informal phrase meaning angry about something or bored with something □ *I'm sick of having to do all his work for him. □ I'm sick of salad – can't we have a hot meal?*
6 make someone sick (a) to make someone angry and upset □ *It makes me sick the way she expects everyone to do what she wants all the time.* (b) to

make someone very jealous □ *She does everything well – it makes me sick!*

sickness /'sɪknɪs/ NOUN, NO PLURAL when someone is ill □ *He had a lot of time off work due to sickness.*

side /saɪd/ NOUN [plural sides]
1 the outer surface or edge of something, especially one that is not the top, bottom, front or back □ *He built a house by the side of the river. □ Go round the side of the building. □ Write on both sides of the paper. □ We sat on opposite sides of the table.* ⮥ *The two soldiers stood on either side of (= both sides of) the king.*
2 the area of something that is near the edge □ *Could you move to the side, please? □ He put the pasta to one side and started making the sauce.*
3 one of the parts or areas of something when it is divided □ *In the UK, people drive on the left hand side of the road. □ We live in the north side of town.* ⮥ *Australia is on the other side of the world.*
4 an edge or flat surface of a shape □ *How many sides does a hexagon have?*
5 the left or right part of someone's body □ *She stood by his side all day. □ Could you lie on your side, please?*
6 side by side next to each other □ *They sat side by side on the sofa.*
7 one of the people or groups who are arguing □ *Both sides agree that discussions are needed.*
8 one of the teams in a competition □ *He was chosen to captain the England side.*
9 if you are on someone's side, you support them in an argument ⮥ *Why do you always take Mum's side?*

sidewalk /'saɪdwɔːk/ NOUN [plural sidewalks] the US word for **pavement**

siege /siːdʒ/ NOUN [plural sieges] a situation in which an army surrounds a place and stops supplies from getting in or people from getting out □ *The port was under siege.*

sigh¹ /saɪ/ VERB [sighs, sighing, sighed] to breathe out noisily, because you feel tired, disappointed, unhappy, etc. □ *She sighed wearily as she looked at the pile of ironing she had to do.*

sigh² /saɪ/ NOUN [plural sighs] a long noisy breath out, often because you are tired, disappointed, unhappy, etc. □ *'I'm afraid there's still no news,' he said with a sigh.* ⮥ *When Phil finally got home we all breathed a huge sigh of relief.*

sight /saɪt/ NOUN [plural sights]
1 no plural the ability to see □ *He lost his sight in an explosion.*
2 no plural when you see something □ *He fainted at the sight of blood.* ⮥ *I caught sight of him, hurrying round a corner.*
3 no plural the place or area you are able to see □ *We watched the ship until it disappeared from sight.* ⮥ *We waved until their car was out of sight.*

4 something that you see □ *Foxes are a familiar sight round here.* □ *I'll never forget the sight of all those people waving flags.*
5 the sights interesting places to visit in a country or area □ *He offered to show me the sights of Hong Kong.*

→ go to **lose sight of something**

sightseeing /ˈsaɪtsiːɪŋ/ NOUN, NO PLURAL
travelling around looking at interesting things and places □ *The hotel organized a sightseeing trip to the Roman amphitheatre.*

sign¹ /saɪn/ NOUN [plural signs]
1 something that shows that something is happening or will happen or that something exists □ **+ of** *There is no sign of spring arriving yet.* □ **+ that** *There are signs that the economy is recovering.* 🖽 *My boss is showing signs of stress.* 🖽 *I can't see much sign of progress.* 🖽 *The fact that he is eating well is a good sign.*
2 an object in a public place with words, symbols or pictures that give information □ *The sign said 'No smoking'.* □ *Follow the signs to the car park.*
3 a symbol with a particular meaning □ *a dollar sign*

sign² /saɪn/ VERB [signs, signing, signed] to write your name on something, for example to agree officially to something, or to prove that something was done by you □ *Please sign the contract and return it to us.* □ *The letter was not signed.* □ *The painting is a signed original.*

signal¹ /ˈsɪgnəl/ NOUN [plural signals] a sign, action or sound that sends a message to someone 🖽 *When I give the signal, turn on the music.* □ **+ to do something** *The troops waited for the signal to attack.*

signal² /ˈsɪgnəl/ VERB [signals, signalling/US signaling, signalled/US signaled] to make a sign, sound or movement to tell someone something □ *You must signal well before the junction.* □ **+ to** *Jo was signalling to us from across the room.*

signature /ˈsɪgnətʃə(r)/ NOUN [plural signatures] your name, written by you, for example on the bottom of a letter or on a document □ *Someone had forged my signature on the form.*

significance /sɪgˈnɪfɪkəns/ NOUN, NO PLURAL the meaning or importance of something □ *I didn't understand the significance of what he said at the time.*

significant /sɪgˈnɪfɪkənt/ ADJECTIVE large or important □ *A significant number of children are failing to reach the required standard.* □ *She is now recognized as one of the most significant novelists of the 20th century.*

signpost /ˈsaɪnpəʊst/ NOUN [plural signposts] a sign by a road showing which direction to go to get to a particular place

silence /ˈsaɪləns/ NOUN [plural silences]
1 *no plural* when it is completely quiet and no sound can be heard □ *For a moment there was absolute silence in the theatre.*
2 a period when there is no sound or no one speaks □ *The players observed two minutes' silence for their former teammate.*

silent /ˈsaɪlənt/ ADJECTIVE
1 not speaking or making any noise 🖽 *The crowd fell silent.*
2 completely quiet □ *the silent churchyard*

silk /sɪlk/ NOUN [plural silks] a soft smooth cloth made from the very soft thin threads produced by a special insect (called a silkworm) □ *The dress was made of ivory silk.* □ *a silk kimono*

silver¹ /ˈsɪlvə(r)/ NOUN [plural silvers]
1 *no plural* a valuable shiny grey metal, used to make jewellery □ *This tray is made of solid silver.*
2 a silver medal (= prize for coming second in a competition or race)

silver² /ˈsɪlvə(r)/ ADJECTIVE
1 made of silver □ *a pair of silver earrings*
2 having the colour of silver □ *silver paint*

similar /ˈsɪmɪlə(r)/ ADJECTIVE two things are similar when they are like each other but not exactly the same □ **+ to** *An alligator is similar to a crocodile, but smaller.*

similarity /ˌsɪmɪˈlærəti/ NOUN [plural similarities] a characteristic that two people or things share □ *There are several similarities between the two novels.*

simmer /ˈsɪmə(r)/ VERB [simmers, simmering, simmered] to cook food slowly by boiling it very gently

simple /ˈsɪmpəl/ ADJECTIVE [simpler, simplest]
1 easy to do, solve or understand □ *a simple sum* □ *The dishwasher came with a set of simple instructions.* □ *This mobile phone is very simple to use.*
2 basic or not complicated □ *Stone Age men could make simple tools.* □ *The simple truth is he's too old for the job.*
3 plain or without any decoration □ *a simple design* □ *I like simple home cooking.*

simply /ˈsɪmpli/ ADVERB
1 only □ *Now, it's simply a question of waiting until something happens.*
2 in a way that is not difficult or complicated □ *I'll explain it simply so that you all understand.*
3 with no decorations or extra details □ *a simply furnished apartment*

sin /sɪn/ NOUN [plural sins] a very bad thing to do, especially one that breaks a religious law □ the sin of pride 🖰 He felt that he had committed a sin.

since¹ /sɪns/ CONJUNCTION

1 from a particular time or event in the past until the present □ Ann's been a lot happier since she changed jobs. □ He's put on weight since I saw him last.
2 because □ I decided to go shopping, since I had some free time.

since² /sɪns/ ADVERB

1 from the time that has already been mentioned until the present □ She joined the choir last month and has been going to practice regularly since. 🖰 I came to London in 1995, and I've lived here ever since.
2 at a later time than the time first mentioned □ They met last year and have since become friends.

since³ /sɪns/ PREPOSITION from a particular time in the past until the present □ The little girl has been missing since Christmas. □ We've been living here since 1986. □ I haven't spoken to Gretta since last week.

sincere /sɪn'sɪə(r)/ ADJECTIVE honest and saying what you really think □ I'm never sure he's being sincere with me.

sincerely /sɪn'sɪəlɪ/ ADVERB

1 in a way that is sincere □ I sincerely hope you're right about this.
2 Yours sincerely used at the end of a letter when you have used the name of the person you are writing to

sing /sɪŋ/ VERB [sings, singing, sang, sung] to make musical sounds with your voice □ She sings in a choir. □ I asked him to sing my favourite song.

singer /'sɪŋə(r)/ NOUN [plural singers] a person who sings, especially as their job □ a folk singer

singing /'sɪŋɪŋ/ NOUN, NO PLURAL the activity of making musical sounds with your voice □ a singing teacher

single¹ /'sɪŋgəl/ ADJECTIVE

1 only one □ I didn't get a single card on my birthday. □ A single shelf held all her belongings.
2 talking about each thing in a group 🖰 He rang me every single day while he was away.
3 not married □ a club for single women
4 for use by one person □ a single room □ a pair of single sheets
5 a single ticket is used for a journey in one direction

single² /'sɪŋgəl/ NOUN [plural singles]

1 a ticket for a journey you make in one direction but not back again □ How much is a single to York? □ Two singles to Kings Cross.
2 a musical CD or record with only one or two songs on it 🖰 a hit single (= very popular song)

singular¹ /'sɪŋgjʊlə(r)/ ADJECTIVE in grammar, a singular form of a word is the form used to talk about one person, thing or group □ 'Child' is the singular form of 'children'.

singular² /'sɪŋgjʊlə(r)/ NOUN the singular the form of a noun, pronoun, adjective or verb that you use to talk about one person, thing or group □ The singular is 'sheep' and the plural is also 'sheep'.

sink¹ /sɪŋk/ VERB [sinks, sinking, sank, sunk]

1 to drop below the surface of water and move down to the bottom, or to make something do this □ The boat sank in a storm. □ She fell in and sank below the surface of the water.
2 to move to a lower position or level □ The sun was sinking towards the horizon. □ **+ into** He sank to his knees.

sink² /sɪŋk/ NOUN [plural sinks] a bowl fixed to the wall in a kitchen or bathroom, used for washing in 🖰 She put the dirty cups in the kitchen sink.

sip¹ /sɪp/ VERB [sips, sipping, sipped] to drink something slowly taking only a small amount at a time □ Russell sipped his coffee.

sip² /sɪp/ NOUN [plural sips] when you sip a drink 🖰 She took a sip of water.

sir /sɜː(r)/ NOUN [plural sirs]

1 a polite way of speaking or writing to a man, especially one you do not know □ Excuse me, sir. Can I help you?
2 Dear Sir a way of beginning a formal letter to a man when you do not know his name
3 a title used before the name of a knight (= a man with a high social rank) □ Sir Paul McCartney

siren /'saɪərən/ NOUN [plural sirens] a device that makes a very loud noise to warn people of something □ I heard police sirens outside.

sister /'sɪstə(r)/ NOUN [plural sisters]

1 a girl or a woman who has the same parents as you 🖰 He had two older sisters. 🖰 She was walking to school with her younger sister.
2 a female nurse who is in charge of part of a hospital □ a ward sister
3 a nun (= a member of a female religious group), often used as a title □ Sister Dorothy

sister-in-law /'sɪstərɪnˌlɔː/ NOUN [plural sisters-in-law] your brother's wife, or your husband's or wife's sister

sit /sɪt/ VERB [sits, sitting, sat]

1 to be in a position where your weight is supported on your bottom, not your legs □ I sat next to my friend. 🖰 Would you please sit still while I get the books out? □ **+ on** He was sitting on the sofa. □ **+ down** They were sitting down waiting for me.
2 to move your body into a position where your weight is supported on your bottom □ He came in

and sat on the floor. □ **+ down** *Sit down now, and get on with your work, please.*

3 if you sit an exam, you do an exam □ *She's sitting her GCSEs next term.*

♦ PHRASAL VERB **sit up** **1** to move from a lying position to a sitting position □ *Can you manage to sit up?* **2** to sit with your back straight ⬛ *Sit up straight and pay attention!*

site /saɪt/ NOUN [*plural* sites]
1 a place where something happens or happened, or a place used for a certain purpose □ **+ of** *the site of a battle* ⬛ *He works on a construction site.* □ *It is one of the most visited archaeological sites in Europe.* □ *The minister visited the crash site.*
2 a website. A computing word ⬛ *an Internet site* □ *The film is posted on video sharing sites like YouTube.*

sitting room /ˈsɪtɪŋ ˌrʊm/ NOUN [*plural* sitting rooms] a room, usually in a house, for sitting and relaxing in

situation /ˌsɪtjuˈeɪʃən/ NOUN [*plural* situations] the things that are happening in a place or affecting someone at a particular time □ *We're in a difficult situation.* ⬛ *She handled the situation very well.* □ *They're trying to improve the situation for part-time workers.*

six /sɪks/ NUMBER [*plural* sixes] the number 6

sixteen /ˌsɪksˈtiːn/ NUMBER the number 16
sixteenth /ˌsɪksˈtiːnθ/ NUMBER 16th written as a word

sixth¹ /sɪksθ/ NUMBER 6th written as a word

sixth² /sɪksθ/ NOUN [*plural* sixths] 1/6; one of six equal parts of something

sixtieth /ˈsɪkstiəθ/ NUMBER 60th written as a word
sixty /ˈsɪksti/ NUMBER [*plural* sixties]
1 the number 60
2 the sixties the years between 1960 and 1969

size /saɪz/ NOUN [*plural* sizes]
1 how big, small, long, wide, etc. something is, □ **+ of** *The hole was the size of a tennis ball.* □ *They are less than 2 centimetres in size.* □ *We were disappointed by the small size of the bedrooms.* ⬛ *It's about the same size as a credit card.* ⬛ *There were boats of every size and shape.* □ *The government wants to reduce class sizes.*
2 one of the measurements that clothes, shoes and other objects are made in □ *Can I try a smaller size?* □ *I'm a size 12.*

skate¹ /skeɪt/ NOUN [*plural* skates]
1 an ice skate
2 a roller skate
skate² /skeɪt/ VERB [skates, skating, skated] to move wearing skates □ *The Russian pair skated well.*

skateboard /ˈskeɪtbɔːd/ NOUN [*plural* skateboards] a long narrow board with wheels on the bottom which you ride by standing on it

skating /ˈskeɪtɪŋ/ NOUN, NO PLURAL the sport or activity of moving over ice wearing ice skates (= boots with a metal blade on the bottom)

skeleton /ˈskelɪtən/ NOUN [*plural* skeletons] the frame of bones inside the body of a person or an animal □ *They found a nearly complete dinosaur skeleton.*

sketch /sketʃ/ NOUN [*plural* sketches] a drawing that is done quickly □ *a pencil sketch* □ *He drew a rough sketch of the house.*

ski¹ /skiː/ NOUN [*plural* skis] one of two long narrow strips of wood or metal that you attach to boots and use for moving over snow ⬛ *a pair of skis*

ski² /skiː/ VERB [skis, skiing, skied] to move over snow on skis □ *They skied down together.* □ *I'm just learning to ski.*

skier /ˈskiːə(r)/ NOUN [*plural* skiers] someone who skis

skiing /ˈskiːɪŋ/ NOUN, NO PLURAL the sport or activity of moving over snow on skis ⬛ *I would love to go skiing.* ⬛ *a skiing holiday*

skilful /ˈskɪlfʊl/ ADJECTIVE showing the ability to do something well □ *He's a very skilful player.* □ *She's very skilful at handling the media.*

skilfully /ˈskɪlfʊli/ ADVERB in a skilful way □ *They had skilfully avoided being caught.* □ *a skilfully edited programme*

skill /skɪl/ NOUN [*plural* skills]
1 an ability to do something that you develop through training and practice ⬛ *It helps children develop their social skills.* ⬛ *Effective communication skills are essential.* ⬛ *They lack basic computer skills.*
2 no plural the ability to do something very well □ *His skill as a writer is in creating interesting characters.* □ **+ in** *He showed great skill in handling the situation.* □ **+ at** *She was known for her skill at motivating workers.*

skilled /skɪld/ ADJECTIVE a skilled person is very good at what they do □ *Amanda's a skilled pianist.* ⬛ *a highly skilled employee*

skin /skɪn/ NOUN [*plural* skins]
1 no plural the outside layer of your body ⬛ *She had blonde hair and very pale skin.* ⬛ *People with dark skin don't burn as easily in the sun.* ⬛ *A moisturizing cream will help prevent dry skin.* □ *skin cancer*
2 the outside layer of some fruits and vegetables □ *banana skins* □ *grape skins*
3 the outside layer of a dead animal which is used for making something □ *the illegal trade in tiger skins*

> ➤ **THESAURUS:** The outside layer of some fruits and vegetables is called the skin. Peaches, tomatoes and cherries have a skin. The skin of some fruits and vegetables is called the peel. Oranges, lemons, and bananas have peel. For some things, for example apples and potatoes, you can talk about either the skin or the peel. In general, when you remove the skin, we usually use the word peel, but when you eat the skin, we usually use the word skin. The hard covering on a nut or an egg is called the shell.

skinny /'skɪnɪ/ ADJECTIVE [skinnier, skinniest] very thin □ She's too skinny.

skip /skɪp/ VERB [skips, skipping, skipped]
1 to move forward by jumping from one foot to the other foot □ He skipped down the road.
2 to jump over a rope that you are turning □ The girls were skipping in the playground.
3 to not do something that you should do □ Children who skip breakfast find it more difficult to concentrate in class. □ He was being bullied and regularly skipped school.

> ➤ **THESAURUS:** If you jump, you push yourself off the ground or other surface with your legs. If you skip, you move forward by jumping from one foot to the other foot, or jump over a rope that you are turning. If you hop, you jump on one leg. When an animal hops, it moves by jumping. Frogs, rabbits and kangaroos all hop.

skirt /skɜːt/ NOUN [plural skirts] a piece of clothing for girls or women that hangs from the waist 🔊 Anja was wearing a black skirt. □ a short skirt

skull /skʌl/ NOUN [plural skulls] the structure of bones that form your head □ He fell out of a tree and fractured his skull.

sky /skaɪ/ NOUN [plural skies] the area above the Earth where you can see the sun, moon, stars and clouds □ There was a beautiful clear blue sky. □ She looked up at the cloudy sky. □ There were several stars in the sky.

skyscraper /'skaɪskreɪpə(r)/ NOUN [plural skyscrapers] a very tall building

slam /slæm/ VERB [slams, slamming, slammed]
1 to shut quickly with a loud noise, or to shut something quickly with a loud noise 🔊 She walked angrily out of the room and slammed the door. 🔊 The gate slammed shut.
2 to put something somewhere with a loud noise □ He slammed the books down on the table.

slap¹ /slæp/ VERB [slaps, slapping, slapped] to hit something or someone with the flat part of your hand □ She slapped him across the face.

slap² /slæp/ NOUN [plural slaps] a hit made with the flat part of your hand

✦ IDIOM **a slap in the face** something someone does which upsets or insults you □ The fare increases are a slap in the face for commuters.

slaughter¹ /'slɔːtə(r)/ VERB [slaughters, slaughtering, slaughtered]
1 to kill an animal, usually for its meat
2 to kill a lot of people very violently

slaughter² /'slɔːtə(r)/ NOUN, NO PLURAL the act of killing a lot of people violently, or of killing animals for meat □ Officials carried out a mass slaughter of cows to prevent the spread of the disease. □ The war has seen the slaughter of innocent civilians.

slave /sleɪv/ NOUN [plural slaves] someone who is owned by another person and has to work for them without being paid □ My parents treat me like a slave.

slavery /'sleɪvərɪ/ NOUN, NO PLURAL
1 the system of owning people and making them work without being paid □ The US did not abolish slavery until 1865.
2 the state of being a owned by another person □ He had been sold into slavery.

sleep¹ /sliːp/ NOUN, NO PLURAL
1 the state when you are resting with your eyes closed and are naturally unconscious □ I really need some sleep. 🔊 I couldn't get to sleep.
2 **go to sleep** (a) to begin to sleep (b) if part of your body goes to sleep, you lose the feeling in it

sleep² /sliːp/ VERB [sleeps, sleeping, slept] to become naturally unconscious and rest with your eyes closed □ I hardly slept at all last night. □ She slept through the fire alarm (= did not wake up). 🔊 After their long walk, they slept soundly (= slept well).

sleepy /'sliːpɪ/ ADJECTIVE [sleepier, sleepiest] feeling tired and wanting to sleep

sleet¹ /sliːt/ NOUN, NO PLURAL a mixture of rain and snow

sleet² /sliːt/ VERB [sleets, sleeting, sleeted] if it is sleeting, sleet is falling

sleeve /sliːv/ NOUN [plural sleeves] the part of a piece of clothing that covers your arm or part of your arm □ a dress with wide sleeves

✦ IDIOM **have something up your sleeve** to have a secret plan □ I haven't persuaded them to come yet, but I've still got a few things up my sleeve.

slender /'slendə(r)/ ADJECTIVE thin in an attractive way □ a slender figure

slept /slept/ PAST TENSE AND PAST PARTICIPLE OF **sleep**²

slice¹ /slaɪs/ NOUN [plural slices] a thin or smaller piece cut from a larger piece of food □ He cut himself a thick slice of chocolate cake. □ a slice of ham

slice² /slaɪs/ VERB [slices, slicing, sliced] to cut something into thin pieces □ *Slice the onions thinly.* □ *a tin of sliced peaches*

slide¹ /slaɪd/ VERB [slides, sliding, slid] to move over a surface quickly and in a smooth way, or to make something do this □ *The kids enjoyed sliding on the ice.* □ *a sliding door* □ *We slid the poles into place.*

> **THESAURUS:** If you slide, you move over a surface quickly and smoothly, or make something do this. If you slip, you slide and lose your balance or fall. For example, you might slip on an icy path or a wet floor. If you trip, you hit your foot on something and fall, or almost fall. For example, you might trip on the edge of a carpet.

slide² /slaɪd/ NOUN [plural slides]
1 a piece of play equipment on which children climb up steps and slide down a smooth sloping surface □ *Megan loves playing on the slide.*
2 a small transparent photograph that you shine light through to look at an image on a screen □ *a slide show*
3 a small clear piece of glass or plastic which you put something on so that you can look at it using a microscope (= scientific instrument for examining things)

slight /slaɪt/ ADJECTIVE [slighter, slightest] small or not important □ *a slight increase in temperature* □ *There's a slight problem with your application.* □ *Lewis has a slight cold.*

slightly /ˈslaɪtlɪ/ ADVERB by only a small amount □ *Adam is slightly taller than Alex.* □ *I only know her slightly.*

slim¹ /slɪm/ ADJECTIVE [slimmer, slimmest] thin in an attractive way □ *His sister's a tall, slim girl with blonde hair.*

slim² /slɪm/ VERB [slims, slimming, slimmed] to become or try to become thinner □ *I can't have any cake, I'm slimming.*

slip¹ /slɪp/ VERB [slips, slipping, slipped]
1 to slide and lose your balance or fall □ *Gran slipped on the ice and broke her hip.*
2 to fall out of position or out of your hands □ *The knife slipped and I nearly cut myself.* □ *I'm sorry, the cup just slipped out of my hands.*
3 to put something somewhere quickly □ *Dad slipped a £10 note in my pocket.*
4 to go somewhere quietly and without anyone noticing you □ *I saw Polly slip out of the room.* □ *They must have slipped away while we were watching the show.*
♦ PHRASAL VERB **slip up** to make a mistake or do something wrong □ *I'm afraid you slipped up on the first question.*

slip² /slɪp/ NOUN [plural slips]
1 a small piece of paper □ *a slip of paper* □ *Fill in the green slip and give it back to me.*
2 a small mistake ☞ *She made a couple of slips in her dance routine*

slipper /ˈslɪpə(r)/ NOUN [plural slippers] a soft shoe for wearing indoors

slippery /ˈslɪpərɪ/ ADJECTIVE a slippery surface is smooth, wet or shiny and not easy to walk on or hold □ *The floor was slippery with grease.*

slogan /ˈsləʊgən/ NOUN [plural slogans] a phrase that is easy to remember and is used to advertise something or to emphasize the opinions of political parties, etc. □ *advertising slogans*

slope¹ /sləʊp/ VERB [slopes, sloping, sloped] to have one end higher than the other □ *The garden slopes upwards.* □ *a sloping roof*

slope² /sləʊp/ NOUN [plural slopes] a surface that slopes □ *a steep slope* □ *a ski slope*

sloppy /ˈslɒpɪ/ ADJECTIVE [sloppier, sloppiest]
1 careless or untidy □ *a sloppy piece of work*
2 sloppy clothes are loose and do not have a clear shape □ *a sloppy jumper*

slot /slɒt/ NOUN [plural slots] a small narrow opening, especially one that you put coins or bank cards into □ *There's a pound coin stuck in the slot.*

slow¹ /sləʊ/ ADJECTIVE [slower, slowest]
1 not fast or not moving or acting quickly □ *a slow march* □ *a slow reader* □ *We made slow progress through the crowds.*
2 not doing something immediately □ *+ to do something* Social services were slow to take any action to protect the child. □ *+ in* He was very slow in coming to the phone.
3 if a clock or watch is slow, it shows a time earlier than the correct time □ *I think your clock's five minutes slow.*

slow² /sləʊ/ VERB [slows, slowing, slowed]
♦ PHRASAL VERB **slow (something) down** to become slower or to make something slower □ *You should slow down as you approach the bend.*

slowly /ˈsləʊlɪ/ ADVERB at a slow speed □ *He drove slowly past the house.* □ *She speaks very slowly.*

slug /slʌg/ NOUN [plural slugs] a creature with a long soft body and no legs, that moves slowly and eats plants □ *Slugs had attacked our bean plants.*

slum /slʌm/ NOUN [plural slums] a part of a town or city where the buildings are dirty and in bad condition □ *She sang about her childhood in the slums of Naples.*

slump /slʌmp/ VERB [slumps, slumping, slumped]
1 to quickly go down to a much lower level □ *Business has slumped in the last few months.*

2 to fall or sit down suddenly because you feel weak, ill or tired □ *He was slumped over his desk, fast asleep.* □ *She suddenly slumped back in her chair.*

smack /smæk/ VERB [smacks, smacking, smacked] to hit someone with your hand flat □ *It is wrong to smack children.*

small /smɔːl/ ADJECTIVE [smaller, smallest]
1 little □ *a small country* ▣ *This coat is too small for you now.* □ *We're only interviewing a small number of applicants.*
2 very young □ *a playground for small children* □ *I used to love these books when I was small.*
3 not important or serious □ *a small problem*

smart /smɑːt/ ADJECTIVE [smarter, smartest]
1 clean and tidy □ *a pair of smart black shoes* □ *She looked really smart in her uniform.*
2 clever □ *a smart answer* □ *He's one of the smartest guys I know.*

smash /smæʃ/ VERB [smashes, smashing, smashed]
1 to break something into pieces, for example by dropping it □ *She smashed one of our best glasses.* □ *Mum, I've smashed a window.* □ *Police had to smash the door down.*
2 to break into pieces □ *The vase fell off the table and smashed.*

smear¹ /smɪə(r)/ VERB [smears, smearing, smeared] to spread a soft or dirty substance on a surface □ *Her face was smeared with mascara.*

smear² /smɪə(r)/ NOUN [plural smears] a dirty mark made by spreading something sticky on something □ *smears of paint*

smell¹ /smel/ VERB [smells, smelling, smelled or smelt]
1 to notice or recognize something by using your nose □ *Can you smell burning?* □ *I could smell his sweaty trainers from across the room.*
2 to have a particular smell □ *Those scones smell delicious.* □ **+ of** *The sheets smelled of lavender.* □ *This chicken smells funny.*
3 to have a bad smell □ *His breath smells.*

> ➤ THESAURUS: When you smell something, you notice or recognize it by using your nose. When you breathe, you take air into and out of your lungs. If you sniff, you breathe in through your nose in order to smell something. You might sniff a piece of food to decide if it smells bad.

smell² /smel/ NOUN [plural smells]
1 the quality you notice by smelling □ *a strong smell of garlic* □ *These lilies have a lovely smell.*
2 no plural the ability to smell things ▣ *The virus made him lose his sense of smell.*

smelly /ˈsmelɪ/ ADJECTIVE [smellier, smelliest] having a strong or bad smell □ *smelly feet*

smelt /smelt/ PAST TENSE AND PAST PARTICIPLE OF **smell¹**

smile¹ /smaɪl/ VERB [smiles, smiling, smiled] to show you are happy or think something is funny by making the corners of your mouth go up □ *The little girl smiled happily up at him.*

> ➤ Remember that you **smile at** someone. You do not 'smile to' someone:
> ✓ She turned and smiled at me.
> ✗ She turned and smiled to me.

> ➤ THESAURUS: If you smile, you show you are happy or think something is funny by making the corners of your mouth go up. If you grin, you give a big smile. If you laugh, you make a sound of enjoyment when you think something is funny. If you giggle, you laugh in a silly or nervous way.

smile² /smaɪl/ NOUN [plural smiles] an expression in which the corners of your mouth go up to show you are happy □ *a broad smile* □ *'Can I help you?' she said with a smile.*

smoke¹ /sməʊk/ NOUN, NO PLURAL the grey or black gas that something produces when it is burning □ *I can smell smoke.* □ *cigarette smoke* ▣ *Firefighters battled thick smoke to rescue the children.* ▣ *A cloud of smoke rose into the air.*

smoke² /sməʊk/ VERB [smokes, smoking, smoked]
1 someone who smokes sucks smoke from cigarettes □ *My parents don't smoke.* □ *Dan was smoking a cigarette.*
2 to produce smoke □ *The chimney was smoking.*

smoker /ˈsməʊkə(r)/ NOUN [plural smokers] someone who smokes cigarettes ▣ *He used to be a heavy smoker* (= someone who smokes a lot of cigarettes).

smoking /ˈsməʊkɪŋ/ NOUN, NO PLURAL the habit of smoking cigarettes ▣ *My Dad wants to stop smoking.* □ *In England smoking is banned in public buildings.*

smoky /ˈsməʊkɪ/ ADJECTIVE [smokier, smokiest] filled with smoke □ *a smoky bar*

smooth /smuːð/ ADJECTIVE [smoother, smoothest]
1 having an even surface □ *She ran her fingers along the smooth surface of the wood.* □ *Babies have beautifully smooth, soft skin.*
2 a smooth substance has no lumps □ *Stir the ingredients until a smooth paste is formed.*
3 happening without any problems ▣ *Young people want a smooth transition from school to work.* □ *His recovery from the operation was relatively smooth.*

4 having no sudden movements □ *Larger boats provide a smoother ride than rowing boats.* □ *In one smooth movement, he climbed onto the horse.*

smother /'smʌðə(r)/ VERB [smothers, smothering, smothered]
1 to cover something with a substance □ *The little boy's hands were smothered in chocolate.* □ *She smothered him with kisses.*
2 to kill someone by putting something over their nose and mouth

smuggle /'smʌgəl/ VERB [smuggles, smuggling, smuggled] to bring something into a country illegally □ *The weapons had been smuggled into the country.*

smuggler /'smʌglə(r)/ NOUN [plural smugglers] someone who brings something into a country illegally

snack /snæk/ NOUN [plural snacks] a small meal, or a small amount of food that you eat between meals ✑ *She had a snack during the morning.* ✑ *Some people eat too many snack foods such as crisps and biscuits.*

snail /sneɪl/ NOUN [plural snails] a small creature with a soft body and a shell on its back

snake /sneɪk/ NOUN [plural snakes] a long thin animal with no legs, which slides along the ground □ *There are several poisonous snakes in the region.*

snap¹ /snæp/ VERB [snaps, snapping, snapped]
1 to break with a sudden, sharp noise or to break something with a sudden, sharp noise □ *The twig snapped.* □ *He snapped off a piece of his biscuit.*
2 to speak to someone in an angry way □ *When I asked for a break, he snapped at me.*
3 if an animal snaps, it tries to bite someone or something

snap² /snæp/ NOUN [plural snaps]
1 a sudden, short sound □ *She shut her purse with a snap.*
2 an informal word for a photograph ✑ *holiday snaps*

snarl /snɑːl/ VERB [snarls, snarling, snarled]
1 to say something in an angry or threatening way □ *'I have no comment,' he snarled.*
2 if an animal snarls, it makes an angry sound and shows its teeth □ *The dog snarled every time he tried to move.*

snatch /snætʃ/ VERB [snatches, snatching, snatched] to take something from someone suddenly and roughly □ *She snatched the book out of my hand.*

sneak /sniːk/ VERB [sneaks, sneaking, sneaked] to go somewhere quietly and secretly □ *Maggie sneaked out of the house.*

sneaker /'sniːkə(r)/ NOUN [plural sneakers] a US word for a type of sports shoe ✑ *Farooq was wearing a pair of sneakers.*

sneeze /sniːz/ VERB [sneezes, sneezing, sneezed] to suddenly blow out air from your nose and mouth in a way that you cannot control □ *Dust always makes me sneeze.*

➤ **THESAURUS:** You might sneeze because you have a cold or if you have dust in your nose. When you yawn, you open your mouth very wide and breathe in, because you are feeling tired or bored. If you snore, you make a loud noise when you breathe while you are sleeping.

sniff /snɪf/ VERB [sniffs, sniffing, sniffed]
1 to breathe in air through your nose noisily □ *He was crying and sniffing.*
2 to breathe in through your nose in order to smell something □ *Tess sniffed the air.*

snore /snɔː(r)/ VERB [snores, snoring, snored] to make a loud noise when you breathe while you are sleeping □ *My Dad snores and you can hear it all round the house.*

snow¹ /snəʊ/ NOUN, NO PLURAL soft white pieces that fall from the sky when it is very cold ✑ *15 centimetres of snow fell in many areas.* ✑ *Heavy snow affected much of the country.* ✑ *The snow was starting to melt.*

snow² /snəʊ/ VERB [snows, snowing, snowed] if it snows, snow falls from the sky □ *It's been snowing all night.*

snowball /'snəʊbɔːl/ NOUN [plural snowballs] a ball of snow that children make and throw at each other ✑ *The children were throwing snowballs.* ✑ *a snowball fight*

snowboarding /'snəʊbɔːdɪŋ/ NOUN, NO PLURAL a sport in which you move over snow while standing on a board

snowman /'snəʊmæn/ NOUN [plural snowmen] a model of a person which children make from snow ✑ *The children have built a snowman.*

snowy /'snəʊɪ/ ADJECTIVE [snowier, snowiest]
covered with snow, or involving snow □ *snowy hills*
□ *snowy weather*

so¹ /səʊ/ ADVERB

1 used to emphasize the word that follows □ *I was
so happy to see her.* □ *I've never seen so many
children.* □ *Thank you so much for all your help.*
2 used to avoid repeating something that has just
been said □ *'Are you coming to the party?' 'I hope
so.'* □ *'How do you know Emma's going camping?'
'Because she said so.'* ⊞ *When she won the
competition, she was the first person over 40 to do
so.*
3 used to say that something is true for something
or someone else □ *She's tired and so am I.* □ *The
accommodation was dreadful, and so was the food.*
4 used to agree with something that you have just
been shown or told □ *'Look, our tomato seeds are
coming up.' 'Oh, so they are!'*
5 or **so** used to show that a number or amount is
not exact □ *There were forty people or so at the
party.* □ *I've been feeling ill for the last week or so.*
6 and **so** on used to show that other similar things
could be added to what you have just said □ *Make
sure you have plenty of pens, pencils, paper and so
on.*
7 so far until now □ *I'm enjoying the job so far.*
8 So what? used to show that you do not think
something is important □ *'Sam will be cross if we're
late.' 'So what? He can't do anything to us.'*

so² /səʊ/ CONJUNCTION

1 used to show that something was the reason for
something else □ *He asked me to come, so I did.*
□ *So they got married and lived happily ever after.*
2 so (that) in order to make something happen
□ *I've washed my jeans so that I can wear them
tomorrow.*

soak /səʊk/ VERB [soaks, soaking, soaked]

1 to put something in liquid for a period of time □ *If
you soak your blouse, the stain might come out.*
2 to make someone or something very wet □ *Heavy
rain soaked the city.*
♦ PHRASAL VERB **soak something up** if something
soaks up a liquid, it takes it in □ *I used a towel to
soak up the spilt milk.*

soap /səʊp/ NOUN [plural soaps] a substance that
you use for washing ⊞ *a bar of soap* □ *He washed
his face with soap and water.*

soar /sɔː(r)/ VERB [soars, soaring, soared]

1 to increase very quickly to a high level □ *The price
of petrol has soared over the last ten years.*
2 to fly high in the air □ *An eagle soared high above
their heads.*

sob /sɒb/ VERB [sobs, sobbing, sobbed] to cry
noisily □ *Lisa lay on her bed, sobbing.*

sober /'səʊbə(r)/ ADJECTIVE not drunk

soccer /'sɒkə(r)/ NOUN, NO PLURAL football □ *The
children were playing soccer.* □ *a soccer ball*

social /'səʊʃəl/ ADJECTIVE

1 to do with society □ *The programme is designed
to tackle crime and other social problems.* □ *The
school attracts students from all social backgrounds.*
2 to do with meeting and being friendly with other
people □ *I always feel nervous in social situations.*
□ *a social club* ⊞ *He didn't have very good social
skills.*

social networking /ˌsəʊʃəl 'netwɜːkɪŋ/ NOUN,
NO PLURAL using websites to meet people and talk to
them

society /sə'saɪətɪ/ NOUN [plural societies]

1 all the people who live in a group or in a particular
country or area □ *Racism still exists in British society.*
□ *Australia is a more multicultural society.* ⊞ *We
have a responsibility to support the weaker members
of society.*
2 an organization for people with a particular
interest □ *She joined the university's debating
society.*

sock /sɒk/ NOUN [plural socks] a covering for
your foot that you wear inside your shoe ⊞ *a pair of
socks* ⊞ *She was wearing black socks.*
♦ IDIOM **pull your socks up** to try to improve your
behaviour or work □ *You'll have to pull your socks
up if you want to pass the exam.*

socket /'sɒkɪt/ NOUN [plural sockets] the place on
a wall where you connect electrical equipment to
the electricity supply □ *an electric socket*

> ➤ THESAURUS: The thing that you connect to a
> socket is called a plug. A plug is attached to a
> piece of electrical equipment by a wire. A
> switch is a thing that you press to make
> something work or stop working. Many sockets
> also have a switch.

sofa /'səʊfə/ NOUN [plural sofas] a long,
comfortable seat for more than one person □ *Dan
and Clare were sitting on the sofa watching
television.*

soft /sɒft/ ADJECTIVE [softer, softest]

1 not hard or firm □ *a nice soft cushion* □ *soft
ground*
2 smooth and pleasant to touch □ *She had soft silky
hair.* □ *soft leather*
3 not loud □ *a soft voice*
4 not bright □ *Her bedroom is decorated in soft
pastel colours.* □ *a soft light*

soft drink /ˌsɒft 'drɪŋk/ NOUN [plural soft drinks]
a cold drink that does not contain alcohol

soften /'sɒfən/ VERB [softens, softening,
softened] to become soft or to make something

soft □ *Soften the clay by working it with your hands.* □ *The cream softens the skin.*

softly /'sɒftlɪ/ ADVERB gently or quietly □ *Snow was falling softly in the moonlight.* □ *She stroked the cat softly.*

software /'sɒftweə(r)/ NOUN, NO PLURAL computer programs. A computing word. ⌑ *We've installed new software.* ⌑ *Users need to download a piece of software.*

soil /sɔɪl/ NOUN, NO PLURAL the top layer of the ground, that you can grow plants in □ *a soil sample* □ *Rice and corn grow well in the rich soil.* □ *He brushed the red, sandy soil off his trousers.*

solar /'səʊlə(r)/ ADJECTIVE
1 to do with the sun □ *a solar eclipse*
2 to do with energy from the sun □ *solar panels*
solar system /'səʊlə ˌsɪstəm/ NOUN [*plural* solar systems] the sun and the planets that move around it

sold /səʊld/ PAST TENSE AND PAST PARTICIPLE OF **sell**

soldier /'səʊldʒə(r)/ NOUN [*plural* soldiers] someone who is in the army □ *Two soldiers from the same regiment were captured.*

sole[1] /səʊl/ ADJECTIVE only □ *Her sole ambition was to be famous.* □ *A young boy was the sole survivor of the accident.*
sole[2] /səʊl/ NOUN [*plural* soles] the bottom part of your foot or of a shoe ⌑ *The sand was hot on the soles of her feet.*
sole[3] /səʊl/ NOUN [*plural* sole] a flat fish that people can eat

solemn /'sɒləm/ ADJECTIVE serious and sometimes sad □ *a solemn expression* □ *a rather solemn little boy*

solicitor /sə'lɪsɪtə(r)/ NOUN [*plural* solicitors] someone whose job is to give advice to people about the law and help them with legal work □ *a firm of solicitors*

solid[1] /'sɒlɪd/ ADJECTIVE
1 firm and with a fixed shape, not in the form of a liquid or a gas ⌑ *They scrambled through the mud to more solid ground.* □ *The river froze solid.*
2 not hollow or with no spaces inside □ *a solid chocolate egg* ⌑ *They had to cut through solid rock.*
3 solid gold, silver, etc. made only of gold, silver, etc. □ *a solid gold pendant*

► THESAURUS: If something is firm, it is not soft. Something which is solid is firm and has a fixed shape, or does not have any spaces inside. Something which is hollow has an empty space inside. A football is hollow. Something which is hard is firm and is not easy to bend or break. Something which is stable is strong and does not move easily.

solid[2] /'sɒlɪd/ NOUN [*plural* solids] something that is not a liquid or a gas □ *This element changes from a solid to a gas when heated.*

solo[1] /'səʊləʊ/ NOUN [*plural* solos] a piece of music or a song for one person to play or sing □ *a guitar solo* □ *Emma sang a solo in the Christmas concert.*
solo[2] /'səʊləʊ/ ADJECTIVE done or performed by one person alone □ *a solo flight* □ *a solo album* □ *He went on to have a career as a solo artist.*

solution /sə'luːʃən/ NOUN [*plural* solutions] an answer to a problem or a question □ *+ to* *It's difficult to offer simple solutions to a complex problem.* ⌑ *We must try to find a peaceful solution.*

► Remember that 'solution' is followed by the preposition **to**:
✓ There is no easy solution **to** the problem.
✗ There is no easy solution of the problem.

solve /sɒlv/ VERB [solves, solving, solved] to find an answer to a problem or a difficult question □ *Solve the puzzle to win a prize.* ⌑ *A new bridge won't solve the traffic problem.* ⌑ *This information could help us to solve the crime.*

solvent[1] /'sɒlvənt/ NOUN [*plural* solvents] something that dissolves another substance. A chemistry word.
solvent[2] /'sɒlvənt/ ADJECTIVE having enough money to pay what you owe □ *At last they were financially solvent.*

some /sʌm/ DETERMINER, PRONOUN
1 used to talk about a number or an amount without saying exactly how many or how much □ *It's all right; I've got some money.* □ *Would you like some more milk?* □ *I've made a cake – would you like some?*
2 used to talk about part of a larger amount or number of things or people □ *+ of* *Some of the apples were rotten.* □ *Some people have brought rain coats and some haven't.*
3 used to talk about a person or a thing when you do not know exactly who or what they are □ *He mentioned some letter that he had received.* □ *Some silly person forgot to close the gate.*

somebody /'sʌmbədɪ/ PRONOUN used to talk about a person when you do not know who they are or it is not necessary to say their name □ *Somebody knocked at the door.* □ *They get money every time somebody downloads a song.* □ *She's somebody who's popular at school.* ⌑ *Let somebody else* (= another person) *do it for a change.*

somehow /'sʌmhaʊ/ ADVERB in a way that is not known or you do not understand □ *Don't worry, we'll manage somehow.* □ *She'd somehow managed to get her finger caught in the mechanism.*

□ *Somehow, it didn't seem very important.* 🔁 *He'll succeed in the end, somehow or other.*

someone /'sʌmwʌn/ PRONOUN used to talk about a person when you do not know who they are or it is not necessary to say their name □ *We'll have to find someone to replace him.* □ *I was having a conversation with someone at work about it.* □ *It could save someone's life.* 🔁 *It's good to have someone else* (= another person) *to blame.*

something /'sʌmθɪŋ/ PRONOUN
1 used to talk about a thing or a fact when you do not know what it is, or when it is not necessary to say what it is □ *I've got something in my eye.* □ *Let's have something to eat before we go.* □ *She told me something else as well.* □ *The roof's leaking and we need to do something about it.*
2 used to show that what you have said is only a guess or an example □ *I think he's an actor or something like that.* □ *She speaks something like ten different languages.* 🔁 *We could take her some flowers or something.*

sometimes /'sʌmtaɪmz/ ADVERB at times, but not always □ *I still see him sometimes.* □ *Sometimes I feel like giving up my job and moving away.*

somewhat /'sʌmwɒt/ ADVERB quite or slightly □ *The wind had died down somewhat.*

somewhere /'sʌmweə(r)/ ADVERB used to talk about a place when you do not know where it is, or when it is not necessary to say where it is □ *Let's go away somewhere for a few days.* □ *They live somewhere near Oxford.* □ *It must be around here somewhere.* □ *Put it somewhere safe.* 🔁 *If you don't like it, we can go somewhere else* (= to another place).

son /sʌn/ NOUN [plural sons] someone's male child 🔁 *They have two young sons.* 🔁 *Her eldest son, Dave, is at university.* □ **+ of** *He's the son of Algerian immigrants.*

song /sɒŋ/ NOUN [plural songs]
1 a piece of music with words that you sing □ *a pop song* □ *This is one of my favourite songs.* 🔁 *She mostly sings folk songs.*
2 no plural songs in general or the activity of singing □ *A blackbird suddenly burst into song.* □ *a song and dance routine*

son-in-law /'sʌnɪnˌlɔː/ NOUN [plural sons-in-law] your daughter's husband

soon /suːn/ ADVERB [sooner, soonest]
1 in a short time from now □ *It will soon be summer.* □ *I hope to see you soon.* □ *Soon we'll be reaching Liverpool* □ *I'd like the work done by Friday, or sooner if you can.* 🔁 *I'll do it as soon as I can.*
2 as soon as immediately □ *As soon as I saw her, I knew something was wrong.* □ *He started shouting at us as soon as we arrived.*

3 sooner or later used to say that you are certain that something will happen at some time in the future □ *Sooner or later there's going to be an accident.*
4 too soon too early □ *It's too soon to tell whether she'll recover.* □ *Help arrived not a moment too soon.*

soothe /suːð/ VERB [soothes, soothing, soothed]
1 to make someone feel calmer or happier □ *She was unable to soothe her crying baby.*
2 to make pain less strong □ *I had a bath to soothe my sore muscles.*

sophisticated /sə'fɪstɪkeɪtɪd/ ADJECTIVE
1 knowing a lot about the world, culture, fashion, etc. □ *a highly sophisticated audience* □ *It's a sophisticated and cosmopolitan city.*
2 using new and clever ideas 🔁 *highly sophisticated software*

sore¹ /sɔː(r)/ ADJECTIVE [sorer, sorest] if a part of your body is sore, it is painful □ *a sore finger* 🔁 *She woke up with a sore throat.* 🔁 *My legs feel sore today.*

sore² /sɔː(r)/ NOUN [plural sores] a red, painful place on your skin □ *The horse had a nasty sore on its leg.*

sorry /'sɒri/ ADJECTIVE [sorrier, sorriest]
1 (I'm) sorry (a) something that you say when you have done something wrong, hurt someone, upset someone, etc. □ *Sorry, I didn't mean to hurt you.* □ *I'm so sorry – I've spilt tea on your carpet.* 🔁 *He broke my chair and he never even said sorry.* (b) something you say to be polite when you have to tell someone something they may not like □ *Sorry, the shop's closing now.* □ *I'm sorry, but this work just isn't good enough.*
2 ashamed about something that you have done and wishing you had not done it □ *She knows how much she upset us, and she's not even sorry.* □ **+ that** *I'm really sorry that I lied to you.* □ **+ about** *I'm sorry about forgetting your birthday.* □ **+ for** *He's truly sorry for spoiling your party.*
3 feeling sympathy for someone □ *I was sorry to hear about your father.* □ **+ for** *I feel really sorry for Anna, having to travel on her own.* □ **+ that** *I was sorry that you didn't get the job.*
4 used to say that you wish a situation could have been different □ **+ that** *I was sorry that I never met her.* □ **+ to do something** *I think they were sorry to leave.*

sort¹ /sɔːt/ NOUN [plural sorts]
1 a type of thing or person □ **+ of** *What sort of books do you read?* □ *We won't tolerate that sort of behaviour here.* □ *It's the sort of shop that might sell matches.* 🔁 *There were all sorts of people there.* 🔁 *She needs to take up a hobby of some sort.* 🔁 *He enjoys skiing and that sort of thing.*
2 sort of similar, but not exactly what has been said □ *I think she'd sort of forgotten about us by then.* □ *The house was sort of cut out of the rock.*

sort² /sɔːt/ VERB [sorts, sorting, sorted] to arrange things or people into groups or into a particular order □ **+ into** We sorted the books into piles by subject.

◆ PHRASAL VERB **sort something out** to arrange or deal successfully with something □ We've sorted out a new system for feeding the cattle. □ Did you manage to sort out Jackie's problem with her computer?

so-so /ˈsəʊsəʊ/ ADJECTIVE not very good but not very bad □ The restaurant looked nice but the meal was so-so.

sought /sɔːt/ PAST TENSE AND PAST PARTICIPLE OF **seek**

soul /səʊl/ NOUN [plural souls]
1 the part of a person that is not their body but which some people believe continues to exist after they die □ the souls of the dead □ God rest his soul.
2 a type of pop music that expresses strong emotions, especially played by Black Americans 🖫 a soul singer 🖫 He grew up listening to soul music.

sound¹ /saʊnd/ NOUN [plural sounds] something that you can hear 🖫 I could hear a faint sound. □ **+ of** We heard the sound of breaking glass. 🖫 Elspeth made a sound of disgust. □ There isn't a sound coming from the children's bedroom.

sound² /saʊnd/ VERB [sounds, sounding, sounded]
1 if something sounds good, bad, etc., it seems that way from what you have heard or read □ Tom's holiday sounds wonderful. □ I don't want to sound too negative. □ I don't think that sounds right. Are you sure? 🖫 That sounds like a good idea.
2 used to talk about a noise that you hear □ His voice sounded shaky. □ All their songs sound exactly the same. 🖫 That sounds like Zoe's voice in the kitchen.
3 to make a noise □ Sound your horn before you turn the corner. □ If the fire alarm sounds, leave the building immediately.

sound³ /saʊnd/ ADVERB sound asleep if someone is sound asleep, they are sleeping and it is difficult to wake them □ At ten o'clock I was still sound asleep.

sound⁴ /saʊnd/ ADJECTIVE [sounder, soundest]
1 strong, firm, or healthy □ The walls of the old church were still sound. □ Her health was pretty sound.
2 good, sensible and that you can trust 🖫 It seemed like sound advice. □ The recommendations are based on scientifically sound evidence.

soup /suːp/ NOUN [plural soups] a liquid food made from meat, fish, or vegetables □ a bowl of chicken soup

sour /ˈsaʊə(r)/ ADJECTIVE [sourer, sourest] sour food has a bitter taste like a lemon, sometimes

because it is bad □ sour plums □ a sour taste 🖫 The milk had gone sour in the sun.

► **THESAURUS:** Sweet food tastes like sugar, or contains sugar. Salty food contains salt, or tastes of salt. Bitter food has a strong taste such as the taste of strong coffee or dark chocolate. Sour food has a sharp taste, like the taste of a lemon. Sometimes sour food tastes unpleasant because it has gone bad, for example sour milk.

source /sɔːs/ NOUN [plural sources] where something begins or comes from 🖫 renewable energy sources □ Nuts are a rich source of protein. □ Tourism is the island's main source of income.

south¹ /saʊθ/ NOUN, NO PLURAL the direction that is to your right when you are facing towards the rising sun

south² /saʊθ/ ADJECTIVE, ADVERB in or towards the south □ the south coast □ The river flows south into the sea.

south-east¹ /ˌsaʊθˈiːst/ NOUN, NO PLURAL the direction between south and east
south-east² /ˌsaʊθˈiːst/ ADJECTIVE, ADVERB in or towards the south-east □ the south-east coast

southern /ˈsʌðən/ ADJECTIVE in or from the south □ the southern states of the USA

South Pole /ˌsaʊθ ˈpəʊl/ NOUN the South Pole the point on the Earth that is furthest South
south-west¹ /ˌsaʊθˈwest/ NOUN, NO PLURAL the direction between south and west
south-west² /ˌsaʊθˈwest/ ADJECTIVE, ADVERB in or towards the south-west

souvenir /ˌsuːvəˈnɪə(r)/ NOUN [plural souvenirs] something that you buy to help you remember a particular place or occasion □ **+ of** We brought back some shells as souvenirs of our holiday. 🖫 a souvenir shop

sow¹ /səʊ/ VERB [sows, sowing, sowed, sown] to put seeds on or in the ground so that they will grow
sow² /saʊ/ NOUN [plural sows] a female pig

► This meaning of **sow** rhymes with **how**.

space¹ /speɪs/ NOUN [plural spaces]
1 no plural the area available to be used □ There isn't enough space to hold a party here. 🖫 Can you make space for one more person? 🖫 We created more space by removing all the shelves. 🖫 I don't have enough disk space.
2 an empty area □ Write your name in the space at the top of the sheet. 🖫 I couldn't find a parking space. 🖫 It is important for cities to have plenty of open spaces.
3 no plural the area outside the Earth's

atmosphere, where the planets and stars are □ *Another rocket was launched into space yesterday.*

➤ Remember that when you say 'space' meaning 'the area outside the Earth's atmosphere', you do not use the word 'the' before it:
✓ *He's always been very interested in space.*
✗ *He's always been very interested in the space.*

space² /speɪs/ VERB [spaces, spacing, spaced] to arrange things so that they have a particular distance or amount of time between them □ *Plants were spaced at intervals of roughly 50 centimetres.* □ *The journeys were spaced over a five year period.*

spacecraft /'speɪskrɑːft/ NOUN [plural spacecraft or spacecrafts] a vehicle that can travel into space

space shuttle /'speɪs ʃʌtəl/ NOUN [plural space shuttles] a vehicle like a plane that can travel into space and come back to Earth to be used again

spade /speɪd/ NOUN [plural spades]
1 a tool with a wide flat part that you use for digging
2 spades one of the four types of playing card, which have the symbol (♠) printed on them □ *the ace of spades*

spaghetti /spə'geti/ NOUN, NO PLURAL a type of pasta that is like long thin string □ *spaghetti with tomato sauce*

spam /spæm/ NOUN, NO PLURAL e-mails that you do not want, especially e-mails trying to sell you things. A computing word.

span¹ /spæn/ NOUN [plural spans] the length of time that something lasts □ *The country had changed completely within a span of twenty years.* 🔂 *Most toddlers have a very short attention span.*

span² /spæn/ VERB [spans, spanning, spanned]
1 to last for a particular period of time □ *His singing career spanned three decades.*
2 to go across an area □ *An old wooden bridge spans the river.*

spare¹ /speə(r)/ ADJECTIVE
1 extra and available to be used □ *I stayed in Fiona's spare room.* □ *I've got a spare ticket for Saturday's concert, if you'd like it.* □ *Neither of us had any spare cash.*
2 spare time time when you do not have to work and can do what you want □ *What do you do in your spare time?*

spare² /speə(r)/ VERB [spares, sparing, spared] to be able to give or lend something to someone because you do not need it yourself □ *Could you spare me a few pounds?* □ *We can't spare anyone to help out today.*

spark /spɑːk/ NOUN [plural sparks] a very small burning piece that is sent out from a fire or made by rubbing two hard surfaces together □ *A shower of sparks shot out of the bonfire.*

sparkle /'spɑːkəl/ NOUN [plural sparkles] points of bright light □ *the sparkle of the sea*

speak /spiːk/ VERB [speaks, speaking, spoke, spoken]
1 to say something □ **+ to** *Could I speak to you for a moment?* □ **+ about** *He never spoke publicly about his marriage.* □ *She was so tired she could hardly speak.* □ *We all sat there, and nobody spoke.*
2 to be able to talk in a particular language □ *Do you speak Greek?*
3 Speaking. something you say when someone on the telephone asks to speak to you □ *'May I speak to Mrs Kennedy?' 'Speaking.'*
♦ PHRASAL VERB **speak up 1** to say something more loudly □ *Could you speak up, please?* **2** to tell people your opinion about something □ *We all thought our boss was being unfair, but nobody was brave enough to speak up.*

speaker /'spiːkə(r)/ NOUN [plural speakers]
1 a piece of equipment that the sound from a radio, CD player, etc. comes out of
2 someone who gives a speech 🔂 *Our guest speaker tonight is from Oxfam.*

spear /spɪə(r)/ NOUN [plural spears] a long thin weapon with a sharp metal point

special /'speʃəl/ ADJECTIVE
1 unusual, and usually better than what is normal 🔂 *We've been saving this wine for a special occasion.* □ *My boyfriend always makes me feel really special.* 🔂 *We've all been making a special effort to be friendly.*
2 meant for or having a particular purpose □ *Special trains will take fans to the match.* □ *a special tool for making rugs*

specialist /'speʃəlɪst/ NOUN [plural specialists] someone who knows a lot about a particular subject □ *My GP has referred me to a heart specialist.*

specially /'speʃəli/ ADVERB for one particular purpose □ *Jo's had her costume specially made for the party.*

species /'spiːʃiːz/ NOUN [plural species] a group of animals or plants whose members have similar features and that can produce young together □ *a rare species of orchid*

specific /spə'sɪfɪk/ ADJECTIVE
1 giving all the details about something in a clear way □ *Sarah's directions weren't very specific.*
2 exactly as has been stated or described □ *Each child has his own specific jobs to do.*

specimen /'spesɪmən/ NOUN [plural specimens] a small amount of blood etc. that can be tested by doctors or scientists □ *a specimen of urine*

spectacle /'spektəkəl/ NOUN [plural spectacles] something that is interesting, exciting or surprising to see □ *The opening ceremony of the games was a wonderful spectacle.*

spectacular /spek'tækjʊlə(r)/ ADJECTIVE very interesting, exciting or surprising □ *a spectacular firework display* □ *The scenery was absolutely spectacular.*

spectator /spek'teɪtə(r)/ NOUN [plural spectators] someone who is watching an event □ *United won the match in front of more than 60,000 spectators.*

sped /sped/ PAST TENSE AND PAST PARTICIPLE OF **speed²** □ *A bullet sped past his ear.*

speech /spiːtʃ/ NOUN [plural speeches]
1 a talk that you give in front of a group of people ⊞ *The bride's father usually makes a speech.*
2 *no plural* the ability to speak ⊞ *He seemed to have lost the power of speech.*
3 *no plural* the particular way that someone speaks □ *She was so tired that her speech was slurred.*

➤ Note that when you speak formally in front of a group of people, you **make a speech**. You can also **give a speech**:
✓ *I had to make/give a speech at the wedding.*
✗ *I had to do a speech at the wedding.*

speed¹ /spiːd/ NOUN [plural speeds]
1 how quickly someone or something moves □ *He was driving at a speed of about 30 miles per hour.* □ *The train was travelling at speed when it hit the rocks on the track.* ⊞ *What's the top speed of this model?*
2 how quickly someone or something works or something happens □ *Our new programs offer accuracy and speed.* □ *The managers are very pleased with the speed of her progress.* ⊞ *You'll gradually pick up speed as you learn the job.*

speed² /spiːd/ VERB [speeds, speeding, sped or speeded] to move, go or pass quickly □ *He sped off down the road on his bike.* □ *The hours sped by as we sat and chatted.*
♦ PHRASAL VERB **speed (something) up** to go faster or make something faster □ *Accepting online applications should speed up the recruitment process.*

speedy /'spiːdɪ/ ADJECTIVE [speedier, speediest] quick or fast □ *Thanks for the speedy reply to my letter.*

spell¹ /spel/ VERB [spells, spelling, spelt or spelled] to say or write the letters of a word in the correct order □ *Could you spell your name for me?* □ *Adam was always good at spelling.*

spell² /spel/ NOUN [plural spells] a set of words that are used to make something magic happen ⊞ *The wicked witch cast a spell on Snow White.*

spelling /'spelɪŋ/ NOUN [plural spellings]
1 the way that a word is spelt □ *'Donut' is the American spelling of 'doughnut'.*
2 *no plural* the ability to spell □ *His spelling is terrible.*

spend /spend/ VERB [spends, spending, spent]
1 to use money to buy things ⊞ *We spent a lot of money on our holiday.* □ *Try to cut down how much you spend.*
2 to pass time doing something ⊞ *Do you spend much time on the computer?* ⊞ *I used to spend hours reading in my room.* ⊞ *I spent ages decorating that cake.* □ *We spent the weekend at my sister's.*

➤ Note that you spend money **on** someone or something:
✓ *She spends a lot of money on clothes.*
✗ *She spends a lot of money for clothes.*

sperm /spɜːm/ NOUN [plural sperm or sperms] a cell from a man that joins with the egg from a woman to make a baby. A biology word.

sphere /sfɪə(r)/ NOUN [plural spheres] a solid object that is the shape of a ball

spice /spaɪs/ NOUN [plural spices] a substance made from a plant that adds flavour to food □ *herbs and spices* □ *Ginger is a spice.*

spicy /'spaɪsɪ/ ADJECTIVE [spicier, spiciest] tasting hot on your tongue □ *spicy food*

spider /'spaɪdə(r)/ NOUN [plural spiders] a small creature with eight legs that uses very thin threads to make a web (= very thin net) for catching insects

spike /spaɪk/ NOUN [plural spikes] a hard, sharp point, usually made of metal or wood □ *There were sharp spikes on top of the wall.*

spill /spɪl/ VERB [spills, spilling, spilt or spilled] to come out of a container by accident or to make something, especially a liquid, do this □ *Careful! You're going to spill your tea.* □ *She spilt a can of paint all over the carpet.* □ *The sack burst and the rice spilled out onto the floor.*

➤ **THESAURUS:** If something **spills**, it comes out of a container by accident or you make something, especially a liquid, do this. If you **pour** a liquid, you make it come out of a container such as a jug or bottle. For example, you might **pour** a glass of orange juice from a bottle. If you **tip** a liquid somewhere, you pour it out of a container. If you **tip** something, it is often less careful than pouring. For example, you might **tip** water into a sink when you have finished using it.

spin /spɪn/ VERB [spins, spinning, spun]
1 to turn round and round very quickly or make something do this □ *The ballerina spun round and round on her toes.* □ *He can spin the basketball on his finger.*
2 to make long, thin threads out of cotton, wool, or other material by pulling it and twisting it

spinach /'spɪnɪdʒ/ NOUN, NO PLURAL a vegetable with large dark green leaves

spinal /'spaɪnəl/ ADJECTIVE to do with the line of bones down the back of a person or animal. A biology word. □ *a spinal injury*

spine /spaɪn/ NOUN [plural spines] the line of bones down the back of a person or animal. A biology word.

spiral /'spaɪərəl/ NOUN [plural spirals] a shape formed by a line that curves round and round a centre point □ *The shell formed a perfect spiral.*

spirit /'spɪrɪt/ NOUN [plural spirits]
1 your attitude or the attitude of a group of people □ **+ of** *The celebration was held in a spirit of friendship.* □ *Her adventurous spirit took her all over the world.* □ *Our town has a strong community spirit.*
2 spirits your mood ᄆ *She was in really high/low spirits (= a happy/sad mood).*
3 a strong alcoholic drink, for example whisky
4 the part of a person that some people believe continues to live after the body dies

spiritual /'spɪrɪtʃuəl/ ADJECTIVE to do with someone's spirit, emotions and thoughts and not their body □ *an intensely spiritual experience*

spit /spɪt/ VERB [spits, spitting, spat] to force liquid or food out of your mouth □ *She took one mouthful and then spat it out on to her plate.*

spite /spaɪt/ NOUN, NO PLURAL
1 in spite of used to say that a fact or event makes something else that happens surprising □ *We decided to go to the seaside in spite of the rain.* □ *He passed his exam in spite of doing no revision.*
2 a feeling of wanting to hurt or upset someone □ *He threw my picture away out of spite.*

splash¹ /splæʃ/ VERB [splashes, splashing, splashed]
1 to put liquid on something with a quick movement □ *Kate splashed some cold water on her face.*
2 to move water around in a noisy way □ *The baby was splashing happily in his bath.*

splash² /splæʃ/ NOUN [plural splashes] the sound that water makes when something hits it □ *Kurt fell into the pool with a loud splash.*

splendid /'splendɪd/ ADJECTIVE very good □ *a splendid idea*

split¹ /splɪt/ VERB [splits, splitting, split]
1 to break or tear apart □ *Your trousers have split down the back.*

2 to break something or tear it apart □ *The lightning had split the tree in two.*
3 to divide a group of people into smaller groups □ *I split the children into two groups.*
4 to end a marriage or relationship □ *I was three when my parents split.* □ *I've just split up with my boyfriend.*

split² /splɪt/ NOUN [plural splits] a tear or break in something □ *There's a long split in the wood.*

spoil /spɔɪl/ VERB [spoils, spoiling, spoilt or spoiled]
1 to make something less good □ *I had an argument with Adrian and it spoilt the whole evening.* □ *Low cloud spoilt the view of the mountains.* □ *The weather was fairly awful but we didn't let it spoil our fun.*
2 to always allow a child to have or do what they want and cause them to become badly behaved □ *She spoils those children.*

spoilt /spɔɪlt/ PAST TENSE AND PAST PARTICIPLE OF spoil

spoke¹ /spəʊk/ PAST TENSE OF speak

spoke² /spəʊk/ NOUN [plural spokes] one of the thin metal pieces that connect the centre of a wheel with the edge

spoken /'spəʊkən/ PAST PARTICIPLE OF speak

sponge /spʌndʒ/ NOUN [plural sponges] a soft object, made from natural or artificial material, that you use to wash your body

sponsor¹ /'spɒnsə(r)/ VERB [sponsors, sponsoring, sponsored]
1 to pay for something such as an event or television programme, often as a way of advertising your company □ *A local company sponsors our football team.*
2 to agree to give someone money for a school, organization, etc. if they do something difficult □ *Will you sponsor me to run in the race?*

sponsor² /'spɒnsə(r)/ NOUN [plural sponsors]
1 a company that gives money to someone or something as a way of advertising the company □ *The company is the official sponsor of the 2008 European Cup.*
2 a person who gives money to a charity (= organization that helps people) if someone else does something difficult □ *How many sponsors have you got?*
• **sponsored** /'spɒnsəd/ ADJECTIVE a sponsored swim/walk, etc. a swim or walk, etc. that you do to get money for a school or charity (= organization that helps people), in which people agree to give you money if you are successful
• **sponsorship** /'spɒnsəʃɪp/ NOUN, NO PLURAL when someone sponsors someone or something ᄆ *Toyota announced a five-year sponsorship deal with the American Football League.*

spoon /spuːn/ NOUN [plural spoons] an object with a handle and a curved part at one end that you use for lifting liquid food to your mouth □ a soup spoon □ a wooden spoon

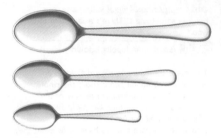

spoonful /ˈspuːnfʊl/ NOUN [plural spoonfuls] the amount a spoon will hold □ Jamila put a spoonful of sugar in her coffee.

sport /spɔːt/ NOUN [plural sports]
1 a particular game or activity □ Football is a very popular sport. ᐸ My Dad has played sports all his life. ᐸ We have very good sports facilities at our school.
2 no plural games and physical activities like football, tennis, and swimming □ Adam loves all kinds of sport. □ She watches a lot of sport on the television.

sports car /spɔːts ˌkɑː(r)/ NOUN [plural sports cars] a small fast car that has two seats and no roof

spot¹ /spɒt/ NOUN [plural spots]
1 a place or position □ This is a lovely spot for a picnic. □ X marks the spot where the treasure is buried. □ She hopes to retain her number one spot in the championship.
2 a round shape that is often part of a pattern □ She wore a pink dress with white spots.
3 a red raised mark on your skin □ Teenagers often suffer from spots.

spot² /spɒt/ VERB [spots, spotting, spotted] to see or notice something or someone □ I suddenly spotted Ian over by the window. □ Social workers spotted signs of neglect in the girl.

spouse /spaʊs/ NOUN [plural spouses] a formal word meaning your husband or wife

sprang /spræŋ/ PAST TENSE OF spring²

spray¹ /spreɪ/ VERB [sprays, spraying, sprayed] to cause a liquid to come out of a container in many very small drops □ She sprayed herself with perfume.

spray² /spreɪ/ NOUN [plural sprays]
1 many very small drops of liquid in the air □ The spray from the waterfall wet their hair.
2 liquid in a container which is forced out in very small drops □ a perfume spray

spread /spred/ VERB [spreads, spreading, spread]
1 to cover a larger area or to affect more and more people, or to make something do this □ The cancer has spread to his lungs. □ The virus spread rapidly in the crowded conditions. □ I don't want to spread alarm. □ Fire spread throughout the building.
2 to arrange something so that it covers a large area □ + out I spread the map out on the table. □ The bird spread its wings and flew off. □ Bits of machinery were spread all over the floor.
3 if information spreads, or you spread it, it becomes known by more and more people □ Rumours spread very quickly in this little village. ᐸ News of his death spread rapidly.
4 to put a layer of a soft substance onto a surface □ She spread her toast thickly with butter.

spring¹ /sprɪŋ/ NOUN [plural springs]
1 the season between winter and summer when plants start to grow □ Daffodils flower in spring. □ There will be an election next spring. □ spring sunshine
2 a twisted piece of wire which goes back to its original shape after you have pushed or pulled it □ The chair had some broken springs in it.
3 a place where water flows out of the ground □ a mountain spring □ spring water

spring² /sprɪŋ/ VERB [springs, springing, sprang, sprung] to move or jump quickly □ He sprang out of bed to answer the door.

sprinkle /ˈsprɪŋkəl/ VERB [sprinkles, sprinkling, sprinkled] to put small drops or pieces of something over a surface □ She sprinkled chocolate chips onto the cake.

sprout /spraʊt/ VERB [sprouts, sprouting, sprouted] to start to grow, or to produce new leaves or flowers □ Buds were sprouting on the sycamore tree.

spruce /spruːs/ NOUN [plural spruces] a tall tree with leaves that look like needles

sprung /sprʌŋ/ PAST PARTICIPLE OF spring²

spun /spʌn/ PAST TENSE AND PAST PARTICIPLE OF spin

spy¹ /spaɪ/ NOUN [plural spies] someone whose job is to discover secret information about another country or company □ a former Russian spy

spy² /spaɪ/ VERB [spies, spying, spied] to work as a spy □ Both men had been spying for the government.
♦ PHRASAL VERB spy on someone to secretly watch what someone is doing □ Hetty spent a lot of time spying on her neighbours.

square¹ /skweə(r)/ NOUN [plural squares]
1 a flat shape with four equal sides and four angles of 90 degrees
2 an open space with buildings on all four sides □ *a tree-lined square* □ *There was a clock in the market square.* □ *Trafalgar Square*
3 the result of multiplying a number by itself. A mathematics word □ *The square of 4 is 16.*

square² /skweə(r)/ ADJECTIVE
1 shaped like a square □ *a square table*
2 measuring a particular amount on each side □ *The room was about 3 metres square.*
3 a square metre/foot/mile, etc. the area of a square which has sides which are a metre, a mile, etc. long □ *The tiles cost £20 a square metre.* □ *The building offers 65,000 square metres of office space.*

squash¹ /skwɒʃ/ VERB [squashes, squashing, squashed]
1 to press something until it is flat □ *Juliet squashed the empty can.* �All the strawberries got squashed at the bottom of the bag.*
2 to put a lot of people or things into a small space □ *I was squashed in the back seat of the car with three other people.* □ *+ into 12 of us squashed into two cars to travel into town.*

squash² /skwɒʃ/ NOUN, NO PLURAL
1 a game in which you hit a small rubber ball against the walls of a court
2 a sweet cold drink with a fruit flavour □ *a glass of orange squash*

squeak /skwi:k/ NOUN [plural squeaks] a very high sound

squeeze /skwi:z/ VERB [squeezes, squeezing, squeezed]
1 to press something tightly □ *She squeezed my hand encouragingly.*
2 to try to move somewhere where there is very little space □ *The cat tried to squeeze itself under the sofa.* □ *He was trying to squeeze into some very tight jeans.*
3 to press something in order to get something out □ *He squeezed the last of the toothpaste out of the tube.* □ *Emma was squeezing a lemon.*

➤ **THESAURUS:** If you **press** something, you push it, or push it firmly against something else. You might **press** a doorbell, for example. If you **squeeze** something, you press it tightly. For example, you squeeze a lemon to remove the juice. If you **squash** something, you press it until it is flat. You might **squash** a box before you put it into the bin, for example. If you **crush** something, you press it so that it is broken or in small pieces. You might **crush** biscuits to use in a cake.

squirrel /ˈskwɪrəl/ NOUN [plural squirrels] a small grey or red animal with a long, thick tail that lives in trees and eats nuts

St /seɪnt, stri:t/ ABBREVIATION
1 saint
2 street

stab /stæb/ VERB [stabs, stabbing, stabbed] to kill or to injure someone by pushing a knife or other sharp object into them □ *The woman was stabbed with a knife.*

stable¹ /ˈsteɪbəl/ ADJECTIVE
1 firm, strong and not moving □ *This will help to keep the shelf stable.*
2 not changing over a period of time 🔸 *The price has remained relatively stable over recent years.* 🔸 *He's in a stable condition in hospital.*

stable² /ˈsteɪbəl/ NOUN [plural stables] a building to keep horses in

stack¹ /stæk/ NOUN [plural stacks] a pile of things □ *a stack of books*

stack² /stæk/ VERB [stacks, stacking, stacked] to put things into a stack □ *Stack the dishes in the sink and I'll wash them later.* 🔸 *He got a job stacking shelves in a supermarket.*

stadium /ˈsteɪdɪəm/ NOUN [plural stadiums or stadia] a large open area for playing sports, with seats around it 🔸 *a football stadium* □ *They will face Real Madrid at the Bernabeu Stadium in the semi-finals.*

staff /stɑ:f/ NOUN, NO PLURAL the people who work for a particular organization 🔸 *Six new members of staff are joining the school this term.* □ *The company has a staff of 150.* □ *There is a shortage of medical staff in many hospitals.*

stage /steɪdʒ/ NOUN [plural stages]
1 the raised area in a theatre where the actors and other performers perform □ *This is their first appearance on stage together.* 🔸 *I loved the stage show.*
2 one part of a process, or a period of time in the development of something □ *+ of The designs are at various stages of development.* 🔸 *The work is still in its early stages.* 🔸 *It's hard to predict what will happen at this stage.*

stagger /ˈstæɡə(r)/ VERB [staggers, staggering, staggered] to walk moving from side to side in a way that looks as if you might fall □ *He staggered across the room and fell into a chair.*

stain¹ /steɪn/ VERB [stains, staining, stained] to leave a mark that is difficult to remove □ *The coffee you spilt has stained the carpet.* □ *+ with His uniform was stained with blood.*

stain² /steɪn/ NOUN [plural stains] a dirty mark on something that is difficult to remove □ *His overalls were covered in oil stains.*

stair /steə(r)/ NOUN [plural **stairs**]
1 stairs a set of steps that go from one level in a building to another 🔁 I climbed the stairs to the second floor. 🔁 A flight of stairs led down to the cellar.
2 one of these steps □ Alice sat on the bottom stair.

staircase /'steəkeɪs/ NOUN [plural **staircases**] a set of stairs 🔁 a spiral staircase (= stairs which curl round and round)

stale /steɪl/ ADJECTIVE [**staler**, **stalest**] not fresh □ stale bread □ The air smelt stale inside the room.

stalk /stɔːk/ NOUN [plural **stalks**] the stem of a flower, leaf or fruit □ an apple stalk

stall /stɔːl/ NOUN [plural **stalls**] a table or a small open shop where people sell things 🔁 a market stall □ a roadside food stall □ The stalls sell fresh fruit and vegetables.

stamp¹ /stæmp/ NOUN [plural **stamps**]
1 a small printed piece of paper that you buy and stick on letters before you post them 🔁 a first-class stamp □ I noticed the Canadian stamp on the envelope.
2 a tool that you use to stamp words, numbers, or a design on something, or the mark it makes 🔁 a rubber stamp □ a date stamp

stamp² /stæmp/ VERB [**stamps, stamping, stamped**]
1 to bring your foot down firmly on the ground □ + **on** He stamped on the brake. 🔁 She stamped her feet to keep them warm.
2 to print letters, numbers, or a design on something □ The official stamped her passport. □ + **with** Each letter is stamped with the date we receive it.

stand¹ /stænd/ VERB [**stands, standing, stood**]
1 to be in a vertical position on your feet, not sitting or lying □ I was so tired I could barely stand. □ I stood on a chair to reach the shelf. □ He was standing next to his brother.
2 to get up onto your feet after sitting or lying □ Everyone stood when the queen entered. □ + **up** Stand up and let me look at you.
3 to be in a particular position □ The train stood outside Waterloo for nearly an hour. □ Durham stands on the River Wear.
4 to put something in a particular position □ I stood the jug on the table.
5 to be able to accept someone or something 🔁 I can't stand her brother, Mark. □ Marie couldn't stand hearing her parents arguing any more.
6 to continue to exist or to be used □ The judge ordered that the sentence should stand. 🔁 His offer of money still stands.

♦ PHRASAL VERBS **stand back** to move a short distance away from someone □ Stand back, please, so that the doctors can get through. **stand by**
1 to be ready to do something □ Teams of doctors are standing by with medical equipment. **2** to do nothing to prevent an unpleasant action or situation □ The government is just standing by while its people starve. **stand for something** if letters stand for something, that thing begins with those letters □ What does BBC stand for? **stand out** to be very easy to see or notice □ The yellow flowers really stood out against the green background. **stand up** to get up onto your feet after sitting or lying □ She stood up and left the room. **stand up for someone/ something** to support someone or something that is being criticized or attacked □ My brother always stands up for me when my parents tell me off.

stand² /stænd/ NOUN [plural **stands**]
1 rows of seats where people sit to watch sports □ Spectators were cheering from the stands.
2 something that an object stands on □ a large mirror on a stand

standard¹ /'stændəd/ NOUN [plural **standards**]
1 a level of quality □ + **of** We hope to improve the standard of medical care. 🔁 The club has set high standards for itself this season. 🔁 Living standards have risen dramatically. 🔁 Standards have been slipping (= getting worse) recently.
2 standards principles about what is acceptable behaviour □ He has high moral standards.

standard² /'stændəd/ ADJECTIVE normal or usual □ the standard charge for postage 🔁 All of this is standard police procedure. □ Chemotherapy is now a standard treatment for cancer.

staple¹ /'steɪpəl/ NOUN [plural **staples**] a type of food or product that you use a lot of □ staples such as milk and bread
staple² /'steɪpəl/ ADJECTIVE a staple food or product is one of the most basic and important ones 🔁 Their staple diet is rice.
staple³ /'steɪpəl/ NOUN [plural **staples**] a bent piece of wire that you push through papers to fasten them together
staple⁴ /'steɪpəl/ VERB [**staples, stapling, stapled**] to fasten papers together with a staple □ Staple the pages together.
● **stapler** /'steɪplə(r)/ NOUN [plural **staplers**] a small tool for stapling papers together

star¹ /stɑː(r)/ NOUN [plural **stars**]
1 a mass of burning gas in the sky that you can see at night as a point of light □ the brightest star in the night sky □ There are billions of stars in our galaxy.

2 a famous person, especially a performer 🔲 *a film star* 🔲 *a pop star* 🔲 *He became one of Hollywood's biggest stars.* □ **+ of** *He was married to Jennifer Aniston, star of the TV show 'Friends'.*

3 a shape with five or more points □ *a six-pointed star* □ *The EU symbol is a circle of gold stars on a blue background.*

star² /stɑː(r)/ VERB [stars, starring, starred] to have the main part in a film □ *Tom Cruise is to star in the sequel.* □ *a new film starring Kate Winslet*

stare¹ /steə(r)/ VERB [stares, staring, stared] to look at someone or something for a long time □ *What are you staring at?*

stare² /steə(r)/ NOUN [plural stares] when you look at someone or something for a long time 🔲 *Tony gave him a blank stare.*

start¹ /stɑːt/ VERB [starts, starting, started]

1 to begin doing something □ **+ to do something** *Suddenly, a bird started to sing.* □ **+ ing** *What time did you start working this morning?* □ *I'm starting a new job next week.*

2 to begin to happen or exist, or to make something happen or exist □ *Work on the new bridge has started at last.* □ *He started an online art gallery.* □ *The fire started in the kitchen.*

3 to begin to work or to make a machine or a vehicle begin to work □ *The car wouldn't start.* □ *I couldn't start the engine.*

♦ PHRASAL VERB **start (something) off** to begin an activity or an event □ *Let's start off with some gentle exercises*

start² /stɑːt/ NOUN [plural starts]

1 the beginning of something 🔲 *Right from the start, I knew I'd be happy here.* □ **+ of** *The runners lined up for the start of the race.*

2 make a start to begin doing something □ *I'm going to make a start on the cooking.*

3 for a start used to give the first of a list of reasons □ *For a start, I'm fed up with sharing a room with my sister.*

startle /'stɑːtəl/ VERB [startles, startling, startled] to suddenly frighten or shock someone □ *He was startled by a loud noise.*

starvation /stɑːˈveɪʃən/ NOUN, NO PLURAL when people are very hungry and have not got enough to eat □ *Thousands of people die of starvation every year.*

starve /stɑːv/ VERB [starves, starving, starved] to die or to suffer because you have not got enough to eat 🔲 *If they don't get food aid, these people are going to starve to death.*

state¹ /steɪt/ NOUN [plural states]

1 the condition that someone or something is in □ *The house was in a very poor state.* □ **+ of** *She's always complaining about the state of our public transport.* 🔲 *I'm still in a state of shock.*

2 a country □ *the state of Israel* 🔲 *There was a meeting between heads of state* (= leaders of countries).

3 the state the government of a country □ *The state should provide help for the sick and elderly.*

4 a part of a country that has its own government □ *New York state* □ **+ of** *the southern Indian state of Andhra Pradesh*

5 the States the US □ *He spent six weeks in the States.*

state² /steɪt/ VERB [states, stating, stated] to formally say or write something □ *The letter clearly states that you must bring some identification with you.* □ *They were given an opportunity to state their views.*

statement /'steɪtmənt/ NOUN [plural statements] something that you say or write, especially formally or officially 🔲 *The police asked me to make a written statement of what I saw.* □ *A statement on his website said he had no plans to leave the band.*

station /'steɪʃən/ NOUN [plural stations]

1 a building where trains or buses stop to allow people to get on and off 🔲 *a railway station* 🔲 *a bus station* □ *I'll meet you at the station.*

2 a building where some types of work take place 🔲 *He was taken to the local police station.* 🔲 *a fire station* 🔲 *We stopped at a petrol station* (= a place that sells petrol). 🔲 *a nuclear power station*

3 a company which makes and broadcasts television or radio programmes 🔲 *a local radio station* 🔲 *The interview was broadcast by a Spanish television station.*

statue /'stætʃuː/ NOUN [plural statues] a large model of a person or animal made out of stone, metal or wood □ **+ of** *a huge statue of the Buddha* □ *a life-size bronze statue*

stay¹ /steɪ/ VERB [stays, staying, stayed]

1 to remain in a place □ *Make sure you stay inside the house.* □ *Would you like to stay for dinner?* 🔲 *He agreed to stay home and look after the children.* 🔲 *Stay there/here!* □ *I stayed in the same job for nearly twenty years.*

2 to continue to be in a particular condition □ *She tried to stay calm as they waited.* □ *I could hardly stay awake.* □ *Things can't stay the same for ever.* 🔲 *At the moment we are very happy together, and I hope it will stay that way.*

3 to spend a period of time in a place □ **+ with** *I'm going to stay with my sister for a few days.* □ **+ in** *We stayed in a wonderful hotel.* 🔲 *I stayed the night at a friend's house.*

♦ PHRASAL VERBS **stay in** to remain in your house □ *I stayed in on Saturday and watched TV.* **stay out** to not come home at night, or to come home very late □ *My parents don't like me staying out late.* **stay up** to not go to bed until later than usual □ *We stayed up to watch the election results.*

stay[2] /steɪ/ NOUN [plural stays] a period of time that you spend at a place □ *The trip includes an overnight stay in Bangkok.*

steady /'stedɪ/ ADJECTIVE [steadier, steadiest]
1 firm and not shaking □ *You need a steady hand.* □ *Can you hold it steady for me?*
2 continuous and gradual 🕮 *We're making steady progress.*
3 not changing □ *I tried to keep a steady pace.*

steak /steɪk/ NOUN [plural steaks] a thick piece of meat or fish, especially meat from a cow □ *He was eating steak and chips.* □ *tuna steaks*

steal /sti:l/ VERB [steals, stealing, stole, stolen] to take something without the owner's permission □ *The thieves stole money and jewellery.* □ *It's wrong to steal.* □ *+ from* *Several valuable paintings were stolen from the house.* □ *a stolen car*

> ➤ Remember that thieves **steal** money and objects. They **rob** people and places: □ *They stole his money and his watch.* □ *They were robbed in the street.* □ *They robbed a bank.*

steam[1] /sti:m/ NOUN, NO PLURAL the gas that is formed when you heat water □ *Steam was rising from the coffee pot.*

steam[2] /sti:m/ VERB [steams, steaming, steamed]
1 to produce steam □ *A kettle was steaming on the stove.* □ *a steaming bowl of soup*
2 to cook food in steam □ *steamed vegetables*

steel[1] /sti:l/ NOUN, NO PLURAL a very hard metal that is a mixture of iron and carbon 🕮 *Many knives and forks are made from stainless steel* (= steel that stays shiny).

steel[2] /sti:l/ ADJECTIVE
1 made from steel □ *steel knives*
2 to do with making steel and steel objects □ *the steel industry*

steep /sti:p/ ADJECTIVE [steeper, steepest] a steep hill or slope goes up or down very quickly □ *a steep hill* □ *The path was too steep for me to cycle up.* 🕮 *It was a steep climb to the top of the hill.*

steer /stɪə(r)/ VERB [steers, steering, steered] to control the direction that a vehicle moves in □ *He steered the car through the narrow streets.* □ *The captain steered out of the harbour.*

steering wheel /'stɪərɪŋ ˌwi:l/ NOUN [plural steering wheels] the wheel a driver holds to control a car's direction

stem /stem/ NOUN [plural stems] the long thin part of a plant, which the leaves grow on

step[1] /step/ NOUN [plural steps]
1 one of a series of actions involved in doing or achieving something 🕮 *These talks are an important step in bringing peace to the region.* 🕮 *For me, that school play was the first step towards becoming an actor.* 🕮 *Step by step* (= gradually) *she is learning to speak again.*
2 the action of lifting your foot off the ground and putting it down again in walking, running or dancing 🕮 *He took a step forward.* □ *I'm sure I heard steps* (= the sound that steps make) *outside.*
3 a flat surface that you walk on to go up or down to a different level, often one of a series □ *The postman left the parcel on the front step.* □ *We climbed the steep steps to the castle.*

step[2] /step/ VERB [steps, stepping, stepped]
1 to take a step □ *He opened the door and stepped out.*
2 to put your foot on something, often by accident □ *+ on* *He stepped on my toe!* □ *+ in* *I stepped in some mud.*

step- /step/ PREFIX step- is added to the beginning of words to show that people are related to you by a second marriage □ *stepfather* □ *stepdaughter*

stepbrother /'stepbrʌðə(r)/ NOUN [plural stepbrothers] the son of a person who has married your mother or father, but who is not your brother

stepdaughter /'stepdɔ:tə(r)/ NOUN [plural stepdaughters] the daughter of your husband or wife, who is not your daughter

stepfather /'stepfɑ:ðə(r)/ NOUN [plural stepfathers] the man who is married to your mother but is not your father

stepmother /'stepmʌðə(r)/ NOUN [plural stepmothers] the woman who is married to your father but is not your mother

stepsister /'stepsɪstə(r)/ NOUN [plural stepsisters] the daughter of a person who has married your mother or father, but who is not your sister

stepson /'stepsʌn/ NOUN [plural stepsons] the son of your husband or wife, who is not your son

stereotype /'steriətaɪp/ NOUN [plural stereotypes] an idea about what a particular type of person is like, which may be wrong or unfair □ *The programme aims to challenge racial stereotypes.*

stern /stɜ:n/ ADJECTIVE [sterner, sternest] very serious and slightly angry □ *He had a stern expression on his face.* □ *a stern warning*

steward /'stjʊəd/ NOUN [plural stewards] a man whose job is to look after passengers on an aeroplane or ship

stick¹ /stɪk/ VERB [sticks, sticking, stuck]
1 to push something thin or sharp into something, or to be pushed into something □ *We stuck pins into the cushion.* □ *Stop sticking your elbows into me!* □ *There was a thorn sticking in my skin.* □ *He stuck his fingers in his ears.*
2 to fix something to something else, or to become fixed to something □ *Never mind, we can always stick the pieces back together.* □ *We stuck labels on the jam jars.* □ *He had a piece of paper stuck on his back.*
3 an informal word meaning to put something somewhere □ *Just stick the shopping on the floor.* □ *He stuck his head round the door to say hello.*
4 to become unable to move □ *The car stuck in the mud.* □ *This drawer keeps sticking.*
➡ go to **stick your nose in/into something**
◆ PHRASAL VERBS **stick out** to come out further than a surface or an edge □ *His ears stick out.* □ *I could see an umbrella sticking out of her bag.*
➡ go to **stick out like a sore thumb**
stick something out to stretch a part of your body forward □ *They stuck out their hands for food.* 🖫 *She stuck her tongue out at me.* **stick to something** if you stick to a plan, decision, etc., you do not change it □ *They promised to stick to our original agreement.*

stick² /stɪk/ NOUN [plural sticks]
1 a thin piece of wood that has come from a tree □ *We searched for sticks to make a fire.*
2 a long thin piece of wood used for a particular purpose □ *a walking stick* □ *a hockey stick*
3 a long thin piece of something □ *a stick of rhubarb*

sticky /'stɪkɪ/ ADJECTIVE [stickier, stickiest]
designed to stick to another surface, or covered with something that can stick to things 🖫 *Mend the book with some sticky tape.* 🖫 *sticky fingers*

stiff /stɪf/ ADJECTIVE [stiffer, stiffest]
1 difficult to bend □ *stiff cardboard* □ *stiff material*
2 if part of your body is stiff, it hurts when you move it 🖫 *I've got a stiff neck.* □ *stiff joints*

still¹ /stɪl/ ADVERB
1 up to a particular time and continuing □ *Are you still living in Tokyo?* □ *By Sunday she still hadn't replied to the invitation.* □ *I'm still hungry.*
2 despite what you have just said or done □ *She's treated me badly but she's still my daughter and I love her.* □ *It was raining but we still decided to go.*
3 used for saying that something is possible even now □ *You can still catch the bus if you leave now.*

still² /stɪl/ ADJECTIVE [stiller, stillest]
1 not moving 🖫 *Keep still while I brush your hair!*
2 a still drink is without bubbles □ *still lemonade*

sting¹ /stɪŋ/ VERB [stings, stinging, stung]
1 if an insect or plant stings you, it hurts your skin when it touches you □ *I was badly stung by the plant.* □ *Bees can sting.*
2 to feel a sudden pain in your eyes or skin, or to make someone feel a sudden pain in their eyes or skin □ *The shampoo made her eyes sting.* □ *Smoke stung his eyes.*

sting² /stɪŋ/ NOUN [plural stings]
1 the sudden pain you feel when an insect or plant stings you □ *a wasp sting*
2 a sudden pain in your eyes or skin

stir /stɜː(r)/ VERB [stirs, stirring, stirred]
1 to mix something with a circular movement □ *He put sugar in his tea and stirred it.*
2 to move slightly, or to make something move slightly □ *The baby stirred in its sleep.* □ *The breeze stirred her hair.*

stitch¹ /stɪtʃ/ NOUN [plural stitches]
1 a piece of thread on cloth that has been sewn □ *She sewed up the hole with small neat stitches.*
2 a piece of thread that a doctor uses to repair injuries to your skin □ *He cut his hand and needed stitches in it.*

stitch² /stɪtʃ/ VERB [stitches, stitching, stitched] to sew □ *I stitched the button on to my coat.*

stock¹ /stɒk/ NOUN [plural stocks]
1 the goods that a shop has available □ *Buy now while stocks last!*
2 out of/in stock not available/available to buy in a particular shop □ *I'm sorry but the item is out of stock at the moment.*
3 stocks shares in a company, which you can buy

stock² /stɒk/ VERB [stocks, stocking, stocked] to have something available to buy □ *Most supermarkets now stock organic products.*

stocking /'stɒkɪŋ/ NOUN [plural stockings] a very thin piece of clothing for a woman's foot and leg □ *a pair of stockings*

stock market /'stɒk ˌmɑːkɪt/ NOUN [plural stock markets] a place where company shares are bought and sold

stole /stəʊl/ PAST TENSE OF **steal**

stolen /'stəʊlən/ PAST PARTICIPLE OF **steal**

stomach /'stʌmək/ NOUN [plural stomachs]
1 the part inside your body where food goes when you have eaten it
2 the front part of your body below your chest □ *a flat stomach*

stomach ache /'stʌmək ˌeɪk/ NOUN [plural stomach aches] a pain in the stomach

stone¹ /stəʊn/ NOUN [plural stones]
1 a small piece of rock 🖫 *The boys were throwing stones into the water.*
2 *no plural* the hard substance that rocks are made of □ *The house was built of stone.*

3 a small piece of valuable rock, used for making jewellery ⏹ The necklace was made of gold and precious stones (= valuable and rare stones).
4 [plural stone] a unit for measuring weight, equal to 6.35 kilograms ☐ I weigh nine stone.
5 the hard piece in the middle of some fruits ☐ a peach stone

stone² /stəʊn/ ADJECTIVE made of stone ☐ stone walls ☐ a stone floor

stood /stʊd/ PAST TENSE AND PAST PARTICIPLE OF **stand¹**

stool /stuːl/ NOUN [plural stools] a seat without a back ☐ She was sitting on a stool in the kitchen.

stop¹ /stɒp/ VERB [stops, stopping, stopped]
1 to prevent something happening or existing or someone from doing something ☐ + ing He'll never succeed but that won't stop him trying. ☐ + from The barriers stop the crowd from pouring into the street. ☐ Nothing seems to stop the violence.
2 to no longer do something ☐ + ing The wound has stopped bleeding. ☐ Please stop this nonsense. ⏹ Stop it! I'm trying to concentrate.
3 to not happen or exist any more ☐ It was lovely when the noise stopped. ☐ We're waiting for the rain to stop.
4 to no longer move or to make something finish moving ☐ A car stopped outside the house. ☐ He stopped the ball with his foot.
5 if a public vehicle stops somewhere, it stays there for a short time for people to get on and off ☐ Does this train stop at Chester?
6 to no longer work ☐ My watch has stopped.

stop² /stɒp/ NOUN [plural stops]
1 a place where a public vehicle stops ⏹ This train calls at all stops to Glasgow.
2 come to a stop to stop moving ☐ The train came to a stop just outside Hull.

store¹ /stɔː(r)/ NOUN [plural stores]
1 a shop ☐ the village store ☐ an online store ⏹ The company opened its first store in 1930. ⏹ The store sells cards and gifts.
2 a supply of something which you keep to use when you need it ☐ + of Squirrels keep a store of food.

store² /stɔː(r)/ VERB [stores, storing, stored] to keep something somewhere ☐ Store the chocolate in a cool dry place. ☐ + away The books had been carefully stored away.

storey /ˈstɔːrɪ/ NOUN [plural storeys] one of the levels in a building ☐ a four-storey carpark

storm /stɔːm/ NOUN [plural storms] a time when there is suddenly a lot of wind and rain ⏹ A huge storm hit New Orleans. ⏹ She waited indoors until the storm had passed. ⏹ a tropical storm

stormy /ˈstɔːmɪ/ ADJECTIVE [stormier, stormiest] with a lot of strong winds and rain ⏹ stormy weather ☐ a stormy night

story /ˈstɔːrɪ/ NOUN [plural stories]
1 a description of events, which can be real or invented ⏹ The teacher was reading a story to the class. ⏹ The film is based on a true story. ⏹ The children were telling each other ghost stories. ☐ + of The book is the story of his life. ☐ + about It's a story about a Jewish boy growing up in London.
2 the US spelling of **storey**

straight¹ /streɪt/ ADJECTIVE [straighter, straightest]
1 not bent or curved ☐ a straight line ☐ straight hair
2 completely horizontal or vertical ☐ That picture isn't straight.
3 honest ⏹ Give me a straight answer!

straight² /streɪt/ ADVERB
1 in a straight line ☐ I was so tired, I couldn't walk straight. ☐ The lion ran straight towards him. ☐ She was looking straight at me.
2 straight on without changing direction ☐ Go straight on at the traffic lights.
3 immediately ☐ I came straight here.
4 straight away immediately ☐ Could you come to my office straight away, please?

straighten /ˈstreɪtən/ VERB [straightens, straightening, straightened] to become straight or to make something straight ☐ The road curved then straightened. ☐ He straightened his tie.

straightforward /ˌstreɪtˈfɔːwəd/ ADJECTIVE easy ☐ a straightforward task

strain¹ /streɪn/ VERB [strains, straining, strained]
1 to injure part of your body by using it too much ☐ You'll strain your eyes reading in the dark.
2 to try hard to do something ☐ He strained to look through a small hole in the wall.
3 to separate solid parts from a liquid ☐ Now strain the pasta.

strain² /streɪn/ NOUN [plural strains]
1 an injury to part of your body because you have used it too much ☐ a muscle strain
2 no plural when something has a lot of pressure on it ☐ The dam had burst under the strain.
3 no plural the bad effects on your mind and body when you have too much work or too many worries ☐ The strain of looking after four young children was too much for her. ☐ He's been under a lot of strain recently.

strand /strænd/ NOUN [plural strands] a thin piece of something such as hair or thread ☐ a strand of hair

stranded /ˈstrændɪd/ ADJECTIVE being in a place that you cannot leave ⏹ She was left stranded without money or passport.

strange /streɪndʒ/ ADJECTIVE [stranger, strangest]

1 unusual □ *She's a very strange woman.* □ *+ that It's strange that he hasn't called.* 🔁 *The strange thing is that the burglars ignored all her jewellery.* 🔁 *That's strange – I wonder why she didn't tell you?*
2 not familiar □ *Being ill in a strange country was quite frightening.*

strangely /'streɪndʒlɪ/ ADVERB

1 in a strange way □ *She looked at me strangely.*
2 used for saying that something is surprising 🔁 *Strangely enough, some actors are quite shy.*

stranger /'streɪndʒə(r)/ NOUN [plural strangers]

1 someone who you do not know □ *Children should never talk to strangers.* 🔁 *How many people would give £5000 to a complete stranger?*
2 someone who is in a place they do not know □ *I'm afraid I don't know where the station is. I'm a stranger here myself.*
3 be no stranger to something to have a lot of experience of something □ *She is no stranger to public attention.*

➤ Remember that a **stranger** is a person you do not know. It is not a person from another country. (The word for this is **foreigner**.)
✓ *Foreigners are usually very welcome in this region.*
✗ *Strangers are usually very welcome in this region.*

strangle /'stræŋgəl/ VERB [strangles, strangling, strangled] to kill someone by putting something around their throat □ *She had been strangled with a piece of rope.*

strap¹ /stræp/ NOUN [plural straps] a long narrow piece of leather or cloth used to hold things, fasten things or hang things on □ *a watch strap* □ *The bag had a shoulder strap.*

strap² /stræp/ VERB [straps, strapping, strapped] to fasten something with a strap □ *I usually strap my bag to my bike.*

strategy /'strætɪdʒɪ/ NOUN [plural strategies] a plan for achieving something □ *a business strategy* □ *He had developed his own strategies for dealing with stress.*

straw /strɔː/ NOUN [plural straws]
1 no plural long dried stems of crops which animals eat or sleep on □ *The cows need fresh straw.*
2 a thin tube used for sucking up a drink
♦ IDIOM the last/final straw the last in a series of unpleasant events, which makes you feel angry or makes you want to stop doing something □ *They all started laughing at her, and it was the last straw.*

strawberry /'strɔːbərɪ/ NOUN [plural strawberries] a soft red fruit with many very small seeds on its surface □ *fresh strawberries* □ *strawberry ice cream*

stray /streɪ/ NOUN [plural strays] a cat or dog that has no home

streak /striːk/ NOUN [plural streaks] a long thin line or mark □ *hair with blonde streaks* □ *There were dirty streaks on the window.*

stream /striːm/ NOUN [plural streams]

1 a very narrow river □ *The children were paddling in the stream.*
2 a flow of something 🔁 *The museum had a steady stream of visitors.* 🔁 *There was a constant stream of traffic.*

street /striːt/ NOUN [plural streets] a road with buildings such as houses and shops on one or both sides 🔁 *Lincoln's main street was full of shoppers.* □ *There are a lot of shops on this street.* □ *She walked down the street to the library.* □ *I live at 32 Montgomery Street.*

➤ **THESAURUS:** A road is a hard, level surface for vehicles to travel along. Road is a general word. A street is a road with buildings such as houses and shops on one side or both sides. A lane is a narrow road, especially in the country. A lane is also a strip of road separated by painted lines. Most roads have two lanes. A motorway is a wide road for vehicles travelling fast over long distances. Most motorways have 3 or more lanes.

strength /streŋθ/ NOUN, NO PLURAL

1 when someone or something is strong 🔁 *He didn't have the strength to lift the box.* □ *The soup gave her a little more strength.* □ *They tested the strength of the metal.*
2 how successful, good or powerful something is □ *The strength of the dollar has caused problems for some companies.* □ *The government should not underestimate the strength of the army.*

strengthen /'streŋθən/ VERB [strengthens, strengthening, strengthened] to become stronger or to make something stronger □ He did exercises to strengthen his muscles. □ The wind strengthened.

stress¹ /stres/ NOUN [plural stresses]
1 no plural the bad effect on your mind or body when you have too much work or too many worries □ A lot of headaches are caused by stress. ⌑ He was suffering from stress and exhaustion. ⌑ Exercise is an effective way to reduce stress. ⌑ Students often have high stress levels around the time of exams.
2 be under stress to have too much work or too many worries □ I've been under a lot of stress recently.
3 the emphasis of a particular part of a word when you are saying it □ In the word 'bedroom' the stress is on 'bed'.

stress² /stres/ VERB [stresses, stressing, stressed]
1 to say that something is important ⌑ Her speech stressed the need for change. □ + that She stressed that she did not blame her father.
2 to emphasize part of a word □ When 'object' is a noun you stress the 'ob'.

stretch /stretʃ/ VERB [stretches, stretching, stretched]
1 to make something longer or wider, especially by pulling □ Stretch this rope between the two posts.
2 to become longer or wider □ This material stretches. □ New shoes usually stretch a little.
3 to push your arms or legs as far as you can □ Amy got out of bed and stretched. □ She stretched her arms over her head. □ + over/across, etc. He stretched across me to get the book.
4 to cover a large area □ The mountains stretch from the north to the south of the country.

stretcher /'stretʃə(r)/ NOUN [plural stretchers] a bed for carrying an ill or injured person □ The stretcher was put into the back of the ambulance.

strict /strɪkt/ ADJECTIVE [stricter, strictest] expecting people to obey your rules □ a strict teacher □ + with He's very strict with the students.

strictly /'strɪktlɪ/ ADVERB
1 exactly ⌑ It's not strictly true. ⌑ They are not refugees, strictly speaking (= used for emphasizing that you are being exact).
2 strictly prohibited/forbidden/banned used to emphasize that something is not allowed □ Smoking is strictly prohibited.

stride /straɪd/ NOUN [plural strides] a long step you take when you walk
♦ IDIOM take something in your stride to deal with something difficult and not allow it to affect you □ She's had a lot of health problems but she's taken them all in her stride.

strike¹ /straɪk/ VERB [strikes, striking, struck]
1 to hit someone or something □ The bomb struck its target. □ My head struck the table. □ The house was struck by lightning.
2 if a thought strikes you, you suddenly think of it □ + that It suddenly struck me that the road would be closed.
3 to refuse to work because of an argument with your employer □ + for They were striking for higher wages. □ + over They are striking over their working conditions.
4 if a clock strikes, it makes a number of sounds to show the time □ The clock struck three.
♦ PHRASAL VERB strike someone as something to seem to someone to have a particular quality □ He didn't strike me as particularly shy.

strike² /straɪk/ NOUN [plural strikes] a period of time when workers refuse to work because of an argument with their employer ⌑ The train drivers are threatening to go on strike.

string /strɪŋ/ NOUN [plural strings]
1 no plural strong thread, used for tying things ⌑ a ball of string
2 a string of something (a) a series of things or a group of things □ a string of disasters □ They have opened a string of nightclubs across Europe. (b) several things which are on a piece of string □ a string of beads
3 a piece of wire used to make a sound on a musical instrument

strip¹ /strɪp/ NOUN [plural strips] a long narrow piece of something □ + of a strip of paper □ a narrow strip of land □ Slice the peppers into strips.

strip² /strɪp/ VERB [strips, stripping, stripped]
1 to remove a layer or covering from something □ + off You need to strip off the old paint first.
2 to remove your clothes □ He stripped and dived into the water. □ + off They stripped off their jackets.

stripe /straɪp/ NOUN [plural stripes] a line of colour □ a T-shirt with black and white stripes

strive /straɪv/ VERB [strives, striving, strove, striven] a formal word meaning to try very hard to achieve something □ The airline must strive to remain competitive.

stroke¹ /strəʊk/ NOUN [plural strokes]
1 a sudden illness in the brain that affects someone's ability to move and speak ⌑ She had a stroke in August.
2 a way of moving your arms and legs when you swim □ I usually do breast stroke.
3 a stroke of luck something you are not expecting which is lucky □ Police solved the crime by an incredible stroke of luck.

stroke² /strəʊk/ VERB [strokes, stroking, stroked] to rub something gently with your hand □ She was stroking the cat.

stroll /strəʊl/ VERB [strolls, strolling, strolled] to walk in a slow, relaxed way □ *We strolled down to the beach.*

strong /strɒŋ/ ADJECTIVE [stronger, strongest]
1 physically powerful □ *He is very strong.* □ *I have strong legs from cycling.*
2 not easy to damage or break □ *We tied the branches together with a strong rope.* □ *They have a very strong relationship.*
3 believed, felt or expressed in a deep and forceful way □ *He has very strong opinions about climate change.* □ *There has been strong opposition to the new airport.*
4 having or using a lot of power or force □ *I felt a strong pull on the rope.* 🖻 *strong winds*
5 very noticeable 🖻 *There was a strong smell of fish in the room.* □ *She speaks with a strong French accent.*
6 a strong drink has a lot of a particular substance in it □ *He drinks really strong coffee.*

struck /strʌk/ PAST TENSE AND PAST PARTICIPLE OF **strike**[1]

structure /ˈstrʌktʃə(r)/ NOUN [plural structures]
1 the way that the parts of something are arranged or organized □ **+ of** *the structure of the story* □ *Crick and Watson discovered the structure of DNA.* □ *a new management structure*
2 something that has been built □ *The bridge was a massive steel structure.*

struggle[1] /ˈstrʌɡəl/ VERB [struggles, struggling, struggled]
1 to try hard to do something that is difficult □ *She struggled to finish the work on time.*
2 to turn and twist your body in order to try to escape □ *The child struggled in his arms.*

struggle[2] /ˈstrʌɡəl/ NOUN [plural struggles] a fight □ *the country's struggle for independence*

stubborn /ˈstʌbən/ ADJECTIVE refusing to change your mind or do what other people tell you □ *a stubborn man* □ *I was frustrated by Tom's stubborn refusal to make any changes.*

stuck /stʌk/ PAST TENSE AND PAST PARTICIPLE OF **stick**[1]

student /ˈstjuːdənt/ NOUN [plural students]
someone who is studying, especially at a college or university □ *a law student* 🖻 *a part-time university student* □ **+ at** *He's a student at Harvard University.*

studio /ˈstjuːdɪəʊ/ NOUN [plural studios]
1 a room from which radio or television programmes are broadcast 🖻 *a TV studio* □ *The programme's recorded in front of a live studio audience.*
2 a place where films are made, or a company that makes films 🖻 *an independent film studio* □ *Hollywood studios*

3 the room that an artist or photographer works in □ *She set up her own photographic studio.*

study[1] /ˈstʌdɪ/ NOUN [plural studies]
1 when you spend time examining something to find out more about it □ *a scientific study* 🖻 *Researchers* conducted a study *on the effects of mobile phones.* 🖻 *A new study shows coffee-drinking does not increase the risk of heart disease.*
2 when you spend time learning about a subject □ **+ of** *the study of history* □ *He completed his undergraduate studies.*
3 a room used for studying or quiet work □ *She sat reading in her study.*

study[2] /ˈstʌdɪ/ VERB [studies, studying, studied]
1 to spend time learning about a subject □ *I'm studying French.* □ **+ for** *Sophie is studying for a degree in politics.* □ **+ to do something** *She's studying to be a teacher.*
2 to look at something carefully □ *He studied the railway timetable.*

stuff[1] /stʌf/ NOUN, NO PLURAL used to talk about a substance, material or a group of objects □ *What's that black oily stuff on the beach?* □ *I've got too much stuff to carry.* □ *I need to buy some stuff for the party.*

stuff[2] /stʌf/ VERB [stuffs, stuffing, stuffed]
1 to push something into a space, often in a quick, careless way □ *He stuffed the letter into his pocket.* □ *I stuffed tissue in my ears to block out the noise.* □ *All his old letters were stuffed into drawers.*
2 to fill something completely □ *She used feathers to stuff the cushions.* □ *Her suitcase was stuffed with clothes.*

stumble /ˈstʌmbəl/ VERB [stumbles, stumbling, stumbled] to almost fall while you are walking □ *He stumbled along the track in the dark.*

stump /stʌmp/ NOUN [plural stumps] the part of something left after the main part has been taken away 🖻 *She sat on a tree stump.*

stun /stʌn/ VERB [stuns, stunning, stunned]
1 if you are stunned by something, it surprises or shocks you very much □ *We were all stunned by the news of the accident.*
2 to make someone unconscious, usually by hitting them on the head

stung /stʌŋ/ PAST TENSE AND PAST PARTICIPLE OF **sting**[1]

stunning /ˈstʌnɪŋ/ ADJECTIVE extremely attractive □ *She looked stunning.*

stunt /stʌnt/ NOUN [plural stunts] something dangerous and exciting that someone does, especially in a film □ *The actor performs all his own stunts.*

stupid /ˈstjuːpɪd/ ADJECTIVE silly and not clever □ *It was a stupid thing to do!* □ *a stupid idea* □ *I felt rather stupid.*

stupidly /ˈstjuːpɪdlɪ/ ADVERB in a stupid way □ I'd rather stupidly forgotten to bring a coat. □ Stupidly, I agreed to do it.

sturdy /ˈstɜːdɪ/ ADJECTIVE [sturdier, sturdiest] strong □ sturdy shoes

sty[1] /staɪ/ NOUN [plural sties] a place where pigs are kept

sty[2] or **stye** /staɪ/ NOUN [plural sties or styes] an infection near your eye that makes it painful and swollen

style /staɪl/ NOUN [plural styles]
1 a particular way of doing something □ a mix of musical styles □ + of She has a wonderful style of writing.
2 the design of something, especially clothes or buildings □ + of a new style of shoe □ We stayed in a traditional style cottage.

stylish /ˈstaɪlɪʃ/ ADJECTIVE attractive and fashionable □ It's one of the city's most stylish hotels. □ She looked stylish in a simple black dress.

subject /ˈsʌbdʒɪkt/ NOUN [plural subjects]
1 the person or thing that a story, a conversation, etc. is about □ + of The affair has been the subject of many rumours. ▣ He raised the subject of (= started talking about) security at the jail. ▣ Can we change the subject (= talk about something different), please?
2 something that you study and learn about at school, university, etc. □ French is my favourite subject at school. □ Fewer students are now studying science subjects.
3 in grammar, the subject of a sentence is the person or thing that does something □ In the sentence 'John plays tennis', 'John' is the subject.

submarine /ˌsʌbməˈriːn/ NOUN [plural submarines] a ship that travels under water

subscribe /səbˈskraɪb/ VERB [subscribes, subscribing, subscribed] to get a product or service by regularly paying money □ One in three Americans subscribe to cable television.

subsequent /ˈsʌbsɪkwənt/ ADJECTIVE happening after something else □ The story is about the soldier's capture and subsequent escape.

substance /ˈsʌbstəns/ NOUN [plural substances] a liquid, a solid or a gas □ Glue is a sticky substance. □ a toxic substance

substitute /ˈsʌbstɪtjuːt/ NOUN [plural substitutes]
1 a person or thing used instead of another ▣ Use lemons as a substitute for limes.
2 a player who replaces another player in a team during a game □ James came on as a substitute at half-time.

subtle /ˈsʌtəl/ ADJECTIVE [subtler, subtlest] slight and difficult to notice or to describe ▣ There have been subtle changes. ▣ There is a subtle difference between the two birds.

subtract /səbˈtrækt/ VERB [subtracts, subtracting, subtracted] to take one number away from another. A mathematics word. □ + from If you subtract 4 from 6, you get 2.

> ➤ **THESAURUS:** If you subtract, you take one number away from another. If you add two numbers, you put them together. If you add 2 and 3, you get 5. If you multiply two numbers, you increase one number by adding it to itself a particular number of times. If you multiply 3 by 5, you get 15. If you divide a number, you find out how many times that number contains another number. If you divide 12 by 3, you get 4.

suburb /ˈsʌbɜːb/ NOUN [plural suburbs] an area of houses at the edge of a town or city □ a suburb of Liverpool

suburban /səˈbɜːbən/ ADJECTIVE to do with areas of houses at the edge of a town or city □ suburban housing

subway /ˈsʌbweɪ/ NOUN [plural subways]
1 a path under a busy road or railway
2 the US word for **underground**[2] (= a railway under the ground)

succeed /səkˈsiːd/ VERB [succeeds, succeeding, succeeded] to achieve something, or to have the effect you want □ If you try hard, I'm sure you'll succeed. □ Ravana's clever plan had succeeded. □ + in She succeeded in getting the job.

> ➤ Note that **succeed** is followed by **in doing** something:
> ✓ She finally succeeded in persuading him.
> ✗ She finally succeeded to persuade him.

success /səkˈses/ NOUN [plural successes]
1 no plural the achievement of what you tried to achieve □ Her success is due to determination and hard work. ▣ He tried, without success, to pull her out of the water. ▣ The project had little chance of success. □ + in Have you had any success in finding a job?
2 something that is popular or has the result that you want ▣ The party had been a great success. ▣ The film was a huge success.

successful /səkˈsesfʊl/ ADJECTIVE
1 having the result you wanted □ a successful election campaign □ The policy has been very successful. □ + in He was successful in his attempt to buy the business.
2 earning or achieving a lot in your work □ a successful businessman ▣ Houlahan had a highly successful career training horses.

3 very popular and making a lot of money 🔁 *He starred in the hugely successful action film 'Die Hard'.*

such /sʌtʃ/ DETERMINER, PRONOUN
1 such used before a phrase with a noun for emphasizing a statement □ *I was such a fool to believe him.* □ *This is such a waste of time.* □ *She's such a nice person.*
2 such as used for giving an example □ *Citrus fruits such as oranges and lemons contain a lot of vitamin C.*
3 similar to someone or something that has already been mentioned □ *Such things are difficult to find.*
4 such ... that used for saying what the result of something is □ *It was such an awful hotel that we decided to leave.*

suck /sʌk/ VERB [sucks, sucking, sucked]
1 to take something into your mouth by pulling in air □ *She was sucking lemonade through a straw.* □ + in *Gerald sucked in his breath.*
2 to hold something in your mouth while making pulling movements with your lips and tongue □ *My sister still sucks her thumb.* □ *She was sucking a sweet.* □ + on *The baby was sucking on a dummy.*

sudden /'sʌdən/ ADJECTIVE
1 happening quickly and unexpectedly □ *The sudden death of his mother changed everything.* □ *Pat felt a sudden urge to laugh.* □ *The attack was so sudden that he wasn't able to defend himself.*
2 all of a sudden suddenly □ *All of a sudden, he started to run towards the door.*

suddenly /'sʌdənli/ ADVERB quickly and unexpectedly □ *Suddenly a woman ran into the room, shouting.* □ *I suddenly felt very tired.*

sue /su:/ VERB [sues, suing, sued] to start a law case to try to get money from a person or organization that has harmed you □ *He sued the company for racial discrimination.*

suffer /'sʌfə(r)/ VERB [suffers, suffering, suffered]
1 to feel pain or unpleasant feelings 🔁 *She suffered a lot of pain after the accident.* □ *I couldn't bear to see him suffering like that.*
2 suffer from something to have a particular illness □ *Her brother suffers from depression.*

suffering /'sʌfərɪŋ/ NOUN, NO PLURAL pain or unpleasant feelings 🔁 *Years of civil war and drought have caused widespread human suffering.*

sugar /'ʃʊgə(r)/ NOUN, NO PLURAL white or brown grains that you add to food and drink to make them taste sweeter 🔁 *Do you take sugar in your tea?*

suggest /sə'dʒest/ VERB [suggests, suggesting, suggested]
1 to mention something as a possibility □ *He suggested a picnic.* □ + that *I suggest that we have*

lunch now. □ + ing *She suggested meeting outside the theatre.*
2 to tell someone about something that they might like or find useful □ *Can you suggest a nice place to stay in Paris?* □ + for *She suggested me for the job.*

➤ Notice the examples in 'suggest' (*sense 1*). You **suggest that** someone **does** something, or you **suggest doing** something. You do not suggest 'to do' something.
✓ *I suggest that we start now.*
✓ *I suggest starting now.*
✗ *I suggest to start now.*

suggestion /sə'dʒestʃən/ NOUN [plural suggestions] an idea that you mention 🔁 *He made several helpful suggestions.* 🔁 *Do you have any suggestions about where we could go for a holiday?* □ + that *He rejected suggestions that he had lied.*

suicide /'su:ɪsaɪd/ NOUN [plural suicides] the act of killing yourself deliberately 🔁 *He committed suicide by jumping off a bridge.*

suit¹ /su:t/ NOUN [plural suits]
1 a jacket and trousers or a jacket and skirt which are made of the same cloth and are worn together 🔁 *He was wearing a suit and tie.*
2 one of the four types of cards in a set used for playing games □ *The four suits are hearts, diamonds, clubs and spades.*

suit² /su:t/ VERB [suits, suiting, suited]
1 if something suits you, it makes you look nice □ *Blue really suits her.* □ *That dress suits you.*
2 to be convenient for someone □ *Would it suit you if I called round this evening?*

suitable /'su:təbəl/ ADJECTIVE right for a purpose, person or occasion □ *Finding suitable accommodation wasn't easy.* □ + for *High-heeled shoes aren't suitable for walking in the country.*
• **suitably** /'su:təblɪ/ ADVERB in a way that is suitable □ *Are you suitably dressed for the cold weather?*

suitcase /'su:tkeɪs/ NOUN [plural suitcases] a big case with a handle, that you carry your clothes in when you are travelling 🔁 *He packed his suitcase and went to the airport.* 🔁 *I unpacked my suitcase as soon as I arrived.*

sulk /sʌlk/ VERB [sulks, sulking, sulked] to show that you are angry by being silent □ *He's sulking because I said he couldn't go out.*

sum /sʌm/ NOUN [plural sums]
1 an amount of money 🔁 *Huge sums were spent on repairing the building.* 🔁 *Some footballers earn vast sums of money.*
2 a simple calculation □ *I was never any good at sums.*

3 the total when you add numbers together □ + *of* *The sum of 2, 3 and 4 is 9.*

summer /'sʌmə(r)/ NOUN [*plural* summers] the season between spring and autumn when the weather is warmest □ *People buy more ice cream in summer.* □ *My sister got married last summer.* □ *summer clothes* □ *summer holidays* □ *Summers are getting hotter.*

summit /'sʌmɪt/ NOUN [*plural* summits] the top of a hill or mountain ⊞ *He reached the summit of Mount Everest in 1970.*

summon /'sʌmən/ VERB [summons, summoning, summoned] to order someone to come □ *The headteacher summoned me to her office.*

sun /sʌn/ NOUN, NO PLURAL
1 the sun the yellow thing in the sky which gives light and heat to the Earth ⊞ *The sun shone brightly into the room.* ⊞ *The sun rose at 7.12 am.* ⊞ *The sun set at 8.24 pm.* □ *The Earth goes round the sun.*
2 the light and heat from the sun □ *We sat in the sun.*

sunbathe /'sʌnbeɪð/ VERB [sunbathes, sunbathing, sunbathed] to lie or sit in the sun so that your skin becomes darker □ *Lots of people were sunbathing on the beach.*

Sunday /'sʌndɪ/ NOUN [*plural* Sundays] the day of the week after Saturday and before Monday □ *I always go to church on Sundays.*

sung /sʌŋ/ PAST PARTICIPLE OF **sing**

sunglasses /'sʌnglɑːsɪz/ PLURAL NOUN dark glasses that protect your eyes from the sun □ *She was wearing a pair of sunglasses.*

sunk /sʌŋk/ PAST PARTICIPLE OF **sink**[1]

sunlight /'sʌnlaɪt/ NOUN, NO PLURAL the light from the sun ⊞ *Driving can be difficult in bright sunlight* ⊞ *Keep babies out of direct sunlight.*

sunny /'sʌnɪ/ ADJECTIVE [sunnier, sunniest] full of light from the sun ⊞ *It's sunny outside.* ⊞ *It's a lovely sunny day.* □ *sunny weather*

sunrise /'sʌnraɪz/ NOUN [*plural* sunrises] the time when the sun appears in the morning □ *I was up at sunrise.*

sunset /'sʌnset/ NOUN [*plural* sunsets] the time when the sun starts to disappear in the evening □ *We left the beach at sunset.*

sunshine /'sʌnʃaɪn/ NOUN, NO PLURAL the light and heat of the sun ⊞ *He was squinting in the bright sunshine.*

suntan /'sʌntæn/ NOUN [*plural* suntans] a brown skin colour that you get because you have been in the sun

super /'suːpə(r)/ ADVERB an informal word meaning very □ *I exercise a bit but I'm not super fit.*

superb /suːˈpɜːb/ ADJECTIVE extremely good □ *a superb performance*

superior[1] /suːˈpɪərɪə(r)/ ADJECTIVE better than something else ⊞ *This product is far superior to earlier versions.*

superior[2] /suːˈpɪərɪə(r)/ NOUN [*plural* superiors] a person who has a higher rank than you at work □ *He made complaints to his superiors.*

superlative[1] /suːˈpɜːlətɪv/ ADJECTIVE in grammar, the superlative form of an adjective or adverb is the form that usually ends with *-est* or is formed with *most*. For example, *hardest, worst* and *most difficult* are superlative forms.

superlative[2] /suːˈpɜːlətɪv/ NOUN [*plural* superlatives] a superlative form of an adjective or adverb

supermarket /'suːpəmɑːkɪt/ NOUN [*plural* supermarkets] a large shop that sells food and other goods

superstar /'suːpəstɑː(r)/ NOUN [*plural* superstars] a very famous actor, singer, person who plays sport, etc.

supervise /'suːpəvaɪz/ VERB [supervises, supervising, supervised] to be in charge of a person or activity □ *Someone has to be there to supervise the children.* □ *He was supervising the road repair work.*

supervision /ˌsuːpəˈvɪʒən/ NOUN, NO PLURAL the act of being in charge of a person or activity □ *The prisoner was kept under close supervision.*

supper /'sʌpə(r)/ NOUN [*plural* suppers] a meal that you eat in the evening □ *He ate his supper and went to bed.*

supply[1] /səˈplaɪ/ NOUN [*plural* supplies]
1 an amount of something that you can use ⊞ *The lack of rain is affecting the city's water supply.* ⊞ *There is a limited supply of housing in the area.* □ + *of* *a supply of food*
2 supplies food, clothes, medicines, etc. that you need to live or to do something □ *A military plane landed with medical supplies for the refugees.*

supply[2] /səˈplaɪ/ VERB [supplies, supplying, supplied] to provide something □ *Wind power could supply up to 20% of the country's electricity.* □ + *with* *The farm supplies several major supermarkets with milk.* □ + *to* *He supplied information to the police.*

support[1] /səˈpɔːt/ VERB [supports, supporting, supported]
1 to agree with an idea, person, etc. and want them to succeed □ *I support the idea in principle.* □ *Teachers did not support the proposal.*
2 to be under something and stop it from falling □ *The roof was supported by wooden beams.*
3 to like a particular sports team and want them to win □ *Which football team do you support?*

4 to provide money for someone or something
□ *She supports her family on a very low wage.*

support² /sə'pɔ:t/ NOUN [plural supports]
1 *no plural* encouragement and help ℗ *He called to offer support as soon as he heard about my accident.*
2 an object under something, which stops it from falling □ *One of the supports of the bridge collapsed.*
3 *no plural* agreement with an idea or person and wanting them to succeed ℗ *The idea has received strong support from all the parties.* ℗ *Klinsmann eventually won massive public support in Germany.* □ *+ for There was not much support for the war.*

supporter /sə'pɔ:tə(r)/ NOUN [plural supporters]
1 someone who likes a sports team and wants them to win □ *a Liverpool supporter*
2 someone who agrees with an idea or person and wants them to succeed ℗ *He was a strong supporter of government policy.*

suppose /sə'pəʊz/ VERB [supposes, supposing, supposed]
1 to think that something is probably true □ *+ that I suppose that all the tickets have been sold now?* ℗ *I don't suppose we'll see him again.* □ *I suppose you'll be going to the concert.*
2 be supposed to do something (a) to be expected to do something, especially because of a rule □ *I'm supposed to look after my little sister on Saturdays.* □ *You're not supposed to walk on the grass.* (b) to be intended or expected to have a particular result or to happen in a particular way □ *The belts are supposed to support your back.* □ *He wasn't supposed to arrive until next week.*
3 I suppose so (a) used to agree to something that you do not want to do or to happen □ *'Could you do the shopping this week?' 'I suppose so.'* (b) used to agree that something is possible, true or correct, but in a way that shows that you are not sure or happy about it □ *'We could always hire a gardener.' 'I suppose so, but it would be rather expensive.'*
4 I suppose used to say that you think something is possible, true or correct, although you are not sure or happy about it □ *We could get a taxi, I suppose.* □ *I suppose I deserve his criticism.* □ *I suppose the weather might improve.*
5 be supposed to be something to be considered by many people to have a particular quality □ *That area is supposed to be really beautiful.* □ *He's supposed to be good at maths.*

supreme /su:'pri:m/ ADJECTIVE most powerful □ *the supreme ruler*

sure /ʃʊə(r)/ ADJECTIVE
1 certain □ *+ that I'm sure that we've met before.* □ *+ about Alex is coming, but I'm not sure about Dan.* □ *+ question word I'm not sure why he was so*

angry. □ *+ of I'll phone you when I'm sure of the date.* □ *Are you sure you want to leave?*
2 make sure (a) to do something to make it certain that something happens □ *Can you make sure all the doors are locked?* (b) to check that something is true □ *I think his birthday's on Saturday, but I'll look in the diary to make sure.*
3 sure to do something certain to happen or be the result of something □ *He's sure to win.*

surely /'ʃʊəlɪ/ ADVERB
1 used to show surprise about something □ *Surely you're going to wash that fruit before you eat it!* □ *Surely he didn't just leave her there!*
2 used to show that you think something will probably happen □ *Surely they'll phone if they're not coming.*

surf /sɜ:f/ NOUN, NO PLURAL the white part at the top of waves on the sea

surface /'sɜ:fɪs/ NOUN [plural surfaces] the outside or top layer of something □ *The leaves had a rough surface.* □ *The temperature of the Earth's surface has risen.* □ *+ of A light wind rippled the surface of the lake.*

surfing /'sɜ:fɪŋ/ NOUN, NO PLURAL the sport of balancing on a board and moving on the sea's waves ℗ *We went surfing in Cornwall.*

surgeon /'sɜ:dʒən/ NOUN [plural surgeons] a doctor who does operations

surgery /'sɜ:dʒərɪ/ NOUN [plural surgeries]
1 *no plural* medical treatments which involve cutting into someone's body □ *heart surgery*
2 a place where you go to see a doctor or a dentist

surname /'sɜ:neɪm/ NOUN [plural surnames] your last name or family name □ *Smith is a common English surname.* □ *What's your surname?*

surplus /'sɜ:pləs/ NOUN [plural surpluses] an extra amount that is more than you need □ *This country produces a surplus of grain.*

surprise¹ /sə'praɪz/ NOUN [plural surprises]
1 *no plural* the feeling caused by something sudden or unexpected □ *He stared at her in surprise.* ℗ *To my surprise, I passed my driving test.*
2 something sudden or unexpected □ *Your letter was a nice surprise.*
3 take/catch someone by surprise to happen unexpectedly, and make you feel surprised □ *The message had taken her by surprise.*

surprise² /sə'praɪz/ VERB [surprises, surprising, surprised]
1 to make someone feel surprise □ *He surprised me by turning up without calling.*
2 to attack someone suddenly and without warning □ *They surprised the enemy from the rear.*

surprised /səˈpraɪzd/ ADJECTIVE having a feeling of surprise 🔁 *Anna looked surprised when I told her.* □ + *that* *I'm surprised that he agreed to come.* □ + *to do something* *I was very surprised to hear that he had left.* □ + *at/by* *She was surprised by the news.*

➤ Notice the prepositions that follow the word **surprised**. You are **surprised at** or **by** something:
✓ *I was surprised at/by his decision.*
✗ *I was surprised about his decision.*

surprising /səˈpraɪzɪŋ/ ADJECTIVE making you feel surprise □ *A surprising number of people voted for him.* 🔁 *It's surprising how many people believe in ghosts.*

surrender /səˈrendə(r)/ VERB [surrenders, surrendering, surrendered] to stop fighting or trying to escape because you know you will not be successful □ *They surrendered to the enemy.*

surround /səˈraʊnd/ VERB [surrounds, surrounding, surrounded] to be or go all around something or someone □ *Fans surrounded the players.* □ *The city is surrounded by hills.*

surroundings /səˈraʊndɪŋz/ PLURAL NOUN the area around a person or place □ *The hotel is set in beautiful surroundings.* □ *He was glad to be back in his own surroundings.*

survival /səˈvaɪvəl/ NOUN, NO PLURAL the fact of continuing to live or exist □ *His survival depended on finding fresh water.*

survive /səˈvaɪv/ VERB [survives, surviving, survived] to continue to live after something bad has happened □ *He didn't survive long after the accident.* □ *Amazingly, the diver survived the shark attack.*

survivor /səˈvaɪvə(r)/ NOUN [plural survivors] someone who continues to live after something bad has happened to them □ *He was the only survivor of the crash which killed the princess.*

suspect¹ /ˈsʌspekt/ NOUN [plural suspects] someone who may have committed a crime □ *terrorist suspects* 🔁 *He's the prime suspect in the murder of Rachel Smith.*

suspect² /səˈspekt/ VERB [suspects, suspecting, suspected]
1 to think that someone may have committed a crime □ *He's suspected of murdering two women.*
2 to think that something might be true □ *I suspect that she is hiding her true feelings.*

suspend /səˈspend/ VERB [suspends, suspending, suspended]
1 to stop something for a period of time □ *All business will be suspended until after New Year.*
2 to hang something □ *The meat was suspended from a hook.*

suspicion /səˈspɪʃən/ NOUN [plural suspicions]
1 a feeling or a belief that someone has done something wrong or illegal 🔁 *He was arrested on suspicion of burglary.*
2 a feeling that something is true 🔁 *I had a strong suspicion that it was broken.*

suspicious /səˈspɪʃəs/ ADJECTIVE
1 feeling or showing that you do not completely trust someone □ *She gave him a suspicious glance.*
2 making you think that a crime might be involved □ *He died in suspicious circumstances.*

swallow¹ /ˈswɒləʊ/ VERB [swallows, swallowing, swallowed] to make food or drink go down your throat □ *Try to swallow the pill.* □ *She swallowed a large mouthful of water.*

swallow² /ˈswɒləʊ/ NOUN [plural swallows] a small bird with long pointed wings and a tail with two points

swam /swæm/ PAST TENSE OF **swim¹**

swamp /swɒmp/ NOUN [plural swamps] an area of land that is always very wet

swan /swɒn/ NOUN [plural swans] a large white bird with a long neck which lives on rivers and lakes

swap¹ /swɒp/ VERB [swaps, swapping, swapped] to exchange one thing for another thing □ *I took the dress back to the shop and swapped it for a bigger size.*

swap² /swɒp/ NOUN [plural swaps] when you swap one thing for another 🔁 *He suggested that we do a swap.*

sway /sweɪ/ VERB [sways, swaying, swayed] to move from side to side □ *The trees swayed in the wind.*

swear /sweə(r)/ VERB [swears, swearing, swore, sworn]
1 to use words that are offensive □ *He was sent off for swearing at the referee.*
2 to promise □ *She swore never to do it again.*

sweat¹ /swet/ NOUN, NO PLURAL the salty liquid that comes out of your skin when you are hot □ *He was dripping with sweat after his run.*

sweat² /swet/ VERB [sweats, sweating, sweated] to give out sweat □ *Exercise makes you sweat.*

sweater /ˈswetə(r)/ NOUN [plural sweaters] a piece of clothing for the top part of your body that you pull over your head □ *He was wearing a blue sweater and jeans.*

➤ THESAURUS: A jumper is the same as a sweater. Sweaters and jumpers are often made of wool. A sweatshirt is a piece of clothing for the top part of your body, made of thick, soft cotton. A cardigan is a piece of clothing for your upper body that is made from wool and fastens with buttons down the front.

sweatshirt /'swetʃɜːt/ NOUN [plural sweatshirts] a piece of clothing for the top part of your body, made of thick, soft cotton

sweep /swiːp/ VERB [sweeps, sweeping, swept]
1 to clean something using a brush □ He swept the floor. □ + up She swept up the broken glass.
2 to move someone or something somewhere with a quick, strong movement □ + away Whole villages were swept away by the flood. □ Tonnes of mud were swept down the hillside.

sweet¹ /swiːt/ ADJECTIVE [sweeter, sweetest]
1 tasting like sugar □ He loves sweet food.
2 kind and friendly □ She seems very sweet. ⓗ It was sweet of him to offer.
3 pleasant in smell or sound □ the sweet smell of flowers
4 attractive and making you feel affection □ a sweet little boy

sweet² /swiːt/ NOUN [plural sweets]
1 a small piece of sweet food, for example chocolate □ a packet of sweets
2 something sweet that people eat at the end of a meal

swell /swel/ VERB [swells, swelling, swelled, swollen] to become bigger in size □ The wasp sting made her finger swell. □ + up My feet swelled up.

swept /swept/ PAST TENSE AND PAST PARTICIPLE OF sweep

swerve /swɜːv/ VERB [swerves, swerving, swerved] to suddenly move to the right or left when you are driving □ The driver had to swerve to avoid hitting a dog.

swift /swɪft/ ADJECTIVE [swifter, swiftest] quick □ I hope she makes a swift recovery.

swim¹ /swɪm/ VERB [swims, swimming, swam, swum] to move through water using your arms and legs □ Can you swim? □ He swam across the river.

swim² /swɪm/ NOUN [plural swims] when you swim ⓗ I think I'll go for a swim.

swimmer /'swɪmə(r)/ NOUN [plural swimmers] someone or something that swims □ an Olympic swimmer ⓗ She was a strong swimmer (= able to swim well).

swimming /'swɪmɪŋ/ NOUN, NO PLURAL the activity or sport of moving through water using your arms and legs □ Swimming is excellent exercise. ⓗ We went swimming at the local pool.

swimming costume /'swɪmɪŋ ˌkɒstjuːm/ NOUN [plural swimming costumes] a piece of clothing that women and girls wear for swimming

swimming pool /'swɪmɪŋ ˌpuːl/ NOUN [plural swimming pools] an area of water made for swimming in

swimming trunks /'swɪmɪŋ ˌtrʌŋks/ PLURAL NOUN a piece of clothing that men and boys wear for swimming

swimsuit /'swɪmsuːt/ NOUN [plural swimsuits] a piece of clothing that women and girls wear for swimming

swing¹ /swɪŋ/ VERB [swings, swinging, swung]
1 to move backwards and forwards through the air, or to make something do this □ You swing your arms when you walk. □ The children were swinging on a rope.
2 to move in a smooth, wide curve, or to make something do this ⓗ The door swung open. □ She sat up and swung her legs over the side of the bed.

swing² /swɪŋ/ NOUN [plural swings] a seat hanging from ropes or chains, that children sit on and move backwards and forwards

switch¹ /swɪtʃ/ VERB [switches, switching, switched] to change from one thing to another thing □ We switched channels to watch the news. □ + from She switched from English to French with no difficulty. □ + to Many families have switched to cheaper gas suppliers.
♦ PHRASAL VERB switch (something) on/off to turn something on or off using a switch □ I switched the light on. □ He'd forgotten to switch off the microphone.

> ➤ THESAURUS: If you turn something on, you move a switch or a device so that a machine starts working or a supply of something starts. You can turn on a light or turn on a tap, for example. If you switch something on, you turn it on, using a switch. You switch on a light, but you cannot switch on a tap. When you open something, you move it to a position that is not shut or fastened. You open a door or a window, for example.

switch² /swɪtʃ/ NOUN [plural switches] a device that you press to make something work or stop working ⓗ I can't find the light switch.

swollen¹ /'swəʊlən/ ADJECTIVE bigger than usual □ He had a swollen ankle after falling downstairs. □ Several swollen rivers burst their banks.

swollen² /'swəʊlən/ PAST PARTICIPLE OF swell

swoop /swuːp/ VERB [swoops, swooping, swooped] to suddenly and quickly move down □ The owl swooped down on its prey.

sword /sɔːd/ NOUN [plural swords] a weapon with a long blade

swore /swɔː(r)/ PAST TENSE OF swear

sworn /swɔːn/ PAST PARTICIPLE OF swear

swum /swʌm/ PAST PARTICIPLE OF swim¹

syllable /ˈsɪləbəl/ NOUN [*plural* syllables] a word or part of a word that is a single sound. For example, *pen* has one syllable and *pen-cil* has two syllables.

symbol /ˈsɪmbəl/ NOUN [*plural* symbols]
1 something that represents a more general idea □ **+ of** *The dove is a symbol of peace.* ⊞ *The statue became a symbol of freedom.*
2 a written sign or a letter that represents something □ **+ for** *H is the chemical symbol for hydrogen*

sympathetic /ˌsɪmpəˈθetɪk/ ADJECTIVE feeling or showing sympathy □ *a sympathetic smile*

sympathy /ˈsɪmpəθɪ/ NOUN [*plural* sympathies] when you feel sorry for someone who is unhappy or suffering □ **+ for** *I have great sympathy for the victims.* □ *She received many letters of sympathy when her husband died.* □ *He expressed his sympathies to the family.*

symptom /ˈsɪmptəm/ NOUN [*plural* symptoms] a sign that someone has a particular illness □ *Sore throat, blocked nose, and sneezing are the usual symptoms of a cold.*

synagogue /ˈsɪnəgɒg/ NOUN [*plural* synagogues] a building where Jewish people go to pray

syrup /ˈsɪrəp/ NOUN [*plural* syrups] a thick, sticky substance made from sugar

system /ˈsɪstəm/ NOUN [*plural* systems]
1 an way of organizing or doing something ⊞ *the country's education system* ⊞ *the US legal system* □ **+ for** *We have a new system for processing applications.*
2 pieces of equipment that work together □ *a computer operating system* □ *There's a problem with the central heating system.*

T*t*

T *or* **t** /tiː/ the 20th letter of the alphabet

table /ˈteɪbəl/ NOUN [*plural* tables]
1 a piece of furniture with a flat surface that you put things on ⊞ *They were sitting at the dining room/kitchen table.*
2 a set of numbers or words that are arranged in rows □ *The table below shows which schools have the best results.*

tablecloth /ˈteɪbəlklɒθ/ NOUN [*plural* tablecloths] a cloth for covering a table
tablespoon /ˈteɪbəlspuːn/ NOUN [*plural* tablespoons] a large spoon, often used for measuring things when you are cooking

tablet /ˈtæblɪt/ NOUN [*plural* tablets] a pill ⊞ *She took a vitamin tablet.* □ *She takes sleeping tablets.*

table tennis /ˈteɪbəl ˌtenɪs/ NOUN, NO PLURAL a game in which people hit a ball over a net which is attached to a table
tabloid /ˈtæblɔɪd/ NOUN [*plural* tabloids] a small newspaper with lots of pictures and not much serious news
tackle /ˈtækəl/ VERB [tackles, tackling, tackled]
1 to deal with something difficult ⊞ *The policy is designed to tackle the problem of pollution.* □ *The government has failed to tackle poverty.*
2 to try to get the ball from another player in games such as football
tactic /ˈtæktɪk/ NOUN [*plural* tactics] a way of doing something to achieve what you want ⊞ *The companies had used the same tactics for promoting their products.* □ *I've got a new tactic for persuading the children to walk.*
tag /tæg/ NOUN [*plural* tags] a small piece of paper, plastic, etc. with information on it which is attached to something else ⊞ *She looked at the price tag on the jacket.*

tail /teɪl/ NOUN [*plural* tails] the part that sticks out from the end of an animal's body ⊞ *The dog wagged his tail.*

take /teɪk/ VERB [takes, taking, took, taken]
1 to get something and often move it from one place to another □ *I took him some food.* □ *Make sure you take a coat with you.* □ *Who's taken all the milk?* □ **+ away** *His passport was taken away*

from him. □ **+ back** *I must take Jo's book back.*
□ **+ out** *He opened the case and took out a jacket.*
2 to accept something that you have been offered □ *She took a biscuit.* □ *Are you going to take the job?* □ *Do you take credit cards?*
3 to go somewhere with someone, especially to look after them or to provide transport for them □ *I took my mother to the hospital.* □ *I take my son swimming every week.*
4 to do or have a particular thing □ *Take a deep breath.* □ *Take a look at his work.* □ *She won't take any responsibility for the business.* □ *Sometimes, you have to take a chance.*
5 to need a particular amount of time to be done □ *I just need to finish this letter – it won't take long.* □ *It took him five years to finish his novel.*
6 to need something □ **+ to do something** *It takes a lot of courage to oppose your friends.* □ *It took five people to lift the piano.*
7 to travel somewhere using a particular form of transport □ *I took a ferry to Stockholm.*
8 to swallow medicine □ *I have to take these antibiotics for a week.*
9 if you take a photograph, you use your camera to make a picture
➔ *go to* **take your** breath **away, take your** mind[1] **off something**

♦ PHRASAL VERBS **take after someone** to be like an older person in your family □ *She's so emotional – she takes after her father.* **take something down** to write something □ *He took down our names.* **take something off** to remove a piece of clothing □ *He took off his jacket.* **take off** if an aircraft takes off, it leaves the ground at the beginning of a flight **take over (something)**
1 to start doing something that someone else was doing □ *Could you take over the cooking while I make a phone call?* □ **+ from** *She took over from Annie as secretary.* **3** to take control of something □ *The business was taken over by a French company.* **take something up**
1 to start doing an activity □ *I've taken up judo.* **2** to use a particular amount of time or space □ *His piano takes up most of the front room.*

> ► THESAURUS: If you take something, you get something and often move it from one place to another. If you take something violently or suddenly, you can say that you **grab** it or **snatch** it. If you **grasp** something, you take hold of it tightly. If you **catch** something, you stop and hold something that is moving through the air. You might catch a ball, for example. If you hold something, you have it in your hand or hands.

taken /'teɪkən/ PAST PARTICIPLE OF **take**

take-off /'teɪkɒf/ NOUN [plural **take-offs**] the time when an aeroplane leaves the ground and goes up into the air □ *Please keep your seat belt fastened during take-off.*

takeover /'teɪkəʊvə(r)/ NOUN [plural **takeovers**] when a company takes control of another company 🔁 *The company accepted a takeover bid.*

tale /teɪl/ NOUN [plural **tales**] a story, often one that is difficult to believe □ *tales of great adventures*

talent /'tælənt/ NOUN [plural **talents**] a natural ability to do something well □ *Sarah had a talent for acting.*

talented /'tæləntɪd/ ADJECTIVE having the ability to do something well □ *She's a talented young artist.*

talk¹ /tɔːk/ VERB [**talks, talking, talked**] to say words in order to communicate □ + **to** *I talked to Molly on the phone yesterday.* □ + **about** *He's always talking about football.* □ *I like him, but he talks too much.*

talk² /tɔːk/ NOUN [plural **talks**]
1 a conversation 🔁 *I need to have a talk with Julie.* □ + **about** *We had a brief talk about school.*
2 when someone talks to a group of people about a particular subject 🔁 *He gave a talk about his work with gorillas.*
3 talks formal meetings between people such as politicians, especially to try to make plans or solve arguments 🔁 *Ministers will be holding talks in Geneva.* □ + **between** *Talks between unions and employers have broken down.*

tall /tɔːl/ ADJECTIVE [**taller, tallest**]
1 bigger in height than most people or things 🔁 *a tall building* □ *He's tall for his age.* □ *tall trees*
2 used when talking about the height of someone or something □ *She's less than five feet tall.*

tame /teɪm/ ADJECTIVE [**tamer, tamest**] a tame animal is no longer wild, and has been trained to be near people

tan¹ /tæn/ VERB [**tans, tanning, tanned**] to get darker skin because you have been in the sun □ *She tans very easily.*

tan² /tæn/ NOUN [plural **tans**] a brown colour on your skin because you have been in the sun □ *Many people want to get a tan even though it is bad for your skin.*

tangle /'tæŋɡəl/ NOUN [plural **tangles**] a mass of wires, hair, string, etc. which are twisted together

tank /tæŋk/ NOUN [plural **tanks**]
1 a large container for liquids or gases 🔁 *The car's fuel tank was empty.* □ *an oxygen tank*
2 a large military vehicle with a gun on top, which moves on metal belts over wheels

tanker /'tæŋkə(r)/ NOUN [plural **tankers**] a ship or truck which carries liquids or gases 🔁 *an oil tanker*

tap¹ /tæp/ NOUN [plural **taps**]
1 a device you use for controlling the flow of water or gas from a pipe 🔁 *She turned on the tap to wash her hands.* 🔁 *The tap is dripping.* 🔁 *I always drink tap water rather than bottled water.* □ *the hot/cold tap*
2 a light knock □ *He felt a tap on his shoulder.*

tap² /tæp/ VERB [**taps, tapping, tapped**]
1 to knock gently □ + **on** *He tapped on the window.* □ *She tapped me on the arm.*
2 to hit your fingers or feet gently against something 🔁 *He tapped his foot in time with the music.*

tape¹ /teɪp/ NOUN [plural **tapes**]
1 a long, thin piece of plastic for recording sounds or pictures, or the case that it is kept in 🔁 *They played a tape of the police interview.*
2 *no plural* a long, thin piece of plastic that is sticky on one side, used for fastening things □ *The door was sealed with yellow police tape.*

tape² /teɪp/ VERB [**tapes, taping, taped**]
1 to record sounds and pictures onto tape □ *I taped the show to watch later.*
2 to fasten something somewhere using tape □ *The note was taped to the car's windscreen.*

target /'tɑːɡɪt/ NOUN [plural **targets**]
1 a level that you are trying to achieve 🔁 *The company won't reach its sales targets.*
2 a mark or object that people aim at when they are shooting 🔁 *I practised until I could hit the target.*
3 a person or thing that someone attacks 🔁 *Old people are an easy target for thieves.* □ *It is believed that the White House was the intended target of the attack.*

task /tɑːsk/ NOUN [plural **tasks**] a job that you have to do 🔁 *The school is facing the difficult task of trying to raise money.* 🔁 *He was so ill that he couldn't even perform simple tasks.* □ + **of** *The teacher gave me the task of helping her to carry the books.*

> ► THESAURUS: **Job** is a general word for the work that someone does regularly for money, or for a piece of work. A **task** is a piece of work that you have to do. A **duty** is something that you do because other people expect you to do it, or because it is morally right to do it. An **exercise** is a piece of written work that you do when you are studying.

taste¹ /teɪst/ NOUN [plural **tastes**]
1 the flavour of something, especially food or drink □ *The seeds have a bitter taste.*

2 *no plural* the ability to recognize flavours
□ *Smoking can affect your sense of taste.*
3 *no plural* the ability to judge if something such as clothing, art or behaviour is good and suitable for a situation 🔁 *He has extremely good taste.*

taste² /teɪst/ VERB [tastes, tasting, tasted]
1 to have a particular flavour □ *This sauce tastes salty.*
2 to experience the flavour of something □ *Can you taste the herbs in this?*
3 to try a small amount of food or drink to judge its flavour □ *Have you tasted this cheese?*

> ➤ THESAURUS: If you **taste** food, you try a small amount of it to judge its flavour. If you **chew** food, you break it up inside your mouth with your teeth. If you **swallow** food, you make it go down your throat. If you **eat** food, you put it in your mouth and swallow it.

tasty /ˈteɪsti/ ADJECTIVE [tastier, tastiest] having a good flavour
tattoo /təˈtuː/ NOUN [plural tattoos] a permanent picture made on someone's skin with ink
taught /tɔːt/ PAST TENSE AND PAST PARTICIPLE OF **teach**

tax¹ /tæks/ NOUN [plural taxes] money you pay to the government from your income or that is added to the price of goods you buy to pay for public services 🔁 *Most pensioners don't pay tax.* □ **+ on** *A company pays tax on its profits.* 🔁 *income tax rates*

tax² /tæks/ VERB [taxes, taxing, taxed] to charge tax on something □ *There are plans to tax the profits of oil companies.* □ *Their income will be taxed at 40%.*

taxi /ˈtæksi/ NOUN [plural taxis] a car with a driver that you pay to take you from one place to another 🔁 *They took a taxi to the airport.* 🔁 *Don't worry, I'll get a taxi home.* 🔁 *a taxi driver*

tea /tiː/ NOUN [plural teas]
1 a drink made by pouring boiling water on dried leaves, or the leaves you use to make this drink 🔁 *Can I have a cup of tea?* 🔁 *She sat and drank her tea.* □ *Two teas and a coffee, please.* □ *Do you serve peppermint tea?*
2 *no plural* a light meal with tea that some people have in the afternoon 🔁 *We stopped in a café for afternoon tea.*
3 *no plural* used by some people to refer to the meal they have in the early evening

teach /tiːtʃ/ VERB [teaches, teaching, taught]
1 to give lessons at a school, college or university □ *She taught at the local school.* □ *He teaches maths.* □ *Students are taught in small classes.*
2 to pass your knowledge, skills or experience on to another person □ **+ to do something** *Parents should teach their children to behave properly.* □ **+ question word** *Will you teach me how to sail a yacht?* □ **+ about** *They teach the children about healthy eating.*

> ➤ THESAURUS: Teach is a general word for passing your knowledge, skills or experience on to another person. If you **instruct** or **train** someone, you tell them how to do something, especially something practical. You might train or instruct someone to use a new computer, for example. Train and coach are used to talk about helping people to improve a skill, often a sport. For example, a person might **train** or **coach** an athlete to compete in the Olympic Games.

teacher /ˈtiːtʃə(r)/ NOUN [plural teachers]
someone who teaches, usually as their job □ *She's an English teacher.* □ *He's the head teacher at the local school.*

teaching /ˈtiːtʃɪŋ/ NOUN, NO PLURAL the work of a teacher □ *teaching methods* □ *language teaching materials* □ *We want to improve the quality of teaching in schools.*

team /tiːm/ NOUN [plural teams]
1 a group of people who play together against another group in a game or a sport □ *the England cricket team* □ *Which football team do you support?* 🔁 *He was selected for the national team.*
2 a group of people who work together □ **+ of** *a team of engineers* □ *the senior management team*

tear¹ /teə(r)/ VERB [tears, tearing, tore, torn]
1 to damage paper, cloth, etc. by pulling it apart or making a hole in it □ *You've torn your sleeve on that barbed wire.* □ *The cat tore a hole in the curtain.*
2 to pull or to remove something using force □ *a page torn from a notebook* □ *Liz tore open the envelope.* □ *He tore off a chunk of bread.*
♦ PHRASAL VERB **tear something up** to pull a piece of paper into many small pieces □ *She tore up the letter.*

tear² /teə(r)/ NOUN [plural tears] the place where something has been torn □ *There was a large tear in the fabric.*

tear³ /tɪə(r)/ NOUN [plural tears]
1 a drop of liquid that comes from your eyes when you cry 🔁 *His mum burst into tears (= started crying).* □ *They cried tears of joy.*
2 in tears crying □ *We were all in tears at the end of the film.*

tease /tiːz/ VERB [teases, teasing, teased] to say or do something to make someone angry or embarrassed, or to make them believe something that is not true, either as a joke or to make them angry □ *I didn't mean what I said. I was only teasing.* □ *Stop teasing the dog!*

teaspoon /ˈtiːspuːn/ NOUN [plural teaspoons] a small spoon used for mixing sugar in tea or for measuring small amounts

technical /ˈteknɪkəl/ ADJECTIVE to do with science and technology □ *Does he have any technical training?*

technician /tek'nɪʃən/ NOUN [*plural* technicians] someone whose job is to do practical work in a laboratory or to use special equipment

technique /tek'ni:k/ NOUN [*plural* techniques] a particular method of doing something □ *traditional painting techniques* 🖰 *We've been using a new technique.* □ *+ for There are improved techniques for language testing.*

technological /ˌteknə'lɒdʒɪkəl/ ADJECTIVE to do with technology □ *technological advances*

technology /tek'nɒlədʒɪ/ NOUN [*plural* technologies] scientific knowledge, methods or equipment used in practical ways 🖰 *The system uses wireless technology.* 🖰 *The company is investing in new technology.*

teenage /'ti:neɪdʒ/ ADJECTIVE aged between 13 and 19 🖰 *a teenage girl* 🖰 *a group of teenage boys* □ *They have a teenage son.*

teenager /'ti:neɪdʒə(r)/ NOUN [*plural* teenagers] someone who is aged between 13 and 19 □ *She's just a typical teenager.* □ *The site's popular with teenagers and young adults.*

teens /ti:nz/ PLURAL NOUN the years of your life between the ages of 13 and 19 □ *He was in his teens when the family moved.* 🖰 *The audience were mostly in their late teens and early twenties.*

teeth /ti:θ/ PLURAL OF **tooth** □ *Look after your teeth.*

telephone[1] /'telɪfəun/ NOUN [*plural* telephones]
1 *no plural* a system for speaking to someone in another place, using equipment connected by wires □ *I spoke to him by telephone yesterday.* 🖰 *Kennedy made a telephone call.*
2 a piece of equipment that you use to make telephone calls 🖰 *The telephone rang.* 🖰 *Isabelle answered the telephone.* 🖰 *Can I use your telephone?*

telephone[2] /'telɪfəun/ VERB [telephones, telephoning, telephoned] to contact someone using the telephone □ *Her mother telephoned the police when she didn't return home.*

telescope /'telɪskəup/ NOUN [*plural* telescopes] a piece of equipment with lenses (= curved pieces of glass) and mirrors inside that makes objects that are far away seem closer or larger

television /'telɪvɪʒən/ NOUN [*plural* televisions]
1 *no plural* a system for sending images and sounds in the form of electrical signals, or programmes broadcast in this way 🖰 *Children watch too much television.* □ *Is there anything good on television tonight?*
2 the equipment which receives these pictures and sounds □ *a new flat-screen television* 🖰 *an old black-and-white television set* 🖰 *He switched on the television.*

➤ Remember that people and things appear **on television**:
    ✓ *He's often on television these days.*
    ✗ *He's often in television these days.*

tell /tel/ VERB [tells, telling, told]
1 to give someone information by speaking □ *Don't tell Mum I've lost my key.* □ *+ that He told the court that he was abroad at the time.* □ *+ question word Can you tell us why you disagree?* 🖰 *He promised to tell the truth.* 🖰 *She accused us of telling lies about her.*
2 to order someone to do something □ *+ to do something He told me to sit down.* 🖰 *I wish you would do as you are told!*
3 if you can tell something, you know that it is true or recognize the characteristics of someone or something 🖰 *I couldn't tell if he was joking or not.* □ *+ that I could tell that she was upset.* 🖰 *Can you tell the difference between butter and margarine?*
4 tell the time to be able to understand the information on a clock or watch

► Note that when you use the word **tell**, meaning 'to speak to someone', you must say the person that you are speaking to:
✓ I told Peter I would come.
✓ I told him I would come.
✗ I told that I would come.

♦ PHRASAL VERB **tell someone off** to speak angrily to someone who has done something wrong □ **+ for** He told me off for wasting water.

temper /'tempə(r)/ NOUN [plural tempers]
1 when someone becomes angry very easily 🔲 My father had a really bad temper. □ He was known for his violent temper.
2 **lose your temper** to become angry □ I'm afraid I lost my temper and shouted at him.
3 a person's mood □ Don't ask him until he's in a better temper.

temperature /'temprətʃə(r)/ NOUN [plural temperatures]
1 how hot or cold a place or a thing is □ Average temperatures in spring are 19–24°C. □ **+ of** a temperature of minus 10°C
2 how hot or cold a person's body is 🔲 Flora woke up with a headache and a high temperature. 🔲 A nurse came in to take his temperature (= to measure it).
3 **have a temperature** if someone has a temperature, their body is hotter than it should be because they are ill

temple /'tempəl/ NOUN [plural temples]
1 a building in which the members of some religions show respect for a god by praying, having religious ceremonies, etc. □ a Hindu temple
2 the area on the side of your head between the side of your eye and your hair □ He rubbed his temples.

temporarily /'tempərərɪlɪ/ ADVERB for a short or limited time only □ The road was temporarily closed. □ He'd repaired the roof temporarily with a piece of plastic. □ The noise seems to have stopped, at least temporarily.

temporary /'tempərərɪ/ ADJECTIVE lasting or used only for a short or limited time □ a temporary job □ The firm hires temporary workers in the summer. 🔲 Some families are living in temporary accommodation.

► THESAURUS: A temporary job only lasts for a short time. A part-time job is a job where you only work for part of the day or part of the working week. A permanent job is a job which lasts forever or for a long time. A full-time job is one where you work for all of the hours of a normal job, not part of the time.

tempt /tempt/ VERB [tempts, tempting, tempted] to make someone want to do something or to have something □ I was very tempted by their offer. □ Special deals are tempting people to switch banks.

ten /ten/ NUMBER [plural tens] the number 10

tenant /'tenənt/ NOUN [plural tenants] someone who pays rent to the owner of a house, building or land to use it □ The table was left by the previous tenants.

tend /tend/ VERB [tends, tending, tended] **tend to do something** to often do something, happen, or be a particular way □ She tends to be a bit moody. □ People tend not to talk about financial problems.

tender /'tendə(r)/ ADJECTIVE
1 tender meat and vegetables are soft and easy to cut □ Cook the beans until tender.
2 kind and gentle □ They shared a tender moment.
3 slightly painful when touched □ The skin is tender and red.

tennis /'tenɪs/ NOUN, NO PLURAL a game played on a court with a net across the middle in which the players hit a small ball over the net using rackets (= objects held in the hand) 🔲 We play tennis every weekend. 🔲 a professional tennis player 🔲 a tennis court

tense[1] /tens/ NOUN [plural tenses] a form of a verb which shows if the action of the verb happens now (the **present tense**), in the past (the **past tense**), or in the future (the **future tense**)

tense[2] /tens/ ADJECTIVE [tenser, tensest]
1 feeling nervous and unable to relax □ He looked tense and exhausted.
2 stretched tight □ tense muscles

tense[3] /tens/ VERB [tenses, tensing, tensed] if you tense your muscles, you stretch them tight

tent /tent/ NOUN [plural tents] a frame covered with cloth which you sleep in when you are camping 🔲 We pitched the tent (= put it up) next to the river.

tenth[1] /tenθ/ NUMBER 10th written as a word

tenth[2] /tenθ/ NOUN [plural tenths] 1/10; one of ten equal parts of something

term /tɜːm/ NOUN [plural terms]
1 one of the periods of time that the school or college year is divided into ■ Students do exams in the summer term.
2 a limited period of time □ the president's term of office □ **+ of** He was sent to prison for a term of 15 years.
3 a word or expression with a particular meaning or used in a particular subject 🔲 Patients don't

understand complicated medical terms. □ **+ for**
What is the term for someone who collects coins?
□ **+ of** 'Darling' is a term of affection.
4 terms the rules of an agreement □ Under the
terms of his contract, he is eligible for a payment of
£2 million.

> ➤ **THESAURUS:** A word is a unit of language that
> is written as a group of letters with spaces on
> either side. A term is a word or expression with
> a particular meaning or used in a particular
> subject. For example, you might talk about a
> scientific term or a cookery term. An expres-
> sion is a word or a phrase. You might talk
> about a German expression, or a humorous
> expression, for example.

terminal /ˈtɜːmɪnəl/ NOUN [plural terminals] a
building where planes, boats, trains or buses arrive at
and leave from 🔁 Smoking is not allowed in the
terminal building. □ Developers want to build a
new terminal at the airport.

terrace /ˈterəs/ NOUN [plural terraces]
1 an area next to a building or on the roof of a
building where you can sit □ They sat and drank
coffee on the terrace at the Hotel Duomo.
2 a row of houses that are joined to each other
3 one of a series of flat areas cut into the side of a
hill, where crops are grown

terrain /təˈreɪn/ NOUN, NO PLURAL a particular type
of land □ rough terrain

terrible /ˈterəbəl/ ADJECTIVE very bad or of
very low quality □ a terrible smell □ He made a
terrible mistake. □ I'm terrible at remembering
names. 🔁 I feel terrible about lying to my
parents.

terribly /ˈterəblɪ/ ADVERB
1 extremely □ I'm terribly sorry I broke your vase.
□ I feel terribly guilty about it.
2 very badly □ His death has affected us
terribly.

terrific /təˈrɪfɪk/ ADJECTIVE excellent □ He's done a
terrific job as team captain. □ The party was
terrific.

terrified /ˈterɪfaɪd/ ADJECTIVE very frightened □ I
was terrified of my history teacher. □ He is
absolutely terrified that someone will break into the
house.

terrify /ˈterɪfaɪ/ VERB [terrifies, terrifying,
terrified] to make someone feel very frightened
□ The thought of dying terrifies me.

territory /ˈterətərɪ/ NOUN [plural territories]
1 the land that a particular country controls 🔁 The
army was in enemy territory. □ The plane wasn't
allowed to land on British territory.
2 the area that an animal thinks is its own □ Cats
don't like other cats going into their territory.

terror /ˈterə(r)/ NOUN, NO PLURAL a feeling of great
fear □ He ran away in terror.

terrorism /ˈterərɪzəm/ NOUN, NO PLURAL
violence used by illegal groups to achieve
political aims □ There has been a rise in global
terrorism.

terrorist /ˈterərɪst/ NOUN [plural terrorists]
someone who uses violence to achieve political
aims 🔁 a terrorist organization □ a suspected
terrorist

test¹ /test/ NOUN [plural tests]
1 an exam, usually a short one □ a spelling test
🔁 You will need to pass a simple maths test. 🔁 I had
to take a test to prove my French was good enough.
🔁 He failed his driving test.
2 something you do to check that something works
correctly, is safe, etc. 🔁 They will be conducting tests
on the new aircraft next year. 🔁 nuclear tests □ an
eye/blood test

> ➤ Remember that you **do** or **take** a test (exam).
> You do not 'make' a test:
> ✓ I had to do a test in my interview.
> ✗ I had to make a test in my interview.

> ➤ **THESAURUS:** A test is a short examination, or
> something you do to check that something
> works correctly. An experiment is a scientific
> test to discover or prove something. An
> investigation is an attempt to find out about
> something such as an accident or a crime. The
> police conduct an investigation when a crime
> has taken place.

test² /test/ VERB [tests, testing, tested]
1 to do something to check that something works
correctly, is safe, etc. □ After driving through water,
you should test the brakes. □ **+ on** The drugs
are tested on volunteers. □ I need to get my eyes
tested.
2 to give someone an exam, usually a short one □ **+
on** Can you test me on my verb endings?

text¹ /tekst/ NOUN [plural texts]
1 a written message sent to a mobile phone 🔁 I sent
a text to my sister. □ She got a text from her
boyfriend.
2 no plural the writing in a book □ The pictures
were nice but the text wasn't very interesting.
3 a book or piece of writing that people study
□ India's ancient texts

text² /tekst/ VERB [texts, texting, texted] to send
a written message to someone's mobile phone
□ Text me when you get to the station.

textbook /ˈtekstbʊk/ NOUN [plural textbooks] a
book about a subject which you use at school or
college □ a biology textbook

text message /'tekst ˌmesɪdʒ/ NOUN [plural text messages] a **text**[1] (= written message sent to a mobile phone)

texture /'tekstʃə(r)/ NOUN [plural textures] the way something feels when you touch it □ *the smooth texture of a baby's skin*

than /ðæn/ CONJUNCTION used when comparing things □ *The test was easier than I expected.* □ *He can swim better than me.* □ *The dress cost more than £200.*

thank /θæŋk/ VERB [thanks, thanking, thanked] to tell someone that you are grateful for something □ + *for* *He thanked me for the birthday present* □ *I must thank Emma for helping me.*

thanks[1] /θæŋks/ EXCLAMATION
1 something you say to show that you are grateful □ *'I've made you a drink.' 'Thanks.'* ⊞ *'Here's an invitation to the party.' 'Oh, thanks very much.'* □ + *for* *Thanks for the present. It's lovely.* □ *Thanks for driving me to the airport.*
2 **no thanks** used as a polite way of saying you do not want something □ *'Do you want to come with us?' 'No thanks, I'm busy on Saturday.'*

thanks[2] /θæŋks/ PLURAL NOUN
1 something you say or do to show that you are grateful □ *He expressed his thanks to everyone who helped.* □ *I got no thanks for helping him.*
2 **thanks to someone/something** because of someone or something □ *We finished the project on time, thanks to everyone's hard work.* □ *Thanks to the strike, our flight was cancelled.*

Thanksgiving /'θæŋksɡɪvɪŋ/ NOUN, NO PLURAL a holiday in the US and Canada in autumn, when families eat a special meal together

thank you /ˈθæŋkjuː/ EXCLAMATION
1 something you say to someone when you are grateful for something they have done or given you ⊞ *'I've made you a cup of coffee.' 'Oh, thank you very much.'* □ + *for* *Thank you for the flowers. They're beautiful.* □ *Thank you for helping me yesterday.*
2 used when answering a question in a polite way □ *'How are you?' 'I'm fine, thank you.'*
3 used as a polite way of accepting or refusing someone's offer □ *'Would you like to come for a meal with us?' 'Thank you. That would be lovely.'* ⊞ *'Do you want another biscuit?' 'No, thank you.'*

> ► Note that you say **thank you for** something or **thank you for** + doing something: □ *Thank you for your help.* □ *Thank you for helping.*

that[1] /ðæt/ CONJUNCTION
1 used after some verbs, adjectives and nouns to start a new part of a sentence □ *He said that he hated sports.* □ *We must make sure that we invite*

enough people. □ *The fact that he earns so much means that he can afford a big house.*
2 used instead of 'who' or 'which' at the beginning of a clause (= part of a sentence) □ *People that know her well say she is very unhappy.* □ *We are working with organizations that provide emergency aid.*

that[2] /ðæt/ ADVERB to the amount or degree mentioned □ *It's a kilometre to the shops. I can't walk that far.* □ *The film wasn't that bad.*

that[3] /ðæt/ PRONOUN [plural those]
1 used to talk about something that you can see or that you have already talked about □ *I don't want to know that.* □ *Who is that at the door?*
2 **that's it** (a) used to say that someone has done something correctly □ *Put the wire through the hole – that's it.* (b) used to show that you are angry and will not continue with something □ *That's it! You can cook your own meals from now on!*

that[4] /ðæt/ DETERMINER [plural those] used to talk about a person or thing that you can see or that you have already talked about □ *Who is that girl over there?* □ *Pass me that towel, please.* □ *I left that job a year ago.*

that'd /'ðætəd/ a short way to say and write that had or that would □ *That'd never happened before.* □ *That'd be nice.*
that'll /'ðætəl/ a short way to say and write that will □ *That'll be too big for you.*
that's /ðæts/ a short way to say and write that is □ *That's not what I meant.*

the /ðə/ DETERMINER
1 used before a noun to refer to a particular person or thing that has been mentioned or is known about □ *The bus arrived late, as usual.* □ *I opened the letter and read it.* □ *The men rode on horses and the women walked.*
2 used before a noun when there is only one of that thing □ *The moon was shining.* □ *Balloons floated up into the air.*
3 used to refer to part of a thing □ *Hold the box at the bottom.* □ *Come to the back of the building.*
4 used in dates □ *the third of June* □ *July the fourth*
5 used before nouns referring to groups of people or things of the same kind □ *the poor* (= poor people) □ *the English* (= English people)

theater /'θɪətə(r)/ NOUN [plural theaters]
1 the US spelling of **theatre**
2 the US word for **cinema**

theatre /'θɪətə(r)/ NOUN [plural theatres] a building where plays are performed ⊞ *We went to the theatre last night.*

theft /θeft/ NOUN [plural thefts] the crime of stealing something ⊞ *car thefts* □ + *of* *The theft of a computer is a serious matter.* □ *She was jailed for theft.*

their /ðeə(r)/ DETERMINER belonging to or to do with them □ *Do you know their address?*

theirs /ðeəz/ PRONOUN used to talk or write about things belonging to or to do with a group of people or things that have already been mentioned □ *They say it belongs to them, but I know it's not theirs.*

them /ðem/ PRONOUN
1 used for talking about two or more people or things that you have already mentioned □ *The girls waved to me and I waved back to them.* □ *'Do you like strawberries?' 'Yes, I love them.'*
2 used to avoid saying 'him' or 'her' □ *If anyone asks where I am, can you tell them I've gone to the dentist's.*

theme /θi:m/ NOUN [*plural* themes] the main idea or subject in a book, film, discussion, etc. 🔁 *The country's history is the central theme of the book.*
theme park /'θi:m ˌpɑ:k/ NOUN [*plural* theme parks] a place where you go for fun, where the entertainments and machines you ride on are based on one subject □ *Disney theme parks*

themselves /ðəm'selvz/ PRONOUN
1 the reflexive form of *they* □ *They'd made themselves a cosy little shelter.*
2 used to show that two or more people do something without any help from other people □ *They'll have to work it out themselves.* 🔁 *They built the shelter all by themselves.*
3 used to emphasize the pronoun *they* □ *They themselves are innocent.*
4 by themselves not with or near other people □ *They sat by themselves and didn't talk to anyone else.*

then /ðen/ ADVERB
1 at that time, in the past or future □ *I didn't know you then.* 🔁 *The rest of the kids should be here by then.* 🔁 *They can deliver the car by March, but we really need it before then.* 🔁 *Max and I met up in June, but I haven't seen him since then.*
2 after that time or next □ *I went for a swim, and then I went home.* □ *Mix in the flour and then the fruit.*
3 because of that □ *If you can't be quiet, then you'll have to leave the room.* □ *'This carpet will last longer.' 'I think we'll buy it then.'*

theory /'θɪərɪ/ NOUN [*plural* theories] an idea which tries to explain why something happens □ **+ about** *There are many theories about why children are getting fatter.* □ **+ of** *Newton's theory of gravity*

there¹ /ðeə(r)/ PRONOUN used to start a statement about something that exists or happens □ *There is a mouse somewhere in this house.* □ *There's too much noise.* □ *There is plenty of milk in the fridge.*

there² /ðeə(r)/ ADVERB
1 at, in or to a place □ *I know someone who lives there.* □ *I'm going there tomorrow.* □ *When I got to work, Clive was already there.*
2 used to show someone something you are pointing to or want them to look at □ *You can leave your coats there.* □ *There's Dad.*

therefore /'ðeəfɔ:(r)/ ADVERB because of that □ *She had been awake all night and therefore was very tired.*

thermometer /θə'mɒmɪtə(r)/ NOUN [*plural* thermometers] an instrument for measuring the temperature of something or someone □ *The nurse used a thermometer to take his temperature.*

these¹ /ði:z/ DETERMINER used to talk about people or things that you have already talked about, or things that you can see, usually near you □ *These cups are dirty.* □ *These athletes train very hard.* □ *These problems could have been avoided.*

these² /ði:z/ PRONOUN used to talk about things that you have already talked about, or that you can see, usually near you □ *I can't eat these.* □ *Are these yours?*

they /ðeɪ/ PRONOUN
1 used to talk or write about two or more people or things that have already been mentioned □ *Apes are not monkeys. They don't have tails.* □ *What did they think of your idea?*
2 people in general, or people in authority □ *They say it's going to be a hot summer.* □ *They've raised taxes again.*

they'd /ðeɪd/ a short way to say and write they had or they would □ *They'd all had their lunch.* □ *They'd like to come with us.*
they'll /ðeɪl/ a short way to say and write they will or they shall □ *They'll be here tomorrow.*
they're /ðeə(r)/ a short way to say and write they are □ *They're going to the park after school.*

they've /ðeɪv/ a short way to say and write they have □ *They've never been skating before.*

thick /θɪk/ ADJECTIVE [thicker, thickest]
1 wide between the opposite sides or surfaces □ *Make sure you wear a thick coat.* □ *There was a thick layer of snow on the ground.*
2 having a particular width between sides or surfaces □ *The ice was 20 centimetres thick.*
3 made up of many parts that are very close together □ *thick hair*
4 a thick liquid does not flow easily □ *thick soup*
5 thick smoke, fog, etc. fills the air and is difficult to see through
6 an informal word meaning stupid

thief /θiːf/ NOUN [plural thieves] someone who steals things 🔁 *car thieves* 🔁 *Thieves stole her handbag.*

thigh /θaɪ/ NOUN [plural thighs] the top part of your leg above your knee

thin /θɪn/ ADJECTIVE [thinner, thinnest]
1 not wide from one side to the other □ *He spread a thin layer of jam on the cake.* □ *Cut the potato into thin slices.*
2 a thin person or animal does not have much fat on their body □ *She is small and thin.*
3 a thin liquid flows very easily □ *They were given a bowl of thin soup.*

thing /θɪŋ/ NOUN [plural things]
1 used to refer to an object without using its name □ *I bought a few things for the party when I was in town.* □ *Where's the thing for opening bottles?*
2 an action or event □ *I hope I haven't done the wrong thing.* □ *The same thing happened to me once.*
3 a fact, belief or idea □ *She said lots of nice things about you.* □ *He asked me a few things about my work.*
4 your things the objects that belong to you □ *He packed up his things and left.*

think /θɪŋk/ VERB [thinks, thinking, thought]
1 to have an opinion about someone or something □ *I think there's too much salt in this soup.* □ **+ that** *I think that you should ask him to leave.* □ **+ about** *What do you think about the death penalty?* □ **+ of** *What do you think of his new girlfriend?*
2 to believe that something is true, although you are not certain □ *I think Anna will be here soon.* □ **+ that** *We thought that there would be more people there.* 🔁 *'Do the trains run on Sunday?' 'I think so.'*
3 to consider something, especially in order to understand it or to decide what to do □ **+ about** *You need to think very carefully about what to do.* □ **+ of** *We need to think of a way to raise money.*
4 to remember someone or something □ **+ about** *I was just thinking about your birthday party.* □ **+ of** *I often think of my mother.*
5 to express words to yourself in your mind □ *I kept thinking, 'I must stay calm.'*

6 if you are thinking of doing something, you are considering doing it □ **+ of** *I'm thinking of starting my own business.* □ **+ about** *They're thinking about moving to Australia.*

third¹ /θɜːd/ NUMBER 3ʳᵈ written as a word □ *That's the third time he's called today.* □ *She came third in an art competition.*

third² /θɜːd/ NOUN [plural thirds] 1/3; one of three equal parts of something □ *The bottle holds a third of a litre.*

Third World¹ /ˌθɜːd ˈwɜːld/ NOUN, NO PLURAL the Third World a slightly old-fashioned name for the countries of the world that are the poorest and least developed □ *The work aims to improve health in the Third World.*

Third World² /ˌθɜːd ˈwɜːld/ ADJECTIVE to do with the countries of the Third World 🔁 *a Third World country*

thirst /θɜːst/ NOUN, NO PLURAL the feeling that you need something to drink □ *He was dying of thirst.*

thirsty /ˈθɜːstɪ/ ADJECTIVE [thirstier, thirstiest] feeling that you need something to drink □ *They were tired, hungry and thirsty.* 🔁 *I felt incredibly thirsty.*

thirteen /ˌθɜːˈtiːn/ NUMBER the number 13

thirteenth /ˌθɜːˈtiːnθ/ NUMBER 13ᵗʰ written as a word

thirtieth /ˈθɜːtɪəθ/ NUMBER 30ᵗʰ written as a word

thirty /ˈθɜːtɪ/ NUMBER [plural thirties]
1 the number 30
2 the thirties the years between 1930 and 1939

this¹ /ðɪs/ DETERMINER [plural these]
1 used to talk about a person or thing that you have already talked about, or something that you can see, usually near you □ *This apple is sour.* □ *I've lived in this country for five years.* □ *This argument went on for weeks.*
2 used to refer to a present period of time, or the one that comes next □ *I went shopping this morning.* □ *I'll be seeing her this weekend.*

this² /ðɪs/ ADVERB to the amount or degree mentioned □ *It wasn't this hot yesterday.* □ *I didn't know we'd used this much fuel already.*

this³ /ðɪs/ PRONOUN
1 used to talk about something that you have already talked about, or that you can see, usually near you □ *I can't eat this.* □ *Where are you going after this?* □ *This is my bedroom.*
2 used to say who you are on the telephone □ *Hello, this is Ollie.*

thorough /ˈθʌrə/ ADJECTIVE done carefully, paying attention to every detail □ *He made a thorough* search. 🔁 *We are conducting a thorough investigation into this incident.*

thoroughly /ˈθʌrəlɪ/ ADVERB
1 with great care and attention to every detail □ *Clean all the kitchen surfaces thoroughly.* □ *The book has been thoroughly researched.*
2 completely 🔁 *We thoroughly enjoyed ourselves.* □ *She was feeling thoroughly fed up.* □ *They thoroughly deserve this victory.*

those¹ /ðəʊz/ DETERMINER used to talk about several people or things already mentioned or that you can see, usually not near you □ *Who are those two boys?* □ *In those days, people didn't have cars.*

those² /ðəʊz/ PRONOUN used to talk about several things already mentioned or that you can see, usually not near you □ *What are those?* □ *Those are just some of the problems we face.*

though¹ /ðəʊ/ ADVERB used to show that what you have just said is surprising or different from what you said before □ *It's a pity we didn't win. It was an exciting match, though.*

though² /ðəʊ/ CONJUNCTION
1 but □ *We only waited for half an hour, though it seemed like hours.* □ *He will continue his political work, though not with the same party.*
2 despite the fact that □ *He went out, though I told him not to.*

thought¹ /θɔːt/ NOUN [plural **thoughts**]
1 an idea, opinion, word or image that you have in your mind □ **+ on** *Do you have any thoughts on the problem of transport?* □ **+ about** *I had a sudden thought about the garden.* □ **+ of** *I can't bear the thought of leaving you all.*
2 no plural the activity of thinking □ *This issue needs some careful thought.*

thought² /θɔːt/ PAST TENSE AND PAST PARTICIPLE OF **think**

thoughtful /ˈθɔːtfʊl/ ADJECTIVE
1 a thoughtful person is kind and thinks of other people □ *It was very thoughtful of you to phone.*
2 if someone looks thoughtful, they look as if they are thinking
• **thoughtfully** /ˈθɔːtfʊlɪ/ ADVERB in a thoughtful way □ *She stared thoughtfully at the letter.* □ *She'd very thoughtfully left drinks and sandwiches for us on the kitchen table for us.*

thousand /ˈθaʊzənd/ NUMBER [plural **thousands**] the number 1,000

thousandth¹ /ˈθaʊzəntθ/ NUMBER 1,000th written as a word
thousandth² /ˈθaʊzəntθ/ NOUN [plural **thousandths**] 1/1,000; one of a thousand equal parts of something

thread¹ /θred/ NOUN [plural **threads**]
1 a long, thin piece of cotton, wool, etc. used for sewing □ *fine silk threads* □ *His name was embroidered in red thread.*
2 a series of messages on a website about a particular subject

thread² /θred/ VERB [**threads, threading, threaded**] to push something long and thin through a hole □ *He threaded a piece of wire through a hole in the top.*

threat /θret/ NOUN [plural **threats**]
1 a warning that someone might hurt you or harm you, especially if you do not do what they say 🔁 *She has received death threats.* □ **+ against** *Rebel leaders have made threats against the president.*
2 something that might cause harm or problems □ **+ to** *These actions are a threat to international peace.*

threaten /ˈθretən/ VERB [**threatens, threatening, threatened**]
1 to say that someone will be harmed or hurt, especially if they do not do something □ *His wife was threatened with a knife.* □ **+ to do something** *The kidnappers have threatened to kill the hostages.*
2 to make problems or harm probable □ *Government cuts threaten the future of the service.*

three /θriː/ NUMBER [plural **threes**] the number 3

threw /θruː/ PAST TENSE OF **throw¹**

thrill¹ /θrɪl/ VERB [**thrills, thrilling, thrilled**] to make someone feel excited and very pleased □ *He thrilled the crowd with some dramatic shots.*

thrill² /θrɪl/ NOUN [plural **thrills**] a feeling of excitement and pleasure, or the thing that gives you that feeling □ *She felt a thrill of excitement.* □ *Getting this job was a real thrill.*

thriller /ˈθrɪlə(r)/ NOUN [plural **thrillers**] a book, film or play with an exciting story, full of danger and frightening events 🔁 *He stars in a new crime thriller set in New York.*

thrive /θraɪv/ VERB [**thrives, thriving, thrived**] to grow strong and healthy, or to become successful □ *The business is thriving.* □ *These guys thrive on competition.*

throat /θrəʊt/ NOUN [plural **throats**]
1 the top part of the tube that goes from your mouth down to your stomach □ *My throat felt dry and I couldn't speak.* □ *He got a piece of food stuck in his throat.* 🔁 *I had a headache and a sore throat.*
2 the front part of your neck □ *He put his hands round her throat.*

throne /θrəʊn/ NOUN [plural thrones] a special chair that a king or queen sits on

through /θruː/ PREPOSITION

1 from one end or side of something to the other □ He walked through the door. □ The pole fits through this hole. □ We walked through the woods.
2 because of something or using something □ He failed his exams through laziness. □ He contacted people through his website.
3 for the whole of a period of time or activity □ We drove through the night. □ We left half way through the film. □ She has lived through some terrible events.

throughout /θruː'aʊt/ PREPOSITION

1 during a whole period of time □ It rained throughout June and July. □ There will be regular news reports throughout the day.
2 in every part of something □ They have stores throughout the country.

throw¹ /θrəʊ/ VERB [throws, throwing, threw, thrown]

1 to make something move through the air by pushing it with your hand □ He threw the ball to me. □ They were throwing stones into the water.
2 to put something somewhere very quickly and without care □ She threw her bag down and switched on the TV. □ I threw a few clothes into a case and set off.
3 to move your body or part of your body into a position quickly and with force □ She threw herself to the floor. □ He threw his arms around me.
‣ PHRASAL VERBS **throw something away**
1 to get rid of something you do not want □ I threw away the rest of the food. **2** to waste something □ She threw away her career to follow her boyfriend. **throw something out** to get rid of something that you do not want □ I've thrown out all my old books. **throw someone out** to force someone to leave a place □ My parents threw me out when I was seventeen.

throw² /θrəʊ/ NOUN [plural throws] an act of throwing something □ That was a great throw!

thrust /θrʌst/ VERB [thrusts, thrusting, thrust] to push something somewhere quickly and with force □ He thrust his hands into his pockets. □ Someone thrust a microphone at him.

thug /θʌg/ NOUN [plural thugs] a violent man □ a gang of thugs

thumb /θʌm/ NOUN [plural thumbs] the short, thick finger that is on the side of your hand □ He injured his right thumb. □ She held it carefully between her thumb and forefinger.

thump /θʌmp/ VERB [thumps, thumping, thumped] to hit someone or something hard,

usually with your hand □ He thumped the table for emphasis.

thunder /'θʌndə(r)/ NOUN, NO PLURAL the loud, deep sound that you hear in a storm after a flash of lightning (= bright light in the sky) 🔁 thunder and lightning 🔁 There was a loud clap of thunder.

thunderstorm /'θʌndəstɔːm/ NOUN [plural thunderstorms] a storm with thunder and lightning (= bright light in the sky) □ Thunderstorms were forecast for the afternoon. □ We arrived in the middle of a thunderstorm.

Thursday /'θɜːzdɪ/ NOUN [plural Thursdays] the day of the week after Wednesday and before Friday □ My piano lessons are on Thursday.

tick¹ /tɪk/ NOUN [plural ticks]

1 a small written mark (✓) used to show that something is correct or to show which things on a list have been dealt with 🔁 He put a tick in the box marked 'No'. □ The girl put a tick next to her name.
2 the regular noise that a clock makes □ + of I could hear the tick of the clock in the hall.

tick² /tɪk/ VERB [ticks, ticking, ticked]

1 to write a tick 🔁 You just tick the boxes.
2 to make a regular noise like a clock □ a ticking clock

ticket /'tɪkɪt/ NOUN [plural tickets] a small piece of printed paper that shows you have paid to do something 🔁 She bought an airline ticket to Paris. 🔁 a single/return ticket □ + for He's got free tickets for the match.

> ➤ THESAURUS: You usually need a ticket to travel on a public vehicle, and to go to the theatre or the cinema. A pass is a ticket that allows you to go into a place or to travel on a vehicle. For example, if you travel by train every day, you might buy a pass instead of buying a new ticket every day. Some people need a pass to show that they work in a particular building and are allowed to enter it. A card is a small flat piece of plastic that you can use in shops and machines to pay for things.

tickle /'tɪkəl/ VERB [tickles, tickling, tickled]

1 to touch someone's body lightly so that they laugh □ She tickled him under the arms.
2 if something tickles you, it causes an uncomfortable, light feeling on your skin □ The grass tickled her nose.

tide /taɪd/ NOUN [plural tides] the regular rise and fall of the level of the sea 🔁 At high tide, the rocks are completely covered. 🔁 You can walk out to the island at low tide.

tidy¹ /'taɪdɪ/ ADJECTIVE [tidier, tidiest]

1 carefully ordered or arranged with everything in

its correct place □ *Everything looked tidy.* 🔁 *He keeps his room tidy.*
2 a tidy person likes to keep things ordered and in their correct place □ *She's the tidiest person I know.*

tidy² /'taɪdɪ/ VERB [tidies, tidying, tidied] to put things back in their correct places and to make something tidy □ *Anne was tidying the kitchen.* □ **+ up** *Are you going to tidy up the mess you've made?* □ **+ away** *He tidied away his tools.*

tie¹ /taɪ/ VERB [ties, tying, tied]
1 to join or to fasten things together using string, rope, etc. □ **+ together** *We tied the boats together.* □ **+ with** *a box tied with white ribbon* □ **+ to** *The riders tied their horses to a tree.* □ *She tied her long hair in a ponytail.* □ *Their hands were tied behind their backs.*
2 to twist pieces of rope, string, etc. together to make a knot 🔁 *Tie a knot in the end of the thread.* □ *He bent down to tie his shoe lace.* □ **+ around** *She had a silk scarf tied around her neck.*
3 if two teams or players tie, they each have the same number of points □ **+ for** *They tied for second place.*
◆ PHRASAL VERB **tie someone/something up** to fasten someone or something with rope, etc. so that they cannot move □ *The boat's tied up in the harbour.* □ *The kidnappers tied them both up.*

tie² /taɪ/ NOUN [plural ties]
1 a narrow piece of cloth worn round your neck under your shirt collar and tied in a knot 🔁 *I have to wear a suit and tie for work*
2 a situation in which two teams or players each have the same number of points □ **+ for** *There was a tie for third place.*

tiger /'taɪgə(r)/ NOUN [plural tigers] a large wild animal related to the cat with yellow fur and black stripes

tight /taɪt/ ADJECTIVE [tighter, tightest]
1 fitting very closely and difficult to move □ *I was wearing very tight jeans.* □ *The top on this jar is very tight.*
2 very firm and strong □ *a tight knot*

tighten /'taɪtən/ VERB [tightens, tightening, tightened] to become firmer and stronger or to make something firmer and stronger □ *He tightened his grip on my arm.* □ *I tightened up the screws.*
tightly /'taɪtlɪ/ ADVERB in a firm and strong way □ *She held her purse tightly.* □ *I pulled the door tightly shut.*

tights /taɪts/ PLURAL NOUN a piece of women's clothing covering the feet, legs and bottom made of very thin material 🔁 *a pair of tights*

tile /taɪl/ NOUN [plural tiles] a piece of hard, flat material such as clay or stone, used for covering roofs, walls or floors □ *red roof tiles* □ *shiny floor tiles*

till¹ /tɪl/ PREPOSITION, CONJUNCTION until □ *We'll probably stay here till the end.* □ *It doesn't get dark till 10 o'clock in the summer.*

till² /tɪl/ NOUN [plural tills] a machine in a shop for counting what customers need to pay and for putting money in □ *She works at a supermarket behind the till.*

tilt /tɪlt/ VERB [tilts, tilting, tilted] to move something so that one side is lower than the other, or to move like this □ *He tilted his head to one side.*

timber /'tɪmbə(r)/ NOUN, NO PLURAL wood that is used for building things such as houses, or a piece of this wood

time¹ /taɪm/ NOUN [plural times]
1 *no plural* the way we measure minutes, hours, days, etc. □ *I was hardly aware of time passing.*
2 a particular moment in a day □ *What's the time?* □ *What would be a good time to meet?* 🔁 *What time does the show start?* 🔁 *Excuse me, have you got the time* (= can you tell me what time it is)? 🔁 *Can Dina tell the time* (= be able to read a clock) yet?
3 *no plural* an amount of time 🔁 *Do you spend a lot of time in London?* 🔁 *Ironing sheets is a complete waste of time.* 🔁 *We spent a long time talking about the past.* 🔁 *It takes a lot of time to learn a language well.*
4 a particular occasion □ *Do you remember the time Michael fell in the river?* □ *I've been to Morocco several times.* 🔁 *Next time you see Billy, can you ask him to call me?* 🔁 *The first time we met, I thought he was really rude.*
5 *no plural* if it is time to do something or for something to happen, it should be done or happen now □ *It's time the children were in bed.* □ *Is it time to plant the tomatoes yet?*
6 **in time** not too late □ *We got there just in time to see the queen.* □ *I hope the present arrives in time for his birthday.*
7 **on time** not early or late □ *The trains are usually on time.*
8 a long enough period 🔁 *We don't have time to contact everyone.* □ *We can play tennis if there's time later.*
9 an experience, or a period in someone's life 🔁 *Did you have a nice time in Brighton?*
10 **all the time** (a) continuously □ *We monitor our staff all the time.* (b) very often □ *I love Crete – we go there all the time.*
11 **one/two etc. at a time** one/two etc. on a particular occasion □ *He ran up the steps three at a time.* □ *One at a time, we went to the front of the class.*
12 **in an hour's/day's/year's, etc. time** after a particular period of time □ *The work should be complete in three week's time.*

➤ Note that you **have** a good/great, etc. time somewhere. You do not 'spend' a good/great, etc. time somewhere:
   ✓ We had a great time in Paris.
   ✗ We spent a great time in Paris.

time² /taɪm/ VERB [times, timing, timed]
1 to arrange for something to happen at a particular time □ The meeting was timed to coincide with his visit.
2 to measure how long something takes □ He timed me running a mile.

times /taɪmz/ PREPOSITION used in mathematics between the numbers you are multiplying □ Two times four is eight.

timetable /'taɪmteɪbəl/ NOUN [plural timetables]
1 a list of the times when public vehicles such as trains or buses arrive or leave
2 a list of the lessons at a school, college, etc. and the times they happen 🔁 We want to see more practical subjects on the school timetable.

➤ **THESAURUS:** A timetable is a list of the times when public vehicles such as trains or buses arrive or leave, or a list of the lessons at a school and the times they happen. A schedule is a plan that shows when things should happen or be done. You might have a schedule for doing a particular job. An agenda is a list of things to be discussed at a meeting. A calendar is a thing that shows all the days, weeks and months of the year.

tin /tɪn/ NOUN [plural tins]
1 a closed metal container which food is sold in □ **+ of** a tin of tuna □ He opened a tin of tomato soup.
2 a metal container with a lid, which you store food or other things in □ **+ of** a tin of biscuits □ a tin of paint
3 no plural a soft, silver metal □ the tin roof of the garage □ a tin bucket

tin opener /'tɪn ˌəʊpənə(r)/ NOUN [plural tin openers] a small tool for opening metal containers of food

tiny /'taɪni/ ADJECTIVE [tinier, tiniest] extremely small □ a baby's tiny hands and feet 🔁 a tiny amount of water

tip¹ /tɪp/ NOUN [plural tips]
1 the point at the end or the top of something □ They used arrows with poison tips. □ Point to it with the tip of your finger.
2 a small extra amount of money for someone who has done a job for you 🔁 Did you leave a tip?
3 a piece of helpful advice □ He gave me some useful tips on laying floor tiles.

tip² /tɪp/ VERB [tips, tipping, tipped]
1 to move something so that it is not flat or vertical, or to move in this way □ Tip the chairs forward against the tables. □ The vehicle tipped onto its side.
2 to pour something from a container □ They just tip the rubbish over the side of the ship. □ She tipped a bucket of water on my head.
3 to give a small extra amount of money to someone who has done a job for you □ She tipped the taxi driver.
◆ PHRASAL VERB **tip (something) over** to push something onto its side or to fall on one side □ She tipped her drink over.

tire /'taɪə(r)/ VERB [tires, tiring, tired] to start feeling that you need a rest □ Grandma tires easily nowadays.
◆ PHRASAL VERB **tire someone out** to make someone feel tired □ Let's go to the park and tire the children out a bit.

tired /'taɪəd/ ADJECTIVE
1 feeling that you need a rest □ You must be tired after your journey. 🔁 I was getting really tired. 🔁 He felt too tired and ill to continue.
2 bored and often annoyed □ **+ of** I'm tired of wearing the same clothes every day. □ I'm tired of people asking me questions.

tissue /'tɪʃuː/ NOUN [plural tissues] a thin, soft piece of paper for cleaning your nose, etc. □ She took out a tissue to wipe her nose.

title /'taɪtəl/ NOUN [plural titles]
1 the name of something such as a book, song or film □ **+ of** What's the title of your poem? □ How did you choose the book's title?
2 a word that you can use before your name, for example Ms or Professor □ Her title is 'Doctor', not 'Mrs'.

➤ **THESAURUS:** Name is a general word for the word or words that you use to refer to a person, animal, place or thing. A title is the name of something, such as a book, song or film. You can also use title to talk about the subject of an essay. A headline is the words that are printed in large letters at the top of a newspaper article.

to¹ /tuː/
1 used before a verb to make the infinitive form □ I want to leave now. □ I forgot to tell him.
2 used as part of the infinitive to show the purpose of something □ I went to get a drink. □ I phoned her to invite her to the party.

to² /tuː/ PREPOSITION
1 used to say where someone or something goes □ We went to the shops. □ I go to work by bus. □ The cup fell to the floor.
2 used to say who is given something, told something, etc. □ Give the letter to Clara. □ I spoke to her several times.

3 connected or fixed □ *The cake was stuck to the tin.* □ *We nailed the picture to the wall.*
4 facing or going in a particular direction □ *He had his back to me.* □ *Keep to the side of the woods.* □ *He pointed to the sign.*
5 used to say how someone's actions affect someone or something □ *He was always kind to me.* □ *What have you done to my car?*
6 from ... to (a) used to show a period of time □ *We are open from 9 to 6.* (b) used to show a range of something □ *Everyone was there, from young to old.*
7 used for saying the time up to 30 minutes before an hour □ *It's ten to three.*

toast /təʊst/ NOUN [*plural* toasts]
1 *no plural* bread that has been made hard and slightly brown by heating □ *I had toast and honey for breakfast.* 🖻 *a piece of toast*
2 when people lift their glasses and drink together to express good wishes to someone 🖻 *I'd like to propose a toast to the bride and groom.*

toaster /ˈtəʊstə(r)/ NOUN [*plural* toasters] a machine for heating bread until it is hard and slightly brown

tobacco /təˈbækəʊ/ NOUN, NO PLURAL the leaves of a plant that are dried and used for smoking □ *tobacco smoke* □ *the tobacco industry*

today¹ /təˈdeɪ/ ADVERB
1 on this day □ *I can't come today.* 🖻 *I spoke to Alan earlier today.* 🖻 *My parents are coming over later today.*
2 at or around the present time □ *People are taller today than they were a hundred years ago.*

today² /təˈdeɪ/ NOUN, NO PLURAL this day □ *Today is Tuesday.* □ *Today's announcement comes as no surprise.*

toe /təʊ/ NOUN [*plural* toes] one of the five parts at the end of your foot □ *Reach up high, standing*

on your toes. 🖻 *He injured his left big toe.* 🖻 *She stubbed* (= hit) *her toe on the end of the bed.*

together /təˈgeðə(r)/ ADVERB
1 with or near each other □ *We work together.* □ *They spent the evening together watching television.* 🖻 *The houses are quite close together.*
2 touching, joined or mixed with each other □ *Mix the sugar and eggs together in a bowl.* □ *She pressed her hands together.* □ *Add all the numbers together.*
3 at the same time □ *All these things happened together.*

toilet /ˈtɔɪlɪt/ NOUN [*plural* toilets]
1 a large bowl that you sit on to get rid of waste from your body 🖻 *I need to go to the toilet.* 🖻 *He flushed the toilet and washed his hands.*
2 a room with a toilet in it 🖻 *a public toilet* □ *Excuse me, where are the ladies' toilets?*

> ➤ **THESAURUS:** A lavatory or a WC is the same as a toilet. Lavatory is a formal word, and quite old-fashioned, and WC is usually used to talk about public toilets. A bathroom is the room where you wash yourself, and usually also contains a toilet.

told /təʊld/ PAST TENSE AND PAST PARTICIPLE OF **tell**
tolerance /ˈtɒlərəns/ NOUN, NO PLURAL when you are willing to accept other people's ideas and behaviour, even when they are different from yours □ *Everyone needs to show tolerance.* 🖻 *His speech was about religious tolerance.*
tolerate /ˈtɒləreɪt/ VERB [tolerates, tolerating, tolerated] to accept something even if you do not like it or agree with it □ *I can't tolerate this noise for much longer.* □ *We will not tolerate aggressive behaviour.*

tomato /təˈmɑːtəʊ/ NOUN [*plural* tomatoes] a soft, red fruit with a lot of juice that is used like a vegetable in salads, sauces, etc. □ *pasta with tomato sauce* □ *a cheese and tomato sandwich*

tomb /tuːm/ NOUN [*plural* tombs] a place where a dead body is buried, often with a stone structure

tomorrow¹ /təˈmɒrəʊ/ NOUN, NO PLURAL the day after today □ *Tomorrow is Wednesday.* 🖻 *He's arriving early tomorrow morning.* 🖻 *Will he be fit for the game tomorrow night?* 🖻 *I'll be back the day after tomorrow.*

tomorrow² /təˈmɒrəʊ/ ADVERB on the day after today □ *Let's have our meeting tomorrow.* □ *We'll be here tomorrow.*

ton /tʌn/ NOUN [*plural* tons]
1 a unit for measuring weight, equal to 1016 kilograms in Britain or 907 kilograms in America □ *a truck carrying 60 tons of coal*
2 tons of an informal phrase meaning a lot of

something □ She's got tons of clothes to choose from. □ I've got tons of things to do.

tone /təʊn/ NOUN [plural tones] the quality of a sound or of someone's voice ☐ I could tell she was angry from her tone of voice. □ a cello with a soft gentle tone

tongue /tʌŋ/ NOUN [plural tongues] the soft part inside your mouth that you can move and that you use to speak, eat and taste □ He ran his tongue across his teeth. ☐ Tim stuck his tongue out at me.

tonight[1] /tə'naɪt/ NOUN, NO PLURAL the night or evening of today □ I'll have to miss tonight's class, I'm afraid.

tonight[2] /tə'naɪt/ ADVERB on the night or evening of today □ I'm going to bed early tonight. □ The show is on BBC1 at 9pm tonight.

tonne /tʌn/ NOUN [plural tonnes] a unit for measuring weight, equal to 1000 kilograms

too /tuː/ ADVERB
1 more than necessary or more than is sensible □ If the water is too hot, add some cold. □ The offer was too good to refuse. □ Don't spend too much. ☐ You're driving much too fast!
2 also □ Can I come too? □ I was really shocked and I think Maria was too.

➤ Note that if something is **too** heavy/hot/old, etc. it is bad. It means that something is more heavy/hot/old, etc. than you want it to be: □ It's too heavy – I can't lift it. □ The weather is too hot – I like it a bit cooler.

took /tʊk/ PAST TENSE OF **take**

tool /tuːl/ NOUN [plural tools] a piece of equipment that you hold in your hand and use to do a particular job □ a set of gardening tools ☐ Keep a basic tool kit in the car.

➤ THESAURUS: There are many different types of tool. A hammer is a tool with a heavy metal or wooden part at the end of a handle, used for hitting nails etc. A drill is a tool for making holes in something hard. Drills are often electric. A saw is a tool with a thin blade used for cutting through wood or metal.

tooth /tuːθ/ NOUN [plural teeth]
1 one of the hard, white parts in your mouth that you use for biting □ He has one front tooth missing. ☐ I brushed my teeth and washed my face. ☐ That cat's got sharp teeth.
2 one of the row of sharp points that form one side of an object such as a comb (= thing used to tidy hair)

toothache /'tuːθeɪk/ NOUN, NO PLURAL a pain in or around your tooth ☐ I had terrible toothache. □ He went to the dentist with toothache.

toothbrush /'tuːθbrʌʃ/ NOUN [plural toothbrushes] a small brush that you use for cleaning your teeth

toothpaste /'tuːθpeɪst/ NOUN, NO PLURAL a cream that you use to clean your teeth

top[1] /tɒp/ NOUN [plural tops]
1 the highest point or part of something □ We climbed to the top of the tower. □ They were waiting at the top of the steps. □ Start reading at the top of the page.
2 the top the most successful position ☐ He's determined to get to the top of his profession.
3 on (the) top on the upper surface of something □ I keep his photograph on top of the TV. □ I like pizza with lots of olives on top.
4 the lid or cover of a container □ Screw the top back on tightly.
5 a piece of clothing for the upper half of your body □ She was wearing green trousers and a black top.

top[2] /tɒp/ ADJECTIVE
1 most important or successful □ Safety is our top priority. ☐ He came top in the exam. □ a top fashion designer
2 in the highest part of something ☐ My office is on the top floor.

topic /'tɒpɪk/ NOUN [plural topics] a subject to study, write or talk about □ + of The storms were the main topic of conversation. □ A range of topics was discussed. □ Immigration can be a sensitive topic.

topple /'tɒpəl/ VERB [topples, toppling, toppled] to fall over or to make something fall over □ I knocked into a table and it toppled over. □ High winds toppled trees.

torch /tɔːtʃ/ NOUN [plural torches] a small electric light that you carry in your hand ☐ Someone shone a torch into the tent.

tore /tɔː(r)/ PAST TENSE OF **tear**[1]

torn /tɔːn/ PAST PARTICIPLE OF **tear**[1]

tornado /tɔː'neɪdəʊ/ NOUN [plural tornadoes] a violent storm with a powerful wind with a circular movement that causes a lot of damage

torture /'tɔːtʃə(r)/ VERB [tortures, torturing, tortured] to hurt someone in a cruel way, usually as a punishment or to get information from them □ He was tortured by his guards.

toss /tɒs/ VERB [tosses, tossing, tossed]
1 to throw something lightly or without care □ Toss the keys over here, would you? □ He tossed aside the magazine.
2 to move repeatedly from side to side ☐ Alice spent the night tossing and turning restlessly.
3 to throw a coin up in the air to see which side it falls on, in order to make a choice □ We decided to toss for the front seat. ☐ Why not just toss a coin?

total[1] /'təʊtəl/ ADJECTIVE
1 complete □ *She was a total stranger.* □ *He showed a total lack of respect.* □ *The job must be done in total secrecy.*
2 including everything ⊞ *Two more people arrived yesterday, bringing the total number of guests to 12.* □ *the total cost of the project*

total[2] /'təʊtəl/ NOUN [plural totals] the number or amount you get when you add everything together □ + *of We've got a total of fifteen cats.* ⊞ *They raised a grand total of £940.* □ *There were thirty people in total.*

total[3] /'təʊtəl/ VERB [totals, totalling/US totaling, totalled/US totaled] to be a particular number or amount when added together □ *Our collection totalled £320.*

totally /'təʊtəli/ ADVERB completely □ *Is she totally deaf?* □ *I agree with you totally.*

> ➤ **Totally** is only used before adjectives with very strong meanings. Before adjectives with less strong meanings, use **very** or **extremely:** □ *I was totally exhausted.* □ *I was very tired.* □ *It's totally ridiculous.* □ *It's very silly.*

touch[1] /tʌtʃ/ VERB [touches, touching, touched]
1 to put your hand or fingers on something □ *Please do not touch the items on the shelf.* □ *Can you touch the ceiling?*
2 if things touch, there is no space between them □ *We stood in a line with our shoulders touching.*

touch[2] /tʌtʃ/ NOUN [plural touches]
1 when you put your hands or fingers on something □ *You can start the engine at the touch of a button.* □ *I felt a touch on my shoulder.*
2 *no plural* the ability to feel □ *The fur was smooth to the touch.*
3 in touch if you are in touch with someone, you communicate with them □ *I wish Sally would get in touch with me.* □ *I hope we can stay in touch.*
4 lose touch to stop communicating with someone, usually not deliberately □ *We lost touch after we left university.*

tough /tʌf/ ADJECTIVE [tougher, toughest]
1 difficult to deal with □ *It was a tough decision.* □ *He had a tough time in that job.*
2 very severe □ *Tough new measures have been introduced to reduce crime.* □ *We're very tough on students who do not work hard enough.*
3 physically or mentally strong □ *You need to be tough to succeed in business.*
4 not easy to cut or damage □ *You'll need a tough pair of shoes for climbing.* □ *The meat was a bit tough.*

tour[1] /tʊə(r)/ NOUN [plural tours] a visit somewhere, stopping several times at places of interest □ + *of We went on a tour of the region.* ⊞ *He takes visitors on guided tours of the city.*

tour[2] /tʊə(r)/ VERB [tours, touring, toured] to go on a tour □ *We're going to tour the wine-making regions of France.* □ *We've hired a car to tour the city.*

tourism /'tʊərɪzəm/ NOUN, NO PLURAL travelling to and visiting places for enjoyment, or the business of providing holiday services ⊞ *the tourism industry* □ *We are trying to promote tourism on the island.*

tourist /'tʊərɪst/ NOUN [plural tourists] a person who is travelling for enjoyment or on holiday □ *a group of foreign tourists* ⊞ *a tourist attraction*

tournament /'tʊənəmənt/ NOUN [plural tournaments] a number of sports matches that make up a big competition ⊞ *a golf tournament* ⊞ *the US Open tennis tournament*

tow /təʊ/ VERB [tows, towing, towed] to pull something behind you with a rope or chain □ *The car broke down and we had to be towed home.*

towards /tə'wɔːdz/ PREPOSITION
1 in the direction of someone or something □ *I ran towards her.* □ *The sign points towards the east.* □ *He moved his chair towards the window*
2 used to talk about the way someone feels about someone or something □ *I found his attitude towards money strange.* □ *She feels a lot of anger towards her family.*
3 near something □ *The bit about Cromwell is towards the end of the book.* □ *I hope to finish my book towards the end of the year.*
4 in order to help to pay for something □ *He made a donation towards the new roof.*

towel /'taʊəl/ NOUN [plural towels] a piece of soft, thick cloth for drying yourself ⊞ *a bath towel* □ *She picked up the wet towel from the bathroom floor.* ⊞ *She dried her hands using a paper towel.*

tower /'taʊə(r)/ NOUN [plural towers] a tall narrow building or part of a building □ *a church tower* □ *the Eiffel Tower*

town /taʊn/ NOUN [plural towns] a place where people live and work, bigger than a village and smaller than a city ⊞ *She comes from a small town in Ohio.* ⊞ *The wedding was in her home town of Hobart.*

town hall /ˌtaʊn 'hɔːl/ NOUN [plural town halls] a building that contains local government offices

toxic /'tɒksɪk/ ADJECTIVE poisonous ⊞ *toxic chemicals* ⊞ *The river is polluted with toxic waste.*

toy /tɔɪ/ NOUN [plural toys] an object made for someone, especially a child, to play with

trace[1] /treɪs/ VERB [traces, tracing, traced]
1 to find someone or something by following

information about where they have been □ *The man has been traced to a village in the south of the country.*

2 to copy a picture by covering it with a sheet of thin paper and drawing over the lines you can see through it

trace[2] /treɪs/ NOUN [*plural* traces] a mark or sign that someone or something leaves behind 🔄 *He disappeared without trace.*

track[1] /træk/ NOUN [*plural* tracks]

1 a rough path or road □ *We followed a narrow track along the edge of the field.*

2 a mark on the ground left by a person, animal or thing that has been there □ *They followed the bear's tracks through the forest.*

3 the long metal pieces that a train moves along □ *Repairs were needed to the track.*

4 an area of ground used for racing, often with a circular path □ *The runners were training on the track.*

5 keep track to continue to have enough information about something □ *I can't keep track of all the new rules.*

6 lose track to no longer have enough information about something □ *I've lost track of the number of times I've given her money.*

track[2] /træk/ VERB [tracks, tracking, tracked] to follow a person, animal or vehicle by looking for their marks or using special equipment □ *They use radar to track the aircraft's movements.*

◆ PHRASAL VERB track someone/something down to find someone or something after looking for them for a long time □ *I'm trying to track down an old friend.* □ *The shop has tracked down the book you ordered.*

tractor /'træktə(r)/ NOUN [*plural* tractors] a powerful vehicle with large wheels, used on farms

trade[1] /treɪd/ NOUN [*plural* trades]

1 *no plural* the buying and selling of goods, services or shares (= parts of a company that you can sell or buy) □ *international trade*

2 a particular area of business □ *She works in the diamond trade.*

3 a job using your hands that involves skill and training 🔄 *He learned the trade from his father.*

trade[2] /treɪd/ VERB [trades, trading, traded] to buy or sell goods, services or shares (= parts of a company that you can sell or buy) □ *+ with We will not trade with corrupt regimes.*

trademark /'treɪdmɑːk/ NOUN [*plural* trademarks] a name, word or symbol that a

company uses on its products and which legally belongs to that company

trader /'treɪdə(r)/ NOUN [*plural* traders] a person or company that buys and sells things

tradition /trə'dɪʃən/ NOUN [*plural* traditions] a custom that has continued for a long time □ *Having special birthday meals is a family tradition.* □ *He does not follow any religious tradition.*

traditional /trə'dɪʃənəl/ ADJECTIVE based on customs that have existed for a long time □ *They wore traditional costumes.*

traffic /'træfɪk/ NOUN, NO PLURAL vehicles that are travelling 🔄 *We were stuck in heavy traffic* (= a lot of traffic).

> ➤ THESAURUS: Vehicle is a general word for something that carries people or goods, especially on roads. Cars, trucks and buses are all vehicles. Traffic is vehicles that are travelling. Transport is vehicles or a system used for taking goods and people from one place to another. For example, public transport includes buses and trains, and any other vehicle which carries people who buy a ticket to travel.

traffic jam /'træfɪk ˌdʒæm/ NOUN [*plural* traffic jams] a long line of vehicles that cannot move because the road is blocked

traffic lights /'træfɪk ˌlaɪts/ PLURAL NOUN a set of red, yellow and green lights that tell vehicles when to stop or go

traffic warden /'træfɪk ˌwɔːdən/ NOUN [*plural* traffic wardens] a person whose job is to check that vehicles have been parked legally

tragedy /'trædʒədɪ/ NOUN [*plural* tragedies]

1 a very sad event, often where people die □ *The train driver did not cause the tragedy.*

2 a story that has a sad ending, especially when the main character dies □ *She is a character in a Shakespeare tragedy.*

tragic /'trædʒɪk/ ADJECTIVE very sad, often because of a death 🔄 *His death was a tragic accident.* □ *Her actions had tragic consequences.*

trail /treɪl/ NOUN [*plural* trails]

1 a series of marks or objects that someone or something leaves when they move somewhere □ *They left a trail of litter behind them.*

2 a path through the countryside

train[1] /treɪn/ NOUN [plural trains] a vehicle that moves on a railway and carries passengers □ *I prefer to travel by train.* 🔊 *I caught the early train.*

> ► THESAURUS: Train is a general word for a vehicle that moves on tracks and carries pasengers. An underground is a railway that is underground, usually in a large city. The underground railway system in London is often called the tube. In American English, an underground is usually called a **subway**. A tram is a type of electric bus that runs on metal tracks in the street.

train[2] /treɪn/ VERB [trains, training, trained]
1 to teach a person or animal to do something □ + *to do something* Veronica has trained her dog to carry her handbag.
2 to learn to do a particular job □ + *as* Andrew trained as a nurse when he left school.
3 to prepare for a sports event □ *The team trains for three hours every day.*

trainer /ˈtreɪnə(r)/ NOUN [plural trainers]
1 someone who teaches people or animals to do something
2 trainers soft shoes that are used for sport

training /ˈtreɪnɪŋ/ NOUN, NO PLURAL
1 the process of training people or being trained □ + *in* We received very little training in how to use the equipment. 🔊 *They run training courses for diving instructors.*
2 preparation for a sports event □ *The team will be in training for the World Cup.*

trait /treɪt/ NOUN [plural traits] a particular characteristic or quality that someone or something has □ *The test is supposed to reveal your character traits.*

traitor /ˈtreɪtə(r)/ NOUN [plural traitors] a person who is not loyal to their friends or country

tram /træm/ NOUN [plural trams] a type of electric bus that runs on metal tracks in the street □ *Trams run from the station to the city centre every 5 minutes.*

transfer[1] /trænsˈfɜː(r)/ VERB [transfers, transferring, transferred] to move someone or something from one place to another □ *She transferred all her photos onto a CD.* □ *I transferred some money into his account.*

transfer[2] /ˈtrænsfɜː(r)/ NOUN [plural transfers]
1 when someone moves to another job or place of work in the same organization □ *The sergeant has asked for a transfer.*
2 the act of moving someone or something from one place to another □ *I am responsible for the transfer of supplies to the new base.*

transform /trænsˈfɔːm/ VERB [transforms, transforming, transformed] to change something completely □ *We could transform this room with a few tins of paint.*

transitive /ˈtrænzɪtɪv/ ADJECTIVE a transitive verb always has an object □ *In the sentence 'I can see Mary.', 'see' is a transitive verb.*

translate /trænsˈleɪt/ VERB [translates, translating, translated] to change words into a different language □ + *into* Can you translate this into French?

translation /trænsˈleɪʃən/ NOUN [plural translations]
1 writing or speech that has been changed into a different language □ + *of* This is a new translation of her novel.
2 *no plural* the process of changing words into a different language

translator /trænsˈleɪtə(r)/ NOUN [plural translators] someone whose job is to change words into a different language

transparent /trænsˈpærənt/ ADJECTIVE if something is transparent, you can see through it □ *The box is made of transparent plastic so that you can see what's inside.*

transplant /ˈtrænsplɑːnt/ NOUN [plural transplants] an operation to put an organ from one person's body into someone else 🔊 *He had a heart transplant.*

transport[1] /ˈtrænspɔːt/ NOUN, NO PLURAL
1 vehicles or a system used for taking people and goods from one place to another 🔊 *Older people have free travel on public transport.* 🔊 *Paris has a very efficient transport system.* 🔊 *Trains are a very safe form of transport.*
2 moving people or things from one place to another □ *The price includes the cost of transport.* □ + *of* The transport of farm animals was banned.

➤ Remember that **transport** cannot be used in the plural:
✓ *Public transport is very good in the capital.*
✗ *Public transports are very good in the capital.*
To talk about one particular type of transport, use the phrase **form of transport**: □ *Train is probably the greenest form of transport.*

transport² /træns'pɔːt/ VERB [transports, transporting, transported] to move something from one place to another □ *The planes were used to transport prisoners.* □ *Red blood cells transport oxygen around the body.*

trap¹ /træp/ NOUN [plural traps]
1 a piece of equipment for catching animals □ *a mouse trap*
2 a clever plan that is designed to trick someone 🔁 *Police set a trap for the thief.*

trap² /træp/ VERB [traps, trapping, trapped]
1 if you are trapped in a bad place or situation, you cannot escape from it □ *Passengers were trapped in the burning bus.* □ *He was trapped in a loveless marriage.*
2 to catch an animal in a trap □ *The animals were trapped for their fur.*

trash /træʃ/ NOUN, NO PLURAL the US word for **rubbish** (= things that have been thrown away)

trauma /'trɔːmə/ NOUN [plural traumas] a very unpleasant experience that upsets someone a lot and for a long time □ *She never recovered from the trauma of losing her son.*

travel¹ /'trævəl/ VERB [travels, travelling/US traveling, travelled/US traveled]
1 to go from one place to another □ *Holly spent the summer travelling in the United States.* □ *Some people have to travel long distances to get to school.* 🔁 *She travels the world in her job.* □ **+ by** *I like travelling by train.*
2 to move at a particular speed □ *How fast does light travel?* □ *The vehicle was travelling too fast.*

travel² /'trævəl/ NOUN, NO PLURAL the activity of going from one place to another 🔁 *Cheap air travel has encouraged more people to fly.* 🔁 *Make sure you have travel insurance if you go abroad.*

travel agency /'trævəl ˌeɪdʒənsɪ/ NOUN [plural travel agencies] a shop or business where you can buy holidays

travel agent /'trævəl ˌeɪdʒənt/ NOUN [plural travel agents]
1 a person whose job is to arrange holidays for people
2 a travel agent's a **travel agency**

traveler /'trævələ(r)/ NOUN [plural travelers] the US spelling of **traveller**

traveler's check /'trævələz ˌtʃek/ NOUN [plural traveler's checks] the US spelling of **traveller's cheque**

traveller /'trævələ(r)/ NOUN [plural travellers] a person who is on a journey 🔁 *Air travellers faced delays due to bad weather.*

traveller's cheque /'trævələz ˌtʃek/ NOUN [plural traveller's cheques] a cheque for a fixed amount that you can change for local money when you are abroad

tray /treɪ/ NOUN [plural trays] a flat object for carrying food, plates, cups, etc. on □ *The waiter was carrying a tray of drinks.*

tread /tred/ VERB [treads, treading, trod, trodden]
1 to put your foot on something □ *Don't tread on the flowers.*
2 **tread water** to stay in one place in water by moving your legs up and down

treason /'triːzən/ NOUN, NO PLURAL the crime of not being loyal to your country, for example by giving away secret information

treasure /'treʒə(r)/ NOUN, NO PLURAL valuable objects, especially if they have been hidden □ *The children were hoping to find some buried treasure.*

treat¹ /triːt/ VERB [treats, treating, treated]
1 to behave in a particular way towards someone □ *I think Debbie treated Steve really badly.* □ *They treat their staff well.*
2 to deal with something in a particular way □ **+ as** *He treated my remark as a joke.* □ *We treat any form of racism very seriously.*
3 to give medicine or medical care to someone who is ill or injured □ *Doctors use all the latest methods to treat their patients.* □ **+ for** *She is being treated for shock.*
4 to buy or do something special for someone □ **+ to** *I treated the children to a pizza on the way home.*

treat² /triːt/ NOUN [plural treats] something special that you do or buy for someone 🔁 *We're having dinner in front of the TV as a special treat.*

treatment /'triːtmənt/ NOUN [plural treatments]
1 medicine or medical care □ *My treatment will last for about a month.* 🔁 *He is receiving treatment for a heart condition.* □ *They are trying out a new treatment for cancer.*
2 *no plural* the way you behave towards someone or deal with something □ *Will I get special treatment if I pay more?*

treaty /'triːtɪ/ NOUN [plural treaties] an official agreement between countries 🔁 *The two countries have signed a peace treaty.*

tree /triː/ NOUN [plural trees] a very tall plant with branches and leaves □ *We planted lots of trees in the garden last autumn.* □ *an apple tree* □ *an oak* tree 🔁 We planted a new tree. 🔁 The children were climbing trees. 🔁 a tree trunk

tremble /'trembəl/ VERB [trembles, trembling, trembled] to shake because you are frightened or excited □ Joe's hand trembled as he dialled the number. □ She was trembling with fear.

tremendous /trɪ'mendəs/ ADJECTIVE
1 very great □ The car was travelling at a tremendous speed.
2 very good □ That's tremendous news!

trench /trentʃ/ NOUN [plural trenches] a long narrow hole dug in the ground

trend /trend/ NOUN [plural trends] a gradual change or development □ There's a new trend towards healthy eating.

trial /'traɪəl/ NOUN [plural trials]
1 a legal process in which a court has to decide if someone is guilty of a crime □ a murder trial 🔁 She's on trial for the killing of her husband. 🔁 He was not given a fair trial.
2 a test that is done to find out how good or effective something is □ The company is carrying out trials on new drugs.

triangle /'traɪæŋgəl/ NOUN [plural triangles] a flat shape with three sides and three angles □ a right-angled triangle

triangular /traɪ'æŋgjʊlə(r)/ ADJECTIVE in the shape of a triangle □ a triangular shape □ a triangular piece of cloth

tribal /'traɪbəl/ ADJECTIVE to do with a group of families who have the same culture and language and have a traditional way of living a long way from cities □ tribal ceremonies

tribe /traɪb/ NOUN [plural tribes] a group of families who have the same culture and language and have a traditional way of living a long way from cities □ the Christian Arab tribes of the Syrian desert

tribute /'trɪbjuːt/ NOUN [plural tributes]
1 a speech or action that shows you admire someone □ The film will be shown as a tribute to its star who died last week.
2 **pay tribute to someone/something** to praise someone or something in public □ They wanted to pay tribute to all the soldiers who had died in the war.

trick[1] /trɪk/ NOUN [plural tricks]
1 an unfair or unpleasant thing that you do to someone as a joke, or in order to get an advantage for yourself 🔁 The children were playing tricks on each other.
2 something that looks like magic which you do to

entertain people 🔁 a magic trick 🔁 Ella was doing card tricks.

trick[2] /trɪk/ VERB [tricks, tricking, tricked] to make someone do what you want by using clever but unfair methods □ **+ into** She was tricked into signing the papers.

trickle /'trɪkəl/ VERB [trickles, trickling, trickled] to flow in a slow, thin stream □ Sweat trickled down his face.

tricky /'trɪkɪ/ ADJECTIVE [trickier, trickiest] difficult to do or to deal with □ a tricky situation

tried /traɪd/ PAST TENSE AND PAST PARTICIPLE OF **try**[1]

trigger[1] /'trɪgə(r)/ NOUN [plural triggers] the part you pull to fire a gun 🔁 He pointed the gun and pulled the trigger.

trigger[2] /'trɪgə(r)/ VERB [triggers, triggering, triggered] to make something start to happen □ The announcement triggered violent protests around the country.

trillion /'trɪljən/ NUMBER [plural trillions] the number 1,000,000,000,000

trim /trɪm/ VERB [trims, trimming, trimmed] to cut a small amount off something □ Get your hair trimmed. □ You'll need to trim that photo to get it into the frame.

trio /'triːəʊ/ NOUN [plural trios] a group of three people or things, especially musicians

trip[1] /trɪp/ NOUN [plural trips] a journey to a place and back again □ There are boat trips around Lake Geneva. 🔁 a shopping trip 🔁 He has made several trips to Japan. □ **+ to** We went on a trip to the zoo.

trip[2] /trɪp/ VERB [trips, tripping, tripped]
1 to hit your foot on something and fall, or almost fall □ **+ over** Caroline tripped over the edge of the carpet. □ Mind you don't trip on the step.
2 to make someone fall by putting your foot in front of them □ **+ up** One of the boys tripped me up.

triumph /'traɪəmf/ NOUN [plural triumphs] a great success in a competition or fight □ It was another triumph for the champions. □ England's only World Cup triumph was in 1966.

trod /trɒd/ PAST TENSE OF **tread**

trodden /'trɒdən/ PAST PARTICIPLE OF **tread**

trolley /'trɒlɪ/ NOUN [plural trolleys] a container on wheels, used for carrying things □ a supermarket trolley

troops /truːps/ PLURAL NOUN soldiers □ The US sent troops to Darfur.

trophy /'trəʊfɪ/ NOUN [plural trophies] a prize such as a silver cup that you get for winning a competition □ *Helen won the junior tennis trophy last year.*

tropical /'trɒpɪkəl/ ADJECTIVE in or to do with hot areas near the equator (= line round the middle of the world) □ *a tropical rainforest*

tropics /'trɒpɪks/ PLURAL NOUN the tropics the hot areas near the equator (= line round the middle of the world). A geography word.

trot /trɒt/ VERB [trots, trotting, trotted] if a horse trots, it moves more quickly than walking, but does not run □ *The horse trotted down the road.*

trouble¹ /'trʌbəl/ NOUN [plural troubles]
1 problems, difficulties or worries □ + *ing She has trouble sleeping.* □ *He had financial troubles.* ᐓ *You'll have no trouble finding a better job.*
2 no plural extra effort ᐓ *He took the trouble to thank everyone.* ᐓ *They went to so much trouble to make our visit pleasant.*
3 no plural a problem with your health or with a machine or piece of equipment □ *She has heart trouble.* □ *The car had engine trouble.*
4 no plural a situation where people are behaving badly, fighting, causing difficulties, etc. ᐓ *Some people at the back of the hall started to cause trouble.*
5 no plural a difficult or dangerous situation ᐓ *Their ship got into trouble during a storm.* ᐓ *The business is in deep trouble.*
6 no plural a situation where you will be punished or blamed ᐓ *We got into trouble for talking in class.* ᐓ *If I'm late home, I'll be in big trouble.*
7 no plural the thing about something that causes problems ᐓ *The trouble is, I already have a meeting on that day.*

trouble² /'trʌbəl/ VERB [troubles, troubling, troubled] if something troubles you, it worries you □ *They were troubled by reports of violence in the area.*

trousers /'traʊzəz/ PLURAL NOUN a piece of clothing for the lower half of your body that covers each leg ᐓ *She was wearing a pair of black trousers.*

truce /truːs/ NOUN [plural truces] an agreement to stop fighting or arguing ᐓ *The political parties called a truce.*

truck /trʌk/ NOUN [plural trucks] a large road vehicle for carrying goods □ *He drove the truck into the yard.* □ *Her Dad's a truck driver.*

true /truː/ ADJECTIVE [truer, truest]
1 real and not invented ᐓ *Is it a true story?* □ + *that Is it true that you're moving to Tokyo?*
2 real and not pretended □ *Ben never showed his true feelings.* □ *She's a true friend.* □ *He had finally*

found true love. □ *He had a false passport to hide his true identity.*
3 come true if something comes true, the thing you have spoken about really happens □ *My wish to travel round the world has finally come true.*

truly /'truːlɪ/ ADVERB really □ *Tell me what you truly want to do.* □ *I'm truly sorry.*

trumpet /'trʌmpɪt/ NOUN [plural trumpets] a metal musical instrument that you blow into □ *Millie is learning to play the trumpet.*

trunk /trʌŋk/ NOUN [plural trunks]
1 the thick main stem of a tree ᐓ *a tree trunk*
2 an elephant's long nose
3 a large box for storing things
4 the main part of a person's body, not including their head, arms or legs
5 the US word for **boot** (= part of a car)

trust¹ /trʌst/ VERB [trusts, trusting, trusted]
1 to believe that someone is honest and loyal □ *The officer picked ten men he knew he could trust.*
2 to feel confident that someone will do something correctly and well or will look after something well □ + *to do something I know I can trust you to choose a suitable present.*

trust² /trʌst/ NOUN, NO PLURAL the belief that someone is honest and loyal ᐓ *The new manager will have to gain the trust of her staff.*

trustworthy /'trʌstwɜːðɪ/ ADJECTIVE able to be trusted □ *I'm sure he's a trustworthy person.*

truth /truːθ/ NOUN [plural truths]
1 the truth the true facts ᐓ *I don't think he is telling the truth.* □ + *about I don't think we'll ever know the truth about what happened.*
2 no plural the quality of being true □ + *in Is there any truth in the rumours that he is leaving?*

➤ Note that you **tell** the **truth**. You do not 'say the truth':
✓ *Tell me the truth: Do you like her?*
✗ *Say the truth: Do you like her?*

try¹ /traɪ/ VERB [tries, trying, tried]
1 to make an effort or an attempt to do something □ **+ to do something** *Please try to understand.* 🔁 *He failed the exam, but he can always try again next year.*
2 to do or use something to see if you like it or if it works or is effective □ *Try this powder for a cleaner wash.* □ *I've never tried Chinese food.* □ **+ ing** *You could try phoning him.*
3 to find out if someone committed a crime by hearing all the evidence (= facts or statements given in a court of law) □ *They will be tried in the European Court of Human Rights.* □ **+ for** *She was tried for murder.*
◆ PHRASAL VERB **try something on** to put on a piece of clothing to see if it fits or what it looks like on you □ *I tried on three summer dresses but I didn't like any of them.*
➡ *go to* **try your luck**

try² /traɪ/ NOUN [plural tries] an attempt to do something 🔁 *I couldn't get the tyre off – could you have a try?*

T-shirt /'tiː.ʃɜːt/ NOUN [plural T-shirts] a piece of clothing made from soft cotton which you wear on the top part of your body □ *She was wearing jeans and a white T-shirt.*

tsunami /tsuː.ˈnɑː.mi/ NOUN [plural tsunamis] a very high, fast wave that is caused by an earthquake (= when the ground shakes) under the sea

tub /tʌb/ NOUN [plural tubs]
1 a container with a lid which has food in it □ *a tub of ice cream*
2 a round, deep container □ *The tub was full of bright red flowers.*

tube /tjuːb/ NOUN [plural tubes]
1 a long, thin pipe □ *He was in hospital with a feeding tube in his stomach.*
2 a container for a soft substance which you press to get the substance out □ **+ of** *a tube of toothpaste*
3 no plural an underground railway system, especially in London □ *We can easily get there by tube.* 🔁 *a tube station*

tuck /tʌk/ VERB [tucks, tucking, tucked] to push the edge of something somewhere to make it tidy or firm □ *Tuck your shirt into your trousers.* □ *She tucked the flap into the envelope.*
◆ PHRASAL VERB **tuck someone in/up** to make someone comfortable in bed by putting the sheets over them □ *She went upstairs to tuck the children in.*

Tuesday /'tjuːz.deɪ/ NOUN [plural Tuesdays] the day of the week after Monday and before Wednesday □ *Kay's coming on Tuesday.*

tug¹ /tʌg/ VERB [tugs, tugging, tugged] to pull something suddenly and firmly □ *She tugged her hand away from mine.* □ *James tugged on the rope.*

tug² /tʌg/ NOUN [plural tugs] a sudden firm pull 🔁 *I gave his arm a tug and he looked at me angrily.*

tuition /tjuː.ˈɪʃ.ən/ NOUN, NO PLURAL teaching something, especially to one person or a small group □ *His parents paid for him to have private tuition in English.* 🔁 *Students have to pay tuition fees.*

tumble /'tʌm.bəl/ VERB [tumbles, tumbling, tumbled] to fall somewhere □ *He tripped and tumbled down the stairs.*

tummy /'tʌm.i/ NOUN [plural tummies] an informal word for stomach

tumour /'tjuː.mə(r)/ NOUN [plural tumours] a group of cells in your body which are not growing in a normal way □ *He had an operation to remove a brain tumour.*

tune¹ /tjuːn/ NOUN [plural tunes] a series of musical notes that sound nice 🔁 *She was playing some tunes on the piano.* 🔁 *a catchy tune* (= one that is easy to remember)

tune² /tjuːn/ VERB [tunes, tuning, tuned] to make small changes to a musical instrument so that it sounds right □ *Ben was tuning his guitar.*

tunnel¹ /'tʌn.əl/ NOUN [plural tunnels] a long underground passage □ *There is a rail tunnel linking England and France.* 🔁 *There were plans to build a tunnel through the Alps.*

tunnel² /'tʌn.əl/ VERB [tunnels, tunnelling/US tunneling, tunnelled/US tunneled] to make an underground passage □ *Will they tunnel under the river or build a bridge over it?*

turkey /'tɜː.ki/ NOUN [plural turkeys]
1 a large bird that lives on farms and is eaten as food

2 no plural the meat from this bird □ roast turkey
□ a turkey sandwich

turmoil /'tɜːmɔɪl/ NOUN, NO PLURAL a state of
worry and confusion □ Her mind was in turmoil.
□ political turmoil

turn[1] /tɜːn/ VERB [turns, turning, turned]
1 to move your body or part of your body to face in
another direction □ He turned and walked away.
□ **+ around** I turned around to look at them. □ **+ to**
She turned to her neighbour and whispered
something. □ He turned his head slightly.
2 to move something so that it faces in another
direction, or to move like this □ The car turned
upside down. □ **+ over** You must not turn the cards
over before the game starts. □ **+ round** He turned
the book round to show us the picture.
3 to make a circular movement around a
central point, or to make something do this □ The
wheels began to turn. □ Turn the handle to the
right.
4 if you turn the page of a book, you move it so that
you can see the next page
5 to change in a particular way □ She took one look
and turned pale. □ Things turned nasty when the
police arrived.
➡ go to **turn your nose up at something**
◆ PHRASAL VERBS **turn something down** to make
a machine produce less sound, heat, etc. □ Could
you turn the music down, please? □ I've turned
down the heating. **turn someone/something
down** to not accept an offer □ He asked her to
marry him but she turned him down. □ I turned
down a job in his company. **turn (someone/
something) into someone/something** to
change into something different or to make
someone or something do this □ His book is being
turned into a movie. □ The caterpillar turns into a
butterfly. **turn something off** to move a switch
so that a machine stops working or a supply of
something is stopped □ Don't forget to turn off the
lights. **turn something on** to move a switch so
that a machine starts working or a supply of
something is started □ I've turned on the heating.
turn out to be found to have a particular reason,
quality or result 🔁 It turned out that she'd never
received the letter. 🔁 The hotel turned out to be
really bad. **turn up** to arrive □ He didn't turn up
for work this morning.

turn[2] /tɜːn/ NOUN [plural turns]
1 the time when you can or must do something,
before or after someone else □ It's your/my turn
next. □ Josh hasn't had a turn yet.
2 take turns/take it in turns if people take
turns, each person does something, one after
the other □ We took it in turns to use the
computer.
3 in turn one after the other □ He tried each of the
dishes in turn.

4 a change of direction or a curve or corner in a road
or path 🔁 Take the first turn on the right. 🔁 a left/
right turn
5 when something is moved in a circle around a
central point □ I gave the screw another turn.

turning /'tɜːnɪŋ/ NOUN [plural turnings] a place
where a car can leave a road and go onto another
road 🔁 Take the second turning on the right.
🔁 We took a wrong turning and ended up on a mud
track.

turtle /'tɜːtəl/ NOUN [plural turtles] an animal that
usually lives in water and has a hard shell

tutor /'tjuːtə(r)/ NOUN [plural tutors] a teacher
who teaches one person or a small group □ He hired
a private tutor to help him learn Japanese.

TV /ˌtiːˈviː/ NOUN [plural TVs] television 🔁 She
switched the TV on. □ What's on TV tonight? 🔁 I
think the children watch too much TV.

twelfth /twelfθ/ NUMBER 12th written as a
word

twelve /twelv/ NUMBER [plural twelves] the
number 12

twentieth /'twentɪəθ/ NUMBER 20th written as a
word

twenty /'twentɪ/ NUMBER [plural twenties]
1 the number 20
2 the twenties the years between 1920 and 1929

twice /twaɪs/ ADVERB two times □ He sneezed
twice. □ I could eat twice that amount. □ I visit my
grandmother twice a week.

twilight /'twaɪlaɪt/ NOUN, NO PLURAL the time in
the evening just before it becomes completely dark

twin[1] /twɪn/ NOUN [plural twins] one of two
children born to the same mother at the same time
□ Paul and Jo are twins. 🔁 Our children are identical
twins (= they look exactly the same).

twin[2] /twɪn/ ADJECTIVE twin sister/brother/
daughters, etc. a sister, brother, etc. who is a twin
□ Bella's my twin sister.

twist[1] /twɪst/ VERB [twists, twisting, twisted]
1 to turn something using your hands □ Twist the
handle hard and then pull it. □ She twisted the lid of
the jar.
2 to turn the top half of your body □ **+ round/
around** Gregory twisted round in his chair to look at
me.
3 to bend something out of its correct shape □ The
front wheel of the bike twisted when it hit the
wall.
4 twist your ankle/knee, etc. to hurt your ankle,
knee, etc. by turning it suddenly
5 if a road or river twists, it has a lot of curves
in it 🔁 The road twisted and turned up the
mountain.

> ► THESAURUS: If you twist something, you turn it, using your hands. You might twist a lid to remove it, for example. If you wind something, you twist or wrap it around something else. For example, you might wind a bandage around your arm if you hurt yourself. If you curl something, you make it form curves. Some women curl their hair.

twist[2] /twɪst/ NOUN [*plural* twists]
1 a piece of something that has been bent □ *She put a twist of lemon in the drink.*
2 a movement in which you turn something □ *Give the lid a twist.*
3 a curve in a road or river
4 a sudden and unexpected change in a story or situation □ *This announcement added a strange new twist to his sudden death.*

twitch /twɪtʃ/ VERB [twitches, twitching, twitched] if part of your body twitches, it moves slightly in a way you cannot control □ *Her eyelid twitched.*

two /tuː/ NUMBER [*plural* twos] the number 2

type[1] /taɪp/ NOUN [*plural* types]
1 used for talking about people or things that have similar qualities and can be considered as a group

🕮 *Research of this type has never been done before.* □ **+ of** *He's the type of person who never worries about anything.* □ *What type of dog have you got?* □ *There are many different types of cancer.*
2 *no plural* printed letters and numbers □ *The title should be in bold type.*

type[2] /taɪp/ VERB [types, typing, typed] to write something using a keyboard on a computer □ *Type your name and then your password.*

typical /ˈtɪpɪkəl/ ADJECTIVE having the usual qualities of a particular person or thing 🕮 *This is a typical example of a 17th-century cottage.* □ *Beth is a typical teenager.* □ *On a typical day, there are over 100,000 lorries on Britain's roads.* □ **+ of** *It was typical of Emily to offer to help.*

typically /ˈtɪpɪkəlɪ/ ADVERB as you would expect from a particular person or thing □ *Typically, Tracy arrived late.* □ *He was behaving in a typically aggressive way.*

tyrant /ˈtaɪrənt/ NOUN [*plural* tyrants] a ruler who uses power in a cruel and unfair way

tyre /ˈtaɪə(r)/ NOUN [*plural* tyres] a piece of rubber around the edge of a wheel, which has air in it 🕮 *We had a flat tyre.*

U*u*

U *or* **u** /ju:/ the 21st letter of the alphabet

ugly /'ʌglɪ/ ADJECTIVE [uglier, ugliest] not pleasant to look at □ *an ugly building* □ *a big ugly monster*

> ➤ People do not often use the word **ugly** to describe people as it sounds unkind. Sometimes the word **plain** (which has the same meaning) is used instead as it sounds less unkind.

UK /ju:'keɪ/ ABBREVIATION United Kingdom

ulcer /'ʌlsə(r)/ NOUN [*plural* ulcers] a small sore area on your skin or inside your body ⊞ *a mouth ulcer*

umbrella /ʌm'brelə/ NOUN [*plural* umbrellas] a frame with cloth over it that you hold above you for shelter when it rains

umpire /'ʌmpaɪə(r)/ NOUN [*plural* umpires] the person in a game such as cricket, who makes sure the players obey the rules

UN /ju:'en/ ABBREVIATION United Nations

un- /ʌn/ PREFIX un- is used at the beginning of words to mean 'not' □ *untidy* □ *unkind*

unable /ʌn'eɪbəl/ ADJECTIVE unable to do something not able to do something □ *He stood completely still, unable to take his eyes off the bear.*

unacceptable /ˌʌnək'septəbəl/ ADJECTIVE something unacceptable cannot be allowed to happen, exist or continue because it is wrong or not of a high enough standard ⊞ *His behaviour is totally unacceptable.* □ *The bank decided that the financial risk was unacceptable.*

unanimous /ju:'nænɪməs/ ADJECTIVE agreed by everyone □ *a unanimous decision*

unbelievable /ˌʌnbɪ'li:vəbəl/ ADJECTIVE
1 used to emphasize how bad, good, extreme, etc. something is □ *Seeing the whales was an unbelievable experience.*
2 difficult to believe □ *an unbelievable story*

uncertain /ʌn'sɜ:tən/ ADJECTIVE
1 not sure what to decide □ **+ about** *I was uncertain about what to do next.*
2 not known ⊞ *The future is uncertain.*

uncle /'ʌŋkəl/ NOUN [*plural* uncles]
1 the brother of one of your parents □ *My aunt and uncle live in Scotland.* □ *Uncle Douglas came to visit.*
2 your aunt's husband

unclear /ˌʌn'klɪə(r)/ ADJECTIVE not obvious or easy to understand □ *It's unclear why she left her job.* ⊔ *The writing was rather unclear.*

uncomfortable /ˌʌn'kʌmftəbəl/ ADJECTIVE
1 not feeling comfortable ⊔ *We were uncomfortable in the heat.*
2 causing you to feel uncomfortable □ *The seats were really uncomfortable.*
3 slightly embarrassed or slightly embarrassing □ **+ about** *I feel uncomfortable about accepting money from her.* □ *There were a lot of uncomfortable silences.*

> ➤ THESAURUS: Something which is uncomfortable does not feel comfortable. For example, a chair might be uncomfortable, or shoes that do not fit properly. If something is painful, it causes you pain. You might describe a toothache as painful. If something is awkward, it is difficult to manage or use. If you write with your left hand, scissors may be awkward to use.

uncomfortably /ˌʌn'kʌmftəblɪ/ ADVERB in an uncomfortable way □ *Tom shifted uncomfortably in his seat.*

unconscious /ˌʌn'kɒnʃəs/ ADJECTIVE in a state like sleep where you are not aware of what is happening around you, because you are seriously ill or injured 🕮 *A brick hit his head and he was knocked unconscious.*

uncontrollable /ˌʌnkən'trəʊləbəl/ ADJECTIVE
not possible to control 🕮 *She suddenly had an uncontrollable urge to kick something.*

uncount noun /ˌʌnkaʊnt 'naʊn/ *or*
uncountable noun /ˌʌnˌkaʊntəbəl 'naʊn/
NOUN [*plural* uncount nouns *or* uncountable nouns] in grammar, a noun that does not have a plural form, e.g. *happiness, water* or *advice*

uncover /ˌʌn'kʌvə(r)/ VERB [uncovers, uncovering, uncovered]
1 to discover something that had been secret or hidden 🕮 *Police have uncovered new evidence about the murder.*
2 to remove a cover from something

under¹ /'ʌndə(r)/ PREPOSITION
1 below something □ *The bag is under the table.* □ *We walked under the bridge.*
2 covered by something □ *I found my glasses under a cushion.* □ *The mountains were under a thick layer of snow.*
3 less than an amount, level or age □ *All the clothes are under £20.* □ *The competition is open to anyone under 30.*
4 controlled by a particular person, government, organization, etc. □ *The country was under military control.*
5 having a particular thing done, or affected by a particular thing 🕮 *Our troops came under attack.* 🕮 *He was under pressure to resign.* 🕮 *I think you should show her some sympathy under the circumstances* (= because of the situation).

➤ THESAURUS: Below means in a lower place or position. A plane might fly below the clouds, or you could stand on the top of a hill and look at what is below you. If something is under something else, it is directly below it. You might put a saucer under a cup, for example. Beneath has a similar meaning to under.

under² /'ʌndə(r)/ ADVERB
1 in or to a lower place □ *We watched the divers go under.*
2 less than an amount, level or age □ *The play equipment is for children aged 6 and under.*

undercover /'ʌndəkʌvə(r)/ ADJECTIVE working or done secretly □ *an undercover police operation*
undergo /ˌʌndə'gəʊ/ VERB [undergoes, undergoing, underwent, undergone] to experience something □ *He underwent an operation to mend his broken leg.*
undergraduate /ˌʌndə'grædʒʊət/ NOUN [*plural* undergraduates] someone who is studying at a

university and has not yet done their degree (= qualification)

underground¹ /'ʌndəgraʊnd/ ADJECTIVE, ADVERB below the surface of the ground □ *Moles live underground.* □ *an underground stream*

underground² /'ʌndəgraʊnd/ NOUN [*plural* undergrounds] a railway that is under the ground, usually in a large city □ *the London Underground*

underline /ˌʌndə'laɪn/ VERB [underlines, underlining, underlined] to draw a line under something □ *Underline all the adjectives in these sentences.*

underpants /'ʌndəpænts/ PLURAL NOUN underwear that men and boys wear under their trousers

understand /ˌʌndə'stænd/ VERB [understands, understanding, understood]
1 to know what something means □ *I can't understand the instructions.* □ *Do you understand German?*
2 to know why something happens, how something works, or the effect or importance of something □ **+ question word** *Doctors still don't understand how the disease spreads.* □ *We didn't understand the importance of his words at the time.*
3 to know why someone behaves and feels the way they do □ *I'll never understand him.* □ *I understood her anger.* □ *I don't understand what you are trying to do.*

➤ THESAURUS: If you understand something, you know what it means, or why it happens or is important. If you realize something, you understand something that you did not know or understand before. If you recognize something, you accept that it is true. If you follow someone, you understand what they are saying. For example, it can be difficult to follow what people say on television if you do not speak the language very well.

understanding¹ /ˌʌndə'stændɪŋ/ NOUN, NO PLURAL knowledge about something 🕮 *Scientists are trying to gain a better understanding of the disease.*

understanding² /ˌʌndə'stændɪŋ/ ADJECTIVE able to understand other people's feelings or to forgive someone because of their situation □ *The illness makes me bad-tempered at times, but my family have been very understanding.*

understood /ˌʌndə'stʊd/ PAST TENSE AND PAST PARTICIPLE OF **understand**
undertake /ˌʌndə'teɪk/ VERB [undertakes, undertaking, undertook, undertaken] undertake to do something a formal word meaning to promise to do something □ *I undertook to ensure their safety.*

underwater /ˈʌndəwɔːtə(r)/ ADJECTIVE, ADVERB under the surface of water □ *an underwater creature* □ *Can you swim underwater?*

underway /ˌʌndərˈweɪ/ ADJECTIVE happening or having started 🖫 *Work on the new motorway got underway last week.*

underwear /ˈʌndəweə(r)/ NOUN, NO PLURAL clothes you wear next to your skin and under your other clothes

> ► THESAURUS: Underwear is a general word for any clothes that you wear under your clothes next to your skin. Pants are underwear that covers your bottom. Both men and women wear pants. Pants for women are also called knickers. A bra is a piece of underwear that women wear to support their breasts. A vest is a piece of underwear without sleeves that covers the top part of your body.

underwent /ˌʌndəˈwent/ PAST TENSE OF undergo

undid /ˌʌnˈdɪd/ PAST TENSE OF undo

undo /ˌʌnˈduː/ VERB [undoes, undoing, undid, undone] to open something that is fastened □ *He undid his jacket.*

unemployed /ˌʌnɪmˈplɔɪd/ ADJECTIVE without a job □ *My Dad's unemployed at the moment.* □ *unemployed miners*

unemployment /ˌʌnɪmˈplɔɪmənt/ NOUN, NO PLURAL
1 the number of people who do not have a job 🖫 *Unemployment has risen again.*
2 not having a job

unexpected /ˌʌnɪkˈspektɪd/ ADJECTIVE surprising because of not being expected □ *an unexpected visitor* □ *an unexpected development*

unfair /ˌʌnˈfeə(r)/ ADJECTIVE
1 not right or reasonable □ *Some of her criticism was very unfair.*
2 when a situation is unfair, people are not treated in an equal way, or do not have equal opportunities 🖫 *His father's fame gives him an unfair advantage.*

unfairly /ˌʌnˈfeəlɪ/ ADVERB in a way that is unfair □ *We have been very unfairly treated.*

unfasten /ˌʌnˈfɑːsən/ VERB [unfastens, unfastening, unfastened] to open something that was fastened □ *She unfastened her coat.*

unfit /ˌʌnˈfɪt/ ADJECTIVE
1 not suitable or not good enough □ *The water is unfit to drink.*
2 not in good physical condition, especially because of not doing enough exercise

unfold /ˌʌnˈfəʊld/ VERB [unfolds, unfolding, unfolded] to spread out something that was folded

unfortunate /ˌʌnˈfɔːtʃənət/ ADJECTIVE caused by bad luck □ *an unfortunate accident*

unfortunately /ˌʌnˈfɔːtʃənətlɪ/ ADVERB used to show that you wish something had not happened or been true □ *Unfortunately, I lost the ring.*

unfriendly /ˌʌnˈfrendlɪ/ ADJECTIVE not friendly □ *His sister was very unfriendly.*

unhappiness /ʌnˈhæpɪnɪs/ NOUN, NO PLURAL the state of being unhappy

unhappy /ʌnˈhæpɪ/ ADJECTIVE [unhappier, unhappiest]
1 sad or causing sadness 🖫 *Ben has been feeling unhappy for a long time.* □ *an unhappy marriage*
2 not pleased or not satisfied □ *+ about* *He was unhappy about the result of the meeting.* 🖫 *We were deeply unhappy about the quality of their work.*

unhealthy /ʌnˈhelθɪ/ ADJECTIVE [unhealthier, unhealthiest]
1 someone who is unhealthy is ill, or does not have good health □ *He looks very unhealthy.*
2 harmful for your health □ *an unhealthy lifestyle*

uniform /ˈjuːnɪfɔːm/ NOUN [plural uniforms] a set of clothes that shows you belong to a particular organization, job or school □ *a bus driver's uniform* 🖫 *school uniform*

union /ˈjuːnjən/ NOUN [plural unions]
1 an organization of workers that tries to get good pay and conditions for its members
2 a group of countries, organizations, etc. that join together

unique /juːˈniːk/ ADJECTIVE completely different from anyone or anything else

> ► THESAURUS: A unique person is different from all other people in some way. A single person is a person who is not married. A lone person is acting on their own. So a lone parent looks after their children without a husband or wife, and a lone criminal commits a crime without any other people. A lonely person is unhappy because they are alone with no friends around them.

unit /ˈjuːnɪt/ NOUN [plural units]
1 a measure used to show an amount or level □ *A metre is a unit of length.* □ *What is the unit of currency in Ecuador?*
2 a single thing that can be part of a larger group of things □ *The book is divided into ten units.*

unite /juːˈnaɪt/ VERB [unites, uniting, united]
1 if people or groups unite, they join together, often to achieve something □ *Workers have united to oppose the pay cuts.*
2 to join people or groups together, often making them them feel that they belong together and have

the same opinions □ *We need a new leader to unite the party.*

United Kingdom / juː ˌnaɪtɪd ˈkɪŋdəm/ NOUN the United Kingdom England, Scotland, Wales and Northern Ireland

United Nations /juː ˌnaɪtɪd ˈneɪʃənz/ NOUN the United Nations an organization of people from most countries of the world, that works to try to solve world problems

United States of America /juː ˈnaɪtɪd ˌsteɪts əv əˈmerɪkə/ NOUN the United States of America the 50 states that make the country of North America

unity /ˈjuːnəti/ NOUN, NO PLURAL when people agree on things and act together □ *She has called for unity within the party.*

universal /ˌjuːnɪˈvɜːsəl/ ADJECTIVE
1 affecting or including everyone in the world □ *English may become a universal language that everyone can learn and use.*
2 relating to everyone in a group □ *There was universal approval of the decision.*

universe /ˈjuːnɪvɜːs/ NOUN the universe everything that exists anywhere, including the Earth, the sun and all the other planets and stars in space □ *Somewhere in the universe there might be another world like ours.*

university /ˌjuːnɪˈvɜːsəti/ NOUN [plural universities] a place where you go to study at the highest level after leaving school 🕮 *I am hoping to go to university.* □ *university students*

unkind /ˌʌnˈkaɪnd/ ADJECTIVE [unkinder, unkindest] cruel and not kind □ *It was unkind of you to tease her.*

unknown /ˌʌnˈnəʊn/ ADJECTIVE
1 not known □ *The man's identity is unknown.*
2 not famous □ *an unknown actor*

unleaded /ˌʌnˈledɪd/ ADJECTIVE unleaded petrol does not have lead (= a soft, grey metal) added to it and so causes less harm to the environment

unless /ənˈles/ CONJUNCTION except when, or except if □ *We always go for a walk on Sundays, unless it's raining.* □ *Don't come unless I phone you.*

unlike /ˌʌnˈlaɪk/ PREPOSITION different from □ *I never saw twins who were so unlike each other.*

unlikely /ˌʌnˈlaɪkli/ ADJECTIVE not expected to happen □ **+ that** *It's unlikely that she'll come.* □ **+ to do something** *We're unlikely to finish the work today.* 🕮 *A victory for England now seems highly unlikely.*

unload /ˌʌnˈləʊd/ VERB [unloads, unloading, unloaded] to take things off or out of a vehicle □ *After we got back from the trip, we had to unload the car.*

unlock /ˌʌnˈlɒk/ VERB [unlocks, unlocking, unlocked] to open something that is locked □ *Unlock this door now!*

unlucky /ˌʌnˈlʌki/ ADJECTIVE having bad luck, causing bad luck or caused by bad luck □ *I'm very unlucky at cards.* □ *It was an unlucky defeat.*

unmarried /ˌʌnˈmærɪd/ ADJECTIVE not married □ *unmarried couples*

unnecessary /ˌʌnˈnesəsəri/ ADJECTIVE not needed □ *Any unnecessary clothing can be given to charity.*

unofficial /ˌʌnəˈfɪʃəl/ ADJECTIVE not done or allowed by anyone in authority □ *Unofficial estimates suggest unemployment is still rising.*

unpleasant /ˌʌnˈplezənt/ ADJECTIVE
1 if something is unpleasant, you do not like it or enjoy it □ *an unpleasant smell* □ *I found skiing a thoroughly unpleasant experience.*
2 not polite, friendly or kind □ **+ to** *He was rather unpleasant to his students.*

unpopular /ˌʌnˈpɒpjʊlə(r)/ ADJECTIVE disliked by many people □ *He is very unpopular at school.*

unreasonable /ˌʌnˈriːzənəbəl/ ADJECTIVE not fair, often because of wanting too much □ *It's unreasonable to expect students to do so much homework.* □ *He accused the unions of making unreasonable demands.*

unreliable /ˌʌnrɪˈlaɪəbəl/ ADJECTIVE not able to be trusted to do something □ *He's totally unreliable.* □ *My car's a bit unreliable.*

unsafe /ˌʌnˈseɪf/ ADJECTIVE dangerous □ *unsafe practices*

unstable /ˌʌnˈsteɪbəl/ ADJECTIVE
1 changing or may change over a period □ *a politically unstable region*
2 not firm or strong □ *This chair seems a bit unstable.*

unsuccessful /ˌʌnsəkˈsesfʊl/ ADJECTIVE not managing to do something you are trying to do 🕮 *Thieves made an unsuccessful attempt to steal the car.* □ *I tried to contact him but was unsuccessful.*

unsuitable /ˌʌnˈsuːtəbəl/ ADJECTIVE not right for a purpose or occasion □ *unsuitable clothing*

unsure /ˌʌnˈʃɔː(r)/ ADJECTIVE not certain □ *I was unsure of the spelling.* □ *I asked if she was coming but he seemed unsure.*

untidy /ˌʌnˈtaɪdi/ ADJECTIVE [untidier, untidiest]
1 not carefully ordered or arranged □ *His flat is always untidy.*
2 an untidy person does not keep their home, office, etc. tidy

until /ənˈtɪl/ PREPOSITION, CONJUNCTION
1 continuing to a particular time but not after that
□ *He'll be here until midday.* □ *I waited until she left.*
2 continuing as far as somewhere □ *Carry on walking until you get to a bridge.*
3 not ... until not before □ *I won't start until you tell me.*

untrue /ˌʌnˈtruː/ ADJECTIVE false, not true □ *His story was completely untrue.*
unused[1] /ˌʌnˈjuːzd/ ADJECTIVE not having been used or not used now □ *unused stamps*
unused[2] /ˌʌnˈjuːst/ ADJECTIVE be unused to sth to have little experience of something □ *I'm unused to cooking my own meals.*

unusual /ˌʌnˈjuːʒuəl/ ADJECTIVE not normal or not ordinary 🔁 *It's unusual for him to arrive late.*
□ *They make some lovely, quite unusual jewellery.*

unwilling /ˌʌnˈwɪlɪŋ/ ADJECTIVE not wanting to do something □ *+ to do something They seem unwilling to help.*

up[1] /ʌp/ ADVERB, PREPOSITION
1 towards or in a higher position □ *I walked up the stairs.* □ *We went up in a helicopter.* □ *He looked up and saw her.* □ *She threw the ball up in the air.*
2 to a greater amount or level □ *Prices have gone up again.* □ *Could you turn the volume up a bit?*
3 if you stand up or sit up, you move your body to a vertical position
4 up to less than or as much as a particular amount or level □ *The hall can hold up to 200 people.*
5 up to him/you, etc. if an action or decision is up to you, you are responsible for doing it or making it □ *It's up to you whether you come or not.*
6 used after verbs to show that something is finished or completely used □ *Eat up all your vegetables.*
7 if you go up to someone, you move close to them, often in order to speak to them □ *He came up to me and asked if I needed any help.*
8 further along a road, river, etc. □ *He lives just up the road from me.*
9 be up to something to be doing something, usually something wrong or secret □ *The children are very quiet – what are they up to?*

up[2] /ʌp/ ADJECTIVE
1 not in bed □ *He's not up yet.* □ *I've been up half the night.*
2 if an amount or level is up, it is higher □ *Profits are up by 25% this year.*
3 if the sun is up, it has risen
4 if something is up, there is a problem. An informal word 🔁 *What's up with you today?* □ *As soon as we reached the house, I knew something was up.*

up[3] /ʌp/ VERB [ups, upping, upped] to increase something □ *The doctors have upped his dose of painkillers.*

update[1] /ʌpˈdeɪt/ VERB [updates, updating, updated]
1 to add the latest information to something
□ *When did we last update the website?*
2 to change something to make it more modern □ *I need to update my wardrobe.*

update[2] /ˈʌpdeɪt/ NOUN [plural updates] the latest information about a subject 🔁 *Dan gave me an update on the situation.*

upgrade /ˈʌpɡreɪd/ NOUN [plural upgrades] a piece of software that makes a computer more powerful. A computing word.

uphill /ˈʌphɪl/ ADJECTIVE
1 going upwards □ *an uphill part of the track*
2 very difficult 🔁 *We face an uphill struggle to finish the job.*

uphold /ʌpˈhəʊld/ VERB [upholds, upholding, upheld] to support or agree with a decision, especially in a court of law □ *The court upheld his complaint.*

upon /əˈpɒn/ PREPOSITION on. A formal word □ *a castle upon a high cliff*

upper /ˈʌpə(r)/ ADJECTIVE
1 being the higher of two things that are the same □ *my upper lip*
2 at the top or towards the top □ *the upper floors of the building*

upset[1] /ʌpˈset/ VERB [upsets, upsetting, upset]
1 to make someone sad or worried □ *I didn't mean to upset you.*
2 to stop something from happening in the right way □ *I don't want to upset your plans.*
3 to knock something over by accident

upset[2] /ʌpˈset/ ADJECTIVE
1 sad or worried about something that has happened □ *He looked upset.* □ *+ that She's upset that no one invited her.* 🔁 *She got upset looking at his photos.*
2 upset stomach/tummy an illness affecting the stomach

upside down /ˌʌpsaɪd ˈdaʊn/ ADJECTIVE, ADVERB with the top part where the bottom should be and the bottom part where the top should be □ *He was holding the book upside down.*

> ► **THESAURUS:** If something is upside down, the top part is where the bottom part should be and the bottom part is where the top part should be. If something, especially clothes, is inside out, the part that should be on the inside is on the outside. If something is back to front, the part that should be at the back is at the front.

upstairs[1] /ˌʌpˈsteəz/ ADVERB to or on a higher level of a building □ *I went upstairs to bed.*

upstairs[2] /'ʌpsteəz/ ADJECTIVE on a higher level of a building □ *an upstairs bedroom*

upward /'ʌpwəd/ ADJECTIVE towards a higher place or position □ *an upward climb*
• **upwards** /'ʌpwədz/ or **upward** /'ʌpwəd/ ADVERB towards a higher place or position □ *He looked upwards and saw the sun.*

urban /'ɜ:bən/ ADJECTIVE to do with a town or city □ *urban areas* □ *urban planning*

urge[1] /ɜ:dʒ/ VERB [urges, urging, urged] to advise someone strongly to do something □ *I urge you to fill in the form as soon as possible.*

urge[2] /ɜ:dʒ/ NOUN [plural urges] a sudden, strong feeling of wanting to do something □ *I felt an urge to shake him.* ☝ *I resisted the urge to tell her* (= did not tell her although I wanted to).

urgent /'ɜ:dʒənt/ ADJECTIVE very serious and needing action now ☝ *There is an urgent need for water and food supplies in the region.* ☝ *He has called for urgent action to stop the killing.*

urinate /'juərɪˌneɪt/ VERB [urinates, urinating, urinated] to pass urine out of your body. A formal word.

US /ˌju:'es/ ABBREVIATION the **United States**

us /ʌs/ PRONOUN used as the object in a sentence to talk or write about yourself and at least one other person □ *Do you want to come with us?* □ *They gave us coffee.* □ *The news surprised all of us.*

USA /ˌju:es'eɪ/ ABBREVIATION the **United States of America**

use[1] /ju:z/ VERB [uses, using, used]
1 to do something with something for a particular purpose □ *Use a knife to open it.* □ *He used words like 'disappointing' and 'shocking'.* □ **+ for** *I use these boxes for storing apples.* □ **+ as** *Dad uses this room as his office.*
2 to take an amount of something from a supply in order to do something with it □ *I've used all the milk now.* □ *You can use the wood from the garage.*
♦ PHRASAL VERB **use something up** to use all of a supply of something □ *We've used up all the paper.*

use[2] /ju:s/ NOUN [plural uses]
1 no plural when you use something □ **+ of** *We do not allow the use of calculators in the exam.* ☝ *We were able to make use of the sports facilities.*
2 the purpose for which something is used □ *This knife has a lot of uses.* □ *They deny that the uranium is for military use.*
3 no plural if something is of use, it is useful or effective □ *Is this coat of any use to you?* ☝ *It's no use asking him for help – he's always busy.*

4 no plural the right or ability to use something □ **+ of** *He offered me the use of his car while he's away.* □ *She lost the use of her legs.*

used /ju:zd/ ADJECTIVE something that is used has been owned and used by someone else □ *He sells used cars.*

used to[1] /'ju:st tu:/ MODAL VERB used to talk about things that happened regularly in the past or things that were true in the past, especially when they no longer happen or are true □ *I used to visit her a lot when she lived in Germany.* □ *The fence used to be painted white.* □ *I used to be a teacher.*

> If you use **used to** in a question or a negative, you should use the form **use to**: □ *Did you use to play the piano?* □ *I didn't use to like many vegetables.*

used to[2] /'ju:st tu:/ ADJECTIVE if you are used to something, you have often seen it or experienced it before, so it does not seem strange, difficult, etc. □ *I'm used to living on my own.* ☝ *Working nights is difficult, but you get used to it.*

useful /'ju:sful/ ADJECTIVE helpful for doing something or achieving something □ *The book gave me some useful information.* □ **+ for** *These little pots are useful for growing seeds.*

useless /'ju:slɪs/ ADJECTIVE having no purpose, or not effective or working correctly □ *This knife's useless – it's completely blunt.* □ *It's useless trying to explain to them.* □ *She wastes her money on useless things.*

user /'ju:zə(r)/ NOUN [plural users] a person who uses something □ *users of public transport*

usual /'ju:ʒuəl/ ADJECTIVE
1 done or happening most often □ *I had my usual coffee this morning.* □ *'What did you talk about?' 'Oh, the usual things.'* □ *My walk to work took longer than usual.*
2 as usual as happens most often □ *He was late as usual.*

usually /'ju:ʒuəlɪ/ ADVERB normally, on most occasions □ *I usually drink tea.* □ *We usually go on holiday in August.* □ *Usually I'm in bed by ten o'clock.*

utter[1] /'ʌtə(r)/ VERB [utters, uttering, uttered] to say something □ *She didn't utter a single word.*

utter[2] /'ʌtə(r)/ ADJECTIVE complete □ *utter silence*
• **utterly** /'ʌtəlɪ/ ADVERB completely □ *I feel utterly exhausted.*

Vv

V¹ *or* **V** /vi:/ the 22nd letter of the alphabet

V² /vi:/ ABBREVIATION volt; a unit for measuring how strong an electric current is

V /vi:/ ABBREVIATION
1 versus; used for saying which two players or teams are competing against each other □ *Arsenal v Manchester United*
2 very □ *v good* (= very good)

vacancy /ˈveɪkənsɪ/ NOUN [*plural* vacancies]
1 an available room in a hotel □ *Sorry, no vacancies.*
2 an available job

vacant /ˈveɪkənt/ ADJECTIVE
1 if something is vacant, it is available because no one else is using it □ *a vacant seat* □ *a vacant office*
2 if a job is vacant, it is available because no one is doing it

vacation /vəˈkeɪʃən/ NOUN [*plural* vacations]
1 the US word for **holiday** ⌷ *We're taking a vacation in the mountains this summer.*
2 on vacation taking a holiday. A US phrase.
3 a part of the year when a university is closed □ *the summer vacation*

vaccinate /ˈvæksɪneɪt/ VERB [vaccinates, vaccinating, vaccinated] to put a substance containing bacteria or a virus into someone's body to protect them from a disease

vaccination /ˌvæksɪˈneɪʃən/ NOUN [*plural* vaccinations] the process of putting a substance containing bacteria or a virus into someone's body in order to protect them from disease

vaccine /ˈvæksiːn/ NOUN [*plural* vaccines] a substance containing bacteria or a virus, which is put into someone's body to protect them against a disease

vacuum¹ /ˈvækjuəm/ NOUN [*plural* vacuums] a space with no air or other gases in it

vacuum² /ˈvækjuəm/ VERB [vacuums, vacuuming, vacuumed] to clean a floor using a vacuum cleaner

vacuum cleaner /ˈvækjuəm ˌkliːnə(r)/ NOUN [*plural* vacuum cleaners] an electrical machine that sucks dust up from the floor

vagina /vəˈdʒaɪnə/ NOUN [*plural* vaginas] the passage in a woman's body that connects her womb (= organ where a baby grows) to the outside of her body. A biology word.

vague /veɪg/ ADJECTIVE [vaguer, vaguest]
1 not clear and without details ⌷ *I have a vague idea of where he lives.* ⌷ *He had a vague memory of seeing her there.*
2 explaining something in a way that is not clear and has no details □ *He was a bit vague about their plans.*

vain /veɪn/ ADJECTIVE [vainer, vainest]
1 very pleased with your appearance and paying too much attention to it
2 unsuccessful ⌷ *I made a vain attempt to reach her.*
3 in vain without achieving what you want to □ *I tried in vain to persuade him.*

valid /ˈvælɪd/ ADJECTIVE
1 legally or officially acceptable and able to be used □ *a valid passport* □ *a valid ticket*
2 reasonable and acceptable □ *a valid excuse* □ *a valid argument*

valley /ˈvælɪ/ NOUN [*plural* valleys] an area of low land between hills, often with a river running through it

valuable /ˈvæljuəbəl/ ADJECTIVE
1 worth a lot of money □ *valuable jewellery*
2 very useful □ *valuable advice* □ *She's a valuable member of the team.*

➤ Note that **valuable** does not have the same meaning as 'expensive'. If something is valuable, you could sell it for a lot of money. If something is expensive, it costs a lot of money: □ *valuable antiques/paintings* □ *expensive food/clothes*

value[1] /ˈvælju:/ NOUN [*plural* values]
1 the amount of money that something is worth □ *The paintings had an estimated value of $1.4 billion.* □ *The house has increased in value.*
2 *no plural* how useful and important something is □ *This food has very little nutritional value.*
3 *no plural* the quality or amount of something compared to its price ⊞ *I thought the hotel was very good value.*

➤ THESAURUS: The cost of a thing is the amount of money you need in order to buy it. If something is worth a particular amount of money, that is how much it would cost to buy. The value of a thing is how much money it is worth. So you can say that a diamond ring has a value of £1000 or that it is worth £1000.

value[2] /ˈvælju:/ VERB [values, valuing, valued]
1 to think something is important and worth having □ *I really value my free time.* □ *I value your advice on the matter.*
2 to say how much something is worth □ *The jewels were valued at three thousand dollars.*

valve /vælv/ NOUN [*plural* valves] something that opens and shuts to control the flow of liquid, air or gas through a pipe

vampire /ˈvæmpaɪə(r)/ NOUN [*plural* vampires] in stories, a dead person who comes out at night and sucks blood from people's necks

van /væn/ NOUN [*plural* vans] a road vehicle, like a small truck, used for carrying goods

➤ THESAURUS: A lorry or a truck is a large vehicle for carrying heavy goods by road. A van is a road vehicle like a small truck, used for carrying goods. People like plumbers or electricians often use a van to carry their tools and equipment.

vanilla /vəˈnɪlə/ NOUN, NO PLURAL a flavour that is used in a lot of sweet foods □ *vanilla ice cream*

vanish /ˈvænɪʃ/ VERB [vanishes, vanishing, vanished] to disappear suddenly, leaving nothing behind □ *He was standing in front of me a moment ago and suddenly he vanished.*

variety /vəˈraɪətɪ/ NOUN [*plural* varieties]
1 *no plural* a lot of different types □ **+ of** *The chairs are available in a variety of colours.*

2 *no plural* the quality of having many different things □ *You need variety in your diet.*
3 a type that is different from other similar things □ *a new variety of rose*

various /ˈveərɪəs/ ADJECTIVE many different □ *There were various types of cheese.* □ *There's been flooding in various parts of the country.*

vary /ˈveərɪ/ VERB [varies, varying, varied]
1 if things of the same type vary, they are all different in some way □ *Prices vary from shop to shop.*
2 if something varies, it changes at different times □ *Snowfall varies throughout the season.*
3 to change something slightly □ *You can vary the quantity that you order.*

vase /vɑ:z/ NOUN [*plural* vases] a decorative container for flowers

vast /vɑ:st/ ADJECTIVE extremely big □ *a vast area of land*

VAT /væt, ˌvi:eɪˈti:/ ABBREVIATION value added tax; a tax on goods and services in the UK

veal /vi:l/ NOUN, NO PLURAL meat from a baby cow

vegetable /ˈvedʒtəbəl/ NOUN [*plural* vegetables] a plant that you can eat, especially one that is not sweet □ *vegetables such as potatoes and carrots*

➤ Note that although the word 'fruit' cannot be used in the plural, the word **vegetable** can:
✓ Eat more fruit and vegetables.
✗ Eat more fruit and vegetable.

vegetarian[1] /ˌvedʒɪˈteərɪən/ NOUN [*plural* vegetarians] someone who does not eat meat or fish

vegetarian[2] /ˌvedʒɪˈteərɪən/ ADJECTIVE not eating or containing meat or fish □ *vegetarian cookery*

vehicle /ˈvi:ɪkəl/ NOUN [*plural* vehicles] something that carries people or goods, especially on roads, for example a car or a truck

veil /veɪl/ NOUN [*plural* veils] a piece of material that covers a woman's head or face

vein /veɪn/ NOUN [*plural* veins] one of the thin tubes inside the body that carry blood back to the heart

velvet /ˈvelvɪt/ NOUN, NO PLURAL a thick cloth that feels very soft on one side

venue /ˈvenju:/ NOUN [*plural* venues] the place where an event happens □ *The castle is used as a wedding venue.*

verb /vɜ:b/ NOUN [*plural* verbs] a word that says what someone or something does. For example, *eat*, *speak* and *be* are verbs.

verbal /ˈvɜ:bəl/ ADJECTIVE spoken and not written □ *a verbal agreement* □ *verbal communication*

verdict /'vɜːdɪkt/ NOUN [plural verdicts] a decision made in a court of law saying if someone is guilty or not guilty of committing a crime 🔁 Eventually the jury reached a verdict.

verge /vɜːdʒ/ NOUN [plural verges] the area at the edge of a road, usually covered in grass
◆ IDIOM on the verge of something going to do something very soon □ The company is on the verge of collapse.

verse /vɜːs/ NOUN [plural verses]
1 a set of lines that form one part of a song or poem
2 no plural poetry and not ordinary writing

version /'vɜːʃən/ NOUN [plural versions]
1 one form of something when other forms of it exist □ I know three versions of this song.
2 one person's description of something that happened 🔁 I've only heard Debbie's version of events.

versus /'vɜːsəs/ PREPOSITION used for saying which two players or teams are competing against each other □ It's Scotland versus France tonight.

vertical /'vɜːtɪkəl/ ADJECTIVE pointing straight up, at an angle of 90° to the ground □ vertical lines

very /'verɪ/ ADVERB
1 to a great degree □ I'm very tired. □ She was very pleased. □ It all happened very quickly.
2 not very good/nice/pleased, etc. not good/nice/pleased, etc. □ She wasn't very pleased.

➤ Very is not used before adjectives which have a strong meaning:
✓ I was very tired.
✗ I was very exhausted.
If you are using an adjective with a strong meaning, put an adverb such as completely or absolutely before it: □ I was completely exhausted.

vest /vest/ NOUN [plural vests]
1 a piece of underwear without sleeves that covers the top part of the body
2 the US word for waistcoat

vet /vet/ NOUN [plural vets] someone whose job is to treat animals that are ill or injured

veto /'viːtəʊ/ NOUN [plural vetoes] when someone officially stops something from happening

via /'vaɪə/ PREPOSITION travelling through a place □ The train goes to London via Birmingham.

vicar /'vɪkə(r)/ NOUN [plural vicars] in the Church of England, a priest

vice /vaɪs/ NOUN [plural vices] a bad habit □ vices such as smoking

vice-president /ˌvaɪs'prezɪdənt/ NOUN [plural vice-presidents] the person who is next in rank after a country's president (= elected leader of a country) □ the vice-president of the United States

vicious /'vɪʃəs/ ADJECTIVE extremely cruel and violent □ a vicious attack

victim /'vɪktɪm/ NOUN [plural victims] someone who is harmed or killed by something bad, such as a crime, disease, flood, etc. □ victims of crime □ victims of the bombing □ murder victims

victorious /vɪk'tɔːrɪəs/ ADJECTIVE successful in a fight or competition

victory /'vɪktərɪ/ NOUN [plural victories] success in a fight or competition □ victory in the Cup Final □ + for The game ended in victory for France.

video¹ /'vɪdɪəʊ/ NOUN [plural videos]
1 a recording of a film or television programme made on videotape
2 a recording of an event that has been made using a video camera
3 a machine for playing videos

video² /'vɪdɪəʊ/ VERB [videos, videoing, videoed]
1 to record a television programme onto videotape
2 to film an event using a video camera

video camera /'vɪdɪəʊ ˌkæmərə/ NOUN [plural video cameras] a piece of equipment that you use to record events onto videotape

video game /'vɪdɪəʊ ˌgeɪm/ NOUN [plural video games] an electronic game in which players move images on a computer or television screen

videotape /'vɪdɪəʊteɪp/ NOUN [plural videotapes] magnetic tape (= long, thin piece of plastic) that pictures and sounds can be recorded on

view /vjuː/ NOUN [plural views]
1 your opinion □ + on What's your view on wind farms? □ + about He made his views about the government very clear.
2 your ability to see things from a place □ The tall man spoilt my view of the concert. 🔁 Eventually, the lion came into view.
3 the things you can see from a place □ There's a fantastic view from the top of the hill.

viewer /'vjuːə(r)/ NOUN [plural viewers] someone who watches television □ The programme attracted more than a million viewers.

vigorous /'vɪgərəs/ ADJECTIVE very active and energetic □ vigorous exercise

villa /'vɪlə/ NOUN [plural villas] a large house, especially one used for holidays

village /'vɪlɪdʒ/ NOUN [plural villages] an area where people live in the countryside, which is smaller than a town □ She lives in a village just outside Stratford.

➤ THESAURUS: A village is an area in the countryside where people live. A town is a place where people live and work, which is bigger than a village. A city is a large important town. Manchester, Bristol and London are all cities. A capital or capital city is the city where the government of a state or country is. London is the capital of the UK, Paris is the capital of France and Beijing is the capital of China.

villager /'vɪlɪdʒə(r)/ NOUN [plural villagers] someone who lives in a village

villain /'vɪlən/ NOUN [plural villains] a bad person in a story, film, etc.

► THESAURUS: A bad person in a story or a film is called a villain. A criminal is someone who has committed a crime. A rogue is a dishonest or badly behaved man or boy.

vine /vaɪn/ NOUN [plural vines] a plant that grapes (= small green or red fruit that grows in groups) grow on

vinegar /'vɪnɪgə(r)/ NOUN, NO PLURAL a sour liquid that is used for giving flavour to food

vineyard /'vɪnjəd/ NOUN [plural vineyards] a place where grapes (= small green or red fruit that grows in groups) are grown to produce wine

violence /'vaɪələns/ NOUN, NO PLURAL
1 actions intended to hurt or kill someone or to damage something □ Something must be done to stop the violence. □ + against violence against women
2 force and strength, often causing damage □ The violence of the storm shocked everyone.

violent /'vaɪələnt/ ADJECTIVE
1 involving actions intended to hurt or kill someone or to damage something □ violent crime □ a violent film
2 with a lot of force and strength, causing damage □ a violent storm □ a violent explosion

violently /'vaɪələntlɪ/ ADVERB in a violent way

violet /'vaɪələt/ ADJECTIVE having a pale purple colour

violin /ˌvaɪə'lɪn/ NOUN [plural violins] a musical instrument with four strings, which you hold under your chin and play by pulling a bow (= long, thin piece of wood with hair stretched along it) across the strings

VIP /ˌviːaɪ'piː/ ABBREVIATION very important person; someone who is treated very well because they are powerful or famous

virtual /'vɜːtʃuəl/ ADJECTIVE
1 almost a particular thing □ He was a virtual prisoner in his own home.
2 using computer images to make something that is not real seem real. A computing word. □ a virtual tour of the museum

virtue /'vɜːtʃuː/ NOUN [plural virtues]
1 a good quality in a person's character □ Patience is a virtue.

2 a way of behaving that is morally good. A formal word. □ a woman of virtue

virus /'vaɪrəs/ NOUN [plural viruses]
1 a very small living thing that can enter the body and cause disease. A biology word.
2 an illness caused by a virus □ He's been off work all week with a virus.
3 a computer program that can send itself to many computers, for example by e-mail, and can destroy files on those computers. A computing word.

visa /'viːzə/ NOUN [plural visas] a document that you need to travel to and work in some countries

visible /'vɪzəbəl/ ADJECTIVE able to be seen □ Is the house visible from the road?

vision /'vɪʒən/ NOUN [plural visions]
1 your ability to see □ poor vision
2 an idea of how something should be in the future □ He talked about his vision for the school.

visit¹ /'vɪzɪt/ VERB [visits, visiting, visited] to go and see a place or person □ We're going to visit my aunt while we're in York. □ We visited a couple of museums.

visit² /'vɪzɪt/ NOUN [plural visits] the act of visiting a place or person 🔁 I'm going to pay him a visit.

visitor /'vɪzɪtə(r)/ NOUN [plural visitors] someone who visits a place or person 🔁 She had two visitors yesterday.

visual /'vɪʒjuəl/ ADJECTIVE to do with seeing □ visual signals

vital /'vaɪtəl/ ADJECTIVE necessary or extremely important □ vital information □ He played a vital role in the project.

vitamin /'vɪtəmɪn/ NOUN [plural vitamins] a substance in food that you need to stay healthy □ Oranges contain vitamin C.

vivid /'vɪvɪd/ ADJECTIVE
1 producing very clear ideas and pictures in your mind □ a vivid description □ vivid memories
2 very bright □ vivid colours

vocabulary /və'kæbjʊlərɪ/ NOUN [plural vocabularies]
1 the range of words that someone knows and uses □ She has a good vocabulary for a child of her age.
2 all the words in a language

voice /vɔɪs/ NOUN [plural voices] the sound you make when you speak or sing □ She has quite a low voice. □ Her singing voice is beautiful. □ I thought I heard voices.

volcano /vɒl'keɪnəʊ/ NOUN [plural volcanoes] a mountain that sometimes sends out hot lava (= liquid rock) through a hole in its top

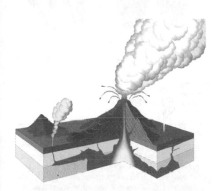

volleyball /'vɒlɪbɔːl/ NOUN, NO PLURAL a game in which two teams hit a ball over a high net with their hands

volume /'vɒljuːm/ NOUN [plural volumes]
1 the level of sound that something makes 🔁 Can you turn the volume down on the TV, please?
2 the space that something takes up or the amount of space that a container has
3 a book, especially a book that is part of a set

voluntary /'vɒlənterɪ/ ADJECTIVE
1 done by choice and not because you have to ☐ She took voluntary redundancy.
2 done without payment 🔁 voluntary work

volunteer[1] /ˌvɒlən'tɪə(r)/ NOUN [plural volunteers]
1 someone who offers to do something ☐ Do I have any volunteers to help me tidy up?
2 someone who does work for no payment
volunteer[2] /ˌvɒlən'tɪə(r)/ VERB [volunteers, volunteering, volunteered] to offer to do something ☐ Dana volunteered to take the children swimming.

vomit /'vɒmɪt/ VERB [vomits, vomiting, vomited] to bring food back up from your stomach through your mouth

vote[1] /vəʊt/ VERB [votes, voting, voted] to make a formal choice by secretly marking a piece of paper or putting your hand up to be counted ☐ + *for* Which candidate did you vote for in the elections? ☐ + *to do something* They voted to reject the offer.
• **voter** /'vəʊtə(r)/ NOUN [plural voters] someone who votes in an election

vote[2] /vəʊt/ NOUN [plural votes] a choice you make by marking a piece of paper or putting your hand up to be counted 🔁 The party that plans to lower taxes will get my vote.

vowel /'vaʊəl/ NOUN [plural vowels]
1 one of the letters a, e, i, o or u
2 a speech sound you make that does not use your lips, teeth, or tongue to stop the flow of air

voyage /'vɔɪɪdʒ/ NOUN [plural voyages] a long journey by sea or in space

vulnerable /'vʌlnərəbəl/ ADJECTIVE easily hurt, upset or made ill ☐ the protection of vulnerable children ☐ After surgery, people are more vulnerable to infection.

Ww

W¹ or **W** /'dʌbəlju:/ the 23rd letter of the alphabet

W² /west/ ABBREVIATION **west²**

wade /weɪd/ VERB [wades, wading, waded] to walk through water or mud □ *We waded across the stream.*

wag /wæg/ VERB [wags, wagging, wagged] if an animal wags its tail, it moves it from side to side □ *The dog ran backwards and forwards, wagging its tail.*

wage /weɪdʒ/ NOUN [plural wages] money that someone is paid for doing their job □ *They pay our wages on Fridays.* □ *a wage increase/cut* □ *What's the average wage?*

wail /weɪl/ VERB [wails, wailing, wailed] to cry loudly □ *A small child was wailing in the next room.*

waist /weɪst/ NOUN [plural waists] the middle part of your body, where you wear a belt

waistcoat /'weɪskəut/ NOUN [plural waistcoats] a short jacket with no sleeves and usually with buttons up the front that is worn over a shirt

wait¹ /weɪt/ VERB [waits, waiting, waited]
1 to stay in a place until something happens, something or someone is ready, etc. □ **+ for** *Several people were already waiting for the bus.* □ *He asked us to wait outside.* □ *We waited patiently for the show to begin.*
2 to not do something until something happens, someone arrives, etc. □ *I will wait until it stops raining before I leave.* □ **+ for** *We'd better wait for Jasmine before we start.*
3 to not do something or get something for a particular period of time □ *I had to wait 6 months for my operation.* □ *I decided to wait a while before making a decision.*
4 can't wait/can hardly wait if you can't wait to do something or for something to happen, you are very excited about it □ *I can't wait for our holiday!*
5 wait a minute/second used to tell someone to stop what they are doing or stay where they are for a short time □ *Wait a minute – I need to get my keys.*
♦ PHRASAL VERB **wait up** to not go to bed until someone comes home □ *I'll be late tonight – don't wait up for me.*

wait² /weɪt/ NOUN [plural waits] a period of time when you are waiting 🔁 *We had a long wait for the bus.*

> ➤ THESAURUS: A **wait** is a period of time when you are waiting. A **delay** is the extra time you have to wait if something happens later than expected. For example, if your train is late, you might have a ten minute **delay**. A **pause** is a short stop or rest. If someone stops talking, there might be a **pause** before someone replies. An **interval** is a period of time between two things. If you go to the theatre, there is often an **interval** in the middle of the play when you can have a drink.

waiter /'weɪtə(r)/ NOUN [plural waiters] someone who brings food to customers in a restaurant

waiting list /'weɪtɪŋ ˌlɪst/ NOUN [plural waiting lists] a list of people who are waiting to get or do something □ *hospital waiting lists*

waitress /'weɪtrɪs/ NOUN [plural waitresses] a woman who brings food to customers in a restaurant

wake /weɪk/ VERB [wakes, waking, woke, woken] to stop sleeping, or to make someone stop sleeping □ *We woke the children early and set off.*
♦ PHRASAL VERB **wake (someone) up** to stop sleeping, or to make someone stop sleeping □ *We were woken up by the dogs.*

walk¹ /wɔ:k/ VERB [walks, walking, walked] to move by putting one foot in front of the other □ *The door opened and Simon walked in.* □ *I think I'll walk to work today.*
♦ PHRASAL VERB **walk out** to leave a place because you are angry or upset □ *I was so angry in the meeting that I walked out.*

> ➤ THESAURUS: **Walk** is a general word. If you **march**, you walk in an angry, confident or determined way. **March** is also used to describe soldiers walking together with the same, regular steps. If you walk slowly, sliding your feet along the ground without lifting them, you **shuffle**. To **crawl** means to move on your hands and knees. Babies **crawl** before they learn to walk.

walk² /wɔːk/ NOUN [plural walks] a journey made by walking 🔊 They went for a walk on the beach. □ It's just a short walk to the shops. □ I need to take the dog for a walk.

wall /wɔːl/ NOUN [plural walls]
1 any of the sides of a room or building □ She hung the new clock on the kitchen wall.
2 a structure made of brick or stone that separates two areas or goes around an area □ A high wall surrounds the school.

wallet /'wɒlɪt/ NOUN [plural wallets] a flat container for money and cards, usually made of leather

> THESAURUS: Men usually carry a wallet. Women often carry money and cards in a purse. A handbag is a woman's bag for carrying things like money and keys. You might carry a purse in your handbag.

wander /'wɒndə(r)/ VERB [wanders, wandering, wandered] to go from one place to another without any clear plan or purpose □ We spent the summer wandering all around southern Italy.

want¹ /wɒnt/ VERB [wants, wanting, wanted]
1 to feel that you would like to have something or do something, or to wish that something will happen □ Do you want some cake? □ Nobody wants higher taxes. □ **+ to do something** I didn't want anyone to know.
2 to need something □ Your hands want a good wash.
3 used to give someone advice or a warning □ Maps? You want to try the library. □ She has a lot of influence. You don't want to upset her.

want² /wɒnt/ NOUN, NO PLURAL the state of being very poor or not having the things you need to live □ Many families are living in severe want.

war /wɔː(r)/ NOUN [plural wars]
1 fighting between two countries or groups, involving armies 🔊 War broke out (= started) between the two countries. 🔊 That was the year that war was declared (= announced). □ **+ between** the war between Britain and Argentina
2 at war fighting a war □ The two countries had been at war for years.

ward /wɔːd/ NOUN [plural wards] a room with beds in a hospital □ the children's ward

warden /'wɔːdən/ NOUN [plural wardens] someone who is in charge of a building and the people in it
wardrobe /'wɔːdrəʊb/ NOUN [plural wardrobes] a tall cupboard that you hang clothes inside
warehouse /'weəhaʊs/ NOUN [plural warehouses] a big building where businesses store large amounts of things □ a furniture warehouse

warfare /'wɔːfeə(r)/ NOUN, NO PLURAL fighting in a war □ modern warfare

warm¹ /wɔːm/ ADJECTIVE [warmer, warmest]
1 quite hot in a way that is pleasant □ a nice warm bath □ Are you warm enough? 🔊 I tried to keep warm by jumping up and down.
2 warm clothes make you feel warm □ a warm winter coat
3 friendly and showing good feelings towards other people 🔊 a warm welcome □ She's a very warm person.

warm² /wɔːm/ VERB [warms, warming, warmed] to make someone or something warm □ She warmed her hands on the radiator. □ I'll just warm the sauce.
♦ PHRASAL VERBS **warm (someone/something) up** to become warm, or to make someone or something warm □ Put a sweater on and you'll soon warm up. □ Could you warm up the soup? **warm up** to make your body ready to do a sport by doing gentle exercises □ It's important to warm up before a run.

warmly /'wɔːmli/ ADVERB
1 in a warm way □ Make sure you're warmly dressed for the walk.
2 showing good feelings □ She spoke very warmly of him.

warmth /wɔːmθ/ NOUN, NO PLURAL
1 pleasant heat, or the state of being pleasantly warm □ the warmth of the fire
2 when someone is friendly and shows good feelings towards other people □ the warmth of her welcome

warn /wɔːn/ VERB [warns, warning, warned] to tell someone about a possible danger or something bad that may happen so that they can avoid it or prepare for it □ **+ about** I warned her about the icy roads. □ **+ that** He warned me that it would be expensive. □ **+ to do something** I warned you to be careful!

warning /'wɔːnɪŋ/ NOUN [plural warnings]
1 a statement that tells you about a possible danger or something bad that may happen 🔊 There are health warnings on all bottles of alcohol. □ There are flood warnings for the region.
2 without warning if something bad happens without warning, it happens suddenly so that you do not know it is going to happen □ The volcano erupted without any warning.

> THESAURUS: Warning is a general word. A threat is a warning that someone might hurt you or harm you, especially if you do not do what they say. An alarm is a loud noise to warn people about something, for example a fire. An alert is a warning about something. For example, if there is going to be very bad weather, there may be an alert to warn people about it.

warrant /'wɒrənt/ NOUN [*plural* warrants] a document that gives the police the right to arrest someone or search their property

warrior /'wɒrɪə(r)/ NOUN [*plural* warriors] especially in the past, a soldier

wary /'weərɪ/ ADJECTIVE [warier, wariest] not wanting to do something or trust someone because you think it might cause problems □ *I am very wary of lending her money.*

was /wɒz/ VERB the past tense of the verb **be**¹ when it is used with **I**, **he**, **she** or **it** □ *I was surprised to see Rosie there.* □ *Mr Brock was my favourite teacher.*

wash¹ /wɒʃ/ VERB [washes, washing, washed]
1 to clean something with water and soap □ *His mum still washes his clothes.* ⓑ *Wash your hands before dinner.*
2 if water washes against something, it flows against it □ *Gentle waves were washing against the boat.*
♦ PHRASAL VERBS **wash something away** if something such as a building, tree or car is washed away, the force of the water carries it away □ *Whole trees were washed away in the storm.* **wash (something) up** to wash the plates, dishes, etc. that you have used for eating □ *It's my turn to wash up.*

> ► **THESAURUS:** If you clean something, you remove the dirt from it. If you wash something, you clean it with soap and water. If you rinse something, you remove dirt or soap from it by putting it in clean water. You rinse your hair to remove the shampoo from it, and you rinse clothes after you have washed them.

wash² /wɒʃ/ NOUN [*plural* washes]
1 when you wash yourself or wash something ⓑ *I'll just have a wash.* □ *Could you give this shirt a wash?*
2 no plural all the clothes that need to be washed □ *Your red shirt is in the wash.*

washbasin /'wɒʃbeɪsən/ NOUN [*plural* washbasins] a bowl with taps (= objects you turn to get water) for washing your hands and face in

washing /'wɒʃɪŋ/ NOUN, NO PLURAL all the clothes that need to be washed

washing machine /'wɒʃɪŋ məˌʃi:n/ NOUN [*plural* washing machines] a piece of electrical equipment that you wash clothes in

washing-up /ˌwɒʃɪŋ'ʌp/ NOUN, NO PLURAL
1 all the dishes, plates, etc. that need to be washed after cooking or eating
2 the activity of washing dishes and plates, etc. after cooking or eating ⓑ *I'll do the washing-up.*

wasn't /'wɒzənt/ a short way to say and write was not □ *He wasn't there.*

wasp /wɒsp/ NOUN [*plural* wasps] an insect with a thin black and yellow body that can sting you (= hurt you when it touches your skin)

waste¹ /weɪst/ VERB [wastes, wasting, wasted]
1 to use too much of something, often in a way that means some of it is thrown away □ *I'm trying not to waste any paper.* □ *We waste too much food.*
2 to use something, especially time or money, in a way that does not have good results ⓑ *You're wasting your time.* ⓑ *He wastes so much money.*

waste² /weɪst/ ADJECTIVE waste products or materials have no use now and can be thrown away □ *waste paper*

waste³ /weɪst/ NOUN, NO PLURAL
1 when too much of something is used, often so that some of it is thrown away □ *You should never throw away food – it's such a waste.*
2 when something, especially time or money, is used in a way that does not have good results ⓑ *I'm not going to clean this area – it's just a* waste of time. ⓑ *The whole course was a complete* waste of money.
3 rubbish or material that cannot be used for anything □ *industrial waste*

watch¹ /wɒtʃ/ VERB [watches, watching, watched]
1 to look at someone or something for a while □ *Max is watching the football.* □ *I watched the children dancing.*
2 to be careful about something □ *Watch you don't trip over that step.*
3 to look after someone or something □ *Could you watch the baby for me while I go and wash my hands?*
♦ PHRASAL VERB **watch out** used for telling someone to be careful □ *Watch out! Don't bang your head!*

watch² /wɒtʃ/ NOUN [*plural* watches]
1 a small clock that you wear on your lower arm
2 keep a watch on something/someone to pay

attention to something or someone, often to make sure that nothing bad happens

water¹ /ˈwɔːtə(r)/ NOUN, NO PLURAL a clear liquid that falls from the sky as rain and is used for drinking, washing, etc. □ *a glass of water*

water² /ˈwɔːtə(r)/ VERB [waters, watering, watered]
1 to water a plant is to pour water on it so it will live and grow
2 if your eyes water, they produce tears □ *The smoke made her eyes water.*

waterfall /ˈwɔːtəfɔːl/ NOUN [plural waterfalls] a place where a river or stream falls over a high rock onto rocks below

waterproof /ˈwɔːtəpruːf/ ADJECTIVE waterproof material does not allow water through it

waters /ˈwɔːtəz/ PLURAL NOUN used for talking about large areas of water, especially areas of the sea which belong to a particular country □ *The boat had entered Australian waters.*

watt /wɒt/ NOUN [plural watts] a unit of electrical power. This is often written **W**.

wave¹ /weɪv/ NOUN [plural waves]
1 a raised line of water that moves across the sea or other area of water □ *The waves were huge.*
2 a movement of the hand to say hello or goodbye or to attract someone's attention □ *She gave a wave as the train left the station.*
3 the form that sound or light takes as it travels through the air □ *sound waves*

wave² /weɪv/ VERB [waves, waving, waved]
1 to move your hand in order to say hello or goodbye or to attract someone's attention □ *She waved goodbye and then got on the train.*
2 to move in the wind □ *Flags were waving in the breeze.*
3 to move something from side to side in the air □ *She waved a handkerchief at me.*

wavelength /ˈweɪvleŋθ/ NOUN [plural wavelengths] the length of radio wave that a radio station uses to broadcast programmes
♦ IDIOM be on the same wavelength to think in the same way as someone else so you are able to understand them □ *My mother and I are just not on the same wavelength.*

wax /wæks/ NOUN, NO PLURAL a solid substance such as bees make, which becomes liquid when you heat it

way /weɪ/ NOUN [plural ways]
1 a method of doing something, or how someone does something □ **+ of** *We are trying out new ways*

of working. □ **+ to do something** *The best way to make new friends is to join a club.* □ **+ that** *I like the way that she sings.* □ *I've found a way to make cakes without eggs.*
2 used to talk about a particular feature or characteristic of something □ *He's like his father in many ways.* □ *In some ways I'd prefer to work full time.*
3 a route from one place to another □ **+ to** *Do you know the way to the station?* □ *Sorry I'm late – I lost my way.* □ *Can you manage to find your way to the main hall?*
4 a distance, or a journey or movement from one place to another □ *It's quite a long way to the coast.* □ *They have come all the way from Brazil*
5 an amount of time □ *The wedding still seems a long way off.*
6 on his/its/my, etc. way coming towards a place □ *Karen is on her way.* □ *Dinner is on its way.*
7 in/out of the way in/not in a position that stops someone seeing something or being able to move easily □ *I couldn't see the stage – there was a pillar in the way.* □ *Could you get out of the way while I'm cooking, please?*
8 used to talk about how much of something has happened or been done □ *We were half way through our dinner when the phone rang.*
9 by the way used to add a piece of information □ *By the way, have you heard the news about Alex?*
10 no way (a) certainly not. An informal phrase. □ *'Are you giving any money towards Carlo's present?' 'No way!'* (b) no possibility □ *There's no way we'll be finished before June.* (c) used to show surprise. An informal phrase. □ *They're getting married? No way!*
11 way of life the things that someone usually does □ *Marriage had changed his whole way of life.*

way out /ˌweɪ ˈaʊt/ NOUN [plural ways out] a door you go through to leave a public building

WC /ˌdʌbəljuːˈsiː/ NOUN [plural WCs] a toilet

we /wiː/ PRONOUN
1 used to talk or write about yourself and at least one other person □ *We left home at about nine o'clock.*
2 people in general □ *We need to do more about global warming.*

weak /wiːk/ ADJECTIVE [weaker, weakest]
1 not physically strong □ *His illness has left him feeling very weak.* □ *She suffers from a weak heart.*
2 not powerful □ *a weak government/leader*
3 not strong in character □ *She's too weak to stand up to her boss.*

4 easy to break □ *The metal bolts were too weak to hold the structure.* □ *a weak bridge*
5 weak liquids contain a lot of water, do not have a strong taste, or do not contain much alcohol □ *a cup of weak tea*

weaken /'wiːkən/ VERB [weakens, weakening, weakened] to become weak or to make someone or something weak □ *The metal has weakened because of rain and age.* □ *The illness weakened her heart.*

weakness /'wiːknɪs/ NOUN [plural weaknesses]
1 no plural when something or someone is not strong or forceful □ *The weakness of the frame made the building dangerous.* □ *I was ashamed of my weakness.*
2 a feature of something that is not of a high quality or standard □ *His main weakness is that he is lazy.* □ *The plan has several major weaknesses.*

wealth /welθ/ NOUN, NO PLURAL when someone has a lot of money and expensive things □ *The wealth of these people is amazing.*
wealthy /'welθɪ/ ADJECTIVE [wealthier, wealthiest] rich □ *a wealthy businessman*

weapon /'wepən/ NOUN [plural weapons] something that is used for fighting, such as a gun or a knife □ *The murder weapon was never found.*

wear /weə(r)/ VERB [wears, wearing, wore, worn]
1 to have clothes, jewellery, etc. on your body □ *Ann was wearing a red hat.* □ *How long have you worn glasses?* □ *He doesn't wear a wedding ring.*
2 if a material or surface wears, it gradually becomes thinner because of being used or rubbed, and if something wears it, it makes it thinner □ *His sleeves had worn through at the elbows.* 🔁 *My chair has worn a hole in the carpet.*

➤ Note that to **wear** clothes is to have them on your body. To say 'to start to wear clothes', use the phrasal verb **put on**:
✓ *I put on my coat and left.*
✗ *I wore my coat and left.*

◆ PHRASAL VERBS **wear off** if a feeling or the effect of something wears off, it gradually disappears □ *The anaesthetic should soon wear off.* **wear (something) out** to use something so much that it becomes damaged and cannot be used any more, or to become damaged in this way □ *These shoes are completely worn out already.* **wear someone out** to make someone very tired □ *Walking so far completely wore me out.*

weary /'wɪərɪ/ ADJECTIVE [wearier, weariest] tired □ *He finally got home, weary after a long day.*

weather /'weðə(r)/ NOUN, NO PLURAL the conditions outside, for example how hot, cold, wet or dry it is 🔁 *cold/hot weather* 🔁 *bad weather* □ *The weather's very warm for October.*

weave /wiːv/ VERB [weaves, weaving, wove, woven]
1 to make cloth by passing threads under and over each other on a frame called a loom (= a machine for making cloth)
2 to make something by twisting long pieces of things together □ *She taught me how to weave baskets.*

web /web/ NOUN [plural webs]
1 a very thin net that a spider makes for catching insects
2 the Web the World Wide Web; all the websites on the Internet. A computing word.

website /'websaɪt/ NOUN [plural websites] a group of connected pages on the Internet about a particular company, organization, subject, etc. A computing word. □ *Rowling's official website* □ *He has his own website.*

we'd /wiːd/ a short way to say and write we had or we would □ *We'd better hurry up.* □ *We'd buy a new car if we had the money.*

wedding /'wedɪŋ/ NOUN [plural weddings] a marriage ceremony □ *I met her at Lucy and John's wedding.* □ *a wedding present*

Wednesday /'wenzdɪ/ NOUN [plural Wednesdays] the day of the week after Tuesday and before Thursday □ *Shall we meet again on Wednesday?*

weed /wiːd/ NOUN [plural weeds] a wild plant that is growing where you do not want it to □ *The garden was full of weeds.*

week /wiːk/ NOUN [plural weeks]
1 a period of seven days □ *Debbie teaches aerobics twice a week.* □ *I'll see you next week.*
2 in/during the week on the five days from Monday to Friday when many people go to work □ *I don't go out much during the week.*

weekday /'wiːkˌdeɪ/ NOUN [plural weekdays] any of the days from Monday to Friday □ *The office is only open on weekdays.*

weekend /ˌwiːk'end/ NOUN [plural weekends] Saturday and Sunday □ *We're going to Oxford for the weekend.* □ *I like to go cycling at the weekend.*

weekly[1] /'wiːklɪ/ ADJECTIVE happening or produced once every week □ *a weekly magazine*

weekly[2] /'wi:klɪ/ ADVERB once every week □ *In those days I used to get paid weekly.*

weep /wi:p/ VERB [weeps, weeping, wept] to cry □ *She wept when she heard the terrible news.*

weigh /weɪ/ VERB [weighs, weighing, weighed]
1 to measure how heavy something is □ *Brenda weighs herself every day.* □ *Weigh the ingredients carefully.*
2 to have a particular weight □ *My suitcase weighed 15 kilograms.*

weight[1] /weɪt/ NOUN [*plural* weights]
1 *no plural* how heavy someone or something is □ *My luggage was above the weight limit.* 🕮 *He has lost a lot of weight* (= got thinner) *recently.* 🕮 *I've put on weight* (= got fatter) *since I stopped cycling.*
2 *no plural* the quality of being heavy □ *The shelf bent under the weight of all those books.*
3 weights heavy objects that you lift to make your muscles stronger □ *I spend ten minutes lifting weights.*

weight[2] /weɪt/ VERB [weights, weighting, weighted] to put something heavy into or onto something □ *We weighted the sheet down with rocks.*

weird /wɪəd/ ADJECTIVE [weirder, weirdest] very strange □ *Something really weird just happened.*

welcome[1] /'welkəm/ ADJECTIVE
1 if someone or something is welcome, you are pleased about it □ *This fall in inflation is welcome news to home owners.* □ *We stopped for a very welcome rest.*
2 if you are welcome somewhere, people like you being there and make you feel happy and comfortable 🕮 *They made us very welcome in their home.* □ *He is not welcome at his parent's house.*
3 welcome to do something if someone is welcome to do something, you are happy to allow them to do it □ *You're welcome to borrow my bike when I'm not using it.*
4 You're welcome. used as a polite reply when someone has thanked you for something □ *'Thank you for all your help.' 'You're welcome.'*

welcome[2] /'welkəm/ EXCLAMATION used for welcoming someone who has arrived somewhere □ **+ to** *Welcome to London!*

welcome[3] /'welkəm/ NOUN [*plural* welcomes] the way that people treat someone when they arrive somewhere 🕮 *We received a very warm welcome in Berlin.*

welcome[4] /'welkəm/ VERB [welcomes, welcoming, welcomed]
1 to meet someone and make them feel that you are happy to see them □ *The whole family came to welcome us at the airport.*
2 to be pleased about something □ *I would welcome the chance of a different job.* □ *We welcome these new plans.*

welfare /'welfeə(r)/ NOUN, NO PLURAL health, happiness and safety □ *The police were concerned for the child's welfare.*

well[1] /wel/ ADVERB [better, best]
1 in a satisfactory, successful or correct way □ *Janet speaks French very well.* □ *Federer played really well.* 🕮 *My students are all doing well.* 🕮 *Our meetings went well.*
2 completely □ *Mix the butter and sugar well before adding the flour.* □ *I know Marie really well.*
3 as well in addition □ *I'd like an ice cream as well.* □ *As well as his family, a lot of his colleagues were there.*
4 may as well/might as well used to make a suggestion because of a situation □ *If you're spending that much on rent, you might as well buy a flat.* □ *We may as well talk to them.*
5 well done used to praise someone for something they have done □ *You passed? Oh, well done!* □ *Well done for remembering the map!*
6 used to form compound adjectives (= adjectives in two parts). When they are used before nouns, they usually have hyphens, e.g. *a well paid job* □ *The business was very well run.* □ *Their staff are well paid.*

well[2] /wel/ EXCLAMATION
1 used at the beginning of a statement, especially a reply, often when you are explaining something, or expressing slight doubt or disagreement □ *'How did you make the sofa?' 'Well, I started with an old bed frame.'* □ *'Do you think he's suitable for the job?' 'Well, I've never worked with him, so it's hard to say.'* □ *'It's a great book, isn't it?' 'Well, I didn't enjoy it as much as you.'*
2 oh well used for accepting a bad situation □ *'Kiera is going to be late.' 'Oh well, we'll have to start without her.'*

well[3] /wel/ ADJECTIVE [better, best] healthy 🕮 *I don't feel very well.* 🕮 *You're looking well.* 🕮 *Get well soon!*

well[4] /wel/ NOUN [*plural* wells] a deep hole in the ground where you can get water, oil or gas □ *an oil well*

we'll /wi:l/ a short way to say and write we will □ *I'm sure we'll meet again.*

well-known /ˌwelˈnəʊn/ ADJECTIVE famous or known by many people □ *a well-known writer*

Welsh[1] /welʃ/ ADJECTIVE
1 belonging to or from Wales
2 to do with the Welsh language

Welsh[2] /welʃ/ NOUN, NO PLURAL
1 the Celtic language of Wales
2 the Welsh the people of Wales

went /went/ PAST TENSE OF **go**[1]

wept /wept/ PAST TENSE AND PAST PARTICIPLE OF **weep**

were /wɜː(r)/ PAST TENSE OF **be**[1] when it is used with **you**, **we** or **they** □ *We were so relieved to see him.*

we're /wɪə(r)/ a short way to say and write we are □ *We're so pleased you could come.*

weren't /wɜːnt/ a short way to say and write were not □ *Weren't the acrobats amazing?*

west[1] /west/ NOUN, NO PLURAL
1 the direction in which the sun goes down
2 the countries in Europe and North America □ *The family moved to the West in 1998.*

west[2] /west/ ADJECTIVE, ADVERB in or towards the west □ *the west coast of America* □ *We travelled west as far as the motorway.*

western[1] /ˈwestən/ ADJECTIVE in or from the west □ *the western hills*

western[2] /ˈwestən/ NOUN [*plural* westerns] a book or film about cowboys (= men who ride horses and look after cows) in North America

westward /ˈwestwəd/ *or* **westwards** /ˈwestwədz/ ADVERB to or towards the west □ *We travelled westwards.*

wet[1] /wet/ ADJECTIVE [wetter, wettest]
1 full of water or covered with water □ *wet clothes* □ *It's easy to slip on a wet floor.* 🔊 *My trousers are soaking wet!*
2 not dried □ *wet paint*
3 raining □ *a wet afternoon*

> ► THESAURUS: If something is wet, it is full of water or covered in water. If something is damp or moist, it is slightly wet. For example, a towel might be damp once you have used it after a bath. If something is soaking, it is very wet.

wet[2] /wet/ VERB [wets, wetting, wet] to make something wet □ *He wet his hair to flatten it down.*

we've /wiːv/ a short way to say and write we have □ *We've got something to tell you.*

whale /weɪl/ NOUN [*plural* whales] a very large mammal that lives in the sea
♦ IDIOM **have a whale of a time** to enjoy yourself

very much □ *The children had a whale of a time at the swimming pool.*

what[1] /wɒt/ DETERMINER, PRONOUN
1 used for asking for information about something □ *What day is it today?* □ *What's your brother's name?* □ *What did that man want?* □ *What shall we do this evening?*
2 used for referring to something □ *This bag is just what I wanted.* □ *I saw what you did.* □ *I had no idea what to do.*
3 **what for** used to ask about the purpose of something or the reason for something □ *What's this handle for?* □ *What did you do that for?*
4 an informal word used when you have not heard someone and want them to repeat what they have said □ *'Could you pass the bread?' 'What?'*
5 an informal word used to ask what someone wants when they speak to you or call to you □ *'Kate!' 'Yes, what?'*
6 used to emphasize your feelings about something □ *What a beautiful view!*

what[2] /wɒt/ EXCLAMATION used to express surprise or shock □ *'The car repairs cost £400.' 'What! I had no idea it would be that much.'*

whatever /wɒtˈevə(r)/ PRONOUN, DETERMINER
1 any, anything or any amount □ *I can give you whatever money you need.* □ *Choose whatever you like from the menu.*
2 used to say that something will always be true and will not be affected by anything else □ *You know we'll always love you, whatever happens.* □ *We'll be going, whatever the weather.*
3 an informal word used to say that you do not care what happens or what you do □ *'Do you want to come with me to the party?' 'Whatever.'*

what'll /ˈwɒtəl/ a short way to say and write what will □ *What'll happen to him?*

what's /wɒts/ a short way to say and write what is or what has □ *What's that noise?* □ *What's she got in her hand?*

what've /ˈwɒtəv/ a short way to say and write what have □ *What've you done with the phone?*

wheat /wiːt/ NOUN, NO PLURAL a plant that produces grain that is used to make flour

wheel[1] /wiːl/ NOUN [*plural* wheels] a round object under a vehicle that turns to make the vehicle move 🔊 *There's a spare wheel in the boot.*

wheel[2] /wiːl/ VERB [wheels, wheeling, wheeled] to push something along on wheels □ *He wheeled the trolley through the airport.*

wheelchair /'wiːltʃeə(r)/ NOUN [plural wheelchairs] a seat with wheels, used by people who cannot walk

when /wen/ ADVERB, CONJUNCTION
1 used for asking about the time something happened or will happen □ When did you get home? □ When do you think they will arrive? □ When will the cakes be ready?
2 used for talking about the time at which something happens or will happen □ I'll go when I've had a shower. □ I'm not sure when the new store will open.
3 used for talking about something that happens at the same time as something else □ I was just going out when the phone rang. □ When I heard the news, I went straight to the airport. □ I was with her when she died.

whenever /wen'evə(r)/ CONJUNCTION, ADVERB
1 at any time □ You can borrow my book whenever you want to.
2 every time □ They go swimming whenever they get the chance.
3 used at the beginning of a question, especially to show that you are surprised □ Whenever did you do all this?

where /weə(r)/ ADVERB, CONJUNCTION
1 used for asking about a place or position □ Where are we going? □ Where did you get that hat? □ Where can I park my car? □ Where do you come from?
2 used for talking about a place or position □ I know where you can buy really good fish. □ He told me where he lives. □ That is the place where I lost my camera.

whereas /weər'æz/ CONJUNCTION used for comparing two things □ He likes going out and meeting people, whereas I'm quite shy.
where's /weəz/ a short way to say and write where is or where has □ Where's the cat? □ Where's he gone?
where've /weəv/ a short way to say and write where have □ Where've the children gone?

wherever /weər'evə(r)/ CONJUNCTION, ADVERB
1 to or in any place □ Wherever he is, I am sure he will come back soon.
2 to or in every place □ He follows me wherever I go.
3 used to ask where someone or something is, especially when you are surprised or angry □ Wherever did you get that hat?

whether /'weðə(r)/ CONJUNCTION
1 used to show that there is a choice between two possibilities □ I couldn't decide whether to have the salmon or the pork. 🔁 I wasn't sure whether or not to tell her.
2 if □ I'm not sure whether they're coming.

which /wɪtʃ/ ADJECTIVE, DETERMINER
1 used for asking or talking about a choice between two or more people or things □ Which hand do you think the coin is in? □ Which person is tallest? □ + of Which of these books is yours?
2 used for referring to something □ I saw the letter which was lying on the table. □ These are the ideas which we must discuss.
3 used for giving extra information about something □ The cars, which were all luxury models, were available for us to use. □ I went to her party, which was very pleasant.

whichever /wɪtʃ'evə(r)/ DETERMINER, PRONOUN any of a group of things or people □ Come on whichever day suits you.

while¹ /waɪl/ CONJUNCTION during the time that □ Will you go to Disneyland while you are in Florida? □ I had a cup of coffee while I was waiting.

➤ Note that the word **while**, meaning 'during the time that' is never followed by a noun:
✓ She got ill while we were on holiday.
✗ She got ill while the holiday.

while² /waɪl/ NOUN a while a period of time □ We waited inside for a while, but the rain didn't stop. 🔁 I haven't seen her for quite a while (= a long time).

whilst /waɪlst/ CONJUNCTION while □ You could look at these magazines whilst you're waiting.
whine /waɪn/ VERB [whines, whining, whined]
1 to talk in a complaining voice □ She's always whining about her job.
2 a dog or other animal whines when it makes a long high sound
whip¹ /wɪp/ NOUN [plural whips] a piece of leather or other material fastened to a handle and used to hit animals or people
whip² /wɪp/ VERB [whips, whipping, whipped]
1 to hit someone or something with a whip
2 to mix food, especially cream, very quickly to make it become thick

➤ THESAURUS: Whip is used particularly to talk about cream. If you beat other food, such as eggs, or a cake mixture together very quickly, you can use the word beat. To whisk means to mix food together to get a lot of air into it, using a whisk (a kitchen tool with curved wire parts). You might whisk egg whites, for example.

whisk¹ /wɪsk/ NOUN [plural whisks] a kitchen tool with curved wire parts, used for mixing things like cream or eggs and getting a lot of air into them.

whisk² /wɪsk/ VERB [whisks, whisking, whisked]
1 to mix food with a whisk
2 to make someone or something move somewhere quickly □ *They whisked us off to meet their cousins.* □ *She whisked away the plates.*

whisky /ˈwɪskɪ/ NOUN [*plural* whiskies] a strong alcoholic drink made from grain, or a glass of this drink

whisper¹ /ˈwɪspə(r)/ VERB [whispers, whispering, whispered] to talk very quietly so that other people cannot hear □ *My friend whispered the answer to me.*

whisper² /ˈwɪspə(r)/ NOUN [*plural* whispers] something said in a very quiet voice □ *She answered in a whisper.*

whistle¹ /ˈwɪsəl/ VERB [whistles, whistling, whistled]
1 to make a high sound or musical notes by blowing air through your lips □ *She was whistling a merry tune.*
2 to make a high sound using a whistle □ *The train whistled as it entered the tunnel.* □ *The referee whistled for the end of the game.*

whistle² /ˈwɪsəl/ NOUN [*plural* whistles]
1 a small object that makes a high sound when you blow in it
2 a piece of equipment that makes a loud, high sound, for example on a train
3 the sound made when someone or something whistles

white¹ /waɪt/ ADJECTIVE
1 having the colour of snow □ *He served the soup in large, white bowls.* □ *This powder will get your washing really white.*
2 white people are of a race that have pale skin □ *He married a white woman.*
3 white tea or coffee has milk in it
4 white wine is a pale yellow colour

white² /waɪt/ NOUN [*plural* whites]
1 *no plural* the colour of snow □ *The white of the walls reflected the sunlight.*
2 the white of an egg is the clear substance around

the yolk (= yellow part) which turns white if it is cooked

who /huː/ PRONOUN
1 used for asking about a person or people □ *Who is your favourite actor?* □ *Who left the door open?* □ *Who are you going to London with?*
2 used for referring to a person or people □ *It was Malcolm who told me the news.* □ *It was the Italians who invented pizza.* □ *I know who has been offered the job.*
3 used for giving extra information about a person or people □ *Emily, who lives next door, is 12 years old.*

who'd /huːd/ a short way to say and write who had or who would □ *It was my Dad who'd told him.* □ *Who'd like another biscuit?*

whoever /huːˈevə(r)/ PRONOUN, CONJUNCTION
1 the person that has done something □ *Would whoever left the gate open please go and close it.*
2 any person □ *Bring whoever you like to the party.*
3 used at the beginning of a question to show that you are surprised □ *Whoever told you I was a doctor?*

whole¹ /həʊl/ ADJECTIVE
1 containing or including every part of something □ *We spent the whole day on the beach.* □ *I drank a whole bottle of milk.* □ *Half the guests were late, and the whole thing was a disaster.*
2 not broken into parts □ *The cake is decorated with whole hazelnuts.*

whole² /həʊl/ ADVERB in one complete piece □ *He swallowed the egg whole.*

whole³ /həʊl/ NOUN, NO PLURAL
1 a complete thing, especially one that is made up of different parts □ *Two halves make a whole.*
2 the whole of something all of something □ *She spent the whole of her life in Wales.* □ *The Olympics will benefit the whole of the country.*
3 on the whole used to talk about what something is usually or mostly like □ *On the whole, I enjoy school.* □ *People were very kind to us on the whole.*

who'll /huːl/ a short way to say and write who will □ *Who'll help me to carry this box?*

whom /huːm/ PRONOUN a formal word, used instead of 'who' when it is the object of a verb or a preposition □ *He phoned his friend Andrew, whom he hadn't seen for years.* □ *To whom should I address the letter?*

who're /ˈhuːə(r)/ a short way to say and write who are □ *Who're you going with?*

who's /huːz/ a short way to say and write who is or who has □ *Who's coming for a walk?* □ *Who's got the TV guide?*

whose /huːz/ ADJECTIVE, PRONOUN
1 used to ask who something belongs to or is connected with □ *Whose bike is this?* □ *Whose is this coat?*

2 used to say that something or someone belongs to someone or is connected to them □ *This is the boy whose family owns the farm.* □ *Cheeky, whose real name was Robert Ritchie, lived in Glasgow.*

who've /huːv/ a short way to say and write who have □ *These are the members who've already paid their subscriptions.*

why /waɪ/ ADVERB
1 used for asking and talking about the reason for something □ *Why were you late?* □ *Why didn't they phone us?* □ *She explained why she had made the decision.* □ *I have no idea why he was so angry.*
2 used for making a suggestion □ *Why don't you ask Claire to come with you?* □ *Why doesn't he ask a doctor about it?*
3 why not ...? (a) used for making a suggestion □ *Why not make some soup with the vegetables?* (b) used for agreeing to a suggestion □ *'Shall we invite Peter?' 'Yes, why not?'*

why've /waɪv/ a short way to say and write why have □ *Why've we got to wait?*

wicked /'wɪkɪd/ ADJECTIVE
1 evil or morally wrong □ *a wicked old witch* □ *Separating children from their parents is wicked.*
2 an informal word meaning very good □ *He scored a wicked goal.*

wide[1] /waɪd/ ADJECTIVE [wider, widest]
1 a large distance from side to side □ *a wide river* □ *Floods affected a wide area.*
2 having a particular width □ *The river is nearly a mile wide at some points.*
3 including many different things ▣ *They sell a wide range of products.* □ *The college offers a wide choice of subjects.*

wide[2] /waɪd/ ADVERB [wider, widest]
1 with a large distance from top to bottom or side to side □ *The tiger opened his mouth wide, showing his enormous teeth.* ▣ *The door was wide open.* ▣ *She stood with her feet wide apart.*
2 wide awake completely awake

widely /'waɪdlɪ/ ADVERB
1 by many people or in many places □ *He was widely believed to be guilty.* □ *The tour was widely advertised.*
2 by a large amount □ *Standards vary widely.*

widen /'waɪdən/ VERB [widens, widening, widened] to make something wider or to become wider □ *The river widens as it reaches the sea.*

widespread /'waɪdspred/ ADJECTIVE found in a lot of places or among a lot of people □ *There is widespread use of these drugs.* □ *There has been widespread criticism of the law.*

widow /'wɪdəʊ/ NOUN [plural widows] a woman whose husband has died

widower /'wɪdəʊə(r)/ NOUN [plural widowers] a man whose wife has died

width /wɪdθ/ NOUN [plural widths] the width of something is how much it measures from side to side □ *This curtain material comes in several different widths.*

wife /waɪf/ NOUN [plural wives] the woman that a man is married to

wig /wɪg/ NOUN [plural wigs] a covering of artificial hair that is worn on the head

wild /waɪld/ ADJECTIVE [wilder, wildest]
1 wild animals or plants live in natural conditions and are not kept by human beings □ *wild salmon* □ *wild flowers*
2 not controlled, and often expressing strong emotions or a lot of energy and excitement ▣ *When he came on stage, the audience went wild.* □ *The children were wild with excitement.* ▣ *wild parties*

wilderness /'wɪldənɪs/ NOUN [plural wildernesses] a wild area of a country with no roads, houses, etc.

wildlife /'waɪldlaɪf/ NOUN, NO PLURAL wild animals, birds, insects and plants

will[1] /wɪl/ MODAL VERB
1 used to talk about the future □ *It will be winter soon.* □ *Will Tom be at the party?* □ *It won't take long to mend the hole.*
2 used to talk about if someone is willing to do something □ *Will you hold this for me?* □ *I'll carry that bag for you.* □ *He won't lend me any money.*
3 used in conditional sentences that start with 'if' □ *If he is rude, I will leave straight away.* □ *If it rains, they will have to work indoors.*

➤ Notice that instead of **will not**, people often say or write the short form **won't**: □ *I won't tell her.*

will[2] /wɪl/ NOUN [plural wills]
1 the mental strength needed to achieve something □ *She has the will to succeed.* ▣ *He had a very strong will.*
2 a legal document that says what you want to happen to your money and possessions when you die ▣ *Have you made a will?*

will[3] /wɪl/ VERB [wills, willing, willed] if you will something to happen, you try to make it happen by wishing for it very much □ *We were willing our team to win.*

willing /'wɪlɪŋ/ ADJECTIVE willing to do something if you are willing to do something, you will do it if you are asked to □ *He'll succeed if he's willing to work hard.* □ *She wasn't willing to accept responsibility.*

win[1] /wɪn/ VERB [wins, winning, won]
1 to beat everyone else in a game, competition, election, etc. ▣ *We played tennis, and Sam won easily.* □ *They won the championship three times.*

2 to defeat the other side in a war, argument, etc.
3 to get something because you have been successful in a game, competition, etc. □ *She won a gold medal at the 2008 Olympics.* □ *The film won two Oscars.*

win² /wɪn/ NOUN [*plural* wins] when someone wins a game, competition, etc. □ *This is the team's third win this season.*

wind¹ /wɪnd/ NOUN [*plural* winds] a current of air 🔊 *Strong winds prevented the aircraft from landing.* 🔊 *The wind blew and snow fell.*

> ➤ **THESAURUS:** Wind is a general word. A light wind is called a breeze. A very strong wind is called a gale. A storm with very strong winds is called a hurricane. A tornado is a violent storm with a powerful wind with a circular movement. Hurricanes and tornadoes often cause a lot of damage.

wind² /waɪnd/ VERB [winds, winding, wound]
1 to twist or wrap something around something else □ **+ round** *A turban is a long piece of cloth that is wound round the head.*
2 if a road, path or river winds somewhere, it has a lot of curves or turns □ **+ through** *A narrow path wound through the valley.*
3 to turn a part of a machine or piece of equipment in order to make it work □ *This watch has a battery, so you don't need to wind it.* □ **+ up** *You wind up this toy car to make it go.*
◆ PHRASAL VERB **wind someone up** an informal word meaning to make someone upset or angry □ *It really winds me up when he's late.*

windmill /'wɪndmɪl/ NOUN [*plural* windmills] a building with large parts on the outside which are turned by the wind and provide power for crushing grain

window /'wɪndəʊ/ NOUN [*plural* windows]
1 an opening in the wall of a building or in a vehicle,

with glass fitted in it 🔊 *Could you open/close the window, please?*
2 an area on a computer screen where you can work or see information. A computing word 🔊 *I opened a new window.*

windscreen /'wɪndskriːn/ NOUN [*plural* windscreens] the window at the front of a car or other vehicle

windshield /'wɪndʃiːld/ NOUN [*plural* windshields] the US word for **windscreen**

windsurfing /'wɪndsɜːfɪŋ/ NOUN, NO PLURAL the sport of moving across the surface of water standing on a narrow board with a sail attached to it

windy /'wɪndɪ/ ADJECTIVE [windier, windiest] with a lot of wind □ *a windy day*

wine /waɪn/ NOUN [*plural* wines] an alcoholic drink usually made from grapes (= small green or purple fruits) 🔊 *a glass of wine* 🔊 *red/white wine*

wing /wɪŋ/ NOUN [*plural* wings]
1 one of the parts of a bird or an insect's body that it uses to fly with 🔊 *The owl flapped its wings.*
2 one of the two long flat parts that stick out at either side of an aircraft

wink¹ /wɪŋk/ VERB [winks, winking, winked] to shut one of your eyes and open it again quickly, as a friendly or secret sign to someone

> ➤ **THESAURUS:** If you wink, you shut and open one eye. If you blink, you close and open your eyes quickly. If you frown, you look as if you are angry, worried or thinking a lot by moving your eyebrows down.

wink² /wɪŋk/ NOUN [*plural* winks] the action of shutting one of your eyes and opening it again quickly

winner /'wɪnə(r)/ NOUN [*plural* winners] someone who wins a race, competition, election, etc. □ *This year's winner gets a £3,000 prize.*

winter /'wɪntə(r)/ NOUN [*plural* winters] the coldest season of the year, between autumn and spring □ *the winter months* □ *a winter coat*

wipe /waɪp/ VERB [wipes, wiping, wiped]
1 to rub the surface of something to clean it or dry it □ *I wiped my face with a tissue.* □ *We wiped all the tables.* 🔊 *Please wipe your feet* (= clean the dirt off your shoes) *before you come in.*
2 to remove something, for example dirt or water, from the surface of something by rubbing it □ *Wipe any mud off the potatoes.*

♦ PHRASAL VERBS **wipe something out** to destroy something completely □ *These elephants are in danger of being wiped out by hunters.* **wipe something up** to clean away a substance, often a liquid, with a cloth □ *Could you wipe that milk up, please?*

wire /'waɪə(r)/ NOUN [plural wires]
1 *no plural* metal that has been made into long, thin pieces, used for fastening things together, or for fences, etc. □ *a wire fence*
2 a piece of wire used for carrying electricity or telephone signals

wisdom /'wɪzdəm/ NOUN, NO PLURAL when someone understands a lot about life and is able to make good decisions and give good advice

wise /waɪz/ ADJECTIVE [wiser, wisest] a wise person understands a lot about life and is able to make good decisions and give good advice

wish¹ /wɪʃ/ VERB [wishes, wishing, wished]
1 to want something to happen, especially to want a situation to change □ *I wish it would stop raining.* □ **+ that** *I wish that I could go with you.*
2 wish to do something a formal word meaning to want to do something □ *Do you wish to pay now or later?*
3 used to say that you hope someone will have something or enjoy something ▣ *We all wish you luck.* □ *I wished her a happy birthday.*

wish² /wɪʃ/ NOUN [plural wishes]
1 what you want to do or to happen ▣ *We must respect his wishes* (= do what he wants).
2 something that you want to happen by magic ▣ *Blow out the candles and make a wish!*
3 best wishes a polite way of ending a letter or e-mail

wit /wɪt/ NOUN, NO PLURAL the ability to say funny and clever things

witch /wɪtʃ/ NOUN [plural witches] a woman in stories who has evil magic powers

➤ THESAURUS: A witch is a woman with magic powers. A man with magic powers is called a wizard. A fairy is an imaginary creature which looks like a small person with wings.

with /wɪð/ PREPOSITION
1 if something or someone is in a place with something or someone else, or doing something with someone or something else, they are together □ *Come with me.* □ *She keeps her diary on the shelf with her other books.* □ *He was playing football with his friends.*
2 using □ *The board was stuck down with glue.* □ *I*

chopped up the wood with an axe. □ *He covered the table with a sheet.*
3 having □ *Who is that man with the curly hair?* □ *The meeting was in the room with the large table.*
4 as the result of □ *He was crying with pain.*
5 against □ *I'm always arguing with my parents.* □ *He was killed in the war with Spain.*
6 used to describe how something happens or is done □ *She agreed with a smile.* □ *He stood with his hands behind his back.*
7 holding or carrying □ *He arrived with a huge bunch of roses.*
8 used to show what something refers to □ *What's wrong with your eye?* □ *I'm really pleased with my new computer.*

withdraw /wɪð'drɔː/ VERB [withdraws, withdrawing, withdrew, withdrawn]
1 to take something away or to stop providing something □ *The council has withdrawn funding for the nursery.* □ *His father has withdrawn consent for the treatment.*
2 to not take part in something, or to say that someone cannot take part in something □ *The government has withdrawn from the negotiations.* □ *He began to withdraw from public life.*
3 to take money out of a bank account □ *I withdrew £100 for the weekend.*
4 If an army withdraws or is withdrawn, it leaves an area ▣ *We plan to withdraw our forces from the area.*

wither /'wɪðə(r)/ VERB [withers, withering, withered] if a plant withers, it becomes dry and starts to die

withhold /wɪð'həʊld/ VERB [withholds, withholding, withheld] to refuse to give something to someone ▣ *She was accused of withholding information from the police.*

within /wɪ'ðɪn/ PREPOSITION
1 in less than a particular amount of time, or during a particular period of time □ *The police were called within minutes of the discovery.* □ *We'll be home within the hour.* □ *Within the last week there have been reports of fighting in the area.*
2 less than a particular distance or amount away from something □ *I have always lived within 20 miles of York.* □ *They are within two points of the championship.*
3 inside a place, group, organization or system □ *They took cover within the castle walls.* □ *I moved to another job within the same company.*

without¹ /wɪ'ðaʊt/ PREPOSITION
1 not having something □ *I prefer my coffee without milk.* □ *It's a kind of bicycle without pedals.* □ *They left us without any food or water.* ▣ *We had to do without knives and forks.*
2 not with someone or something □ *Don't leave without me!*

3 not doing something □ *+ ing He left without saying goodbye.*

without² /wɪ'ðaʊt/ ADVERB do/go without to manage when you do not have something □ *We only have two blankets, so the children will have to do without.*

withstand /wɪð'stænd/ VERB [withstands, withstanding, withstood] to not be harmed by something □ *The buildings are designed to withstand earthquakes.*

witness¹ /'wɪtnɪs/ NOUN [*plural* witnesses]
1 someone who sees an event such as an accident or a crime happening, and can tell other people about it □ *+ to Were there any witnesses to the accident?*
2 someone who answers questions in a court about what they know about a crime

witness² /'wɪtnɪs/ VERB [witnesses, witnessing, witnessed] to see something happening □ *Several people witnessed the shooting.*

witty /'wɪtɪ/ ADJECTIVE [wittier, wittiest] clever and funny □ *My brother is very witty.* □ *a witty remark*
wives /waɪvz/ PLURAL OF **wife**
wizard /'wɪzəd/ NOUN [*plural* wizards] in stories, a man with magic powers
woke /wəʊk/ PAST TENSE OF **wake**
woken /'wəʊkən/ PAST PARTICIPLE OF **wake**
wolf /wʊlf/ NOUN [*plural* wolves] a wild animal like a large dog

woman /'wʊmən/ NOUN [*plural* women] an adult female person □ *There were three other women in the office.*

womb /wuːm/ NOUN [*plural* wombs] the organ inside a woman's or female animal's body where her babies grow. A biology word.

won /wʌn/ PAST TENSE AND PAST PARTICIPLE OF **win**¹

wonder¹ /'wʌndə(r)/ VERB [wonders, wondering, wondered]
1 to want to know something □ *+ question word I wonder what Jack has bought me for Christmas.* □ *I wonder whether Susie is coming?*
2 used to ask someone something in a polite way □ *I wonder if you could tell me where the post office is?*

wonder² /'wʌndə(r)/ NOUN [*plural* wonders]
1 *no plural* a feeling of great admiration and surprise □ *The comet filled people with wonder.* □ *We stared in wonder at the castle.*
2 something that makes you feel admiration and surprise □ *Now we can keep in touch all the time, with the wonders of modern technology.*
3 no wonder used to say that something does not surprise you □ *It's no wonder she gets cross if you behave like that.*

wonderful /'wʌndəfʊl/ ADJECTIVE extremely good □ *We had a wonderful view of the mountains.* □ *This job is a wonderful opportunity for her.*

won't /wəʊnt/ a short way to say and write will not □ *He won't tell me what he saw.*

wood /wʊd/ NOUN [*plural* woods]
1 the hard substance that trees are made of □ *a piece of wood* □ *a wood floor* □ *They were chopping wood for the fire.*
2 *also* woods an area where a lot of trees grow closely together □ *We went for a walk in the woods.*

wooden /'wʊdən/ ADJECTIVE made of wood □ *wooden toys* □ *a wooden chair*

wool /wʊl/ NOUN, NO PLURAL cloth or thread made from the hair of sheep ⊞ *a ball of wool* □ *a wool coat*

woollen /'wʊlən/ ADJECTIVE made of wool □ *a woollen blanket*

word /wɜːd/ NOUN [*plural* words]
1 a unit of language that is written as a group of letters with spaces on either side □ *She asked me how to pronounce the word 'catastrophe'.* □ *He always uses lots of long words.*
2 words something that someone says □ *What were her exact words?* ⊞ *Tell us what happened in your own words.*
3 *no plural* a short conversation ⊞ *I'll have a word with my Dad and see if we can borrow the car.* ⊞ *I want a word with you.*
4 *no plural* a promise ⊞ *He gave me his word that he would be there.* ⊞ *I will always keep my word.*
5 in other words used when you say something in a different way in order to explain it □ *We are spending more than we earn at the moment. In other words, we need more money.*
6 not believe/understand, etc. a word to not believe/understand, etc. any of what is said or written □ *I couldn't hear a word of what he was saying.* □ *She doesn't speak a word of English.*

7 take someone's word for it to believe what someone says about something □ *The movie's great, but you don't have to take my word for it – go and see it yourself.*
8 word for word using exactly the same words □ *He copied the essay word for word from the Internet.*

wore /wɔː(r)/ PAST TENSE OF **wear**

work¹ /wɜːk/ VERB [works, working, worked]
1 to do something that needs effort or energy □ **+ on** *She's working on another novel.* □ **+ to do something** *We have been working to improve conditions for the homeless.* 🔁 *We all need to work hard to make this event a success.*
2 to have a job that you are paid to do □ **+ for** *He works for a shipping company.* □ **+ as** *I was working as a nurse at the time.*
3 to operate correctly □ *My e-mail isn't working at the moment.*
4 to be successful or effective □ *The new treatment seems to be working.* 🔁 *Our plan worked well.*
5 to operate a machine or a piece of equipment □ *I don't know how to work the heating.*

◆ PHRASAL VERBS **work out 1** if a plan or a situation works out, it is successful □ *I hope everything works out for you.* **2** to end in a particular way □ *The arrangement worked out well for me.* **3** to do exercises to make your body stronger □ *I work out four times a week.* **work something out 1** to be able to understand something or make a decision about something □ **+ question word** *There was a message on the back, but I couldn't work out what it said.* □ *I worked out how to put the tent up.* **2** to calculate something □ *I've worked out how much tax I owe.* □ *The doctors have worked out the correct dose for me.*

work² /wɜːk/ NOUN [plural works]
1 *no plural* an activity that needs effort 🔁 *It was hard work clearing up after the party.* 🔁 *There's still a lot of work to do before the website will be ready.*
2 *no plural* someone's job, or the place they go to do it 🔁 *I go to work at 8.* □ *I usually go to the gym before work.* □ *My work involves talking to doctors.*
3 *no plural* the things that you create or do when you are working □ *I've done a lot of work with young people.* □ *Hand your work in to the teacher.*
4 something produced by an artist, musician, writer etc. □ *Her early works are quite different.*
5 get/set to work to start working □ *We set to work on the garden.*

worker /ˈwɜːkə(r)/ NOUN [plural workers]
someone who works for a company or organization, but who is not a manager □ *steel workers*
workforce /ˈwɜːkfɔːs/ NOUN, NO PLURAL all the people who work in a country or in a particular company

working /ˈwɜːkɪŋ/ ADJECTIVE
1 to do with your job 🔁 *They demanded better working conditions.* 🔁 *He'd spent his whole working life in the same job.* 🔁 *He wanted to reduce his working hours.*
2 having a job □ *working mothers*

work of art /ˌwɜːk əv ˈɑːt/ NOUN [plural works of art] something which an artist has painted or made □ *The gallery owns the country's best-known works of art.*

workout /ˈwɜːkaʊt/ NOUN [plural workouts] an occasion when you do exercises to make yourself stronger
workplace /ˈwɜːkpleɪs/ NOUN [plural workplaces] a building or room where people work
workshop /ˈwɜːkʃɒp/ NOUN [plural workshops]
1 a meeting to learn more about something by discussing it and doing practical exercises □ *a drama workshop*
2 a place where things are built or repaired

world /wɜːld/ NOUN [plural worlds]
1 the world the Earth or all the people living on it □ *He is the tallest man in the world.* □ *The whole world is affected by global warming.* □ *He longed to travel the world.* □ *She really wants to change the world.*
2 the people and things involved in a particular activity □ *He is famous in the world of antiques.*
3 an area of the world or a group of countries with a particular characteristic □ *the Arab world* □ *Many of the goods we import are from the developing world.*

worm /wɜːm/ NOUN [plural worms] a long, thin, soft creature with no bones or legs which lives in soil
worn /wɔːn/ PAST PARTICIPLE OF **wear**

worried /ˈwʌrɪd/ ADJECTIVE thinking a lot about problems or bad things that could happen □ **+ about** *I'm worried about what will happen if I fail my exams.* □ **+ that** *He is worried that Amy won't like him.*

worry¹ /ˈwʌri/ VERB [worries, worrying, worried]
1 to keep thinking about a problem or something bad that might happen □ **+ about** *A lot of young people worry about the future.*
2 to make someone feel worried 🔁 *It worries me that I might not be able to find a job.*
3 Don't worry (a) said when trying to make someone feel less worried □ *Don't worry. I'm sure things will improve.* **(b)** used to tell someone that they do not need to do something □ *Don't worry about getting the milk. I can get it on my way home.*

worry² /ˈwʌri/ NOUN [plural worries]
1 something that makes you worried 🔁 *Lack of money is a real worry at the moment.*
2 *no plural* the feeling of being worried □ *Some medical tests can lead to unnecessary worry.*

worse[1] /wɜːs/ ADJECTIVE
1 of a lower standard, or more unpleasant 🔂 *The situation will get worse.* □ *+ than The damage was worse than expected.*
2 more ill □ *I felt worse yesterday.*

worse[2] /wɜːs/ ADVERB
1 more badly, or more severely □ *+ than His headache had returned worse than ever.*
2 not as well □ *+ than Some of the children were treated worse than others.*

worship[1] /'wɜːʃɪp/ VERB [worships, worshipping, worshipped]
1 to show respect for a god by praying, having religious ceremonies, etc
2 to admire someone so much that you do not see their faults □ *She worshipped her husband.*

worship[2] /'wɜːʃɪp/ NOUN, NO PLURAL religious services and other ways of showing respect for a god 🔂 *a place of worship (= a church, mosque, etc.)*

worst[1] /wɜːst/ ADJECTIVE the worst most severe, most unpleasant, or most difficult □ *It was the worst storm we'd ever seen.*

worst[2] /wɜːst/ ADVERB most badly □ *I scored worst in the test.* □ *The area worst affected by the floods was the North.*

worth[1] /wɜːθ/ ADJECTIVE
1 having a particular value □ *The ring is worth £1000.*
2 used for saying that something is useful, important or enjoyable □ *The museum is worth a visit.* □ *+ ing It is worth asking a solicitor for advice.* 🔂 *The project was hard work but it was worth it.*

worth[2] /wɜːθ/ NOUN, NO PLURAL
1 £10/$50, etc. worth of something an amount of something that costs £10/$50, etc. to buy □ *£10,000 worth of jewellery was stolen in the robbery.*
2 a week's/a month's, etc. worth of something an amount for a week/month, etc. □ *A month's worth of rain fell in less than 24 hours.*
3 how useful someone or something is 🔂 *Since joining the team, he has proved his worth.*

worthless /'wɜːθlɪs/ ADJECTIVE
1 not important or not useful □ *He felt worthless.*
2 having no financial value □ *The necklace is worthless.*

worthwhile /ˌwɜːθ'waɪl/ ADJECTIVE if something is worthwhile, it is useful or enjoyable although you have to spend time or effort doing it □ *a worthwhile project*

worthy /'wɜːðɪ/ ADJECTIVE [worthier, worthiest]
1 deserving respect or support □ *The German team were worthy winners.* 🔂 *She gives a lot of money to worthy causes.*
2 be worthy of something a formal phrase

meaning to deserve something □ *The offer is certainly worthy of consideration.*

would /wʊd/ MODAL VERB
1 used to say what might happen in a particular situation □ *What would you do if you won a million dollars?* □ *What would happen if there was a fire?*
2 used as the past tense of will[1] to talk about what was going to happen □ *I didn't think she would agree.* □ *He said he would come later.*
3 used as the past tense of will[1] to talk about if someone or something was willing or able to do something □ *My camera wouldn't work.* □ *She wouldn't help me.*
4 used for talking about what you think is true, or what you think the reason for something is □ *You would find it hard to get another job.* □ *It would be difficult to manage without a car.* □ *Why would he want to hurt them?*
5 would you used in polite questions and offers □ *Would you like a drink?* □ *Would you mind helping me with these boxes?*
6 would like/prefer, etc. used to say what you want or what you want to do □ *I would like to see a different doctor.* □ *I would really like a hot shower.*

wouldn't /'wʊdənt/ a short way to say and write would not □ *She wouldn't go.*

would've /'wʊdəv/ a short way to say and write would have □ *It would've been nice to see her.*

wound[1] /waʊnd/ PAST TENSE AND PAST PARTICIPLE OF wind[2]

wound[2] /wuːnd/ NOUN [plural wounds] an injury, especially where the skin is broken □ *gunshot wounds*

wound[3] /wuːnd/ VERB [wounds, wounding, wounded] to injure a person or an animal, especially in a way that breaks their skin □ *She was seriously wounded in the attack.*

wove /wəʊv/ PAST TENSE OF weave

woven /'wəʊvən/ PAST PARTICIPLE OF weave

wow /waʊ/ EXCLAMATION an informal word used to express surprise or admiration □ *Wow! You look great!*

wrap /ræp/ VERB [wraps, wrapping, wrapped] to cover something by putting paper or another material around it □ *Would you like the chocolates wrapped?* □ *We wrapped all the glasses in paper.*
♦ PHRASAL VERB **wrap something up** to cover something with paper or another material, especially a present □ *We wrapped up the toys.*

wreck[1] /rek/ VERB [wrecks, wrecking, wrecked]
1 to destroy or badly damage something □ *He wrecked all our new furniture.* □ *A knee injury has wrecked his chance of playing in the final.*
2 if a ship is wrecked, it is damaged and sinks

wreck[2] /rek/ NOUN [plural wrecks]
1 a ship that has sunk
2 a badly damaged vehicle that has crashed

wreckage /'rekɪdʒ/ NOUN, NO PLURAL the damaged pieces left after a vehicle has been destroyed □ *He was trapped in the wreckage for over an hour.*

wrestle /'resəl/ VERB [wrestles, wrestling, wrestled] to fight with someone by holding them and trying to throw them to the ground

wriggle /'rɪgəl/ VERB [wriggles, wriggling, wriggled] to make short, twisting movements □ *Stop wriggling about in your chair and sit still!*

wrinkle /'rɪŋkəl/ NOUN [plural wrinkles]
1 a line in your skin, caused by getting older
2 a line where something such as a piece of cloth is slightly folded

wrist /rɪst/ NOUN [plural wrists] the part of your body where your arm joins your hand

write /raɪt/ VERB [writes, writing, wrote, written]
1 to form letters, words or numbers, usually on paper using a pen or pencil □ *Write your name and address on the top of the paper.*
2 to use words to make a story, essay, book, letter, song, etc. □ *She has written four novels.* □ *I wrote a note and left it on the table.* □ **+ about** *She writes about gardening.*
3 to send a letter or a message to someone □ **+ to** *I wrote to the manager to complain.* □ *We'll write in a week or two.*
4 if you write music, you put the symbols for the notes on special paper □ *He wrote his second symphony when he was fifteen.*
♦ PHRASAL VERB **write something down** to write something on a piece of paper, especially so that you do not forget it □ *I wrote down his phone number.*

writer /'raɪtə(r)/ NOUN [plural writers] someone who writes books, plays, newspaper articles, etc. as a job

writing /'raɪtɪŋ/ NOUN [plural writings]
1 *no plural* the forming of letters and words on paper or other surfaces so that they can be read
2 *no plural* your writing is the way you write
3 the things that a writer has written

written /'rɪtən/ PAST PARTICIPLE OF **write**

wrong[1] /rɒŋ/ ADJECTIVE
1 if something is wrong, there is a problem □ **+ with** *Is there something wrong with David? He doesn't look happy.* □ *What's wrong? I thought you'd be pleased to see me.*
2 not correct □ *That was the wrong answer.* □ *We made the wrong decision.* □ *You're looking in the wrong place.* □ **+ about** *He was wrong about Helen.*
3 not morally right □ *She has done nothing wrong.* □ **+ to do something** *It would be wrong to deceive him.*
4 not suitable □ **+ with** *If you want flowers, what's wrong with roses?* □ **+ for** *The dress was wrong for a wedding.*

wrong[2] /rɒŋ/ ADVERB
1 in a way that is not correct □ *I think I have spelt your name wrong.* □ *He guessed wrong.*
2 **go wrong** (a) to stop working correctly □ *My watch has gone wrong.* (b) to stop being successful □ *Everything went wrong after Nik left.*

wrong[3] /rɒŋ/ NOUN, NO PLURAL behaviour that is not morally correct 🖩 *He doesn't know the difference between right and wrong.* □ *I accept that I did wrong.*

wrongly /'rɒŋlɪ/ ADVERB not correctly □ *The plug had been fitted wrongly so the machine did not work.* □ *She was wrongly accused of fraud.*

wrote /rəʊt/ PAST TENSE OF **write**

X*x*

X *or* **x** /eks/ the 24th letter of the alphabet

Xmas /'eksməs/ NOUN an informal short way of writing **Christmas**[1]

X-ray /'eksreɪ/ NOUN [*plural* X-rays] a special kind of photograph that shows the inside parts of someone's body

Yy

Y or **y** /waɪ/ the 25th letter of the alphabet

yacht /jɒt/ NOUN [*plural* yachts] a boat with sails that you use for racing or for pleasure

yard¹ /jɑːd/ NOUN [*plural* yards] a unit for measuring length, equal to 3 feet

yard² /jɑːd/ NOUN [*plural* yards]
1 an area of land, often with a fence or wall around it, and often used for a particular purpose □ *The dogs have a large exercise yard.*
2 a US word for a garden next to a house

yawn /jɔːn/ VERB [yawns, yawning, yawned] to open your mouth very wide and breathe in, because you are feeling tired or bored

yeah /jeə/ EXCLAMATION an informal way of saying yes

year /jɪə(r)/ NOUN [*plural* years]
1 a period of 365 or 366 days, marking the length of time it takes for the Earth to go around the sun, especially the period from 1 January to 31 December □ *We're going to America next year.* □ *I spent a year working in Paris.* □ *In recent years, the building has not been used much.*
2 three/sixteen/fifty, etc. years old used to talk about the age of someone or something □ *He's only twelve years old.* □ *Our house is almost three hundred years old.*
3 a three/sixteen/fifty year-old a person who is a particular age □ *You're acting like a five year-old!*
4 years a long period of time ⑤ *I haven't been to Madrid for years.*
5 the students at a school, college, etc. who start in the same year □ *He was in my year at school.* □ *We studied the Egyptians in year 3.*

> ➤ When saying how old someone is, do not say 'years'. Say only the number or a number + 'years old':
> ✓ She is eight.
> ✓ She is eight years old.
> ✗ She is eight years.

yearly /ˈjɪəlɪ/ ADJECTIVE, ADVERB happening or done every year □ *our yearly holiday* □ *Accounts must be prepared yearly.*

yeast /jiːst/ NOUN, NO PLURAL a substance that is used to make bread rise

yell /jel/ VERB [yells, yelling, yelled] to shout something loudly □ *'Let me go!' she yelled.*

yellow¹ /ˈjeləʊ/ ADJECTIVE having the colour of the sun or a lemon □ *The garden was full of bright yellow flowers.*

yellow² /ˈjeləʊ/ NOUN, NO PLURAL the colour of the sun or a lemon

yes /jes/ EXCLAMATION
1 used to agree with someone, agree to do something, or to give a positive answer □ *'Are these shoes all right?' 'Yes, they're lovely.'* □ *'Could you help me with my homework?' 'Yes, no problem.'* □ *'Would you like a cup of coffee?' 'Yes, please.'*
2 used to disagree with a negative statement □ *'You haven't washed your hair.' 'Yes I have.'*

yesterday /ˈjestədeɪ/ ADVERB, NOUN, NO PLURAL the day before today □ *I saw Kim yesterday.* □ *He called me yesterday morning.* □ *Yesterday was her birthday.*

yet¹ /jet/ ADVERB
1 used in questions or negative statements to mean before now or before the time you are talking about □ *Have you read her new book yet?* □ *We haven't paid them any money yet.*
2 used in questions and negative statements to mean that something will not happen immediately but will happen in the future □ *Please don't leave yet.* □ *You can't go in yet.*
3 used to emphasize how often something exists or happens ⑤ *Yet again, they have let us down.* ⑤ *Apparently, Richard has bought yet another bicycle.*

yet² /jet/ CONJUNCTION used to say something surprising after what has been said before □ *He was pleasant, yet failed to offer any real help.* □ *We claim to live in a civilized society, and yet children live in poverty here.* □ *The decorations were colourful yet tasteful.*

yield /jiːld/ VERB [yields, yielding, yielded]
1 to produce something useful □ *Discussions have failed to yield results.* □ *The investment yielded a good profit.*
2 to produce a particular amount of a crop
3 to be forced to do something or agree to something, or to be defeated □ *The government*

yielded to pressure and delayed the tax rise. □ *The army yielded to enemy forces.*

yoga /ˈjəʊɡə/ NOUN, NO PLURAL a type of exercise for the body and the mind, which involves stretching your body and doing breathing exercises

you /juː/ PRONOUN used to talk or write about the person or people that you are talking to □ *Do you like pizza?* □ *I'll ring you tomorrow night.* □ *Max is taller than you.*

you'd /juːd/ a short way to say and write you had or you would □ *You'd better be careful.* □ *You'd be sorry if she left.*

you'll /juːl/ a short way to say and write you will □ *You'll never guess what happened next!*

young¹ /jʌŋ/ ADJECTIVE [younger, youngest] not old □ *a young boy* □ *You're too young to stay up so late.*

young² /jʌŋ/ PLURAL NOUN
1 the babies that an animal or bird has □ *a bird feeding its young*
2 the young young people

your /jɔː(r)/ DETERMINER
1 belonging to or to do with you □ *Can I borrow your pen?*
2 belonging to or to do with people in general □ *Your school days are the happiest days of your life.*

you're /jɔː(r)/ a short way to say and write you are □ *You're early!*

yours /jɔːz/ PRONOUN
1 used to talk or write about things belonging to or to do with the person or people you are talking to □ *Which glass is yours?*
2 used at the end of a letter, before your name □ *I look forward to hearing from you. Yours, Amy.*

yourself /jɔːˈself/ PRONOUN [plural yourselves]
1 the reflexive form of you □ *Careful you don't cut yourself on that knife.* □ *You'll have to dry yourselves on your T-shirts.*
2 used to show that you do something without any help from other people □ *Did you really make that skirt yourself?* ⊞ *Have you done this work all by yourself?*
3 used to emphasize the pronoun you □ *You cannot film the concert yourselves, but you can buy a video.*
4 by yourself not with or near other people □ *It can be lonely living by yourself.*

youth /juːθ/ NOUN [plural youths]
1 a young man □ *a gang of youths*
2 no plural the time in your life when you are young □ *She spent most of her youth abroad.*
3 no plural young people □ *the youth of today*

you've /juːv/ a short way to say and write you have □ *You've left the door open again.*

Zz

Z or **z** /zed/ the 26th letter of the alphabet

zebra /'zebrə/ NOUN [*plural* zebras] an animal like a horse with black and white stripes

zebra crossing /ˌzebrə 'krɒsɪŋ/ NOUN [*plural* zebra crossings] a place where you can cross a road, marked with black and white stripes

zero /'zɪərəʊ/ NOUN [*plural* zeros]
1 nothing or the number 0 □ *There are six zeros in one million.*
2 *no plural* the temperature at which water freezes □ *It was three degrees below zero.*

zip¹ /zɪp/ NOUN [*plural* zips] a device for fastening clothes or bags that has two rows of small metal or plastic parts that fit tightly together when a sliding piece is pulled along them
zip² /zɪp/ VERB [zips, zipping, zipped]
1 to fasten something with a zip □ *Zip up your jacket; it's cold.*
2 to make the information on a computer file fit into a much smaller space, so that it can be sent or stored more easily. A computing word □ *I'll zip the file before I send it to you.*
3 to move somewhere very quickly, or to do something very quickly □ *The bullet zipped by his head.* □ *He zipped through the answers.*

zodiac /'zəʊdiæk/ NOUN the zodiac the twelve signs of the groups of stars that some people believe influence your life 🕮 *What sign of the zodiac are you?*

zone /zəʊn/ NOUN [*plural* zones] an area that has a particular feature or where a particular thing happens 🕮 *This is a danger zone because of avalanches.* □ *a smoke-free zone* □ *a war zone*

zoo /zuː/ NOUN [*plural* zoos] a place where wild animals are kept for people to look at

zoom /zuːm/ VERB [zooms, zooming, zoomed] to go somewhere very fast, especially with a loud noise □ *The rocket zoomed up into the air.*